DICTIONARY

Collins

An Imprint of HarperCollins*Publishers*

HarperCollins Publishers
Westerhill Road
Bishopbriggs
Glasgow
G64 2QT
Great Britain

First Edition 2005

© HarperCollins Publishers
2005

ISBN 0-00-719156-1

Collins® is a registered
trademark of HarperCollins
Publishers Limited

Scrabble® is a registered
trademark of J. W. Spear &
Sons Ltd., a subsidiary of
Mattel, Inc
© 2005 Mattel, Inc

www.collins.co.uk

A catalogue record for this
book is available from the
British Library

Typeset by Wordcraft,
Glasgow

Printed in Italy by Legoprint
S.P.A.

Introduction

Collins Gem Scrabble Dictionary – Every Word Counts

The *Collins Gem Scrabble Dictionary* is the ideal reference book for people who play Scrabble on the move. Its handy size makes it the perfect companion to Travel Scrabble.

This dictionary doesn't include every word eligible for Scrabble, but contains the most commonly used of the 260,000 words in *Collins Scrabble Words 2005*, the definitive Scrabble wordlist. The concise definitions in the *Gem Scrabble Dictionary* allow players to check the meaning of words, as well as using the book for settling arguments during games.

The *Collins Gem Scrabble Dictionary* only contains words of up to eight letters in length, plus their inflections, as these are the words most likely to be used in Scrabble. As the dictionary is designed for family play, it does not include offensive terms. Such words are included in *Collins Scrabble Words 2005*, the complete wordlist for tournaments and club competitions.

Word order
In the *Collins Gem Scrabble Dictionary*, all words are listed in alphabetical order, rather than being grouped at the base form as in a conventional dictionary. Where words are inflections of a base form, only the base form will have a definition, but the inflections will be listed alphabetically as individual entries for easy reference during a game.

Special Scrabble words
To help players learn and use some of the rarer and higher-scoring words in the game, the *Collins Gem Scrabble Dictionary* includes a number of special panel entries.

These are unusual words which are particularly useful in Scrabble, either because they use the high-scoring 'power tiles' (J, Q, X and Z) or because they have only two or three letters. There are also panel entries at the start of every letter section, which offer advice on useful words beginning with that letter.

The *Collins Gem Scrabble Dictionary* is designed to be useful to new players and veterans alike – we hope you enjoy using it!

Forming Words

The key to successful Scrabble is awareness of the various opportunities for forming words on the board. At the end of a game, the Scrabble board looks like a completed crossword – but like an American crossword, with blocks of letters in which many short words are contained, rather than a British crossword where words intersect each other without overlap. Indeed, Scrabble was invented by a crossword enthusiast, Alfred Butts; as Mr Butts was American, the US type of crossword was the model for the game.

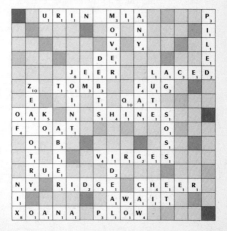

The board looks like this because Scrabble words don't have to be formed by simply intersecting existing words as in a British crossword, or by adding letters to them. The other methods are 'hooking' and 'tagging', and allow more than one word to be created at a time, giving a higher score.

Hooking
Hooking is a Scrabble term for the act of 'hanging' one word on another, changing the first word in the process. When you form a word by hooking, you add a letter to the beginning or end of a word already on the board, transforming it into a longer word as you do so. The 'hook' is the letter that enables you to attach one word to another, as in the following example:

Adding an S to the end of a noun is the easiest and most obvious way to hook onto a word on the board. In this example, you get the points for COMETS (10) as well as for SERPENT (7):

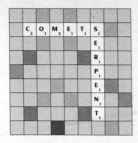

Hooking allows you to benefit from high-scoring 'power tiles' played by other players. Whenever your opponents use one of these tiles, look out for opportunities to hook onto the word so that you can take advantage of the high-scoring letter, as in the example below:

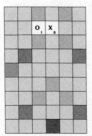 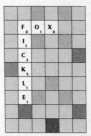

Here you get the 13 points for FOX as well as those for FICKLE. So you can see that hooking is generally a much more profitable method of word-formation than simply playing a word through one that is already on the board.

Obviously, only certain words can be hooked onto. Some words cannot form other words by having a single letter added to their front or back; these are knows as blockers, as they prevent other players from adding words to the board by hooking.

Tagging
Playing a word parallel to one already on the board, so that one or more tiles are in contact, is known as tagging, or parallel play. Tagging is more difficult than hooking because you need to form one additional word for each tile in contact with the word already on the board. In most circumstances, these will be two-letter words, which is why these short words are so vital to the game. The more two-letter words you know, the greater your opportunities for fitting words onto the board through tagging – and of running up some impressive scores!

Consider the following example:

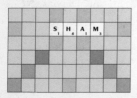

By playing HEXES, you can also create the words SH, HE, AX and ME, all of which are valid in Scrabble, and each of which will give you an additional score to add to the points you'll score from HEXES.

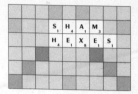

In theory, you could form eight words at once by tagging (though this is unlikely to happen very often!). Try to learn as many two-letter words as possible; while they may not score many points on their own, they are invaluable in allowing you to tag onto words to earn some very respectable scores.

The panel entries in this dictionary contain a number of unusual two-letter words: learning these is an excellent method of improving your game immediately!

ABBREVIATIONS USED IN THIS DICTIONARY

AD	anno Domini	meteorol	meteorology
adj	adjective	mil	military
adv	adverb	n	noun
anat	anatomy	N	North
archit	architecture	naut	nautical
astrol	astrology	NZ	New Zealand
Aust	Australia(n)	obs	obsolete
BC	before Christ	offens	offensive
biol	biology	orig	originally
Brit	British	photog	photography
chem	chemistry	pl	plural
C of E	Church of England	prep	preposition
conj	conjunction	pron	pronoun
E	East	psychol	psychology
eg	for example	®	trademark
esp	especially	RC	Roman Catholic
etc	et cetera	S	South
fem	feminine	S Afr	South African
foll	followed	Scot	Scottish
geom	geometry	sing	singular
hist	history	US	United States
interj	interjection	usu	usually
lit	literary	v	verb
masc	masculine	W	West
med	medicine	zool	zoology

Aa

A forms a two-letter word when followed by any one of A, B, D, E, G, H, I, M, N, R, S, T, W, X and Y – 15 letters out of 26 – so it's a really useful tile. There are also a number of short high-scoring words beginning with A. **Axe** (10 points) and **adze** (14 points) are good examples, but don't forget their US variants, **ax** (9 points) and **adz** (13 points). Also remember their plurals and the verb form **axed** (12 points). **Aye** (6) and **ay** (5) are handy for tight corners.

a *adj* indefinite article, used before a noun being mentioned for the first time

aa *n* (**aas**). Aa is a type of volcanic rock. Aa scores 2 points, and is a good way of getting rid of annoying multiples of A.

aah *interj* Aah is a sound people make when they're pleased or amazed. Aah scores 6 points.

aal *adj* Aal is a Scots word for **all**. Aal scores 3 points.

aardvark *n* (*pl* **-s**) S African anteater with long ears and snout

aardvarks *v* ▷ **aardvark**

ab *n* (*pl* **-s**) *informal* (usually plural) abdominal muscle

aba *noun* (**abas**). Cloth made from goat or camel hair. This is a useful word to remember for when you have more than one A on your rack. Aba scores 5 points.

aback *adv* startled or disconnected

abacus (*pl* **-es**) *n* beads on a wire frame, used for doing calculations

abacuses *n* ▷ **abacus**

abalone (*pl* **-s**) *n* edible sea creature with a shell lined with mother of pearl

abalones *n* ▷ **abalone**

abandon *v* (**-s**, **-ing**, **-ed**) desert or leave (one's wife, children, etc) ▶ *n* lack of inhibition > **abandonment** *n* (*pl* **-s**)

abandoned *v* ▷ **abandon**

abandoning *v* ▷ **abandon**

abandonment *n* ▷ **abandon**

abandonments *n* ▷ **abandon**

abandons *v* ▷ **abandon**

abase *v* (**-ses**, **-sing**, **-sed**) humiliate or degrade (oneself) > **abasement** *n* (*pl* **-s**)

abased *v* ▷ **abase**

abasement *n* ▷ **abase**

abasements *n* ▷ **abase**

abases *v* ▷ **abase**

abashed *adj* embarrassed and ashamed

abasing *v* ▷ **abase**

abate *v* (**-tes**, **-ting**, **-ted**) make or become less strong > **abatement** *n* (*pl* **-s**)

abated *v* ▷ **abate**

abatement *n* ▷ **abate**

abatements *n* ▷ **abate**

abates *v* ▷ **abate**

abating *v* ▷ **abate**

abattoir (*pl* **-s**) *n* place where animals are killed for food

abattoirs *n* ▷ **abattoir**

abb *noun* (**abbs**). Abb is yarn used in weaving. Remember this word for when you have two Bs on your rack, as there will probably already be an A on the board that you can use. Abb scores 7 points.

abbess n (pl **-es**) nun in charge of a convent
abbesses n ▷ abbess
abbey n (pl **-s**) dwelling place of, or a church belonging to, a community of monks or nuns
abbeys n ▷ abbey
abbot n (pl **-s**) head of an abbey of monks
abbots n ▷ abbot
abdicate v (**-tes, -ting, -ted**) give up (the throne or a responsibility) > **abdication** n (pl **-s**)
abdicated v ▷ abdicate
abdicates v ▷ abdicate
abdicating v ▷ abdicate
abdication n ▷ abdicate
abdications n ▷ abdicate
abdomen n (pl **-s**) part of the body containing the stomach and intestines > **abdominal** adj
abdomens n ▷ abdomen
abdominal adj ▷ abdomen
abduct v (**-s, -ing, -ed**) carry off, kidnap > **abduction** n (pl **-s**) > **abductor** n (pl **-s**)
abducted v ▷ abduct
abducting v ▷ abduct
abduction n ▷ abduct
abductions n ▷ abduct
abductor n ▷ abduct
abductors n ▷ abduct
abducts v ▷ abduct
aberrant adj showing aberration
abet v (**-s, -ting, -ted**) help or encourage in wrongdoing > **abettor** n (pl **-s**)
abets v ▷ abet
abetted v ▷ abet
abetting v ▷ abet
abettor n ▷ abet
abettors n ▷ abet
abeyance n (pl **-s**) not in use
abeyances n ▷ abeyance
abhor v (**-s, -rring, -rred**) detest utterly > **abhorrence** n (pl **-s**)
abhorred v ▷ abhor
abhorrence n ▷ abhor

abhorrences n ▷ abhor
abhorring v ▷ abhor
abhors v ▷ abhor
abide v (**-des, -ding, -ded**) endure, put up with
abided v ▷ abide
abides v ▷ abide
abiding adj lasting ▶ v ▷ abide
abilities n ▷ ability
ability n (pl **-ties**) competence, power
abject adj utterly miserable > **abjectly** adv
abjectly adv ▷ abject
abjure v (**-res, -ring, -red**) deny or renounce on oath
abjured v ▷ abjure
abjures v ▷ abjure
abjuring v ▷ abjure
ablative n (pl **-s**) case of nouns in Latin and other languages, indicating source, agent, or instrument of action
ablatives n ▷ ablative
ablaze adj burning fiercely
able adj (**-r, -st**) capable, competent > **ably** adv
abler adj ▷ able
ablest adj ▷ able
ablution n (pl **-s**) (usually plural) act of washing
ablutions n ▷ ablution
ably adv ▷ able
abnormal adj not normal or usual > **abnormally** adv > **abnormality** n (pl **-ties**)
abnormalities n ▷ abnormal
abnormality n ▷ abnormal
abnormally adv ▷ abnormal
aboard adv, prep on, in, onto, or into (a ship, train, or plane)
abode n (pl **-s**) home, dwelling
abodes n ▷ abode
abolish v (**-shes, -shing, -shed**) do away with > **abolition** n (pl **-s**)
abolished v ▷ abolish
abolishes v ▷ abolish
abolishing v ▷ abolish
abolition n ▷ abolish
abolitions n ▷ abolish

abort v (-s, -ing, -ed) have an abortion
or perform an abortion on
aborted v ▷ abort
aborting v ▷ abort
abortion n (pl -s) operation to end a
pregnancy
abortions n ▷ abortion
abortive adj unsuccessful
aborts v ▷ abort
abound v (-s, -ing, -ed) be plentiful
>**abounding** adj
abounded v ▷ abound
abounding v, adj ▷ abound
abounds v ▷ abound
about prep concerning, on the subject
of ▶ adv nearly, approximately
above adv, prep over or higher (than)
abrasion n (pl -s) scraped area on
the skin
abrasions n ▷ abrasion
abrasive adj harsh and unpleasant
in manner ▶ n (pl -s) substance for
cleaning or polishing by rubbing
abrasives n ▷ abrasive
abreast adv, adj side by side
abridge v (-ges, -ging, -ged) shorten
by using fewer words >**abridgment,**
abridgement n (pl -s)
abridged v ▷ abridge
abridgement n ▷ abridge
abridgements n ▷ abridge
abridges v ▷ abridge
abridging v ▷ abridge
abridgment n ▷ abridge
abridgments n ▷ abridge
abroad adv to or in a foreign country
abrogate v (-tes, -ting, -ted) cancel
(a law or agreement) formally
>**abrogation** n (pl -s)
abrogated v ▷ abrogate
abrogates v ▷ abrogate
abrogating v ▷ abrogate
abrogation n ▷ abrogate
abrogations n ▷ abrogate
abrupt adj (-er, -est) sudden,
unexpected >**abruptly** adv
>**abruptness** n (pl -es)
abrupter adj ▷ abrupt

abruptest adj ▷ abrupt
abruptly adv ▷ abrupt
abruptness n ▷ abrupt
abruptnesses n ▷ abrupt
abs n ▷ ab
abscess n (pl -es) inflamed swelling
containing pus
abscesses n ▷ abscess
abscond v (-s, -ing, -ed) leave secretly
absconded v ▷ abscond
absconding v ▷ abscond
absconds v ▷ abscond
abseil v (-s, -ing, -ed) go down a steep
drop by a rope fastened at the top and
tied around one's body
abseiled v ▷ abseil
abseiling v ▷ abseil
abseils v ▷ abseil
absence n (pl -s) being away
absences n ▷ absence
absent adj not present ▶ v (-s, -ing,
-ed) stay away >**absently** adv
absented v ▷ absent
absentee n (pl -s) person who should
be present but is not
absentees n ▷ absentee
absenting v ▷ absent
absently adv ▷ absent
absents v ▷ absent
absinthe n (pl -s) strong green
aniseed-flavoured liqueur
absinthes n ▷ absinthe
absolute adj complete, perfect
absolution n ▷ absolve
absolutions n ▷ absolve
absolve v (-ves, -ving, -ved)
declare to be free from blame or sin
>**absolution** n (pl -s)
absolved v ▷ absolve
absolves v ▷ absolve
absolving v ▷ absolve
absorb v (-s, -ing, -ed) soak up
(a liquid) >**absorption** n (pl -s)
>**absorbency** n (pl -s)
absorbed v ▷ absorb
absorbencies n ▷ absorb
absorbency n ▷ absorb
absorbing v ▷ absorb

absorbs v ▷ absorb
absorption n ▷ absorb
absorptions n ▷ absorb
abstain v (-s, -ing, -ed) choose not to do something ▶ **abstainer** n (pl -s)
abstained v ▷ abstain
abstainer n ▷ abstain
abstainers n ▷ abstain
abstaining v ▷ abstain
abstains v ▷ abstain
abstract adj (-er, -est) existing as a quality or idea rather than a material object ▶ n (pl -s) summary ▶ v (-s, -ing, -ed) summarize > **abstraction** n (pl -s)
abstracted v ▷ abstract
abstracter adj ▷ abstract
abstractest adj ▷ abstract
abstracting v ▷ abstract
abstraction n ▷ abstract
abstractions n ▷ abstract
abstracts n, v ▷ abstract
abstruse adj (-r, -st) not easy to understand
abstruser adj ▷ abstruse
abstrusest adj ▷ abstruse
absurd adj (-er, -est) incongruous or ridiculous > **absurdly** adv > **absurdity** n (pl -ties)
absurder adj ▷ absurd
absurdest adj ▷ absurd
absurdities n ▷ absurd
absurdity n ▷ absurd
absurdly adv ▷ absurd
abundance n ▷ abundant
abundances n ▷ abundant
abundant adj plentiful > **abundantly** adv > **abundance** n (pl -s)
abundantly adv ▷ abundant
abuse v (-ses, -sing, -sed) use wrongly ▶ n (pl -s) prolonged ill-treatment > **abuser** n (pl -s) > **abusive** adj > **abusively** adv > **abusiveness** n (pl -es)
abused v ▷ abuse
abuser n ▷ abuse
abusers n ▷ abuse
abuses v, n ▷ abuse
abusing v ▷ abuse

abusive adj ▷ abuse
abusively adv ▷ abuse
abusiveness n ▷ abuse
abusivenesses n ▷ abuse
abut v (-s, -tting, -tted) be next to or touching
abuts v ▷ abut
abutted v ▷ abut
abutting v ▷ abut

| **aby** verb (**abys abying abought**). Aby is an old word meaning to pay a penalty. If someone plays this word, remember that it can be expanded to **baby**, **abysmal** or **abyss**. Aby scores 8 points.

abysmal adj informal extremely bad, awful > **abysmally** adv
abysmally adv ▷ abysmal
abyss n (pl -es) very deep hole or chasm
abysses n ▷ abyss
acacia n (pl -s) tree or shrub with yellow or white flowers
acacias n ▷ acacia
academic adj of an academy or university ▶ n (pl -s) lecturer or researcher at a university > **academically** adv
academically adv ▷ academic
academies n ▷ academy
academy n (pl -mies) society to advance arts or sciences
acanthus n (pl -es) prickly plant
acanthuses n ▷ acanthus
accede v (-des, -ding, -ded) consent or agree (to)
acceded v ▷ accede
accedes v ▷ accede
acceding v ▷ accede
accent n (pl -s) distinctive style of pronunciation of a local, national, or social group ▶ v (-s, -ing, -ed) place emphasis on
accented v ▷ accent
accenting v ▷ accent
accents n, v ▷ accent
accept v (-s, -ing, -ed) receive willingly > **acceptance** n (pl -s)
acceptance n ▷ accept

acceptances n ▷ **accept**
accepted v ▷ **accept**
accepting v ▷ **accept**
accepts v ▷ **accept**
access n (pl -es) means of or right to approach or enter ▶ v (-es, -ing, -ed) obtain (data) from a computer
accessed v ▷ **access**
accesses n, v ▷ **access**
accessing v ▷ **access**
accident n (pl -s) mishap, often causing injury
accidents n ▷ **accident**
acclaim v (-s, -ing, -ed) applaud, praise ▶ n (pl -s) enthusiastic approval
 > **acclamation** n (pl -s)
acclaimed v ▷ **acclaim**
acclaiming v ▷ **acclaim**
acclaims v, n ▷ **acclaim**
acclamation n ▷ **acclaim**
acclamations n ▷ **acclaim**
accolade n (pl -s) award, honour, or praise
accolades n ▷ **accolade**
accord n (pl -s) agreement, harmony ▶ v (-s, -ing, -ed) fit in with
accorded v ▷ **accord**
according v ▷ **accord**
accords v ▷ **accord**
accost v (-s, -ing, -ed) approach and speak to, often aggressively
accosted v ▷ **accost**
accosting v ▷ **accost**
accosts v ▷ **accost**
account n (pl -s) report, description ▶ v (-s, -ing, -ed) judge to be
accounted v ▷ **account**
accounting v ▷ **account**
accounts n, v ▷ **account**
accrual n ▷ **accrue**
accruals n ▷ **accrue**
accrue v (-crues, -cruing, -crued) increase gradually ▶ **accrual** n (pl -s)
accrued v ▷ **accrue**
accrues v ▷ **accrue**
accruing v ▷ **accrue**
accuracies n ▷ **accurate**
accuracy n ▷ **accurate**

accurate adj exact, correct
 > **accurately** adv > **accuracy** n (pl -cies)
accurately adv ▷ **accurate**
accursed adj under a curse
accusation n ▷ **accuse**
accusations n ▷ **accuse**
accusatory adj ▷ **accuse**
accuse v (-ses, -sing, -sed) charge with wrongdoing ▶ **accused** n
 > **accuser** n (pl -s) > **accusing** adj
 > **accusation** n (pl -s) > **accusatory** adj
accused v, n ▷ **accuse**
accuser n ▷ **accuse**
accusers n ▷ **accuse**
accuses v ▷ **accuse**
accusing v, adj ▷ **accuse**
accustom v (-s, -ing, -ed) make used to
accustomed v ▷ **accustom**
accustoming v ▷ **accustom**
accustoms v ▷ **accustom**
ace n (pl -s) playing card with one symbol on it ▶ adj informal excellent
acerbic adj harsh or bitter > **acerbity** n (pl -ties)
acerbities n ▷ **acerbic**
acerbity n ▷ **acerbic**
aces n ▷ **ace**
acetate n (pl -s) CHEM salt or ester of acetic acid
acetates n ▷ **acetate**
acetic adj of or involving vinegar
acetone n (pl -s) colourless liquid used as a solvent
acetones n ▷ **acetone**
ache n (pl -s) dull continuous pain ▶ v (-ches, -ching, -ched) be in or cause continuous dull pain
ached n ▷ **ache**
aches n, v ▷ **ache**
achieve v (-ves, -ving, -ved) gain by hard work or ability
achieved v ▷ **achieve**
achieves v ▷ **achieve**
achieving v ▷ **achieve**
aching v ▷ **ache**
acid n (pl -s) CHEM one of a class of compounds, corrosive and sour when

dissolved in water, that combine with a base to form a salt ▶ *adj* containing acid ▷ **acidic** *adj* ▷ **acidify** *v* ▷ **acidity** *n* (*pl* **-ties**)

acidic *adj* ▷ **acid**

acidify *v* ▷ **acid**

acidities *n* ▷ **acid**

acidity *n* ▷ **acid**

acids *n* ▷ **acid**

acme *n* (*pl* **-s**) highest point of achievement or excellence

acmes *n* ▷ **acme**

acne *n* (*pl* **-s**) pimply skin disease

acnes *n* ▷ **acne**

acolyte *n* (*pl* **-s**) follower or attendant

acolytes *n* ▷ **acolyte**

aconite *n* (*pl* **-s**) poisonous plant with hoodlike flowers

aconites *n* ▷ **aconite**

acorn *n* (*pl* **-s**) nut of the oak tree

acorns *n* ▷ **acorn**

acoustic *adj* of sound and hearing > **acoustically** *adv*

acoustically *adv* ▷ **acoustic**

acquaint *v* (**-s, -ing, -ed**) make familiar, inform > **acquainted** *adj*

acquainted *v, adj* ▷ **acquaint**

acquainting *v* ▷ **acquaint**

acquaints *v* ▷ **acquaint**

acquire *v* (**-res, -ring, -red**) gain, get

acquired *v* ▷ **acquire**

acquires *v* ▷ **acquire**

acquiring *v* ▷ **acquire**

acquit *v* (**-s, -tting, -tted**) pronounce (someone) innocent ▶ **acquittal** *n* (*pl* **-s**)

acquits *v* ▷ **acquit**

acquittal *n* ▷ **acquit**

acquittals *n* ▷ **acquit**

acquitted *v* ▷ **acquit**

acquitting *v* ▷ **acquit**

acre *n* (*pl* **-s**) measure of land, 4840 square yards (4046.86 square metres)

acreage *n* (*pl* **-s**) land area in acres

acreages *n* ▷ **acreage**

acres *n* ▷ **acre**

acrid *adj* (**-er, -est**) pungent, bitter

acrider *adj* ▷ **acrid**

acridest *adj* ▷ **acrid**

acrobat *n* (*pl* **-s**) person skilled in gymnastic feats requiring agility and balance > **acrobatic** *adj*

acrobats *n* ▷ **acrobat**

acronym *n* (*pl* **-s**) word formed from the initial letters of other words, such as NASA

acronyms *n* ▷ **acronym**

across *adv, prep* from side to side (of)

acrostic *n* (*pl* **-s**) lines of writing in which the first or last letters of each line spell a word or saying

acrostics *n* ▷ **acrostic**

acrylic *n* (*pl* **-s**) ▶ *adj* (synthetic fibre, paint, etc) made from acrylic acid

acrylics *n* ▷ **acrylic**

act *n* (*pl* **-s**) thing done ▶ *v* (**-s, -ing, -ed**) do something

acted *v* ▷ **act**

acting *n* (*pl* **-s**) art of an actor ▶ *adj* temporarily performing the duties of ▶ *v* ▷ **act**

actings *n* ▷ **acting**

actinium *n* (*pl* **-s**) CHEM radioactive chemical element

actiniums *n* ▷ **actinium**

action *n* (*pl* **-s**) process of doing something

actions *n* ▷ **action**

activate *v* (**-tes, -ting, -ted**) make active > **activation** *n* (*pl* **-s**) > **activator** *n* (*pl* **-s**)

activated *v* ▷ **activate**

activates *v* ▷ **activate**

activating *v* ▷ **activate**

activation *n* ▷ **activate**

activations *n* ▷ **activate**

activator *n* ▷ **activate**

activators *n* ▷ **activate**

active *adj* moving, working > **actively** *adv*

actively *adv* ▷ **active**

activism *n* ▷ **activist**

activisms *n* ▷ **activist**

activist *n* (*pl* **-s**) person who works energetically to achieve political or social goals > **activism** *n* (*pl* **-s**)

activists n ▷ activist
activities n ▷ activity
activity n (pl -ties) state of being active

actor n (pl -s) person who acts in a play, film, etc
actors n ▷ actor
actress n (pl -es) woman who acts in a play, film, etc
actresses n ▷ actress
acts n, v ▷ act

actual adj existing in reality
> **actuality** n (pl -ties)
actualities n ▷ actual
actuality n ▷ actual
actually adv really, indeed
actuarial adj ▷ actuary
actuaries n ▷ actuary
actuary n (pl -ries) statistician who calculates insurance risks
> **actuarial** adj

actuate v (-tes, -ting, -ted) start up (a device)
actuated v ▷ actuate
actuates v ▷ actuate
actuating v ▷ actuate
acuities n ▷ acuity
acuity n (pl -ties) keenness of vision or thought
acumen n (pl -s) ability to make good judgments
acumens n ▷ acumen
acute adj (-r, -st) severe ▶ n (pl -s) accent (´) over a letter to indicate the quality or length of its sound, as in café
> **acutely** adv > **acuteness** n (pl -s)
acutely adv ▷ acute
acuteness n ▷ acute
acutenesses n ▷ acute
acuter adj ▷ acute
acutes n ▷ acute
acutest adj ▷ acute

ad n (pl -s) informal advertisement
adage n (pl -s) wise saying, proverb
adages n ▷ adage
adagio n (pl -s) ▶ adv MUSIC (piece to be played) slowly and gracefully
adagios n ▷ adagio

adamant adj unshakable in determination or purpose
> **adamantly** adv
adamantly adv ▷ adamant
adapt v (-s, -ing, -ed) alter for new use or new conditions > **adaptable** adj
> **adaptability** n (pl -ties)
adaptabilities n ▷ adapt
adaptability n ▷ adapt
adaptable adj ▷ adapt
adapted v ▷ adapt
adapter n ▷ adaptor
adapters n ▷ adaptor
adapting v ▷ adapt
adaptor, adapter n (pl -s) device for connecting several electrical appliances to a single socket
adaptors n ▷ adapt
adapts v ▷ adapt
add v (-s, -ing, -ed) combine (numbers or quantities)
added v ▷ add
addenda n ▷ addendum
addendum n (pl -da) addition
adder n (pl -s) small poisonous snake
adders n ▷ adder
addict n (pl -s) person who is unable to stop taking drugs > **addicted** adj
> **addiction** n (pl -s)
addicted adj ▷ addict
addiction n ▷ addict
addictions n ▷ addict
addicts n ▷ addict
adding v ▷ add
addition n (pl -s) adding
> **additional** adj > **additionally** adv
additional adj ▷ addition
additionally adv ▷ addition
additions n ▷ addition
additive n (pl -s) something added, esp. to a foodstuff, to improve it or prevent deterioration
additives n ▷ additive
addled adj confused or unable to think clearly
address n (pl -es) place where a person lives ▶ v (-es, -ing, -ed) mark the destination, as on an envelope

addressed v ▷ address
addresses n, v ▷ address
addressing v ▷ address
adds v ▷ add
adduce v (-ces, -cing, -ced) mention something as evidence or proof
adduced v ▷ adduce
adduces v ▷ adduce
adducing v ▷ adduce
adenoid n (pl -s) (usually plural) mass of tissue at the back of the throat
adenoids n ▷ adenoid
adept adj (-er, -est) ▷ n (pl -s) very skilful (person)
adepter adj ▷ adept
adeptest adj ▷ adept
adepts n ▷ adept
adequacies n ▷ adequate
adequacy n ▷ adequate
adequate adj sufficient, enough
> **adequately** adv ▷ adequacy n (pl -ies)
adequately adv ▷ adequate
adhere v (-res, -ring, -red) stick (to)
> **adherence** n (pl -ces)
adhered v ▷ adhere
adherence n ▷ adhere
adherences n ▷ adhere
adherent n (pl -s) devotee, follower
adherents n ▷ adherent
adheres v ▷ adhere
adhering v ▷ adhere
adhesion n (pl -s) sticking (to)
adhesions n ▷ adhesion
adhesive n (pl -s) substance used to stick things together ▶ adj able to stick to things
adhesives n ▷ adhesive
adieu interj lit farewell, goodbye
adipose adj of or containing fat
adjacent adj near or next (to)
adjoin v (-s, -ing, -ed) be next to
> **adjoining** adj
adjoined v ▷ adjoin
adjoining v, adj ▷ adjoin
adjoins v ▷ adjoin
adjourn v (-s, -ing, -ed) close (a court) at the end of a session
> **adjournment** n (pl -s)

adjourned v ▷ adjourn
adjourning v ▷ adjourn
adjournment n ▷ adjourn
adjournments n ▷ adjourn
adjourns v ▷ adjourn
adjudge v (-ges, -ging, -ged) declare (to be)
adjudged v ▷ adjudge
adjudges v ▷ adjudge
adjudging v ▷ adjudge
adjunct n (pl -s) subordinate or additional person or thing
adjuncts n ▷ adjunct
adjure v (-res, -ring, -red) command (to do)
adjured v ▷ adjure
adjures v ▷ adjure
adjuring v ▷ adjure
adjust v (-s, -ing, -ted) adapt to new conditions > **adjustable** adj
> **adjuster** n (pl -s) > **adjustment** n (pl -s)
adjustable adj ▷ adjust
adjusted v ▷ adjust
adjuster n ▷ adjust
adjusters n ▷ adjust
adjustment n ▷ adjust
adjustments n ▷ adjust
adjusts v ▷ adjust
adjutant n (pl -s) army officer in charge of routine administration
adjutants n ▷ adjutant
admin n (pl -s) informal administration
admins n ▷ admin
admirable adj ▷ admire
admirably adv ▷ admire
admiral n (pl -s) highest naval rank
admirals n ▷ admiral
admiration n ▷ admire
admirations n ▷ admire
admire v (-res, -ring, -red) regard with esteem and approval > **admirable** adj
> **admirably** adv > **admiration** n (pl -s) > **admirer** n (pl -s) > **admiring** adj
> **admiringly** adv
admired v ▷ admire
admirer n ▷ admire
admirers n ▷ admire

admires v ▷ admire
admiring v, adj ▷ admire
admiringly adv ▷ admire
admit v (-s, -tting, -tted) confess, acknowledge
admits v ▷ admit
admitted v ▷ admit
admitting v ▷ admit
admonish v (-es, -ing, -ed) reprove sternly > **admonition** n (pl -s)
admonished v ▷ admonish
admonishes n ▷ admonish
admonishing v ▷ admonish
admonition n ▷ admonish
admonitions n ▷ admonish
ado n (pl -s) lit fuss, trouble
adobe n (pl -s) sun-dried brick
adobes n ▷ adobe
adopt v (-s, -ing, -ed) take (someone else's child) as one's own > **adoption** n (pl -s)
adopted v ▷ adopt
adopting v ▷ adopt
adoption n ▷ adopt
adoptions n ▷ adopt
adoptive adj related by adoption
adopts v ▷ adopt
adorable adj ▷ adore
adoration n ▷ adore
adorations n ▷ adore
adore v (-res, -ring, -red) love intensely > **adorable** adj > **adoration** n (pl -s) > **adoring** adj > **adoringly** adv
adored v ▷ adore
adores v ▷ adore
adoring v, adj ▷ adore
adoringly adv ▷ adore
adorn v (-s, -ing, -ed) decorate, embellish > **adornment** n (pl -s)
adorned v ▷ adorn
adorning v ▷ adorn
adornment n ▷ adorn
adornments n ▷ adorn
adorns v ▷ adorn
ados n ▷ ado
adrenal adj near the kidneys
adrift adj, adv drifting
adroit adj quick and skilful

admires *v* ▷ admire
> **adroitly** adv > **adroitness** n
adroitly adv ▷ adroit
adroitness n ▷ adroit
ads n ▷ ad
adsorb v (-s, -ing, -ed) (of a gas or vapour) condense and form a thin film on a surface > **adsorption** n (pl -s)
adsorbed v ▷ adsorb
adsorbing v ▷ adsorb
adsorbs v ▷ adsorb
adsorption n ▷ adsorb
adsorptions n ▷ adsorb
adult adj fully grown, mature ▶ n (pl -s) adult person or animal > **adulthood** n (pl -s)
adulterer n ▷ adultery
adulterers n ▷ adultery
adulteress n ▷ adultery
adulteresses n ▷ adultery
adulteries n ▷ adultery
adulterous adj ▷ adultery
adultery n (pl -teries) sexual unfaithfulness of a husband or wife > **adulterer** n (pl -s) > **adulteress** n (pl -es) > **adulterous** adj
adulthood n ▷ adult
adulthoods n ▷ adult
adults n ▷ adult
advance v (-ces, -cing, -ced) go or bring forward ▶ n (pl -s) forward movement ▶ adj done or happening before an event
advanced adj at a late stage in development ▶ v ▷ advance
advances v, n ▷ advance
advancing v ▷ advance
advent n (pl -s) arrival
advents n ▷ advent
adverb n (pl -s) word that adds information about a verb, adjective, or other adverb > **adverbial** adj
adverbial adj ▷ adverb
adverbs n ▷ adverb
adverse adj unfavourable
> **adversely** adv
adversely adv ▷ adverse
advert n (pl -s) informal advertisement
adverts n ▷ advert

advice n (pl -s) recommendation as to what to do

advices n ▷ advice

advise v (-ses, -sing, -sed) offer advice to

advised adj considered, thought-out ▶ v ▷ advise

adviser, advisor n (pl -s) person who offers advice, e.g. on careers to students or school pupils

advisers n ▷ adviser

advises v ▷ advise

advising v ▷ advise

advisor n ▷ adviser

advisors n ▷ adviser

advisory adj giving advice

advocaat n (pl -s) liqueur with a raw egg base

advocaats n ▷ advocaat

advocacies n ▷ advocate

advocacy n ▷ advocate

advocate v (-tes, -ting, -ted) propose or recommend ▶ n (pl -s) person who publicly supports a cause >**advocacy** n (pl -cies)

advocated v ▷ advocate

advocates v, n ▷ advocate

advocating v ▷ advocate

adz n ▷ adze

adze, adz n (pl adzes) tool with an arched blade at right angles to the handle

adzes n ▷ adze

ae adj. Ae is a Scots word that means **one**. This is a useful word to remember when you want to form words in two directions at once. Ae scores 2 points.

aegis n (pl -es) sponsorship, protection

aegises n ▷ aegis

aeon n (pl -s) immeasurably long period of time

aeons n ▷ aeon

aerate v (-tes, -ting, -ted) put gas into (a liquid), as when making a fizzy drink >**aeration** n (pl -s)

aerated v ▷ aerate

aerates v ▷ aerate

aerating v ▷ aerate

aeration n ▷ aerate

aerations n ▷ aerate

aerial adj in, from, or operating in the air ▶ n (pl -ls) metal pole, wire, etc, for receiving or transmitting radio or TV signals

aerials n ▷ aerial

aerobic adj ▷ aerobics

aerobics n exercises designed to increase the amount of oxygen in the blood >**aerobic** adj

aerofoil n (pl -s) part of an aircraft, such as the wing, designed to give lift

aerofoils n ▷ aerofoil

aerogram n (pl -s) airmail letter on a single sheet of paper that seals to form an envelope

aerograms n ▷ aerogram

aerosol n (pl -s) pressurized can from which a substance can be dispensed as a fine spray

aerosols n ▷ aerosol

aesthete n (pl -s) person who has or affects an extravagant love of art >**aestheticism** n (pl -s)

aesthetes n ▷ aesthete

aestheticism n ▷ aesthete

aestheticisms n ▷ aesthete

aether n (pl -s) ▷ ether

aethers n ▷ aether

aetiology n (pl -gies) ▷ etiology

afar adv from or at a great distance

affabilities n ▷ affable

affability n ▷ affable

affable adj friendly and easy to talk to >**affably** adv >**affability** n (pl -ties)

affably adv ▷ affable

affair n (pl -s) event or happening

affairs n ▷ affair

affect[1] v (-s, -ing, -ed) act on, influence

affect[2] v (-s, -ing, -ed) put on a show of

affected adj displaying affectation ▶ v ▷ affect[1, 2]

affecting v ▷ affect[1, 2]

affects v ▷ affect[1, 2]

affinities n ▷ affinity

affinity n (pl -ties) close connection or liking

affirm v (-s, -ing, -ed) declare to be true >**affirmation** n (pl -s)

affirmation n ▷ affirm

affirmations n ▷ affirm

affirmed v ▷ affirm

affirming v ▷ affirm

affirms v ▷ affirm

affix v (-xes, -xing, -xed) attach or fasten ▶ n (pl -xes) word or syllable added to a word to change its meaning

affixed v ▷ affix

affixes v, n ▷ affix

affixing v ▷ affix

afflict v (-s, -ing, -ed) give pain or grief to >**affliction** n (pl -s)

afflicted v ▷ afflict

afflicting v ▷ afflict

affliction n ▷ afflict

afflictions n ▷ afflict

afflicts v ▷ afflict

affluent adj having plenty of money

afford v (-s, -ing, -ed) have enough money to buy >**affordable** adj

affordable adj ▷ afford

afforded v ▷ afford

affording v ▷ afford

affords v ▷ afford

afforest v (-s, -ing, -ed) plant trees on >**afforestation** n (pl -s)

afforestation n ▷ afforest

afforestations n ▷ afforest

afforested v ▷ afforest

afforesting v ▷ afforest

afforests v ▷ afforest

affray n (pl -s) BRIT, AUST & NZ LAW noisy fight, brawl

affrays n ▷ affray

affront v (-s, -ing, -ed) ▶ n (pl -s) insult

affronted v ▷ affront

affronting v ▷ affront

affronts v, n ▷ affront

afghan adj of Afghanistan or its language

afield adv far away

aflame adj burning

afloat adv, adj floating

afoot adv, adj happening, in operation

afraid adj frightened

afresh adv again, anew

aft adv at or towards the rear of a ship or aircraft

after prep following in time or place ▶ conj at a later time than ▶ adv at a later time

afters pl n BRIT informal dessert

again adv once more

against prep in opposition or contrast to

agape adj (of the mouth) wide open

agaric n (pl -s) fungus with gills on the underside of the cap, such as a mushroom

agarics n ▷ agaric

agate n (pl -s) semiprecious form of quartz with striped colouring

agates n ▷ agate

age n (pl -s) length of time a person or thing has existed ▶ v (-s, ageing or aging, -d) make or grow old >**ageing, aging** n (pl -s) adj

aged v, adj old

ageing v, n adj ▷ age

ageings n ▷ age

ageless adj apparently never growing old

agencies n ▷ agency

agency n (pl -cies) organization providing a service

agenda n (pl -s) list of things to be dealt with, esp. at a meeting

agendas n ▷ agenda

agent n (pl -s) person acting on behalf of another

agents n ▷ agent

ages n, v ▷ age

aggro n (pl -s) BRIT, AUST & NZ slang aggressive behaviour

aggros n ▷ aggro

aghast adj overcome with amazement or horror

agile adj (-r, -st) nimble, quick-moving >**agility** n (pl -ties)

agiler adj ▷ agile

agilest adj ▷ agile
agilities n ▷ agile
agility n ▷ agile
aging v, n adj ▷ age
agings n ▷ age
agitate v (-tes, -ting, -ted) disturb or excite > **agitation** n (pl -s) > **agitator** n (pl -s)
agitated adj ▷ agitate
agitates v ▷ agitate
agitating v ▷ agitate
agitation n ▷ agitate
agitations n ▷ agitate
agitator n ▷ agitate
agitators n ▷ agitate
aglow adj glowing
agnostic n (pl -s) person who believes that it is impossible to know whether God exists ▶ adj of agnostics > **agnosticism** n (pl -s)
agnosticism n ▷ agnostic
agnosticisms n ▷ agnostic
agnostics n ▷ agnostic
ago adv in the past
agog adj eager or curious
agonies n ▷ agony
agonize v (-zes, -zing, -zed) worry greatly > **agonizing** adj
agonized v ▷ agonize
agonizes v ▷ agonize
agonizing v, adj ▷ agonize
agony n (pl -nies) extreme physical or mental pain
agrarian adj of land or agriculture
agree v (-s, -ing, -d) be of the same opinion
agreed v ▷ agree
agreeing v ▷ agree
agrees v ▷ agree
agronomies n ▷ agronomy
agronomist n ▷ agronomy
agronomists n ▷ agronomy
agronomy n (pl -mies) science of soil management and crop production > **agronomist** n (pl -s)
aground adv onto the bottom of shallow water
ague n (pl -s) old-fashioned periodic fever with shivering
agues n ▷ ague

ah interj. Ah is a sound people make to show pleasure or pain. Ah scores 5 points, and is a good word to form as a result of playing a longer word.
ahead adv in front
ahoy interj shout used at sea to attract attention
ai n (**ais**). An ai is a three-toed sloth. Although ai only scores 2 points, it's a useful word to remember when you're trying to form several words at once.
aid v (-s, -ing, -ed) ▶ n (pl -s) (give) assistance or support
aide n (pl -s) assistant
aided v ▷ aid
aides n ▷ aide
aiding v ▷ aid
aids v, n ▷ aid
ail v (-s, -ing, -ed) trouble, afflict
ailed v ▷ ail
aileron n (pl -s) movable flap on an aircraft wing which controls rolling
ailerons n ▷ aileron
ailing adj sickly ▶ v ▷ ail
ailment n (pl -s) illness
ailments n ▷ ailment
ails v ▷ ail
aim v (-s, -ing, -ed) point (a weapon or missile) or direct (a blow or remark) at a target ▶ n (pl -s) aiming
aimed v ▷ aim
aiming v ▷ aim
aimless adj having no purpose > **aimlessly** adv
aimlessly adv ▷ aimless
aims v, n ▷ aim
air n (pl -s) mixture of gases forming the earth's atmosphere ▶ v (-s, -ing, -ed) make known publicly
airborne adj carried by air
airbrush n (pl -es) atomizer spraying paint by compressed air
airbrushes n ▷ airbrush
aircraft n any machine that flies, such as an aeroplane

aired v ▷ **air**

airfield n (pl **-s**) place where aircraft can land and take off

airfields n ▷ **airfield**

airier adj ▷ **airy**

airiest adj ▷ **airy**

airily adv ▷ **airy**

airing n (pl **-s**) exposure to air for drying or ventilation ▶ v ▷ **air**

airings n ▷ **airing**

airless adj stuffy

airlift n (pl **-s**) transport of troops or cargo by aircraft when other routes are blocked ▶ v (**-s, -ing, -ed**) transport by airlift

airlifted v ▷ **airlift**

airlifting v ▷ **airlift**

airlifts n, v ▷ **airlift**

airline n (pl **-s**) company providing scheduled flights for passengers and cargo

airliner n (pl **-s**) large passenger aircraft

airliners n ▷ **airliner**

airlines n ▷ **airline**

airlock n (pl **-s**) air bubble blocking the flow of liquid in a pipe

airlocks n ▷ **airlock**

airmail n (pl **-s**) system of sending mail by aircraft

airmails n ▷ **airmail**

airman n (pl **airmen**) member of the air force

airmen n ▷ **airman**

airplay n (pl **-s**) broadcast performances of a record on radio

airplays n ▷ **airplay**

airport n (pl **-s**) airfield for civilian aircraft, with facilities for aircraft maintenance and passengers

airports n ▷ **airport**

airs n, v ▷ **air**

airship n (pl **-s**) lighter-than-air self-propelled aircraft

airships n ▷ **airship**

airspace n (pl **-s**) atmosphere above a country, regarded as its territory

airspaces n ▷ **airspace**

airstrip n (pl **-s**) cleared area where aircraft can take off and land

airstrips n ▷ **airstrip**

airtight adj sealed so that air cannot enter

airy adj (**-rier, -riest**) well-ventilated > **airily** adv

aisle n (pl **-s**) passageway separating seating areas in a church, theatre, etc, or row of shelves in a supermarket

aisles n ▷ **aisle**

ajar adj, adv (of a door) partly open

akimbo adv with hands on hips and elbows outwards

akin adj similar, related

■ **al** conj. Al is an old word for **if** or **although**. Al scores 2 points.

alacrities n ▷ **alacrity**

alacrity n (pl **-ies**) speed, eagerness

alarm n (pl **-s**) sudden fear caused by awareness of danger ▶ v (**-s, -ing, -ed**) fill with fear > **alarming** adj

alarmed v ▷ **alarm**

alarming v, adj ▷ **alarm**

alarmist n (pl **-s**) person who alarms others needlessly

alarmists n ▷ **alarmist**

alarms n, v ▷ **alarm**

alas adv unfortunately, regrettably

albeit conj even though

albino n (pl **-nos**) person or animal with white skin and hair and pink eyes

albinos n ▷ **albino**

album n (pl **-s**) book with blank pages for keeping photographs or stamps in

albumen n (pl **-s**) egg white

albumens n ▷ **albumen**

albumin n (pl **-s**) protein found in blood plasma, egg white, milk, and muscle

albumins n ▷ **albumin**

albums n ▷ **album**

alchemies n ▷ **alchemy**

alchemist n ▷ **alchemy**

alchemists n ▷ **alchemy**

alchemy n (pl **-ies**) medieval form of chemistry concerned with trying to turn base metals into gold and to find the elixir of life ▷ **alchemist** n (pl **-s**)

alcohol n (pl **-s**) colourless flammable liquid present in intoxicating drinks

alcohols n ▷ **alcohol**

alcopop n (pl **-s**) BRIT, AUST & S AFR informal alcoholic drink that tastes like a soft drink

alcopops n ▷ **alcopop**

alcove n (pl **-s**) recess in the wall of a room

alcoves n ▷ **alcove**

aldehyde n (pl **-s**) one of a group of chemical compounds derived from alcohol by oxidation

aldehydes n ▷ **aldehyde**

alder n (pl **-s**) tree related to the birch

alderman n (pl **-men**) formerly, senior member of a local council

aldermen n ▷ **alderman**

alders n ▷ **alder**

ale n (pl **-s**) kind of beer

alert adj (**-er, -est**) watchful, attentive ▶ n (pl **-s**) warning of danger ▶ v (**-s, -ing, -ed**) warn of danger ▶ **alertness** n (pl **-es**)

alerted v ▷ **alert**

alerter adj ▷ **alert**

alertest adj ▷ **alert**

alerting v ▷ **alert**

alertness n ▷ **alert**

alertnesses n ▷ **alert**

alerts n, v ▷ **alert**

ales n ▷ **ale**

alfalfa n (pl **-s**) kind of plant used to feed livestock

alfalfas n ▷ **alfalfa**

alfresco adv, adj in the open air

alga n (pl **-e**) (usually plural) plant which lives in or near water and has no true stems, leaves, or roots

algae n ▷ **alga**

algebra n (pl **-s**) branch of mathematics using symbols to represent numbers > **algebraic** adj

algebraic adj ▷ **algebra**

algebras n ▷ **algebra**

alias adv also known as ▶ n (pl **-ses**) false name

aliases n ▷ **alias**

alibi n (pl **-s**) plea of being somewhere else when a crime was committed

alibis n ▷ **alibi**

alien adj foreign ▶ n (pl **-s**) foreigner

alienate v (**-tes, -ting, -ted**) cause to become hostile ▶ **alienation** n (pl **-s**)

alienated v ▷ **alienate**

alienates v ▷ **alienate**

alienating v ▷ **alienate**

alienation n ▷ **alienate**

alienations n ▷ **alienate**

aliens n ▷ **alien**

alight¹ v (**-s, -ing, -ed**) step out of (a vehicle)

alight² adj on fire

alighted v ▷ **alight¹**

alighting v ▷ **alight¹**

alights v ▷ **alight¹**

align v (**-s, -ing, -ed**) bring (a person or group) into agreement with the policy of another ▶ **alignment** n (pl **-s**)

aligned v ▷ **align**

aligning v ▷ **align**

alignment n ▷ **align**

alignments n ▷ **align**

aligns v ▷ **align**

alike adj like, similar ▶ adv in the same way

alimonies n ▷ **alimony**

alimony n (pl **-nies**) allowance paid under a court order to a separated or divorced spouse

aliquot MATHS adj of or denoting an exact divisor of a number ▶ n (pl **-s**) exact divisor

aliquots n ▷ **aliquot**

alive adj living, in existence

alkali n (pl **-s**) substance which combines with acid and neutralizes it to form a salt > **alkaline** adj
▶ **alkalinity** n (pl **-ties**)

alkaline adj ▷ **alkali**

alkalinities n ▷ **alkali**

alkalinity n ▷ **alkali**

alkalis n ▷ **alkali**

alkaloid n (pl **-s**) any of a group of organic compounds containing nitrogen

alkaloids n ▷ **alkaloid**

all adj whole quantity or number (of) ▶ adv wholly, entirely

allay v (-s, -ing, -ed) reduce (fear or anger)

allayed v ▷ **allay**

allaying v ▷ **allay**

allays v ▷ **allay**

allege v (-ges, -ging, -ged) state without proof > **alleged** adj
> **allegedly** adv

alleged v, adj ▷ **allege**

allegedly adv ▷ **allege**

alleges v ▷ **allege**

alleging v ▷ **allege**

allegorical adj ▷ **allegory**

allegories n ▷ **allegory**

allegory n (pl -ries) story with an underlying meaning as well as the literal one > **allegorical** adj

allegro n (pl -s) ▶ adv MUSIC (piece to be played) in a brisk lively manner

allegros n ▷ **allegro**

allergen n (pl -s) substance capable of causing an allergic reaction

allergens n ▷ **allergen**

allergic adj having or caused by an allergy

allergies n ▷ **allergy**

allergy n (pl -gies) extreme sensitivity to a substance, which causes the body to react to it

alley n (pl -s) narrow street or path

alleys n ▷ **alley**

alliance n (pl -s) state of being allied

alliances n ▷ **alliance**

allied v, adj ▷ **ally**

allies n, v ▷ **ally**

allocate v (-tes, -ting, -ted) assign to someone or for a particular purpose
> **allocation** n (pl -s)

allocated v ▷ **allocate**

allocates v ▷ **allocate**

allocating v ▷ **allocate**

allocation n ▷ **allocate**

allocations n ▷ **allocate**

allot v (-s, -tting, -tted) assign as a

share or for a particular purpose

allots v ▷ **allot**

allotted v ▷ **allot**

allotting v ▷ **allot**

allow v (-s, -ing, -ed) permit
> **allowable** adj

allowable adj ▷ **allow**

allowed v ▷ **allow**

allowing v ▷ **allow**

allows v ▷ **allow**

alloy n (pl -s) mixture of two or more metals ▶ v (-s, -ing, -ed) mix (metals)

alloyed v ▷ **alloy**

alloying v ▷ **alloy**

alloys n, v ▷ **alloy**

allspice n (pl -s) spice made from the berries of a tropical American tree

allspices n ▷ **allspice**

allude v (-des, -ding, -ded) (foll. by to) refer indirectly to

alluded v ▷ **allude**

alludes v ▷ **allude**

alluding v ▷ **allude**

allure n (pl -s) attractiveness ▶ v (-s, -ing, -ed) entice or attract
> **alluring** adj

allured v ▷ **allure**

allures n, v ▷ **allure**

alluring v, adj ▷ **allure**

allusion n (pl -s) indirect reference
> **allusive** adj

allusions n ▷ **allusion**

allusive adj ▷ **allusion**

alluvial adj ▷ **alluvium**

alluvium n (pl -s) fertile soil deposited by flowing water ▶ **alluvial** adj

alluviums n ▷ **alluvium**

ally n (pl -lies) country, person, or group with an agreement to support another ▶ v (-lies, -lying, -lied) > **allied** adj

allying v ▷ **ally**

almanac n (pl -s) yearly calendar with detailed information on anniversaries, phases of the moon, etc

almanacs n ▷ **almanac**

almighty adj having absolute power

almond n (pl -s) edible oval-shaped nut which grows on a small tree

almonds n ▷ almond
almoner n (pl -s) BRIT formerly, a hospital social worker
almoners n ▷ almoner
almost adv very nearly
alms pl n old-fashioned gifts to the poor
aloe n (pl -s) plant with fleshy spiny leaves
aloes n ▷ aloe
aloft adv in the air
alone adj, adv without anyone or anything else
along prep over part or all the length of ▶ adv forward
aloof adj distant or haughty in manner > aloofness n (pl -es)
aloofness n ▷ aloof
aloofnesses n ▷ aloof
alopecia n (pl -s) loss of hair
alopecias n ▷ alopecia
aloud adv in an audible voice
alpaca n (pl -s) Peruvian llama
alpacas n ▷ alpaca
alpha n (pl -s) first letter in the Greek alphabet
alphabet n (pl -s) set of letters used in writing a language
alphabets n ▷ alphabet
alphas n ▷ alpha
alpine adj of high mountains ▶ n (pl -s) mountain plant
alpines n ▷ alpine
already adv before the present time
alright adj, interj all right
also adv in addition, too
altar n (pl -s) table used for Communion in Christian churches
altars n ▷ altar
alter v (-s, -ing, -ed) make or become different > alteration n (pl -s)
alteration n ▷ alter
alterations n ▷ alter
altered v ▷ alter
altering v ▷ alter
alters v ▷ alter
although conj despite the fact that
altitude n (pl -s) height above sea level
altitudes n ▷ altitude

alto n (pl -s) MUSIC (singer with) the highest adult male voice
altos n ▷ alto
altruism n (pl -s) unselfish concern for the welfare of others > altruistic adj > altruistically adv
altruisms n ▷ altruism
altruistic adj ▷ altruism
altruistically adv ▷ altruism
alumna ▷ alumnus
alumnae ▷ alumnus
alumni n ▷ alumnus
alumnus n (pl -ni) graduate of a college > alumna ▶ n fem (pl -nae)
always adv at all times
alyssum n (pl -s) garden plant with small yellow or white flowers
alyssums n ▷ alyssum
am v ▷ be
amalgam n (pl -s) blend or combination
amalgams n ▷ amalgam
amandla n S AFR political slogan calling for power to the Black population
amaranth n (pl -s) imaginary flower that never fades
amaranths n ▷ amaranth
amass v (-ses, -sing, -sed) collect or accumulate
amassed v ▷ amass
amasses v ▷ amass
amassing v ▷ amass
amateur n (pl -s) person who engages in a sport or activity as a pastime rather than as a profession
amateurs n ▷ amateur
amatory adj relating to romantic or sexual love
amaze v (-zes, -zing, -zed) surprise greatly, astound > amazing adj > amazingly adv > amazement n (pl -s)
amazed v ▷ amaze
amazement n ▷ amaze
amazements n ▷ amaze
amazes v ▷ amaze
amazing v, adj ▷ amaze
amazingly adv ▷ amaze

amazon n (pl -s) strong and powerful woman ▷ **amazonian** adj

amazonian adj ▷ **amazon**

amazons n ▷ **amazon**

amber n (pl -s) clear yellowish fossil resin ▶ adj brownish-yellow

ambers n ▷ **amber**

ambience n (pl -s) atmosphere of a place

ambiences n ▷ **ambience**

ambient adj surrounding

ambit n (pl -s) limits or boundary

ambition n (pl -s) desire for success > **ambitious** adj > **ambitiously** adv

ambitions n ▷ **ambition**

ambitious adj ▷ **ambition**

ambitiously adv ▷ **ambition**

ambits n ▷ **ambit**

amble v (-les, -ling, -led) walk at a leisurely pace ▶ n (pl -s) leisurely walk or pace

ambled v ▷ **amble**

ambles v, n ▷ **amble**

ambling v ▷ **amble**

ambrosia n (pl -s) MYTH food of the gods > **ambrosial** adj

ambrosial adj ▷ **ambrosia**

ambrosias n ▷ **ambrosia**

ambush n (pl -es) act of waiting in a concealed position to make a surprise attack ▶ v (-es, -ing, -ed) attack from a concealed position

ambushed v ▷ **ambush**

ambushes n, v ▷ **ambush**

ambushing v ▷ **ambush**

amen interj so be it: used at the end of a prayer

amenable adj likely or willing to cooperate

amend v (-s, -ing, -ed) make small changes to correct or improve (something) > **amendment** n (pl -s)

amended v ▷ **amend**

amending v ▷ **amend**

amendment n ▷ **amend**

amendments n ▷ **amend**

amends v ▷ **amend**

amenities n ▷ **amenity**

amenity n (pl -ties) useful or enjoyable feature

amethyst n (pl -s) bluish-violet variety of quartz used as a gemstone

amethysts n ▷ **amethyst**

amiabilities n ▷ **amiable**

amiability n ▷ **amiable**

amiable adj friendly, pleasant-natured > **amiably** adv > **amiability** n (pl -ties)

amiably adv ▷ **amiable**

amicable adj friendly > **amicably** adv

amicably adv ▷ **amicable**

amid, amidst prep in the middle of, among

amidst prep ▷ **amid**

amiss adv wrongly, badly ▶ adj wrong, faulty

amities n ▷ **amity**

amity n (pl -ties) friendship

ammeter n (pl -s) instrument for measuring electric current

ammeters n ▷ **ammeter**

ammonia n (pl -s) strong-smelling alkaline gas containing hydrogen and nitrogen

ammonias n ▷ **ammonia**

ammonite n (pl -s) fossilized spiral shell of an extinct sea creature

ammonites n ▷ **ammonite**

amnesia n (pl -s) loss of memory > **amnesiac** adj, n (pl -s)

amnesiac adj, n ▷ **amnesia**

amnesiacs n ▷ **amnesia**

amnesias n ▷ **amnesia**

amnesties n ▷ **amnesty**

amnesty n (pl -ties) general pardon for offences against a government

amoeba n (pl -bae, -bas) microscopic single-celled animal able to change its shape

amoebae n ▷ **amoeba**

amoebas n ▷ **amoeba**

amok adv in a violent frenzy

among, amongst prep in the midst of

amongst prep ▷ **among**

amoral adj without moral standards > **amorality** n (pl -ties)

amoralities n ▷ amoral
amorality n ▷ amoral
amorous adj feeling, showing, or relating to sexual love > **amorously** adv
amorously adv ▷ amorous
amortize v (-zes, -zing, -zed) pay off (a debt) gradually by periodic transfers to a sinking fund
amortized v ▷ amortize
amortizes v ▷ amortize
amortizing v ▷ amortize
amount n (pl -s) extent or quantity ▶ v (-s, -ing, -ed) (foll. by **to**) be equal or add up to
amounted v ▷ amount
amounting v ▷ amount
amounts n, v ▷ amount
amour n (pl -s) (secret) love affair
amours n ▷ amour
amp n (pl -s) ampere
ampere n (pl -s) basic unit of electric current
amperes n ▷ ampere
amphora n (pl -ae) two-handled ancient Greek or Roman jar
amphorae n ▷ amphora
ample adj (-r, -st) more than sufficient > **amply** adv
ampler adj ▷ ample
amplest adj ▷ ample
amplification n ▷ amplify
amplifications n ▷ amplify
amplified v ▷ amplify
amplifies v ▷ amplify
amplify v (-fies, -fying, -fied) increase the strength of (a current or sound signal) > **amplification** n (pl -s)
amplifying v ▷ amplify
amply adv ▷ ample
ampoule n (pl -s) small sealed glass vessel containing liquid for injection
ampoules n ▷ ampoule
amps n ▷ amp
amputate v (-tes, -ting, -ted) cut off (a limb or part of a limb) for medical reasons > **amputation** n (pl -s)
amputated v ▷ amputate
amputates v ▷ amputate

amputating v ▷ amputate
amputation n ▷ amputate
amputations n ▷ amputate
amuck adv ▷ amok
amulet n (pl -s) something carried or worn as a protection against evil
amulets n ▷ amulet
amuse v (-ses, -sing, -sed) cause to laugh or smile > **amusing** adj
amused v ▷ amuse
amuses v ▷ amuse
amusing v, adj ▷ amuse
an adj form of **a** used before vowels, and sometimes before **h**
anaconda n (pl -s) large S American snake which kills by constriction
anacondas n ▷ anaconda
anaemia n (pl -s) deficiency in the number of red blood cells
anaemias n ▷ anaemia
anaemic adj having anaemia
anagram n (pl -s) word or phrase made by rearranging the letters of another word or phrase
anagrams n ▷ anagram
anal adj of the anus
analogical adj ▷ analogy
analogies n ▷ analogy
analogue n (pl -s) something that is similar in some respects to something else ▶ adj displaying information by means of a dial
analogues n ▷ analogue
analogy n (pl -gies) similarity in some respects > **analogical** adj
analyse v (-ses, -sing, -sed) make an analysis of (something)
analysed v ▷ analyse
analyses v ▷ analyse ▶ n ▷ analysis
analysing v ▷ analyse
analysis n (pl -ses) separation of a whole into its parts for study and interpretation > **analytical, analytic** adj > **analytically** adv
analyst n (pl -s) person skilled in analysis
analysts n ▷ analyst
analytic adj ▷ analysis

analytical *adj* ▷ **analysis**

analytically *adv* ▷ **analysis**

anarchic *adj* ▷ **anarchy**

anarchies *n* ▷ **anarchy**

anarchy *n* (*pl* **-ies**) lawlessness and disorder > **anarchic** *adj*

anathema *n* (*pl* **-s**) detested person or thing

anathemas *n* ▷ **anathema**

anatomical *adj* ▷ **anatomy**

anatomically *adv* ▷ **anatomy**

anatomies *n* ▷ **anatomy**

anatomy *n* (*pl* **-mies**) science of the structure of the body > **anatomical** *adj* > **anatomically** *adv*

ancestor *n* (*pl* **-s**) person from whom one is descended > **ancestral** *adj*

ancestors *n* ▷ **ancestor**

ancestral *adj* ▷ **ancestor**

ancestries *n* ▷ **ancestry**

ancestry *n* (*pl* **-ries**) lineage or descent

anchor *n* (*pl* **-s**) heavy hooked device attached to a boat by a cable and dropped overboard to fasten the ship to the sea bottom ▷ *v* (**-s, -ing, -ed**) fasten with or as if with an anchor

anchored *v* ▷ **anchor**

anchoring *v* ▷ **anchor**

anchors *n, v* ▷ **anchor**

anchovies *n* ▷ **anchovy**

anchovy *n* (*pl* **-vies**) small strong-tasting fish

ancient *adj* dating from very long ago

ancients *pl n* people who lived very long ago

and *conj* in addition to

andante *n* (*pl* **-s**) ▷ *adv* MUSIC (piece to be played) moderately slowly

andantes *n* ▷ **andante**

andiron *n* (*pl* **-s**) iron stand for supporting logs in a fireplace

andirons *n* ▷ **andiron**

android *n* (*pl* **-s**) robot resembling a human

androids *n* ▷ **android**

anecdotal *adj* ▷ **anecdote**

anecdote *n* (*pl* **-s**) short amusing account of an incident > **anecdotal** *adj*

anecdotes *n* ▷ **anecdote**

anemone *n* (*pl* **-s**) plant with white, purple, or red flowers

anemones *n* ▷ **anemone**

aneurism *n* ▷ **aneurysm**

aneurisms *n* ▷ **aneurysm**

aneurysm, aneurism *n* (*pl* **-s**) permanent swelling of a blood vessel

aneurysms *n* ▷ **aneurysm**

anew *adv* once more

angel *n* (*pl* **-s**) spiritual being believed to be an attendant or messenger of God > **angelic** *adj* > **angelically** *adv*

angelic *adj* ▷ **angel**

angelica *n* (*pl* **-s**) aromatic plant

angelically *adv* ▷ **angel**

angelicas *n* ▷ **angelica**

angels *n* ▷ **angel**

angelus *n* (*pl* **-es**) (in the Roman Catholic Church) prayers recited in the morning, at midday, and in the evening

angeluses *n* ▷ **angelus**

anger *n* (*pl* **-s**) fierce displeasure or extreme annoyance ▷ *v* (**-s, -ing, -ed**) make (someone) angry

angered *v* ▷ **anger**

angering *v* ▷ **anger**

angers *n, v* ▷ **anger**

angina *n* (*pl* **-s**) heart disorder causing sudden severe chest pains

anginas *n* ▷ **angina**

angle¹ *n* (*pl* **-s**) space between or shape formed by two lines or surfaces that meet ▷ *v* (**-s, -ing, -ed**) bend or place (something) at an angle

angle² *v* (**-s, -ing, -ed**) fish with a hook and line ▷ **angling** ▷ **angle¹, ²**

angled *v* ▷ **angle¹, ²**

angler *n* (*pl* **-s**) person who fishes with a hook and line

anglers *n* ▷ **angler**

angles *n* ▷ **angle¹** ▷ *v* ▷ **angle¹, ²**

angling *n* ▷ **angle²** ▷ *v* ▷ **angle¹, ²**

anglings *n* ▷ **angle²**

angora *n* (*pl* **-s**) variety of goat, cat, or rabbit with long silky hair

angoras *n* ▷ **angora**

angrier *adj* ▷ **angry**

angriest adj ▷ angry

angrily adv ▷ angry

angry adj (**-rier, -riest**) full of anger
>**angrily** adv

angst n (pl **-s**) feeling of anxiety

angstrom n (pl **-s**) unit of length used
to measure wavelengths

angstroms n ▷ angstrom

angsts n ▷ angst

anguish n (pl **-es**) great mental pain
>**anguished** adj

anguished adj ▷ anguish

anguishes n ▷ anguish

angular adj (of a person) lean and bony
>**angularity** n (pl **-ties**)

angularities n ▷ angular

angularity n ▷ angular

aniline n (pl **-s**) colourless oily liquid
obtained from coal tar and used for
making dyes, plastics, and explosives

anilines n ▷ aniline

animal n (pl **-s**) living creature with
specialized sense organs and capable
of voluntary motion, esp. one other
than a human being ▶ adj of animals

animals n ▷ animal

animate v (**-tes, -ting, -ted**) give life
to ▶ adj having life >**animated** adj
>**animator** n (pl **-s**)

animated v, adj ▷ animate

animates v ▷ animate

animating v ▷ animate

animator n ▷ animate

animators n ▷ animate

animism n (pl **-s**) belief that natural
objects possess souls >**animist** n (pl
-s), adj >**animistic** adj

animisms n ▷ animism

animist n, adj ▷ animism

animistic adj ▷ animism

animists n ▷ animism

animus n (pl **-es**) hatred, animosity

animuses n ▷ animus

anion n (pl **-s**) ion with negative charge

anions n ▷ anion

anise n (pl **-s**) plant with liquorice-
flavoured seeds

aniseed n (pl **-s**) liquorice-flavoured

seeds of the anise plant

aniseeds n ▷ aniseed

anises n ▷ anise

ankle n (pl **-s**) joint between the foot
and leg

ankles n ▷ ankle

anklet n (pl **-s**) ornamental chain worn
round the ankle

anklets n ▷ anklet

annal n (pl **-s**) yearly record of events

annals n ▷ annal

anneal v (**-s, -ing, -ed**) toughen (metal
or glass) by heating and slow cooling

annealed v ▷ anneal

annealing v ▷ anneal

anneals v ▷ anneal

annelid n (pl **-s**) worm with a
segmented body, such as an
earthworm

annelids n ▷ annelid

annex v (**-es, -ing, -ed**) seize (territory)
>**annexation** n (pl **-s**)

annexation n ▷ annex

annexations n ▷ annex

annexe n (pl **-s**) extension to a building

annexed v ▷ annex

annexes v ▷ annex ▶ n ▷ annexe

annexing v ▷ annex

annotate v (**-tes, -ting, -ted**)
add notes to (a written work)
>**annotation** n (pl **-s**)

annotated v ▷ annotate

annotates v ▷ annotate

annotating v ▷ annotate

annotation n ▷ annotate

annotations n ▷ annotate

announce v (**-ces, -cing, -ced**) make
known publicly >**announcement** n
(pl **-s**)

announced v ▷ announce

announcement n ▷ announce

announcements n ▷ announce

announces v ▷ announce

announcing v ▷ announce

annoy v (**-s, -ing, -ed**) irritate or
displease >**annoyance** n (pl **-s**)

annoyance n ▷ annoy

annoyances n ▷ annoy

annoyed v ▷ annoy
annoying v ▷ annoy
annoys v ▷ annoy
annual adj happening once a year ▶ n (pl **-s**) plant that completes its life cycle in a year ▶ **annually** adv
annually adv ▷ annual
annuals n ▷ annual
annuities n ▷ annuity
annuity n (pl **-ties**) fixed sum paid every year
annul v (**-ls, -lling, -lled**) declare (something, esp. a marriage) invalid ▷ **annulment** n ▷ annul
annular adj ring-shaped
annulled v ▷ annul
annulling v ▷ annul
annulment n ▷ annul
annulments n ▷ annul
annuls v ▷ annul
anode n (pl **-s**) ELECTRICITY positive electrode in a battery, valve, etc
anodes n ▷ anode
anodize v (**-zes, -zing, -zed**) coat (metal) with a protective oxide film by electrolysis
anodized v ▷ anodize
anodizes v ▷ anodize
anodizing v ▷ anodize
anodyne n (pl **-s**) something that relieves pain or distress ▶ adj relieving pain or distress
anodynes n ▷ anodyne
anoint v (**-s, -ing, -ed**) smear with oil as a sign of consecration
anointed v ▷ anoint
anointing v ▷ anoint
anoints v ▷ anoint
anomalies n ▷ anomaly
anomalous adj ▷ anomaly
anomaly n (pl **-lies**) something that deviates from the normal, irregularity ▶ **anomalous** adj
anon adv obs in a short time, soon
anorak n (pl **-s**) light waterproof hooded jacket
anoraks n ▷ anorak
anorexia n (pl **-s**) psychological

disorder characterized by fear of becoming fat and refusal to eat ▷ **anorexic** adj, n
anorexias n ▷ anorexia
anorexic n ▷ anorexia
another adj, pron one more
answer n (pl **-s**) reply to a question, request, letter, etc ▶ v (**-s, -ing, -ed**) give an answer (to)
answered v ▷ answer
answering v ▷ answer
answers n, v ▷ answer
ant n (pl **-s**) small insect living in highly organized colonies
antacid n (pl **-s**) substance that counteracts acidity, esp. in the stomach
antacids n ▷ antacid
ante n (pl **-s**) player's stake in poker ▶ v (**-tes, -teing, -ted** or **-teed**) place (one's stake) in poker
anteater n (pl **-s**) mammal which feeds on ants by means of a long snout
anteaters n ▷ anteater
anted v ▷ ante
antedate v (**-tes, -ting, -ted**) precede in time
antedated v ▷ antedate
antedates v ▷ antedate
antedating v ▷ antedate
anteed v ▷ ante
anteing v ▷ ante
antelope n (pl **-s**) deerlike mammal with long legs and horns
antelopes n ▷ antelope
antenna n insect's feeler (pl **-e**); aerial (pl **-s**)
antennae n ▷ antenna
antennas n ▷ antenna
anterior adj to the front
anteroom n (pl **-s**) small room leading into a larger one, often used as a waiting room
anterooms n ▷ anteroom
antes n, v ▷ ante
anthem n (pl **-s**) song of loyalty, esp. to a country
anthems n ▷ anthem

anther n (pl -s) part of a flower's stamen containing pollen

anthers n ▷ anther

anthraces n ▷ anthrax

anthrax n (pl -thraces) dangerous disease of cattle and sheep, communicable to humans

antibodies n ▷ antibody

antibody n (pl -dies) protein produced in the blood, which destroys bacteria

antics pl n absurd acts or postures

antidote n (pl -s) substance that counteracts a poison

antidotes n ▷ antidote

antigen n (pl -s) substance, usu. a toxin, causing the blood to produce antibodies

antigens n ▷ antigen

antihero n (pl -roes) central character in a book, film, etc, who lacks the traditional heroic virtues

antiheroes n ▷ antihero

antimonies n ▷ antimony

antimony n (pl -ies) CHEM brittle silvery-white metallic element

antiphon n (pl -s) hymn sung in alternate parts by two groups of singers > antiphonal adj

antiphonal adj ▷ antiphon

antiphons n ▷ antiphon

antique n (pl -s) object of an earlier period, valued for its beauty, workmanship, or age ▸ adj made in an earlier period

antiques n ▷ antique

antler n (pl -s) branched horn of male deer

antlers n ▷ antler

antonym n (pl -s) word that means the opposite of another

antonyms n ▷ antonym

ants n ▷ ant

anus n (pl -es) opening at the end of the alimentary canal, through which faeces are discharged

anuses n ▷ anus

anvil n (pl -s) heavy iron block on which metals are hammered into particular shapes

anvils n ▷ anvil

anxieties n ▷ anxiety

anxiety n (pl -ties) state of being anxious

anxious adj worried and tense > anxiously adv

anxiously adv ▷ anxious

any adj, pron one or some, no matter which ▸ adv at all > anything pron

anybody pron anyone

anyhow adv anyway

anyone pron any person

anything pron ▷ any

anyway adv at any rate, nevertheless

anywhere adv in, at, or to any place

aorta n (pl -s) main artery of the body, carrying oxygen-rich blood from the heart

aortas n ▷ aorta

apace adv lit swiftly

apart adv to or in pieces

apathetic adj ▷ apathy

apathies n ▷ apathy

apathy n (pl -thies) lack of interest or enthusiasm > apathetic adj

ape n (pl -s) tailless monkey such as the chimpanzee or gorilla ▸ v (apes, aping, aped) imitate

aped v ▷ ape

aperient adj having a mild laxative effect ▸ n mild laxative

aperients n ▷ aperient

aperitif n (pl -s) alcoholic drink taken before a meal

aperitifs n ▷ aperitif

aperture n (pl -s) opening or hole

apertures n ▷ aperture

apes n, v ▷ ape

apex n (pl -es) highest point

apexes n ▷ apex

aphasia n (pl -s) disorder of the central nervous system that affects the ability to speak and understand words

aphasias n ▷ aphasia

aphid , aphis n (pl aphids) small insect which sucks the sap from plants

aphids n ▷ aphid

aphis n ▷ aphid
aphorism n (pl **-s**) short clever saying expressing a general truth
aphorisms n ▷ aphorism
apiaries n ▷ apiary
apiary n (pl **-ries**) place where bees are kept
apiece adv each
aping v ▷ ape
aplomb n (pl **-s**) calm self-possession
aplombs n ▷ aplomb
apogee n (pl **-s**) point of the moon's or a satellite's orbit that is farthest from the earth
apogees n ▷ apogee
apologies n ▷ apology
apology n (pl **-gies**) expression of regret for wrongdoing
apoplexies n ▷ apoplexy
apoplexy n (pl **-xies**) MED stroke
apostasies n ▷ apostasy
apostasy n (pl **-sies**) abandonment of one's religious faith or other belief ▶ **apostate** n (pl **-s**) adj
apostate n, adj ▷ apostasy
apostates n ▷ apostasy
apostle n (pl **-s**) ardent supporter of a cause or movement ▶ **apostolic** adj
apostles n ▷ apostle
apostolic adj ▷ apostle
appal v (**-s**, **-lling**, **-lled**) dismay, terrify
appalled v ▷ appal
appalling v ▷ appal
appals v ▷ appal
apparel n (pl **-s**) old-fashioned clothing
apparels n ▷ apparel
apparent adj readily seen, obvious ▶ **apparently** adv
apparently adv ▷ apparent
appeal v (**-s**, **-ing**, **-ed**) make an earnest request ▶ n (pl **-s**) earnest request ▷ **appealing** adj
appealed v ▷ appeal
appealing v, adj ▷ appeal
appeals v, n ▷ appeal
appear v (**-s**, **-ing**, **-ed**) become visible or present
appeared v ▷ appear

appearing v ▷ appear
appears v ▷ appear
appease v (**-s**, **-ing**, **-ed**) pacify (a person) by yielding to his or her demands ▷ **appeasement** n (pl **-s**)
appeased v ▷ appease
appeasement n ▷ appeal
appeasements n ▷ appeal
appeases v ▷ appease
appeasing v ▷ appease
append v (**-s**, **-ing**, **-ed**) join on, add
appended v ▷ append
appendices n ▷ appendix
appending v ▷ append
appendix n (pl **-dices**, **-dixes**) separate additional material at the end of a book
appendixes n ▷ appendix
appends v ▷ append
appetite n (pl **-s**) desire for food or drink
appetites n ▷ appetite
applaud v (**-s**, **-ing**, **-ed**) show approval of by clapping one's hands
applauded v ▷ applaud
applauding v ▷ applaud
applauds v ▷ applaud
applause n (pl **-s**) approval shown by clapping one's hands
applauses n ▷ applause
apple n (pl **-s**) round firm fleshy fruit that grows on trees
apples n ▷ apple
applied adj (of a skill, science, etc) put to practical use ▼ v ▷ apply
applies v ▷ apply
appliqué n (pl **-s**) kind of decoration in which one material is cut out and attached to another
appliqués n ▷ appliqué
apply v (**-plies**, **-plying**, **-plied**) make a formal request
applying v ▷ apply
appoint v (**-s**, **-ing**, **-ed**) assign to a job or position
appointed v ▷ appoint
appointing v ▷ appoint
appoints v ▷ appoint
apposite adj suitable, apt

appraisal n ▷ appraise
appraisals n ▷ appraise
appraise v (-ses, -sing, -sed) estimate the value or quality of ▶ **appraisal** n (pl -s)
appraised v ▷ appraise
appraises v ▷ appraise
appraising v ▷ appraise
apprise v (-ses, -sing, -sed) make aware (of)
apprised v ▷ apprise
apprises v ▷ apprise
apprising v ▷ apprise
approach v (-es, -ing, -ed) come near or nearer (to) ▶ n (pl -es) approaching or means of approaching > **approachable** adj
approachable adj ▷ approach
approached v ▷ approach
approaches v, n ▷ approach
approaching v ▷ approach
approval n (pl -s) consent
approvals n ▷ approval
approve v (-ves, -ving, -ved) consider good or right
approved v ▷ approve
approves v ▷ approve
approving v ▷ approve
apricot n (pl -s) yellowish-orange juicy fruit like a small peach ▶ adj yellowish-orange
apricots n ▷ apricot
apron n (pl -s) garment worn over the front of the body to protect the clothes
aprons n ▷ apron
apropos adj, adv appropriate(ly)
apse n (pl -s) arched or domed recess, esp. in a church
apses n ▷ apse
apt adj having a specified tendency > **aptly** adv > **aptness** n (pl -es)
aptitude n (pl -s) natural ability
aptitudes n ▷ aptitude
aptly adv ▷ apt
aptness n ▷ apt
aptnesses n ▷ apt
aqualung n (pl -s) mouthpiece attached to air cylinders, worn for underwater swimming

aqualungs n ▷ aqualung
aquaria n ▷ aquarium
aquarium n (pl -s, -ria) tank in which fish and other underwater creatures are kept
aquariums n ▷ aquarium
aquatic adj living in or near water
aquatics pl n water sports
aquatint n (pl -s) print like a watercolour, produced by etching copper
aquatints n ▷ aquatint
aqueduct n (pl -s) structure carrying water across a valley or river
aqueducts n ▷ aqueduct
aqueous adj of, like, or containing water
aquiline adj (of a nose) curved like an eagle's beak

> **ar** n (ars). Ar is the letter R. This is a good two-letter word to remember because it uses two very common tiles, and so is easy to fit on the board. Ar scores 2 points.

arable adj suitable for growing crops on
arachnid n (pl -s) eight-legged invertebrate, such as a spider, scorpion, tick, or mite
arachnids n ▷ arachnid
arbiter n (pl -s) person empowered to judge in a dispute
arbiters n ▷ arbiter
arboreal adj of or living in trees
arbour n (pl -s) glade sheltered by trees
arbours n ▷ arbour
arc n (pl -s) part of a circle or other curve ▶ v (-s, -ing, -ed) form an arc
arcade n (pl -s) covered passageway lined with shops
arcades n ▷ arcade
arcane adj mysterious and secret
arced v ▷ arc
arch¹ n (pl -es) curved structure supporting a bridge or roof ▶ v (-es, -ing, -ed) (cause to) form an arch
arch² adj (-er, -est) superior, knowing > **archly** adv > **archness** n (pl -es)
archaic adj ancient > **archaism** ▶ n (pl

-s) archaic word or phrase
archaism n ▷ archaic
archaisms n ▷ archaic
arched v ▷ arch¹
archer n (pl -s) person who shoots
with a bow and arrow ▶ adj ▷ arch²
>archery n (pl -ries)
archeries n ▷ archer
archers n ▷ archer
archery n ▷ archer
arches n, v ▷ arch¹
archest adj ▷ arch²
arching v ▷ arch¹
archival adj ▷ archive
archive n (pl -s) (often pl) collection of
records or documents ▷ archival adj
archives n ▷ archive
archly adv ▷ arch²
archness n ▷ arch²
archnesses n ▷ arch²
archway n (pl -s) passageway under
an arch
archways n ▷ archway
arcing v ▷ arc
arcs n, v ▷ arc
arctic n (pl -s) area around the North
Pole ▶ adj of this region
arctics n ▷ arctic
ardent adj passionate **>ardently** adv
ardently adv ▷ ardent
ardour n (pl -s) passion
ardours n ▷ ardour
arduous adj hard to accomplish,
strenuous **>arduously** adv
arduously adv ▷ arduous
are¹ v ▷ be
are² n (pl -s) unit of measure, 100
square metres
area n (pl -s) part or region
areas n ▷ area
arena n (pl -s) seated enclosure for
sports events
arenas n ▷ arena
areola n (pl -lae, -las) small circular
area, such as the coloured ring around
the human nipple
areolae n ▷ areola
areolas n ▷ areola

ares n ▷ are
argon n (pl -s) CHEM inert gas found
in the air
argons n ▷ argon
argot n (pl -s) slang or jargon
argots n ▷ argot
argue v (-gues, -guing, -gued) try to
prove by giving reasons **>arguable** adj
>arguably adv
arguable adj ▷ argue
arguably adv ▷ argue
argued v ▷ argue
argues v ▷ argue
arguing v ▷ argue
argument n (pl -s) quarrel
arguments n ▷ argument
aria n (pl -s) elaborate song for solo
voice, esp. one from an opera
arias n ▷ aria
arid adj parched, dry **>aridity** n (pl -ties)
aridities n ▷ arid
aridity n ▷ arid
aright adv rightly
arise v (arises, arising, arose, arisen)
come about
arisen v ▷ arise
arises v ▷ arise
arising v ▷ arise
ark n (pl -s) OLD TESTAMENT boat built by
Noah, which survived the Flood
arks n ▷ ark
arm¹ n (pl -s) either of the upper limbs
from the shoulder to the wrist
arm² v (-s, -ing, -ed) supply with
weapons
armada n (pl -s) large number of
warships
armadas n ▷ armada
armament n (pl -s) military weapons
armaments n ▷ armament
armature n (pl -s) revolving structure
in an electric motor or generator,
wound with coils carrying the current
armatures n ▷ armature
armchair n (pl -s) upholstered chair
with side supports for the arms
armchairs n ▷ armchair
armed v ▷ arm²

armful n (pl -s) as much as can be held in the arms

armfuls n ▷ armful

armhole n (pl -s) opening in a garment through which the arm passes

armholes n ▷ armhole

armies n ▷ army

arming v ▷ arm²

armour n (pl -s) metal clothing formerly worn to protect the body in battle

armourer n (pl -s) maker, repairer, or keeper of arms or armour

armourers n ▷ armourer

armouries n ▷ armoury

armours n ▷ armour

armoury n (pl -ries) place where weapons are stored

armpit n (pl -s) hollow under the arm at the shoulder

armpits n ▷ armpit

arms pl n weapons ▶ n ▷ arm¹ ▶ v ▷ arm²

army n (pl -mies) military land forces of a nation

aroma n (pl -s) pleasant smell > **aromatic** adj

aromas n ▷ aroma

aromatic adj ▷ aroma

arose v ▷ arise

around prep, adv on all sides (of)

arouse v (-ses, -sing, -sed) stimulate, make active

aroused v ▷ arouse

arouses v ▷ arouse

arousing v ▷ arouse

arpeggio n (pl -s) MUSIC notes of a chord played or sung in quick succession

arpeggios n ▷ arpeggio

arraign v (-s, -ing, -ed) bring (a prisoner) before a court to answer a charge > **arraignment** n (pl -s)

arraigned v ▷ arraign

arraigning v ▷ arraign

arraignment n ▷ arraign

arraignments n ▷ arraign

arraigns v ▷ arraign

arrange v (-ges, -ging, -ged) plan > **arrangement** n (pl -s)

arranged v ▷ arrange

arrangement n ▷ arrange

arrangements n ▷ arrange

arranges v ▷ arrange

arranging v ▷ arrange

arrant adj utter, downright

arras n (pl -es) tapestry wall-hanging

arrases n ▷ arras

array n (pl -s) impressive display or collection poetic ▶ v (-s, -ing, -ed) arrange in order

arrayed v ▷ array

arraying v ▷ array

arrays n, v ▷ array

arrear n (p-s) (usually plural) money owed

arrears n ▷ arrear

arrest v (-s, -ing, -ed) take (a person) into custody ▶ n (pl -s) act of taking a person into custody

arrested v ▷ arrest

arresting v ▷ arrest

arrests n, v ▷ arrest

arrival n (pl -s) arriving

arrivals n ▷ arrival

arrive v (-ves, -ving, -ved) reach a place or destination

arrived v ▷ arrive

arrives v ▷ arrive

arriving v ▷ arrive

arrogance n ▷ arrogant

arrogances n ▷ arrogant

arrogant adj proud and overbearing > **arrogantly** adv > **arrogance** n (pl -s)

arrogantly adv ▷ arrogant

arrogate v (-tes, -ting, -ted) claim or seize without justification

arrogated v ▷ arrogate

arrogates v ▷ arrogate

arrogating v ▷ arrogate

arrow n (pl -s) pointed shaft shot from a bow

arrows n ▷ arrow

arsenal n (pl -s) place where arms and ammunition are made or stored

arsenals n ▷ arsenal

arsenic n (pl -s) toxic grey element > **arsenical** adj

arsenical adj ▷ **arsenic**
arsenics n ▷ **arsenic**
arson n (pl -s) crime of intentionally setting property on fire ▷ **arsonist** n (pl -s)
arsonist n ▷ **arson**
arsonists n ▷ **arson**
arsons n ▷ **arson**
art n (pl -s) creation of works of beauty, esp. paintings or sculpture
artefact n (pl -s) something made by human beings
artefacts n ▷ **artefact**
arterial adj of an artery
arteries n ▷ **artery**
artery n (pl -ries) one of the tubes carrying blood from the heart
artful adj cunning, wily ▷ **artfully** adv ▷ **artfulness** n (pl -es)
artfully adv ▷ **artful**
artfulness n ▷ **artful**
artfulnesses n ▷ **artful**
article n (pl -s) written piece in a magazine or newspaper
articled adj bound (as an apprentice) by a written contract
articles n ▷ **article**
artier adj ▷ **arty**
artiest adj ▷ **arty**
artifice n (pl -s) clever trick
artifices n ▷ **artifice**
artisan n (pl -s) skilled worker, craftsman
artisans n ▷ **artisan**
artist n (pl -s) person who produces works of art, esp. paintings or sculpture ▷ **artistic** adj ▷ **artistically** adv
artiste n (pl -s) professional entertainer such as a singer or dancer
artistes n ▷ **artiste**
artistic adj ▷ **artist**
artistically adv ▷ **artist**
artistries n ▷ **artistry**
artistry n (pl -ries) artistic skill
artists n ▷ **artist**
artless adj free from deceit or cunning ▷ **artlessly** adv
artlessly adv ▷ **artless**

arts n ▷ **art**
arty adj (-tier, -tiest) informal having an affected interest in art
as conj while, when ▷ adv, conj used to indicate amount or extent in comparisons ▷ prep in the role of, being
asbestos n (pl -es) fibrous mineral which does not burn
asbestoses n ▷ **asbestos**
ascend v (-s, -ing, -ed) go or move up
ascended v ▷ **ascend**
ascending v ▷ **ascend**
ascends v ▷ **ascend**
ascent n (pl -s) ascending
ascents n ▷ **ascent**
ascetic n (pl -s) ▷ adj (person) abstaining from worldly pleasures and comforts ▷ **asceticism** n (pl -s)
asceticism n ▷ **ascetic**
asceticisms n ▷ **ascetic**
ascetics n ▷ **ascetic**
ascribe v (-bes, -bing, -bed) attribute, as to a particular origin ▷ **ascription** n (pl -s)
ascribed v ▷ **ascribe**
ascribes v ▷ **ascribe**
ascribing v ▷ **ascribe**
ascription n ▷ **ascribe**
ascriptions n ▷ **ascribe**
aseptic adj free from harmful bacteria
asexual adj without sex ▷ **asexually** adv
asexually adv ▷ **asexual**
ash[1] n (pl -es) powdery substance left when something is burnt
ash[2] n (pl -es) tree with grey bark
ashamed adj feeling shame
ashen adj pale with shock
ashes n ▷ **ash**[1,2]
ashlar n (pl -s) square block of hewn stone used in building
ashlars n ▷ **ashlar**
ashore adv towards or on land
ashram n (pl -s) religious retreat where a Hindu holy man lives
ashrams n ▷ **ashram**
ashtray n (pl -s) receptacle for tobacco ash and cigarette butts
ashtrays n ▷ **ashtray**

aside *adv* to one side ▸ *n* (*pl* **-s**) remark not meant to be heard by everyone present

asides *n* ▷ **aside**

asinine *adj* stupid, idiotic

ask *v* (**-s, -ing, -ed**) say or write (something) in a form that requires an answer

askance *adv* with an oblique glance

asked *v* ▷ **ask**

askew *adv, adj* to one side, crooked

asking *v* ▷ **ask**

asks *v* ▷ **ask**

aslant *adv, prep* at a slant (to), slanting (across)

asleep *adj* sleeping

asp *n* (*pl* **-s**) small poisonous snake

aspect *n* (*pl* **-s**) feature or element

aspects *n* ▷ **aspect**

aspen *n* (*pl* **-s**) kind of poplar tree

aspens *n* ▷ **aspen**

asperities *n* ▷ **asperity**

asperity *n* (*pl* **-ties**) roughness of temper

asphalt *n* (*pl* **-s**) black hard tarlike substance used for road surfaces etc

asphalts *n* ▷ **asphalt**

asphodel *n* (*pl* **-s**) plant with clusters of yellow or white flowers

asphodels *n* ▷ **asphodel**

asphyxia *n* (*pl* **-s**) suffocation

aspic *n* (*pl* **-s**) savoury jelly used to coat meat, eggs, fish, etc

aspics *n* ▷ **aspic**

aspirant *n* (*pl* **-s**) person who aspires

aspirants *n* ▷ **aspirant**

aspirate PHONETICS *v* (**-tes, -ting, -ted**) pronounce with an h sound ▸ *n* (*pl* **-s**) h sound

aspirated *v* ▷ **aspirate**

aspirates *v, n* ▷ **aspirate**

aspirating *v* ▷ **aspirate**

aspire *v* (**-res, -ring, -red**) (*foll. by* **to**) yearn (for), hope (to do or be)

aspired *v* ▷ **aspire**

aspires *v* ▷ **aspire**

aspirin *n* (*pl* **-s**) drug used to relieve pain and fever

aspiring *v* ▷ **aspire**

aspirins *n* ▷ **aspirin**

asps *n* ▷ **asp**

ass *n* (*pl* **-es**) donkey

assagai *n* (*pl* **-s**) ▷ **assegai**

assagais *n* ▷ **assagai**

assail *v* (**-s, -ing, -ed**) attack violently > **assailant** (*pl* **-s**)

assailant *n* ▷ **assail**

assailants *n* ▷ **assail**

assailed *v* ▷ **assail**

assailing *v* ▷ **assail**

assails *v* ▷ **assail**

assassin *n* (*pl* **-s**) person who murders a prominent person

assassins *n* ▷ **assassin**

assault *n* (*pl* **-s**) violent attack ▸ *v* (**-s, -ing, -ed**) attack violently

assaulted *v* ▷ **assault**

assaulting *v* ▷ **assault**

assaults *n, v* ▷ **assault**

assay *n* (*pl* **-s**) analysis of a substance, esp. a metal, to ascertain its purity ▸ *v* (**-s, -ing, -ed**)

assayed *v* ▷ **assay**

assaying *v* ▷ **assay**

assays *n, v* ▷ **assay**

assegai *n* (*pl* **-s**) slender spear used in S Africa

assegais *n* ▷ **assegai**

assemble *v* (**-bles, -bling, -bled**) collect or congregate

assembled *v* ▷ **assemble**

assembles *v* ▷ **assemble**

assemblies *n* ▷ **assembly**

assembling *v* ▷ **assemble**

assembly *n* (*pl* **-blies**) assembled group

assent *n* (*pl* **-s**) agreement or consent ▸ *v* (**-s, -ing, -ed**) agree or consent

assented *v* ▷ **assent**

assenting *v* ▷ **assent**

assents *n, v* ▷ **assent**

assert *v* (**-s, -ing, -ed**) declare forcefully > **assertion** (*pl* **-s**) > **assertive** *adj* > **assertively** *adv*

asserted *v* ▷ **assert**

asserting *v* ▷ **assert**

assertion *n* ▷ **assert**

assertions n ▷ assert
assertive adj ▷ assert
assertively adv ▷ assert
asserts v ▷ assert
asses n ▷ ass
assess v (-es, -ing, -ed) judge the worth or importance of ▷ **assessment** n (pl -s) ▷ **assessor** n (pl -s)
assessed v ▷ assess
assesses v ▷ assess
assessing v ▷ assess
assessment n ▷ assess
assessments n ▷ assess
assessor n ▷ assess
assessors n ▷ assess
asset n (pl -s) valuable or useful person or thing
assets n ▷ asset
assign v (-s, -ing, -ed) appoint (someone) to a job or task
assigned v ▷ assign
assigning v ▷ assign
assigns v ▷ assign
assist v (-s, -ing, -ed) give help or support ▷ **assistance** n (pl -s)
assistance n ▷ assist
assistances n ▷ assist
assisted v ▷ assist
assisting v ▷ assist
assists v ▷ assist
assizes pl n BRIT court sessions formerly held in each county of England and Wales
assorted adj consisting of various types mixed together
assuage v (-ges, -ging, -ged) relieve (pain, grief, thirst, etc)
assuaged v ▷ assuage
assuages v ▷ assuage
assuaging v ▷ assuage
assume v (-mes, -ming, -med) take to be true without proof
assumed v ▷ assume
assumes v ▷ assume
assuming v ▷ assume
assure v (-res, -ring, -red) promise or guarantee
assured adj confident ▶ v ▷ assure

assures v ▷ assure
assuring v ▷ assure
astatine n (pl -s) CHEM radioactive nonmetallic element
astatines n ▷ astatine
aster n (pl -s) plant with daisy-like flowers
asterisk n (pl -s) star-shaped symbol (*) used in printing or writing to indicate a footnote etc ▶ v (-s, -ing, -ed) mark with an asterisk
asterisked v ▷ asterisk
asterisking v ▷ asterisk
asterisks n, v ▷ asterisk
astern adv at or towards the stern of a ship
asteroid n (pl -s) any of the small planets that orbit the sun between Mars and Jupiter
asteroids n ▷ asteroid
asters n ▷ aster
asthma n (pl -s) illness causing difficulty in breathing ▷ **asthmatic** adj, n (pl -s)
asthmas n ▷ asthma
asthmatic adj, n ▷ asthma
asthmatics n ▷ asthma
astir adj old-fashioned out of bed
astonish v (-es, -ing, -ed) surprise greatly ▷ **astonishment** n (pl -s)
astonished v ▷ astonish
astonishes v ▷ astonish
astonishing v ▷ astonish
astonishment n ▷ astonish
astonishments n ▷ astonish
astound v (-s, -ing, -ed) overwhelm with amazement ▷ **astounding** adj
astounded v ▷ astound
astounding v, adj ▷ astound
astounds v ▷ astound
astral adj of stars
astray adv off the right path
astride adv, prep with a leg on either side (of)
astute adj perceptive or shrewd ▷ **astutely** adv ▷ **astuteness** n (pl -es)
astutely adv ▷ astute
astuteness n ▷ astute

astutenesses n ▷ **astute**

asunder adv obs or poetic into parts or pieces

asylum n (pl -s) refuge or sanctuary

asylums n ▷ **asylum**

at prep indicating position in space or time, movement towards an object, etc

atavism n (pl -s) recurrence of a trait present in distant ancestors > **atavistic** adj

atavisms n ▷ **atavism**

atavistic adj ▷ **atavism**

ate v ▷ **eat**

atheism n (pl -s) belief that there is no God > **atheist** n (pl -s) > **atheistic** adj

atheisms n ▷ **atheism**

atheist n ▷ **atheism**

atheistic adj ▷ **atheism**

atheists n ▷ **atheism**

athlete n (pl -s) person trained in or good at athletics

athletes n ▷ **athlete**

athletic adj physically fit or strong > **athletically** adv > **athleticism** n (pl -s)

athletically adv ▷ **athletic**

athleticism n ▷ **athletic**

athleticisms n ▷ **athletic**

athwart prep across ▶ adv transversely

atlas n (pl -es) book of maps

atlases n ▷ **atlas**

atoll n (pl -s) ring-shaped coral reef enclosing a lagoon

atolls n ▷ **atoll**

atom n (pl -s) smallest unit of matter which can take part in a chemical reaction

atomic adj of or using atomic bombs or atomic energy

atomize v (-zes, -zing, -zed) reduce to atoms or small particles

atomized v ▷ **atomize**

atomizer n (pl -s) device for discharging a liquid in a fine spray

atomizers n ▷ **atomizer**

atomizes n ▷ **atomize**

atomizing v ▷ **atomize**

atoms n ▷ **atom**

atonal adj (of music) not written in an established key

atone v (-nes, -ning, -ned) make amends (for sin or wrongdoing) > **atonement** n (pl -s)

atoned v ▷ **atone**

atonement n ▷ **atone**

atonements n ▷ **atone**

atones v ▷ **atone**

atoning v ▷ **atone**

atop prep lit on top of

atria n ▷ **atrium**

atrium n (pl **atria**) upper chamber of either half of the heart

atrocities n ▷ **atrocity**

atrocity n (pl -ties) wickedness

atrophied v ▷ **atrophy**

atrophies n, v ▷ **atrophy**

atrophy n (pl -phies) wasting away of an organ or part ▶ v (-phies, -phying, -phied) (cause to) waste away

atrophying v ▷ **atrophy**

attach v (-es, -ing, -ed) join, fasten, or connect > **attachment** n (pl -s)

attaché n (pl -s) specialist attached to a diplomatic mission

attached v, adj ▷ **attach**

attaches v ▷ **attach**

attachés n ▷ **attaché**

attaching v ▷ **attach**

attachment n ▷ **attach**

attachments n ▷ **attach**

attack v (-s, -ing, -ed) launch a physical assault (against) ▶ n (pl -s) act of attacking > **attacker** n (pl -s)

attacked v ▷ **attack**

attacker n ▷ **attack**

attackers n ▷ **attack**

attacking v ▷ **attack**

attacks v, n ▷ **attack**

attain v (-s, -ing, -ed) achieve or accomplish (a task or aim) > **attainable** adj

attainable adj ▷ **attain**

attained v ▷ **attain**

attaining v ▷ **attain**

attains v ▷ **attain**

attar n (pl -s) fragrant oil made from roses

attars n ▷ attar

attempt v (-s, -ing, -ed) try, make an effort ▶ (-s) effort or endeavour

attempted v ▷ attempt

attempting v ▷ attempt

attempts v, n ▷ attempt

attend v (-s, -ing, -ed) be present at

attended v ▷ attend

attending v ▷ attend

attends v ▷ attend

attest v (-s, -ing, -ed) affirm the truth of, be proof of ▷ attestation n (pl -s)

attestation n ▷ attest

attestations n ▷ attest

attested v ▷ attest

attesting v ▷ attest

attests v ▷ attest

attic n (pl -s) space or room within the roof of a house

attics n ▷ attic

attire n (pl -s) formal fine or formal clothes

attired adj dressed in a specified way

attires n ▷ attire

attitude n (pl -s) way of thinking and behaving

attitudes n ▷ attitude

attorney n (pl -s) person legally appointed to act for another

attorneys n ▷ attorney

attract v (-s, -ing, -ed) arouse the interest or admiration of

attracted v ▷ attract

attracting v ▷ attract

attracts v ▷ attract

attune v (-nes, -ning, -ned) adjust or accustom (a person or thing)

attuned v ▷ attune

attunes n ▷ attune

attuning v ▷ attune

atypical adj not typical

auburn adj (of hair) reddish-brown

auction n (pl -s) public sale in which articles are sold to the highest bidder ▶ v (-s, -ing, -ed) sell by auction

auctioned v ▷ auction

auctioning v ▷ auction

auctions n, v ▷ auction

audibilities n ▷ audible

audibility n ▷ audible

audible adj loud enough to be heard > **audibly** adv ▷ audibility n (pl -ties)

audibly adv ▷ audible

audience n (pl -s) group of spectators or listeners

audiences n ▷ audience

audio adj of sound or hearing > **audiovisual** adj (esp. of teaching aids) involving both sight and hearing

audiovisual adj ▷ audio

audit n (pl -s) official examination of business accounts ▶ v (-s, -ing, -ted) examine (business accounts) officially > **auditor** n (pl -s)

audited v ▷ audit

auditing v ▷ audit

audition n (pl -s) test of a performer's ability for a particular role or job ▶ v (-s, -ing, -ed) test or be tested in an audition

auditioned v ▷ audition

auditioning v ▷ audition

auditions n, v ▷ audition

auditor n ▷ audit

auditors n ▷ audit

auditory adj of or relating to hearing

audits n, v ▷ audit

auf n (aufs). An auf is an elf-child left in place of a human baby. Auf scores 6 points.

auger n (pl -s) tool for boring holes

augers n ▷ auger

aught pron obs anything whatever

augment v (-s, -ing, -ed) increase or enlarge > **augmentation** n (pl -s)

augmentation n ▷ augment

augmentations n ▷ augment

augmented v ▷ augment

augmenting v ▷ augment

augments v ▷ augment

augur v (-s, -ing, -ed) be a sign of (future events)

augured v ▷ augur

auguries n ▷ augury

auguring v ▷ augur

augurs v ▷ augur

augury n (pl -ries) foretelling of the future

august adj dignified and imposing

auk n (pl -s) northern sea bird with short wings and black-and-white plumage

auks n ▷ auk

aunt n (pl -s) father's or mother's sister

auntie, aunty n (pl -ties) informal aunt

aunties n ▷ auntie

aunts n ▷ aunt

aunty n ▷ auntie

aura n (pl -s) distinctive air or quality of a person or thing

aural adj of or using the ears or hearing

auras n ▷ aura

aureola n ▷ aureole

aureolas n ▷ aureole

aureole, aureola n (pl -s) halo

aureoles n ▷ aureole

auricle n (pl -s) upper chamber of the heart > **auricular** adj

auricles n ▷ auricle

auricular adj ▷ auricle

aurochs n (pl aurochs) recently extinct European wild ox

aurora n (pl -ras, -rae) bands of light sometimes seen in the sky in polar regions

aurorae n ▷ aurora

auroras n ▷ aurora

auspice n (pl -s) (usually plural) patronage or guidance

auspices n ▷ auspice

austere adj (-r, -st) stern or severe > **austerely** adv > **austerity** n (pl -ties)

austerely adv ▷ austere

austerer adj ▷ austere

austerest adj ▷ austere

austerities n ▷ austere

austerity n ▷ austere

autarchies n ▷ autarchy

autarchy n (pl -chies) absolute power or autocracy

autarkies n ▷ autarky

autarky n (pl -kies) policy of economic self-sufficiency

author n (pl -s) writer of a book etc > **authorship** n (pl -s)

authors n ▷ author

authorship n ▷ author

authorships n ▷ author

autism n PSYCHIATRY disorder, usu. of children, characterized by lack of response to people and limited ability to communicate > **autistic** adj

autisms n ▷ autism

autistic adj ▷ autism

autocrat n (pl -s) ruler with absolute authority > **autocratic** adj > **autocratically** adv

autocratic adj ▷ autocrat

autocratically adv ▷ autocrat

autocrats n ▷ autocrat

autocue n (pl -s)® electronic television prompting device displaying a speaker's script, unseen by the audience

autocues n ▷ autocue

autogiro, autogyro n (pl -ros) self-propelled aircraft resembling a helicopter but with an unpowered rotor

autogiros n ▷ autogiro

autogyro n ▷ autogiro

autogyros n ▷ autogiro

automat n (pl -s) vending machine

automate v (-tes, -ting, -ted) make (a manufacturing process) automatic > **automation** n (pl -s)

automated v ▷ automate

automates v ▷ automate

automating v ▷ automate

automation n ▷ automate

automations n ▷ automate

automats n ▷ automat

autonomies n ▷ autonomy

autonomous adj ▷ autonomy

autonomy n (pl -mies) self-government > **autonomous** adj

autopsies n ▷ autopsy

autopsy n (pl -sies) examination of a corpse to determine the cause of death

autumn n (pl -s) season between summer and winter > **autumnal** adj

autumnal adj ▷ autumn

autumns n ▷ autumn

avail v (-s, -ing, -ed) be of use or

advantage (to) ▶ n (pl -s) use or
advantage
availed v ▷ avail
availing v ▷ avail
avails v, n ▷ avail
avarice n (pl -s) greed for wealth
> avaricious adj
avarices n ▷ avarice
avaricious adj ▷ avarice
avast interj NAUT stop
avatar n (pl -s) HINDUISM appearance
of a god in animal or human form
avatars n ▷ avatar
avenge v (-ges, -ging, -ged) take
revenge in retaliation for (harm done)
or on behalf of (a person harmed)
> avenger n (pl -s)
avenged v ▷ avenge
avenger n ▷ avenge
avengers n ▷ avenge
avenges v ▷ avenge
avenging v ▷ avenge
avenue n (pl -s) wide street
avenues n ▷ avenue
aver v (-s, -rring, -rred) state to be true
average n (pl -s) typical or normal
amount or quality ▶ adj usual
or typical ▶ v (-ges, -ging, -ged)
calculate the average of
averaged v ▷ average
averages n, v ▷ average
averaging v ▷ average
averred v ▷ aver
averring v ▷ aver
avers v ▷ aver
averse adj (usu. foll. by **to**) disinclined
or unwilling
aversion n (pl -s) strong dislike
aversions n ▷ aversion
avert v (-s, -ing, -ed) turn away
averted v ▷ avert
averting v ▷ avert
averts v ▷ avert
aviaries n ▷ aviary
aviary n (pl -ries) large cage or
enclosure for birds
aviation n (pl -s) art of flying aircraft
> aviator n (pl -s)

aviations n ▷ aviation
aviator n ▷ aviation
aviators n ▷ aviation
avid adj (-er, -est) keen or enthusiastic
> avidly adv > avidity n (pl -ties)
avider adj ▷ avid
avidest adj ▷ avid
avidities n ▷ avid
avidity n ▷ avid
avidly adv ▷ avid
avocado n (pl -dos) pear-shaped
tropical fruit with a leathery green skin
and yellowish-green flesh
avocados n ▷ avocado
avocet n (pl -s) long-legged wading
bird with a long slender upward-
curving bill
avocets n ▷ avocet
avoid v (-s, -ing, -ed) prevent
from happening > avoidable adj
> avoidance n (pl -s)
avoidable adj ▷ avoid
avoidance n ▷ avoid
avoidances n ▷ avoid
avoided v ▷ avoid
avoiding v ▷ avoid
avoids v ▷ avoid
avow v (-s, -ing, -ed) state or affirm
> avowal n (pl -s) > avowed adj
> avowedly adv
avowal n ▷ avow
avowals n ▷ avow
avowed v, adj ▷ avow
avowedly adv ▷ avow
avowing v ▷ avow
avows v ▷ avow
await v (-s, -ing, -ed) wait for
awaited v ▷ await
awaiting v ▷ await
awaits v ▷ await
awake v (awakes, awaking, awoke,
awoken) emerge or rouse from sleep
▶ adj not sleeping
awaken v (-s, -ing, -ed) awake
awakened v ▷ awaken
awakening v ▷ awaken
awakens v ▷ awaken
awakes v ▷ awake

awaking v ▷ awake

award v (-s, -ing, -ed) give (something, such as a prize) formally ▶ n (pl -s) something awarded, such as a prize

awarded v ▷ award

awarding v ▷ award

awards v, n ▷ award

aware adj having knowledge, informed >**awareness** n (pl -es)

awareness n ▷ aware

awarenesses n ▷ aware

awash adv washed over by water

away adv from a place ▶ adj not present

awe n (pl -s) wonder and respect mixed with dread ▶ v (awes, awing, awed) fill with awe

awed v ▷ awe

awes n, v ▷ awe

awesome adj inspiring awe

awful adj (-ler, -llest) very bad or unpleasant

awfuller adj ▷ awful

awfullest adj ▷ awful

awfully adv in an unpleasant way

awhile adv for a brief time

awing v ▷ awe

awkward adj (-er, -est) clumsy or ungainly >**awkwardly** adv >**awkwardness** n (pl -es)

awkwarder adj ▷ awkward

awkwardest adj ▷ awkward

awkwardly adv ▷ awkward

awkwardness n ▷ awkward

awkwardnesses n ▷ awkward

awl n (pl -s) pointed tool for piercing wood, leather, etc

awls n ▷ awl

awning n (pl -s) canvas roof supported by a frame to give protection against the weather

awnings n ▷ awning

awoke v ▷ awake

awoken v ▷ awake

awry adv, adj with a twist to one side, askew

ax n ▷ axe

axe, ax n (pl **axes**) tool with a sharp blade for felling trees or chopping wood informal ▶ v (axes, axing, axed) informal dismiss (employees), restrict (expenditure), or terminate (a project)

axed v ▷ axe

axes n, v ▷ axe, axis

axial adj ▷ axis

axil n (pl -s) angle where the stalk of a leaf joins a stem

axils n ▷ axil

axing v ▷ axe

axiom n (pl -s) generally accepted principle

axioms n ▷ axiom

axis n (pl **axes**) (imaginary) line round which a body can rotate or about which an object or geometrical figure is symmetrical >**axial** adj

axle n (pl -s) shaft on which a wheel or pair of wheels turns

axles n ▷ axle

axolotl n (pl -s) aquatic salamander of central America

axolotis n ▷ axolotl

ay interj ▷ aye

aye, ay interj yes ▶ n (pl -s) affirmative vote or voter

ayes n ▷ aye

ays n ▷ aye

azalea n (pl -s) garden shrub grown for its showy flowers

azaleas n ▷ azalea

azimuth n (pl -s) arc of the sky between the zenith and the horizon

azimuths n ▷ azimuth

> **azo** adj. Azo describes a kind of chemical. Azo scores 12 points, and so is a very high-scoring word for only three letters.

> **azulejo** n (**azulejos**). An azulejo is a painted and glazed tile. Azulejo scores 23 points, and if you are lucky enough to have all seven letters needed for it, you'll get the 50-point bonus for using all of your tiles.

azure adj, n (pl -s) (of) the colour of a clear blue sky

azures n ▷ azure

Bb

B forms a two-letter word with every vowel except U – and with Y as well. With a B in your rack, you can play lots of short everyday words that will give you relatively high scores. The best of these is **box** (12 points), but don't forget **bay** (8), **by** (7), **bow** (8), **boy** (8), **buy** (8) and **bye** (8).

ba n (**bas**). A ba is the human soul in Egyptian mythology, shown in paintings as a bird with a human head. Ba scores 4 points.

baa v (**-s, -ing, -ed**) make the characteristic bleating sound of a sheep ▸ n (pl **-s**) cry made by a sheep
baaed v ▷ **baa**
baaing v ▷ **baa**
baas v, n ▷ **baa**
babble v (**-les, -ling, -led**) talk excitedly or foolishly ▸ n (pl **-s**) muddled or foolish speech
babbled v ▷ **babble**
babbles v, n ▷ **babble**
babbling v ▷ **babble**
babe n (pl **-s**) baby
babel n (pl **-s**) confused mixture of noises or voices
babels n ▷ **babel**
babes n ▷ **babe**
babies n ▷ **baby**
baby n (pl **-bies**) very young child or animal ▸ adj comparatively small of its type ▸ **babyish** adj
babyish adj ▷ **baby**
baccarat n (pl **-s**) card game involving gambling
baccarats n ▷ **baccarat**
bach NZ n (pl **-es**) small holiday cottage

▸ v (**-es, -ing, -ed**) look after oneself when one's spouse is away
bached v ▷ **bach**
bachelor n (pl **-s**) unmarried man
bachelors n ▷ **bachelor**
baches n, ▷ **bach**
baching v ▷ **bach**
bacilli n ▷ **bacillus**
bacillus n (pl **-li**) rod-shaped bacterium
back n (pl **-s**) rear part of the human body, from the neck to the pelvis ▸ v (**-s, -ing, -ed**) (cause to) move backwards ▸ adv at, to, or towards the rear
backbone n (pl **-s**) spinal column
backbones n ▷ **backbone**
backchat n (pl **-s**) informal impudent replies
backchats n ▷ **backchat**
backdate v (**-tes, -ting, -ted**) make (a document) effective from a date earlier than its completion
backdated v ▷ **backdate**
backdates v ▷ **backdate**
backdating v ▷ **backdate**
backdrop n (pl **-s**) painted curtain at the back of a stage set
backdrops n ▷ **backdrop**
backed v ▷ **back**
backer n (pl **-s**) person who gives financial support
backers n ▷ **backer**
backfire v (**-res, -ring, -red**) (of a plan)

fail to have the desired effect
backfired v ▷ backfire
backfires v ▷ backfire
backfiring v ▷ backfire
backhand n (pl -s) TENNIS ETC stroke played with the back of the hand facing the direction of the stroke
backhands n ▷ backhand
backing n (pl -s) support ▶ v ▷ back
backings n ▷ backing
backlash n (pl -es) sudden and adverse reaction
backlashes n ▷ backlash
backlog n (pl -s) accumulation of things to be dealt with
backlogs n ▷ backlog
backpack n (pl -s) large pack carried on the back
backpacks n ▷ backpack
backs n, v ▷ back
backside n (pl -s) informal buttocks
backsides n ▷ backside
backup n (pl -s) support or reinforcement
backups n ▷ backup
backward adj directed towards the rear > **backwardness** n (pl -es)
backwardness n ▷ backward
backwardnesses n ▷ backward
backwash n (pl -es) water washed backwards by the motion of a boat
backwashes n ▷ backwash
backwood n (pl -s) (usually plural) remote sparsely populated area
backwoods n ▷ backwood
bacon n salted or smoked pig meat
bacons n ▷ bacon
bacteria pl n (sing -rium) large group of microorganisms, many of which cause disease > **bacterial** adj
bacterial adj ▷ bacteria
bacterium n ▷ bacteria
bad adj (worse, worst) of poor quality > **badly** adv > **badness** n (pl -es)
bade v ▷ bid
badge n (pl -s) emblem worn to show membership, rank, etc

badger n (pl -s) nocturnal burrowing mammal of Europe, Asia, and N America with a black and white head ▶ v (-s, -ing, -ed) pester or harass
badgered v ▷ badger
badgering v ▷ badger
badgers n, v ▷ badger
badges n ▷ badge
badinage n (pl -s) playful and witty conversation
badinages n ▷ badinage
badly adv ▷ bad
badness n ▷ bad
badnesses n ▷ bad
baffle v (-les, -ling, -led) perplex or puzzle ▶ n (pl -s) device to limit or regulate the flow of fluid, light, or sound > **bafflement** n
baffled v ▷ baffle
bafflement n ▷ baffle
baffles v, n ▷ baffle
baffling v ▷ baffle
bag n (pl -s) flexible container with an opening at one end ▶ v (-s, -gging, -gged) put into a bag
bagel n (pl -s) hard ring-shaped bread roll
bagels n ▷ bagel
baggage n (pl -s) suitcases packed for a journey
baggages n ▷ baggage
bagged v ▷ bag
baggier adj ▷ baggy
baggiest adj ▷ baggy
bagging v ▷ bag
baggy adj (-ggier, -ggiest) (of clothes) hanging loosely
bagpipes pl n musical wind instrument with reed pipes and an inflatable bag
bags n, v ▷ bag

■ **bah** interj. Bah is something people say when they are annoyed or disgusted. Bah scores 8 points.

bail¹ n (pl -s) LAW money deposited with a court as security for a person's reappearance in court ▶ v (-s, -ing, -ed) pay bail for (a person)

bail², **bale** v (-s, -ing, -ed) (foll. by **out**) remove (water) from (a boat) *informal*

bail³ n (pl -s) CRICKET either of two wooden bars across the tops of the stumps
bailed v ▷ **bail¹, ²**

bailey n (pl -s) outermost wall or court of a castle
baileys n ▷ **bailey**

bailiff n (pl -s) sheriff's officer who serves writs and summonses
bailiffs n ▷ **bailiff**
bailing v ▷ **bail¹, ²**
bails n ▷ **bail¹, ³** v ▷ **bail¹, ²**

bairn n (pl -s) SCOT child
bairns n ▷ **bairn**

bait n (pl -s) piece of food on a hook or in a trap to attract fish or animals ▶ v (-s, -ing, -ed) put a piece of food on or in (a hook or trap)
baited v ▷ **bait**
baiting v ▷ **bait**
baits n, v ▷ **bait**

baize n (pl -s) woollen fabric used to cover billiard and card tables
baizes n ▷ **baize**

bake v (-kes, -king, -ked) cook by dry heat as in an oven
baked v ▷ **bake**

baker n (pl -s) person whose business is to make or sell bread, cakes, etc
bakeries n ▷ **bakery**
bakers n ▷ **baker**

bakery n (pl -eries) place where bread, cakes, etc are baked or sold
bakes v ▷ **bake**
baking v ▷ **bake**

bakkie n (pl -s) S AFR small truck
bakkies n ▷ **bakkie**

balance n (pl -s) state in which a weight or amount is evenly distributed ▶ v (-ces, -cing, -ced) weigh in a balance
balanced v ▷ **balance**
balances n, v ▷ **balance**
balancing v ▷ **balance**
balconies n ▷ **balcony**
balcony n (pl -nies) platform on the

outside of a building with a rail along the outer edge

bald adj (-er, -est) having little or no hair on the scalp ▷ **baldness** n (pl -es)
balder adj ▷ **bald**
baldest adj ▷ **bald**

balding adj becoming bald
baldness n ▷ **bald**
baldnesses n ▷ **bald**

bale¹ n (pl -s) large bundle of hay or goods tightly bound together ▶ v (-les, -ling, -led) make or put into bales
bale² v ▷ **bail²**
baled n ▷ **bale¹, ²**

baleful adj vindictive or menacing ▷ **balefully** adv
balefully adv ▷ **baleful**
bales n, v ▷ **bale¹, ²**
baling v ▷ **bale¹, ²**

balk, **baulk** v (-s, -ing, -ed) be reluctant to (do something)
balked v ▷ **balk**
balking v ▷ **balk**
balks v ▷ **balk**

ball¹ n (pl -s) round or nearly round object, esp. one used in games ▶ v (-lls, -lling, -lled) form into a ball
ball² n (pl -s) formal social function for dancing ▷ **ballroom** n (pl -s)

ballad n (pl -s) narrative poem or song
ballads n ▷ **ballad**

ballast n (pl -s) substance, such as sand, used to stabilize a ship when it is not carrying cargo
ballasts n ▷ **ballast**
balled v ▷ **ball¹**

ballet n (pl -s) classical style of expressive dancing based on conventional steps
ballets n ▷ **ballet**
balling v ▷ **ball¹**

balloon n (pl -s) inflatable rubber bag used as a plaything or decoration ▶ v (-s, -ing, -ed) fly in a balloon ▷ **balloonist** n (pl -s)
ballooned v ▷ **balloon**
ballooning v ▷ **balloon**
balloonist n ▷ **balloon**

balloonists n ▷ **balloon**
balloons n, v ▷ **balloon**
ballot n (pl -**s**) method of voting ▶ v
(-**lots**, -**loting**, -**loted**) vote or ask for
a vote from
balloted v ▷ **ballot**
balloting v ▷ **ballot**
ballots n, v ▷ **ballot**
ballroom n ▷ **ball²**
ballrooms n ▷ **ball²**
balls n ▷ **ball¹, ²** ▶ v ▷ **ball¹**
ballyhoo n (pl -**s**) exaggerated fuss
ballyhoos n ▷ **ballyhoo**
balm n (pl -**s**) aromatic substance used
for healing and soothing
balmier adj ▷ **balmy**
balmiest adj ▷ **balmy**
balms n ▷ **balm**
balmy adj (-**mier**, -**miest**) (of weather)
mild and pleasant
baloney, boloney n (pl -**s**) informal
nonsense
baloneys n ▷ **baloney**
balsa n (pl -**s**) very light wood from a
tropical American tree
balsam n (pl -**s**) soothing ointment
balsams n ▷ **balsam**
balsas n ▷ **balsa**
baluster n (pl -**s**) set of posts
supporting a rail
balusters n ▷ **baluster**
bamboo n (pl -**s**) tall treelike tropical
grass with hollow stems
bamboos n ▷ **bamboo**
ban v (-**s**, -**nning**, -**nned**) prohibit
or forbid officially ▶ n (pl -**s**) official
prohibition
banal adj (-**er**, -**est**) ordinary and
unoriginal > **banality** n (pl -**ties**)
banaler adj ▷ **banal**
banalest adj ▷ **banal**
banalities n ▷ **banal**
banality n ▷ **banal**
banana n (pl -**s**) yellow crescent-
shaped fruit
bananas n ▷ **banana**
band¹ n (pl -**s**) group of musicians
playing together > **bandsman** n (pl

-**men**)
band² n (pl -**s**) strip of some material,
used to hold objects
bandage n (pl -**s**) piece of material
used to cover a wound or wrap an
injured limb ▶ v (-**ges**, -**ging**, -**ged**)
cover with a bandage
bandaged v ▷ **bandage**
bandages n, v ▷ **bandage**
bandaging v ▷ **bandage**
bandana n ▷ **bandanna**
bandanas n ▷ **bandanna**
bandanna, bandana n (pl -**s**) large
brightly coloured handkerchief or
neckerchief
bandannas n ▷ **bandanna**
bandied v ▷ **bandy**
bandier adj ▷ **bandy**
bandies n ▷ **bandy**
bandiest n ▷ **bandy**
bandit n (pl -**s**) robber, esp. a member
of an armed gang > **banditry** n (pl -**ries**)
banditries n ▷ **bandit**
banditry n ▷ **bandit**
bandits n ▷ **bandit**
bands n ▷ **band¹, ²**
bandsman n ▷ **band¹**
bandsmen n ▷ **band¹**
bandy adj (-**dier**, -**diest**) ▶ v (-**dies**,
-**dying**, -**died**) exchange (words) in a
heated manner
bandying v ▷ **bandy**
bane n (pl -**s**) person or thing that
causes misery or distress > **baneful** adj
baneful adj ▷ **bane**
banes n ▷ **bane**
bang n (pl -**s**) short loud explosive noise
▶ v (-**s**, -**ging**, -**ged**) hit or knock, esp.
with a loud noise ▶ adv precisely
banged v ▷ **bang**
banger n (pl -**s**) informal BRIT & AUST old
decrepit car
bangers n ▷ **banger**
banging v ▷ **bang**
bangle n (pl -**s**) bracelet worn round
the arm or the ankle
bangles n ▷ **bangle**
bangs n, v ▷ **bang**

banish v (-es, -ing, -ed) send (someone) into exile > **banishment** n (pl -s)

banished v ▷ banish

banishes v ▷ banish

banishing v ▷ banish

banishment n ▷ banish

banishments n ▷ banish

banjo n (pl -jos, -joes) guitar-like musical instrument with a circular body

banjoes n ▷ banjo

banjos n ▷ banjo

bank[1] n (pl -s) institution offering services such as the safekeeping and lending of money ▶ v (-s, -ing, -ed) deposit (cash or cheques) in a bank > **banking** n (pl -s)

bank[2] n (pl -s) raised mass, esp. of earth ▶ v (-s, -ing, -ed) form into a bank

bank[3] n (pl -s) arrangement of switches, keys, oars, etc in a row or in tiers

banked v ▷ bank[1, 2]

banker n (pl -s) manager or owner of a bank

bankers n ▷ banker

banking v ▷ bank[1, 2] ▷ n ▷ bank[1]

bankings n ▷ bank[1]

banknote n (pl -s) piece of paper money

banknotes n ▷ banknote

bankrupt n (pl -s) person declared by a court to be unable to pay his or her debts ▶ adj financially ruined ▶ v (-s, -ing, -ed) make bankrupt > **bankruptcy** n (pl -cies)

bankruptcies n ▷ bankrupt

bankruptcy n ▷ bankrupt

bankrupted v ▷ bankrupt

bankrupting v ▷ bankrupt

bankrupts n, v ▷ bankrupt

banks n ▷ bank[1, 2, 3] ▶ v ▷ bank[1, 2]

banksia n (pl -s) Australian evergreen tree or shrub

banksias n ▷ banksia

banned v ▷ ban

banner n (pl -s) long strip of cloth displaying a slogan, advertisement, etc

banners n ▷ banner

banning v ▷ ban

banns pl n public declaration, esp. in a church, of an intended marriage

banquet n (pl -s) elaborate formal dinner

banquets n ▷ banquet

bans v, n ▷ ban

banshee n (pl -s) (in Irish folklore) female spirit whose wailing warns of a coming death

banshees n ▷ banshee

bantam n (pl -s) small breed of chicken

bantams n ▷ bantam

banter v (-s, -ing, -ed) tease jokingly ▶ n (pl -s) teasing or joking conversation

bantered v ▷ banter

bantering v ▷ banter

banters v, n ▷ banter

baobab n (pl -s) African tree with a thick trunk and angular branches

baobabs n ▷ baobab

baptism n (pl -s) Christian religious ceremony in which a person is immersed in or sprinkled with water as a sign of being cleansed from sin and accepted into the Church > **baptismal** adj

baptismal adj ▷ baptism

baptisms n ▷ baptism

baptist n (pl -s) member of a Protestant denomination that believes in adult baptism by immersion

baptists n ▷ baptist

baptize v (-zes, -zing, -zed) perform baptism on

baptized v ▷ baptize

baptizes v ▷ baptize

baptizing v ▷ baptize

bar[1] n (pl -s) rigid length of metal, wood, etc ▶ v (-s, -rring, -rred) secure with a bar > **barman** (pl -men), **barmaid** (pl -s) ▶ n

bar[2] n (pl -s) unit of atmospheric pressure

barb n (pl -s) cutting remark

> **barbed** adj

barbaric adj cruel or brutal

barbecue n (pl -s) grill on which food is cooked over hot charcoal, usu. outdoors ▶ v (-cues, -cuing, -cued) cook (food) on a barbecue
  barbecued v ▷ barbecue
  barbecues n, v ▷ barbecue
  barbecuing v ▷ barbecue
  barbed adj ▷ barb

barber n (pl -s) person who cuts men's hair and shaves beards
  barbers n ▷ barber
  barbs n ▷ barb

bard n (pl -s) lit poet
  bards n ▷ bard

bare adj (-r, -st) unclothed, naked ▶ v (-res, -ring, -red) uncover
  > **bareness** n (pl -es)

bareback adj, adv (of horse-riding) without a saddle
  bared v ▷ bare

barely adv only just
  bareness n ▷ bare
  barenesses n ▷ bare
  barer adj ▷ bare
  bares v ▷ bare
  barest adj ▷ bare

bargain n (pl -s) agreement establishing what each party will give, receive, or perform in a transaction ▶ v (-s, -ing, -ed) negotiate the terms of an agreement
  bargained v ▷ bargain
  bargaining v ▷ bargain
  bargains n, v ▷ bargain

barge n (pl -s) flat-bottomed boat used to transport freight ▶ v (-ges, -ging, -ged) informal push violently
  barged v ▷ barge
  barges n, v ▷ barge
  barging v ▷ barge
  baring v ▷ bare

barista n (pl -s) person who makes and sells coffee in a coffee bar
  baristas n ▷ barista

baritone n (pl -s) (singer with) the second lowest adult male voice

baritones n ▷ baritone

barium n (pl -s) CHEM soft white metallic element
  bariums n ▷ barium

bark[1] n (pl -s) loud harsh cry of a dog ▶ v (-s, -ing, -ed) (of a dog) make its typical cry
  barked v ▷ bark[1]
  barking v ▷ bark[1]
  barks n, v ▷ bark[1] ▶ n ▷ bark[2]

bark[2] n (pl -s) tough outer layer of a tree

barley n (pl -s) tall grasslike plant cultivated for grain
  barleys n ▷ barley
  barmaid n ▷ bar[1]
  barmaids n ▷ bar[1]
  barman n ▷ bar[1]
  barmen n ▷ bar[1]
  barmier adj ▷ barmy
  barmiest adj ▷ barmy

barmy adj (-mier, -miest) slang insane

barn n (pl -s) large building on a farm used for storing grain

barnacle n (pl -s) shellfish that lives attached to rocks, ship bottoms, etc
  barnacles n ▷ barnacle

barney n (pl -s) informal noisy fight or argument
  barneys n ▷ barney
  barns n ▷ barn

baron n (pl -s) member of the lowest rank of nobility ▶ **baroness** n (pl -es)
  > **baronial** adj
  baroness n ▷ baron
  baronesses n ▷ baron

baronet n (pl -s) commoner who holds the lowest hereditary British title
  baronets n ▷ baronet
  baronial adj ▷ baron
  barons n ▷ baron

baroque n (pl -s) highly ornate style of art, architecture, or music from the late 16th to the early 18th century ▶ adj ornate in style
  baroques n ▷ baroque

barque n (pl -s) sailing ship, esp. one with three masts
  barques n ▷ barque

barrack v (**-s, -ing, -ed**) criticize loudly or shout against (a team or speaker)
barracked v ▷ **barrack**
barracking v ▷ **barrack**
barracks v ▷ **barrack** ▶ *pl* n building used to accommodate military personnel
barrage n (*pl* **-s**) continuous delivery of questions, complaints, etc
barrages n ▷ **barrage**
barred v ▷ **bar**[1]
barrel n (*pl* **-s**) cylindrical container with rounded sides and flat ends
barrels n ▷ **barrel**
barren *adj* (**-er, -est**) (of a woman or female animal) incapable of producing offspring > **barrenness** n (*pl* **-es**)
barrener *adj* ▷ **barren**
barrenest *adj* ▷ **barren**
barrenness n ▷ **barren**
barrennesses n ▷ **barren**
barrier n (*pl* **-s**) anything that prevents access, progress, or union
barriers n ▷ **barrier**
barring v ▷ **bar**[1] ▶ *prep* except for
barrow[1] n (*pl* **-s**) wheelbarrow
barrow[2] n (*pl* **-s**) mound of earth over a prehistoric tomb
barrows n ▷ **barrow**[1, 2]
bars ▷ **bar**[1, 2] ▶ v ▷ **bar**[1]
barter v (**-s, -ing, -ed**) trade (goods) in exchange for other goods ▶ n (*pl* **-s**) trade by the exchange of goods
bartered v ▷ **barter**
bartering v ▷ **barter**
barters v, n ▷ **barter**
basalt n (*pl* **-s**) dark volcanic rock > **basaltic** *adj*
basaltic *adj* ▷ **basalt**
basalts n ▷ **basalt**
base[1] n (*pl* **-s**) bottom or supporting part of anything ▶ v (**-es, -sing, -sed**) (foll. by **on** or **upon**) use as a basis (for) > **baseless** *adj*
base[2] *adj* (**-r, -st**) dishonourable or immoral > **baseness** n (*pl* **-es**)
baseball n (*pl* **-s**) team game in which runs are scored by hitting a ball with a

bat then running round four bases
baseballs n ▷ **baseball**
based v ▷ **base**[1]
baseless *adj* ▷ **base**[1]
basement n (*pl* **-s**) partly or wholly underground storey of a building
basements n ▷ **basement**
baseness n ▷ **base**[2]
basenesses n ▷ **base**[2]
baser *adj* ▷ **base**[2]
bases ▷ **base**[1], **basis** ▶ v ▷ **base**[1]
basest *adj* ▷ **base**[2]
bash *informal* v (**-es, -ing, -ed**) hit violently or forcefully ▶ n (*pl* **-es**) heavy blow
bashed v ▷ **bash**
bashes v, n ▷ **bash**
bashful *adj* shy or modest > **bashfully** *adv* > **bashfulness** n (*pl* **-es**)
bashfully *adv* ▷ **bashful**
bashfulness n ▷ **bashful**
bashfulnesses n ▷ **bashful**
bashing v ▷ **bash**
basic *adj* of or forming a base or basis > **basically** *adv*
basically *adv* ▷ **basic**
basics *pl* n fundamental principles, facts, etc
basil n (*pl* **-s**) aromatic herb used in cooking
basilica n (*pl* **-s**) rectangular church with a rounded end and two aisles
basilicas n ▷ **basilica**
basilisk n (*pl* **-s**) legendary serpent said to kill by its breath or glance
basilisks n ▷ **basilisk**
basils n ▷ **basil**
basin n (*pl* **-s**) round open container
basing v ▷ **base**[1]
basins n ▷ **basin**
basis n (*pl* **-ses**) fundamental principles etc from which something is started or developed
bask v (**-s, -ing, -ed**) lie in or be exposed to something, esp. pleasant warmth
basked v ▷ **bask**
basket n (*pl* **-s**) container made of interwoven strips of wood or cane

> **basketwork** n (pl **-s**)

baskets n ▷ basket

basketwork n ▷ basket

basketworks n ▷ basket

basking v ▷ bask

basks v ▷ bask

bass¹ n (pl **-es**) (singer with) the lowest adult male voice ▶ adj of the lowest range of musical notes

bass² n (pl **bass**) edible sea fish

basses n ▷ bass¹

bassoon n (pl **-s**) low-pitched woodwind instrument

bassoons n ▷ bassoon

bastard n (pl **-s**) offens obnoxious or despicable person

bastards n ▷ bastard

baste¹ v (**-es**, **-ting**, **-ted**) moisten (meat) during cooking with hot fat

baste² v (**-es**, **-ting**, **-ted**) sew with loose temporary stitches

basted v ▷ baste¹, ²

bastes v ▷ baste¹, ²

basting v ▷ baste¹, ²

bastion n (pl **-s**) projecting part of a fortification

bastions n ▷ bastion

bat¹ n (pl **-s**) any of various types of club used to hit the ball in certain sports ▶ v (**-s**, **-tting**, **-tted**) strike with or as if with a bat

bat² n (pl **-s**) nocturnal mouselike flying animal

batch n (pl **-es**) group of people or things dealt with at the same time

batches n ▷ batch

bath n (pl **-s**) large container in which to wash the body ▶ pl public swimming pool ▶ v (**-s**, **-ing**, **-ed**) wash in a bath

bathe v (**-thes**, **-thing**, **-thed**) swim in open water for pleasure > **bather** n (pl **-s**)

bathed v ▷ bath, bathe

bather n ▷ bathe

bathers n ▷ bathe

bathes v ▷ bath, bathe

bathing v ▷ bath, bathe

bathos n (pl **-es**) sudden ludicrous change in speech or writing from a serious subject to a trivial one

bathoses n ▷ bathos

bathroom n (pl **-s**) room with a bath, sink, and usu. a toilet

bathrooms n ▷ bathe

baths n, v ▷ bath

batik n (pl **-s**) process of printing fabric using wax to cover areas not to be dyed

batiks n ▷ batik

batman n (pl **-men**) officer's servant in the armed forces

batmen n ▷ batman

baton n (pl **-s**) thin stick used by the conductor of an orchestra

batons n ▷ baton

bats n ▷ bat¹, ², ▶ v ▷ bat¹

batsman n (pl **-men**) CRICKET person who bats or specializes in batting

batsmen n ▷ batsman

batted v ▷ bat¹

batten n (pl **-s**) strip of wood fixed to something, esp. to hold it in place

battens n ▷ batten

batter¹ v (**-s**, **-ing**, **-ed**) hit repeatedly

batter² n (pl **-s**) mixture of flour, eggs, and milk, used in cooking

battered v ▷ batter¹

batteries n ▷ battery

battering v ▷ batter¹

batters v, n ▷ batter¹, ²

battery n (pl **-ries**) device that produces electricity in a torch, radio, etc ▶ adj kept in series of cages for intensive rearing

battier adj ▷ batty

battiest adj ▷ batty

batting v ▷ bat¹

battle n (pl **-s**) fight between large armed forces ▶ v (**battles**, **battling**, **battled**) struggle

battled v ▷ battle

battles n, v ▷ battle

battling v ▷ battle

batty adj (**-tier**, **-tiest**) slang eccentric or crazy

bauble n (pl **-s**) trinket of little value

baubles n ▷ **bauble**

bauera n (pl -s) small evergreen Australian shrub

baueras n ▷ **bauera**

baulk v (-s, -ing, -ed) ▷ **balk**

baulked v ▷ **baulk**

baulking v ▷ **baulk**

baulks v ▷ **baulk**

bauxite n (pl -s) claylike substance that is the chief source of aluminium

bauxites n ▷ **bauxite**

bawdier adj ▷ **bawdy**

bawdiest adj ▷ **bawdy**

bawdy adj (-dier, -diest) (of writing etc) containing humorous references to sex

bawl v (-s, -ing, -ed) shout or weep noisily

bawled v ▷ **bawl**

bawling v ▷ **bawl**

bawls v ▷ **bawl**

bay[1] n (pl -s) stretch of coastline that curves inwards

bay[2] n (pl -s) recess in a wall

bay[3] v (-s, -ing, -ed) howl in deep prolonged tones

bay[4] n (pl -s) Mediterranean laurel tree

bay[5] adj, n (pl -s) reddish-brown (horse)

bayed v ▷ **bay**[3]

baying v ▷ **bay**[3]

bayonet n (pl -s) sharp blade that can be fixed to the end of a rifle ▶ v (-nets, -neting, -neted) stab with a bayonet

bayoneted v ▷ **bayonet**

bayoneting v ▷ **bayonet**

bayonets n, v ▷ **bayonet**

bays n ▷ **bay**[1, 2, 3, 4, 5]

bazaar n (pl -s) sale in aid of charity

bazaars n ▷ **bazaar**

bazooka n (pl -s) portable rocket launcher that fires an armour-piercing projectile

bazookas n ▷ **bazooka**

be v (present sing 1st person **am**) (2nd person **are**) (3rd person **is**) (present pl **are**) (past sing 1st person **was**) (2nd person **were**) (3rd person **was**) (past pl **were**) (present participle **being**) (past participle

been) exist or live

beach n (pl -es) area of sand or pebbles on a shore ▶ v (-es, -ing, -ed) run or haul (a boat) onto a beach

beached v ▷ **beach**

beaches n, v ▷ **beach**

beaching v ▷ **beach**

beacon n (pl -s) fire or light on a hill or tower, used as a warning

beacons n ▷ **beacon**

bead n (pl -s) small piece of plastic, wood, etc, pierced for threading on a string to form a necklace etc ▶ **beaded** adj

beaded adj ▷ **bead**

beadier adj ▷ **beady**

beadiest adj ▷ **beady**

beading n (pl -s) strip of moulding used for edging furniture

beading n ▷ **beading**

beads n ▷ **bead**

beady adj (-ier, -iest) small, round, and glittering

beagle n (pl -s) small hound with short legs and drooping ears

beagles n ▷ **beagle**

beak[1] n (pl -s) projecting horny jaws of a bird ▶ **beaky** adj (-kier, -kiest)

beak[2] n (pl -s) BRIT, AUST & NZ slang judge, magistrate, or headmaster

beaker n (pl -s) large drinking cup

beakers n ▷ **beaker**

beakier adj ▷ **beak**[1]

beakiest adj ▷ **beak**[1]

beaks n ▷ **beak**[1, 2]

beaky adj ▷ **beak**[1]

beam n (pl -s) broad smile ▶ v (-s, -ing, -ed) smile broadly

beamed v ▷ **beam**

beaming v ▷ **beam**

beams n, v ▷ **beam**

bean n (pl -s) seed or pod of various plants, eaten as a vegetable or used to make coffee etc

beanie n (pl -s) close-fitting woollen hat

beanies n ▷ **beanie**

beans n ▷ **bean**

bear¹ v (**bears, bearing, bore, borne**) support or hold up (*passive* **born**)
> **bearable** adj

bear² n (pl **-s**) large heavy mammal with a shaggy coat
> **bearable** adj ▷ **bear¹**

beard n (pl **-s**) hair growing on the lower parts of a man's face
> **bearded** adj

bearded adj ▷ **beard**

beards n ▷ **beard**

bearer n (pl **-s**) person who carries, presents, or upholds something

bearers n ▷ **bearer**

bearing n (pl **-s**) relevance (to) ▶ pl sense of one's own relative position
▶ v ▷ **bear¹**

bearings n ▷ **bearing**

bears v ▷ **bear¹** ▶ n ▷ **bear²**

bearskin n (pl **-s**) tall fur helmet worn by some British soldiers

bearskins n ▷ **bearskin**

beast n (pl **-s**) large wild animal

beastliness n ▷ **beastly**

beastlinesses n ▷ **beastly**

beastly adj unpleasant or disagreeable
> **beastliness** n (pl **-es**)

beasts n ▷ **beast**

beat v (**beats, beating, beat, beaten** or **beat**) hit hard and repeatedly ▶ n (pl **-s**) regular throb

beaten v ▷ **beat**

beatific adj displaying great happiness

beatification n ▷ **beatify**

beatifications n ▷ **beatify**

beatified v ▷ **beatify**

beatifies v ▷ **beatify**

beatify v (**-fies, -fying, -fied**) RC CHURCH declare (a dead person) to be among the blessed in heaven: the first step towards canonization
> **beatification** n (pl **-s**)

beatifying v ▷ **beatify**

beating v ▷ **beat**

beats v, n ▷ **beat**

beau n (pl **beaux, beaus**) boyfriend or admirer

beaus n ▷ **beau**

beauties n ▷ **beauty**

beautification n ▷ **beautify**

beautified v ▷ **beautify**

beautifies v ▷ **beautify**

beautify v (**-fies, -fying, -fied**) make beautiful > **beautification** n

beautifying v ▷ **beautify**

beauty n (pl **-ties**) combination of all the qualities of a person or thing that delight the senses and mind

beaux n ▷ **beau**

beaver n (pl **-s**) amphibious rodent with a big flat tail

beavers n ▷ **beaver**

becalmed adj (of a sailing ship) motionless through lack of wind

became v ▷ **become**

because conj on account of the fact that

beck n (pl **-s**) N ENGLISH stream

beckon v (**-s, -ing, -ed**) summon with a gesture

beckoned v ▷ **beckon**

beckoning v ▷ **beckon**

beckons v ▷ **beckon**

becks n ▷ **beck**

become v (**-coming, -came, -come**) come to be

becoming adj attractive or pleasing
▶ v ▷ **become**

bed n (pl **-s**) piece of furniture on which to sleep > **bedroom** n (pl **-s**)

bedding n (pl **-s**) sheets and covers that are used on a bed

beddings n ▷ **bedding**

bedevil v (**-s, -lling, -lled**) harass, confuse, or torment

bedevilled v ▷ **bedevil**

bedevilling v ▷ **bedevil**

bedevils v ▷ **bedevil**

bedlam n (pl **-s**) noisy confused situation

bedlams n ▷ **bedlam**

bedpan n (pl **-s**) shallow bowl used as a toilet by bedridden people

bedpans n ▷ **bedpan**

bedrock n (pl **-s**) solid rock beneath the surface soil

bedrocks n ▷ **bedrock**

bedroom n ▷ **bed**

bedrooms n ▷ **bed**

beds n ▷ **bed**

bedsit, bedsitter n (pl -**s**) furnished sitting room with a bed

bedsits n ▷ **bedsit**

bedsitter n ▷ **bedsit**

bedsitters n ▷ **bedsit**

bee n (pl -**s**) insect that makes wax and honey

beech n (pl -**es**) tree with a smooth greyish bark

beeches n ▷ **beech**

beef n (pl **beeves**) flesh of a cow, bull, or ox

beefier adj ▷ **beefy**

beefiest adj ▷ **beefy**

beefy adj (-**fier**, -**fiest**) like beef

beehive n (pl -**s**) structure in which bees live

beehives n ▷ **beehive**

been v ▷ **be**

beep n (pl -**s**) high-pitched sound, like that of a car horn ▶ v (-**s**, -**ing**, -**ed**) (cause to) make this noise

beeped v ▷ **beep**

beeping v ▷ **beep**

beeps n, v ▷ **beep**

beer n (pl -**s**) alcoholic drink brewed from malt and hops ▶ **beery** (-**rier**, -**riest**) ▶ adj

beerier adj ▷ **beer**

beeriest adj ▷ **beer**

beers n ▷ **beer**

beery adj ▷ **beer**

bees n ▷ **bee**

beeswax n (pl -**es**) wax secreted by bees, used in polishes etc

beeswaxes n ▷ **beeswax**

beet n (pl -**s**) plant with an edible root and leaves

beetle n (pl -**s**) insect with a hard wing cover on its back

beetles n ▷ **beetle**

beetroot n (pl -**s**) type of beet plant with a dark red root

beetroots n ▷ **beetroot**

beets n ▷ **beet**

beeves n ▷ **beef**

befall v (-**s**, -**ing**, -**fell**, -**fallen**) old-fashioned happen to (someone)

befallen v ▷ **befall**

befalling v ▷ **befall**

befalls v ▷ **befall**

befell v ▷ **befall**

befit v (-**s**, -**tting**, -**tted**) be appropriate or suitable for ▷ **befitting** adj

befits v ▷ **befit**

befitted v ▷ **befit**

befitting v, adj ▷ **befit**

before conj, prep adv indicating something earlier in time, in front of, or preferred to

befriend v (-**s**, -**ing**, -**ed**) become friends with

befriended v ▷ **befriend**

befriending v ▷ **befriend**

befriends v ▷ **befriend**

beg v (-**s**, -**ging**, -**gged**) solicit (for money or food), esp. in the street

began v ▷ **begin**

begat v ▷ **beget**

beget v (-**gets**, -**getting**, -**got** or -**gat**, -**gotten** or -**got**) old-fashioned cause or create

begets v ▷ **beget**

begetting v ▷ **beget**

beggar n (pl -**s**) person who lives by begging ▶ **beggarly** adj ▶ **beggarliness** n

beggarliness n ▷ **beggar**

beggarly adj ▷ **beggar**

beggars n ▷ **beggar**

begged v ▷ **beg**

begging v ▷ **beg**

begin v (-**gins**, -**ginning**, -**gan**, -**gun**) start ▷ **beginning** n (pl -**s**)

beginner n (pl -**s**) person who has just started learning to do something

beginners n ▷ **begin**

beginning v, n ▷ **begin**

beginnings n ▷ **begin**

begins v ▷ **begin**

begonia n (pl -**s**) tropical plant with waxy flowers

begonias n ▷ **begonia**

begot v ▷ **beget**

begotten v ▷ **beget**

begrudge v (-**grudges**, -**grudging**, -**grudged**) envy (someone) the possession of something

begrudged v ▷ **begrudge**

begrudges v ▷ **begrudge**

begrudging v ▷ **begrudge**

begs v ▷ **beg**

beguile v (-**guiles**, -**guiling**, -**guiled**) cheat or mislead > **beguiling** adj

beguiled v ▷ **beguile**

beguiles v ▷ **beguile**

beguiling v, adj ▷ **beguile**

begun v ▷ **begin**

behalf n in the interest of or for the benefit of

behave v (-**haves**, -**having**, -**haved**) act or function in a particular way

behaved v ▷ **behave**

behaves v ▷ **behave**

behaving v ▷ **behave**

behead v (-**s**, -**ing**, -**ed**) remove the head from

beheaded v ▷ **behead**

beheading v ▷ **behead**

beheads v ▷ **behead**

beheld v ▷ **behold**

behest n (pl -**s**) order or earnest request

behests n ▷ **behest**

behind prep, adv indicating position to the rear, lateness, responsibility, etc ▶ n (pl -**s**) informal buttocks

behinds n ▷ **behind**

behold v (-**holds**, -**holding**, -**held**) old-fashioned look (at) > **beholder** n (pl -**s**)

beholden adj indebted or obliged

beholder n ▷ **behold**

beholders n ▷ **behold**

beholding v ▷ **behold**

beholds v ▷ **behold**

behove v (-**hoves**, -**hoving**, -**hoved**) old-fashioned be necessary or fitting for

behoved v ▷ **behove**

behoves v ▷ **behove**

behoving v ▷ **behove**

beige adj pale brown

being n (pl -**s**) state or fact of existing

▶ v ▷ **be**

beings n ▷ **being**

belabour v (-**s**, -**ing**, -**ed**) attack verbally or physically

belaboured v ▷ **belabour**

belabouring v ▷ **belabour**

belabours v ▷ **belabour**

belated adj late or too late > **belatedly** adv

belatedly v ▷ **belated**

belch v (-**es**, -**ing**, -**ed**) expel wind from the stomach noisily through the mouth ▶ n (pl -**es**) act of belching

belched v ▷ **belch**

belches v, n ▷ **belch**

belching v ▷ **belch**

belfries n ▷ **belfry**

belfry n (pl -**fries**) part of a tower where bells are hung

belie v (-**lies**, -**lying**, -**lied**) show to be untrue

belied v ▷ **belie**

belief n (pl -**s**) faith or confidence

beliefs n ▷ **belief**

belies v ▷ **belie**

believable adj ▷ **believe**

believe v (-**lieves**, -**lieving**, -**lieved**) accept as true or real > **believable** adj > **believer** n (pl -**s**)

believed v ▷ **believe**

believer n ▷ **believe**

believers n ▷ **believe**

believes v ▷ **believe**

believing v ▷ **believe**

belittle v (-**les**, -**ling**, -**led**) treat as having little value or importance

belittled v ▷ **belittle**

belittles v ▷ **belittle**

belittling v ▷ **belittle**

bell n (pl -**s**) hollow, usu. metal, cup-shaped instrument that emits a ringing sound when struck

bellbird n (pl -**s**) Australasian bird with bell-like call

bellbirds n ▷ **bellbird**

belle n (pl -**s**) beautiful woman, esp. the most attractive woman at a function

belles n ▷ **belle**

bellied v ▷ **belly**
bellies n, v ▷ **belly**
bellow v (**-s, -ing, -ed**) make a low deep cry like that of a bull ▶ n (pl **-s**) loud deep roar
bellowed v ▷ **bellow**
bellowing v ▷ **bellow**
bellows v, n ▷ **bellow** ▶ n pl **-s** instrument for pumping a stream of air into something
bells n ▷ **bell**
belly n (pl **-lies**) part of the body of a vertebrate which contains the intestines ▶ v (**-lies, -lying, -lied**) (cause to) swell out
bellyful n (pl **-s**) slang more than one can tolerate
bellyfuls n ▷ **bellyful**
bellying v ▷ **belly**
belong v (**-s, -ing, -ed**) (foll. by **to**) be the property of
belonged v ▷ **belong**
belonging v ▷ **belong**
belongs v ▷ **belong**
beloved adj dearly loved ▶ n (pl **-s**) person dearly loved
beloveds n ▷ **beloved**
below prep, adv at or to a position lower than, under
belt n (pl **-s**) band of cloth, leather, etc, worn usu. around the waist ▶ v (**-s, -ing, -ed**) fasten with a belt
belted v ▷ **belt**
belting v ▷ **belt**
belts n, v ▷ **belt**
belying v ▷ **belie**
bemoan v (**-s, -ing, -ed**) express sorrow or dissatisfaction about
bemoaned v ▷ **bemoan**
bemoaning v ▷ **bemoan**
bemoans v ▷ **bemoan**
bemused adj puzzled or confused
bench n (pl **-es**) long seat
benches n ▷ **bench**
bend v (**-s, -ing, bent**) (cause to) form a curve ▶ n curved part ▶ **bendy** adj (**-dier, -diest**)
bendier adj ▷ **bend**

bendiest adj ▷ **bend**
bending v ▷ **bend**
bends v ▷ **bend** ▶ n pl informal decompression sickness
bendy adj ▷ **bend**
beneath adv, prep below
benefit n (pl **-s**) something that improves or promotes ▶ v (**-s, -fiting, -fited**) do or receive good
benefited v ▷ **benefit**
benefiting v ▷ **benefit**
benefits n, v ▷ **benefit**
benign adj showing kindliness
▷ **benignly** adv
benignly adv ▷ **benign**
bent v ▷ **bend** ▶ adj curved ▶ n (pl **-s**) personal inclination or aptitude
bento n (pl **-s**) thin lightweight box divided into compartments, which contain small separate dishes comprising a Japanese meal
bentos n ▷ **bento**
bents n ▷ **bent**
benzene n (pl **-s**) flammable poisonous liquid used as a solvent, insecticide, etc
benzenes n ▷ **benzene**
bequeath v (**-s, -ing, -ed**) dispose of (property) as in a will
bequeathed v ▷ **bequeath**
bequeathing v ▷ **bequeath**
bequeaths v ▷ **bequeath**
bequest n (pl **-s**) legal gift of money or property by someone who has died
bequests n ▷ **bequest**
berate v (**-ates, -ating, -ated**) scold harshly
berated v ▷ **berate**
berates v ▷ **berate**
berating v ▷ **berate**
bereaved adj having recently lost a close friend or relative through death
▷ **bereavement** n (pl **-s**)
bereavement n ▷ **bereaved**
bereavements n ▷ **bereaved**
bereft adj (foll. by **of**) deprived
beret n (pl **-s**) round flat close-fitting brimless cap
berets n ▷ **beret**

berg¹ n (pl **-s**) iceberg

berg² n (pl **-s**) S AFR mountain

bergamot n (pl **-s**) small Asian tree, the fruit of which yields an oil used in perfumery

bergamots n ▷ bergamot

bergs n ▷ berg¹ ², ²

beriberi n (pl **-s**) disease caused by vitamin B deficiency

beriberis n ▷ beriberi

berk n (pl **-s**) BRIT, AUST & NZ slang stupid person

berks n ▷ berk

berm n (pl **-s**) NZ narrow grass strip between the road and the footpath in a residential area

berms n ▷ berm

berries n ▷ berry

berry n (pl **-ries**) small soft stoneless fruit

berserk adj violent or destructive

berth n (pl **-s**) bunk in a ship or train ▷ v (**-s, -ing, -ed**) dock (a ship)

berthed v ▷ berth

berthing v ▷ berth

berths n, v ▷ berth

beryl n (pl **-s**) hard transparent mineral

beryls n ▷ beryl

beseech v (**-seeches, -seeching, -sought** or **-seeched**) ask earnestly; beg

beseeched v ▷ beseech

beseeches v ▷ beseech

beseeching v ▷ beseech

beset v (**-sets, -setting, -set**) trouble or harass constantly

besets v ▷ beset

besetting v ▷ beset

beside prep at, by, or to the side of

besides adv, prep in addition

besiege v (**-sieges, -sieging, -sieged**) surround with military forces

besieged v ▷ besiege

besieges v ▷ besiege

besieging v ▷ besiege

besotted adj infatuated

besought v ▷ beseech

bespeak v (**-speaks, -speaking,**

-spoke, -spoken) indicate or suggest

bespeaking v ▷ bespeak

bespeaks v ▷ bespeak

bespoke v ▷ bespeak ▷ adj (esp. of a suit) made to the customer's specifications

bespoken v ▷ bespeak

best adj most excellent of a particular group etc ▷ adv in a manner surpassing all others ▷ n (pl **-s**) most outstanding or excellent person, thing, or group in a category

bestial adj brutal or savage
> bestiality n (pl **-ities**)

bestialities n ▷ bestial

bestiality n ▷ bestial

bestir v (**-stirs, -stirring, -stirred**) cause (oneself) to become active

bestirred v ▷ bestir

bestirring v ▷ bestir

bestirs v ▷ bestir

bestow v (**-s, -ing, -ed**) present (a gift) or confer (an honour) ▷ bestowal n (pl **-s**)

bestowal n ▷ bestow

bestowals n ▷ bestow

bestowed v ▷ bestow

bestowing v ▷ bestow

bestows v ▷ bestow

bestridden v ▷ bestride

bestride v (**-strides, -striding, -strode, -stridden**) have or put a leg on either side of

bestrides v ▷ bestride

bestriding v ▷ bestride

bestrode v ▷ bestride

bests n ▷ best

bet n (pl **-s**) the act of staking a sum of money or other stake on the outcome of an event ▷ v (**-s, -tting, bet** or **betted**) make or place (a bet)

betel n (pl **-s**) Asian climbing plant, the leaves and nuts of which can be chewed

betels n ▷ betels

betide v (**-tides, -tiding, -tided**) happen (to)

betided v ▷ betide

betides v ▷ betide
betiding v ▷ betide
betoken v (-s, -ing, -ed) indicate or signify
betokened v ▷ betoken
betokening v ▷ betoken
betokens v ▷ betoken
betray v (-s, -ing, -ed) hand over or expose (one's nation, friend, etc) treacherously to an enemy >betrayal n (pl -s) >betrayer n (pl -s)
betrayal n ▷ betray
betrayals n ▷ betray
betrayed v ▷ betray
betrayer n ▷ betray
betrayers n ▷ betray
betraying v ▷ betray
betrays v ▷ betray
bets n, v ▷ bet
betted v ▷ bet
better adj more excellent than others ▶ adv in a more excellent manner ▶ pl n one's superiors ▶ v (-s, -ing, -ed) improve upon
bettered v ▷ better
bettering v ▷ better
betters n, v ▷ better
betting v ▷ bet
bettong n (pl -s) short-nosed rat kangaroo
bettongs n ▷ bettong
between prep, adv indicating position in the middle, alternatives, etc
betwixt prep, adv old-fashioned between
bevel n (pl -s) slanting edge ▶ v (-s, -elling, -elled) cut a bevel on (a piece of timber etc)
bevelled v ▷ bevel
bevelling v ▷ bevel
bevels n, v ▷ bevel
beverage n (pl -s) drink
beverages n ▷ beverage
bevies n ▷ bevy
bevy n (pl bevies) flock or group
bewail v (-s, -ing, -ed) express great sorrow over
bewailed v ▷ bewail

bewailing v ▷ bewail
bewails v ▷ bewail
beware v (-wares, -waring, -wared) be on one's guard (against)
bewared v ▷ beware
bewares v ▷ beware
bewaring v ▷ beware
bewilder v (-s, -ing, -ed) confuse utterly >bewildering adj >bewilderment n (pl -s)
bewildered v ▷ bewilder
bewildering v, adj ▷ bewilder
bewilderment n ▷ bewilder
bewilderments n ▷ bewilder
bewilders v ▷ bewilder
bewitch v (-es, -ing, -ed) attract and fascinate >bewitching adj
bewitched v ▷ bewitch
bewitches v ▷ bewitch
bewitching v, adj ▷ bewitch
 bey n (**beys**). A bey was an official in the Ottoman empire, and scores 8 points
beyond prep at or to a point on the other side of ▶ adv at or to the far side of something
 bez n (**bezes**). A bez is the second spike of a deer's antler. This is a really handy word when you have Z on your rack. Bez scores 14 points.
 bezique n (**beziques**). Bezique is a card game; if you're lucky enough to be able to play it, you'll score 27 points.
bi adj, n (pl -s) short for bisexual
biannual adj occurring twice a year >biannually adv
biannually adv ▷ biannual
bias n (pl -es) mental tendency, esp. prejudice ▶ v (-ases, -asing, -ased or -asses, -assing, -assed) cause to have a >biased, biassed adj
biased v, adj ▷ bias
biases n, v ▷ bias
biasing v ▷ bias
biassed v, adj ▷ bias
biasses n, v ▷ bias
biassing v ▷ bias

bib n (pl -s) piece of cloth or plastic worn to protect a young child's clothes when eating

bible n (pl -s) book regarded as authoritative >**biblical** adj

bibles n ▷ bible

biblical adj ▷ bible

bibs n ▷ bib

bibulous adj addicted to alcohol

biceps n (pl -es) muscle with two origins, esp. the muscle that flexes the forearm

bicepses n ▷ biceps

bicker v (-s, -ing, -ed) argue over petty matters

bickered v ▷ bicker

bickering v ▷ bicker

bickers v ▷ bicker

bicycle n (pl -s) vehicle with two wheels, one behind the other, pedalled by the rider

bicycles n ▷ bicycle

bid v (bids, bidding, bade, bidden) say (a greeting) (past bid) ▶ n (pl -s) offer of a specified amount >**bidder** n (pl -s)

biddable adj obedient

bidden v ▷ bid

bidder n ▷ bid

bidders n ▷ bid

bidding n (pl -s) command ▶ v ▷ bid

bide v (bides, biding, bided) wait patiently for an opportunity

bided v ▷ bide

bides v ▷ bide

bidet n (pl -s) low basin for washing the genital area

bidets n ▷ bidet

biding v ▷ bide

bids v, n ▷ bid

biennial adj occurring every two years ▶ n (pl -s) plant that completes its life cycle in two years

biennials n ▷ biennial

bier n (pl -s) stand on which a corpse or coffin rests before burial

biers n ▷ bier

bifocals pl n spectacles with lenses permitting near and distant vision

big adj (bigger, biggest) of considerable size, height, number, or capacity ▶ adv on a grand scale

bigamies n ▷ bigamy

bigamist n ▷ bigamy

bigamists n ▷ bigamy

bigamous adj ▷ bigamy

bigamously adv ▷ bigamy

bigamy n (pl -mies) crime of marrying a person while still legally married to someone else >**bigamist** n (pl -s) >**bigamous** adj >**bigamously** adv

bigger adj ▷ big

biggest adj ▷ big

bighead n (pl -s) informal conceited person >**bigheaded** adj

bigheaded n ▷ bighead

bigheads n ▷ bighead

bigot n (pl -s) person who is intolerant, esp. regarding religion or race >**bigoted** adj >**bigotry** n (pl -tries)

bigoted adj ▷ bigot

bigotries n ▷ bigot

bigotry n ▷ bigot

bigots n ▷ bigot

bigwig n (pl -s) informal important person

bigwigs n ▷ bigwig

> **bijou** n (**bijoux**). A bijou is an intricate trinket. The plural form, bijoux, uses an X and allows you to score 22 points.

bike n (pl -s) informal bicycle or motorcycle

bikes n ▷ bike

bikini n (pl -s) woman's brief two-piece swimming costume

bikinis n ▷ bikini

bilberries n ▷ bilberry

bilberry n (pl -berries) bluish-black edible berry

bilbies n ▷ bilby

bilby n (pl -bies) Australian marsupial with long pointed ears and grey fur

bile n (pl -s) bitter yellow fluid secreted by the liver

biles n ▷ bile

bilge n (pl -s) informal nonsense

bilges n ▷ bilge
bilious adj sick, nauseous
 >**biliousness** n
biliousness n ▷ bilious
bill¹ n (pl -s) statement of money owed for goods or services supplied ▶ v (-s, -ing, -ed) send or present a bill to
bill² n (pl -s) bird's beak
 billed v ▷ bill¹
billet v (-lets, -leting, -leted) assign a lodging to (a soldier) ▶ n (pl -s) accommodation for a soldier in civil lodgings
 billeted v ▷ billet
 billeting v ▷ billet
 billets v, n ▷ billet
billhook n (pl -s) tool with a hooked blade, used for chopping etc
 billhooks n ▷ billhook
 billies n ▷ billy
 billing v ▷ bill¹
billion n (pl -s) one thousand million
 >**billionth** adj
 billions n ▷ billion
 billionth adj ▷ billion
billow n (pl -s) large sea wave ▶ v (-s, -ing, -ed) rise up or swell out
 >**billowy, billowing** adj
 billowed v ▷ billow
 billowing v, adj ▷ billow
 billows n, v ▷ billow
 billowy adj ▷ billow
 bills n ▷ bill¹, ², ▶ v ▷ bill¹
billy, billycan n (pl -llies, -s) metal can or pot for cooking on a camp fire
 billycan n ▷ billy
 billycans n ▷ billy
biltong n (pl -s) S AFR strips of dried meat
 biltongs n ▷ biltong
bimbo n (pl -s) slang attractive but empty-headed young person, esp. a woman
 bimbos n ▷ bimbo
bin n (pl -s) container for rubbish or for storing grain, coal, etc
binary adj composed of two parts
bind v (binds, binding, bound) make

secure with or as if with a rope ▶ n (pl -s) informal annoying situation
binder n (pl -s) firm cover for holding loose sheets of paper together
 binders n ▷ binder
binding n (pl -s) anything that binds or fastens ▶ v ▷ bind
 bindings n ▷ binding
bindweed n (pl -s) plant that twines around a support
 bindweeds n ▷ bindweed
binge n (pl -s) informal bout of excessive indulgence, esp. in drink
 binges n ▷ binge
bingo n (pl -s) gambling game in which numbers are called out and covered by the players on their individual cards
 bingos n ▷ bingo
binomial n (pl -s) ▶ adj (mathematical expression) consisting of two terms
 binomials n ▷ binomial
 bins n ▷ bin
 biologies n ▷ biology
 biologist n ▷ biology
 biologists n ▷ biology
biology n (pl -gies) study of living organisms >**biologist** n (pl -s)
bionic adj having a part of the body that is operated electronically
 biopsies n ▷ biopsy
biopsy n (pl -sies) examination of tissue from a living body
biped n (pl -s) animal with two feet
 bipeds n ▷ biped
biplane n (pl -s) aeroplane with two sets of wings, one above the other
 biplanes n ▷ biplane
birch n (pl -es) tree with thin peeling bark
 birches n ▷ birch
bird n (pl -s) creature with feathers and wings, most types of which can fly
birdie n (pl -s) GOLF score of one stroke under par for a hole
 birdies n ▷ birdie
 birds n ▷ bird
biretta n (pl -s) stiff square cap worn by the Catholic clergy

birettas n ▷ biretta
birth n (pl -s) process of bearing young; childbirth
birthday n (pl -s) anniversary of the day of one's birth
  birthdays n ▷ birthday
births n ▷ birth
bis n ▷ bi
biscuit n (pl -s) small flat dry sweet or plain cake
  biscuits n ▷ biscuit
bisect v (-s, -ing, -ed) divide into two equal parts
  bisected v ▷ bisect
  bisecting v ▷ bisect
  bisects v ▷ bisect
bisexual adj sexually attracted to both men and women ▶ **bisexuality** n (pl -ties)
  bisexualities n ▷ bisexual
  bisexuality n ▷ bisexual
bishop n (pl -s) clergyman who governs a diocese
  bishops n ▷ bishop
bismuth n (pl -s) CHEM pinkish-white metallic element
  bismuths n ▷ bismuth
bison n (pl bison) large hairy animal of the cattle family, native to N America and Europe
bistro n (pl -s) small restaurant
  bistros n ▷ bistro
bit n[1] (pl -s) small piece, portion, or quantity
bit n[2] (pl -s) metal mouthpiece on a bridle
bit n[3] v ▷ bite
bit n[4] (pl -s) MATHS COMPUTERS single digit of binary notation, either 0 or 1
bitch n (pl -es) female dog, fox, or wolf ▶ v (-es, -ing, -ed) informal complain or grumble > **bitchy** adj (-ier, -iest) > **bitchiness** n
  bitched v ▷ bitch
  bitches n, v ▷ bitch
  bitchier adj ▷ bitch
  bitchiest adj ▷ bitch
  bitching v ▷ bitch

bitchy adj ▷ bitch
bite v (bites, biting, bit, bitten) grip, tear, or puncture the skin, as with the teeth or jaws ▶ n (pl -s) act of biting
  biter n (pl -s)
  biter n ▷ bite
  biters n ▷ bite
  bites v, n ▷ bite
biting adj piercing or keen ▶ v ▷ bite
  bits n ▷ bit[1, 2, 4]
  bitten v ▷ bite
bitter adj (-er, -est) having a sharp unpleasant taste ▶ n (pl -s) beer with a slightly bitter taste ▶ pl bitter-tasting alcoholic drink > **bitterly** adv > **bitterness** n (pl -es)
  bitterer adj ▷ bitter
  bitterest adj ▷ bitter
  bitterly adv ▷ bitter
bittern n (pl -s) wading marsh bird with a booming call
  bitterness n ▷ bitter
  bitternesses n ▷ bitter
  bitterns n ▷ bittern
  bitters n ▷ bitter
bitumen n (pl -s) black sticky substance obtained from tar or petrol
  bitumens n ▷ bitumen
bivalve n (pl -s) ▶ adj (marine mollusc) with two hinged segments to its shell
  bivalves n ▷ bivalve
bivouac n (pl -s) temporary camp in the open air ▶ v (-acs, -acking, -acked) camp in a bivouac
  bivouacked v ▷ bivouac
  bivouacking v ▷ bivouac
  bivouacs n, v ▷ bivouac
bizarre adj odd or unusual > **bizarrely** adv > **bizarreness** n (pl -es)
  bizarrely adv ▷ bizarre
  bizarreness n ▷ bizarre
  bizarrenesses n ▷ bizarre
blab v (-s, -bbing, -bbed) reveal (secrets) indiscreetly
  blabbed v ▷ blab
  blabbing v ▷ blab
  blabs v ▷ blab
black adj (-er, -est) of the darkest

colour, like coal ▶ n (pl -s) darkest
colour ▶ v (-s, -ing, -ed) make black
> **blackness** n (pl -es)
blackboy n (pl -s) Australian plant
with grasslike leaves and a spike of
small white flowers
blackboys n ▷ blackboy
blacked v ▷ black
blacken v (-s, -ing, -ed) make or
become black
blackened v ▷ blacken
blackening v ▷ blacken
blackens v ▷ blacken
blacker adj ▷ black
blackest adj ▷ black
blacking v ▷ black
blackleg n (pl -s) person who
continues to work during a strike
blacklegs n ▷ blackleg
blackness n ▷ black
blackout n (pl -s) extinguishing of
all light as a precaution against an
air attack
blackouts n ▷ blackout
blacks n, v ▷ black
bladder n (pl -s) sac in the body where
urine is held
bladders n ▷ bladder
blade n (pl -s) cutting edge of a weapon
or tool
blades n ▷ blade
blame v (-mes, -ming, -med) consider
(someone) responsible for ▶ n (pl -s)
responsibility for something that is
wrong > **blameless** adj
blamed v ▷ blame
blameless adj ▷ blame
blames v, n ▷ blame
blaming v ▷ blame
blanch v (-es, -ing, -ed) become
white or pale
blanched v ▷ blanch
blanches v ▷ blanch
blanching v ▷ blanch
bland adj (-er, -est) dull and
uninteresting > **blandly** adv
blander adj ▷ bland
blandest adj ▷ bland

blandly adv ▷ bland
blank adj not written on ▶ n (pl -s)
empty space > **blankly** adv
blanket n (pl -s) large thick cloth used
as covering for a bed ▶ v (-s, -ing, -ed)
cover as with a blanket
blanketed v ▷ blanket
blanketing v ▷ blanket
blankets n, v ▷ blanket
blankly adv ▷ blank
blanks n ▷ blank
blare v (-res, -ring, -red) sound loudly
and harshly ▶ n (pl -s) loud harsh noise
blared v ▷ blare
blares v, n ▷ blare
blaring v ▷ blare
blarney n (pl -s) flattering talk
blarneys n ▷ blarney
blasé adj indifferent or bored through
familiarity
blast n (pl -s) explosion ▶ v (-s,
-ing, -ed) blow up (a rock etc) with
explosives
blasted v ▷ blast
blasting v ▷ blast
blastoff n (pl -s) launching of a rocket
blastoffs n ▷ blastoff
blasts n, v ▷ blast
blatant adj glaringly obvious
> **blatantly** adv
blatantly adv ▷ blatant
blaze[1] n (pl -s) strong fire or flame ▶ v
(-s, -zing, -d) burn or shine brightly
blaze[2] n (pl -s) mark made on a tree to
indicate a route
blazed v ▷ blaze[1]
blazer n (pl -s) lightweight jacket,
often in the colours of a school etc
blazers n ▷ blazer
blazes n ▷ blaze[1, 2] ▶ v ▷ blaze[1]
blazing v ▷ blaze[1]
blazon v (-s, -ing, -ed) proclaim
publicly
blazoned v ▷ blazon
blazoning v ▷ blazon
blazons v ▷ blazon
bleach ▶ v (-es, -ing, -ed) make or
become white or colourless ▶ n (pl -es)

bleaching agent
bleached v ▷ **bleach**
bleaches v, n ▷ **bleach**
bleaching v ▷ **bleach**

bleak adj (**-er, -est**) exposed and barren > **bleakly** adv > **bleakness** n (pl **-es**)
bleaker adj ▷ **bleak**
bleakest adj ▷ **bleak**
bleakly adv ▷ **bleak**
bleakness n ▷ **bleak**
bleaknesses n ▷ **bleak**
blearier adj ▷ **bleary**
bleariest adj ▷ **bleary**
blearily adv ▷ **bleary**
bleariness n ▷ **bleary**
blearinesses n ▷ **bleary**
bleary adj (**-rier, -riest**) with eyes dimmed, by tears or tiredness > **blearily** adv > **bleariness** n (pl **-es**)
bleat v (**-s, -ing, -ed**) (of a sheep, goat, or calf) utter its plaintive cry ▶ n (pl **-s**) cry of sheep, goats, and calves
bleated v ▷ **bleat**
bleating v ▷ **bleat**
bleats v, n ▷ **bleat**
bled v ▷ **bleed**
bleed v (**-s, -ing, bled**) lose or emit blood
bleeding v ▷ **bleed**
bleeds v ▷ **bleed**
bleep n (pl **-s**) short high-pitched sound made by an electrical device ▶ v (**-s, -ing, -ed**) make a bleeping sound
bleeped v ▷ **bleep**
bleeper n (pl **-s**) small portable radio receiver that makes a bleeping signal
bleepers n ▷ **bleeper**
bleeping v ▷ **bleep**
bleeps v, n ▷ **bleep**
blemish n (pl **-es**) defect or stain ▶ v (**-es, -ing, -ed**) spoil or tarnish
blemished v ▷ **blemish**
blemishes n, v ▷ **blemish**
blemishing v ▷ **blemish**
blench v (**-es, -ing, -ed**) shy away, as in fear
blenched v ▷ **blench**
blenches v ▷ **blench**

blenching v ▷ **blench**
blend v (**-s, -ing, -ed**) mix or mingle (components or ingredients) ▶ n (pl **-s**) mixture
blended v ▷ **blend**
blender n (pl **-s**) electrical appliance for puréeing vegetables etc
blenders n ▷ **blender**
blending v ▷ **blend**
blends v, n ▷ **blend**
bless v (**-es, -ing, -ed**) make holy by means of a religious rite
blessed adj holy ▶ v ▷ **blessed** > **blessedness** n
blessedness n ▷ **blessed**
blesses v ▷ **bless**
blessing n (pl **-s**) invoking of divine aid ▶ v ▷ **bless**
blessings n ▷ **blessing**
blether SCOT v (**-s, -ing, -ed**) talk, esp. foolishly or at length ▶ n (pl **-s**) conversation
blethered v ▷ **blether**
blethering v ▷ **blether**
blethers v, n ▷ **blether**
blew v ▷ **blow¹**
blight n (pl **-s**) person or thing that spoils or prevents growth ▶ v (**-s, -ing, -ed**) frustrate or disappoint
blighted v ▷ **blight**
blighter n (pl **-s**) informal irritating person
blighters n ▷ **blighter**
blighting v ▷ **blight**
blights n, v ▷ **blight**
blimp n (pl **-s**) small airship
blimps n ▷ **blimp**
blind adj (**-er, -est**) unable to see ▶ v (**-s, -ing, -ed**) deprive of sight ▶ n (pl **-s**) covering for a window > **blindly** adv > **blindness** n (pl **-es**)
blinded v ▷ **blind**
blinder adj ▷ **blind**
blindest adj ▷ **blind**
blinding v ▷ **blind**
blindly adv ▷ **blind**
blindness n ▷ **blind**
blindnesses n ▷ **blind**

blinds v, n ▷ blind

blink v (**-s, -ing, -ed**) close and immediately reopen (the eyes) ▶ n (pl **-s**) act of blinking
blinked v ▷ blink

blinkers pl n leather flaps on a horse's bridle to prevent sideways vision
blinking v ▷ blink
blinks v, n ▷ blink

blip n (pl **-s**) spot of light on a radar screen indicating the position of an object
blips n ▷ blip

bliss n (pl **-es**) perfect happiness > blissful adj > blissfully adv
blisses n ▷ bliss
blissful adj ▷ bliss
blissfully adv ▷ bliss

blister n (pl **-s**) small bubble on the skin ▶ v (**-s, -ing, -ed**) (cause to) have blisters
blistered v ▷ blister
blisters n, v ▷ blister

blithe adj (**-r, -st**) casual and indifferent > blithely adv > blitheness n (pl **-es**)
blithely adv ▷ blithe
blitheness n ▷ blithe
blithenesses n ▷ blithe
blither adj ▷ blithe
blithest adj ▷ blithe

blitz n (pl **-es**) violent and sustained attack by aircraft ▶ v (**-s, -ing, -ed**) attack suddenly and intensively
blitzed v ▷ blitz
blitzes n, v ▷ blitz
blitzing v ▷ blitz

blizzard n (pl **-s**) blinding storm of wind and snow
blizzards n ▷ blizzard

bloat v (**-s, -ing, -ed**) cause to swell, as with liquid or air
bloated v ▷ bloat

bloater n (pl **-s**) BRIT salted smoked herring
bloaters n ▷ bloater
bloating v ▷ bloat
bloats v ▷ bloat

blob n (pl **-s**) soft mass or drop

blobs n ▷ blob

bloc n (pl **-s**) people or countries combined by a common interest

block n (pl **-s**) large solid piece of wood, stone, etc ▶ v (**-s, -ing, -ed**) obstruct or impede by introducing an obstacle > blockage n (pl **-s**)

blockade n (pl **-s**) sealing off of a place to prevent the passage of goods ▶ v (**-ades, -ading, -aded**) impose a blockade on
blockaded n ▷ blockade
blockades n, v ▷ blockade
blockading n ▷ blockade
blockage n ▷ block
blockages n ▷ block
blocked v ▷ block

blockie n (pl **-s**) AUST owner of a small property, esp. a farm
blockies n ▷ blockie
blocking v ▷ block
blocks n, v ▷ block
blocs n ▷ bloc

blog n (pl **-s**) > weblog
blogs n ▷ blog

bloke n (pl **-s**) informal man
blokes n ▷ bloke

blonde, blond adj, n (pl **-es, -s**) fair-haired (person)
blondes n ▷ blonde
blonds n ▷ blonde

blood n (pl **-s**) red fluid that flows around the body > bloodless adj > bloodlessness n
bloodied v ▷ bloody
bloodies v ▷ bloody
bloodily adv ▷ bloody
bloodiness n ▷ bloody
bloodinesses n ▷ bloody
bloodless adj ▷ blood
bloodlessness n ▷ blood
bloods n ▷ blood

bloody adj covered with blood ▶ adj, adv slang extreme or extremely ▶ v (**-dies, -dying, -died**) stain with blood > bloodily adv > bloodiness n (pl **-es**)
bloodying v ▷ bloody

bloom n (pl **-s**) blossom on a flowering

plant ▶ v (-s, -ing, -ed) bear flowers
bloomed v ▷ **bloom**
bloomer n (pl -s) BRIT informal stupid mistake
bloomers n ▷ **bloomer** ▶ pl n woman's baggy knickers
blooming v ▷ **bloom**
blooms n, v ▷ **bloom**
blooper n (pl -s) CHIEFLY US informal stupid mistake
bloopers n ▷ **blooper**
blossom n (pl -s) flowers of a plant ▶ v (-s, -ing, -ed) (of plants) flower
blossomed v ▷ **blossom**
blossoming v ▷ **blossom**
blossoms n, v ▷ **blossom**
blot n (pl -s) spot or stain ▶ v (-s, -tting, -tted) cause a blemish in or on
> **blotter** n (pl -s)
blotch n (pl -es) discoloured area or stain ▶ **blotchy** adj
blotches n ▷ **blotch**
blotchy adj ▷ **blotch**
blots n, v ▷ **blot**
blotted v ▷ **blot**
blotter n ▷ **blot**
blotters n ▷ **blot**
blotting v ▷ **blot**
blotto adj BRIT, AUST & NZ slang extremely drunk
blouse n (pl -s) woman's shirtlike garment
blouses n ▷ **blouse**
blow[1] v (-s, -ing, blew, blown) (of air, the wind, etc) move ▶ **blower** n (pl -s)
blow[2] n (pl -s) hard hit
blower n ▷ **blow**[1]
blowers n ▷ **blow**[1]
blowie n (pl blowies) AUST informal bluebottle
blowier n ▷ **blowy**
blowies n ▷ **blowie**
blowiest n ▷ **blowy**
blowing v ▷ **blow**[1]
blown v ▷ **blow**[1]
blowout n (pl -s) sudden loss of air in a tyre
blowouts n ▷ **blowout**

blows v ▷ **blow**[1] ▶ n ▷ **blow**[2]
blowsier n ▷ **blowsy**
blowsiest n ▷ **blowsy**
blowsy adj (-sier, -siest) fat, untidy, and red-faced
blowy adj (-wier, -wiest) windy
blubber n fat of whales, seals, etc ▶ v (-s, -ing, -ed) sob without restraint
blubbered v ▷ **blubber**
blubbering v ▷ **blubber**
blubbers n, v ▷ **blubber**
bludge informal v (-ges, -ging, -ged) AUST & NZ evade work ▶ n (pl -s) AUST easy task
bludged v ▷ **bludge**
bludgeon n (pl -s) short thick club ▶ v (-s, -ing, -ed) hit with a bludgeon
bludgeoned v ▷ **bludgeon**
bludgeoning v ▷ **bludgeon**
bludgeons n, v ▷ **bludgeon**
bludger n (pl -s) person who scrounges
bludgers n ▷ **bludger**
bludges v, n ▷ **bludge**
bludging v ▷ **bludge**
blue n (pl -s) colour of a clear unclouded sky ▶ pl feeling of depression ▶ adj (bluer, bluest) of the colour blue
> **bluish** adj
bluebell n (pl -s) flower with blue bell-shaped flowers
bluebells n ▷ **bluebell**
bluer adj ▷ **blue**
blues n ▷ **blue**
bluest adj ▷ **blue**
bluff[1] v (-s, -ing, -ed) pretend to be confident in order to influence (someone) ▶ n (pl -s) act of bluffing
bluff[2] n (pl -s) steep cliff or bank ▶ adj good-naturedly frank and hearty
bluffed v ▷ **bluff**[1]
bluffing v ▷ **bluff**[1]
bluffs v, n ▷ **bluff**[1, 2]
bluish adj ▷ **blue**
blunder n (pl -s) clumsy mistake ▶ v (-s, -ing, -ed) make a blunder
blundered v ▷ **blunder**
blundering v ▷ **blunder**
blunders n, v ▷ **blunder**

blunt adj (-er, -est) not having a sharp edge or point ▸ v (-s, -ing, -ed) make less sharp ▸ **bluntly** adv ▸ **bluntness** n (pl -es)

blunted v ▷ blunt

blunter adj ▷ blunt

bluntest adj ▷ blunt

blunting v ▷ blunt

bluntly adv ▷ blunt

bluntness n ▷ blunt

bluntnesses n ▷ blunt

blunts v ▷ blunt

blur v (-s, -rring, -rred) make or become vague or less distinct ▸ n (pl -s) something vague, hazy, or indistinct ▸ **blurry** adj (-rier, -rriest)

blurb n (pl -s) promotional description, as on the jacket of a book

blurbs n ▷ blurb

blurred v ▷ blur

blurrier adj ▷ blur

blurriest adj ▷ blur

blurring v ▷ blur

blurry adj ▷ blur

blurs v, n ▷ blur

blurt v (-s, -ing, -ed) (foll. by **out**) utter suddenly and involuntarily

blurted v ▷ blurt

blurting v ▷ blurt

blurts v ▷ blurt

blush v (-es, -ing, -ed) become red in the face, esp. from embarrassment or shame ▸ n (pl -es) reddening of the face

blushed v ▷ blush

blushes v, n ▷ blush

blushing v ▷ blush

bluster v (-s, -ing, -ed) speak loudly or in a bullying way ▸ n (pl -s) empty threats or protests

blustered v ▷ bluster

blusteriness n ▷ blustery

blustering v ▷ bluster

blusters v, n ▷ bluster

blustery adj (of weather) rough and windy

bo or **boh** interjection. Bo is an exclamation used to startle someone. Bo scores 4 points, while boh scores 8.

boa n (pl -s) large nonvenomous snake

boab n (pl -s) AUST informal ▷ **baobab**

boabs n ▷ **boab**

boar n (pl -s) uncastrated male pig

board n (pl -s) long flat piece of sawn timber ▸ v (-s, -ing, -ed) go aboard (a train, aeroplane, etc)

boarded v ▷ **board**

boarder n (pl -s) person who pays rent in return for accommodation in someone else's home

boarders n ▷ **boarder**

boarding v ▷ **board**

boards n, v ▷ **board**

boars n ▷ **boar**

boas n ▷ **boa**

boast v (-s, -ing, -ed) speak too proudly about one's talents etc ▸ n (pl -s) bragging statement ▷ **boastful** adj ▷ **boastfully** adv ▷ **boastfulness** n

boasted v ▷ **boast**

boastful adj ▷ **boast**

boastfully adv ▷ **boast**

boastfulness n ▷ **boast**

boasting v ▷ **boast**

boasts v, n ▷ **boast**

boat n (pl -s) small vehicle for travelling across water ▷ **boating** n

boater n (pl -s) flat straw hat

boaters n ▷ **boater**

boating n ▷ **boat**

boats n ▷ **boat**

boatswain n (pl -s) ▷ **bosun**

boatswains n ▷ **bosun**

bob¹ v (-s, -bbing, -bbed) move up and down repeatedly ▸ n (pl -s) short abrupt movement

bob² n (pl -s) hairstyle in which the hair is cut short evenly all round the head ▸ v (-s, -bbing, -bbed) cut (the hair) in a bob

bobbed v ▷ bob¹, ²

bobbies n ▷ **bobby**

bobbin n (pl -s) reel on which thread is wound

bobbing v ▷ bob¹, ²

bobbins n ▷ bobbin

bobble n (pl -s) small ball of material, usu. for decoration

bobbles n ▷ bobble

bobby n (pl -bies) BRIT informal policeman

bobotie n (pl -s) S AFR dish of curried mince

boboties n ▷ bobotie

bobs v, n ▷ bob[1, 2]

bode v (-des, -ding, -ded) be an omen of (good or ill)

boded v ▷ bode

bodes v ▷ bode

bodice n (pl -s) upper part of a dress

bodices n ▷ bodice

bodies n ▷ body

bodily adj relating to the body ▶ adv by taking hold of the body

boding v ▷ bode

bodkin n (pl -s) blunt large-eyed needle

bodkins n ▷ bodkin

body n (pl -dies) entire physical structure of an animal or human

bodywork n (pl -s) outer shell of a motor vehicle

bodyworks n ▷ bodywork

boffin n (pl -s) BRIT, AUST, NZ & S AFR informal scientist or expert

boffins n ▷ boffin

bog n (pl -s) wet spongy ground ▷ **boggy** adj (-gier, -giest)

bogan n (pl -s) AUST DATED & NZ slang youth who dresses and behaves rebelliously

bogans n ▷ bogan

bogey, bogy n (pl bogeys, bogies) something that worries or annoys

bogeys n ▷ bogey

boggier adj ▷ bog

boggiest adj ▷ bog

boggle v (-les, -ling, -led) be surprised, confused, or alarmed

boggled v ▷ boggle

boggles v ▷ boggle

boggling v ▷ boggle

boggy adj ▷ bog

bogies n ▷ bogey

bogong, bugong n (pl -s) large nocturnal Australian moth

bogongs n ▷ bogong

bogs n ▷ bog

bogus adj not genuine

bogy n (pl -gies) ▷ bogey

bohemian n (pl -s) ▶ adj (person) leading an unconventional life

bohemians n ▷ bohemian

boil[1] v (-s, -ing, -ed) (cause to) change from a liquid to a vapour so quickly that bubbles are formed ▶ n (pl -s) state or action of boiling

boil[2] n (pl -s) red pus-filled swelling on the skin

boiled v ▷ boil[1]

boiler n (pl -s) piece of equipment which provides hot water

boilers n ▷ boiler

boiling v ▷ boil[1]

boils v, n ▷ boil[1, 2]

bold adj (-er, -est) confident and fearless ▷ **boldly** adv ▷ **boldness** n (pl -es)

bolder adj ▷ bold

boldest adj ▷ bold

boldly adv ▷ bold

boldness n ▷ bold

boldnesses n ▷ bold

bole n (pl -s) tree trunk

bolero n (pl -s) (music for) traditional Spanish dance

boleros n ▷ bolero

boles n ▷ bole

bollard n (pl -s) short thick post used to prevent the passage of motor vehicles

bollards n ▷ bollard

boloney n (pl -s) ▷ baloney

boloneys n ▷ boloney

bolshie, bolshy adj informal difficult or rebellious

bolshy adj ▷ bolshie

bolster v (-s, -ing, -ed) support or strengthen ▶ n (pl -s) long narrow pillow

bolstered v ▷ bolster

bolstering v ▷ bolster

bolsters v, n ▷ bolster

bolt n (pl -s) sliding metal bar for fastening a door etc ▶ v (-s, -ing, -ed) run away suddenly
bolted v ▷ bolt
bolting v ▷ bolt
bolts n, v ▷ bolt

bomb n (pl -s) container fitted with explosive material ▶ v (-s, -ing, -ed) attack with bombs

bombard v (-s, -ing, -ed) attack with heavy gunfire or bombs
> **bombardment** n (pl -s)
bombarded v ▷ bombard
bombarding v ▷ bombard
bombardment n ▷ bombard
bombardments n ▷ bombard
bombards n ▷ bombard

bombast n (pl -s) pompous language
> **bombastic** adj
bombastic adj ▷ bombast
bombasts n ▷ bombast
bombed v ▷ bomb

bomber n (pl -s) aircraft that drops bombs
bombers n ▷ bomber
bombing v ▷ bomb
bombs n, v ▷ bomb

bonanza n (pl -s) sudden good luck or wealth
bonanzas n ▷ bonanza

bond n (pl -s) something that binds, fastens or holds together ▶ pl something that restrains or imprisons ▶ v (-s, -ing, -ed) bind > **bonded** adj

bondage n (pl -s) slavery
bondages n ▷ bondage
bonded v, adj ▷ bond
bonding v ▷ bond
bonds n, v ▷ bond

bone n (pl -s) any of the hard parts in the body that form the skeleton ▶ v (-nes, -ning, -ned) remove the bones from (meat for cooking etc)
> **boneless** adj
boned v ▷ bone
boneless adj ▷ bone
bones n, v ▷ bone

bonfire n (pl -s) large outdoor fire

bonfires n ▷ bonfire

bongo n (pl -gos, -goes) small drum played with the fingers
bongoes n ▷ bongo
bongos n ▷ bongo

bonhomie n (pl -s) cheerful friendliness
bonhomies n ▷ bonhomie
bonier adj ▷ bony
boniest adj ▷ bony
boning v ▷ bone

bonito n (pl -s) small tunny-like marine food fish
bonitos n ▷ bonito

bonnet n (pl -s) metal cover over a vehicle's engine
bonnets n ▷ bonnet
bonnier adj ▷ bonny
bonniest adj ▷ bonny
bonnily adv ▷ bonny

bonny adj (-nier, -niest) SCOT beautiful
> **bonnily** adv

bonsai n (pl bonsai) ornamental miniature tree or shrub

bonus n (pl -es) something given, paid, or received above what is due or expected
bonuses n ▷ bonus

bony adj (-nier, -niest) having many bones

boo interj shout of disapproval ▶ v (-s, -ing, -ed) shout `boo' to show disapproval

boob slang n (pl -s) foolish mistake
boobies n ▷ booby

boobook n (pl -s) small spotted Australian brown owl
boobooks n ▷ boobook
boobs n ▷ boob

booby n (pl -bies) foolish person
booed v ▷ boo

boogie v (-s, -ing, -d) informal dance to fast pop music
boogied v ▷ boogie
boogieing v ▷ boogie
boogies v ▷ boogie
booing v ▷ boo

book n (pl -s) number of pages bound

together between covers ▶ *pl* record
of transactions of a business or society
▶ *v* (**-s, -ing, -ed**) reserve (a place,
passage, etc) in advance
booked *n* ▷ **book**
booking *v* ▷ **book**

booklet *n* (*pl* **-s**) thin book with paper
covers
booklets *n* ▷ **booklet**

bookmark *n* (*pl* **-s**) strip of material
used to mark a place in a book ▶ *v* (**-s,
-ing, -ed**) COMPUTERS identify and
store (a website) so that one can return
to it quickly and easily
bookmarked *v* ▷ **bookmark**
bookmarking *v* ▷ **bookmark**
bookmarks *n, v* ▷ **bookmark**
books *n, v* ▷ **book**

bookworm *n* (*pl* **-s**) person devoted
to reading
bookworms *n* ▷ **bookworm**

boom[1] *v* (**-s, -ing, -ed**) make a loud
deep echoing sound ▶ *n* (*pl* **-s**) loud
deep echoing sound

boom[2] *n* (*pl* **-s**) pole to which the foot
of a sail is attached
boomed *v* ▷ **boom**[1]

boomer *n* (*pl* **-s**) AUST large male
kangaroo
boomers *n* ▷ **boomer**
booming *v* ▷ **boom**[1, 2]
booms *v, n* ▷ **boom**[1, 2]

boon *n* (*pl* **-s**) something helpful or
beneficial
boongaries *n* ▷ **boongary**

boongary *n* (*pl* **-garies**) tree kangaroo
of NE Queensland, Australia
boons *n* ▷ **boon**

boor *n* (*pl* **-s**) rude or insensitive
person ▶ **boorish** *adj* ▷ **boorishly** *adv*
▷ **boorishness** *n*
boorishly *adv* ▷ **boor**
boorishness *n* ▷ **boor**
boors *n* ▷ **boor**
boos *v* ▷ **boo**

boost *n* (*pl* **-s**) encouragement or help
▶ *v* (**-s, -ing, -ed**) improve
boosted *v* ▷ **boost**

booster *n* (*pl* **-s**) small additional
injection of a vaccine
boosters *n* ▷ **booster**
boosting *v* ▷ **boost**
boosts *n, v* ▷ **boost**

boot *n* (*pl* **-s**) outer covering for the foot
that extends above the ankle ▶ *v* (**-s,
-ing, -ed**) *informal* kick
booted *v* ▷ **boot**

bootee *n* (*pl* **-s**) baby's soft shoe
bootees *n* ▷ **bootee**

booth *n* (*pl* **-s**) small partly enclosed
cubicle
booths *n* ▷ **booth**
booties *n* ▷ **booty**
booting *v* ▷ **boot**

bootleg *adj* produced, distributed,
or sold illicitly ▶ *v* (**-legs, -legging,
-legged**) make, carry, or sell (illicit
goods) > **bootlegger** *n* (*pl* **-s**)
bootlegged *v* ▷ **bootleg**
bootlegger *n* ▷ **bootleg**
bootleggers *n* ▷ **bootleg**
bootlegging *v* ▷ **bootleg**
bootlegs *v* ▷ **bootleg**
boots *n, v* ▷ **boot**

booty *n* (*pl* **-ties**) valuable articles
obtained as plunder

booze *v* (**-zes, -zing, -zed**), ▶ *n* (*pl* **-s**)
informal (consume) alcoholic drink
> **boozy** *adj* (**-zier, -ziest**) > **boozily** *adv*
boozed *v* ▷ **booze**

boozer *n* (*pl* **-s**) *informal* person who is
fond of drinking
boozers *n* ▷ **booze**
boozes *v, n* ▷ **booze**
boozier *adj* ▷ **booze**
booziest *adj* ▷ **booze**
boozily *adv* ▷ **booze**
boozing *v* ▷ **booze**
boozy *adj* ▷ **booze**

bop *v* (**-s, -pping, -pped**) *informal*
dance to pop music
bopped *v* ▷ **bop**
bopping *v* ▷ **bop**
bops *v* ▷ **bop**

bora *n* (*pl* **-s**) AUST Aboriginal ceremony
boras *n* ▷ **bora**

borax n (pl -es) white mineral used in making glass

boraxes n ▷ borax

border n (pl -s) dividing line between political or geographical regions ▶ v (-s, -ing, -ed) provide with a border

bordered v ▷ border

bordering v ▷ border

borders n, v ▷ border

bore¹ v (-res, -ring, -red) make (a hole) with a drill etc ▶ n (pl -s) (diameter of) the hollow of a gun barrel or other tube

bore² v (-res, -ring, -red) make weary by being dull or repetitious ▶ n (pl -s) dull or repetitious person or thing > **bored** adj > **boredom** n (pl -s)

bore³ n (pl -s) high wave in a narrow estuary, caused by the tide

bore⁴ v ▷ bear¹

bored v, n ▷ bore¹, ²

boredom n ▷ bore²

boredoms n ▷ bore²

boree n (pl -s) AUST ▷ myall

borees n ▷ boree

bores n bore¹, ², ³ ▶ v ▷ bore¹, ²

boring v ▷ bore¹, ²

born v ▷ bear¹ ▶ adj possessing certain qualities from birth

borne v ▷ bear¹

boron n CHEM element used in hardening steel

boronia n (pl -s) Australian aromatic flowering shrub

boronias n ▷ boronia

borons n ▷ boron

borough n (pl -s) CHIEFLY BRIT town or district with its own council

boroughs n ▷ borough

borrow v (-s, -ing, -ed) obtain (something) temporarily > **borrower** n (pl -s)

borrowed v ▷ borrow

borrower n ▷ borrow

borrowers n ▷ borrow

borrowing v ▷ borrow

borrows v ▷ borrow

borstal n (pl -s) (formerly in Britain) prison for young criminals

borstals n ▷ borstal

borzoi n (pl -s) tall dog with a long silky coat

borzois n ▷ borzoi

bosh n (pl -es) BRIT, AUST & NZ informal empty talk, nonsense

boshes n ▷ bosh

bosom n (pl -s) chest of a person, esp. the female breasts ▶ adj very dear

bosoms n ▷ bosom

boss¹ n (pl -es) person in charge of or employing others ▶ v (-es, -ing, -ed) be domineering towards > **bossy** adj > **bossiness** n

boss² n (pl -es) raised knob or stud

bossed v ▷ boss¹

bosses n ▷ boss¹, ² ▶ v ▷ boss¹

bossiness n ▷ boss¹

bossing v ▷ boss¹

bossy adj ▷ boss¹

bosun n (pl -s) officer responsible for the maintenance of a ship

bosuns n ▷ bosun

botanic adj ▷ botany

botanical adj ▷ botany

botanies n ▷ botany

botanist n ▷ botany

botanists n ▷ botany

botany n (pl -ies) study of plants > **botanical, botanic** adj > **botanist** n (pl -s)

botch v (-es, -ing, -ed) spoil through clumsiness ▶ n (pl -es) badly done piece of work or repair

botched v ▷ botch

botches v, n ▷ botch

botching v ▷ botch

both adj, pron two considered together

bother v (-s, -ing, -ed) take the time or trouble ▶ n (pl -s) trouble, fuss, or difficulty > **bothersome** adj

bothered v ▷ bother

bothering v ▷ bother

bothers v, n ▷ bother

bothersome adj ▷ bother

bottle n (pl -s) container for holding liquids ▶ v (-les, -ling, -led) put in a bottle

bottled v ▷ bottle

bottles n, v ▷ bottle

bottling v ▷ bottle

bottom n (pl -s) lowest, deepest, or farthest removed part of a thing ▶ adj lowest or last ▷ **bottomless** adj

bottomless adj ▷ bottom

bottoms n ▷ bottom

botulism n (pl -s) severe food poisoning

botulisms n ▷ botulism

boudoir n (pl -s) woman's bedroom or private sitting room

boudoirs n ▷ boudoir

bough n (pl -s) large branch of a tree

boughs n ▷ bough

bought v ▷ buy

boulder n (pl -s) large rounded rock

boulders n ▷ boulder

bounce v (-ces, -cing, -ced) (of a ball etc) rebound from an impact slang ▶ n (pl -s) act of rebounding

bounced v ▷ bounce

bouncer n (pl -s) person employed at a disco etc to remove unwanted people

bouncers n ▷ bouncer

bounces v, n ▷ bounce

bouncing v ▷ bounce ▶ adj vigorous and robust

bound¹ v ▷ bind ▶ adj destined or certain

bound² v (-s, -ing, -ed) move forwards by jumps ▶ n (pl -s) jump upwards or forwards

bound³ v (-s, -ing, -ed) form a boundary of ▶ pl n limit

bound⁴ adj going or intending to go towards

boundaries n ▷ boundary

boundary n (pl -ries) dividing line that indicates the farthest limit

bounded v ▷ bound², 3

bounding v ▷ bound², 3

bounds v, n ▷ bound², 3

bounteous adj ▷ bounty

bounties n ▷ bounty

bountiful adj ▷ bounty

bounty n (pl -ties) generosity

> **bountiful, bounteous** adj

bouquet n (pl -s) bunch of flowers

bouquets n ▷ bouquet

bourbon n (pl -s) whiskey made from maize

bourbons n ▷ bourbon

bout n (pl -s) period of activity or illness

boutique n (pl -s) small clothes shop

boutiques n ▷ boutique

bouts n ▷ bout

bovine adj relating to cattle

bow¹ v (-s, -ing, -ed) lower (one's head) or bend (one's knee or body) as a sign of respect or shame ▶ n (pl -s) movement made when bowing

bow² n (pl -s) knot with two loops and loose ends

bow³ n (pl -s) front end of a ship

bowed v ▷ bow¹

bowel n (pl -s) intestine, esp. the large intestine ▶ pl innermost part

bowels n ▷ bowel

bower n (pl -s) shady leafy shelter

bowers n ▷ bower

bowing v ▷ bow¹

bowl¹ n (pl -s) round container with an open top

bowl² n (pl -s) large heavy ball ▶ pl game played on smooth grass with wooden bowls ▶ v (-s, -ing, -ed) CRICKET send (a ball) towards the batsman

bowled v ▷ bowl²

bowler¹ n CRICKET player who sends (a ball) towards the batsman

bowler² n (pl -s) stiff felt hat with a rounded crown

bowlers n ▷ bowler¹, ²

bowling n game in which bowls are rolled at a group of pins ▶ v ▷ bowl²

bowls n ▷ bowl¹, ² ▶ v ▷ bowl²

bows v ▷ bow¹ ▶ n ▷ bow¹, ², 3

box¹ n (pl -es) container with a firm flat base and sides ▶ v (-es, -ing, -ed) put into a box

box² v (-es, -ing, -ed) fight (an opponent) in a boxing match

box³ n (pl -es) evergreen tree with shiny

leaves bark

boxed v ▷ **box**¹, ²

boxer n (pl **-s**) person who participates in the sport of boxing

boxers n ▷ **boxer**

boxes v ▷ **box**¹, ², ³ ▶ n ▷ **box**¹, ², ³

boxing n sport of fighting with the fists ▶ v ▷ **box**¹, ²

boy n (pl **-s**) male child ▶ **boyish** adj ▷ **boyhood** n (pl **-s**)

boycott v (**-s, -ing, -ed**) refuse to deal with (an organization or country) ▶ n (pl **-s**) instance of boycotting

boycotted v ▷ **boycott**

boycotting v ▷ **boycott**

boycotts v, n ▷ **boycott**

boyhood n ▷ **boy**

boyhoods n ▷ **boy**

boyish n ▷ **boy**

boys n ▷ **boy**

bra n (pl **-s**) woman's undergarment for supporting the breasts

brace n (pl **-s**) object fastened to something to straighten or support it ▶ pl straps worn over the shoulders to hold up trousers ▶ v (**-ces, -cing, -ced**) steady or prepare (oneself) for something unpleasant

braced n, v ▷ **brace**

bracelet n (pl **-s**) ornamental chain or band for the wrist

bracelets n ▷ **bracelet**

braces n, v ▷ **brace**

bracing adj refreshing and invigorating ▶ v ▷ **brace**

bracken n (pl **-s**) large fern

brackens n ▷ **bracken**

bracket n (pl **-s**) either of a pair of characters used to enclose a section of writing ▶ v (**-s, -ing, -ed**) put in brackets

bracketed v ▷ **bracket**

bracketing v ▷ **bracket**

brackets n, v ▷ **bracket**

brackish adj (of water) slightly salty ▷ **brackishness**

brackishness n ▷ **bracket**

bract n (pl **-s**) leaf at the base of a flower

bracts n ▷ **bract**

brag v (**-s, -gging, -gged**) speak arrogantly and boastfully ▶ **braggart** n (pl **-s**)

braggart n ▷ **brag**

braggarts n ▷ **brag**

bragged v ▷ **brag**

bragging v ▷ **brag**

brags v ▷ **brag**

braid v (**-s, -ing, -ed**) interweave (hair, thread, etc) ▶ n (pl **-s**) length of hair etc that has been braided

braided v ▷ **braid**

braiding v ▷ **braid**

braids v, n ▷ **braid**

braille n (pl **-s**) system of writing for the blind, consisting of raised dots interpreted by touch

brailles n ▷ **braille**

brain n (pl **-s**) soft mass of nervous tissue in the head ▶ v (**-s, -ing, -ed**) hit (someone) hard on the head

brained v ▷ **brain**

brainier adj ▷ **brainy**

brainiest adj ▷ **brainy**

braininess n ▷ **brainy**

braininesses n ▷ **brainy**

braining v ▷ **brain**

brains n, v ▷ **brain**

brainy adj (**-nier, -niest**) informal clever ▷ **braininess** n (pl **-es**)

braise v (**-ses, -sing, -sed**) cook slowly in a covered pan with a little liquid

braised v ▷ **braise**

braises v ▷ **braise**

braising v ▷ **braise**

brake n (pl **-s**) device for slowing or stopping a vehicle ▶ v (**-kes, -king, -ked**) slow down or stop by using a brake

braked v ▷ **brake**

brakes n, v ▷ **brake**

braking v ▷ **brake**

bramble n (pl **-s**) prickly shrub that produces blackberries

brambles n ▷ **bramble**

bran n (pl **-s**) husks of cereal grain

branch n (pl **-es**) secondary stem of

a tree ▶ v (-es, -ing, -ed) (of stems, roots, etc) divide, then develop in different directions

branched v ▷ branch

branches n, v ▷ branch

branching v ▷ branch

brand n (pl -s) particular product ▶ v (-s, -ing, -ed) mark with a brand

branded v ▷ brand

brandies n ▷ brandy

branding v ▷ brand

brandish v (-es, -ing, -ed) wave (a weapon etc) in a threatening way

brandished v ▷ brandish

brandishes v ▷ brandish

brandishing v ▷ brandish

brands n, v ▷ brand

brandy n (pl -dies) alcoholic spirit distilled from wine

brans n ▷ bran

bras n ▷ bra

brash adj offensively loud, showy, or self-confident >**brashness** n

brashness n ▷ brash

brass n (pl -es) alloy of copper and zinc

brasses n ▷ brass

brassier adj ▷ brassy

brassiest adj ▷ brassy

brassiness adj ▷ brassy

brassinesses adj ▷ brassy

brassy adj (-sier, -siest) brazen or flashy >**brassiness** n (pl -es)

brat n (pl -s) unruly child

brats n ▷ brat

bravado n (pl -oes) showy display of self-confidence

bravadoes n ▷ bravado

brave adj (-r, -st) having or showing courage, resolution, and daring ▶ n (pl -s) Native American warrior ▶ v (-ves, -ving, -ved) confront with resolution or courage >**bravery** n (pl -ries)

braved v ▷ brave

braver adj ▷ brave

braveries n ▷ brave

bravery n ▷ brave

braves n, v ▷ brave

bravest adj ▷ brave

braving v ▷ brave

bravo interj well done!

bravl n (pl -s) noisy fight ▶ v (-s, -ing, -ed) fight noisily

brawled v ▷ brawl

brawling v ▷ brawl

brawls n, v ▷ brawl

brawn n (pl -s) physical strength >**brawny** (-nier, -niest) ▶ adj

brawnier adj ▷ brawn

brawniest adj ▷ brawn

brawns n ▷ brawn

brawny adj ▷ brawn

bray v (-s, -ing, -ed) (of a donkey) utter its loud harsh sound ▶ n (pl -s) donkey's loud harsh sound

brayed v ▷ bray

braying v ▷ bray

brays v, n ▷ bray

brazen adj shameless and bold ▶ v (-s, -ing, -ed) >**brazenly** adv >**brazenness** n (pl -es)

brazened v ▷ brazen

brazening v ▷ brazen

brazenly adv ▷ brazen

brazenness n ▷ brazen

brazennesses n ▷ brazen

brazens v ▷ brazen

brazier n (pl -s) portable container for burning charcoal or coal

braziers n ▷ brazier

breach n (pl -es) breaking of a promise, obligation, etc ▶ v (-es, -ing, -ed) break (a promise, law, etc)

breached v ▷ breach

breaches n, v ▷ breach

breaching v ▷ breach

bread n (pl -s) food made by baking a mixture of flour and water or milk

breads n ▷ bread

breadth n (pl -s) extent of something from side to side

breadths n ▷ breadth

break v (-s, -ing, broke, broken) separate or become separated into two or more pieces ▶ n (pl -s) act or result of breaking >**breakable** adj >**breakage** n (pl -s)

breakable adj ▷ break
breakage n ▷ break
breakages n ▷ break
breaker n (pl -s) large wave
breakers n ▷ breaker
breaking v ▷ break
breaks v, n ▷ break
bream n (pl **bream**) freshwater fish with silvery scales
breast n (pl -s) either of the two soft fleshy milk-secreting glands on a woman's chest
breasts n ▷ breast
breath n (pl -s) taking in and letting out of air during breathing
> **breathless** adj ▷ **breathlessly** adv
> **breathlessness** n
breathe v (-thes, -thing, -thed) take in oxygen and give out carbon dioxide
> **breathing** n (pl -s)
breathed v ▷ breathe
breather n (pl -s) informal short rest
breathers n ▷ breather
breathes v ▷ breathe
breathing v, n ▷ breathe
breathings n ▷ breathe
breathless adj ▷ breath
breathlessly adv ▷ breath
breathlessness n ▷ breath
breaths n ▷ breath
bred v ▷ breed
breech n (pl -es) buttocks
breeches pl n trousers extending to just below the knee ▶ n ▷ breech
breed v (-s, -ing, bred) produce new or improved strains of (domestic animals or plants) ▶ n (pl -s) group of animals etc within a species that have certain clearly defined characteristics
> **breeder** n (pl -s)
breeder n ▷ breed
breeders n ▷ breed
breeding n (pl -s) result of good upbringing or training ▶ v ▷ breed
breedings n ▷ breeding
breeds v, n ▷ breed
breeze n (pl -s) gentle wind ▶ v (-zes, -zing, -zed) move quickly or casually

breezed v ▷ breeze
breezes n, v ▷ breeze
breezier adj ▷ breezy
breeziest adj ▷ breezy
breezily adv ▷ breezy
breezing v ▷ breeze
breezy adj (-zier, -ziest) windy
> **breezily** adv
brethren pl n old-fashioned (used in religious contexts) brothers
brevities n ▷ brevity
brevity n (pl -ities) shortness
brew v (-s, -ing, -ed) make (beer etc) by steeping, boiling, and fermentation ▶ n (pl -s) beverage produced by brewing
brewed v ▷ brew
brewer n (pl -s) person or company that brews beer
breweries n ▷ brewery
brewers n ▷ brewer
brewery n (pl -eries) place where beer etc is brewed
brewing v ▷ brewer
brews v, n ▷ brew
briar[1], **brier** n (pl -s) European shrub with a hard woody root
briar[2] n (pl -s) ▷ brier[1]
briars n ▷ briar[1, 2]
bribe v (-bes, -bing, -bed) offer or give something to someone to gain favour, influence, etc ▶ n (pl -s) something given or offered as a bribe > **bribery** n (pl -ries)
bribed v ▷ bribe
bribes v, n ▷ bribe
bribing v ▷ bribe
brick n (pl -s) (rectangular block of) baked clay used in building ▶ v (-s, -ing, -ed) (foll. by **up** or **over**) build, enclose, or fill with bricks
bricked v ▷ brick
bricking v ▷ brick
bricks n, v ▷ brick
bridal adj ▷ bride
bride n (pl -s) woman who has just been or is about to be married
> **bridal** adj

brides n ▷ **bride**
bridge[1] n (pl -s) structure for crossing a river etc ▶ v (-ges, -ging, -ged) build a bridge over (something)
bridge[2] n (pl -s) card game based on whist, played between two pairs
bridged v ▷ **bridge**[1, 2] v ▷ **bridge**[1]
bridges n ▷ **bridge**[1, 2] v ▷ **bridge**[1]
bridging v ▷ **bridge**[1]
bridle n (pl -s) headgear for controlling a horse ▶ v (-les, -ling, -led) show anger or indignation
bridled v ▷ **bridle**
bridles n, v ▷ **bridle**
bridling v ▷ **bridle**
brief adj (-er, -est) short in duration ▶ n (pl -s) condensed statement or written synopsis (also **briefing**) (pl -s) ▶ pl men's or women's underpants ▶ v (-s, -ing, -ed) give information and instructions to (a person) > **briefly** adv
briefed v ▷ **brief**
briefer adj ▷ **brief**
briefest adj ▷ **brief**
briefing v, n ▷ **brief**
briefings n ▷ **brief**
briefly adv ▷ **brief**
briefs n, v ▷ **brief**
brier[1], **briar** n (pl -s) wild rose with long thorny stems
brier[2] n (pl -s) ▷ **briar**[1]
briers n ▷ **brier**[1, 2]
brig n (pl -s) two-masted square-rigged ship
brigade n (pl -s) army unit smaller than a division
brigades n ▷ **brigade**
brigalow n (pl -s) AUST type of acacia tree
brigalows n ▷ **brigalow**
brigand n (pl -s) lit bandit
brigands n ▷ **brigand**
bright adj (-er, -est) emitting or reflecting much light > **brightly** adv > **brightness** n (pl -es) > **brighten** v (-s, -ing, -ed)
brighten v ▷ **bright**
brightened v ▷ **bright**

brightening v ▷ **bright**
brightens v ▷ **bright**
brighter adj ▷ **bright**
brightest adj ▷ **bright**
brightly adj ▷ **bright**
brightness n ▷ **bright**
brightnesses n ▷ **bright**
brigs n ▷ **brig**
brim n (pl -s) upper rim of a cup etc ▶ v (-s, -mming, -mmed) be full to the brim
brimmed v ▷ **brim**
brimming v ▷ **brim**
brims n, v ▷ **brim**
brine n (pl -s) salt water
brines n ▷ **brine**
bring v (-s, -ing, **brought**) carry, convey, or take to a designated place or person
bringing v ▷ **bring**
brings v ▷ **bring**
brinier adj ▷ **briny**
briniest adj ▷ **briny**
brinjal n (pl -s) S AFR aubergine
brinjals n ▷ **brinjal**
brink n (pl -s) edge of a steep place
brinks n ▷ **brink**
briny (-ier, -iest) adj very salty
brisk adj (-er, -est) lively and quick > **briskly** adv
brisker adj ▷ **brisk**
briskest adj ▷ **brisk**
brisket n (pl -s) beef from the breast of a cow
briskets n ▷ **brisket**
briskly adv ▷ **brisk**
bristle n (pl -s) short stiff hair ▶ v (-les, -ling, -led) (cause to) stand up like bristles > **bristly** adj (-lier, -liest)
bristled v ▷ **bristle**
bristles n, v ▷ **bristle**
bristlier adj ▷ **bristle**
bristliest adj ▷ **bristle**
bristling v ▷ **bristle**
bristly adj ▷ **bristle**
brit n (pl -s) informal British person
brits n ▷ **brit**
brittle adj (-er, -st) hard but easily

broken > **brittleness** n (pl -es)

brittleness n ▷ brittle

brittlenesses n ▷ brittle

brittler adj ▷ brittle

brittlest adj ▷ brittle

broach v (-es, -ing, -ed) introduce (a topic) for discussion

broached v ▷ broach

broaches v ▷ broach

broaching v ▷ broach

broad adj (-er, -est) having great breadth or width > **broadly** adv

> **broaden** (-s, -ing, -ed)

broaden v ▷ broad

broadened v ▷ broad

broadening v ▷ broad

broadens v ▷ broad

broader adj ▷ broad

broadest adj ▷ broad

broadly adv ▷ broad

brocade n (pl -s) rich fabric woven with a raised design

brocades n ▷ brocade

broccoli n (pl -s) type of cabbage with greenish flower heads

broccolis n ▷ broccoli

brochure n (pl -s) booklet that contains information about a product or service

brochures n ▷ brochure

broekies pl n S AFR informal underpants

brogue[1] n (pl -s) sturdy walking shoe

brogue[2] n (pl -s) strong accent, esp. Irish

brogues n ▷ brogue[1, 2]

broil v (-s, -ing, -ed) AUST, NZ, US & CANADIAN cook by direct heat under a grill

broiled v ▷ broil

broiling v ▷ broil

broils v ▷ broil

broke v ▷ break ▶ adj informal having no money

broken v ▷ break ▶ adj fractured or smashed

broker n (pl -s) agent who buys or sells goods, securities, etc

brokers n ▷ broker

brolga n (pl -s) large grey Australian crane with a trumpeting call

brolgas n ▷ brolga

brollies n ▷ brolly

brolly n (pl -lies) informal umbrella

bromide n (pl -s) chemical compound used in medicine and photography

bromides n ▷ bromide

bromine n (pl -s) CHEM dark red liquid element that gives off a pungent vapour

bromines n ▷ bromine

bronchi n ▷ bronchus

bronchus n (pl bronchi) either of the two branches of the windpipe

bronco n (pl -s) (in the US) wild or partially tamed pony

broncos n ▷ bronco

bronze n (pl -s) alloy of copper and tin ▶ adj made of, or coloured like, bronze ▶ v (-zes, -zing, -zed) (esp. of the skin) make or become brown-

bronzed v ▷ bronze

bronzes n, v ▷ bronze

bronzing v ▷ bronze

brooch n (pl -es) ornament with a pin, worn fastened to clothes

brooches n ▷ brooch

brood n (pl -s) number of birds produced at one hatching ▶ v (-s, -ing, -ed) think long and unhappily > **broody** adj moody and sullen informal

brooded v ▷ brood

brooding v ▷ brood

broods n, v ▷ brood

broody adj ▷ brood

brook[1] n (pl -s) small stream

brook[2] v (-s, -ing, -ed) bear or tolerate

brooked v ▷ brook[2]

brooking v ▷ brook[2]

brooks n ▷ brook[1] ▶ v ▷ brook[2]

broom n (pl -s) long-handled sweeping brush

brooms n ▷ broom

broth n (pl -s) soup, usu. containing vegetables

brothel n (pl -s) house where men pay

to have sex with prostitutes
brothels n ▷ **brothel**

brother n (pl **-s**) boy or man with
the same parents as another person
▷ **brotherly** adj
brotherly adj ▷ **brother**
brothers ▷ **brother**
broths n ▷ **broth**
brought v ▷ **bring**

brow n (pl **-s**) part of the face from the
eyes to the hairline

browbeat v (**-s**, **-ing**, **-beat**, **-en**)
frighten (someone) with threats
browbeaten v ▷ **browbeat**
browbeating v ▷ **browbeat**
browbeats v ▷ **browbeat**

brown n (pl **-s**) colour of earth or wood
▶ adj (**-er**, **-est**) of the colour brown ▶ v
(**-s**, **-ing**, **-ed**) make or become brown
▷ **brownish** adj
browned v ▷ **brown**
browner adj ▷ **brown**
brownest adj ▷ **brown**
browning v ▷ **brown**
brownish adj ▷ **brown**
browns n, v ▷ **brown**
brows v ▷ **brow**

browse v (**-ses**, **-sing**, **-sed**) look
through (a book or articles for sale) in
a casual manner ▶ n (pl **-s**) instance
of browsing
browsed v ▷ **browse**

browser n (pl **-s**) COMPUTERS software
package that enables a user to read
hypertext, esp. on the Internet
browsers n ▷ **browser**
browses v, n ▷ **browse**
browsing v ▷ **browse**

bruise n (pl **-s**) discoloured area on
the skin caused by an injury ▶ v (**-ses**,
-sing, **-sed**) cause a bruise on
bruised v ▷ **bruise**

bruiser n (pl **-s**) strong tough person
bruisers n ▷ **bruiser**
bruises n, v ▷ **bruise**
bruising v ▷ **bruise**
brumbies n ▷ **brumby**

brumby n (pl **-bies**) AUST wild horse

brunch n (pl **-es**) informal breakfast
and lunch combined
brunches n ▷ **brunch**

brunette n (pl **-s**) girl or woman with
dark brown hair
brunettes n ▷ **brunette**

brunt n (pl **-s**) main force or shock of a
blow, attack, etc
brunts n ▷ **brunt**

brush¹ n (pl **-es**) device made of
bristles, wires, etc used for cleaning,
painting, etc ▶ v (**-es**, **-ing**, **-ed**) clean,
scrub, or paint with a brush

brush² n (pl **-es**) thick growth of shrubs
brushed v ▷ **brush**¹
brushes v ▷ **brush**¹ ▶ n ▷ **brush**¹, ²
brushing v ▷ **brush**¹

brusque adj (**-r**, **-st**) blunt or curt in
manner or speech ▷ **brusquely** adv
▷ **brusqueness** n (pl **-es**)
brusquely adv ▷ **brusque**
brusqueness n ▷ **brusque**
brusquenesses n ▷ **brusque**
brusquer adj ▷ **brusque**
brusquest adj ▷ **brusque**

brutal adj cruel and vicious
▷ **brutally** adv ▷ **brutality** n (pl **-ties**)
▷ **brutalize** v (**-zes**, **-zing**, **-zed**)
brutalities n ▷ **brutal**
brutality n ▷ **brutal**
brutalized v ▷ **brutal**
brutalizes v ▷ **brutal**
brutalizing v ▷ **brutal**
brutally adv ▷ **brutal**

brute n (pl **-s**) brutal person ▶ adj
wholly instinctive or physical, like
an animal
brutes n ▷ **brute**

brutish adj of or like an animal
▷ **brutishly** adv ▷ **brutishness** n (pl **-es**)
brutishly adv ▷ **brutish**
brutishness n ▷ **brutish**
brutishnesses n ▷ **brutish**

bubble n (pl **-s**) ball of air in a liquid
or solid ▶ v (**-les**, **-ling**, **-led**) form
bubbles
bubbled v ▷ **bubble**
bubbles n, v ▷ **bubble**

bubblier adj ▷ bubbly
bubbliest adj ▷ bubbly
bubbling v ▷ bubble
bubbly adj (-lier, -liest) excited and lively
buck[1] n (pl **-s**) male of the goat, hare, kangaroo, rabbit, and reindeer ▶ v (**-s, -ing, -ed**) (of a horse etc) jump with legs stiff and back arched
buck[2] n (pl **-s**) US, CANADIAN, AUST & NZ slang dollar
bucked v ▷ buck[1]
bucket n (pl **-s**) open-topped round container with a handle ▶ v (**-s, -ing, -ed**) rain heavily ▷ **bucketful** n (pl **-s**)
bucketed v ▷ bucket
bucketful v ▷ bucket
bucketfuls n ▷ bucket
bucketing v ▷ bucket
buckets n, v ▷ bucket
bucking v ▷ buck[1]
buckle n (pl **-s**) clasp for fastening a belt or strap ▶ v (**-les, -ling, -led**) fasten or be fastened with a buckle
buckled v ▷ buckle
buckles n, v ▷ buckle
buckling v ▷ buckle
bucks v ▷ buck[1] ▶ n ▷ buck[1, 2]
buckshee adj slang free
bucolic adj of the countryside or country life
bud n (pl **-s**) swelling on a tree or plant that develops into a leaf or flower ▶ v (**-s, -dding, -dded**) produce buds
budded v ▷ bud
buddies n ▷ buddy
budding adj beginning to develop or grow ▶ v ▷ bud
buddleia n (pl **-s**) shrub with long spikes of purple flowers
buddleias n ▷ buddleia
buddy n (pl **-dies**) informal friend
budge v (**-ges, -ging, -ged**) move slightly
budged v ▷ budge
budges v ▷ budge
budget n (pl **-s**) financial plan for a period of time ▶ v (**-ets, -eting, -eted**) plan the expenditure of (money or time) ▶ adj cheap ▷ **budgetary** adj
budgeted v ▷ budget
budgeting v ▷ budget
budgets n, v ▷ budget
budgies n ▷ budgie
budging v ▷ budge
buds n, v ▷ bud
buff[1] adj dull yellowish-brown ▶ v (**-s, -ing, -ed**) clean or polish with soft material
buff[2] n (pl **-s**) informal expert on or devotee of a given subject
buffalo n (pl **-oes**) type of cattle
buffaloes n ▷ buffalo
buffed v ▷ buff[1]
buffer n (pl **-s**) something that lessens shock or protects from damaging impact, circumstances, etc
buffers n ▷ buffer
buffet[1] n (pl **-s**) counter where drinks and snacks are served
buffet[2] v (**-s, -feting, -feted**) knock against or about
buffeted v ▷ buffet[2]
buffeting v ▷ buffet[2]
buffets n ▷ buffet[1] ▶ v ▷ buffet[2]
buffing v ▷ buff[1]
buffoon n (pl **-s**) clown or fool ▷ **buffoonery** n (pl **-ries**)
buffooneries n ▷ buffoon
buffoonery n ▷ buffoon
buffoons n ▷ buffoon
buffs v ▷ buff[1] ▶ n ▷ buff[1, 2]
bug n (pl **-s**) small insect ▶ v (**-s, -gging, -gged**) informal irritate (someone)
bugbear n (pl **-s**) thing that causes obsessive anxiety
bugbears n ▷ bugbear
bugged v ▷ bug
bugging v ▷ bug
bugle n (pl **-s**) instrument like a small trumpet ▷ **bugler** n (pl **-s**)
bugler n ▷ bugle
buglers n ▷ bugle
bugles n ▷ bugle
bugong n ▷ bogong
bugongs n ▷ bogong

bugs n, v ▷ bug

build v (builds, building, built) make, construct, or form by joining parts or materials ▶ n (pl -s) shape of the body > **builder** n (pl -s)

builder ▷ build

builders ▷ build

building v ▷ build ▶ n (pl -s) structure with walls and a roof

buildings n ▷ building

builds v, n ▷ build

built v ▷ build

bulb n (pl -s) onion-shaped root which grows into a flower or plant

bulbous adj round and fat

bulbs n ▷ bulb

bulge n (pl -s) swelling on a normally flat surface ▶ v (-ges, -ging, -ged) swell outwards > **bulging** adj

bulged v ▷ bulge

bulges n, v ▷ bulge

bulging v, adj ▷ bulge

bulimia n (pl -s) disorder characterized by compulsive overeating followed by vomiting > **bulimic** adj, n (pl -s)

bulimias n ▷ bulimia

bulimic adj, n ▷ bulimia

bulimics n ▷ bulimia

bulk n (pl -s) size or volume, esp. when great > **bulky** adj (-kier, -kiest)

bulkhead n (pl -s) partition in a ship or aeroplane

bulkheads n ▷ bulkhead

bulkier adj ▷ bulk

bulkiest adj ▷ bulk

bulks n ▷ bulk

bulky adj ▷ bulk

bull¹ n (pl -s) male of some animals, such as cattle, elephants, and whales

bull² n (pl -s) informal complete nonsense

bull³ n papal decree

bulldog n (pl -s) thickset dog with a broad head and a muscular body

bulldogs n ▷ bulldog

bullet n (pl -s) small piece of metal fired from a gun

bulletin n (pl -s) short official report or

announcement

bulletins n ▷ bulletin

bullets n ▷ bullet

bullied v ▷ bully

bullies n, v ▷ bully

bullion n (pl -s) gold or silver in the form of bars

bullions n ▷ bullion

bullock n (pl -s) castrated bull

bullocks n ▷ bullock

bulls ▷ bull¹, ², ³

bully n (pl -lies) person who hurts, persecutes, or intimidates a weaker person ▶ v (-lies, -lying, -lied) hurt, intimidate, or persecute (a weaker person)

bullying v ▷ bully

bulrush n (pl -es) tall stiff reed

bulrushes n ▷ bulrush

bulwark n (pl -s) wall used as a fortification

bulwarks n ▷ bulwark

bum¹ n (pl -s) slang buttocks or anus

bum² informal n (pl -s) disreputable idler ▶ adj of poor quality

bumble v (-bles, -bling, -bled) speak, do, or move in a clumsy way > **bumbling** adj, n

bumbled v ▷ bumble

bumbles v ▷ bumble

bumbling v, adj, n ▷ bumble

bumf, bumph n (pl -s) informal official documents or forms

bumfs n ▷ bumf

bump v (-s, -ing, -ed) knock or strike with a jolt ▶ n (pl -s) dull thud from an impact or collision > **bumpy** adj (-pier, -piest)

bumped v ▷ bump

bumper¹ n (pl -s) bar on the front and back of a vehicle to protect against damage

bumper² adj unusually large or abundant

bumpers n ▷ bumper¹

bumph n ▷ bumf

bumphs n ▷ bumf

bumpier adj ▷ bump

bumpiest adj ▷ **bump**
bumping v ▷ **bump**
bumpkin n (pl **-s**) awkward simple country person
bumpkins n ▷ **bumpkin**
bumps v, n ▷ **bump**
bumpy adj ▷ **bump**
bums n ▷ **bum**[1, 2]
bun n (pl **-s**) small sweet bread roll or cake
bunch n (pl **-es**) number of things growing, fastened, or grouped together ▶ v (**-es, -ing, -ed**) group or be grouped together in a bunch
bunched v ▷ **bunch**
bunches n, v ▷ **bunch**
bunching v ▷ **bunch**
bundle n (pl **-s**) number of things gathered loosely together ▶ v (**-dles, -dling, -dled**) cause to go roughly or unceremoniously
bundled v ▷ **bundle**
bundles n, v ▷ **bundle**
bundling v ▷ **bundle**
bung n (pl **-s**) stopper for a cask etc ▶ v (**-s, -ing, -ed**) (foll. by **up**) informal close with a bung
bungalow n (pl **-s**) one-storey house
bungalows n ▷ **bungalow**
bunged v ▷ **bung**
bunging v ▷ **bung**
bungle v (**-gles, -gling, -gled**) spoil through incompetence ▶ **bungler** n (pl **-s**) ▷ **bungling** adj, n
bungled v ▷ **bungle**
bungler n ▷ **bungle**
bunglers n ▷ **bungle**
bungles v ▷ **bungle**
bungling v, adj n ▷ **bungle**
bungs n, v ▷ **bung**
bunion n (pl **-s**) inflamed swelling on the big toe
bunions n ▷ **bunion**
bunk[1] n (pl **-s**) narrow shelflike bed
bunk[2] n (pl **-s**) ▷ **bunkum**
bunk[3] slang n (pl **-s**) BRIT make a hurried and secret departure ▶ v (**-s, -ing, -ed**) BRIT, NZ G-S AFR be absent

without permission
bunked v ▷ **bunk**[3]
bunker n (pl **-s**) sand-filled hollow forming an obstacle on a golf course
bunkers n ▷ **bunker**
bunking v ▷ **bunk**[3]
bunks n ▷ **bunk**[1, 2, 3] ▶ v ▷ **bunk**[3]
bunkum n (pl **-s**) nonsense
bunkums n ▷ **bunkum**
bunnies n ▷ **bunny**
bunny n (pl **-nies**) child's word for a rabbit
buns n ▷ **bun**
bunting n (pl **-s**) decorative flags
buntings n ▷ **bunting**
bunya n (pl **-s**) tall dome-shaped Australian coniferous tree
bunyas n ▷ **bunya**
bunyip n (pl **-s**) AUST legendary monster said to live in swamps and lakes
bunyips n ▷ **bunyip**
buoy n (pl **-s**) floating marker anchored in the sea ▶ v (**-s, -ing, -ed**) prevent from sinking
buoyancy n ▷ **buoyant**
buoyant adj able to float ▶ **buoyancy** n
buoyed v ▷ **buoy**
buoying v ▷ **buoy**
buoys n, v ▷ **buoy**
bur n (pl **-s**) ▷ **burr**[1]
burble v (**-bles, -bling, -bled**) make a bubbling sound
burbled v ▷ **burble**
burbles v ▷ **burble**
burbling v ▷ **burble**
burden[1] n (pl **-s**) heavy load ▶ v (**-s, -ing, -ed**) put a burden on ▷ **burdensome** adj
burden[2] n (pl **-s**) theme of a speech etc
burdened v ▷ **burden**[1]
burdening v ▷ **burden**[1]
burdens v ▷ **burden**[1] ▶ n ▷ **burden**[1, 2]
burdensome adj ▷ **burden**[1]
bureau n (pl **-reaus, -reaux**) office that provides a service

bureaus n ▷ bureau

bureaux n ▷ bureau

burgeon v (-s, -ing, -ed) develop or grow rapidly

burgeoned v ▷ burgeon

burgeoning v ▷ burgeon

burgeons v ▷ burgeon

burgh n (pl -s) Scottish borough

burghs n ▷ burgh

burglar n (pl -s) person who enters a building to commit a crime, esp. theft > **burglary** n (pl -glaries) > **burgle** v (-les, -ling, -led)

burglaries n ▷ burglar

burglars n ▷ burglar

burglary n ▷ burglar

burgled v ▷ burglar

burgles v ▷ burglar

burgling v ▷ burglar

burgundy adj dark-purplish red

burial n (pl -s) burying of a dead body

burials n ▷ burial

buried v ▷ bury

buries v ▷ bury

burlier adj ▷ burly

burliest adj ▷ burly

burly adj (-lier, -liest) (of a person) broad and strong

burn¹ v (-s, -ing, -t or -ed) be or set on fire ▶ n (pl -s) injury or mark caused by fire or exposure to heat

burn² n (pl -s) SCOT small stream

burned v ▷ burn

burning adj intense ▶ v ▷ burn¹

burnish v (-es, -ing, -ed) make smooth and shiny by rubbing

burnished v ▷ burnish

burnishes v ▷ burnish

burnishing v ▷ burnish

burns n ▷ burn¹,² v ▷ burn¹

burnt v ▷ burn¹

burp v (-s, -ing, -ed) ▶ n (pl -s) informal belch

burped v ▷ burp

burping v ▷ burp

burps v, n ▷ burp

burr¹, bur n (pl -s) head of a plant with prickles or hooks

burr² n (pl -s) soft trilling sound given to the letter r in some dialects

burrow n (pl -s) hole dug in the ground by a rabbit etc ▶ v (-s, -ing, -ed) dig holes in the ground

burrowed v ▷ burrow

burrowing v ▷ burrow

burrows n, v ▷ burrow

burrs n ▷ burr¹,²

burs n ▷ burr¹

bursar n (pl -s) treasurer of a school, college, or university

bursaries n ▷ bursary

bursars n ▷ bursar

bursary n (pl -ries) scholarship

burst v (-s, -ing, burst) (cause to) break open or apart noisily and suddenly ▶ n (pl -s) instance of breaking open suddenly

bursting v ▷ burst

bursts v, n ▷ burst

bury v (-ries, -rying, -ried) place in a grave

burying v ▷ bury

bus n (pl buses) large motor vehicle for carrying passengers ▶ v (-sses, -ssing, -ssed) travel or transport by bus

busbies n ▷ busby

busby n (pl -bies) tall fur hat worn by some soldiers

buses n ▷ bus

bush n (pl -es) dense woody plant, smaller than a tree

bushbabies n ▷ bushbaby

bushbaby n (pl -babies) small African tree-living mammal with large eyes

bushel n (pl -s) obsolete unit of measure equal to 8 gallons (36.4 litres)

bushels n ▷ bushel

bushes n ▷ bush

bushier adj ▷ bushy

bushiest adj ▷ bushy

bushy adj (-shier, -shiest) (of hair) thick and shaggy

busied v ▷ busy

busier adj ▷ busy

busies v ▷ busy

busiest adj ▷ busy

business n (pl -es) purchase and sale of goods and services ▷ **businessman** n (pl -men), **businesswoman** (pl -women)

businesses n ▷ **business**

businessman n ▷ **business**

businessmen n ▷ **business**

businesswoman n ▷ **business**

businesswomen n ▷ **business**

busk v (-s, -ing, -ed) act as a busker

busked v ▷ **busk**

busker n (pl -s) street entertainer

buskers n ▷ **busker**

busking v ▷ **busk**

busks v ▷ **busk**

bussed v ▷ **bus**

busses v ▷ **bus**

bussing v ▷ **bus**

bust[1] n (pl -s) woman's bosom

bust[2] informal v (-s, -ing, bust or busted) burst or break ▶ adj broken

bustard n (pl -s) bird with long strong legs, a heavy body, a long neck, and speckled plumage

bustards n ▷ **bustard**

busted v ▷ **bust**[2]

busting v ▷ **bust**[2]

bustle[1] v (-les, -ling, -led) hurry with a show of activity or energy ▶ n (pl -s) energetic and noisy activity ▷ **bustling** adj

bustle[2] n (pl -s) cushion or framework formerly worn under the back of a woman's skirt to hold it out

bustled v ▷ **bustle**[1]

bustles v ▷ **bustle**[1] n ▷ **bustle**[1, 2]

bustling v, adj ▷ **bustle**[1]

busts n ▷ **bust**[1, 2]

busy adj (-sier, -siest) actively employed ▶ v (-sies, -sying, -sied) keep (someone, esp. oneself) busy ▷ **busily** adv

busybodies n ▷ **busybody**

busybody n (pl -bodies) meddlesome or nosy person

busying v ▷ **busy**

but conj contrary to expectation ▶ prep except ▶ adv only

butane n (pl -s) gas used for fuel

butanes n ▷ **butane**

butch adj (-er, -est) slang markedly or aggressively masculine

butcher n (pl -s) person who slaughters animals or sells their meat ▶ v (-s, -ing, -ed) kill and prepare (animals) for meat ▷ **butchery** n (pl -ries) adj ▷ **butch**

butchered v ▷ **butcher**

butcheries n ▷ **butcher**

butchering v ▷ **butcher**

butchers n, v ▷ **butcher**

butchery n ▷ **butcher**

butchest adj ▷ **butch**

butler n (pl -s) chief male servant

butlers n ▷ **butler**

butt[1] n (pl -s) thicker end of something

butt[2] n (pl -s) person or thing that is the target of ridicule

butt[3] v (-s, -ing, -ed) strike with the head or horns

butt[4] n (pl -s) large cask

butted v ▷ **butt**[3]

butter n (pl -s) edible fatty solid made by churning cream ▶ v (-s, -ing, -ed) put butter on ▷ **buttery** adj

buttered v ▷ **butter**

buttering v ▷ **butter**

butters n, v ▷ **butter**

buttery adj ▷ **butter**

butting v ▷ **butt**[3]

buttock n (pl -s) either of the two fleshy masses that form the human rump

buttocks n ▷ **buttock**

button n (pl -s) small disc or knob sewn to clothing, which can be passed through a slit in another piece of fabric to fasten them ▶ v (-s, -ing, -ed) fasten with buttons

buttoned v ▷ **button**

buttoning v ▷ **button**

buttons n, v ▷ **button**

buttress n (pl -es) structure to support a wall ▶ v (-es, -ing, -ed) support with, or as if with, a buttress

buttressed v ▷ **buttress**

buttresses n, v ▷ buttress
buttressing v ▷ buttress
butts n ▷ butt¹, ², ⁴ ▶ v ▷ butt³
buxom adj (-er, -est) (of a woman) healthily plump and full-bosomed
buxomer adj ▷ buxom
buxomest adj ▷ buxom
buy v (-s, -ing, bought) acquire by paying money for ▶ n (pl -s) thing acquired through payment
buyer n (pl -s) customer
buyers n ▷ buyer
buying v ▷ buy
buys v, n ▷ buy
buzz n (pl -es) rapidly vibrating humming sound informal ▶ v (-es, -ing, -ed) make a humming sound > buzzer n (pl -s)
buzzard n (pl -s) bird of prey of the hawk family
buzzards n ▷ buzzard
buzzed v ▷ buzz
buzzer n ▷ buzz
buzzers n ▷ buzz
buzzes n, v ▷ buzz
buzzing v ▷ buzz
by prep indicating the doer of an action,

nearness, movement past, time before or during which, etc ▶ adv near
bye interj informal goodbye
byelaw n ▷ bylaw
byelaws n ▷ bylaw
bygone adj past or former
bylaw, byelaw n (pl -s) rule made by a local authority
bylaws n ▷ bylaw
bypass n (pl -es) main road built to avoid a city ▶ v (-es, -ing, -ed) go round or avoid
bypassed v ▷ bypass
bypasses n, v ▷ bypass
bypassing v ▷ bypass
byre n (pl -s) BRIT shelter for cows
byres n ▷ byre
byte n (pl -s) COMPUTERS group of bits processed as one unit of data
bytes n ▷ byte
byway n (pl -s) minor road
byways n ▷ byway
byword n (pl -s) person or thing regarded as a perfect example of something
bywords n ▷ byword

Cc

C can be a tricky letter to use, especially as it only forms a single two-letter word **ch**. But if you remember this, you won't waste time racking your brains for two-letter words. There are, however, plenty of good three-letter words beginning with C. **Cox** scores 12 points, while **caw**, **cow** and **coy** are each worth 8. It's also a good idea to remember the short words starting with C that don't contain any vowels: **cly** and **cwm** as well as **ch**.

cab n (pl -s) taxi

cabal n (pl -s) small group of political plotters
cabals n ▷ cabal

cabaret n (pl -s) dancing and singing show in a nightclub
cabarets n ▷ cabaret

cabbage n (pl -s) vegetable with a large head of green leaves
cabbages n ▷ cabbage

cabbie, cabby n (pl -bies) informal taxi driver
cabbies n ▷ cabbie
cabby n ▷ cabbie

caber n (pl -s) tree trunk tossed in competition at Highland games
cabers n ▷ caber

cabin n (pl -s) compartment in a ship or aircraft

cabinet n (pl -s) piece of furniture with drawers or shelves
cabinets n ▷ cabinet
cabins n ▷ cabin

cable n (pl -s) strong thick rope ▶ v (-les, -ling, -led) send (someone) a message by cable
cabled v ▷ cable
cables n, v ▷ cable
cabling v ▷ cable

caboodle n informal the whole lot
cabs n ▷ cab

cacao n (pl -s) tropical tree with seed pods from which chocolate and cocoa are made
cacaos n ▷ cacao

cache n (pl -s) hidden store of weapons or treasure
caches n ▷ cache

cachet n (pl -s) prestige, distinction
cachets n ▷ cachet

cackle v (-les, -ling, -led) laugh shrilly ▶ n (pl -s) cackling noise
cackled v ▷ cackle
cackles v, n ▷ cackle
cackling v ▷ cackle
cacti n ▷ cactus

cactus n (pl -tuses, -ti) fleshy desert plant with spines but no leaves
cactuses n ▷ cactus

cad n (pl -s) old-fashioned dishonourable man > **caddish** adj

cadaver n (pl -s) corpse
cadavers n ▷ cadaver

caddie, caddy n (pl -dies) person who carries a golfer's clubs ▶ v (-dies, -dying, -died) act as a caddie
caddies n ▷ caddie
caddish adj ▷ cad

caddy n (pl -dies) small container for tea ▷ caddie

cadence n (pl -s) rise and fall in the pitch of the voice

cadences n ▷ **cadence**

cadenza n (pl **-s**) complex solo passage in a piece of music

cadenzas n ▷ **cadenza**

cadet n (pl **-s**) young person training for the armed forces or police

cadets n ▷ **cadet**

cadge v (**cadges, cadging, cadged**) informal get (something) by taking advantage of someone's generosity > **cadger** n (pl **-s**)

cadged v ▷ **cadge**

cadger n ▷ **cadge**

cadgers n ▷ **cadge**

cadges n ▷ **cadge**

cadging v ▷ **cadge**

cadmium n (pl **-s**) CHEM bluish-white metallic element used in alloys

cadmiums n ▷ **cadmium**

cadre n (pl **-s**) small group of people selected and trained to form the core of a political organization or military unit

cadres n ▷ **cadre**

cads n ▷ **cad**

caeca n ▷ **caecum**

caecum n (pl **-ca**) pouch at the beginning of the large intestine

caesium n (pl **-s**) CHEM silvery-white metallic element used in photocells

caesiums n ▷ **caesium**

café n (pl **-s**) small or inexpensive restaurant serving light refreshments

cafés n ▷ **café**

caffeine n (pl **-s**) stimulant found in tea and coffee

caffeines n ▷ **caffeine**

caftan n (pl **-s**) ▷ **kaftan**

caftans n ▷ **kaftan**

cage n (pl **-s**) enclosure of bars or wires, for keeping animals or birds

caged adj kept in a cage

cages n ▷ **cage**

cagey adj (**-gier, -giest**) informal reluctant to go into details

cagier adj ▷ **cagey**

cagiest adj ▷ **cagey**

cagoule n (pl **-s**) BRIT lightweight hooded waterproof jacket

cagoules n ▷ **cagoule**

cahoots pl n informal conspiring together

cairn n (pl **-s**) mound of stones erected as a memorial or marker

cairns n ▷ **cairn**

cajole v (**-les, -ling, -led**) persuade by flattery > **cajolery** n (pl **-ries**)

cajoled v ▷ **cajole**

cajoleries n ▷ **cajole**

cajolery n ▷ **cajole**

cajoles v ▷ **cajole**

cajoling v ▷ **cajole**

cake n (pl **-s**) sweet food baked from a mixture of flour, eggs, etc ▷ v (**cakes, caking, caked**) form into a hardened mass or crust

caked v ▷ **cake**

cakes n, v ▷ **cake**

caking v ▷ **cake**

calamine n (pl **-s**) pink powder consisting chiefly of zinc oxide, used in skin lotions and ointments

calamines n ▷ **calamine**

calamities n ▷ **calamity**

calamitous adj ▷ **calamity**

calamity n (pl **-ties**) disaster > **calamitous** adj

calcification n ▷ **calcify**

calcified v ▷ **calcify**

calcifies v ▷ **calcify**

calcify v (**-fies, -fying, -fied**) harden by the depositing of calcium salts > **calcification** n (pl **-s**)

calcifications n ▷ **calcify**

calcifying v ▷ **calcify**

calcium n (pl **-s**) CHEM silvery-white metallic element found in bones, teeth, limestone, and chalk

calciums n ▷ **calcium**

calculus n (pl **-ses**) branch of mathematics dealing with infinitesimal changes to a variable number or quantity

calculuses n ▷ **calculus**

calendar n (pl **-s**) chart showing a year divided up into months, weeks, and days

calendars n ▷ **calendar**

calf¹ n (pl **calves**) young cow, bull, elephant, whale, or seal

calf² n (pl **calves**) back of the leg between the ankle and knee

calibre n (pl **-s**) person's ability or worth

calibres n ▷ **calibre**

calico n (pl **-coes**) white cotton fabric

calicoes n ▷ **calico**

caliph n (pl **-s**) HIST Muslim ruler

caliphs n ▷ **caliph**

call v (**-s, -ing, -ed**) name ▶ n (pl **-s**) cry, shout > **caller** n (pl **-s**)

called v ▷ **call**

caller n ▷ **call**

callers n ▷ **call**

calling n (pl **-s**) vocation, profession ▶ v ▷ **call**

callings n ▷ **calling**

calliper n (pl **-s**) metal splint for supporting the leg

callipers n ▷ **calliper**

callous adj showing no concern for other people's feelings > **callously** adv > **callousness** n

callously adv ▷ **callous**

callousness n ▷ **callous**

callow adj (**-er, -est**) young and inexperienced > **callowness** n (pl **-es**)

callower adj ▷ **callow**

callowest adj ▷ **callow**

callowness n ▷ **callow**

callownesses n ▷ **callow**

calls v, n ▷ **call**

callus n (pl **-es**) area of thick hardened skin

calluses n ▷ **callus**

calm adj (**-er, -est**) not agitated or excited ▶ n (pl **-s**) peaceful state ▶ v (**-s, -ing, -ed**) (often foll. by **down**) make or become calm > **calmly** adv > **calmness** n (pl **-es**)

calmed v ▷ **calm**

calmer adj ▷ **calm**

calmest adj ▷ **calm**

calming v ▷ **calm**

calmly adv ▷ **calm**

calmness adv ▷ **calm**

calmnesses adv ▷ **calm**

calms n, v ▷ **calm**

calorie n (pl **-s**) unit of measurement for the energy value of food

calories n ▷ **calorie**

calumnies n ▷ **calumny**

calumny n (pl **-nies**) false or malicious statement

calve v (**calves, calving, calved**) give birth to a calf

calved v ▷ **calve**

calves n ▷ **calve** ▶ n ▷ **calf¹, ²**

calving v ▷ **calve**

calyces n ▷ **calyx**

calypso n (pl **-s**) West Indian song with improvised topical lyrics

calypsos n ▷ **calypso**

calyx n (pl **-yxes, -yces**) outer leaves that protect a flower bud

calyxes n ▷ **calyx**

cam n (pl **-s**) device that converts a circular motion to a to-and-fro motion

camber n (pl **-s**) slight upward curve to the centre of a surface

cambers n ▷ **camber**

cambric n (pl **-s**) fine white linen fabric

cambrics n ▷ **cambric**

came v ▷ **come**

camel n (pl **-s**) humped mammal that can survive long periods without food or water in desert regions

camellia n (pl **-s**) evergreen ornamental shrub with white, pink, or red flowers

camellias n ▷ **camellia**

camels n ▷ **camel**

cameo n (pl **-s**) brooch or ring with a profile head carved in relief

cameos n ▷ **cameo**

camera n (pl **-s**) apparatus used for taking photographs or pictures for television or cinema

cameras n ▷ **camera**

camisole n (pl **-s**) woman's bodice-like garment

camisoles n ▷ **camisole**

camomile n (pl **-s**) aromatic plant,

used to make herbal tea

camomiles n ▷ **camomile**

camp¹ n (pl -s) (place for) temporary lodgings consisting of tents, huts, or cabins ▶ v (-s, -ing, -ed) stay in a camp > **camper** n (pl -s)

camp² adj (-er, -est) informal effeminate or homosexual

campaign n (pl -s) series of coordinated activities designed to achieve a goal ▶ v (-s, -ing, -ed) take part in a campaign

campaigned v ▷ **campaign**

campaigning v ▷ **campaign**

campaigns n, v ▷ **campaign**

camped v ▷ **camp¹**

camper n ▷ **camp¹** ▶ adj ▷ **camp²**

campers n ▷ **camp¹**

campest adj ▷ **camp²**

camphor n (pl -s) aromatic crystalline substance used medicinally and in mothballs

camphors n ▷ **camphor**

camping v ▷ **camp¹**

campion n (pl -s) red, pink, or white wild flower

campions n ▷ **campion**

camps n, v ▷ **camp¹**

campus n (pl -es) grounds of a university or college

campuses n ▷ **campus**

cams n ▷ **cam**

camshaft n (pl -s) part of an engine consisting of a rod to which cams are fixed

camshafts n ▷ **camshaft**

can¹ v (past could) be able to

can² n (pl -s) metal container for food or liquids ▶ v (-s, -nning, -nned) put (something) into a can

canal n (pl -s) artificial waterway

canals n ▷ **canal**

canapé n (pl -s) small piece of bread or toast with a savoury topping

canapés n ▷ **canapé**

canaries n ▷ **canary**

canary n (pl -ries) small yellow songbird often kept as a pet

canasta n (pl -s) card game like rummy, played with two packs

canastas n ▷ **canasta**

cancan n (pl -s) lively high-kicking dance performed by a female group

cancans n ▷ **cancan**

cancel v (-cels, -celling, -celled) stop (something that has been arranged) from taking place > **cancellation** n (pl -s)

cancellation n ▷ **cancel**

cancellations n ▷ **cancel**

cancelled v ▷ **cancel**

cancelling v ▷ **cancel**

cancels v ▷ **cancel**

cancer n (pl -s) serious disease resulting from a malignant growth or tumour > **cancerous** adj

cancerous adj ▷ **cancer**

cancers n ▷ **cancer**

candela n (pl -s) unit of luminous intensity

candelas n ▷ **candela**

candid adj (-er, -est) honest and straightforward > **candidly** adv > **candidness** n (pl -es)

candider adj ▷ **candid**

candidest adj ▷ **candid**

candidly adv ▷ **candid**

candidness n ▷ **candid**

candidnesses n ▷ **candid**

candied adj coated with sugar

candies n ▷ **candy**

candle n (pl -s) stick of wax enclosing a wick, which is burned to produce light

candles n ▷ **candle**

candour n (pl -s) honesty and straightforwardness

candours n ▷ **candour**

candy n (pl -dies) US sweet or sweets

cane n (pl -s) stem of the bamboo or similar plant ▶ v (-nes, -ning, -ned) beat with a cane

caned v ▷ **cane**

canes n, v ▷ **cane**

canine adj of or like a dog ▶ n (pl -s) sharp pointed tooth between the incisors and the molars

canines n ▷ **canine**
caning v ▷ **cane**
canister n (pl **-s**) metal container
canisters n ▷ **canister**
canker n (pl **-s**) ulceration, ulcerous disease
cankers n ▷ **canker**
cannabis n (pl **-es**) Asian plant with tough fibres
cannabises n ▷ **cannabis**
canned adj preserved in a can ▶ v ▷ **can²**
canneries n ▷ **cannery**
cannery n (pl **-ries**) factory where food is canned
cannibal n (pl **-s**) person who eats human flesh > **cannibalism** n
cannibals n ▷ **cannibal**
cannier adj ▷ **canny**
canniest adj ▷ **canny**
cannily adv ▷ **canny**
canning v ▷ **can²**
cannon n (pl **-s**) large gun on wheels
cannons n ▷ **cannon**
cannot v can not
canny adj (**-nier**, **-niest**) shrewd, cautious > **cannily** adv
canoe n (pl **-s**) light narrow open boat propelled by a paddle or paddles > **canoeist** n (pl **-s**)
canoeing n sport of rowing in a canoe
canoeist n ▷ **canoe**
canoeists n ▷ **canoe**
canoes n ▷ **canoe**
canon¹ n (pl **-s**) priest serving in a cathedral
canon² n (pl **-s**) Church decree regulating morals or religious practices > **canonical** adj
canonical adj ▷ **canon²**
canonization n ▷ **canonize**
canonizations n ▷ **canonize**
canonize v (**-izes**, **-izing**, **-ized**) declare (a person) officially to be a saint > **canonization** n (pl **-s**)
canonized v ▷ **canonize**
canonizes v ▷ **canonize**
canonizing v ▷ **canonize**

canons n ▷ **canon¹, ²**
canoodle v (**-les**, **-ling**, **-led**) slang kiss and cuddle
canoodled v ▷ **canoodle**
canoodles v ▷ **canoodle**
canoodling v ▷ **canoodle**
canopied adj covered with a canopy
canopies n ▷ **canopy**
canopy n (pl **-pies**) covering above a bed, door, etc
cans n, v ▷ **can²**
cant¹ n (pl **-s**) insincere talk
cant² n (pl **-s**) tilted position ▶ v (**-s**, **-ing**, **-ed**) tilt, overturn
cantata n (pl **-s**) musical work consisting of arias, duets, and choruses
cantatas n ▷ **cantata**
canted v ▷ **cant²**
canteen n (pl **-s**) restaurant attached to a workplace or school
canteens n ▷ **canteen**
canter n (pl **-s**) horse's gait between a trot and a gallop ▶ v (**-s**, **-ing**, **-ed**) move at a canter
cantered v ▷ **canter**
cantering v ▷ **canter**
canters n, v ▷ **canter**
canticle n (pl **-s**) short hymn with words from the Bible
canticles n ▷ **canticle**
canting v ▷ **cant²**
canto n (pl **-s**) main division of a long poem
canton n (pl **-s**) political division of a country, esp. Switzerland
cantons n ▷ **canton**
cantor n (pl **-s**) man employed to lead services in a synagogue
cantors n ▷ **cantor**
cantos n ▷ **canto**
cants n ▷ **cant¹, ²** ▶ v ▷ **cant²**
canvas n (pl **-es**) heavy coarse cloth used for sails and tents, and for oil painting
canvases n ▷ **canvas**
canvass v (**-es**, **-ing**, **-ed**) try to get votes or support (from) ▶ n (pl **-es**)

canvassing

canvassed v ▷ **canvass**

canvasses v, n ▷ **canvass**

canvassing v ▷ **canvass**

canyon n (pl -s) deep narrow valley

canyons n ▷ **canyon**

cap n (pl -s) soft close-fitting covering for the head ▶ v (-s, -pping, -pped) cover or top with something

capabilities n ▷ **capable**

capability n ▷ **capable**

capable adj (foll. by **of**) having the ability (for) > **capably** adv > **capability** n (pl -**ties**)

capably adv ▷ **capable**

capacities n ▷ **capacity**

capacity n (pl -**ties**) ability to contain, absorb, or hold

cape¹ n (pl -s) short cloak

cape² n (pl -s) large piece of land that juts out into the sea

caper n (pl -s) high-spirited prank ▶ v (-s, -ing, -ed) skip about

capered v ▷ **caper**

capering v ▷ **caper**

capers pl n pickled flower buds of a Mediterranean shrub used in sauces ▶ n ▷ **caper** ▶ v ▷ **caper**

capes n ▷ **cape¹, ²**

capital¹ n (pl -s) chief city of a country ▶ adj involving or punishable by death

capital² n (pl -s) top part of a pillar

capitals n ▷ **capital¹, ²**

capon n (pl -s) castrated cock fowl fattened for eating

capons n ▷ **capon**

capped v ▷ **cap**

capping v ▷ **cap**

caprice n (pl -s) sudden change of attitude

caprices n ▷ **caprice**

caps n, v ▷ **cap**

capsicum n (pl -s) kind of pepper used as a vegetable or as a spice

capsicums n ▷ **capsicum**

capsize v (-zes, -zing, -zed) (of a boat) overturn accidentally

capsized v ▷ **capsize**

capsizes v ▷ **capsize**

capsizing v ▷ **capsize**

capstan n (pl -s) rotating cylinder round which a ship's rope is wound

capstans n ▷ **capstan**

capsule n (pl -s) soluble gelatine case containing a dose of medicine

capsules n ▷ **capsule**

captain n (pl -s) commander of a ship or civil aircraft ▶ v (-s, -ing, -ed) be captain of > **captaincy** n (pl -**cies**)

captaincies n ▷ **captain**

captaincy n ▷ **captain**

captained v ▷ **captain**

captaining v ▷ **captain**

captains n, v ▷ **captain**

caption n (pl -s) title or explanation accompanying an illustration ▶ v (-s, -ing, -ed) provide with a caption

captioned v ▷ **caption**

captioning v ▷ **caption**

captions n, v ▷ **caption**

captious adj tending to make trivial criticisms > **captiously** adv > **captiousness** n

captiously adv ▷ **captious**

captiousness n ▷ **captious**

captive n (pl -s) person kept in confinement ▶ adj kept in confinement > **captivity** n (pl -**ties**)

captives n ▷ **captive**

captivities n ▷ **captive**

captivity n ▷ **captive**

captor n (pl -s) person who captures a person or animal

captors n ▷ **captor**

capture v (-res, -ring, -red) take by force ▶ n (pl -s) capturing

captured v ▷ **capture**

captures v, n ▷ **capture**

capturing v ▷ **capture**

car n (pl -s) motor vehicle designed to carry a small number of people

carafe n (pl -s) glass bottle for serving water or wine

carafes n ▷ **carafe**

caramel n (pl -s) chewy sweet made from sugar and milk

caramels n ▷ caramel
carapace n (pl -s) hard upper shell of tortoises and crustaceans
carapaces n ▷ carapace
carat n (pl -s) unit of weight of precious stones
carats n ▷ carat
caravan n (pl -s) large enclosed vehicle for living in, designed to be towed by a car or horse
caravans n ▷ caravan
caraway n (pl -s) plant whose seeds are used as a spice
caraways n ▷ caraway
carbide n (pl -s) compound of carbon with a metal
carbides n ▷ carbide
carbine n (pl -s) light automatic rifle
carbines n ▷ carbine
carbon n (pl -s) nonmetallic element occurring as charcoal, graphite, and diamond, found in all organic matter
carbons n ▷ carbon
carcase n ▷ carcass
carcases n ▷ carcass
carcass, carcase n (pl -casses, -cases) dead body of an animal
carcasses n ▷ carcass
card n (pl -s) piece of thick stiff paper or cardboard used for identification, reference, or sending greetings or messages ▶ v (pl any card game, or card games in general
cardiac adj of the heart
cardigan n (pl -s) knitted jacket
cardigans n ▷ cardigan
cardinal n (pl -s) any of the high-ranking clergymen of the RC Church who elect the Pope and act as his counsellors ▶ adj fundamentally important
cardinals n ▷ cardinal
cards n ▷ card
care v (-res, -ring, -red) be concerned ▶ n (pl -s) careful attention, caution > **careful** adj (-ller, -llest) > **carefully** adv > **carefulness** n (pl -es) > **careless** adj > **carelessly** adv

> **carelessness** n (pl -es)
> **cared** v ▷ care
careen v (-s, -ing, -ed) tilt over to one side
careened v ▷ careen
careening v ▷ careen
careens v ▷ careen
career n (pl -s) series of jobs in a profession or occupation that a person has through their life ▶ v (-s, -ing, -ed) rush in an uncontrolled way
careered v ▷ career
careering v ▷ career
careers n, v ▷ career
carefree adj without worry or responsibility
careful adj ▷ care
carefuller adj ▷ care
carefullest adj ▷ care
carefully adv ▷ care
carefulness n ▷ care
carefulnesses n ▷ care
careless adj ▷ care
carelessly adv ▷ care
carelessness n ▷ care
carelessnesses n ▷ care
cares v, n ▷ care
caress n (pl -es) gentle affectionate touch or embrace ▶ v (-es, -ing, -ed) touch gently and affectionately
caressed v ▷ caress
caresses n, v ▷ caress
caressing v ▷ caress
caret n (pl -s) symbol (∧) indicating a place in written or printed matter where something is to be inserted
carets n ▷ caret
careworn adj showing signs of worry
cargo n (pl -es) goods carried by a ship, aircraft, etc
cargoes n ▷ cargo
caribou n (pl -bou or -bous) large N American reindeer
caribous n ▷ caribou
caries n (pl caries) tooth decay
carillon n (pl -s) set of bells played by keyboard or mechanically
carillons n ▷ carillon

caring v ▷ care

cark v (**-s, -ing, -ed**) AUST & NZ *slang* die

carked v ▷ cark

carking v ▷ cark

carks v ▷ cark

carmine adj vivid red

carnage n (pl **-s**) extensive slaughter of people

carnages n ▷ carnage

carnal adj of a sexual or sensual nature ▷ **carnally** adv

carnally adv ▷ carnal

carnival n (pl **-s**) festive period with processions, music, and dancing in the street

carnivals n ▷ carnival

carob n (pl **-s**) pod of a Mediterranean tree, used as a chocolate substitute

carobs n ▷ carob

carol n (pl **-s**) joyful Christmas hymn ▶ v (**-ls, -lling, -lled**) sing carols

carolled v ▷ carol

carolling v ▷ carol

carols n, v ▷ carol

carotid adj, n (pl **-s**) (of) either of the two arteries supplying blood to the head

carotids n ▷ carotid

carouse v (**-ses, -sing, -sed**) have a merry drinking party

caroused v ▷ carouse

carousel n (pl **-s**) revolving conveyor belt for luggage or photographic slides

carousels n ▷ carousel

carouses v ▷ carouse

carousing v ▷ carouse

carp¹ n (pl **carp**) large freshwater fish

carp² v (**-s, -ing, -ed**) complain, find fault

carped v ▷ carp²

carpel n (pl **-s**) female reproductive organ of a flowering plant

carpels n ▷ carpel

carpet n (pl **-s**) heavy fabric for covering floors ▶ v (**-s, -ing, -ed**) cover with a carpet

carpeted v ▷ carpet

carpeting v ▷ carpet

carpets n, v ▷ carpet

carpi n ▷ carpus

carping v ▷ carp²

carps v ▷ carp²

carpus n (pl **-pi**) set of eight bones of the wrist

carriage n (pl **-s**) one of the sections of a train for passengers

carriages n ▷ carriage

carried v ▷ carry

carrier n (pl **-s**) person or thing that carries something

carriers n ▷ carrier

carries v ▷ carry

carrion n (pl **-s**) dead and rotting flesh

carrions n ▷ carrion

carrot n (pl **-s**) long tapering orange root vegetable

carrots n ▷ carrot

carroty adj (of hair) reddish-orange

carry v (**-ries, -rying, -ried**) take from one place to another

carrying v ▷ carry

cars n ▷ car

cart n (pl **-s**) open two-wheeled horse-drawn vehicle for carrying goods or passengers ▶ v (**-s, -ing, -ed**) carry, usu. with some effort

carted v ▷ cart

cartel n (pl **-s**) association of competing firms formed to fix prices

cartels n ▷ cartel

carting v ▷ cart

carton n (pl **-s**) container made of cardboard or waxed paper

cartons n ▷ carton

cartoon n (pl **-s**) humorous or satirical drawing ▷ **cartoonist** n (pl **-s**)

cartoonist n ▷ cartoon

cartoonists n ▷ cartoon

cartoons n ▷ cartoon

carts v ▷ cart

carve v (**carves, carving, carved**) cut to form an object ▷ **carving** n (pl **-s**)

carved v ▷ carve

carves v ▷ carve

carving v, n ▷ carve

carvings n ▷ carve
caryatid n (pl **-s**) supporting column in the shape of a female figure
caryatids n ▷ caryatid
casbah n (pl **-s**) citadel of a N African city
casbahs n ▷ casbah
cascade n (pl **-s**) waterfall ▶ v (**-cades, -cading, -caded**) flow or fall in a cascade
cascaded v ▷ cascade
cascades n, v ▷ cascade
cascading v ▷ cascade
case¹ n (pl **-s**) instance, example
case² n (pl **-s**) container, protective covering ▶ v (**-ses, -sing, -sed**) slang inspect (a building) with the intention of burgling it
cased v ▷ case²
casement n (pl **-s**) window that is hinged on one side
casements n ▷ casement
cases n ▷ case¹, ², v ▷ case²
cash n banknotes and coins ▶ v (**-es, -ing, -ed**) obtain cash for
cashed v ▷ cash
cashes v ▷ cash
cashew n (pl **-s**) edible kidney-shaped nut
cashews n ▷ cashew
cashier¹ n (pl **-s**) person responsible for handling cash in a bank, shop, etc
cashier² v (**-s, -ing, -ed**) dismiss with dishonour from the armed forces
cashiered v ▷ cashier²
cashiering v ▷ cashier²
cashiers n ▷ cashier¹ ▶ v ▷ cashier²
cashing v ▷ cash
cashmere n (pl **-s**) fine soft wool obtained from goats
cashmeres n ▷ cashmere
casing n (pl **-s**) protective case, covering ▶ v ▷ case²
casings n ▷ casing
casino n (pl **-s**) public building or room where gambling games are played
casinos n ▷ casino
cask n barrel used to hold

alcoholic drink
casket n (pl **-s**) small box for valuables
caskets n ▷ casket
casks n ▷ cask
cassava n (pl **-s**) starch obtained from the roots of a tropical American plant, used to make tapioca
cassavas n ▷ cassava
cassette n (pl **-s**) plastic case containing a reel of film or magnetic tape
cassettes n ▷ cassette
cassock n (pl **-s**) long tunic, usu. black, worn by priests
cassocks n ▷ cassock
cast n (pl **-s**) actors in a play or film collectively ▶ v (**casts, casting, cast**) select (an actor) to play a part in a play or film
castaway n (pl **-s**) shipwrecked person
castaways n ▷ castaway
caste n (pl **-s**) any of the hereditary classes into which Hindu society is divided
castes n ▷ caste
casting v ▷ cast
castle n (pl **-s**) large fortified building, often built as a ruler's residence
castles n ▷ castle
castoff adj, n (pl **-s**) discarded (person or thing)
castoffs n ▷ castoff
castor n (pl **-s**) small swivelling wheel fixed to the bottom of a piece of furniture for easy moving
castors n ▷ castor
castrate v (**-tes, -ting, -ted**) remove the testicles of ▷ castration n (pl **-s**)
castrated v ▷ castrate
castrates v ▷ castrate
castrating v ▷ castrate
castration n ▷ castrate
castrations n ▷ castrate
casts n, v ▷ cast
casual adj careless, nonchalant ▷ casually adv
casually adv ▷ casual
casualties n ▷ casualty

casualty n (pl **-ties**) person killed or injured in an accident or war

cat n (pl **-s**) small domesticated furry mammal

catalyse v (**-lyses, -lysing, -lysed**) speed up (a chemical reaction) by a catalyst

catalysed v ▷ catalyse

catalyses v ▷ catalyse

catalysing v ▷ catalyse

catalysis n ▷ catalyst

catalyst n (pl **-s**) substance that speeds up a chemical reaction without itself changing > **catalysis** n > **catalytic** adj > **catalytically** adv

catalysts n ▷ catalyst

catalytic adj ▷ catalyst

catalytically adv ▷ catalyst

catapult n (pl **-s**) Y-shaped device with a loop of elastic, used by children for firing stones ▶ v (**-s, -ing, -ed**) shoot forwards or upwards violently

catapulted v ▷ catapult

catapulting v ▷ catapult

catapults n, v ▷ catapult

cataract n (pl **-s**) eye disease in which the lens becomes opaque

cataracts n ▷ cataract

catarrh n (pl **-s**) excessive mucus in the nose and throat, during or following a cold > **catarrhal** adj

catarrhal adj ▷ catarrh

catarrhs n ▷ catarrh

catcall n (pl **-s**) derisive whistle or cry

catcalls n ▷ catcall

catch v (**-ches, -ching, caught**) seize, capture ▶ n (pl **-es**) device for fastening a door, window, etc

catches v, n ▷ catch

catchier adj ▷ catchy

catchiest adj ▷ catchy

catchiness n ▷ catchy

catchinesses n ▷ catchy

catching adj infectious ▶ v ▷ catch

catchy adj (**-chier, -chiest**) (of a tune) pleasant and easily remembered > **catchiness** n (pl **-es**)

categories n ▷ category

category n (pl **-ries**) class, group

cater v (**-s, -ing, -ed**) provide what is needed or wanted, esp. food or services > **caterer** n (pl **-s**)

catered v ▷ cater

caterer n ▷ cater

caterers n ▷ cater

catering v ▷ cater

caters v ▷ cater

catfish n (pl **-fish, -fishes**) fish with whisker-like barbels round the mouth

catfishes n ▷ catfish

catgut n (pl **-s**) strong cord used to string musical instruments and sports rackets

catguts n ▷ catgut

catheter n (pl **-s**) tube inserted into a body cavity to drain fluid

catheters n ▷ catheter

cathode n (pl **-s**) negative electrode, by which electrons leave a circuit

cathodes n ▷ cathode

catholic adj (of tastes or interests) covering a wide range > **catholicism** n (pl **-s**)

catholicism n ▷ catholic

catholicisms n ▷ catholic

cation n (pl **-s**) positively charged ion

cations n ▷ cation

catkin n (pl **-s**) drooping flower spike of certain trees

catkins n ▷ catkin

catnap n (pl **-s**) ▶ v (**-naps, -napping, -napped**) doze

catnapped v ▷ catnap

catnapping v ▷ catnap

catnaps n, v ▷ catnap

cats n ▷ cat

cattier adj ▷ catty

cattiest adj ▷ catty

cattily adv ▷ catty

cattiness n ▷ catty

cattinesses n ▷ catty

cattle pl n domesticated cows and bulls

catty adj (**-tier, -tiest**) informal spiteful > **cattily** adv > **cattiness** n (pl **-es**)

catwalk n (pl **-s**) narrow pathway or

platform
catwalks n ▷ catwalk
caucus n (pl **-es**) local committee or faction of a political party
caucuses n ▷ caucus
caught v ▷ catch
cauldron n (pl **-s**) large pot used for boiling
cauldrons n ▷ cauldron
caulk v (**-s, -ing, -ed**) fill in (cracks) with paste etc
caulked v ▷ caulk
caulking v ▷ caulk
caulks v ▷ caulk
causal adj of or being a cause
> **causally** adv
causally adv ▷ causal
cause n (pl **-s**) something that produces a particular effect ▶ v (**-ses, -sing, -sed**) be the cause of
caused v ▷ cause
causes n, v ▷ cause
causeway n (pl **-s**) raised path or road across water or marshland
causeways n ▷ causeway
causing v ▷ cause
caustic adj capable of burning by chemical action > **caustically** adv
caustically adv ▷ caustic
caution n (pl **-s**) care, esp. in the face of danger ▶ v (**-s, -ing, -ed**) warn, advise
cautioned v ▷ caution
cautioning v ▷ caution
cautions n, v ▷ caution
cautious adj showing caution
> **cautiously** adv
cautiously adv ▷ cautious
cavalier adj showing haughty disregard ▶ n (pl **-s**) (**C-**) supporter of Charles I in the English Civil War
> **cavalierly** adv
cavalierly adv ▷ cavalier
cavaliers n ▷ cavalier
cavalries n ▷ cavalry
cavalry n (pl **-ries**) part of the army orig. on horseback, but now often using fast armoured vehicles
cave n (pl **-s**) hollow in the side of a hill or cliff

caveat n (pl **-s**) warning
caveats n ▷ caveat
caveman n (pl **-men**) prehistoric cave dweller
cavemen n ▷ caveman
cavern n (pl **-s**) large cave
> **cavernous** adj
cavernous adj ▷ cavern
caverns n ▷ cavern
caves n ▷ cave
caviar, caviare n (pl **-s**) salted sturgeon roe, regarded as a delicacy
caviare n ▷ caviar
caviares n ▷ caviar
caviars n ▷ caviar
cavil v (**-ils, -illing, -illed**) make petty objections ▶ n (pl **-s**) petty objection
cavilled v ▷ cavil
cavilling v ▷ cavil
cavils v, n ▷ cavil
caving n sport of exploring caves
cavities n ▷ cavity
cavity n (pl **-ties**) hollow space
cavort v (**-s, -ing, -ed**) skip about
cavorted v ▷ cavort
cavorting v ▷ cavort
cavorts v ▷ cavort
caw n (pl **-s**) cry of a crow, rook, or raven ▶ v (**-s, -ing, -ed**) make this cry
cawed v ▷ caw
cawing v ▷ caw
caws n, v ▷ caw

> **cay** n (**cays**) A cay is a small low island. Cay scores 8 points.

cayman n (pl **-s**) S American reptile similar to an alligator
caymans n ▷ cayman

> **caz** adj. Caz is a slang word for **casual**. It's a great word to have up your sleeve as it scores 14 points.

> **cazique** n (**caziques**). A cazique is a chief among certain American Indian tribes. Cazique scores 27 points, and will earn you a 50-point bonus if you manage to use all of your tiles to form it.

cease v (**ceases, ceasing, ceased**)

bring or come to an end ▶ **ceaseless** adj ▶ **ceaselessly** adv

ceased v ▷ **cease**

ceaseless adj ▷ **cease**

ceaselessly adv ▷ **cease**

ceases v ▷ **cease**

ceasing v ▷ **cease**

cedar n (pl **-s**) evergreen coniferous tree

cedars n ▷ **cedar**

cede v (**cedes, ceding, ceded**) surrender (territory or legal rights)

ceded v ▷ **cede**

cedes v ▷ **cede**

cedilla n (pl **-s**) character (¸) placed under a c in some languages, to show that it is pronounced s, not k

cedillas n ▷ **cedilla**

ceding v ▷ **cede**

ceilidh n (pl **-s**) informal social gathering for singing and dancing, esp. in Scotland

ceilidhs n ▷ **ceilidh**

ceiling n (pl **-s**) inner upper surface of a room

ceilings n ▷ **ceiling**

celeriac n (pl **-s**) variety of celery with a large turnip-like root

celeriacs n ▷ **celeriac**

celeries n ▷ **celery**

celerities n ▷ **celerity**

celerity n (pl **-ties**) swiftness

celery n (pl **-ries**) vegetable with long green crisp edible stalks

celibacies n ▷ **celibacy**

celibacy n ▷ **celibate**

celibate adj unmarried or abstaining from sex, esp. because of a religious vow of chastity ▶ n (pl **-s**) celibate person ▶ **celibacy** n (pl **-cies**)

celibates n ▷ **celibate**

cell n (pl **-s**) smallest unit of an organism that is able to function independently

cellar n (pl **-s**) underground room for storage

cellars n ▷ **cellar**

cellist n ▷ **cello**

cellists n ▷ **cello**

cello n (pl **-s**) large low-pitched instrument of the violin family ▶ **cellist** n (pl **-s**)

cellos n ▷ **cello**

cells n ▷ **cell**

cellular adj of or consisting of cells

cement n (pl **-s**) fine grey powder mixed with water and sand to make mortar or concrete ▶ v (**-s, -ing, -ed**) join, bind, or cover with cement

cemented v ▷ **cement**

cementing v ▷ **cement**

cements n, v ▷ **cement**

cemeteries n ▷ **cemetery**

cemetery n (pl **-ries**) place where dead people are buried

cenotaph n (pl **-s**) monument honouring soldiers who died in a war

cenotaphs n ▷ **cenotaph**

censer n (pl **-s**) container for burning incense

censers n ▷ **censer**

censor n (pl **-s**) person authorized to examine films, books, etc, to ban or cut anything considered obscene or objectionable ▶ v (**-s, -ing, -ed**) ban or cut parts of (a film, book, etc) ▶ **censorship** n (pl **-s**)

censored v ▷ **censor**

censoring v ▷ **censor**

censors n, v ▷ **censor**

censorship n ▷ **censor**

censorships n ▷ **censor**

censure n (pl **-s**) severe disapproval ▶ v (**-res, -ring, -red**) criticize severely

censured v ▷ **censure**

censures n, v ▷ **censure**

censuring v ▷ **censure**

census n (pl **-es**) official count of a population

censuses n ▷ **census**

cent n (pl **-s**) hundredth part of a monetary unit such as the dollar or euro

centaur n (pl **-s**) mythical creature with the head, arms, and torso of a man, and the lower body and legs of a horse

centaurs n ▷ centaur

central adj of, at, or forming the centre > **centrally** adv > **centrality** n
centrality n ▷ central
centrally adv ▷ central

centre n (pl -s) middle point or part ▶ v (-res, -ring, -red) put in the centre of something

centred v ▷ centre
centres n, v ▷ centre
centring v ▷ centre

centrist n (pl -s) person favouring political moderation
centrists n ▷ centrist

cents n ▷ cent
centuries n ▷ century

century n (pl -ries) period of 100 years

   cep n (**ceps**). A cep is an edible
   fungus. Cep scores 7 points.

ceramic n (pl -s) hard brittle material made by heating clay to a very high temperature ▶ pl art of producing ceramic objects ▶ adj made of ceramic
ceramics n ▷ ceramic

cereal n (pl -s) grass plant with edible grain, such as oat or wheat
cereals n ▷ cereal
cerebra n ▷ cerebrum
cerebral adj of the brain
cerebrum n (pl -brums, -bra) main part of the brain
cerebrums n ▷ cerebrum
ceremonial adj of ceremony
ceremonially adv ▷ ceremony
ceremonials n ▷ ceremony
ceremonies n ▷ ceremony
ceremony n (pl -nies) formal act or ritual > **ceremonial** adj, n (pl -s) > **ceremonially** adv
cerise adj cherry-red
certain adj (-er, -est) positive and confident > **certainly** adv
certainer adj ▷ certain
certainest adj ▷ certain
certainly adv ▷ certain
certification n ▷ certify
certifications n ▷ certify

certified v ▷ certify
certifies v ▷ certify
certify v (-fies, -fying, -fied) confirm, attest to > **certification** n (pl -s)
certifying v ▷ certify
cervical adj ▷ cervix
cervices n ▷ cervix
cervix n (pl -ixes, -ices) narrow entrance of the womb > **cervical** adj
cervixes n ▷ cervix
cesspit, cesspool n (pl -s) covered tank or pit for sewage
cesspits n ▷ cesspit
cesspool n ▷ cesspit
cesspools n ▷ cesspit
cetacean n (pl -s) fish-shaped sea mammal such as a whale or dolphin
cetaceans n ▷ cetacean

   ch pron. This is an old dialect form
   of I. It's the only two-letter word
   that can be formed with the letter
   C, and it's a good word to remember
   because it doesn't use any vowels. Ch
   scores 7 points.

   cha n (**chas**). Cha is a slang word for
   tea. Cha scores 8 points.

chafe v (chafes, chafing, chafed) make sore or worn by rubbing
chafed v ▷ chafe
chafes v ▷ chafe
chaff¹ n (pl -s) grain husks
chaff² v (-s, -ing, -ed) old-fashioned tease good-naturedly
chaffed v ▷ chaff²
chaffing v ▷ chaff²
chaffs n ▷ chaff¹ ▶ v ▷ chaff²
chafing v ▷ chafe
chagrin n (pl -s) annoyance and disappointment
chagrins n ▷ chagrin
chain n (pl -s) flexible length of connected metal links ▶ v (-s, -ing, -ed) restrict or fasten with or as if with a chain
chained v ▷ chain
chaining v ▷ chain
chains n, v ▷ chain
chair n (pl -s) seat with a back, for one

person ▸ v (-s, -ing, -ed) preside over (a meeting)

chaired v ▷ chair

chairing v ▷ chair

chairman, chairwoman n (pl -men, -women) person in charge of a company's board of directors or a meeting (also **chairperson**) (pl -s)

chairmen n ▷ chairman

chairperson n ▷ chairman

chairpersons n ▷ chairman

chairs n, v ▷ chair

chairwoman n ▷ chairman

chairwomen n ▷ chairman

chaise n (pl -s) HIST light horse-drawn carriage

chaises ▷ chaise

chalet n (pl -s) kind of Swiss wooden house with a steeply sloping roof

chalets ▷ chalet

chalice n (pl -s) large goblet

chalices ▷ chalice

chalk n (pl -s) soft white rock consisting of calcium carbonate ▸ v (-s, -ing, -ed) draw or mark with chalk > **chalky** adj (-kier, -kiest)

chalked v ▷ chalk

chalkier adj ▷ chalk

chalkiest adj ▷ chalk

chalking v ▷ chalk

chalks n, v ▷ chalk

chalky adj ▷ chalk

chamber n (pl -s) hall used for formal meetings   old-fashioned ▸ pl set of rooms used as offices by a barrister

chambers n ▷ chamber

chamfer v (-s, -ing, -ed) bevel the edge of

chamfered v ▷ chamfer

chamfering v ▷ chamfer

chamfers v ▷ chamfer

chamois n (pl -ois) small mountain antelope

chamomile n (pl -s) ▷ camomile

chamomiles n ▷ camomile

champ[1] v (-s, -ing, -ed) chew noisily

champ[2] n (pl -s) ▷ champion

champed v ▷ champ[1]

champing v ▷ champ[1]

champion n (pl -s) overall winner of a competition (foll. by **of**) ▸ v (-s, -ing, -ed) support ▸ adj   dialect excellent > **championship** n (pl -s)

championed v ▷ champion

championing v ▷ champion

champions n, v ▷ champion

championship n ▷ champion

championships n ▷ champion

champs v ▷ champ[1] ▸ n ▷ champ[2]

chance n (pl -s) likelihood, probability ▸ v (**chances, chancing, chanced**) risk, hazard

chanced v ▷ chance

chancel n (pl -s) part of a church containing the altar and choir

chancels n ▷ chancel

chances n, v ▷ chance

chancier adj ▷ chancy

chanciest adj ▷ chancy

chancing v ▷ chance

chancy adj (-cier, -ciest) uncertain, risky

chandler n (pl -s) dealer, esp. in ships' supplies

chandlers n ▷ chandler

change n (pl -s) becoming different ▸ v (-ges, -ging, -ged) make or become different

changed v ▷ change

changes n, v ▷ change

changing v ▷ change

channel n (pl -s) band of broadcasting frequencies ▸ v (-nels, -nelling, -nelled) direct or convey through a channel

channelled v ▷ channel

channelling v ▷ channel

channels n, v ▷ channel

chant v (-s, -ing, -ed) utter or sing (a slogan or psalm) ▸ n (pl -s) rhythmic or repetitious slogan

chanted v ▷ chant

chanter n (pl -s) (on bagpipes) pipe on which the melody is played

chanters n ▷ chanter

chanting v ▷ chant

chants v, n ▷ **chant**

chaos n complete disorder or confusion > **chaotic** adj
> **chaotically** adv

chaotic adj ▷ **chaos**

chaotically adv ▷ **chaos**

chap n (pl -s) informal man or boy

chapati, chapatti n (pl -s) (in Indian cookery) flat thin unleavened bread

chapatis n ▷ **chapati**

chapatti n ▷ **chapati**

chapattis n ▷ **chapati**

chapel n (pl -s) place of worship with its own altar, within a church

chapels n ▷ **chapel**

chaplain n (pl -s) clergyman attached to a chapel, military body, or institution > **chaplaincy** n (pl -cies)

chaplaincies n ▷ **chaplain**

chaplaincy n ▷ **chaplain**

chaplains n ▷ **chaplain**

chaplet n (pl -s) garland for the head

chaplets n ▷ **chaplet**

chapped adj (of the skin) raw and cracked, through exposure to cold

chaps n ▷ **chap**

chapter n (pl -s) division of a book

chapters n ▷ **chapter**

char¹ v (-rs, -rring, -rred) blacken by partial burning

char² BRIT informal n (pl -s) charwoman ▶ v (-rs, -rring, -rred) clean other people's houses as a job

char³ BRIT old-fashioned slang tea

charade n (pl -s) absurd pretence ▶ pl game in which one team acts out a word or phrase, which the other team has to guess

charades n ▷ **charade**

charcoal n (pl -s) black substance formed by partially burning wood

charcoals n ▷ **charcoal**

charge v (-ges, -ging, -ged) ask as a price ▶ n (pl **charges**) price charged
> **chargeable** adj

chargeable adj ▷ **charge**

charged v ▷ **charge**

charger n (pl -s) device for charging an accumulator

chargers n ▷ **charger**

charges v, n ▷ **charge**

charging v ▷ **charge**

charier adj ▷ **chary**

chariest adj ▷ **chary**

chariot n (pl -s) two-wheeled horse-drawn vehicle used in ancient times in wars and races

chariots n ▷ **chariot**

charisma n (pl -s) person's power to attract or influence people
> **charismatic** ▶ adj

charismas n ▷ **charisma**

charismatic adj ▷ **charisma**

charitable adj ▷ **charity**

charitably adv ▷ **charity**

charities n ▷ **charity**

charity n (pl -ties) organization that gives help, such as money or food, to those in need > **charitable** adj
> **charitably** adv

charladies n ▷ **charlady**

charm n (pl -s) attractive quality ▶ v (-s, -ing, -ed) attract, delight
> **charmer** n (pl -s)

charmed v ▷ **charm**

charmer n ▷ **charm**

charmers n ▷ **charm**

charming adj attractive ▶ v ▷ **charm**

charms n, v ▷ **charm**

charred v ▷ **char¹, ²**

charring v ▷ **char¹, ²**

chars v ▷ **char¹, ²** n ▷ **char²**

chart n (pl -s) graph, table, or diagram showing information ▶ v (-s, -ing, -ed) plot the course of

charted v ▷ **chart**

charter n (pl -s) document granting or demanding certain rights ▶ v (-s, -ing, -ed) hire by charter

chartering v ▷ **charter**

charters n, v ▷ **charter**

charting v ▷ **chart**

charts n, v ▷ **chart**

chary adj (-rier, -riest) wary, careful

chase¹ v (-ses, -sing, -sed) run after quickly in order to catch or drive away

▶ n (pl **-s**) chasing, pursuit

chase² v (**-ses, -sing, -sed**) engrave or emboss (metal)

chased v ▷ **chase¹, ²**

chaser n (pl **-s**) milder drink drunk after one stronger one

chasers n ▷ **chaser**

chases v ▷ **chase¹, ²** ▶ n ▷ **chase¹**

chasing v ▷ **chase¹, ²**

chasm n (pl **-s**) deep crack in the earth

chasms n ▷ **chasm**

chassis n (pl **-sis**) frame, wheels, and mechanical parts of a vehicle

chaste adj (**-r, -st**) abstaining from sex outside marriage or altogether
> **chastely** adv > **chasteness** n (pl **-es**)
> **chastity** n (pl **-ties**)

chastely adv ▷ **chaste**

chasten v (**-s, -ing, -ed**) subdue by criticism

chastened v ▷ **chasten**

chasteness n ▷ **chaste**

chastenesses n ▷ **chaste**

chastening v ▷ **chasten**

chastens v ▷ **chasten**

chaster adj ▷ **chaste**

chastest adj ▷ **chaste**

chastise v (**-ses, -sing, -sed**) scold severely > **chastisement** n (pl **-s**)

chastised v ▷ **chastise**

chastisement n ▷ **chastise**

chastisements n ▷ **chastise**

chastises v ▷ **chastise**

chastising v ▷ **chastise**

chastities n ▷ **chaste**

chastity n ▷ **chaste**

chat n (pl **-s**) informal conversation ▶ v (**-ts, -tting, -tted**) have an informal conversation > **chatty** adj (**-tier, -tiest**) > **chattily** adv > **chattiness** n (pl **-es**)

chateau n (pl **-teaux, -teaus**) French castle

chateaus n ▷ **chateau**

chateaux n ▷ **chateau**

chatroom n (pl **-s**) site on the Internet where users have group discussions by e-mail

chatrooms n ▷ **chatroom**

chats n, v ▷ **chat**

chatted v ▷ **chat**

chattel n (pl **-s**) (usually plural) possessions

chattels n ▷ **chattel**

chatter v (**-s, -ing, -ed**) speak quickly and continuously about unimportant things ▶ n (pl **-s**) idle talk

chattered v ▷ **chatter**

chattering v ▷ **chatter**

chatters v, n ▷ **chatter**

chattier adj ▷ **chat**

chattiest adj ▷ **chat**

chattily adv ▷ **chat**

chattiness n ▷ **chat**

chattinesses n ▷ **chat**

chatting v ▷ **chat**

chatty adj ▷ **chat**

cheap adj (**-er, -est**) costing relatively little > **cheaply** adv

cheapen v (**-s, -ing, -ed**) lower the reputation of

cheapened v ▷ **cheapen**

cheapening v ▷ **cheapen**

cheapens v ▷ **cheapen**

cheaper adj ▷ **cheap**

cheapest adj ▷ **cheap**

cheaply adv ▷ **cheap**

cheat v (**-s, -ing, -ed**) act dishonestly to gain profit or advantage ▶ n (pl **-s**) person who cheats

cheated v ▷ **cheat**

cheating v ▷ **cheat**

cheats v, n ▷ **cheat**

check v (**-s, -ing, -ed**) examine, investigate ▶ n (pl **-s**) test to ensure accuracy or progress

checked v ▷ **check**

checking v ▷ **check**

checkout n (pl **-s**) counter in a supermarket, where customers pay

checkouts n ▷ **checkout**

checks v, n ▷ **check**

checkup n (pl **-s**) thorough medical examination

checkups n ▷ **checkup**

cheddar n (pl **-s**) firm orange or

yellowy-white cheese
cheddars n ▷ cheddar
cheek n (pl -s) either side of the face below the eye ▶ v (-s, -ing, -ed) BRIT, AUST & NZ informal speak impudently to
cheeked v ▷ cheek
cheekier adj ▷ cheeky
cheekiest adj ▷ cheeky
cheekily adv ▷ cheeky
cheekiness n ▷ cheeky
cheekinesses n ▷ cheeky
cheeking v ▷ cheek
cheeks n, v ▷ cheek
cheeky adj (-kier, -kiest) impudent, disrespectful > **cheekily** adv > **cheekiness** n (pl -es)
cheep n (pl -s) young bird's high-pitched cry ▶ v (-s, -ing, -ed) utter a cheep
cheeped v ▷ cheep
cheeping v ▷ cheep
cheeps n, v ▷ cheep
cheer v (-s, -ing, -ed) applaud or encourage with shouts ▶ n (pl -s) shout of applause or encouragement > **cheerful** adj (-ller, -llest) > **cheerfully** adv > **cheerfulness** n (pl -es) > **cheery** adj (-rier, -riest) > **cheerily** adv
cheered v ▷ cheer
cheerful adj ▷ cheer
cheerfuller adj ▷ cheer
cheerfullest adj ▷ cheer
cheerfully adv ▷ cheer
cheerfulness n ▷ cheer
cheerfulnesses n ▷ cheer
cheerier adj ▷ cheer
cheeriest adj ▷ cheer
cheerily adv ▷ cheer
cheering v ▷ cheer
cheerio interj informal goodbye ▶ n (pl -s) AUST & NZ small red cocktail sausage
cheerios n ▷ cheerio
cheers v, n ▷ cheer
cheery adj ▷ cheer
cheese n (pl -s) food made from

coagulated milk curd > **cheesy** adj (-sier, -siest) > **cheesily** adv > **cheesiness** n (pl -es)
cheeses n ▷ cheese
cheesier adj ▷ cheese
cheesiest adj ▷ cheese
cheesily adv ▷ cheese
cheesiness n ▷ cheese
cheesinesses n ▷ cheese
cheesy adj ▷ cheese
cheetah n (pl -s) large fast-running spotted African wild cat
cheetahs n ▷ cheetah
chef n (pl -s) cook in a restaurant
chefs n ▷ chef
chemical n (pl -s) substance used in or resulting from a reaction involving changes to atoms or molecules ▶ adj of chemistry or chemicals > **chemically** adv
chemically adv ▷ chemical
chemicals n ▷ chemical
chemise n (pl -s) old-fashioned woman's loose-fitting slip
chemises n ▷ chemise
chemist n (pl -s) shop selling medicines and cosmetics
chemists n ▷ chemist
chenille n (pl -s) (fabric of) thick tufty yarn
chenilles n ▷ chenille
cheque n (pl -s) written order to one's bank to pay money from one's account
chequer n (pl -s) piece used in Chinese chequers ▶ pl game of draughts
chequers n ▷ chequer
cheques n ▷ cheque
cherish v (-es, -ing, -ed) cling to (an idea or feeling)
cherished v ▷ cherish
cherishes v ▷ cherish
cherishing v ▷ cherish
cheroot n (pl -s) cigar with both ends cut flat
cheroots n ▷ cheroot
cherries n ▷ cherry
cherry n (pl -ries) small red or black fruit with a stone ▶ adj deep red

cherub n (pl -s, -bim) angel, often represented as a winged child > **cherubic** ▶ adj

cherubic adj ▷ **cherub**

cherubim n ▷ **cherub**

cherubs n ▷ **cherub**

chervil n (pl -s) aniseed-flavoured herb

chervils n ▷ **chervil**

chess n (pl -es) game for two players with 16 pieces each, played on a chequered board of 64 squares

chesses n ▷ **chess**

chessman n (pl -men) piece used in chess

chessmen n ▷ **chessman**

chest n (pl -s) front of the body, from neck to waist

chestnut n (pl -s) reddish-brown edible nut informal ▶ adj (of hair or a horse) reddish-brown

chestnuts n ▷ **chestnut**

chests n ▷ **chest**

chevron n (pl -s) V-shaped pattern, esp. on the sleeve of a military uniform to indicate rank

chevrons n ▷ **chevron**

chew v (-s, -ing, -ed) grind (food) between the teeth

chewed v ▷ **chew**

chewier adj ▷ **chewy**

chewiest adj ▷ **chewy**

chewing v ▷ **chew**

chews v ▷ **chew**

chewy adj (-wier, -wiest) requiring a lot of chewing

▎**chi** n (**chis**). Chi is a letter of the Greek alphabet, and is worth 8 points.

chianti n (pl -s) dry red Italian wine

chiantis n ▷ **chianti**

chic adj (-er, -est) stylish, elegant ▶ n (pl -s) stylishness, elegance

chicane n (pl -s) obstacle in a motor-racing circuit

chicanes n ▷ **chicane**

chicer adj ▷ **chic**

chicest adj ▷ **chic**

chick n (pl -s) baby bird

chicken n (pl -s) domestic fowl ▶ adj slang cowardly

chickens n ▷ **chicken**

chickpea n (pl -s) edible yellow pealike seed

chickpeas n ▷ **chickpea**

chicks n ▷ **chick**

chicories n ▷ **chicory**

chicory n (pl -ries) plant whose leaves are used in salads

chics n ▷ **chic**

chid v ▷ **chide**

chidden v ▷ **chide**

chide v (chiding, chided or chid) (chid or chidden) rebuke, scold

chided v ▷ **chide**

chiding v ▷ **chide**

chief n (pl -s) head of a group of people ▶ adj most important

chiefly adv especially

chiefs n ▷ **chief**

chiffon n (pl -s) fine see-through fabric

chiffons n ▷ **chiffon**

chignon n (pl -s) knot of hair pinned up at the back of the head

chignons n ▷ **chignon**

child n (pl children) young human being, boy or girl > **childhood** n (pl -s) > **childless** adj > **childlessness** n (pl -es)

childhood n ▷ **child**

childhoods n ▷ **child**

childish adj immature, silly > **childishly** adv > **childishness** n (pl -es)

childishly adv ▷ **childish**

childishness n ▷ **childish**

childishnesses n ▷ **childish**

childless adj ▷ **child**

childlessness n ▷ **child**

childlessnesses n ▷ **child**

children n ▷ **child**

chili n ▷ **chilli**

chilies n ▷ **chilli**

chilis n ▷ **chilli**

chill n (pl -s) feverish cold ▶ v (-s, -ing, -ed) make (something) cool or cold ▶ adj unpleasantly cold

chilled v ▷ **chill**

chilli, chili n (pl -is, -es) small red or green hot-tasting capsicum pod, used in cooking

chillier adj ▷ **chilly**

chillies n ▷ **chilli**

chilliest adj ▷ **chilly**

chilliness n ▷ **chilly**

chilling v ▷ **chill**

chillis n ▷ **chilli**

chills n, v ▷ **chill**

chilly adj (-lier, -liest) moderately cold > **chilliness** n (pl -es)

chime n (pl -s) musical ringing sound of a bell or clock ▶ v (-mes, -ming, -med) make a musical ringing sound

chimed v ▷ **chime**

chimera n (pl -s) unrealistic hope or idea

chimeras n ▷ **chimera**

chimes n, v ▷ **chime**

chiming v ▷ **chime**

chimney n (pl -s) hollow vertical structure for carrying away smoke from a fire

chimneys n ▷ **chimney**

chimps n ▷ **chimp**

chin n (pl -s) part of the face below the mouth

china n (pl -s) fine earthenware or porcelain

chinas n ▷ **china**

chine n (pl -s) cut of meat including part of the backbone

chines n ▷ **chine**

chink¹ n (pl -s) small narrow opening

chink² v (-s, -ing, -ed) ▶ n (pl -s) (make) a light ringing sound

chinked v ▷ **chink²**

chinking v ▷ **chink²**

chinks n ▷ **chink¹, ²** v ▷ **chink²**

chins n ▷ **chin**

chintz n (pl -es) printed cotton fabric with a glazed finish

chintzes n ▷ **chintz**

chinwag n (pl -s) BRIT, AUST & NZ informal chat

chinwags n ▷ **chinwag**

chip n (pl -s) strip of potato, fried in deep fat ▶ v (-s, -pping, -pped) break small pieces from

chipmunk n (pl -s) small squirrel-like N American rodent with a striped back

chipmunks n ▷ **chipmunk**

chipped v ▷ **chip**

chippie n (pl -s) BRIT, AUST & NZ informal carpenter

chippies n ▷ **chippie**

chipping v ▷ **chip**

chips n, v ▷ **chip**

chirp v (-s, -ing, -ed) (of a bird or insect) make a short high-pitched sound ▶ n (pl -s) chirping sound

chirped v ▷ **chirp**

chirpier adj ▷ **chirpy**

chirpiest adj ▷ **chirpy**

chirpily adv ▷ **chirpy**

chirpiness n ▷ **chirpy**

chirpinesses n ▷ **chirpy**

chirping v ▷ **chirp**

chirps v, n ▷ **chirp**

chirpy adj (-pier, -piest) informal lively and cheerful > **chirpily** adv > **chirpiness** n (pl -es)

chisel n (pl -s) metal tool with a sharp end for shaping wood or stone ▶ v (-ls, -lling, -lled) carve or form with a chisel

chiselled v ▷ **chisel**

chiselling v ▷ **chisel**

chisels n, v ▷ **chisel**

chit¹ n (pl -s) short official note, such as a receipt

chit² n (pl -s) BRIT, AUST & NZ old-fashioned pert or impudent girl

chitchat n (pl -s) chat, gossip

chitchats n ▷ **chitchat**

chits n ▷ **chit¹, ²**

chivalries n ▷ **chivalry**

chivalrous adj ▷ **chivalry**

chivalrously adv ▷ **chivalry**

chivalry n (pl -ries) courteous behaviour, esp. by men towards women > **chivalrous** adj > **chivalrously** adv

chives pl n herb with a mild onion flavour

chivvied v ▷ chivvy

chivvies v ▷ chivvy

chivvy v (-vies, -vying, -vied) *informal* harass, nag

    chivvying v ▷ chivvy

chloride n (pl -s) compound of chlorine and another substance

    chlorides n ▷ chloride

chlorine n (pl -s) strong-smelling greenish-yellow gaseous element, used to disinfect water

    chlorines n ▷ chlorine

chock n (pl -s) block or wedge used to prevent a heavy object from moving

    chocks n ▷ chock

choice n (pl -s) choosing ▶ adj (-r, -st) of high quality

    choicer adj ▷ choice

    choices n ▷ choice

    choicest adj ▷ choice

choir n (pl -s) organized group of singers, esp. in church

    choirs n ▷ choir

choke v (-kes, -king, -ked) hinder or stop the breathing of (a person) by strangling or smothering ▶ n (pl -s) device controlling the amount of air that is mixed with the fuel in a petrol engine

    choked v ▷ choke

choker n (pl -s) tight-fitting necklace

    chokers n ▷ choke

    chokes v, n ▷ choke

    choking v ▷ choke

cholera n (pl -s) serious infectious disease causing severe vomiting and diarrhoea

    choleras n ▷ cholera

choleric adj bad-tempered

chomp v (-s, -ing, -ed) chew noisily

    chomped v ▷ chomp

    chomping v ▷ chomp

    chomps v ▷ chomp

chook n (pl -s) AUST & NZ hen or chicken

    chooks n ▷ chook

choose v (-ses, -sing, chose, chosen) select from a number of alternatives

chooses v ▷ choose

choosier adj ▷ choosy

choosiest adj ▷ choosy

choosing v ▷ choose

choosy adj (-sier, -siest) *informal* fussy, hard to please

chop[1] v (-ps, -pping, -pped) cut with a blow from an axe or knife ▶ n (pl -s) cutting or sharp blow

chop[2] v (-ps, -pping, -pped) change one's mind repeatedly

    chopped v ▷ chop[1, 2]

chopper n (pl -s) *informal* helicopter

    choppers n ▷ chopper

    choppier adj ▷ choppy

    choppiest adj ▷ choppy

    choppiness n ▷ choppy

    choppinesses n ▷ choppy

    chopping v ▷ chop[1, 2]

choppy adj (-ppier, -ppiest) (of the sea) fairly rough ▷ **choppiness** n (pl -es)

chops pl n BRIT, AUST & NZ *informal* jaws, cheeks ▶ v ▷ chop[1, 2] ▶ n ▷ chop[1]

choral adj of a choir

chorale n (pl -s) slow stately hymn tune

    chorales n ▷ chorale

chord[1] n (pl -s) MATHS straight line joining two points on a curve

chord[2] n (pl -s) simultaneous sounding of three or more musical notes

    chords n ▷ chord[1, 2]

chore n (pl -s) routine task

    chores n ▷ chore

chortle v (-tles, -tling, -tled) chuckle in amusement ▶ n (pl -s) amused chuckle

    chortled v ▷ chortle

    chortles v, n ▷ chortle

    chortling v ▷ chortle

chorus n (pl -es) large choir ▶ v (-es, -ing, -ed) sing or say together

    chorused v ▷ chorus

    choruses n, v ▷ chorus

    chorusing v ▷ chorus

chose v ▷ choose

chosen v ▷ choose

chow n (pl -s) thick-coated dog with a curled tail, orig. from China

chowder n (pl -s) thick soup containing clams or fish
chowders n ▷ chowder
chows n ▷ chow

christen v (-s, -ing, -ed) baptize
>**christening** n (pl -s)
christened v ▷ christen
christening v, n ▷ christen
christenings v, n ▷ christen
christens v ▷ christen

chrome n ▷ chromium
chromes n ▷ chromium

chromium, chrome n (pl -s) CHEM grey metallic element used in steel alloys and for electroplating
chromiums n ▷ chromium

chronic adj (of an illness) lasting a long time >**chronically** adv
chronically adv ▷ chronic

chub n (pl chub) European freshwater fish of the carp family
chubbier adj ▷ chubby
chubbiest adj ▷ chubby
chubbiness n ▷ chubby
chubbinesses n ▷ chubby
chubby adj (-bier, -biest) plump and round >**chubbiness** n (pl -es)

chuck[1] v (-s, -ing, -ed) informal throw
chuck[2] n (pl -s) cut of beef from the neck to the shoulder
chucked v ▷ chuck[1]
chucking v ▷ chuck[1]
chuckle v (-les, -ling, -led) laugh softly ▶ n (pl -s) soft laugh
chuckled v ▷ chuckle
chuckles v, n ▷ chuckle
chuckling v ▷ chuckle
chucks v ▷ chuck[1] ▶ n ▷ chuck[2]
chuffed adj informal very pleased

chug n (pl -s) short dull sound like the noise of an engine ▶ v (-s, -gging, -gged) operate or move with this sound
chugged v ▷ chug
chugging v ▷ chug
chugs n, v ▷ chug

chukka n (pl -s) period of play in polo
chukkas n ▷ chukka

chum informal n (pl -s) close friend ▶ v (-s, -mming, -mmed) form a close friendship with >**chummy** adj (-mmier, -mmiest) n >**chumminess** n (pl -es)
chummed v ▷ chum
chummier adj ▷ chum
chummiest adj ▷ chum
chumminess n ▷ chum
chumminesses n ▷ chum
chumming v ▷ chum
chummy adj ▷ chum

chump n (pl -s) informal stupid person
chumps n ▷ chump
chums n, v ▷ chum

chunk n (pl -s) thick solid piece
chunkier adj ▷ chunky
chunkiest adj ▷ chunky
chunkiness n ▷ chunky
chunkinesses n ▷ chunky
chunks n ▷ chunk
chunky adj (-kier, -kiest) (of a person) broad and heavy >**chunkiness** n (pl -es)

church n (pl -es) building for public Christian worship
churches n ▷ church

churlish adj surly and rude >**churlishly** adv >**churlishness** n (pl -es)
churlishly adv ▷ churlish
churlishness n ▷ churlish
churlishnesses n ▷ churlish

churn n (pl -s) machine in which cream is shaken to make butter ▶ v (-s, -ing, -ed) stir (cream) vigorously to make butter
churned v ▷ churn
churning v ▷ churn
churns n, v ▷ churn

chute[1] n (pl -s) steep slope down which things may be slid
chutes n ▷ chute[1, 2]

chutney n (pl -s) pickle made from fruit, vinegar, spices, and sugar
chutneys n ▷ chutney

cicada n (pl -s) large insect that makes

a high-pitched drone
cicadas n ▷ **cicada**
cicatrices n ▷ **cicatrix**
cicatrix n (pl **-trices**) scar
cid n (**cids**) A cid is a hero or
commander. Cid scores 6 points.
cider n (pl **-s**) alcoholic drink made
from fermented apple juice
ciders n ▷ **cider**
cigar n (pl **-s**) roll of cured tobacco
leaves for smoking
cigars n ▷ **cigar**
cinch n (pl **-es**) informal easy task
cinches n ▷ **cinch**
cinder n (pl **-s**) piece of material that
will not burn, left after burning coal
cinders n ▷ **cinder**
cinema n (pl **-s**) place for showing films
> **cinematic** adj
cinemas n ▷ **cinema**
cinematic adj ▷ **cinema**
cinnamon n (pl **-s**) spice obtained
from the bark of an Asian tree
cinnamons n ▷ **cinnamon**
cipher, cypher n (pl **-s**) system of
secret writing
ciphers n ▷ **cipher**
circa prep LATIN approximately, about
circle n (pl **-s**) perfectly round
geometric figure, line, or shape ▶ v
(**-les, -ling, -led**) move in a circle
(round)
circled v ▷ **circle**
circles n, v ▷ **circle**
circlet n (pl **-s**) circular ornament worn
on the head
circlets n ▷ **circlet**
circling v ▷ **circle**
circuit n (pl **-s**) complete route or
course, esp. a circular one
circuits n ▷ **circuit**
circular adj in the shape of a circle ▶ n
(pl **-s**) letter for general distribution
> **circularity** n (pl **-ties**)
circularities n ▷ **circular**
circularity n ▷ **circular**
circulars n ▷ **circular**
circus n (pl **-es**) (performance given

by) a travelling company of acrobats,
clowns, performing animals, etc
circuses n ▷ **circus**
cirri n ▷ **cirrus**
cirrus n (pl **-ri**) high wispy cloud
cistern n (pl **-s**) water tank, esp. one
that holds water for flushing a toilet
cisterns n ▷ **cistern**
citadel n (pl **-s**) fortress in a city
citadels n ▷ **citadel**
citation n ▷ **cite**
citations n ▷ **cite**
cite v (**-tes, -ting, -ted**) quote, refer to
> **citation** n (pl **-s**)
cited v ▷ **cite**
cites v ▷ **cite**
cities n ▷ **city**
citing v ▷ **cite**
citizen n (pl **-s**) native or naturalized
member of a state or nation
> **citizenship** n (pl **-s**)
citizens n ▷ **citizen**
citizenship n ▷ **citizen**
citizenships n ▷ **citizen**
city n (pl **-ties**) large or important town
civet n (pl **-s**) spotted catlike African
mammal
civets n ▷ **civet**
civic adj of a city or citizens
civics n study of the rights and
responsibilities of citizenship
civil adj relating to the citizens of a
state as opposed to the armed forces or
the Church > **civilly** adv
civilian n (pl **-s**) ▶ adj (person) not
belonging to the armed forces
civilians n ▷ **civilian**
civilities n ▷ **civility**
civility n (pl **-ities**) polite or courteous
behaviour
civilize v (**-izes, -izing, -ized**) refine or
educate (a person)
civilized v ▷ **civilize**
civilizes v ▷ **civilize**
civilizing v ▷ **civilize**
civilly adv ▷ **civil**
civvies pl n BRIT, AUST & NZ slang
ordinary clothes that are not part of

a uniform

clack n (pl **-s**) sound made by two hard objects striking each other ▶ v (**-s**, **-ing**, **-ed**) make this sound
clacked v ▷ clack
clacking v ▷ clack
clacks n, v ▷ clack

clad v (**-s**, **-dding**, clad) ▷ clothe

cladding n (pl **-s**) material used to cover the outside of a building ▶ v ▷ clad
claddings n ▷ cladding
clads v ▷ clad

claim v (**-s**, **-ing**, **-ed**) assert as a fact ▶ n (pl **-s**) assertion that something is true > **claimant** n (pl **-s**)
claimant n ▷ claim
claimants n ▷ claim
claimed v ▷ claim
claiming v ▷ claim
claims v, n ▷ claim

clam n (pl **-s**) edible shellfish with a hinged shell ▶ v (**-s**, **-mming**, **-mmed**) informal stop talking, esp. through nervousness

clamber v (**-s**, **-ing**, **-ed**) climb awkwardly
clambered v ▷ clamber
clambering v ▷ clamber
clambers v ▷ clamber
clammed v ▷ clam
clammier v ▷ clam
clammiest v ▷ clam
clamming v ▷ clam

clammy adj (**-mmier**, **-mmiest**) unpleasantly moist and sticky

clamorous adj ▷ clamour
clamorously adv ▷ clamour
clamorousness n ▷ clamour
clamorousnesses n ▷ clamour

clamour n (pl **-s**) loud protest ▶ v (**-s**, **-ing**, **-ed**) make a loud noise or outcry > **clamorous** adj ▷ clamour > **clamorously** adv > **clamorousness** n (pl **-es**)
clamoured v ▷ clamour
clamouring v ▷ clamour
clamours n, v ▷ clamour

clamp n (pl **-s**) tool with movable jaws for holding things together tightly ▶ v (**-s**, **-ing**, **-ed**) fasten with a clamp
clamped v ▷ clamp
clamping v ▷ clamp
clamps n, v ▷ clamp
clams v, n ▷ clam

clan n (pl **-s**) group of families with a common ancestor, esp. among Scottish Highlanders

clang v (**-s**, **-ing**, **-ed**) make a loud ringing metallic sound ▶ n (pl **-s**) ringing metallic sound
clanged v ▷ clang

clanger n (pl **-s**) informal obvious mistake
clangers n ▷ clanger
clanging v ▷ clang

clangour n (pl **-s**) loud continuous clanging sound
clangours n ▷ clangour
clangs v, n ▷ clang

clank n (pl **-s**) harsh metallic sound ▶ v (**-s**, **-ing**, **-ed**) make such a sound
clanked v ▷ clank
clanking v ▷ clank
clanks n, v ▷ clank

clannish adj (of a group) tending to exclude outsiders > **clannishness** n (pl **-es**)
clannishness n ▷ clannish
clannishnesses n ▷ clannish
clans n ▷ clan

clap v (**claps**, **clapping**, **clapped**) applaud by hitting the palms of one's hands sharply together ▶ n (pl **-s**) act or sound of clapping
clapped v ▷ clap

clapper n (pl **-s**) piece of metal inside a bell, which causes it to sound when struck against the side
clappers n ▷ clapper
clapping v ▷ clap
claps v, n ▷ clap

claptrap n (pl **-s**) informal foolish or pretentious talk
claptraps n ▷ claptrap

claret n (pl **-s**) dry red wine from Bordeaux

clarets n ▷ **claret**
clarification n ▷ **clarify**
clarifications n ▷ **clarify**
clarified v ▷ **clarify**
clarifies v ▷ **clarify**
clarify v (**-fies, -fying, -fied**) make (a matter) clear and unambiguous > **clarification** n (pl **-s**)
clarifying v ▷ **clarify**
clarinet n (pl **-s**) keyed woodwind instrument with a single reed > **clarinettist** n (pl **-s**)
clarinets n ▷ **clarinet**
clarinettist n ▷ **clarinet**
clarinettists n ▷ **clarinet**
clarion n (pl **-s**) obsolete high-pitched trumpet
clarions n ▷ **clarion**
clarities n ▷ **clarity**
clarity n (pl **-ities**) clearness
clash v (**-es, -ing, -ed**) come into conflict ▶ n (pl **-es**) fight, argument
clashed v ▷ **clash**
clashes n, v ▷ **clash**
clashing v ▷ **clash**
clasp n (pl **-s**) device for fastening things ▶ v (**-s, -ing, -ed**) grasp or embrace firmly
clasped v ▷ **clasp**
clasping v ▷ **clasp**
clasps n, v ▷ **clasp**
class n (pl **-es**) group of people sharing a similar social position ▶ v (**-es, -ing, -ed**) place in a class
classed v ▷ **class**
classes n, v ▷ **class**
classic adj being a typical example of something ▶ n (pl **-s**) author, artist, or work of art of recognized excellence ▶ pl study of ancient Greek and Roman literature and culture
classics n ▷ **classic**
classier adj ▷ **classy**
classiest adj ▷ **classy**
classifiable adj ▷ **classify**
classification n ▷ **classify**
classifications n ▷ **classify**
classified v ▷ **classify**

classifies v ▷ **classify**
classify v (**-fies, -fying, -fied**) divide into groups with similar characteristics > **classifiable** adj > **classification** n (pl **-s**)
classifying v ▷ **classify**
classing v ▷ **class**
classy adj (**-sier, -siest**) informal stylish and elegant
clatter v (**-s, -ing, -ed**) ▶ n (pl **-s**) (make) a rattling noise
clattered v ▷ **clatter**
clattering v ▷ **clatter**
clatters v, n ▷ **clatter**
clause n (pl **-s**) section of a legal document
clauses n ▷ **clause**
clavicles n ▷ **clavicle**
claw n (pl **-s**) sharp hooked nail of a bird or beast ▶ v (**-s, -ing, -ed**) tear with claws or nails
clawed v ▷ **claw**
clawing v ▷ **claw**
claws n, v ▷ **claw**
clay n (pl **-s**) fine-grained earth, soft when moist and hardening when baked, used to make bricks and pottery > **clayey** adj
clayey adj ▷ **clay**
claymore n (pl **-s**) large two-edged sword formerly used by Scottish Highlanders
claymores n ▷ **claymore**
clays n ▷ **clay**
clean adj (**-er, -est**) free from dirt or impurities ▶ v (**-s, -ing, -ed**) make (something) free from dirt ▶ adv not standard completely ▶ cleaner n (pl **-s**) > **cleanly** adv > **cleanliness** n (pl **-es**)
cleaned v ▷ **clean**
cleaner n, adj ▷ **clean**
cleaners n ▷ **clean**
cleanest adj ▷ **clean**
cleaning v ▷ **clean**
cleanliness n ▷ **clean**
cleanlinesses n ▷ **clean**
cleanly adv ▷ **clean**
cleans v ▷ **clean**

cleanse v (-ses, -sing, -sed) make clean > **cleanser** n (pl -s)

cleansed v ▷ **cleanse**

cleanser n ▷ **cleanse**

cleansers n ▷ **cleanse**

cleanses v ▷ **cleanse**

cleansing v ▷ **cleanse**

clear adj (-er, -est) free from doubt or confusion ▶ adv out of the way ▶ v (-s, -ing, -ed) make or become clear > **clearly** adv

clearances n ▷ **clear**

cleared v ▷ **clear**

clearer adj ▷ **clear**

clearest adj ▷ **clear**

clearing n (pl -s) treeless area in a wood ▶ v ▷ **clear**

clearings n ▷ **clearing**

clearly adv ▷ **clear**

clears v ▷ **clear**

clearway n (pl -s) stretch of road on which motorists may stop only in an emergency

clearways n ▷ **clearway**

cleat n (pl -s) wedge

cleats n ▷ **cleat**

cleavage n (pl -s) space between a woman's breasts, as revealed by a low-cut dress

cleavages n ▷ **cleavage**

cleave[1] v (-ves, -ving, cleft, -ved or clove, -ved or cloven) split apart

cleave[2] v (-ves, -ving, cleft, cleft) cling or stick

cleaved v ▷ **cleave**[1]

cleaver n (pl -s) butcher's heavy knife with a square blade

cleavers n ▷ **cleaver**

cleaves v ▷ **cleave**[1, 2]

cleaving v ▷ **cleave**[1, 2]

clef n (pl -s) MUSIC symbol at the beginning of a stave to show the pitch

clefs n ▷ **clef**

cleft n (pl -s) narrow opening or crack ▶ v ▷ **cleave**[1, 2]

clefts n ▷ **cleft**

clematis n (pl -es) climbing plant with large colourful flowers

clematises n ▷ **clematis**

clemencies n ▷ **clemency**

clemency n (pl -cies) kind or lenient treatment

clement adj (of weather) mild

clench v (-es, -ing, -ed) close or squeeze (one's teeth or fist) tightly

clenched v ▷ **clench**

clenches v ▷ **clench**

clenching v ▷ **clench**

clergies n ▷ **clergy**

clergy n (pl -gies) priests and ministers as a group > **clergyman** n (pl -men)

clergyman n ▷ **clergy**

clergymen n ▷ **clergy**

cleric n (pl -s) member of the clergy

clerical adj of clerks or office work .

clerics n ▷ **cleric**

clerk n (pl -s) employee in an office, bank, or court who keeps records, files, and accounts

clerks n ▷ **clerk**

clever adj (-er, -est) intelligent, quick at learning > **cleverly** adv > **cleverness** n (pl -es)

cleverer adj ▷ **clever**

cleverest adj ▷ **clever**

cleverly adv ▷ **clever**

cleverness n ▷ **clever**

clevernesses n ▷ **clever**

cliché n (pl -s) expression or idea that is no longer effective because of overuse > **clichéd** adj

clichéd n ▷ **cliché**

clichés n ▷ **cliché**

click n (pl -s) short sharp sound ▶ v (-s, -ing, -ed) make this sound

clicked v ▷ **click**

clicking v ▷ **click**

clicks n, v ▷ **click**

client n (pl -s) person who uses the services of a professional person or company

clients n ▷ **client**

cliff n (pl -s) steep rock face, esp. along the sea shore

cliffs n ▷ **cliff**

climactic adj ▷ **climax**

climate n (pl -s) typical weather conditions of an area > **climatic** adj
climates n ▷ climate
climatic adj ▷ climate

climax n (pl -es) most intense point of an experience, series of events, or story > **climactic** adj
climaxes n ▷ climax

climb v (-s, -ing, -ed) go up, ascend ▶ n (pl -s) climbing > **climber** n (pl -s)
climbed v ▷ climb
climber n ▷ climb
climbers n ▷ climb
climbing v ▷ climb
climbs v, n ▷ climb

clime n (pl -s) *poetic* place or its climate
climes n ▷ clime

clinch v (-es, -ing, -ed) settle (an argument or agreement) decisively
clinched v ▷ clinch
clincher n (pl -s) *informal* something decisive
clinchers n ▷ clincher
clinches n ▷ clinch
clinching v ▷ clinch

cling v (-s, -ing, clung) hold tightly or stick closely
clinging v ▷ cling
clings v ▷ cling

clinic n (pl -s) building where outpatients receive medical treatment or advice
clinical adj of a clinic > **clinically** adv
clinically adv ▷ clinic
clinics n ▷ clinic

clink¹ v (-s, -ing, -ed) ▶ n (pl -s) (make) a light sharp metallic sound
clink² n (pl -s) BRIT, AUST & NZ *slang* prison
clinked v ▷ clink¹
clinker n (pl -s) fused coal left over in a fire or furnace
clinkers n ▷ clinker
clinking v ▷ clink¹
clinks n ▷ clink¹, ² v ▷ clink¹

clip¹ v (-s, -pping, -pped) cut with shears or scissors *informal* ▶ n (-s)

short extract of a film

clip² n device for attaching or holding things together ▶ v (-s, -pping, -pped) attach or hold together with a clip
clipped v ▷ clip¹, ²
clipper n (pl -s) fast commercial sailing ship
clippers pl n tool for clipping ▶ n ▷ clipper
clipping n (pl -s) something cut out, esp. an article from a newspaper ▶ v ▷ clip¹, ²
clippings n ▷ clipping
clips n, v ▷ clip¹, ²

clique n (pl -s) small exclusive group
cliques n ▷ clique
clitoral adj ▷ clitoris

clitoris n (pl -es) small sexually sensitive organ at the front of the vulva > **clitoral** adj
clitorises n ▷ clitoris

cloak n (pl -s) loose sleeveless outer garment ▶ v (-s, -ing, -ed) cover or conceal
cloaked v ▷ cloak
cloaking v ▷ cloak
cloaks n, v ▷ cloak

clobber¹ v (-s, -ing, -ed) *informal* hit
clobber² n (pl -s) BRIT, AUST & NZ *informal* belongings, esp. clothes
clobbered v ▷ clobber¹
clobbering v ▷ clobber¹
clobbers v ▷ clobber¹ ▶ n ▷ clobber²

cloche n (pl -s) cover to protect young plants
cloches n ▷ cloche

clock n (pl -s) instrument for showing the time
clocks n ▷ clock

clod n (pl -s) lump of earth
clods n ▷ clod

clog v (-s, -gging, -gged) obstruct ▶ n (pl -s) wooden or wooden-soled shoe
clogged v ▷ clog
clogging v ▷ clog
clogs v, n ▷ clog

cloister n (pl -s) covered pillared arcade, usu. in a monastery

cloisters n ▷ cloister

clone n (pl -s) animal or plant produced artificially from the cells of another animal or plant, and identical to the original informal ▶ v (-nes, -ning, -ned) produce as a clone
cloned v ▷ clone
clones n, v ▷ clone
cloning v ▷ clone

close¹ v (-ses, -sing, -sed) shut ▶ n (pl -s) end, conclusion

close² adj (-r, -st) near ▶ adv closely, tightly ▷ **closely** adv ▷ **closeness** n (pl -es)
closed v ▷ close¹
closely adv ▷ close²
closeness n ▷ close²
closenesses n ▷ close²
closer adj ▷ close²
closes v, n ▷ close¹
closest adj ▷ close²

closet n (pl -s) us cupboard ▶ adj private, secret ▶ v (-s, -ing, -ed) shut (oneself) away in private
closeted v ▷ closet
closeting v ▷ closet
closets n, v ▷ closet
closeure v ▷ close¹
closure n (pl -s) closing
closures n ▷ closure

clot n (pl -s) soft thick lump formed from liquid ▶ v (-s, -tting, -tted) form soft thick lumps

cloth n (pl -s) (piece of) woven fabric

clothe v (-thes, -thing, -thed or clad) put clothes on
clothed v ▷ clothe
clothes pl n articles of dress ▶ v ▷ clothe
clothing n clothes collectively ▶ v ▷ clothe
cloths n ▷ cloth
clots n, v ▷ clot
clotted v ▷ clot
clotting v ▷ clot

cloud n (pl -s) mass of condensed water vapour floating in the sky ▶ v (-s, -ing, -ed) (foll. by over) become cloudy

> **cloudless** adj
clouded v ▷ cloud
cloudier adj ▷ cloud
cloudiest adj ▷ cloud
cloudiness n ▷ cloudy
cloudinesses n ▷ cloudy
clouding v ▷ cloud
cloudless adj ▷ cloud
clouds n, v ▷ cloud

cloudy adj (-dier, -diest) having a lot of clouds > **cloudiness** n (pl -es)

clout informal n (pl -s) hard blow ▶ v (-s, -ed, -ing) hit hard
clouted v ▷ clout
clouting v ▷ clout
clouts n, v ▷ clout

clove¹ n (pl -s) dried flower bud of a tropical tree, used as a spice
clove² n (pl -s) segment of a bulb of garlic
clove³ v ▷ cleave¹
cloven v ▷ cleave¹
clover n (pl -s) plant with three-lobed leaves
clovers n ▷ clover
cloves n ▷ clove¹, ²

clown n (pl -s) comic entertainer in a circus ▶ v (-s, -ing, -ed) behave foolishly > **clownish** adj > **clownishly** adv > **clownishness** n (pl -es)
clowned v ▷ clown
clowning v ▷ clown
clownish adj ▷ clown
clownishly adv ▷ clown
clownishness n ▷ clown
clownishnesses n ▷ clown
clowns n, v ▷ clown

club n (pl -s) association of people with common interests ▶ v (-s, -bbing, -bbed) hit with a club
clubbed v ▷ club
clubbing v ▷ club
clubs n, v ▷ club

cluck n (pl -s) low clicking noise made by a hen ▶ v (-s, -ing, -ed) make this noise
clucked v ▷ cluck

clucks n, v ▷ cluck

clue n (pl -s) something that helps to solve a mystery or puzzle

clueless adj stupid

clues n ▷ clue

clump n (pl -s) small group of things or people ▶ v (-s, -ing, -ed) walk heavily

clumped v ▷ clump

clumping v ▷ clump

clumps n, v ▷ clump

clumsier adj ▷ clumsy

clumsiest adj ▷ clumsy

clumsily adv ▷ clumsy

clumsiness n ▷ clumsy

clumsy adj (-sier, -siest) lacking skill or physical coordination > **clumsily** adv > **clumsiness** n

clung v ▷ cling

clunk n (pl -s) dull metallic sound ▶ v (-s, -ing, -ed) make such a sound

clunked v ▷ clunk

clunking v ▷ clunk

clunks n, v ▷ clunk

cluster n (pl -s) small close group ▶ v (-s, -ing, -ed) gather in clusters

clustered v ▷ cluster

clustering v ▷ cluster

clusters n, v ▷ cluster

clutch¹ v (-es, -ing, -ed) grasp tightly (foll. by at) ▶ n (pl -es) device enabling two revolving shafts to be connected and disconnected, esp. in a motor vehicle

clutch² n (pl -es) set of eggs laid at the same time

clutched v ▷ clutch¹

clutches v ▷ clutch¹ ▶ n ▷ clutch¹, ²

clutching v ▷ clutch¹

clutter v (-s, -ing, -ed) scatter objects about (a place) untidily ▶ n (pl -s) untidy mess

cluttered v ▷ clutter

cluttering v ▷ clutter

clutters v, n ▷ clutter

> **cly** verb (**clys, clying, clyed**). Cly is an old word meaning steal. The various forms of this word can be useful when you are short of vowels. Cly scores 8 points.

coach n (pl -es) long-distance bus ▶ v (-es, -ing, -ed) train, teach

coached v ▷ coach

coaches n, v ▷ coach

coaching v ▷ coach

coal n (pl -s) black rock consisting mainly of carbon, used as fuel

coalesce v (-ces, -cing, -ced) come together, merge > **coalescence** n (pl -s)

coalesced v ▷ coalesce

coalescence n ▷ coalesce

coalescences n ▷ coalesce

coalesces v ▷ coalesce

coalescing v ▷ coalesce

coals n ▷ coal

coarse adj (-r, -st) rough in texture > **coarsely** adv > **coarseness** n (pl -s)

coarsen v (-s, -ing, -ed)

coarsely adv ▷ coarse

coarsened v ▷ coarse

coarseness n ▷ coarse

coarsenesses n ▷ coarse

coarsening v ▷ coarse

coarsens v ▷ coarse

coarser adj ▷ coarse

coarsest adj ▷ coarse

coast n (pl -s) place where the land meets the sea ▶ v (-s, -ing, -ed) move by momentum, without the use of power > **coastal** adj

coastal adj ▷ coast

coasted v ▷ coast

coaster n (pl -s) small mat placed under a glass

coasters n ▷ coaster

coasting v ▷ coast

coasts n, v ▷ coast

coat n (pl -s) outer garment with long sleeves ▶ v (-s, -ing, -ed) cover with a layer

coated v ▷ coat

coating n (pl -s) covering layer ▶ v ▷ coat

coatings n ▷ coating

coats n, v ▷ coat

coax v (-es, -ing, -ed) persuade gently

coaxed v ▷ coax

coaxes v ▷ **coax**

coaxial adj (of a cable) transmitting by means of two concentric conductors separated by an insulator

coaxing v ▷ **coax**

cob n (pl -s) stalk of an ear of maize

cobalt n (pl -s) CHEM brittle silvery-white metallic element

cobalts n ▷ **cobalt**

cobber n (pl -s) AUST & OLD-FASHIONED NZ informal friend

cobbers n ▷ **cobber**

cobble n (pl -s) cobblestone

cobbler n (pl -s) shoe mender

cobblers n ▷ **cobbler**

cobbles n ▷ **cobble**

cobia n (pl -s) large dark-striped game fish of tropical and subtropical seas

cobias n ▷ **cobia**

cobra n (pl -s) venomous hooded snake of Asia and Africa

cobras n ▷ **cobra**

cobs n ▷ **cob**

cobweb n (pl -s) spider's web

cobwebs n ▷ **cobweb**

cocaine n (pl -s) addictive drug used as a narcotic and as an anaesthetic

cocaines n ▷ **cocaine**

coccyges n ▷ **coccyx**

coccyx n (pl -yges) bone at the base of the spinal column

cock n (pl -s) male bird, esp. of domestic fowl ▶ v (-s, -ing, -ed) draw back (the hammer of a gun) to firing position

cockade n (pl -s) feather or rosette worn on a hat as a badge

cockades n ▷ **cockade**

cockatoo n (pl -s) crested parrot of Australia or the East Indies

cockatoos n ▷ **cockatoo**

cocked v ▷ **cock**

cockerel n (pl -s) young domestic cock

cockerels n ▷ **cockerel**

cockeyed adj informal crooked, askew

cockier adj ▷ **cocky**

cockiest adj ▷ **cocky**

cockily adv ▷ **cocky**

cockiness n ▷ **cocky**

cockinesses n ▷ **cocky**

cocking v ▷ **cock**

cockle n (pl -s) edible shellfish

cockles n ▷ **cockle**

cockney n (pl -s) native of the East End of London

cockneys n ▷ **cockney**

cockpit n (pl -s) pilot's compartment in an aircraft

cockpits n ▷ **cockpit**

cocks n, v ▷ **cock**

cocksure adj overconfident, arrogant

cocktail n (pl -s) mixed alcoholic drink

cocktails n ▷ **cocktail**

cocky adj (-kier, -kiest) conceited and overconfident ▷ **cockily** adv ▷ **cockiness** n (pl -es)

cocoa n (pl -s) powder made from the seed of the cacao tree

cocoas n ▷ **cocoa**

coconut n (pl -s) large hard fruit of a type of palm tree

coconuts n ▷ **coconut**

cocoon n (pl -s) silky protective covering of a silkworm ▶ v (-s, -ing, -ed) wrap up tightly for protection

cocooned v ▷ **cocoon**

cocooning v ▷ **cocoon**

cocoons n, v ▷ **cocoon**

cod n (pl cod) large food fish of the North Atlantic

coda n (pl -s) final part of a musical composition

codas n ▷ **coda**

coddle v (-les, -ling, -led) pamper, overprotect

coddled v ▷ **coddle**

coddles v ▷ **coddle**

coddling v ▷ **coddle**

code n (pl -s) system of letters, symbols, or prearranged signals by which messages can be communicated secretly or briefly ▶ v (-des, -ding, -ded) put into code

coded v ▷ **code**

codeine n (pl -s) drug used as a

painkiller

codeines v ▷ codeine

codes n, v ▷ code

codex n (pl **codices**) volume of manuscripts of an ancient text

codger n (pl **-s**) BRIT, AUST & NZ informal old man

codgers n ▷ codger

codices n ▷ codex

codicil n (pl **-s**) addition to a will

codicils n ▷ codicil

codification n ▷ codify

codifications n ▷ codify

codified v ▷ codify

codifies v ▷ codify

codify v (**-fies**, **-fying**, **-fied**) organize (rules or procedures) systematically > **codification** n (pl **-s**)

codifying v ▷ codify

coding v ▷ code

coerce v (**-ces**, **-cing**, **-ced**) compel, force > **coercion** > **coercive** adj

coerced v ▷ coerce

coerces v ▷ coerce

coercing v ▷ coerce

coercion n ▷ coerce

coercive adj ▷ coerce

coeval adj, n (pl **-s**) contemporary

coevals n ▷ coeval

coexist v (**-s**, **-ing**, **-ed**) exist together, esp. peacefully despite differences > **coexistence** n

coexisted v ▷ coexist

coexistence n ▷ coexist

coexisting v ▷ coexist

coexists v ▷ coexist

coffee n (pl **-s**) drink made from the roasted and ground beans of a tropical shrub ▶ adj medium-brown

coffees n ▷ coffee

coffer n (pl **-s**) chest for valuables ▶ pl store of money

coffers n ▷ coffer

coffin n (pl **-s**) box in which a corpse is buried or cremated

coffins n ▷ coffin

cog n (pl **-s**) one of the teeth on the rim of a gearwheel

cogencies n ▷ cogent

cogency n ▷ cogent

cogent adj forcefully convincing > **cogency** (pl **-cies**) > **cogently** adv

cogently adv ▷ cogent

cogitate v (**-tes**, **-ting**, **-ted**) think deeply about > **cogitation** n (pl **-s**)

cogitated v ▷ cogitate

cogitates v ▷ cogitate

cogitating v ▷ cogitate

cogitation n ▷ cogitate

cogitations n ▷ cogitate

cognac n (pl **-s**) French brandy

cognacs n ▷ cognac

cognate adj derived from a common original form

cogs n ▷ cog

cohabit v (**-s**, **-ing**, **-ed**) live together as husband and wife without being married > **cohabitation** n (pl **-s**)

cohabitation n ▷ cohabit

cohabitations n ▷ cohabit

cohabited v ▷ cohabit

cohabiting v ▷ cohabit

cohabits v ▷ cohabit

cohere v (**-res**, **-ring**, **-red**) hold or stick together

cohered v ▷ cohere

coherence n ▷ coherent

coherences n ▷ coherent

coherent adj logical and consistent > **coherence** n (pl **-s**) > **coherently** adv

coherently adv ▷ coherent

coheres v ▷ cohere

cohering v ▷ cohere

cohesion n (pl **-s**) sticking together

cohesions n ▷ cohesion

cohesive adj sticking together to form a whole

cohort n (pl **-s**) band of associates

cohorts n ▷ cohort

coiffeur n ▷ coiffure

coiffeurs n ▷ coiffure

coiffeuse n ▷ coiffure

coiffeuses n ▷ coiffure

coiffure n (pl **-s**) hairstyle > **coiffeur, coiffeuse** n (pl **-s**) hairdresser

coiffures n ▷ coiffure

coil v (-s, -ing, -ed) wind in loops ▶ n (pl -s) something coiled
 coiled v ▷ coil
 coiling v ▷ coil
 coils v, n ▷ coil
coin n (pl -s) piece of metal money ▶ v (-s, -ing, -ed) invent (a word or phrase)
 coinage n (pl -s) coins collectively
 coinages n ▷ coinage
coincide v (-des, -ding, -ded) happen at the same time
 coincided v ▷ coincide
 coincides v ▷ coincide
 coinciding v ▷ coincide
 coined v ▷ coin
 coining v ▷ coin
 coins n, v ▷ coin
coir n (pl -s) coconut fibre, used for matting
 coirs n ▷ coir
coital adj ▷ coitus
coition n ▷ coitus
 coitions n ▷ coitus
coitus (pl -es), **coition** (pl -s) n sexual intercourse > coital adj
 coituses n ▷ coitus
coke¹ n (pl -s) solid fuel left after gas has been distilled from coal
coke² n (pl -s) slang cocaine
 cokes n ▷ coke¹, ²
col n (pl -s) high mountain pass
cola n (pl -s) dark brown fizzy soft drink
colander n (pl -s) perforated bowl for straining or rinsing foods
 colanders n ▷ colander
 colas n ▷ cola
cold adj (-er, -est) lacking heat ▶ n (pl -s) lack of heat > coldly adv
 > coldness n (pl -es)
 colder adj ▷ cold
 coldest adj ▷ cold
 coldly adv ▷ cold
 coldness n ▷ cold
 coldnesses n ▷ cold
 colds n ▷ cold
coleslaw n (pl -s) salad dish of shredded raw cabbage in a dressing
 coleslaws n ▷ coleslaw

coley n (pl -s) codlike food fish of the N Atlantic
 coleys n ▷ coley
colic n (pl -s) severe pains in the stomach and bowels > colicky adj (-kier, -kiest)
 colickier adj ▷ colic
 colickiest adj ▷ colic
 colicky adj ▷ colic
 colics n ▷ colic
colitis n (pl -es) inflammation of the colon
 colitises n ▷ colitis
collage n (pl -s) art form in which various materials or objects are glued onto a surface
 collages n ▷ collage
collapse v (-ses, -sing, -sed) fall down suddenly ▶ n (pl -s) collapsing > collapsible adj
 collapsed v ▷ collapse
 collapses v, n ▷ collapse
 collapsible adj ▷ collapse
 collapsing v ▷ collapse
collar n (pl -s) part of a garment round the neck ▶ v (-s, -ing, -ed) BRIT, AUST & NZ informal seize, arrest
 collared v ▷ collar
 collaring v ▷ collar
 collars n, v ▷ collar
collate v (-tes, -ting, -ted) gather together, examine, and put in order
 collated v ▷ collate
 collates v ▷ collate
 collating v ▷ collate
collect¹ v (-s, -ing, -ed) gather together > collector n (pl -s)
collect² n (pl -s) short prayer
 collecting v ▷ collect¹
 collects v ▷ collect¹ ▶ n ▷ collect²
colleen n (pl -s) IRISH girl
 colleens n ▷ colleen
college n (pl -s) place of higher education > collegiate adj
 colleges n ▷ college
 collegiate adj ▷ college
collide v (-des, -ding, -ded) crash together violently > collision n (pl -s)

collided v ▷ collide

collides v ▷ collide

colliding v ▷ collide

collie n (pl -s) silky-haired sheepdog

collier n (pl -s) coal miner

collieries n ▷ colliery

colliers n ▷ collier

colliery n (pl -lieries) coal mine

collies n ▷ collie

collision n ▷ collide

collisions n ▷ collide

colloid n (pl -s) suspension of particles in a solution

colloids n ▷ colloid

collude v (-ludes, -luding, -luded) act in collusion

colluded v ▷ collude

colludes v ▷ collude

colluding v ▷ collude

cologne n (pl -s) mild perfume

colognes n ▷ cologne

colon¹ n (pl -s) punctuation mark (:)

colon² n (pl -s) part of the large intestine connected to the rectum

colonel n (pl -s) senior commissioned army or air-force officer

colonels n ▷ colonel

colonial adj, n (pl -s) (inhabitant) of a colony

colonials n ▷ colonial

colonies n ▷ colony

colonist n (pl -s) settler in a colony

colonists n ▷ colonist

colonization n ▷ colonize

colonizations n ▷ colonize

colonize v (-zes, -zing, -zed) make into a colony **colonization** n (pl -s)

colonized v ▷ colonize

colonizes v ▷ colonize

colonizing v ▷ colonize

colons n ▷ colon¹,²

colony n (pl -nies) group of people who settle in a new country but remain under the rule of their homeland

colossal adj very large **> colossally** adv

colossally adv ▷ colossal

colossi n ▷ colossus

colossus n (pl -si, -suses) huge statue

colossuses n ▷ colossus

colour n (pl -s) appearance of things as a result of reflecting light ▶ pl flag of a country or regiment SPORT ▶ v (-s, -ing, -ed) apply colour to **> colourless** adj **> colourlessly** adv

coloured adj having colour ▶ v ▷ colour

colouring v ▷ colour

colourless adj ▷ colour

colourlessly adv ▷ colour

colours n, v ▷ colour

cols n ▷ col

colt n (pl -s) young male horse

colts n ▷ colt

column n (pl -s) pillar

columns n ▷ column

coma n (pl -s) state of deep unconsciousness

comas n ▷ coma

comatose adj in a coma

comb n (pl -s) toothed implement for arranging the hair ▶ v (-s, -ing, -ed) use a comb on

combat n (pl -s, -ing, -ed) fight, struggle **> combatant** n (pl -s) **> combative** adj **> combativeness** n

combatant n ▷ combat

combatants n ▷ combat

combated v ▷ combat

combating v ▷ combat

combats n, v ▷ combat

combed v ▷ comb

combine v (-nes, -ning, -ned) join together ▶ n (pl -s) association of people or firms for a common purpose

combined v ▷ combine

combines v, n ▷ combine

combing v ▷ comb

combining v ▷ combine

combs n, v ▷ comb

come v (-es, -ming, came, come) move towards a place, arrive

comeback n (pl -s) informal return to a former position

comebacks n ▷ comeback

comedian, comedienne n (pl -s) entertainer who tells jokes

comedians n ▷ comedian
comedienne n ▷ comedian
comediennes n ▷ comedian
comedies n ▷ comedy
comedown n (pl -s) decline in status
comedowns n ▷ comedown
comedy n (pl -dies) humorous play, film, or programme
comelier adj ▷ comely
comeliest adj ▷ comely
comeliness n ▷ comely
comelinesses n ▷ comely
comely adj (-lier, -liest) old-fashioned nice-looking >comeliness n (pl -es)
comes v ▷ come
comet n (pl -s) heavenly body with a long luminous tail
comets n ▷ comet
comfier adj ▷ comfy
comfiest adj ▷ comfy
comfit n (pl -s) old-fashioned sugar-coated sweet
comfits n ▷ comfit
comfort n (pl -s) physical ease or wellbeing ▶ v (-s, -ing, -ed) soothe, console >comforter n (pl -s)
comforted v ▷ comfort
comforter n ▷ comfort
comforters n ▷ comfort
comforting v ▷ comfort
comforts n, v ▷ comfort
comfrey n (pl -s) tall plant with bell-shaped flowers
comfreys n ▷ comfrey
comfy adj (-fier, -fiest) informal comfortable
comic adj humorous, funny ▶ n (pl -s) comedian
comical adj amusing >comically adv
comically adv ▷ comical
comics n ▷ comic
coming v ▷ come
comma n (pl -s) punctuation mark (,)
command v (-s, -ing, -ed) order ▶ n (pl -s) authoritative instruction that something must be done
commanded v ▷ command
commanding v ▷ command

commando n (pl -dos, -does) (member of) a military unit trained for swift raids in enemy territory
commandoes n ▷ commando
commandos n ▷ commando
commands v, n ▷ command
commas n ▷ comma
commence v (-ces, -cing, -ced) begin >commencement n (pl -s)
commenced v ▷ commence
commencement n ▷ commence
commencements n ▷ commence
commences v ▷ commence
commencing v ▷ commence
commend v (-s, -ing, -ed) praise >commendable adj >commendably adv >commendation n (pl -s)
commendable adj ▷ commend
commendably adv ▷ commend
commendation n ▷ commend
commendations n ▷ commend
commended v ▷ commend
commending v ▷ commend
commends v ▷ commend
comment n (pl -s) remark ▶ v (-s, -ing, -ed) make a comment
commented v ▷ comment
commenting v ▷ comment
comments n, v ▷ comment
commerce n (pl -s) buying and selling, trade
commerces n ▷ commerce
commit v (-s, -tting, -tted) perform (a crime or error)
commits v ▷ commit
committed v ▷ commit
committing v ▷ commit
commode n (pl -s) seat with a hinged flap concealing a chamber pot
commodes n ▷ commode
common adj (-er, -est) occurring often ▶ n (pl -s) area of grassy land belonging to a community >commonly adv
commoner n (pl -s) person who does not belong to the nobility ▶ adj ▷ common
commoners n ▷ commoner

commonest adj ▷ **common**
commonly adv ▷ **common**
commons n ▷ **common**
communal adj shared
> **communally** adv
communally n ▷ **communal**
commune[1] n (pl -s) group of people who live together and share everything
commune[2] v (-nes, -ning, -ned) (foll. by with) feel very close (to)
  communed v ▷ **commune**[2]
  communes n ▷ **commune**[1] ▶ v ▷ **commune**[2]
  communing v ▷ **commune**[2]
commute v (-tes, -ting, -ted) travel daily to and from work
  commuted v ▷ **commute**
commuter n (pl -s) person who commutes to and from work
  commuters n ▷ **commuter**
  commutes v ▷ **commute**
  commuting v ▷ **commute**
compact[1] adj (-er, -est) closely packed ▶ n (pl -s) small flat case containing a mirror and face powder ▶ v (-s, -ing, -ed) pack closely together
  > **compactly** adv > **compactness** n (pl -es)
compact[2] n (pl -s) contract, agreement
  compacted v ▷ **compact**[1]
  compacter adj ▷ **compact**[1]
  compactest adj ▷ **compact**[1]
  compacting v ▷ **compact**[1]
  compactly adv ▷ **compact**[1]
  compactness n ▷ **compact**[1]
  compactnesses n ▷ **compact**[1]
  compacts n ▷ **compact**[1, 2] ▶ v ▷ **compact**[1]
company n (pl -nies) business organization
comparability n ▷ **compare**
comparable adj ▷ **compare**
compare v (-res, -ring, -red) examine (things) and point out the resemblances or differences (foll. by to) (foll. by with) > **comparable** adj

> **comparability** n
compared v ▷ **compare**
compares v ▷ **compare**
comparing v ▷ **compare**
compass n (pl -es) instrument for showing direction, with a needle that points north ▶ pl hinged instrument for drawing circles
  compasses n ▷ **compass**
compel v (-s, -lling, -lled) force (to be or do)
  compelled v ▷ **compel**
  compelling v ▷ **compel**
  compels v ▷ **compel**
compere n (pl -s) person who presents a stage, radio, or television show ▶ v (-res, -ring, -red) be the compere of
  compered v ▷ **compere**
  comperes n, v ▷ **compere**
  compering v ▷ **compere**
compete v (-tes, -ting, -ted) try to win or achieve (a prize, profit, etc)
  > **competitive** adj > **competitively** adv
  > **competitiveness** n > **competitor** n (pl -s)
  competed v ▷ **compete**
  competes v ▷ **compete**
  competing v ▷ **compete**
  competitive adj ▷ **compete**
  competitively adv ▷ **compete**
  competitiveness n ▷ **compete**
  competitor n ▷ **compete**
  competitors n ▷ **compete**
compilation n ▷ **compile**
  compilations n ▷ **compile**
compile v (-s, -ling, -led) collect and arrange (information), esp. to make a book > **compilation** n (pl -s)
  > **compiler** n (pl -s)
  compiled v ▷ **compile**
  compiler n ▷ **compile**
  compilers n ▷ **compile**
  compiles v ▷ **compile**
  compiling v ▷ **compile**
complain v (-s, -ing, -ed) express resentment or displeasure
  complained v ▷ **complain**
  complaining v ▷ **complain**

complains v ▷ complain
complete adj thorough, absolute ▶ v (-pletes, -pleting, -pleted) finish > completely adv > completeness n (pl -es)
completed v ▷ complete
completely adv ▷ complete
completeness n ▷ complete
completenesses n ▷ complete
completes v ▷ complete
completing v ▷ complete
complex adj (-er, -est) made up of parts ▶ n (pl -es) whole made up of parts > complexity n (pl -ities)
complexer adj ▷ complex
complexes n ▷ complex
complexest adj ▷ complex
complexities n ▷ complex
complexity n ▷ complex
complied v ▷ comply
complies v ▷ comply
compline n (pl -s) last service of the day in the Roman Catholic Church
complines n ▷ compline
comply v (-plies, -plying, -plied) (foll. by with) act in accordance with
complying v ▷ comply
comport v (-s, -ing, -ed) formal behave (oneself) in a specified way
comported v ▷ comport
comporting v ▷ comport
comports v ▷ comport
compose v (-ses, -sing, -sed) put together
composed v ▷ compose
composer n (pl -s) person who writes music
composers n ▷ composer
composes v ▷ compose
composing ▷ compose
compost n (pl -s) decayed plants used as a fertilizer
composts n ▷ compost
compote n (pl -s) fruit stewed with sugar
compotes n ▷ compote
compound¹ n (pl -s) ▶ adj (thing, esp. chemical) made up of two or more combined parts or elements ▶ v (-s, -ing, -ed) combine or make by combining
compound² n (pl -s) fenced enclosure containing buildings
compounded v ▷ compound¹
compounding v ▷ compound¹
compounds v ▷ compound¹ ▶ n ▷ compound¹, ²
compress v (-es, -ing, -ed) squeeze together ▶ n (pl -es) pad applied to stop bleeding or cool inflammation > compression n (pl -s)
compressed v ▷ compress
compresses v, n ▷ compress
compressing v ▷ compress
compression n ▷ compress
compressions n ▷ compress
comprise v (-ises, -ising, -ised) be made up of or make up
comprised v ▷ comprise
comprises v ▷ comprise
comprising v ▷ comprise
computation n ▷ compute
computations n ▷ compute
compute v (-putes, -puting, -puted) calculate, esp. using a computer > computation n (pl -s)
computed v ▷ compute
computer n (pl -s) electronic machine that stores and processes data
computers n ▷ computer
computes v ▷ compute
computing v ▷ compute
comrade n (pl -s) fellow member of a union or socialist political party > comradeship n
comrades n ▷ comrade
comradeship n ▷ comrade
con¹ informal n (pl -s) confidence trick ▶ v (-s, -nning, -nned) deceive, swindle
con² n (pl -s) ▷ pro¹
concave adj curving inwards
conceal v (-s, -ing, -ed) cover and hide > concealment n (pl -s)
concealed v ▷ conceal
concealing v ▷ conceal

concealment n ▷ conceal
concealments n ▷ conceal
conceals v ▷ conceal
concede v (-des, -ding, -ded) admit
to be true
conceded v ▷ concede
concedes v ▷ concede
conceding v ▷ concede
conceit n (pl -s) too high an
opinion of oneself > **conceited** adj
> **conceitedly** adv > **conceitedness** n
(pl -s)
conceited adj ▷ conceit
conceitedly adv ▷ conceit
conceitedness adv ▷ conceit
conceitednesses n ▷ conceit
conceits n ▷ conceit
conceive v (-ves, -ving, -ved)
imagine, think
conceived v ▷ conceive
conceives v ▷ conceive
conceiving v ▷ conceive
concept n (pl -s) abstract or general
idea
concepts n ▷ concept
concern n (pl -s) anxiety, worry ▶ v (-s,
-ing, -ed) worry (someone)
concerns n, v ▷ concern
concert n (pl -s) musical
entertainment
concerti n ▷ concerto
concerto n (pl -tos, -ti) large-scale
composition for a solo instrument and
orchestra
concertos n ▷ concerto
concerts n ▷ concert
conch n (pl -s) shellfish with a large
spiral shell
conchs n ▷ conch
concise adj (-r, -st) brief and to the
point > **concisely** adv > **concision** (pl
-s), **conciseness** (pl -es) n
concisely adv ▷ concise
conciseness n ▷ concise
concisenesses n ▷ concise
conciser adj ▷ concise
concisest adj ▷ concise
concision n ▷ concise

concisions n ▷ concise
conclave n (pl -s) secret meeting
conclaves n ▷ conclave
conclude v (-des, -ding, -ded) decide
by reasoning
concluded v ▷ conclude
concludes v ▷ conclude
concluding v ▷ conclude
concoct v (-s, -ing, -ed) make up (a
story or plan) > **concoction** n (pl -s)
concocted v ▷ concoct
concocting v ▷ concoct
concoction n ▷ concoct
concoctions n ▷ concoct
concocts v ▷ concoct
concord n (pl -s) state of peaceful
agreement, harmony
concords n ▷ concord
concrete n (pl -s) mixture of cement,
sand, stone, and water, used in
building ▶ adj made of concrete
concretes n ▷ concrete
concur v (-rs, -rring, -rred) agree
> **concurrence** n (pl -s)
concurred v ▷ concur
concurrence n ▷ concur
concurrences n ▷ concur
concurring v ▷ concur
concurs v ▷ concur
condemn v (-s, -ing, -ed) express
disapproval of > **condemnation** n (pl
-s) > **condemnatory** adj
condemnation n ▷ condemn
condemnations n ▷ condemn
condemnatory adj ▷ condemn
condemned v ▷ condemn
condemning v ▷ condemn
condemns v ▷ condemn
condensation n ▷ condense
condensations n ▷ condense
condense v (-s, -ing, -ed, -densing,
-densed) make shorter
> **condensation** n (pl -s)
condensed v ▷ condense
condenses v ▷ condense
condensing v ▷ condense
condom n (pl -s) rubber sheath
worn on the penis or in the vagina

during sexual intercourse to prevent conception or infection

condoms n ▷ **condom**

condone v (**-nes, -ning, -ned**) overlook or forgive (wrongdoing)

condoned v ▷ **condone**

condones v ▷ **condone**

condoning v ▷ **condone**

condor n (pl **-s**) large vulture of S America

condors n ▷ **condor**

conduct n (pl **-s**) management of an activity ▶ v (**-s, -ing, -ed**) carry out (a task)

conducted v ▷ **conduct**

conducting v ▷ **conduct**

conducts n, v ▷ **conduct**

conduit n (pl **-s**) channel or tube for fluid or cables

conduits n ▷ **conduit**

cone n (pl **-s**) object with a circular base, tapering to a point

cones n ▷ **cone**

coney n (pl **-s**) ▷ **cony**

coneys n ▷ **coney**

confab n (pl **-s**) informal conversation (also **confabulation**)

confabs n ▷ **confab**

confabulation n ▷ **confab**

confabulations n ▷ **confab**

confer v (**-rs, -rring, -rred**) discuss together

conferred v ▷ **confer**

conferring v ▷ **confer**

confers v ▷ **confer**

confess v (**-es, -ing, -ed**) admit (a fault or crime)

confessed v ▷ **confess**

confesses v ▷ **confess**

confessing v ▷ **confess**

confetti n small pieces of coloured paper thrown at weddings

confide v (**-des, -ding, -ded**) tell someone (a secret)

confided v ▷ **confide**

confides v ▷ **confide**

confiding v ▷ **confide**

confine v (**-nes, -ning, -ned**) keep within bounds

confined v ▷ **confine**

confines pl n boundaries, limits ▶ v ▷ **confine**

confining v ▷ **confine**

confirm v (**-s, -ing, -ed**) prove to be true

confirming v ▷ **confirm**

confirms v ▷ **confirm**

conflate v (**-tes, -ting, -ted**) combine or blend into a whole > **conflation** n (pl **-s**)

conflated v ▷ **conflate**

conflates v ▷ **conflate**

conflating v ▷ **conflate**

conflation n ▷ **conflate**

conflations n ▷ **conflate**

conflict n (pl **-s**) disagreement ▶ v (**-s, -ing, -ed**) be incompatible

conflicted v ▷ **conflict**

conflicting v ▷ **conflict**

conflicts n, v ▷ **conflict**

conform v (**-s, -ing, -ed**) comply with accepted standards or customs (foll. by **to** or **with**)

conformed v ▷ **conform**

conforming v ▷ **conform**

conforms v ▷ **conform**

confound v (**-s, -ing, -ed**) astound, bewilder

confounding v ▷ **confound**

confounds v ▷ **confound**

confront v (**-s, -ing, -ed**) come face to face with

confronted v ▷ **confront**

confronting v ▷ **confront**

confronts v ▷ **confront**

confuse v (**-ses, -sing, -sed**) mix up > **confusion** n (pl **-s**)

confused v ▷ **confuse**

confuses v ▷ **confuse**

confusing v ▷ **confuse**

confusion n ▷ **confuse**

confusions n ▷ **confuse**

confute v (**-tes, -ting, -ted**) prove wrong

confuted v ▷ **confute**

confutes v ▷ **confute**

confuting v ▷ confute

conga n (pl -s) dance performed by a number of people in single file

congas n ▷ conga

congeal v (-s, -ing, -ed) (of a liquid) become thick and sticky

congealed v ▷ congeal

congealing v ▷ congeal

congeals v ▷ congeal

conger n (pl -s) large sea eel

congers n ▷ conger

congress n (pl -es) formal meeting for discussion > **congressional** adj

congresses n ▷ congress

congressional n ▷ congress

conical adj cone-shaped

conies n ▷ cony

conifer n cone-bearing tree, such as the fir or pine > **coniferous** adj

coniferous adj ▷ conifer

conifers n ▷ conifer

conjugal adj of marriage > **conjugally** adv

conjugally adv ▷ conjugal

conjure v (-res, -ring, -red) perform tricks that appear to be magic > **conjuror** n (pl -s)

conjured v ▷ conjure

conjures v ▷ conjure

conjuring v ▷ conjure

conjuror n ▷ conjure

conjurors n ▷ conjure

conk n (pl -s) BRIT, AUST & NZ slang nose

conker n (pl -s) informal nut of the horse chestnut

conkers n ▷ conker

conks n ▷ conk

connect v (-s, -ing, -ed) join together > **connection, connexion** n (pl -s) relationship, association > **connective** adj

connected v ▷ connect

connecting v ▷ connect

connection n ▷ connect

connections n ▷ connect

connective n ▷ connect

connects v ▷ connect

conned v ▷ con¹

connexion n ▷ connect

connexions n ▷ connect

conning v ▷ con¹

connivance n ▷ connive

connivances n ▷ connive

connive v (-ves, -ving, -ved) (foll. by at) allow (wrongdoing) by ignoring it > **connivance** n (pl -s)

connived v ▷ connive

connives v ▷ connive

conniving v ▷ connive

conquer v (-s, -ing, -ed) defeat > **conqueror** n (pl -s)

conquered v ▷ conquer

conquering v ▷ conquer

conqueror n ▷ conquer

conquerors n ▷ conquer

conquers v ▷ conquer

conquest n (pl -s) conquering

conquests n ▷ conquer

cons n ▷ con¹, ²

consent n (pl -s) agreement, permission ▶ v (-s, -ing, -ed) (foll. by to) permit, agree to

consented v ▷ consent

consenting v ▷ consent

consents v, n ▷ consent

conserve v (-ves, -ving, -ved) protect from harm, decay, or loss ▶ n (pl -s) jam containing large pieces of fruit

conserved v ▷ conserve

conserves v, n ▷ conserve

conserving v ▷ conserve

consider v (-s, -ing, -ed) regard as

considered v ▷ consider

considers v ▷ consider

consign v (-s, -ing, -ed) put somewhere

consigned v ▷ consign

consigning v ▷ consign

consigns v ▷ consign

consist v (-s, -ing, -ed) be made up of

consisted v ▷ consist

consisting v ▷ consist

consists v ▷ consist

console¹ v (-les, -ling, -led) comfort in distress

console² n (pl -s) panel of controls for
electronic equipment
consoled v ▷ **console¹**
consoles v ▷ **console¹** ▶ n ▷ **console²**
consoling v ▷ **console¹**
consommé n (pl -s) thin clear meat
soup
consommés n ▷ **consommé**
consort v (-s, -ing, -ed) (foll. by with)
keep company (with) ▶ n (pl -s)
husband or wife of a monarch
consorted v ▷ **consort**
consorting v ▷ **consort**
consorts v, n ▷ **consort**
conspire v (-res, -ring, -red) plan a
crime together in secret
conspired v ▷ **conspire**
conspires v ▷ **conspire**
conspiring v ▷ **conspire**
constancies n ▷ **constant**
constancy n ▷ **constant**
constant adj continuous ▶ n (pl -s)
unvarying quantity > **constantly** adv
> **constancy** n (pl -cies)
constantly adv ▷ **constant**
constants n ▷ **constant**
construe v (-rues, -ruing, -rued)
interpret
construed v ▷ **construe**
construes v ▷ **construe**
construing v ▷ **construe**
consul n (pl -s) official representing
a state in a foreign country
> **consular** adj > **consulship** n (pl -s)
consular adj ▷ **consul**
consuls n ▷ **consul**
consulship n ▷ **consul**
consulships n ▷ **consul**
consult v (-s, -ing, -ed) go to for advice
or information
consulted v ▷ **consult**
consulting v ▷ **consult**
consults v ▷ **consult**
consume v (-mes, -ming, -med) eat
or drink
consumed v ▷ **consume**
consumer n (pl -s) person who buys
goods or uses services

consumers n ▷ **consumer**
consumes v ▷ **consume**
consuming v ▷ **consume**
contact n (pl -s) communicating ▶ v
(-s, -ing, -ed) get in touch with
contacted v ▷ **contact**
contacting v ▷ **contact**
contacts n, v ▷ **contact**
contain v (-s, -ing, -ed) hold or be
capable of holding
contained v ▷ **contain**
containing v ▷ **contain**
contains v ▷ **contain**
contempt n (pl -s) dislike and
disregard
contempts n ▷ **contempt**
contend v (-s, -ing, -ed) (foll. by with)
deal with
contended v ▷ **contend**
contending v ▷ **contend**
contends v ▷ **contend**
content¹ n (pl -s) meaning or
substance of a piece of writing ▶ v
what something contains
content² adj satisfied with things
as they are ▶ v (-s, -ing, -ed) make
(someone) content ▶ n happiness
and satisfaction > **contented** adj
> **contentedly** adv > **contentment** n
contented v, adj ▷ **content²**
contentedly adv ▷ **content²**
contenting v ▷ **content²**
contentment n ▷ **content²**
contents n ▷ **content¹** ▶ v
▷ **content²**
contest n (pl -s) competition or
struggle ▶ v (-s, -ing, -ed) dispute,
object to > **contestant** n (pl -s)
contestant n ▷ **contest**
contestants n ▷ **contest**
contested v ▷ **contest**
contesting v ▷ **contest**
contests n, v ▷ **contest**
context n (pl -s) circumstances of an
event or fact > **contextual** adj
contexts n ▷ **context**
contextual adj ▷ **context**
continue v (-nues, -nuing, -nued)

(cause to) remain in a condition or place
continued v ▷ continue
continues v ▷ continue
continuing v ▷ continue
continuo n (pl **-s**) MUSIC continuous bass part, usu. played on a keyboard instrument
continuos n ▷ continuo
contort v (**-s, -ing, -ed**) twist out of shape > **contortion** n (pl **-s**)
contorted v ▷ contort
contorting v ▷ contort
contortion n ▷ contort
contortions n ▷ contort
contorts v ▷ contort
contour n (pl **-s**) outline
contours n ▷ contour
contract n (pl **-s**) (document setting out) a legal agreement ▶ v (**-s, -ing, -ed**) make a formal agreement (to do something) > **contraction** n (pl **-s**) > **contractual** adj > **contractually** adv
contracted v ▷ contract
contracting v ▷ contract
contraction n ▷ contract
contractions n ▷ contract
contracts n, v ▷ contract
contractual adj ▷ contract
contractually adv ▷ contract
contraries n ▷ contrary
contrarily adv ▷ contrary
contrariness n ▷ contrary
contrariwise adv ▷ contrary
contrary n (pl **-aries**) complete opposite ▶ adj opposed, completely different ▶ adv in opposition
> **contrarily** adv > **contrariness** n > **contrariwise** adv
contrast n (pl **-s**) obvious difference ▶ v (**-s, -ing, -ed**) compare in order to show differences (foll. by **with**)
contrasted v ▷ contrast
contrasting v ▷ contrast
contrasts n, v ▷ contrast
contrite adj sorry and apologetic > **contritely** adv > **contrition** n
contritely adv ▷ contrite

contrition n ▷ contrite
contrive v (**-ves, -ving, -ved**) make happen
contrives v ▷ contrive
contriving v ▷ contrive
control n (pl **-s**) power to direct something ▶ pl instruments used to operate a machine ▶ v (**-s, -lling, -lled**) have power over > **controllable** adj > **controller** n (pl **-s**)
controllable adj ▷ control
controlled v ▷ control
controller n ▷ control
controllers n ▷ control
controlling v ▷ control
controls n, v ▷ control
convene v (**-nes, -ning, -ned**) gather or summon for a formal meeting
convened v ▷ convene
convener, convenor n (pl **-s**) person who calls a meeting
conveners n ▷ convener
convenes v ▷ convene
convening v ▷ convene
convenor n ▷ convener
convenors n ▷ convener
convent n (pl **-s**) building where nuns live
convents n ▷ convent
converge v (**-ges, -ging, -ged**) meet or join > **convergence** n
converged v ▷ converge
converges v ▷ converge
converging v ▷ converge
converse¹ v (**-ses, -sing, -sed**) have a conversation
converse² adj, n (pl **-s**) opposite or contrary > **conversely** adv
conversed v ▷ converse¹
conversely adv ▷ converse²
converses v ▷ converse¹ ▶ n ▷ converse²
conversing v ▷ converse¹
convert v (**-s, -ing, ed**) change in form, character, or function ▶ n (pl **-s**) person who has converted to a different belief or religion
converted v ▷ convert

converting v ▷ **convert**

converts v, n ▷ **convert**

convex adj curving outwards

convey v (-s, -ing, -ed) communicate (information)

conveyed v ▷ **convey**

conveying v ▷ **convey**

conveys v ▷ **convey**

convict v (-s, -ing, -ed) declare guilty ▶ n (pl -s) person serving a prison sentence

convicted v ▷ **convict**

convicting v ▷ **convict**

convicts v, n ▷ **convict**

convince v (-ces, -cing, -ced) persuade by argument or evidence > **convincing** adj > **convincingly** adv

convinced v ▷ **convince**

convinces v ▷ **convince**

convincing v, adj ▷ **convince**

convincingly adv ▷ **convince**

convoke v (-kes, -king, -ked) call together

convoked v ▷ **convoke**

convokes v ▷ **convoke**

convoking v ▷ **convoke**

convoy n (pl -s) group of vehicles or ships travelling together

convoys n ▷ **convoy**

convulse v (-ses, -sing, -sed) (of part of the body) undergo violent spasms informal ▶ **convulsive** adj > **convulsively** adv

convulsed v ▷ **convulse**

convulses v ▷ **convulse**

convulsing v ▷ **convulse**

convulsive adj ▷ **convulse**

convulsively adv ▷ **convulse**

cony, coney n (pl -nies, -neys) BRIT rabbit

coo v (-s, -ing, -ed) (of a dove or pigeon) make a soft murmuring sound

cooed v ▷ **coo**

cooee interj BRIT, AUST & NZ call to attract attention

cooing v ▷ **coo**

cook v (-s, -ing, -ed) prepare (food) by heating ▶ n (pl -s) person who

cooks food

cooked v ▷ **cook**

cooker n (pl -s) CHIEFLY BRIT apparatus for cooking heated by gas or electricity

cookers n ▷ **cooker**

cookery n art of cooking

cookie n (pl -s) US biscuit

cookies n ▷ **cookie**

cooking v ▷ **cook**

cooks v, n ▷ **cook**

cool adj (-er, -est) moderately cold ▶ v (-s, -ing, -ed) make or become cool ▶ n (pl -s) coolness > **coolly** adv > **coolness** n (pl -es)

coolant n (pl -s) fluid used to cool machinery while it is working

coolants n ▷ **coolant**

cooled v ▷ **cool**

cooler n (pl -s) container for making or keeping things cool ▶ adj ▷ **cool**

coolers n ▷ **cooler**

coolest adj ▷ **cool**

coolibah n (pl -s) Australian eucalypt that grows beside rivers

coolibahs n ▷ **coolibah**

cooling v ▷ **cool**

coolly adv ▷ **cool**

coolness n ▷ **cool**

coolnesses n ▷ **cool**

cools v, n ▷ **cool**

coomb, coombe n (pl -s) S ENGLISH short valley or deep hollow

coombe n ▷ **coomb**

coombes n ▷ **coomb**

coombs n ▷ **coomb**

coop[1] n (pl -s) cage or pen for poultry

coop[2] n (pl -s) BRIT, US & AUST (shop run by) a cooperative society

cooper n (pl -s) person who makes or repairs barrels

coopers n ▷ **cooper**

coops n ▷ **coop**[1, 2]

coopt v (-s, -ing, -ed) add (someone) to a group by the agreement of the existing members

coopted v ▷ **coopt**

coopting v ▷ **coopt**

coopts v ▷ **coopt**

coos v ▷ **coo**

coot n (pl **-s**) small black water bird

coots n ▷ **coot**

cop slang n (pl **-s**) policeman ▶ v (**-s, -pping, -pped**) take or seize

cope¹ v (**-pes, -ping, -ped**) (often foll. by **with**) deal successfully (with)

cope² n (pl **-s**) large ceremonial cloak worn by some Christian priests

coped v ▷ **cope**¹

copes v ▷ **cope**¹ ▶ n ▷ **cope**²

copied v ▷ **copy**

copies n, v ▷ **copy**

coping v ▷ **cope**¹ ▶ n (pl **-s**) sloping top row of a wall

copings n ▷ **coping**

copious adj abundant, plentiful
> **copiously** adv

copiously adv ▷ **copious**

copped v ▷ **cop**

copper¹ n (pl **-s**) soft reddish-brown metal

copper² n (pl **-s**) BRIT slang policeman

coppers n ▷ **copper**¹, ²

coppice, copse n (pl **-s**) small group of trees growing close together

coppices n ▷ **coppice**

copping v ▷ **cop**

copra n (pl **-s**) dried oil-yielding kernel of the coconut

copras n ▷ **copra**

cops n, v ▷ **cop**

copse n ▷ **coppice**

copses n ▷ **coppice**

copulate v (**-tes, -ting, -ted**) have sexual intercourse > **copulation** n (pl **-s**)

copulated v ▷ **copulate**

copulates v ▷ **copulate**

copulating v ▷ **copulate**

copulation n ▷ **copulate**

copulations n ▷ **copulate**

copy n (pl **copies**) thing made to look exactly like another ▶ v (**-pies, -pying, -pied**) make a copy of

copying v ▷ **copy**

coquette n (pl **-s**) woman who flirts

> **coquettish** adj

coquettes n ▷ **coquette**

coquettish adj ▷ **coquette**

coracle n (pl **-s**) small round boat of wicker covered with skins

coracles n ▷ **coracle**

coral n (pl **-s**) hard substance formed from the skeletons of very small sea animals ▶ adj orange-pink

corals n ▷ **coral**

cord n (pl **-s**) thin rope or thick string
▶ pl corduroy trousers

cordial adj warm and friendly ▶ n (pl **-s**) drink with a fruit base > **cordially** adv
> **cordiality** n (pl **-ties**)

cordialities n ▷ **cordial**

cordiality n ▷ **cordial**

cordially adv ▷ **cordial**

cordials n ▷ **cordial**

cordite n (pl **-s**) explosive used in guns and bombs

cordites n ▷ **cordite**

cordon n (pl **-s**) chain of police, soldiers, etc, guarding an area

cordons n ▷ **cordon**

cords n ▷ **cord**

corduroy n (pl **-s**) cotton fabric with a velvety ribbed surface

corduroys n ▷ **corduroy**

core n (pl **-s**) central part of certain fruits, containing the seeds ▶ v (**-res, -ring, -red**) remove the core from

cored v ▷ **core**

corella n (pl **-s**) white Australian cockatoo

corellas n ▷ **corella**

cores n, v ▷ **core**

corgi n (pl **-s**) short-legged sturdy dog

corgis n ▷ **corgi**

coring v ▷ **core**

cork n (pl **-s**) thick light bark of a Mediterranean oak ▶ v (**-s, -ing, -ed**) seal with a cork

corkage n (pl **-s**) restaurant's charge for serving wine bought elsewhere

corkages n ▷ **corkage**

corked v ▷ **cork**

corking v ▷ **cork**

corks n, v ▷ **cork**

corm n (pl -s) bulblike underground stem of certain plants
corms n ▷ **corm**

corn[1] n (pl -s) cereal plant such as wheat or oats

corn[2] n (pl -s) painful hard skin on the toe

cornea n (pl -neas, -neae) transparent membrane covering the eyeball
> **corneal** adj
corneae n ▷ **cornea**
corneal adj ▷ **cornea**
corneas n ▷ **cornea**

corner n (pl -s) area or angle where two converging lines or surfaces meet SPORT ▶ v (-s, -ing, -ed) force into a difficult or inescapable position
cornered v ▷ **corner**
cornering v ▷ **corner**
corners n, v ▷ **corner**

cornet n (pl -s) brass instrument similar to the trumpet
cornets n ▷ **cornet**

cornice n (pl -s) decorative moulding round the top of a wall
cornices n ▷ **cornice**
cornier adj ▷ **corny**
corniest adj ▷ **corny**
corns n ▷ **corn**[1,2]

corny (-nier, -niest) adj slang unoriginal or oversentimental

corolla n (pl -s) petals of a flower collectively
corollas n ▷ **corolla**

corona n (pl -nas, -nae) ring of light round the moon or sun
coronae n ▷ **corona**
coronaries n ▷ **coronary**

coronary adj of the arteries surrounding the heart ▶ n (pl -ries)
coronas n ▷ **corona**

coroner n (pl -s) BRIT, AUST & NZ official responsible for the investigation of violent, sudden, or suspicious deaths
coroners n ▷ **coroner**

coronet n (pl -s) small crown
coronets n ▷ **coronet**

corpora n ▷ **corpus**

corporal[1] n (pl -s) noncommissioned officer in an army

corporal[2] adj of the body
> **corporally** adv
corporally adv ▷ **corporal**[2]
corporals n ▷ **corporal**[1]

corps n (pl **corps**) military unit with a specific function

corpse n (pl -s) dead body
corpses n ▷ **corpse**

corpus n (pl **corpora**) collection of writings, esp. by a single author

corral US n (pl -s) enclosure for cattle or horses ▶ v (-rals, -ralling, -ralled) put in a corral
corralled v ▷ **corral**
corralling v ▷ **corral**
corrals n, v ▷ **corral**

correct adj free from error, true ▶ v (-s, -ing, -ed) put right > **correctly** adv > **correctness** n
corrected v ▷ **correct**
correcting v ▷ **correct**
correctly adv ▷ **correct**
correctness n ▷ **correct**
corrects v ▷ **correct**

corridor n (pl -s) passage in a building or train
corridors n ▷ **corridor**

corrode v (-rodes, -roding, -roded) eat or be eaten away by chemical action or rust > **corrosion** n > **corrosive** adj > **corrosively** adv > **corrosiveness** n (pl -es)
corroded v ▷ **corrode**
corrodes v ▷ **corrode**
corroding v ▷ **corrode**
corrosion n ▷ **corrode**
corrosive n ▷ **corrode**
corrosively adv ▷ **corrode**
corrosiveness n ▷ **corrode**
corrosivenesses n ▷ **corrode**

corrupt adj (-er, -est) open to or involving bribery ▶ v (-s, -ing, -ed) make corrupt > **corruptly** adv > **corruption** n (pl -s) > **corruptible** adj
corrupted v ▷ **corrupt**

corrupter n (pl -s) ▷ **corrupt**
corruptest adj ▷ **corrupt**
corruptible adj ▷ **corrupt**
corrupting v ▷ **corrupt**
corruption n ▷ **corrupt**
corruptions n ▷ **corrupt**
corruptly adv ▷ **corrupt**
corrupts v ▷ **corrupt**
corsage n (pl -s) small bouquet worn on the bodice of a dress
corsages n ▷ **corsage**
corsair n (pl -s) pirate
corsairs n ▷ **corsair**
corset n (pl -s) women's close-fitting undergarment worn to shape the torso
corsets n ▷ **corset**
cortege n (pl -s) funeral procession
corteges n ▷ **cortege**
cortex n (pl -tices) ANAT outer layer of the brain or other internal organ
> **cortical** adj
cortical adj ▷ **cortex**
cortices n ▷ **cortex**
corundum n (pl -s) hard mineral used as an abrasive
corundums n ▷ **corundum**
corvette n (pl -s) lightly armed escort warship
corvettes n ▷ **corvette**
cosh n (pl -s) BRIT heavy blunt weapon ▶ v (-es, -ing, -ed) hit with a cosh
coshed v, n ▷ **cosh**
coshes v ▷ **cosh**
coshing v ▷ **cosh**
cosier adj ▷ **cosy**
cosies n ▷ **cosy**
cosiest adj ▷ **cosy**
cosily adv ▷ **cosy**
cosine n (pl -s) (in trigonometry) ratio of the length of the adjacent side to that of the hypotenuse in a right-angled triangle
cosines n ▷ **cosine**
cosiness n ▷ **cosy**
cosinesses n ▷ **cosy**
cosmetic n (pl -s) preparation used to improve the appearance of a person's skin ▶ adj improving the appearance only
cosmetics n ▷ **cosmetic**
cosmic adj of the whole universe
> **cosmically** adv
cosmically adv ▷ **cosmic**
cosmos n (pl **cosmos**) the universe
cossack n (pl -s) member of a S Russian people famous as horsemen and dancers
cossacks n ▷ **cossack**
cosset v (-s, -ing, -ed) pamper
cosseted v ▷ **cosset**
cosseting v ▷ **cosset**
cossets v ▷ **cosset**
cost n (pl -s) amount of money, time, labour, etc, required for something ▶ pl expenses of a lawsuit ▶ v (-s,-ing, cost) have as its cost
costing v ▷ **cost**
costlier adj ▷ **costly**
costliest adj ▷ **costly**
costliness n ▷ **costly**
costlinesses n ▷ **costly**
costly adj (-lier, -liest) expensive
> **costliness** n (pl -es)
costs n, v ▷ **cost**
costume n (pl -s) style of dress of a particular place or time, or for a particular activity
costumes n ▷ **costume**
cosy adj (-sier, -siest) warm and snug ▶ n (pl -sies) cover for keeping things warm > **cosily** adv > **cosiness** n (pl -es)
cot n (pl -s) baby's bed with high sides
cote n (pl -s) shelter for birds or animals
coterie n (pl -s) exclusive group, clique
coteries n ▷ **coterie**
cotes n ▷ **cote**
cots n ▷ **cot**
cottage n (pl -s) small house in the country
cottages n ▷ **cottage**
cotter n (pl -s) pin or wedge used to secure machine parts
cotters n ▷ **cotter**
cotton n (pl -s) white downy fibre covering the seeds of a tropical plant

> **cottony** adj

cottons n ▷ cotton

cottony adj ▷ cotton

couch n (pl -es) piece of upholstered furniture for seating more than one person ▶ v (-es, -ing, -ed) express in a particular way

couched v ▷ couch

couches n, v ▷ couch

couching v ▷ couch

cougan n (pl -s) AUST slang drunk and rowdy person

cougans n ▷ cougan

cougar n (pl -s) puma

cougars n ▷ cougar

cough v (-s, -ing, -ed) expel air from the lungs abruptly and noisily ▶ n (pl -s) act or sound of coughing

coughed v ▷ cough

coughing v ▷ cough

coughs v, n ▷ cough

could v ▷ can¹

coulomb n (pl -s) SI unit of electric charge

coulombs n ▷ coulomb

coulter n (pl -s) blade at the front of a ploughshare

coulters n ▷ coulter

council n (pl -s) group meeting for discussion or consultation ▶ adj of or by a council

councils n ▷ council

counsel n (pl -s) advice or guidance ▶ v (-sels, -selling, -selled) give guidance to > **counsellor** n (pl -s)

counselled v ▷ counsel

counselling v ▷ counsel

counsellor n ▷ counsel

counsellors n ▷ counsel

counsels n, v ▷ counsel

count¹ v (-s, -ing, -ed) say numbers in order ▶ n (pl -s) counting

count² n (pl -s) European nobleman

counted v ▷ count¹

counter¹ n (pl -s) long flat surface in a bank or shop, on which business is transacted

counter² v (-s, -ing, -ed) oppose,

retaliate against ▶ adv in the opposite direction ▶ n (pl -s) opposing or retaliatory action

countered v ▷ counter

countering v ▷ counter

counters n ▷ counter¹, ² ▶ v ▷ counter²

countess n (pl -es) woman holding the rank of count or earl

countesses n ▷ countess

counties n ▷ county

counting v ▷ count¹

countries n ▷ country

country n (pl -tries) nation

counts v ▷ count¹ ▶ n ▷ count¹, ²

county n (pl -ties) (in some countries) division of a country

coup n (pl -s) successful action

coupé n (pl -s) sports car with two doors and a sloping fixed roof

coupés n ▷ coupé

couple n (pl -s) two people who are married or romantically involved ▶ v (-ples, -pling, -pled) connect, associate

coupled v ▷ couple

couples n, v ▷ couple

couplet n (pl -s) two consecutive lines of verse, usu. rhyming and of the same metre

couplets n ▷ couplet

coupling n (pl -s) device for connecting things, such as railway carriages ▶ v ▷ couple

couplings n ▷ coupling

coupon n (pl -s) piece of paper entitling the holder to a discount or gift

coupons n ▷ coupon

coups n ▷ coup

courage n (pl -s) ability to face danger or pain without fear > **courageous** adj > **courageously** adv

courageous adj ▷ courage

courageously adv ▷ courage

courages n ▷ courage

courier n (pl -s) person employed to look after holiday-makers

couriers n ▷ courier

course n (pl -s) series of lessons or medical treatment ▶ v (-ses, -sing, -sed) (of liquid) run swiftly

coursed v ▷ course

courses n, v ▷ course

coursing v ▷ course

court n (pl -s) body which decides legal cases ▶ v (-s, -ing, -ed) old-fashioned try to gain the love of

courted v ▷ court

courtesies n ▷ courtesy

courtesy n (pl -sies) politeness, good manners

courtier n (pl -s) attendant at a royal court

courtiers n ▷ courtier

courting v ▷ court

courtlier adj ▷ courtly

courtliest adj ▷ courtly

courtliness n ▷ courtly

courtlinesses n ▷ courtly

courtly adj (-lier, -liest) ceremoniously polite > courtliness n (pl -es)

courts n, v ▷ court

cousin n (pl -s) child of one's uncle or aunt

cousins n ▷ cousin

couture n (pl -s) high-fashion designing and dressmaking

coutures n ▷ couture

cove n (pl -s) small bay or inlet

coven n (pl -s) meeting of witches

covenant n (pl -s) contract ▶ v (-s, -ing, -ed) agree by a covenant

covenanted v ▷ covenant

covenanting v ▷ covenant

covenants n, v ▷ covenant

covens n ▷ coven

cover v (-s, -ing, -ed) place something over, to protect or conceal ▶ n (pl -s) anything that covers

coverage n amount or extent covered

covered v ▷ cover

covering v ▷ cover

coverlet n (pl -s) bed cover

coverlets v ▷ coverlet

covers v, n ▷ cover

covert adj concealed, secret ▶ n (pl -s) thicket giving shelter to game birds or animals > covertly adv

covertly adv ▷ covert

coverts n ▷ covert

coves n ▷ cove

covet v (-s, -ing, -ed) long to possess (what belongs to someone else) > covetous adj > covetousness n (pl -es)

coveted v ▷ covet

coveting v ▷ covet

covetous adj ▷ covet

covetousness n ▷ covet

covetousnesses n ▷ covet

covets v ▷ covet

covey n (pl -s) small flock of grouse or partridge

coveys n ▷ covey

cow¹ n (pl -s) mature female of cattle and of certain other mammals, such as the elephant or seal

cow² v (-s, -ing, -ed) intimidate, subdue

coward n (pl -s) person who lacks courage > cowardly adj > cowardliness n (pl -es)

cowardliness n ▷ coward

cowardlinesses n ▷ coward

cowardly adj ▷ coward

cowards n ▷ coward

cowboy n (pl -s) (in the US) ranch worker who herds and tends cattle, usu. on horseback

cowboys n ▷ cowboy

cowed v ▷ cow²

cower v (-s, -ing, -ed) cringe in fear

cowered v ▷ cower

cowering v ▷ cower

cowers v ▷ cower

cowing v ▷ cow²

cowl n (pl -s) loose hood

cowling n (pl -s) cover on an engine

cowlings n ▷ cowling

cowls n ▷ cowl

cowrie n (pl -s) brightly-marked sea shell

cowries n ▷ cowrie

cows n ▷ cow¹ ▶ v ▷ cow²

cowslip n (pl -s) small yellow wild European flower

cowslips n ▷ cowslip

cox n (pl -es) coxswain ▶ v (-es, -ing, -ed) act as cox of (a boat)

coxed v ▷ cox

coxes n, v ▷ cox

coxing v ▷ cox

coxswain n (pl -s) person who steers a rowing boat

coxswains n ▷ coxswain

coy adj (-er, -est) affectedly shy or modest > coyly adv > coyness n (pl -es)

coyer adj ▷ coy

coyest adj ▷ coy

coyly adv ▷ coy

coyness n ▷ coy

coynesses n ▷ coy

coyote n (pl -s) prairie wolf of N America

coyotes n ▷ coyote

coypu n (pl -s) beaver-like aquatic rodent native to S America, bred for its fur

coypus n ▷ coypu

> coz n (cozes). Coz is an old word for cousin, and a good one to know as it scores 14 points.

cozen v (-s, -ing, -ed) lit cheat, trick

cozened v ▷ cozen

cozening v ▷ cozen

cozens v ▷ cozen

crab n (pl -s) edible shellfish with ten legs, the first claw modified into pincers

crabbed adj (of handwriting) hard to read (also crabby; -ier, -iest)

crabbier adj ▷ crabbed

crabbiest adj ▷ crabbed

crabby adj ▷ crabbed

crabs n ▷ crab

crack v (-s, -ing, -ed) break or split partially ▶ n (pl -s) sudden sharp noise ▶ adj informal first-rate, excellent

cracked v ▷ crack

cracker n (pl -s) thin dry biscuit

crackers n ▷ cracker ▶ adj slang insane

cracking adj very good ▶ v ▷ crack

crackle v (-les, -ling, -led) make small sharp popping noises ▶ n (pl -les) crackling sound

crackled v ▷ crackle

crackles v, n ▷ crackle

crackling v ▷ crackle

crackpot n (pl -s) ▶ adj informal eccentric (person)

crackpots n ▷ crackpot

cracks v ▷ crack

cradle n (pl -s) baby's bed on rockers ▶ v (-dles, -dling, -dled) hold gently as if in a cradle

cradled v ▷ cradle

cradles v, n ▷ cradle

cradling v ▷ cradle

craft n (pl -s) occupation requiring skill with the hands

craftier adj ▷ crafty

craftiest adj ▷ crafty

craftily adv ▷ crafty

craftiness n ▷ crafty

craftinesses n ▷ crafty

crafts n ▷ craft

crafty adj (-tier, -tiest) skilled in deception > craftily adv > craftiness n (pl -es)

crag n (pl -s) steep rugged rock > craggy (-ggier, -ggiest)

craggier adj ▷ crag

craggiest adj ▷ crag

craggy adj ▷ crag

crags n ▷ crag

cram v (-s, -mming, -mmed) force into too small a space

crammed v ▷ cram

cramming v ▷ cram

cramp¹ n (pl -s) painful muscular contraction

cramp² v (-s, -ing, -ed) confine, restrict

cramped v ▷ cramp²

cramping v ▷ cramp²

crampon n (pl -s) spiked plate strapped to a boot for climbing on ice

crampons n ▷ **crampon**
cramps n ▷ **cramp¹** ▶ v ▷ **cramp²**
crams v ▷ **cram**
crane n (pl -s) machine for lifting and moving heavy weights ▶ v (-nes, -ning, -ned) stretch (one's neck) to see something
craned v ▷ **crane**
cranes n, v ▷ **crane**
crania n ▷ **cranium**
cranial adj ▷ **cranium**
craning v ▷ **crane**
cranium n (pl -niums, -nia) ANAT skull > **cranial** adj
craniums n ▷ **cranium**
crank n (pl -s) arm projecting at right angles from a shaft, for transmitting or converting motion informal ▶ v (-s, -ing, -ed) start (an engine) with a crank
cranked v ▷ **crank**
crankier adj ▷ **cranky**
crankiest adj ▷ **cranky**
cranking v ▷ **crank**
cranks n, v ▷ **crank**
cranky adj (-kier, -kiest) informal eccentric
crannies n ▷ **cranny**
cranny n (pl -nies) narrow opening
crape n (pl -s) ▷ **crepe**
crapes n ▷ **crape**
craps n gambling game played with two dice
crash n (pl -es) collision involving a vehicle or vehicles ▶ v (-es, -ing, -ed) (cause to) collide violently with a vehicle, a stationary object, or the ground
crashed v ▷ **crash**
crashes n, v ▷ **crash**
crashing v ▷ **crash**
crass adj (-er, -est) stupid and insensitive > **crassly** adv > **crassness** n (pl -es)
crasser adj ▷ **crass**
crassest adj ▷ **crass**
crassly adv ▷ **crass**
crassness n ▷ **crass**

crassnesses n ▷ **crass**
crate n (pl -s) large wooden container for packing goods
crater n (pl -s) very large hole in the ground or in the surface of the moon
craters n ▷ **crater**
crates n ▷ **crate**
cravat n (pl -s) man's scarf worn like a tie
cravats n ▷ **cravat**
crave v (-ves, -ving, -ved) desire intensely > **craving** n (pl -s)
craved v ▷ **crave**
craven adj cowardly
craves v ▷ **crave**
craving v ▷ **crave**
cravings n ▷ **crave**
crawfish n (pl crawfish) ▷ **crayfish**
crawl v (-s, -ing, -ed) move on one's hands and knees ▶ n (pl -s) crawling motion or pace > **crawler** n (pl -s)
crawled v ▷ **crawl**
crawler n ▷ **crawl**
crawlers n ▷ **crawl**
crawling v ▷ **crawl**
crawls n, v ▷ **crawl**
crayfish n (pl crayfish) edible shellfish like a lobster
crayon v (-s, -ing, -ed) ▶ n (pl -s) (draw or colour with) a stick or pencil of coloured wax or clay
crayoned v ▷ **crayon**
crayoning v ▷ **crayon**
crayons n, v ▷ **crayon**
craze n (pl -s) short-lived fashion or enthusiasm
crazed adj wild and uncontrolled
crazes n ▷ **craze**
crazier adj ▷ **crazy**
craziest adj ▷ **crazy**
crazily adv ▷ **crazy**
craziness n ▷ **crazy**
crazinesses n ▷ **crazy**
crazy adj (-zier, -ziest) ridiculous > **crazily** adv > **craziness** n (pl -es)
creak v, n (pl -s) (make) a harsh squeaking sound > **creaky** adj (-kier, -kiest)

creakier adj ▷ creak
creakiest adj ▷ creak
creaks n ▷ creak
creaky adj ▷ creak
cream n (pl -s) fatty part of milk ▶ v (-s, -ing, -ed) beat to a creamy consistency > **creamy** adj (pl -mier, -miest) > **creaminess** n
creamed v ▷ cream
creamier adj ▷ cream
creamiest adj ▷ cream
creaminess n ▷ cream
creaming v ▷ cream
creams n, v ▷ cream
creamy adj ▷ cream
crease n (pl -s) line made by folding or pressing ▶ v (-ses, -sing, -sed) crush or line
creased v ▷ crease
creases n, v ▷ crease
creasing v ▷ crease
create v (-s, -ting, -ted) make, cause to exist > **creation** n (pl -s) > **creator** n (pl -s)
created v ▷ create
creates v ▷ create
creating v ▷ create
creation n ▷ create
creations n ▷ create
creative adj imaginative or inventive > **creatively** adv > **creativity** n (pl -ties)
creatively adv ▷ creative
creativities n ▷ creative
creativity n ▷ create
creator n ▷ create
creators n ▷ create
creature n (pl -s) animal, person, or other being
creatures n ▷ creature
crèche n (pl -s) place where small children are looked after while their parents are working, shopping, etc
crèches n ▷ crèche
credence n (pl -s) belief in the truth or accuracy of a statement
credences n ▷ credence
credibilities n ▷ credible
credibility n ▷ credible

credible adj believable > **credibly** adv > **credibility** n (pl -ties)
credibly adv ▷ credible
credit n (pl -s) system of allowing customers to receive goods and pay later ▶ v (-s, -ing, -ed) enter as a credit in an account
credited v ▷ credit
crediting v ▷ credit
creditor n (pl -s) person to whom money is owed
creditors n ▷ creditor
credits n, v ▷ credit
creed n (pl -s) statement or system of (Christian) beliefs or principles
creeds n ▷ creed
creek n (pl -s) narrow inlet or bay AUST, NZ, US & CANADIAN
creeks n ▷ creek
creel n (pl -s) wicker basket used by anglers
creels n ▷ creel
creep v (-s, -ing, crept) move quietly and cautiously ▶ n (pl -s) slang obnoxious or servile person
creeper n (pl -s) creeping plant
creepers n ▷ creeper
creepier adj ▷ creepy
creepiest adj ▷ creepy
creepily adv ▷ creepy
creepiness n ▷ creepy
creepinesses n ▷ creepy
creeping v ▷ creep
creeps n, n ▷ creep
creepy adj (-pier, -piest) informal causing a feeling of fear or disgust > **creepily** adv > **creepiness** n (pl -es)
cremate v (-tes, -ting, -ted) burn (a corpse) to ash > **cremation** n (pl -s)
cremated v ▷ cremate
cremates v ▷ cremate
cremating v ▷ cremate
cremation n ▷ cremate
cremations n ▷ cremate
creole n (pl -s) language developed from a mixture of languages
creoles n ▷ creole
creosote n (pl -s) dark oily liquid made

from coal tar and used for preserving wood ▶ (**-sotes, -soting, -soted**) treat with creosote

creosoted v ▷ **creosote**

creosotes n, v ▷ **creosote**

creosoting v ▷ **creosote**

crepe, crape n (pl **-s**) fabric or rubber with a crinkled texture

crepes n ▷ **crepe**

crept v ▷ **creep**

crescent n (pl **-s**) (curved shape of) the moon as seen in its first or last quarter

crescents n ▷ **crescent**

cress n (pl **-es**) plant with strong-tasting leaves, used in salads

cresses n ▷ **cress**

crest n (pl **-s**) top of a mountain, hill, or wave ▷ **crested** adj

crested adj ▷ **crest**

crests n ▷ **crest**

cretin n (pl **-s**) informal stupid person > **cretinous** adj

cretinous adj ▷ **cretin**

cretins n ▷ **cretin**

crevasse n (pl **-s**) deep open crack in a glacier

crevasses n ▷ **crevasse**

crevice n (pl **-s**) narrow crack or gap in rock

crevices n ▷ **crevice**

crew n (pl **-s**) people who work on a ship or aircraft informal ▶ v (**-s, -ing, -ed**) serve as a crew member (on)

crewed v ▷ **crew**

crewel n (pl **-s**) fine worsted yarn used in embroidery

crewels n ▷ **crewel**

crewing v ▷ **crew**

crews n, v ▷ **crew**

crib n (pl **-s**) piece of writing stolen from elsewhere ▶ v (**-s, -bbing, -bbed**) copy (someone's work) dishonestly

cribbage n (pl **-s**) card game for two to four players

cribbages n ▷ **cribbage**

cribbed v ▷ **crib**

cribbing v ▷ **crib**

cribs n, v ▷ **crib**

crick n (pl **-s**) muscle spasm or cramp in the back or neck ▶ v (**-s, -ing, -ed**) cause a crick in

cricked v ▷ **crick**

cricket[1] n (pl **-s**) outdoor game played with bats, a ball, and wickets by two teams of eleven ▷ **cricketer** n (pl **-s**)

cricket[2] n (pl **-s**) chirping insect like a grasshopper

cricketer n ▷ **cricket**[1]

cricketers n ▷ **cricket**[1]

crickets n ▷ **cricket**[1, 2]

cricking v ▷ **crick**

cricks n, v ▷ **crick**

cried v ▷ **cry**

cries v ▷ **cry**

crime n (pl **-s**) unlawful act

crimes n ▷ **crime**

criminal n (pl **-s**) person guilty of a crime ▶ adj of crime > **criminally** adv > **criminality** n (pl **-ties**)

criminalities n ▷ **criminal**

criminality n ▷ **criminal**

criminally adv ▷ **criminal**

criminals n ▷ **criminal**

crimp v (**-s, -ing, -ed**) fold or press into ridges

crimped v ▷ **crimp**

crimping v ▷ **crimp**

crimps v ▷ **crimp**

crimson adj deep purplish-red

cringe v (**-ges, -ging, -ged**) flinch in fear

cringed v ▷ **cringe**

cringes n ▷ **cringe**

cringing v ▷ **cringe**

crinkle v (**-les, -ling, -led**) ▶ n (pl **-s**) wrinkle, crease, or fold

crinkled v ▷ **crinkle**

crinkles v, n ▷ **crinkle**

crinkling v ▷ **crinkle**

cripple n (pl **-s**) person who is lame or disabled ▶ v (**-les, -ling, -led**) make lame or disabled

crippled v ▷ **cripple**

cripples n, v ▷ **cripple**

crippling v ▷ **cripple**

crises n ▷ **crisis**

crisis n (pl -ses) crucial stage, turning point

crisp adj (-er, -est) fresh and firm ▶ n (pl -s) BRIT very thin slice of potato fried till crunchy > **crisply** adv > **crispness** n (pl -es)

crisper adj ▷ **crisp**

crispest adj ▷ **crisp**

crispier adj ▷ **crisp**

crispiest adj ▷ **crisp**

crisply adv ▷ **crisp**

crispness n ▷ **crisp**

crispnesses n ▷ **crisp**

crisps n ▷ **crisp**

crispy adj (-pier, -piest) hard and crunchy

critic n (pl -s) professional judge of any of the arts

critical adj very important or dangerous > **critically** adv

critically adv ▷ **critical**

critics n ▷ **critic**

critique n (pl -s) critical essay

critiques n ▷ **critique**

croak v (-s, -ing, -ed) (of a frog or crow) give a low hoarse cry ▶ n (pl -s) low hoarse sound

croaked v ▷ **croak**

croakier adj ▷ **croaky**

croakiest adj ▷ **croaky**

croakiness n ▷ **croaky**

croaking v ▷ **croak**

croaks v, n ▷ **croak**

croaky adj (-kier, -kiest) hoarse > **croakiness** n

crochet v (-s, -ing, -ed) make by looping and intertwining yarn with a hooked needle ▶ n (pl -s) work made in this way

crocheted v ▷ **crochet**

crocheting v ▷ **crochet**

crochets v, n ▷ **crochet**

crock[1] n (pl -s) earthenware pot or jar

crock[2] n (pl -s) BRIT, AUST & NZ informal old or decrepit person or thing

crockery n dishes

crocks n ▷ **crock**[1, 2]

crocus n (pl -cuses) small plant with

yellow, white, or purple flowers in spring

crocuses n ▷ **crocus**

croft n (pl -s) small farm worked by one family in Scotland > **crofter** n (pl -s)

crofter n ▷ **croft**

crofters n ▷ **croft**

crofts n ▷ **croft**

cromlech n (pl -s) BRIT circle of prehistoric standing stones

cromlechs n ▷ **cromlech**

crone n (pl -s) witchlike old woman

crones n ▷ **crone**

cronies n ▷ **crony**

crony n (pl -nies) close friend

crook n (pl -s) informal criminal ▶ adj AUST & NZ slang unwell, injured

crooked adj bent or twisted > **crookedly** adv > **crookedness** n

crookedly adv ▷ **crooked**

crookedness n ▷ **crooked**

crooks n ▷ **crook**

croon v (-s, -ing, -ed) sing, hum, or speak in a soft low tone

crooned v ▷ **croon**

crooner n (pl -s) male singer of sentimental ballads

crooners n ▷ **crooner**

crooning v ▷ **croon**

croons v ▷ **croon**

crop n (pl -s) cultivated plant ▶ v (-s, -pping, -pped) cut very short

cropped v ▷ **crop**

cropping v ▷ **crop**

crops n, v ▷ **crop**

croquet n (pl -s) game played on a lawn in which balls are hit through hoops

croquets n ▷ **croquet**

crosier n (pl -s) ▷ **crozier**

crosiers n ▷ **crosier**

cross v (-es, -ing, -ed) move or go across (something) ▶ n (pl -es) structure, symbol, or mark of two intersecting lines ▶ adj (-er, -est) angry, annoyed > **crossly** adv > **crossness** n (pl -es)

crossbar n (pl -s) horizontal bar across goalposts or on a bicycle

crossbars n ▷ crossbar

crossbow n (pl -s) weapon consisting of a bow fixed across a wooden stock

crossbows n ▷ crossbow

crossed v ▷ cross

crosser adj ▷ cross

crosses v, n ▷ cross

crossest adj ▷ cross

crossing n (pl -s) place where a street may be crossed safely ▶ v ▷ cross

crossings n ▷ crossing

crossly adv ▷ cross

crossness n ▷ cross

crossnesses n ▷ cross

crotch n (pl -es) part of the body between the tops of the legs

crotches n ▷ crotch

crotchet n (pl -s) musical note half the length of a minim

crotchets n ▷ crotchet

crouch v (-es, -ing, -ed) bend low with the legs and body close ▶ n (pl -es) this position

crouched v ▷ crouch

crouches v, n ▷ crouch

crouching v ▷ crouch

croup¹ n (pl -s) throat disease of children, with a cough

croup² n (pl -s) hind quarters of a horse

croupier n (pl -s) person who collects bets and pays out winnings at a gambling table in a casino

croupiers n ▷ croupier

croups n ▷ croup¹, ²

crouton n (pl -s) small piece of fried or toasted bread served in soup

croutons n ▷ crouton

crow¹ n (pl -s) large black bird with a harsh call

crow² v (-s, -ing, -ed) (of a cock) make a shrill squawking sound

crowbar n (pl -s) iron bar used as a lever

crowbars n ▷ crowbar

crowd n (pl -s) large group of people or things ▶ v (-s, -ing, -ed) gather together in large numbers

crowded v ▷ crowd

crowding v ▷ crowd

crowds n, v ▷ crowd

crowed v ▷ crow²

crowing v ▷ crow²

crown n (pl -s) monarch's headdress of gold and jewels ▶ v (-s, -ing, -ed) put a crown on the head of (someone) to proclaim him or her monarch

crowned v ▷ crown

crowning v ▷ crown

crowns n, v ▷ crown

crows n ▷ crow¹ ▶ v ▷ crow²

crozier n (pl -s) bishop's hooked staff

croziers n ▷ crozier

crucial adj very important
> crucially adv

crucially adv ▷ crucial

crucible n (pl -s) pot in which metals are melted

crucibles n ▷ crucible

crucified v ▷ crucify

crucifies v ▷ crucify

crucifix n (pl -es) model of Christ on the Cross

crucifixes n ▷ crucify

crucify v (-fies, -fying, -fied) put to death by fastening to a cross

crucifying v ▷ crucify

crude adj (-r, -st) rough and simple
> crudely adv > crudeness n (pl -es)
> crudity n (pl -ties)

crudely adv ▷ crude

crudeness n ▷ crude

crudenesses n ▷ crude

cruder adj ▷ crude

crudest adj ▷ crude

crudities n ▷ crude

crudity n ▷ crude

cruel adj (-ller, -llest) delighting in others' pain > cruelly adv > cruelty n (pl -ties)

crueller adj ▷ cruel

cruellest adj ▷ cruel

cruelly adv ▷ cruel

cruelties n ▷ cruel

cruelty n ▷ cruel

cruet n (pl -s) small container for salt, pepper, etc, at table

cruets n ▷ cruet

cruise n (pl **-s**) sail for pleasure ▶ v (**-ses, -sing, -sed**) sail from place to place for pleasure
cruised n ▷ cruise

cruiser n (pl **-s**) fast warship
cruisers n ▷ cruiser
cruises n, v ▷ cruise
cruising v ▷ cruise

crumb n (pl **-s**) small fragment of bread or other dry food

crumble v (**-bles, -bling, -bled**) break into fragments ▶ n (pl **-s**) pudding of stewed fruit with a crumbly topping
> **crumbly** adj (**-lier, -liest**)
crumbled v ▷ crumble
crumbles v, n ▷ crumble
crumblier adj ▷ crumble
crumbliest adj ▷ crumble
crumbling v ▷ crumble
crumbly adj ▷ crumble
crumbs n ▷ crumb

crummier adj ▷ crummy
crummiest adj ▷ crummy

crummy adj (**-mier, -miest**) slang of poor quality

crumpet n (pl **-s**) round soft yeast cake, eaten buttered
crumpets n ▷ crumpet

crumple v (**-les, -ling, -led**) crush, crease > **crumpled** adj
crumpled v, adj ▷ crumple
crumples v ▷ crumple
crumpling v ▷ crumple

crunch v (**-es, -ing, -ed**) bite or chew with a noisy crushing sound ▶ n (pl **-es**) crunching sound informal
> **crunchy** adj (**-chier, -chiest**)
crunched v ▷ crunch
crunches v, n ▷ crunch
crunchier adj ▷ crunch
crunchiest adj ▷ crunch
crunching v ▷ crunch
crunchy adj ▷ crunch

crupper n (pl **-s**) strap that passes from the back of a saddle under a horse's tail
cruppers n ▷ crupper

crusade n (pl **-s**) medieval Christian war to recover the Holy Land from the Muslims ▶ v (**-des, -ding, -ded**) take part in a crusade
crusaded v ▷ crusade

crusader n (pl **-s**) person who took part in the medieval Christian war to recover the Holy Land from the Muslims
crusaders n ▷ crusader
crusades n, v ▷ crusade
crusading v ▷ crusade

crush v (**-es, -ing, -ed**) compress so as to injure, break, or crumple ▶ n (pl **-es**) dense crowd
crushed v ▷ crush
crushes v, n ▷ crush
crushing v ▷ crush

crust n (pl **-s**) hard outer part of something, esp. bread ▶ v (**-s, -ing, -ed**) cover with or form a crust
crusted v ▷ crust
crustier adj ▷ crusty
crustiest adj ▷ crusty
crusting v ▷ crust
crusts n, v ▷ crust

crusty adj (**-tier, -tiest**) having a crust

crutch n (pl **-es**) long sticklike support with a rest for the armpit, used by a lame person
crutches n ▷ crutch

crux n (pl **-es**) crucial or decisive point
cruxes n ▷ crux

cry v (**cries, crying, cried**) shed tears ▶ n (pl **cries**) fit of weeping
crybabies n ▷ crybaby

crybaby n (pl **-bies**) person, esp. a child, who cries too readily
crying v ▷ cry

crypt n (pl **-s**) vault under a church, esp. one used as a burial place

cryptic adj obscure in meaning, secret
> **cryptically** adv
crypts n ▷ crypt

crystal n (pl **-s**) (single grain of) a symmetrically shaped solid formed naturally by some substances ▶ adj bright and clear
crystals n ▷ crystal

cub n (pl -s) young wild animal such as a bear or fox ▶ v (-s, -bbing, -bbed) give birth to cubs
cubbed v ▷ cub
cubbing v ▷ cub

cube n (pl -s) object with six equal square sides ▶ v (-bes, -bing, -bed) cut into cubes
cubed v ▷ cube
cubes n, v ▷ cube

cubic adj having three dimensions

cubicle n (pl -s) enclosed part of a large room, screened for privacy
cubicles n ▷ cubicle
cubing v ▷ cube

cubism n (pl -s) style of art in which objects are represented by geometrical shapes > **cubist** adj, n (pl -s)
cubisms n ▷ cubism
cubist n ▷ cubism
cubists n ▷ cubism
cubs n, v ▷ cub

cuckold n (pl -s) man whose wife has been unfaithful ▶ v (-s, -ing, -ed) be unfaithful to (one's husband)
cuckolded v ▷ cuckold
cuckolding v ▷ cuckold
cuckolds n, v ▷ cuckold

cuckoo n (pl -s) migratory bird with a characteristic two-note call, which lays its eggs in the nests of other birds ▶ adj informal insane or foolish
cuckoos n ▷ cuckoo

cucumber n (pl -s) long green-skinned fleshy fruit used in salads
cucumbers n ▷ cucumber

cud n (pl -s) partially digested food which a ruminant brings back into its mouth to chew again

cuddle v (-les, -ling, -led) ▶ n (pl -s) hug > **cuddly** adj (-lier, -liest)
cuddled v ▷ cuddle
cuddles n, v ▷ cuddle
cuddlier adj ▷ cuddle
cuddliest adj ▷ cuddle
cuddling v ▷ cuddle
cuddly adj ▷ cuddle

cudgel n (pl -s) short thick stick used

as a weapon
cudgels n ▷ cudgel
cuds n ▷ cud

cue¹ n (pl -s) signal to an actor or musician to begin speaking or playing ▶ v (cues, cueing, cued) give a cue to

cue² n long tapering stick used in billiards, snooker, or pool ▶ v (cues, cueing, cued) hit (a ball) with a cue
cued v ▷ cue¹, ²
cueing v ▷ cue¹, ²
cues n, v ▷ cue¹, ²

cuff¹ n (pl -s) end of a sleeve

cuff² BRIT, AUST & NZ v (-s, -ing, -ed) hit with an open hand ▶ n (pl -s) blow with an open hand
cuffed v ▷ cuff²
cuffing v ▷ cuff²
cuffs n ▷ cuff¹, ² ▶ v ▷ cuff²

cuisine n (pl -s) style of cooking
cuisines n ▷ cuisine

culinary adj of kitchens or cookery

cull v (-s, -ing, -ed) choose, gather ▶ n (pl -s) culling
culled v ▷ cull
culling v ▷ cull
culls v, n ▷ cull

culottes pl n women's knee-length trousers cut to look like a skirt
culpabilities n ▷ culpable
culpability n ▷ culpable

culpable adj deserving blame > **culpability** n (pl -ties) > **culpably** adv
culpably adv ▷ culpable

culprit n (pl -s) person guilty of an offence or misdeed
culprits n ▷ culprit

cult n (pl -s) specific system of worship
cults n ▷ cult

cultural adj ▷ culture
culturally adv ▷ culture

culture n (pl -s) ideas, customs, and art of a particular society > **cultural** adj > **culturally** adv
cultured adj showing good taste or manners
cultures n ▷ culture

culvert n (pl -s) drain under a road

or railway

culverts n ▷ **culvert**

cumin, cummin n (pl **-s**) sweet-smelling seeds of a Mediterranean plant, used in cooking

cumins n ▷ **cumin**

cummin n ▷ **cumin**

cummins n ▷ **cummin**

cumuli n ▷ **cumulus**

cumulus n (pl **-li**) thick white or dark grey cloud

cunjevoi n AUST plant of tropical Asia and Australia with small flowers, cultivated for its edible rhizome

cunjevois n ▷ **cunjevoi**

cunning adj clever at deceiving ▶ n (pl **-s**) cleverness at deceiving > **cunningly** adv

cunningly adv ▷ **cunning**

cunnings n ▷ **cunning**

cup n (pl **-s**) small bowl-shaped drinking container with a handle ▶ v (**-s, -pping, -pped**) form (one's hands) into the shape of a cup > **cupful** n (pl **-s**)

cupboard n (pl **-s**) piece of furniture or alcove with a door, for storage

cupboards n ▷ **cupboard**

cupful n ▷ **cup**

cupfuls n ▷ **cup**

cupidities n ▷ **cupidity**

cupidity n (pl **-ties**) greed for money or possessions

cupola n (pl **-s**) domed roof or ceiling

cupolas n ▷ **cupola**

cupped v ▷ **cup**

cupping v ▷ **cup**

cups n, v ▷ **cup**

cur n (pl **-s**) lit mongrel dog

curable adj ▷ **cure**

curaçao n (pl **-s**) orange-flavoured liqueur

curaçaos n ▷ **curaçao**

curacies n ▷ **curacy**

curacy n (pl **-cies**) work or position of a curate

curare n (pl **-s**) poisonous resin of a S American tree, used as a muscle

relaxant in medicine

curares n ▷ **curare**

curate n (pl **-s**) clergyman who assists a parish priest

curates n ▷ **curate**

curative adj, n (pl **-s**) (something) able to cure

curatives n ▷ **curative**

curator n (pl **-s**) person in charge of a museum or art gallery > **curatorship** n (pl **-s**)

curators n ▷ **curator**

curatorship n ▷ **curator**

curatorships n ▷ **curator**

curb n (pl **-s**) something that restrains ▶ v (**-s, -ing, -ed**) control, restrain

curbed v ▷ **curb**

curbing v ▷ **curb**

curbs n, v ▷ **curb**

curd n (pl **-s**) coagulated milk, used to make cheese

curdle v (**-dles, -dling, -dled**) turn into curd, coagulate

curdled v ▷ **curdle**

curdles v ▷ **curdle**

curdling v ▷ **curdle**

curds n ▷ **curd**

cure v (**-res, -ring, -red**) get rid of (an illness or problem) ▶ n (pl **-s**) (treatment causing) curing of an illness or person > **curable** adj

cured v ▷ **cure**

cures v, n ▷ **cure**

curettage n ▷ **curette**

curettages n ▷ **curette**

curette n (pl **-s**) surgical instrument for scraping tissue from body cavities ▶ v (**-ttes, -tting, -tted**) scrape with a curette > **curettage** n (pl **-s**)

curetted v ▷ **curette**

curettes n, v ▷ **curette**

curetting v ▷ **curette**

curfew n (pl **-s**) law ordering people to stay inside their homes after a specific time at night

curfews n ▷ **curfew**

curie n (pl **-s**) standard unit of radioactivity

curies n ▷ **curie**

curing v ▷ **cure**

curio n (pl -s) rare or unusual object valued as a collector's item

curios n ▷ **curio**

curious adj eager to learn or know
> **curiously** adv

curiously adv ▷ **curious**

curl n (pl -s) curved piece of hair ▶ v (-s, -ing, -ed) make (hair) into curls or (of hair) grow in curls > **curler** n (pl -s) > **curly** adj (-lier, -liest)

curled v ▷ **curl**

curler n ▷ **curl**

curlers n ▷ **curl**

curlew n (pl -s) long-billed wading bird

curlews n ▷ **curlew**

curlier adj ▷ **curl**

curliest adj ▷ **curl**

curling n game like bowls, played with heavy stones on ice ▶ v ▷ **curl**

curls n, v ▷ **curl**

curly adj ▷ **curl**

currant n (pl -s) small dried grape

currants n ▷ **currant**

currencies n ▷ **currency**

currency n (pl -cies) money in use in a particular country

current adj of the immediate present ▶ n (pl -s) flow of water or air in one direction > **currently** adv

currently adv ▷ **current**

currents n ▷ **current**

curried v ▷ **curry**[1, 2]

curries n ▷ **curry**[1] ▶ v ▷ **curry**[1, 2]

curry[1] n (pl -ries) Indian dish of meat or vegetables in a hot spicy sauce ▶ v (-ries, -rying, -ried) prepare (food) with curry powder

curry[2] v (-ries, -rrying, -ried) groom (a horse)

currying v ▷ **curry**[1, 2]

curs n ▷ **cur**

curse v (-ses, -sing, -sed) swear (at) ▶ n (pl -s) swearword > **cursed** adj

cursed adj, v ▷ **curse**

curses v, n ▷ **curse**

cursing v ▷ **curse**

cursive adj, n (pl -s) (handwriting) done with joined letters
> **cursively** adv

cursively adv ▷ **cursive**

cursives n ▷ **cursive**

cursor n (pl -s) movable point of light that shows a specific position on a visual display unit

cursorily adv ▷ **cursory**

cursoriness n ▷ **cursory**

cursors n ▷ **cursor**

cursory adj quick and superficial
> **cursorily** adv > **cursoriness** n

curt adj (-er, -est) brief and rather rude
> **curtly** adv > **curtness** n (pl -es)

curtail v (-s, -ing, -ed) cut short
> **curtailment** n (pl -s)

curtailed v ▷ **curtail**

curtailing v ▷ **curtail**

curtailment v ▷ **curtail**

curtailments n ▷ **curtail**

curtails v ▷ **curtail**

curtain n (pl -s) piece of cloth hung at a window or opening as a screen ▶ v (-s, -ing, -ed) provide with curtains

curtained v ▷ **curtain**

curtaining v ▷ **curtain**

curtains n, v ▷ **curtain**

curter adj ▷ **curt**

curtest adj ▷ **curt**

curtly adv ▷ **curt**

curtness n ▷ **curt**

curtnesses n ▷ **curt**

curtsey n ▷ **curtsy**

curtseyed v ▷ **curtsy**

curtseying v ▷ **curtsy**

curtseys v, n ▷ **curtsy**

curtsied v ▷ **curtsy**

curtsies n, v ▷ **curtsy**

curtsy, curtsey n (pl -sies, -seys) woman's gesture of respect made by bending the knees and bowing the head ▶ v (-sies, -seys, -sying or -sied, or -seying, -seyed) make a curtsy

curtsying v ▷ **curtsy**

curve n (pl -s) continuously bending line with no straight parts ▶ v (-ves, -ving, -ved) form or move in a curve

> **curvy** adj (-vier, -viest)
curved v ▷ curve
curves n, v ▷ curve
curvier adj ▷ curve
curviest adj ▷ curve
curving v ▷ curve
curvy adj ▷ curve
cuscus n (pl -ses) large Australian nocturnal possum
cuscuses n ▷ cuscus
cushier adj ▷ cushy
cushiest adj ▷ cushy
cushion n (pl -s) bag filled with soft material, to make a seat more comfortable ▶ v (-s, -ing, -ed) lessen the effects of
cushioned v ▷ cushion
cushioning v ▷ cushion
cushions n, v ▷ cushion
cushy adj (-shier, -shiest) informal easy
cusp n (pl -s) pointed end, esp. on a tooth
cusps n ▷ cusp
cuss informal n (pl -es) curse, oath ▶ v (-es, -ing, -ed) swear (at)
cussed adj informal obstinate ▶ v ▷ cuss **cussedly** adv ▷ **cussedness** n (pl -es)
cussedly adv ▷ cussed
cussedness n ▷ cussed
cussednesses n ▷ cussed
cusses n, v ▷ cuss
cussing v ▷ cuss
custard n (pl -s) sweet yellow sauce made from milk and eggs
custards n ▷ custard
custodial adj ▷ custody
custodies n ▷ custody
custody n (pl -dies) protective care
> **custodial** adj
custom n (pl -s) long-established activity or action ▶ pl duty charged on imports or exports
customer n (pl s) person who buys goods or services
customers n ▷ customer
customs n ▷ custom

cut v (-s, -tting, cut) open up, penetrate, wound, or divide with a sharp instrument ▶ n (pl -s) stroke or incision made by cutting
cute adj (-r, -st) appealing or attractive
> **cutely** adv > **cuteness** n (pl -es)
cutely adv ▷ cute
cuteness n ▷ cute
cutenesses n ▷ cute
cuter adj ▷ cute
cutest adj ▷ cute
cuticle n (pl -s) skin at the base of a fingernail or toenail
cuticles n ▷ cuticle
cutlass n (pl -es) curved one-edged sword formerly used by sailors
cutlasses n ▷ cutlass
cutler n (pl -s) maker of cutlery
cutlers n ▷ cutler
cutlery n knives, forks, and spoons
cutlet n (pl -s) small piece of meat like a chop
cutlets n ▷ cutlet
cuts v, n ▷ cut
cutter n (pl -s) person or tool that cuts
cutters n ▷ cutter
cutting n (pl -s) article cut from a newspaper or magazine ▶ adj (of a remark) hurtful ▶ v ▷ cut
> **cuttingly** adv
cuttingly adv ▷ cutting
cuttings n ▷ cutting
cyanide n (pl -s) extremely poisonous chemical compound
cyanides n ▷ cyanide
cyclamen n (pl -s) plant with red, pink, or white flowers
cyclamens n ▷ cyclamen
cycle v (-les, -ling, -led) ride a bicycle ▶ n (pl -s) BRIT, AUST & NZ bicycle
cycled v ▷ cycle
cycles v, n ▷ cycle
cyclic adj ▷ cyclical
cyclical, cyclic adj occurring in cycles
> **cyclically** adv
cyclically adv ▷ cyclical
cycling v ▷ cycle
cyclist n (pl -s) person who rides a

bicycle
cyclists n ▷ **cyclist**
cyclone n (pl -s) violent wind moving round a central area
cyclones n ▷ **cyclone**
cygnet n (pl -s) young swan
cygnets n ▷ **cygnet**
cylinder n (pl -s) solid or hollow body with straight sides and circular ends > **cylindrical** adj
cylinders n ▷ **cylinder**
cylindrical adj ▷ **cylinder**
cymbal n (pl -s) percussion instrument consisting of a brass plate which is struck against another or hit with a stick
cymbals n ▷ **cymbal**
cynic n (pl -s) person who believes that people always act selfishly > **cynical** adj > **cynically** adv > **cynicism** n
cynical adj ▷ **cynic**
cynically adv ▷ **cynic**
cynicism n ▷ **cynic**
cynics n ▷ **cynic**
cynosure n (pl -s) centre of attention
cynosures n ▷ **cynosure**

cypher n (pl -s) ▷ **cipher**
cyphers n ▷ **cypher**
cypress n (pl -es) evergreen tree with dark green leaves
cypresses n ▷ **cypress**
cyst n (pl -s) (abnormal) sac in the body containing fluid or soft matter > **cystic** adj
cystic adj ▷ **cyst**
cystitis n inflammation of the bladder
cysts n ▷ **cyst**
cytological adj ▷ **cytology**
cytologically adv ▷ **cytology**
cytologies n ▷ **cytology**
cytologist n ▷ **cytology**
cytologists n ▷ **cytology**
cytology n (pl -logies) study of plant and animal cells > **cytological** adj > **cytologically** adv > **cytologist** n (pl -s)
czar n (pl -s) ▷ **tsar** > **czarism** n > **czarist** adj, n (pl -s)
czarism n ▷ **czar**
czarist n ▷ **czar**
czarists n ▷ **czar**
czars n ▷ **czar**

Dd

D only starts a handful of two-letter words, but it does form a two-letter word before every vowel except U. There are plenty of good three-letter words beginning with D, particularly those with a Y or W: **day**, **dye** and **dew** are worth 7 points each, for example.

da n (**das.**) A da is a Burmese knife. Da scores 3 points.

dab[1] v (**-s, -bbing, -bbed**) pat lightly ▸ n (pl **-s**) small amount of something soft or moist

dab[2] n (pl **-s**) small European flatfish with rough scales
  dabbed v ▷ **dab**[1]
  dabbing v ▷ **dab**[1]

dabble v (**-les, -ling, -led**) be involved in something superficially > **dabbler** n (pl **-s**)
  dabbled v ▷ **dabble**
  dabbler n ▷ **dabble**
  dabblers n ▷ **dabble**
  dabbles v ▷ **dabble**
  dabbling v ▷ **dabble**
  dabs n ▷ **dab**[1] [2] ▷ v[1]

dace n (pl **dace**) small European freshwater fish

dad n (pl **-s**) informal father
  daddies n ▷ **daddy**

daddy n (pl **-dies**) informal father

dado n (pl **-does, -dos**) lower part of an interior wall, below a rail, decorated differently from the upper part
  dadoes n ▷ **dado**
  dados n ▷ **dado**
  dads n ▷ **dad**

daffodil n (pl **-s**) yellow trumpet-shaped flower that blooms in spring
  daffodils n ▷ **daffodil**

daft adj (**-er, -est**) informal foolish or crazy > **daftness** n (pl **-es**)
  dafter adj ▷ **daft**
  daftest adj ▷ **daft**
  daftness n ▷ **daft**
  daftnesses n ▷ **daft**

dag NZ n (pl **-s**) dried dung on a sheep's rear ▸ v (**-s, -gging, -gged**) remove the dags from a sheep

dagga n (pl **-s**) S AFR informal cannabis
  daggas n ▷ **dagga**
  dagged v ▷ **dag**

dagger n (pl **-s**) short knifelike weapon with a pointed blade
  daggers n ▷ **dagger**
  daggier adj ▷ **daggy**
  daggiest adj ▷ **daggy**
  dagging v ▷ **dag**

daggy adj (**-gier, -ggiest**) NZ informal amusing
  dags n, v ▷ **dag**

dahlia n (pl **-s**) brightly coloured garden flower
  dahlias n ▷ **dahlia**
  dailies n ▷ **daily**

daily adj occurring every day or every weekday ▸ adv every day ▸ n (pl **-lies**) daily newspaper
  daintier adj ▷ **dainty**
  daintiest adj ▷ **dainty**
  daintily adv ▷ **dainty**

dainty adj (**-tier, -tiest**) delicate or elegant > **daintily** adv

daiquiri n (pl **-s**) iced drink containing

rum, lime juice, and sugar
daiquiris n ▷ **daiquiri**
dairies n ▷ **dairy**
dairy n (pl **-ies**) place for the processing or sale of milk and its products ▶ adj of milk or its products
dais n (pl **-es**) raised platform in a hall, used by a speaker
daises n ▷ **dais**
daisies n ▷ **daisy**
daisy n (pl **-sies**) small wild flower with a yellow centre and white petals

| **dak** n (**daks**.) A dak is an old Indian mail or transport system. This is a good word to know if you have a K on your rack but can't think of a longer word in which to use it. Dak scores 8 points.

dale n (pl **-s**) (esp. in N England) valley
dales n ▷ **dale**
dallied v ▷ **dally**
dallies v ▷ **dally**
dally v (**-lies, -lying, -lied**) waste time
dallying v ▷ **dally**
dam[1] n (pl **-s**) barrier built across a river to create a lake ▶ v (**-s, -mming, -mmed**) build a dam across (a river)
dam[2] n (pl **-s**) mother of an animal such as a sheep or horse
damage v (**-ges, -ging, -ged**) harm, spoil ▶ n (pl **-s**) harm to a person or thing ▶ pl money awarded as compensation for injury or loss
damaged v ▷ **damage**
damages v, n ▷ **damage**
damaging v ▷ **damage**
damask n (pl **-s**) fabric with a pattern woven into it, used for tablecloths etc
damasks n ▷ **damask**
dame n (pl **-s**) CHIEFLY US & CANADIAN slang woman
dames n ▷ **dame**
dammed v ▷ **dam**[1]
damming v ▷ **dam**[1]
damn interj slang exclamation of annoyance ▶ adv, adj (also **damned**) slang extreme(ly) ▶ v (**-s, -ing, -ed**) condemn as bad or worthless

> **damnation** interj, n (pl **-s**)
damnable adj annoying
> **damnably** adv
damnably adv ▷ **damnable**
damnation interj, n ▷ **damn**
damnations n ▷ **damn**
damned v ▷ **damn**
damning adj proving or suggesting guilt ▶ v ▷ **damn**
damns v ▷ **damn**
damp adj (**-er, -est**) slightly wet ▶ n (pl **-s**) slight wetness, moisture ▶ v (**-s, -ing, -ed**) (also **dampen**) (**-s, -ing, -ed**) make damp (foll. by down)
> **damply** adv **dampness** n
damped v ▷ **damp**
dampen v ▷ **dampen**
dampened v ▷ **dampen**
dampening v ▷ **dampen**
dampens v ▷ **dampen**
damper n (pl **-s**) movable plate to regulate the draught in a fire ▶ adj ▷ **damp**
dampers n ▷ **damper**
dampest adj ▷ **damp**
damping v ▷ **damp**
damply adv ▷ **damp**
dampness n ▷ **damp**
damps v, n ▷ **damp**
damsel n (pl **-s**) old-fashioned young woman
damsels n ▷ **damsel**
damson n (pl **-s**) small blue-black plumlike fruit
damsons n ▷ **damson**
dance v (**-ces, -cing, -ced**) move the feet and body rhythmically in time to music ▶ n (pl **-s**) series of steps and movements in time to music
> **dancer** n (pl **-s**)
danced v ▷ **dance**
dancer n ▷ **dance**
dancers n ▷ **dance**
dances v, n ▷ **dance**
dancing v ▷ **dance**
dander n (pl **-s**) slang anger
danders n ▷ **dander**

dandier adj ▷ **dandy**
dandies n ▷ **dandy**
dandiest adj ▷ **dandy**
dandified adj ▷ **dandy**
dandle v (**-dles, -dling, -dled**) move (a child) up and down on one's knee
dandled v ▷ **dandle**
dandles v ▷ **dandle**
dandling v ▷ **dandle**
dandruff n (pl **-s**) loose scales of dry dead skin shed from the scalp
dandruffs n ▷ **dandruff**
dandy n (pl **-dies**) man who is overconcerned with the elegance of his appearance ▶ adj (**-dier, -diest**) informal very good ▷ **dandified** adj
danger n (pl **-s**) possibility of being injured or killed ▷ **dangerous** adj ▷ **dangerously** adv
dangerous adj ▷ **danger**
dangerously adv ▷ **danger**
dangers n ▷ **danger**
dangle v (**-gles, -gling, -gled**) hang loosely
dangled v ▷ **dangle**
dangles v ▷ **dangle**
dangling v ▷ **dangle**
dank adj (**-er, -est**) unpleasantly damp and chilly ▷ **dankly** adv ▷ **dankness** n (pl **-es**)
danker adj ▷ **dank**
dankest adj ▷ **dank**
dankly adv ▷ **dank**
dankness n ▷ **dank**
danknesses n ▷ **dank**
dapper adj (**-er, -est**) (of a man) neat in appearance ▷ **dapperly** adv ▷ **dapperness** n (pl **-es**)
dapperer adj ▷ **dapper**
dapperest adj ▷ **dapper**
dapperly adv ▷ **dapper**
dapperness n ▷ **dapper**
dappernesses n ▷ **dapper**
dappled adj marked with spots of a different colour
dare v (**-res, -ring, -red**) be courageous enough to try (to do something) ▶ n (pl **-s**) challenge to do something risky

dared v ▷ **dare**
dares v, n ▷ **dare**
daring adj willing to take risks ▶ n courage to do dangerous things ▶ v ▷ **dare** ▷ **daringly** adv
daringly adv ▷ **daring**
dark adj (**-er, -est**) having little or no light ▶ n (pl **-s**) absence of light ▷ **darkly** adv ▷ **darkness** n (pl **-es**) ▷ **darken** v (**-s, -ing, -ed**)
darken v ▷ **dark**
darkened v ▷ **dark**
darkening v ▷ **dark**
darkens v ▷ **dark**
darker adj ▷ **dark**
darkest adj ▷ **dark**
darkly adv ▷ **dark**
darkness n ▷ **dark**
darknesses n ▷ **dark**
darkroom n (pl **-s**) darkened room for processing photographic film
darkrooms n ▷ **darkroom**
darks n ▷ **dark**
darling n (pl **-s**) much-loved person ▶ adj much-loved
darlings n ▷ **darling**
darn¹ v (**-s, -ing, -ed**) mend (a garment) with a series of interwoven stitches ▶ n (pl **-s**) patch of darned work
darn² interj, adv adj, v (**-s, -ing, -ed**) euphemistic damn
darned v ▷ **darn**¹, ²
darning v ▷ **darn**¹, ²
darns v ▷ **darn**¹, ² n ▷ **darn**¹
dart n (pl **-s**) small narrow pointed missile that is thrown or shot, esp. in the game of darts ▶ pl game in which darts are thrown at a circular numbered board ▶ v (**-s, -ing, -ed**) move or direct quickly and suddenly
darted v ▷ **dart**
darting v ▷ **dart**
darts n, v ▷ **dart**
dash v (**-es, -ing, -ed**) move quickly ▶ n (pl **-es**) sudden quick movement
dashed v ▷ **dash**
dashes v, n ▷ **dash**
dashing adj stylish and attractive ▶ v

▷ **dash** > **dashingly** adv

dashingly adv ▷ **dashing**

dassie n (pl -s) S AFR type of hoofed rodent-like animal (also **hyrax**)

dassies n ▷ **dassie**

dasyure n (pl -s) small marsupial of Australia, New Guinea, and adjacent islands

dasyures n ▷ **dasyure**

data pl n (sing **datum**) information consisting of observations, measurements, or facts

date¹ n (pl -s) specified day of the month ▶ v (-tes, -ting, -ted) mark with the date

date² n (pl -s) dark-brown sweet-tasting fruit of the date palm

dated adj old-fashioned v ▷ **date**¹

dates n ▷ **date**¹, ² v ▷ **date**¹

dating v ▷ **date**¹

dative n (pl -s) (in certain languages) the form of the noun that expresses the indirect object

datives n ▷ **dative**

datum n (pl **data**) single piece of information in the form of a fact or statistic

daub v (-s, -ing, -ed) smear or spread quickly or clumsily

daubed v ▷ **daub**

daubing v ▷ **daub**

daubs v ▷ **daub**

daughter n (pl -s) female child
> **daughterly** adj

daughterly adj ▷ **daughter**

daughters n ▷ **daughter**

daunting adj intimidating or worrying ▷ **dauntingly** adv

dauntingly adv ▷ **daunting**

dauphin n (pl -s) (formerly) eldest son of the king of France

dauphins n ▷ **dauphin**

davit n (pl -s) crane, usu. one of a pair, at a ship's side, for lowering and hoisting a lifeboat

davits n ▷ **davit**

| **daw** n (**daws**). A daw is another name for a **jackdaw**. Daw scores 7 points.

dawdle v (-dles, -dling, -dled) walk slowly, lag behind

dawdled v ▷ **dawdle**

dawdles v ▷ **dawdle**

dawdling v ▷ **dawdle**

dawn n (pl -s) daybreak ▶ v (-s, -ing, -ed) begin to grow light

dawned v ▷ **dawn**

dawning v ▷ **dawn**

dawns n, v ▷ **dawn**

day n (pl -s) period of 24 hours

daybreak n time in the morning when light first appears

daydream n (pl -s) pleasant fantasy indulged in while awake ▶ v (-s, -ing, -ed) indulge in idle fantasy
> **daydreamer** n (pl -s)

daydreamed v ▷ **daydream**

daydreamer n ▷ **daydream**

daydreamers n ▷ **daydream**

daydreaming v ▷ **daydream**

daydreams n, v ▷ **daydream**

daylight n (pl -s) light from the sun

daylights n ▷ **daylight**

days n ▷ **day**

daze v (-zes, -zing, -zed) stun, by a blow or shock ▶ n (pl -s) state of confusion or shock

dazed v ▷ **daze**

dazes v, n ▷ **daze**

dazing v ▷ **daze**

dazzle v (-les, -ling, -led) impress greatly ▶ n (pl -s) bright light that dazzles > **dazzling** adj > **dazzlingly** adv

dazzled v ▷ **dazzle**

dazzles v, n ▷ **dazzle**

dazzling v, adj ▷ **dazzle**

dazzlingly adv ▷ **dazzle**

| **de** prep. De means of or from. This is a useful little word to fit in when trying to form several words at once. De scores 3 points.

deacon n (pl -s) CHRISTIANITY ordained minister ranking immediately below a priest

deacons n ▷ **deacon**

dead adj (-er, -est) no longer alive ▶ n (pl -s) period during which coldness or darkness is most intense ▶ *adv* extremely

deadbeat *n* (*pl* -s) *informal* lazy useless person
> **deadbeats** *n* ▷ **deadbeat**

deaden *v* (-s, -ing, -ed) make less intense
> **deadened** *v* ▷ **deaden**
> **deadening** *v* ▷ **deaden**
> **deadens** *v* ▷ **deaden**
> **deader** *adj* ▷ **dead**
> **deadest** *adj* ▷ **dead**
> **deadlier** *adj* ▷ **deadly**
> **deadliest** *adj* ▷ **deadly**

deadline *n* (*pl* -s) time limit
> **deadlines** *n* ▷ **deadline**
> **deadliness** *n* ▷ **deadly**
> **deadlinesses** *n* ▷ **deadly**

deadlock *n* (*pl* -s) point in a dispute at which no agreement can be reached
> **deadlocked** *adj*
> **deadlocked** *adj* ▷ **deadlock**
> **deadlocks** *n* ▷ **deadlock**

deadly *adj* (-lier, -liest) likely to cause death ▶ *adv* extremely > **deadliness** *n* (*pl* -es)

deadpan *adj*, *adv* showing no emotion or expression
> **deads** *n* ▷ **dead**

deaf *adj* (-er, -est) unable to hear
> **deafness** *n* (*pl* -es)

deafen *v* (-s, -ing, -ed) make deaf, esp. temporarily
> **deafened** *v* ▷ **deafen**
> **deafening** *v* ▷ **deafen**
> **deafens** *v* ▷ **deafen**
> **deafer** *adj* ▷ **deaf**
> **deafest** *adj* ▷ **deaf**
> **deafness** *n* ▷ **deaf**
> **deafnesses** *n* ▷ **deaf**

deal[1] *n* (*pl* -s) agreement or transaction ▶ *v* (-s, -ling, dealt) inflict (a blow) on
> **dealer** *n* ▷ **deal**[1]

deal[2] *n* (*pl* -s) plank of fir or pine wood
> **dealer** *n* ▷ **deal**[1]
> **dealers** *n* ▷ **deal**[1]
> **dealing** *v* ▷ **deal**[1]

dealings *pl n* transactions or business relations

deals *v* ▷ **deal**[1] ▶ *n* ▷ **deal**[1, 2]
> **dealt** *v* ▷ **deal**[1]

dean *n* (*pl* -s) chief administrative official of a college or university faculty
> **deaneries** *n* ▷ **deanery**

deanery *n* (*pl* -eries) office or residence of a dean
> **deans** *n* ▷ **dean**

dear *n* (*pl* -s) someone regarded with affection ▶ *adj* (-er, -est) much-loved ▶ *dearly adv* > **dearness** *n* (*pl* -es)
> **dearer** *adj* ▷ **dear**
> **dearest** *adj* ▷ **dear**
> **dearly** *adv* ▷ **dear**
> **dearness** *n* ▷ **dear**
> **dearnesses** *n* ▷ **dear**
> **dears** *n* ▷ **dear**

dearth *n* (*pl* -s) inadequate amount, scarcity
> **dearths** *n* ▷ **dearth**

death *n* (*pl* -s) permanent end of life in a person or animal

deathly *adj*, *adv* like death
> **deaths** *n* ▷ **death**

deb *n* (*pl* -s) *informal* debutante

debacle *n* (*pl* -s) disastrous failure
> **debacles** *n* ▷ **debacle**

debar *v* (-bars, -barring, -barred) prevent, bar
> **debarred** *v* ▷ **debar**
> **debarring** *v* ▷ **debar**
> **debars** *v* ▷ **debar**

debase *v* (-ses, -sing, -sed) lower in value, quality, or character
> **debasement** *n* (*pl* -s)
> **debased** *v* ▷ **debase**
> **debasement** *n* ▷ **debase**
> **debasements** *n* ▷ **debase**
> **debases** *v* ▷ **debase**
> **debasing** *v* ▷ **debase**

debate *n* (*pl* -s) discussion ▶ *v* (-tes, -ting, -ted) discuss formally
> **debated** *v* ▷ **debate**
> **debates** *n*, *v* ▷ **debate**
> **debating** *v* ▷ **debate**

debauch *v* (-es, -ing, -ed) make (someone) bad or corrupt, esp. sexually

> **debauchery** n (pl **-eries**)
debauched v ▷ debauch
debaucheries n ▷ debauch
debauchery n ▷ debauch
debauches v ▷ debauch
debauching v ▷ debauch
debilities n ▷ debility

debility n (pl **-ities**) weakness, infirmity
debit n (pl **-s**) acknowledgment of a sum owing by entry on the left side of an account ▶ v (**-s**, **-ing**, **-ed**) charge (an account) with a debt
debited v ▷ debit
debiting v ▷ debit
debits n, v ▷ debit

debonair adj (of a man) charming and refined

debouch v (**-es**, **-ing**, **-ed**) move out from a narrow place to a wider one
debouched v ▷ debouch
debouches v ▷ debouch
debouching v ▷ debouch

debris n fragments of something destroyed
debs n ▷ deb

debt n (pl **-s**) something owed, esp. money > **debtor** n (pl **-s**)
debtor n ▷ debt
debtors n ▷ debt
debts n ▷ debt

debunk v (**-s**, **-ing**, **-ed**) informal expose the falseness of
debunked v ▷ debunk
debunking v ▷ debunk
debunks v ▷ debunk

debut n (pl **-s**) first public appearance of a performer
debuts n ▷ debut

decade n (pl **-s**) period of ten years
decades n ▷ decade

decagon n (pl **-s**) geometric figure with ten faces > **decagonal** adj
decagonal adj ▷ decagon
decagons n ▷ decagon

decamp v (**-s**, **-ing**, **-ed**) depart secretly or suddenly
decamped v ▷ decamp
decamping v ▷ decamp
decamps v ▷ decamp

decant v (**-s**, **-ing**, **-ed**) pour (a liquid) from one container to another
decanted v ▷ decant
decanting v ▷ decant
decants v ▷ decant

decanter n (pl **-s**) stoppered bottle for wine or spirits
decanters n ▷ decanter
decanting v ▷ decant
decants v ▷ decant

decay v (**-s**, **-ing**, **-ed**) become weaker or more corrupt ▶ n (pl **-s**) process of decaying
decayed v ▷ decay
decaying v ▷ decay
decays v, n ▷ decay

decease n (pl **-s**) formal death
deceased adj formal dead
deceases n ▷ decease

deceit n (pl **-s**) behaviour intended to deceive > **deceitful** adj
> **deceitfully** adv
deceitful adj ▷ deceit
deceitfully adv ▷ deceit
deceits n ▷ deceit

deceive v (**-ves**, **-ving**, **-ved**) mislead by lying > **deceiver** n (pl **-s**)
deceived v ▷ deceive
deceiver n ▷ deceive
deceivers n ▷ deceive
deceives v ▷ deceive
deceiving v ▷ deceive
decencies n ▷ decency
decency n ▷ decent

decent adj (**-er**, **-est**) (of a person) polite and morally acceptable
> **decently** adv > **decency** n (pl **-cies**)
decenter adj ▷ decent
decentest adj ▷ decent
decently adv ▷ decent

decibel n (pl **-s**) unit for measuring the intensity of sound

decibels n ▷ decibel
decide v (-cides, -ciding, -cided) (cause to) reach a decision
decided adj unmistakable ▶ v
  ▷ decide > decidedly adv
  decidedly adv ▷ decided
  decides v ▷ decide
  deciding v ▷ decide
decimal n (pl -s) fraction written in the form of a dot followed by one or more numbers ▶ adj relating to or using powers of ten > **decimalization** n (pl -s)
  > decimally adv
  decimalization n ▷ decimal
  decimalizations n ▷ decimal
  decimally adv ▷ decimal
  decimals n ▷ decimal
decimate v (-tes, -ting, -ted) destroy or kill a large proportion of > decimation n (pl -s)
  decimated v ▷ decimate
  decimates v ▷ decimate
  decimating v ▷ decimate
  decimation n ▷ decimate
  decimations n ▷ decimate
decipher v (-s, -ing, -ed) work out the meaning of (something illegible or in code) > decipherable adj
  decipherable adj ▷ decipher
  deciphered v ▷ decipher
  deciphering v ▷ decipher
  deciphers v ▷ decipher
decision n (pl -s) judgment, conclusion, or resolution
  decisions n ▷ decision
decisive adj having a definite influence > decisively adv
  > decisiveness n (pl -es)
  decisively adv ▷ decisive
  decisiveness n ▷ decisive
  decisivenesses n ▷ decisive
deck n (pl -s) area of a ship that forms a floor
decking n wooden platform in a garden
  decks n ▷ deck
declaim v (-s, -ing, -ed) speak loudly and dramatically > declamation n (pl -s) > declamatory adj

declaimed v ▷ declaim
declaiming v ▷ declaim
declaims v ▷ declaim
declamation n ▷ declaim
declamations n ▷ declaim
declamatory adj ▷ declaim
declaration n ▷ declare
declarations n ▷ declare
declaratory adj ▷ declare
declare v (-res, -ring, -red) state firmly and forcefully > declaration n (pl -s) > declaratory adj
  declared v ▷ declare
  declares v ▷ declare
  declaring v ▷ declare
decline v (-nes, -ning, -ned) become smaller, weaker, or less important ▶ n (pl -s) gradual weakening or loss
  declined v ▷ decline
  declines v, n ▷ decline
  declining v ▷ decline
declutch v (-es, -ing, -ed) disengage the clutch of a motor vehicle
  declutched v ▷ declutch
  declutches v ▷ declutch
  declutching v ▷ declutch
decoct v (-s, -ing, -ed) extract the essence from (a substance) by boiling > decoction n (pl -s)
  decocted v ▷ decoct
  decocting v ▷ decoct
  decoction n ▷ decoct
  decoctions n ▷ decoct
  decocts v ▷ decoct
decode v (-des, -ding, -ded) convert from code into ordinary language > decoder n (pl -s)
  decoded v ▷ decode
  decoder n ▷ decode
  decoders n ▷ decode
  decodes v ▷ decode
  decoding v ▷ decode
decor n (pl -s) style in which a room or house is decorated
decorate v (-tes, -ting, -ted) make more attractive by adding something ornamental > decoration n (pl -s) > decorative adj > decorator n (pl -s)

decorated v ▷ decorate

decorates v ▷ decorate

decorating v ▷ decorate

decoration n ▷ decorate

decorations n ▷ decorate

decorator n ▷ decorate

decorators n ▷ decorate

decorous adj polite, calm, and sensible in behaviour > **decorously** adv > **decorousness** n (pl -es)

decorously adv ▷ decorous

decorousness n ▷ decorous

decorousnesses n ▷ decorous

decors n ▷ decor

decorum n (pl -s) polite and socially correct behaviour

decorums n ▷ decorum

decoy n (pl -s) person or thing used to lure someone into danger ▶ v (-s, -ing, -ed) lure away by means of a trick

decoyed v ▷ decoy

decoying v ▷ decoy

decoys n, v ▷ decoy

decrease v (-creases, -creasing, -creased) make or become less ▶ n (pl -s) lessening, reduction

decreased v ▷ decrease

decreases v, n ▷ decrease

decreasing v ▷ decrease

decree n (pl -s) law made by someone in authority ▶ v (-s, -ing, -creed) order by decree

decreed v ▷ decree

decreeing v ▷ decree

decrees n, v ▷ decree

decrepit adj weakened or worn out by age or long use > **decrepitude** n (pl -s)

decrepitude n ▷ decrepit

decrepitudes n ▷ decrepit

decried v ▷ decry

decries v ▷ decry

decry v (-cries, -crying, -cried) express disapproval of

decrying v ▷ decry

dedicate v (-tes, -ting, -ted) commit (oneself or one's time) wholly to a special purpose or cause > **dedication** n (pl -s)

dedicates v ▷ dedicate

dedicating v ▷ dedicate

dedication n ▷ dedicate

dedications n ▷ dedicate

deduce v (-ces, -cing, -ced) reach (a conclusion) by reasoning from evidence > **deducible** adj

deduced v ▷ deduce

deduces v ▷ deduce

deducible adj ▷ deduce

deducing v ▷ deduce

deduct v (-s, -ing, -ed) subtract

deducted v ▷ deduct

deducting v ▷ deduct

deducts v ▷ deduct

deed n (pl -s) something that is done

deeds n ▷ deed

deem v (-s, -ing, -ed) consider, judge

deemed v ▷ deem

deeming v ▷ deem

deems v ▷ deem

deep adj (-er, -est) extending or situated far down, inwards, backwards, or sideways ▶ **deepen** v (-s, -ing, -ed)

deepen v ▷ deep

deepened v ▷ deep

deepening v ▷ deep

deepens v ▷ deep

deeper adj ▷ deep

deepest adj ▷ deep

deepfreeze n (pl -s) ▷ freezer

deeply adv profoundly or intensely

deer n (pl deer) large wild animal, the male of which has antlers

deface v (-ces, -cing, -ced) deliberately spoil the appearance of > **defacement** n (pl -s)

defaced v ▷ deface

defacement n ▷ deface

defacements n ▷ deface

defaces v ▷ deface

defacing v ▷ deface

defamation n ▷ defame

defamations n ▷ defame

defamatory adj ▷ defame

defame v (-mes, -ming, -med) attack the good reputation of > **defamation** n

(pl -s) > defamatory adj
defamed v ▷ defame
defames v ▷ defame
defaming v ▷ defame
default n (pl -s) failure to do something ▶ v (-s, -ing, -ed) fail to fulfil an obligation > **defaulter** n (pl -s)
defaulted v ▷ default
defaulter n ▷ default
defaulters n ▷ default
defaulting v ▷ default
defaults n, v ▷ default
defeat v (-s, -ing, -ed) win a victory over ▶ n (pl -s) defeating
defeated v ▷ defeat
defeating v ▷ defeat
defeats v ▷ defeat
defecate v (-tes, -ting, -ted) discharge waste from the body through the anus > **defecation** n (pl -s)
defecated v ▷ defecate
defecates v ▷ defecate
defecating v ▷ defecate
defecation n ▷ defecate
defecations n ▷ defecate
defect n (pl -s) imperfection, blemish ▶ v (-s, -ing, -ed) desert one's cause or country to join the opposing forces > **defection** n (pl -s) > **defector** n (pl -s)
defected v ▷ defect
defecting v ▷ defect
defection n ▷ defect
defections n ▷ defect
defector n ▷ defect
defectors n ▷ defect
defects n, v ▷ defect
defence n (pl -s) resistance against attack > **defenceless** adj
defenceless adj ▷ defence
defences n ▷ defence
defend v (-s, -ing, -ed) protect from harm or danger
defended v ▷ defend
defender n (pl -s) person who supports someone or something in the face of criticism
defenders n ▷ defender
defending v ▷ defend

defends v ▷ defend
defer[1] v (-s, -rring, -rred) delay (something) until a future time > **deferment, deferral** n (pl -s)
defer[2] v (-s, -rring, -rred) (foll. by to) comply with the wishes (of)
deferment n ▷ defer[1]
deferments n ▷ defer[1]
deferral n ▷ defer[1]
deferrals n ▷ defer[1]
deferred v ▷ defer[1, 2]
deferring v ▷ defer[1, 2]
defers v ▷ defer[1, 2]
defiance n ▷ defy
defiances n ▷ defy
defiant adj ▷ defy
defiantly adv ▷ defy
deficit n (pl -s) amount by which a sum of money is too small
deficits n ▷ deficit
defied v ▷ defy
defies v ▷ defy
defile[1] v (-les, -ling, -led) treat (something sacred or important) without respect > **defilement** n (pl -s)
defile[2] n (pl -s) narrow valley or pass
defiled v ▷ defile[1]
defilement n ▷ defile[1]
defilements n ▷ defile[1]
defiles v ▷ defile[1] ▶ n ▷ defile[1, 2]
defiling v ▷ defile[1]
definable adj ▷ define
define v (-nes, -ning, -ned) state precisely the meaning of > **definable** adj
defined v ▷ define
defines v ▷ define
defining v ▷ define
definite adj firm, clear, and precise > **definitely** adv
definitely adv ▷ definite
deflate v (-tes, -ting, -ted) (cause to) collapse through the release of air
deflated v ▷ deflate
deflates v ▷ deflate
deflating v ▷ deflate
deflect v (-s, -ing, -ed) (cause to) turn aside from a course > **deflection** n (pl

-s) > **deflector** n (pl -s)

deflected v ▷ **deflect**

deflecting v ▷ **deflect**

deflection n ▷ **deflect**

deflections n ▷ **deflect**

deflector n ▷ **deflect**

deflectors n ▷ **deflect**

deflects v ▷ **deflect**

deflower v (-s, -ing, -d) lit deprive (a woman) of her virginity

deflowered v ▷ **deflower**

deflowering v ▷ **deflower**

deflowers v ▷ **deflower**

deform v (-s, -ing, -ed) put out of shape or spoil the appearance of > **deformation** n (pl -s) > **deformity** n (pl -ties)

deformation n ▷ **deform**

deformations n ▷ **deform**

deformed v ▷ **deform**

deforming v ▷ **deform**

deformities n ▷ **deform**

deformity n ▷ **deform**

deforms v ▷ **deform**

defraud v (-s, -ing, -ed) cheat out of money, property, etc

defrauded v ▷ **defraud**

defrauding v ▷ **defraud**

defrauds v ▷ **defraud**

defray v (-s, -ing, -ed) provide money for (costs or expenses)

defrayed v ▷ **defray**

defraying v ▷ **defray**

defrays v ▷ **defray**

defrock v (-s, -ing, -ed) deprive (a priest) of priestly status

defrocked v ▷ **defrock**

defrocking v ▷ **defrock**

defrocks v ▷ **defrock**

defrost v (-s, -ing, -ed) make or become free of ice

defrosted v ▷ **defrost**

defrosting v ▷ **defrost**

defrosts v ▷ **defrost**

deft adj quick and skilful in movement > **deftly** adv > **deftness** n (pl -es)

deftly adv ▷ **deft**

deftness n ▷ **deft**

deftnesses n ▷ **deft**

defunct adj no longer existing or operative

defuse v (-ses, -sing, -sed) remove the fuse of (an explosive device)

defused v ▷ **defuse**

defuses v ▷ **defuse**

defusing v ▷ **defuse**

defy v (-fies, -fying, -fied) resist openly and boldly > **defiance** n (pl -s) > **defiant** adj > **defiantly** adv

defying v ▷ **defy**

degradation n ▷ **degrade**

degradations n ▷ **degrade**

degrade v (-des, -ding, -ded) reduce to dishonour or disgrace CHEM > **degradation** n (pl -s)

degraded v ▷ **degrade**

degrades v ▷ **degrade**

degrading v ▷ **degrade**

degree n (pl -s) stage in a scale of relative amount or intensity

degrees n ▷ **degree**

deification n ▷ **deify**

deifications n ▷ **deify**

deified v ▷ **deify**

deifies v ▷ **deify**

deify v (-fies, -fying, -fied) treat or worship as a god > **deification** n (pl -s)

deifying v ▷ **deify**

deign v (-s, -ing, -ed) agree (to do something), but as if doing someone a favour

deigned v ▷ **deign**

deigning v ▷ **deign**

deigns v ▷ **deign**

deities n ▷ **deity**

deity n (pl -ties) god or goddess

dejected adj unhappy > **dejectedly** adv > **dejection** n (pl -s)

dejectedly adv ▷ **dejected**

dejection n ▷ **dejected**

dejections n ▷ **dejected**

dekko n (pl -s) BRIT, AUST & NZ slang look

dekkos n ▷ **dekko**

delay v (-s, -ing, -ed) put off to a later time ▶ n (pl -s) act of delaying

delayed v ▷ **delay**

delaying v ▷ delay

delays v, n ▷ delay

delegate n (pl -s) person chosen to represent others, esp. at a meeting ▶ v (-tes, -ting, -ted) entrust (duties or powers) to someone

delegated v ▷ delegate

delegates n, v ▷ delegate

delegating v ▷ delegate

delete v (-tes, -ting, -ted) remove (something written or printed) > **deletion** n (pl -s)

deleted v ▷ delete

deletes v ▷ delete

deleting v ▷ delete

deletion n ▷ delete

deletions n ▷ delete

delicacies n ▷ delicacy

delicacy n (pl -cies) being delicate

delicate adj fine or subtle in quality or workmanship > **delicately** adv

delicately adv ▷ delicate

delight n (pl -s) (source of) great pleasure ▶ v (-s, -ing, -ed) please greatly > **delightful** adj > **delightfully** adv

delighted v ▷ delight

delightful adj ▷ delight

delightfully adv ▷ delight

delighting v ▷ delight

delights n, v ▷ delight

delimit v (-s, -ing, -ed) mark or lay down the limits of > **delimitation** n (pl -s)

delimitation n ▷ delimit

delimitations n ▷ delimit

delimited v ▷ delimit

delimiting v ▷ delimit

delimits v ▷ delimit

delirious adj ▷ delirium

deliriously adv ▷ delirium

delirium n (pl -s) state of excitement and mental confusion, often with hallucinations ▶ **delirious** adj > **deliriously** adv

deliriums n ▷ delirium

deliver v (-s, -ing, -ed) carry (goods etc) to a destination

delivered v ▷ deliver

deliveries n ▷ delivery

delivering v ▷ deliver

delivers v ▷ deliver

delivery n (pl -eries) delivering

dell n (pl -s) CHIEFLY BRIT small wooded hollow

dells n ▷ dell

delta n (pl -s) fourth letter in the Greek alphabet

deltas n ▷ delta

delude v (-des, -ding, -ded) deceive

deluded v ▷ delude

deludes v ▷ delude

deluding v ▷ delude

deluge n (pl -s) great flood ▶ v (-ges, -ging, -ged) flood

deluged v ▷ deluge

deluges n, v ▷ deluge

deluging v ▷ deluge

delusion n (pl -s) mistaken idea or belief ▶ **delusive** adj

delusions n ▷ delusion

delusive adj ▷ delusion

delve v (-ves, -ving, -ved) research deeply (for information)

delved v ▷ delve

delves v ▷ delve

delving v ▷ delve

demand v (-s, -ing, -ed) request forcefully ▶ n (pl -s) forceful request

demanded v ▷ demand

demands v, n ▷ demand

demean v (-s, -ing, -ed) do something unworthy of one's status or character

demeaned v ▷ demean

demeaning v ▷ demean

demeans v ▷ demean

demented adj mad > **dementedly** adv

dementedly adv ▷ demented

dementia n (pl -s) state of serious mental deterioration

dementias n ▷ dementia

demerit n (pl -s) fault, disadvantage

demerits n ▷ demerit

demesne n (pl -s) land surrounding a house

demesnes n ▷ demesne

demijohn n (pl -s) large bottle with a

short neck, often encased in wicker
demijohns n ▷ **demijohn**

demise n (pl -**s**) eventual failure (of
something successful)
demises n ▷ **demise**

demo n (pl -**s**) informal demonstration,
organized expression of public opinion

demob v (-**s**, -**bbing**, -**bbed**) BRIT, AUST
& NZ informal demobilize
demobbed v ▷ **demob**
demobbing v ▷ **demob**
demobs v ▷ **demob**

democrat n (pl -**s**) advocate of
democracy
democrats n ▷ **democrat**

demolish v (-**es**, -**ing**, -**ed**) knock
down or destroy (a building)
> **demolition** n (pl -**s**)
demolished v ▷ **demolish**
demolishes v ▷ **demolish**
demolishing v ▷ **demolish**
demolition n ▷ **demolish**
demolitions n ▷ **demolish**

demon n (pl -**s**) evil spirit
demoniac adj ▷ **demonic**
demoniacal adj ▷ **demonic**
demoniacally adv ▷ **demonic**

demonic adj evil > **demoniac**,
demoniacal adj appearing
to be possessed by a devil
> **demoniacally** adv
demons n ▷ **demon**
demos n ▷ **demo**

demote v (-**tes**, -**ting**, -**ted**) reduce in
status or rank > **demotion** n (pl -**s**)
demoted v ▷ **demote**
demotes v ▷ **demote**
demoting v ▷ **demote**
demotion n ▷ **demote**
demotions n ▷ **demote**

demur v (-**s**, -**rring**, -**rred**) show
reluctance

demure adj (-**r**, -**st**) quiet, reserved,
and rather shy > **demurely** adv
demurely adv ▷ **demure**
demurer adj ▷ **demure**
demurest adj ▷ **demure**
demurred v ▷ **demure**

demurring v ▷ **demur**
demurs v ▷ **demur**

den n (pl -**s**) home of a wild animal

denature v (-**res**, -**ring**, -**red**) change
the nature of
denatured v ▷ **denature**
denatures v ▷ **denature**
denaturing v ▷ **denature**

deniable adj ▷ **deny**
deniably adv ▷ **deny**

denial n (pl -**s**) statement that
something is not true
denials n ▷ **denial**
denied v ▷ **deny**

denier n (pl -**s**) unit of weight used to
measure the fineness of nylon or silk
deniers n ▷ **denier**
denies v ▷ **deny**

denim n (pl -**s**) hard-wearing cotton
fabric, usu. blue ▶ pl jeans made of
denim
denims n ▷ **denim**

denizen n (pl -**s**) inhabitant
denizens n ▷ **denizen**

denotation n ▷ **denote**
denotations n ▷ **denote**

denote v (-**tes**, -**ting**, -**ted**) be a sign of
> **denotation** n (pl -**s**)
denoted v ▷ **denote**
denotes v ▷ **denote**
denoting v ▷ **denote**

denounce v (-**ces**, -**cing**, -**ced**) speak
vehemently against
denounced v ▷ **denounce**
denounces v ▷ **denounce**
denouncing v ▷ **denounce**
dens n ▷ **den**

dense adj (-**r**, -**st**) closely packed
> **densely** adv
densely adv ▷ **dense**
denser adj ▷ **dense**
densest adj ▷ **dense**
densities n ▷ **density**

density n (pl -**ties**) degree to which
something is filled or occupied

dent n (pl -**s**) hollow in the surface of
something, made by hitting it ▶ v (-**s**,
-**ing**, -**ed**) make a dent in

dental adj of teeth or dentistry

dented v ▷ dent

dentine n (pl -s) hard dense tissue forming the bulk of a tooth

dentines n ▷ dentine

denting v ▷ dent

dentist n (pl -s) person qualified to practise dentistry

dentists n ▷ dentist

dents n, v ▷ dent

denture n (pl -s) false tooth

dentures n ▷ denture

denude v (-des, -ding, -ded) remove the covering or protection from

denuded v ▷ denude

denudes v ▷ denude

denuding v ▷ denude

deny v (-nies, -nying, -nied) declare to be untrue > **deniable** adj > **deniably** adv

denying v ▷ deny

depart v (-s, -ing, -ed) leave > **departed** n > **departure** n (pl -s)

departed adj euphemistic dead ▶ v ▷ depart

departing v ▷ depart

departs v ▷ depart

departure n ▷ depart

departures n ▷ depart

depend v (-s, -ing, -ed) (foll. by on) put trust (in) > **dependable** adj > **dependably** adv > **dependability** n (pl -ities)

dependabilities n ▷ depend

dependability n ▷ depend

dependable adj ▷ depend

dependably adv ▷ depend

depended v ▷ depend

depending v ▷ depend

depends v ▷ depend

depict v (-s, -ing, -ed) produce a picture of > **depiction** n (pl -s)

depicted v ▷ depict

depicting v ▷ depict

depiction n ▷ depict

depictions n ▷ depict

depicts v ▷ depict

deplete v (-tes, -ting, -ted) use up

> **depletion** n (pl -s)

depleted v ▷ deplete

depletes v ▷ deplete

depleting v ▷ deplete

depletion n ▷ deplete

depletions n ▷ deplete

deplore v (-res, -ring, -red) condemn strongly

deplored v ▷ deplore

deplores v ▷ deplore

deploring v ▷ deplore

deploy v (-s, -ing, -ed) organize (troops or resources) into a position ready for immediate action

> **deployment** n (pl -s)

deployed v ▷ deploy

deploying v ▷ deploy

deployment n ▷ deploy

deployments n ▷ deploy

deploys v ▷ deploy

deport v (-s, -ing, -ed) remove forcibly from a country > **deportation** n (pl -s)

> **deportee** n (pl -s)

deportation n ▷ deport

deportations n ▷ deport

deported v ▷ deport

deportee n ▷ deport

deportees n ▷ deport

deporting v ▷ deport

deports v ▷ deport

depose v (-ses, -sing, -sed) remove from an office or position of power

deposed v ▷ depose

deposes v ▷ depose

deposing v ▷ depose

deposit v (-s, -ing, -ed) put down ▶ n (pl -s) sum of money paid into a bank account > **depositor** n (pl -s)

deposited v ▷ deposit

depositing v ▷ deposit

depositor n ▷ deposit

depositories n ▷ deposit

depositors n ▷ deposit

deposits v, n ▷ deposit

depot n (pl -s) building where goods or vehicles are kept when not in use

depots n ▷ depot

depraved adj morally bad

>**depravity** n (pl -**ities**)
depravities n ▷ **depraved**
depravity n ▷ **depraved**
depress v (-**es**, -**ing**, -**ed**) make sad
>**depressing** adj ▷ **depressingly** adv
depressed v ▷ **depress**
depresses v ▷ **depress**
depressing v, adj ▷ **depress**
depressingly adv ▷ **depress**
deprivation n ▷ **deprive**
deprivations n ▷ **deprive**
deprive v (-**ves**, -**ving**, -**ved**) (foll. by
of) prevent from (having or enjoying)
>**deprivation** n (pl -**s**)
deprived adj lacking adequate
living conditions, education, etc ▶ v
▷ **deprive**
deprives v ▷ **deprive**
depriving v ▷ **deprive**
depth n (pl -**s**) distance downwards,
backwards, or inwards
depths n ▷ **depth**
depute v (-**tes**, -**ting**, -**ted**) appoint
(someone) to act on one's behalf
deputed v ▷ **depute**
deputes v ▷ **depute**
deputies n ▷ **deputy**
deputing v ▷ **depute**
deputize v (-**izes**, -**izing**, -**ized**) act
as deputy
deputized v ▷ **deputize**
deputizes v ▷ **deputize**
deputizing v ▷ **deputize**
deputy n (pl -**ties**) person appointed to
act on behalf of another
derail v (-**s**, -**ing**, -**ed**) cause (a train) to
go off the rails >**derailment** n (pl -**s**)
derailed v ▷ **derail**
derailing v ▷ **derail**
derailment n ▷ **derail**
derailments n ▷ **derail**
derails v ▷ **derail**
deranged adj insane or uncontrolled
>**derangement** n (pl -**s**)
derangement n ▷ **deranged**
derangements n ▷ **deranged**
derbies n ▷ **derby**
derby n (pl -**bies**) sporting event

between teams from the same area ▶ n
any of various horse races
derelict adj unused and falling into
ruins ▶ n (pl -**s**) social outcast, vagrant
derelicts n ▷ **derelict**
deride v (-**des**, -**ding**, -**ded**) treat with
contempt or ridicule >**derision** n (pl -**s**)
derided v ▷ **deride**
derides v ▷ **deride**
deriding v ▷ **deride**
derision n ▷ **deride**
derisions n ▷ **deride**
derisive adj mocking, scornful
>**derisively** adv >**derisiveness** n (pl -**es**)
derisively adv ▷ **derisive**
derisiveness n ▷ **derisive**
derisivenesses n ▷ **derisive**
derisory adj too small or inadequate
to be considered seriously
derivation n ▷ **derive**
derivations n ▷ **derive**
derive v (-**ves**, -**ving**, -**ved**) (foll.
by from) take or develop (from)
>**derivation** n (pl -**s**)
derived v ▷ **derive**
derives v ▷ **derive**
deriving v ▷ **derive**
derrick n (pl -**s**) simple crane
derricks n ▷ **derrick**
derv n (pl -**s**) BRIT diesel oil, when used
for road transport
dervish n (pl -**es**) member of a Muslim
religious order noted for a frenzied
whirling dance
dervishes n ▷ **dervish**
dervs n ▷ **derv**
descant n (pl -**s**) MUSIC tune played or
sung above a basic melody
descants n ▷ **descant**
descend v (-**s**, -**ing**, -**ed**) move down
(a slope etc)
descended v ▷ **descend**
descending v ▷ **descend**
descends v ▷ **descend**
descent n (pl -**s**) descending
descents n ▷ **descent**
describe v (-**bes**, -**bing**, -**bed**) give an
account of (something or someone)

in words
described v ▷ describe
describes v ▷ describe
describing v ▷ describe
descried v ▷ descry
descries v ▷ descry
descry v (**-cries, -crying, -cried**) catch sight of
descrying v ▷ descry
deselect v (**-s, -ing, -ed**) BRIT POLITICS refuse to select (an MP) for re-election > **deselection** n (pl **-s**)
deselected v ▷ deselect
deselecting v ▷ deselect
deselection n ▷ deselect
deselections n ▷ deselect
deselects v ▷ deselect
desert[1] n (pl **-s**) region with little or no vegetation because of low rainfall
desert[2] v (**-s, -ing, -ed**) abandon (a person or place) without intending to return > **deserter** n (pl **-s**) > **desertion** n (pl **-s**)
deserted v ▷ desert[2]
deserter n ▷ desert[2]
deserters n ▷ desert[2]
deserting v ▷ desert[2]
desertion n ▷ desert[2]
desertions n ▷ desert[2]
deserts n ▷ desert[1] ▶ pl n the punishment one deserves ▶ v ▷ desert[2]
deserve v (**-ves, -ving, -ved**) be entitled to or worthy of
deserved adj rightfully earned ▶ v ▷ deserve > **deservedly** adv
deservedly adv ▷ deserved
deserves v ▷ deserve
design v (**-s, -ing, -ed**) work out the structure or form of (something), by making a sketch or plans ▶ n (pl **-s**) preliminary drawing
designed v ▷ design
designer n (pl **-s**) person who draws up original sketches or plans from which things are made ▶ adj designed by a well-known designer
designers n ▷ designer
designs v, n ▷ design

desire v (**-sires, -siring, -sired**) want very much ▶ n (pl **-s**) wish, longing
desired v ▷ desire
desires v, n ▷ desire
desiring v ▷ desire
desist v (**-s, -ing, -ed**) (foll. by **from**) stop (doing something)
desisted v ▷ desist
desisting v ▷ desist
desists v ▷ desist
desk n (pl **-s**) piece of furniture with a writing surface and drawers
desks n ▷ desk
desktop adj (of a computer) small enough to use at a desk
desolate adj uninhabited and bleak ▶ v (**-lates, -lating, -lated**) deprive of inhabitants > **desolately** adv > **desolateness** n (pl **-es**)
desolateness n (pl **-es**)
desolation n (pl **-s**)
desolated v ▷ desolate
desolately adv ▷ desolate
desolateness n ▷ desolate
desolatenesses n ▷ desolate
desolates v ▷ desolate
desolating v ▷ desolate
desolation n ▷ desolate
desolations n ▷ desolate
despair n (pl **-s**) total loss of hope ▶ v (**-s, -ing, -ed**) lose hope > **despairingly** adv
despaired v ▷ despair
despairing v ▷ despair
despairingly adv ▷ despair
despairs n, v ▷ despair
despatch v (**-es, -ing, -ed**) ▶ n (pl **-es**) ▷ dispatch
despatched v ▷ despatch
despatches v, n ▷ despatch
despatching v ▷ despatch
despise v (**-ses, -sing, -sed**) regard with contempt
despised v ▷ despise
despises v ▷ despise
despising v ▷ despise
despite prep in spite of
despoil v (**-s, -ing, -ed**) formal plunder > **despoliation** n (pl **-s**)

despoiled v ▷ despoil

despoiling v ▷ despoil

despoils v ▷ despoil

despoliation n ▷ despoil

despoliations n ▷ despoil

despot n (pl -s) person in power who acts unfairly or cruelly > **despotic** adj > **despotically** adv

despotic adj ▷ despot

despotically adv ▷ despot

despots n ▷ despot

dessert n (pl -s) sweet course served at the end of a meal

desserts n ▷ dessert

destined adj certain to be or to do something

destinies n ▷ destiny

destiny n (pl -nies) future marked out for a person or thing

destroy v (-s, -ing, -ed) ruin, demolish

destroyed v ▷ destroy

destroying v ▷ destroy

destroys v ▷ destroy

detach v (-es, -ing, -ed) disengage and separate > **detachable** adj

detachable adj ▷ detach

detached adj BRIT, AUST & S AFR (of a house) not joined to another house ▶ v ▷ detach

detaches v ▷ detach

detaching v ▷ detach

detail n (pl -s) individual piece of information ▶ v (-s, -ing, -ed) list fully

detailed v ▷ detail

detailing v ▷ detail

details n, v ▷ detail

detain v (-s, -ing, -ed) delay (someone) > **detainee** n (pl -s)

detained v ▷ detain

detainee n ▷ detain

detainees n ▷ detain

detaining v ▷ detain

detains v ▷ detain

detect v (-s, -ing, -ed) notice > **detectable** adj > **detection** n (pl -s)

detectable adj ▷ detect

detected v ▷ detect

detecting v ▷ detect

detection n ▷ detect

detections n ▷ detect

detector n (pl -s) instrument used to find something

detectors n ▷ detector

detects v ▷ detect

detente n (pl -s) easing of tension between nations

detentes n ▷ detente

deter v (-ters, -terring, -terred) discourage (someone) from doing something by instilling fear or doubt

deterred v ▷ deter

deterring v ▷ deter

deters v ▷ deter

detest v (-s, -ing, -ed) dislike intensely > **detestable** adj > **detestably** adv > **detestation** n (pl -s)

detestable adj ▷ detest

detestably adv ▷ detest

detestation n ▷ detest

detestations n ▷ detest

detested v ▷ detest

detesting v ▷ detest

detests v ▷ detest

dethrone v (-nes, -ning, -ned) remove from a throne or position of power

dethroned v ▷ dethrone

dethrones v ▷ dethrone

dethroning v ▷ dethrone

detonate v (-tes, -ting, -ted) explode > **detonation** n (pl -s)

detonated v ▷ detonate

detonates v ▷ detonate

detonating v ▷ detonate

detonation n ▷ detonate

detonations n ▷ detonate

detour n (pl -s) route that is not the most direct one

detours n ▷ detour

detract v (-s, -ing, -ed) (foll. by from) make (something) seem less good > **detractor** n (pl -s)

detracted v ▷ detract

detracting v ▷ detract

detractor n ▷ detract

detractors n ▷ detract

detracts v ▷ detract

detrimental adj ▷ detract

detrimentally adv ▷ detract

detriments n ▷ detract

detritus n loose mass of stones and silt worn away from rocks

deuce n (pl -s) TENNIS score of forty all

deuces n ▷ deuce

> **deus** n (**di**). Deus is a Latin word for a god. Its plural, di, is a very handy word to know when trying to form several words at once. Di scores 3 points.

devaluation n ▷ devalue

devaluations n ▷ devalue

devalue v (-lues, -luing, -lued) reduce the exchange value of (a currency)
> **devaluation** n (pl -s)

devalued v ▷ devalue

devalues v ▷ devalue

devaluing v ▷ devalue

develop v (-s, -ing, -ed) grow or bring to a later, more elaborate, or more advanced stage > **development** n (pl -s)

developed v ▷ develop

developing v ▷ develop

development n ▷ develop

developments n ▷ develop

develops v ▷ develop

deviance n ▷ deviant

deviances n ▷ deviant

deviant n (pl -s), adj (person) deviating from what is considered acceptable behaviour > **deviance** n (pl -s)

deviants n ▷ deviant

deviate v (-tes, -ting, -ted) differ from others in belief or thought
> **deviation** n (pl -s)

deviated v ▷ deviate

deviates v ▷ deviate

deviating v ▷ deviate

deviation n ▷ deviate

deviations n ▷ deviate

device n (pl -s) machine or tool used for a specific task

devices n ▷ device

devil n (pl -s) evil spirit informal ▶ v (-ils, -illing, -illed) prepare (food) with a highly flavoured spiced mixture

devilish adj cruel or unpleasant ▶ adv (also **devilishly**) informal extremely

devilishly adv ▷ devilish

devilled v ▷ devil

devilling v ▷ devil

devilries n ▷ devilry

devilry n (pl -ries) mischievousness

devils n, v ▷ devil

devious adj insincere and dishonest
> **deviously** adv > **deviousness** n

deviously adv ▷ devious

deviousness n ▷ devious

devise v (-ses, -sing, -sed) work out (something) in one's mind

devised v ▷ devise

devises v ▷ devise

devising v ▷ devise

devoid adj (foll. by **of**) completely lacking (in)

devolve v (-ves, -ving, -ved) (foll. by **on** or **to**) pass (power or duties) or (of power or duties) be passed to a successor or substitute

devolved v ▷ devolve

devolves v ▷ devolve

devolving v ▷ devolve

devote v (-tes, -ting, -ted) apply or dedicate to a particular purpose

devoted adj showing loyalty or devotion ▶ v ▷ devote
> **devotedly** adv

devotedly adv ▷ devoted

devotee n (pl -s) person who is very enthusiastic about something

devotees n ▷ devotee

devotes v ▷ devote

devoting v ▷ devote

devotion n (pl -s) strong affection for or loyalty to someone or something ▶ pl prayers > **devotional** adj

devotional adj ▷ devotion

devotions adj ▷ devotion

devour v (-s, -ing, -ed) eat greedily

devoured v ▷ devour

devouring v ▷ devour

devours v ▷ devour

devout adj deeply religious
> **devoutly** adv > **devoutness** n (pl -es)

devoutly adv ▷ **devout**

devoutness n ▷ **devout**

devoutnesses n ▷ **devout**

dew n (pl -s) drops of water that form on the ground at night from vapour in the air ▷ **dewy** adj (-wier, -wiest)

dewier adj ▷ **dew**

dewiest adj ▷ **dew**

dewlap n (pl -s) loose fold of skin hanging under the throat in dogs, cattle, etc

dewlaps n ▷ **dewlap**

dews n ▷ **dew**

dewy adj ▷ **dew**

▐ **dex** n (**dexes**). Dex is a slang word for a kind of amphetamine. This is an easy way to pick up a some points after another player has used an X. Dex scores 11 points.

dextrose n (pl -s) glucose occurring in fruit, honey, and the blood of animals

dextroses n ▷ **dextrose**

▐ **dey** n (**deys**). A dey is an Ottoman governor. Dey scores 7 points.

diabetes n disorder in which an abnormal amount of urine containing an excess of sugar is excreted ▷ **diabetic** n (pl -s), adj

diabetic n, adj ▷ **diabetes**

diabetics n ▷ **diabetes**

diabolic adj of the Devil

diadem n (pl -s) old-fashioned crown

diadems n ▷ **diadem**

diagonal adj from corner to corner ▶ n (pl -s) diagonal line ▷ **diagonally** adv

diagonally adv ▷ **diagonal**

diagonals n ▷ **diagonal**

diagram n (pl -s) sketch showing the form or workings of something ▷ **diagrammatic** adj

diagrammatic adj ▷ **diagram**

diagrams n ▷ **diagram**

dial n (pl -s) face of a clock or watch ▶ v (-s, -lling, -lled) operate the dial or buttons on a telephone in order to contact (a number)

dialect n (pl -s) form of a language spoken in a particular area ▷ **dialectal** adj ▷ **dialectally** adv

dialectal adj ▷ **dialect**

dialectally adv ▷ **dialect**

dialects n ▷ **dialect**

dialled v ▷ **dial**

dialling v ▷ **dial**

dialogue n (pl -s) conversation between two people, esp. in a book, film, or play

dialogues n ▷ **dialogue**

dials n, v ▷ **dial**

dialyses n ▷ **dialysis**

dialysis n (pl -ses) MED filtering of blood through a membrane to remove waste products

diamanté adj decorated with artificial jewels or sequins

diameter n (pl -s) (length of) a straight line through the centre of a circle or sphere

diameters n ▷ **diameter**

diamond n (pl -s) exceptionally hard, usu. colourless, precious stone

diamonds n ▷ **diamond**

diaper n (pl -s) US nappy

diapers n ▷ **diaper**

diaries n ▷ **diary**

diarist n ▷ **diary**

diarists n ▷ **diary**

diary n (pl -ries) (book for) a record of daily events, appointments, or observations ▷ **diarist** n (pl -s)

diatribe n (pl -s) bitter critical attack

diatribes n ▷ **diatribe**

dibble n (pl -s) small hand tool used to make holes in the ground for seeds or plants

dibbles n ▷ **dibble**

dice n (pl **dice**) small cube each of whose sides has a different number of spots (1 to 6), used in games of chance ▶ v (-ces, -cing, -ced) cut (food) into small cubes

diced v ▷ **dice**

dices v ▷ **dice**

dicey adj (-cier, -ciest) informal dangerous or risky

dicier v ▷ **dicey**

diciest v ▷ **dicey**

dicing v ▷ dice
dickier adj ▷ dicky²
dickies n ▷ dicky¹
dickiest adj ▷ dicky²
dicky¹ n (pl -kies) false shirt front
dicky² adj (-kier, -kiest) informal
shaky or weak
dicta n ▷ dictum
dictate v (-tes, -ting, -ted) say aloud
for someone else to write down (foll. by
to) ▶ n (pl -s) authoritative command
>**dictation** n (pl -s)
dictated v ▷ dictate
dictates v, n ▷ dictate
dictating v ▷ dictate
dictation n ▷ dictate
dictations n ▷ dictate
dictator n (pl -s) ruler who has
complete power >**dictatorship** n (pl -s)
dictators n ▷ dictator
dictatorship n ▷ dictator
dictatorships n ▷ dictator
diction n (pl -s) manner of
pronouncing words and sounds
dictions n ▷ diction
dictum n (pl -tums, -ta) formal
statement
dictums n ▷ dictum
did v ▷ do
didactic adj intended to instruct
>**didactically** adv
didactically adv ▷ didactic
diddle v (-dles, -dling, -dled) informal
swindle
diddled v ▷ diddle
diddles v ▷ diddle
diddling v ▷ diddle
die¹ v (dies, dying, died) (of a person,
animal, or plant) cease all biological
activity permanently
die² n (pl -s) shaped block used to cut
or form metal
died v ▷ die¹
diehard n (pl -s) person who resists
change
diehards n ▷ diehard
diereses n ▷ dieresis
dies v ▷ die¹ ▶ n ▷ die²

diesel n (pl -s) diesel engine
diesels n ▷ diesel
diet¹ n (pl -s) food that a person or
animal regularly eats ▶ v (-s, -ing,
-ed) follow a special diet so as to lose
weight ▶ adj (of food) suitable for a
weight-reduction diet >**dietary** adj
>**dieter** n (pl -s)
diet² n (pl -s) parliament of some
countries
dietary adj ▷ diet
dieted v ▷ diet
dieter n ▷ diet
dieters n ▷ diet
dietetic adj prepared for special
dietary requirements
dieting v ▷ diet
diets v ▷ diet¹ ▶ n ▷ diet¹, ²
differ v (-s, -ing, -ed) be unlike
differed v ▷ differ
differing v ▷ differ
differs v ▷ differ
diffuse v (-ses, -sing, -sed) spread
over a wide area ▶ adj widely spread
>**diffusely** adv >**diffuseness** n
>**diffusion** n (pl -s)
diffused v ▷ diffuse
diffusely adv ▷ diffuse
diffuseness n ▷ diffuse
diffuses v ▷ diffuse
diffusing v ▷ diffuse
diffusion n ▷ diffuse
diffusions n ▷ diffuse
dig v (digs, digging, dug) cut into,
break up, and turn over or remove
(earth), esp. with a spade ▶ n (pl -s)
digging ▶ pl (pl -s) BRIT, AUST & S AFR
informal lodgings
digest v (-s, -ing, -ed) subject to
a process of digestion ▶ n (pl -s)
shortened version of book, report, or
article >**digestible** adj >**digestibility** n
(pl -ties) >**digestive** adj
>**digestively** adv
digested v ▷ digest
digestibilities n ▷ digest
digestibility n ▷ digest
digestible adj ▷ digest

digesting v ▷ digest
digestive adj ▷ digest
digestively adv ▷ digest
digests v, n ▷ digest
digger n (pl -s) machine used for digging
  diggers n ▷ digger
  digging v ▷ dig
  diggings n ▷ dig
digit n (pl -s) finger or toe
digital adj displaying information as numbers rather than with hands and a dial > **digitally** adv
  digitally adv ▷ digital
  digits n ▷ digit
dignified n ▷ dignify
dignifies n ▷ dignify
dignify v (-s, -ing, -ed) add distinction to
  dignifying v ▷ dignify
  dignities n ▷ dignify
dignity n (pl -ties) serious, calm, and controlled behaviour or manner
digress v (-es, -ing, -ed) depart from the main subject in speech or writing > **digression** n (pl -s)
  digressed v ▷ digress
  digresses v ▷ digress
  digressing v ▷ digress
  digression n ▷ digress
  digressions n ▷ digress
  digs v, n ▷ dig
dike n (pl -s) ▷ dyke
  dikes n ▷ dike
dilatation n ▷ dilate
  dilatations n ▷ dilate
dilate v (-lates, -lating, -lated) make or become wider or larger > **dilation, dilatation** n (pl -s)
  dilated v ▷ dilate
  dilates v ▷ dilate
  dilating v ▷ dilate
  dilation n ▷ dilate
  dilations n ▷ dilate
  dilatorily adv ▷ dilatory
  dilatoriness n ▷ dilatory
  dilatorinesses n ▷ dilatory
dilatory adj tending or intended to waste time > **dilatorily** adv
> **dilatoriness** n (pl -es)
dilemma n (pl -s) situation offering a choice between two equally undesirable alternatives
  dilemmas n ▷ dilemma
  diligence n ▷ diligent
diligent adj careful and persevering in carrying out duties > **diligently** adv
> **diligence** n
  diligently adv ▷ diligent
dill n (pl -s) sweet-smelling herb
  dills n ▷ dill
dilute v (-tes, -ting, -ted) make (a liquid) less concentrated, esp. by adding water > **dilution** n (pl -s)
  diluted v ▷ dilute
  dilutes v ▷ dilute
  diluting v ▷ dilute
  dilution n ▷ dilute
  dilutions n ▷ dilute
diluvial, diluvian adj of a flood, esp. the great Flood described in the Old Testament
  diluvian adj ▷ diluvial
dim adj (dimmer, dimmest) badly lit ▶ v (-s, -mming, -mmed) make or become dim > **dimly** adv > **dimness** n (pl -es)
dime n (pl -s) coin of the US and Canada, worth ten cents
  dimes n ▷ dime
diminish v (-es, -ing, -ed) make or become smaller, fewer, or less > **diminution** n (pl -s)
  diminished v ▷ diminish
  diminishes v ▷ diminish
  diminishing v ▷ diminish
  diminution n ▷ diminish
  diminutions n ▷ diminish
  dimly adv ▷ dim
  dimmed v ▷ dim
dimmer n (pl -s) device for dimming an electric light ▶ adj ▷ dim
  dimmers n ▷ dimmer
  dimmest adj ▷ dim
  dimming v ▷ dim
  dimness n ▷ dim

dimnesses *n* ▷ **dim**

dimple *n (pl -s)* small natural dent, esp. in the cheeks or chin ▶ *v (-ples, -pling, -pled)* produce dimples by smiling

dimpled *v* ▷ **dimple**

dimples *v* ▷ **dimple**

dimpling *v* ▷ **dimple**

dims *v* ▷ **dim**

din *n (pl -s)* loud unpleasant confused noise ▶ *v (-ns, -nning, -nned)* (foll. by **into**) instil (something) into someone by constant repetition

dinar *n (pl -s)* monetary unit of various Balkan, Middle Eastern, and North African countries

dinars *n* ▷ **dinar**

dine *v (-nes, -ning, -ned)* eat dinner

dined *v* ▷ **dine**

diner *n (pl -s)* person eating a meal

diners *n* ▷ **diner**

dines *v* ▷ **dine**

ding *n (pl -s)* AUST & NZ *informal* small dent in a vehicle

dinghies *n* ▷ **dinghy**

dinghy *n (pl -ghies)* small boat, powered by sails, oars, or a motor

dingier *adj* ▷ **dingy**

dingiest *adj* ▷ **dingy**

dinginess *n* ▷ **dingy**

dingo *n (pl -goes)* Australian wild dog

dingoes *n* ▷ **dingo**

dings *n* ▷ **ding**

dingy *adj (-gier, -giest)* BRIT, AUST & NZ dull and drab ▷ **dinginess** *n*

dining *v* ▷ **dine**

dinkier *adj* ▷ **dinky**

dinkiest *adj* ▷ **dinky**

dinkum *adj* AUST & NZ *informal* genuine or right

dinky *adj (-kier, -kiest)* BRIT, AUST & NZ *informal* small and neat

dinned *v* ▷ **din**

dinner *n (pl -s)* main meal of the day, eaten either in the evening or at midday

dinners *n* ▷ **dinner**

dinning *v* ▷ **din**

dinosaur *n (pl -s)* type of extinct prehistoric reptile, many of which were of gigantic size

dinosaurs *n* ▷ **dinosaur**

dins *n, v* ▷ **din**

dint *n (pl -s)* means

dints *n* ▷ **dint**

diocesan *adj* ▷ **diocese**

diocese *n (pl -s)* district over which a bishop has control ▷ **diocesan** *adj*

dioceses *n* ▷ **diocese**

diode *n (pl -s)* semiconductor device for converting alternating current to direct current

diodes *n* ▷ **diode**

dioptre *n (pl -s)* unit for measuring the refractive power of a lens

dioptres *n* ▷ **dioptre**

dioxide *n (pl -s)* oxide containing two oxygen atoms per molecule

dioxides *n* ▷ **dioxide**

dip *v (-s, -pping, -pped)* plunge quickly or briefly into a liquid ▶ *n (pl -s)* dipping

diploma *n (pl -s)* qualification awarded by a college on successful completion of a course

diplomas *n* ▷ **diploma**

diplomat *n (pl -s)* official engaged in diplomacy

diplomats *n* ▷ **diplomat**

dipped *v* ▷ **dip**

dipper *n (pl -s)* ladle used for dipping

dippers *n* ▷ **dipper**

dipping *v* ▷ **dip**

dips *v, n* ▷ **dip**

diptych *n (pl -s)* painting on two hinged panels

diptychs *n* ▷ **diptych**

dire *adj (-er, -est)* disastrous, urgent, or terrible ▷ **direly** *adv* ▷ **direness** *n (pl -es)*

direct *adj (-er, -est)* shortest, straight ▶ *adv* in a direct manner ▶ *v (-s, -ing, -ed)* lead and organize ▷ **directness** *n*

directed *v* ▷ **direct**

directing *v* ▷ **direct**

directly *adv* in a direct manner ▶ *conj* as soon as

directness *n* ▷ **direct**

director n (pl -s) person or thing that directs or controls ▷ **directorial** adj ▷ **directorship** n (pl -s)
directorial adj ▷ director
directors n ▷ director
directorship n ▷ director
directorships n ▷ director
directs v ▷ direct
direly adv ▷ dire
direness n ▷ dire
direnesses n ▷ dire
direr adj ▷ dire
direst adj ▷ dire
dirge n (pl -s) slow sad song of mourning
dirges n ▷ dirge
dirk n (pl -s) dagger, formerly worn by Scottish Highlanders
dirks n ▷ dirk
dirndl n (pl -s) full gathered skirt originating from Tyrolean peasant wear
dirndls n ▷ dirndl
dirt n (pl -s) unclean substance, filth
dirtied v ▷ dirty
dirtier adj ▷ dirty
dirties v ▷ dirty
dirtiest adj ▷ dirty
dirtily adv ▷ dirty
dirtiness n ▷ dirty
dirts n ▷ dirt
dirty (-tier, -tiest) covered or marked with dirt ▶ v (-ties, -tying, -tied) make dirty ▷ **dirtily** adv ▷ **dirtiness** n
dirtying v ▷ dirty
disable v (-les, -ling, -led) make ineffective, unfit, or incapable ▷ **disablement** n
disabled adj lacking a physical power, such as the ability to walk ▶ v ▷ disable
disablement n ▷ disable
disables v ▷ disable
disabling v ▷ disable
disabuse v (-ses, -sing, -sed) (foll. by of) rid (someone) of a mistaken idea
disabused v ▷ disabuse

disabuses v ▷ disabuse
disabusing v ▷ disabuse
disagree v (-s, -ing, -d) argue or have different opinions ▷ **disagreement** n (pl -s)
disagreed v ▷ disagree
disagreeing v ▷ disagree
disagreement n ▷ disagree
disagreements n ▷ disagree
disagrees v ▷ disagree
disallow v (-s, -ing, -ed) reject as untrue or invalid
disallowed v ▷ disallow
disallowing v ▷ disallow
disallows v ▷ disallow
disarm v (-s, -ing, -ed) deprive of weapons ▷ **disarmament** n (pl -s)
disarmament n ▷ disarm
disarmaments n ▷ disarm
disarmed v ▷ disarm
disarms v ▷ disarm
disarray n (pl -s) confusion and lack of disc-ipline
disarrays n ▷ disarray
disaster n (pl -s) occurrence that causes great distress or destruction ▷ **disastrous** adj ▷ **disastrously** adv
disasters n ▷ disaster
disastrous adj ▷ disaster
disastrously adv ▷ disaster
disavow v (-s, -ing, -ed) deny connection with or responsibility for ▷ **disavowal** n (pl -s)
disavowal n ▷ disavow
disavowals n ▷ disavow
disavowed v ▷ disavow
disavowing v ▷ disavow
disavows v ▷ disavow
disband v (-s, -ing, -ed) (cause to) cease to function as a group
disbanded v ▷ disband
disbanding v ▷ disband
disbands v ▷ disband
disburse v (-ses, -sing, -sed) pay out ▷ **disbursement** n (pl -s)
disbursed v ▷ disburse
disbursement n ▷ disburse
disbursements n ▷ disburse

disburses v ▷ disburse
disbursing v ▷ disburse

disc n (pl -s) flat circular object

discard v (-s, -ing, -ed) get rid of (something or someone) as useless or undesirable
discarded v ▷ discard
discarding v ▷ discard
discards v ▷ discard

discern v (-s, -ing, -ed) see or be aware of (something) clearly > **discernible** adj > **discernibly** adv > **discernment** n (pl -s)
discerned v ▷ discern
discernible adj ▷ discern
discernibly adv ▷ discern
discernment n ▷ discern
discernments n ▷ discern
discerns v ▷ discern

disciple n (pl -s) follower of the doctrines of a teacher, esp. Jesus Christ
disciples n ▷ disciple

disclose v (-ses, -sing, -sed) make known > **disclosure** n (pl -s)
disclosed v ▷ disclose
discloses v ▷ disclose
disclosing v ▷ disclose
disclosure n ▷ disclose
disclosures n ▷ disclose

disco n (pl -s) nightclub where people dance to amplified pop records

discord n (pl -s) lack of agreement or harmony between people > **discordant** adj > **discordantly** adv > **discordance** n (pl -s)
discordance n ▷ discord
discordances n ▷ discord
discordant adj ▷ discord
discordantly adv ▷ discord
discords n ▷ discord
discos n ▷ disco

discotheque n (pl -s) ▷ disco

discount v (-s, -ing, -ed) take no account of (something) because it is considered to be unreliable, prejudiced, or irrelevant ► n (pl -s) deduction from the full price of something
discounted v ▷ discount

discounting v ▷ discount
discounts v, n ▷ discount

discover v (-s, -ing, -ed) be the first to find or to find out about > **discoverer** n (pl -s)
discovered v ▷ discover
discoverer n ▷ discover
discoverers n ▷ discover
discovering v ▷ discover
discovers v ▷ discover

discreet adj (-er, -est) careful to avoid embarrassment, esp. by keeping confidences secret > **discreetly** adv > **discreetness** n (pl -es)
discreeter adj ▷ discreet
discreetest adj ▷ discreet
discreetly adv ▷ discreet
discreetness n ▷ discreet
discreetnesses n ▷ discreet

discrete adj (-r, -st) separate, distinct > **discretely** adv > **discreteness** n (pl -es)
discretely adv ▷ discrete
discreteness n ▷ discrete
discretenesses n ▷ discrete
discreter adj ▷ discrete
discretest adj ▷ discrete

discs n ▷ disc

discus n (pl -es) heavy disc-shaped object thrown in sports competitions
discuses n ▷ discus

discuss v (-es, -ing, -ed) consider (something) by talking it over > **discussion** n (pl -s)
discussed v ▷ discuss
discusses v ▷ discuss
discussing v ▷ discuss
discussion n ▷ discuss
discussions n ▷ discuss

disdain n (pl -s) feeling of superiority and dislike ► v (-s, -ing, -ed) refuse with disdain > **disdainful** adj > **disdainfully** adv
disdained v ▷ disdain
disdainful adj ▷ disdain
disdainfully adv ▷ disdain
disdaining v ▷ disdain
disdains n, v ▷ disdain

disease n (pl -s) illness, sickness

>**diseased** adj
diseased n ▷ disease
diseases n ▷ disease
disgorge v (-ges, -ging, -ged) empty out, discharge
disgorged v ▷ disgorge
disgorges v ▷ disgorge
disgorging v ▷ disgorge
disgrace n (pl -s) condition of shame, loss of reputation, or dishonour ▶ v (-ces, -cing, -ced) bring shame upon (oneself or others) >**disgraceful** adj >**disgracefully** adv
disgraced v ▷ disgrace
disgraceful adj ▷ disgrace
disgracefully adv ▷ disgrace
disgraces n, v ▷ disgrace
disgracing v ▷ disgrace
disguise v (-ses, -sing, -sed) change the appearance or manner in order to conceal the identity of (someone or something) ▶ n (pl -s) mask, costume, or manner that disguises
disguised v ▷ disguise
disguises v, n ▷ disguise
disguising v ▷ disguise
disgust n (pl -s) great loathing or distaste ▶ v (-s, -ing, -ed) sicken, fill with loathing
disgusted v ▷ disgust
disgusting v ▷ disgust
disgusts v ▷ disgust
dish n (pl -es) shallow container used for holding or serving food
dishes n ▷ dish
disinter v (-s, -rring, -rred) dig up
disinterred v ▷ disinter
disinterring v ▷ disinter
disinters v ▷ disinter
disk n (pl -s) COMPUTERS storage device, consisting of a stack of plates coated with a magnetic layer, which rotates rapidly as a single unit
disks n ▷ disk
dislike v (-kes, -king, -ked) consider unpleasant or disagreeable ▶ n (pl -s) feeling of not liking something or someone

disliked v ▷ dislike
dislikes v, n ▷ dislike
disliking v ▷ dislike
dislodge v (-ges, -ging, -ged) remove (something) from a previously fixed position
dislodged v ▷ dislodge
dislodges v ▷ dislodge
dislodging v ▷ dislodge
disloyal adj not loyal, deserting one's allegiance >**disloyalty** n (pl -ties)
disloyalties n ▷ disloyal
dismal adj gloomy and depressing >**dismally** adv >**dismalness** n (pl -es)
dismally adv ▷ dismal
dismalness n ▷ dismal
dismalnesses n ▷ dismal
dismay v (-s, -ing, -ed) fill with alarm or depression ▶ n (pl -s) alarm mixed with sadness
dismayed v ▷ dismay
dismaying v ▷ dismay
dismays v, n ▷ dismay
dismiss v (-es, -ing, -ed) remove (an employee) from a job >**dismissal** n (pl -s)
dismissal n ▷ dismiss
dismissals n ▷ dismiss
dismissed v ▷ dismiss
dismisses v ▷ dismiss
dismissing v ▷ dismiss
dismount v (-s, -ing, -ed) get off a horse or bicycle
dismounted v ▷ dismount
dismounting v ▷ dismount
dismounts v ▷ dismount
disobedience n ▷ disobey
disobedient adj ▷ disobey
disobediently adv ▷ disobey
disobey v (-s, -ing, -ed) neglect or refuse to obey >**disobedient** adj >**disobediently** adv >**disobedience** n
disobeyed v ▷ disobey
disobeying v ▷ disobey
disobeys v ▷ disobey
disorder n (pl -s) state of untidiness and disorganization
disorders n ▷ disorder
disown v (-s, -ing, -ed) deny any

connection with (someone)
disowned v ▷ disown
disowning v ▷ disown
disowns v ▷ disown
dispatch v (-es, -ing, -ed) send off to a destination or to perform a task ▶ n (pl -es) official communication or report, sent in haste
dispatched v ▷ dispatch
dispatches v, n ▷ dispatch
dispatching v ▷ dispatch
dispel v (-ls, -lling, -lled) destroy or remove
dispelled v ▷ dispel
dispelling v ▷ dispel
dispels v ▷ dispel
dispense v (-ses, -sing, -sed) distribute in portions > **dispenser** n (pl -s)
dispensed v ▷ dispense
dispenser n ▷ dispense
dispensers n ▷ dispense
dispenses v ▷ dispense
dispensing v ▷ dispense
dispersal n ▷ disperse
dispersals n ▷ disperse
disperse v (-ses, -sing, -sed) scatter over a wide area > **dispersal**, **dispersion** n (pl -s)
dispersed v ▷ disperse
disperses v ▷ disperse
dispersing v ▷ disperse
dispersion n ▷ disperse
dispersions n ▷ disperse
dispirit v (-s, -ing, -ed) make downhearted
dispirited v ▷ dispirit
dispiriting v ▷ dispirit
dispirits v ▷ dispirit
displace v (-ces, -cing, -ced) move from the usual location > **displacement** n (pl -s)
displaced v ▷ displace
displacement n ▷ displace
displacements n ▷ displace
displaces v ▷ displace
displacing v ▷ displace
display v (-s, -ing, -ed) make visible or noticeable ▶ n (pl -s) displaying

displayed v ▷ display
displaying v ▷ display
displays v, n ▷ display
disport v (-s, -ing, -ed) indulge oneself in pleasure
disported v ▷ disport
disporting v ▷ disport
disports v ▷ disport
disposal n (pl -s) getting rid of something
disposals n ▷ disposal
dispose v (-poses, -posing, -posed) place in a certain order
disposed adj willing or eager ▶ v ▷ dispose
disposes v ▷ dispose
disposing v ▷ dispose
disprove v (-ves, -ving, -ved) show (an assertion or claim) to be incorrect
disproved v ▷ disprove
disproves v ▷ disprove
disproving v ▷ disprove
dispute n (pl -s) disagreement, argument ▶ v (-tes, -ting, -ted) argue about (something)
disputed v ▷ dispute
disputes n, v ▷ dispute
disputing v ▷ dispute
disquiet n (pl -s) feeling of anxiety ▶ v (-s, -ing, -ed) make (someone) anxious > **disquietude** n (pl -s)
disquieted v ▷ disquiet
disquieting v ▷ disquiet
disquiets v, n ▷ disquiet
disquietude n ▷ disquiet
disquietudes n ▷ disquiet
disrobe v (-bes, -bing, -bed) undress
disrobed v ▷ disrobe
disrobes v ▷ disrobe
disrobing v ▷ disrobe
disrupt v (-s, -ing, -ed) interrupt the progress of > **disruption** n (pl -s) > **disruptive** adj
disrupted v ▷ disrupt
disrupting v ▷ disrupt
disruption n ▷ disrupt
disruptions n ▷ disrupt
disruptive adj ▷ disrupt
disrupts v ▷ disrupt

dissect v (-s, -ing, -ed) cut open (a corpse) to examine it > **dissection** n (pl -s)
dissected v ▷ **dissect**
dissecting v ▷ **dissect**
dissection n ▷ **dissect**
dissections n ▷ **dissect**
dissects v ▷ **dissect**
dissension n ▷ **dissent**
dissensions n ▷ **dissent**
dissent v (-s, -ing, -ed) disagree ▶ n (pl -s) disagreement > **dissension** n (pl -s) > **dissenter** n (pl -s)
dissented v ▷ **dissent**
dissenter n ▷ **dissent**
dissenters n ▷ **dissent**
dissenting v ▷ **dissent**
dissents v ▷ **dissent**
dissolve v (-ves, -ving, -ved) (cause to) become liquid
dissolved v ▷ **dissolve**
dissolves v ▷ **dissolve**
dissolving v ▷ **dissolve**
dissuade v (-des, -ding, -ded) deter (someone) by persuasion from doing something > **dissuasion** n (pl -s)
dissuaded v ▷ **dissuade**
dissuades v ▷ **dissuade**
dissuading v ▷ **dissuade**
dissuasion n ▷ **dissuade**
dissuasions n ▷ **dissuade**
distaff n (pl -s) rod on which wool etc is wound for spinning
distaffs n ▷ **distaff**
distance n (pl -s) space between two points
distances n ▷ **distance**
distant adj far apart > **distantly** adv
distantly adv ▷ **distant**
distaste n (pl -s) dislike, disgust
distastes n ▷ **distaste**
distend v (-s, -ing, -ed) (of part of the body) swell > **distension** n (pl -s)
distended v ▷ **distend**
distending v ▷ **distend**
distends v ▷ **distend**
distension n ▷ **distend**
distensions n ▷ **distend**
distil v (-tils, -tilling, -tilled) subject to or obtain by distillation

distilled v ▷ **distil**
distilling v ▷ **distil**
distils v ▷ **distil**
distinct adj (-er, -est) not the same > **distinctly** adv > **distinctness** n (pl -es)
distincter adj ▷ **distinct**
distinctest adj ▷ **distinct**
distinctly adv ▷ **distinct**
distinctness n ▷ **distinct**
distinctnesses n ▷ **distinct**
distort v (-s, -ing, -ed) misrepresent (the truth or facts) > **distortion** n (pl -s)
distorted v ▷ **distort**
distorting v ▷ **distort**
distortion n ▷ **distort**
distortions n ▷ **distort**
distorts v ▷ **distort**
distract v (-s, -ing, -ed) draw the attention of (a person) away from something > **distraction** n (pl -s)
distracting v ▷ **distract**
distraction n ▷ **distract**
distractions n ▷ **distract**
distracts v ▷ **distract**
distrait adj absent-minded or preoccupied
distress n (pl -es) extreme unhappiness ▶ v (-es, -ing, -ed) upset badly > **distressing** adj > **distressingly** adv
distresses n, adj ▷ **distress**
distressing v, adj ▷ **distress**
distressingly adv ▷ **distress**
district n (pl -s) area of land regarded as an administrative or geographical unit
districts n ▷ **district**
distrust v (-s, -ing, -ed) regard as untrustworthy ▶ n (pl -s) feeling of suspicion or doubt > **distrustful** adj
distrusted v ▷ **distrust**
distrustful adj ▷ **distrust**
distrusting v ▷ **distrust**
distrusts v, n ▷ **distrust**
disturb v (-s, -ing, -ed) intrude on > **disturbance** n (pl -s) > **disturbing** adj > **disturbingly** adv
disturbance n ▷ **disturb**
disturbances n ▷ **disturb**

disturbing v, adj ▷ disturb

disturbingly adv ▷ disturb

disturbs v ▷ disturb

disunite v (-tes, -ting, -ted) cause disagreement among > **disunity** n (pl -ities)

disunited v ▷ disunite

disunites v ▷ disunite

disunities n ▷ disunite

disuniting v ▷ disunite

disunity n ▷ disunite

disuse n (pl -s) state of being no longer used > **disused** adj

disused adj ▷ disuse

disuses n ▷ disuse

ditch n (pl -es) narrow channel dug in the earth for drainage or irrigation ▶ v (-es, -ing, -ed) slang abandon

ditched v ▷ ditch

ditches n, v ▷ ditch

ditching v ▷ ditch

dither v (-s, -ing, -ed) be uncertain or indecisive ▶ n (pl -s) state of indecision or agitation > **ditherer** n (pl -s) > **dithery** adj

dithered v ▷ dither

dithering v ▷ dither

dithers v, n ▷ dither

dithery adj ▷ dither

ditties n ▷ ditty

ditto n (pl -tos) the same ▶ adv in the same way

dittos n ▷ ditto

ditty n (pl -ties) short simple poem or song

diuretic n (pl -s) drug that increases the flow of urine

diuretics n ▷ diuretic

diurnal adj happening during the day or daily > **diurnally** adv

diurnally adv ▷ diurnal

diva n (pl -s) distinguished female singer

divan n (pl -s) low backless bed

divans n ▷ divan

divas n ▷ diva

dive v (-ves, -ving, -ved) plunge headfirst into water (foll. by in or into) ▶ n (pl -s) diving

dived v ▷ dive

diver n (pl -s) person who works or explores underwater

diverge v (-ges, -ging, -ged) separate and go in different directions > **divergence** n (pl -s) > **divergent** adj

diverged v ▷ diverge

divergence n ▷ diverge

divergences n ▷ diverge

divergent adj ▷ diverge

diverges v ▷ diverge

diverging v ▷ diverge

divers adj old-fashioned various ▶ n ▷ diver

diverse adj having variety, assorted > **diversely** adv > **diversify** v (-fies, -fying, -fied) > **diversification** n

diversely adv ▷ diverse

diversification n ▷ diverse

diversified v ▷ diverse

diversifies v ▷ diverse

diversify v ▷ diverse

diversifying v ▷ diverse

divert v (-s, -ing, -ed) change the direction of

diverted v ▷ divert

diverting v ▷ divert

diverts v ▷ divert

dives v, n ▷ dive

divest v (-s, -ing, -ed) strip (of clothes)

divested v ▷ divest

divesting v ▷ divest

divests v ▷ divest

divide v (-des, -ding, -ded) separate into parts ▶ n (pl -s) division, split

divided v ▷ divide

dividend n (pl -s) sum of money representing part of the profit made, paid by a company to its shareholders

dividends n ▷ dividend

divider n (pl -s) screen used to divide a room into separate areas ▶ pl compasses with two pointed arms, used for measuring or dividing lines

dividers n ▷ divider

divides v, n ▷ divide

dividing v ▷ divide

divinations n ▷ divine

divine adj (-r, -st) of God or a god ▶ v (-nes, -ning, -ned) discover (something) by intuition or guessing > **divinely** adv
divined v ▷ divine
divinely adv ▷ divine
diviner adj ▷ divine
divines v ▷ divine
divinest adj ▷ divine
diving v ▷ dive
divining v ▷ divine
divinities n ▷ divinity
divinity n study of religion (pl -ties)
divisibilities n ▷ division
divisibility n ▷ division
divisible adj ▷ division
division n (pl -s) dividing, sharing out > **divisible** adj > **divisibility** n -ties
divisions n ▷ division
divisive adj tending to cause disagreement > **divisively** adv > **divisiveness** n (pl -es)
divisively adv ▷ divisive
divisiveness n ▷ divisive
divisivenesses n ▷ divisive
divisor n (pl -s) number to be divided into another number
divisors n ▷ divisor
divorce n (pl -s) legal ending of a marriage ▶ v (-ces, -cing, -ced) legally end one's marriage (to)
divorcé n ▷ divorcée
divorced v ▷ divorce
divorcée, masc **divorcé** n (pl -s) person who is divorced
divorcées n ▷ divorcée
divorces n, v ▷ divorce
divorcés n ▷ divorcée
divorcing v ▷ divorce
divulge v (-ges, -ging, -ged) make known, disclose > **divulgence** n (pl -s)
divulged v ▷ divulge
divulgence n ▷ divulge
divulgences n ▷ divulge
divulges v ▷ divulge
divulging v ▷ divulge
dizzied v ▷ dizzy
dizzier adj ▷ dizzy

dizzies v ▷ dizzy
dizziest adj ▷ dizzy
dizzily adv ▷ dizzy
dizziness n ▷ dizzy
dizzinesses n ▷ dizzy
dizzy adj (-zier, -ziest) having or causing a whirling sensation ▶ v (-zies, -zying, -zied) make dizzy > **dizzily** adv > **dizziness** n (pl -es)
do v (does, doing, did, done) perform or complete (a deed or action) ▶ n (pl -s) informal party, celebration
docile adj (-r, -st) (of a person or animal) easily controlled > **docilely** adv > **docility** n (pl -ties)
docilely adv ▷ docile
dociler adj ▷ docile
docilest adj ▷ docile
docilities n ▷ docile
docility n ▷ docile
dock[1] n (pl -s) enclosed area of water where ships are loaded, unloaded, or repaired ▶ v (-s, -ing, -ed) bring or be brought into dock
dock[2] v (-s, -ing, -ed) deduct money from (a person's wages)
dock[3] n (pl -s) enclosed space in a court of law where the accused person sits or stands
dock[4] n (pl -s) weed with broad leaves
docked v ▷ dock
docker n (pl -s) BRIT person employed to load and unload ships
dockers n ▷ docker
docket n (pl -s) label on a package or other delivery, stating contents, delivery instructions, etc
dockets n ▷ dock
docking v ▷ dock
docks n ▷ dock[1, 3, 4] ▶ v ▷ dock[1, 2]
dockyard n (pl -s) place where ships are built or repaired
dockyards n ▷ dockyard
doctor n (pl -s) person licensed to practise medicine ▶ v (-s, -ing, -ed) alter in order to deceive > **doctoral** adj
doctoral adj ▷ doctor

doctored v ▷ doctor

doctoring v ▷ doctor

doctors n, v ▷ doctor

doctrine n (pl -s) body of teachings of a religious, political, or philosophical group

doctrines n ▷ doctrine

document n (pl -s) piece of paper providing an official record of something ▶ v (-s, -ing, -ed) record or report (something) in detail >**documentation** n (pl -s)

documentation n ▷ document

documentations n ▷ document

documented v ▷ document

documenting v ▷ document

documents n, v ▷ document

dodder v (-s, -ing, -ed) move unsteadily >**doddery** adj (-rier, -riest)

doddered v ▷ dodder

dodderier adj ▷ dodder

dodderiest adj ▷ dodder

doddering v ▷ dodder

dodders v ▷ dodder

doddery adj ▷ dodder

dodge v (-ges, -ging, -ged) avoid (a blow, being seen, etc) by moving suddenly ▶ n (pl -s) cunning or deceitful trick

dodged v ▷ dodge

dodger n (pl -s) person who evades a responsibility or duty

dodgers n ▷ dodger

dodges v, n ▷ dodge

dodgier adj ▷ dodgy

dodgiest adj ▷ dodgy

dodging v ▷ dodge

dodgy adj (-gier, -giest) informal dangerous, risky

dodo n (pl -s, -es) large flightless extinct bird

dodoes n ▷ dodo

dodos n ▷ dodo

doe n (pl -s) female deer, hare, or rabbit

does n ▷ doe ▶ v ▷ do

doff v (-s, -ing, -ed) take off or lift (one's hat) in polite greeting

doffed v ▷ doff

doffing v ▷ doff

doffs v ▷ doff

dog n (pl -s) domesticated four-legged mammal of many different breeds ▶ v (-s, -gging, -gged) follow (someone) closely

dogcart n (pl -s) light horse-drawn two-wheeled cart

dogcarts n ▷ dogcart

doge n (pl -s) (formerly) chief magistrate of Venice or Genoa

dogeared adj (of a book) having pages folded down at the corner

doges n ▷ doge

dogfight n (pl -s) close-quarters combat between fighter aircraft

dogfights n ▷ dogfight

dogfish n (pl -es) small shark

dogfishes n ▷ dogfish

dogged adj obstinately determined ▶ v ▷ dog >**doggedly** adv >**doggedness** n (pl -es)

doggedly adv ▷ dogged

doggedness n ▷ dogged

doggednesses n ▷ dogged

doggerel n (pl -s) poorly written poetry, usu. comic

doggerels n ▷ doggerel

doggie n ▷ doggy

doggies n ▷ doggy

dogging v ▷ dog

doggo adv informal in hiding and keeping quiet

doggy, doggie n (pl -ggies) child's word for a dog

doghouse n (pl -s) us kennel

doghouses n ▷ doghouse

dogleg n (pl -s) sharp bend

doglegs n ▷ dogleg

dogma n (pl -s) doctrine or system of doctrines proclaimed by authority as true >**dogmatic** adj habitually stating one's opinions forcefully or arrogantly >**dogmatically** adv >**dogmatism** n (pl -s)

dogmas n ▷ dogma

dogmatic adj ▷ dogma

dogmatically adv ▷ dogma

dogmatism n ▷ **dogma**

dogmatisms n ▷ **dogma**

dogs n, v ▷ **dog**

dogsbodies n ▷ **dogsbody**

dogsbody n (pl -bodies) informal person who carries out boring tasks for others

▌**doh** interj. Doh is a sound people make when things go wrong. Doh scores 7 points.

doilies n ▷ **doily**

doily n (pl -lies) decorative lacy paper mat, laid on a plate

doing v ▷ **do**

doldrums pl n depressed state of mind

dole n (pl -s) BRIT, AUST & NZ informal money received from the state while unemployed ▶ v (-les, -ling, -led) (foll. by **out**) distribute in small quantities

doled v ▷ **dole**

doleful adj dreary, unhappy
> **dolefully** adv > **dolefulness** n

dolefully adv ▷ **doleful**

dolefulness n ▷ **doleful**

doles v, n ▷ **dole**

doling v ▷ **dole**

doll n (pl -s) small model of a human being, used as a toy

dollar n (pl -s) standard monetary unit of many countries

dollars n ▷ **dollar**

dollies n ▷ **dolly**

dollop n (pl -s) informal lump (of food)

dollops n ▷ **dollop**

dolls n ▷ **doll**

dolly n (pl -lies) child's word for a doll

dolmen n (pl -s) prehistoric monument consisting of a horizontal stone supported by vertical stones

dolmens n ▷ **dolmen**

dolomite n (pl -s) mineral consisting of calcium magnesium carbonate

dolomites n ▷ **dolomite**

dolorous adj sad, mournful
> **dolorously** adv

dolorously adv ▷ **dolorous**

dolphin n (pl -s) sea mammal of the whale family, with a beaklike snout

dolphins n ▷ **dolphin**

dolt n (pl -s) stupid person > **doltish** adj
> **doltishness** n (pl -es)

doltish adj ▷ **dolt**

doltishness n ▷ **dolt**

doltishnesses n ▷ **dolt**

dolts n ▷ **dolt**

domain n (pl -s) field of knowledge or activity

domains n ▷ **domain**

dome n (pl -s) rounded roof built on a circular base > **domed** adj

domes n ▷ **dome**

domestic adj of one's own country or a specific country ▶ n (pl -s) person whose job is to do housework in someone else's house
> **domestically** adv > **domesticity** n

domestically adv ▷ **domestic**

domesticity n ▷ **domestic**

domestics n ▷ **domestic**

domicile n (pl -s) place where one lives

domiciles n ▷ **domicile**

dominance n ▷ **dominant**

dominances n ▷ **dominant**

dominant adj having authority or influence > **dominance** n (pl -s)

dominate v (-tes, -ting, -ted) control or govern > **domination** n (pl -s)

dominated v ▷ **dominate**

dominates v ▷ **dominate**

dominating v ▷ **dominate**

domination n ▷ **dominate**

dominations n ▷ **dominate**

dominion n (pl -s) control or authority

dominions n ▷ **dominion**

domino n (pl -noes) small rectangular block marked with dots, used in dominoes ▶ pl game in which dominoes with matching halves are laid together

dominoes n ▷ **domino**

don¹ v (-ns, -nning, -nned) put on (clothing)

don² n (pl -s) BRIT member of the teaching staff at a university or college

donate v (-tes, -ting, -ted) give, esp. to a charity or organization

donated v ▷ **donate**

donates v ▷ donate

donating v ▷ donate

donation n (pl -s) donating

donations n ▷ donation

done v ▷ do

donga n (pl -s) S AFR, AUST & NZ steep-sided gully created by soil erosion

dongas n ▷ donga

donkey n (pl -s) long-eared member of the horse family

donkeys n ▷ donkey

donned v ▷ don¹

donning v ▷ don¹

donnish adj serious and academic
 > **donnishness** n ▷ donnish

donnishness n ▷ donnish

donnishnesses n ▷ donnish

donor n (pl -s) MED person who gives blood or organs for use in the treatment of another person

donors n ▷ donor

dons v ▷ don¹ ▶ n ▷ don²

doodle v (-les, -ling, -led) scribble or draw aimlessly ▶ n (pl -s) shape or picture drawn aimlessly

doodled v ▷ doodle

doodles v, n ▷ doodle

doodling v ▷ doodle

doom n (pl -s) death or a terrible fate ▶ v (-s, -ing, -ed) destine or condemn to death or a terrible fate

doomed v ▷ doom

dooming v ▷ doom

dooms n, v ▷ doom

doomsday n (pl -s) CHRISTIANITY day on which the Last Judgment will occur

doomsdays n ▷ doomsday

door n (pl -s) hinged or sliding panel for closing the entrance to a building, room, etc

doormat n (pl -s) mat for wiping dirt from shoes before going indoors

doormats n ▷ doormat

doors n ▷ door

doorway n (pl -s) opening into a building or room

doorways n ▷ doorway

dope n (pl -s) slang illegal drug, usu.

cannabis ▶ v (-pes, -ping, -ped) give a drug to, esp. in order to improve performance in a race

doped v ▷ dope

dopes n, v ▷ dope

dopey, dopy (-pier, -piest) adj half-asleep, drowsy

dopier adj ▷ dopey

dopiest adj ▷ dopey

doping v ▷ dope

dopy adj ▷ dopey

dorb n ▷ dorba

dorba, dorb n (pl -s) AUST slang stupid, inept, or clumsy person

dorbas n ▷ dorba

dorbs n ▷ dorba

dories n ▷ dory

dork n (pl -s) slang stupid person

dorks n ▷ dork

dormancy n ▷ dormant

dormant adj temporarily quiet, inactive, or not being used > **dormancy** n

dormer n (pl -s) window that sticks out from a sloping roof

dormers n ▷ dormer

dormice n ▷ dormouse

dormouse n (pl -mice) small mouselike rodent with a furry tail

dorp n (pl -s) S AFR small town

dorps n ▷ dorp

dorsal adj of or on the back

dory n (pl -ries) spiny-finned edible sea fish

dos n ▷ do

dosage n (pl -s) size of a dose

dosages n ▷ dosage

dose n (pl -s) specific quantity of a medicine taken at one time informal ▶ v (-ses, -sing, -sed) give a dose to

dosed v ▷ dose

doses n, v ▷ dose

dosing v ▷ dose

doss v (-es, -ing, -ed) slang sleep in an uncomfortable place

dossed v ▷ doss

dosses v ▷ doss

dossier n (pl -s) collection of documents about a subject or person

dossiers n ▷ dossier

dossing v ▷ doss

dot n (pl -s) small round mark ▶ v (-s, -tting, -tted) mark with a dot

dotage n (pl -s) weakness as a result of old age

dotages n ▷ dotage

dotcom n (pl -s) company that does most of its business on the Internet

dotcoms n ▷ dotcom

dote v (-tes, -ting, -ted) love to an excessive degree

doted v ▷ dote

dotes v ▷ dote

doting v ▷ dote

dots n, v ▷ dot

dotted v ▷ dot

dottier adj ▷ dotty

dottiest adj ▷ dotty

dottily adv ▷ dotty

dottiness n ▷ dotty

dottinesses n ▷ dotty

dotting v ▷ dot

dotty adj (-tier, -tiest) slang rather eccentric > **dottily** adv > **dottiness** n (pl -es)

double adj as much again in number, amount, size, etc ▶ adv twice over ▶ n (pl -s) twice the number, amount, size, etc ▶ pl game between two pairs of players ▶ v (-bles, -bling, -bled) make or become twice as much or as many > **doubly** adv

doubled v ▷ double

doubles n, v ▷ double

doublet n (pl -s) HIST man's close-fitting jacket, with or without sleeves

doublets n ▷ doublet

doubling v ▷ double

doubloon n (pl -s) former Spanish gold coin

doubloons n ▷ doubloon

doubly adv ▷ double

doubt n (pl -s) uncertainty about the truth, facts, or existence of something ▶ v (-s, -ing, -ed) question the truth of > **doubter** n (pl -s)

doubted v ▷ doubt

doubter n ▷ doubt

doubters n ▷ doubt

doubtful adj unlikely > **doubtfully** adv

doubtfully adv ▷ doubtful

doubting v ▷ doubt

doubts n, v ▷ doubt

douche n (pl -s) (instrument for applying) a stream of water directed onto or into the body for cleansing or medical purposes ▶ v (-es, -ing, -ed) cleanse or treat by means of a douche

douched v ▷ douche

douches n, v ▷ douche

douching v ▷ douche

dough n (pl -s) thick mixture of flour and water or milk, used for making bread etc

doughnut n (pl -s) small cake of sweetened dough fried in deep fat

doughnuts n ▷ doughnut

doughs n ▷ dough

doughtier adj ▷ doughty

doughtiest adj ▷ doughty

doughtily adv ▷ doughty

doughtiness n ▷ doughty

doughtinesses n ▷ doughty

doughty adj (-tier, -tiest) old-fashioned brave and determined > **doughtily** adv > **doughtiness** n (pl -es)

dour adj (-er, -est) sullen and unfriendly > **dourly** adv > **dourness** n (pl -es)

dourer adj ▷ dour

dourest adj ▷ dour

dourly adv ▷ dour

dourness n ▷ dour

dournesses n ▷ dour

douse v (-ses, -sing, -sed) drench with water or other liquid

doused v ▷ douse

douses v ▷ douse

dousing v ▷ douse

dove n (pl -s) bird with a heavy body, small head, and short legs

dovecot n ▷ dovecote

dovecote, dovecot n (pl -s) structure for housing pigeons

dovecotes n ▷ dovecote

dovecots n ▷ dovecote

doves n ▷ dove

dovetail n (pl -s) joint containing wedge-shaped tenons ▶ v (-s, -ing, -ed) fit together neatly

dovetailed v ▷ dovetail

dovetailing v ▷ dovetail

dovetails v ▷ dovetail

> **dow** n (dows). A dow is an Arab ship. Dow scores 7 points.

dowager n (pl -s) widow possessing property or a title obtained from her husband

dowagers n ▷ dowager

dowdier adj ▷ dowdy

dowdiest adj ▷ dowdy

dowdily adv ▷ dowdy

dowdiness n ▷ dowdy

dowdy adj (-dier, -diest) dull and old-fashioned > **dowdily** adv > **dowdiness** n

dowel n (pl -s) wooden or metal peg that fits into two corresponding holes to join two adjacent parts

dowels n ▷ dowel

dower n (pl -s) life interest in a part of her husband's estate allotted to a widow by law

dowers n ▷ dower

down¹ prep, adv indicating movement to or position in a lower place ▶ adv indicating completion of an action, lessening of intensity, etc ▶ adj depressed, unhappy ▶ v (-s, -ing, -ed) informal drink quickly
>**downiness** n > **downy** adj (-nier, -niest)

down² n soft fine feathers
>**downiness** n > **downy** adj (-nier, -niest)

downbeat adj informal gloomy

downcast adj sad, dejected

downed v ▷ down¹

downfall n (pl -s) (cause of) a sudden loss of position or reputation

downfalls n ▷ downfall

downhill adj going or sloping down ▶ adv towards the bottom of a hill

downier adj ▷ down²

downiest adj ▷ down²

downiness n ▷ down²

downing v ▷ down¹

download v (-s, -ing, -ed) transfer (data) from the memory of one computer to that of another, especially over the Internet ▶ n (pl -s) file transferred in such a way

downloaded v ▷ download

downloading v ▷ download

downloads v, n ▷ download

downpour n (pl -s) heavy fall of rain

downpours n ▷ downpour

downs pl n low grassy hills, esp. in S England ▶ v ▷ down¹ ▶ n ▷ down²

downward adj, adv (descending) from a higher to a lower level, condition, or position

downy adj ▷ down²

dowries n ▷ dowry

dowry n (pl -ries) property brought by a woman to her husband at marriage

dowse v (-ses, -sing, -sed) search for underground water or minerals using a divining rod

dowsed v ▷ dowse

dowses v ▷ dowse

dowsing v ▷ dowse

doxologies n ▷ doxology

doxology n (pl -gies) short hymn of praise to God

> **doy** n (doys). Doy is a dialect word for a beloved person. Doy scores 7 points.

doyen n (pl -s) senior member of a group, profession, or society
> **doyenne** n fem

doyenne n ▷ doyen

doyennes n ▷ doyen

doyens n ▷ doyen

doze v (-zes, -zing, -zed) sleep lightly or briefly ▶ n (pl -s) short sleep

dozed v ▷ doze

dozen adj, n (pl -s) twelve > **dozenth** adj

dozens n ▷ dozen

dozenth adj ▷ dozen

dozes v, n ▷ doze

dozier adj ▷ dozy

doziest adj ▷ dozy

dozily adv ▷ dozy

doziness n ▷ dozy

dozing v ▷ **doze**

dozy adj (**-zier, -ziest**) feeling sleepy
> **dozily** adv ▷ **doziness** adv

drab adj (**-bber, -bbest**) dull and dreary
> **drably** adv ▷ **drabness** n (**-es**)
 drabber adj ▷ **drab**
 drabbest adj ▷ **drab**
 drably adv ▷ **drab**
 drabness n ▷ **drab**
 drabnesses n ▷ **drab**

drachm n (**pl -s**) BRIT one eighth of a
fluid ounce

drachma n (**pl -mas, -mae**) former
monetary unit of Greece
 drachmae n ▷ **drachma**
 drachmas n ▷ **drachma**
 drachms n ▷ **drachm**

draft n (**pl -s**) plan, sketch, or drawing
of something US & AUST. ▶ v (**-s, -ing,
-ed**) draw up an outline or plan of
 drafted v ▷ **draft**
 drafting v ▷ **draft**
 drafts n, v ▷ **draft**

drag v (**-s, -gging, -gged**) pull with
force, esp. along the ground (foll. by **on**
or **out**) ▶ n (**pl -s**) person or thing that
slows up progress
 dragged v ▷ **drag**
 dragging v ▷ **drag**

dragnet n (**pl -s**) net used to scour the
bottom of a pond or river to search for
something
 dragnets n ▷ **dragnet**

dragon n (**pl -s**) mythical fire-
breathing monster like a huge lizard
 dragons n ▷ **dragon**

dragoon n (**pl -s**) heavily armed
cavalryman ▶ v (**-s, -ing, -ed**) coerce,
force
 dragooned v ▷ **dragoon**
 dragooning v ▷ **dragoon**
 dragoons n, v ▷ **dragoon**
 drags v, n ▷ **drag**

drain n (**pl -s**) pipe or channel that
carries off water or sewage ▶ v (**-s, -ing,
-ed**) draw off or remove liquid from
drainage n (**pl -s**) system of drains
 drainages n ▷ **drainage**

drained v ▷ **drain**
draining v ▷ **drain**
drains n, v ▷ **drain**

drake n (**pl -s**) male duck
 drakes n ▷ **drake**

dram n (**pl -s**) small amount of a strong
alcoholic drink, esp. whisky

drama n (**pl -s**) serious play for theatre,
television, or radio
 dramas n ▷ **drama**

dramatic adj of or like drama
> **dramatically** adv
 dramatically adv ▷ **dramatic**
 drams n ▷ **dram**
 drank v ▷ **drink**

drape v (**-pes, -ping, -ped**) cover with
material, usu. in folds ▶ n (**pl -s**) AUST,
US & CANADIAN piece of cloth hung at a
window or opening as a screen
 draped v ▷ **drape**

draper n (**pl -s**) BRIT person who sells
fabrics and sewing materials
 draperies n ▷ **drapery**
 drapers n ▷ **draper**

drapery n (**pl -ries**) fabric or clothing
arranged and draped
 drapes v, n ▷ **drape**
 draping v ▷ **drape**

drastic adj strong and severe
> **drastically** adv
 drastically adv ▷ **drastic**

draught n (**pl -s**) current of cold air,
esp. in an enclosed space ▶ pl game
for two players using a chessboard
and twelve draughts each ▶ adj (of an
animal) used for pulling heavy loads
 draughtier adj ▷ **draughty**
 draughtiest adj ▷ **draughty**
 draughtiness n ▷ **draughty**
 draughtinesses n ▷ **draughty**
 draughts n ▷ **draught**

draughty adj (**-tier, -tiest**) exposed
to draughts of air ▶ **draughtiness** n
(**pl -es**)

draw v (**-s, -ing, drew, drawn**) sketch
(a figure, picture, etc) with a pencil or
pen ▶ n (**pl -s**) raffle or lottery
drawback n (**pl -s**) disadvantage

drawbacks n ▷ **drawback**

drawer n (pl **-s**) sliding box-shaped part of a piece of furniture, used for storage ▶ pl old-fashioned undergarment worn on the lower part of the body
drawers n (pl **-s**) sliding box-shaped part of a piece of furniture, used for storage ▶ pl old-fashioned undergarment worn on the lower part of the body

drawing n (pl **-s**) picture or plan made by means of lines on a surface ▶ v ▷ **draw**

drawl v (**-s**, **-ing**, **-ed**) speak slowly, with long vowel sounds ▶ n (pl **-s**) drawling manner of speech
drawled v ▷ **drawl**
drawling v ▷ **drawl**
drawls v ▷ **drawl**
drawls n ▷ **drawl**
drawn v ▷ **draw** ▶ adj haggard, tired, or tense in appearance
draws n, v ▷ **draw**

dray n (pl **-s**) low cart used for carrying heavy loads
drays n ▷ **dray**

dread v (**-s**, **-ing**, **-ed**) anticipate with apprehension or fear ▶ n (pl **-s**) great fear
dreaded v ▷ **dread**

dreadful adj very disagreeable or shocking > **dreadfully** adv
dreadfully adv ▷ **dreadful**
dreading v ▷ **dread**
dreads v, n ▷ **dread**

dream n (pl **-s**) imagined series of events experienced in the mind while asleep informal ▶ v (**-s**, **-ing**, **-ed** or **-t**) see imaginary pictures in the mind while asleep (often foll. by of or about) (foll. by of) ▶ adj ideal > **dreamer** n (pl **-s**)
dreamed v ▷ **dream**
dreamer n ▷ **dream**
dreamers n ▷ **dream**
dreamier adj ▷ **dreamy**
dreamiest adj ▷ **dreamy**
dreamily adv ▷ **dreamy**
dreaminess n ▷ **dreamy**
dreaminesses n ▷ **dreamy**
dreaming v ▷ **dream**
dreams n, v ▷ **dream**
dreamt v ▷ **dream**

dreamy adj (**-mier**, **-miest**) vague or impractical informal > **dreamily** adv > **dreaminess** n (pl **-es**)
drearier adj ▷ **dreary**
dreariest adj ▷ **dreary**
drearily adv ▷ **dreary**
dreariness n ▷ **dreary**
drearinesses n (pl **-es**)

dreary adj (**-rier**, **-riest**) dull, boring > **drearily** adv > **dreariness** n (pl **-es**)

dredge[1] v (**-ges**, **-ging**, **-ged**) clear or search (a river bed or harbour) by removing silt or mud

dredge[2] v (**-ges**, **-ging**, **-ged**) sprinkle (food) with flour etc
dredged v ▷ **dredge**[1, 2]

dredger n (pl **-s**) boat fitted with machinery for dredging
dredgers n ▷ **dredger**
dredges v ▷ **dredge**[1, 2]
dredging v ▷ **dredge**[1, 2]

dregs pl n solid particles that settle at the bottom of some liquids

drench v (**-es**, **-ing**, **-ed**) make completely wet
drenched v ▷ **drench**
drenches v ▷ **drench**
drenching v ▷ **drench**

dress n (pl **-es**) one-piece garment for a woman or girl, consisting of a skirt and bodice and sometimes sleeves ▶ v (**-es**, **-ing**, **-ed**) put clothes on

dressage n (pl **-s**) training of a horse to perform manoeuvres in response to the rider's body signals
dressages n ▷ **dressage**
dressed v ▷ **dress**

dresser[1] n (pl **-s**) piece of furniture with shelves and with cupboards, for storing or displaying dishes

dresser[2] n (pl **-s**) THEATRE person employed to assist actors with their costumes
dressers n ▷ **dresser**[1, 2]
dresses n, v ▷ **dress**
dressier adj ▷ **dressy**
dressiest adj ▷ **dressy**
dressiness n ▷ **dressy**

dressinesses n ▷ dressy

dressing n (pl -s) sauce for salad ▶ v ▷ dress

dressings n ▷ dressing

dressy adj (-sier, -siest) (of clothes) elegant > **dressiness** n (pl -es)

drew v ▷ draw

drey n (pl -s) squirrel's nest

dreys n ▷ drey

dribble v (-les, -ling, -led) (allow to) flow in drops ▶ n (pl -s) small quantity of liquid falling in drops > **dribbler** n (pl -s)

dribbled v ▷ dribble

dribbler n ▷ dribble

dribblers n ▷ dribble

dribbles v, n ▷ dribble

dribbling v ▷ dribble

dried v ▷ dry

drier¹ adj ▷ dry

drier² n (pl -s) ▷ dryer

driers n ▷ drier²

dries v ▷ dry

driest adj ▷ dry

drift v (-s, -ing, -ed) be carried along by currents of air or water ▶ n (pl -s) something piled up by the wind or current, such as a snowdrift

drifted v ▷ drift

drifter n (pl -s) person who moves aimlessly from place to place or job to job

drifters n ▷ drifter

drifting v ▷ drift

drifts v, n ▷ drift

drill¹ n (pl -s) tool or machine for boring holes ▶ v (-s, -ing, -ed) bore a hole in (something) with or as if with a drill

drill² n (pl -s) machine for sowing seed in rows

drill³ n (pl -s) hard-wearing cotton cloth

drilled v ▷ drill¹

drilling v ▷ drill¹

drills n ▷ drill¹, ², ³ ▶ v ▷ drill¹

drily adv ▷ dry

drink v (-s, -ing, drank, drunk)

swallow (a liquid) ▶ n (pl -s) (portion of) a liquid suitable for drinking > **drinkable** adj ▷ drinker n (pl -s)

drinkable adj ▷ drink

drinker n ▷ drink

drinkers n ▷ drink

drinking v ▷ drink

drinks v, n ▷ drink

drip v (-s, -pping, -pped) (let) fall in drops ▶ n (pl -s) falling of drops of liquid

dripped v ▷ drip

dripping n (pl -s) fat that comes from meat while it is being roasted or fried ▶ v ▷ drip

drippings n ▷ dripping

drips v, n ▷ drip

drive v (-ves, -ving, drove, driven) guide the movement of (a vehicle) ▶ n (pl -s) journey by car, van, etc; path for vehicles (also **driveway**) (pl -s)

drivel n (pl -s) foolish talk ▶ v (-s, -lling, -lled) speak foolishly

drivelled v ▷ drivel

drivelling v ▷ drivel

drivels v, n ▷ drivel

driven v ▷ drive

driver n (pl -s) person who drives a vehicle

drivers n ▷ driver

drives v, n ▷ drive

driveway n ▷ drive

driveways n ▷ drive

driving v ▷ drive

drizzle n (pl -s) very light rain ▶ v (-zles, -zling, -zled) rain lightly > **drizzly** adj

drizzled v ▷ drizzle

drizzles n, v ▷ drizzle

drizzling v ▷ drizzle

drizzly adj ▷ drizzle

droll adj (-er, -est) quaintly amusing > **drolly** adv > **drollery** n (pl -ries)

drollness n (pl -es)

droller adj ▷ droll

drolleries n ▷ droll

drollery n ▷ droll

drollest adj ▷ droll

drollness n ▷ droll

drollnesses n ▷ droll

drolly adv ▷ **droll**

drone[1] n (pl **-s**) male bee

drone[2] v (**-nes, -ned, -ning**) ▶ n (pl **-s**) (make) a monotonous low dull sound

  droned v ▷ **drone**[1], [2] ▶ v ▷ **drone**[2]

  drones n ▷ **drone**[1], [2]

drongo n (pl **-gos**) tropical songbird with a glossy black plumage, a forked tail, and a stout bill

  drongos n ▷ **drongo**

  droning v ▷ **drone**[2]

drool v (**-s, -ing, -ed**) (foll. by over) show excessive enthusiasm (for)

  drooled v ▷ **drool**

  drooling v ▷ **drool**

  drools v ▷ **drool**

droop v (**-s, -ing, -ed**) hang downwards loosely > **droopy** adj (**-pier, -piest**)

  drooped v ▷ **droop**

  droopier adj ▷ **droop**

  droopiest adj ▷ **droop**

  drooping v ▷ **droop**

  droops v ▷ **droop**

  droopy adj ▷ **droop**

drop v (**-s, -pping, -pped**) (allow to) fall vertically ▶ n (pl **-s**) small quantity of liquid forming a round shape ▶ pl liquid medication applied in small drops > **droplet** n (pl **-s**)

  droplet n ▷ **drop**

  droplets n ▷ **drop**

dropout n (pl **-s**) person who rejects conventional society

  dropouts n ▷ **dropout**

  dropped v ▷ **drop**

  dropping v ▷ **drop**

  drops v, n ▷ **drop**

  dropsical adj ▷ **dropsy**

dropsy n (pl **-sies**) illness in which watery fluid collects in the body > **dropsical** adj

dross n (pl **-es**) scum formed on the surfaces of molten metals

  drosses n ▷ **dross**

drought n (pl **-s**) prolonged shortage of rainfall

  droughts n ▷ **drought**

drove[1] v ▷ **drive**

drove[2] n (pl **-s**) very large group, esp. of people

drover n (pl **-s**) person who drives sheep or cattle

  drovers n ▷ **drover**

  droves n ▷ **drove**[2]

drown v (**-s, -ing, -ed**) die or kill by immersion in liquid

  drowned v ▷ **drown**

  drowning v ▷ **drown**

  drowns v ▷ **drown**

drowse v (**-ses, -sing, -sed**) be sleepy, dull, or sluggish > **drowsy** adj (**-sier, -siest**) > **drowsily** adv > **drowsiness** n (pl **-es**)

  drowsed v ▷ **drowse**

  drowses v ▷ **drowse**

  drowsier adj ▷ **drowse**

  drowsiest adj ▷ **drowse**

  drowsily adv ▷ **drowse**

  drowsiness n ▷ **drowse**

  drowsinesses n ▷ **drowse**

  drowsing v ▷ **drowse**

  drowsy adj ▷ **drowse**

drubbing n (pl **-s**) utter defeat in a contest etc

  drubbings n ▷ **drubbing**

drudge n (pl **-s**) person who works hard at uninteresting tasks > **drudgery** n (pl **-eries**)

  drudgeries n ▷ **drudge**

  drudgery n ▷ **drudge**

  drudges n ▷ **drudge**

drug n (pl **-s**) substance used in the treatment or prevention of disease ▶ v (**-s, -gging, -gged**) give a drug to (a person or animal) to cause sleepiness or unconsciousness

  drugged v ▷ **drug**

  drugging v ▷ **drug**

  drugs v, n ▷ **drug**

druid n (pl **-s**) member of an ancient order of Celtic priests > **druidic, druidical** adj

  druidic adj ▷ **druid**

  druidical adj ▷ **druid**

  druids adj ▷ **druid**

drum n (pl **-s**) percussion instrument

sounded by striking a membrane stretched across the opening of a hollow cylinder ▶ v (-s, -mming, -mmed) play (music) on a drum

drummed v ▷ drum

drummer n (pl -s) person who plays a drum or drums

drummers n ▷ drummer

drumming v ▷ drum

drums n, v ▷ drum

drunk v ▷ drink ▶ adj (-er, -est) intoxicated with alcohol to the extent of losing control over normal functions ▶ n (pl -s) person who is drunk or who frequently gets drunk

drunkard n (pl -s) person who frequently gets drunk

drunkards n ▷ drunkard

drunken adj drunk or frequently drunk
> drunkenly adv > drunkenness n (pl -es)

drunkenly adv ▷ drunken

drunkenness n ▷ drunken

drunkennesses n ▷ drunken

drunker adj ▷ drunk

drunkest adj ▷ drunk

drunks n ▷ drunk

dry adj (drier, driest or dryer, dryest) lacking moisture ▶ v (dries, drying, dried) make or become dry > drily, dryly adv > dryness n (pl -es)

dryad n (pl -s) wood nymph

dryads n ▷ dryad

dryer n (pl -s) apparatus for removing moisture ▶ adj ▷ dry

dryers n ▷ dryer

dryest adj ▷ dry

drying v ▷ dry

dryly adv ▷ dry

dryness n ▷ dry

drynesses n ▷ dry

dso n (dsos) Dso is one of several spelling for a Tibetan animal bred from yaks and cattle. The other forms are **dzo, zho** and **zo**, and it's worth remembering all of them. Dso scores 4 points.

dual adj having two parts, functions, or aspects > duality n (pl -ties)

> dually adv

dualities n ▷ dual

duality n ▷ dual

dually adv ▷ dual

dub[1] v (-s, -bbing, -bbed) give (a person or place) a name or nickname

dub[2] v (-s, -bbing, -bbed) provide (a film) with a new soundtrack, esp. in a different language

dubbed v ▷ dub[1, 2]

dubbin n (pl -s) BRIT thick grease applied to leather to soften and waterproof it

dubbing v ▷ dub[1, 2]

dubbins n ▷ dubbin

dubieties n ▷ dubious

dubiety n ▷ dubious

dubious adj feeling or causing doubt
> dubiously adv > dubiousness n (pl -es) > dubiety n (pl -ties)

dubiously adv ▷ dubious

dubiousness n ▷ dubious

dubiousnesses adv ▷ dubious

dubs v ▷ dub[1, 2]

ducal adj of a duke

ducat n (pl -s) former European gold or silver coin

ducats n ▷ ducat

duchess n (pl -es) woman who holds the rank of duke

duchesse n (pl -s) NZ dressing table with a mirror

duchesses n ▷ duchess duchesse

duchies n ▷ duchy

duchy n (pl -chies) territory of a duke or duchess

duck[1] n (pl -s) water bird with short legs, webbed feet, and a broad blunt bill

duck[2] v (-s, -ing, -ed) move (the head or body) quickly downwards, to avoid being seen or to dodge a blow

ducked v ▷ duck[2]

ducking v ▷ duck[2]

duckling n (pl -s) baby duck

ducklings n ▷ duckling

ducks n ▷ duck[1] ▶ v ▷ duck[2]

duct n (pl -s) tube, pipe, or channel through which liquid or gas is conveyed

ductile adj (of a metal) able to be

shaped into sheets or wires
ducts n ▷ duct

dud informal n (pl **-s**) ineffectual person or thing ▶ adj bad or useless

dude n (pl **-s**) US informal man
dudes n ▷ dude

dudgeon n (pl **-s**) anger, resentment
dudgeons n ▷ dudgeon

duds n ▷ dud

due adj expected or scheduled to be present or arrive ▶ n (pl **-s**) something that is owed or required ▶ pl charges for membership of a club or organization ▶ adv directly or exactly

duel n (pl **-s**) formal fight with deadly weapons between two people, to settle a quarrel ▶ v (**-s, -lling, -lled**) fight in a duel > **duellist** n (pl **-s**)

duelled v ▷ duel

duelling v ▷ duel

duellist n ▷ duel

duellists n ▷ duel

duels n, v ▷ duel

dues n ▷ due

duet n (pl **-s**) piece of music for two performers

duets n ▷ duet

duff n (pl **-er, -est**) CHIEFLY BRIT broken or useless

duffel, duffle n (pl **-s**) heavy woolen cloth

duffels n ▷ duffel

duffer n (pl **-s**) informal dull or incompetent person ▶ adj ▷ duff

duffers n ▷ duffer

duffest adj ▷ duff

duffle n ▷ duffel

duffles n ▷ duffel

dug¹ v ▷ dig

dug² n (pl **-s**) teat or udder

dugite n (pl **-s**) medium-sized Australian venomous snake
· **dugites** n ▷ dugite

dugong n (pl **-s**) whalelike mammal of tropical waters

dugongs n ▷ dugong

dugout n (pl **-s**) BRIT (at a sports ground) covered bench where

managers and substitutes sit
dugouts n ▷ dugout

dugs n ▷ dug²

duke n (pl **-s**) nobleman of the highest rank > **dukedom** n (pl **-s**)

dukedom n ▷ duke

dukedoms n ▷ duke

dukes n ▷ duke

dulcet adj (of a sound) soothing or pleasant

dulcimer n (pl **-s**) tuned percussion instrument consisting of a set of strings stretched over a sounding board and struck with hammers

dulcimers n ▷ dulcimer

dull adj (**-er, -est**) not interesting ▶ v (**-s, -ing, -ed**) make or become dull > **dullness** n (pl **-es**) > **dully** adv

dullard n (pl **-s**) dull or stupid person

dullards n ▷ dullard

dulled v ▷ dull

duller adj ▷ dull

dullest adj ▷ dull

dulling v ▷ dull

dullness n ▷ dull

dullnesses n ▷ dull

dulls v ▷ dull

dully adv ▷ dull

duly adv in a proper manner

dumb adj (**-er, -est**) lacking the power to speak > **dumbly** adv > **dumbness** n (pl **-es**)

dumbbell n (pl **-s**) short bar with a heavy ball or disc at each end, used for physical exercise

dumbbells n ▷ dumbbell

dumber adj ▷ dumb

dumbest adj ▷ dumb

dumbly adv ▷ dumb

dumbness n ▷ dumb

dumbnesses n ▷ dumb

dumdum n (pl **-s**) soft-nosed bullet that expands on impact and causes serious wounds

dumdums n ▷ dumdum

dummies n ▷ dummy

dummy n (pl **-mies**) figure representing the human form, used for displaying clothes etc ▶ *adj* imitation, substitute

dump *v* (**-s, -ing, -ed**) drop or let fall in a careless manner ▶ *n* (*pl* **-s**) place where waste materials are left

dumped *v* ▷ dump

dumpier *adj* ▷ dumpy

dumpiest *adj* ▷ dumpy

dumpily *adv* ▷ dumpy

dumpiness *n* ▷ dumpy

dumpinesses *n* ▷ dumpy

dumping *v* ▷ dump

dumpling *n* (*pl* **-s**) small ball of dough cooked and served with stew

dumplings *n* ▷ dumpling

dumps *v, n* ▷ dump

dumpy *adj* (**-ier, -iest**) short and plump > **dumpily** *adv* > **dumpiness** *n* (*pl* **-es**)

dun (**-nner, -nnest**) *adj* brownish-grey

dunce *n* (*pl* **-s**) person who is stupid or slow to learn

dunces *n* ▷ dunce

dune *n* (*pl* **-s**) mound or ridge of drifted sand

dunes *n* ▷ dune

dung *n* (*pl* **-s**) faeces from animals such as cattle

dungeon *n* (*pl* **-s**) underground prison cell

dungeons *n* ▷ dungeon

dungs *n* ▷ dung

dunk *v* (**-s, -ing, -ed**) dip (a biscuit or bread) in a drink or soup before eating it

dunked *v* ▷ dunk

dunking *v* ▷ dunk

dunks *v* ▷ dunk

dunner *adj* ▷ dun

dunnest *adj* ▷ dun

dunnies *n* ▷ dunny

dunny *n* (*pl* **-nies**) AUST & OLD-FASHIONED NZ *informal* toilet

duo *n* (*pl* **-s**) pair of performers

duodena *n* ▷ duodenum

duodenal *adj* ▷ duodenum

duodenum *n* (*pl* **-na, -nums**) first part of the small intestine, just below the stomach > **duodenal** *adj*

duodenums *n* ▷ duodenum

duos *n* ▷ duo

dupe *v* (**-pes, -ping, -ped**) deceive or cheat ▶ *n* (*pl* **-s**) person who is easily deceived

duped *v* ▷ dupe

dupes *v, n* ▷ dupe

duping *v* ▷ dupe

duple *adj* MUSIC having two beats in a bar

duplex *n* (*pl* **-es**) CHIEFLY US apartment on two floors

duplexes *n* ▷ duplex

durabilities *n* ▷ durable

durability *n* ▷ durable

durable *adj* long-lasting > **durability** *n* (*pl* **-ties**) > **durably** *adv*

durables *pl n* goods that require infrequent replacement

durably *adv* ▷ durable

duration *n* (*pl* **-s**) length of time that something lasts

durations *n* ▷ duration

duress *n* (*pl* **-es**) compulsion by use of force or threats

duresses *n* ▷ duress

during *prep* throughout or within the limit of (a period of time)

dusk *n* (*pl* **-s**) time just before nightfall, when it is almost dark

duskier *adj* ▷ dusky

duskiest *adj* ▷ dusky

duskily *adv* ▷ dusky

duskiness *n* ▷ dusky

duskinesses *n* ▷ dusky

dusks *n* ▷ dusk

dusky *adj* (**duskier, duskiest**) dark in colour > **duskily** *adv* > **duskiness** *n* (*pl* **-es**)

dust *n* (*pl* **-s**) small dry particles of earth, sand, or dirt ▶ *v* (**-s, -ing, -ed**) remove dust from (furniture) by wiping

dustbin *n* (*pl* **-s**) large container for household rubbish

dustbins *n* ▷ dustbin

dusted *v* ▷ dust

duster *n* (*pl* **-s**) cloth used for dusting

dusters *n* ▷ duster

dustier adj ▷ dusty

dustiest adj ▷ dusty

dusting v ▷ dust

dustman n (pl -men) BRIT man whose job is to collect household rubbish

dustmen n ▷ dustman

dustpan n (pl -s) short-handled shovel into which dust is swept from floors

dustpans n ▷ dustpan

dusts n, v ▷ dust

dusty adj (-tier, -tiest) covered with dust

dutiabilities n ▷ dutiable

dutiability n ▷ dutiable

dutiable adj (of goods) requiring payment of duty > **dutiability** n (pl -ties)

duties n ▷ duty

dutiful adj doing what is expected > **dutifully** adv

dutifully adv ▷ dutiful

duty n (pl -ties) work or a task performed as part of one's job

duvet n (pl -s) kind of quilt used in bed instead of a top sheet and blankets

duvets n ▷ duvet

dux n (duces). A dux is the top pupil in a school. This is a handy word to have ready if someone else has played a word containing X. Dux scores 11 points.

dwang n (pl -s) NZ & S AFR short piece of wood inserted in a timber-framed wall

dwangs n ▷ dwang

dwarf n (pl -rfs, -rves) person who is smaller than average ▶ adj (of an animal or plant) much smaller than the usual size for the species ▶ v (-s, -ing or -ed) cause (someone or something) to seem small by being much larger

dwarfed v ▷ dwarf

dwarfing v ▷ dwarf

dwarfs n, v ▷ dwarf

dwarves n ▷ dwarf

dwell v (dwells, dwelling, dwelt or dwelled) live, reside

dwelled v ▷ dwell

dweller n (pl -s) person who lives in a specified place

dwellers n ▷ dweller

dwelling n (pl -s) place of residence ▶ v ▷ dwell

dwellings n ▷ dwelling

dwells v ▷ dwell

dwelt v ▷ dwell

dwindle v (-les, -ling, -led) grow less in size, strength, or number

dwindled v ▷ dwindle

dwindles v ▷ dwindle

dwindling v ▷ dwindle

dye n (pl -s) colouring substance ▶ v (dyes, dyeing, dyed) colour (hair or fabric) by applying a dye ▶ **dyer** n (pl -s)

dyed v ▷ dye

dyeing v ▷ dye

dyer n ▷ dye

dyers n ▷ dye

dyes n, v ▷ dye

dying v ▷ die¹

dyke n (pl -s) wall built to prevent flooding

dykes n ▷ dyke

dynamic adj full of energy, ambition, and new ideas > **dynamically** adv

dynamically adv ▷ dynamic

dynamics n branch of mechanics concerned with the forces that change or produce the motions of bodies

dynamism n (pl -s) great energy and enthusiasm

dynamisms n ▷ dynamism

dynamite n (pl -s) explosive made of nitroglycerine ▶ v (-tes, -ting, -ted) blow (something) up with dynamite

dynamited v ▷ dynamite

dynamites n, v ▷ dynamite

dynamiting v ▷ dynamite

dynamo n (pl -s) device for converting mechanical energy into electrical energy

dynamos n ▷ dynamo

dynastic adj ▷ dynasty

dynasties n ▷ dynasty

dynasty n (pl -ties) sequence of hereditary rulers > **dynastic** adj

dyslexia n (pl -s) disorder causing impaired ability to read > **dyslexic** adj

dyslexias n ▷ dyslexia

dyslexic adj ▷ dyslexia

Ee

E is the most common tile in the game and, while it is only worth one point, as the most frequent letter in English it is extremely useful. Many words contain two or more Es, so, unlike many tiles, it's good to have several Es on your rack. Keep in mind three-letter words formed by two Es either side of a consonant, like **eye**, **ewe** and **eve** (6 points each), and **eke** (7). E can also be handy for getting rid of double consonants: think of words like **egg** or **ebb** (each 5 points). E also combines well with K: as well as **eke**, we have **elk** and **eek** (both 7), and **ewk** (10). If you have an X on your rack, E offers you all kinds of options: just think of all the words that begin with ex-, like **exhaust** (17), which will give you a 50-point bonus if you use all of your tiles to form it. And don't forget **ex** itself, a nice little word that earns you 9 points.

ea n (**eas**). Ea is a dialect word for a river. This word won't earn you many points, but it does provide many opportunities to play longer words that form ea in the process. Ea scores 2 points.

each adj, pron every (one) taken separately

eager adj (**-er, -est**) showing or feeling great desire, keen > **eagerly** adv
> **eagerness** n (pl **-es**)
eagerer adj ▷ **eager**
eagerest adj ▷ **eager**
eagerly adv ▷ **eager**
eagerness n ▷ **eager**
eagernesses n ▷ **eager**

eagle n (pl **-s**) large bird of prey with keen eyesight
eagles n ▷ **eagle**

eaglet n (pl **-s**) young eagle
eaglets n ▷ **eaglet**

ear¹ n (pl **-s**) organ of hearing, esp. the external part of it

ear² n (pl **-s**) head of corn

earache n (pl **-s**) pain in the ear
earaches n ▷ **earache**

earbash v (**-es, -ing, -ed**) AUST & NZ informal talk incessantly
> **earbashing** n (pl **-s**)
earbashed n ▷ **earbash**
earbashes n ▷ **earbash**
earbashing v, n ▷ **earbash**
earbashings n ▷ **earbash**

eardrum n (pl **-s**) thin piece of skin inside the ear which enables one to hear sounds
eardrums n ▷ **eardrum**

earl n (pl **-s**) British nobleman ranking next below a marquess > **earldom** n (pl **-s**)
earldom n ▷ **earl**
earldoms n ▷ **earl**
earlier adj, adv ▷ **early**
earliest adj, adv ▷ **early**
earls n ▷ **earl**

early adj, adv (**-lier, -liest**) before the expected or usual time

earmark v (**-s, -ing, -ed**) set (something) aside for a specific purpose
earmarked v ▷ **earmark**
earmarking v ▷ **earmark**

earmarks v ▷ earmark

earn v (-s, -ing, -ed) obtain by work or merit

earned v ▷ earn

earnest¹ adj serious and sincere
> earnestly adv

earnest² n (pl -s) part payment given in advance, esp. to confirm a contract

earnestly adv ▷ earnest¹

earnests n ▷ earnest²

earning v ▷ earn

earnings pl n money earned

earns v ▷ earn

earphone n (pl -s) receiver for a radio etc, held to or put in the ear

earphones n ▷ earphone

earring n (pl -s) ornament for the lobe of the ear

earrings n ▷ earring

ears n ▷ ear¹, ²

earshot n (pl -s) hearing range

earshots n ▷ earshot

earth n (pl -s) land, the ground ▶ v (-s, -ing, -ed) connect (a circuit) to earth

earthed v ▷ earth

earthen adj made of baked clay or earth

earthier adj ▷ earthy

earthiest adj ▷ earthy

earthing v ▷ earth

earthly adj conceivable or possible

earths n, v ▷ earth

earthy adj (-thier, -thiest) coarse or crude

earwig n (pl -s) small insect with a pincer-like tail

earwigs n ▷ earwig

ease n (pl -s) freedom from difficulty, discomfort, or worry ▶ v (-ses, -sing, -sed) give bodily or mental ease to

eased v ▷ ease

easel n (pl -s) frame to support an artist's canvas or a blackboard

easels n ▷ easel

eases n, v ▷ ease

easier adj ▷ easy

easiest adj ▷ easy

easily adv ▷ easy

easiness n ▷ easy

easinesses n ▷ easy

easing v ▷ ease

east n (pl -s) (direction towards) the part of the horizon where the sun rises ▶ adj to or in the east ▶ adv in, to, or towards the east > easterly adj > eastern adj > eastward adj, adv > eastwards adv

easterly adj ▷ east

eastern adj ▷ east

easts n ▷ east

eastward adj, adv ▷ east

eastwards adv ▷ east

easy adj (-ier, -iest) not needing much work or effort > easily adv > easiness n (pl -es)

eat v (-s, -ing, ate, -en) take (food) into the mouth and swallow it

eatable adj fit or suitable for eating

eaten v ▷ eat

eating v ▷ eat

eats v ▷ eat

eaves pl n overhanging edges of a roof

ebb v (-s, -ing, -ed) (of tide water) flow back ▶ n (pl -s) flowing back of the tide

ebbed v ▷ ebb

ebbing v ▷ ebb

ebbs v, n ▷ ebb

ebonies n ▷ ebony

ebony n (pl -ies) hard black wood ▶ adj deep black

echelon n (pl -s) level of power or responsibility

echelons n ▷ echelon

echidna n (pl -nas, -nae) Australian spiny egg-laying mammal

echidnae n ▷ echidna

echidnas n ▷ echidna

echo n (pl -es) repetition of sounds by reflection of sound waves off a surface ▶ v (-es, -ing, -ed) repeat or be repeated as an echo

echoed v ▷ echo

echoes v, n ▷ echo

echoing v ▷ echo

éclair n (pl -s) finger-shaped pastry filled with cream and covered with

chocolate
éclairs n ▷ **éclair**
éclat n brilliant success
eclectic adj selecting from various
styles, ideas, or sources >**eclecticism** n
(pl -s)
eclecticism n ▷ **eclectic**
eclecticisms n ▷ **eclectic**
eclipse n (pl -s) temporary obscuring of
one star or planet by another ▶ v (-ses,
-sing, -sed) surpass or outclass
eclipsed v ▷ **eclipse**
eclipses n, v ▷ **eclipse**
eclipsing v ▷ **eclipse**
ecliptic n (pl -s) apparent path of
the sun
ecliptics n ▷ **ecliptic**
ecologies n ▷ **ecology**
ecologist n ▷ **ecology**
ecologists n ▷ **ecology**
ecology n (pl -ies) study of the
relationships between living things
and their environment >**ecologist** n
(pl -s)
economic adj of economics
economies n ▷ **economy**
economy n (pl -ies) system of
interrelationship of money, industry,
and employment in a country
ecru adj pale creamy-brown
ecstasies n ▷ **ecstasy**
ecstasy n (pl -ies) state of
intense delight >**ecstatic** adj
>**ecstatically** adv
ecstatic adj ▷ **ecstasy**
ecstatically adv ▷ **ecstasy**
eczema n (pl s) skin disease causing
intense itching
eczemas n ▷ **eczema**
eddied v ▷ **eddy**
eddies n, v ▷ **eddy**
eddy n (pl eddies) circular movement
of air, water, etc ▶ v (eddies, eddying,
eddied) move with a circular motion
eddying v ▷ **eddy**
edge n (pl -s) border or line where
something ends or begins ▶ v (-ges,
-ging, -ged) provide an edge or

border for
edged v ▷ **edge**
edges n, v ▷ **edge**
edgeways adv with the edge forwards
or uppermost
edgier adj ▷ **edgy**
edgiest adj ▷ **edgy**
edging v ▷ **edge**
edgy adj (-gier, -giest) (-giest nervous
or irritable
edibilities n ▷ **edible**
edibility n ▷ **edible**
edible adj fit to be eaten >**edibility** n
(pl -ties)
edict n (pl -s) order issued by an
authority
edicts n ▷ **edict**
edification n ▷ **edify**
edifications n ▷ **edify**
edifice n (pl -s) large building
edifices n ▷ **edifice**
edified v ▷ **edify**
edifies v ▷ **edify**
edify v (-fies, -fying, -fied) improve
morally by instruction >**edification** n
(pl -s)
edifying v ▷ **edify**
edit v (-s, -ing, -ed) prepare (a book,
film, etc) for publication or broadcast
edited v ▷ **edit**
editing v ▷ **edit**
edition n (pl -s) number of copies of a
new publication printed at one time
editions n ▷ **edition**
editor n (pl -s) person who edits
editors n ▷ **editor**
edits v ▷ **edit**
educate v (-tes, -ting, -ted) teach
>**education** n (pl -s) >**educational** adj
>**educationally** adv
educated v ▷ **educate**
educates v ▷ **educate**
educating v ▷ **educate**
educational adj ▷ **educate**
educationally adv ▷ **educate**
educations n ▷ **educate**
eel n (pl -s) snakelike fish
eels n ▷ **eel**

eerie *adj* (**-r, -st**) uncannily frightening or disturbing ▷ **eerily** *adv*

eerier *adj* ▷ **eerie**

eeriest *adj* ▷ **eerie**

eerily *adv* ▷ **eerie**

ef *n* (**efs**). Ef is the letter F, and is a handy word to know when you want to play a longer word parallel to a word that's already on the board. Ef scores 5 points.

efface *v* (**-ces, -cing, -ced**) remove by rubbing ▷ **effacement** *n* (*pl* **-s**)

effaced *v* ▷ **efface**

effacement *n* ▷ **efface**

effacements *n* ▷ **efface**

effaces *v* ▷ **efface**

effacing *v* ▷ **efface**

effect *n* (*pl* **-s**) change or result caused by someone or something ▶ *pl* personal belongings ▶ *v* (**-s, -ing, -ed**) cause to happen, accomplish

effected *v* ▷ **effect**

effecting *v* ▷ **effect**

effects *n, v* ▷ **effect**

effete *adj* powerless, feeble

effigies *n* ▷ **effigy**

effigy *n* (*pl* **-ies**) image or likeness of a person

effluent *n* (*pl* **-s**) liquid discharged as waste

effluents *n* ▷ **effluent**

effort *n* (*pl* **-s**) physical or mental exertion ▷ **effortless** *adj*

effortless *adj* ▷ **effort**

efforts *n* ▷ **effort**

effusion *n* (*pl* **-s**) unrestrained outburst

effusions *n* ▷ **effusion**

effusive *adj* openly emotional, demonstrative ▷ **effusively** *adv*

effusively *adv* ▷ **effusive**

egg¹ *n* (*pl* **-s**) oval or round object laid by the females of birds and other creatures, containing a developing embryo

egg² *v* (**-s, -ing, -ed**) encourage or incite, esp. to do wrong

egged *v* ▷ **egg²**

egghead *n* (*pl* **-s**) *informal* intellectual person

eggheads *n* ▷ **egghead**

egging *v* ▷ **egg²**

eggplant *n* (*pl* **-s**) US, CANADIAN, AUST & NZ aubergine

eggplants *n* ▷ **eggplant**

eggs *n, v* ▷ **egg¹, ²**

ego *n* (*pl* **-s**) the conscious mind of an individual

egoism, egotism *n* (*pl* **-s**) excessive concern for one's own interests ▷ **egoist, egotist** *n* (*pl* **-s**) ▷ **egoistic, egotistic** *adj*

egoisms *n* ▷ **egoism**

egoist *n* ▷ **egoism**

egoistic *adj* ▷ **egoism**

egoists *n* ▷ **egoism**

egos *n* ▷ **ego**

egotism *n* ▷ **egoism**

egotisms *n* ▷ **egoism**

egotist *n* ▷ **egoism**

egotistic *adj* ▷ **egoism**

egotists *n* ▷ **egoism**

egress *n* (*pl* **-es**) departure

egresses *n* ▷ **egress**

egret *n* (*pl* **-s**) lesser white heron

egrets *n* ▷ **egret**

eider *n* (*pl* **-s**) Arctic duck

eiders *n* ▷ **eider**

eight *adj, n* (*pl* **-s**) one more than seven

eighteen *adj, n* (*pl* **-s**) eight and ten ▷ **eighteenth** *adj, n* (*pl* **-s**)

eighteens *n* ▷ **eighteen**

eighteenth *adj, n* ▷ **eighteen**

eighteenths *n* ▷ **eighteen**

eighth *adj, n* (*pl* **-s**) (of) number eight in a series

eighths *n* ▷ **eighth**

eighties *n* ▷ **eighty**

eightieth *n* ▷ **eighty**

eightieths *n* ▷ **eighty**

eights *n* ▷ **eight**

eighty *adj, n* (*pl* **-ies**) eight times ten ▷ **eightieth** *adj, n* (*pl* **-s**)

either *adj, pron* one or the other (of two) ▶ *conj* used preceding two or more possibilities joined by *or* ▶ *adv* likewise

eject v (**-s, -ing, -ed**) force out, expel
> **ejection** n (pl **-s**) > **ejector** n (pl **-s**)
ejected v ▷ eject
ejecting v ▷ eject
ejection n ▷ eject
ejections n ▷ eject
ejector n ▷ eject
ejectors n ▷ eject
ejects v ▷ eject

eke v (**ekes, eking, eked**) (usu. foll. by
out) make (a living) with difficulty
eked v ▷ eke
ekes v ▷ eke
eking v ▷ eke

élan n (pl **-s**) style and vigour
eland n (pl **-s**) large antelope of
southern Africa
elands n ▷ eland
élans n ▷ élan

elapse v (**-ses, -sing, -sed**) (of time)
pass by
elapsed v ▷ elapse
elapses v ▷ elapse
elapsing v ▷ elapse

elastic adj resuming normal shape
after distortion ▶ n (pl **-s**) tape or fabric
containing interwoven strands of
flexible rubber > **elasticity** n (pl **-ties**)
elasticities n ▷ elastic
elasticity n ▷ elastic
elastics n ▷ elastic

elate v (**-tes, -ting, -ted**) make
extremely happy and excited
> **elation** n (pl **-s**)
elated v ▷ elate
elates v ▷ elate
elating v ▷ elate
elation n ▷ elate
elations n ▷ elate

elbow n (pl **-s**) joint between the upper
arm and the forearm ▶ v (**-s, -ing, -ed**)
shove or strike with the elbow
elbowed v ▷ elbow
elbowing v ▷ elbow
elbows n, v ▷ elbow

elder[1] adj older ▶ n (pl **-s**) older person
elder[2] n (pl **-s**) small tree with white
flowers and black berries

elderly adj (fairly) old
elders n ▷ elder[1, 2]
eldest adj oldest
eldritch adj SCOT weird, uncanny
elect v (**-s, -ing, -ed**) choose by voting
▶ adj appointed but not yet in office
elected v ▷ elect
electing v ▷ elect
election n (pl **-s**) choosing of
representatives by voting
elections n ▷ election
elective adj chosen by election
elector n (pl **-s**) someone who has
the right to vote in an election
> **electoral** adj ▷ elector
electoral adj ▷ elector
electors n ▷ elector
electric adj produced by, transmitting,
or powered by electricity
electron n (pl **-s**) elementary particle
in all atoms that has a negative
electrical charge
electrons n ▷ electron
elects v ▷ elect
elegance n ▷ elegant
elegances n ▷ elegant
elegant adj pleasing or graceful in
dress, style, or design ▶ **elegance** n
(pl **-s**)
elegiac adj mournful or plaintive
elegies n ▷ elegy
elegy n (pl **-ies**) mournful poem, esp. a
lament for the dead
element n (pl **-s**) component part ▶ pl
basic principles of something
elements n ▷ element
elephant n (pl **-s**) huge four-footed
thick-skinned animal with ivory tusks
and a long trunk
elephants n ▷ elephant
elevate v (**-tes, -ting, -ted**) raise in
rank or status
elevated v ▷ elevate
elevates v ▷ elevate
elevating v ▷ elevate
elevator n (pl **-s**) AUST, US & CANADIAN
lift for carrying people

elevators n ▷ elevator

eleven adj, n (pl **-s**) one more than ten

elevens n ▷ eleven

eleventh adj, n (pl **-s**) (of) number
eleven in a series

elevenths n ▷ eleventh

elf n (pl **elves**) (in folklore) small
mischievous fairy

elfin adj small and delicate

elicit v (**-s, -ing, -ed**) bring about (a
response or reaction)

elicited v ▷ elicit

eliciting v ▷ elicit

elicits v ▷ elicit

elide v (**-des, -ding, -ded**) omit (a
vowel or syllable) from a spoken word
> **elision** n (pl **-s**)

elided v ▷ elide

elides v ▷ elide

eliding v ▷ elide

eligibilities n ▷ eligible

eligibility n ▷ eligible

eligible adj meeting the requirements
or qualifications needed > **eligibility** n
(pl **-ties**)

elision n ▷ elide

elisions n ▷ elide

elite n (pl **-s**) most powerful, rich, or
gifted members of a group

elites n ▷ elite

elitism n (pl **-s**) belief that society
should be governed by a small group of
superior people > **elitist** n, adj (pl **-s**)

elitisms n ▷ elitism

elitist n ▷ elitism

elitists n ▷ elitism

elixir n (pl **-s**) imaginary liquid that
can prolong life or turn base metals
into gold

elixirs n ▷ elixir

elk n (pl **-s**) large deer of N Europe
and Asia

elks n ▷ elk

ellipse n (pl **-s**) oval shape

ellipses n ▷ ellipse ▷ ellipsis

ellipsis n (pl **-pses**) omission of letters
or words in a sentence

elm n (pl **-s**) tree with serrated leaves

elms n ▷ elm

elongate v (**-tes, -ting, -ted**) make or
become longer > **elongation** n (pl **-s**)

elongated v ▷ elongate

elongates v ▷ elongate

elongating v ▷ elongate

elongation n ▷ elongate

elongations n ▷ elongate

elope v (**-s, -ing, -ed**) (of two people)
run away secretly to get married
> **elopement** n (pl **-s**)

eloped v ▷ elope

elopement n ▷ elope

elopements n ▷ elope

elopes v ▷ elope

eloping v ▷ elope

else adv in addition or more

elude v (**-s, -ing, -ed**) escape from by
cleverness or quickness

eluded v ▷ elude

eludes v ▷ elude

eluding v ▷ elude

elusive adj difficult to catch or
remember

elver n (pl **-s**) young eel

elvers n ▷ elver

elves n ▷ elf

emanate v (**-tes, -ting, -ted**) issue,
proceed from a source > **emanation** n
(pl **-s**)

emanated v ▷ emanate

emanates v ▷ emanate

emanating v ▷ emanate

emanation n ▷ emanate

emanations n ▷ emanate

embalm v (**-s, -ing, -ed**) preserve
(a corpse) from decay by the use of
chemicals etc

embalmed v ▷ embalm

embalming v ▷ embalm

embalms v ▷ embalm

embargo n (pl **-oes**) order by a
government prohibiting trade with a
country ▶ v (**-oes, -oing, -oed**) put an
embargo on

embargoed v ▷ embargo

embargoes n, v ▷ embargo

embargoing v ▷ embargo

embark v (-s, -ing, -ed) board a ship or aircraft (foll. by **on**) ▷ **embarkation** n (-s)

embarkation n ▷ embark

embarkations n ▷ embark

embarked v ▷ embark

embarking v ▷ embark

embarks v ▷ embark

embassies n ▷ embassy

embassy n (pl -ies) offices or official residence of an ambassador

embed v (-s, -dding, -dded) fix firmly in something solid

embedded adj (of a journalist) assigned to accompany an active military unit ▶ v ▷ embed

embedding v ▷ embed

embeds v ▷ embed

ember n (pl -s) glowing piece of wood or coal in a dying fire

embers n ▷ ember

embezzle v (-s, -ing, -ed) steal money that has been entrusted to one > **embezzlement** n (pl -s) > **embezzler** n (pl -s)

embezzled v ▷ embezzle

embezzlement n ▷ embezzle

embezzlements n ▷ embezzle

embezzler n ▷ embezzle

embezzlers n ▷ embezzle

embezzles v ▷ embezzle

embezzling v ▷ embezzle

emblazon v (-s, -ing, -ed) decorate with bright colours

emblazoned v ▷ emblazon

emblazoning v ▷ emblazon

emblazons v ▷ emblazon

emblem n (pl -s) object or design that symbolizes a quality, type, or group > **emblematic** adj

emblematic adj ▷ emblem

emblems n ▷ emblem

embodied v ▷ embody

embodies v ▷ embody

embodiment n ▷ embody

embodiments n ▷ embody

embody v (-dies, -dying, -died) be an example or expression of

> **embodiment** n (pl -s)

embodying v ▷ embody

embolden v (-s, -ing, -ed) encourage (someone)

emboldened v ▷ embolden

emboldening v ▷ embolden

emboldens v ▷ embolden

embolism n (pl -s) blocking of a blood vessel by a blood clot or air bubble

embolisms n ▷ embolism

embossed adj (of a design or pattern) standing out from a surface

embrace v (-ces, -cing, -ced) clasp in the arms, hug ▶ n (pl -s) act of embracing

embraced v ▷ embrace

embraces v, n ▷ embrace

embracing v ▷ embrace

embroil v (-s, -ing, -ed) involve (a person) in problems

embroiled v ▷ embroil

embroiling v ▷ embroil

embroils v ▷ embroil

embryo n (pl -s) unborn creature in the early stages of development > **embryology** n (pl -gies)

embryologies n ▷ embryo

embryology n ▷ embryo

embryos n ▷ embryo

emend v (-s, -ing, -ed) remove errors from > **emendation** n (pl -s)

emendation n ▷ emend

emendations n ▷ emend

emended v ▷ emend

emending v ▷ emend

emends v ▷ emend

emerald n (pl -s) bright green precious stone ▶ adj bright green

emeralds n ▷ emerald

emerge v (-ges, -ging, -ged) come into view > **emergence** n (pl -s) > **emergent** adj

emerged v ▷ emerge

emergence n ▷ emerge

emergences n ▷ emerge

emergent adj ▷ emerge

emerges v ▷ emerge

emerging v ▷ emerge

emeries n ▷ **emery**

emeritus adj retired, but retaining an honorary title

emery n (pl-**ries**) hard mineral used for smoothing and polishing

emetic n (pl-**s**) substance that causes vomiting ▶ adj causing vomiting

emetics n ▷ **emetic**

emigrant n ▷ **emigrate**

emigrants n ▷ **emigrate**

emigrate v (-**tes**, -**ting**, -**ted**) go and settle in another country > **emigrant** n (pl-**s**) > **emigration** n (pl-**s**)

emigrated v ▷ **emigrate**

emigrates v ▷ **emigrate**

emigrating v ▷ **emigrate**

emigration n ▷ **emigrate**

emigrations n ▷ **emigrate**

émigré n (pl-**s**) someone who has left his native country for political reasons

émigrés n ▷ **émigré**

eminence n (pl-**s**) position of superiority or fame

eminences n ▷ **eminence**

eminent adj distinguished, well-known > **eminently** adv

eminently adv ▷ **eminent**

emir n (pl-**s**) Muslim ruler

emirate n (pl-**s**) country ruled by an emir

emirates n ▷ **emirate**

emirs n ▷ **emir**

emissaries n ▷ **emissary**

emissary n (pl-**ies**) agent sent on a mission by a government

emission n ▷ **emit**

emissions n ▷ **emit**

emit v (-**s**, -**tting**, -**tted**) give out (heat, light, or a smell) > **emission** n (pl-**s**)

emits v ▷ **emit**

emitted v ▷ **emit**

emitting v ▷ **emit**

emoticon n (pl-**s**) COMPUTERS ▷ **smiley**

emoticons n ▷ **emoticon**

emotion n (pl-**s**) strong feeling

emotions n ▷ **emotion**

emotive adj tending to arouse emotion

empathies n ▷ **empathy**

empathy n (pl-**thies**) ability to understand someone else's feelings as if they were one's own

emperor n (pl-**s**) ruler of an empire > **empress** n fem (pl-**es**)

emperors n ▷ **emperor**

emphases n ▷ **emphasis**

emphasis n (pl-**ses**) special importance or significance > **emphasize** or (-**s**, -**ing**, -**ed**)

emphasize v ▷ **emphasis**

emphasized v ▷ **emphasis**

emphasizes v ▷ **emphasis**

emphasizing v ▷ **emphasis**

emphatic adj showing emphasis > **emphatically** adv

emphatically adv ▷ **emphatic**

empire n (pl-**s**) group of territories under the rule of one state or person

empires n ▷ **empire**

employ v (-**s**, -**ing**, -**ed**) hire (a person) ▶ n (pl-**s**) > **employee** n (pl-**s**)

employed v ▷ **employ**

employee n ▷ **employ**

employees n ▷ **employ**

employer n (pl-**s**) person or organization that employs someone

employers n ▷ **employer**

employing v ▷ **employ**

employs v, n ▷ **employ**

emporia n ▷ **emporium**

emporium n (pl-**riums**, -**ria**) old-fashioned large general shop

emporiums n ▷ **emporia**

empower v (-**s**, -**ing**, -**ed**) enable, authorize

empowered v ▷ **empower**

empowering v ▷ **empower**

empowers v ▷ **empower**

empress n ▷ **emperor**

empresses n ▷ **emperor**

emptied v ▷ **empty**

emptier adj ▷ **empty**

empties pl n empty boxes, bottles, etc ▶ v ▷ **empty**

emptiest adj ▷ **empty**

emptiness n ▷ **empty**

emptinesses v ▷ **empty**

empty adj (**-tier, -tiest**) containing nothing ▶ v (**-ties, -tying, -tied**) make or become empty > **emptiness** n (pl **-es**)

emptying v ▷ **empty**

emu n (pl **-s**) large Australian flightless bird with long legs

emulate v (**-tes, -ting, -ted**) attempt to equal or surpass by imitating > **emulation** n (pl **-s**)

emulated v ▷ **emulate**

emulates v ▷ **emulate**

emulating v ▷ **emulate**

emulation n ▷ **emulate**

emulations n ▷ **emulate**

emulsified v ▷ **emulsify**

emulsifier n ▷ **emulsify**

emulsifiers n ▷ **emulsify**

emulsifies v ▷ **emulsify**

emulsify v (**-fies, -fying, -fied**) (of two liquids) join together or join (two liquids) together > **emulsifier** n (pl **-s**)

emulsifying v ▷ **emulsify**

emulsion n (pl **-s**) light-sensitive coating on photographic film ▶ v (**-s, -ing, -ed**) paint with emulsion paint

emulsioned v ▷ **emulsion**

emulsioning v ▷ **emulsion**

emulsions n, v ▷ **emulsion**

emus n ▷ **emu**

enable v (**-les, -ling, -led**) provide (a person) with the means, opportunity, or authority (to do something)

enabled v ▷ **enable**

enables v ▷ **enable**

enabling v ▷ **enable**

enact v (**-s, -ing, -ed**) establish by law > **enactment** n (pl **-s**)

enacted v ▷ **enact**

enacting v ▷ **enact**

enactment n ▷ **enact**

enactments n ▷ **enact**

enacts v ▷ **enact**

enamel n (pl **-s**) glasslike coating applied to metal etc to preserve the surface ▶ v (**-s, -lling, -lled**) cover with enamel

enamelled v ▷ **enamel**

enamelling v ▷ **enamel**

enamels n, v ▷ **enamel**

encamp v (**-s, -ing, -ed**) set up in a camp > **encampment** n (pl **-s**)

encamped v ▷ **encamp**

encamping v ▷ **encamp**

encampment n ▷ **encamp**

encampments n ▷ **encamp**

encamps v ▷ **encamp**

enchant v (**-s, -ing, -ed**) delight and fascinate > **enchantment** n (pl **-s**) > **enchanter** n (pl **-s**) > **enchantress** n fem (pl **-es**)

enchanted v ▷ **enchant**

enchanter n ▷ **enchant**

enchanters n ▷ **enchant**

enchanting v ▷ **enchant**

enchantment n ▷ **enchant**

enchantments n ▷ **enchant**

enchantress n ▷ **enchant**

enchantresses n ▷ **enchant**

enchants v ▷ **enchant**

encircle v (**-s, -ling, -led**) form a circle around > **encirclement** n (pl **-s**)

encircled v ▷ **encircle**

encirclement n ▷ **encircle**

encirclements n ▷ **encircle**

encircles v ▷ **encircle**

encircling v ▷ **encircle**

enclave n (pl **-s**) part of a country entirely surrounded by foreign territory

enclaves n ▷ **enclave**

enclose v (**-s, -sing, -sed**) surround completely > **enclosure** n (pl **-s**)

enclosed v ▷ **enclose**

encloses v ▷ **enclose**

enclosing v ▷ **enclose**

enclosure n ▷ **enclose**

enclosures n ▷ **enclose**

encomia n ▷ **encomium**

encomium n (pl **-miums, -mia**) formal expression of praise

encore interj again, once more ▶ n (pl **-s**) extra performance due to enthusiastic demand

encores n ▷ **encore**

encroach v (-es, -ing, -ed) intrude gradually on a person's rights or land
> **encroachment** n (pl -s)
encroached v ▷ encroach
encroaches v ▷ encroach
encroaching v ▷ encroach
encroachment n ▷ encroach
encroachments n ▷ encroach

encrust v (-s, -ing, -ed) cover with a layer of something
encrusted v ▷ encrust
encrusting v ▷ encrust
encrusts v ▷ encrust

encumber v (-s, -ing, -ed) hinder or impede
encumbered v ▷ encumber
encumbering v ▷ encumber
encumbers v ▷ encumber

end n (pl -s) furthest point or part ▶ v (-s, -ing, -ed) bring or come to a finish
> **ending** n (pl -s) > **endless** adj
endanger v (-s, -ing, -ed) put in danger
endangered v ▷ endanger
endangering v ▷ endanger
endangers v ▷ endanger

endear v (-s, -ing, -ed) cause to be liked > **endearing** adj
endeared v ▷ endear
endearing v, adj ▷ endear
endears v ▷ endear
ended v ▷ end

endemic adj present within a localized area or peculiar to a particular group of people
ending v, n ▷ end
endings n ▷ end

endive n (pl -s) curly-leaved plant used in salads
endives n ▷ endive
endless adj ▷ end

endorse v (-ses, -sing, -sed) give approval to > **endorsement** n (pl -s)
endorsed v ▷ endorse
endorsement n ▷ endorse
endorsements n ▷ endorse
endorses v ▷ endorse
endorsing v ▷ endorse

endow v (-s, -ing, -ed) provide permanent income for
> **endowment** n (pl -s)
endowed v ▷ endow
endowing v ▷ endow
endowment v ▷ endow
endowments v ▷ endow
endows v ▷ endow
ends n, v ▷ end

endurable adj ▷ endure
endure v (-res, -ring, -red) bear (hardship) patiently > **endurable** adj
endured v ▷ endure
endures v ▷ endure
enduring v ▷ endure

endways adv having the end forwards or upwards

enema n (pl -s) medicine injected into the rectum to empty the bowels
enemas n ▷ enema
enemies n ▷ enemy

enemy n (pl -mies) hostile person or nation, opponent

energetic adj > energy
energetically adv > energy
energies n > energy

energize v (-zes, -zing, -zed) give vigour to
energized v ▷ energize
energizes v ▷ energize
energizing v ▷ energize

energy n (pl -gies) capacity for intense activity > **energetic** adj
> **energetically** adv

enervate v (-tes, -ting, -ted) deprive of strength or vitality > **enervation** n (pl -s)
enervated v ▷ enervate
enervates v ▷ enervate
enervating v ▷ enervate
enervation n ▷ enervate
enervations n ▷ enervate

enfeeble v (-les, -ling, -led) weaken
enfeebled v ▷ enfeeble
enfeebles v ▷ enfeeble
enfeebling v ▷ enfeeble

enfold v (-s, -ing, -ed) cover by wrapping something around

enfolded v ▷ enfold
enfolding v ▷ enfold
enfolds v ▷ enfold
enforce v (-ces, -cing, -ced)
impose obedience (to a law etc)
> **enforceable** adj > **enforcement** n
(pl -s)
enforced v ▷ enforce
enforcement n ▷ enforce
enforcements n ▷ enforce
enforces v ▷ enforce
enforcing v ▷ enforce
engage v (-ges, -ging, -ged) take part,
participate > **engagement** n (pl -s)
engaged adj pledged to be married
▶ v ▷ engage
engagement n ▷ engage
engagements n ▷ engage
engages v ▷ engage
engaging adj charming ▶ v ▷ engage
engender v (-s, -ing, -ed) produce,
cause to occur
engendered v ▷ engender
engendering v ▷ engender
engenders v ▷ engender
engine n (pl -s) any machine which
converts energy into mechanical work
engineer n (pl -s) person trained in
any branch of engineering ▶ v (-s, -ing,
-ed) plan in a clever manner
engineered v ▷ engineer
engineers n, v ▷ engineer
engines v ▷ engine
engrave v (-ves, -ving, -ved) carve
(a design) onto a hard surface
> **engraver** n (pl -s)
engraved v ▷ engrave
engraver n ▷ engrave
engravers n ▷ engrave
engraves v ▷ engrave
engross v (-es, -ing, -ed) occupy the
attention of (a person) completely
engrossed v ▷ engross
engrosses v ▷ engross
engrossing v ▷ engross
engulf v (-s, -ing, -ed) cover or
surround completely
engulfed v ▷ engulf

engulfing v ▷ engulf
engulfs v ▷ engulf
enhance v (-ced, -cing, -ced) increase
in quality, value, or attractiveness
> **enhancement** n (pl -s)
enhanced v ▷ enhance
enhancement n ▷ enhance
enhancements n ▷ enhance
enhances v ▷ enhance
enhancing v ▷ enhance
enigma n (pl -s) puzzling thing
or person > **enigmatic** adj
> **enigmatically** adv
enigmas n ▷ enigma
enigmatic adj ▷ enigma
enigmatically adv ▷ enigma
enjoin v (-s, -ing, -ed) order (someone)
to do something
enjoined v ▷ enjoin
enjoining v ▷ enjoin
enjoins v ▷ enjoin
enjoy v (-s, -ing, -ed) take joy in
> **enjoyable** adj > **enjoyment** n (pl -s)
enjoyable adj ▷ enjoy
enjoyed v ▷ enjoy
enjoying v ▷ enjoy
enjoyment n ▷ enjoy
enjoyments n ▷ enjoy
enjoys v ▷ enjoy
enlarge v (-ges, -ging, -ged)
make or grow larger (foll. by **on**)
> **enlargement** n (pl -s)
enlarged v ▷ enlarge
enlargement n ▷ enlarge
enlargements n ▷ enlarge
enlarges v ▷ enlarge
enlarging v ▷ enlarge
enlist v (-s, -ing, -ed) enter the armed
forces > **enlistment** n (pl -s)
enlisted v ▷ enlist
enlisting v ▷ enlist
enlistment n ▷ enlist
enlistments n ▷ enlist
enlists v ▷ enlist
enliven v (-s, -ing, -ed) make lively
or cheerful
enlivened v ▷ enliven
enlivening v ▷ enliven

enlivens v ▷ enliven
enmeshed adj deeply involved
enmities n ▷ enmity
enmity n (pl -ies) ill will, hatred
ennoble v (-s, -ing, -ed) make noble, elevate
  ennobled v ▷ ennoble
  ennobles v ▷ ennoble
  ennobling v ▷ ennoble
ennui n (pl -s) boredom, dissatisfaction
  ennuis n ▷ ennui
enormities n ▷ enormity
enormity n (pl -ties) great wickedness
enormous adj very big, vast
enough adj as much or as many as necessary ► pron sufficient quantity ► adv sufficiently
enquire v (-res, -ring, -red) ▷ inquire
  > enquiry n (pl -ries)
  enquired v ▷ enquire
  enquires v ▷ enquire
  enquiries n ▷ enquire
  enquiring v ▷ enquire
  enquiry n ▷ enquire
enrich v (-es, -ing, -ed) improve in quality
  enriched v ▷ enrich
  enriches v ▷ enrich
  enriching v ▷ enrich
enrol v (-s, -lling, -lled) (cause to) become a member > **enrolment** n (pl -s)
  enrolled v ▷ enrol
  enrolling v ▷ enrol
  enrolment n ▷ enrol
  enrolments n ▷ enrol
  enrols v ▷ enrol
ensconce v (-ces, -cing, -ced) settle firmly or comfortably
  ensconced v ▷ ensconce
  ensconces v ▷ ensconce
  ensconcing v ▷ ensconce
ensemble n (pl -s) all the parts of something taken together
  ensembles n ▷ ensemble
enshrine v (-nes, -ning, -ned) cherish or treasure
  enshrined v ▷ enshrine

enshrines v ▷ enshrine
enshrining v ▷ enshrine
ensign n (pl -s) naval flag
  ensigns n ▷ ensign
enslave v (-ves, -ving, -ved) make a slave of (someone) > **enslavement** n (pl -s)
  enslaved v ▷ enslave
  enslavement n ▷ enslave
  enslavements n ▷ enslave
  enslaves v ▷ enslave
  enslaving v ▷ enslave
ensnare v (-res, -ring, -red) catch in or as if in a snare
  ensnared v ▷ ensnare
  ensnares v ▷ ensnare
  ensnaring v ▷ ensnare
ensue v (-sues, -suing, -sued) come next, result
  ensued v ▷ ensue
  ensues v ▷ ensue
  ensuing v ▷ ensue
ensure v (-res, -ring, -red) make certain or sure
  ensured v ▷ ensure
  ensures v ▷ ensure
  ensuring v ▷ ensure
entail v (-s, -ing, -ed) bring about or impose inevitably
  entailed v ▷ entail
  entailing v ▷ entail
  entails v ▷ entail
entangle v (-les, -ling, -led) catch or involve in or as if in a tangle
  > **entanglement** n (pl -s)
  entangled v ▷ entangle
  entanglement n ▷ entangle
  entanglements n ▷ entangle
  entangles v ▷ entangle
  entangling v ▷ entangle
entente n (pl -s) friendly understanding between nations
  ententes n ▷ entente
enter v (-s, -ing, -ed) come or go in
  entered v ▷ enter
enteric adj intestinal
  entering v ▷ enter
  enters v ▷ enter

enthral v (-s, -lling, -lled) hold the attention of > **enthralling** adj
enthralled v ▷ enthral
enthralling v, adj ▷ enthral
enthrals v ▷ enthral
enthuse v (-s, -sing, -ed) (cause to) show enthusiasm
enthused v ▷ enthuse
enthuses v ▷ enthuse
enthusing v ▷ enthuse
entice v (-ces, -cing, -ced) attract by exciting hope or desire, tempt > **enticement** n (pl -s)
enticed v ▷ entice
enticement n ▷ entice
enticements n ▷ entice
entices v ▷ entice
enticing v ▷ entice
entire adj including every detail, part, or aspect of something > **entirely** adv > **entirety** n (pl -ties)
entirely adv ▷ entire
entireties n ▷ entire
entirety n ▷ entire
entities n ▷ entity
entitle v (-les, -ling, -led) give a right to > **entitlement** n (pl -s)
entitled v ▷ entitle
entitlement n ▷ entitle
entitlements n ▷ entitle
entitles v ▷ entitle
entitling v ▷ entitle
entity n (pl -ties) separate distinct thing
entrails pl n intestines
entrance¹ n (pl -s) way into a place
entrance² v (-ces, -cing, -ced) delight
entranced v ▷ entrance
entrances n ▷ entrance¹ ▶ v ▷ entrance²
entrancing v ▷ entrance
entrant n (pl -s) person who enters a university, contest, etc
entrants n ▷ entrant
entreat v (-s, -ing, -ed) ask earnestly
entreated v ▷ entreat
entreaties v ▷ entreaty
entreating v ▷ entreat

entreats v ▷ entreat
entreaty n (pl -ties) earnest request
entrée n (pl -s) dish served before a main course
entrées n ▷ entrée
entrench v (-s, -ing, -ed) establish firmly > **entrenchment** n (pl -s)
entrenched v ▷ entrench
entrenches v ▷ entrench
entrenching v ▷ entrench
entrenchment n ▷ entrench
entrenchments n ▷ entrench
entries n ▷ entry
entropies n ▷ entropy
entropy n (pl -ies) lack of organization
entrust v (-s, -ing, -ed) put into the care or protection of
entrusted v ▷ entrust
entrusting v ▷ entrust
entrusts v ▷ entrust
entry n (pl -ies) entrance
entwine v (-s, -ing, -ed) twist together or around
entwined v ▷ entwine
entwines v ▷ entwine
entwining v ▷ entwine
envelop v (-s, -ing, -ed) wrap up, enclose > **envelopment** n (pl -s)
envelope n (pl -s) folded gummed paper cover for a letter
enveloped v ▷ envelop
envelopes n ▷ envelope
enveloping v ▷ envelop
envelopment n ▷ envelop
envelopments n ▷ envelop
envelops v ▷ envelop
enviable adj arousing envy, fortunate
envied v ▷ envy
envies n, v ▷ envy
envious adj full of envy
environs pl n surrounding area, esp. of a town
envisage v (-ges, -ging, -ged) conceive of as a possibility
envisaged v ▷ envisage
envisages v ▷ envisage
envisaging v ▷ envisage
envoy n (pl -s) messenger

envoys n ▷ **envoy**

envy n (pl -**vies**) feeling of discontent aroused by another's good fortune ▶ v (-**vies**, -**vying**, -**vied**) grudge (another's good fortune, success, or qualities)

envying v ▷ **envy**

enzyme n (pl -**s**) any of a group of complex proteins that act as catalysts in specific biochemical reactions

enzymes n ▷ **enzyme**

eolithic adj of the early part of the Stone Age

epic n (pl -**s**) long poem, book, or film about heroic events or actions ▶ adj very impressive or ambitious

epics n ▷ **epic**

epicure n (pl -**s**) person who enjoys good food and drink

epicures n ▷ **epicure**

epidemic n (pl -**s**) widespread occurrence of a disease

epidemics n ▷ **epidemic**

epidural adj, n (pl -**s**) (of) spinal anaesthetic injected to relieve pain during childbirth

epidurals n ▷ **epidural**

epigram n (pl -**s**) short witty remark or poem > **epigrammatic** adj

epigrammatic adj ▷ **epigram**

epigrams n ▷ **epigram**

epigraph n (pl -**s**) quotation at the start of a book

epigraphs n ▷ **epigraph**

epilepsies n ▷ **epilepsy**

epilepsy n (pl -**sies**) disorder of the nervous system causing loss of consciousness and sometimes convulsions

epilogue n (pl -**s**) short speech or poem at the end of a literary work, esp. a play

epilogues n ▷ **epilogue**

epiphanies n ▷ **epiphany**

epiphany n (pl -**nies**) a moment of great or sudden realization

episode n (pl -**s**) incident in a series of incidents

episodes n ▷ **episode**

episodic adj occurring at irregular intervals

epistle n (pl -**s**) letter, esp. of an apostle > **epistolary** adj

epistles n ▷ **epistle**

epistolary adj ▷ **epistle**

epitaph n (pl -**s**) commemorative inscription on a tomb

epitaphs n ▷ **epitaph**

epithet n (pl -**s**) descriptive word or name

epithets n ▷ **epithet**

epitome n (pl -**s**) typical example

epitomes n ▷ **epitome**

epoch n (pl -**s**) period of notable events

epochs n ▷ **epoch**

equable adj even-tempered > **equably** adv

equably adv ▷ **equable**

equal adj identical in size, quantity, degree, etc ▶ n (pl -**s**) person or thing equal to another ▶ v (-**s**, -**lling**, -**lled**) be equal to > **equally** adv

equalities n ▷ **equality**

equality n (pl -**ties**) state of being equal

equalization n ▷ **equalize**

equalizations n ▷ **equalize**

equalize v (-**zes**, -**zing**, -**zed**) make or become equal > **equalization** n (pl -**s**)

equalized v ▷ **equalize**

equalizes v ▷ **equalize**

equalizing v ▷ **equalize**

equalled v ▷ **equal**

equalling v ▷ **equal**

equally adv ▷ **equal**

equals n, v ▷ **equal**

equate v (-**tes**, -**ting**, -**ted**) make or regard as equivalent

equated v ▷ **equate**

equates v ▷ **equate**

equating v ▷ **equate**

equation n (pl -**s**) mathematical statement that two expressions are equal

equations n ▷ **equation**

equator n (pl -**s**) imaginary circle round the earth, equidistant from the

poles > **equatorial** adj
equatorial adj ▷ **equator**
equators n ▷ **equator**
equerries n ▷ **equerry**
equerry n (pl -ries) BRIT officer who acts as an attendant to a member of a royal family
equine adj of or like a horse
equinoctial adj ▷ **equinox**
equinox n (pl -es) time of year when day and night are of equal length
> **equinoctial** adj
equinoxes n ▷ **equinox**
equip v (-s, -pping, -pped) provide with supplies, components, etc
equipped v ▷ **equip**
equipping v ▷ **equip**
equips v ▷ **equips**
equities n ▷ **equity**
equity n (pl -ties) fairness ▶ pl interest of ordinary shareholders in a company
era n (pl -s) period of time considered as distinctive
eras n ▷ **era**
erase v (-ses, -sing, -sed) rub out
erased v ▷ **erase**
eraser n (pl -s) object for erasing something written
erasers n ▷ **eraser**
erases v ▷ **erase**
erasing v ▷ **erase**
erasure n (pl -s) erasing
erasures n ▷ **erasure**
ere prep, conj poetic before
erect v (-s, -ing, -ed) build ▶ adj upright > **erection** n (pl -s)
erected v ▷ **erect**
erectile adj capable of becoming erect from sexual excitement
erecting v ▷ **erect**
erection n ▷ **erect**
erections n ▷ **erect**
erects v ▷ **erect**
erg n (pl -s) unit of work or energy
ergot n (pl -s) fungal disease of cereal
ergots n ▷ **ergot**
ergs n ▷ **erg**
ermine n (pl -s) stoat in northern

regions
ermines n ▷ **ermine**
erode v (-s, -ing, -ed) wear away
> **erosion** n (pl -s)
eroded v ▷ **erode**
erodes v ▷ **erode**
eroding v ▷ **erode**
erosion n ▷ **erode**
erosions n ▷ **erode**
erotic adj relating to sexual pleasure or desire > **eroticism** n (pl -s)
erotica n sexual literature or art
eroticism n ▷ **erotic**
eroticisms n ▷ **erotic**
err v (-s, -ing, -ed) make a mistake
errand n (pl -s) short trip to do something for someone
errands n ▷ **errand**
errant adj behaving in a manner considered to be unacceptable
errata n ▷ **erratum**
erratic adj irregular or unpredictable
> **erratically** adv
erratically adv ▷ **erratic**
erratum n (pl -ta) error in writing or printing
erred v ▷ **err**
erring v ▷ **err**
error n (pl -s) mistake, inaccuracy, or misjudgment
errors n ▷ **error**
errs v ▷ **err**
ersatz adj made in imitation
erudite adj having great academic knowledge > **erudition** n (pl -s)
erudition v ▷ **erudite**
eruditions n ▷ **erudite**
erupt v (-s, -ing, -ed) eject (steam, water, or volcanic material) violently
> **eruption** n (pl -s)
erupted v ▷ **erupt**
erupting v ▷ **erupt**
eruption n ▷ **erupt**
eruptions n ▷ **erupt**
erupts v ▷ **erupt**
escalate v (-tes, -ting, -ted) increase in extent or intensity > **escalation** n (pl -s)

escalated v ▷ escalate

escalates v ▷ escalate

escalating v ▷ escalate

escalation n ▷ escalate

escalations n ▷ escalate

escalope n (pl **-s**) thin slice of meat, esp. veal

escalopes n ▷ escalope

escapade n (pl **-s**) mischievous adventure

escapades n ▷ escapade

escape v (**-pes, -ping, -ped**) get free (of) ▶ n (pl **-s**) act of escaping

escaped v ▷ escape

escapee n (pl **-s**) person who has escaped

escapees n ▷ escape

escapes v, n ▷ escape

escaping v ▷ escape

escapism n (pl **-s**) taking refuge in fantasy to avoid unpleasant reality

escapisms n ▷ escapism

eschew v (**-s, -ing, -ed**) abstain from, avoid

eschewed v ▷ eschew

eschewing v ▷ eschew

eschews v ▷ eschew

escort n (pl **-s**) people or vehicles accompanying another person for protection or as an honour ▶ v (**-s, -ing, -ed**) act as an escort to

escorted v ▷ escort

escorting v ▷ escort

escorts n, v ▷ escort

escudo n (pl **-dos**) former monetary unit of Portugal

escudos n ▷ escudo

esoteric adj understood by only a small number of people with special knowledge

espalier n (pl **-s**) shrub or fruit tree trained to grow flat

espaliers n ▷ espalier

esparto n (pl **-s**) grass of S Europe and N Africa used for making rope etc

espartos n ▷ esparto

especial adj formal special

espied v ▷ espy

espies v ▷ espy

espousal n ▷ espouse

espousals n ▷ espouse

espouse v (**-ses, -sing, -sed**) adopt or give support to (a cause etc)
> **espousal** n (pl **-s**)

espoused v ▷ espouse

espouses v ▷ espouse

espousing v ▷ espouse

espresso n (pl **-s**) strong coffee made by forcing steam or boiling water through ground coffee beans

espressos n ▷ espresso

esprit n (pl **-s**) spirit, liveliness, or wit

esprits n ▷ esprit

espy v (**-pies, -pying, -pied**) catch sight of

espying v ▷ espy

esquire n (pl **-s**) courtesy title placed after a man's name

esquires n ▷ esquire

essay n (pl **-s**) short literary composition ▶ v (**-s, -ing, -ed**) attempt > **essayist** n (pl **-s**)

essayed v ▷ essay

essaying v ▷ essay

essayist n ▷ essay

essayists n ▷ essay

essays n, v ▷ essay

essence n (pl **-s**) most important feature of a thing which determines its identity

essences n ▷ essence

estate n (pl **-s**) landed property

estates n ▷ estate

esteem n (pl **-s**) high regard ▶ v (**-s, -ing, -ed**) think highly of

esteemed v ▷ esteem

esteeming v ▷ esteem

esteems n, v ▷ esteem

ester n (pl **-s**) CHEM compound produced by the reaction between an acid and an alcohol

esters n ▷ ester

estimate v (**-tes, -ting, -ted**) calculate roughly ▶ n (pl **-s**) approximate calculation

estimated v ▷ estimate

estimates v, n ▷ **estimate**
estimating v ▷ **estimate**
estuaries n ▷ **estuary**
estuary n (pl **-ries**) mouth of a river
etch v (**-es, -ing, -ed**) wear away or cut
the surface of (metal, glass, etc) with
acid > **etching** n (pl **-s**)
etched v ▷ **etch**
etches v ▷ **etch**
etching v, n ▷ **etch**
eternal adj without beginning or end
> **eternally** adv
eternally adv ▷ **eternal**
eternities n ▷ **eternity**
eternity n (pl **-ies**) infinite time
ether n (pl **-s**) colourless sweet-
smelling liquid used as an anaesthetic
ethereal adj extremely delicate
ethers n ▷ **ether**
ethic n (pl **-s**) moral principle
> **ethical** adj > **ethically** adv
ethical adj ▷ **ethic**
ethically adv ▷ **ethic**
ethics n ▷ **ethic**
ethnic adj relating to a people or
group that shares a culture, religion,
or language
ethos n (pl **-es**) distinctive spirit and
attitudes of a people, culture, etc
ethoses n ▷ **ethos**
ethyl adj of, consisting of, or
containing the hydrocarbon group
C_2H_5
ethylene n (pl **-s**) poisonous gas used
as an anaesthetic and as fuel
ethylenes n ▷ **ethylene**
etiolate v (**-tes, -ting, -ted**) become
pale and weak
etiolated v ▷ **etiolate**
etiolates v ▷ **etiolate**
etiolating v ▷ **etiolate**
etiologies n ▷ **etiology**
etiology n (pl **-ies**) study of the
causes of diseases
étude n (pl **-s**) short musical
composition for a solo instrument,
esp. intended as a technical exercise
études n ▷ **étude**

eugenics n (pl study of methods of
improving the human race
eulogies n ▷ **eulogy**
eulogistic adj ▷ **eulogy**
eulogize v (**-zes, -zing, -zed**) praise
(a person or thing) highly in speech
or writing
eulogized v ▷ **eulogize**
eulogizes v ▷ **eulogize**
eulogizing v ▷ **eulogize**
eulogy n (pl **-ies**) speech or writing in
praise of a person > **eulogistic** adj
eunuch n (pl **-s**) castrated man, esp.
(formerly) a guard in a harem
eunuchs n ▷ **eunuch**
euphonies n ▷ **euphony**
euphony n (pl **-nies**) pleasing sound
euphoria n (pl **-s**) sense of elation
> **euphoric** adj
euphorias n ▷ **euphoria**
euphoric adj ▷ **euphoria**
eureka interj exclamation of triumph
at finding something
euro n (pl **-s**) unit of the single currency
of the European Union
euros n ▷ **euro**
evacuate v (**-tes, -ting, -ted**) send
(someone) away from a place of danger
> **evacuation** n (pl **-s**) > **evacuee** n
(pl **-s**)
evacuated v ▷ **evacuate**
evacuates v ▷ **evacuate**
evacuating v ▷ **evacuate**
evacuation n ▷ **evacuate**
evacuations n ▷ **evacuate**
evacuee n ▷ **evacuate**
evacuees n ▷ **evacuate**
evade v (**-des, -ding, -ded**) get away
from or avoid > **evasion** n (pl **-s**)
evaded v ▷ **evade**
evades v ▷ **evade**
evading v ▷ **evade**
evaluate v (**-tes, -ting, -ted**) find or
judge the value of > **evaluation** n (pl **-s**)
evaluated v ▷ **evaluate**
evaluates v ▷ **evaluate**
evaluating v ▷ **evaluate**
evaluation n ▷ **evaluate**

evaluations n ▷ evaluate

evasion n ▷ evade

evasions n ▷ evade

evasive adj not straightforward
> **evasively** adv

evasively adv ▷ evasive

eve n (pl -s) evening or day before some special event

even (-er, -est) adj flat or smooth (foll. by with) ▶ adj equally ▶ v (-s, -ing, -ed) make even

evened v ▷ even

evener adj ▷ even

evenest adj ▷ even

evening n (pl -s) end of the day or early part of the night ▶ adj of or in the evening ▶ v ▷ even

evenings n ▷ evening

evens n ▷ even

evensong n (pl -s) evening prayer

evensongs n ▷ evensong

event n (pl -s) anything that takes place

eventful adj full of exciting incidents

eventing n (pl -s) BRIT, AUST & NZ riding competitions, usu. involving cross-country, jumping, and dressage

eventings n ▷ eventing

events n ▷ event

eventual adj ultimate

ever adv at any time > **everlasting** adj

everlasting adj ▷ ever

evermore adv for all time to come

every adj each without exception

everyday adj usual or ordinary

everyone pron every person

eves n ▷ eve

evict v (-s, -ing, -ed) legally expel (someone) from his or her home
> **eviction** n (pl -s)

evicted v ▷ evict

evicting v ▷ evict

eviction n ▷ evict

evictions n ▷ evict

evicts v ▷ evict

evidence n (pl -s) ground for belief ▶ v (-s, -ing, -ed) demonstrate, prove

evidenced v ▷ evidence

evidences n, v ▷ evidence

evidencing v ▷ evidence

evident adj easily seen or understood
> **evidently** adv

evidently adv ▷ evident

evil n (pl -s) wickedness ▶ adj (-ller, -llest) harmful > **evilly** adv

evildoer n (pl -s) wicked person

evildoers n ▷ evildoer

eviller adj ▷ evil

evillest adj ▷ evil

evilly adv ▷ evil

evils n ▷ evil

evince v (-ces, -cing, -ced) make evident

evinced v ▷ evince

evinces v ▷ evince

evincing v ▷ evince

evocation n ▷ evoke

evocations n ▷ evoke

evocative adj ▷ evoke

evoke v (-kes, -king, -ked) call or summon up (a memory, feeling, etc) > **evocation** n (pl -s)
> **evocative** adj

evoked v ▷ evoke

evokes v ▷ evoke

evoking v ▷ evoke

evolve v (-ves, -ving, -ved) develop gradually

evolved v ▷ evolve

evolves v ▷ evolve

evolving v ▷ evolve

ewe n (pl -s) female sheep

ewer n (pl -s) large jug with a wide mouth

ewers n ▷ ewer

ewes n ▷ ewe

> **ewk** n (**ewks**). Ewk is a dialect word for *itch*. It's a handy little word and a good one to remember in case you end up with both K and W, as you're very likely to be able to play it from an E already on the board. Ewk scores 10 points.

ex n (pl -es) informal former wife or husband

exact adj (-er, -est) correct and

complete in every detail ▶ v (-s, -ing, -ed) demand (payment or obedience) > **exactness** n (pl -es) > **exactitude** n (pl -s)

exacted v ▷ **exact**

exacter adj ▷ **exact**

exactest adj ▷ **exact**

exacting adj making rigorous or excessive demands ▶ v ▷ **exact**

exactitude n ▷ **exact**

exactitudes n ▷ **exact**

exactly adv precisely, in every respect

exactness n ▷ **exact**

exactnesses n ▷ **exact**

exacts v ▷ **exact**

exalt v (-s, -ing, -ed) praise highly > **exalted** adj > **exaltation** n (pl -s)

exaltation n ▷ **exalt**

exaltations n ▷ **exalt**

exalted v, adj ▷ **exalt**

exalting v ▷ **exalt**

exalts v ▷ **exalt**

examine v (-nes, -ning, -ned) look at closely > **examinee** n (pl -s) > **examiner** n (pl -s)

examined v ▷ **examine**

examinee n ▷ **examine**

examinees n ▷ **examine**

examiner n ▷ **examine**

examiners n ▷ **examine**

examines v ▷ **examine**

examining v ▷ **examine**

example n (pl -s) specimen typical of its group

examples n ▷ **example**

exams n ▷ **exam**

excavate v (-tes, -ting, -ted) unearth buried objects from (a piece of land) methodically to learn about the past > **excavation** n (pl -s)

excavated v ▷ **excavate**

excavates v ▷ **excavate**

excavating v ▷ **excavate**

excavation n ▷ **excavate**

excavations n ▷ **excavate**

exceed v (-s, -ing, -ed) be greater than

exceeded v ▷ **exceed**

exceeding v ▷ **exceed**

exceeds v ▷ **exceed**

excel v (-s, -lling, -lled) be superior to

excelled v ▷ **excel**

excelling v ▷ **excel**

excels v ▷ **excel**

except prep (sometimes foll. by **for**) other than, not including ▶ v (-s, -ing, -ed) not include

excepted v ▷ **except**

excepts v ▷ **except**

excerpt n (pl -s) passage taken from a book, speech, etc

excerpts n ▷ **excerpt**

excess n (pl -es) state or act of exceeding the permitted limits > **excessive** adj > **excessively** adv

excesses n ▷ **excess**

excessive adj ▷ **excess**

excessively adv ▷ **excess**

exchange v (-ges, -ging, -ged) give or receive (something) in return for something else ▶ n (pl -s) act of exchanging > **exchangeable** adj

exchangeable adj ▷ **exchange**

exchanged v ▷ **exchange**

exchanges v, n ▷ **exchange**

exchanging v ▷ **exchange**

excise v (-ses, -sing, -sed) cut out or away > **excision** n (pl -s)

excised v ▷ **excise**

excises v ▷ **excise**

excising v ▷ **excise**

excision n ▷ **excise**

excisions n ▷ **excise**

excite v (-s, -ing, -ed) arouse to strong emotion > **excitement** n (pl -s)

excited v ▷ **excite**

excitement n ▷ **excite**

excitements n ▷ **excite**

excites v ▷ **excite**

exciting v ▷ **excite**

exclaim v (-s, -ing, -ed) speak suddenly, cry out > **exclamation** n > **exclamatory** adj

exclaimed v ▷ **exclaim**

exclaiming v ▷ **exclaim**

exclaims v ▷ **exclaim**

exclamation n ▷ exclaim
exclamations n ▷ exclaim
exclamatory adj ▷ exclaim
exclude v (-s, -ing, -ed) keep out, leave
out ▶ **exclusion** n (pl -s)
excluded v ▷ exclude
excludes v ▷ exclude
excluding v ▷ exclude
exclusion n ▷ exclude
exclusions n ▷ exclude
excreta n excrement
excrete v (-tes, -ting, -ted) discharge
(waste matter) from the body
▷ **excretion** n (pl -s) ▷ **excretory** adj
excreted v ▷ excrete
excretes v ▷ excrete
excreting v ▷ excrete
excretion n ▷ excrete
excretions n ▷ excrete
excretory adj ▷ excrete
excusable adj ▷ excuse
excuse n (pl -s) explanation offered
to justify (a fault etc) ▶ v (-ses,
-sing, -sed) put forward a reason
or justification for (a fault etc)
▷ **excusable** adj
excused v ▷ excuse
excuses n, v ▷ excuse
excusing v ▷ excuse
execute v (-tes, -ting, -ted) put
(a condemned person) to death
▷ **execution** n (pl -s) ▷ **executioner** n
(pl -s)
executed v ▷ execute
executes v ▷ execute
executing v ▷ execute
execution n ▷ execute
executioner n ▷ execute
executioners n ▷ execute
executions n ▷ execute
executor n (pl -s) person appointed to
perform the instructions of a will
executors n ▷ executor
exegeses n ▷ exegesis
exegesis n (pl -ses) explanation of a
text, esp. of the Bible
exemplar n (pl -s) person or thing to
be copied, model

exemplars n ▷ exemplar
exempt adj not subject to an
obligation etc ▶ v (-s, -ing, -ed)
release from an obligation etc
▷ **exemption** n (pl -s)
exempted v ▷ exempt
exempting v ▷ exempt
exemption n ▷ exempt
exemptions n ▷ exempt
exempts v ▷ exempt

> **exequy** n (**exequies**). An exequy is
> a funeral rite. This is a great word if
> you have the tiles for it, combining
> X and Q. Even better, if you have all
> the letters for the plural, exequies,
> and can play it, you'll score an extra
> 50 points for using all your tiles.
> Exequy scores 25 points.

exercise n (pl -s) activity to train the
body or mind ▶ v (-ses, -sing, -sed)
make use of
exercised v ▷ exercise
exercises n, v ▷ exercise
exercising v ▷ exercise
exert v (-s, -ing, -ed) use (influence,
authority, etc) forcefully or effectively
▷ **exertion** n (pl -s)
exerted v ▷ exert
exerting v ▷ exert
exertion n ▷ exert
exertions n ▷ exert
exerts v ▷ exert
exes ▷ ex
exeunt v LATIN they go out: used as a
stage direction
exhalation n ▷ exhale
exhalations n ▷ exhale
exhale v (-les, -ling, -led) breathe out
▷ **exhalation** n (pl -s)
exhaled v ▷ exhale
exhales v ▷ exhale
exhaling v ▷ exhale
exhaust v (-s, -ing, -ed) tire out ▶ n
(pl -s) gases ejected from an engine as
waste products
exhausted v ▷ exhaust
exhausting v ▷ exhaust
exhausts v, n ▷ exhaust

exhibit | 194

exhibit v (**-s, -ing, -ed**) display to the public ► n (pl **-s**) object exhibited to the public LAW > **exhibitor** n (pl **-s**)
exhibited v ▷ **exhibit**
exhibiting v ▷ **exhibit**
exhibitor n ▷ **exhibit**
exhibitors n ▷ **exhibit**
exhibits v, n ▷ **exhibit**
exhort v (**-s, -ing, -ed**) urge earnestly >**exhortation** n (pl **-s**)
exhortation n ▷ **exhort**
exhortations n ▷ **exhort**
exhorted v ▷ **exhort**
exhorting v ▷ **exhort**
exhorts v ▷ **exhort**
exhumation n ▷ **exhume**
exhumations n ▷ **exhume**
exhume v (**-mes, -ming, -med**) dig up (something buried, esp. a corpse) >**exhumation** n (pl **-s**)
exhumed v ▷ **exhume**
exhumes v ▷ **exhume**
exhuming v ▷ **exhume**
exigencies n ▷ **exigency**
exigency n (pl **-cies**) urgent demand or need > **exigent** adj
exigent adj ▷ **exigency**
exiguous adj scanty or meagre
exile n (pl **-s**) prolonged, usu. enforced, absence from one's country ► v (**-les, -ling, -led**) expel from one's country
exiled v ▷ **exile**
exiles n, v ▷ **exile**
exiling v ▷ **exile**
exist v (**-s, -ing, -ed**) have being or reality > **existence** n (pl **-s**) >**existent** adj
existed v ▷ **exist**
existence n ▷ **exist**
existences n ▷ **exist**
existent adj ▷ **exist**
existing v ▷ **exist**
exists v ▷ **exist**
exit n (pl **-s**) way out ► v (**-s, -ing, -ed**) go out
exited v ▷ **exit**
exiting v ▷ **exit**

exits n, v ▷ **exit**

> **exo** adj. Exo is an informal Australian way of saying **excellent**. This is a great little word as it allows you to combine X with two of the most common tiles in the game, E and O. Exo scores 10 points.

exocrine adj relating to a gland, such as the sweat gland, that secretes externally through a duct
exodus n (pl **-es**) departure of a large number of people
exoduses n ▷ **exodus**
exorcism n ▷ **exorcize**
exorcisms n ▷ **exorcize**
exorcist n ▷ **exorcize**
exorcists n ▷ **exorcize**
exorcize v (**-zes, -zing, -zed**) expel (evil spirits) by prayers and religious rites > **exorcism** n (pl **-s**) > **exorcist** n (pl **-s**)
exorcized v ▷ **exorcize**
exorcizes v ▷ **exorcize**
exorcizing v ▷ **exorcize**
exotic adj having a strange allure or beauty ► n (pl **-s**) non-native plant >**exotically** adv
exotica pl n (collection of) exotic objects
exotically adv ▷ **exotic**
exotics n ▷ **exotic**
expand v (**-s, -ing, -ed**) make or become larger (foll. by **on**) > **expansion** n (pl **-s**)
expanded v ▷ **expand**
expanding v ▷ **expand**
expands v ▷ **expand**
expanse n (pl **-s**) uninterrupted wide area
expanses n ▷ **expanse**
expansion n ▷ **expand**
expansions n ▷ **expand**
expats n ▷ **expat**
expect v (**-s, -ing, -ed**) regard as probable
expected v ▷ **expect**
expecting v ▷ **expect**
expects v ▷ **expect**

expedite v (-s, -ing, -ed) hasten the progress of
expedited v ▷ expedite
expedites v ▷ expedite
expediting v ▷ expedite

expel v (-s, -lling, -lled) drive out with force > **expulsion** n (pl -s)
expelled v ▷ expel
expelling v ▷ expel
expels v ▷ expel

expend v (-s, -ing, -ed) spend, use up
expended v ▷ expend
expending v ▷ expend
expends v ▷ expend

expense n (pl -s) cost ▶ pl charges, outlay incurred
expenses n ▷ expense

expert n (pl -s) person with extensive skill or knowledge in a particular field ▶ adj skilful or knowledgeable
experts n ▷ expert

expiate v (-tes, -ting, -ted) make amends for > **expiation** n (pl -s)
expiated v ▷ expiate
expiates v ▷ expiate
expiating v ▷ expiate
expiation n ▷ expiate
expiations n ▷ expiate
expiration n ▷ expire
expirations n ▷ expire

expire v (-res, -ring, -red) finish or run out lit > **expiration** n (pl -s)
expired v ▷ expire
expires v ▷ expire
expiries n ▷ expiry
expiring v ▷ expire

expiry n (pl -ies) end, esp. of a contract period

explain v (-s, -ing, -ed) make clear and intelligible > **explanation** n (pl -s) > **explanatory** adj
explained v ▷ explain
explaining v ▷ explain
explains v ▷ explain
explanation n ▷ explain
explanations n ▷ explain
explanatory adj ▷ explain

explicit adj precisely and clearly

expressed > **explicitly** adv
explicitly adv ▷ explicit

explode v (-des, -ding, -ded) burst with great violence, blow up > **explosion** n (pl -s)
exploded v ▷ explode
explodes v ▷ explode
exploding v ▷ explode

exploit v (pl -s) take advantage of for one's own purposes ▶ n (pl -s) notable feat or deed > **exploitation** n (pl -s) > **exploiter** n (pl -s)
exploitation n ▷ exploit
exploitations n ▷ exploit
exploited v ▷ exploit
exploiter n ▷ exploit
exploiters n ▷ exploit
exploiting v ▷ exploit
exploits v, n ▷ exploit
exploration n ▷ explore
explorations n ▷ explore
exploratory adj ▷ explore

explore v (-s, -ing, -ed) investigate > **exploration** n (pl -s) > **exploratory** adj > **explorer** n (pl -s)
explored v ▷ explore
explorer n ▷ explore
explorers n ▷ explore
explores v ▷ explore
exploring v ▷ explore
explosion n ▷ explode
explosions n ▷ explode

expo n (pl -s) informal exposition, large public exhibition

exponent n (pl -s) person who advocates an idea, cause, etc
exponents n ▷ exponent

export n (pl -s) selling or shipping of goods to a foreign country ▶ v (-s, -ing, -ed) sell or ship (goods) to a foreign country > **exporter** n (pl -s)
exported v ▷ export
exporter n ▷ export
exporters n ▷ export
exporting v ▷ export
exports n, v ▷ export
expos n ▷ expo

expose v (-ses, -sing, -sed) uncover or

reveal > **exposure** n (pl **-s**) exposing

exposé n (pl **-s**) bringing of a crime, scandal, etc to public notice

exposed v ▷ **expose**

exposes v ▷ **expose**

exposés n ▷ **exposé**

exposing v ▷ **expose**

exposition n ▷ **expound**

expositions n ▷ **expound**

exposure n ▷ **expose**

exposures n ▷ **expose**

expound v (**-s, -ing, -ed**) explain in detail ▸ **exposition** n (pl **-s**) explanation

expounded v ▷ **expound**

expounding v ▷ **expound**

expounds v ▷ **expound**

express v (**-es, -ing, -ed**) put into words ▸ adj explicitly stated ▸ n (pl **-es**) fast train or bus stopping at only a few stations ▸ adv by express delivery

expressed v ▷ **express**

expresses v, n ▷ **express**

expressing v ▷ **express**

expulsion n ▷ **expel**

expulsions n ▷ **expel**

expunge v (**-ges, -ging, -ged**) delete, erase, blot out

expunged v ▷ **expunge**

expunges v ▷ **expunge**

expunging v ▷ **expunge**

extant adj still existing

extend v (**-s, -ing, -ed**) draw out or be drawn out, stretch (foll. by **to**) > **extendable** adj

extendable adj ▷ **extend**

extended v ▷ **extend**

extending v ▷ **extend**

extends v ▷ **extend**

extensor n (pl **-s**) muscle that extends a part of the body

extensors n ▷ **extensor**

extent n (pl **-s**) range over which something extends, area

extents n ▷ **extent**

exterior n (pl **-s**) part or surface on the outside ▸ adj of, on, or coming from the outside

exteriors n ▷ **exterior**

external adj of, situated on, or coming from the outside > **externally** adv

externally adv ▷ **external**

extinct adj having died out
> **extinction** n (pl **-s**)

extinction n ▷ **extinct**

extinctions n ▷ **extinct**

extol v (**-s, -lling, -lled**) praise highly

extolled v ▷ **extol**

extolling v ▷ **extol**

extols v ▷ **extol**

extort v (**-s, -ing, -ed**) get (something) by force or threats > **extortion** n (pl **-s**)

extorted v ▷ **extort**

extorting v ▷ **extort**

extortion n ▷ **extort**

extortions n ▷ **extort**

extorts v ▷ **extort**

extra adj more than is usual, expected or needed ▸ n (pl **-s**) additional person or thing ▸ adv unusually or exceptionally

extract v (**-s, -ing, -ed**) pull out by force ▸ n (pl **-s**) something extracted, such as a passage from a book etc
> **extraction** n (pl **-s**) ▸ **extractor** (pl **-s**)

extracted v ▷ **extract**

extracting v ▷ **extract**

extraction n ▷ **extract**

extractions n ▷ **extract**

extractor n ▷ **extract**

extractors n ▷ **extract**

extracts v, n ▷ **extract**

extras n ▷ **extra**

extreme adj of a high or the highest degree or intensity ▸ n (pl **-s**) either of the two limits of a scale or range
> **extremely** adv

extremely adv ▷ **extreme**

extremes n ▷ **extreme**

extrude v (**-des, -ding, -ded**) squeeze or force out > **extrusion** n (pl **-s**)

extruded v ▷ **extrude**

extrudes v ▷ **extrude**

extruding v ▷ **extrude**

extrusion n ▷ **extrude**

extrusions n ▷ extrude

exude v (-des, -ding, -ded) (of a liquid or smell) seep or flow out slowly and steadily

exuded v ▷ exude

exudes v ▷ exude

exuding v ▷ exude

exult v (-s, -ing, -ed) be joyful or jubilant > **exultation** n (pl -s) > **exultant** adj

exultant adj ▷ exult

exultation n ▷ exult

exultations n ▷ exult

exulted v ▷ exult

exulting v ▷ exult

exults v ▷ exult

eye n (pl -s) organ of sight ▶ v (-s, -ing or eying, -d) look at carefully or warily > **eyeless** adj

eyeball n (pl -s) ball-shaped part of the eye

eyeballs n ▷ eyeball

eyebrow n (pl -s) line of hair on the bony ridge above the eye

eyebrows n ▷ eyebrow

eyed v ▷ eye

eyeglass n (pl -es) lens for aiding defective vision

eyeglasses n ▷ eyeglass

eyeing v ▷ eye

eyelash n (pl -es) short hair that grows out from the eyelid

eyelashes n ▷ eyelash

eyeless adj ▷ eye

eyelet n (pl -s) small hole for a lace or cord to be passed through

eyelets n ▷ eyelet

eyelid n (pl -s) fold of skin that covers the eye when it is closed

eyelids n ▷ eyelid

eyeliner n (pl -s) cosmetic used to outline the eyes

eyeliners n ▷ eyeliner

eyes n, v ▷ eye

eyesight n (pl -s) ability to see

eyesights n ▷ eyesight

eyesore n (pl -s) ugly object

eyesores n ▷ eyesore

eying v ▷ eye

eyrie n (pl -s) nest of an eagle

eyries n ▷ eyrie

Ff

F can be an awkward letter in Scrabble: there are only two two-letter words beginning with F, for example (**fa** and **fy**). But if you're aware of this, you won't waste time trying to think of other two-letter words. There are also quite a few words that combine F with X or Z, allowing high scores particularly if you can hit a bonus square with them. **Fax**, **fix** and **fox** are good examples (13 points each), and don't forget **fez** (15). If you have a blank tile, you can use it for the second Z in **fuzz** (15) or **fuzzy** (19). **Fey**, **fly** and **fry** can also be useful (9 each).

fa n (**fas**). Fa is the musical note F. This word isn't going to win you a game on its own, but it's useful when you're trying to form several words at once. Fa scores 5 points.
fab adj Fab is a short form of **fabulous**. Fab scores 8 points.
fable n (pl **-s**) story with a moral
fabled adj made famous in legend
　fables n ▷ fable
fabric n (pl **-s**) knitted or woven cloth
　fabrics n ▷ fabric
fabulous adj informal excellent
　>**fabulously** adv
fabulously adv ▷ fabulous
facade n (pl **-s**) front of a building
　facades n ▷ facade
face n (pl **-s**) front of the head ▶ v (**-ces**, **-cing**, **-ced**) look or turn towards
　faced v ▷ face
faceless adj impersonal, anonymous
　faces n, v ▷ face
facet n (pl **-s**) aspect
　facets n ▷ facet
facia n (pl **-ciae**) ▷ fascia
　faciae n ▷ fascia
facial adj of the face ▶ n (pl **-s**) beauty treatment for the face
　facials n ▷ facial

facile adj (of a remark, argument, etc) superficial and showing lack of real thought
facilities n ▷ facility
facility n (pl **-ties**) skill ▶ pl means or equipment for an activity
facing v ▷ face
facing n (pl **-s**) lining or covering for decoration or reinforcement ▶ pl contrasting collar and cuffs on a jacket
　facings n ▷ facing
fact n (pl **-s**) event or thing known to have happened or existed ▷ **factual** adj
faction n (pl **-s**) (dissenting) minority group within a larger body
　factions n ▷ faction
factious adj of or producing factions
factor n (pl **-s**) element contributing to a result
　factories n ▷ factory
　factors n ▷ factor
factory n (pl **-ies**) building where goods are manufactured
factotum n (pl **-s**) person employed to do all sorts of work
　factotums n ▷ factotum
　facts n ▷ fact
factual adj ▷ fact
　faculties n ▷ faculty

faculty n (pl **-ties**) physical or mental ability

fad n (pl **-s**) short-lived fashion >**faddy** (**-ier, -iest**), **faddish** adj
  faddier adj ▷ **fad**
  faddiest adj ▷ **fad**
  faddish adj ▷ **fad**
  faddy adj ▷ **fad**

fade v (**-des, -ding, -ded**) (cause to) lose brightness, colour, or strength
  faded v ▷ **fade**
  fades v ▷ **fade**
  fading v ▷ **fade**
  fads n ▷ **fad**

faecal adj ▷ **faeces**

faeces pl n waste matter discharged from the anus >**faecal** ▷ adj

fag¹ n (pl **-s**) informal boring task BRIT ▶(**-s, -gging, -gged**) BRIT do menial chores in a public school

fag² n BRIT slang cigarette
  fagged v ▷ **fag¹**
  fagging v ▷ **fag¹**

faggot n (pl **-s**) BRIT, AUST & NZ ball of chopped liver, herbs, and bread
  faggots n ▷ **faggot**
  fags n, v ▷ **fag¹, ²**

faïence n (pl **-s**) tin-glazed earthenware
  faïences n ▷ **faïence**

fail v (**-s, -ing, -ed**) be unsuccessful ▶ n (pl **-s**) instance of not passing an exam or test
  failed v ▷ **fail**

failing n (pl **-s**) weak point ▶ prep in the absence of ▶ v ▷ **fail**
  failings n ▷ **failing**
  fails n, v ▷ **fail**

failure n (pl **-s**) act or instance of failing
  failures n ▷ **failure**

fain adv obs gladly

faint adj lacking clarity, brightness, or volume ▶ v (**-s, -ing, -ed**) lose consciousness temporarily ▶ n (pl **-s**) temporary loss of consciousness
  fainted v ▷ **faint**
  fainting v ▷ **faint**
  faints n, v ▷ **faint**

fair¹ adj (**-er, -est**) unbiased and reasonable ▶ adv fairly >**fairness** (pl **-s**)

fair² n (pl **-s**) travelling entertainment with sideshows, rides, and amusements
  fairer adj ▷ **fair¹**
  fairest adj ▷ **fair¹**
  fairies n ▷ **fairy**

fairly adv moderately
  fairness n ▷ **fair¹**
  fairnesses n ▷ **fair¹**
  fairs n ▷ **fair¹, ²**

fairway n (pl **-s**) GOLF smooth area between the tee and the green
  fairways n ▷ **fairway**

fairy n (pl **-ries**) imaginary small creature with magic powers >**fairyland** (pl **-s**)
  fairyland n ▷ **fairy**
  fairylands n ▷ **fairy**

faith n (pl **-s**) strong belief, esp. without proof

faithful adj loyal >**faithfully** adv
  faithfully adv ▷ **faithful**
  faiths n ▷ **faith**

fake v (**-kes, -king, -ked**) cause something not genuine to appear real or more valuable by fraud ▶ n (pl **-s**) person, thing, or act that is not genuine ▶ adj not genuine
  faked v ▷ **fake**
  fakes v, n ▷ **fake**
  faking v ▷ **fake**

fakir n (pl **-s**) Muslim who spurns worldly possessions
  fakirs n ▷ **fakir**

falcon n (pl **-s**) small bird of prey
  falconer n ▷ **falconry**
  falconers n ▷ **falconry**
  falconries n ▷ **falconry**

falconry n (pl **-ries**) art of training falcons >**falconer** n (pl **-s**)
  falcons n ▷ **falcon**

fall v (**-s, -ing, fell, fallen**) drop from a higher to lower place through the force of gravity ▶ n (pl **-s**) falling
  fallacies n ▷ **fallacy**

fallacious *adj* ▷ **fallacy**

fallacy *n* (*pl* **-cies**) false belief
> **fallacious** *adj*

fallen *v* ▷ **fall**

fallibilities *n* ▷ **fallible**

fallibility *n* ▷ **fallible**

fallible *adj* (of a person) liable to make
mistakes ▷ **fallibility** *n* (*pl* **-ties**)

falling *v* ▷ **fall**

fallout *n* (*pl* **-s**) radioactive particles
spread as a result of a nuclear explosion

fallouts *n* ▷ **fallout**

fallow *adj* (of land) ploughed but left
unseeded to regain fertility

falls *v, n* ▷ **fall**

false *adj* (**-r, -st**) not true or correct
> **falsely** *adv* > **falseness** *n* (*pl* **-es**)
> **falsity** *n* (*pl* **-ies**)

falsely *adv* ▷ **false**

falseness *n* ▷ **false**

falsenesses *n* ▷ **false**

falser *adj* ▷ **false**

falsest *adj* ▷ **false**

falsetto *n* (*pl* **-tos**) voice pitched
higher than one's natural range

falsettos *n* ▷ **falsetto**

falsification *n* ▷ **falsify**

falsifications *n* ▷ **falsify**

falsified *v* ▷ **falsify**

falsifies *v* ▷ **falsify**

falsify *v* (**-fies, -fying, -fied**) alter
fraudulently > **falsification** *n* (*pl* **-s**)

falsifying *v* ▷ **falsify**

falsities *n* ▷ **false**

falsity *n* ▷ **false**

falter *v* (**-s, -ing, -ed**) be hesitant,
weak, or unsure

faltered *v* ▷ **falter**

faltering *v* ▷ **falter**

falters *v* ▷ **falter**

fame *n* (*pl* **-s**) state of being widely
known or recognized

famed *adj* famous

fames *n* ▷ **fame**

familial *adj* ▷ **family**

familiar *adj* well-known ▶ *n* (*pl* **-s**)
demon supposed to attend a witch

> **familiarly** *adv* > **familiarity** *n* (*pl* **-ties**)

familiarly *adv* ▷ **familiar**

familiars *n* ▷ **familiar**

families *n* ▷ **family**

family *n* (*pl* **-lies**) group of parents
and their children ▶ *adj* suitable
for parents and children together
> **familial** *adj*

famine *n* (*pl* **-s**) severe shortage of food

famines *n* ▷ **famine**

famished *adj* very hungry

famous *adj* very well-known

famously *adv* informal excellently

fan[1] *n* (*pl* **-s**) hand-held or mechanical
object used to create a current of air for
ventilation or cooling ▶ *v* (**-s, -nning,
-nned**) blow or cool with a fan

fan[2] *n* (*pl* **-s**) informal devotee of a pop
star, sport, or hobby

fanatic *n* (*pl* **-s**) person who is
excessively enthusiastic about
something > **fanatical** *adj*
> **fanatically** *adv* > **fanaticism** *n* (*pl* **-s**)

fanatical *adj* ▷ **fanatic**

fanatically *adv* ▷ **fanatic**

fanaticism *n* ▷ **fanatic**

fanaticisms *n* ▷ **fanatic**

fanatics *n* ▷ **fanatic**

fanbase *n* (*pl* **-s**) body of admirers of a
particular pop singer, sports team, etc

fanbases *n* ▷ **fanbase**

fancied *v* ▷ **fancy**

fancier *adj* ▷ **fancy**

fancies *n, v* ▷ **fancy**

fanciest *adj* ▷ **fancy**

fanciful *adj* not based on fact
> **fancifully** *adv*

fancifully *adv* ▷ **fanciful**

fancy *adj* (**-cier, -ciest**) elaborate, not
plain ▶ *n* (*pl* **-cies**) sudden irrational
liking or desire ▶ *v* (**-cies, -cying,
-cied**) *informal* be sexually attracted to
> **fancying** *v* ▷ **fancy**

fandango *n* (*pl* **-os**) lively Spanish
dance

fandangos *n* ▷ **fandango**

fanfare *n* (*pl* **-s**) short loud tune played
on brass instruments

fanfares n ▷ fanfare

fang n (pl -s) snake's tooth which injects poison

fangs n ▷ fang

fanned v ▷ fan

fanning n ▷ fan

fans n, v ▷ fan

fantail n (pl -s) small New Zealand bird with a tail like a fan

fantails n ▷ fantail

fantasia n (pl -s) musical composition of an improvised nature

fantasias n ▷ fantasia

fantasies n ▷ fantasy

fantasy n (pl -sies) far-fetched notion

far adv (**farther** or **further**) (**farthest** or **furthest**) at, to, or from a great distance ▶ adj remote in space or time

farad n (pl -s) unit of electrical capacitance

farads n ▷ farad

farce n (pl -s) boisterous comedy

farces n ▷ farce

farcical adj ludicrous >**farcically** adv

farcically adv ▷ farcical

fare n (pl -s) charge for a passenger's journey ▶ v (-res, -ring, -red) get on (as specified)

fared v ▷ fare

fares n, v ▷ fare

farewell interj goodbye ▶ n (pl -s) act of saying goodbye and leaving ▶ v (-s, -ing, -ed) NZ say goodbye

farewelled v ▷ farewell

farewelling v ▷ farewell

farewells n, v ▷ farewell

faring v ▷ fare

farm n (pl -s) area of land for growing crops or rearing livestock ▶ v (-s, -ing, -ed) cultivate (land) >**farmhouse** n (pl -s) ▶ **farmyard** n (pl -s)

farmed v ▷ farm

farmer n (pl -s) person who owns or runs a farm

farmers n ▷ farmer

farmhouse n ▷ farm

farmhouses n ▷ farm

farming v ▷ farm

farms n, v ▷ farm

farmyard n ▷ farm

farmyards n ▷ farm

farrago n (pl -gos, -goes) jumbled mixture of things

farragoes n ▷ farrago

farragos n ▷ farrago

farrier n (pl -s) person who shoes horses

farriers n ▷ farrier

farrow n (pl -s) litter of piglets ▶ v (-s, -ing, -ed) (of a sow) give birth

farrowed v ▷ farrow

farrowing v ▷ farrow

farrows n, v ▷ farrow

farther, farthest adv, adj ▷ far

farthing n (pl -s) former British coin equivalent to a quarter of a penny

farthings n ▷ farthing

fascia n (pl -e, -s) outer surface of a dashboard

fasciae n ▷ fascia

fascias n ▷ fascia

fascism n (pl -s) right-wing totalitarian political system characterized by state control and extreme nationalism >**fascist** adj, n (pl -s)

fascisms n ▷ fascism

fascist n ▷ fascism

fascists n ▷ fascist

fashion n (pl -s) style in clothes, hairstyle, etc, popular at a particular time ▶ v (-s, -ing, -ed) form or make into a particular shape

fashioned v ▷ fashion

fashioning v ▷ fashion

fashions n, v ▷ fashion

fast[1] adj (-er, -est) (capable of) acting or moving quickly ▶ adv quickly

fast[2] v (-s, -ing, -ed) go without food, esp. for religious reasons ▶ n (pl -s) period of fasting

fasted v ▷ fast[2]

fasten v (-s, -ing, -ed) make or become firmly fixed or joined

fastened v ▷ fasten

fastener n (pl -s) device that fastens

fasteners n ▷ **fastener**
fastens v ▷ **fasten**
faster adj ▷ **fast**[1]
fastest adj ▷ **fast**[1]
fasting v ▷ **fast**[2]
fastness n (pl **-es**) fortress, safe place
fastnesses n ▷ **fastness**
fasts v, n ▷ **fast**[2]
fat adj (**-er, -est**) having excess flesh on the body ▶ n (pl **-s**) extra flesh on the body >**fatness** n (pl **-es**)
fatal adj causing death or ruin >**fatally** adv
fatalism n (pl **-s**) belief that all events are predetermined and people are powerless to change their destinies >**fatalist** n (pl **-s**) >**fatalistic** adj
fatalisms n ▷ **fatalism**
fatalist n ▷ **fatalism**
fatalistic adj ▷ **fatalism**
fatalists n ▷ **fatalism**
fatalities n ▷ **fatality**
fatality n (pl **-ties**) death caused by an accident or disaster
fatally adv ▷ **fatal**
fate n (pl **-s**) power supposed to predetermine events
fated adj destined
fateful adj having important, usu. disastrous, consequences
fates n ▷ **fate**
fathead n (pl **-s**) informal stupid person >**fat-headed** adj
fatheaded adj ▷ **fathead**
fatheads n ▷ **fathead**
father n (pl **-s**) male parent ▶ v (**-s, -ing, -ed**) be the father of (offspring) >**fatherhood** n (pl **-s**) >**fatherless** adj >**fatherly** adj
fathered v ▷ **father**
fatherhood n ▷ **father**
fathering v ▷ **father**
fatherless adj ▷ **father**
fatherly adj ▷ **father**
fathers n, v ▷ **father**
fathom n (pl **-s**) unit of length, used in navigation, equal to six feet (1.83 metres) ▶ v (**-s, -ing, -ed**) understand

fathomable adj ▷ **fathom**
fathomable adj ▷ **fathom**
fathomed v ▷ **fathom**
fathoming v ▷ **fathom**
fathoms n, v ▷ **fathom**
fatigue n (pl **-s**) extreme physical or mental tiredness ▶ v (**-gues, -guing, -gued**) tire out
fatigued v ▷ **fatigue**
fatigues v, n ▷ **fatigue**
fatiguing v ▷ **fatigue**
fatness n ▷ **fat**
fatnesses n ▷ **fat**
fats n ▷ **fat**
fatten v (**-s, -ing, -ed**) (cause to) become fat
fattened v ▷ **fatten**
fattening v ▷ **fatten**
fattens v ▷ **fatten**
fattier adj ▷ **fatty**
fattiest adj ▷ **fatty**
fatty adj (**-ier, -iest**) containing fat
fatuities n ▷ **fatuous**
fatuity n ▷ **fatuous**
fatuous adj foolish >**fatuously** adv >**fatuity** n (pl **-s**)
fatuously adv ▷ **fatuous**
faucet n (pl **-s**) us tap
faucets n ▷ **faucet**
fault n (pl **-s**) responsibility for something wrong ▶ v (**-s, -ing, -ed**) criticize or blame >**faulty** adj (**-tier, -tiest**) >**faultless** adj >**faultlessly** adv
faulted v ▷ **fault**
faultier adj ▷ **fault**
faultiest adj ▷ **fault**
faulting v ▷ **fault**
faultless adj ▷ **fault**
faultlessly adv ▷ **fault**
faults v ▷ **fault**
faulty adj ▷ **fault**
faun n (pl **-s**) (in Roman legend) creature with a human face and torso and a goat's horns and legs
fauna n (pl **-as, -ae**) animals of a given place or time
faunae n ▷ **fauna**
faunas n ▷ **fauna**

fauns n ▷ faun

favour n (pl -s) approving attitude ▶ v (-s, -ing, -ed) prefer

favoured v ▷ favour

favouring v ▷ favour

favours n, v ▷ favour

> **faw** n (faws). A faw is a gypsy. This is a good word for taking advantage of a nearby bonus square. Faw scores 9 points.

fawn¹ n (pl -s) young deer ▶ adj light yellowish-brown

fawn² v (-s, -ing, -ed) (foll. by **on**) seek attention from (someone) by insincere flattery

fawned v ▷ fawn²

fawning v ▷ fawn²

fawns n, v ▷ fawn¹, ²

fax n (pl -es) electronic system for sending facsimiles of documents by telephone ▶ v (-xes, -xing, -xed) send (a document) by this system

faxed n ▷ fax

faxes n, v ▷ fax

faxing v ▷ fax

> **fay** n (fays). A fay is a fairy. This is a fairly high-scoring short word that can be helpful in a tight game. Fay scores 9 points.

fealties n ▷ fealty

fealty n (pl -ties) (in feudal society) subordinate's loyalty to his ruler or lord

fear n (pl -s) distress or alarm caused by impending danger or pain ▶ v (-s, -ing, -ed) be afraid of (something or someone) > **fearless** adj > **fearlessly** adv

feared v ▷ fear

fearful adj feeling fear informal > **fearfully** adv

fearfully adv ▷ fearful

fearing v ▷ fear

fearless adj ▷ fear

fearlessly adv ▷ fear

fears n, v ▷ fear

fearsome adj terrifying

feasibilities n ▷ feasible

feasibility n ▷ feasible

feasible adj able to be done, possible > **feasibly** adv > **feasibility** n (pl -s)

feasibly adv ▷ feasible

feast n (pl -s) lavish meal ▶ v (-s, -ing, -ed) eat a feast

feasted v ▷ feast

feasting v ▷ feast

feasts n, v ▷ feast

feat n (pl -s) remarkable, skilful, or daring action

feather n (pl -s) one of the barbed shafts forming the plumage of birds ▶ v (-s, -ing, -ed) fit or cover with feathers > **feathered** adj > **feathery** adj (-rier, -riest)

feathered v, adj ▷ feather

featherier adj ▷ feather

featheriest adj ▷ feather

feathering v ▷ feather

feathers n, v ▷ feather

feathery adj ▷ feather

feats n ▷ feat

feature n (pl -s) part of the face, such as the eyes ▶ v (-res, -ring, -red) have as a feature or be a feature in > **featureless** adj

featured v ▷ feature

featureless adj ▷ feature

features n, v ▷ feature

featuring v ▷ feature

febrile adj feverish

feckless adj ineffectual or irresponsible

fecund adj fertile > **fecundity** n (pl -ties)

fecundities n ▷ fecund

fecundity n ▷ fecund

fed v ▷ feed

federal adj of a system in which power is divided between one central government and several regional governments > **federalism** n (pl -s) > **federalist** n (pl -s)

federalism n ▷ federal

federalisms n ▷ federal

federalist n ▷ federal

federalists n ▷ federal

federate v (-tes, -ting, -ted) unite in

a federation

federated v ▷ **federate**

federates v ▷ **federate**

federating v ▷ **federate**

fedora n (pl -s) man's soft hat with a brim

fedoras n ▷ **fedora**

fee n (pl -s) charge paid to be allowed to do something

feeble adj (-r, -st) lacking physical or mental power ▶ **feebleness** n (pl -es) >**feebly** adv

feebleness n ▷ **feeble**

feeblenesses n ▷ **feeble**

feebler adj ▷ **feeble**

feeblest adj ▷ **feeble**

feebly adv ▷ **feeble**

feed v (-s, -ing, fed) give food to ▶ n (pl -s) act of feeding

feedback n (pl -s) information received in response to something done

feedbacks n ▷ **feedback**

feeder n (pl -s) road or railway line linking outlying areas to the main traffic network

feeders n ▷ **feeder**

feeding v ▷ **feed**

feeds v, n ▷ **feed**

feel v (-s, -ing, felt) have a physical or emotional sensation of ▶ n (pl -s) act of feeling

feeler n (pl -s) organ of touch in some animals

feelers n ▷ **feeler**

feeling n (pl -s) emotional reaction

feelings n ▷ **feeling** ▶ v ▷ **feel**

feels v, n ▷ **feel**

fees n ▷ **fee**

feet n ▷ **foot**

feign v (-s, -ing, -ed) pretend

feigned v ▷ **feign**

feigning v ▷ **feign**

feigns v ▷ **feign**

feint[1] n (pl -s) sham attack or blow meant to distract an opponent ▶ v (-s, -ing, -ed) make a feint

feint[2] n (pl -s) narrow lines on ruled

paper

feinted v ▷ **feint**[1]

feinting v ▷ **feint**[1]

feints n, v ▷ **feint**[1, 2]

feldspar n (pl -s) hard mineral that is the main constituent of igneous rocks

feldspars n ▷ **feldspar**

felicities n ▷ **felicity**

felicitous adj ▷ **felicity**

felicity n (pl -ties) happiness (pl -ties) >**felicitous** adj

feline adj of cats ▶ n (pl -s) member of the cat family

felines n ▷ **feline**

fell[1] v ▷ **fall**

fell[2] v (-s, -ing, -ed) cut down (a tree)

fell[3] adj (-er, -est) deadly

fell[4] n (pl -s) SCOT & N ENGLISH mountain, hill, or moor

felled v ▷ **fell**[2]

feller adj ▷ **fell**[3]

fellest adj ▷ **fell**[3]

felling v ▷ **fell**[2]

felloe n (pl -s) (segment of) the rim of a wheel

felloes n ▷ **felloe**

fellow n (pl -s) man or boy ▶ adj in the same group or condition

fellows n ▷ **fellow**

fells v, n ▷ **fell**[2, 4]

felon n (pl -s) CRIMINAL LAW (formerly) person guilty of a felony

felonies n ▷ **felony**

felonious adj ▷ **felony**

felons n ▷ **felon**

felony n (pl -nies) serious crime >**felonious** adj

felspar n (pl -s) ▷ **feldspar**

felspars n ▷ **felspar**

felt[1] v ▷ **feel**

felt[2] n (pl -s) matted fabric made by bonding fibres by pressure

felts n ▷ **felt**[2]

female adj of the sex which bears offspring ▶ n (pl -s) female person or animal

females n ▷ **female**

feminine adj having qualities

traditionally regarded as suitable for, or typical of, women >**femininity** n (pl **-ties**)

femininities n ▷ **feminine**

femininity n ▷ **feminine**

feminism n (pl **-s**) advocacy of equal rights for women >**feminist** adj, n (pl **-s**)

feminisms n ▷ **feminism**

feminist n ▷ **feminism**

feminists n ▷ **feminism**

femoral adj of the thigh

femur n (pl **-s**) thighbone

femurs n ▷ **femur**

fen n (pl **-s**) BRIT low-lying flat marshy land

fence n (pl **-s**) barrier of posts linked by wire or wood, enclosing an area ▶ v (**-ces, -cing, -ced**) enclose with or as if with a fence

fenced v ▷ **fence**

fencer n ▷ **fencing**

fencers n ▷ **fencing**

fences n, v ▷ **fence**

fencing n (pl **-s**) sport of fighting with swords ▶ v ▷ **fence** >**fencer** n (pl **-s**)

fencings n ▷ **fencing**

fend v (**-s, -ing, -ed**) provide (for oneself)

fended v ▷ **fend**

fender n (pl **-s**) low metal frame in front of a fireplace

fenders n ▷ **fender**

fending v ▷ **fend**

fends v ▷ **fend**

fennel n (pl **-s**) fragrant plant whose seeds, leaves, and root are used in cookery

fennels n ▷ **fennel**

fens n ▷ **fen**

feral adj wild

ferment n (pl **-s**) commotion, unrest ▶ v (**-s, -ing, -ed**) undergo or cause to undergo fermentation

fermented v ▷ **ferment**

fermenting v ▷ **ferment**

ferments n, v ▷ **ferment**

fern n (pl **-s**) flowerless plant with fine fronds

ferns n ▷ **fern**

ferret n (pl **-s**) tamed polecat used to catch rabbits or rats ▶ v (**-s, -ing, -ed**) hunt with ferrets

ferreted v ▷ **ferret**

ferreting v ▷ **ferret**

ferrets n, v ▷ **ferret**

ferric, ferrous adj of or containing iron

ferried v ▷ **ferry**

ferries n, v ▷ **ferry**

ferrous adj ▷ **ferric**

ferry n (pl **-ries**) boat for transporting people and vehicles ▶ v (**-ries, -rying, -ried**) carry by ferry >**ferryman** n (pl **-men**)

ferrying v ▷ **ferry**

ferryman n ▷ **ferry**

ferrymen n ▷ **ferry**

fertile adj capable of producing young, crops, or vegetation >**fertility** n (pl **-ties**)

fertilities n ▷ **fertile**

fertility n ▷ **fertile**

fervent, fervid adj intensely passionate and sincere >**fervently** adv

fervently adv ▷ **fervent**

fervid adj ▷ **fervent**

fervour n (pl **-s**) intensity of feeling

fervours n ▷ **fervour**

fescue n (pl **-s**) pasture and lawn grass with stiff narrow leaves

fescues n ▷ **fescue**

fester v (**-s, -ing, -ed**) grow worse and increasingly hostile

festered v ▷ **fester**

festering v ▷ **fester**

festers v ▷ **fester**

festival n (pl **-s**) organized series of special events or performances

festivals n ▷ **festival**

festive adj of or like a celebration

festoon v (**-s, -ing, -ed**) hang decorations in loops

festooned v ▷ **festoon**

festooning v ▷ **festoon**

festoons v ▷ **festoon**

feta n (pl -s) white salty Greek cheese
  fetal adj ▷ **fetus**
  fetas n ▷ **feta**
fetch v (-es, -ing, -ed) go after and bring back informal
  fetched v ▷ **fetch**
  fetches v ▷ **fetch**
  fetching v ▷ **fetch** ▶ adj attractive
fete n (pl -s) gala, bazaar, etc. usu. held outdoors ▶ v (-tes, -ting, -ted) honour or entertain regally
  feted v ▷ **fete**
  fetes n, v ▷ **fete**
fetid adj (-er, -est) stinking
  fetider adj ▷ **fetid**
  fetidest adj ▷ **fetid**
  feting v ▷ **fete**
fetish n (pl -es) form of behaviour in which sexual pleasure is derived from looking at or handling an inanimate object > **fetishism** n (pl -s) > **fetishist** (pl -s) n
  fetishes n ▷ **fetish**
  fetishism n ▷ **fetish**
  fetishisms n ▷ **fetish**
  fetishist n ▷ **fetish**
  fetishists n ▷ **fetish**
fetlock n (pl -s) projection behind and above a horse's hoof
  fetlocks n ▷ **fetlock**
fetter n (pl -s) chain or shackle for the foot ▶ pl restrictions ▶ v (-s, -ing, -ed) restrict
  fettered v ▷ **fetter**
  fettering v ▷ **fetter**
  fetters n, v ▷ **fetter**
fettle n (pl -s) state of health or spirits
  fettles n ▷ **fettle**
fetus n (pl -tuses) embryo of a mammal in the later stages of development > **fetal** adj
  fetuses n ▷ **fetus**
feu n (pl -s) (in Scotland) right of use of land in return for a fixed annual payment
feud n (pl -s) long bitter hostility between two people or groups ▶ v (-s, -ing, -ed) carry on a feud

feudal adj of or like feudalism
  feuded v ▷ **feud**
  feuding v ▷ **feud**
  feuds n ▷ **feud**
  feus n ▷ **feu**
fever n (pl -s) (illness causing) high body temperature > **fevered** adj
  fevered adj ▷ **fever**
feverish adj suffering from fever > **feverishly** adv
  feverishly adv ▷ **feverish**
  fevers n ▷ **fever**
few adj (-er, -est) not many
  fewer adj ▷ **few**
  fewest adj ▷ **few**
fey adj (-er, -est) whimsically strange
  feyer adj ▷ **fey**
  feyest adj ▷ **fey**
fez n (pl **fezzes**) brimless tasselled cap, orig. from Turkey
  fezzes n ▷ **fez**
fiancé n (pl -**cés**) man engaged to be married > **fiancée** n fem (pl -**cées**)
  fiancée n ▷ **fiancé**
  fiancées n ▷ **fiancé**
  fiancés n ▷ **fiancé**
fiasco n (pl -**cos**, -**coes**) ridiculous or humiliating failure
  fiascoes n ▷ **fiasco**
  fiascos n ▷ **fiasco**
fiat n (pl -s) arbitrary order
  fiats n ▷ **fiat**
fib n (pl -s) trivial lie ▶ v (-s, -**bbing**, -**bbed**) tell a lie > **fibber** n (pl -s)
  fibbed v ▷ **fib**
  fibber n ▷ **fib**
  fibbers n ▷ **fib**
  fibbing v ▷ **fib**
fibre n (pl -s) thread that can be spun into yarn > **fibrous** adj
  fibres n ▷ **fibre**
fibro n (pl -s) AUST mixture of cement and asbestos fibre, used in sheets for building (also **fibrocement**)
fibroid n (pl -s) benign tumour composed of fibrous connective tissue
  fibroids n ▷ **fibroid**
  fibros n ▷ **fibro**

fibrous adj ▷ **fibre**

fibs n, v ▷ **fib**

fibula n (pl -lae, -las) slender outer bone of the lower leg

fibulae n ▷ **fibula**

fibulas n ▷ **fibula**

fiche n (pl -s) sheet of film for storing publications in miniaturized form

fiches n ▷ **fiche**

fickle adj changeable, inconstant > **fickleness** n (pl -ess)

fickleness n ▷ **fickle**

ficklenesses n ▷ **fickle**

fiction n (pl -s) literary works of the imagination, such as novels > **fictional** adj

fictional adj ▷ **fiction**

fictions n ▷ **fiction**

fiddle n (pl -s) violin informal ▶ v (-les, -ling, -led) play the violin

fiddled v ▷ **fiddle**

fiddles n, v ▷ **fiddle**

fiddlier adj ▷ **fiddly**

fiddliest adj ▷ **fiddly**

fiddling v ▷ **fiddle** ▶ adj trivial

fiddly adj (-lier, -liest) awkward to do or use

fidelities n ▷ **fidelity**

fidelity n (pl -ies) faithfulness

fidget v (-s, -ing, -ed) move about restlessly ▶ n (pl -s) person who fidgets ▶ pl restlessness > **fidgety** adj (-tier, -tiest)

fidgeted v ▷ **fidget**

fidgetier adj ▷ **fidget**

fidgetiest adj ▷ **fidget**

fidgeting v ▷ **fidget**

fidgets v, n ▷ **fidget**

fidgety adj ▷ **fidget**

fief n (pl -s) HIST land granted by a lord in return for war service

fiefs n ▷ **fief**

field n (pl -s) enclosed piece of agricultural land ▶ v (-s, -ing, -ed) SPORT catch and return (a ball)

fielded v ▷ **field**

fielder n (pl -s) SPORT player whose task is to field the ball

fielders n ▷ **fielder**

fielding v ▷ **field**

fields n, v ▷ **field**

fiend n (pl -s) evil spirit informal > **fiendish** adj > **fiendishly** adv

fiendish adj ▷ **fiend**

fiendishly adv ▷ **fiend**

fiends n ▷ **fiend**

fierce adj (-r, -st) wild or aggressive > **fiercely** adv > **fierceness** n (pl -es)

fiercely adv ▷ **fierce**

fierceness n ▷ **fierce**

fiercenesses n ▷ **fierce**

fiercer adj ▷ **fierce**

fiercest adj ▷ **fierce**

fierier adj ▷ **fiery**

fieriest adj ▷ **fiery**

fiery adj (-rier, -riest) consisting of or like fire

fiesta n (pl -s) religious festival, carnival

fiestas n ▷ **fiesta**

fife n (pl -s) small high-pitched flute

fifes n ▷ **fife**

fifteen adj, n (pl -s) five and ten > **fifteenth** adj, n (pl -s)

fifteens n ▷ **fifteen**

fifteenth adj, n ▷ **fifteen**

fifth adj, n (pl -s) (of) number five in a series

fifths n ▷ **fifth**

fifties n ▷ **fifty**

fiftieth adj, n ▷ **fifty**

fiftieths n ▷ **fifty**

fifty adj, n (pl -ties) five times ten > **fiftieth** adj, n (pl -s)

fig n (pl -s) soft pear-shaped fruit

fight v (-s, -ing, fought) struggle (against) in battle or physical combat ▶ n (pl -s) aggressive conflict between two (groups of) people

fighter n (pl -s) boxer

fighters n ▷ **fighter**

fighting v ▷ **fight**

fights n, v ▷ **fight**

figment n (pl -s) something imagined

figments n ▷ **figment**

figs n ▷ **fig**

figure | 208

figure n (pl -s) numerical symbol
MATHS ▶ v (-res, -ring, -red) consider, conclude
figured v ▷ figure
figures n, v ▷ figure
figurine n (pl -s) statuette
figurines n ▷ figurine
figuring v ▷ figure

filament n (pl -s) fine wire in a light bulb that gives out light
filaments n ▷ filament
filbert n (pl -s) hazelnut
filberts n ▷ filbert
filch v (-es, -ing, -ed) steal (small amounts)
filched v ▷ filch
filches v ▷ filch
filching v ▷ filch

file¹ n (pl -s) box or folder used to keep documents in order ▶ v (-les, -ling, -led) place (a document) in a file
file² n (pl -s) tool with a roughened blade for smoothing or shaping ▶ v (-les, -ling, -led) shape or smooth with a file
filed v ▷ file¹, ²
files n, v ▷ file¹, ²
filial adj of or befitting a son or daughter
filigree n (pl -s) delicate ornamental work of gold or silver wire ▶ adj made of filigree
filigrees n ▷ filigree
filing v ▷ file¹, ²
filings pl n shavings removed by a file
fill v (-s, -ing, -ed) make or become full
filled v ▷ fill
filler n (pl -s) substance that fills a gap or increases bulk
fillers n ▷ filler
fillet n (pl -s) boneless piece of meat or fish ▶ v (-s, -ing, -ed) remove the bones from
filleted v ▷ fillet
filleting v ▷ fillet
fillets n, v ▷ fillet
fillies n ▷ filly
filling n (pl -s) substance that fills a gap

or cavity, esp. in a tooth ▶ adj (of food) substantial and satisfying ▶ v ▷ fill
fillings n ▷ filling
fillip n (pl -s) something that adds stimulation or enjoyment
fillips n ▷ fillip
fills v ▷ fill
filly n (pl -llies) young female horse
film n (pl -s) sequence of images projected on a screen, creating the illusion of movement ▶ v (-s, -ing, -ed) photograph with a movie or video camera ▶ adj connected with films or the cinema
filmed v ▷ film
filmier adj ▷ filmy
filmiest adj ▷ filmy
filming v ▷ film
films n, v ▷ film
filmy adj (-mier, -miest) very thin, delicate
filter n (pl -s) material or device permitting fluid to pass but retaining solid particles ▶ v (-s, -ing, -ed) remove impurities from (a substance) with a filter
filtered v ▷ filter
filtering v ▷ filter
filters n, v ▷ filter
filth n (pl -s) disgusting dirt > filthy adj (-thier, -thiest) > filthiness n (pl -es)
filthier adj ▷ filth
filthiest adj ▷ filth
filthiness n ▷ filth
filthinesses n ▷ filth
filths n ▷ filth
filthy adj ▷ filth
filtrate n (pl -s) filtered gas or liquid ▶ v (-tes, -ting, -ted) remove impurities with a filter > filtration n (pl -s)
filtrated v ▷ filtrate
filtrates n, v ▷ filtrate
filtrating v ▷ filtrate
filtration n ▷ filtrate
filtrations n ▷ filtrate
fin n (pl -s) projection from a fish's body enabling it to balance and swim
finagle v (-les, -ling, -led) get or

achieve by craftiness or trickery
finagled v ▷ **finagle**
finagles v ▷ **finagle**
finagling v ▷ **finagle**
final adj at the end ▶ n (pl **-s**) deciding contest between winners of previous rounds in a competition ▶ pl BRIT & S AFR last examinations in an educational course > **finally** adv
> **finality** n (pl **-ties**)
finale (pl **-s**) n concluding part of a dramatic performance or musical work
finales n ▷ **finale**
finalist (pl **-s**) n competitor in a final
finalists n ▷ **finalist**
finalities n ▷ **final**
finality n ▷ **final**
finalize v (**-zes**, **-zing**, **-zed**) put into final form
finalized v ▷ **finalize**
finalizes v ▷ **finalize**
finalizing v ▷ **finalize**
finally adv ▷ **final**
finals n ▷ **final**
finance v (**-ces**, **-cing**, **-ced**) provide or obtain funds for ▶ n (pl **-s**) management of money, loans, or credits ▶ pl money resources
> **financial** adj > **financially** adv
financed v ▷ **finance**
finances v, n ▷ **finance**
financial adj ▷ **finance**
financially adv ▷ **finance**
financing v ▷ **finance**
finch n (pl **-es**) small songbird with a short strong beak
finches n ▷ **finch**
find v (**-s**, **-ing**, **found**) discover by chance ▶ n (pl **-s**) person or thing found, esp. when valuable > **finder** n (pl **-s**)
finder n ▷ **find**
finders n ▷ **find**
finding n (pl **-s**) conclusion from an investigation ▶ v ▷ **find**
findings n ▷ **finding**
finds v, n ▷ **find**
fine[1] adj (**-r**, **-st**) very good > **finely** adv

> **fineness** n (pl **-es**)
fine[2] n (pl **-s**) payment imposed as a penalty ▶ v (**-nes**, **-ning**, **-ned**) impose a fine on
fined v ▷ **fine**[2]
finely adv ▷ **fine**[1]
fineness n ▷ **fine**[1]
finenesses n ▷ **fine**[1]
finer adj ▷ **fine**[1]
fineries n ▷ **finery**
finery n (pl **-ries**) showy clothing
fines v, n ▷ **fine**[1, 2]
finesse n (pl **-s**) delicate skill
finesses n ▷ **finesse**
finest adj ▷ **fine**[1]
finger n (pl **-s**) one of the four long jointed parts of the hand ▶ v (**-s**, **-ing**, **-ed**) touch or handle with the fingers
fingered v ▷ **finger**
fingers n, v ▷ **finger**
finickier adj ▷ **finicky**
finickiest adj ▷ **finicky**
finicky adj (**-kier**, **-kiest**) excessively particular, fussy
fining v ▷ **fine**
finish v (**-es**, **-ing**, **-ed**) bring to an end, stop ▶ n (pl **-es**) end, last part
finished v ▷ **finish**
finishes n ▷ **finish**
finishing v ▷ **finish**
finite adj having limits in space, time, or size
fins n ▷ **fin**
fiord n (pl **-s**) ▷ **fjord**
fiords n ▷ **fiord**
fir n (pl **-s**) pyramid-shaped tree with needle-like leaves and erect cones
fire n (pl **-s**) state of combustion producing heat, flames, and smoke ▶ v (**-res**, **-ring**, **-red**) operate (a weapon) so that a bullet or missile is released
firearm n (pl **-s**) rifle, pistol, or shotgun
firearms n ▷ **firearms**
fired v ▷ **fire**
firedamp n (pl **-s**) explosive gas, composed mainly of methane, formed in mines
firedamps n ▷ **firedamp**

fireflies n ▷ firefly

firefly n (pl -flies) beetle that glows in the dark

fires n, v ▷ fire

firewall n (pl -s) COMPUTERS computer that prevents unauthorized access to a computer network from the Internet

firewalls n ▷ firewall

firework n (pl -s) device containing chemicals that is ignited to produce spectacular explosions and coloured sparks ▶ pl show of fireworks

fireworks n ▷ firework

firing v ▷ fire

firm[1] adj (-er, -est) not soft or yielding ▶ adv in an unyielding manner ▶ v (-s, -ing, -ed) make or become firm
> **firmly** adv **firmness** n (pl -es)

firm[2] n (pl -s) business company

firmed v ▷ firm[1]

firmer adj ▷ firm[1]

firmest adj ▷ firm[1]

firming v ▷ firm[1]

firmly adv ▷ firm[1]

firmness n ▷ firm[1]

firmnesses n ▷ firm[1]

firms v, n ▷ firm[1, 2]

firs n ▷ fir

first adj earliest in time or order ▶ n (pl -s) person or thing coming before all others ▶ adv before anything else
> **firstly** adv

firstly adv ▷ first

firsts n ▷ first

firth n (pl -s) narrow inlet of the sea, esp. in Scotland

firths n ▷ firth

fiscal adj of government finances, esp. taxes

fish n (pl fish, fishes) cold-blooded vertebrate with gills, that lives in water ▶ v (-es, -ing, -ed) try to catch fish

fished v ▷ fish

fisheries n ▷ fishery

fishery n (pl -ries) area of the sea used for fishing

fishes n, v ▷ fish

fishier adj ▷ fishy

fishiest adj ▷ fishy

fishing v ▷ fish

fishmeal n (pl -s) dried ground fish used as animal feed or fertilizer

fishmeals n ▷ fishmeal

fishnet n (pl -s) open mesh fabric resembling netting

fishnets n ▷ fishnet

fishwife n (pl -wives) coarse scolding woman

fishwives n ▷ fishwife

fishy adj (-shier, -shiest) of or like fish

fissile adj capable of undergoing nuclear fission

fission n (pl -s) splitting
> **fissionable** adj

fissionable adj ▷ fission

fissions n ▷ fission

fissure n (pl -s) long narrow cleft or crack

fissures n ▷ fissure

fist n (pl -s) clenched hand

fists n ▷ fist

fit[1] v (-s, -tting, -tted) be appropriate or suitable for ▶ adj appropriate ▶ n (-tter, -ttest) (pl -s) way in which something fits > **fitness** n (pl -es)

fit[2] n (pl -s) sudden attack or convulsion, such as an epileptic seizure

fitful adj occurring in irregular spells
> **fitfully** adv

fitfully adv ▷ fitful

fitment n (pl -s) detachable part of the furnishings of a room

fitments n ▷ fitment

fitness n ▷ fit[1]

fitnesses n ▷ fit[1]

fits v, n ▷ fit[1, 2]

fitted v ▷ fit[1]

fitter n (pl -s) person skilled in the installation and adjustment of machinery ▶ adj ▷ fit[1]

fitters n ▷ fitter

fittest adj ▷ fit[1]

fitting adj appropriate, suitable ▶ n (pl -s) accessory or part ▶ pl furnishings and accessories in a building ▶ v ▷ fit

fittings n ▷ fitting

five adj, n (pl **-s**) one more than four

fiver n (pl **-s**) informal five-pound note
fivers n ▷ fiver

fives n ball game resembling squash but played with bats or the hands ▶ n ▷ five

fix v (**-xes, -xing, -xed**) make or become firm, stable, or secure ▶ n (pl **-es**) informal difficult situation >**fixed** adj >**fixedly** adv steadily

fixated adj obsessed

fixation n (pl **-s**) obsessive interest in something
fixations n ▷ fixation

fixative n (pl **-s**) liquid used to preserve or hold things in place
fixatives n ▷ fixative

fixed v, adj ▷ fix
fixedly adv ▷ fix

fixer n (pl **-s**) solution used to make a photographic image permanent slang
fixers n ▷ fixer
fixes v, n ▷ fix
fixing v ▷ fix

fixture n (pl **-s**) permanently fitted piece of household equipment
fixtures n ▷ fixture

fizz v (**-es, -ing, -ed**) make a hissing or bubbling noise ▶ n (pl **-es**) hissing or bubbling noise >**fizzy** adj (**-zier, -ziest**)
fizzed v ▷ fizz
fizzes v ▷ fizz
fizzier adj ▷ fizz
fizziest adj ▷ fizz
fizzing v ▷ fizz

fizzle v (**-les, -ling, -led**) make a weak hissing or bubbling sound
fizzled v ▷ fizzle
fizzles v ▷ fizzle
fizzling v ▷ fizzle
fizzy adj ▷ fizz

fjord n (pl **-s**) long narrow inlet of the sea between cliffs, esp. in Norway
fjords n ▷ fjord

flab n (pl **-s**) informal unsightly body fat
flabbier adj ▷ flabby
flabbiest adj ▷ flabby

flabby adj (**-bier, -biest**) having flabby flesh

flabs n ▷ flab

flaccid adj (**-er, -est**) soft and limp >**flaccidity** n (pl **-ties**)
flaccider adj ▷ flaccid
flaccidest adj ▷ flaccid
flaccidities n ▷ flaccid
flaccidity n ▷ flaccid

flag¹ n (pl **-s**) piece of cloth attached to a pole as an emblem or signal ▶ v (**-s, -gging, -gged**) mark with a flag or sticker

flag² v (**-s, -gging, -gged**) lose enthusiasm or vigour

flag³, flagstone (pl **-s**) n flat paving-stone

flagged adj paved with flagstones ▶ v ▷ flag¹,²
flagged v ▷ flag¹,²
flagging v ▷ flag¹,²

flagon n (pl **-s**) wide bottle for wine or cider
flagons n ▷ flagon

flagpole, flagstaff (pl **-s**) n pole for a flag
flagpoles n ▷ flagpole

flagrant adj openly outrageous >**flagrantly** adv
flagrantly adv ▷ flagrant
flagrants n ▷ flag¹,²,³

flagship n (pl **-s**) admiral's ship
flagships n ▷ flagship
flagstaff n ▷ flagpole
flagstaffs n ▷ flagpole
flagstone n ▷ flag³
flagstones n ▷ flag³

flail v (**-s, -ing, -ed**) wave about wildly ▶ n (pl **-s**) tool formerly used for threshing grain by hand
flailed v ▷ flail
flailing v ▷ flail
flails v, n ▷ flail

flair n (pl **-s**) natural ability
flairs n ▷ flair

flak n (pl **-s**) anti-aircraft fire

flake¹ n (pl **-s**) small thin piece, esp. chipped off something informal ▶ v

(**-kes, -king, -ked**) peel off in flakes
▷ **flaky** *adj* (**-kier, -kiest**)

flake² *n* (*pl* **-s**) (in Australia) the commercial name for the meat of the gummy shark
flaked *v* ▷ **flake**
flakes *v, n* ▷ **flake¹, ²**
flakier *adj* ▷ **flaky**
flakiest *adj* ▷ **flaky**
flaking *v* ▷ **flake¹**
flaks *n* ▷ **flak**
flaky *adj* ▷ **flake¹**

flambé *v* (**-bés, -béing, -béed**) cook or serve (food) in flaming brandy
flambéed *v* ▷ **flambé**
flambéing *v* ▷ **flambé**
flambés *v* ▷ **flambé**

flame *n* (*pl* **-s**) luminous burning gas coming from burning material ▷ *v*
(**-mes, -ming, -med**) burn brightly
flamed *v* ▷ **flame**

flamenco *n* (*pl* **-s**) rhythmical Spanish dance accompanied by a guitar and vocalist
flamencos *n* ▷ **flamenco**
flames *n, v* ▷ **flame**
flaming *v* ▷ **flame**

flamingo *n* (*pl* **-s, -es**) large pink wading bird with a long neck and legs
flamingoes *n* ▷ **flamingo**
flamingos *n* ▷ **flamingo**

flan *n* (*pl* **-s**) open sweet or savoury tart
flange *n* (*pl* **-s**) projecting rim or collar
flanges *n* ▷ **flange**

flank *n* (*pl* **-s**) part of the side between the hips and ribs ▷ *v* (**-s, -ing, -ed**) be at or move along the side of
flanked *v* ▷ **flank**
flanking *v* ▷ **flank**
flanks *n, v* ▷ **flank**

flannel *n* (*pl* **-s**) BRIT small piece of cloth for washing the face ▷ *pl* trousers made of flannel ▷ *v* (**-s, -lling, -lled**) *informal* talk evasively
flannelled *v* ▷ **flannel**
flannelling *v* ▷ **flannel**
flannels *n, v* ▷ **flannel**
flans *n* ▷ **flan**

flap *v* (**-s, -pping, -pped**) move back and forwards or up and down ▷ *n* (*pl* **-s**) action or sound of flapping
flapjack *n* (*pl* **-s**) chewy biscuit made with oats
flapjacks *n* ▷ **flapjack**
flapped *v* ▷ **flap**
flapping *v* ▷ **flap**
flaps *v, n* ▷ **flap**

flare *v* (**-res, -ring, -red**) blaze with a sudden unsteady flame ▷ *n* (*pl* **-s**) sudden unsteady flame ▷ *pl* flared trousers
flared *adj* (of a skirt or trousers) becoming wider towards the hem
▷ *v* ▷ **flare**
flares *v, n* ▷ **flare**
flaring *v* ▷ **flare**

flash *n* (*pl* **-es**) sudden burst of light or flame ▷ *v* (**-es, -ing, -ed**) (cause to) burst into flame
flashed *v* ▷ **flash**

flasher *n* (*pl* **-s**) *slang* man who exposes himself indecently
flashers *n* ▷ **flasher**
flashes *n, v* ▷ **flash**
flashier *adj* ▷ **flashy**
flashiest *adj* ▷ **flashy**

flashing *n* (*pl* **-s**) watertight material used to cover joins in a roof ▷ *v* ▷ **flash**
flashings *n* ▷ **flashing**

flashy *adj* (**-shier, -shiest**) vulgarly showy

flask *n* (*pl* **-s**) flat bottle for carrying alcoholic drink in the pocket
flasks *n* ▷ **flask**

flat¹ *adj* (**-tter, -ttest**) level and horizontal ▷ *adv* in or into a flat position ▷ *n* (*pl* **-s**) MUSIC symbol lowering the pitch of a note by a semitone ▷ **flatly** *adv* ▷ **flatness** *n* (*pl* **-es**) ▷ **flatten** *v* (**-s, -ing, -ed**)

flat² *n* (*pl* **-s**) set of rooms for living in which are part of a larger building ▷ *v* (**-s, -tting, -tted**) AUST & NZ live in a flat

flatfish *n* (*pl* **-fish, -fishes**) sea fish, such as the sole, which has a flat body
flatfishes *n* ▷ **flatfish**

flatlet n (pl **-s**) BRIT, AUST & S AFR small flat
flatlets n ▷ flatlet
flatly adv ▷ flat¹
flatmate n (pl **-s**) person with whom one shares a flat
flatmates n ▷ flatmate
flatness n ▷ flat¹
flatnesses n ▷ flat¹
flats n, v ▷ flat¹, ²
flatted v ▷ flat²
flatten v ▷ flat¹
flattened v ▷ flat¹
flattening v ▷ flat¹
flatter¹ v (**-s, -ing, -ed**) praise insincerely ▷ flatterer n (pl **-s**) ▷ flattery (pl **-ries**)
flatter² adj ▷ flat¹
flattered v ▷ flatter¹
flatterer n ▷ flatter¹
flatterers n ▷ flatter¹
flatteries n ▷ flatter¹
flattering v ▷ flatter¹
flatters v ▷ flatter¹
flattery n ▷ flatter¹
flattest adj ▷ flat¹
flattie n (pl **-s**) NZ & S AFR informal flat tyre
flatties n ▷ flattie
flatting v ▷ flat²
flaunt v (**-s, -ing, -ed**) display (oneself or one's possessions) arrogantly
flaunted v ▷ flaunt
flaunting v ▷ flaunt
flaunts v ▷ flaunt
flautist n (pl **-s**) flute player
flautists n ▷ flautist
flavour n (pl **-s**) distinctive taste ▶ v (**-s, -ing, -ed**) give flavour to ▷ flavourless adj
flavoured v ▷ flavour
flavourless adj ▷ flavour
flavours n, v ▷ flavour
flaw n (pl **-s**) imperfection or blemish ▷ flawed adj ▷ flawless adj
flawed adj ▷ flaw
flawless adj ▷ flaw
flaws n ▷ flaw

flax n (pl **-es**) plant grown for its stem fibres and seeds
flaxen adj (of hair) pale yellow
flaxes n ▷ flax
flay v (**-s, -ing, -ed**) strip the skin off
flayed v ▷ flay
flaying v ▷ flay
flays v ▷ flay
flea n (pl **-s**) small wingless jumping bloodsucking insect
fleapit n (pl **-s**) informal shabby cinema or theatre
fleapits n ▷ fleapit
fleas n ▷ flea
fleck n (pl **-s**) small mark, streak, or speck ▶ v (**-s, -ing, -ed**) speckle
flecked n ▷ fleck
flecking v ▷ fleck
flecks v ▷ fleck
fled v ▷ flee
fledged adj (of young birds) able to fly
flee v (**-s, -ing, fled**) run away (from)
fleece n (pl **-s**) sheep's coat of wool BRIT ▶ v (**-ces, -cing, -ced**) defraud or overcharge
fleeced v ▷ fleece
fleeces n, v ▷ fleece
fleecier adj ▷ fleecy
fleeciest adj ▷ fleecy
fleecing v ▷ fleece
fleecy adj (**-cier, -ciest**) made of or like fleece
fleeing v ▷ flee
flees v ▷ flee
fleet¹ n (pl **-s**) number of warships organized as a unit
fleet² adj swift in movement
fleeting adj rapid and soon passing ▷ fleetingly adv
fleetingly adv ▷ fleeting
fleets n ▷ fleet¹
flesh n (pl **-es**) soft part of a human or animal body informal
fleshes n ▷ flesh
fleshier adj ▷ fleshy
fleshiest adj ▷ fleshy
fleshly adj carnal
fleshy adj (**-shier, -shiest**) plump

flew *n* ▷ **fly**[1]

flex *n* (*pl* **-xes**) flexible insulated electric cable ▶ *v* (**-xes, -xing, -xed**) bend

flexed *v* ▷ **flex**

flexes *n, v* ▷ **flex**

flexibilities *n* ▷ **flexible**

flexibility *n* ▷ **flexible**

flexible *adj* easily bent > **flexibly** *adv* > **flexibility** *n* (*pl* **-ties**)

flexibly *adv* ▷ **flexible**

flexing *v* ▷ **flex**

flick *v* (**-s, -ing, -ed**) touch or move with the finger or hand in a quick movement ▶ *n* (*pl* **-s**) tap or quick stroke ▶ *pl* slang the cinema

flicked *v* ▷ **flick**

flicker *v* (**-s, -ing, -ed**) shine unsteadily or intermittently ▶ *n* (*pl* **-s**) unsteady brief light

flickered *v* ▷ **flicker**

flickering *v* ▷ **flicker**

flickers *v, n* ▷ **flicker**

flicking *v* ▷ **flick**

flicks *v, n* ▷ **flick**

flier[1] *adj* ▷ **fly**[3]

flier[2] *n* ▷ **flyer**

fliers *n* ▷ **flyer**

flies *v, n* ▷ **fly**[1, 2]

fliest *adj* ▷ **fly**[3]

flight[1] *n* (*pl* **-s**) journey by air

flight[2] *n* (*pl* **-s**) act of running away

flightier *adj* ▷ **flighty**

flightiest *adj* ▷ **flighty**

flights *n* ▷ **flight**[1, 2]

flighty *adj* (**-tier, -tiest**) frivolous and fickle

flimsier *adj* ▷ **flimsy**

flimsiest *adj* ▷ **flimsy**

flimsily *adv* ▷ **flimsy**

flimsiness *n* ▷ **flimsy**

flimsinesses *n* ▷ **flimsy**

flimsy *adj* (**-sier, -siest**) not strong or substantial > **flimsily** *adv* > **flimsiness** *n* (*pl* **-es**)

flinch *v* (**-es, -ing, -ed**) draw back or wince, as from pain

flinched *v* ▷ **flinch**

flinches *v* ▷ **flinch**

flinching *v* ▷ **flinch**

fling *v* (**-s, -ing, flung**) throw, send, or move forcefully or hurriedly ▶ *n* (*pl* **-s**) spell of self-indulgent enjoyment

flinging *v* ▷ **fling**

flings *v, n* ▷ **fling**

flint *n* (*pl* **-s**) hard grey stone

flintier *adj* ▷ **flinty**

flintiest *adj* ▷ **flinty**

flints *n* ▷ **flint**

flinty (**-tier, -tiest**) *adj* cruel

flip *v* (**-s, -pping, -pped**) throw (something small or light) carelessly ▶ *adj* informal flippant

flippancies *n* ▷ **flippant**

flippancy *n* ▷ **flippant**

flippant *adj* treating serious things lightly > **flippancy** *n* (*pl* **-cies**)

flipped *v* ▷ **flip**

flipper (*pl* **-s**) *n* limb of a sea animal adapted for swimming

flippers *n* ▷ **flipper**

flipping *v* ▷ **flip**

flips *v* ▷ **flip**

flirt *v* (**-s, -ing, -ed**) behave as if sexually attracted to someone ▶ *n* (*pl* **-s**) person who flirts > **flirtation** *n* (*pl* **-s**) > **flirtatious** *adj*

flirtation *n* ▷ **flirt**

flirtations *n* ▷ **flirt**

flirtatious *adj* ▷ **flirt**

flirted *v* ▷ **flirt**

flirting *v* ▷ **flirt**

flirts *v, n* ▷ **flirt**

flit *v* (**-s, -tting, -tted**) move lightly and rapidly ▶ *n* (*pl* **-s**) act of flitting

flits *v, n* ▷ **flit**

flitted *v* ▷ **flit**

flitting *v* ▷ **flit**

float *v* (**-s, -ing, -ed**) rest on the surface of a liquid ▶ *n* (*pl* **-s**) light object used to help someone or something float

floated *v* ▷ **float**

floating *adj* moving about, changing ▶ *v* ▷ **float**

floats *v, n* ▷ **float**

flock[1] *n* (*pl* **-s**) number of animals of one kind together ▶ *v* (**-s, -ing, -ed**) gather in a crowd

flock² n (pl **-s**) wool or cotton waste used as stuffing ▶ adj (of wallpaper) with a velvety raised pattern

flocked v ▷ **flock¹**

flocking v ▷ **flock¹**

flocks n, v ▷ **flock¹, ²**

floe n (pl **-s**) sheet of floating ice

floes n ▷ **floe**

flog v (**-s, -gging, -gged**) beat with a whip or stick ▶ **flogging** n (pl **-s**)

flogged v ▷ **flog**

flogging v, n ▷ **flog**

floggings n ▷ **flog**

flogs v ▷ **flog**

flood n (pl **-s**) overflow of water onto a normally dry area ▶ v (**-s, -ing, -ed**) cover or become covered with water

flooded v ▷ **flood**

flooding v ▷ **flood**

floods n, v ▷ **flood**

floor n (pl **-s**) lower surface of a room ▶ v (**-s, -ing, -ed**) knock down

floored adj covered with a floor ▶ v ▷ **floor**

flooring n (pl **-s**) material for floors ▶ v ▷ **floor**

floorings n ▷ **flooring**

floors n, v ▷ **floor**

floozies n ▷ **floozy**

floozy n (pl **-zies**) old-fashioned slang disreputable woman

flop v (**-s, -pping, -pped**) bend, fall, or collapse loosely or carelessly ▶ n (pl **-s**) informal failure

flopped v ▷ **flop**

floppier adj ▷ **floppy**

floppies n ▷ **floppy**

floppiest adj ▷ **floppy**

flopping v ▷ **flop**

floppy adj (**-pier, -ppiest**) hanging downwards, loose ▶ n (pl **-ppies**) COMPUTERS a flexible magnetic disk that stores information

flops v, n ▷ **flop**

flora n (pl **-s**) plants of a given place or time

floral adj consisting of or decorated with flowers

floras n ▷ **flora**

floret n (pl **-s**) small flower forming part of a composite flower head

florets n ▷ **floret**

florid adj (**-er, -est**) with a red or flushed complexion

florider adj ▷ **florid**

floridest adj ▷ **florid**

florin n (pl **-s**) former British and Australian coin

florins n ▷ **florin**

florist n (pl **-s**) seller of flowers

florists n ▷ **florist**

floss n (pl **-es**) fine silky fibres

flosses n ▷ **floss**

flotilla n (pl **-s**) small fleet or fleet of small ships

flotillas n ▷ **flotilla**

flotsam n (pl **-s**) floating wreckage

flotsams n ▷ **flotsam**

flounce¹ v (**-ces, -cing, -ced**) go with emphatic movements ▶ n (pl **-s**) flouncing movement

flounce² n (pl **-s**) ornamental frill on a garment

flounced v ▷ **flounce**

flounces v, n ▷ **flounce¹, ²**

flouncing v ▷ **flounce**

flounder¹ v (**-s, -ing, -ed**) move with difficulty, as in mud

flounder² n (pl **-s**) edible flatfish

floundered v ▷ **flounder**

floundering v ▷ **flounder**

flounders v, n ▷ **flounder¹, ²**

flour n (pl **-s**) powder made by grinding grain, esp. wheat ▶ v (**-s, -ing, -ed**) sprinkle with flour ▷ **floury** adj (**-rier, -riest**)

floured v ▷ **flour**

flourier adj ▷ **flour**

flouriest adj ▷ **flour**

flouring v ▷ **flour**

flourish v (**-es, -ing, -ed**) be active, successful, or widespread ▶ n (pl **-es**) dramatic waving motion ▷ **flourishing** adj

flourished v ▷ **flourish**

flourishes v, n ▷ flourish

flourishing n, adj ▷ flourish

flours n, v ▷ flour

floury adj ▷ flour

flout v (**-s, -ing, -ed**) deliberately disobey (a rule, law, etc)

flouted v ▷ flout

flouting v ▷ flout

flouts v ▷ flout

flow v (**-s, -ing, -ed**) (of liquid) move in a stream ▶ n (pl **-s**) act, rate, or manner of flowing

flowed v ▷ flow

flower n (pl **-s**) part of a plant that produces seeds ▶ v (**-s, -ing, -ed**) produce flowers, bloom

flowered adj decorated with a floral design ▶ v ▷ flower

flowerier adj ▷ flowery

floweriest adj ▷ flowery

flowering v ▷ flower

flowers n, v ▷ flower

flowery adj (**-rier, -riest**) decorated with a floral design

flowing v ▷ flow

flown v ▷ fly¹

flows v, n ▷ flow

flue n (pl **-s**) passage or pipe for smoke or hot air

fluencies n ▷ fluent

fluency n ▷ fluent

fluent adj able to speak or write with ease > **fluently** adv > **fluency** n (pl **-ies**)

fluently adv ▷ fluent

flues n ▷ flue

fluff n (pl **-s**) soft fibres ▶ v (**-s, -ing, -ed**) make or become soft and puffy > **fluffy** adj (**-fier, -fiest**)

fluffed v ▷ fluff

fluffier adj ▷ fluff

fluffiest adj ▷ fluff

fluffing v ▷ fluff

fluffs n, v ▷ fluff

fluffy adj ▷ fluff

fluid n (pl **-s**) substance able to flow and change its shape; a liquid or a gas ▶ adj able to flow or change shape easily > **fluidity** n (pl **-ies**)

fluidities n ▷ fluid

fluidity n ▷ fluid

fluids n ▷ fluid

fluke¹ n (pl **-s**) accidental stroke of luck

fluke² (pl **-s**) n flat triangular point of an anchor

fluke³ (pl **-s**) n parasitic worm

flukes n ▷ fluke¹, ², ³

flume n (pl **-s**) narrow sloping channel for water

flumes n ▷ flume

flummox v (**-xes, -xing, -xed**) puzzle or confuse

flummoxed v ▷ flummox

flummoxes v ▷ flummox

flummoxing v ▷ flummox

flung v ▷ fling

flunk v (**flunks, flunking, flunked**) US, AUST, NZ & S AFR *informal* fail

flunked v ▷ flunk

flunkey n ▷ flunky

flunkeys n ▷ flunky

flunkies n ▷ flunky

flunking v ▷ flunk

flunks v ▷ flunk

flunky, flunkey n (pl **-kies, -keys**) servile person

fluoride n (pl **-s**) compound containing fluorine

fluorides n ▷ fluoride

fluorine n (pl **-s**) CHEM toxic yellow gas, most reactive of all the elements

fluorines n ▷ fluorine

flurried v ▷ flurry

flurries n, v ▷ flurry

flurry n (pl **-ries**) sudden commotion ▶ v (**-ries, -rying, -ried**) confuse

flurrying v ▷ flurry

flus n ▷ flu

flush¹ v (**-es, -ing, -ed**) blush or cause to blush ▶ n (pl **-es**) blush

flush² adj level with the surrounding surface

flush³ v (**-es, -ing, -ed**) drive out of a hiding place

flush⁴ n (pl **-es**) (in card games) hand all of one suit

flushed v ▷ flush¹, ³

flushes v, n ▷ **flush¹, ³, 4**

flushing v ▷ **flush¹, ³**

fluster v (**-s, -ing, -ed**) make nervous or upset ▶ n (pl **-s**) nervous or upset state

flustered v ▷ **fluster**

flustering v ▷ **fluster**

flusters v, n ▷ **fluster**

flute n (pl **-s**) wind instrument consisting of a tube with sound holes and a mouth hole in the side

fluted adj having decorative grooves

flutes n ▷ **flute**

flutter v (**-s, -ing, -ed**) wave rapidly ▶ n (pl **-s**) flapping movement

fluttered v ▷ **flutter**

fluttering v ▷ **flutter**

flutters v, n ▷ **flutter**

fluvial adj of rivers

flux n (pl **-es**) constant change or instability

fluxes n ▷ **flux**

fly¹ v (**flying, flew, flown**) move through the air on wings or in an aircraft ▶ n (pl **flies**) (often pl) BRIT fastening at the front of trousers ▶ pl space above a stage, used for storage

fly² n (pl **flies**) two-winged insect

fly³ adj (**flier, fliest**) slang sharp and cunning

flyer, flier (pl **-s**) n small advertising leaflet

flyers n ▷ **flyer**

flying adj hurried and brief ▶ v ▷ **fly**

flyleaf n (pl **-leaves**) blank leaf at the beginning or end of a book

flyleaves n ▷ **flyleaf**

flyover n (pl **-s**) road passing over another by a bridge

flyovers n ▷ **flyover**

flypaper n (pl **-s**) paper with a sticky poisonous coating, used to kill flies

flypapers n ▷ **flypaper**

flywheel (pl **-s**) n heavy wheel regulating the speed of a machine

flywheels n ▷ **flywheel**

foal n (pl **-s**) young of a horse or related animal ▶ v (**-s, -ing, -ed**) give birth to a foal

foaled v ▷ **foal**

foaling v ▷ **foal**

foals n, v ▷ **foal**

foam n (pl **-s**) mass of small bubbles on a liquid ▶ v (**-s, -ing, -ed**) produce foam > **foamy** adj (**-ier, -iest**)

foamed v ▷ **foam**

foamier adj ▷ **foam**

foamiest adj ▷ **foam**

foaming v ▷ **foam**

foams n, v ▷ **foam**

foamy adj ▷ **foam**

fob n (pl **-s**) short watch chain

fobs n ▷ **fob**

focal adj of or at a focus

foci n ▷ **focus**

focus n (pl **-cuses, -ci**) point at which light or sound waves converge ▶ v (**-cuses** or **-cusses, -cusing** or **-cussing, -cused** or **-cussed**) bring or come into focus

focused v ▷ **focus**

focuses n, v ▷ **focus**

focusing v ▷ **focus**

focussed v ▷ **focus**

focussing v ▷ **focus**

fodder n (pl **-s**) feed for livestock

fodders n ▷ **fodder**

foe n (pl **foes**) enemy, opponent

foes n ▷ **foe**

foetid adj (**-er, -est**) ▷ **fetid**

foetider adj ▷ **foetid**

foetidest adj ▷ **foetid**

foetus n (pl **-tuses**) ▷ **fetus**

foetuses n ▷ **foetus**

fog n (pl **-s**) mass of condensed water vapour in the lower air, often greatly reducing visibility ▶ v (**-s, -gging, -gged**) cover with steam > **foggy** adj (**-ier, -iest**)

fogey, fogy n (pl **-geys, -gies**) old-fashioned person

fogeys n ▷ **fogey**

fogged v ▷ **fog**

foggier adj ▷ **fog**

foggiest adj ▷ **fog**

fogging v ▷ **fog**

foggy adj ▷ fog

foghorn n (pl **-s**) large horn sounded to warn ships in fog

foghorns n ▷ foghorn

fogies n ▷ fogey

fogs n ▷ fog

fogy n ▷ fogey

foible n (pl **-s**) minor weakness or slight peculiarity

foibles n ▷ foible

foil[1] v (**-s**, **-ing**, **-ed**) ruin (someone's plan)

foil[2] n (pl **-s**) metal in a thin sheet, esp: for wrapping food

foil[3] n (pl **-s**) light slender flexible sword tipped with a button

foiled v ▷ foil

foiling v ▷ foil

foils v, n ▷ foil[1, 2, 3]

foist v (**-s**, **-ing**, **-ed**) (foll. by **on** or **upon**) force or impose on

foisted v ▷ foist

foisting v ▷ foist

foists v ▷ foist

fold[1] v (**-s**, **-ing**, **-ed**) bend so that one part covers another ▶ n (pl **-s**) folded piece or part

fold[2] n (pl **-s**) BRIT, AUST & S AFR enclosure for sheep

folded v ▷ fold

folder n (pl **-s**) piece of folded cardboard for holding loose papers

folders n ▷ folder

folding v ▷ fold

folds v, n ▷ fold[1, 2]

foliage n (pl **-s**) leaves

foliages n ▷ foliage

folio n (pl **-s**) sheet of paper folded in half to make two leaves of a book

folios n ▷ folio

folk n (pl **-s**) people in general ▶ pl relatives

folklore n (pl **-s**) traditional beliefs and stories of a people

folklores n ▷ folklore

folks n ▷ folk

folksier adj ▷ folksy

folksiest adj ▷ folksy

folksy adj (**-sier**, **-siest**) simple and unpretentious

follicle n (pl **-s**) small cavity in the body, esp. one from which a hair grows

follicles n ▷ follicle

follies n ▷ folly

follow v (**-s**, **-ing**, **-ed**) go or come after

followed v ▷ follow

follower n (pl **-s**) disciple or supporter

followers n ▷ follower

follows v ▷ follow

folly n (pl **-llies**) foolishness

foment v (**-s**, **-ing**, **-ed**) encourage or stir up (trouble)

fomented v ▷ foment

fomenting v ▷ foment

foments v ▷ foment

fond adj (**-er**, **-est**) tender, loving > **fondly** adv > **fondness** n (pl **-es**)

fondant n (pl **-s**) (sweet made from) flavoured paste of sugar and water

fondants n ▷ fondant

fonder adj ▷ fond

fondest adj ▷ fond

fondle v (**-les**, **-ling**, **-led**) caress

fondled v ▷ fondle

fondles v ▷ fondle

fondling v ▷ fondle

fondly adv ▷ fond

fondness n ▷ fond

fondnesses n ▷ fond

fondue n (pl **-s**) Swiss dish of a hot melted cheese sauce into which pieces of bread are dipped

fondues n ▷ fondue

font[1] n (pl **-s**) bowl in a church for baptismal water

font[2] (pl **-s**) n set of printing type of one style and size

fonts n ▷ font[1, 2]

food n (pl **-s**) what one eats, solid nourishment

foodie n (pl **-s**) informal gourmet

foodies n ▷ foodie

foods n ▷ food

fool[1] n (pl **-s**) person lacking sense or judgment HIST ▶ v (**-s**, **-ing**, **-ed**) deceive (someone)

fool² (pl **-s**) n dessert of puréed fruit mixed with cream
fooled v ▷ **fool**
fooleries n ▷ **foolery**
foolery n (pl **-ries**) foolish behaviour
fooling v ▷ **fool**
foolish adj (**-er, -est**) unwise, silly, or absurd > **foolishly** adv > **foolishness** n (pl **-es**)
foolisher adj ▷ **foolish**
foolishest adj ▷ **foolish**
foolishly adv ▷ **foolish**
foolishness n ▷ **foolish**
foolishnesses n ▷ **foolish**
fools n, v ▷ **fool¹, ²**
foolscap n (pl **-s**) size of paper, 34.3 x 43.2 centimetres
foolscaps n ▷ **foolscap**
foot n (pl **feet**) part of the leg below the ankle
footage n amount of film used
footages n ▷ **footage**
football n (pl **-s**) game played by two teams of eleven players kicking a ball in an attempt to score goals > **footballer** n (pl **-s**)
footballer n ▷ **football**
footballs n ▷ **football**
footfall n (pl **-s**) sound of a footstep
footfalls n ▷ **footfall**
foothold n (pl **-s**) secure position from which progress may be made
footholds n ▷ **foothold**
footing n (pl **-s**) basis or foundation
footings n ▷ **footing**
footling adj CHIEFLY BRIT informal trivial
footman n (pl **-men**) male servant in uniform
footmen n ▷ **footman**
footnote n note printed at the foot of a page
footnotes n ▷ **footnote**
footpath n (pl **-s**) narrow path for walkers only
footpaths n ▷ **footpath**
footsie n (pl **-s**) informal flirtation involving the touching together of feet

footsies n ▷ **footsie**
footstep n step in walking
footsteps n ▷ **footstep**
footwear n (pl **-s**) anything worn to cover the feet
footwears n ▷ **footwear**
footwork n (pl **-s**) skilful use of the feet, as in sport or dancing
footworks n ▷ **footwork**
fop n (pl **-s**) man excessively concerned with fashion > **foppery** n (pl **-ies**) > **foppish** adj
fopperies n ▷ **fop**
foppery n ▷ **fop**
foppish n ▷ **fop**
fops n ▷ **fop**
for prep indicating a person intended to benefit from or receive something, span of time or distance, person or thing represented by someone, etc ▶ conj because
forage v (**-ges, -ging, -ged**) search about (for) ▶ n (pl **-s**) food for cattle or horses
foraged v ▷ **forage**
forages v, n ▷ **forage**
foraging v ▷ **forage**
foray n (pl **-s**) brief raid or attack
forays n ▷ **foray**
forbade v ▷ **forbid**
forbear v (**-s, -ing, forbore, forborne**) cease or refrain (from doing something)
forbearing v ▷ **forbear**
forbears n ▷ **forbear**
forbid v (**-s, -dding, -bade, -bidden**) prohibit, refuse to allow > **forbidden** adj
forbidden v, adj ▷ **forbid**
forbids v ▷ **forbid**
forbore v ▷ **forbear**
forborne v ▷ **forbear**
force n (pl **-s**) strength or power ▶ v (**-ces, -cing, -ced**) compel, make (someone) do something
forced adj compulsory ▶ v ▷ **force**
forceful adj emphatic and confident > **forcefully** adv

forcefully adv ▷ **forceful**

forceps pl n surgical pincers

forces n, v ▷ **force**

forcible adj involving physical force or violence > **forcibly** adv

forcibly adv ▷ **forcible**

forcing v ▷ **force**

ford n (pl -s) shallow place where a river may be crossed ► v (-s, -ing, -ed) cross (a river) at a ford

forded v ▷ **ford**

fording v ▷ **ford**

fords n, v ▷ **ford**

fore adj in, at, or towards the front ► n (pl -s) front part

forearm[1] n (pl -s) arm from the wrist to the elbow

forearm[2] v (-s, -ing, -ed) prepare beforehand

forearmed v ▷ **forearm**[2]

forearming v ▷ **forearm**[2]

forearms n, v ▷ **forearm**[1,2]

forebear n (pl -s) ancestor

forebears n ▷ **forebear**

forecast v (-casts, -casting, -cast or -casted) predict (weather, events, etc) ► n (pl -s) prediction

forecasted v ▷ **forecast**

forecasting v ▷ **forecast**

forecasts n, v ▷ **forecast**

forego v (-goes, -going, -went, -gone) ▷ **forgo**

foregoes v ▷ **forego**

foregone v ▷ **forego**

forehand n (pl -s) TENNIS ETC stroke played with the palm of the hand facing forward

forehands n ▷ **forehand**

forehead n (pl -s) part of the face above the eyebrows

foreheads n ▷ **forehead**

foreign adj not of, or in, one's own country > **foreigner** n (pl -s)

foreigner n ▷ **foreign**

foreigners n ▷ **foreign**

foreleg n (pl -s) either of the front legs of an animal

forelegs n ▷ **foreleg**

forelock n (pl -s) lock of hair over the forehead

forelocks n ▷ **forelock**

foreman n (pl -men) person in charge of a group of workers

foremast n (pl -s) mast nearest the bow of a ship

foremasts n ▷ **foremast**

foremen n ▷ **foreman**

foremost adj, adv first in time, place, or importance

forename n (pl -s) first name

forenames n ▷ **forename**

forenoon n (pl -s) CHIEFLY US & CANADIAN morning

forenoons n ▷ **forenoon**

forensic adj used in or connected with courts of law

foreplay n (pl -s) sexual stimulation before intercourse

foreplays n ▷ **foreplay**

fores n ▷ **fore**

foresail n (pl -s) main sail on the foremast of a ship

foresails n ▷ **foresail**

foresaw v ▷ **foresee**

foresee v (-sees, -seeing, -saw, -seen) see or know beforehand > **foreseeable** adj

foreseeable adj ▷ **foresee**

foreseeing v ▷ **foresee**

foreseen v ▷ **foresee**

foresees v ▷ **foresee**

foreskin n (pl -s) fold of skin covering the tip of the penis

foreskins n ▷ **foreskin**

forest n (pl -s) large area with a thick growth of trees > **forested** adj

forested adj ▷ **forest**

forester n (pl -s) person skilled in forestry

forestries n ▷ **forestry**

forestry n (pl -ries) science of planting and caring for trees

forests n ▷ **forest**

foretell v (-s, -ing, -told) tell or indicate beforehand

foretelling v ▷ **foretell**

foretells v ▷ foretell
foretold v ▷ foretell
forever adv without end
forewarn v (-s, -ing, -ed) warn beforehand
forewarning v ▷ forewarn
forewarns v ▷ forewarn
forewent v ▷ forego
foreword n (pl -s) introduction to a book
forewords n ▷ foreword
forfeit n (pl -s) thing lost or given up as a penalty for a fault or mistake ▶ v (-s, -ing, -ed) lose as a forfeit ▶ adj lost as a forfeit >**forfeiture** n (pl -s)
forfeited v ▷ forfeit
forfeiting v ▷ forfeit
forfeits n, v ▷ forfeit
forfeiture n ▷ forfeit
forfeitures n ▷ forfeit
forgave ▷ forgive
forge¹ n (pl -s) place where metal is worked, smithy ▶ v (-ges, -ging, -ged) make a fraudulent imitation of (something)
forge² v (-ges, -ging, -ged) advance steadily
forged n ▷ forge¹, ²
forger n (pl -s) person who makes an illegal copy of something
forgeries n ▷ forgery
forgers n ▷ forger
forgery n (pl -ries) illegal copy of something
forges v, n ▷ forge¹, ²
forget v (-s, -getting, -got, -gotten) fail to remember
forgets v ▷ forget
forgetting v ▷ forget
forging v ▷ forge¹, ²
forgive v (-giving, -gave, -given) cease to blame or hold resentment against, pardon >**forgiveness** n (pl -es)
forgiven v ▷ forgive
forgiveness n ▷ forgive
forgivenesses n ▷ forgive
forgiving v ▷ forgive

forgo v (-goes, -going, -went, -gone) do without or give up
forgoes v ▷ forgo
forgoing v ▷ forgo
forgone v ▷ forgo
forgot v ▷ forget
forgotten v ▷ forget
fork n (pl -s) tool for eating food, with prongs and a handle ▶ v (-s, -ing, -ed) pick up, dig, etc with a fork >**forked** adj
forked v, adj ▷ fork
forking v ▷ fork
forks n, v ▷ fork
forlorn adj lonely and unhappy >**forlornly** adv
forlornly adv ▷ forlorn
form n (pl -s) shape or appearance ▶ v (-s, -ing, -ed) give a (particular) shape to or take a (particular) shape >**formless** adj
formal adj of or characterized by established conventions of ceremony and behaviour >**formally** adv
formalin n (pl -s) solution of formaldehyde in water, used as a disinfectant or a preservative for biological specimens
formalins n ▷ formalin
formally adv ▷ formal
format n (pl -s) style in which something is arranged ▶ v (-s, -matting, -matted) arrange in a format
formats n, v ▷ format
formatted v ▷ format
formatting v ▷ format
formed v ▷ form
former adj of an earlier time, previous >**formerly** adv
formerly adv ▷ former
forming v ▷ form
formless adj ▷ form
forms n, v ▷ form
formula n (pl -s, -e) group of numbers, letters, or symbols expressing a scientific or mathematical rule

>**formulaic** adj

formulae n ▷ formula

formulaic adj ▷ formula

formulas n ▷ formula

forsake v (-sakes, -saking, -sook, -saken) withdraw support or friendship from

forsaken v ▷ forsake

forsakes v ▷ forsake

forsaking v ▷ forsake

forsook v ▷ forsake

forsooth adv obs indeed

forswear v (-s, -sing, -swore, -sworn) renounce or reject

forswearing v ▷ forswear

forswears v ▷ forswear

forswore v ▷ forswear

forsworn v ▷ forswear

fort n (pl -s) fortified building or place

forte[1] n (pl -s) thing at which a person excels

forte[2] adv MUSIC loudly

fortes n ▷ forte

forth adv forwards, out, or away

forties n ▷ forty

fortieth adj, n ▷ forty

fortieths n ▷ forty

fortification n ▷ fortify

fortifications n ▷ fortify

fortified v ▷ fortify

fortifies v ▷ fortify

fortify v (-fies, -fying, -fied) make (a place) defensible, as by building walls
>**fortification** n (pl -s)

fortifying v ▷ fortify

fortress n (pl -es) large fort or fortified town

fortresses n ▷ fortress

forts n ▷ fort

fortune n (pl -s) luck, esp. when favourable ▶ pl person's destiny

fortunes n ▷ fortune

forty adj, n (pl -ties) four times ten
>**fortieth** adj, n (pl -s)

forum n (pl -ums) meeting or medium for open discussion or debate

forums n ▷ forum

forward adj directed or moving ahead

▶ n (pl -s) attacking player in various team games, such as soccer or hockey
▶ adv forwards ▶ v (-s, -ing, -ed) send (a letter etc) on to an ultimate destination

forwarded v ▷ forward

forwarding v ▷ forward

forwards adv towards or at a place further ahead in space or time ▶ n, v
▷ forward

fossick v (-s, -ing, -ed) AUST & NZ search, esp. for gold or precious stones

fossicked v ▷ fossick

fossicking v ▷ fossick

fossicks v ▷ fossick

fossil n (pl -s) hardened remains of a prehistoric animal or plant preserved in rock

fossils n ▷ fossil

foster v (-s, -ing, -ed) promote the growth or development of ▶ adj of or involved in fostering a child

fostered v ▷ foster

fostering v ▷ foster

fosters v ▷ foster

fought v ▷ fight

foul adj (-er, -est) loathsome or offensive ▶ n (pl -s) SPORT violation of the rules ▶ v (-s, -ing, -ed) make dirty or polluted

fouled v ▷ foul

fouler adj ▷ foul

foulest adj ▷ foul

fouling v ▷ foul

fouls n, v ▷ foul

found[1] v ▷ find

found[2] v (-s, -ing, -ed) establish or bring into being (foll. by on or upon)
>**founder** n (pl -s)

found[3] v (-s, -ing, -ed) cast (metal or glass) by melting and setting in a mould

founded v ▷ found[2,3]

founder[1] n ▷ found[2]

founder[2] v (-s, -ing, -ed) break down or fail

foundered v ▷ founder

foundering v ▷ founder

founders¹ n ▷ **found²**
founders² v ▷ **founder**
  founding v ▷ **found², 3**
  foundries n ▷ **foundry**
foundry n (pl -ries) place where metal
is melted and cast
  founds v ▷ **found², 3**
fount¹ n (pl -s) lit fountain
fount² n (pl -s) set of printing type of
one style and size
fountain n (pl -s) jet of water
  fountains n ▷ **fountain**
  founts n ▷ **fount¹, 2**
four adj, n (pl -s) one more than three
  fours n ▷ **four**
foursome n group of four people
  foursomes n (pl -s) ▷ **foursome**
fourteen adj, n (pl -s) four and ten
  >**fourteenth** adj, n (pl -s)
  fourteens n ▷ **fourteen**
  fourteenth adj, n ▷ **fourteen**
  fourteenths n ▷ **fourteen**
fourth adj, n (pl -s) (of) number four in
a series ▶ n quarter
  fourths n ▷ **fourth**
fowl n (pl -s) domestic cock or hen
  fowls n ▷ **fowl**
fox n (pl -es) reddish-brown bushy-
tailed animal of the dog family ▶ v (-es,
-ing, -ed) informal perplex or deceive
  foxed v ▷ **fox**
  foxes n, v ▷ **fox**
foxglove n (pl -s) tall plant with purple
or white flowers
  foxgloves n ▷ **foxglove**
foxhole n (pl -s) MIL small pit dug for
protection
  foxholes n ▷ **foxhole**
foxhound n (pl -s) dog bred for
hunting foxes
  foxhounds n ▷ **foxhound**
  foxier adj ▷ **foxy**
  foxiest adj ▷ **foxy**
  foxing v ▷ **fox**
foxtrot n (pl -s) ballroom dance with
slow and quick steps
  foxtrots n ▷ **foxtrot**
foxy adj (-xier, -xiest) of or like a fox,

esp. in craftiness

┃ **foy** n (**foys**). Foy is an old dialect
┃ word meaning a farewell meal
┃ or gift. This unusual word can be
┃ useful when there is little space
┃ to form longer words. Foy scores
┃ 9 points.

foyer n (pl -s) entrance hall in a theatre,
cinema, or hotel
  foyers n ▷ **foyer**
fracas n (pl -es) noisy quarrel
  fracases n ▷ **fracas**
fraction n (pl -s) numerical
quantity that is not a whole number
  >**fractional** adj >**fractionally** adv
  fractional adj ▷ **fraction**
  fractionally adv ▷ **fraction**
  fractions n ▷ **fraction**
fracture n (pl -s) breaking, esp. of a
bone ▶ v (-res, -ring, -red) break
  fractured v ▷ **fracture**
  fractures n, v ▷ **fracture**
  fracturing v ▷ **fracture**
fragile adj easily broken or damaged
  >**fragility** n (pl -ties)
  fragilities n ▷ **fragile**
  fragility n ▷ **fragile**
fragment n (pl -s) piece broken off
▶ v (-s, -ing, -ed) break into pieces
  >**fragmentary** adj >**fragmentation** n
  (pl -s)
  fragmentary adj ▷ **fragment**
  fragmentation n ▷ **fragment**
  fragmentations n ▷ **fragment**
  fragmented v ▷ **fragment**
  fragmenting v ▷ **fragment**
  fragments n, v ▷ **fragment**
fragrant adj sweet-smelling
frail adj (-er, -est) physically weak
  frailer adj ▷ **frail**
  frailest adj ▷ **frail**
  frailties n ▷ **frailty**
frailty n (pl -ties) physical or moral
weakness
frame n (pl -s) structure giving shape
or support ▶ v (-mes, -ming, -med)
put together, construct
  framed v ▷ **frame**

frames n, v ▷ **frame**

framing v ▷ **frame**

franc n (pl **-s**) monetary unit of Switzerland, various African countries, and formerly of France and Belgium

francium n (pl **-s**) CHEM radioactive metallic element

franciums n ▷ **francium**

francs n ▷ **franc**

frank adj (**-er**, **-est**) honest and straightforward in speech or attitude ▶ n (pl **-s**) official mark on a letter permitting delivery ▶ v (**-s**, **-ing**, **-ed**) put such a mark on (a letter) > **frankly** adv > **frankness** n (pl **-es**)

franked v ▷ **frank**

franker adj ▷ **frank**

frankest adj ▷ **frank**

franking v ▷ **frank**

frankly adv ▷ **frank**

frankness n ▷ **frank**

franknesses n ▷ **frank**

franks n, v ▷ **frank**

frantic adj distracted with rage, grief, joy, etc ▶ **frantically** adv

frantically adv ▷ **frantic**

frau n (pl **-s**) married German woman

fraud n (pl **-s**) (criminal) deception, swindle ▶ **fraudulent** adj > **fraudulence** n (pl **-s**)

frauds n ▷ **fraud**

fraudulence n ▷ **fraud**

fraudulences n ▷ **fraud**

fraudulent adj ▷ **fraud**

fraught adj (**-er**, **-est**) tense or anxious

fraughter adj ▷ **fraught**

fraughtest adj ▷ **fraught**

fräulein n (pl **-s**) unmarried German woman

fräuleins n ▷ **fräulein**

fraus n ▷ **frau**

fray[1] n (pl **-s**) BRIT, AUST & NZ noisy quarrel or conflict

fray[2] v (**-s**, **-ing**, **-ed**) make or become ragged at the edge

frayed v ▷ **fray**[2]

fraying v ▷ **fray**[2]

frays n, v ▷ **fray**[1, 2]

frazzle n (pl **-s**) informal exhausted state

frazzles n ▷ **frazzle**

freak n (pl **-s**) abnormal person or thing ▶ adj abnormal ▶ **freakish** adj

freakish adj ▷ **freak**

freaks n ▷ **freak**

freckle n (pl **-s**) small brown spot on the skin

freckled adj marked with freckles

freckles n ▷ **freckle**

free adj (**freer**, **freest**) able to act at will, not compelled or restrained ▶ v (**frees**, **freeing**, **freed**) release, liberate > **freely** adv

freed v ▷ **free**

freedom n (pl **-s**) being free

freedoms n ▷ **freedom**

freehand adj drawn without guiding instruments

freehold n (pl **-s**) tenure of land for life without restrictions > **freeholder** n (pl **-s**)

freeholder n ▷ **freehold**

freeholders n ▷ **freehold**

freeholds n ▷ **freehold**

freeing v ▷ **free**

freely adv ▷ **free**

freer adj ▷ **free**

frees v ▷ **free**

freesia n (pl **-s**) plant with fragrant tubular flowers

freesias n ▷ **freesia**

freest adj ▷ **free**

freeway n (pl **-s**) US & AUST motorway

freeways n ▷ **freeway**

freeze v (**-zes**, **-zing**, **froze**, **frozen**) change from a liquid to a solid by the reduction of temperature, as water to ice ▶ n period of very cold weather

freezer n (pl **-s**) insulated cabinet for cold-storage of perishable foods

freezers n ▷ **freezer**

freezes v ▷ **freeze**

freezing adj informal very cold ▶ v ▷ **freeze**

freight n (pl **-s**) commercial transport

of goods ▶ v (-s, -ing, -ed) send by
freight
freighted v ▷ freight
freighting v ▷ freight
freights n, v ▷ freight
frenetic adj uncontrolled, excited
> **frenetically** adv
frenetically adv ▷ frenetic
frenzied adj ▷ frenzy
frenziedly adv ▷ frenzy
frenzies n ▷ frenzy
frenzy n (pl -zies) violent mental
derangement > **frenzied** adj
> **frenziedly** adv
frequent adj happening often
▶ v (-s, -ing, -ed) visit habitually
> **frequently** adv
frequented v ▷ frequent
frequenting v ▷ frequent
frequently adv ▷ frequent
frequents v ▷ frequent
fresco n (pl -coes, -cos) watercolour
painting done on wet plaster on a wall
frescoes n ▷ fresco
frescos n ▷ fresco
fresh adj (-er, -est) newly made,
acquired, etc > **freshly** adv
> **freshness** n (pl -es)
freshen v (-s, -ing, -ed) make or
become fresh or fresher
freshened v ▷ freshen
freshening v ▷ freshen
freshens v ▷ freshen
fresher n (pl -s) first-year student
▶ adj ▷ fresh
freshers n ▷ fresher
freshest adj ▷ fresh
freshly adv ▷ fresh
freshman n (pl -men) BRIT & US first-
year student
freshmen n ▷ freshman
freshness n ▷ fresh
freshnesses n ▷ fresh
fret[1] v (-s, -tting, -tted) be worried
fret[2] n (pl -s) small bar on the
fingerboard of a guitar etc
fretful adj irritable
frets n ▷ fret[1, 2]

fretsaw n (pl -s) fine saw with a
narrow blade, used for fretwork
fretsaws n ▷ fretsaw
fretted v ▷ fret[1]
fretting v ▷ fret[1]
fretwork n (pl -s) decorative carving
in wood
fretworks n ▷ fretwork
friable adj easily crumbled
friar n (pl -s) member of a male Roman
Catholic religious order
friaries n ▷ friary
friars n ▷ friar
friary n (pl -ries) house of friars
friction n (pl -s) resistance met
with by a body moving over another
> **frictional** adj
frictional adj ▷ friction
frictions n ▷ friction
fridge n (pl -s) apparatus in which food
and drinks are kept cool
fridges n ▷ fridge
fried v ▷ fry[1]
friend n (pl -s) person whom one
knows well and likes > **friendless** adj
> **friendship** n (pl -s)
friendless adj ▷ friend
friendlier adj ▷ friendly
friendlies n ▷ friendly
friendliest adj ▷ friendly
friendliness n ▷ friendly
friendlinesses n ▷ friendly
friendly adj (-lier, -liest) showing
or expressing liking ▶ n (pl -lies)
SPORT match played for its own sake
and not as part of a competition
> **friendliness** n (pl -es)
friends n ▷ friend
friendship n ▷ friend
friendships n ▷ friend
fries v, n ▷ fry[1]
frieze n (pl -s) ornamental band on
a wall
friezes n ▷ frieze
frigate n (pl -s) medium-sized fast
warship
frigates n ▷ frigate
fright n (pl -s) sudden fear or alarm

frighten v (-s, -ing, -ed) scare or terrify > **frightening** adj

frightened v ▷ **frighten**

frightened v ▷ **frighten**

frightening v, adj ▷ **frighten**

frights n ▷ **fright**

frigid adj (of a woman) sexually unresponsive > **frigidity** n (pl -ties)

frigidities n ▷ **frigid**

frigidity n ▷ **frigid**

frill n (pl -s) gathered strip of fabric attached at one edge ▶ pl superfluous decorations or details > **frilled** adj > **frilly** adj (-ier, -iest)

frilled adj ▷ **frill**

frillier adj ▷ **frill**

frilliest adj ▷ **frill**

frills n ▷ **frill**

frilly adj ▷ **frill**

fringe n (pl -es) hair cut short and hanging over the forehead ▶ v (-ges, -ging, -ged) decorate with a fringe ▶ adj (of theatre) unofficial or unconventional > **fringed** adj

fringed v, adj ▷ **fringe**

fringes n, v ▷ **fringe**

fringing v ▷ **fringe**

fripperies n ▷ **frippery**

frippery n (pl -ries) useless ornamentation

frisk v (-s, -ing, -ed) move or leap playfully

frisked v ▷ **frisk**

friskier adj ▷ **frisky**

friskiest adj ▷ **frisky**

frisking v ▷ **frisk**

frisks v ▷ **frisk**

frisky adj (-kier, -kiest) lively or high-spirited

frisson n (pl -s) shiver of fear or excitement

frissons n ▷ **frisson**

fritter n (pl -s) piece of food fried in batter

fritters n ▷ **fritter**

frizz v (-es, -ing, -ed) form (hair) into stiff wiry curls > **frizzy** adj (-zier, -ziest)

frizzed v ▷ **frizz**

frizzes v ▷ **frizz**

frizzier adj ▷ **frizz**

frizziest adj ▷ **frizz**

frizzing v ▷ **frizz**

frizzle v (-les, -ling, -led) cook or heat until crisp and shrivelled

frizzled v ▷ **frizzle**

frizzles v ▷ **frizzle**

frizzling v ▷ **frizzle**

frizzy adj ▷ **frizz**

frock n (pl -s) dress

frocks n ▷ **frock**

frog n (pl -s) smooth-skinned tailless amphibian with long back legs used for jumping

frogman n (pl -men) swimmer with a rubber suit and breathing equipment for working underwater

frogmen n ▷ **frogman**

frogs n ▷ **frog**

frolic v (-lics, -licking, -licked) run and play in a lively way ▶ n (pl -s) lively and merry behaviour

frolicked v ▷ **frolic**

frolicking v ▷ **frolic**

frolics v, n ▷ **frolic**

from prep indicating the point of departure, source, distance, cause, change of state, etc

frond n (pl -s) long leaf or leaflike part of a fern, palm, or seaweed

fronds n ▷ **frond**

front n (pl -s) fore part ▶ adj of or at the front ▶ v (-s, -ing, -ed) face (onto) > **frontal** adj

frontage n (pl -s) facade of a building

frontages n ▷ **frontage**

frontal adj ▷ **front**

fronted v ▷ **front**

frontier n (pl -s) area of a country bordering on another

frontiers n ▷ **frontier**

fronting v ▷ **front**

fronts n, v ▷ **front**

frost n (pl -s) white frozen dew or mist ▶ v (-s, -ing, -ed) become covered with frost

frosted v ▷ **frost** ▶ adj (of glass)

having a rough surface to make it opaque

frostier adj ▷ **frosty**
frostiest adj ▷ **frosty**
frostily adv ▷ **frosty**
frostiness n ▷ **frosty**
frostinesses n ▷ **frosty**
frosting v ▷ **frost** ▶ n (pl **-s**) CHIEFLY US sugar icing
frostings n ▷ **frosting**
frosts n, v ▷ **frost**
frosty adj (**-tier, -tiest**) characterized or covered with frost > **frostily** adv > **frostiness** n (pl **-es**)
froth n (pl **-s**) mass of small bubbles ▶ v (**-s, -ing, -ed**) foam > **frothy** adj (**-thier, -thiest**)
frothed v ▷ **froth**
frothier adj ▷ **froth**
frothiest adj ▷ **froth**
frothing v ▷ **froth**
froths n, v ▷ **froth**
frothy adj ▷ **froth**
frowiest adj ▷ **frowzy**
frown v (**-s, -ing, -ed**) wrinkle one's brows in worry, anger, or thought ▶ n (pl **-s**) frowning expression
frowned v ▷ **frown**
frowning v ▷ **frown**
frowns v, n ▷ **frown**
frowsier adj ▷ **frowzy**
frowsiest adj ▷ **frowzy**
frowstier adj ▷ **frowsty**
frowstiest adj ▷ **frowsty**
frowsty adj (**-ier, -iest**) BRIT stale or musty
frowzier adj ▷ **frowzy**
frowzy, frowsy adj (**-zier, -ziest**) dirty or unkempt
froze v ▷ **freeze**
frozen v ▷ **freeze**
frugal adj thrifty, sparing > **frugally** adv > **frugality** n (pl **-ties**)
frugalities n ▷ **frugal**
frugality n ▷ **frugal**
frugally adv ▷ **frugal**
fruit n (pl **-s**) part of a plant containing seeds, esp. if edible ▶ v (**-s, -ing, -ed**)

bear fruit
fruited v ▷ **fruit**
fruitful adj useful or productive > **fruitfully** adv
fruitfully adv ▷ **fruitful**
fruitier adj ▷ **fruity**
fruitiest adj ▷ **fruity**
fruiting v ▷ **fruit**
fruition n (pl **-s**) fulfilment of something worked for or desired
fruitions n ▷ **fruition**
fruits n, v ▷ **fruit**
fruity adj (**-tier, -tiest**) of or like fruit
frump n (pl **-s**) dowdy woman > **frumpy** adj (**-pier, -piest**)
frumpier adj ▷ **frump**
frumpiest adj ▷ **frump**
frumps n ▷ **frump**
frumpy adj ▷ **frump**
fry¹ v (**fries, frying, fried**) cook or be cooked in fat or oil ▶ n (pl **fries**) potato chip
fry² pl n young fishes
frying v ▷ **fry**
fuchsia n (pl **-s**) ornamental shrub with hanging flowers
fuchsias n ▷ **fuchsia**
fuddle v (**-les, -ling, -led**) cause to be intoxicated or confused > **fuddled** adj
fuddled v, adj ▷ **fuddle**
fuddles v ▷ **fuddle**
fuddling v ▷ **fuddle**
fudge¹ n (pl **-s**) soft caramel-like sweet
fudge² v (**-ges, -ging, -ged**) avoid making a firm statement or decision
fudged v ▷ **fudge**²
fudges n, v ▷ **fudge**¹, ²
fudging v ▷ **fudge**²
fuel n (pl **-s**) substance burned or treated to produce heat or power ▶ v (**-s, -lling, -lled**) provide with fuel
fuelled v ▷ **fuel**
fuelling v ▷ **fuel**
fuels n, v ▷ **fuel**
fug n (pl **-s**) hot stale atmosphere > **fuggy** adj (**-ggier, -ggiest**)
fuggier adj ▷ **fug**
fuggiest adj ▷ **fug**

fuggy adj ▷ **fug**

fugitive n (pl -s) person who flees, esp. from arrest or pursuit ▶ adj fleeing

fugitives n ▷ **fugitive**

fugs n ▷ **fug**

fugue n (pl -s) musical composition in which a theme is repeated in different parts

fugues n ▷ **fugue**

fulcra n ▷ **fulcrum**

fulcrum n (pl -crums, -cra) pivot about which a lever turns

fulcrums n ▷ **fulcrum**

fulfil v (-s, -lling, -lled) bring about the achievement of (a desire or promise) >**fulfilment** n (pl -s)

fulfilled n ▷ **fulfil**

fulfilling v ▷ **fulfil**

fulfilment n ▷ **fulfil**

fulfilments n ▷ **fulfil**

fulfils v ▷ **fulfil**

full adj (-er, -est) containing as much or as many as possible ▶ adv completely >**fully** adv >**fullness** n (pl -es)

fuller adj ▷ **full**

fullest adj ▷ **full**

fullness n ▷ **full**

fullnesses n ▷ **full**

fully adv ▷ **full**

fulmar n (pl -s) Arctic sea bird

fulmars n ▷ **fulmar**

fulsome adj distastefully excessive or insincere

fumble v (-les, -ling, -led) handle awkwardly ▶ n (pl -s) act of fumbling

fumbled v ▷ **fumble**

fumbles n, v ▷ **fumble**

fumbling v ▷ **fumble**

fume v (-s, -ing, -ed) be very angry ▶ pl n pungent smoke or vapour

fumed v ▷ **fume**

fumes v, n ▷ **fume**

fumigate v (-tes, -ting, -ted) disinfect with fumes >**fumigation** n (pl -s)

fumigated v ▷ **fumigate**

fumigates v ▷ **fumigate**

fumigating v ▷ **fumigate**

fumigation n ▷ **fumigate**

fumigations n ▷ **fumigate**

fuming v ▷ **fume**

fun n (pl -s) enjoyment or amusement

function n (pl -s) purpose something exists for ▶ v (-s, -ing, -ed) operate or work

functioned v ▷ **function**

functioning v ▷ **function**

functions n, v ▷ **function**

fund n (pl -s) stock of money for a special purpose ▶ pl money resources ▶ v (-s, -ing, -ed) provide money to >**funding** n (pl -s)

funded v ▷ **fund**

fundi n (pl -s) S AFR expert or boffin

funding v, n ▷ **fund**

fundings n ▷ **fund**

fundis n ▷ **fundi**

funds n, v ▷ **fund**

funeral n (pl -s) ceremony of burying or cremating a dead person

funerals n ▷ **funeral**

funerary adj of or for a funeral

funereal adj gloomy or sombre

funfair n (pl -s) entertainment with machines to ride on and stalls

funfairs n ▷ **funfair**

fungal adj ▷ **fungus**

fungi n ▷ **fungus**

fungous adj ▷ **fungus**

fungus n (pl -gi, -guses) plant without leaves, flowers, or roots, such as a mushroom or mould ▶ **fungal, fungous** adj

funguses n ▷ **fungus**

funk¹ n (pl -s) style of dance music with a strong beat

funk² informal n nervous or fearful state ▶ v (-s, -ing, -ed) avoid (doing something) through fear

funked v ▷ **funk**

funkier adj ▷ **funky**

funkiest adj ▷ **funky**

funking v ▷ **funk**

funks n, v ▷ **funk¹, ²**

funky adj (-kier, -kiest) (of music) having a strong beat

funnel n (pl -s) cone-shaped tube for

pouring liquids into a narrow opening ▶ v (-s, -lling, -lled) (cause to) move through or as if through a funnel

funnelled v ▷ funnel

funnelling v ▷ funnel

funnels n, v ▷ funnel

funnier adj ▷ funny

funniest adj ▷ funny

funnily adv ▷ funny

funny adj (-nier, -niest) comical, humorous ▶ **funnily** adv

funs n ▷ fun

fur n (pl -s) soft hair of a mammal ▶ v (-s, -rring, -rred) cover or become covered with fur ▶ **furry** (-rier, -riest) ▶ adj

furbish v (-es, -ing, -ed) smarten up

furbished v ▷ furbish

furbishes v ▷ furbish

furbishing v ▷ furbish

furies n ▷ fury

furious adj very angry ▶ **furiously** adv

furiously adv ▷ furious

furl v (-s, -ing, -ed) roll up and fasten (a sail, umbrella, or flag)

furled v ▷ furl

furling v ▷ furl

furlong n (pl -s) unit of length equal to 220 yards (201.168 metres)

furlongs n ▷ furlong

furlough n (pl -s) leave of absence

furloughs n ▷ furlough

furls v ▷ furl

furnace n (pl -s) enclosed chamber containing a very hot fire

furnaces n ▷ furnace

furnish v (-es, -ing, -ed) provide (a house or room) with furniture

furnished v ▷ furnish

furnishes v ▷ furnish

furnishing v ▷ furnish

furore n (pl -s) very excited or angry reaction

furores n ▷ furore

furred v ▷ fur

furrier n (pl -s) dealer in furs ▶ adj ▷ fur

furriers n ▷ furrier

furriest adj ▷ fur

furring v ▷ fur

furrow n (pl -s) trench made by a plough ▶ v (-s, -ing, -ed) make or become wrinkled

furrowed v ▷ furrow

furrowing v ▷ furrow

furrows n, v ▷ furrow

furry adj ▷ fur

furs n, v ▷ fur

further adv in addition ▶ adj additional ▶ v (-s, -ing, -ed) assist the progress of > **furtherance** n ▷ further

furtherance n ▷ further

furtherances n ▷ further

furthered v ▷ further

furthering v ▷ further

furthers v ▷ further

furthest adv to the greatest distance or extent ▶ adj most distant

furtive adj sly and secretive > **furtively** adv

furtively adv. ▷ furtive

fury n (pl -ries) wild anger

furze n (pl -s) gorse

furzes n ▷ furze

fuse[1] n (pl -s) cord containing an explosive for detonating a bomb

fuse[2] n (pl -s) safety device for electric circuits, containing a wire that melts and breaks the connection when the circuit is overloaded ▶ v (-ses, -sing, -sed) (cause to) fail as a result of a blown fuse

fused v ▷ fuse

fuselage n (pl -s) body of an aircraft

fuselages n ▷ fuselage

fuses v, n ▷ fuse

fusilier n (pl -s) soldier of certain regiments

fusiliers n ▷ fusilier

fusing v ▷ fuse

fusion n (pl -s) melting ▶ adj of a style of cooking that combines traditional Western techniques and ingredients with those used in Eastern cuisine

fusions n ▷ fusion

fuss n (pl -es) needless activity or worry ▶ v (-es, -ing, -ed) make a fuss

fussed v ▷ **fuss**
fusses n, v ▷ **fuss**
fussier adj ▷ **fussy**
fussiest adj ▷ **fussy**
fussily adv ▷ **fussy**
fussiness n ▷ **fussy**
fussinesses n ▷ **fussy**
fussing v ▷ **fuss**
fussy adj (**-sier, -siest**) inclined to fuss
>**fussily** adv >**fussiness** n (pl **-es**)
fustier adj ▷ **fusty**
fustiest adj ▷ **fusty**
fustiness n ▷ **fusty**
fustinesses n ▷ **fusty**
fusty adj (**-tier, -tiest**) stale-smelling
>**fustiness** n (pl **-es**)
futile adj unsuccessful or useless
>**futility** n (pl **-ties**)
futilities n ▷ **futile**
futility n ▷ **futile**
futon n (pl **-s**) Japanese-style bed
futons n ▷ **futon**

future n (pl **-s**) time to come ▶ adj yet
to come or be
futures n ▷ **future**
fuzz¹ n (pl **-es**) mass of fine or curly
hairs or fibres
fuzz² n slang police
fuzzes n ▷ **fuzz¹**
fuzzier adj ▷ **fuzzy**
fuzziest adj ▷ **fuzzy**
fuzzily adv ▷ **fuzzy**
fuzziness n ▷ **fuzzy**
fuzzinesses n ▷ **fuzzy**
fuzzy adj (**-zier, -ziest**) of, like, or
covered with fuzz >**fuzzily** adv
>**fuzziness** n (pl **-es**)

> **fy** interj. Fy is an old word that
> people said when they were
> disgusted or dismayed. This very
> unusual word can be really useful
> when you're trying to form words in
> more than one direction. Fy scores
> 8 points.

Gg

Only three two-letter words begin with G (**gi**, **go** and **gu**). Knowing these will save you worrying about other possibilities. There are quite a few short words beginning with G that use Y, which can prove very useful. These include **gay**, **gey**, **goy** and **guy** (7 points each), as well as **gym** and **gyp** (9 points each).

gab n (pl -s) ▶ v (-s, -ing, -ed) informal talk or chatter

gababouts n ▷ gadabout

gabbed v ▷ gab

gabbier adj ▷ gabby

gabbiest adj ▷ gabby

gabbing v ▷ gab

gabble v (-les, -ling, -led) speak rapidly and indistinctly ▶ n (pl -s) rapid indistinct speech

gabbled v ▷ gabble

gabbles v, n ▷ gabble

gabbling v ▷ gabble

gabby adj (-bier, -biest) informal talkative

gable n (pl -s) triangular upper part of a wall between sloping roofs > **gabled** adj

gabled adj ▷ gable

gables n ▷ gable

gabs n, v ▷ gab

gad v (-s, -dding, -dded) go around in search of pleasure

gadabout n (pl -s) pleasure-seeker

gadded v ▷ gad

gadding v ▷ gad

gadflies n ▷ gadfly

gadfly n (pl -flies) fly that bites cattle

gadget n (pl -s) small mechanical device or appliance

gadgetries n ▷ gadgetry

gadgetry n (pl -ries) gadgets

gadgets n ▷ gadget

gads v ▷ gad

gaff n (pl -s) stick with an iron hook for landing large fish

gaffe n (pl -s) social blunder

gaffer n (pl -s) BRIT informal foreman or boss

gaffers n ▷ gaffer

gaffes n ▷ gaffe

gaffs n ▷ gaff

gag¹ v (-s, -gging, -gged) choke or retch ▶ n (pl -s) cloth etc put into or tied across the mouth

gag² n (pl -s) informal joke

gaga adj slang senile

gagged v ▷ gag¹

gagging v ▷ gag¹

gaggle n (pl -s) informal disorderly crowd

gaggles n ▷ gaggle

gags v, n ▷ gag¹, ²

gaieties n ▷ gaiety

gaiety n (pl -ties) cheerfulness

gaily adv merrily

gain v (-s, -ing, -ed) acquire or obtain ▶ n (pl -s) profit or advantage

gained v ▷ gain

gainful adj useful or profitable > **gainfully** adv

gainfully adv ▷ gainful

gaining v ▷ gain

gains v, n ▷ gain

gainsaid v ▷ **gainsay**

gainsay v (**-s, -ing, -said**) deny or contradict

gainsaying v ▷ **gainsay**

gainsays v ▷ **gainsay**

gait n (pl **-s**) manner of walking

gaiter n (pl **-s**) cloth or leather covering for the lower leg

gaiters n ▷ **gaiter**

gaits n ▷ **gait**

gala n (pl **-s**) festival

galactic adj ▷ **galaxy**

galas n ▷ **gala**

galaxies n ▷ **galaxy**

galaxy n (pl **-xies**) system of stars
  > **galactic** adj

gale n (pl **-s**) strong wind

gales n ▷ **gale**

gall¹ n (pl **-s**) informal impudence

gall² v (**-s, -ing, -ed**) annoy

gall³ n (pl **-s**) abnormal outgrowth on a tree or plant

gallant adj (**-er, -est**) brave and noble
  > **gallantly** adv

gallanter adj ▷ **gallant**

gallantest adj ▷ **gallant**

gallantly adv ▷ **gallant**

galled v ▷ **gall²**

galleon n (pl **-s**) large three-masted sailing ship of the 15th–17th centuries

galleons n ▷ **galleon**

galleries n ▷ **gallery**

gallery n (pl **-ries**) room or building for displaying works of art

galley n (pl **-s**) kitchen of a ship or aircraft

galleys n ▷ **galley**

galling v ▷ **gall²**

gallium n (pl **-s**) CHEM soft grey metallic element used in semiconductors

galliums n ▷ **gallium**

gallon n (pl **-s**) liquid measure of eight pints, equal to 4.55 litres

gallons n ▷ **gallon**

gallop n (pl **-s**) horse's fastest pace ▶ v (**-s, -ing, -ed**) go or ride at a gallop

galloped v ▷ **gallop**

galloping v ▷ **gallop**

gallops n, v ▷ **gallop**

gallows n (pl **-ses**) wooden structure used for hanging criminals

gallowses n ▷ **gallows**

galls v, n ▷ **gall¹, ², ³**

galore adv in abundance

galoshes pl n BRIT, AUST & NZ waterproof overshoes

galumph v (**-s, -ing, -ed**) BRIT, AUST & NZ informal leap or move about clumsily

galumphed v ▷ **galumph**

galumphing v ▷ **galumph**

galumphs v ▷ **galumph**

galvanic adj of or producing an electric current generated by chemical means

gambit n (pl **-s**) opening line or move intended to secure an advantage CHESS

gambits n ▷ **gambit**

gamble v (**-les, -ling, -led**) play games of chance to win money ▶ n (pl **-s**) risky undertaking > **gambler** n (pl **-s**)
  > **gambling** n (pl **-s**)

gambled v ▷ **gamble**

gambler n ▷ **gamble**

gamblers n ▷ **gamble**

gambles v, n ▷ **gamble**

gambling v, n ▷ **gamble**

gamblings n ▷ **gamble**

gamboge n (pl **-s**) gum resin used as a yellow pigment and purgative

gamboges n ▷ **gamboge**

gambol v (**-s, -bolling, -bolled**) jump about playfully, frolic ▶ n (pl **-s**) frolic

gambolled v ▷ **gambol**

gambolling v ▷ **gambol**

gambols v, n ▷ **gambol**

game¹ n (pl **-s**) amusement or pastime ▶ v (**-mes, -ming, -med**) gamble ▶ adj (**-er, -est**) brave > **gamely** adv

game² adj (**-er, -est**) BRIT, AUST & NZ lame, crippled

gamed v ▷ **game¹**

gamely adv ▷ **game¹**

gamer n person who plays computer games ▶ adj ▷ **game¹, ²**

gamers n ▷ **gamer**

games n, v ▷ **game¹**
gamest adj ▷ **game¹, ²**
gamete n (pl -s) BIOL reproductive cell
gametes n ▷ **gamete**
gamine n (pl -s) slim boyish young woman
gamines n ▷ **gamine**
gaming n gambling ▶ v ▷ **game¹**
gamma n (pl -s) third letter of the Greek alphabet
gammas n ▷ **gamma**
gammier adj ▷ **gammy**
gammiest adj ▷ **gammy**
gammon n (pl -s) cured or smoked ham
gammons n ▷ **gammon**
gammy adj (-mier, -miest) ▷ **game²**
gamut n (pl -s) whole range or scale (of music, emotions, etc)
gamuts n ▷ **gamut**
gander n (pl -s) male goose
ganders n ▷ **gander**
gang n (pl -s) (criminal) group
gangland n (pl -s) criminal underworld
ganglands n ▷ **gangland**
gangling adj lanky and awkward
ganglion n (pl -s) group of nerve cells
ganglions n ▷ **ganglion**
gangrene n (pl -s) decay of body tissue as a result of disease or injury
> **gangrenous** adj
gangrenes n ▷ **gangrene**
gangs n ▷ **gang**
gangster n (pl -s) member of a criminal gang
gangsters n ▷ **gangster**
gangway n (pl -s) passage between rows of seats
gangways n ▷ **gangway**
gannet n (pl -s) large sea bird
gannets n ▷ **gannet**
gantries n ▷ **gantry**
gantry n (pl -ries) structure supporting something such as a crane or rocket
gaol n (pl -s) ▷ **jail**
gaols n ▷ **gaol**

gap n (pl -s) break or opening
> **gappy** adj (-pier, -piest)
gape v (-pes, -ping, -ped) stare in wonder ▶ n ▷ **gaping** adj
gaped v ▷ **gape**
gapes v ▷ **gape**
gaping v, adj ▷ **gape**
gappier adj ▷ **gap**
gappiest adj ▷ **gap**
gappy adj ▷ **gap**
gaps n ▷ **gap**
garage n (pl -s) building used to house cars ▶ v (-ges, -ging, -ged) put or keep a car in a garage
garaged v ▷ **garage**
garages n, v ▷ **garage**
garaging v ▷ **garage**
garb n (pl -s) clothes ▶ v (-s, -ing, -ed) clothe
garbage n (pl -s) rubbish
garbages n ▷ **garbage**
garbed v ▷ **garb**
garbing v ▷ **garb**
garbled adj (of a story etc) jumbled and confused
garbs n, v ▷ **garb**
garden n (pl -s) piece of land for growing flowers, fruit, or vegetables ▶ pl ornamental park ▶ v (-s, -ing, -ed) cultivate a garden ▶ **gardener** n (pl -s)
> **gardening** n (pl -s)
gardened v ▷ **garden**
gardenia n (pl -s) large fragrant white waxy flower
gardenias n ▷ **gardenia**
gardening v ▷ **garden**
gardens n, v ▷ **garden**
garfish n (pl -fishes) freshwater fish with a long body and very long toothed jaws
garfishes n ▷ **garfish**
gargle v (-les, -ling, -led) wash the throat with (a liquid) by breathing out slowly through the liquid ▶ n (pl -s) liquid used for gargling
gargled v ▷ **gargle**
gargles v, n ▷ **gargle**
gargling v ▷ **gargle**

gargoyle n (pl -s) waterspout carved in the form of a grotesque face, esp. on a church

gargoyles n ▷ gargoyle

garish adj crudely bright or colourful > **garishly** adv > **garishness** n (pl -es)

garishly adv ▷ garish

garishness n ▷ garish

garishnesses n ▷ garish

garland n (pl -s) wreath of flowers worn or hung as a decoration ▶ v (-s, -ing, -ed) decorate with garlands

garlanded v ▷ garland

garlanding v ▷ garland

garlands n, v ▷ garland

garlic n (pl -s) pungent bulb of a plant of the onion family, used in cooking

garlics n ▷ garlic

garment n (pl -s) article of clothing ▶ pl clothes

garments n ▷ garment

garner v (-s, -ing, -ed) collect or store

garnered v ▷ garner

garnering v ▷ garner

garners v ▷ garner

garnet n (pl -s) red semiprecious stone

garnets n ▷ garnet

garnish v (-es, -ing, -ed) decorate (food) ▶ n (pl -es) decoration for food

garnished v ▷ garnish

garnishes v, n ▷ garnish

garnishing v ▷ garnish

garotte, garotte n (pl -s) Spanish method of execution by strangling ▶ v (-tes, -ting, -ted) kill by this method

garotted v ▷ garrotte

garottes n, v ▷ garrotte

garotting v ▷ garrotte

garret n (pl -s) attic in a house

garrets n ▷ garret

garrison n (pl -s) troops stationed in a town or fort ▶ v (-s, -ing, -ed) station troops in

garrisoned v ▷ garrison

garrisoning v ▷ garrison

garrisons n, v ▷ garrison

garrotte, garotte n (pl -s) Spanish method of execution by strangling ▶ v (-tes, -ting, -ted) kill by this method

garrotted v ▷ garrotte

garrottes n, v ▷ garrotte

garrotting v ▷ garrotte

garter n (pl -s) band worn round the leg to hold up a sock or stocking

garters n ▷ garter

gas n (pl gases, gasses) airlike substance that is not liquid or solid ▶ v poison or render unconscious with gas

gasbag n (pl -s) informal person who talks too much

gasbags n ▷ gasbag

gaseous adj of or like gas

gases n, v ▷ gas

gash v (-es, -ing, -ed) make a long deep cut in ▶ n (pl -es) long deep cut

gashed v ▷ gash

gashes v, n ▷ gash

gashing v ▷ gash

gasket n (pl -s) piece of rubber etc placed between the faces of a metal joint to act as a seal

gaskets n ▷ gasket

gasoline n (pl -s) US petrol

gasolines n ▷ gasoline

gasp v (-s, -ing, -ed) draw in breath sharply or with difficulty ▶ n (pl -s) convulsive intake of breath

gasped v ▷ gasp

gasping v ▷ gasp

gasps v, n ▷ gasp

gassed v ▷ gas

gasses n, v ▷ gas

gassier adj ▷ gassy

gassiest adj ▷ gassy

gassing v ▷ gas

gassy adj (-sier, -siest) filled with gas

gastric adj of the stomach

gate n (pl -s) movable barrier, usu. hinged, in a wall or fence

gâteau n (pl -teaux) rich elaborate cake

gâteaux n ▷ gâteau

gates n ▷ gate

gateway n (pl -s) entrance with a gate

gateways n ▷ gateway

gather v (-s, -ing, -ed) assemble

gathered v ▷ gather

gathers pl n gathered folds in material

▶ v ▷ gather

gauche adj (-r, -st) socially awkward
>**gaucheness** n (pl -es)
gauchenesses n ▷ gauche
gaucher adj ▷ gauche
gauchest adj ▷ gauche
gaucho n (pl -s) S American cowboy
gauchos n ▷ gaucho
gaudier adj ▷ gaudy
gaudiest adj ▷ gaudy
gaudily adv ▷ gaudy
gaudiness n ▷ gaudy
gaudinesses n ▷ gaudy
gaudy adj (-dier, -diest) vulgarly
bright or colourful >**gaudily** adv
>**gaudiness** n (pl -es)
gauge v (-ges, -ging, -ged) estimate
or judge ▶ n (pl -s) measuring
instrument
gauged v ▷ gauge
gauges v, n ▷ gauge
gauging v ▷ gauge
gaunt adj (-er, -est) lean and haggard
>**gauntness** n (pl -es)
gaunter adj ▷ gaunt
gauntest adj ▷ gaunt
gauntlet n (pl -s) heavy glove with
a long cuff
gauntlets n ▷ gauntlet
gauntness n ▷ gaunt
gauntnesses n ▷ gaunt
gauze n (pl -s) transparent loosely-
woven fabric, often used for surgical
dressings >**gauzy** adj (-zier, -ziest)
gauzes n ▷ gauze
gauzier adj ▷ gauze
gauziest adj ▷ gauze
gauzy adj ▷ gauze
gave v ▷ give
gavel n (pl -s) small hammer banged
on a table by a judge, auctioneer, or
chairman to call for attention
gavels n ▷ gavel
gavotte n (pl -s) old formal dance
gavottes n ▷ gavotte
gawk v (-s, -ing, -ed) stare stupidly
gawked v ▷ gawk

gawkier adj ▷ gawky
gawkiest adj ▷ gawky
gawkiness n ▷ gawky
gawkinesses n ▷ gawky
gawking v ▷ gawk
gawks v ▷ gawk
gawky adj (-ier, -iest) clumsy or
awkward >**gawkiness** n (pl -es)
gawp v (-s, -ing, -ed) slang stare
stupidly
gawped v ▷ gawp
gawping v ▷ gawp
gawps v ▷ gawp
gay adj (-er, -est) homosexual ▶ n (pl
-s) homosexual
gayer adj ▷ gay
gayest adj ▷ gay
gayness n (pl -es) homosexuality
gaynesses n ▷ gayness
gays n ▷ gay
gaze v (-zes, -zing, -zed) look fixedly
▶ n (pl -s) fixed look
gazebo n (pl -bos, -boes)
summerhouse with a good view
gazeboes n ▷ gazebo
gazebos n ▷ gazebo
gazed v ▷ gaze
gazelle n (pl -s) small graceful antelope
gazelles n ▷ gazelle
gazes v, n ▷ gaze
gazette n (pl -s) official publication
containing announcements
gazettes n ▷ gazette
gazing v ▷ gaze
gazump v (-s, -ing, -ed) BRIT & AUST
raise the price of a property after
verbally agreeing it with (a prospective
buyer)
gazumped v ▷ gazump
gazumping v ▷ gazump
gazumps v ▷ gazump
gear n (pl -s) set of toothed wheels
connecting with another or with a rack
to change the direction or speed of
transmitted motion ▶ v (-s, -ing, -ed)
prepare or organize for something
gearbox n (pl -es) case enclosing a set
of gears in a motor vehicle

gearboxes n ▷ **gearbox**
geared v ▷ **gear**
gearing v ▷ **gear**
gears n, v ▷ **gear**
gecko n (pl **-os, -oes**) small tropical lizard
geckoes n ▷ **gecko**
geckos n ▷ **gecko**
geebung n (pl **-s**) Australian tree or shrub with an edible but tasteless fruit
geebungs n ▷ **geebung**
geek n (pl **-s**) informal boring, unattractive person ▷ **geeky** adj (**-kier, -kiest**)
geekier adj ▷ **geek**
geekiest adj ▷ **geek**
geeks n ▷ **geek**
geeky adj ▷ **geek**
geelbek n (pl **-s**) S AFR edible marine fish
geelbeks n ▷ **geelbek**
geese n ▷ **goose**
geezer n (pl **-s**) BRIT, AUST & NZ informal man
geezers n ▷ **geezer**
geisha n (pl **-sha, -shas**) (in Japan) professional female companion for men
geishas n ▷ **geisha**
gel n (pl **-s**) jelly-like substance, esp. one used to secure a hairstyle ▷ v (**-s, gelling, gelled**) form a gel
gelatine, gelatin n (pl **-s**) substance made by boiling animal bones
gelatines n ▷ **gelatine**
geld v (**gelds, gelding, gelded**) castrate
gelded v ▷ **geld**
gelding n (pl **-s**) castrated horse ▷ v ▷ **geld**
geldings n ▷ **gelding**
gelds v ▷ **geld**
gelled v ▷ **gel**
gelling v ▷ **gel**
gels n, v ▷ **gel**
gem n (pl **-s**) precious stone or jewel
gemfish (pl **-es**) n Australian food fish with a delicate flavour

gemfishes n ▷ **gemfish**
gems n ▷ **gem**
gen n (pl **-s**) informal information
gendarme n (pl **-s**) member of the French police force
gendarmes n ▷ **gendarme**
gender n (pl **-s**) state of being male or female
genders n ▷ **gender**
gene n (pl **-s**) part of a cell which determines inherited characteristics
genera n ▷ **genus**
general adj common or widespread ▶ n (pl **-s**) very senior army officer ▷ **generally** adv
generally adv ▷ **general**
generals n ▷ **general**
generate v (**-tes, -ting, -ted**) produce or bring into being
generated v ▷ **generate**
generates v ▷ **generate**
generating v ▷ **generate**
generic adj of a class, group, or genus > **generically** adv
generically adv ▷ **generic**
generosities n ▷ **generous**
generosity n ▷ **generous**
generous adj free in giving > **generously** adv > **generosity** n (pl **-ties**)
generously adv ▷ **generous**
genes n ▷ **gene**
geneses n ▷ **genesis**
genesis n (pl **-ses**) beginning or origin
genetic adj of genes or genetics
geneticist n ▷ **genetics**
geneticists n ▷ **genetics**
genetics n study of heredity and variation in organisms > **geneticist** n (pl **-s**)
genial adj cheerful and friendly > **genially** adv > **geniality** n (pl **-ties**)
genialities n ▷ **genial**
geniality n ▷ **genial**
genially adv ▷ **genial**
genie n (pl **-s**) (in fairy tales) servant who appears by magic and grants wishes

genies n ▷ genie

genital adj of the sexual organs or reproduction

genitalia n ▷ genitals

genitals, genitalia pl n external sexual organs

genitive n (pl -s) grammatical case indicating possession or association

genitives n ▷ genitive

genius n (pl -es) (person with) exceptional ability in a particular field

geniuses n ▷ genius

genocide n (pl -s) murder of a race of people

genocides n ▷ genocide

genre n (pl -s) style of literary, musical, or artistic work

genres n ▷ genre

gens n ▷ gen

gent n (pl -s) BRIT, AUST & NZ informal gentleman

genteel adj (-er, -est) affectedly proper and polite ▷ **genteelly** adv

genteeler adj ▷ genteel

genteelest adj ▷ genteel

genteelly adv ▷ genteel

gentian n (pl -s) mountain plant with deep blue flowers

gentians n ▷ gentian

gentile adj, n (pl -s) non-Jewish (person)

gentiles n ▷ gentile

gentle adj (-r, -st) mild or kindly ▷ **gentleness** n (pl -es) ▷ **gently** adv

gentleness n ▷ gentle

gentlenesses n ▷ gentle

gentler adj ▷ gentle

gentlest adj ▷ gentle

gently adv ▷ gentle

gentries n ▷ gentry

gentry n (pl -ies) people just below the nobility in social rank

gents n men's public toilet ▶ n ▷ gent

genuine adj not fake, authentic ▷ **genuinely** adv ▷ **genuineness** n (-es)

genuinely adv ▷ genuine

genuineness n ▷ genuine

genuinenesses n ▷ genuine

genus n (pl genera) group into which a family of animals or plants is divided

geological adj ▷ geology

geologically adv ▷ geology

geologies n ▷ geology

geologist n ▷ geology

geologists n ▷ geology

geology n (pl -gies) study of the earth's origin, structure, and composition
> **geological** adj ▷ **geologically** adv
> **geologist** n (pl -s)

geometric adj ▷ geometry

geometrical adj ▷ geometry

geometrically adv ▷ geometry

geometries n ▷ geometry

geometry n (pl -ries) branch of mathematics dealing with points, lines, curves, and surfaces
> **geometric, geometrical** adj
> **geometrically** adv

geranium n (pl -s) cultivated plant with red, pink, or white flowers

geraniums n ▷ geranium

gerbil n (pl -s) burrowing desert rodent of Asia and Africa

gerbils n ▷ gerbil

germ n (pl -s) microbe, esp. one causing disease

germane adj relevant to

germinal adj of or in the earliest stage of development

germs n ▷ germ

gerund n (pl -s) noun formed from a verb

gerunds n ▷ gerund

gesture n (pl -s) movement to convey meaning ▶ v (-res, -ring, -red) gesticulate

gestured v ▷ gesture

gestures n, v ▷ gesture

gesturing v ▷ gesture

get v (-s, -tting, got) obtain or receive

getaway adj, n (pl -s) (used in) escape

getaways n ▷ getaway

gets v ▷ get

getting v ▷ get

gey adv. Gey is a Scots word meaning **very**. If you have a G and a

Y, it's highly likley that there will be an E you can use somewhere on the board. Gey scores 7 points.

geyser n (pl -s) spring that discharges steam and hot water BRIT & S AFR

geysers n ▷ geyser

ghastlier adj ▷ ghastly

ghastliest adj ▷ ghastly

ghastliness n ▷ ghastly

ghastlinesses n ▷ ghastly

ghastly adj (-lier, -liest) informal unpleasant >**ghastliness** n (pl -es)

ghat n (pl -s) (in India) steps leading down to a river

ghats n ▷ ghat

ghee n (pl -s) (in Indian cookery) clarified butter

ghees n ▷ ghee

gherkin n (pl -s) small pickled cucumber

gherkins n ▷ gherkin

ghetto n (pl -s, -es) slum area inhabited by a deprived minority

ghettoes n ▷ ghetto

ghettos n ▷ ghetto

ghillie n (pl -s) ▷ gillie

ghillies n ▷ ghillie

ghost n (pl -s) disembodied spirit of a dead person ▶ v (-s, -ing, -ed) ghostwrite >**ghostly** adj (-ier, -iest)

ghosted v ▷ ghost

ghosting v ▷ ghost

ghostlier adj ▷ ghost

ghostliest adj ▷ ghost

ghostly adj ▷ ghost

ghosts n, v ▷ ghost

ghoul n (pl -s) person with morbid interests >**ghoulish** adj

ghoulish adj ▷ ghoul

ghouls n ▷ ghoul

gi n. A gi is a suit worn by judo or karate practitioners. Gi is one of only three two-letter words beginning with G, and so is worth knowing. Gi scores 3 points.

giant n (pl -s) mythical being of superhuman size ▶ adj huge

giants n ▷ giant

gibber[1] v (-s, -ing, -ed) speak or utter rapidly and unintelligibly

gibber[2] n (pl -s) AUST boulder

gibbered v ▷ gibber[1]

gibbering v ▷ gibber[1]

gibbers n, v ▷ gibber[1, 2]

gibbet n (pl -s) gallows for displaying executed criminals

gibbets n ▷ gibbet

gibbon n (pl -s) agile tree-dwelling ape of S Asia

gibbons n ▷ gibbon

gibbous adj (of the moon) more than half but less than fully illuminated

gibe v, n (pl -s) ▷ jibe[1]

gibes n ▷ gibe

giblets pl n gizzard, liver, heart, and neck of a fowl

gidday, g'day interj AUST & NZ expression of greeting

giddier adj ▷ giddy

giddiest adj ▷ giddy

giddily adv ▷ giddy

giddiness n ▷ giddy

giddinesses n ▷ giddy

giddy adj (-dier, -diest) having or causing a feeling of dizziness >**giddily** adv >**giddiness** n (pl -es)

gift n (pl -s) present ▶ v (-s, -ing, -ed) make a present of

gifted adj talented ▶ v ▷ gift

gifting v ▷ gift

gifts n, v ▷ gift

gig[1] n (pl -s) single performance by pop or jazz musicians ▶ v (-s, -gging, -gged) play a gig or gigs

gig[2] n (pl -s) light two-wheeled horse-drawn carriage

gigantic adj enormous

gigged v ▷ gig[1]

gigging v ▷ gig[1]

giggle v (-les, -ling, -led) laugh nervously or foolishly ▶ n (pl -s) such a laugh >**giggly** adj (-lier, -liest)

giggled v ▷ giggle

giggles v, n ▷ giggle

gigglier adj ▷ giggle

giggliest adj ▷ giggle

giggling v ▷ **giggle**
giggly adj ▷ **giggle**
gigolo n (pl -**s**) man paid by an older woman to be her escort or lover
gigolos n ▷ **gigolo**
gigot n (pl -**s**) CHIEFLY BRIT leg of lamb or mutton
gigots n ▷ **gigot**
gigs n, v, ▷ **gig¹, ²**
gild v (-**s**, -**ing**, -**ed** or **gilt**) put a thin layer of gold on
gilded v ▷ **gild**
gilding v ▷ **gild**
gilds v ▷ **gild**
gill n (pl -**s**) liquid measure of quarter of a pint, equal to 0.142 litres
gillie n (pl -**s**) (in Scotland) attendant for hunting or fishing
gillies n ▷ **gillie**
gills pl n breathing organs in fish and other water creatures ▶ v ▷ **gill**
gilt adj covered with a thin layer of gold ▶ n (pl -**s**) thin layer of gold used as decoration ▶ v ▷ **gild**
gilts n ▷ **gilt**
gimbals pl n set of pivoted rings which allow nautical instruments to remain horizontal at sea
gimcrack adj showy but cheap
gimlet n (pl -**s**) small tool with a screwlike tip for boring holes in wood
gimlets n ▷ **gimlet**
gimmick n (pl -**s**) something designed to attract attention or publicity ▷ **gimmickry** n (pl -**ries**) ▷ **gimmicky** adj (-**kier**, -**kiest**)
gimmicked adj ▷ **gimmick**
gimmickiest adj ▷ **gimmick**
gimmickries n ▷ **gimmick**
gimmickry n ▷ **gimmick**
gimmicks n ▷ **gimmick**
gimmicky adj ▷ **gimmick**
gin¹ n (pl -**s**) spirit flavoured with juniper berries
gin² n (pl -**s**) wire noose used to trap small animals
ginger n (pl -**s**) root of a tropical plant, used as a spice ▷ **gingery** adj

gingerly adv cautiously
gingers n ▷ **ginger**
gingery adj ▷ **ginger**
gingham n (pl -**s**) cotton cloth, usu. checked or striped
ginghams n ▷ **gingham**
ginkgo n (pl -**es**) ornamental Chinese tree
ginkgoes n ▷ **ginkgo**
gins n ▷ **gin¹, ², ³**
ginseng n (pl -**s**) (root of) a plant believed to have tonic and energy-giving properties
ginsengs n ▷ **ginseng**
gipsies n ▷ **gipsy**
gipsy n (pl -**sies**) ▷ **gypsy**
giraffe n (pl -**s**) African ruminant mammal with a spotted yellow skin and long neck and legs
giraffes n ▷ **giraffe**
gird v (-**s**, -**ing**; **girded** or **girt**) put a belt round
girded v ▷ **gird**
girder n (pl -**s**) large metal beam
girders n ▷ **girder**
girding v ▷ **gird**
girdle¹ n (pl -**s**) woman's elastic corset ▶ v (-**les**, -**ling**, -**led**) surround or encircle
girdle² n (pl -**s**) SCOT griddle
girdled v ▷ **girdle¹**
girdles v, n ▷ **girdle¹, ²**
girdling v ▷ **girdle¹**
girds v ▷ **gird**
girl n (pl -**s**) female child informal ▷ **girlhood** n ▷ **girlish** adj
girlhood n ▷ **girl**
girlhoods n ▷ **girl**
girlie, girly adj informal featuring photographs of naked or scantily clad women
girlish adj ▷ **girl**
girls n ▷ **girl**
girly n ▷ **girlie**
giro n (pl -**s**) (in some countries) system of transferring money within a post office or bank directly from one account to another

giros n ▷ **giro**
girt v ▷ **gird**
girth n (pl -s) measurement round something
girths n ▷ **girth**
gist n (pl -s) substance or main point of a matter
gists n ▷ **gist**
give v (-s, giving, gave, given) present (something) to another person ▶ n (pl -s) resilience or elasticity
giveaway n (pl -s) something that reveals hidden feelings or intentions ▶ adj very cheap or free
giveaways n ▷ **giveaway**
given v ▷ **give**
gives v, n ▷ **give**
giving v ▷ **give**
gizzard n (pl -s) part of a bird's stomach
gizzards n ▷ **gizzard**

> **gju** n (**gjus**). A gju (also spelt **gu**) is a kind of violin from Shetland. This unusual term is a great little word, especially when there's not much space on the board. Gju scores 11 points.

glacé adj preserved in a thick sugary syrup
glacial adj of ice or glaciers
glacier n (pl -s) slow-moving mass of ice formed by accumulated snow
glaciers n ▷ **glacier**
glad adj (-dder, -ddest) pleased and happy > **gladly** adv **gladness** n (pl -es)
gladden v (-s, -ing, -ed) make glad
gladdened v ▷ **gladden**
gladdening v ▷ **gladden**
gladdens v ▷ **gladden**
gladder adj ▷ **glad**
gladdest adj ▷ **glad**
glade n (pl -s) open space in a forest
glades n ▷ **glade**
gladly adv ▷ **glad**
gladness n ▷ **glad**
gladnesses n ▷ **glad**
glamour n (pl -s) alluring charm or fascination
glamours n ▷ **glamour**

glance v (-ces, -cing, -ced) look rapidly or briefly ▶ n (pl -s) brief look
glanced v ▷ **glance**
glances v, n ▷ **glance**
glancing adj hitting at an oblique angle ▶ v ▷ **glance**
gland n (pl -s) organ that produces and secretes substances in the body
> **glandular** adj
glands n ▷ **gland**
glandular adj ▷ **gland**
glare v (-res, -ring, -red) stare angrily ▶ n (pl -s) angry stare
glared v ▷ **glare**
glares v, n ▷ **glare**
glaring adj conspicuous ▶ v ▷ **glare**
> **glaringly** adv
glaringly adv ▷ **glaring**
glass n (pl -es) hard brittle, usu. transparent substance consisting of metal silicates or similar compounds ▶ pl spectacles
glasses n ▷ **glass**
glassier adj ▷ **glassy**
glassiest adj ▷ **glassy**
glassy adj (-sier, -siest) like glass
glaucoma n (pl -s) eye disease
glaucomas n ▷ **glaucoma**
glaze v (-zes, -zing, -zed) fit or cover with glass ▶ n (pl -s) transparent coating
glazed v ▷ **glaze**
glazes v, n ▷ **glaze**
glazier (pl -s) n person who fits windows with glass
glaziers n ▷ **glazier**
glazing n ▷ **glaze**
gleam n (pl -s) small beam or glow of light ▶ v (-s, -ing, -ed) emit a gleam
> **gleaming** adj
gleamed v ▷ **gleam**
gleaming v, adj ▷ **gleam**
gleams n, v ▷ **gleam**
glean v (-s, -ing, -ed) gather (facts etc) bit by bit ▶ **gleaner** n (pl -s)
gleaned v ▷ **glean**
gleaner n ▷ **glean**
gleaners n ▷ **glean**

gleaning v ▷ glean
gleans v ▷ glean
glee n (pl -s) triumph and delight
  > gleeful adj > gleefully adv
gleeful adj ▷ glee
gleefully adv ▷ glee
glees n ▷ glee
glen n (pl -s) deep narrow valley, esp.
  in Scotland
glens n ▷ glen
glib adj (-bber, -bbest) fluent but
  insincere or superficial > glibly adv
  > glibness n (pl -es)
glibber adj ▷ glib
glibbest adj ▷ glib
glibly adv ▷ glib
glibness n ▷ glib
glibnesses n ▷ glib
glide v (-des, -ding, -ded) move easily
  and smoothly ▶ n (pl -s) smooth easy
  movement
glided v ▷ glide
glider n AUST flying phalanger
gliders n ▷ glider
glides n ▷ glide
gliding n sport of flying gliders ▶ v
  ▷ glide
glimmer v (-s, -ing, -ed) shine faintly,
  flicker ▶ n (pl -s) faint gleam
glimmered v ▷ glimmer
glimmering v ▷ glimmer
glimmers v, n ▷ glimmer
glimpse n (pl -s) brief or incomplete
  view ▶ v (-ses, -sing, -sed) catch a
  glimpse of
glimpsed v ▷ glimpse
glimpses n, v ▷ glimpse
glimpsing v ▷ glimpse
glint v (-s, -ing, -ed) gleam brightly ▶ n
  (pl -s) bright gleam
glinted v ▷ glint
glinting v ▷ glint
glints v, n ▷ glint
glisten v (-s, -ing, -ed) gleam by
  reflecting light
glistened v ▷ glisten
glistening v ▷ glisten
glistens v ▷ glisten

glitch n (pl -es) small problem that
  stops something from working
  properly
glitches n ▷ glitch
glitter v (-s, -ing, -ed) shine with
  bright flashes ▶ n (pl -s) sparkle or
  brilliance
glittered v ▷ glitter
glittering v ▷ glitter
glitters v, n ▷ glitter
gloaming n (pl -s) SCOT poetic twilight
gloamings n ▷ gloaming
gloat v (-s, -ing, -ed) regard one's
  own good fortune or the misfortune
  of others with smug or malicious
  pleasure
gloated v ▷ gloat
gloating v ▷ gloat
gloats v ▷ gloat
glob n (pl -s) rounded mass of thick
  fluid
global adj worldwide > globally adv
globally adv ▷ global
globe n (pl -s) sphere with a map of the
  earth on it
globes n ▷ globe
globs n ▷ glob
globular adj ▷ globule
globule n (pl -s) small round drop
  > globular adj
globules n ▷ globule
gloom n (pl -s) melancholy or
  depression > gloomy adj (-mier,
  -miest) > gloomily adv
gloomier adj ▷ gloom
gloomiest adj ▷ gloom
gloomily adv ▷ gloom
glooms n ▷ gloom
gloomy adj ▷ gloom
gloried v ▷ glory
glories v, n ▷ glory
glorification n ▷ glorify
glorifications n ▷ glorify
glorified v ▷ glorify
glorifies v ▷ glorify
glorify v (-fies, -fying, -fied) make
  (something) seem more worthy than it
  is > glorification n (pl -s)

glorifying v ▷ glorify

glorious adj brilliantly beautiful
> **gloriously** adv

gloriously adv ▷ glorious

glory n (pl -ries) praise or honour ▶ v
(-ries, -rying, -ied) (foll. by in) triumph
or exalt

glorying v ▷ glory

gloss¹ n (pl -es) surface shine or lustre

gloss² n (pl -es) explanatory comment
added to the text of a book ▶ v (-es,
-ing, -ed) add glosses to

glossaries n ▷ glossary

glossary n (pl -ries) list of special or
technical words with definitions

glossed v ▷ gloss¹, ²

glosses n, v ▷ gloss¹, ²

glossier adj ▷ glossy

glossiest adj ▷ glossy

glossily adv ▷ glossy

glossiness n ▷ glossy

glossinesses n ▷ glossy

glossing v ▷ gloss²

glossy adj (-sier, -siest) smooth and
shiny > **glossily** adv > **glossiness** n
(pl -es)

glottal adj of the glottis

glottides n ▷ glottis

glottis n (pl -tises, -tides) vocal cords
and the space between them

glottises n ▷ glottis

glove n (pl -s) covering for the hand
with individual sheaths for each finger
and the thumb

gloved adj covered by a glove or gloves

gloves n ▷ glove

glow v (-s, -ing, -ed) emit light
and heat without flames ▶ n (pl -s)
glowing light

glowed v ▷ glow

glower v (-s, -ing, -ed) ▶ n (pl -s) scowl

glowered v ▷ glower

glowering v ▷ glower

glowers v, n ▷ glower

glowing v ▷ glow

glows v, n ▷ glow

glowworm n (pl -s) insect giving out
a green light

glowworms n ▷ glowworm

gloxinia n (pl -s) tropical plant with
large bell-shaped flowers

gloxinias n ▷ gloxinia

glucose n (pl -s) kind of sugar found
in fruit

glucoses n ▷ glucose

glue n (pl -s) natural or synthetic sticky
substance used as an adhesive ▶ v
(**glues, gluing** or **glueing, glued**)
fasten with glue > **gluey** adj

glued v ▷ glue

glueing v ▷ glue

glues n, v ▷ glue

gluey adj ▷ glue

gluing v ▷ glue

glum adj (-mmer, -mmest) sullen or
gloomy > **glumly** adv

glumly adv ▷ glum

glummer adj ▷ glum

glummest adj ▷ glum

glut n (pl -s) excessive supply ▶ v (-s,
-tting, -tted) oversupply

gluten n (pl -s) protein found in cereal
grain

glutens n ▷ gluten

gluts n, v ▷ glut

glutted v ▷ glut

glutting v ▷ glut

glutton n (pl -s) greedy person
> **gluttonous** adj > **gluttony** n (pl -nies)

gluttonies n ▷ glutton

gluttonous adj ▷ glutton

gluttons n ▷ glutton

gluttony n ▷ glutton

gnarled adj rough, twisted, and
knobbly

gnash v (-es, -ing, -ed) grind (the
teeth) together in anger or pain

gnashed v ▷ gnash

gnashes v ▷ gnash

gnashing v ▷ gnash

gnat n (pl -s) small biting two-winged
fly

gnats n ▷ gnat

gnaw v (-s, -ing, -ed or **gnawn**) bite or
chew steadily

gnawed v ▷ gnaw

gnawing v ▷ gnaw

gnawn v ▷ gnaw

gnaws v ▷ gnaw

gneiss n (pl -es) coarse-grained metamorphic rock

gneisses n ▷ gneiss

gnome n (pl -s) imaginary creature like a little old man

gnomes n ▷ gnome

gnomic adj of pithy sayings

gnu n (pl -s) oxlike S African antelope

gnus n ▷ gnu

go v (going, went, gone) move to or from a place (pl gos) ▶ n attempt

goad v (-s, -ing, -ed) provoke (someone) to take some kind of action, usu. in anger ▶ n (pl -s) spur or provocation

goaded v ▷ goad

goading v ▷ goad

goads v, n ▷ goad

goal n (pl -s) SPORT posts through which the ball or puck has to be propelled to score

goalie n (pl -s) informal goalkeeper

goalies n ▷ goalie

goalpost (pl -s) n one of the two posts marking the limit of a goal

goalposts n ▷ goalpost

goals n ▷ goal

goanna n (pl -s) large Australian lizard

goannas n ▷ goanna

goat n (pl -s) sure-footed ruminant animal with horns

goatee n (pl -s) pointed tuftlike beard

goatees n ▷ goatee

goats n ▷ goat

gob n (pl -s) lump of a soft substance

gobbet n (pl -s) lump, esp. of food

gobbets n ▷ gobbet

gobble¹ v (-les, -ling, -led) eat hastily and greedily

gobble² n (pl -s) rapid gurgling cry of the male turkey ▶ v (-les, -ling, -led) make this noise

gobbled v ▷ gobble¹, ²

gobbles v, n ▷ gobble¹, ²

gobbling v ▷ gobble¹, ²

gobies n ▷ goby

goblet n (pl -s) drinking cup without handles

goblets n ▷ goblet

goblin n (pl -s) (in folklore) small malevolent creature

goblins n ▷ goblin

gobs n ▷ gob

goby n (pl -bies) small spiny-finned fish

god n (pl -s) spirit or being worshipped as having supernatural power ▷ godlike adj

godchild n (pl -s) child for whom a person stands as godparent ▷ goddaughter n (pl -s) ▷ godson n (pl -s)

goddaughter n ▷ godchild

goddaughters n ▷ godchild

goddess n fem (pl -s) female god

goddesses n ▷ goddess

godetia n (pl -s) plant with showy flowers

godetias n ▷ godetia

godlier adj ▷ godly

godliest adj ▷ godly

godlike adj ▷ god

godliness n ▷ godly

godlinesses n ▷ godly

godly adj (-lier, -liest) devout or pious ▷ godliness n (pl -es)

gods n ▷ god

godsend n (pl -s) something unexpected but welcome

godsends n ▷ godsend

godson n ▷ godchild

godsons n ▷ godchild

gogga n (pl -s) S AFR informal any small insect

goggas n ▷ gogga

goggle v (-les, -ling, -led) (of the eyes) bulge

goggled v ▷ goggle

goggles pl n protective spectacles ▶ v ▷ goggle

goggling v ▷ goggle

going n (pl -s) condition of the ground for walking or riding over ▶ adj thriving ▶ v ▷ go

goings n ▷ going

goitre n (pl -s) swelling of the thyroid gland in the neck

goitres n ▷ goitre

gold n (pl -s) yellow precious metal ▶ adj made of gold

golden adj made of gold

goldfish n (pl -es) orange fish kept in ponds or aquariums

goldfishes n ▷ goldfish

golds n ▷ gold

golf n (pl -s) outdoor game in which a ball is struck with clubs into a series of holes ▶ v (-s, -ing, -ed) play golf > **golfer** n ▷ golfer

golfed v ▷ golf

golfer n ▷ golf

golfers n ▷ golf

golfing v ▷ golf

golfs n, v ▷ golf

golliwog n (pl -s) soft black-faced doll

golliwogs n ▷ golliwog

gonad n (pl -s) organ producing reproductive cells, such as a testicle or ovary

gonads n ▷ gonad

gondola n (pl -s) long narrow boat used in Venice

gondolas n ▷ gondola

gone v ▷ go

goner n (pl -s) informal person or thing beyond help or recovery

goners n ▷ goner

gong n (pl -s) rimmed metal disc that produces a note when struck

gongs n ▷ gong

good adj (better, best) giving pleasure ▶ n benefit ▶ pl merchandise > **goodness** n (pl -es)

goodbye interj, n (pl -s) expression used on parting

goodbyes n ▷ goodbye

goodies n ▷ goody

goodly adj considerable

goodness n ▷ good

goodnesses n ▷ good

goodwill n (pl -s) kindly feeling

goodwills n ▷ goodwill

goody n (pl -dies) informal hero in a book or film

gooey adj (gooier, gooiest) informal sticky and soft

goof informal (pl -s) mistake ▶ v (-s, -ing, -ed) make a mistake

goofed v ▷ goof

goofing v ▷ goof

goofs n, v ▷ goof

googlies n ▷ googly

googly n (pl -lies) CRICKET ball that spins unexpectedly from off to leg on the bounce

gooier adj ▷ gooey

gooiest adj ▷ gooey

goon n (pl -s) informal stupid person

goons n ▷ goon

goose n (pl geese) web-footed bird like a large duck

gopher n (pl -s) American burrowing rodent

gophers n ▷ gopher

gore¹ n (pl -s) blood from a wound

gore² v (-res, -ring, -red) pierce with horns

gored v ▷ gore²

gores n, v ▷ gore¹, ²

gorge n (pl -s) deep narrow valley ▶ v (-ges, -ging, -ged) eat greedily

gorged v ▷ gorge

gorgeous adj strikingly beautiful or attractive informal > **gorgeously** adv

gorgeously adv ▷ gorgeous

gorges n, v ▷ gorge

gorging v ▷ gorge

gorgon n (pl -s) terrifying or repulsive woman

gorgons n ▷ gorgon

gorier adj ▷ gory

goriest adj ▷ gory

gorilla n (pl -s) largest of the apes, found in Africa

gorillas n ▷ gorilla

goring v ▷ gore²

gormless adj informal stupid

gorse n (pl -s) prickly yellow-flowered shrub

gorses n ▷ gorse

gory adj (**-rier, -riest**) horrific or bloodthirsty

gos n ▷ **go**

goshawk n (pl **-s**) large hawk

goshawks n ▷ **goshawk**

gosling n (pl **-s**) young goose

goslings n ▷ **gosling**

gospel n (pl **-s**) any of the first four books of the New Testament

gospels n ▷ **gospel**

gossamer n (pl **-s**) very fine fabric

gossamers n ▷ **gossamer**

gossip n (pl **-s**) idle talk, esp. about other people ▶ v (**-s, -ing, -ed**) engage in gossip > **gossipy** adj

gossiped v ▷ **gossip**

gossiping v ▷ **gossip**

gossips n, v ▷ **gossip**

gossipy adj ▷ **gossip**

got v ▷ **get**

gouache n (pl **-s**) (painting using) watercolours mixed with glue

gouaches n ▷ **gouache**

gouge v (**-ges, -ging, -ged**) scoop or force out ▶ n (pl **-s**) hole or groove

gouged v ▷ **gouge**

gouges v, n ▷ **gouge**

gouging v ▷ **gouge**

goulash n (pl **-es**) rich stew seasoned with paprika

goulashes n ▷ **goulash**

gourd n (pl **-s**) fleshy fruit of a climbing plant

gourds n ▷ **gourd**

gourmand n (pl **-s**) person who is very keen on food and drink

gourmands n ▷ **gourmand**

gourmet n (pl **-s**) connoisseur of food and drink

gourmets n ▷ **gourmet**

gout n (pl **-s**) disease causing inflammation of the joints

gouts n ▷ **gout**

govern v (**-s, -ing, -ed**) rule, direct, or control > **governable** adj

governable adj ▷ **govern**

governed v ▷ **govern**

governing v ▷ **govern**

governor n (pl **-s**) official governing a province or state

governors n ▷ **governor**

governs v ▷ **govern**

gown n (pl **-s**) woman's long formal dress

gowns n ▷ **gown**

gox n (**goxes**) Gox is a short word meaning gaseous oxygen. This unusual word can come in very useful, especially if you can use it to hit a bonus square. Gox scores 11 points.

goy n (pl **-im, -s**) slang Jewish word for a non-Jew

goyim n ▷ **goy**

goys n ▷ **goy**

grab v (**-s, -bbing, -bbed**) grasp suddenly, snatch ▶ n sudden snatch

grabbed v ▷ **grab**

grabbing v ▷ **grab**

grabs v ▷ **grab**

grace n (pl **-s**) beauty and elegance ▶ v (**-ces, -cing, -ced**) add grace to > **graceful** adj > **gracefully** adv > **graceless** adj

graced v ▷ **grace**

graceful adj ▷ **grace**

gracefully adv ▷ **grace**

graceless adj ▷ **grace**

graces v, n ▷ **grace**

gracing v ▷ **grace**

gracious adj kind and courteous > **graciously** adv

graciously adv ▷ **gracious**

grade n (pl **-s**) place on a scale of quality, rank, or size ▶ v (**-des, -ding, -ded**) arrange in grades

graded v ▷ **grade**

grades n, v ▷ **grade**

gradient n (pl **-s**) (degree of) slope

gradients n ▷ **gradient**

grading v ▷ **grade**

gradual adj occurring, developing, or moving in small stages > **gradually** adv

gradually adv ▷ **gradual**

graduate v (-tes, -ting, -ted) receive a degree or diploma ► n (pl -s) holder of a degree ▷ **graduation** n (pl -s)
graduated v ▷ graduate
graduates v, n ▷ graduate
graduating v ▷ graduate
graduation n ▷ graduate
graduations n ▷ graduate
graffiti pl n words or drawings scribbled or sprayed on walls etc
graft¹ n (pl -s) surgical transplant of skin or tissue ► v (-s, -ing, -ed) transplant (living tissue) surgically
graft² BRIT informal n hard work ► v work hard ▷ **grafter** n (pl -s)
grafted v ▷ graft¹, ²
grafter n ▷ graft
grafters n ▷ graft
grafting v ▷ graft¹, ²
grafts n, v ▷ graft¹, ²
grain n (pl -s) seedlike fruit of a cereal plant ▷ **grainy** adj (-nier, -niest)
grainier adj ▷ grain
grainiest adj ▷ grain
grains n ▷ grain
grainy adj ▷ grain
gram, gramme n (pl -s) metric unit of mass equal to one thousandth of a kilogram
grammar n (pl -s) branch of linguistics dealing with the form, function, and order of words ▷ **grammarian** n (pl -s)
grammarian n ▷ grammar
grammarians n ▷ grammar
grammars n ▷ grammar
grammes n ▷ gram
grampus n (pl -es) dolphin-like mammal
grampuses n ▷ grampus
grams n ▷ gram
gran n (pl -s) BRIT, AUST & NZ informal grandmother
granaries n ▷ granary
granary n (pl -ries) storehouse for grain
grand adj large or impressive, imposing ► n (pl -s) slang thousand pounds or dollars

grandee n (pl -s) person of high station
grandees n ▷ grandee
grandeur n (pl -s) magnificence
grandeurs n ▷ grandeur
grands n ▷ grand
grandson n (pl -s) male grandchild
grandsons n ▷ grandson
grange n (pl -s) BRIT country house with farm buildings
granges n ▷ grange
granite n (pl -s) very hard igneous rock often used in building
granites n ▷ granite
grannies n ▷ granny
granny, grannie n (pl -nnies) informal grandmother
grans n ▷ gran
grant v (-s, -ing, -ed) consent to fulfil (a request) ► n (pl -s) sum of money provided by a government for a specific purpose, such as education
granted v ▷ grant
granting v ▷ grant
grants v, n ▷ grant
granular adj of or like grains
granule n (pl -s) small grain
granules n ▷ granule
grape n (pl -s) small juicy green or purple berry, eaten raw or used to produce wine, raisins, currants, or sultanas
grapes n ▷ grape
graph n (pl -s) drawing showing the relation of different numbers or quantities plotted against a set of axes
graphic adj vividly descriptive ▷ **graphically** adv
graphically adv ▷ graphic
graphics pl n diagrams, graphs, etc, esp. as used on a television programme or computer screen
graphite n (pl -s) soft black form of carbon, used in pencil leads
graphites n ▷ graphite
graphs n ▷ graph
grapnel n (pl -s) device with several hooks, used to grasp or secure things
grapnels n ▷ grapnel

grapple v (-les, -ling, -led) try to cope with (something difficult)
  grappled v ▷ grapple
  grapples v ▷ grapple
  grappling v ▷ grapple

grasp v (-s, -ing, -ed) grip something firmly ▶ n (pl -s) grip or clasp
  grasped v ▷ grasp

grasping adj greedy or avaricious
  ▶ v ▷ grasp
  grasps v, n ▷ grasp

grass n (pl -es) common type of plant with jointed stems and long narrow leaves, including cereals and bamboo ▶ v (-es, -ing, -ed) cover with grass > **grassy** adj (-ier, -iest)
  grassed v ▷ grass
  grasses n, v ▷ grass
  grassier adj ▷ grass
  grassiest adj ▷ grass
  grassing v ▷ grass
  grassy adj ▷ grass

grate¹ v (-tes, -ting, -ted) rub into small bits on a rough surface > **grater** n (pl -s)

grate² n (pl -s) framework of metal bars for holding fuel in a fireplace
  grated v ▷ grate¹

grateful adj feeling or showing gratitude > **gratefully** adv
  gratefully adv ▷ grateful
  grater n ▷ grate¹
  graters n ▷ grate¹
  grates v, n ▷ grate¹, ²

gratification n ▷ gratify
  gratifications n ▷ gratify
  gratified v ▷ gratify
  gratifies v ▷ gratify

gratify v (-fies, -fying, -fied) satisfy or please > **gratification** n (pl -s)
  gratifying v ▷ gratify

grating n (pl -s) framework of metal bars covering an opening ▶ adj harsh or rasping ▶ v ▷ grate¹
  gratings n ▷ grating

gratis adv, adj free, for nothing
  gratuities n ▷ gratuity

gratuity n (pl -ies) money given for services rendered, tip

grave¹ n (pl -s) hole for burying a corpse

grave² adj causing concern > **gravely** adv

grave³ n (pl -s) accent (`) over a vowel to indicate a special pronunciation

gravel n (pl -s) mixture of small stones and coarse sand

gravelly adj covered with gravel
  gravels n ▷ gravel
  gravely adv ▷ grave²

graven adj carved or engraved
  graves n ▷ grave¹, ³

gravid adj MED pregnant
  gravies n ▷ gravy
  gravities n ▷ gravity

gravity n (pl -ies) force of attraction of one object for another, esp. of objects to the earth

gravy n (pl -ies) juices from meat in cooking

gray adj (-er, -est) CHIEFLY US grey
  grayer adj ▷ gray
  grayest adj ▷ gray

grayling n (pl -s) fish of the salmon family
  graylings n ▷ grayling

graze¹ v (-zes, -zing, -zed) feed on grass

graze² v (-zes, -zing, -zed) scratch or scrape the skin ▶ n (pl -s) slight scratch or scrape
  grazed v ▷ graze¹, ²
  grazes v, n ▷ graze¹, ²
  grazing v ▷ graze¹, ²

grease n (pl -s) soft melted animal fat ▶ v (-ses, -sing, -sed) apply grease to
  greased v ▷ grease
  greases n, v ▷ grease
  greasier adj ▷ greasy
  greasiest adj ▷ greasy
  greasiness n ▷ greasy
  greasinesses n ▷ greasy
  greasing v ▷ grease

greasy adj (-sier, -siest) covered with or containing grease > **greasiness** n (pl -s)

great adj (**-er**, **-est**) large in size or number informal > **greatly** adv > **greatness** n (pl **-es**)

greater adj ▷ **great**

greatest adj ▷ **great**

greatly adv ▷ **great**

greatness n ▷ **great**

greatnesses n ▷ **great**

greave n (pl **-s**) piece of armour for the shin

greaves n ▷ **greave**

grebe n (pl **-s**) diving water bird

grebes n ▷ **grebe**

greed n (pl **-s**) excessive desire for food, wealth, etc > **greedy** adj (**-dier**, **-diest**) > **greedily** adv > **greediness** n (pl **-es**)

greedier adj ▷ **greed**

greediest adj ▷ **greed**

greedily adv ▷ **greed**

greediness n ▷ **greed**

greedinesses n ▷ **greed**

greeds n ▷ **greed**

greedy adj ▷ **greed**

green adj (**-er**, **-est**) of a colour between blue and yellow ▶ n (pl **-s**) colour between blue and yellow ▶ pl green vegetables ▶ v (**-s**, **-ing**, **-ed**) make or become green > **greenness** n (pl **-es**) > **greenish**, **greeny** adj

greened v ▷ **green**

greener adj ▷ **green**

greeneries n ▷ **greenery**

greenest adj ▷ **green**

greenflies n ▷ **greenfly**

greenery n (pl **-ries**) vegetation

greenest adj ▷ **green**

greenflies n ▷ **greenfly**

greenfly n (pl **-flies**) green aphid, a common garden pest

greening v ▷ **green**

greenish adj ▷ **green**

greenness n ▷ **green**

greennesses n ▷ **green**

greens n, v ▷ **green**

greeny adj ▷ **green**

greet v (**-s**, **-ing**, **-ed**) meet with expressions of welcome > **greeting** n (pl **-s**)

greeted v ▷ **greet**

greeting v, n ▷ **greet**

greetings n ▷ **greet**

greets v ▷ **greet**

gremlin n (pl **-s**) imaginary being blamed for mechanical malfunctions

gremlins n ▷ **gremlin**

grenade n (pl **-s**) small bomb thrown by hand or fired from a rifle

grenades n ▷ **grenade**

grew v ▷ **grow**

grey adj (**-er**, **-est**) of a colour between black and white ▶ n (pl **-s**) grey colour

greyer adj ▷ **grey**

greyest adj ▷ **grey**

greying adj (of hair) turning grey > **greyish** adj > **greyness** n (pl **-es**)

greyish adj ▷ **grey**

greyness n ▷ **grey**

greynesses n ▷ **grey**

greys n ▷ **grey**

grid n (pl **-s**) network of horizontal and vertical lines, bars, etc

griddle n (pl **-s**) flat iron plate for cooking

griddles n ▷ **griddle**

gridiron n (pl **-s**) frame of metal bars for grilling food

gridirons n ▷ **gridiron**

gridlock n (pl **-s**) situation where traffic is not moving > **gridlocked** adj

gridlocked adj ▷ **gridlock**

gridlocks n ▷ **gridlock**

grids n ▷ **grid**

grief n (pl **-s**) deep sadness

griefs n ▷ **grief**

grieve v (**-ves**, **-ving**, **-ved**) (cause to) feel grief

grieved v ▷ **grieve**

grieves v ▷ **grieve**

grieving adj ▷ **grieve**

grievous adj very severe or painful

griffin n (pl **-s**) mythical monster with an eagle's head and wings and a lion's body

griffins n ▷ **griffin**

grill n (pl **-s**) device on a cooker that radiates heat downwards ▶ v (**-s**, **-ing**, **-ed**) cook under a grill

grille, **grill** n (pl **-s**) grating over an

opening
grilled v ▷ grill
grilles n ▷ grille
grilling n (pl -s) relentless questioning
▶ v ▷ grill
grillings n ▷ grilling
grills¹ n, v ▷ grill
grills² n ▷ grille
grilse n (pl -s) salmon on its first return
from the sea to fresh water
grilses n ▷ grilse
grim adj (-mmer, -mmest) stern
> **grimly** adv > **grimness** n (pl -es)
grimace n (pl -s) ugly or distorted
facial expression of pain, disgust, etc
▶ v (-ces, -cing, -ced) make a grimace
grimaced v ▷ grimace
grimaces n, v ▷ grimace
grimacing v ▷ grimace
grime n (pl -s) ingrained dirt ▶ v
(-mes, -ming, -med) make very dirty
> **grimy** adj (-mier, -miest)
grimed v ▷ grime
grimes n, v ▷ grime
grimier adj ▷ grime
grimiest adj ▷ grime
griming v ▷ grime
grimly adv ▷ grim
grimmer adj ▷ grim
grimmest adj ▷ grim
grimness n ▷ grim
grimnesses n ▷ grim
grimy adj ▷ grime
grin v (-s, -nning, -nned) smile broadly,
showing the teeth ▶ n (-s) broad smile
grind v (-s, -ing, ground) crush or
rub to a powder ▶ n (pl -s) informal
hard work
grinding v ▷ grind
grinds v, n ▷ grind
grinned v ▷ grin
grinning v ▷ grin
grins n, v ▷ grin
grip n (pl -s) firm hold or grasp us ▶ v
(-s, -pping, -pped) grasp or hold
tightly > **gripping** adj
gripe v (-pes, -ping, -ped) informal
complain persistently ▶ n (pl -s)

informal complaint
griped v ▷ gripe
gripes n, v ▷ gripe
griping v ▷ gripe
gripped v ▷ grip
gripping v, adj ▷ grip
grips n, v ▷ grip
grislier adj ▷ grisly
grisliest adj ▷ grisly
grisly adj (-lier, -liest) horrifying or
ghastly
grist n (pl -s) grain for grinding
gristle n (pl -s) tough stringy animal
tissue found in meat > **gristly** adj
(-lier, -liest)
gristles n ▷ gristle
gristlier adj ▷ gristle
gristliest adj ▷ gristle
gristly adj ▷ gristle
grists n ▷ grist
grit n (pl -s) rough particles of sand
▶ pl coarsely ground grain ▶ v (-s,
-tting, -tted) spread grit on (an icy
road etc) > **gritty** adj (-ttier, -ttiest)
> **grittiness** n (pl -es)
grits n ▷ grit
gritted v ▷ grit
grittier adj ▷ grit
grittiest adj ▷ grit
grittiness n ▷ grit
grittinesses n ▷ grit
gritting v ▷ grit
gritty adj ▷ grit
grizzle v (-les, -ling, -led) BRIT, AUST &
NZ informal whine or complain
grizzled adj grey-haired ▶ v ▷ grizzle
grizzles v ▷ grizzle
grizzlies n ▷ grizzly
grizzling v ▷ grizzle
grizzly n (pl -lies) large American bear
groan n (pl -s) deep sound of grief or
pain ▶ v (-s, -ing, -ed) utter a groan
groaned v ▷ groan
groaning v ▷ groan
groans n, v ▷ groan
groat n (pl -s) HIST fourpenny piece
groats n ▷ groat
grocer n (pl -s) shopkeeper selling

foodstuffs
groceries n ▷ grocery
grocers n ▷ grocer
grocery n (pl -ries) business or premises of a grocer ▶ pl goods sold by a grocer
grog n (pl -s) BRIT, AUST & NZ spirit, usu. rum, and water
groggier adj ▷ groggy
groggiest adj ▷ groggy
groggy adj (-gier, -giest) informal faint, shaky, or dizzy
grogs n ▷ grog
groin n (pl -s) place where the legs join the abdomen
groins n ▷ groin
grommet n (pl -s) ring or eyelet
grommets n ▷ grommet
groom n (pl -s) person who looks after horses ▶ v (-s, -ing, -ed) make or keep one's clothes and appearance neat and tidy
groomed v ▷ groom
grooming v ▷ groom
grooms n, v ▷ groom
groove n (pl -s) long narrow channel in a surface
grooves n ▷ groove
grope v (-pes, -ping, -ped) feel about or search uncertainly > **groping** n (pl -s)
groped v ▷ grope
gropes v ▷ grope
groping v, n ▷ grope
gropings n ▷ grope
gross adj flagrant ▶ n (pl -es) twelve dozen ▶ v (-es, -ing, -ed) make as total revenue before deductions > **grossly** adv > **grossness** n (pl -es)
grossed v ▷ gross
grosses n, v ▷ gross
grossing v ▷ gross
grossly adv ▷ gross
grossness n ▷ gross
grossnesses n ▷ gross
grottier adj ▷ grotty
grottiest adj ▷ grotty
grotto n (pl -toes, -tos) small picturesque cave

grottoes n ▷ grotto
grottos n ▷ grotto
grotty adj (-ttier, -ttiest) informal nasty or in bad condition
grouch informal v (-es, -ing, -ed) grumble or complain ▶ n (pl -es) person who is always complaining > **grouchy** adj (-chier, -chiest)
grouched v ▷ grouch
grouches v, n ▷ grouch
grouchier adj ▷ grouch
grouchiest adj ▷ grouch
grouching v ▷ grouch
grouchy adj ▷ grouch
ground¹ n (pl -s) surface of the earth ▶ pl enclosed land round a house ▶ v (-s, -ing, -ed) base or establish
ground² v ▷ grind
grounded v ▷ ground¹
grounds n, v ▷ ground¹
group n (pl -s) number of people or things regarded as a unit ▶ v (-s, -ing, -ed) place or form into a group
grouped v ▷ group
grouping v ▷ group
groups n, v ▷ group
grouse¹ n (pl -s) stocky game bird
grouse² v (-ses, -sing, -sed) grumble or complain ▶ n (pl -s) complaint
groused v ▷ grouse²
grouses n, v ▷ grouse¹, ²
grousing v ▷ grouse²
grout n (pl -s) thin mortar ▶ v (-s, -ing, -ed) fill up with grout
grouted v ▷ grout
grouting v ▷ grout
grouts n, v ▷ grout
grove n (pl -s) small group of trees
grovel v (-s, -elling, -elled) behave humbly in order to win a superior's favour
grovelled v ▷ grovel
grovelling v ▷ grovel
grovels v ▷ grovel
groves n ▷ grove
grow v (-s, -ing, grew, grown) develop physically
growing v ▷ grow

growl v (-s, -ing, -ed) make a low rumbling sound ▶ n (pl -s) growling sound

growled v ▷ growl

growling v ▷ growl

growls v, n ▷ growl

grown v ▷ grow

grownup adj, n (pl -s) adult

grownups n ▷ grownup

grows v ▷ grow

growth n (pl -s) growing

growths n ▷ growth

groyne n (pl -s) wall built out from the shore to control erosion

groynes n ▷ groyne

grub n (pl -s) legless insect larva ▶ v (-s, -bbing, -bbed) search carefully for something by digging or by moving things about

grubbed v ▷ grub

grubbier adj ▷ grubby

grubbiest adj ▷ grubby

grubbiness n ▷ grubby

grubbinesses n ▷ grubby

grubbing v ▷ grub

grubby adj (-bbier, -bbiest) dirty > grubbiness n (pl -es)

grubs n, v ▷ grub

grudge v (-ges, -ging, -ged) be unwilling to give or allow ▶ n (pl -s) resentment

grudged v ▷ grudge

grudges v, n ▷ grudge

grudging v ▷ grudge

gruel n (pl -s) thin porridge

gruels n ▷ gruel

gruesome adj (-er, -est) causing horror and disgust

gruesomer adj ▷ gruesome

gruesomest adj ▷ gruesome

gruff adj (-er, -est) rough or surly in manner or voice > gruffly adv > gruffness n (pl -es)

gruffer adj ▷ gruff

gruffest adj ▷ gruff

gruffly adv ▷ gruff

gruffness n ▷ gruff

gruffnesses n ▷ gruff

grumble v (-les, -ling, -led) complain ▶ n (pl -s) complaint > grumbler n (pl -s) > grumbling adj, n (pl -s)

grumbled v ▷ grumble

grumbler n ▷ grumble

grumblers n ▷ grumble

grumbles v, n ▷ grumble

grumbling v ▷ grumble

grumblings n ▷ grumble

grumpier adj ▷ grumpy

grumpiest adj ▷ grumpy

grumpily adv ▷ grumpy

grumpiness n ▷ grumpy

grumpinesses n ▷ grumpy

grumpy adj (-pier, -piest) bad-tempered > grumpily adv > grumpiness n (pl -es)

grunge n (pl -s) style of rock music with a fuzzy guitar sound

grunges n ▷ grunge

grunt v (-s, -ing, -ed) make a low short gruff sound, like a pig ▶ n (pl -s) pig's sound

grunted v ▷ grunt

grunting v ▷ grunt

grunts v, n ▷ grunt

gryphon n (pl -s) ▷ griffin

gryphons n ▷ gryphon

gu n (gus) A gu (also spelt **gju**) is a kind of violin from Shetland. This is one of only three two-letter words beginning with G, and so is a good one to remember. Gu scores 3 points.

guano n (pl -s) dried sea-bird manure, used as fertilizer

guanos n ▷ guano

guard v (-s, -ing, -ed) watch over to protect or to prevent escape ▶ n (pl -s) person or group that guards

guarded adj cautious or noncommittal ▶ v ▷ guard > guardedly adv

guardedly adv ▷ guarded

guardian n (pl -s) keeper or protector > guardianship n (pl -s)

guardians n ▷ guardian

guardianship n ▷ guardian

guardianships n ▷ **guardian**
guarding v ▷ **guard**
guards v, n ▷ **guard**
guava n (pl -s) yellow-skinned tropical American fruit
guavas n ▷ **guava**
gudgeon n (pl -s) small freshwater fish
gudgeons n ▷ **gudgeon**
guess v (-es, -ing, -ed) estimate or draw a conclusion without proper knowledge ▶ n (pl -es) estimate or conclusion reached by guessing
guessed v ▷ **guess**
guesses v, n ▷ **guess**
guessing v ▷ **guess**
guest n (pl -s) person entertained at another's house or at another's expense ▶ v (-s, -ing, -ed) appear as a visiting player or performer
guested v ▷ **guest**
guesting v ▷ **guest**
guests n, v ▷ **guest**
guff n (pl -s) BRIT, AUST & NZ slang nonsense
guffaw n (pl -s) crude noisy laugh ▶ v (-s, -ing, -ed) laugh in this way
guffawed v ▷ **guffaw**
guffawing v ▷ **guffaw**
guffaws n, v ▷ **guffaw**
guffs n ▷ **guff**
guidance n (pl -s) leadership, instruction, or advice
guidances n ▷ **guidance**
guide n (pl -s) person who conducts tour expeditions ▶ v (-s, -ing, -ed) act as a guide for
guided v ▷ **guide**
guides n, v ▷ **guide**
guiding v ▷ **guide**
guild n (pl -s) organization or club
guilder n (pl -s) former monetary unit of the Netherlands
guilders n ▷ **guilder**
guilds n ▷ **guild**
guile n (pl -s) cunning or deceit ▷ **guileful** adj ▷ **guileless** adj
guileful adj ▷ **guile**
guileless adj ▷ **guile**

guiles n ▷ **guile**
guilt n (pl -s) fact or state of having done wrong
guiltier adj ▷ **guilty**
guiltiest adj ▷ **guilty**
guiltily adv ▷ **guilty**
guilts n ▷ **guilt**
guilty adj (-tier, -tiest) responsible for an offence or misdeed > **guiltily** adv
guinea n (pl -s) former British monetary unit worth 21 shillings (1.05 pounds)
guineas n ▷ **guinea**
guise n (pl -s) false appearance
guises n ▷ **guise**
guitar n (pl -s) stringed instrument with a flat back and a long neck, played by plucking or strumming > **guitarist** n
guitarist n ▷ **guitar**
guitarists n ▷ **guitar**
guitars n ▷ **guitar**
gulch n (pl -es) US deep narrow valley
gulches n ▷ **gulch**
gulf n (pl -s) large deep bay
gulfs n ▷ **gulf**
gull n (pl -s) long-winged sea bird
gullet n (pl -s) muscular tube through which food passes from the mouth to the stomach
gullets n ▷ **gullet**
gullibilities n ▷ **gullible**
gullibility n ▷ **gullible**
gullible adj easily tricked > **gullibility** n (pl -ties)
gullies n ▷ **gully**
gulls n ▷ **gull**
gully n (pl -lies) channel cut by running water
gulp v (-s, -ing, -ed) swallow hastily ▶ n (pl -s) gulping
gulped v ▷ **gulp**
gulping v ▷ **gulp**
gulps v, n ▷ **gulp**
gum¹ n (pl -s) firm flesh in which the teeth are set
gum² n (pl -s) sticky substance obtained from certain trees ▶ v (-s, -mming, -mmed) stick with gum

gumboot n (pl **-s**) CHIEFLY BRIT Wellington boot
gumboots n ▷ gumboot
gumdrop n (pl **-s**) hard jelly-like sweet
gumdrops n ▷ gumdrop
gummed v ▷ gum²
gummier adj ▷ gummy¹, ²
gummiest adj ▷ gummy¹, ²
gumming v ▷ gum²
gummy¹ adj (**-mier, -mmiest**) toothless
gummy² adj (**-mier, -mmiest**) sticky
gumption n (pl **-s**) informal resourcefulness
gumptions n ▷ gumption
gums n ▷ gum¹, ²
gun n (pl **-s**) weapon with a metal tube from which missiles are fired by explosion ▶ v (**-s, -nning, -nned**) cause (an engine) to run at high speed
gunboat n (pl **-s**) small warship
gunboats n ▷ gunboat
gunge n (pl **-s**) informal sticky unpleasant substance > **gungy** adj (**-gier, -giest**)
gunges n ▷ gunge
gungier adj ▷ gunge
gungiest adj ▷ gunge
gungy adj ▷ gunge
gunman n (pl **-men**) armed criminal
gunmen n ▷ gunman
gunmetal n (pl **-s**) alloy of copper, tin, and zinc ▶ adj dark grey
gunmetals n ▷ gunmetal
gunned v ▷ gun
gunnel n ▷ gunwale
gunnels n ▷ gunwale
gunner n (pl **-s**) artillery soldier
gunneries n ▷ gunnery
gunners n ▷ gunner
gunnery n (pl **-ries**) use or science of large guns
gunnies n ▷ gunny
gunning v ▷ gun
gunny n (pl **-nies**) strong coarse fabric used for sacks
guns n, v ▷ gun
gunshot n (pl **-s**) shot or range of a gun

gunshots n ▷ gunshot
gunwale, gunnel n (pl **-s**) top of a ship's side
gunwales n ▷ gunwale
gunyah n (pl **-s**) AUST hut or shelter in the bush
gunyahs n ▷ gunyah
guppies n ▷ guppy
guppy n (pl **-pies**) small colourful aquarium fish
gurgle v (**-les, -ling, -led**) ▶ n (pl **-s**) (make) a bubbling noise
gurgled v ▷ gurgle
gurgles v, n ▷ gurgle
gurgling v ▷ gurgle
guru n (pl **-s**) Hindu or Sikh religious teacher or leader
gurus n ▷ guru
gush v (**-es, -ing, -ed**) flow out suddenly and profusely ▶ n (pl **-es**) sudden copious flow
gushed v ▷ gush
gusher n (pl **-s**) spurting oil well
gushers n ▷ gusher
gushes v, n ▷ gush
gushing v ▷ gush
gusset n (pl **-s**) piece of material sewn into a garment to strengthen it
gussets n ▷ gusset
gust n (pl **-s**) sudden blast of wind ▶ v (**-s, -ing, -ed**) blow in gusts > **gusty** adj (**-tier, -tiest**)
gusted v ▷ gust
gustier adj ▷ gust
gustiest adj ▷ gust
gusting v ▷ gust
gusto n (pl **-s**) enjoyment or zest
gustos n ▷ gusto
gusts n, v ▷ gust
gusty adj ▷ gust
gut n (pl **-s**) intestine ▶ pl internal organs ▶ v (**-s, -tting, -tted**) remove the guts from ▶ adj basic or instinctive
guts n ▷ gut
gutsier adj ▷ gutsy
gutsiest adj ▷ gutsy
gutsy adj (**-sier, -siest**) informal courageous

gutted adj BRIT, AUST & NZ informal
disappointed and upset ▶ v ▷ **gut**
gutter n (pl -s) shallow channel for
carrying away water from a roof or
roadside ▶ v (-s, -ing, -ed) (of a candle)
burn unsteadily, with wax running
down the sides
guttered v ▷ **gutter**
gutters n, v ▷ **gutter**
gutting v ▷ **gut**
guttural adj (of a sound) produced at
the back of the throat
guy¹ n (pl -s) informal man or boy
guy² n (pl -s) rope or chain to steady or
secure something
guys n ▷ **guy**¹, ²
guzzle v (-les, -ling, -led) eat or drink
greedily
guzzled v ▷ **guzzle**
guzzles v ▷ **guzzle**
guzzling v ▷ **guzzle**
gybe v (-bes, -bing, -bed) (of a fore-
and-aft sail) swing suddenly from one
side to the other
gybed v ▷ **gybe**

gybes v ▷ **gybe**
gybing v ▷ **gybe**
gym n (pl -s) gymnasium
gymkhana n (pl -s) horse-riding
competition
gymkhanas n ▷ **gymkhana**
gymnast n (pl -s) expert in gymnastics
gymnasts n ▷ **gymnast**
gyms n ▷ **gym**
gypsies n ▷ **gypsy**
gypsum n (pl -s) chalklike mineral
used to make plaster of Paris
gypsums n ▷ **gypsum**
gypsy n (pl -sies) member of a
travelling people found throughout
Europe
gyrate v (-tes, -ting, -ted) rotate
or spiral about a point or axis
> **gyration** n (pl -s)
gyrated v ▷ **gyrate**
gyrates v ▷ **gyrate**
gyrating v ▷ **gyrate**
gyration n ▷ **gyrate**
gyrations n ▷ **gyrate**
gyratory adj gyrating

Hh

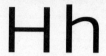

H forms a two-letter word in front of every vowel except U (and you can make **uh** with U), making it a versatile tile when you want to form words in more than one direction. As H is worth 4 points on its own, you can earn some very high scores by doing this: even **ha, he, hi** and **ho** will give 5 points each. There are lots of good short words beginning with H, like **haw, hew, how, hay, hey** and **hoy** (9 each).

ha interj. Ha is a sound people make to express triumph or surprise. This gives a reasonable score for a two-letter word, and is a good one to form when making a longer word in another direction at the same time. Ha scores 5 points.

habit n (pl **-s**) established way of behaving

habitat n (pl **-s**) natural home of an animal or plant

habitats n ▷ **habitat**

habits n ▷ **habit**

habitual adj done frequently and repeatedly > **habitually** adv

habitually adv ▷ **habitual**

habitué n (pl **-s**) frequent visitor to a place

habitués n ▷ **habitué**

hacienda n (pl **-s**) ranch or large estate in Latin America

haciendas n ▷ **hacienda**

hack¹ v (-s, -ing, -ed) cut or chop violently BRIT & NZ informal

hack² n (pl **-es**) (inferior) writer or journalist

hacked v ▷ **hack¹**

hacker n (pl **-s**) slang computer enthusiast, esp. one who breaks into the computer system of a company or government

hackers n ▷ **hacker**

hacking v ▷ **hack¹**

hackles pl n hairs on the neck and back of an animal

hackney n (pl **-s**) BRIT taxi

hackneys n ▷ **hackney**

hacks v ▷ **hack¹** ▷ n ▷ **hack²**

hacksaw n (pl **-s**) small saw for cutting metal

hacksaws n ▷ **hacksaw**

had v ▷ **have**

haddock n (pl **-s**) edible sea fish of N Atlantic

haddocks n ▷ **haddock**

hadj n (pl **-es**) ▷ **hajj**

hadjes n ▷ **hadj**

hafnium n (pl **-s**) CHEM metallic element found in zirconium ores

hafniums n ▷ **hafnium**

haft n (pl **-s**) handle of an axe, knife, or dagger

hafts n ▷ **haft**

hag n (pl **-s**) ugly old woman

haggard adj looking tired and ill

haggis n (pl **-es**) Scottish dish made from sheep's offal, oatmeal, suet, and seasonings, boiled in a bag made from the sheep's stomach

haggises n ▷ **haggis**

haggle v (-les, -ling, -led) bargain or wrangle over a price

haggled v ▷ **haggle**
haggles v ▷ **haggle**
haggling v ▷ **haggle**
hags n ▷ **hag**

hail¹ n (pl -s) (shower of) small pellets of ice ▶ v (-s, -ing, -ed) fall as or like hail ▷ **hailstone** n (pl -s)
hail² v (-s, -ing, -ed) call out to, greet
hailed v ▷ **hail¹, ²**
hailing v ▷ **hail¹, ²**
hails v ▷ **hail¹, ²** ▶ n ▷ **hail¹**
hailstone n ▷ **hail¹**
hailstones n ▷ **hail¹**

hair n (pl -s) threadlike growth on the skin
hairclip n (pl -s) small bent metal hairpin
hairclips n ▷ **hairclip**
hairdo n (pl -s) informal hairstyle
hairdos n ▷ **hairdo**
hairgrip n BRIT ▷ **hairclip**
hairgrips n ▷ **hairgrip**
hairier adj ▷ **hairy**
hairiest adj ▷ **hairy**
hairiness n ▷ **hairy**
hairinesses n ▷ **hairy**
hairline n (pl -s) edge of hair at the top of the forehead ▶ adj very fine or narrow
hairlines n ▷ **hairline**
hairpin n (pl -s) U-shaped wire used to hold the hair in place
hairpins n ▷ **hairpin**
hairs n ▷ **hair**
hairy adj (-rier, -riest) covered with hair ▷ **hairiness** n (pl -es)

> **haj** n. Haj is the same as **hajj**. This is a very useful word, especially when there isn't much space on the board. Remember that this spelling doesn't have a plural form. Haj scores 13 points.

hajj n (pl -es) pilgrimage a Muslim makes to Mecca
hajjes n ▷ **hajj**
haka n (pl -s) NZ ceremonial Maori dance with chanting
hakas n ▷ **haka**

hake n (pl hakes) edible sea fish of N hemisphere AUST
hakea n (pl -s) Australian tree or shrub with hard woody fruit
hakeas n ▷ **hakea**
hakes n ▷ **hake**
halal n (pl -s) meat from animals slaughtered according to Muslim law
halals n ▷ **halal**
halberd n (pl -s) HIST spear with an axe blade
halberds n ▷ **halberd**
halcyon adj peaceful and happy
hale adj (-ler, -lest) healthy, robust
haler adj ▷ **hale**
halest adj ▷ **hale**
half n (pl halves) either of two equal parts ▶ adj denoting one of two equal parts ▶ adv to the extent of half
halflife n (pl -lives) time taken for half the atoms in radioactive material to decay
halflives n ▷ **halflife**
halftime n (pl -s) SPORT short rest period between two halves of a game
halftimes n ▷ **halftime**
halftone n (pl -s) illustration showing lights and shadows by means of very small dots
halftones n ▷ **halftone**
halfway adv, adj at or to half the distance
halfwit n (pl -s) foolish or stupid person
halfwits n ▷ **halfwit**
halibut n (pl -s) large edible flatfish of N Atlantic
halibuts n ▷ **halibut**
hall n (pl -s) (also hallway) entrance passage
hallmark n (pl -s) typical feature ▶ v (-s, -ing, -ed) stamp with a hallmark
hallmarked v ▷ **hallmark**
hallmarking v ▷ **hallmark**
hallmarks n, v ▷ **hallmark**
hallo interj ▷ **hello**
hallowed adj regarded as holy
halls n ▷ **hall**

halo n (pl **-loes, -los**) ring of light round the head of a sacred figure
haloes n ▷ **halo**

halogen n (pl **-s**) CHEM any of a group of nonmetallic elements including chlorine and iodine
halogens n ▷ **halogen**
halos n ▷ **halo**

halt v (**-s, -ing, -ed**) come or bring to a stop ▶ n (pl **-s**) temporary stop
halted v ▷ **halt**

halter n (pl **-s**) strap round a horse's head with a rope to lead it with
halters n ▷ **halter**

halting adj hesitant, uncertain ▶ v ▷ **halt**
halts n, v ▷ **halt**

halve v (**-ves, -ving, -ved**) divide in half
halved v ▷ **halve**
halves v ▷ **halve** ▶ n ▷ **half**
halving v ▷ **halve**

halyard n (pl **-s**) rope for raising a ship's sail or flag
halyards n ▷ **halyard**

ham[1] n (pl **-s**) smoked or salted meat from a pig's thigh
ham[2] informal n (pl **-s**) amateur radio operator ▶ v (**-s, -mming, -mmed**) overact

hamlet n (pl **-s**) small village
hamlets n ▷ **hamlet**
hammed v ▷ **ham**[2]

hammer n (pl **-s**) tool with a heavy metal head and a wooden handle, used to drive in nails etc ▶ v (**-s, -ing, -ed**) hit (as if) with a hammer
hammered v ▷ **hammer**
hammering v ▷ **hammer**
hammers n, v ▷ **hammer**
hamming v ▷ **ham**[2]

hammock n (pl **-s**) hanging bed made of canvas or net
hammocks n ▷ **hammock**

hamper[1] v (**-s, -ing, -ed**) make it difficult for (someone or something) to move or progress
hamper[2] n (pl **-s**) large basket with a lid

hampered v ▷ **hamper**[1]
hampering v ▷ **hamper**[1]
hampers v, n ▷ **hamper**[1, 2]
hams n, v ▷ **ham**[1, 2]

hamster n (pl **-s**) small rodent with a short tail and cheek pouches
hamsters n ▷ **hamster**

hand n (pl **-s**) part of the body at the end of the arm, consisting of a palm, four fingers, and a thumb ▶ v (**-s, -ing, -ed**) pass, give

handbag n (pl **-s**) woman's small bag for carrying personal articles in
handbags n ▷ **handbag**

handbill n (pl **-s**) small printed notice
handbills n ▷ **handbill**

handbook n (pl **-s**) small reference or instruction book
handbooks n ▷ **handbook**

handcuff n (pl **-s**) one of a linked pair of metal rings designed to be locked round a prisoner's wrists by the police ▶ v (**-s, -ing, -ed**) put handcuffs on
handcuffed v ▷ **handcuff**
handcuffing v ▷ **handcuff**
handcuffs n, v ▷ **handcuff**
handed v ▷ **hand**

handful n (pl **-s**) amount that can be held in the hand
handfuls n ▷ **handful**

handheld adj (of a film camera) held rather than mounted, as in close-up action shots ▶ n (pl **-s**) computer that can be held in the hand
handhelds n ▷ **handheld**

handicap n (pl **-s**) physical or mental disability ▶ v (**-s, -pping, -pped**) make it difficult for (someone) to do something
handicapped v ▷ **handicap**
handicapping v ▷ **handicap**
handicaps n, v ▷ **handicap**
handier adj ▷ **handy**
handiest adj ▷ **handy**
handily adv ▷ **handy**
handing v ▷ **hand**

handle n (pl **-s**) part of an object that

is held so that it can be used ▶ v (**-les,
-ling, -led**) hold, feel, or move with
the hands

handled v ▷ handle

handler n (pl **-s**) person who controls
an animal

handlers n ▷ handler

handles n, v ▷ handle

handling v ▷ handle

handout n (pl **-s**) clothing, food, or
money given to a needy person

handouts n ▷ handout

hands n, v ▷ hand

handsome adj (esp. of a man) good-
looking

handy adj (**-dier, -diest**) convenient,
useful > **handily** adv

handyman n (pl **-men**) man who is
good at making or repairing things

handymen n ▷ handyman

hang v (**-s, -ing, hung** or **-ed**) attach or
be attached at the top with the lower
part free; suspend or be suspended by
the neck until dead

hangar n (pl **-s**) large shed for storing
aircraft

hangars n ▷ hangar

hangdog adj guilty, ashamed

hanged v ▷ hang

hanger n (pl **-s**) curved piece of wood,
wire, or plastic, with a hook, for
hanging up clothes (also **coat hanger**)

hangers n ▷ hanger

hangi n (pl **-s**) NZ Maori oven
consisting of a hole in the ground filled
with hot stones

hanging v ▷ hang

hangis n ▷ hangi

hangman n (pl **-men**) man who
executes people by hanging

hangmen n ▷ hangman

hangover n (pl **-s**) headache and
nausea as a result of drinking too
much alcohol

hangovers n ▷ hangover

hangs v ▷ hang

hangup n (pl **-s**) informal emotional or
psychological problem

hangups n ▷ hangup

hank n (pl **-s**) coil, esp. of yarn

hanker v (**-s, -ing, -ed**) (foll. by **after** or
for) desire intensely

hankered v ▷ hanker

hankering v ▷ hanker

hankers v ▷ hanker

hankie n ▷ hanky

hankies n ▷ hanky

hanks n ▷ hank

hanky, hankie n (pl **-kies**) informal
handkerchief

hapless adj unlucky

happen v (**-s, -ing, -ed**) take place,
occur

happened v ▷ happen

happens v ▷ happen

happier adj ▷ happy

happiest adj ▷ happy

happily adv ▷ happy

happiness n ▷ happy

happy adj (**-pier, -piest**) feeling
or causing joy > **happily** adv
> **happiness** n (pl **-es**)

harangue v (**-gues, -guing, -gued**)
address angrily or forcefully ▶ n (pl **-s**)
angry or forceful speech

harangued v ▷ harangue

harangues v, n ▷ harangue

haranguing v ▷ harangue

harass v (**-es, -ing, -ssed**) annoy or
trouble constantly > **harassed** adj
> **harassment** n (pl **-s**)

harassed v, adj ▷ harass

harasses v ▷ harass

harassing v ▷ harass

harassment n ▷ harass

harbour n (pl **-s**) sheltered port ▶ v
(**-s, -ing, -ed**) maintain secretly in
the mind

harboured v ▷ harbour

harbouring v ▷ harbour

harbours n, v ▷ harbour

hard adj firm, solid, or rigid ▶ adv with
great energy or effort > **harden** v (**-s,
-ing, -ed**) > **hardness** n (pl **-es**)

harden v ▷ hard

hardened v ▷ hard

hardening v ▷ hard
hardens v ▷ hard
hardier adj ▷ hardy
hardiest adj ▷ hardy
hardiness n ▷ hardy
hardinesses n ▷ hardy
hardly adv scarcely or not at all
hardness n ▷ hard
hardnesses n ▷ hard
hardship n (pl -s) suffering
hardships n ▷ hardship
hardware n (pl -s) metal tools or implements
hardwares n ▷ hardware
hardwood n (pl -s) wood of a broadleaved tree such as oak or ash
hardwoods n ▷ hardwood
hardy adj (-dier, -diest) able to stand difficult conditions > **hardiness** n (pl -es)
hare n (pl -s) animal like a large rabbit, with longer ears and legs ▶ v (-res, -ring, -red) (usu. foll. by **off**) run (away) quickly
harebell n (pl -s) blue bell-shaped flower
harebells n ▷ harebell
hared v ▷ hare
harelip n (pl -s) slight split in the upper lip
harelips n ▷ harelip
harem n (pl -s) (apartments of) a Muslim man's wives and concubines
harems n ▷ harem
hares v, n ▷ hare
haring v ▷ hare
hark v (-s, -ing, -ed) old-fashioned listen
harked v ▷ hark
harking v ▷ hark
harks v ▷ hark
harlot n (pl -s) lit prostitute
harlots n ▷ harlot
harm v (-s, -ing, -ed) injure physically, mentally, or morally ▶ n (pl -s) physical, mental, or moral injury > **harmful** adj > **harmless** adj
harmed v ▷ harm
harmful adj ▷ harm

harming v ▷ harm
harmless adj ▷ harm
harmonic adj of harmony
harmonies n ▷ harmony
harmonious adj ▷ harmony
harmoniously adv ▷ harmony
harmony n (pl -nies) peaceful agreement and cooperation > **harmonious** adj > **harmoniously** adv
harms v, n ▷ harm
harness n (pl -es) arrangement of straps for attaching a horse to a cart or plough ▶ v (-es, -ing, -ed) put a harness on
harnessed v ▷ harness
harnesses n, v ▷ harness
harnessing v ▷ harness
harp n (pl -s) large triangular stringed instrument played with the fingers > **harpist** n (pl -s)
harpies n ▷ harpy
harpist n ▷ harp
harpists n ▷ harp
harpoon n (pl -s) barbed spear attached to a rope used for hunting whales ▶ v (-s, -ing, -ed) spear with a harpoon
harpooned v ▷ harpoon
harpooning v ▷ harpoon
harpoons n, v ▷ harpoon
harps n ▷ harp
harpy n (pl -pies) nasty or bad-tempered woman
harridan n (pl -s) nagging or vicious woman
harridans n ▷ harridan
harried v ▷ harry
harrier n (pl -s) cross-country runner
harriers n ▷ harrier
harries v ▷ harry
harrow n (pl -s) implement used to break up lumps of soil ▶ v (-s, -ing, -ed) draw a harrow over
harrowed v ▷ harrow
harrows n, v ▷ harrow
harry v (-ries, -rying, -ried) keep asking (someone) to do something, pester

harrying v ▷ **harry**

harsh adj severe and difficult to cope with > **harshly** adv > **harshness** n (pl **-es**)

harshly adv ▷ **harsh**

harshness n ▷ **harsh**

harshnesses n ▷ **harsh**

hart n (pl **-s**) adult male deer

harts n ▷ **hart**

harvest n (pl **-s**) (season for the) gathering of crops ▶ v (**-s, -ing, -ed**) gather (a ripened crop) > **harvester** n (pl **-s**)

harvested v ▷ **harvest**

harvester n ▷ **harvest**

harvesters n ▷ **harvest**

harvesting v ▷ **harvest**

harvests n, v ▷ **harvest**

has v ▷ **have**

hash[1] n (pl **-es**) dish of diced cooked meat and vegetables reheated

hash[2] n (pl **-es**) informal hashish

hashes n ▷ **hash**[1, 2]

hashish n (pl **-es**) drug made from the cannabis plant, smoked for its intoxicating effects

hashishes n ▷ **hashish**

hasp n (pl **-s**) clasp that fits over a staple and is secured by a bolt or padlock, used as a fastening

hasps n ▷ **hasp**

hassle informal n (pl **-s**) trouble, bother ▶ v (**-les, -ling, -led**) bother or annoy

hassled v ▷ **hassle**

hassles n, v ▷ **hassle**

hassling v ▷ **hassle**

hassock n (pl **-s**) cushion for kneeling on in church

hassocks n ▷ **hassock**

haste n (pl **-s**) (excessive) quickness

hasten v (**-s, -ing, -ed**) (cause to) hurry

hastened v ▷ **hasten**

hastening n ▷ **hasten**

hastens n ▷ **hasten**

hastes n ▷ **haste**

hastier adj ▷ **hasty**

hastiest adj ▷ **hasty**

hastily adv ▷ **hasty**

hasty adj (**-tier, -tiest**) (too) quick > **hastily** adv

hat n (pl **-s**) covering for the head, often with a brim, usu. worn to give protection from the weather

hatch[1] v (**-es, -ing, -ed**) (cause to) emerge from an egg

hatch[2] n (pl **-es**) hinged door covering an opening in a floor or wall

hatched v ▷ **hatch**[1]

hatches v ▷ **hatch**[1] ▶ n ▷ **hatch**[2]

hatchet n (pl **-s**) small axe

hatchets n ▷ **hatchet**

hatching v ▷ **hatch**[1]

hatchway n (pl **-s**) opening in the deck of a ship

hatchways n ▷ **hatchway**

hate v (**-tes, -ting, -ted**) dislike intensely ▶ n (pl **-s**) intense dislike > **hater** n (pl **-s**)

hated v ▷ **hate**

hateful adj causing or deserving hate

hater n ▷ **hate**

haters n ▷ **hate**

hates v, n ▷ **hate**

hating v ▷ **hate**

hatred n (pl **-s**) intense dislike

hatreds n ▷ **hatred**

hats n ▷ **hat**

haughtier adj ▷ **haughty**

haughtiest adj ▷ **haughty**

haughtily adv ▷ **haughty**

haughtiness n ▷ **haughty**

haughtinesses n ▷ **haughty**

haughty adj (**-tier, -tiest**) proud, arrogant > **haughtily** adv > **haughtiness** n (pl **-es**)

haul v (**-s, -ing, -ed**) pull or drag with effort ▶ n (pl **-s**) amount gained by effort or theft

haulage n (pl **-s**) (charge for) transporting goods

haulages n ▷ **haulage**

hauled v ▷ **haul**

haulier n (pl **-s**) firm or person that transports goods by road

hauliers n ▷ **haulier**

hauling v ▷ **haul**

hauls v, n ▷ **haul**

haunch n (pl -**es**) human hip or fleshy hindquarter of an animal
haunches n ▷ **haunch**

haunt v (-**s**, -**ing**, -**ed**) visit in the form of a ghost ▶ n (pl -**s**) place visited frequently

haunted adj frequented by ghosts ▶ v ▷ **haunt**

haunting adj memorably beautiful or sad ▶ v ▷ **haunt**
haunts v, n ▷ **haunt**

hauteur n (pl -**s**) haughtiness
hauteurs n ▷ **hauteur**

have v (**has**, **having**, **had**) possess, hold

haven n (pl -**s**) place of safety
havens n ▷ **haven**
having v ▷ **have**

havoc n (pl -**s**) disorder and confusion
havocs n ▷ **havoc**

haw n (pl -**s**) hawthorn berry

hawk[1] n (pl -**s**) bird of prey with a short hooked bill and very good eyesight
> **hawkish, hawklike** adj

hawk[2] v (-**s**, -**ing**, -**ed**) offer (goods) for sale in the street or door-to-door
> **hawker** n (pl -**s**)

hawk[3] v (-**s**, -**ing**, -**ed**) cough noisily
hawked v ▷ **hawk**[2, 3]
hawker n ▷ **hawk**[2]
hawkers n ▷ **hawk**[2, 3]
hawking v ▷ **hawk**[2, 3]
hawkish adj ▷ **hawk**[1]
hawks n ▷ **hawk**[1] ▶ v ▷ **hawk**[2, 3]
hawklike adj ▷ **hawk**[1]
haws n ▷ **haw**

hawser n (pl -**s**) large rope used on a ship
hawsers n ▷ **hawser**

hawthorn n (pl -**s**) thorny shrub or tree
hawthorns n ▷ **hawthorn**

hay n (pl **hays**) grass cut and dried as fodder
hays n ▷ **hay**

haystack n (pl -**s**) large pile of stored hay
haystacks n ▷ **haystack**

haywire adj informal not functioning properly

hazard n (pl -**s**) something that could be dangerous ▶ v (-**s**, -**ing**, -**ed**) put in danger > **hazardous** adj
hazarded v ▷ **hazard**
hazarding v ▷ **hazard**
hazardous adj ▷ **hazard**
hazards n, v ▷ **hazard**

haze n (pl -**s**) mist, often caused by heat

hazel n (pl -**s**) small tree producing edible nuts ▶ adj (of eyes) greenish-brown > **hazelnut** n (pl -**s**)
hazelnut n ▷ **hazel**
hazelnuts n ▷ **hazel**
hazels n ▷ **hazel**
hazes n ▷ **haze**
hazier adj ▷ **hazy**
haziest adj ▷ **hazy**
hazy adj (-**zier**, -**ziest**) not clear, misty

he pron refers to: male person or animal ▶ n (pl -**s**) male person or animal

head n (pl -**s**) upper or front part of the body, containing the sense organs and the brain ▶ adj chief, principal ▶ v (-**s**, -**ing**, -**ed**) be at the top or front of

headache n (pl -**s**) continuous pain in the head
headaches n ▷ **headache**
headed v ▷ **head**

header n (pl -**s**) striking a ball with the head
headers n ▷ **header**

headhunt v (-**s**, -**ing**, -**ed**) (of a company) approach and offer a job to (a person working for a rival company)
> **headhunter** n (pl -**s**)
headhunted v ▷ **headhunt**
headhunter n ▷ **headhunt**
headhunters n ▷ **headhunt**
headhunting v ▷ **headhunt**
headhunts v ▷ **headhunt**
headier adj ▷ **heady**
headiest adj ▷ **heady**

heading n (pl -**s**) title written or printed at the top of a page ▶ v ▷ **head**
headings n ▷ **heading**

headland n (pl -**s**) area of land jutting

out into the sea
headlands n ▷ **headland**

headline n (pl -s) title at the top of a newspaper article, esp. on the front page

headlong adv, adj with the head first

heads adv informal with the side of a coin which has a portrait of a head on it uppermost ▶ n, v ▷ **head**

headway n (pl -s) progress
headways n ▷ **headway**

headwind n (pl -s) wind blowing against the course of an aircraft or ship
headwinds n ▷ **headwind**

heady adj (-dier, -diest) intoxicating or exciting

heal v (-s, -ing, -ed) make or become well >**healer** n (pl -s)
healed v ▷ **heal**
healer n ▷ **heal**
healers n ▷ **heal**
healing v ▷ **heal**
heals v ▷ **heal**

health n (pl -s) normal (good) condition of someone's body
healthier adj ▷ **healthy**
healthiest adj ▷ **healthy**
healthily adv ▷ **healthy**
healths n ▷ **health**

healthy adj (-thier, -thiest) having good health >**healthily** adv

heap n (pl -s) pile of things one on top of another ▶ v (-s, -ing, -ed) gather into a pile
heaped v ▷ **heap**
heaping v ▷ **heap**
heaps n, v ▷ **heap**

hear v (-s, -ing, heard) perceive (a sound) by ear ▶ v **hearer** n (pl -s)
heard v ▷ **hear**
hearer n ▷ **hear**
hearers n ▷ **hear**

hearing n (pl -s) ability to hear ▶ v ▷ **hear**
hearings n ▷ **hearing**
hears n ▷ **hear**

hearsay n (pl -s) gossip, rumour
hearsays n ▷ **hearsay**

hearse n (pl -s) funeral car used to carry a coffin
hearses n ▷ **hearse**

heart n (pl -s) organ that pumps blood round the body

hearten v (-s, -ing, -ed) encourage, make cheerful
heartened v ▷ **hearten**
heartening v ▷ **hearten**
heartens v ▷ **hearten**

hearth n (pl -s) floor of a fireplace
hearths n ▷ **hearth**

heartier adj ▷ **hearty**
heartiest adj ▷ **hearty**
heartily adv ▷ **hearty**
hearts n ▷ **heart**

hearty adj (-tier, -tiest) substantial, nourishing >**heartily** adv

heat v (-s, -ing, -ed) make or become hot ▶ n (pl -s) state of being hot >**heater** n (pl -s)
heated v ▷ **heat** ▶ adj angry and excited >**heatedly** adv
heatedly adv ▷ **heated**
heater n ▷ **heat**
heaters n ▷ **heat**

heath n (pl -s) BRIT area of open uncultivated land

heathen adj, n (pl -s) (of) a person who does not believe in an established religion
heathens n ▷ **heathen**

heather n (pl -s) low-growing plant with small purple, pinkish, or white flowers, growing on heaths and mountains
heathers n ▷ **heather**
heaths n ▷ **heath**
heating v ▷ **heat**
heats v, n ▷ **heat**

heave v (-ves, -ving, -ved) lift with effort ▶ n (pl -s) heaving
heaved v ▷ **heave**

heaven n (pl -s) place believed to be the home of God, where good people go when they die
heavenly adj of or like heaven
heavens n ▷ **heaven**

heaves v, n ▷ **heave**
heavier adj ▷ **heavy**
heaviest adj ▷ **heavy**
heavily adv ▷ **heavy**
heaviness n ▷ **heavy**
heavinesses n ▷ **heavy**
heaving v ▷ **heave**
heavy adj (-vier, -viest) of great weight > **heavily** adv > **heaviness** n (pl -es)
heckle v (-les, -ling, -led) interrupt (a public speaker) with comments, questions, or taunts > **heckler** n (pl -s)
heckled v ▷ **heckle**
heckler n ▷ **heckle**
hecklers n ▷ **heckle**
heckles v ▷ **heckle**
heckling v ▷ **heckle**
hectare n (pl -s) one hundred ares or 10 000 square metres (2.471 acres)
hectares n ▷ **hectare**
hectic adj rushed or busy
hector v (-s, -ing, -ed) bully
hectored v ▷ **hector**
hectoring v ▷ **hector**
hectors v ▷ **hector**
hedge n (pl -s) row of bushes forming a barrier or boundary ▶ v (-ges, -ging, -ged) be evasive or noncommittal
hedged v ▷ **hedge**
hedgehog n (pl -s) small mammal with a protective covering of spines
hedgehogs n ▷ **hedgehog**
hedgerow n (pl -s) bushes forming a hedge
hedgerows n ▷ **hedgerow**
hedges n, v ▷ **hedge**
hedging v ▷ **hedge**
hedonism n (pl -s) doctrine that pleasure is the most important thing in life > **hedonist** n (pl -s) > **hedonistic** adj
hedonisms n ▷ **hedonism**
hedonist n ▷ **hedonism**
hedonistic n ▷ **hedonism**
hedonists n ▷ **hedonism**
heed n (pl -s) careful attention ▶ v (-s, -ing, -ed) pay careful attention to

heeded v ▷ **heed**
heeding v ▷ **heed**
heedless adj taking no notice of
heeds v, n ▷ **heed**
heel[1] n (pl -s) back part of the foot ▶ v (-s, -ing, -ed) repair the heel of (a shoe)
heel[2] v (-s, -ing, -ed) (foll. by over) lean to one side
heeled v ▷ **heel**[1, 2]
heeler n (pl -s) AUST & NZ dog that herds cattle by biting at their heels
heelers n ▷ **heeler**
heeling v ▷ **heel**[1, 2]
heels n ▷ **heel**[1] ▶ v ▷ **heel**[1, 2]
heftier adj ▷ **hefty**
heftiest adj ▷ **hefty**
hefty adj (-tier, -tiest) large, heavy, or strong
hegemonies n ▷ **hegemony**
hegemony n (pl -nies) political domination
hegira n (pl -s) Mohammed's flight from Mecca to Medina in 622 AD
hegiras n ▷ **hegira**
heifer n (pl -s) young cow
heifers n ▷ **heifer**
height n (pl -s) distance from base to top
heighten v (-s, -ing, -ed) make or become higher or more intense
heightened v ▷ **heighten**
heightening v ▷ **heighten**
heightens v ▷ **heighten**
heights n ▷ **height**
heinous adj evil and shocking
heir n (pl -s) person entitled to inherit property or rank > **heiress** n fem (pl -es)
heiresses n ▷ **heiress**
heirloom n (pl -s) object that has belonged to a family for generations
heirlooms n ▷ **heirloom**
heirs n ▷ **heir**
held v ▷ **hold**[1]
helical adj spiral
helices n ▷ **helix**
heliport n (pl -s) airport for helicopters
heliports n ▷ **heliport**
helium n (pl -s) CHEM very light

colourless odourless gas

heliums n ▷ **helium**

helix n (pl **-ices, -ixes**) spiral

helixes n ▷ **helix**

hell n (pl **-s**) place believed to be where wicked people go when they die
> **hellish** adj

hellbent adj (foll. by **on**) intent

hellish adj ▷ **hell**

hello interj expression of greeting or surprise

hells n ▷ **hell**

helm n (pl **-s**) tiller or wheel for steering a ship

helmet n (pl **-s**) hard hat worn for protection

helmets n ▷ **helmet**

helms n ▷ **helm**

help v (**-s, -ing, -ed**) make something easier, better, or quicker for (someone)
▶ n (pl **-s**) assistance or support
> **helper** n (pl **-s**) > **helpful** adj

helped v ▷ **help**

helper n ▷ **help**

helpers n ▷ **help**

helpful adj ▷ **help**

helping n (pl **-s**) single portion of food
▶ v ▷ **help**

helpings n ▷ **helping**

helpless adj weak or incapable
> **helplessly** adv

helplessly adv ▷ **helpless**

helpline n (pl **-s**) telephone line set aside for callers to contact an organization for help with a problem

helplines n ▷ **helpline**

helpmate n (pl **-s**) companion and helper, esp. a husband or wife

helpmates n ▷ **helpmate**

helps v, n ▷ **help**

hem n (pl **-s**) bottom edge of a garment, folded under and stitched down ▶ v (**-s, -mming, -mmed**) provide with a hem

hemline n (pl **-s**) level to which the hem of a skirt hangs

hemlines n ▷ **hemline**

hemlock n (pl **-s**) poison made from a plant with spotted stems and small

white flowers

hemlocks n ▷ **hemlock**

hemmed v ▷ **hem**

hemming v ▷ **hem**

hemp n (pl **-s**) (also **cannabis**) Asian plant with tough fibres

hemps n ▷ **hemp**

hems n, v ▷ **hem**

hen n (pl **-s**) female domestic fowl

hence conj for this reason ▶ adv from this time

henchman n (pl **-men**) person employed to carry out orders

henchmen n ▷ **henchman**

henna n (pl **-s**) reddish dye made from a shrub or tree ▶ v (**-s, -ing, -ed**) dye (the hair) with henna

hennaed v ▷ **henna**

hennaing v ▷ **henna**

hennas n, v ▷ **henna**

henries n ▷ **henry**

henry n (pl **-ries, -rys**) unit of electrical inductance

henrys n ▷ **henry**

hens n ▷ **hen**

heptagon n (pl **-s**) geometric figure with seven sides

heptagons n ▷ **heptagon**

her pron refers to a female person or animal or anything personified as feminine when the object of a sentence or clause ▶ adj belonging to her

herald n (pl **-s**) person who announces important news ▶ v (**-s, -ing, -ed**) signal the approach of

heralded v ▷ **herald**

heraldic adj ▷ **heraldry**

heralding v ▷ **herald**

heraldries n ▷ **heraldry**

heraldry n (pl **-ries**) study of coats of arms and family trees > **heraldic** adj

heralds n, v ▷ **herald**

herb n (pl **-s**) plant used for flavouring in cookery, and in medicine
> **herbal** adj

herbal adj ▷ **herb**

herbs n ▷ herb

herd n (pl -s) group of animals feeding and living together ▶ v (-s, -ing, -ed) collect into a herd

herded v ▷ herd

herding v ▷ herd

herds n, v ▷ herd

herdsman n (pl -men) man who looks after a herd of animals

herdsmen n ▷ herdsman

here adv in, at, or to this place or point

hereby adv by means of or as a result of this

heredities n ▷ heredity

heredity n (pl -ties) passing on of characteristics from one generation to another

herein adv in this place, matter, or document

heresies n ▷ heresy

heresy n (pl -sies) opinion contrary to accepted opinion or belief

heretic n (pl -s) person who holds unorthodox opinions >heretical ▶ adj

heretical n ▷ heretic

heretics n ▷ heretic

herewith adv with this

heritage n (pl -s) something inherited

heritages n ▷ heritage

hermetic adj sealed so as to be airtight >hermetically adv

hermetically adv ▷ hermetic

hermit n (pl -s) person living in solitude, esp. for religious reasons

hermits n ▷ hermit

hernia n (pl -s) protrusion of an organ or part through the lining of the surrounding body cavity

hernias n ▷ hernia

hero n (pl -es) principal character in a film, book, etc ▷ heroine n fem (pl -s) >heroism n (pl -s)

heroes n ▷ hero

heroic adj courageous >heroically adv

heroically adv ▷ heroic

heroics pl n extravagant behaviour

heroin n (pl -s) highly addictive drug derived from morphine

heroine n ▷ hero

heroines n ▷ hero

heroins n ▷ heroin

heroism n ▷ hero

heroisms n ▷ hero

heron n (pl -s) long-legged wading bird

herons n ▷ heron

herpes n (pl -es) any of several inflammatory skin diseases, including shingles and cold sores

herpeses n ▷ herpes

herring n (pl -s) important food fish of northern seas

herrings n ▷ herring

hertz n (pl -es) PHYSICS unit of frequency

hertzes n ▷ hertz

hes n ▷ he

hesitancies n ▷ hesitant

hesitancy n ▷ hesitant

hesitant adj undecided or wavering >hesitantly adv >hesitancy n (pl -cies)

hesitantly adv ▷ hesitant

hesitate v (-tes, -ting, -ted) be slow or uncertain in doing something >hesitation n (pl -s)

hesitated v ▷ hesitate

hesitates v ▷ hesitate

hesitating v ▷ hesitate

hesitation n ▷ hesitate

hesitations n ▷ hesitate

hessian n (pl -s) coarse jute fabric

hessians n ▷ hessian

hew v (-s, -ing, -ed or hewn) cut with an axe

hewed v ▷ hew

hewing v ▷ hew

hewn v ▷ hew

hews v ▷ hew

> **hex** n (**hexes**). A hex is a curse or spell. This is a really useful word to remember when you have an X, as there is likely to be an E or H on the board already.

hexagon n (pl -s) geometrical figure with six sides >hexagonal adj

hexagonal adj ▷ hexagon

hexagons n ▷ hexagon

hey interj expression of surprise or for catching attention

heyday n (pl -s) time of greatest success, prime

heydays n ▷ **heyday**

hi interj. Hi is an informal word for **hello**. This everyday word is worth keeping in mind when you want to form a word adjacent to a parallel word below or above. Hi scores 5 points.

hiatus n (pl -tuses, -tus) pause or interruption in continuity

hiatuses n ▷ **hiatus**

hibiscus n (pl -cuses) tropical plant with large brightly coloured flowers

hibiscuses n ▷ **hibiscus**

hiccough n, v ▷ **hiccup**

hiccoughed v ▷ **hiccup**

hiccoughing v ▷ **hiccup**

hiccoughs n, v ▷ **hiccup**

hiccup, hiccough n (pl -s) spasm of the breathing organs with a sharp coughlike sound informal ▶ v (-s, -pping, -pped) make a hiccup

hiccupped v ▷ **hiccup**

hiccupping v ▷ **hiccup**

hiccups n, v ▷ **hiccup**

hick n (pl -s) US, AUST & NZ informal unsophisticated country person

hickories n ▷ **hickory**

hickory n (pl -ries) N American nut-bearing tree

hicks n ▷ **hick**

hid v ▷ **hide¹**

hidden v ▷ **hide¹**

hide¹ v (-des, -ding, hid, hidden) put (oneself or an object) somewhere difficult to see or find ▶ n (pl -s) place of concealment, esp. for a bird-watcher

hide² n (pl -s) skin of an animal

hideous adj ugly, revolting > **hideously** adv

hideously adv ▷ **hideous**

hideout n (pl -s) place to hide in

hideouts n ▷ **hideout**

hides v ▷ **hide¹** ▶ n ▷ **hide¹, ²**

hiding n (pl -s) slang severe beating

▶ v ▷ **hide¹**

hidings n ▷ **hiding**

high adj (-er, -est) of a great height ▶ adv at or to a high level > **highly** adv

highbrow adj, n (pl -s) intellectual and serious (person)

highbrows n ▷ **highbrow**

higher adj ▷ **high**

highest adj ▷ **high**

highly adv ▷ **high**

highway n (pl -s) US, AUST & NZ main road

highways n ▷ **highway**

hijack v (-s, -ing, -ed) of a great height seize control of (an aircraft or other vehicle) while travelling > **hijacker** n (pl -s)

hijacked v ▷ **hijack**

hijacker n ▷ **hijack**

hijackers n ▷ **hijack**

hijacking v ▷ **hijack**

hijacks v ▷ **hijack**

hike n (pl -s) long walk in the country, esp. for pleasure ▶ v (-kes, -king, -ked) go for a long walk > **hiker** n (pl -s)

hiked v ▷ **hike**

hiker n ▷ **hike**

hikers n ▷ **hike**

hikes n, v ▷ **hike**

hiking v ▷ **hike**

hill n (pl -s) raised part of the earth's surface, less high than a mountain > **hilly** adj (-lier, -lliest)

hillier adj ▷ **hill**

hilliest adj ▷ **hill**

hillock n (pl -s) small hill

hillocks n ▷ **hillock**

hills n ▷ **hill**

hilly adj ▷ **hill**

hilt n (pl -s) handle of a sword or knife

hilts n ▷ **hilt**

him pron refers to a male person or animal when the object of a sentence or clause

hind¹ adj (-er, -most) situated at the back

hind² n (pl -s) female deer

hinder adj ▷ **hind¹** ▶ v (-s, -ing, -ed) get in the way of > **hindrance** n (pl -s)

hindered v ▷ hinder
hindering v ▷ hinder
hinders v ▷ hinder
hindmost adj ▷ hind[1]
hindrance n ▷ hinder
hindrances n ▷ hinder
hinds n ▷ hind[2]

hinge n (pl -s) device for holding together two parts so that one can swing freely ▶ v (-ges, -ging, -ged) (foll. by on) depend (on)
hinged v ▷ hinge
hinges v, n ▷ hinge
hinging v ▷ hinge

hint n (pl -s) indirect suggestion ▶ v (-s, -ing, -ed) suggest indirectly
hinted v ▷ hint
hinting v ▷ hint
hints n, v ▷ hint

hip[1] n (pl -s) either side of the body between the pelvis and the thigh
hip[2] n (pl -s) rosehip
hippie adj, n (pl -s) ▷ hippy
hippies n ▷ hippy
hippo n (pl -s) informal hippopotamus
hippos n ▷ hippo
hippy adj, n (pl -pies) (esp. in the 1960s) (of) a person whose behaviour and dress imply a rejection of conventional values
hips n ▷ hip[1, 2]
hire v (-res, -ring, -red) pay to have temporary use of ▶ n (pl -s) hiring
hired v ▷ hire
hireling n (pl -s) person who works only for wages
hirelings n ▷ hireling
hires v, n ▷ hire
hiring v ▷ hire
hirsute adj hairy
his pron, adj (something) belonging to him
hiss n (pl -es) sound like that of a long s (as an expression of contempt) ▶ v (-es, -ing, -ed) utter a hiss
hissed v ▷ hiss
hisses n, v ▷ hiss
hissing v ▷ hiss

historic adj famous or significant in history
histories n ▷ history
history n (pl -ries) (record or account of) past events and developments
hit v (-s, -tting, hit) strike, touch forcefully ▶ n (pl -s) hitting ▶ adj sometimes successful and sometimes not
hitch n (pl -es) minor problem ▶ v (-es, -ing, -ed) informal obtain (a lift) by hitchhiking
hitched v ▷ hitch
hitches n, v ▷ hitch
hitching v ▷ hitch
hither adv old-fashioned to or towards this place
hitherto adv until this time
hits n, v ▷ hit
hitting v ▷ hit
hive n (pl -s) ▷ beehive
hives n ▷ hive

hm or **hmm** interj. This is a noise that people make when they are thinking or considering something. Both forms of this word are useful because neither contains a vowel, which is great if you have no vowels on your rack. Hm scores 5 points, while hmm scores 8.

ho interj. Ho is a noise people make when they laugh. This little word is useful when you want to go in two directions at once. It's also worth remembering that ho is oh backwards: if you can't use one, you might be able to use the other. Ho scores 5 points.

hoard n (pl -s) store hidden away for future use ▶ v (-s, -ing, -ed) save or store ▶ hoarder n (pl -s)
hoarded v ▷ hoard
hoarder n ▷ hoard
hoarders n ▷ hoard
hoarding n (pl -s) large board for displaying advertisements ▶ v ▷ hoard
hoardings n ▷ hoarding

hoards n, v ▷ hoard
hoarier adj ▷ hoary
hoariest adj ▷ hoary
hoarse adj (**-ser**, **-sest**) (of a voice) rough and unclear > **hoarsely** adv > **hoarseness** n (pl **-es**)
hoarsely adv ▷ hoarse
hoarseness n ▷ hoarse
hoarsenesses n ▷ hoarse
hoarsest adj ▷ hoarse
hoarsest adj ▷ hoarse
hoary adj (**-rier**, **-riest**) grey or white(-haired)
hoax n (pl **-es**) deception or trick ▶ v (**-es**, **-ing**, **-ed**) deceive or play a trick upon > **hoaxer** n
hoaxed v ▷ hoax
hoaxer n ▷ hoax
hoaxers n ▷ hoax
hoaxes n, v ▷ hoax
hoaxing v ▷ hoax
hob n (pl **-s**) BRIT flat top part of a cooker, or a separate flat surface, containing gas or electric rings for cooking on
hobbies n ▷ hobby
hobble v (**-les**, **-ling**, **-led**) walk lamely
hobbled v ▷ hobble
hobbles v ▷ hobble
hobbling v ▷ hobble
hobby n (pl **-bies**) activity pursued in one's spare time
hobnob v (**-s**, **-nobbing**, **-nobbed**) (foll. by **with**) be on friendly terms (with)
hobnobbed v ▷ hobnob
hobnobbing v ▷ hobnob
hobnobs v ▷ hobnob
hobo n (pl **-s**) US, AUST & NZ tramp or vagrant
hobos n ▷ hobo
hobs n ▷ hob
hock¹ n (pl **-s**) joint in the back leg of an animal such as a horse that corresponds to the human ankle
hock² n BRIT white German wine
hock³ v (**-s**, **-ing**, **-ed**) informal pawn
hocked v ▷ hock
hockey n (pl **-s**) team game played on a field with a ball and curved sticks
hockeys n ▷ hockey
hocking v ▷ hock
hocks n ▷ hock¹, ² ▶ v ▷ hock³
hod n (pl **-s**) open wooden box attached to a pole, for carrying bricks or mortar
hods n ▷ hod
hoe n (pl **-s**) long-handled tool used for loosening soil or weeding ▶ v (**-s**, **-ing**, **-d**) scrape or weed with a hoe
hoed v ▷ hoe
hoeing v ▷ hoe
hoes n, v ▷ hoe
hog n (pl **-s**) castrated male pig informal ▶ v (**-s**, **-gging**, **-gged**) informal take more than one's share of
hogged v ▷ hog
hogging v ▷ hog
hogmanay n (pl **-s**) (in Scotland) New Year's Eve
hogmanays n ▷ hogmanay
hogs n, v ▷ hog
hogshead n (pl **-s**) large cask
hogsheads n ▷ hogshead
hogwash n (pl **-es**) informal nonsense
hogwashes n ▷ hogwash
hoick v (**-s**, **-ing**, **-ed**) raise abruptly and sharply
hoicked v ▷ hoick
hoicking v ▷ hoick
hoicks v ▷ hoick
hoist v (**-s**, **-ing**, **-ed**) raise or lift up ▶ n (pl **-s**) device for lifting things
hoisted v ▷ hoist
hoisting v ▷ hoist
hoists v, n ▷ hoist
hold¹ v (**-s**, **-ing**, **held**) keep or support in or with the hands or arms ▶ n (pl **-s**) act or way of holding > **holder** n (pl **-s**)
hold² n (pl **-s**) cargo compartment in a ship or aircraft
holdall n (pl **-s**) large strong travelling bag
holdalls n ▷ holdall
holder n ▷ hold¹
holders n ▷ hold¹
holding n (pl **-s**) property, such as land or stocks and shares ▶ v ▷ hold¹

holds n ▷ hold¹, ² ▶ v ▷ hold¹
holdup n (pl -s) armed robbery
holdups n ▷ holdup
hole n (pl -s) area hollowed out in a solid ▶ v (-les, -ling, -led) make holes in
holed v ▷ hole
holes n, v ▷ hole
holiday n (pl -s) time spent away from home for rest or recreation
holidays n ▷ holiday
holier adj ▷ holy
holiest adj ▷ holy
holiness n (pl -es) state of being holy
holinesses n ▷ holiness
holing v ▷ hole
holisms n ▷ holism
holistic adj considering the complete person, physically and mentally, in the treatment of an illness ▷ holism n (pl -s)
hollies n ▷ holly
hollow adj having a hole or space inside ▶ n (pl -s) cavity or space ▶ v (-s, -ing, -ed) form a hollow in
hollowed v ▷ hollow
hollowing v ▷ hollow
hollows n, v ▷ hollow
holly n (pl -llies) evergreen tree with prickly leaves and red berries
hologram n (pl -s) three-dimensional photographic image
holograms n ▷ hologram
holster n (pl -s) leather case for a pistol, hung from a belt
holsters n ▷ holster
holy adj (-lier, -liest) of God or a god
homage n (pl -s) show of respect or honour towards someone or something
homages n ▷ homage
home n (pl -s) place where one lives ▶ adj of one's home, birthplace, or native country SPORT ▶ adv to or at home ▶ v (-mes, -ming, -med) (foll. by in or in on) direct towards (a point or target) ▶ homeward adj, adv
> homewards adv
homed v ▷ home

homeland n (pl -s) country from which a person's ancestors came
homelands n ▷ homeland
homeless adj having nowhere to live ▶ pl n people who have nowhere to live
> homelessness n (pl -es)
homelessness n ▷ homeless
homelessnesses n ▷ homeless
homelier adj ▷ homely
homeliest adj ▷ homely
homely adj (-lier, -liest) simple, ordinary, and comfortable
homemade adj made at home or on the premises
homes n, v ▷ home
homesick adj sad because missing one's home and family
> homesickness n (pl -es)
homesickness n ▷ homesick
homesicknesses n ▷ homesick
homeward adj, adv ▷ home
homewards adv ▷ home
homework n (pl -s) school work done at home
homeworks n ▷ homework
homicidal adj ▷ homicide
homicide n (pl -s) killing of a human being ▶ homicidal adj
homicides n ▷ homicide
homilies n ▷ homily
homily n (pl -lies) speech telling people how they should behave
homing v ▷ home
hominid n (pl -s) man or any extinct forerunner of man
hominids n ▷ hominid
homonym n (pl -s) word spelt or pronounced the same as another, but with a different meaning
homonyms n ▷ homonym
hone v (-nes, -ning, -ned) sharpen
honed v ▷ hone
hones v ▷ hone
honest adj (-er, -est) truthful and moral > honestly adv
honester adj ▷ honest
honestest adj ▷ honest
honesties n ▷ honesty

honestly adv ▷ honest

honesty n (pl **-ties**) quality of being honest

honey n (pl **-s**) sweet edible sticky substance made by bees from nectar
honeys n ▷ honey

hongi n (pl **-s**) NZ Maori greeting in which people touch noses
hongis n ▷ hongi
honing v ▷ hone

honk n (pl **-s**) sound made by a car horn ▶ v (**-s, -ing, -ed**) (cause to) make this sound
honked v ▷ honk
honking v ▷ honk
honks n, v ▷ honk

honorary adj held or given only as an honour

honour n (pl **-s**) sense of honesty and fairness ▶ v (**-s, -ing, -ed**) give praise and attention to
honoured v ▷ honour
honouring v ▷ honour
honours n, v ▷ honour ▶ pl n university degree of a higher standard than an ordinary degree

hood¹ n (pl **-s**) head covering, often attached to a coat or jacket
hood² n (pl **-s**) CHIEFLY US slang hoodlum
hooded adj (of a garment) having a hood

hoodlum n (pl **-s**) slang violent criminal, gangster
hoodlums n ▷ hoodlum

hoodoo n (pl **-s**) (cause of) bad luck
hoodoos n ▷ hoodoo
hoods n ▷ hood¹, ²

hoodwink v (**-s, -ing, -ed**) trick, deceive
hoodwinked v ▷ hoodwink
hoodwinking v ▷ hoodwink
hoodwinks v ▷ hoodwink

hoof n (pl **hooves, hoofs**) horny covering of the foot of a horse, deer, etc
hoofs n ▷ hoof

hook n (pl **-s**) curved piece of metal, plastic, etc, used to hang, hold, or pull something ▶ v (**-s, -ing, -ed**) fasten or catch (as if) with a hook

hookah n (pl **-s**) oriental pipe in which smoke is drawn through water and a long tube
hookahs n ▷ hookah

hooked adj bent like a hook ▶ v ▷ hook

hooker n (pl **-s**) CHIEFLY US slang prostitute
hookers n ▷ hooker
hooking v ▷ hook
hooks n, v ▷ hook

hookup n (pl **-s**) linking of radio or television stations
hookups n ▷ hookup

hookworm n (pl **-s**) blood-sucking worm with hooked mouthparts
hookworms n ▷ hookworm

hooligan n (pl **-s**) rowdy young person
> **hooliganism** n (pl **-s**)
hooliganism n ▷ hooligan
hooliganisms n ▷ hooligan
hooligans n ▷ hooligan

hoon n AUST & NZ slang loutish youth who drives irresponsibly
hoons n ▷ hoon

hoop n (pl **-s**) rigid circular band, used esp. as a child's toy or for animals to jump through in the circus

hoopla n (pl **-s**) fairground game in which hoops are thrown over objects in an attempt to win them
hooplas n ▷ hoopla
hoops n ▷ hoop

hooray interj ▷ hurrah

hoot n (pl **-s**) sound of a car horn ▶ v (**-s, -ing, -ed**) sound (a car horn)
hooted v ▷ hoot

hooter n (pl **-s**) device that hoots
hooters n ▷ hooter
hooting v ▷ hoot
hoots n, v ▷ hoot

hoover n® (pl **-s**) vacuum cleaner ▶ v (**-s, -ing, -ed**) clean with a vacuum cleaner
hoovered v ▷ hoover
hoovering v ▷ hoover
hoovers n, v ▷ hoover

hooves n ▷ hoof

hop¹ v (**-s, -pping, -pped**) jump on one foot ▶ n (pl **-s**) instance of hopping

hop² n (pl **-s**) (often pl) climbing plant, the dried flowers of which are used to make beer

hope v (**-pes, -ping, -ped**) want (something) to happen or be true ▶ n (pl **-s**) expectation of something desired > **hopeless** adj

hoped v ▷ hope

hopeful adj having, expressing, or inspiring hope ▶ n (pl **-s**) person considered to be on the brink of success

hopefuls n ▷ hopeful

hopeless adj ▷ hope

hopes v, n ▷ hope

hoping v ▷ hope

hopped v ▷ hop¹

hopper n (pl **-s**) container for storing substances such as grain or sand

hoppers n ▷ hopper

hopping v ▷ hop¹

hops n ▷ hop¹, ², v ▷ hop¹

horde n (pl **-s**) large crowd

hordes n ▷ horde

horizon n (pl **-s**) apparent line that divides the earth and the sky

horizons n ▷ horizon ▶ pl n limits of scope, interest, or knowledge

hormonal adj ▷ hormone

hormone n (pl **-s**) substance secreted by certain glands which stimulates certain organs of the body > **hormonal** adj

hormones n ▷ hormone

horn n (pl **-s**) one of a pair of bony growths sticking out of the heads of cattle, sheep, etc > **horned** adj

hornbeam n (pl **-s**) tree with smooth grey bark

hornbeams n ▷ hornbeam

hornbill n bird with a bony growth on its large beak

hornbills n ▷ hornbill

horned n ▷ horn

hornet n (pl **-s**) large wasp with a severe sting

hornets n ▷ hornet

hornpipe n (pl **-s**) (music for) a solo dance, traditionally performed by sailors

hornpipes n ▷ hornpipe

horns n ▷ horn

horny adj (**-nier, -niest**) of or like horn

horrible adj disagreeable, unpleasant > **horribly** adv

horribly adv ▷ horrible

horrid adj disagreeable, unpleasant

horrific adj causing horror

horrified v ▷ horrify

horrifies v ▷ horrify

horrify v (**-fies, -fying, -fied**) cause to feel horror or shock

horrifying v ▷ horrify

horror n (pl **-s**) (thing or person causing) terror or hatred

horrors n ▷ horror

horse n (pl **-s**) large animal with hooves, a mane, and a tail, used for riding and pulling carts etc

horseflies n ▷ horsefly

horsefly n (pl **-flies**) large bloodsucking fly

horseman n (pl **-men**) person riding a horse

horsemen n ▷ horseman

horses n ▷ horse

horsey, horsy adj (**-sier, -siest**) very keen on horses

horsier adj ▷ horsey

horsiest adj ▷ horsey

horsy adj ▷ horsey

hosanna interj exclamation of praise to God

hose¹ n (pl **-s**) flexible pipe for conveying liquid ▶ v (**-ses, -sing, -sed**) water with a hose

hose² n (pl **-s**) stockings, socks, and tights

hosed v ▷ hose¹

hoses n ▷ hose¹, ², v ▷ hose¹

hosieries n ▷ hosiery

hosiery n (pl **-ries**) stockings, socks, and tights collectively

hosing v ▷ **hose**[1]

hospice n (pl -s) nursing home for the terminally ill

hospices n ▷ **hospice**

hospital n (pl -s) place where people who are ill are looked after and treated

hospitals n ▷ **hospital**

host[1] n (pl -s) man who entertains guests, esp. in his own home ▶ v (-s, -ing, -ed) be the host of

host[2] n (pl -s) large number

hostage n (pl -s) person who is illegally held prisoner until certain demands are met by other people

hostages n ▷ **hostage**

hosted v ▷ **host**[1]

hostel n (pl -s) building providing accommodation at a low cost for a specific group of people such as students, travellers, homeless people, etc

hostelries n ▷ **hostelry**

hostelry n (pl -ries) old-fashioned or facetious inn, pub

hostels n ▷ **hostel**

hostess n (pl -es) woman who entertains guests, esp. in her own home

hostesses n ▷ **hostess**

hostile adj unfriendly

hosting v ▷ **host**[1]

hosts n ▷ **host**[1], [2] ▶ v ▷ **host**[1]

hot adj (-ter, -test) having a high temperature in trouble > **hotly** adv

hotbed n (pl -s) any place encouraging a particular activity

hotbeds n ▷ **hotbed**

hotel n (pl -s) commercial establishment providing lodging and meals

hotelier n (pl -s) owner or manager of a hotel

hoteliers n ▷ **hotelier**

hotels n ▷ **hotel**

hotfoot adv informal quickly and eagerly

hothouse n (pl -s) greenhouse

hothouses n ▷ **hothouse**

hotline n (pl -s) direct telephone link for emergency use

hotlines n ▷ **hotline**

hotly adv ▷ **hot**

hotplate n (pl -s) heated metal surface on an electric cooker

hotplates n ▷ **hotplate**

hotter adj ▷ **hot**

hottest adj ▷ **hot**

hound n (pl -s) hunting dog ▶ v (-s, -ing, -ed) pursue relentlessly

hounded v ▷ **hound**

hounding v ▷ **hound**

hounds n, v ▷ **hound**

hour n (pl -s) twenty-fourth part of a day, sixty minutes

houri n (pl -s) ISLAM any of the nymphs of paradise

houris n ▷ **houri**

hourly adj, adv (happening) every hour

hours pl n period regularly appointed for work or business ▶ n ▷ **hour**

house n (pl -s) building used as a home ▶ v (-ses, -sing, -sed) give accommodation to

housed v ▷ **house**

houses n, v ▷ **house**

housing n (pl -s) (providing of) houses ▶ v ▷ **house**

housings n ▷ **housing**

hovea n (pl -s) Australian plant with purple flowers

hoveas n ▷ **hovea**

hovel n (pl -s) small dirty house or hut

hovels n ▷ **hovel**

hover v (-s, -ing, -red) (of a bird etc) remain suspended in one place in the air

hovered v ▷ **hover**

hovering v ▷ **hover**

hovers v ▷ **hover**

how adv in what way, by what means

howdah n (pl -s) canopied seat on an elephant's back

howdahs n ▷ **howdah**

however adv nevertheless

howitzer n (pl -s) large gun firing shells at a steep angle

howitzers n ▷ **howitzer**

howl n (pl **-s**) loud wailing cry ▶ v (**-s**, **-ing**, **-ed**) utter a howl

howled v ▷ **howl**

howler n (pl **-s**) informal stupid mistake

howlers n ▷ **howler**

howling v ▷ **howl**

howls n, v ▷ **howl**

hox v (**hoxes hoxing hoxed**.) This is a word found in Shakespeare's plays, and means to cut a horse's hamstring. This unusual word is a handy one to remember if you draw an X. Hox scores 12 points.

hoyden n (pl **-s**) old-fashioned wild or boisterous girl

hoydens n ▷ **hoyden**

hub n (pl **-s**) centre of a wheel, through which the axle passes

hubbies n ▷ **hubby**

hubbub n (pl **-s**) confused noise of many voices

hubbubs n ▷ **hubbub**

hubby n (pl **-bbies**) informal husband

hubris n (pl **-es**) formal pride, arrogance

hubrises n ▷ **hubris**

hubs n ▷ **hub**

huckster n (pl **-s**) person using aggressive methods of selling

hucksters n ▷ **huckster**

huddle v (**-les**, **-ling**, **-led**) hunch (oneself) through cold or fear ▶ n (pl **-s**) small group

huddled v ▷ **huddle**

huddles n, v ▷ **huddle**

huddling v ▷ **huddle**

hue n (pl **-s**) colour, shade

hues n ▷ **hue**

huff n (pl **-s**) passing mood of anger or resentment ▶ v (**-s**, **-ing**, **-ed**) blow or puff heavily ▶ **huffy** adj (**-fier**, **-ffiest**) > **huffily** adv

huffed v ▷ **huff**

huffier adj ▷ **huff**

huffiest adj ▷ **huff**

huffily adv ▷ **huff**

huffing v ▷ **huff**

huffs n, v ▷ **huff**

huffy adj ▷ **huff**

hug v (**-s**, **-gging**, **-gged**) clasp tightly in the arms, usu. with affection ▶ n (pl **-s**) tight or fond embrace

huge adj (**-r**, **-st**) very big > **hugely** adv

huger adj ▷ **huge**

hugest adj ▷ **huge**

hugged v ▷ **hug**

hugging v ▷ **hug**

hugs n, v ▷ **hug**

huh interj exclamation of derision, bewilderment, or inquiry

hui n (pl **-es**) NZ meeting of Maori people

huies n ▷ **hui**

hula n (pl **-s**) swaying Hawaiian dance

hulas n ▷ **hula**

hulk n (pl **-s**) body of an abandoned ship

hulking adj bulky, unwieldy

hulks n ▷ **hulk**

hull n (pl **-s**) main body of a boat ▶ v (**-s**, **-ing**, **-ed**) remove the hulls from

hulled v ▷ **hull**

hulling v ▷ **hull**

hulls n, v ▷ **hull**

hum v (**-s**, **-mming**, **-mmed**) make a low continuous vibrating sound ▶ n (pl **-s**) humming sound

human adj of or typical of people ▶ n (pl **-s**) human being

humane adj (**-r**, **-st**) kind or merciful > **humanely** adv

humanely adv ▷ **humane**

humaner adj ▷ **humane**

humanest adj ▷ **humane**

humanism n (pl **-s**) belief in human effort rather than religion > **humanist** n (pl **-s**)

humanisms n ▷ **humanism**

humanist n ▷ **humanism**

humanists n ▷ **humanism**

humanity n (pl **-ties**) human race

humanize v (**-zes**, **-zing**, **-zed**) make human or humane

humanized v ▷ **humanize**

humanizes v ▷ **humanize**

humanizing v ▷ **humanize**

humanly adv by human powers or means

humans n ▷ **human**

humble adj (-r, -st) conscious of one's failings ▶ v (-les, -ling, -led) cause to feel humble, humiliate > **humbly** adv

humbled v ▷ **humble**

humbler adj ▷ **humble**

humbles v ▷ **humble**

humblest adj ▷ **humble**

humbling v ▷ **humble**

humbly adv ▷ **humble**

humbug n (pl -s) BRIT hard striped peppermint sweet

humbugs n ▷ **humbug**

humdrum adj ordinary, dull

humeri n ▷ **humerus**

humerus n (pl -meri) bone from the shoulder to the elbow

humid adj (-er, -est) damp and hot > **humidity** n (pl -ties) > **humidify** v (-fies, -fying, -fied)

humider adj ▷ **humid**

humidest adj ▷ **humid**

humidified v ▷ **humid**

humidifies v ▷ **humid**

humidifying v ▷ **humid**

humidities n ▷ **humid**

humidity n ▷ **humid**

humilities n ▷ **humility**

humility n (pl -ties) quality of being humble

hummed v ▷ **hum**

humming v ▷ **hum**

hummock n (pl -s) very small hill

hummocks n ▷ **hummock**

humorist n (pl -s) writer or entertainer who uses humour in his or her work

humorists n ▷ **humorist**

humorous adj ▷ **humour**

humorously adj ▷ **humour**

humour n (pl -s) ability to say or perceive things that are amusing ▶ v (-s, -ing, -ed) be kind and indulgent to > **humorous** adj > **humorously** adv

humoured v ▷ **humour**

humouring v ▷ **humour**

humours n, v ▷ **humour**

hump n (pl -s) raised piece of ground ▶ v (-s, -ing, -ed) slang carry or heave

humped v ▷ **hump**

humping v ▷ **hump**

humps n, v ▷ **hump**

hums v, n ▷ **hum**

humus n (pl -es) decomposing vegetable and animal mould in the soil

humuses n ▷ **humus**

hunch n (pl -es) feeling or suspicion not based on facts ▶ v (-es, -ing, -ed) draw (one's shoulders) up or together

hunched v ▷ **hunch**

hunches n, v ▷ **hunch**

hunching v ▷ **hunch**

hundred adj ten times ten ▶ n (pl -s) (often pl) large but unspecified number > **hundredth** adj, n (pl -s)

hundreds n ▷ **hundred**

hundredth n ▷ **hundred**

hundredths n ▷ **hundred**

hung v ▷ **hang** ▶ adj (of a parliament or jury) with no side having a clear majority

hunger n (pl -s) discomfort or weakness from lack of food ▶ v (-s, -ing, -ed) (foll. by for) want very much

hungered v ▷ **hunger**

hungering v ▷ **hunger**

hungers n, v ▷ **hunger**

hungrier adj ▷ **hungry**

hungriest adj ▷ **hungry**

hungrily adv ▷ **hungry**

hungry adj (-rier, -riest) desiring food (foll. by for) > **hungrily** adv

hunk n (pl -s) large piece

hunks n ▷ **hunk**

hunt v (-s, -ing, -ed) seek out and kill (wild animals) for food or sport ▶ n (pl -s) hunting

huntaway n (pl -s) NZ sheepdog trained to drive sheep by barking

huntaways n ▷ **huntaway**

hunted v ▷ **hunt**

hunter n (pl -s) person or animal that hunts wild animals for food or sport

hunters n ▷ **hunter**

hunting v ▷ **hunt**

hunts v, n ▷ hunt

huntsman n (pl -**men**) man who hunts wild animals, esp. foxes

huntsmen n ▷ huntsman

hurdle n (pl -**s**) SPORT light barrier for jumping over in some races ▶ v (-**les**, -**ling**, -**led**) jump over (something) > **hurdler** n (pl -**s**)

hurdled v ▷ hurdle

hurdler n ▷ hurdle

hurdlers n ▷ hurdle

hurdles n, v ▷ hurdle ▶ pl n race involving hurdles

hurdling v ▷ hurdle

hurl v (-**s**, -**ing**, -**ed**) throw or utter forcefully

hurled v ▷ hurl

hurley n ▷ hurling

hurleys n ▷ hurling

hurling, hurley n (pl -**s**) Irish game like hockey ▶ v ▷ hurl

hurlings n ▷ hurling

hurls v ▷ hurl

hurrah, hurray interj exclamation of joy or applause

hurried v ▷ hurry

hurriedly adv ▷ hurry

hurries v, n ▷ hurry

hurry v (-**ries**, -**rying**, -**ried**) (cause to) move or act very quickly ▶ n (pl -**ries**) doing something quickly or the need to do something quickly > **hurriedly** adv

hurrying v ▷ hurry

hurt v (-**s**, -**ing**, **hurt**) cause physical or mental pain to ▶ n (pl -**s**) physical or mental pain

hurtful adj unkind

hurting v ▷ hurt

hurtle v (-**les**, -**ling**, -**led**) move quickly or violently

hurtled v ▷ hurtle

hurtles v ▷ hurtle

hurtling v ▷ hurtle

hurts v, n ▷ hurt

husband n (pl -**s**) woman's partner in marriage ▶ v (-**s**, -**ing**, -**ed**) use economically

husbanded v ▷ husband

husbanding v ▷ husband

husbands n, v ▷ husband

hush v (-**es**, -**ing**, -**ed**) make or be silent ▶ n (pl -**es**) stillness or silence

hushed v ▷ hush

hushes v, n ▷ hush

hushing v ▷ hush

husk n (pl -**s**) outer covering of certain seeds and fruits ▶ v (-**s**, -**ing**, -**ed**) remove the husk from

husked v ▷ husk

huskier adj ▷ husky¹

huskies n ▷ husky²

huskiest adj ▷ husky¹

huskily adv ▷ husky¹

husking v ▷ husk

husks n, v ▷ husk

husky¹ adj (-**kier**, -**kiest**) slightly hoarse > **huskily** adv

husky² n (pl -**kies**) Arctic sledge dog with thick hair and a curled tail

hussar n (pl -**s**) HIST lightly armed cavalry soldier

hussars n ▷ hussar

hussies n ▷ hussy

hussy n (pl -**sies**) immodest or promiscuous woman

hustings pl n political campaigns and speeches before an election

hustle v (-**les**, -**ling**, -**led**) push about, jostle ▶ n (pl -**les**) lively activity or bustle

hustled v ▷ hustle

hustles v, n ▷ hustle

hustling v ▷ hustle

hut n (pl -**s**) small house, shelter, or shed

hutch n (pl -**es**) cage for pet rabbits etc

hutches n ▷ hutch

huts n ▷ hut

hyacinth n (pl -**s**) sweet-smelling spring flower that grows from a bulb

hyacinths n ▷ hyacinth

hyaena n (pl -**s**) ▷ hyena

hyaenas n ▷ hyaena

hybrid n (pl -**s**) offspring of two plants or animals of different species ▶ adj of mixed origin

hybrids n ▷ hybrid

hydra n (pl -s) mythical many-headed water serpent

hydrant n (pl -s) outlet from a water main with a nozzle for a hose
hydrants n ▷ hydrant

hydras n ▷ hydra

hydrate n (pl -tes) chemical compound of water with another substance
hydrates n ▷ hydrate

hydro¹ n (pl -s) hotel offering facilities for hydropathy

hydrogen n (pl -s) CHEM light flammable colourless gas that combines with oxygen to form water
hydrogens n ▷ hydrogen

hydros n ▷ hydro¹

hyena n (pl -s) scavenging doglike mammal of Africa and S Asia
hyenas n ▷ hyena

hygiene n (pl -s) principles and practice of health and cleanliness
▷ **hygienic** adj ▷ **hygienically** adv
hygienic adj ▷ hygiene
hygienically adj ▷ hygiene

hymen n (pl -s) membrane partly covering the opening of a girl's vagina, which breaks before puberty or at the first occurrence of sexual intercourse
hymens n ▷ hymen

hymn n (pl -s) Christian song of praise sung to God or a saint

hymnal n (pl -s) book of hymns (also **hymn book**)

hymnals n ▷ hymnal

hymns n ▷ hymn

hype n (pl -s) intensive or exaggerated publicity or sales promotion ▶ v (-pes, -ping, -ped) promote (a product) using intensive or exaggerated publicity
hyped v ▷ hype

hyper adj informal overactive or overexcited
hypes n, v ▷ hype

hyphen n (pl -s) punctuation mark (-) indicating that two words or syllables are connected
hyphens n ▷ hyphen

hyping v ▷ hype

hypnoses n ▷ hypnosis

hypnosis n (pl -noses) artificially induced state of relaxation in which the mind is more than usually receptive to suggestion

hypnotic adj of or (as if) producing hypnosis

hyraces n ▷ hyrax

hyrax n (pl -raxes or -races) type of hoofed rodent-like animal of Africa and Asia
hyraxes n ▷ hyrax

hysteria n (pl -s) state of uncontrolled excitement, anger, or panic
▷ **hysterical** adj ▷ **hysterically** adv
hysterias n ▷ hysteria
hysterical adj ▷ hysteria
hysterically adj ▷ hysteria

I i

The letter I can prove a difficult tile to use effectively in Scrabble. It's one of the most common tiles in the game, so you often end up with two or more on your rack, but it can be hard to get rid of. Where I does come in very useful, though, is in the number of everyday short words that can be formed from it, which are very helpful when you need to form short words in addition to the main word that you want to play. These words include **in**, **is**, **it** (2 points each), **id** (3) and **if** (5). Other handy words are **icy** (8), **ivy** (9) and **imp** (7). Don't forget the three-letter words that use K: **ilk**, **ink** and **irk** (7 each).

ibex n (pl **-es**) wild goat of N with large backward-curving horns
ibexes n ▷ **ibex**

ibis n (pl **-es**) large wading bird with long legs
ibises n ▷ **ibis**

ice n (pl **-s**) frozen water ▶ v (**ices**, **icing**, **iced**) (foll. by **up** or **over**) become covered with ice
iceberg n (pl **-s**) large floating mass of ice
icebergs n ▷ **iceberg**
icebox n (pl **-es**) US refrigerator
iceboxes n ▷ **icebox**
icecap n (pl **-s**) mass of ice permanently covering an area
icecaps n ▷ **icecap**
iced adj covered with icing ▶ v ▷ **ice**
ices v, n ▷ **ice**
ich pron. Ich is an old dialect form of I. This is a useful little word that is worth remembering because of its unusual combination of letters and relatively high score. Ich scores 8 points.

icicle n (pl **-s**) tapering spike of ice hanging where water has dripped
icicles n ▷ **icicle**
icier adj ▷ **icy**

iciest adj ▷ **icy**
icily adv ▷ **icy**
iciness n ▷ **icy**
icinesses n ▷ **icy**
icing n (pl **-s**) mixture of sugar and water etc, used to cover and decorate cakes
icings n ▷ **icing**

ick interj. Ick is something that people say when they encounter something unpleasant or disgusting. Ick is a good word to remember because, in addition to being useful when there's little space, it's one of the highest-scoring three-letter word beginning with I. Ick scores 9 points.

icon n (pl **-s**) picture of Christ or another religious figure, regarded as holy in the Orthodox Church
icons n ▷ **icon**

icy adj (**icier**, **iciest**) very cold ▷ **icily** adv ▷ **iciness** n (pl **-es**)

id n (pl **-s**) PSYCHOANALYSIS the mind's instinctive unconscious energies
ide n (**ides**). An ide is a kind of fish. This combination of letters is a good one to keep in mind because

it is both a suffix that can be added to words already on the board and a word in its own right. Ide scores 4 points.

idea n (pl **-s**) plan or thought formed in the mind

ideal adj most suitable ▶ n (pl **-s**) conception of something that is perfect >**idealist** n (pl **-s**) >**idealistic** adj >**ideally** adv

idealism n (pl **-s**) tendency to seek perfection in everything

idealisms n ▷ **idealism**

idealist n ▷ **ideal**

idealistic adj ▷ **ideal**

idealists n ▷ **ideal**

idealization n (pl **-s**)

idealizations n ▷ **idealize**

idealize v (**-izes**, **-izing**, **-ized**) regard or portray as perfect or nearly perfect >**idealization** n (pl **-s**)

idealized v ▷ **idealize**

idealizes v ▷ **idealize**

idealizing v ▷ **idealize**

ideally adv ▷ **ideal**

ideals n ▷ **ideal**

ideas n ▷ **idea**

idem pron, adj LATIN the same: used to refer to an article, chapter, or book already quoted

identifiable adj ▷ **identify**

identification n ▷ **identify**

identifications n ▷ **identify**

identified v ▷ **identify**

identifies v ▷ **identify**

identify v (**-fies**, **-fying**, **-fied**) prove or recognize as being a certain person or thing >**identifiable** adj >**identification** n (pl **-s**)

identifying v ▷ **identify**

identities n ▷ **identity**

identity n (pl **-ties**) state of being a specified person or thing

ideological adj ▷ **ideology**

ideologies n ▷ **ideology**

ideologist n ▷ **ideology**

ideologists n ▷ **ideology**

ideology n (pl **-gies**) body of ideas and beliefs of a group, nation, etc >**ideological** adj >**ideologist** n (pl **-s**)

idiocies n ▷ **idiocy**

idiocy n (pl **-cies**) utter stupidity

idiom n (pl **-s**) group of words which when used together have a different meaning from the words individually >**idiomatic** adj >**idiomatically** adv

idiomatic adj ▷ **idiom**

idiomatically adv ▷ **idiom**

idioms n ▷ **idiom**

idiot n (pl **-s**) foolish or stupid person >**idiotic** adj >**idiotically** adv

idiotic adj ▷ **idiot**

idiotically adv ▷ **idiot**

idiots n ▷ **idiot**

idle adj not doing anything ▶ v (**-les**, **-ling**, **-led**) (usu. foll. by **away**) spend (time) doing very little >**idleness** n (pl **-s**) >**idler** n (pl **-s**) >**idly** adv

idled v ▷ **idle**

idleness n ▷ **idle**

idlenesses n ▷ **idle**

idler n ▷ **idle**

idlers n ▷ **idle**

idles v ▷ **idle**

idling v ▷ **idle**

idly adv ▷ **idle**

idol n (pl **-s**) object of excessive devotion

idolatries n ▷ **idolatry**

idolatrous adj ▷ **idolatry**

idolatry n (pl **-ries**) worship of idols >**idolatrous** adj

idolize v (**-izes**, **-izing**, **-ized**) love or admire excessively

idolized v ▷ **idolize**

idolizes v ▷ **idolize**

idolizing v ▷ **idolize**

idols n ▷ **idol**

ids n ▷ **id**

idyll n (pl **-s**) scene or time of great peace and happiness >**idyllic** adj >**idyllically** adv

idyllic adj ▷ **idyll**

idyllically adj ▷ **idyll**

idylls n ▷ **idyll**

if conj on the condition or supposition

that ▶ n (pl -s) uncertainty or doubt
iff conj. Iff is a word used in logic to mean if and only if. This word is worth remembering: not only can it come in handy when there isn't much space on the board, but it's also one of the highest-scoring three-letter word beginning with I. Iff scores 9 points.
iffy adj informal doubtful, uncertain
ifs n ▷ if
igloo n (pl -loos) dome-shaped Inuit house made of snow and ice
igloos n ▷ igloo
igneous adj (of rock) formed as molten rock cools and hardens
ignite v (-tes, -ting, -ted) catch fire or set fire to
ignited v ▷ ignite
ignites v ▷ ignite
igniting v ▷ ignite
ignition n (pl -s) system that ignites the fuel-and-air mixture to start an engine
ignitions n ▷ ignition
ignoble adj dishonourable
ignominies n ▷ ignominy
ignominious adj ▷ ignominy
ignominiously adv ▷ ignominy
ignominy n (pl -nies) humiliating disgrace > ignominious adj > ignominiously adv
ignorance n ▷ ignorant
ignorant adj lacking knowledge > ignorance n (pl -s)
ignore v (-res, -ring, -red) refuse to notice, disregard deliberately
ignored v ▷ ignore
ignores v ▷ ignore
ignoring v ▷ ignore
iguana n (pl -s) large tropical American lizard
iguanas n ▷ iguana
ileum n (pl -s) lowest part of the small intestine
ileums n ▷ ileum
ilk n (pl -s) type
ilks n ▷ ilk

ill adj not in good health ▶ n (pl -s) evil, harm ▶ adv badly ▶ **illness** n (pl -s)
illegal adj against the law
> illegally adv ▷ illegality n (pl -ties)
illegalities n ▷ illegal
illegality n ▷ illegal
illegally adv ▷ illegal
illicit adj illegal
illness n ▷ ill
illnesses n ▷ ill
ills n ▷ ill
illusion n (pl -s) deceptive appearance or belief
illusions n ▷ illusion
illusory adj seeming to be true, but actually false
image n (pl -s) mental picture of someone or something
imageries n ▷ imagery
imagery n (pl -ries) images collectively, esp. in the arts
images n ▷ image
imaginable adj ▷ imagine
imagine v (-nes, -ning, -ned) form a mental image of > imaginable adj
imagined v ▷ imagine
imagines v ▷ imagine ▶ n ▷ imago
imagining v ▷ imagine
imago n (pl -goes, -gines) sexually mature adult insect
imagoes n ▷ imago
imam n (pl -s) leader of prayers in a mosque
imams n ▷ imam
imbecile n (pl -s) stupid person ▶ adj (also **imbecilic**) stupid or senseless > imbecility n (pl -ties)
imbeciles n ▷ imbecile
imbecilic adj ▷ imbecile
imbecilities n ▷ imbecile
imbecility n ▷ imbecile
imbibe v (-bes, -bing, -bed) drink (alcoholic drinks)
imbibed v ▷ imbibe
imbibes v ▷ imbibe
imbibing v ▷ imbibe
imbue v (-ues, -uing, -ued) (usu. foll. by with) fill or inspire with (ideals or

principles)
imbued v ▷ imbue
imbues v ▷ imbue
imbuing v ▷ imbue
imitate v (-tes, -ting, -ted) take as
a model >imitative adj >imitator n
(pl -s)
imitated v ▷ imitate
imitates v ▷ imitate
imitating v ▷ imitate
imitative adj ▷ imitate
imitator n ▷ imitate
imitators n ▷ imitate
immanence n ▷ immanent
immanences n ▷ immanent
immanent adj present within
and throughout something
>immanence n (pl -s)
immature adj not fully developed
>immaturity n (pl -ties)
immaturities n ▷ immature
immaturity n ▷ immature
immense adj extremely large
>immensity n (pl -ties)
immensities n ▷ immense
immensity n ▷ immense
immerse v (-ses, -sing, -sed) involve
deeply, engross >immersion n (pl -s)
immersed v ▷ immerse
immerses v ▷ immerse
immersing v ▷ immerse
immersion n ▷ immerse
immersions n ▷ immerse
imminence n ▷ imminent
imminences n ▷ imminent
imminent adj about to happen
>imminently adv >imminence n (pl -s)
imminently adv ▷ imminent
immobile adj not moving
>immobility n (pl -ties)
immobilies adj ▷ immobile
immobility n ▷ immobile
immolate v (-tes, -ting, -ted) kill as a
sacrifice >immolation n (pl -s)
immolated v ▷ immolate
immolates v ▷ immolate
immolating v ▷ immolate
immolation n ▷ immolate

immolations n ▷ immolate
immoral adj morally wrong, corrupt
>immorality n (pl -ties)
immoralities n ▷ immoral
immorality n ▷ immoral
immortal adj living forever ▶ n (pl -s)
person whose fame will last for all time
>immortality n (pl -s) >immortalize v
(-zes, -zing, -zed)
immortalities n ▷ immortal
immortality n ▷ immortal
immortalized v ▷ immortal
immortalizes v ▷ immortal
immortalizing v ▷ immortal
immortals n ▷ immortal
immune adj protected against a
specific disease
immunities n ▷ immunity
immunity n (pl -ties) ability to resist
disease
immunization n ▷ immunize
immunizations n ▷ immunize
immunize v (-izes, -izing,
-ized) make immune to a disease
>immunization n (pl -s)
immunized v ▷ immunize
immunizes v ▷ immunize
immunizing v ▷ immunize
imp n (pl -s) (in folklore) mischievous
small creature with magical powers
impact n (pl -s) strong effect ▶ v (-s,
-ing, -ed) press firmly into something
impacted v ▷ impact
impacting v ▷ impact
impacts n, v ▷ impact
impair v (-s, -ing, -ed) weaken or
damage >impairment n (pl -s)
impaired v ▷ impair
impairing v ▷ impair
impairment n ▷ impair
impairments n ▷ impair
impairs v ▷ impair
impala n (pl -s) southern African
antelope
impalas n ▷ impala
impale v (-les, -ling, -led) pierce with
a sharp object
impaled v ▷ impale

impales v ▷ impale
impaling v ▷ impale
impart v (**-s, -ing, -ed**) communicate (information)
imparted v ▷ impart
imparting v ▷ impart
imparts v ▷ impart
impasse n (pl **-s**) situation in which progress is impossible
impasses n ▷ impasse
impeach v (**-es, -ing, -ed**) charge with a serious crime against the state > **impeachment** n (pl **-s**)
impeached v ▷ impeach
impeaches v ▷ impeach
impeaching v ▷ impeach
impeachment n ▷ impeach
impeachments n ▷ impeach
impede v (**-des, -ding, -ded**) hinder in action or progress
impeded v ▷ impede
impedes v ▷ impede
impeding v ▷ impede
impel v (**-s, -lling, -lled**) push or force (someone) to do something
impelled v ▷ impel
impelling v ▷ impel
impels v ▷ impel
imperial adj of or like an empire or emperor
imperialist adj, n ▷ imperial
imperil v (**-s, -lling, -lled**) put in danger
imperilled v ▷ imperil
imperilling v ▷ imperil
imperils v ▷ imperil
impetigo n (pl **-s**) contagious skin disease
impetigos n ▷ impetigo
impetus n (pl **-es**) incentive, impulse
impetuses n ▷ impetus
impinge v (**-ges, -ging, -ged**) (foll. by on) affect or restrict
impinged v ▷ impinge
impinges v ▷ impinge
impinging v ▷ impinge
impious adj showing a lack of respect or reverence

impish adj mischievous
implant n (pl **-s**) MED something put into someone's body, usu. by surgical operation ▶ v (**-s, -ing, -ed**) put (something) into someone's body, usu. by surgical operation > **implantation** n (pl **-s**)
implantation n ▷ implant
implantations n ▷ implant
implanted v ▷ implant
implanting v ▷ implant
implants n, v ▷ implant
implicit adj expressed indirectly > **implicitly** adv
implicitly adv ▷ implicit
implied v ▷ imply
implies v ▷ imply
implore v (**-res, -ring, -red**) beg earnestly
implored v ▷ implore
implores v ▷ implore
imploring v ▷ implore
imply v (**-lies, -lying, -lied**) indicate by hinting, suggest
implying v ▷ imply
import v (**-s, -ing, -ed**) bring in (goods) from another country ▶ n (pl **-s**) something imported > **importation** n (pl **-s**) > **importer** n (pl **-s**)
importation n ▷ import
importations n ▷ import
imported v ▷ import
importer n ▷ import
importers n ▷ import
importing v ▷ import
imports v, n ▷ import
impose v (**-ses, -sing, -sed**) force the acceptance of
imposed v ▷ impose
imposes v ▷ impose
imposing adj grand, impressive ▶ v ▷ impose
imposter, impostor n (pl **-s**) person who cheats or swindles by pretending to be someone else
imposters n ▷ imposter
impostor n ▷ imposter
impostors n ▷ imposter

impotence n ▷ **impotent**
impotences n ▷ **impotent**
impotent adj powerless
>**impotence** n (pl **-s**) >**impotently** adv
>**impotently** adv ▷ **impotent**
impound v (**-s, -ing, -ed**) take legal
possession of, confiscate
impounded v ▷ **impound**
impounding v ▷ **impound**
impounds v ▷ **impound**
impress v (**-es, -ing, -ed**) affect
strongly, usu. favourably
impressed v ▷ **impress**
impresses v ▷ **impress**
impressing v ▷ **impress**
imprint n (pl **-s**) mark made by printing
or stamping ▶ v (**-s, -ing, -ed**) produce
(a mark) by printing or stamping
imprinted v ▷ **imprint**
imprinting v ▷ **imprint**
imprints n, v ▷ **imprint**
imprison v (**-s, -ing, -ed**) put in prison
>**imprisonment** n (pl **-s**)
imprisoned v ▷ **imprison**
imprisoning v ▷ **imprison**
imprisonment n ▷ **imprison**
imprisons v ▷ **imprison**
improper adj indecent
improve v (**-ves, -ving, -ved**) make or
become better >**improvement** n (pl **-s**)
improved v ▷ **improve**
improves v ▷ **improve**
improving v ▷ **improve**
imps n ▷ **imp**
impudence n ▷ **impudent**
impudences n ▷ **impudent**
impudent adj cheeky, disrespectful
>**impudently** adv >**impudence** n (pl **-s**)
impugn v (**-s, -ing, -ed**) challenge the
truth or validity of
impugned v ▷ **impugn**
impugning v ▷ **impugn**
impugns v ▷ **impugn**
impulse n (pl **-s**) sudden urge to do
something >**impulsive** adj acting or
done without careful consideration
>**impulsively** adv
impulses n ▷ **impulse**

impulsive adj ▷ **impulse**
impulsively adv ▷ **impulse**
impunities n ▷ **impunity**
impunity n (pl **-ties**) without
punishment
impure adj having dirty or unwanted
substances mixed in >**impurity** n
(pl **-ties**)
impurities n ▷ **impure**
impurity n ▷ **impure**
imputation n ▷ **impute**
imputations n ▷ **impute**
impute v (**-tes, -ting, -ted**) attribute
responsibility to >**imputation** n (pl **-s**)
imputed v ▷ **impute**
imputes v ▷ **impute**
imputing v ▷ **impute**
in prep indicating position inside, state
or situation, etc ▶ adv indicating
position inside, entry into, etc ▶ adj
fashionable
inane adj senseless, silly >**inanity** n
(pl **-ties**)
inanities n ▷ **inane**
inanity n ▷ **inane**
inboard adj (of a boat's engine) inside
the hull
inborn adj existing from birth, natural
inbred adj produced as a result of
inbreeding
inbuilt adj present from the start
incense[1] v (**-ses, -sing, -sed**) make
very angry
incense[2] n (pl **incenses**) substance
that gives off a sweet perfume when
burned
incensed v ▷ **incense**[1]
incenses v ▷ **incense**[1] ▶ n ▷ **incense**[2]
incensing v ▷ **incense**[1]
incest n (pl **-s**) sexual intercourse
between two people too closely related
to marry >**incestuous** adj
incests n ▷ **incest**
incestuous adj ▷ **incest**
inch n (pl **-es**) unit of length equal
to one twelfth of a foot or 2.54
centimetres ▶ v (**-ches, -ching, -ched**)
move slowly and gradually

inched v ▷ inch
inches v, n ▷ inch
inching v ▷ inch
inchoate adj just begun and not yet properly developed
incident n (pl -s) something that happens
incidents n ▷ incident
incise v (-ses, -sing, -sed) cut into with a sharp tool ▷ incision n (pl -s)
incised v ▷ incise
incises v ▷ incise
incising v ▷ incise
incision n ▷ incise
incisions n ▷ incise
incisive adj direct and forceful
incisor n (pl -s) front tooth, used for biting into food
incisors n ▷ incisor
incite v (-tes, -ting, -ted) stir up, provoke >incitement n (pl -s)
incited v ▷ incite
incitement n ▷ incite
incitements n ▷ incite
incites v ▷ incite
inciting v ▷ incite
incline v (-nes, -ning, -ned) lean, slope ▶ n (pl -s) slope
inclined v ▷ incline
inclines v, n ▷ incline
inclining v ▷ incline
include v (-des, -ding, -ded) have as part of the whole ▷ inclusion n (pl -s)
included v ▷ include
includes v ▷ include
including v ▷ include
inclusion n ▷ include
inclusions n ▷ include
income n (pl -s) amount of money earned from work, investments, etc
incomes n ▷ income
incoming adj coming in
increase v (-ses, -sing, -sed) make or become greater in size, number, etc ▶ n (pl -s) rise in number, size, etc >increasingly adv
increased v ▷ increase
increases v, n ▷ increase

increasing v ▷ increase
increasingly adv ▷ increase
incubate v (-tes, -ting, -ted) (of a bird) hatch (eggs) by sitting on them ▷ incubation n (pl -s)
incubated v ▷ incubate
incubates v ▷ incubate
incubating v ▷ incubate
incubation n ▷ incubate
incubations n ▷ incubate
incubi n ▷ incubus
incubus n (pl -bi, -buses) (in folklore) demon believed to have sex with sleeping women
incubuses n ▷ incubus
incur v (-s, -rring, -rred) cause (something unpleasant) to happen
incurred v ▷ incur
incurring v ▷ incur
incurs v ▷ incur
indebted adj owing gratitude for help or favours >indebtedness n (pl -es)
indebtedness n ▷ indebted
indebtednesses n ▷ indebted
indecencies n ▷ indecent
indecency n ▷ indecent
indecent adj morally or sexually offensive >indecently adv
>indecency n (pl -cies)
indecently adv ▷ indecent
indeed adv really, certainly ▶ interj expression of indignation or surprise
indent v (-s, -ing, -ed) start (a line of writing) further from the margin than the other lines
indented v ▷ indent
indenting v ▷ indent
indents v ▷ indent
index n (pl -dices) alphabetical list of names or subjects dealt with in a book ▶ v (-dexes, -dexing, -dexed) provide (a book) with an index
indexed v ▷ index
indexes v ▷ index
indexing v ▷ index
indicate v (-tes, -ting, -ted) be a sign or symptom of ▷ indication n (pl -s)
indicated v ▷ indicate

indicates v ▷ **indicate**
indicating v ▷ **indicate**
indication n ▷ **indicate**
indications n ▷ **indicate**
indices n ▷ **index**
indict v (-s, -ing, -ed) formally charge with a crime > **indictable** adj > **indictment** n (pl -s)
indictable adj ▷ **indict**
indicted v ▷ **indict**
indicting v ▷ **indict**
indictment n ▷ **indict**
indictments n ▷ **indict**
indicts v ▷ **indict**
indie adj informal (of rock music) released by an independent record company
indigence n ▷ **indigent**
indigences n ▷ **indigent**
indigent adj extremely poor > **indigence** n (pl -s)
indigo adj deep violet-blue ▶ n (pl -s) dye of this colour
indigos n ▷ **indigo**
indirect adj done or caused by someone or something else
indium n (pl -s) CHEM soft silvery-white metallic element
indiums n ▷ **indium**
indolence n ▷ **indolent**
indolences n ▷ **indolent**
indolent adj lazy > **indolence** n (pl -s)
indoor adj inside a building > **indoors** adv
indoors adv ▷ **indoor**
induce v (-ces, -cing, -ced) persuade or influence
induced v ▷ **induce**
induces v ▷ **induce**
inducing v ▷ **induce**
induct v (-s, -ing, -ed) formally install (someone, esp. a clergyman) in office
inducted v ▷ **induct**
inducting v ▷ **induct**
inducts v ▷ **induct**
indulge v (-ges, -ging, -ged) allow oneself pleasure > **indulgent** adj > **indulgently** adv

indulged v ▷ **indulge**
indulgent adj ▷ **indulge**
indulgently adj ▷ **indulge**
indulges v ▷ **indulge**
indulging v ▷ **indulge**
industries n ▷ **industry**
industrious adj ▷ **industry**
industry n (pl -tries) manufacture of goods > **industrious** adj hard-working
inedible adj not fit to be eaten
inept adj clumsy, lacking skill > **ineptitude** n (pl -s)
ineptitude n ▷ **inept**
ineptitudes n ▷ **inept**
inert adj without the power of motion or resistance > **inertness** n (pl -es)
inertia n (pl -s) feeling of unwillingness to do anything
inertias n ▷ **inertia**
inertness n ▷ **inert**
inertnesses n ▷ **inert**
inexpert adj lacking skill
infamies n ▷ **infamous**
infamous adj well-known for something bad > **infamously** adv > **infamy** n (pl -mies)
infamously adv ▷ **infamous**
infamy n ▷ **infamous**
infancies n ▷ **infancy**
infancy n (pl -cies) early childhood
infant n (pl -s) very young child
infantries n ▷ **infantry**
infantry n (pl -ries) soldiers who fight on foot
infants n ▷ **infant**
infect v (-s, -ing, -ed) affect with a disease > **infection** n (pl -s)
infected v ▷ **infect**
infecting v ▷ **infect**
infection n ▷ **infect**
infections n ▷ **infect**
infects v ▷ **infect**
infer v (-s, -rring, -rred) work out from evidence > **inference** n (pl -s)
inference n ▷ **infer**
inferences n ▷ **infer**
inferior adj lower in quality, position, or status ▶ n (pl -s) person of lower

position or status ▷ **inferiority** n
(pl **-ties**)
inferiorities n ▷ **inferior**
inferiority n ▷ **inferior**
inferiors n ▷ **inferior**
infernal adj of hell informal
  ▷ **infernally**
infernally adv ▷ **infernal**
inferno n (pl **-s**) intense raging fire
infernos n ▷ **inferno**
inferred v ▷ **infer**
inferring v ▷ **infer**
infers v ▷ **infer**
infest v (**-s, -ing, -ed**) inhabit or
overrun in unpleasantly large numbers
  ▷ **infestation** n (pl **-s**)
infestation n ▷ **infest**
infestations n ▷ **infest**
infested ▷ **infest**
infesting v ▷ **infest**
infests v ▷ **infest**
infidel n (pl **-s**) person with no religion
infidels n ▷ **infidel**
infinite adj without any limit or end
  ▷ **infinitely** adv
infinitely adv ▷ **infinite**
infinities n ▷ **infinity**
infinity n (pl **-ties**) endless space, time,
or number
infirm adj physically or mentally weak
  ▷ **infirmity** n (pl **-ties**)
infirmities n ▷ **infirm**
infirmity n ▷ **infirm**
inflame v (**-mes, -ming, -med**) make
angry or excited
inflamed adj (of part of the
body) red, swollen, and painful
because of infection ▶ v ▷ **inflame**
  ▷ **inflammation** n (pl **-s**)
inflames v ▷ **inflame**
inflaming v ▷ **inflame**
inflammation n ▷ **inflamed**
inflammations n ▷ **inflamed**
inflate v (**-tes, -ting, -ted**) expand by
filling with air or gas
inflated v ▷ **inflate**
inflates v ▷ **inflate**
inflating v ▷ **inflate**

inflict v (**-s, -ing, -ed**) impose
(something unpleasant) on
  ▷ **infliction** n (pl **-s**)
inflicted v ▷ **inflict**
inflicting v ▷ **inflict**
infliction n ▷ **inflict**
inflictions n ▷ **inflict**
inflicts v ▷ **inflict**
influx n (pl **-es**) arrival or entry of many
people or things
influxes n ▷ **influx**
info n (pl **-s**) informal information
inform v (**-s, -ing, -ed**) tell
informal adj relaxed and friendly
  ▷ **informally** adv ▷ **informality** n (pl **-s**)
informalities n ▷ **informal**
informality n ▷ **informal**
informally adv ▷ **informal**
informed v ▷ **inform**
informer n (pl **-s**) person who informs
to the police
informers n ▷ **informer**
informing v ▷ **inform**
informs v ▷ **inform**
infos n ▷ **info**
infrared adj of or using rays below the
red end of the visible spectrum
infringe v (**-ges, -ging, -ged**) break (a
law or agreement) ▷ **infringement** n
(pl **-s**)
infringed v ▷ **infringe**
infringement n ▷ **infringe**
infringements n ▷ **infringe**
infringes v ▷ **infringe**
infringing v ▷ **infringe**
infuse v (**-ses, -sing, -sed**) fill (with
an emotion or quality) ▷ **infusion** n (pl
-s) infusing
infused v ▷ **infuse**
infuses v ▷ **infuse**
infusing v ▷ **infuse**
infusion n ▷ **infuse**
infusions n ▷ **infuse**
ingénue n (pl **-s**) naive young woman,
esp. as a role played by an actress
ingénues n ▷ **ingénue**
ingest v (**-ts, -ing, -ed**) take (food or
liquid) into the body ▷ **ingestion** n

(pl **-s**)
ingested v ▷ ingest
ingesting v ▷ ingest
ingestion n ▷ ingest
ingestions n ▷ ingest
ingests v ▷ ingest
ingot n (pl **-s**) oblong block of cast metal
ingots n ▷ ingot
ingress n (pl **-es**) act or right of entering
ingresses n ▷ ingress
inhabit v (**-s, -ing, -ed**) live in
>**inhabitable** adj >**inhabitant** n (pl **-s**)
inhabitant n ▷ inhabit
inhabitants n ▷ inhabit
inhabited v ▷ inhabit
inhabiting v ▷ inhabit
inhabits v ▷ inhabit
inhalant n (pl **-s**) medical preparation inhaled to help breathing problems
inhalants n ▷ inhalant
inhale v (**-les, -ling, -led**) breathe in (air, smoke, etc) >**inhalation** n (pl **-s**)
inhaled v ▷ inhale
inhaler n (pl **-s**) container for an inhalant
inhalers n ▷ inhaler
inhales v ▷ inhale
inhaling v ▷ inhale
inherent adj existing as an inseparable part >**inherently** adv
inherently adv ▷ inherent
inherit v (**-s, -ing, -ed**) receive (money etc) from someone who has died
>**inheritance** n (pl **-s**) >**inheritor** n (pl **-s**)
inheritance n ▷ inherit
inheritances n ▷ inherit
inherited v ▷ inherit
inheriting v ▷ inherit
inheritor n ▷ inherit
inheritors n ▷ inherit
inherits v ▷ inherit
inhibit v (**-s, -ing, -ed**) restrain (an impulse or desire) >**inhibited** adj
inhibited v, adj ▷ inhibit
inhibiting v ▷ inhibit

inhibits v ▷ inhibit
inhuman adj cruel or brutal
inhumane adj cruel or brutal
>**inhumanity** n (pl **-ties**)
inhumanities n ▷ inhumane
inhumanity n ▷ inhumane
inimical adj unfavourable or hostile
iniquities n ▷ iniquity
iniquitous adj ▷ iniquity
iniquity n (pl **-ties**) injustice or wickedness >**iniquitous** adj
initial adj first, at the beginning ▶ n (pl **-s**) first letter, esp. of a person's name ▶ v (**-s, -lling, -lled**) sign with one's initials >**initially** adv
initialled v ▷ initial
initialling v ▷ initial
initially adv ▷ initial
initials n, v ▷ initial
initiate v (**-tes, -ting, -ted**) begin or set going ▶ n (pl **-s**) recently initiated person >**initiation** n (pl **-s**) >**initiator** n (pl **-s**)
initiated v ▷ initiate
initiates v, n ▷ initiate
initiating v ▷ initiate
inject v (**-s, -ing, -ed**) put (a fluid) into the body with a syringe >**injection** n (pl **-s**)
injected v ▷ inject
injecting v ▷ inject
injection n ▷ inject
injections n ▷ inject
injects v ▷ inject
injure v (**-res, -ring, -red**) hurt physically or mentally >**injury** n (pl **-ries**) >**injurious** adj
injured v ▷ injure
injures v ▷ injure
injuries n ▷ injure
injuring v ▷ injure
injurious adj ▷ injure
injury n ▷ injure
ink n (pl **-s**) coloured liquid used for writing or printing ▶ v (**-s, -ing, -ed**) (foll. by **in**) mark in ink (something already marked in pencil)
inked v ▷ ink

inking v ▷ **ink**

inkling n (pl **-s**) slight idea or suspicion

inklings n ▷ **inkling**

inks v, n ▷ **ink**

inky adj dark or black

inlaid adj set in another material so that the surface is smooth

inland adj, adv in or towards the interior of a country, away from the sea

inlay n (pl **-s**) inlaid substance or pattern

inlays n ▷ **inlay**

inlet n (pl **-s**) narrow strip of water extending from the sea into the land

inlets n ▷ **inlet**

inmate n (pl **-s**) person living in an institution such as a prison

inmates n ▷ **inmate**

inmost adj innermost

inn n (pl **-s**) pub or small hotel, esp. in the country ▶ **innkeeper** n (pl **-s**)

innards pl n informal internal organs

innate adj being part of someone's nature, inborn

inner adj happening or located inside

innings n SPORT player's or side's turn of batting

innkeeper n ▷ **inn**

innkeepers n ▷ **inn**

innocence n ▷ **innocent**

innocences n ▷ **innocent**

innocent adj not guilty of a crime ▶ n (pl **-s**) innocent person, esp. a child ▷ **innocently** adv ▷ **innocence** n (pl **-s**)

innocently adv ▷ **innocent**

innocents n ▷ **innocent**

inns n ▷ **inn**

innuendo n (pl **-does**) (remark making) an indirect reference to something rude or unpleasant

innuendoes n ▷ **innuendo**

input n (pl **-s**) resources put into a project etc ▶ v (**-s, -tting, -put**) enter (data) in a computer

inputs v, n ▷ **input**

inputting v, n ▷ **input**

inquest n (pl **-s**) official inquiry into a sudden death

inquests n ▷ **inquest**

inquire v (**-res, -ring, -red**) seek information or ask (about) ▷ **inquirer** n (pl **-s**)

inquired v ▷ **inquire**

inquirer n ▷ **inquire**

inquirers n ▷ **inquire**

inquires v ▷ **inquire**

inquiries n ▷ **inquiry**

inquiring v ▷ **inquire**

inquiry n (pl **-ries**) question

inroads pl n start affecting or reducing

insane adj mentally ill ▷ **insanely** adv ▷ **insanity** n (pl **-ties**)

insanely adv ▷ **insane**

insanities n ▷ **insane**

insanity n ▷ **insane**

inscribe v (**-bes, -bing, -bed**) write or carve words on

inscribed v ▷ **inscribe**

inscribes v ▷ **inscribe**

inscribing v ▷ **inscribe**

insect n (pl **-s**) small animal with six legs and usu. wings, such as an ant or fly

insects n ▷ **insect**

insecure adj anxious, not confident

insert v (**-s, -ing, -ed**) put inside or include ▶ n (pl **-s**) something inserted ▷ **insertion** n (pl **-s**)

inserted v ▷ **insert**

inserting v ▷ **insert**

insertion n ▷ **insert**

insertions n ▷ **insert**

inserts v, n ▷ **insert**

inset n (pl **-s**) small picture inserted within a larger one

insets n ▷ **inset**

inshore adj close to the shore ▶ adj, adv towards the shore

inside prep in or to the interior of ▶ adj on or of the inside ▶ adv on, in, or to the inside, indoors ▶ n (pl **-s**) inner side, surface, or part

insider n (pl **-s**) member of a group who has privileged knowledge about it

insiders n ▷ **insider**

insides n ▷ **inside** ▶ pl n informal

stomach and bowels

insight n (pl -s) deep understanding

insights n ▷ insight

insignia n (pl -s) badge or emblem of honour or office

insignias n ▷ insignia

insipid adj lacking interest, spirit, or flavour

insist v (-s, -ing, -ed) demand or state firmly > **insistent** adj making persistent demands > **insistently** adv > **insistence** n (pl -s)

insisted v ▷ insist

insistence n ▷ insist

insistences n ▷ insist

insistent adj ▷ insist

insistently adv ▷ insist

insisting v ▷ insist

insists v ▷ insist

insole n (pl -s) inner sole of a shoe or boot

insolence n ▷ insolent

insolences n ▷ insolent

insolent adj rude and disrespectful > **insolence** n (pl -s) > **insolently** adv

insolently adv ▷ insolent

insoles n ▷ insole

insomnia n (pl -s) inability to sleep > **insomniac** n (pl -s)

insomniac n ▷ insomnia

insomniacs n ▷ insomnia

insomnias n ▷ insomnia

inspect v (-s, -ing, -ed) check closely or officially > **inspection** n (pl -s)

inspected v ▷ inspect

inspecting v ▷ inspect

inspection n ▷ inspect

inspections n ▷ inspect

inspects v ▷ inspect

inspire v (-res, -ring, -red) fill with enthusiasm, stimulate

inspired v ▷ inspire

inspires v ▷ inspire

inspiring v ▷ inspire

install v (-lls, -lling, -lled) put in and prepare (equipment) for use

installed v ▷ install

installing v ▷ install

installs v ▷ install

instance n (pl -s) particular example
▶ v (-ces, -cing, -ced) mention as an example

instanced v ▷ instance

instances n, v ▷ instance

instancing v ▷ instance

instant n (pl -s) very brief time ▶ adj happening at once > **instantly** adv

instantly adv ▷ instant

instants n ▷ instant

instead adv as a replacement or substitute

instep n (pl -s) part of the foot forming the arch between the ankle and toes

insteps n ▷ instep

instil v (-s, -lling, -lled) introduce (an idea etc) gradually into someone's mind

instilled v ▷ instil

instilling v ▷ instil

instils v ▷ instil

instinct n (pl -s) inborn tendency to behave in a certain way > **instinctive** adj > **instinctively** adv

instinctive adj ▷ instinct

instinctively adv ▷ instinct

instincts n ▷ instinct

instruct v (-s, -ing, -ed) order to do something > **instructor** n (pl -s)

instructed v ▷ instruct

instructing v ▷ instruct

instructor n ▷ instruct

instructors n ▷ instruct

instructs v ▷ instruct

insular adj not open to new ideas, narrow-minded > **insularity** n (pl -ties)

insularities n ▷ insular

insularity n ▷ insular

insulate v (-tes, -ting, -ted) prevent or reduce the transfer of electricity, heat, or sound by surrounding or lining with a nonconducting material > **insulation** n (pl -s) > **insulator** n (pl -s)

insulated v ▷ insulate

insulates v ▷ insulate

insulating v ▷ insulate

insulation n ▷ insulate

insulations *n* ▷ insulate

insulator *n* ▷ insulate

insulators *n* ▷ insulate

insulin *n* (pl -s) hormone produced in the pancreas that controls the amount of sugar in the blood

insulins *n* ▷ insulin

insult *v* (-s, -ing, -ed) behave rudely to, offend ► *n* (pl -s) insulting remark or action > insulting *adj*

insulted *v* ▷ insult

insulting *v, adj* ▷ insult

insults *v, n* ▷ insult

insure *v* (-res, -ring, -red) protect by insurance

insured *v* ▷ insure

insures *v* ▷ insure

insuring *v* ▷ insure

intact *adj* not changed or damaged in any way

intaglio *n* (pl -s) (gem carved with) an engraved design

intaglios *n* ▷ intaglio

intake *n* (pl -kes) amount or number taken in

intakes *n* ▷ intake

integer *n* (pl -s) positive or negative whole number or zero

integers *n* ▷ integer

integral *adj* being an essential part of a whole ► *n* (pl -s) MATHS sum of a large number of very small quantities

integrals *n* ▷ integral

intend *v* (-s, -ing, -ed) propose or plan (to do something)

intended *v* ▷ intend

intending *v* ▷ intend

intends *v* ▷ intend

intense *adj* of great strength or degree > intensity *n* (pl -ties)

intensities *n* ▷ intense

intensity *n* ▷ intense

intent *n* (pl -s) intention ► *adj* paying close attention > intently *adv* > intentness *n* (pl -s)

intently *adv* ▷ intent

intentness *n* ▷ intent

intentnesses *n* ▷ intent

intents *n* ▷ intent

inter *v* (-s, -rring, -rred) bury (a corpse) > interment *n* (pl -s)

interact *v* (-s, -ing, -ed) act on or in close relation with each other > interaction *n* (pl -s) > interactive *adj*

interacted *v* ▷ interact

interacting *v* ▷ interact

interaction *n* ▷ interact

interactions *n* ▷ interact

interactive *adj* ▷ interact

interacts *v* ▷ interact

intercom *n* (pl -s) internal communication system with loudspeakers

intercoms *n* ▷ intercom

interest *n* (pl -s) desire to know or hear more about something ► *v* (-s, -ing, -ed) arouse the interest of > interesting *adj* > interestingly *adv*

interesting *v, adj* ▷ interest

interestingly *adv* ▷ interest

interests *n, v* ▷ interest

interim *adj* temporary or provisional

interior *n* (pl -s) inside ► *adj* inside, inner

interiors *n* ▷ interior

interment *n* ▷ inter

interments *n* ▷ inter

intern *v* (-s, -ing, -ed) imprison, esp. during a war ► *n* (pl -s) trainee doctor in a hospital > internment *n* (pl -s)

internal *adj* of or on the inside > internally *adv*

internally *adv* ▷ internal

interned *v* ▷ intern

internee *n* (pl -s) person who is interned

internees *n* ▷ internee

interning *v* ▷ intern

internment *n* ▷ intern

internments *n* ▷ intern

interns *v, n* ▷ intern

interred *v* ▷ inter

interring *v* ▷ inter

inters *v* ▷ inter

interval *n* (pl -s) time between two particular moments or events

intervals n ▷ interval
intimacies n ▷ intimate¹
intimacy n ▷ intimate¹
intimate¹ adj having a close personal relationship ▸ n (pl -s) close friend >intimately adv >intimacy n (pl -cies)
intimate² v (-tes, -ting, -ted) hint at or suggest >intimation n (pl -s)
intimated v ▷ intimate²
intimately adv ▷ intimate¹
intimates n ▷ intimate¹ ▸ v ▷ intimate²
intimating v ▷ intimate²
intimation n ▷ intimate²
intimations n ▷ intimate²
into prep indicating motion towards the centre, result of a change, division, etc
intone v (-nes, -ning, -ned) speak or recite in an unvarying tone of voice
intoned v ▷ intone
intones v ▷ intone
intoning v ▷ intone
intranet n (pl -s) COMPUTERS internal network that makes use of Internet technology
intranets n ▷ intranet
intrepid adj fearless, bold >intrepidity n (pl -ties)
intrepidities n ▷ intrepid
intrepidity n ▷ intrepid
intrigue v (-gues, -guing, -gued) make interested or curious ▸ n (pl -gues) secret plotting >intriguing adj
intrigued v ▷ intrigue
intrigues v, n ▷ intrigue
intriguing v, adj ▷ intrigue
intrude v (-des, -ding, -ded) come in or join without being invited >intrusion n (pl -s) >intrusive adj
intruded v ▷ intrude
intruder n (pl -s) person who enters a place without permission
intruders n ▷ intruder
intrudes v ▷ intrude
intruding v ▷ intrude
intrusion n ▷ intrude
intrusions n ▷ intrude

intrusive adj ▷ intrude
inundate v (-tes, -ting, -ted) flood >inundation n (pl -s)
inundated v ▷ inundate
inundates v ▷ inundate
inundating v ▷ inundate
inundation n ▷ inundate
inundations n ▷ inundate
inured adj accustomed, esp. to hardship or danger
invade v (-des, -ding, -ded) enter (a country) by military force >invader n (pl -s)
invaded v ▷ invade
invader n ▷ invade
invaders n ▷ invade
invades v ▷ invade
invading v ▷ invade
invalid¹ adj, n (pl -s) disabled or chronically ill (person) ▸ v (-s, -ing, -ed) (often foll. by out) dismiss from active service because of illness or injury >invalidity n (pl -ties)
invalid² adj having no legal force
invalided v ▷ invalid¹
invaliding v ▷ invalid¹
invalidities n ▷ invalid¹
invalidity n ▷ invalid¹
invalids n, v ▷ invalid¹
invasion n (pl -s) invading
invasions n ▷ invasion
inveigh v (-s, -ing, -ed) (foll. by against) criticize strongly
inveighed v ▷ inveigh
inveighing v ▷ inveigh
inveighs v ▷ inveigh
inveigle v (-les, -ling, -led) coax by cunning or trickery
inveigled v ▷ inveigle
inveigles v ▷ inveigle
inveigling v ▷ inveigle
invent v (-s, -ing, -ed) think up or create (something new)
invented v ▷ invent
inventing v ▷ invent
invents v ▷ invent
inverse adj reversed in effect, sequence, direction, etc

> **inversely** *adv*
inversely *adv* ▷ **inverse**
inversion *n* ▷ **invert**
inversions *n* ▷ **invert**
invert *v* (**-s, -ing, -ed**) turn upside down or inside out > **inversion** *n* (*pl* **-s**)
inverted *v* ▷ **invert**
inverting *v* ▷ **invert**
inverts *v* ▷ **invert**
invest *v* (**-s, -ing, -ed**) spend (money, time, etc) on something with the expectation of profit
invested *v* ▷ **invest**
investing *v* ▷ **invest**
invests *v* ▷ **invest**
invitation *n* ▷ **invite**
invitations *n* ▷ **invite**
invite *v* (**-tes, -ting, -ted**) request the company of ▶ *n* (*pl* **-s**) *informal* invitation > **invitation** *n* (*pl* **-s**)
invited *v* ▷ **invite**
invites *v, n* ▷ **invite**
inviting *adj* tempting, attractive ▶ *v* ▷ **invite**
invocation *n* ▷ **invoke**
invocations *n* ▷ **invoke**
invoice *v* (**-ces, -cing, -ced**) ▶ *n* (*pl* **-s**) (present with) a bill for goods or services supplied
invoiced *v* ▷ **invoice**
invoices *n, v* ▷ **invoice**
invoicing *v* ▷ **invoice**
invoke *v* (**-kes, -king, -ked**) put (a law or penalty) into operation > **invocation** *n* (*pl* **-s**)
invoked *v* ▷ **invoke**
invokes *v* ▷ **invoke**
invoking *v* ▷ **invoke**
involve *v* (**-lves, -lving, -lved**) include as a necessary part > **involved** *adj* complicated > **involvement** *n* (*pl* **-s**)
involved *v, adj* ▷ **involve**
involvement *n* ▷ **involve**
involvements *n* ▷ **involve**
involves *v* ▷ **involve**
involving *v* ▷ **involve**
inward *adj* directed towards the middle ▶ *adv* (*also* **inwards**) towards

the inside or middle > **inwardly** *adv*
inwardly *adv* ▷ **inward**
inwards *adv* ▷ **inward**

io *n* (**ios**). An io is a cry of joy or grief. While io doesn't earn many points, it's useful when you want to form words in more than one direction: I and O are two of the most common tiles in the game, so there's a good chance that you'll be able to use io when forming a word in another direction. Io scores 2 points.

iodine *n* (*pl* **-s**) CHEM bluish-black element used in medicine and photography
iodines *n* ▷ **iodine**
iodize *v* (**-zes, -zing, -zed**) treat with iodine
iodized *n* ▷ **iodize**
iodizes *n* ▷ **iodize**
iodizing *n* ▷ **iodize**
ion *n* (*pl* **-s**) electrically charged atom > **ionic** *adj*
ionic *adj* ▷ **ion**
ionization *n* ▷ **ionize**
ionizations *n* ▷ **ionize**
ionize *v* (**-izes, -izing, -ized**) change into ions > **ionization** *n* (*pl* **-s**)
ionized *v* ▷ **ionize**
ionizes *v* ▷ **ionize**
ionizing *v* ▷ **ionize**
ions *n* ▷ **ion**
iota *n* (*pl* **-s**) very small amount
iotas *n* ▷ **iota**
irate *adj* very angry
ire *n* (*pl* **-s**) *lit* anger
ires *n* ▷ **ire**
iridium *n* (*pl* **-s**) CHEM very hard corrosion-resistant metal
iridiums *n* ▷ **iridium**
iris *n* (*pl* **-ses**) coloured circular membrane of the eye containing the pupil
irises *n* ▷ **iris**
irk *v* (**-s, -ing, -ed**) irritate, annoy
irked *v* ▷ **irk**
irking *v* ▷ **irk**
irks *v* ▷ **irk**

irksome adj irritating, annoying
iron n (pl -s) strong silvery-white
metallic element, widely used for
structural and engineering purposes
▶ adj made of iron ▶ v (-s, -ing, -ed)
smooth (clothes or fabric) with an iron
ironbark n (pl -s) Australian
eucalyptus with hard rough bark
　ironbarks n ▷ ironbark
　ironed v ▷ iron
ironic, ironical adj using irony
　>**ironically** adv
　ironical adj ▷ ironic
　ironically adv ▷ ironic
　ironies n ▷ irony
ironing n (pl -s) clothes to be ironed
▶ v ▷ iron
　ironings n ▷ ironing
　irons n, v ▷ iron ▶ pl n chains, restraints
irony n (pl -nies) mildly sarcastic use
of words to imply the opposite of
what is said
irrigate v (-tes, -ting, -ted) supply
(land) with water by artificial channels
or pipes >**irrigation** n (pl -s)
　irrigated v ▷ irrigate
　irrigates v ▷ irrigate
　irrigating v ▷ irrigate
　irrigation n ▷ irrigate
　irrigations n ▷ irrigate
irritant n (pl -s) ▶ adj (person or thing)
causing irritation
　irritants n ▷ irritant
irritate v (-tes, -ting, -ted) annoy,
anger >**irritation** n (pl -s)
　irritated v ▷ irritate
　irritates v ▷ irritate
　irritating v ▷ irritate
　irritation n ▷ irritate
　irritations n ▷ irritate
is v ▷ be

　ish n (**ishes**). An ish is a word for
　an issue in Scots law. If you have
　I, S and H on your rack, remember
　that as well as adding **ish** to the end
　of many words, you can also play
　those letters as a word in its own
　right. Ish scores 6 points.

island n (pl -s) piece of land surrounded
by water
islander n (pl -s) person who lives on
an island
　islanders n ▷ islander
　islands n ▷ island
isle n (pl -s) poetic island
　isles n ▷ isle
islet n small island
　islets n ▷ islet

　ism n (**isms**). An ism is an informal
　word for a belief or doctrine. While
　ism can be added to the ends of
　many words as a suffix, it's worth
　remembering as a word in its own
　right. Ism scores 5 points.

isobar n (pl -s) line on a map
connecting places of equal
atmospheric pressure
　isobars n ▷ isobar
isolate v (-tes, -ting, -ted) place apart
or alone >**isolation** n (pl -s)
　isolated v ▷ isolate
　isolates v ▷ isolate
　isolating v ▷ isolate
　isolation n ▷ isolate
　isolations n ▷ isolate
isomer n (pl -s) substance whose
molecules contain the same atoms as
another but in a different arrangement
　isomers n ▷ isomer
isotherm n (pl -s) line on a map
connecting points of equal
temperature
　isotherms n ▷ isotherm
isotope n (pl -s) one of two or more
atoms with the same number of protons
in the nucleus but a different number
of neutrons
　isotopes n ▷ isotope
issue n (pl -s) topic of interest or
discussion ▶ v (-sues, -suing, -sued)
make (a statement etc) publicly
　issued v ▷ issue
　issues n, v ▷ issue
　issuing v ▷ issue
isthmus n (pl -muses) narrow strip of
land connecting two areas of land

isthmuses n ▷ **isthmus**
it pron refers to a nonhuman, animal, plant, or inanimate object > **its** adj, pron belonging to it
italic adj (of printing type) sloping to the right
italics pl n this type, used for emphasis
itch n (pl **-es**) skin irritation causing a desire to scratch ▶ v (**-es, -ing, -ed**) have an itch > **itchy** adj
itched v ▷ **itch**
itches n, v ▷ **itch**
itching v ▷ **itch**
itchy adj ▷ **itch**
item n (pl **-s**) single thing in a list or collection > **itemize** v (**-izes, -izing, -ized**) make a list of
itemized n ▷ **item**
itemizes n ▷ **item**

itemizing n ▷ **item**
items n ▷ **item**
iterate v (**-tes, -ting, -ted**) repeat > **iteration** n (pl **-s**)
iterated v ▷ **iterate**
iterates v ▷ **iterate**
iterating v ▷ **iterate**
iteration n ▷ **iterate**
iterations n ▷ **iterate**
itself pron ▷ **it**
ivies n ▷ **ivy**
ivories n ▷ **ivory**
ivory n (pl **-ries**) hard white bony substance forming the tusks of elephants ▶ adj yellowish-white
ivy n (pl **ivies**) evergreen climbing plant
iwi n (pl **-s**) NZ Maori tribe
iwis n ▷ **iwi**

Jj

J is one of the best tiles to have in Scrabble, as it is worth 8 points on its own. J also forms a number of words with X and Z, allowing you to earn some huge scores if you get the right tiles to go with it. Even better, some of these words are seven letters in length, so the right combination of tiles will give you a 50-point bonus if you are lucky enough to have it on your rack. On the other hand, J isn't the easiest tile to use when forming words in different directions. There's only one two-letter word that begins with J: **jo**. If you remember this, however, you won't waste time trying to think of others. As J has such a high value, look out for double- and triple-letter squares when playing it. There are plenty of good three-letter words starting with J: **jab** (12 points), **jam** (12), **jar** (10), **jaw** (13), **jay** (13), **jet** (10), **jib** (12), **job** (12), **jog** (11), **jot** (10), **joy** (13), **jug** (11) and **jut** (10). In addition to these, there are other fantastic words beginning with J. **Jazz** (19) is very useful – you'll need a blank tile for the second Z, but if you can form it, you may also be able to play **jazzes** (21) or **jazzy** (23). **Jinx** (18) is also handy, and don't forget **jukebox** (27), which can be formed from **box** or **ox** if someone has played those.

jab v (-s, -bbing, -bbed) poke sharply
▶ n (pl -s)
  jabbed v ▷ jab
jabber v (-s, -ing, -ed) talk rapidly or incoherently
  jabbered v ▷ jabber
  jabbering v ▷ jabber
  jabbers v ▷ jabber
  jabbing v ▷ jab
jabiru n (pl -s) large white-and-black Australian stork
  jabirus n ▷ jabiru
  jabs v, n ▷ jab
jack n (pl -s) device for raising a motor vehicle or other heavy object
jackal n (pl -s) doglike wild animal of Africa and Asia
  jackals n ▷ jackal
jackaroo, jackeroo n (pl -roos) AUST trainee on a sheep station

  jackaroos n ▷ jackaroo
jackass n (pl -es) fool
  jackasses n ▷ jackass
jackboot n (pl -s) high military boot
  jackboots n ▷ jackboot
jackdaw n (pl -s) black-and-grey Eurasian bird of the crow family
  jackdaws n ▷ jackdaw
  jackeroo n ▷ jackaroo
  jackeroos n ▷ jackaroo
jacket n (pl -s) short coat
  jackets n ▷ jacket
jackpot n (pl -s) largest prize that may be won in a game
  jackpots n ▷ jackpot
  jacks n ▷ jack
jacuzzi n® (pl -s) circular bath with a device that swirls the water
  jacuzzis n ▷ jacuzzi

jade n (pl -s) ornamental semiprecious stone, usu. dark green ▸ adj bluish-green

jaded adj tired and unenthusiastic

jades n ▷ jade

jagged adj having an uneven edge with sharp points

jaguar n (pl -s) large S American spotted cat

jaguars n ▷ jaguar

jail n (pl -s) prison ▸ v (-s, -ing, -ed) send to prison > **jailer** n (pl -s)

jailbird n (pl -s) informal person who has often been in prison

jailbirds n ▷ jailbird

jailed v ▷ jail

jailer n ▷ jail

jailers n ▷ jail

jailing v ▷ jail

jails n, v ▷ jail

jalopies n ▷ jalopy

jalopy n (pl -pies) informal old car

jam[1] v (-s, -mming, -mmed) pack tightly into a place ▸ n (pl -s) hold-up of traffic

jam[2] n food made from fruit boiled with sugar

jamb n (pl -s) side post of a door or window frame

jamboree n (pl -s) large gathering or celebration

jamborees n ▷ jamboree

jambs n ▷ jamb

jammed v ▷ jam[1]

jamming v ▷ jam[1]

jams v ▷ jam[1] ▸ n ▷ jam[1, 2]

jandal n (pl -s) NZ sandal with a strap between the toes

jandals n ▷ jandal

jangle v (-les, -ling, -led) (cause to) make a harsh ringing noise

jangled v ▷ jangle

jangles v ▷ jangle

jangling v ▷ jangle

janitor n (pl -s) caretaker of a school or other building

janitors n ▷ janitor

janizar or **janizary** n (**janizars**, **janizaries**). A janizar was an elite soldier in the armies of the Ottoman Empire. This is a very useful word, and will earn you a 50-point bonus if you are able to use all your letters in playing it. Also, if janizar is already on the board, you have an opportunity to earn a good score by adding an S, Y or IES. Janizar scores 23 points.

japan n (pl -s) very hard varnish, usu. black ▸ v (-s, -nning, -nned) cover with this varnish

japanned v ▷ japan

japanning v ▷ japan

japans n, v ▷ japan

jape n (pl -s) old-fashioned joke or prank

japes n ▷ jape

japonica n (pl -s) shrub with red flowers

japonicas n ▷ japonica

jar[1] n (pl -s) wide-mouthed container, usu. round and made of glass

jar[2] v (-s, -rring, -rred) have a disturbing or unpleasant effect ▸ n (pl -s) jolt or shock

jargon n (pl -s) specialized technical language of a particular subject

jargons n ▷ jargon

jarrah n (pl -s) Australian eucalypt yielding valuable timber

jarrahs n ▷ jarrah

jarred v ▷ jar[2]

jarring v ▷ jar[2]

jars v ▷ jar[2] ▸ n ▷ jar[1, 2]

jasmine n (pl -s) shrub with sweet-smelling yellow or white flowers

jasmines n ▷ jasmine

jasper n (pl -s) red, yellow, dark green, or brown variety of quartz

jaspers n ▷ jasper

jaundice n (pl -s) disease marked by yellowness of the skin

jaundices n ▷ jaundice

jaunt n (pl -s) short journey for pleasure

jauntier adj ▷ **jaunty**
jauntiest adj ▷ **jaunty**
jauntily adv ▷ **jaunty**
jaunts n ▷ **jaunt**
jaunty adj (**-tier, -tiest**) sprightly and cheerful > **jauntily** adv
javelin n (pl **-s**) light spear thrown in sports competitions
javelins n ▷ **javelin**
jaw n (pl **-s**) one of the bones in which the teeth are set ▶ v (**-s, -ing, -ed**) slang talk lengthily

> **jawbox** n (**jawboxes**). Jawbox is a Scots word for a sink. Watch out for opportunities to form this if someone else has played either jaw or box, and if jawbox itself is on the board, you can earn 27 points just by making it plural with es. Jawbox scores 25 points.

jawed v ▷ **jaw**
jawing v ▷ **jaw**
jaws n, v ▷ **jaw** ▶ pl n mouth
jay n (pl **-s**) bird with a pinkish body and blue-and-black wings
jays ▷ **jay**
jazz n (pl **-es**) kind of music with an exciting rhythm, usu. involving improvisation
jazzes n ▷ **jazz**
jazzier adj ▷ **jazzy**
jazziest adj ▷ **jazzy**
jazzy adj (**-zier, -ziest**) flashy or showy
jealous adj fearful of losing a partner or possession to a rival > **jealously** adv
> **jealousy** n (pl **-sies**)
jealousies n ▷ **jealous**
jealously adv ▷ **jealous**
jealousy n ▷ **jealous**
jeans pl n casual denim trousers
jeer v (**-s, -ing, -ed**) scoff or deride ▶ n (pl **-s**) cry of derision
jeered v ▷ **jeer**
jeering v ▷ **jeer**
jeers v, n ▷ **jeer**
jejune adj simple or naive
jell v (**-s, -ing, -ed**) form into a jelly-like substance

jelled v ▷ **jell**
jellied adj prepared in a jelly
jellies n ▷ **jelly**
jelling v ▷ **jell**
jells v ▷ **jell**
jelly n (pl **-llies**) soft food made of liquid set with gelatine
jemmies n ▷ **jemmy**
jemmy n (pl **-mmies**) short steel crowbar used by burglars
jennies n ▷ **jenny**
jenny n (pl **-nies**) female ass or wren
jeopardies n ▷ **jeopardy**
jeopardized n ▷ **jeopardy**
jeopardizes n ▷ **jeopardy**
jeopardizing n ▷ **jeopardy**
jeopardy n (pl **-dies**) danger
jerboa n (pl **-s**) small mouselike rodent with long hind legs
jerboas n ▷ **jerboa**
jerk v (**-s, -ing, -ed**) move or throw abruptly ▶ n (pl **-s**) sharp or abruptly stopped movement
jerked v ▷ **jerk**
jerkily adv ▷ **jerky**
jerkin n (pl **-s**) sleeveless jacket
jerkiness n ▷ **jerky**
jerkinesses n ▷ **jerky**
jerking v ▷ **jerk**
jerkins n ▷ **jerkin**
jerks v, n ▷ **jerk**
jerky adj sudden or abrupt > **jerkily** adv
> **jerkiness** n (pl **-s**)

> **jerque** v (**jerques, jerquing, jerqued**) ▶ n (**jerquer, jerquers, jerquing, jerquings**). Jerque means to search a ship for smuggled goods. If you have all the tiles for jerques, jerquer or jerqued, you'll get a 50-point bonus for using all your letters, which will give you a fantastic score. Jerque scores 22 points.

jersey n (pl **-s**) knitted jumper
jerseys n ▷ **jersey**
jest n (pl **-s**) ▶ v (**-s, -ing, -ed**) joke
jested v ▷ **jest**
jester n (pl **-s**) HIST professional clown

at court

jesters n ▷ **jester**

jesting v ▷ **jest**

jests n, v ▷ **jest**

jet¹ n (pl **-s**) aircraft driven by jet propulsion ▶ v (**-s, -tting, -tted**) fly by jet aircraft

jet² n (pl **-s**) hard black mineral

jetboat n (pl **-s**) motorboat propelled by a jet of water

jetboats n ▷ **jetboat**

jets n ▷ **jet**¹, ² ▶ v ▷ **jet**¹

jetsam n (pl **-s**) goods thrown overboard to lighten a ship

jetsams n ▷ **jetsam**

jetted v ▷ **jet**¹

jetties n ▷ **jetty**

jetting v ▷ **jet**¹

jettison v (**-s, -ing, -ed**) abandon

jettisoned v ▷ **jettison**

jettisoning v ▷ **jettison**

jettisons v ▷ **jettison**

jetty n (pl **-ties**) small pier

> **jeu** n (**jeux**). Jeu is the French word for **game** or **play**. The plural form, jeux, is a great little word, using both J and X particularly if you can play it on a double- or triple-word square. Jeux scores 18 points.

jewel n (pl **-s**) precious stone

jeweller n (pl **-s**) dealer in jewels

jewellers n ▷ **jeweller**

jewels n ▷ **jewel**

jewfish n (pl **jewfish**) AUST freshwater catfish

> **jezail** n (**jezails**). A jezail is a kind of heavy Afghan musket. This word is potentially a very high scorer, as its plural uses seven tiles. If you can play all of these at once, you'll earn the 50-point bonus for a total of 73 points! Jezail scores 22 points.

jib¹ n (pl **-s**) triangular sail set in front of a mast

jib² v (**-s, -bbing, -bbed**) (of a horse, person, etc) stop suddenly and refuse to go on

jib³ n (pl **-s**) projecting arm of a crane or derrick

jibbed v ▷ **jib**²

jibbing v ▷ **jib**²

jibe¹ n (pl **-s**) ▶ v (**-jibes, -jibing, -jibed**) taunt or jeer

jibed v ▷ **jibe**¹

jibes n, v ▷ **jibe**¹

jibing v ▷ **jibe**¹

jibs n ▷ **jib**¹,³ ▶ v ▷ **jib**²

jiffies n ▷ **jiffy**

jiffy n (pl **-ffies**) informal very short period of time

jig n (pl **-s**) type of lively dance ▶ v (**-s, -gging, -gged**) make jerky up-and-down movements

jigged v ▷ **jig**

jigging v ▷ **jig**

jiggle v (**-ggles, -ggling, -ggled**) move up and down with short jerky movements

jiggled v ▷ **jiggle**

jiggles v ▷ **jiggle**

jiggling v ▷ **jiggle**

jigs n, v ▷ **jig**

jigsaw n (pl **-s**) (also **jigsaw puzzle**) picture cut into interlocking pieces, which the user tries to fit together again

jigsaws n ▷ **jigsaw**

jihad n (pl **-s**) Islamic holy war against unbelievers

jihads n ▷ **jihad**

jilt v (**-s, -ing, -ed**) leave or reject (one's lover)

jilted v ▷ **jilt**

jilting v ▷ **jilt**

jilts v ▷ **jilt**

jingle n (pl **-s**) catchy verse or song used in a radio or television advert ▶ v (**-les, -ling, -led**) (cause to) make a gentle ringing sound

jingled v ▷ **jingle**

jingles n, v ▷ **jingle**

jingling v ▷ **jingle**

jingoism n (pl **-s**) aggressive nationalism ▷ **jingoistic** adj

jingoisms n ▷ **jingoism**

jingoistic adj ▷ **jingoism**

jinks pl n boisterous merrymaking

jinn n ▷ jinni

jinni n (pl jinn) spirit in Muslim mythology

jinx n (pl -es) person or thing bringing bad luck ▶ v (-xes, -xing, -xed) be or put a jinx on

jinxed v ▷ jinx

jinxes n, v ▷ jinx

jinxing v ▷ jinx

jitters pl n worried nervousness

jittery adj nervous

jive n (pl -s) lively dance of the 1940s and '50s ▶ v (-ves, -ving, -ved) dance the jive

jived v ▷ jive

jives n, v ▷ jive

jiving v ▷ jive

> **jiz** n (**jizes**). Jiz is an old word for a wig. This is a very useful word for when you find yourself with J and Z and nothing else that looks promising: there will almost certainly be an I on the board around which you can form jiz. Jiz scores 19 points.

> **jizz** n (**jizzes**). A jizz is the combination of characteristics used to identify a bird or plant species. A blank tile is required to form jizz because it contains two Zs. If **jiz** is already on the board, a blank or a blank and ES will earn you 19 or 21 points. Jizz scores 19 points.

> **jo** n (**joes**). Jo is a Scots word for a sweetheart. This is the only two-letter word that starts with J, and is worth remembering for that reason. It's also a good word to form when playing in more than one direction at once. Jo scores 9 points.

job n (pl -s) occupation or paid employment

jobbing adj doing individual jobs for payment

jobless adj, pl n unemployed (people)

jobs n ▷ job

jockey n (pl -s) (professional) rider of racehorses ▶ v (-ys, -ying, -yed)

manoeuvre to obtain an advantage

jockeyed v ▷ jockey

jockeying v ▷ jockey

jockeys n, v ▷ jockey

jocose adj playful or humorous

jocular adj fond of joking ▷ **jocularity** n (pl -ties) ▷ **jocularly** adv

jocularities n ▷ jocular

jocularity n ▷ jocular

jocularly adv ▷ jocular

jocund adj lit merry or cheerful

jodhpurs pl n riding trousers, loose-fitting above the knee but tight below

joey n (pl -ys) AUST young kangaroo

joeys n ▷ joey

jog v (-s, -gging, -gged) run at a gentle pace, esp. for exercise ▶ n (pl -s) slow run ▷ **jogger** n (pl -s) ▷ **jogging** n (pl -s)

jogged v ▷ jog

jogger n ▷ jog

joggers n ▷ jog

jogging n, v ▷ jog

joggings n ▷ jog

joggle v (-les, -ling, -led) shake or move jerkily

joggled v ▷ joggle

joggles v ▷ joggle

joggling v ▷ joggle

jogs n, v ▷ jog

join v (-s, -ing, -ed) become a member (of) ▶ n (pl -s) place where two things are joined

joined v ▷ join

joiner n (pl -s) maker of finished woodwork

joineries n ▷ joinery

joiners n ▷ joiner

joinery n (pl -ries) joiner's work

joining v ▷ join

joins n, v ▷ join

joint adj shared by two or more ▶ n (pl -s) place where bones meet but can move ▶ v (-s, -ing, -ed) divide meat into joints ▷ **jointed** adj ▷ **jointly** adv

jointed v, adj ▷ joint

jointing v ▷ joint

jointly adv ▷ joint

joints n, v ▷ joint

joist n (pl -s) horizontal beam that helps support a floor or ceiling
joists n ▷ joist

jojoba n (pl -s) shrub of SW North America whose seeds yield oil used in cosmetics
jojobas n ▷ jojoba

joke n (pl -s) thing said or done to cause laughter ▶ v (-kes, -king, -ked) make jokes > **jokey** adj > **jokingly** adv
joked v ▷ joke

joker n (pl -s) person who jokes
jokers n ▷ joker
jokes n, v ▷ joke
jokey adj ▷ joke
joking v ▷ joke
jokingly adv ▷ joke

jollied v ▷ jolly
jollier adj ▷ jolly
jollies v ▷ jolly
jolliest adj ▷ jolly
jollifications n ▷ jolly
jollities n ▷ jolly
jollity n ▷ jolly

jolly adj (-lier, -lliest) (of a person) happy and cheerful ▶ v (-llies, -llying, -llied) try to keep (someone) cheerful by flattery or coaxing > **jollity** n (pl -ties)
jollying v ▷ jolly

jolt n (pl -s) unpleasant surprise or shock ▶ v (-s, -ing, -ed) surprise or shock
jolted v ▷ jolt
jolting v ▷ jolt
jolts n, v ▷ jolt

jonquil n (pl -s) fragrant narcissus
jonquils n ▷ jonquil

josh v (-es, -ing, -ed) CHIEFLY US slang tease
joshed v ▷ josh
joshes v ▷ josh
joshing v ▷ josh

jostle v (-les, -ling, -led) knock or push against
jostled v ▷ jostle
jostles v ▷ jostle
jostling v ▷ jostle

jot v (-s, -tting, -tted) write briefly ▶ n (pl -s) very small amount
jots v, n ▷ jot
jotted v ▷ jot

jotter n (pl -s) notebook
jotters n ▷ jotter
jotting v ▷ jot

jottings pl n notes jotted down

joule n (pl -s) PHYSICS unit of work or energy
joules n ▷ joule

journal n (pl -s) daily newspaper or magazine
journals n ▷ journal

journey n (pl -s) act or process of travelling from one place to another ▶ v (-s, -ing, -ed) travel
journeyed v ▷ journey
journeying v ▷ journey
journeys n, v ▷ journey

joust HIST n (pl -s) combat with lances between two mounted knights ▶ v (-s, -ing, -ed) fight on horseback using lances
jousted v ▷ joust
jousting v ▷ joust
jousts n, v ▷ joust

jovial adj happy and cheerful > **jovially** adv > **joviality** n (pl -ties)
jovialities n ▷ jovial
joviality n ▷ jovial
jovially adv ▷ jovial

jowl¹ n (pl -s) lower jaw

jowl² n (pl -s) fatty flesh hanging from the lower jaw
jowls n > **jowl¹, ²** pl n cheeks

joy n (pl -s) feeling of great delight or pleasure > **joyful** adj > **joyless** adj
joyful adj ▷ joy
joyless adj ▷ joy

joyous adj extremely happy and enthusiastic
joys n ▷ joy

joystick n (pl -s) control device for an aircraft or computer
joysticks n ▷ joystick

jubilant adj feeling or expressing great joy > **jubilantly** adv > **jubilation** n (pl -s)

jubilantly adv ▷ jubilant
jubilation n ▷ jubilant
jubilations n ▷ jubilant
jubilee n (pl -s) special anniversary, esp. 25th (**silver jubilee**) or 50th (**golden jubilee**)
jubilees n ▷ jubilee
judder v (-s, -ing, -ed) vibrate violently ▶ n (pl -s) violent vibration
juddered v ▷ judder
juddering v ▷ judder
judders v, n ▷ judder
judge n (pl -s) public official who tries cases and passes sentence in a court of law ▶ v (-dges, -dging, -dged) act as a judge
judged v ▷ judge
judgement n ▷ judgment
judgemental adj ▷ judgment
judgements n ▷ judgment
judges n, v ▷ judge
judging v ▷ judge
judgment, judgement n (pl -s) opinion reached after careful thought >**judgmental, judgemental** adj
judgmental adj ▷ judgment
judgments n ▷ judgment
judicial adj of or by a court or judge >**judicially** adv
judicially adv ▷ judicial
judo n sport in which two opponents try to throw each other to the ground
jug n (pl -s) container for liquids, with a handle and small spout
juggle v (-les, -ling, -led) throw and catch (several objects) so that most are in the air at the same time >**juggler** n (pl -s)
juggled v ▷ juggle
juggler n ▷ juggle
jugglers n ▷ juggle
juggles v ▷ juggle
juggling v ▷ juggle
jugs n ▷ jug
jugular n (pl -s) one of three large veins of the neck that return blood from the head to the heart
jugulars n ▷ jugular

juice n (pl -s) liquid part of vegetables, fruit, or meat
juices n ▷ juice
juicier adj ▷ juicy
juiciest adj ▷ juicy
juicy adj (-cier, -ciest) full of juice
jujitsu n (pl -s) Japanese art of wrestling and self-defence
jujitsus n ▷ jujitsu
juju n (pl -s) W African magic charm or fetish
jujus n ▷ juju
jukebox n (pl -es) coin-operated machine on which records, CDs, or videos can be played
jukeboxes n ▷ jukebox
julep n (pl -s) sweet alcoholic drink
juleps n ▷ julep
jumble n (pl -s) confused heap or state ▶ v (-les, -ling, -led) mix in a disordered way
jumbled v ▷ jumble
jumbles n, v ▷ jumble
jumbling v ▷ jumble
jumbo adj informal very large ▶ n (pl -s) (also **jumbo jet**) large jet airliner
jumbos n ▷ jumbo
jumbuck n (pl -s) AUST old-fashioned slang sheep
jumbucks n ▷ jumbuck
jump v (-s, -ing, -ed) leap or spring into the air using the leg muscles ▶ n (pl -s) act of jumping
jumped v ▷ jump
jumper n (pl -s) sweater or pullover
jumpers n ▷ jumper
jumpier adj ▷ jumpy
jumpiest adj ▷ jumpy
jumping v ▷ jump
jumps v, n ▷ jump
jumpy adj (-pier, -piest) nervous
junction n (pl -s) place where routes, railway lines, or roads meet
junctions n ▷ junction
juncture n (pl -s) point in time, esp. a critical one
junctures n ▷ juncture
jungle n (pl -s) tropical forest of dense

tangled vegetation

jungles n ▷ jungle

junior adj of lower standing ▶ n (pl **-s**) junior person

juniors n ▷ junior

juniper n (pl **-s**) evergreen shrub with purple berries

junipers n ▷ juniper

junk¹ n (pl **-s**) discarded or useless objects

junk² n (pl **-s**) flat-bottomed Chinese sailing boat

junket n (pl **-s**) excursion by public officials paid for from public funds

junkets n ▷ junket

junkie, junky n (pl **-ies**) slang drug addict

junkies n ▷ junkie

junks n ▷ junk¹, ²

junky n ▷ junkie

junta n (pl **-s**) group of military officers holding power in a country, esp. after a coup

juntas n ▷ junta

juries n ▷ jury

jurist n (pl **-s**) expert in law

jurists n ▷ jurist

juror n (pl **-s**) member of a jury

jurors n ▷ juror

jury n (pl **-ries**) group of people sworn

to deliver a verdict in a court of law

just adv very recently ▶ adj fair or impartial in action or judgment
> **justly** adv > **justness** n (pl **-s**)

justice n (pl **-s**) quality of being just

justices n ▷ justice

justifiable adj ▷ justify

justifiably adv ▷ justify

justification n ▷ justify

justifications n ▷ justify

justified v ▷ justify

justifies v ▷ justify

justify v (**-fies**, **-fying**, **-fied**) prove right or reasonable > **justifiable** adj
> **justifiably** adv > **justification** n (pl **-s**)

justifying v ▷ justify

justly adv ▷ just

justness n ▷ just

justnesses n ▷ just

jut v (**-s**, **-tting**, **-tted**) project or stick out

jute n (pl **-s**) plant fibre, used for rope, canvas, etc

jutes n ▷ jute

juts v ▷ jut

jutted v ▷ jut

jutting v ▷ jut

juvenile adj young ▶ n (pl **-s**) young person or child

juveniles n ▷ juvenile

Kk

Worth 5 points, K is a valuable tile to have in your rack. However, it's not the most useful tile for forming words in different directions at the same time. There are only three two-letter words beginning with K: **ka**, **ko** and **ky**. Remembering these will stop you wasting time trying to think of others. There aren't very many three-letter words either, but remember **kak** (11 points), **keg** (8), **key** (10), **kid** (8), **kin** (7), **kip** (9) and **kit** (7).

ka n (**kas**). A ka is a supernatural being in ancient Egyptian mythology. This is worth remembering as, along with **ko** and **ky**, it's one of only three two-letter words starting with K. Ka scores 6 points.

kaftan n (pl **-s**) long loose Eastern garment
  kaftans n ▷ kaftan

kaiser n (pl **-s**) HIST German or Austro-Hungarian emperor
  kaisers n ▷ kaiser

kak n (pl **s** AFR slang faeces

kale n (pl **-s**) cabbage with crinkled leaves
  kales n ▷ kale

kamikaze n (pl **-s**) (in World War II) Japanese pilot who performed a suicide mission ▶ adj (of an action) undertaken in the knowledge that it will kill or injure the person performing it
  kamikazes n ▷ kamikaze

kangaroo n (pl **-s**) Australian marsupial which moves by jumping with its powerful hind legs
  kangaroos n ▷ kangaroo

kaolin n (pl **-s**) fine white clay used to make porcelain and in some medicines

kaolins n ▷ kaolin

kapok n (pl **-s**) fluffy fibre from a tropical tree, used to stuff cushions etc
  kapoks n ▷ kapok

kaput adj informal ruined or broken

karaoke n (pl **-s**) form of entertainment in which people sing over a prerecorded backing tape
  karaokes n ▷ karaoke

karate n (pl **-s**) Japanese system of unarmed combat using blows with the feet, hands, elbows, and legs
  karates n ▷ karate

karma n (pl **-s**) BUDDHISM HINDUISM person's actions affecting his or her fate in the next reincarnation
  karmas n ▷ karma

karri n (pl **-s**) Australian eucalypt
  karris n ▷ karri

katipo n (pl **-s**) small poisonous New Zealand spider
  katipos n ▷ katipo

kayak n (pl **-s**) Inuit canoe made of sealskins stretched over a frame
  kayaks n ▷ kayak

kebab n (pl **-s**) dish of small pieces of meat grilled on skewers
  kebabs n ▷ kebab

kedgeree n (pl **-s**) dish of fish with rice and eggs

kedgerees n ▷ kedgeree

keel n (pl -s) main lengthways timber or steel support along the base of a ship
keels n ▷ keel

keen¹ adj (-er, -est) eager or enthusiastic > **keenly** adv
> **keenness** n

keen² v (-s, -ing, -ed) wail over the dead
keened v ▷ keen²
keener adj ▷ keen¹
keenest adj ▷ keen¹
keening v ▷ keen²
keenly adv ▷ keen¹
keenness n ▷ keen¹
keens v ▷ keen²

keep v (-s, -ing, kept) have or retain possession of ▶ n (-s) cost of food and everyday expenses
keeper n (pl -s) person who looks after animals in a zoo
keepers n ▷ keeper
keeping v ▷ keep ▶ n (-s) care or charge
keepings n ▷ keeping
keeps v ▷ keep ▶ n ▷ keep
keepsake n (pl -s) gift treasured for the sake of the giver
keepsakes n ▷ keepsake

keg n (pl -s) small metal beer barrel
kegs n ▷ keg

kelp n (pl -s) large brown seaweed
kelpie n (pl -s) Australian sheepdog with a smooth coat and upright ears
kelpies n ▷ kelpie
kelps n ▷ kelp

kelvin n (pl -s) SI unit of temperature
kelvins n ▷ kelvin

ken v (-s, -nning, -nned or kent) SCOT know

kendo n (pl -s) Japanese sport of fencing using wooden staves
kendos n ▷ kendo
kenned v ▷ ken

kennel n (pl -s) hutlike shelter for a dog
kennels n ▷ kennel
kenning v ▷ ken
kens n ▷ ken

kent v ▷ ken

kept v ▷ keep

keratin n (pl -s) fibrous protein found in the hair and nails
keratins n ▷ keratin

kerb n (pl -s) edging to a footpath
kerbs n ▷ kerb

kerchief n (pl -s) piece of cloth worn over the head or round the neck
kerchiefs n ▷ kerchief

kernel n (pl -s) seed of a nut, cereal, or fruit stone
kernels n ▷ kernel

kerosene n (pl -s) US, CANADIAN, AUST & NZ liquid mixture distilled from petroleum and used as a fuel or solvent
kerosenes n ▷ kerosene

kestrel n (pl -s) type of small falcon
kestrels n ▷ kestrel

ketch n (pl -es) two-masted sailing ship
ketches n ▷ ketch

ketchup n (pl -s) thick cold sauce, usu. made of tomatoes
ketchups n ▷ ketchup

kettle n (pl -s) container with a spout and handle used for boiling water
kettles n ▷ kettle

> **kex** (**kexes**). A kex is a hollow-stemmed plant. This is a great three-letter word, combining K with X. If you have these letters on your rack, you can be confident that there will be, or will soon be, an E on the board, around which you can form kex. Kex scores 14 points.

key n (pl -s) device for operating a lock by moving a bolt ▶ adj of great importance ▶ v (-s, -ing, -ed) enter (text) using a keyboard
keyboard n (pl -s) set of keys on a piano, computer, etc ▶ v (-s, -ing, -ed) enter (text) using a keyboard
keyboarded v ▷ keyboard
keyboarding v ▷ keyboard
keyboards n, v ▷ keyboard
keyed v ▷ key

keyhole n (pl **-s**) opening for inserting a key into a lock

keyholes n ▷ **keyhole**

keying v ▷ **key**

keynote n (pl **-s**) dominant idea of a speech etc

keynotes n ▷ **keynote**

keys n, v ▷ **key**

keystone n (pl **-s**) most important part of a process, organization, etc

keystones n ▷ **keystone**

khaki adj dull yellowish-brown ▶ n (pl **-s**) hard-wearing fabric of this colour used for military uniforms

khakis n ▷ **khaki**

khi n (**khis**). Khi is a letter of the Greek alphabet, also spelt **chi**. This is one of the higher-scoring three-letter words starting with K, and so is worth remembering. Khi scores 10 points.

kibbutz n (pl **-im**) communal farm or factory in Israel

kibbutzim n ▷ **kibbutz**

kick v (**-s, -ing, -ed**) drive, push, or strike with the foot ▶ n (pl **kicks**) thrust or blow with the foot

kickback informal n (pl **-s**) money paid illegally for favours done

kickbacks n ▷ **kickback**

kicked v ▷ **kick**

kicking n, v ▷ **kick**

kicks n, v ▷ **kick**

kid¹ n (pl **-s**) informal child

kid² v (**-s, -dding, -dded**) informal tease or deceive (someone)

kidded v ▷ **kid²**

kidding v ▷ **kid²**

kidnap v (**-s, -pping, -pped**) seize and hold (a person) to ransom > **kidnapper** n (pl **-s**)

kidnapped n ▷ **kidnap**

kidnapper n ▷ **kidnap**

kidnappers n ▷ **kidnap**

kidnapping n ▷ **kidnap**

kidnaps n ▷ **kidnap**

kidney n (pl **-s**) either of the pair of organs that filter waste products from the blood to produce urine

kidneys n ▷ **kidney**

kids n ▷ **kid¹** ▶ v ▷ **kid²**

kill v (**-s, -ing, -ed**) cause the death of informal ▶ n (pl **-s**) act of killing > **killer** n (pl **killers**)

killed v ▷ **kill**

killer n ▷ **kill**

killers n ▷ **kill**

killing informal adj very tiring ▶ n (pl **-s**) sudden financial success ▶ v ▷ **kill**

killings n ▷ **killing**

killjoy n (pl **-s**) person who spoils others' pleasure

killjoys n ▷ **killjoy**

kills v, n ▷ **kill**

kiln n (pl **-s**) oven for baking, drying, or processing pottery, bricks, etc

kilns n ▷ **kiln**

kilobyte n (pl **-s**) COMPUTERS 1024 units of information

kilobytes n ▷ **kilobyte**

kilogram, kilogramme n (pl **-s**) one thousand grams

kilogrammes n ▷ **kilogram**

kilograms n ▷ **kilogram**

kilowatt n (pl **-s**) ELECTRICITY one thousand watts

kilowatts n ▷ **kilowatt**

kilt n (pl **-s**) knee-length pleated tartan skirt worn orig. by Scottish Highlanders > **kilted** adj

kilted n ▷ **kilt**

kilts n ▷ **kilt**

kimono n (pl **-s**) loose wide-sleeved Japanese robe, fastened with a sash

kimonos n ▷ **kimono**

kin, kinsfolk n person's relatives collectively > **kinship** n (pl **-s**) ▶ n

kind¹ adj (**-er, -est**) considerate, friendly, and helpful > **kindness** n (pl **-es**) > **kindliness** n (pl **-es**)

kind² n (pl **-s**) class or group with common characteristics

kinder adj n ▷ **kind¹**

kindest adj ▷ **kind¹**

kindhearted adj ▷ **kind¹**

kindies n ▷ **kindy**

kindle v (-les, -ling, -led) set (a fire) alight
kindled v ▷ **kindle**
kindles v ▷ **kindle**
kindliness n (pl -es) ▷ **kind¹**
kindlinesses n ▷ **kind¹**
kindling n (pl -s) dry wood or straw for starting fires ▶ v ▷ **kindle**
kindly adj having a warm-hearted nature ▶ adv in a considerate way
kindness n (pl -es) ▷ **kind¹**
kindnesses n ▷ **kind¹**
kindred adj having similar qualities ▶ n (pl -s) ▷ **kin**
kinds n ▷ **kind²**
kindy, kindie n (pl -dies) AUST & NZ informal kindergarten
kinetic adj relating to or caused by motion
king n (pl kings) male ruler of a monarchy >**kingship** n (pl -s)
kingdom n (pl -s) state ruled by a king or queen
kingdoms n ▷ **kingdom**
kingpin n (pl -s) most important person in an organization
kingpins n ▷ **kingpin**
kings n ▷ **king**
kingship n (pl -s) ▷ **king**
kingships n ▷ **king**
kink n (pl -s) twist or bend in rope, wire, hair, etc
kinks n ▷ **kink**
kinky adj slang given to unusual sexual practices
kinships n ▷ **kin**
kiosk n (pl -s) small booth selling drinks, cigarettes, newspapers, etc
kiosks n ▷ **kiosk**
kip informal n (pl -s) sleep ▶ v (-s, -pping, -pped) sleep
kipped v ▷ **kip**
kipper n (pl -s) cleaned, salted, and smoked herring
kippers n ▷ **kipper**
kipping v ▷ **kip**
kips v ▷ **kip**
kirk n (pl -s) SCOT church

kirks n ▷ **kirk**
kismet n (pl -s) fate or destiny
kismets n ▷ **kismet**
kiss v (-es, -ing, -ed) touch with the lips in affection or greeting ▶ n (pl -es) touch with the lips
kissed v ▷ **kiss**
kisser n (pl -s) slang mouth or face
kissers n ▷ **kisser**
kisses v, n ▷ **kiss**
kissing v ▷ **kiss**
kist n (pl -s) S AFR large wooden chest
kists n ▷ **kist**
kit n (pl -s) outfit or equipment for a specific purpose
kitbag n (pl -s) bag for a soldier's or traveller's belongings
kitbags n ▷ **kitbag**
kitchen n (pl -s) room used for cooking
kitchens n ▷ **kitchen**
kitches n ▷ **kitch**
kite n (pl -s) light frame covered with a thin material flown on a string in the wind
kites n ▷ **kite**
kith n (pl -s) friends and relatives
kiths n ▷ **kith**
kits n ▷ **kit**
kitsch n (pl -es) art or literature with popular sentimental appeal
kitten n (pl -s) young cat
kittens n ▷ **kitten**
kitties n ▷ **kitty**
kitty n (pl -ties) communal fund
kiwi n (pl -s) New Zealand flightless bird with a long beak and no tail
kiwis n ▷ **kiwi**
klaxon n (pl -s) loud horn used on emergency vehicles as a warning signal
klaxons n ▷ **klaxon**
kloof n (pl kloofs) S AFR mountain pass or gorge
kloofs n ▷ **kloof**
knack n (pl knacks) skilful way of doing something
knacker n (pl -s) BRIT buyer of old horses for killing

knackers n ▷ knacker

knacks n ▷ knack

knapsack n (pl -s) soldier's or traveller's bag worn strapped on the back

knapsacks n ▷ knapsack

knave n (pl -s) jack at cards obs

knaves n ▷ knave

knead v (-s, -ing, -ed) work (dough) into a smooth mixture with the hands

kneaded v ▷ knead

kneading v ▷ knead

kneads v ▷ knead

knee n (pl knees) joint between thigh and lower leg ▶ v (-s, -ing, -d) strike or push with the knee

kneecap n (pl kneecaps) bone in front of the knee ▶ v (-pping, -pped) shoot in the kneecap

kneed v ▷ knee

kneeing v ▷ knee

kneejerk adj (of a reply or reaction) automatic and predictable

kneel v (-s, -ing, -ed or knelt) fall or rest on one's knees

kneeled v ▷ kneel

kneeling v ▷ kneel

kneels v ▷ kneel

knees n, v ▷ knee

knell n (pl -s) sound of a bell, esp. at a funeral or death

knells n ▷ knell

knelt v ▷ kneel

knew v ▷ know

knickers pl n woman's or girl's undergarment covering the lower trunk and having legs or legholes

knife n (pl knives) cutting tool or weapon consisting of a sharp-edged blade with a handle ▶ v (-fes, -fing, -fed) cut or stab with a knife

knifed v ▷ knife

knifes v ▷ knife

knifing v ▷ knife

knight n (pl -s) man who has been given a knighthood ▶ v (-s, -ing, -ed) award a knighthood to > **knightly** adj

knighted v ▷ knight

knighting v ▷ knight

knights n, v ▷ knight

knit v (-s, -tting, -tted or knit) make (a garment) by interlocking a series of loops in wool or other yarn > **knitting** n (pl -s)

knits v ▷ knit

knitted v ▷ knit

knitting v ▷ knit

knittings n ▷ knit

knitwear n (pl -s) knitted clothes, such as sweaters

knitwears n ▷ knitwear

knives n ▷ knife

knob n (pl -s) rounded projection, such as a switch on a radio

knobblier adj ▷ knobbly

knobbliest adj ▷ knobbly

knobbly adj (-lier, -liest) covered with small bumps

knobs n ▷ knob

knock v (-s, -ing, -ed) give a blow or push to ▶ n (pl -s) blow or rap

knocked v ▷ knock

knocker n (pl -s) metal fitting for knocking on a door

knockers n ▷ knocker

knocking v ▷ knock

knockout n (pl -s) blow that renders an opponent unconscious

knockouts n ▷ knockout

knocks v, n ▷ knob

knoll n (pl -s) small rounded hill

knolls n ▷ knoll

knot n (pl -s) fastening made by looping and pulling tight strands of string, cord, or rope ▶ v (-s, -tting, -tted) tie with or into a knot

knots n ▷ knot

knotted n ▷ knot

knotting n ▷ knot

knotty adj full of knots

know v (-s, -ing, knew, known) be or feel certain of the truth of (information etc) > **knowable** adj

knowing v ▷ know ▶ adj suggesting secret knowledge

known v ▷ know

knows v ▷ **know**

knuckle n (pl **-s**) bone at the finger joint

knuckles n ▷ **knuckle**

ko n (**kos**). A ko is a Maori digging-stick. This is worth remembering as, along with ka and ky, it's one of only three two-letter words starting with K. Ko scores 6 points.

koala n (pl **-s**) tree-dwelling Australian marsupial with dense grey fur

koalas n ▷ **koala**

kohl n (pl **-s**) cosmetic powder used to darken the edges of the eyelids

kohls n ▷ **kohl**

koori n (pl **-s**) Australian Aborigine

kooris n ▷ **koori**

kopje, koppie n (pl **-s**) S AFR small hill

kopjes n ▷ **kopje**

kosher adj conforming to Jewish religious law, esp. (of food) to Jewish dietary law ▶ n (pl **-s**) kosher food

koshers n ▷ **kosher**

kow n (**kows**). A kow is a Scots word for a bunch of twigs. Kow is relatively high-scoring for a three-letter word, and so can be a good one to form when playing in more than one direction. Kow scores 10 points.

kowhai n (pl **-s**) New Zealand tree with clusters of yellow flowers

kowhais n ▷ **kowhai**

kowtow v (**-s, -ing, -ed**) be servile (towards)

kowtowed v ▷ **kowtow**

kowtowing v ▷ **kowtow**

kowtows v ▷ **kowtow**

kraal n (pl **-s**) S African village surrounded by a strong fence

kraals n ▷ **kraal**

krill n small shrimplike sea creature(s)

krypton n (pl **-s**) CHEM colourless gas present in the atmosphere and used in fluorescent lights

kryptons n ▷ **krypton**

kudos n (pl **-es**) fame or credit

kudoses n ▷ **kudoses**

kugel n (pl **-s**) S AFR rich, fashion-conscious, materialistic young woman

kugels n ▷ **kugel**

kumara n (pl **-s**) NZ tropical root vegetable with yellow flesh

kumaras n ▷ **kumara**

kumquat n (pl **-s**) citrus fruit resembling a tiny orange

kumquats n ▷ **kumquat**

Ll

L can be a difficult letter to use well, especially when you need to play short words. Just three two-letter words begin with L: **la**, **li** and **lo**. Knowing this will save you valuable time in a game, especially when you are trying to fit words into a crowded board. There aren't a great number of three-letter words either, but don't forget common words like **lab** (5 points), **law** (6), **lay** (6), **low** (6) and **lye** (6). Try to remember the three-letter words that combine L with X: **lax**, **lex**, **lox** and **lux** (10 points each). These are particularly useful towards the end of a game if you have an X but little opportunity to play it.

la n (**las**). In music, la is the sixth note of a major scale. La is also spelt **lah**. La scores 2 points.

label n (pl -**s**) piece of card or other material fixed to an object to show its ownership, destination, etc ▶ v (-**s**, -**lling**, -**lled**) give a label to
  labels n ▷ **label**

labia pl n (sing -**bium**) four liplike folds of skin forming part of the female genitals

labial adj of the lips
  labium n ▷ **labia**

labor n (pl -**s**) ▶ v US & AUST ▷ **labour**
  labored v ▷ **labour**
  laboring v ▷ **labour**
  labors n, v ▷ **labour**

labour US & AUST, **labor** n (pl -**s**) physical work or exertion ▶ v (-**s**, -**ing**, -**ed**) work hard

laboured adj uttered or done with difficulty ▶ v ▷ **labour**

labourer n (pl -**s**) person who labours, esp. someone doing manual work for wages
  labourers n ▷ **labourer**
  labouring v ▷ **labour**
  labours n, v ▷ **labour**

labrador n (pl -**s**) large retriever dog with a usu. gold or black coat
  labradors n ▷ **labrador**

laburnum n (pl -**s**) ornamental tree with yellow hanging flowers
  laburnums n ▷ **laburnum**

lace n (pl -**s**) delicate decorative fabric made from threads woven into an open weblike pattern ▶ v (-**ces**, -**cing**, -**ced**) fasten with laces
  laced v ▷ **lace**

lacerate v (-**tes**, -**ting**, -**ted**) tear (flesh) > **laceration** n (pl -**s**)
  lacerated v ▷ **lacerate**
  lacerates v ▷ **lacerate**
  lacerating v ▷ **lacerate**
  lacerations v ▷ **laceration**
  laces n, v ▷ **lace**
  lacing v ▷ **lace**

lack n (pl -**s**) shortage or absence of something needed or wanted ▶ v (-**s**, -**ing**, -**ed**) need or be short of (something)
  lacked v ▷ **lack**

lackey n (pl -**s**) servile follower
  lackeys n ▷ **lackey**
  lacking v ▷ **lack**
  lacks n, v ▷ **lack**

laconic adj using only a few words, terse > **laconically** adv

laconically adv ▷ **laconic**

lacquer n (pl **-s**) hard varnish for wood or metal

lacquers n ▷ **lacquer**

lacrimal adj of tears or the glands which produce them

lacrosse n (pl **-s**) sport in which teams catch and throw a ball using long sticks with a pouched net at the end, in an attempt to score goals

lactic adj of or derived from milk

lactose n (pl **-s**) white crystalline sugar found in milk

lactoses n ▷ **lactose**

lacuna n (pl **-e**) gap or missing part, esp. in a document or series

lacy adj fine, like lace

lad n (pl **-s**) boy or young man

ladder n (pl **-s**) frame of two poles connected by horizontal steps used for climbing ▶ v (**-s, -ing, -ed**) have or cause to have such a line of undone stitches

laddered v ▷ **ladder**

laddering v ▷ **ladder**

ladders n, v ▷ **ladder**

laden adj loaded

ladle n (pl **-s**) spoon with a long handle and a large bowl, used for serving soup etc ▶ v (**-les, -ling, -led**) serve out

ladled v ▷ **ladle**

ladles n, v ▷ **ladle**

ladling v ▷ **ladle**

lads n ▷ **lad**

lady n (pl **-dies**) woman regarded as having characteristics of good breeding or high rank

ladybird n (pl **-s**) small red beetle with black spots

ladybirds n ▷ **ladybird**

ladylike adj polite and dignified

lag¹ v (**-s, -gging, -gged**) go too slowly, fall behind ▶ n (pl **-s**) delay between events

lag² v (**-s, -gging, -gged**) wrap (a boiler, pipes, etc) with insulating material

lag³ n (pl **-s**) BRIT, AUST & NZ slang

convict

lager n (pl **-s**) light-bodied beer

lagers n ▷ **lager**

laggard n (pl **-s**) person who lags behind

laggards n ▷ **laggard**

lagging n (pl **-s**) insulating material ▶ v ▷ **lag¹, ²**

laggings n ▷ **lagging**

lagoon n (pl **-s**) body of water cut off from the open sea by coral reefs or sand bars

lagoons n ▷ **lagoon**

lags n ▷ **lag¹, ³**

laid v ▷ **lay¹**

lain v ▷ **lie²**

lair n (pl **-s**) resting place of an animal

laird n (pl **-s**) Scottish landowner

lairds n ▷ **laird**

lairs n ▷ **lair**

laities n ▷ **laity**

laity n (pl **-ties**) people who are not members of the clergy

lake¹ n (pl **-s**) expanse of water entirely surrounded by land ▶ **lakeside** n (pl **-s**)

lake² n (pl **-s**) red pigment

lakes n ▷ **lake¹, ²**

lakesides n ▷ **lake¹**

lama n (pl **-s**) Buddhist priest in Tibet or Mongolia

lamas n ▷ **lama**

lamb n (pl **-s**) young sheep ▶ v (**-s, -ing, -ed**) (of sheep) give birth to a lamb or lambs ▶ **lambskin** n

lambast, lambaste v (**-s, -ing, -ed**) beat or thrash

lambasted v ▷ **lambast**

lambasting v ▷ **lambast**

lambasts v ▷ **lambast**

lambed v ▷ **lamb**

lambent adj lit (of a flame) flickering softly

lambing v ▷ **lamb**

lambs n, v ▷ **lamb**

lambskin v ▷ **lamb**

lame adj (**-er, -est**) having an injured or disabled leg or foot ▶ v (**-mes, -ming, -med**) make lame ▶ **lamely** adv

> **lameness** n (pl **-s**)

lamé n (pl **-s**) ▸ adj (fabric) interwoven with gold or silver thread

lamed v ▸ **lame**

lamely adv ▸ **lame**

lamenesses n ▸ **lame**

lament v (**-s, -ing, -ed**) feel or express sorrow (for) ▸ n (pl **-s**) passionate expression of grief > **lamentation** n (pl **-s**)

lamentations v ▸ **lament**

lamented adj grieved for ▸ v ▸ **lament**

lamenting v ▸ **lament**

laments v, n ▸ **lament**

lamer adj ▸ **lame**

lames v ▸ **lame**

lamés n ▸ **lamé**

lamest adj ▸ **lame**

laminate v (**-tes, -ting, -ted**) make (a sheet of material) by sticking together thin sheets ▸ n (pl **-s**) laminated sheet > **laminated** adj

laminated v, adj ▸ **laminate**

laminates v, n ▸ **laminate**

laminating v ▸ **laminate**

laming v ▸ **lame**

lamp n (pl **-s**) device which produces light from electricity, oil, or gas > **lampshade** (pl **-s**) n

lampoon n (pl **-s**) humorous satire ridiculing someone ▸ v (**-s, -ing, -ed**) satirize or ridicule

lampooned v ▸ **lampoon**

lampooning v ▸ **lampoon**

lampoons n, v ▸ **lampoon**

lamppost n (pl **-s**) post supporting a lamp in the street

lampposts n ▸ **lamppost**

lamprey n (pl **-s**) eel-like fish with a round sucking mouth

lampreys n ▸ **lamprey**

lamps n ▸ **lamp**

lampshades n ▸ **lamp**

lance n (pl **-s**) long spear used by a mounted soldier ▸ v (**-ces, -cing, -ced**) pierce (a boil or abscess) with a lancet

lanced v ▸ **lance**

lancer n (pl **-s**) formerly, cavalry soldier armed with a lance

lancers n ▸ **lancer**

lances n, v ▸ **lance**

lancet n (pl **-s**) pointed two-edged surgical knife

lancets n ▸ **lancet**

lancing v ▸ **lance**

land n (pl **-s**) solid part of the earth's surface ▸ v (**-s, -ing, -ed**) come or bring to earth after a flight, jump, or fall > **landless** adj

landau n (pl **-s**) four-wheeled carriage with two folding hoods

landaus n ▸ **landau**

landed adj possessing or consisting of lands ▸ v ▸ **land**

landfall n (pl **-s**) ship's first landing after a voyage

landfalls n ▸ **landfall**

landing n (pl **-s**) floor area at the top of a flight of stairs ▸ v ▸ **land**

landings n ▸ **landing**

landladies n ▸ **landlady**

landlady n (pl **-dies**) woman who rents out land, houses, etc

landless v ▸ **land**

landlord n (pl **-s**) man who rents out land, houses, etc

landlords n ▸ **landlord**

landmark n (pl **-s**) prominent object in or feature of a landscape

landmarks n ▸ **landmark**

lands n, v ▸ **land**

landward adj nearest to or facing the land ▸ adv (also **landwards**) towards land

landwards adv ▸ **landward**

lane n (pl **-s**) narrow road

lanes n ▸ **lane**

language n (pl **-s**) system of sounds, symbols, etc for communicating thought

languages n ▸ **language**

languid adj lacking energy or enthusiasm > **languidly** adv

languidly adv ▸ **languid**

languish v (**-es, -ing, -ed**) suffer

neglect or hardship
languished v ▷ **languish**
languishes v ▷ **languish**
languishing v ▷ **languish**
languor n (pl -s) state of dreamy relaxation ▷ **languorous** adj
languorous adj ▷ **languor**
languors n ▷ **languor**
lank adj (-er, -est) (of hair) straight and limp
lanker adj ▷ **lank**
lankest adj ▷ **lank**
lankier adj ▷ **lanky**
lankiest adj ▷ **lanky**
lanky adj (-kier, -kiest) ungracefully tall and thin
lanolin n (pl -s) grease from sheep's wool used in ointments etc
lanolins n ▷ **lanolin**
lantana n (pl -s) shrub with orange or yellow flowers, considered a weed in Australia
lantanas n ▷ **lantana**
lantern n (pl -s) light in a transparent protective case
lanterns n ▷ **lantern**
lanyard n (pl -s) cord worn round the neck to hold a knife or whistle
lanyards n ▷ **lanyard**
lap[1] n (pl -s) part between the waist and knees of a person when sitting
lap[2] n (pl -s) single circuit of a racecourse or track ▷ v (-s, -pping, -pped) overtake an opponent so as to be one or more circuits ahead
lap[3] v (-s, -pping, -pped) (of waves) beat softly against (a shore etc)
lapel n (pl -s) part of the front of a coat or jacket folded back towards the shoulders
lapels n ▷ **lapel**
lapidary adj of or relating to stones
lapped v ▷ **lap**[2,3]
lapping v ▷ **lap**[2,3]
laps n ▷ **lap**[1,2,3], v ▷ **lap**[2,3]
lapse n (pl -s) temporary drop in a standard, esp. through forgetfulness or carelessness ▷ v (-ses, -sing, -sed)

drop in standard ▷ **lapsed** adj
lapsed v ▷ **lapse**
lapses n, v ▷ **lapse**
lapsing v ▷ **lapse**
laptop adj (of a computer) small enough to fit on a user's lap ▶ n (pl -s) computer small enough to fit on a user's lap
laptops n ▷ **laptop**
lapwing n (pl -s) plover with a tuft of feathers on the head
lapwings n ▷ **lapwing**
larboard adj, n (pl -s) old-fashioned port (side of a ship)
larboards n ▷ **larboard**
larcenies n ▷ **larceny**
larceny n (pl -nies) LAW theft
larch n (pl -es) deciduous coniferous tree
larches n ▷ **larch**
lard n (pl -s) soft white fat obtained from a pig ▶ v (-s, -ing, -ed) insert strips of bacon in (meat) before cooking
larded v ▷ **lard**
larder n (pl -s) storeroom for food
larders n ▷ **larder**
larding v ▷ **lard**
lards n, v ▷ **lard**
large adj (-r, -st) great in size, number, or extent ▷ **largely** adv ▷ **largish** adj
largely adv ▷ **large**
larger adj ▷ **large**
largess n (pl -es) ▷ **largesse**
largesse, largess n (pl -(e)s) generous giving, esp. of money
largesses n ▷ **largesse**
largest adj ▷ **large**
largish adj ▷ **large**
largo n (pl -s) ▶ adv MUSIC (piece to be played) in a slow and dignified manner
largos n ▷ **largo**
lariat n (pl -s) lasso
lariats n ▷ **lariat**
lark[1] n (pl -s) small brown songbird, skylark
lark[2] n (pl -s) informal harmless piece of mischief or fun

larks n ▷ **lark**[1, 2]

larkspur n (pl **-s**) plant with spikes of blue, pink, or white flowers with spurs
    larkspurs n ▷ **larkspur**

larrikin n (pl **-s**) AUST & NZ old-fashioned slang mischievous or unruly person
    larrikins n ▷ **larrikin**

larva n (pl **-e**) insect in an immature stage, often resembling a worm
    > **larval** adj
    larval adj ▷ **larva**

laryngeal adj ▷ **larynx**

larynges n ▷ **larynx**

larynx n (pl **-nges**) part of the throat containing the vocal cords
    > **laryngeal** adj

lasagnas n ▷ **lasagne**

lasagne, lasagna n (pl **-s**) pasta in wide flat sheets
    lasagnes n ▷ **lasagne**

laser n (pl **-s**) device that produces a very narrow intense beam of light, used for cutting very hard materials and in surgery etc
    lasers n ▷ **laser**

lash[1] n (pl **-es**) eyelash ▶ v (**-es, -ing, -ed**) hit with a whip

lash[2] v (**-es, -ing, -ed**) fasten or bind tightly with cord etc
    lashed v ▷ **lash**[1, 2]
    lashes n ▷ **lash**[1] ▶ v ▷ **lash**[1, 2]
    lashing v ▷ **lash**[1, 2]

lashings pl n old-fashioned large amounts

lass, lassie n (pl **-es, -s**) SCOT & N ENGLISH girl
    lasses n ▷ **lass**
    lassies n ▷ **lass**

lasso n (pl **-s, -es**) rope with a noose for catching cattle and horses ▶ v (**-s, -ing, -ed**) catch with a lasso
    lassoed v ▷ **lasso**
    lassoes n ▷ **lasso**
    lassoing v ▷ **lasso**
    lassos n, v ▷ **lasso**

last[1] adj, adv coming at the end or after all others ▶ adj only remaining ▶ n (pl **-s**) last person or thing > **lastly** adv

last[2] v (**-s, -ing, -ed**) continue
    > **lasting** adj

last[3] n (pl **-s**) model of a foot on which shoes and boots are made or repaired
    lasted v ▷ **last**[2]
    lasting v, adj ▷ **last**[2]
    lastly adv ▷ **last**[1]
    lasts n ▷ **last**[1, 3] ▶ v ▷ **last**[2]

latch n (pl **-es**) fastening for a door with a bar and lever ▶ v (**-es, -ing, -ed**) fasten with a latch
    latched v ▷ **latch**
    latches n, v ▷ **latch**
    latching v ▷ **latch**

late adj (**-r, -st**) after the normal or expected time ▶ adv after the normal or expected time > **lateness** n (pl **-es**)

lately adv in recent times
    latencies n ▷ **latent**
    lateness n ▷ **late**
    latenesses n ▷ **late**

latent adj hidden and not yet developed > **latency** n (pl **-cies**)
    later adj ▷ **late**

lateral adj of or relating to the side or sides > **laterally** adv
    latest adj ▷ **late**

latex n (pl **-es**) milky fluid found in some plants, esp. the rubber tree, used in making rubber
    latexes n ▷ **latex**

lath n (pl **-s**) thin strip of wood used to support plaster, tiles, etc

lathe n (pl **-s**) machine for turning wood or metal while it is being shaped

lather n (pl **-s**) froth of soap and water ▶ v (**-s, -ing, -ed**) make frothy
    lathered v ▷ **lather**
    lathering v ▷ **lather**
    lathers n, v ▷ **lather**
    lathes n ▷ **lathe**
    laths n ▷ **lath**

latitude n (pl **-s**) angular distance measured in degrees N or S of the equator
    latitudes n ▷ **latitude**

latrine n (pl **-s**) toilet in a barracks or camp

latrines n ▷ **latrine**
latter adj second of two ▷ **latterly** adv
latterly adv ▷ **latter**
lattice n (pl **-s**) framework of intersecting strips of wood, metal, etc ▷ **latticed** adj
latticed adj ▷ **lattice**
lattices n ▷ **lattice**
laud v (**-s**, **-ing**, **-ed**) praise or glorify ▷ **laudably** adv
laudable adj praiseworthy
laudably adv ▷ **laudable**
laudanum n (pl **-s**) opium-based sedative
laudanums n ▷ **laudanum**
lauded v ▷ **laud**
lauding v ▷ **laud**
lauds v ▷ **laud**
laugh v (**-s**, **-ing**, **-ed**) make inarticulate sounds with the voice expressing amusement, merriment, or scorn ▶ n (pl **-s**) act or instance of laughing
laughable adj ▷ **laugh**
laughed v ▷ **laugh**
laughing v ▷ **laugh**
laughs v, n ▷ **laugh**
laughter n (pl **-s**) sound or action of laughing
laughters n ▷ **laughter**
launch¹ v (**-es**, **-ing**, **-ed**) put (a ship or boat) into the water, esp. for the first time ▶ n (pl **-s**) launching ▷ **launcher** n (pl **-s**)
launch² n (pl **-s**) open motorboat
launched v ▷ **launch¹**
launchers n ▷ **launch¹**
launches n ▷ **launch¹** ▶ n ▷ **launch¹,²**
launching v ▷ **launch¹**
launder v (**-s**, **-ing**, **-ed**) wash and iron (clothes and linen)
laundered v ▷ **launder**
laundering v ▷ **launder**
launders v ▷ **launder**
laundries n ▷ **laundry**
laundry n (pl **-ries**) clothes etc for washing or which have recently been washed

laureate adj (of a poet) appointed to the court of Britain
laurel n (pl **-s**) glossy-leaved shrub, bay tree ▶ pl wreath of laurel, an emblem of victory or merit
laurels n ▷ **laurel**
lava n (pl **-s**) molten rock thrown out by volcanoes, which hardens as it cools
lavatories n ▷ **lavatory**
lavatory n (pl **-ries**) toilet
lavender n (pl **-s**) shrub with fragrant flowers ▶ adj bluish-purple
lavenders n ▷ **lavender**
lavish adj great in quantity or richness ▶ v (**-es**, **-ing**, **-ed**) give or spend generously ▷ **lavishly** adv
lavished v ▷ **lavish**
lavishes v ▷ **lavish**
lavishing v ▷ **lavish**
lavishly adv ▷ **lavish**
law n (pl **-s**) rule binding on a community ▷ **lawfully** adv ▷ **lawlessness** n (pl **-es**)
lawful adj allowed by law
lawfully adv ▷ **law**
lawless adj breaking the law, esp. in a violent way
lawlessness n ▷ **law**
lawlessnesses n ▷ **law**
lawn¹ n (pl **-s**) area of tended and mown grass
lawn² n (pl **-s**) fine linen or cotton fabric
lawns n ▷ **lawn¹, ²**
laws n ▷ **law**
lawsuit n (pl **-s**) court case brought by one person or group against another
lawsuits n ▷ **lawsuit**
lawyer n (pl **-s**) professionally qualified legal expert
lawyers n ▷ **lawyer**
lax adj not strict ▷ **laxity** n (pl **-ties**)
laxative n (pl **-s**) ▶ adj (medicine) inducing the emptying of the bowels
laxatives n ▷ **laxative**
laxities n ▷ **lax**
laxity n ▷ **lax**

lay¹ v (**-s, -ing, laid**) cause to lie

lay² v ▷ **lie²**

lay³ adj of or involving people who are not clergymen

lay⁴ n (pl **-s**) short narrative poem designed to be sung

layabout n (pl **-s**) lazy person
   layabouts n ▷ **layabout**

layer n (pl **-s**) single thickness of some substance, as a cover or coating on a surface ▶ v (**-s, -ing, -ed**) form a layer
   >**layered** adj
   layered v, adj ▷ **layer**
   layering v ▷ **layer**
   layers n, v ▷ **layer**

layette n (pl **-s**) clothes for a newborn baby
   layettes n ▷ **layette**
   laying v ▷ **lay¹**

layman n (pl **-men**) person who is not a member of the clergy
   laymen n ▷ **layman**

layout n (pl **-s**) arrangement, esp. of matter for printing or of a building
   layouts n ▷ **layout**
   lays v ▷ **lay¹** ▶ n ▷ **lay⁴**

laze v (**-zes, -zing, -zed**) be idle or lazy ▶ n (pl **-s**) time spent lazing
   lazed v ▷ **laze**
   lazes v, n ▷ **laze**
   lazily adv ▷ **lazy**
   laziness adv ▷ **lazy**
   lazinesses adv ▷ **lazy**
   lazing v ▷ **laze**

lazy adj (**-zier, -ziest**) not inclined to work or exert oneself >**lazily** adv
   >**laziness** n (pl **-s**)

lea n (pl **-s**) poetic meadow

leach v (**-es, -ing, -ed**) remove or be removed from a substance by a liquid passing through it
   leached v ▷ **leach**
   leaches v ▷ **leach**
   leaching v ▷ **leach**

lead¹ v (**-s, -ing, led**) guide or conduct ▶ n (pl **-s**) first or most prominent place ▶ adj acting as a leader or lead

lead² n (pl **-s**) soft heavy grey metal

leaded adj (of windows) made from many small panes of glass held together by lead strips

leaden adj heavy or sluggish

leader n (pl **-s**) person who leads
   >**leadership** n (pl **-s**)
   leaders n ▷ **leader**
   leaderships n ▷ **leader**

leading adj principal
   leads v ▷ **lead¹, ²** ▶ n ▷ **lead¹**

leaf n (pl **leaves**) flat usu. green blade attached to the stem of a plant >**leafy** (**-fier, -fiest**) ▶ adj ▷ **leafless** adj
   leafier adj ▷ **leaf**
   leafiest adj ▷ **leaf**
   leafless adj ▷ **leaf**

leaflet n (pl **-s**) sheet of printed matter for distribution
   leaflets n ▷ **leaflet**
   leafy adj ▷ **leaf**

league¹ n (pl **-s**) association promoting the interests of its members

league² n obs measure of distance, about three miles
   leagues n ▷ **league¹, ²**

leak n (pl **-s**) hole or defect that allows the escape or entrance of liquid, gas, radiation, etc ▶ v (**-s, -ing, -ed**) let liquid etc in or out >**leaky** (**-kier, -kiest**) ▶ adj

leakage n (pl **-s**) act or instance of leaking
   leakages n ▷ **leakage**
   leaked v ▷ **leak**
   leakier adj ▷ **leak**
   leakiest adj ▷ **leak**
   leaking v ▷ **leak**
   leaks n, v ▷ **leak**
   leaky adj (**-kier, -kiest**) ▷ **leak**

lean¹ v (**-ing, -ed** or **leant**) rest against

lean² adj (**-er, -est**) thin but healthy-looking ▶ n (pl **-s**) lean part of meat >**leanness** n (pl **-es**)
   leaner adj ▷ **lean²**
   leanest adj ▷ **lean²**

leaning n (pl **-s**) tendency ▶ v ▷ **lean¹**
   leanings n ▷ **leaning**
   leanness n ▷ **lean²**

leannesses n ▷ **lean²**

leans v, n ▷ **lean¹**

leant n ▷ **lean¹**

leap v (**-s, -ing, leapt** or **-ed**) make a sudden powerful jump ▶ n (pl **-s**) sudden powerful jump

leaped v ▷ **leap**

leapfrog n game in which a player vaults over another bending down

leapfrogs n ▷ **leapfrog**

leaping v ▷ **leap**

leaps v, n ▷ **leap**

leapt v ▷ **leap**

learn v (**-s, -ing, -ed** or **learnt**) gain skill or knowledge by study, practice, or teaching > **learner** n (pl **-s**)

learned adj erudite, deeply read

learner n ▷ **learn**

learners n ▷ **learn**

learning n (pl **-s**) knowledge got by study ▶ v ▷ **learn**

learnings n ▷ **learning**

learns v ▷ **learn**

leas n ▷ **lea**

lease n (pl **-s**) contract by which land or property is rented for a stated time by the owner to a tenant ▶ v (**-ses, -sing, -sed**) let or rent by lease > **leaseholder** n (pl **-s**)

leased v ▷ **lease**

leaseholder n ▷ **lease**

leaseholders n ▷ **lease**

leases n, v ▷ **lease**

leash n (pl **-es**) lead for a dog

leashes n ▷ **leash**

leashing v ▷ **leash**

least adj ▷ **little** smallest ▶ n smallest one ▶ adv in the smallest degree

leather n (pl **-s**) material made from specially treated animal skins ▶ adj made of leather ▶ v (**-s, -ing, -ed**) beat or thrash

leathered v ▷ **leather**

leatherier adj ▷ **leathery**

leatheriest adj ▷ **leathery**

leathering v ▷ **leather**

leathers n, v ▷ **leather**

leathery adj (**-rier, -riest**) like leather, tough

leave¹ v (**-s, -ing, left**) go away from

leave² n (pl **-s**) permission to be absent from work or duty

leaven n (pl **-s**) substance that causes dough to rise ▶ v (**-s, -ing, -ed**) raise with leaven

leavened v ▷ **leaven**

leavening v ▷ **leaven**

leavens n, v ▷ **leaven**

leaves v ▷ **leave**

leaving v ▷ **leave**

lecher n (pl **-s**) man who has or shows excessive sexual desire > **lechery** n (pl **-ries**)

lecheries n ▷ **lecher**

lechers n ▷ **lecher**

lectern n (pl **-s**) sloping reading desk, esp. in a church

lecterns n ▷ **lectern**

lecture n (pl **-s**) informative talk to an audience on a subject ▶ v (**-s, -ing, -ed**) give a talk

lectured v ▷ **lecture**

lecturer n (pl **-s**) person who lectures, esp. in a university or college

lecturers n ▷ **lecturer**

lectures n, v ▷ **lecture**

lecturing v ▷ **lecture**

ledge n (pl **-s**) narrow shelf sticking out from a wall

ledger n (pl **-s**) book of debit and credit accounts of a firm

ledgers n ▷ **ledger**

ledges n ▷ **ledge**

lee n (pl **-s**) sheltered part or side ▶ adv towards this side

leech n (pl **-es**) species of bloodsucking worm

leeches n ▷ **leech**

leek n (pl **-s**) vegetable of the onion family with a long bulb and thick stem

leeks n ▷ **leek**

leer v (**-s, -ing, -ed**) look or grin at in a sneering or suggestive manner ▶ n (pl **-s**) sneering or suggestive look or grin

leered v ▷ **leer**

leerier adj ▷ **leery**

leeriest adj ▷ **leery**

leering v ▷ **leer**

leers v, n ▷ **leer**

leery adj informal (**-rier, -riest**) suspicious or wary (of)

lees pl n sediment of wine ▶ n ▷ **lee**

leeward adj, n (pl **-s**) (on) the lee side

leewards n ▷ **leeward**

leeway n (pl **-s**) room for free movement within limits

leeways n ▷ **leeway**

left¹ adj of the side that faces west when the front faces north ▶ adv on or towards the left ▶ n (pl **-s**) left hand or part

left² v ▷ **leave¹**

leftist n (pl **-s**) ▶ adj (person) of the political left

leftists n ▷ **leftist**

leftover n (pl **-s**) unused portion of food or material

leftovers n ▷ **leftover**

lefts n ▷ **left¹**

leg n (pl **-s**) one of the limbs on which a person or animal walks, runs, or stands

legacies n ▷ **legacy**

legacy n (pl **-cies**) thing left in a will

legal adj established or permitted by law ▶ **legally** adv **legality** n (pl **-ties**) > **legalization** n (pl **-s**)

legalities n ▷ **legal**

legality n ▷ **legal**

legalization n ▷ **legal**

legalizations n ▷ **legal**

legalize v (**-zes, -zing, -zed**) make legal

legalized adv ▷ **legalize**

legalizes adv ▷ **legalize**

legalizing adv ▷ **legalize**

legally adv ▷ **legal**

legate n (pl **-s**) messenger or representative, esp. from the Pope

legatee n (pl **-s**) recipient of a legacy

legatees n ▷ **legatee**

legates n ▷ **legate**

legation n (pl **-s**) diplomatic minister and his staff

legations n ▷ **legation**

legato n (pl **-s**) ▶ adv MUSIC (piece to be played) smoothly

legatos n ▷ **legato**

legend n (pl **-s**) traditional story or myth

legends n ▷ **legend**

leggier adj ▷ **leggy**

leggiest adj ▷ **leggy**

leggings pl n covering of leather or other material for the legs

leggy adj (**-gier, -giest**) having long legs

legibilities n ▷ **legible**

legibility n ▷ **legible**

legible adj easily read ▶ **legibility** n (pl **-ties**) > **legibly** adv

legibly adv ▷ **legible**

legion n (pl **-s**) large military force >**legionary** adj, n (pl **-ries**)

legionaries n ▷ **legion**

legionary n ▷ **legion**

legions n ▷ **legion**

legless adj without legs

legs n ▷ **leg**

leguaan n (pl **-s**) large S African lizard

leguaans n ▷ **leguaan**

legume n (pl **-s**) pod of a plant of the pea or bean family ▶ pl peas or beans

legumes n ▷ **legume**

lei n (pl **-s**) (in Hawaii) garland of flowers

leis n ▷ **lei**

leisure n (pl **-s**) time for relaxation or hobbies

leisured adj with plenty of spare time

leisures n ▷ **leisure**

lekker adj S AFR slang attractive or nice

lemming n (pl **-s**) rodent of arctic regions, reputed to run into the sea and drown during mass migrations

lemmings n ▷ **lemming**

lemon n (pl **-s**) yellow oval fruit that grows on trees ▶ adj pale-yellow

lemonade n (pl **-s**) lemon-flavoured soft drink, often fizzy

lemonades n ▷ **lemonade**

lemons n ▷ **lemon**

lemur n (pl **-s**) nocturnal animal like a small monkey, found in Madagascar
lemurs n ▷ **lemur**

lend v (**-s, -ing, lent**) give the temporary use of > **lender** n (pl **-s**)
lender n ▷ **lend**
lenders n ▷ **lend**
lending v ▷ **lend**
lends v ▷ **lend**

length n (pl **-s**) extent or measurement from end to end > **lengthily** adv
> **lengthways, lengthwise** adj, adv
lengthen v (**-s, -ing, -ed**) make or become longer
lengthened v ▷ **lengthen**
lengthening v ▷ **lengthen**
lengthens v ▷ **lengthen**
lengthier adj ▷ **length**
lengthiest adj ▷ **length**
lengthily adv ▷ **length**
lengths n ▷ **length**
lengthways adj, adv ▷ **length**
lengthwise adj, adv ▷ **lengthen**
lengthy adj (**-thier, -thiest**) very long or tiresome

leniencies n ▷ **lenient**
leniency n ▷ **lenient**
lenient adj tolerant, not strict or severe
> **leniency** n (pl **-cies**) > **leniently** adv
leniently adv ▷ **lenient**

lens n (pl **-es**) piece of glass or similar material with one or both sides curved, used to bring together or spread light rays in cameras, spectacles, telescopes, etc
lenses n ▷ **lens**
lent v ▷ **lend**

lentil n (pl **-s**) edible seed of a leguminous Asian plant
lentils n ▷ **lentil**

lento n (pl **-s**) ▶ adv MUSIC (piece to be played) slowly
lentos n ▷ **lento**

leonine adj like a lion

leopard n (pl **-s**) large spotted carnivorous animal of the cat family
leopards n ▷ **leopard**

leotard n (pl **-s**) tight-fitting garment covering the upper body, worn for dancing or exercise
leotards n ▷ **leotard**

leper n (pl **-s**) person suffering from leprosy
lepers n ▷ **leper**
leprosies n ▷ **leprosy**

leprosy n (pl **-sies**) disease attacking the nerves and skin, resulting in loss of feeling in the affected parts
> **leprous** adj
leprous adj ▷ **leprosy**

lesbian n (pl **-s**) homosexual woman
▶ adj of homosexual women
lesbianism n (pl **-s**)
lesbianisms n ▷ **lesbian**
lesbians n ▷ **lesbian**

lesion n (pl **-s**) structural change in an organ of the body caused by illness or injury
lesions n ▷ **lesion**

less adj smaller in extent, degree, or duration ▶ **little** ▶ pron smaller part or quantity ▶ adv to a smaller extent or degree ▶ prep after deducting, minus

lessee n (pl **-s**) person to whom a lease is granted
lessees n ▷ **lessee**

lessen v (**-s, -ing, -ed**) make or become smaller or not as much
lessened v ▷ **lessen**
lessening v ▷ **lessen**
lessens v ▷ **lessen**

lesser adj not as great in quantity, size, or worth

lesson n (pl **-s**) single period of instruction in a subject
lessons n ▷ **lesson**

lest conj so as to prevent any possibility that

let¹ v (**-s, -tting, let**) allow, enable, or cause

let² n (pl **-s**) TENNIS minor infringement or obstruction of the ball requiring a replay of the point

letdown n (pl **-s**) disappointment
letdowns n ▷ **letdown**

lethal adj deadly

lethargic adj ▷ **lethargy**
lethargically adv ▷ **lethargy**
lethargies n ▷ **lethargy**
lethargy n (pl **-gies**) sluggishness or dullness ▷ **lethargic** adj
> **lethargically** adv
lets v ▷ **let**[1] ▷ n ▷ **let**[2]
letter n (pl **-s**) written message, usu. sent by post ▶ pl literary knowledge or ability > **lettering** n (pl **-s**)
lettered adj learned
lettering n ▷ **letter**
letterings n ▷ **letter**
letters n ▷ **letter**
letting v ▷ **let**[1]
lettuce n (pl **-s**) plant with large green leaves used in salads
lettuces n ▷ **lettuce**
levee n (pl **-s**) us natural or artificial river embankment
levees n ▷ **levee**
level adj (**-ller**, **-llest**) horizontal ▶ v (**-s**, **-lling**, **-lled**, **-ller**) make even or horizontal ▶ n (pl **-s**) horizontal line or surface
levelled v ▷ **level**
leveller adj, v ▷ **level**
levellest adj ▷ **level**
levelling v ▷ **level**
levels v, n ▷ **level**
lever n (pl **-s**) handle used to operate machinery ▶ v (**-s**, **-ing**, **-ed**) prise or move with a lever
leverage n (pl **-s**) action or power of a lever
leverages n ▷ **leverage**
levered v ▷ **lever**
leveret n (pl **-s**) young hare
leverets n ▷ **leveret**
levering v ▷ **lever**
levers n, v ▷ **lever**
levied v ▷ **levy**
levies v, n ▷ **levy**
levitate v (**-tes**, **-ting**, **-ted**) rise or cause to rise into the air
levitated v ▷ **levitate**
levitates v ▷ **levitate**
levitating v ▷ **levitate**

levities n ▷ **levity**
levity n (pl **-ties**) inclination to make a joke of serious matters
levy v (**-vies**, **-ing**, **-vied**) impose and collect (a tax) ▶ n (pl **-vies**) imposition or collection of taxes
levying v ▷ **levy**
lewd adj (**-er**, **-est**) lustful or indecent
> **lewdly** adv > **lewdness** n (pl **-es**)
lewder adj ▷ **lewd**
lewdest adj ▷ **lewd**
lewdly adv ▷ **lewd**
lewdness n ▷ **lewd**
lewdnesses n ▷ **lewd**

> **lex** n (**leges**). A lex is a system or body of laws. This is a really handy word when you have L and X, as there is likely to be an E available on the board. Lex scores 10 points.

lexical adj relating to the vocabulary of a language
lexicographies n ▷ **lexicon**
lexicography n ▷ **lexicon**
lexicon n (pl **-s**) dictionary
> **lexicography** n (pl **-phies**)
lexicons n ▷ **lexicon**

> **li** n (**lis**). The li is a Chinese unit of length. This low-scoring word is worth knowing for when you want to form words in more than one direction at the same time. Li scores 2 points.

liable adj legally obliged or responsible
liaise v (**-ses**, **-sing**, **-sed**) establish and maintain communication (with)
liaised v ▷ **liaise**
liaises v ▷ **liaise**
liaising v ▷ **liaise**
liaison n (pl **-s**) communication and contact between groups
liaisons n ▷ **liaison**
liana n (pl **-s**) climbing plant in tropical forests
lianas n ▷ **liana**
liar n (pl **-s**) person who tells lies
liars n ▷ **liar**
libation n (pl **-s**) drink poured as an offering to the gods

libations n ▷ **libation**
libel n (pl **-s**) published statement falsely damaging a person's reputation ▶ v (**-s, -lling, -lled**) falsely damage the reputation of (someone) > **libellous** adj
libelled v ▷ **libel**
libelling v ▷ **libel**
libellous adj ▷ **libel**
libels n, v ▷ **libel**
liberal adj having social and political views that favour progress and reform ▶ n (pl **-s**) person who has liberal ideas or opinions > **liberally** adv
> **liberalization** n (pl **-s**)
liberalization n ▷ **liberal**
liberalizations n ▷ **liberal**
liberally adv ▷ **liberal**
liberals n ▷ **liberal**
liberate v (**-tes, -ting, -ted**) set free
> **liberation** n (pl **-s**) > **liberator** n (pl **-s**)
liberated v ▷ **liberate**
liberates v ▷ **liberate**
liberating v ▷ **liberate**
liberation n ▷ **liberate**
liberations n ▷ **liberate**
liberator n ▷ **liberate**
liberators n ▷ **liberate**
liberties n ▷ **liberty**
liberty n (pl **-ties**) freedom
libido n (pl **-s**) psychic energy
libidos n ▷ **libido**
libraries n ▷ **library**
library n (pl **-ries**) room or building where books are kept
libretti n ▷ **libretto**
librettist n ▷ **libretto**
librettists n ▷ **libretto**
libretto n (pl **-ttos, -tti**) words of an opera > **librettist** n (pl **-s**)
librettos n ▷ **libretto**
lice n (pl ▷ **louse**
licence n (pl **-s**) document giving official permission to do something
licences n ▷ **licence**
license v (**-ses, -sing, -sed**) grant a licence to > **licensed** adj
licensed v, adj ▷ **license**
licensee n (pl **-s**) holder of a licence,

esp. to sell alcohol
licensees n ▷ **licensee**
licenses v ▷ **license**
licensing v ▷ **license**
lichen n (pl **-s**) small flowerless plant forming a crust on rocks, trees, etc
lichens n ▷ **lichen**
licit adj lawful, permitted
lick v (**-s, -ing, -ed**) pass the tongue over ▶ n (pl **-s**) licking
licked v ▷ **lick**
licking v ▷ **lick**
licks v, n ▷ **lick**
licorices n ▷ **licorice**
lid n (pl **-s**) movable cover
lido n (pl **-s**) open-air centre for swimming and water sports
lidos n ▷ **lido**
lids n ▷ **lid**
lie¹ v (**-s, lying, lied**) make a deliberately false statement ▶ n (pl **-s**) deliberate falsehood
lie² v (**-s, lying, lay, lain**) place oneself or be in a horizontal position ▶ n (pl **-s**) way something lies
lied¹ v ▷ **lie¹**
lied² n (pl **lieder**) MUSIC setting for voice and piano of a romantic poem
liege adj bound to give or receive feudal service ▶ n (pl **-s**) lord
lieges n ▷ **liege**
lien n (pl **-s**) LAW right to hold another's property until a debt is paid
liens n ▷ **lien**
lies v, n ▷ **lie¹, ²**
life n (pl **lives**) state of living beings, characterized by growth, reproduction, and response to stimuli
> **lifelike** adj
lifeboat n (pl **-s**) boat used for rescuing people at sea
lifeboats adj ▷ **lifeboat**
lifeless adj dead
lifelike adj ▷ **life**
lifeline n (pl **-s**) means of contact or support
lifelines n ▷ **lifeline**
lifelong adj lasting all of a person's life

lifetime n (pl -s) length of time a
person is alive
  lifetimes n ▷ lifetime

lift v (lifts, lifting, lifted) move
upwards in position, status, volume,
etc ▶ n (pl **lifts**) cage raised and
lowered in a vertical shaft to transport
people or goods *informal* ▷ **liftoff** n
moment a rocket leaves the ground
  lifted v ▷ lift
  lifting v ▷ lift
  lifts v, n ▷ lift

ligament n (pl -s) band of tissue
joining bones
  ligaments n ▷ ligament

ligature n (pl -s) link, bond, or tie
  ligatures n ▷ ligature

light¹ n (pl -s) electromagnetic
radiation by which things are visible
▶ pl traffic lights ▶ adj bright ▶ v (-s,
-ing, lit) ignite

light² adj (-er, -est) not heavy,
weighing relatively little ▶ adv with
little equipment or luggage ▶ v (-s,
-ing, -ed, lit) (esp. of birds) settle after
flight > **lightly** adv > **lightness** n (pl -s)
  lighted v ▷ light²

lighten¹ v (-s, -ing, -ed) make less dark

lighten² v (-s, -ing, -ed) make less
heavy or burdensome
  lightened v ▷ lighten¹, ²
  lightening v ▷ lighten¹, ²
  lightens v ▷ lighten¹, ²

lighter¹ n (pl -s) device for lighting
cigarettes etc

lighter² n (pl -s) flat-bottomed boat for
unloading ships
  lighter adj ▷ light²
  lighters n ▷ lighter¹, ²
  lightest adj ▷ light²

lighting n (pl -s) apparatus for and use
of artificial light in theatres, films, etc
▶ v ▷ light¹, ²
  lightings n ▷ lighting
  lightly adv ▷ light²
  lightness n ▷ light²
  lightnesses n ▷ light²

lights pl n lungs of animals as animal

food ▶ n ▷ light¹ ▶ v ▷ light¹, ²

ligneous adj of or like wood

lignite n (pl -s) woody textured rock
used as fuel
  lignites n ▷ lignite

like¹ prep, conj adj, pron indicating
similarity, comparison, etc

like² v (-s, -ing, -ed) find enjoyable
> **likeable, likable** adj > **liking** n
fondness
  liked v ▷ like
  likelier adj ▷ likely
  likeliest adj ▷ likely

likely adj (-lier, -liest) tending or
inclined ▶ adv probably

liken v (-s, -ing, -ed) compare
  likened v ▷ liken

likeness n (pl -es) resemblance
  likening v ▷ liken
  likens v ▷ liken
  likes v ▷ like

likewise adv similarly
  liking v ▷ like

lilac n (pl -s) shrub with pale mauve or
white flowers ▶ adj light-purple
  lilacs n ▷ lilac

lilt n (pl -s) pleasing musical quality in
speaking > **lilting** adj
  lilting adj ▷ lilt
  lilts n ▷ lilt

lily n (pl -lies) plant which grows from
a bulb and has large, often white,
flowers

limb n (pl -s) arm, leg, or wing

limber adj pliant or supple

limbo n (pl -s) West Indian dance in
which dancers lean backwards to pass
under a bar
  limbos n ▷ limbo
  limbs n ▷ limb

lime¹ n (pl -s) calcium compound used
as a fertilizer or in making cement

lime² n (pl -s) small green citrus fruit

lime³ n (pl -s) deciduous tree with
heart-shaped leaves and fragrant
flowers
  limelights n ▷ lime

limerick n (pl -s) humorous verse of

five lines

limericks n ▷ **limerick**

limes n ▷ **lime**[1, 2, 3]

limey n (pl **-s**) us slang British person

limeys n ▷ **limey**

limit n (pl **-s**) ultimate extent, degree, or amount of something ▶ v (**-s, -ing, -ed**) restrict or confine ▷ **limitation** n (pl **-s**) ▷ **limitless** adj

limitation n ▷ **limit**

limitations n ▷ **limit**

limited v ▷ **limit**

limiting v ▷ **limit**

limitless v ▷ **limit**

limits n, v ▷ **limit**

limp[1] v (**-s, -ing, -ed**) walk with an uneven step ▶ n (pl **-s**) limping walk

limp[2] (**-er, -est**) adj without firmness or stiffness ▷ **limply** adv

limped v ▷ **limp**[1]

limper adj ▷ **limp**[2]

limpest adj ▷ **limp**[2]

limpet n (pl **-s**) shellfish which sticks tightly to rocks

limpets n ▷ **limpet**

limpid adj clear or transparent ▷ **limpidity** n (pl **-ties**)

limpidities n ▷ **limpid**

limpidity n ▷ **limpid**

limping v ▷ **limp**[1]

limply adv ▷ **limp**[2]

limps v, n ▷ **limp**[1]

linchpin, lynchpin n (pl **-s**) pin to hold a wheel on its axle

linchpins n ▷ **linchpin**

linctus n (pl **-es**) syrupy cough medicine

linctuses n ▷ **linctus**

linden n (pl **-s**) ▷ **lime**[3]

lindens n ▷ **linden**

line[1] n (pl **-s**) long narrow mark ▶ pl words of a theatrical part ▶ v (**-s, -ing, -ed**) mark with lines

line[2] v (**-nes, -ning, -ned**) give a lining to

lineage n (pl **-s**) descent from an ancestor

lineages n ▷ **lineage**

linear adj of or in lines

lined v ▷ **line**[1, 2]

linen n (pl **-s**) cloth or thread made from flax

linens n ▷ **linen**

liner[1] n (pl **-s**) large passenger ship or aircraft

liner[2] n something used as a lining

liners n ▷ **liner**[1, 2]

lines n, v ▷ **line**[1, 2]

linesman n (pl **-men**) (in some sports) an official who helps the referee or umpire

linesmen n ▷ **linesman**

ling[1] n slender food fish

ling[2] n (pl **lings**) heather

linger v (**-s, -ing, -ed**) delay or prolong departure

lingered v ▷ **linger**

lingerie n (pl **-s**) women's underwear or nightwear

lingeries n ▷ **lingerie**

lingering v ▷ **linger**

lingers v ▷ **linger**

lingo n (pl **-s**) informal foreign or unfamiliar language or jargon

lingos n ▷ **lingo**

lings n ▷ **ling**[2]

lingual adj of the tongue

linguist n (pl **-s**) person skilled in foreign languages

linguists n ▷ **linguist**

liniment n (pl **-s**) medicated liquid rubbed on the skin to relieve pain or stiffness

liniments n ▷ **liniment**

lining n (pl **-s**) layer of cloth attached to the inside of a garment etc ▶ v ▷ **line**[1, 2]

linings n ▷ **lining**

link n (pl **-s**) any of the rings forming a chain ▶ v (**-s, -ing, -ed**) connect with or as if with links ▷ **linkage** n (pl **-s**)

linkage n ▷ **link**

linkages n ▷ **link**

linked v ▷ **link**

linking v ▷ **link**

links pl n golf course, esp. one by the

sea ▶ n, v ▷ **link**

linnet n (pl -**s**) songbird of the finch family

linnets n ▷ **linnet**

linoleum n (pl -**s**) floor covering of hessian or jute with a smooth decorative coating of powdered cork

linoleums n ▷ **linoleum**

linseed n (pl -**s**) seed of the flax plant

linseeds n ▷ **linseeds**

lint n (pl -**s**) soft material for dressing a wound

lintel n (pl -**s**) horizontal beam at the top of a door or window

lintels n ▷ **lintel**

lints n ▷ **lint**

lion n (pl -**s**) large animal of the cat family, the male of which has a shaggy mane > **lioness** n fem

lioness n ▷ **lion**

lions n ▷ **lion**

lip n (pl -**s**) either of the fleshy edges of the mouth

lips n ▷ **lip**

lipstick n (pl -**s**) cosmetic in stick form, for colouring the lips

liquefaction n ▷ **liquefy**

liquefactions n ▷ **liquefy**

liquefied v ▷ **liquefy**

liquefies v ▷ **liquefy**

liquefy v (-**fies**, -**fying**, -**fied**) make or become liquid > **liquefaction** n (pl -**s**)

liquefying v ▷ **liquefy**

liqueur n (pl -**s**) flavoured and sweetened alcoholic spirit

liqueurs n ▷ **liqueur**

liquid n (pl -**s**) substance in a physical state which can change shape but not size ▶ adj of or being a liquid

liquids n ▷ **liquid**

liquor n (pl -**s**) alcoholic drink, esp. spirits

liquors n ▷ **liquor**

lira n (pl -**re**, -**ras**) monetary unit of Turkey and formerly of Italy

liras n ▷ **lira**

lire n ▷ **lira**

lisle n (pl -**s**) strong fine cotton thread

or fabric

lisles n ▷ **lisle**

lisp n (pl -**s**) speech defect in which s and z are pronounced th ▶ v (-**s**, -**ing**, -**ed**) speak or utter with a lisp

lisped v ▷ **lisp**

lisping v ▷ **lisp**

lisps n, v ▷ **lisp**

lissom, lissome adj supple, agile

lissome adj ▷ **lissom**

list¹ n (pl -**s**) item-by-item record of names or things, usu. written one below another ▶ v (-**s**, -**ing**, -**ed**) make a list of

list² v (-**s**, -**ing**, -**ed**) (of a ship) lean to one side ▶ n (pl -**s**) leaning to one side

listed v ▷ **list**¹, ²

listen v (-**s**, -**ing**, -**ed**) concentrate on hearing something > **listener** n (pl -**s**)

listened v ▷ **listen**

listener n ▷ **listen**

listeners n ▷ **listen**

listening v ▷ **listen**

listens v ▷ **listen**

listing v ▷ **list**¹, ²

listless adj lacking interest or energy > **listlessly** adv

listlessly adv ▷ **listless**

lists n, v ▷ **list**¹, ²

lit v ▷ **light**¹, ²

litanies n ▷ **litany**

litany n (pl -**nies**) prayer with responses from the congregation

literacies n ▷ **literacy**

literacy n (pl -**cies**) ability to read and write

literal adj according to the explicit meaning of a word or text, not figurative > **literally** adv

literally adv ▷ **literal**

literary adj of or knowledgeable about literature

literate adj able to read and write

literati pl n literary people

lithe adj (-**ther**, -**thest**) flexible or supple, pliant

lither adj ▷ **lithe**

lithest adj ▷ **lithe**

lithium n (pl -s) CHEM chemical element, the lightest known metal

litigant n (pl -s) person involved in a lawsuit
  litigants n ▷ **litigant**

litigate v (-tes, -ting, -ted) bring or contest a law suit
  litigated v ▷ **litigate**
  litigates v ▷ **litigate**
  litigating v ▷ **litigate**

litmus n (pl -es) blue dye turned red by acids and restored to blue by alkalis
  litmuses n ▷ **litmus**

litotes n ironical understatement used for effect

litre n (pl -s) unit of liquid measure equal to 1000 cubic centimetres or 1.76 pints
  litres n ▷ **litre**

litter n (pl -s) untidy rubbish dropped in public places ▶ v (-s, -ing, -ed) strew with litter
  littered v ▷ **litter**
  littering v ▷ **litter**
  litters n, v ▷ **litter**

little adj small or smaller than average ▶ adv not a lot ▶ n small amount, extent, or duration

littoral adj of or by the seashore ▶ n (pl -s) coastal district
  littorals n ▷ **littoral**

liturgical adj ▷ **liturgy**

liturgies n ▷ **liturgy**

liturgy n (pl -gies) prescribed form of public worship ▷ **liturgical** adj

live¹ v (-s, -ing, -ed) be alive

live² adj living, alive ▶ adv in the form of a live performance ▷ **liveliness** n (pl -es)
  lived v ▷ **live¹**
  liveliness n ▷ **live²**
  livelinesses n ▷ **live²**

lively adj full of life or vigour

liver¹ n (pl -s) organ secreting bile

liver² n (pl -s) person who lives in a specified way
  liveried adj ▷ **livery**

liverish adj having a disorder of the liver

livers n ▷ **liver¹, ²**

livery n (pl -ries) distinctive dress, esp. of a servant or servants ▷ **liveried** adj

lives v ▷ **live¹** ▶ n ▷ **life**

livid adj informal (-er, -est) angry or furious
  livider adj ▷ **livid**
  lividest adj ▷ **livid**

living adj possessing life, not dead or inanimate ▶ n (pl -s) condition of being alive ▶ v ▷ **live**
  livings n ▷ **living**

lizard n (pl -s) four-footed reptile with a long body and tail
  lizards n ▷ **lizard**

llama n (pl -s) woolly animal of the camel family used as a beast of burden in S America
  llamas n ▷ **llama**

> **lo** interj. Lo is a command that means look! Along with **la** and **li**, lo is one of just three two-letter words that begin with L. Lo scores 2 points.

loach n (pl -es) carplike freshwater fish
  loaches n ▷ **loach**

load n (pl -s) burden or weight ▶ pl informal lots ▶ v (-s, -ing, -ed) put a load on or into

loaded adj (of a question) containing a hidden trap or implication ▶ v ▷ **load**
  loading v ▷ **load**
  loads n, v ▷ **load**

loaf¹ n (pl loaves) shaped mass of baked bread

loaf² v (-s, -ing, -ed) idle, loiter ▷ **loafer** n (pl -s)
  loafed v ▷ **loaf²**
  loafer n ▷ **loaf²**
  loafers n ▷ **loaf²**
  loafing v ▷ **loaf²**
  loafs v ▷ **loaf²**

loam n (pl -s) fertile soil
  loams n ▷ **loam**

loan n (pl -s) money lent at interest ▶ v (-s, -ing, -ed) lend
  loaned v ▷ **loan**

loaning v ▷ **loan**

loans n, v ▷ **loan**

loath, loth adj unwilling or reluctant (to)

loathe v (-s, -thing, -thed) hate, be disgusted by ▷ **loathing** n (pl -s) > **loathsome** adj

loathed v ▷ **loathe**

loathes v ▷ **loathe**

loathing v, n ▷ **loathe**

loathings n ▷ **loathe**

loathsome adj ▷ **loathe**

loaves n ▷ **loaf**[1]

lob SPORT n (pl -s) ball struck or thrown in a high arc ▷ v (-s, -bbing, -bbed) strike or throw (a ball) in a high arc

lobbed v ▷ **lob**

lobbied v ▷ **lobby**

lobbies n, v ▷ **lobby**

lobbing v ▷ **lob**

lobby n (pl -bies) corridor into which rooms open ▷ v (-bies, -ing, -bied) try to influence (legislators) in the formulation of policy > **lobbyist** n

lobbying v ▷ **lobby**

lobe n (pl -s) rounded projection > **lobed** adj

lobed v ▷ **lobe**

lobelia n (pl -s) garden plant with blue, red, or white flowers

lobelias n ▷ **lobelia**

lobes n ▷ **lobe**

lobola n (pl -s) S AFR (in African custom) price paid by a bridegroom's family to his bride's family

lobolas n ▷ **lobola**

lobotomies n ▷ **lobotomy**

lobotomy n (pl -mies) surgical incision into a lobe of the brain to treat mental disorders

lobs n, v ▷ **lob**

lobster n (pl -s) shellfish with a long tail and claws, which turns red when boiled

lobsters n ▷ **lobster**

local adj of or existing in a particular place ▷ n (pl -s) person belonging to a particular district > **locally** adv

locale n (pl -s) scene of an event

localities n ▷ **locality**

locality n (pl -ties) neighbourhood or area

localize v (-zes, -zing, -zed) restrict to a particular place

localized v ▷ **localize**

localizes v ▷ **localize**

localizing v ▷ **localize**

locally adv ▷ **local**

locals n ▷ **local**

locate v (-s, -ing, -ed) discover the whereabouts of

located v ▷ **locate**

locates v ▷ **locate**

locating v ▷ **locate**

location n (pl -s) site or position

locations n ▷ **location**

loch n (pl -s) SCOT lake

lochs n ▷ **loch**

loci n ▷ **locus**

lock[1] n (pl -s) appliance for fastening a door, case, etc ▷ v (-s, -ing, -ed) fasten or become fastened securely

lock[2] n (pl -s) strand of hair

locked v ▷ **lock**[1]

locker n (pl -s) small cupboard with a lock

lockers n ▷ **locker**

locket n (pl -s) small hinged pendant for a portrait etc

lockets n ▷ **locket**

locking v ▷ **lock**[1]

lockjaw n (pl -s) tetanus

lockjaws n ▷ **lockjaw**

lockout n (pl -s) closing of a workplace by an employer to force workers to accept terms

lockouts n ▷ **lockout**

locks n ▷ **lock**[1, 2] ▷ v ▷ **lock**[1]

lockup n (pl -s) prison

lockups n ▷ **lockup**

locum n (pl -s) temporary stand-in for a doctor or clergyman

locums n ▷ **locum**

locus n (pl -ci) area or place where something happens

locust n (pl -s) destructive African

insect that flies in swarms and eats crops
locusts n ▷ **locust**

lode n (pl -s) vein of ore
lodes n ▷ **lode**

lodestar n (pl -s) star used in navigation or astronomy as a point of reference
lodestars n ▷ **lodestar**

lodge n (pl -s) CHIEFLY BRIT gatekeeper's house ▶ v (-dges, -dging, -dged) live in another's house at a fixed charge
> **lodger** n (pl -s)
lodged v ▷ **lodge**
lodger n ▷ **lodge**
lodgers n ▷ **lodge**
lodges n, v ▷ **lodge**

lodging n (pl -s) temporary residence ▶ pl rented room or rooms in another person's house ▶ v ▷ **lodge**
lodgings n ▷ **lodging**

loft n (pl -s) space between the top storey and roof of a building ▶ v (-s, -ing, -ed) SPORT strike, throw, or kick (a ball) high into the air
lofted v ▷ **loft**
loftier adj ▷ **lofty**
loftiest adj ▷ **lofty**
loftily adv haughtily
lofting v ▷ **loft**
lofts n, v ▷ **loft**
lofty adj (-tier, -tiest) of great height

log¹ n (pl -s) portion of a felled tree stripped of branches ▶ v (-s, -gging, -gged) saw logs from a tree

logbook n (pl -s) book recording the details about a car or a ship's journeys
logbooks n ▷ **logbook**
logged v ▷ **log¹**

loggia n (pl -s) covered gallery at the side of a building
loggias n ▷ **loggia**

logging n (pl -s) work of cutting and transporting logs ▶ v ▷ **log¹**
loggings n ▷ **logging**

logic n (pl -s) philosophy of reasoning
> **logically** adv ▷ **logician** n (pl -s)
logical adj of logic

logically adv ▷ **logic**
logician n ▷ **logic**
logicians n ▷ **logic**
logics n ▷ **logic**

logo n (pl -s) emblem used by a company or other organization
logos n ▷ **logo**
logs n ▷ **log¹**

loin n (pl -s) part of the body between the ribs and the hips
loins n ▷ **loin**

loiter v (-s, -ing, -ed) stand or wait aimlessly or idly
loitered v ▷ **loiter**
loitering v ▷ **loiter**
loiters v ▷ **loiter**

loll v (-s, -ing, -ed) lounge lazily
lolled v ▷ **loll**
lollies n ▷ **loll**
lolling v ▷ **loll**

lollipop n (pl -s) boiled sweet on a small wooden stick
lollipops n ▷ **lollipop**
lolls v ▷ **loll**

lolly n (pl -llies) informal lollipop or ice lolly

lone adj solitary ▶ **lonesome** adj lonely
loneliness n ▷ **lonely**
lonelinesses n ▷ **lonely**
lonely adj sad because alone
> **loneliness** n (pl -s)

loner n (pl -s) informal person who prefers to be alone
loners n ▷ **loner**
lonesome adj ▷ **lone**

long¹ adj (-er, -est) having length, esp. great length, in space or time ▶ adv for an extensive period

long² v (-s, -ing, -ed) have a strong desire (for)
longed v ▷ **long²**
longer adj ▷ **long¹**
longest adj ▷ **long¹**

longhand n (pl -s) ordinary writing, not shorthand or typing
longhands n ▷ **longhand**

longing n (pl -s) yearning ▶ v ▷ **long²**
> **longingly** adv

longingly adv ▷ **longing**
longings n ▷ **longing**
longs v ▷ **long²**
loo n (pl -s) informal toilet
loofah n (pl -s) sponge made from the dried pod of a gourd
loofahs n ▷ **loofah**
look v (-s, -ing, -ed) direct the eyes or attention (towards) ▶ n (pl -s) instance of looking
looked v ▷ **look**
looking v ▷ **look**
lookout n (pl -s) guard
lookouts n ▷ **lookout**
looks v, n ▷ **look**
loom¹ n (pl -s) machine for weaving cloth
loom² v (-s, -ing, -ed) appear dimly
loomed v ▷ **loom²**
looming v ▷ **loom²**
looms n ▷ **loom¹** v ▷ **loom²**
loonier adj ▷ **loony**
loonies n ▷ **loony**
looniest adj ▷ **loony**
loony slang adj (-nier, -niest) foolish or insane ▶ n (pl -nies) foolish or insane person
loop n (pl -s) rounded shape made by a curved line or rope crossing itself ▶ v (-s, -ing, -ed) form or fasten with a loop
looped v ▷ **loop**
loophole n (pl -s) means of evading a rule without breaking it
loopholes n ▷ **loophole**
looping v ▷ **loop**
loops n, v ▷ **loop**
loos n ▷ **loo**
loose adj (-r, -est) not tight, fastened, fixed, or tense ▶ adv in a loose manner ▶ v (-s, -sing, -sed) free ▷ **loosely** adv ▷ **looseness** n (pl -s)
loosed v ▷ **loose**
loosely adv ▷ **loose**
loosen v (-s, -ing, -ed) make loose
loosened v ▷ **loosen**
looseness n ▷ **loose**
loosenesses n ▷ **loose**

loosening v ▷ **loosen**
loosens v ▷ **loosen**
looser adj ▷ **loose**
looses v ▷ **loose**
loosest adj ▷ **loose**
loosing v ▷ **loose**
loot n, v (-s, -ing, -ed) plunder ▶ n (pl -s) informal money ▷ **looter** n (pl -s) ▷ **looting** n
looted v ▷ **loot**
looter n ▷ **loot**
looters n ▷ **loot**
looting v, n ▷ **loot**
lootings n ▷ **loot**
loots v, n ▷ **loot**
lop v (-s, -pping, -pped) cut away twigs and branches
lope v (-s, -ing, -ed) run with long easy strides
loped v ▷ **lope**
lopes v ▷ **lope**
loping v ▷ **lope**
lopsided adj greater in height, weight, or size on one side
lord n (pl -s) person with power over others, such as a monarch or master
lordlier adj ▷ **lordly**
lordliest adj ▷ **lordly**
lordly adj (-lier, -liest) imperious, proud
lords n ▷ **lord**
lordship n the position or authority of a lord
lore n (pl -s) body of traditions on a subject
lores n ▷ **lore**
lorikeet n (pl -s) small brightly coloured Australian parrot
lorikeets n ▷ **lorikeet**
lorries n ▷ **lorry**
lorry n (pl -rries) BRIT & S AFR large vehicle for transporting loads by road
lose v (-ses, -sing, lost) come to be without, esp. by accident or carelessness
loser n (pl -s) person or thing that loses
losers n ▷ **loser**
loses v ▷ **lose**

losing v ▷ **lose**

loss n (pl **-es**) losing

losses n ▷ **loss**

lost v ▷ **lose** ▶ adj unable to find one's way

lot pron great number ▶ n (pl **-s**) collection of people or things

loth adj ▷ **loath**

lotion n (pl **-s**) medical or cosmetic liquid for use on the skin

lotions n ▷ **lotion**

lots n ▷ **lot**

lottery n (pl **-ries**) method of raising money by selling tickets that win prizes by chance

lotto n (pl **-s**) game of chance like bingo

lottos n ▷ **lotto**

lotus n (pl **-es**) legendary plant whose fruit induces forgetfulness

lotuses n ▷ **lotus**

loud adj (**-er, -est**) relatively great in volume > **loudly** adv > **loudness** n (pl **-es**)

louder adj ▷ **loud**

loudest adj ▷ **loud**

loudly adv ▷ **loud**

loudness n ▷ **loud**

loudnesses n ▷ **loud**

lough n (pl **-s**) IRISH loch

loughs n ▷ **lough**

lounge n (pl **-s**) living room in a private house ▶ v (**-s, -ging, -ged**) sit, lie, or stand in a relaxed manner

lounged v ▷ **lounge**

lounges n, v ▷ **lounge**

lounging v ▷ **lounge**

lour v (**-s, -ing, -ed**) ▷ **lower²**

loured v ▷ **lour**

louring v ▷ **lour**

lours v ▷ **lour**

louse n (pl **lice, louses**) wingless parasitic insect

louses n ▷ **louse**

lousier adj ▷ **lousy**

lousiest adj ▷ **lousy**

lousy adj (**-sier, -siest**) slang mean or unpleasant

lout n (pl **-s**) crude, oafish, or aggressive

person > **loutish** adj

loutish adj ▷ **lout**

louts n ▷ **lout**

louvre n (pl **-s**) one of a set of parallel slats slanted to admit air but not rain > **louvred** adj

louvred adj ▷ **louvre**

louvres n ▷ **louvre**

lovable adj ▷ **love**

love v (**-s, -ving, -ved**) have a great affection for ▶ n (pl **-s**) great affection > **lovable, loveable** adj > **loveless** adj > **lovemaking** n (pl **-s**)

loveable adj ▷ **love**

lovebird n (pl **-s**) small parrot

lovebirds n ▷ **lovebird**

loved v ▷ **love**

loveless adj ▷ **love**

lovelier adj ▷ **lovely**

loveliest adj ▷ **lovely**

lovelorn adj miserable because of unhappiness in love

lovely adj (**-lier, -liest**) very attractive

lovemaking n ▷ **love**

lovemakings n ▷ **love**

lover n (pl **-s**) person having a sexual relationship outside marriage

lovers n ▷ **lover**

loves v, n ▷ **love**

loving adj affectionate, tender ▶ v ▷ **love** > **lovingly** adv

lovingly adv ▷ **loving**

low¹ adj not tall, high, or elevated ▶ adv in or to a low position, level, or degree ▶ n (pl **-s**) low position, level, or degree > **lowland** n (pl **-s**)

low² n (pl **-s**) cry of cattle, moo ▶ v (**-s, -ing, -ed**) moo

lowbrow n (pl **-s**) ▶ adj (person) with nonintellectual tastes and interests

lowbrows n ▷ **lowbrow**

lowdown n (pl **-s**) informal inside information

lowdowns n ▷ **lowdown**

lowed v ▷ **low²**

lower¹ adj (**-est**) below one or more other things ▶ v (**-s, -ing, -ed**) cause or allow to move down

lower², **lour** v (of the sky or weather) look gloomy or threatening

lowered v ▷ **lower¹, ²**

lowering v ▷ **lower¹, ²**

lowers v ▷ **lower¹, ²**

lowest adj ▷ **low¹**

lowing v ▷ **low²**

lowland n (pl -s) low-lying country

lowlands n ▷ **lowland**

lowlier adj ▷ **lowly**

lowliest adj ▷ **lowly**

lowliness n ▷ **lowly**

lowlinesses n ▷ **lowly**

lowly adj (-lier, -liest) modest, humble >**lowliness** n (pl -s)

lows ▷ **low¹, ²** ▷ v ▷ **low²**

> **lox** n (**loxes**). Lox is a kind of smoked salmon. This is a good word if you get have an X and L in the late stages of the game: there's likely to be a usable O on the board already. Lox scores 10 points.

loyal adj (-ler, -lest) faithful to one's friends, country, or government
> **loyally** adv ▷ **loyalty** n (pl -ties)
> **loyalist** n (pl -s)

loyalist n ▷ **loyal**

loyalists n ▷ **loyal**

loyaller adj ▷ **loyal**

loyallest adj ▷ **loyal**

loyally adv ▷ **loyal**

loyalties n ▷ **loyal**

loyalty n ▷ **loyal**

lozenge n (pl -s) medicated tablet held in the mouth until it dissolves

lozenges n ▷ **lozenge**

lucerne n (pl -s) fodder plant like clover, alfalfa

lucernes n ▷ **lucerne**

lucid adj clear and easily understood
> **lucidly** adv ▷ **lucidity** n (pl -ties)

lucidities n ▷ **lucid**

lucidity n ▷ **lucid**

lucidly adv ▷ **lucid**

luck n (pl -s) fortune, good or bad

luckily adv fortunately

luckless adj having bad luck

lucks n having bad luck

lucky adj having or bringing good luck

lucre n (pl -s) facetious money

luderick n (pl -s) Australian fish, usu. black or dark brown in colour

ludericks n ▷ **luderick**

ludo n (pl -s) game played with dice and counters on a board

lug¹ v (-s, -gging, -gged) carry or drag with great effort

lug² n (pl -s) projection serving as a handle

luggage n (pl -s) traveller's cases, bags, etc

luggages n projection serving as a handle ▷ **luggage**

lugs v ▷ **lug¹** ▷ n ▷ **lug²**

lugworm n (pl -s) large worm used as bait

lugworms n ▷ **lugworm**

lukewarm adj moderately warm, tepid

lull v (-s, -ing, -ed) soothe (someone) by soft sounds or motions ▷ n brief time of quiet in a storm etc

lullabies n ▷ **lullaby**

lullaby n (pl -bies) quiet song to send a child to sleep

lulled v ▷ **lull**

lulling v ▷ **lull**

lulls v, n ▷ **lull**

lumbago n (pl -s) pain in the lower back

lumbagos n ▷ **lumbago**

lumbar adj relating to the lower back

lumber¹ n (pl -s) BRIT unwanted disused household articles ▷ v (-s, -ing, -ed) informal burden with something unpleasant

lumber² v move heavily and awkwardly ▷ **lumbering** adj

lumbered v ▷ **lumber¹, ²**

lumbering v ▷ **lumber¹, ²** ▷ adj ▷ **lumber²**

lumbers n¹ ▷ v ▷ **lumber¹, ²**

luminary n (pl -ies) famous person

luminescent adj ▷ **luminous**

luminosities n ▷ **luminous**

luminosity n ▷ **luminous**

luminous adj reflecting or giving off light ▸ **luminosity** n (pl -s) ▸ **luminescent** adj

lump¹ n (pl -s) shapeless piece or mass ▸ v (-s, -ing, -ed) consider as a single group ▸ **lumpy** adj (-pier, -piest)

lump² v informal tolerate or put up with it

lumped v ▷ **lump¹, ²**

lumpier adj ▷ **lump¹**

lumpiest adj ▷ **lump¹**

lumping v ▷ **lump¹, ²**

lumps n, v ▷ **lump¹, ²**

lumpy adj ▷ **lump¹**

lunacies n ▷ **lunatic**

lunar adj relating to the moon

lunatic adj foolish and irresponsible ▸ n (pl -s) foolish or annoying person ▸ **lunacy** n (pl -cies)

lunatics n ▷ **lunatic**

lunch n (pl **lunches**) meal taken in the middle of the day ▸ v (-es, -ing, -ed) eat lunch

lunched v ▷ **lunch**

luncheon n (pl -s) formal lunch

luncheons n ▷ **luncheon**

lunches n, v ▷ **lunch**

lunching v ▷ **lunch**

lung n (pl -s) organ that allows an animal or bird to breathe air: humans have two lungs in the chest

lunge n (pl -s) sudden forward motion ▸ v (-s, -ging, -ged) move with or make a lunge

lunged v ▷ **lunge**

lunges n, v ▷ **lunge**

lungfish n freshwater bony fish with an air-breathing lung of South America and Australia

lunging v ▷ **lunge**

lungs n ▷ **lung**

lupin n (pl -s) garden plant with tall spikes of flowers

lupine adj like a wolf

lupins n ▷ **lupin**

lurch v (-es, -ing, -ed) tilt or lean suddenly to one side ▸ n (pl -es) lurching movement

lurched v ▷ **lurch**

lurcher n (pl -s) crossbred dog trained to hunt silently

lurchers n ▷ **lurcher**

lurches v, n ▷ **lurch**

lurching v ▷ **lurch**

lure v (-s, -red, -ring) tempt or attract by the promise of reward ▸ n (pl -s) person or thing that lures

lured v ▷ **lure**

lures v, n ▷ **lure**

lurid adj (-er, -est) vivid in shocking detail, sensational ▸ **luridly** adv

lurider adj ▷ **lurid**

luridest adj ▷ **lurid**

luridly adv ▷ **lurid**

luring v ▷ **lure**

lurk v (-s, -ing, -ed) lie hidden or move stealthily, esp. for sinister purposes

lurked v ▷ **lurk**

lurking v ▷ **lurk**

lurks v ▷ **lurk**

luscious adj extremely pleasurable to taste or smell

lush¹ adj (-er, -est) (of grass etc) growing thickly and healthily

lush² n (pl -es) slang alcoholic

lusher adj ▷ **lush¹**

lushes n ▷ **lush²**

lushest adj ▷ **lush¹**

lust n (pl -s) strong sexual desire ▸ v (-s, -ing, -ed) have passionate desire (for) ▸ **lustful** adj ▸ **lusty** adj vigorous, healthy ▸ **lustily** adv

lusted v ▷ **lust**

lustful adj ▷ **lust**

lustier adj ▷ **lusty**

lustiest adj ▷ **lusty**

lustily adv ▷ **lust**

lusting v ▷ **lust**

lustre n (pl -s) gloss, sheen

lustres n ▷ **lustre**

lustrous adj shining, luminous

lusts n, v ▷ **lust**

lusty adj (-tier, -tiest) vigorous, healthy

lute n (pl -s) ancient guitar-like musical instrument with a body shaped like a half pear

lutes n ▷ lute

> **lux** n (**lux.**) A lux is a unit of illumination. This is a great word to know when you have an X but little opportunity to play it. Lux scores 10 points.

luxury n (pl **-ries**) enjoyment of rich, very comfortable living ▶ adj of or providing luxury

> **luz** n (**luzzes**) In traditional Jewish writings, the luz was a bone that was supposed to be indestructible. This very unusual word is very useful, especially if you have a Z at the end of a game when there is little opportunity to use it in a longer word. Luz scores 12 points.

lychee n (pl **-s**) Chinese fruit with a whitish juicy pulp

lychees n ▷ lychee

lye n (pl **-s**) caustic solution obtained by leaching wood ash

lyes n ▷ lye

lying v ▷ lie¹, ²

lymph n (pl **-s**) colourless bodily fluid

consisting mainly of white blood cells

> **lymphatic** adj

lymphatic adj ▷ lymph

lymphs n ▷ lymph

lynch v (**-es, -ing, -ed**) put to death without a trial

lynched v ▷ lynch

lynches v ▷ lynch

lynching v ▷ lynch

lynchpin n ▷ linchpin

lynchpins n ▷ linchpin

lynx n (pl **-es**) animal of the cat family with tufted ears and a short tail

lynxes n ▷ lynx

lyre n (pl **-s**) ancient musical instrument like a U-shaped harp

lyres n ▷ lyre

lyric adj (of poetry) expressing personal emotion in songlike style ▶ n (pl **-s**) short poem in a songlike style

> **lyrical** adj lyric

lyrical adj ▷ lyric

lyricist n (pl **-s**) person who writes the words of songs or musicals

lyricists n ▷ lyricist

lyrics n ▷ lyric

Mm

M is a very useful letter when you need to form short words as it starts a two-letter word with every vowel, as well as with Y and with another M. Remembering this allows you to use M effectively when you're forming a word parallel to, and in contact with, a word that is already on the board. M also combines well with X and Z, so there is a lot of potential for high-scoring words. Keep **max**, **mix** and **mux** (12 points each) in mind, as well as **miz** and **muz** (14 each). It's also worth remembering the three-letter words ending in W: **maw**, **mew** and **mow** (8 points each).

ma n (pl **-s**) informal mother

mac n (pl **-s**) BRIT informal mackintosh

macabre adj strange and horrible, gruesome

macadam n (pl **-s**) road surface of pressed layers of small broken stones

macadams n ▷ macadam

macaroni n (pl **-s**) pasta in short tube shapes

macaronis n ▷ macaroni

macaroon n (pl **-s**) small biscuit or cake made with ground almonds

macaroons n ▷ macaroon

macaw n (pl **-s**) large tropical American parrot

macaws n ▷ macaw

mace¹ n (pl **-s**) ceremonial staff of office

mace² n (pl **-s**) spice made from the dried husk of the nutmeg

macerate v (**-tes**, **-ting**, **-ted**) soften by soaking > **maceration** n (pl **-s**)

macerated v ▷ macerate

macerates v ▷ macerate

macerating v ▷ macerate

maceration n ▷ macerate

macerations n ▷ macerate

maces n ▷ mace¹, ²

machete n (pl **-s**) broad heavy knife used for cutting or as a weapon

machetes n ▷ machete

machine n (pl **-s**) apparatus, usu. powered by electricity, designed to perform a particular task ▶ v (**-nes**, **-ning**, **-ned**) make or produce by machine

machined v ▷ machine

machines n, v ▷ machine

machining v ▷ machine

machismo n (pl **-s**) exaggerated or strong masculinity

machismos n ▷ machismo

macho adj strongly or exaggeratedly masculine

mackerel n edible sea fish

macramé n (pl **-s**) ornamental work of knotted cord

macramés n ▷ macramé

macs n ▷ mac

mad adj (**madder**, **maddest**) mentally deranged, insane > **madly** adv > **madness** n (pl **-es**) > **madman** n (pl **-men**) > **madwoman** n (pl **-women**)

madam n (pl **madams**) polite form of address to a woman

madame n (pl **mesdames**) French title equivalent to Mrs

madams n ▷ madam

madcap adj foolish or reckless

madden v (-s, -ed, -ing) infuriate or
irritate ▷ **maddening** adj
maddened v ▷ **madden**
maddening v ▷ **madden** ▶ adj
▷ **madden**
maddens v ▷ **madden**
madder n (pl -s) climbing plant ▶ adj
▷ **mad**
maddest adj ▷ **mad**
made v ▷ **make**
madeira n (pl -s) fortified white wine
madeiras n ▷ **madeira**
madly adv ▷ **mad**
madman n ▷ **mad**
madmen n ▷ **mad**
madness n ▷ **mad**
madnesses n ▷ **madness**
madonna n (pl -s) the Virgin Mary
madonnas n ▷ **madonna**
madrigal n (pl -s) 16th–17th-century
part song for unaccompanied voices
madrigals n ▷ **madrigal**
madwoman n ▷ **mad**
madwomen n ▷ **mad**
maestri n ▷ **maestro**
maestro n (pl -tri, -tros) outstanding
musician or conductor
maestros n ▷ **maestro**
mafia n (pl -s) international secret
criminal organization
mafias n ▷ **mafia**
mafiosi n ▷ **mafioso**
mafioso n (pl -sos, -si) member of
the Mafia
mafiosos n ▷ **mafioso**
magazine n (pl -s) periodical
publication with articles by different
writers
magazines n ▷ **magazine**
magenta adj deep purplish-red
maggot n (pl -s) larva of an insect
▷ **maggoty** adj
maggots n ▷ **maggot**
maggoty adj ▷ **maggot**
magi pl n wise men from the East who
came to worship the infant Jesus
magic n (pl -s) supposed art of invoking
supernatural powers to influence

events ▶ adj (also **magical**) of, using, or
like magic ▷ **magically** adv
magical adj ▷ **magic**
magically adv ▷ **magic**
magician n (pl -s) conjuror
magicians n ▷ **magician**
magics n ▷ **magic**
magma n (pl -s) molten rock inside the
earth's crust
magmas n ▷ **magma**
magnate n (pl -s) influential or
wealthy person, esp. in industry
magnates n ▷ **magnate**
magnesia n (pl -s) white tasteless
substance used as an antacid and a
laxative; magnesium oxide
magnesias n ▷ **magnesia**
magnet n (pl -s) piece of iron or steel
capable of attracting iron and pointing
north when suspended
magnetic adj having the properties of
a magnet ▷ **magnetically** adv
magnetically adv ▷ **magnetic**
magneto n (pl -s) apparatus for
ignition in an internal-combustion
engine
magnets n ▷ **magnet**
magnification n ▷ **magnify**
magnifications n ▷ **magnify**
magnified v ▷ **magnify**
magnifies v ▷ **magnify**
magnify v (-fies, -fied, -fied) increase
in apparent size, as with a lens
▷ **magnification** n (pl -s)
magnifying v ▷ **magnify**
magnolia n (pl -s) shrub or tree with
showy white or pink flowers
magnolias n ▷ **magnolia**
magnum n (pl s) large wine bottle
holding about 1.5 litres
magnums n ▷ **magnum**
magpie n (pl -s) black-and-white bird
magpies n ▷ **magpie**
mahoganies n ▷ **mahogany**
mahogany n (pl -nies) hard reddish-
brown wood of several tropical trees
mahout n (pl s) (in India and the East
Indies) elephant driver or keeper

mahouts n ▷ **mahout**

maid (also **maidservant**) n (pl **-s**) female servant

maiden n (pl **-s**) lit young unmarried woman ▶ adj unmarried

maidenly adj modest

maidens n ▷ **maiden**

maids n ▷ **maid**

maidservant n ▷ **maid**

maidservants n ▷ **maid**

mail[1] n (pl **-s**) letters and packages transported and delivered by the post office ▶ v (**-s**, **-ing**, **-ed**) send by mail

mail[2] n (pl **-s**) flexible armour of interlaced rings or links

mailbox n (pl **-es**) US, CANADIAN & AUST box into which letters and parcels are delivered

mailboxes n ▷ **mailbox**

mailed v ▷ **mail**[1]

mailing v ▷ **mail**[1]

mails ▷ **mail**[1, 2] ▶ v ▷ **mail**[2]

mailshot n (pl **-s**) BRIT posting of advertising material to many selected people at once

mailshots n ▷ **mailshot**

maim v (**-s**, **-ing**, **-ed**) cripple or mutilate

maimed v ▷ **maim**

maiming v ▷ **maim**

maims v ▷ **maim**

main adj chief or principal ▶ n (pl **-s**) principal pipe or line carrying water, gas, or electricity

mainland n (pl **-s**) stretch of land which forms the main part of a country

mainlands n ▷ **mainland**

mainly adv for the most part, chiefly

mainmast n (pl **-s**) chief mast of a ship

mainmasts n ▷ **mainmast**

mains n ▷ **main**

mainsail n (pl **-s**) largest sail on a mainmast

mainsails n ▷ **mainsail**

mainstay n (pl **-s**) chief support

mainstays n ▷ **mainstay**

maintain v (**-s**, **-ing**, **-ed**) continue or keep in existence

maintained v ▷ **maintain**

maintaining v ▷ **maintain**

maintains v ▷ **maintain**

maize n (pl **-s**) type of corn with spikes of yellow grains

maizes n ▷ **maize**

majestic adj ▷ **majesty**

majestically adv ▷ **majesty**

majesties n ▷ **majesty**

majesty n (pl **-ties**) stateliness or grandeur > **majestic** adj > **majestically** adv

major adj greater in number, quality, or extent ▶ n (pl **-s**) middle-ranking army officer ▶ v (**-s**, **-ing**, **-ed**) (foll. by **in**) US, CANADIAN, S AFR, AUST & NZ do one's principal study in (a particular subject)

majored v ▷ **major**

majoring v ▷ **major**

majorities n ▷ **majority**

majority n (pl **-ties**) greater number

majors n, v ▷ **major**

make v (**-kes**, **-king**, **made**) create, construct, or establish ▶ n (pl **-s**) brand, type, or style > **maker** n (pl **-s**)

maker n ▷ **make**

makers n ▷ **make**

makes n, v ▷ **make**

makeup n (pl **-s**) cosmetics

makeups n ▷ **makeup**

making v ▷ **make** ▶ n (pl **-s**) creation or production

makings n ▷ **making**

maladies n ▷ **malady**

malady n (pl **-dies**) disease or illness

malaise n (pl **-s**) vague feeling of unease, illness, or depression

malaises n ▷ **malaise**

malaria n (pl **-s**) infectious disease caused by the bite of some mosquitoes > **malarial** adj

malarial adj ▷ **malaria**

malarias n ▷ **malaria**

male adj of the sex which can fertilize female reproductive cells ▶ n (pl **males**) male person or animal

males n ▷ **male**

malice n (pl **-s**) desire to cause

harm to others ▷ **malicious** *adj*
▷ **maliciously** *adv*
malices *n* ▷ **malice**
malicious *adj* ▷ **malice**
maliciously *adj* ▷ **malice**
malign *v* (-s, -ing, -ed) slander or
defame ▶ *adj* evil in influence or effect
▷ **malignity** *n* (*pl* -ties) evil disposition
maligned *v* ▷ **malign**
maligning *v* ▷ **malign**
malignities *n* ▷ **malign**
malignity *n* ▷ **malign**
maligns *v* ▷ **malign**
malinger *v* (-s, -ing, -ed) feign illness
to avoid work ▷ **malingerer** *n* (*pl* -s)
malingered *v* ▷ **malinger**
malingerer *n* ▷ **malinger**
malingerers *n* ▷ **malinger**
malingering *v* ▷ **malinger**
malingers *v* ▷ **malinger**
mall *n* (*pl* -s) street or shopping area
closed to vehicles
mallard *n* wild duck
mallee *n* (*pl* -s) AUST low-growing
eucalyptus in dry regions
mallees *n* ▷ **mallee**
mallet *n* (*pl* -s) (wooden) hammer
mallets *n* ▷ **mallet**
mallow *n* (*pl* -s) plant with pink or
purple flowers
mallows *n* ▷ **mallow**
malls *n* ▷ **mall**
malt *n* (*pl* -s) grain, such as barley,
prepared for use in making beer or
whisky
maltreat *v* (-s, -ing, -ed) treat badly
▷ **maltreatment** *n* (*pl* -s)
maltreated *v* ▷ **maltreat**
maltreating *v* ▷ **maltreat**
maltreatment *n* ▷ **maltreat**
maltreatments *n* ▷ **maltreat**
maltreats *v* ▷ **maltreat**
malts *n* ▷ **malt**
mama *n* (*pl* -s) old-fashioned mother
mamas *n* ▷ **mama**
mamba *n* (*pl* -s) deadly S African snake
mambas *n* ▷ **mamba**
mamma *n* (*pl* -s) ▷ **mama**

mammal *n* (*pl* -s) animal of
the type that suckles its young
▷ **mammalian** *adj*
mammalian *adj* ▷ **mammal**
mammals *n* ▷ **mammal**
mammary *adj* of the breasts or milk-
producing glands
mammas *n* ▷ **mamma**
mammon *n* (*pl* -s) wealth regarded as
a source of evil
mammons *n* ▷ **mammon**
mammoth *n* (*pl* -s) extinct elephant-
like mammal ▶ *adj* colossal
mammoths *n* ▷ **mammoth**
man *n* (*pl* **men**) adult male ▶ *v* (-s,
-nning, -nned) supply with sufficient
people for operation or defence
▷ **manhood** *n* (*pl* -s)
mana *n* NZ authority, influence
manacle *n* (*pl* -s) handcuff or fetter ▶ *v*
(-les, -ling, -led) handcuff or fetter
manacled *v* ▷ **manacle**
manacles *n*, *v* ▷ **manacle**
manacling *v* ▷ **manacle**
manage *v* (-ges, -ging, -ged)
succeed in doing ▷ **manageable** *adj*
▷ **management** *n* (*pl* -s) managers
collectively
manageable *adj* ▷ **manage**
managed *v* ▷ **manage**
management *n* ▷ **manage**
managements *n* ▷ **manage**
manager *n* (*pl* -s) person in charge of
a business, institution, actor, sports
team, etc ▷ **managerial** *adj*
manageresses *n* ▷ **manager**
managerial *adj* ▷ **manager**
managers *n* ▷ **manager**
manages *v* ▷ **manage**
managing *v* ▷ **manage**
manas *n* ▷ **mana**
manatee *n* (*pl* -s) large tropical plant-
eating aquatic mammal
manatees *n* ▷ **manatee**
mandarin *n* (*pl* -s) high-ranking
government official
mandarins *n* ▷ **mandarin**
mandate *n* (*pl* -s) official or

authoritative command ▶ v (-tes, -ting, -ted) give authority to

mandated v ▷ mandate

mandates n, v ▷ mandate

mandating v ▷ mandate

mandible n (pl -s) lower jawbone or jawlike part

mandibles n ▷ mandible

mandolin n (pl s) musical instrument with four pairs of strings

mandolins n ▷ mandolin

mandrake n (pl -s) plant with a forked root, formerly used as a narcotic

mandrakes n ▷ mandrake

mandrel n (pl -s) shaft on which work is held in a lathe

mandrels n ▷ mandrel

mandrill n (pl -s) large blue-faced baboon

mandrills n ▷ mandrill

mane n (pl -s) long hair on the neck of a horse, lion, etc

manes n ▷ mane

manful adj determined and brave > **manfully** adv

manfully adv ▷ manful

mange n (pl -s) skin disease of domestic animals

manger n (pl -s) eating trough in a stable or barn

mangers n ▷ manger

mangier adj ▷ mangy

mangiest adj ▷ mangy

mangle[1] v (-les, -ling, -led) destroy by crushing and twisting

mangle[2] n (pl -s) machine with rollers for squeezing water from washed clothes ▶ v (-les, -ling, -led) put through a mangle

mangled v ▷ mangle[1, 2]

mangles v ▷ mangle[1, 2] ▶ n ▷ mangle[2]

mangling v ▷ mangle[1, 2]

mango n (pl -goes, -gos) tropical fruit with sweet juicy yellow flesh

mangoes n ▷ mango

mangos n ▷ mango

mangrove n (pl-s) tropical tree with exposed roots, which grows beside water

mangroves n ▷ mangrove

mangy adj (-gier, -giest) having mange

manhole n (pl -s) hole with a cover, through which a person can enter a drain or sewer

manholes n ▷ manhole

manhood n ▷ man

manhoods n ▷ man

mania n (pl -s) extreme enthusiasm > **maniacal** ▶ adj

maniac n (pl -s) mad person

maniacal adj ▷ mania

maniacs n ▷ mania

manias n ▷ mania

manic adj affected by mania

manicure n (pl -s) cosmetic care of the fingernails and hands ▶ v (-res, -ring, -red) care for (the fingernails and hands) in this way > **manicurist** n (pl -s)

manicured v ▷ manicure

manicures n, v ▷ manicure

manicuring v ▷ manicure

manicurist n ▷ manicure

manicurists n ▷ manicure

manifest adj easily noticed, obvious ▶ v (-s, -ing, -ed) show plainly ▶ n (pl -s) list of cargo or passengers for customs > **manifestation** n (pl -s)

manifestation n ▷ manifest

manifestations n ▷ manifest

manifested v ▷ manifest

manifesting v, n ▷ manifest

manifests v ▷ manifest

manifold adj numerous and varied ▶ n (pl -s) pipe with several outlets, esp. in an internal-combustion engine

manifolds n ▷ manifold

manikin n (pl -s) little man or dwarf

manikins n ▷ manikin

manila, manilla n (pl-s) strong brown paper used for envelopes

manilas n ▷ manila

manillas n ▷ manila

mankind n (pl -s) human beings collectively

mankinds n ▷ mankind

manlier adj ▷ manly

manliest adj ▷ manly

manliness n ▷ manly

manlinesses n ▷ manly

manly adj (-lier, -liest) (possessing qualities) appropriate to a man > **manliness** n (pl -es)

manna n (pl -s) BIBLE miraculous food which sustained the Israelites in the wilderness

mannas n ▷ manna

manned v ▷ man

manner n (pl -s) way a thing happens or is done > **mannered** adj affected

mannered adj ▷ manner

mannerisms n ▷ manner

manners n ▷ manner

mannikin n (pl -s) ▷ manikin

mannikins n ▷ mannikin

manning v ▷ man

mannish adj (of a woman) like a man

manor n (pl -s) BRIT large country house and its lands > **manorial** adj

manorial adj ▷ manor

manors n ▷ manor

manpower n (pl -s) available number of workers

manpowers n ▷ manpower

manqué adj would-be

mans v ▷ man

manse n (pl -s) house provided for a minister in some religious denominations

manses n ▷ manse

mansion n (pl -s) large house

mansions n ▷ mansion

mantel n (pl -s) structure round a fireplace

mantels n ▷ mantel

mantes n ▷ mantis

mantilla n (pl -s) (in Spain) a lace scarf covering a woman's head and shoulders

mantillas n ▷ mantilla

mantis n (pl -tises, -tes) carnivorous insect like a grasshopper

mantises n ▷ mantis

mantle n (pl -s) loose cloak

mantles n ▷ mantle

mantra n (pl -s) HINDUISM BUDDHISM any sacred word or syllable used as an object of concentration

mantras n ▷ mantra

manual adj of or done with the hands ▶ n (pl -s) handbook > **manually** adv

manually adv ▷ manual

manuals n ▷ manual

manure n (pl -s) animal excrement used as a fertilizer

manures n ▷ manure

many adj (more, most) numerous ▶ n large number

map n (pl -s) representation of the earth's surface or some part of it, showing geographical features ▶ v (-s, -pping, -pped) make a map of

maple n (pl -s) tree with broad leaves, a variety of which (**sugar maple**) yields sugar

maples n ▷ maple

mapped v ▷ map

mapping v ▷ map

maps n, v ▷ map

mar v (-s, -rring, -rred) spoil or impair

marabou n (pl -s) large black-and-white African stork

marabous n ▷ marabou

maraca n (pl -s) shaken percussion instrument made from a gourd containing dried seeds etc

maracas n ▷ maraca

marae n (pl -s) NZ enclosed space in front of a Maori meeting house

maraes n ▷ marae

marathon n (pl -s) long-distance race of 26 miles 385 yards (42.195 kilometres)

marathons n ▷ marathon

marauders n ▷ marauder

marble n (pl -s) kind of limestone with a mottled appearance, which can be highly polished > **marbled** adj having a mottled appearance like marble

marbled adj ▷ marble

marbles n ▷ marble

march¹ v (-es, -ing, -ed) walk with a military step ▶ n (pl -es) action of marching ▷ marcher n (pl -s)

march² n (pl -es) border or frontier

marched v ▷ march¹

marches v ▷ march¹ ▶ n ▷ march¹, ²

marching v ▷ march¹

mare n (pl -s) female horse or zebra

mares n ▷ mare

marge n (pl -s) informal margarine

marges n ▷ marge

margin n (pl -s) edge or border ▷ marginal adj insignificant, unimportant ▷ marginally adv

marginal adj ▷ margin

margins n ▷ margin

marigold n (pl -s) plant with yellow or orange flowers

marigolds n ▷ marigold

marina n (pl -s) harbour for yachts and other pleasure boats

marinade n (pl -s) seasoned liquid in which fish or meat is soaked before cooking ▶ v (-des, -ding, -ded) ▷ marinate

marinaded v ▷ marinade

marinades n, v ▷ marinade

marinading v ▷ marinade

marinas n ▷ marina

marinate v (-tes, -ting, -ted) soak in marinade

marinated v ▷ marinate

marinates v ▷ marinate

marinating v ▷ marinate

marine adj of the sea or shipping ▶ n (pl -s) (esp. in Britain and the US) soldier trained for land and sea combat

mariner n (pl -s) sailor

mariners n ▷ mariner

marines n ▷ marine

marital adj relating to marriage

maritime adj relating to shipping

marjoram n (pl -s) aromatic herb used for seasoning food and in salads

marjorams n ▷ marjoram

mark n (pl -s) line, dot, scar, etc visible on a surface ▶ v (-s, -ing, -ed) make

a mark on ▷ marked adj noticeable ▷ markedly adv ▷ marker n (pl -s)

marked v, adj ▷ mark

markedly adv ▷ mark

marker n ▷ mark

markers n ▷ mark

market n (pl -s) assembly or place for buying and selling ▶ v (-s, -ing, -ed) offer or produce for sale ▷ marketable adj

marketable adj ▷ market

markets n, v ▷ market

marking v ▷ mark

marks n, v ▷ mark

marksman n (pl -men) person skilled at shooting ▷ marksmanship n (pl -s)

marksmanship n ▷ marksman

marksmanships n ▷ marksman

marksmen n ▷ marksman

marl n (pl -s) soil formed of clay and lime, used as fertilizer

marlin n large food and game fish of warm and tropical seas, with a very long upper jaw

marls n ▷ marl

marmoset n (pl -s) small bushy-tailed monkey

marmosets n ▷ marmoset

marmot n (pl -s) burrowing rodent

marmots n ▷ marmot

maroon¹ adj reddish-purple

maroon² v (-s, -ing, -ed) abandon ashore, esp. on an island

marooned v ▷ maroon

marooning v ▷ maroon

maroons v ▷ maroon

marquee n (pl -s) large tent used for a party or exhibition

marquees n ▷ marquee

marquess n (pl -es) BRIT nobleman of the rank below a duke

marquesses n ▷ marquess

marquis n (pl -es) (in some European countries) nobleman of the rank above a count

marquises n ▷ marquis

marred v ▷ mar

marriage n (pl -s) state of being

married ▷ **marriageable** adj
marriageable adj ▷ **marriage**
marriages n ▷ **marriage**
married v ▷ **marry**
marries v ▷ **marry**
marring v ▷ **mar**
marrow n (pl **-s**) fatty substance inside bones
marrows n ▷ **marrow**
marry v (**-ries, -ing, -ried**) take as a husband or wife
marrying v ▷ **marry**
mars v ▷ **mar**
marsala n (pl **-s**) dark sweet wine
marsalas n ▷ **marsala**
marsh n (pl **-s**) low-lying wet land >**marshy** adj (**-shier, -shiest**)
marshal n (pl **-s**) officer of the highest rank ▶ v (**-s, -shalling, -shalled**) arrange in order
marshalled v ▷ **marshal**
marshalling v ▷ **marshal**
marshals n, v ▷ **marshal**
marshes n ▷ **marsh**
marshier adj ▷ **marsh**
marshiest adj ▷ **marsh**
marshy adj ▷ **marsh**
mart n (pl **-s**) market
marten n (pl **-s**) weasel-like animal
martens n ▷ **marten**
martial adj of war, warlike
martian adj of Mars ▶ n (pl **-s**) supposed inhabitant of Mars
martians n ▷ **martian**
martin n (pl **-s**) bird with a slightly forked tail
martinet n (pl **-s**) person who maintains strict discipline
martinets n ▷ **martinet**
martini n (pl **-s**) cocktail of vermouth and gin
martinis n ▷ **martini**
martins n ▷ **martin**
marts n ▷ **mart**
martyr n (pl **-s**) person who dies or suffers for his or her beliefs ▶ v (**-s, -ing, -ed**) make a martyr of >**martyrdom** n (pl **-s**)

martyrdom n ▷ **martyr**
martyrdoms n ▷ **martyr**
martyred v ▷ **martyr**
martyring v ▷ **martyr**
martyrs n, v ▷ **martyr**
marvel v (**-s, -velling, -velled**) be filled with wonder ▶ n wonderful thing
marvelled v ▷ **marvel**
marvelling v ▷ **marvel**
marvels n, v ▷ **marvel**
marzipan n (pl **-s**) paste of ground almonds, sugar, and egg whites
marzipans n ▷ **marzipan**
mas n ▷ **ma**
mascara n (pl **-s**) cosmetic for darkening the eyelashes
mascaras n ▷ **mascara**
mascot n (pl **-s**) person, animal, or thing supposed to bring good luck
mascots n ▷ **mascot**
mash n (pl **-es**) informal mashed potatoes ▶ v (**-es, -ing, -ed**) crush into a soft mass
mashed v ▷ **mash**
mashes n, v ▷ **mash**
mashing v ▷ **mash**
mask n (pl **-s**) covering for the face, as a disguise or protection ▶ v (**-s, -ing, -ed**) cover with a mask
masked v ▷ **mask**
masking v ▷ **mask**
masks n, v ▷ **mask**
mason n (pl **-s**) person who works with stone
masonic adj of Freemasonry
masonry n (pl **-ries**) stonework
masons n ▷ **mason**
masque n (pl **-s**) HIST 16th–17th-century form of dramatic entertainment
masques n ▷ **masque**
mass n (pl **-es**) coherent body of matter ▶ adj large-scale ▶ v (**-es, -ing, -ed**) form into a mass
massacre n (pl **-s**) indiscriminate killing of large numbers of people ▶ v (**-res, -ring, -red**) kill in large numbers
massacred v ▷ **massacre**
massacres n, v ▷ **massacre**

massacring v ▷ massacre

massage n (pl **-s**) rubbing and kneading of parts of the body to reduce pain or stiffness ▶ v (**-ges, -ging, -ged**) give a massage to

massaged v ▷ massage

massages n, v ▷ massage

massaging v ▷ massage

massed v ▷ mass

masses n, v ▷ mass

masseur, fem, **masseuse** n (pl **-s**) person who gives massages

masseurs n ▷ masseur

masseuse n ▷ masseur

masseuses n ▷ masseur

massif n (pl **-s**) connected group of mountains

massifs n ▷ massif

massing v ▷ mass

massive adj large and heavy

mast[1] n (pl **-s**) tall pole for supporting something, esp. a ship's sails

mast[2] n (pl **-s**) fruit of the beech, oak, etc, used as pig fodder

master n (pl **-s**) person in control, such as an employer or an owner of slaves or animals ▶ adj overall or controlling ▶ v (**-s, -ing, -ed**) acquire knowledge of or skill in

mastered v ▷ master

masteries n ▷ mastery

mastering v ▷ master

masterly adj showing great skill

masters n, v ▷ master

mastery n (pl **-ries**) expertise

mastic n (pl **-s**) gum obtained from certain trees

mastics n ▷ mastic

mastiff n (pl **-s**) large dog

mastiffs n ▷ mastiff

mastitis n (pl **-es**) inflammation of a breast or udder

mastitises n ▷ mastitis

mastodon n (pl **-s**) extinct elephant-like mammal

mastodons n ▷ mastodon

mastoid n (pl **-s**) projection of the bone behind the ear

mastoids n ▷ mastoid

masts n ▷ mast[1, 2]

mat n (pl **-s**) piece of fabric used as a floor covering or to protect a surface ▶ v (**-s, -tting, -tted**) tangle or become tangled into a dense mass

matador n (pl **-s**) man who kills the bull in bullfights

matadors n ▷ matador

match[1] n (pl **-es**) contest in a game or sport ▶ v (**-es, -ing, -ed**) be exactly like, equal to, or in harmony with

match[2] n small stick with a tip which ignites when scraped on a rough surface ▶ **matchbox** n (pl **-es**)

matchbox n ▷ match[2]

matchboxes n ▷ match[2]

matched v ▷ match[1]

matches v ▷ match[1] ▶ n ▷ match[1, 2]

matching v ▷ match[1]

mate[1] n (pl **-s**) informal friend ▶ v (**-tes, -ting, -ted**) pair (animals) or (of animals) be paired for reproduction

mate[2] n (pl **-s**) checkmate ▶ v (**-tes, -ting, -ted**) CHESS checkmate

mated v ▷ mate[1, 2]

material n (pl **-s**) substance of which a thing is made ▶ adj of matter or substance > **materialist** adj, n > **materialistic** adj

materialist adj, n (pl **-s**) ▷ material

materialistic adj ▷ material

materialists n ▷ material

materials n ▷ material

maternal adj of a mother ▶ adj of or for pregnant women

mates n, v ▷ mate[1, 2]

matey adj (**-tier, -tiest**) BRIT informal friendly or intimate

maths n informal mathematics

matier adj ▷ matey

matiest adj ▷ matey

matilda n AUST HIST swagman's bundle of belongings

matildas n ▷ matilda

matinée n (pl **-s**) afternoon performance in a theatre or cinema

matinées n ▷ matinée

mating v ▷ **mate**[1, 2]

matins pl n early morning service in various Christian Churches

matrices n ▷ **matrix**

matrix n (pl -**trices**) substance or situation in which something originates, takes form, or is enclosed

matron n (pl -**s**) staid or dignified married woman > **matronly** adj

matrons n ▷ **matron**

mats n, v ▷ **mat**

matt adj dull, not shiny

matted v ▷ **mat**

matter n (pl -**s**) substance of which something is made ▶ v (-**s**, -**ing**, -**ed**) be of importance

mattered v ▷ **matter**

mattering v ▷ **matter**

matters n, v ▷ **matter**

matting v ▷ **mat**

mattock n (pl -**s**) large pick with one of its blade ends flattened for loosening soil

mattocks n ▷ **mattock**

mattress n (pl -**es**) large stuffed flat case, often with springs, used on or as a bed

mattresses n ▷ **mattress**

maturation n ▷ **mature**

maturations n ▷ **mature**

mature adj fully developed or grown-up ▶ v (-**res**, -**ring**, -**red**) make or become mature > **maturation** n (pl -**s**)

matured v ▷ **mature**

matures v ▷ **mature**

maturing v ▷ **mature**

maturities n ▷ **maturity**

maturity n (pl -**ties**) state of being mature

maudlin adj foolishly or tearfully sentimental

maul v (-**s**, -**ing**, -**ed**) handle roughly

mauled v ▷ **maul**

mauling v ▷ **maul**

mauls v ▷ **maul**

maunder v (-**s**, -**ing**, -**ed**) talk or act aimlessly or idly

maundered v ▷ **maunder**

maundering v ▷ **maunder**

maunders v ▷ **maunder**

mauve adj (-**r**, -**est**) pale purple

mauver adj ▷ **mauve**

mauvest adj ▷ **mauve**

maverick n (pl -**s**) ▶ adj independent and unorthodox (person)

mavericks n ▷ **maverick**

maw n (pl -**s**) animal's mouth, throat, or stomach

mawkish adj foolishly sentimental

maws n ▷ **maw**

max n (**maxes**). Max is a short form of **maximum**. This is a useful word, particularly if you find yourself near the end of the game, with limited opportunity to play it. Max scores 12 points.

maxim n (pl -**s**) general truth or principle

maxima n ▷ **maximum**

maximal adj ▷ **maxim**

maximize v (-**zes**, -**zing**, -**zed**) increase to a maximum

maximized v ▷ **maximize**

maximizes v ▷ **maximize**

maximizing v ▷ **maximize**

maxims n ▷ **maxim**

maximum adj, n (pl -**s**, -**ma**) greatest possible (amount or number) > **maximal** adj

maximums n ▷ **maximum**

may[1] v (past tense **might**) used as an auxiliary to express possibility, permission, opportunity, etc

may[2] n (pl -**s**) ▷ **hawthorn**

maybe adv perhaps, possibly

mayday n (pl -**s**) international radio distress signal

maydays n ▷ **mayday**

mayflies n ▷ **mayfly**

mayfly n (pl -**lies**) short-lived aquatic insect

mayhem n (pl -**s**) violent destruction or confusion

mayhems n ▷ **mayhem**

mayor n (pl -**s**) head of a municipality

mayoress n (pl -**es**) mayor's wife

mayoresses n ▷ **mayoress**

mayors n ▷ **mayor**

maypole n (pl -s) pole set up for dancing round on the first day of May to celebrate spring

maypoles n ▷ **maypole**

mays n ▷ **may²**

maze n (pl -s) complex network of paths or lines designed to puzzle

mazes n ▷ **maze**

mazurka n (pl -s) lively Polish dance

mazurkas n ▷ **mazurka**

me pron ▷ **I**

mead n (pl -s) alcoholic drink made from honey

meadow n (pl -s) piece of grassland

meadows n ▷ **meadow**

meads n ▷ **mead**

meagre adj scanty or insufficient

meal¹ n (pl -s) occasion when food is served and eaten

meal² n (pl -s) grain ground to powder > **mealy -lier, -liest**) ▶ adj

mealie n (pl -s) S AFR maize

mealier adj ▷ **meal²**

mealies n ▷ **mealie**

mealiest adj ▷ **meal²**

meals n ▷ **meal¹, ²**

mealy adj ▷ **meal²**

mean¹ v (-s, -ing, meant) intend to convey or express > **meaningful** adj > **meaningless** adj

mean² adj (-er, -est) miserly, ungenerous, or petty > **meanly** adv > **meanness** n (pl -es)

mean³ n (pl -s) middle point between two extremes ▶ pl method by which something is done ▶ adj intermediate in size or quantity

meander v (-s, -ing, -ed) follow a winding course ▶ n (pl -s) winding course

meandered v ▷ **meander**

meandering v ▷ **meander**

meanders v, n ▷ **meander**

meaner adj ▷ **mean²**

meanest adj ▷ **mean²**

meaning n (pl -s) sense, significance

meaningful adj ▷ **mean¹**

meaningless adj ▷ **mean¹**

meanings n ▷ **meaning**

meanly adv ▷ **mean²**

meanness n ▷ **mean²**

meannesses n ▷ **mean²**

means v ▷ **mean¹** ▶ n ▷ **mean³**

meantime n (pl -s) intervening period ▶ adv meanwhile

meantimes n ▷ **meantime**

measles n infectious disease producing red spots

measly adj informal meagre

measurable adj ▷ **measure**

measure n (pl -s) size or quantity ▶ v (-res, -ring, -red) determine the size or quantity of > **measurable** adj

measured adj slow and steady ▶ v ▷ **measure**

measures n, v ▷ **measure**

measuring v ▷ **measure**

meat n (pl -s) animal flesh as food

meatier adj ▷ **meaty**

meatiest adj ▷ **meaty**

meats n ▷ **meat**

meaty adj (-tier, -tiest) (tasting) of or like meat

mechanic n (pl -s) person skilled in repairing or operating machinery

medal n (pl -s) piece of metal with an inscription etc, given as a reward or memento

medals n ▷ **medal**

meddle v (-les, -ling, -led) interfere annoyingly > **meddler** n (pl -s) > **meddlesome** adj

meddled v ▷ **meddle**

meddler n ▷ **meddle**

meddlers n ▷ **meddle**

meddles v ▷ **meddle**

meddlesome adj ▷ **meddle**

meddling v ▷ **meddle**

media n (pl -iae) ▷ **medium** the mass media collectively

mediae n ▷ **media**

mediaeval adj ▷ **medieval**

medial adj of or in the middle

median adj, n (pl -s) middle (point

or line)
medians n ▷ **median**
mediate v (**-tes, -ting, -ted**) intervene in a dispute to bring about agreement > **mediation** n (pl **-s**) > **mediator** n (pl **-s**)
mediated v ▷ **mediate**
mediates v ▷ **mediate**
mediating v ▷ **mediate**
mediation n ▷ **mediate**
mediations n ▷ **mediate**
mediator n ▷ **mediate**
mediators n ▷ **mediate**
medic n (pl **-s**) informal doctor or medical student
medical adj of the science of medicine ▶ n (pl **-s**) informal medical examination > **medically** adv
medically adv ▷ **medical**
medicals n ▷ **medical**
medicate v (**-tes, -ting, -ted**) treat with a medicinal substance
medicated v ▷ **medicate**
medicates v ▷ **medicate**
medicating v ▷ **medicate**
medicine n (pl **-s**) substance used to treat disease
medicines n ▷ **medicine**
medics n ▷ **medic**
medieval adj of the Middle Ages
mediocre adj average in quality > **mediocrity** n (pl **-ties**)
mediocrities n ▷ **mediocre**
mediocrity n ▷ **mediocre**
meditate v (**-tes, -ting, -ted**) reflect deeply, esp. on spiritual matters > **meditation** n (pl **-s**) > **meditative** adj > **meditatively** adv > **meditator** n (pl **-s**)
meditated v ▷ **meditate**
meditates v ▷ **meditate**
meditating v ▷ **meditate**
meditation n ▷ **meditate**
meditations n ▷ **meditate**
meditative adj ▷ **meditate**
meditatively adv ▷ **meditate**
meditator n ▷ **meditate**
meditators n ▷ **meditate**

medium adj midway between extremes, average ▶ n (pl **-dia, -diums**) middle state, degree, or condition
mediums n ▷ **medium**
medlar n (pl **-s**) apple-like fruit of a small tree, eaten when it begins to decay
medlars n ▷ **medlar**
medley n (pl **-s**) miscellaneous mixture
medleys n ▷ **medley**
medulla n (pl **-las, -lae**) marrow, pith, or inner tissue
medullae n ▷ **medulla**
medullas n ▷ **medulla**
meek adj (**-er, -est**) submissive or humble ▶ **meekly** adv > **meekness** n (pl **-es**)
meeker adj ▷ **meek**
meekest adj ▷ **meek**
meekly adv ▷ **meek**
meekness n ▷ **meek**
meeknesses n ▷ **meek**
meerkat n (pl **-s**) S African mongoose
meerkats n ▷ **meerkat**
meet[1] v (**-s, meeting, met**) come together (with) ▶ n (pl **-s**) meeting, esp. a sports meeting
meet[2] adj (**-er, -est**) obs fit or suitable
meeter adj ▷ **meet**[2]
meetest adj ▷ **meet**[2]
meeting n (pl **-s**) coming together ▶ v ▷ **meet**[1]
meets v, n ▷ **meek**[1]
megabyte n (pl **-s**) COMPUTERS 2^{20} or 1 048 576 bytes
megabytes n ▷ **megabyte**
megalith n (pl **-s**) great stone, esp. as part of a prehistoric monument > **megalithic** adj
megalithic adj ▷ **megalith**
megaliths n ▷ **megalith**
megapode n (pl **-s**) bird of Australia, New Guinea, and adjacent islands
megapodes n ▷ **megapode**
megaton n (pl **-s**) explosive power equal to that of one million tons of TNT
megatons n ▷ **megaton**
melange n (pl **-s**) mixture

melanges n ▷ melange
melanin n (pl -s) dark pigment found in the hair, skin, and eyes of humans and animals
melanins n ▷ melanin
mêlée n (pl -s) noisy confused fight or crowd
mêlées n ▷ mêlée
mellow adj soft, not harsh ▶ v (-s, -ing, -ed) make or become mellow
mellowed v ▷ mellow
mellowing v ▷ mellow
mellows v ▷ mellow
melodic adj of melody
melody n (pl -dies) series of musical notes which make a tune
melon n (pl -s) large round juicy fruit with a hard rind
melons n ▷ melon
melt v (-s, -ing, -ed) (cause to) become liquid by heat
meltdown n (pl -s) (in a nuclear reactor) melting of the fuel rods, with the possible release of radiation
meltdowns n ▷ meltdown
melted v ▷ melt
melting v ▷ melt
melts v ▷ melt
member n (pl -s) individual making up a body or society > **membership** n (pl -s)
members n ▷ member
membership n ▷ member
memberships n ▷ member
membrane n (pl -s) thin flexible tissue in a plant or animal body > **membranous** adj
membranes n ▷ membrane
membranous adj ▷ membrane
memento n (pl -tos, -toes) thing serving to remind, souvenir
mementoes n ▷ memento
mementos n ▷ memento
memoir n (pl -s) biography or historical account based on personal knowledge ▶ pl collection of these
memoirs n ▷ memoir
memorial n (pl -s) something serving

to commemorate a person or thing ▶ adj serving as a memorial
memorize v (-zes, -zing, -zed) commit to memory
memorized v ▷ memorize
memorizes v ▷ memorize
memorizing v ▷ memorize
memory n (pl -ries) ability to remember
memos n ▷ memo
men n ▷ man
menace n (pl -s) threat ▶ v (-ces, -cing, -ced) threaten, endanger > **menacing** adj
menaced v ▷ menace
menaces n, v ▷ menace
menacing v, adj ▷ menace
ménage n (pl -s) household
ménages n ▷ ménage
mend v (-s, -ing, -ed) repair or patch ▶ n (pl -s) mended area
mended v ▷ mend
mending v ▷ mend
mends v, n ▷ mend
menhir n (pl -s) single upright prehistoric stone
menhirs n ▷ menhir
menial adj involving boring work of low status ▶ n (pl -s) person with a menial job
menials n ▷ menial
menisci n ▷ meniscus
meniscus n (pl -ci) curved surface of a liquid
mental adj of, in, or done by the mind > **mentally** adv
mentally adv ▷ mental
menthol n (pl -s) organic compound found in peppermint, used medicinally
menthols n ▷ menthol
mention v (-s, -ing, -ed) refer to briefly ▶ n (pl -s) brief reference to a person or thing
mentioned v ▷ mention
mentioning v ▷ mention
mentions v, n ▷ mention
mentor n (pl -s) adviser or guide
mentors n ▷ mentor

menu n (pl -s) list of dishes to be served, or from which to order

menus n ▷ menu

merchant n (pl -s) person engaged in trade, wholesale trader

merchants n ▷ merchant

merciful adj compassionate

merciless adj ▷ mercy

mercuries n ▷ mercury

mercury n (pl -ries) CHEM silvery liquid metal

mercy n (pl -cies) compassionate treatment of an offender or enemy who is in one's power > **merciless** adj

mere¹ adj (-r, -st) nothing more than > **merely** adv

mere² n (pl -s) BRIT obs lake

merely adv ▷ mere¹

merer adj ▷ mere¹

meres n ▷ mere²

merest adj ▷ mere¹

merge v (-ges, -ging, -ged) combine or blend

merged v ▷ merge

merger n (pl -s) combination of business firms into one

mergers n ▷ merger

merges v ▷ merge

merging v ▷ merge

meridian n (pl -s) imaginary circle of the earth passing through both poles

meridians n ▷ meridian

meringue n (pl -s) baked mixture of egg whites and sugar

meringues n ▷ meringue

merino n (pl -s) breed of sheep with fine soft wool

merinos n ▷ merino

merit n (pl -s) excellence or worth ▶ pl admirable qualities ▶ v (-s, -ing, -ed) deserve

merited v ▷ merit

meriting v ▷ merit

merits n, v ▷ merit

merlin n (pl -s) small falcon

merlins n ▷ merlin

mermaid n (pl -s) imaginary sea creature with the upper part of a woman and the lower part of a fish

mermaids n ▷ mermaid

merrier adj ▷ merry

merriest adj ▷ merry

merrily adv ▷ merry

merriment n ▷ merry

merriments n ▷ merry

merry adj (-rier, -rriest) cheerful or jolly > **merrily** adv > **merriment** n (pl -s)

mesdames n ▷ madame

mesh n (pl -es) network or net ▶ v (-es, -ing, -ed) (of gear teeth) engage

meshed v ▷ mesh

meshes n, v ▷ mesh

meshing v ▷ mesh

meson n (pl -s) elementary atomic particle

mesons n ▷ meson

mess n (pl -es) untidy or dirty confusion ▶ v (-es, -ing, -ed) muddle or dirty

message n (pl -s) communication sent

messages n ▷ message

messagings n ▷ message

messed v ▷ mess

messes n, v ▷ mess

messiah n (pl -s) promised deliverer > **messianic** adj

messiahs n ▷ messiah

messianic adj ▷ messiah

messier adj ▷ messy

messiest adj ▷ messy

messieurs n ▷ monsieur

messily adv ▷ messy

messing v ▷ mess

messy adj (-ssier, -ssiest) dirty, confused, or untidy > **messily** adv

met v ▷ meet¹

metal n (pl -s) chemical element, such as iron or copper, that is malleable and capable of conducting heat and electricity > **metallic** adj

metallic adj ▷ metal

metals n ▷ metal

metaphor n (pl -s) figure of speech in which a term is applied to something it does not literally denote in order to imply a

resemblance > **metaphorical** adj
> **metaphorically** adv
metaphorically adv ▷ **metaphor**
metaphors n ▷ **metaphor**

mete v (-**tes**, -**ting**, -**ted**) (usu. with **out**) deal out as punishment
meted v ▷ **mete**

meteor n (pl -**s**) small fast-moving heavenly body, visible as a streak of incandescence if it enters the earth's atmosphere

meteoric adj of a meteor
meteors n ▷ **meteor**

meter n (pl -**s**) instrument for measuring and recording something, such as the consumption of gas or electricity ▷ v (-**s**, -**ing**, -**ed**) measure by meter
meters n, v ▷ **meter**
metes v ▷ **mete**

methane n (pl -**s**) colourless inflammable gas
methanes n ▷ **methane**

methanol n (pl -**s**) colourless poisonous liquid used as a solvent and fuel (also **methyl alcohol**)
methanols n ▷ **methanol**

methinks v (past tense **methought**) obs it seems to me

method n (pl -**s**) way or manner
methods n ▷ **method**

meths n informal methylated spirits

methyl n (pl -**s**) (compound containing) a saturated hydrocarbon group of atoms
methyls n ▷ **methyl**

métier n (pl -**s**) profession or trade
métiers n ▷ **métier**

meting v ▷ **mete**

metonymies n ▷ **metonymy**

metonymy n (pl -**mies**) figure of speech in which one thing is replaced by another associated with it, such as 'the Crown' for 'the queen'

metre n (pl -**s**) basic unit of length equal to about 1.094 yards (100 centimetres)
metres n ▷ **metre**

metric adj of the decimal system of weights and measures based on the metre

metrical adj of measurement

mettle n (pl -**s**) courage or spirit
mettles n ▷ **mettle**

mew n (pl -**s**) cry of a cat ▷ v (-**s**, -**ing**, -**ed**) utter this cry
mewed v ▷ **mew**
mewing v ▷ **mew**
mews n, v ▷ **mew**

mezquit n (**mezquit**) (A). A mezquit is a small spiny tree or shrub. With its combination of Q and Z, mezquit is a very high-scoring word. As it contains seven letters, mezquit can earn you a bonus of 50 points if you manage to use all the letters on your rack to form it. Mezquit scores 28 points.

miaow n (pl -**s**) ▷ v (-**s**, -**ing**, -**wed**)
▷ **mew**
miaowed v ▷ **miaow**
miaowing v ▷ **miaow**
miaows v, n ▷ **miaow**

miasma n (pl -**mata**) unwholesome or foreboding atmosphere
miasmata n ▷ **miasma**

mica n (pl -**s**) glasslike mineral used as an electrical insulator
micas n ▷ **mica**
mice n ▷ **mouse**

microbe n (pl -**s**) minute organism, esp. one causing disease
> **microbial** adj
microbes n ▷ **microbe**
microbial adj ▷ **microbe**

micron n (pl -**s**) one millionth of a metre
microns n ▷ **micron**

mid adj intermediate, middle

midday n (pl -**s**) noon
middays n ▷ **midday**

midden n (pl -**s**) BRIT & AUST dunghill or rubbish heap
middens n ▷ **midden**

middle adj equidistant from two extremes ▷ n (pl -**s**) middle point or part

middles n ▷ middle

middling adj mediocre

midge n (pl -s) small mosquito-like insect

midges n ▷ midge

midget n (pl -s) very small person or thing

midgets n ▷ midget

midland n (pl -s) BRIT, AUST & US middle part of a country

midlands n ▷ midland

midnight n (pl -s) twelve o'clock at night

midnights n ▷ midnight

midriff n (pl -s) middle part of the body

midriffs n ▷ midriff

midway adv halfway

midwife n (pl -wives) trained person who assists at childbirth
> **midwifery** n (pl -ries)

midwiferies n ▷ midwife

midwifery n ▷ midwife

midwives n ▷ midwife

mien n (pl -s) lit person's bearing, demeanour, or appearance

miens n ▷ mien

miffed adj informal offended or upset

might¹ v ▷ may

might² n (pl -s) power or strength

mightier adj ▷ mighty

mightiest adj ▷ mighty

mightily adv ▷ mighty

mighty adj (-tier, -tiest) powerful
▶ adv US G AUST informal very
> **mightily** adv

migraine n (pl -s) severe headache, often with nausea and visual disturbances

migraines n ▷ migraine

migrant n (pl -s) person or animal that moves from one place to another ▶ adj moving from one place to another

migrants n ▷ migrant

migrate v (-tes, -ting, -ted) move from one place to settle in another
> **migration** n (pl -s)

migrated v ▷ migrate

migrates v ▷ migrate

migrating v ▷ migrate

migration n ▷ migrate

migrations n ▷ migrate

mike n (pl -s) informal microphone

mikes n ▷ mike

milch adj CHIEFLY BRIT (of a cow) giving milk

mild adj (-er, -est) not strongly flavoured ▶ **mildly** adv > **mildness** n (pl -es)

milder adj ▷ mild

mildest adj ▷ mild

mildew n (pl -s) destructive fungus on plants or things exposed to damp
> **mildewed** adj

mildewed adj ▷ mildew

mildews n ▷ mildew

mildly adv ▷ mild

mildness n ▷ mild

mildnesses n ▷ mild

mile n (pl -s) unit of length equal to 1760 yards or 1.609 kilometres

mileage n (pl -s) distance travelled in miles

mileages n ▷ mileage

miles n ▷ mile

milieu n (pl -x, -s) environment or surroundings

milieus n ▷ milieu

milieux n ▷ milieu

militancies n ▷ militant

militancy n ▷ militant

militant adj aggressive or vigorous in support of a cause ▶ **militancy** n (pl -cies)

militants n ▷ militant

militaries n ▷ military

militarist n ▷ military

militarists n ▷ military

militarized adj ▷ military

military adj of or for soldiers, armies, or war ▶ n (pl -ries) armed services
> **militarist** n (pl -s) > **militarized** adj

militate v (-tes, -ting, -ted) (usu. with **against** or **for**) have a strong influence or effect

militated v ▷ militate

militates v ▷ **militate**

militating v ▷ **militate**

militia n (pl -**s**) military force of trained citizens for use in emergency only

militias n ▷ **militia**

milk n (pl -**s**) white fluid produced by female mammals to feed their young ▶ v (-**s**, -**ing**, -**ed**) draw milk from > **milky** adj (-**kier**, -**kiest**)

milked v ▷ **milk**

milkier adj ▷ **milk**

milkiest adj ▷ **milk**

milking v ▷ **milk**

milkmaid n (pl -**s**) (esp. in former times) woman who milks cows

milkmaids n ▷ **milkmaid**

milkman n (pl -**men**) BRIT, AUST & NZ man who delivers milk to people's houses

milkmen n ▷ **milkman**

milks n, v ▷ **milk**

milksop n (pl -**s**) feeble man

milksops n ▷ **milk**

milky adj ▷ **milk**

mill n (pl -**s**) factory ▶ v (-**s**, -**ing**, -**ed**) grind, press, or process in or as if in a mill

milled v ▷ **mill**

millennia n ▷ **mill**

millenniums n ▷ **mill**

miller n (pl -**s**) person who works in a mill

millers n ▷ **miller**

millet n (pl -**s**) type of cereal grass

millets n ▷ **millet**

millibar n (pl -**s**) unit of atmospheric pressure

millibars n ▷ **millibar**

milliner n (pl -**s**) maker or seller of women's hats ▷ **millinery** n (pl -**ries**)

millineries n ▷ **milliner**

milliners n ▷ **milliner**

millinery n ▷ **milliner**

milling v ▷ **mill**

million n (pl -**s**) one thousand thousands > **millionth** adj, n (pl -**s**)

millions n ▷ **million**

millionths n ▷ **million**

mills n, v ▷ **mill**

milt n (pl -**s**) sperm of fish

milts n ▷ **milt**

mime n (pl -**s**) acting without the use of words ▶ v (-**mes**, -**ming**, -**med**) act in mime

mimed v ▷ **mime**

mimes n, v ▷ **mime**

mimic v (-**ics**, -**icking**, -**icked**) imitate (a person or manner), esp. for satirical effect ▶ n (pl -**s**) person or animal that is good at mimicking > **mimicry** n (pl -**ries**)

mimicked v ▷ **mimic**

mimicking v ▷ **mimic**

mimicry n ▷ **mimic**

mimics n, v ▷ **mimic**

miming v ▷ **mime**

mina n ▷ **myna**

minaret n (pl -**s**) tall slender tower of a mosque

minarets n ▷ **minaret**

minas n ▷ **myna**

mince v (-**ces**, -**cing**, -**ced**) cut or grind into very small pieces ▶ n (pl -**s**) minced meat

minced v ▷ **mince**

mincer n (pl -**s**) machine for mincing meat

mincers n ▷ **mince**

minces v, n ▷ **mince**

mincing adj affected in manner ▶ v ▷ **mince**

mind n (pl -**s**) thinking faculties ▶ v (-**s**, -**ing**, -**ed**) take offence at

minded adj having an inclination as specified ▶ v ▷ **mind**

minder n (pl -**s**) informal aide or bodyguard

minders n ▷ **minder**

mindful adj heedful

minding v ▷ **mind**

mindless adj stupid

minds n, v ▷ **mind**

mine[1] pron belonging to me

mine[2] n (pl -**s**) deep hole for digging out coal, ores, etc ▶ v (-**nes**, -**ning**, -**ned**) dig for minerals

mined v ▷ mine

miner n (pl -s) person who works in a mine

mineral n (pl -s) naturally occurring inorganic substance, such as metal
▶ adj of, containing, or like minerals

minerals n ▷ mineral

miners n ▷ miner

mines n, v ▷ mine

minger n (pl -s) BRIT informal unattractive person

mingers n ▷ minger

mingier adj ▷ mingy

mingiest adj ▷ mingy

minging adj BRIT informal unattractive or unpleasant

mingle v (-les, -ling, -led) mix or blend

mingled v ▷ mingle

mingles v ▷ mingle

mingling v ▷ mingle

mingy adj (-gier, -giest) informal miserly

mini n (pl -s) ▶ adj (something) small or miniature

minibar n (pl -s) selection of drinks and confectionery provided in a hotel room

minibus n (pl -es) small bus

minibuses n ▷ minibus

minicab n (pl -s) BRIT ordinary car used as a taxi

minicabs n ▷ minicab

minidisc n (pl -s) small recordable compact disc

minidiscs n ▷ minidisc

minier adj ▷ mini

miniest adj ▷ mini

minim n (pl -s) MUSIC note half the length of a semibreve

minima n ▷ minimum

minimal adj minimum

minimize v (-zes, -zing, -zed) reduce to a minimum

minimized v ▷ minimize

minimizes v ▷ minimize

minimizing v ▷ minimize

minims n ▷ minim

minimum adj, n (pl -mums, -ma) least possible (amount or number)

minimums n ▷ minimum

mining v ▷ mine

minion n (pl -s) servile assistant

minions n ▷ minion

minis n ▷ mini

minister n (pl -s) head of a government department ▶ v (-s, -ing, -ed) (foll. by **to**) attend to the needs of
> **ministerial** adj

ministered v ▷ minister

ministerial adj ▷ minister

ministering v ▷ minister

ministers n, v ▷ minister

ministries n ▷ ministry

ministry n (pl -tries) profession or duties of a clergyman

mink n stoatlike animal

minnow n (pl -s) small freshwater fish

minnows n ▷ minnow

minor adj lesser ▶ n (pl -s) person regarded legally as a child

minorities n ▷ minority

minority n (pl -ties) lesser number

minors n ▷ minor

minster n (pl -s) BRIT cathedral or large church

minsters n ▷ minster

minstrel n (pl -s) medieval singer or musician

minstrels n ▷ minstrel

mint¹ n (pl -s) plant with aromatic leaves used for seasoning and flavouring

mint² n place where money is coined
▶ v (-s, -ing, -ed) make (coins)

minted v ▷ mint²

minting v ▷ mint²

mints n ▷ mint¹, ² v ▷ mint²

minuet n (pl -s) stately dance

minuets n ▷ minuet

minus prep, adj indicating subtraction
▶ adj less than zero ▶ n (pl -es) sign (-) denoting subtraction or a number less than zero

minuses n ▷ minus

minute¹ n (pl -s) 60th part of an hour or degree ▶ pl record of the proceedings of a meeting ▶ v (-tes,

-ting, -ted) record in the minutes
minute² adj (-r, -st) very small
> **minutely** adv
minuted v ▷ **minute¹**
minutely adv ▷ **minute²**
minuter adj ▷ **minute²**
minutes n, v ▷ **minute¹**
minutest adj ▷ **minute²**
minutiae pl n trifling or precise details
minuting v ▷ **minute¹**
minx n (pl -es) bold or flirtatious girl
minxes n ▷ **minx**
miracle n (pl -s) wonderful
supernatural event > **miraculous** adj
> **miraculously** adv
miracles n ▷ **miracle**
miraculous adj ▷ **miracle**
miraculously adv ▷ **miracle**
mirage n (pl -s) optical illusion, esp.
one caused by hot air
mirages n ▷ **mirage**
mire n (pl -s) swampy ground
mires n ▷ **mire**
mirror n (pl -s) coated glass surface
for reflecting images ▶ v (-s, -ing, -ed)
reflect in or as if in a mirror
mirrored v ▷ **mirror**
mirroring v ▷ **mirror**
mirrors n, v ▷ **mirror**
mirth n (pl -s) laughter, merriment, or
gaiety > **mirthful** adj > **mirthless** adj
mirthful adv ▷ **mirth**
mirthless adj ▷ **mirth**
mirths n ▷ **mirth**
miscarried v ▷ **miscarry**
miscarries v ▷ **miscarry**
miscarry v (-ries, -rying, -ried) have
a miscarriage
miscarrying v ▷ **miscarry**
miscast v (-s, -ing, -cast) cast
(a role or actor) in (a play or film)
inappropriately
miscasting v ▷ **miscast**
miscasts v ▷ **miscast**
mischief n (pl -s) annoying but not
malicious behaviour
mischiefs n ▷ **mischief**
miscible adj able to be mixed

misdeed n (pl -s) wrongful act
misdeeds n ▷ **misdeed**
miser n (pl -s) person who hoards
money and hates spending it
> **miserly** adj
miseries adj ▷ **misery**
miserly adj ▷ **miser**
misers n ▷ **miser**
misery n (pl -ries) great unhappiness
misfire
misfire v (-res, -ring, -red) (of a
firearm or engine) fail to fire correctly
misfired v ▷ **misfire**
misfires v ▷ **misfire**
misfiring v ▷ **misfire**
misfit n (pl -s) person not suited to his
or her social environment
misfits n ▷ **misfit**
mishap n (pl -s) minor accident
mishaps n ▷ **mishap**
misjudge v (-ges, -ging, -ged) judge
wrongly or unfairly > **misjudgment**,
misjudgement n (pl -s)
misjudged v ▷ **misjudge**
misjudgement n ▷ **misjudge**
misjudges v ▷ **misjudge**
misjudging v ▷ **misjudge**
misjudgment n ▷ **misjudge**
mislaid v ▷ **mislay**
mislay v (-s, -ing, -laid) lose
(something) temporarily
mislaying v ▷ **mislay**
mislays v ▷ **mislay**
mislead v (-s, -ing, -led) give
false or confusing information to
> **misleading** adj
misleading v, adj ▷ **mislead**
misleads v ▷ **mislead**
misled v ▷ **mislead**
misnomer n (pl -s) incorrect or
unsuitable name
misnomers n ▷ **misnomer**
misogynies n ▷ **misogyny**
misogynist n ▷ **misogyny**
misogynists n ▷ **misogyny**
misogyny n (pl -nies) hatred of
women > **misogynist** n (pl -s)
misplace v (-ces, -cing, -ced) mislay

misplaced v ▷ **misplace**

misplaces v ▷ **misplace**

misplacing v ▷ **misplace**

misprint n (pl **-s**) printing error

misprints n ▷ **misprint**

miss v (**-es, -ing, -ed**) fail to notice, hear, hit, reach, find, or catch ▶ n (pl **-es**) fact or instance of missing

missal n (pl **-s**) book containing the prayers and rites of the Mass

missals n ▷ **missal**

missed v ▷ **miss**

misses v, n ▷ **miss**

missile n (pl **-s**) object or weapon thrown, shot, or launched at a target

missiles n ▷ **missile**

missing adj lost or absent ▶ v ▷ **miss**

mission n (pl **-s**) specific task or duty

missionaries n ▷ **mission**

missions n ▷ **mission**

missive n (pl **-s**) letter

missives n ▷ **missive**

misspent adj wasted or misused

mist n (pl **-s**) thin fog

mistake n (pl **-s**) error or blunder ▶ v (**-takes, -taking, -took, -taken**) misunderstand

mistaken v ▷ **mistake**

mistakes n, v ▷ **mistake**

mistaking v ▷ **mistake**

mister n (pl **-s**) an informal form of address for a man

misters n ▷ **mister**

mistier adj ▷ **misty**

mistiest adj ▷ **misty**

mistook v ▷ **mistake**

mistral n (pl **-s**) strong dry northerly wind of S France

mistrals n ▷ **mistral**

mistress n (pl **-es**) woman who has a continuing sexual relationship with a married man

mistresses n ▷ **mistress**

mistrial n (pl **-s**) LAW trial made void because of some error

mistrials n ▷ **mistrial**

mistrust v (**-s, -ing, -ed**) have doubts or suspicions about ▶ n (pl **-s**) lack of trust > **mistrustful** adj

mistrusted v ▷ **mistrust**

mistrustful adj ▷ **mistrust**

mistrusting v ▷ **mistrust**

mistrusts v, n ▷ **mistrust**

mists n ▷ **mist**

misty adj full of mist

misuse n (pl **-s**) incorrect, improper, or careless use ▶ v (**-ses, -sing, -sed**) use wrongly

misused v ▷ **misuse**

misuses n, v ▷ **misuse**

misusing v ▷ **misuse**

mite n (pl **-s**) very small spider-like animal

mites n ▷ **mite**

mitigate v (**-tes, -ting, -ted**) make less severe > **mitigation** n (pl **-s**)

mitigated v ▷ **mitigate**

mitigates v ▷ **mitigate**

mitigating v ▷ **mitigate**

mitigation n ▷ **mitigate**

mitigations n ▷ **mitigate**

mitre n (pl **-s**) bishop's pointed headdress ▶ v (**-res, -ring, -red**) join with a mitre joint

mitred v ▷ **mitre**

mitres n, v ▷ **mitre**

mitring v ▷ **mitre**

mitt n (pl **-s**) baseball catcher's glove

mitten n (pl **-s**) glove with one section for the thumb and one for the four fingers together

mittens n ▷ **mitten**

mitts n ▷ **mitt**

mix v (**-es, -ing, -ed**) combine or blend into one mass ▶ n (pl **-es**) mixture > **mixed** v > **mixup** n (pl **-s**) > **mixer** n (pl **-s**)

mixed v, adj ▷ **mix**

mixer n ▷ **mix**

mixers n ▷ **mix**

mixes v, n ▷ **mix**

mixing v ▷ **mix**

mixture n (pl **-s**) something mixed

mixtures n ▷ **mixture**

mixup n ▷ **mix**

mixups n ▷ **mix**

miz n (**mizzes**) Miz is an informal short form of **misery**. This is a useful word, giving a high score for three letters. Remember that you'll need a blank tile for the second Z if you want to form the plural. Miz scores 14 points.

mnemonic n (pl -s) ▶ adj (something, such as a rhyme) intended to help the memory

mnemonics n ▷ **mnemonic**

mo n (**mos**) Mo is an informal short form of **moment**. This word can come in handy when you are trying to play words in more than one direction at once. Mo scores 4 points.

moa n (pl -s) large extinct flightless New Zealand bird

moan n (pl -s) low cry of pain ▶ v (-s, -ing, -ed) make or utter with a moan

moaned v ▷ **moan**

moaning v ▷ **moan**

moans n, v ▷ **moan**

moas n ▷ **moa**

moat n (pl -s) deep wide ditch, esp. round a castle

moats n ▷ **moat**

mob n (pl -s) disorderly crowd ▶ v (-s, -bbing, -bbed) surround in a mob to acclaim or attack

mobbed v ▷ **mob**

mobbing v ▷ **mob**

mobile adj able to move ▶ n (pl -s) hanging structure designed to move in air currents ▶ **mobility** n (pl -ties)

mobiles n ▷ **mobile**

mobilities n ▷ **mobile**

mobility n ▷ **mobile**

mobilization n ▷ **mobilize**

mobilizations n ▷ **mobilize**

mobilize v (-zes, -zing, -zed) (of the armed services) prepare for active service > **mobilization** n (pl -s)

mobilized v ▷ **mobilize**

mobilizes v ▷ **mobilize**

mobilizing v ▷ **mobilize**

mobs n, v ▷ **mob**

moccasin n (pl -s) soft leather shoe

moccasins n ▷ **moccasin**

mocha n (pl -s) kind of strong dark coffee

mochas n ▷ **mocha**

mock v (-s, -ing, -ed) make fun of ▶ adj sham or imitation

mocked v ▷ **mock**

mockeries n ▷ **mockery**

mockery n (pl -ries) derision

mocking v ▷ **mock**

mocks pl n informal (in England and Wales) practice exams taken before public exams ▶ v ▷ **mock**

mode n (pl -s) method or manner

model n (pl -s) (miniature) representation ▶ v (-s, -elling, -elled) make a model of

modelled n ▷ **model**

modelling v ▷ **model**

models n ▷ **model**

modem n (pl -s) device for connecting two computers by a telephone line

modems n ▷ **modem**

moderate adj not extreme ▶ n (pl -s) person of moderate views ▶ v (-tes, -ting, -ted) make or become less violent or extreme > **moderately** adv > **moderation** n (pl -s)

moderated v ▷ **moderate**

moderately adv ▷ **moderate**

moderates n, v ▷ **moderate**

moderating v ▷ **moderate**

moderation n ▷ **moderate**

moderations n ▷ **moderate**

moderators n ▷ **moderate**

modern adj (-er, -est) of present or recent times ▶ **modernity** n (pl -ties)

moderner adj ▷ **modern**

modernest adj ▷ **modern**

modernisms n ▷ **modernism**

modernist n ▷ **modernism**

modernists n ▷ **modernism**

modernities n ▷ **modern**

modernity n ▷ **modern**

modes n ▷ **mode**

modest adj (-er, -est) not vain or

boastful > **modestly** adv > **modesty** n (pl **-s**)

modester adj ▷ modest

modestest adj ▷ modest

modesties n ▷ modesty

modestly adv ▷ modest

modesty n ▷ modest

modicum n (pl **-s**) small quantity

modicums n ▷ modicum

modified v ▷ modify

modifier n (pl **-s**) word that qualifies the sense of another

modifiers n ▷ modifier

modify v (**-fies, -fying, -fied**) change slightly > **modification** n (pl **-s**)

modish adj in fashion

modulate v (**-tes, -ting, -ted**) vary in tone > **modulation** n (pl **-s**) > **modulator** n (pl **-s**)

modulated v ▷ modulate

modulates v ▷ modulate

modulating v ▷ modulate

modulation n ▷ modulate

modulations n ▷ modulate

module n (pl **-s**) self-contained unit, section, or component with a specific function

modules n ▷ module

mogul n (pl **-s**) important or powerful person

moguls n ▷ mogul

mohair n (pl **-s**) fine hair of the Angora goat

mohairs n ▷ mohair

mohican n (pl **-s**) punk hairstyle with shaved sides and a stiff central strip of hair, often brightly coloured

mohicans n ▷ mohican

moieties n ▷ moiety

moiety n (pl **-ties**) half

moist adj (**-er, -est**) slightly wet

moisten v (**-s, -ing, -ed**) make or become moist

moistened v ▷ moisten

moistening v ▷ moisten

moistens v ▷ moisten

moister adj ▷ moist

moistest adj ▷ moist

moisture n (pl **-s**) liquid diffused as vapour or condensed in drops

moistures n ▷ moisture

moisturized v ▷ moisten

moisturizes v ▷ moisten

moisturizing v ▷ moisten

molar n (pl **-s**) large back tooth used for grinding

molars n ▷ molar

molasses n dark syrup, a by-product of sugar refining

mole[1] n (pl **-s**) small dark raised spot on the skin

mole[2] n (pl **-s**) small burrowing mammal

mole[3] n (pl **-s**) unit of amount of substance

mole[4] n (pl **-s**) breakwater

molecular adj ▷ molecule

molecule n (pl **-s**) simplest freely existing chemical unit, composed of two or more atoms > **molecular** ▶ adj

molecules n ▷ molecule

moles n ▷ mole[1, 2, 3, 4]

molest v (**-s, -ing, -ed**) interfere with sexually > **molester** n (pl **-s**) > **molestation** n (pl **-s**)

molested v ▷ molest

molester n ▷ molest

molesters n ▷ molest

molesting v ▷ molest

molests v ▷ molest

moll n (pl **-s**) slang gangster's female accomplice

mollified v ▷ mollify

mollifies v ▷ mollify

mollify v (**-fies, -fying, -fied**) pacify or soothe

mollifying v ▷ mollify

molls n ▷ moll

mollusc n (pl **-s**) soft-bodied, usu. hard-shelled, animal, such as a snail or oyster

molluscs n ▷ mollusc

molten adj liquefied or melted

moment n (pl **-s**) short space of time

momenta n ▷ momentum

moments n ▷ moment

momentum n (pl **-ta**) impetus of a moving body

monarch n (pl **-s**) sovereign ruler of a state > **monarchical** adj

monarchical adj ▷ **monarch**

monarchies n ▷ **monarchy**

monarchs n ▷ **monarch**

monarchy n (pl **-chies**) government by or a state ruled by a sovereign

monastic adj of monks, nuns, or monasteries

monetary adj of money or currency

money n (pl **-s**) medium of exchange, coins or banknotes > **moneyed,** **monied** adj rich

moneyed adj ▷ **money**

moneys n ▷ **money**

mongoose n (pl **-s**) stoatlike mammal of Asia and Africa that kills snakes

mongooses n ▷ **money**

mongrel n (pl **-s**) animal, esp. a dog, of mixed breed ▶ adj of mixed breed or origin

mongrels n ▷ **mongrel**

monied adj ▷ **money**

monitor n (pl **-s**) person or device that checks, controls, warns, or keeps a record of something ▶ v (**-s, -ing, -ed**) watch and check on

monitored v ▷ **monitor**

monitoring v ▷ **monitor**

monitors n, v ▷ **monitor**

monk n (pl **-s**) member of an all-male religious community bound by vows > **monkish** adj

monkey n (pl **-s**) long-tailed primate ▶ v (**-s, -ing, -ed**) (usu. foll. by **about** or **around**) meddle or fool

monkeyed v ▷ **monkey**

monkeying v ▷ **monkey**

monkeys n, v ▷ **monkey**

monkish adj ▷ **monk**

monks n ▷ **monk**

monocle n (pl **-s**) eyeglass for one eye only

monocles n ▷ **monocle**

monogamies n ▷ **monogamy**

monogamy n (pl **-mies**) custom of

being married to one person at a time

monogram n (pl **-s**) design of combined letters, esp. a person's initials

monograms n ▷ **monogram**

monolith n (pl **-s**) large upright block of stone > **monolithic** adj

monolithic adj ▷ **monolith**

monoliths n ▷ **monolith**

monopolies n ▷ **monopoly**

monopolized v ▷ **monopoly**

monopolizes v ▷ **monopoly**

monopolizes v ▷ **monopoly**

monopoly n (pl **-lies**) exclusive possession of or right to do something

monorail n (pl **-s**) single-rail railway

monorails n ▷ **monorail**

monotheisms n ▷ **monorail**

monotone n (pl **-s**) unvaried pitch in speech or sound > **monotony** n (pl **-s**)

monotones n ▷ **monotone**

monotonies n ▷ **monotone**

monotonously adv ▷ **monotonous**

monsieur n (pl **messieurs**) French title of address equivalent to sir or Mr

monsoon n (pl **-s**) seasonal wind of SE Asia

monsoons n ▷ **monsoon**

monster n (pl **-s**) imaginary, usu. frightening, beast ▶ adj huge

monsters n ▷ **monster**

montage n (pl **-s**) (making of) a picture composed from pieces of others

montages n ▷ **montage**

month n (pl **-s**) one of the twelve divisions of the calendar year

monthlies n ▷ **month**

monthly adj happening or payable once a month ▶ adv once a month ▶ n (pl **-lies**) monthly magazine

months n ▷ **month**

monument n (pl **-s**) something, esp. a building or statue, that commemorates something

monuments n ▷ **monument**

moo n (pl **-s**) long deep cry of a cow ▶ v (**-s, -ing, -ed**) make this noise

mooch v (**-es, -ing, -ed**) slang loiter about aimlessly

mooched v ▷ **mooch**

mooches v ▷ **mooch**

mooching v ▷ **mooch**

mood[1] n (pl **-s**) temporary (gloomy) state of mind

mood[2] n GRAMMAR form of a verb indicating whether it expresses a fact, wish, supposition, or command

moodier adj ▷ **moody**

moodiest adj ▷ **moody**

moodily adv ▷ **moody**

moods n ▷ **mood**[1, 2]

moody adj (**-dier, -iest**) sullen or gloomy > **moodily** adv

mooed v ▷ **moo**

mooing v ▷ **moo**

moon n (pl **-s**) natural satellite of the earth ▶ v (**-s, -ing, -ed**) (foll. by **about** or **around**) be idle in a listless or dreamy way

mooned v ▷ **moon**

mooning v ▷ **moon**

moons n, v ▷ **moon**

moor[1] n (pl **-s**) BRIT tract of open uncultivated ground covered with grass and heather

moor[2] v (**-s, -ing, -ed**) secure (a ship) with ropes etc ▶ **mooring** n (pl **-s**)

moored v ▷ **moor**[2]

moorhen n (pl **-s**) small black water bird

moorhens n ▷ **moorhen**

mooring v, n ▷ **moor**[2]

moors n ▷ **moor**[1] ▶ v ▷ **moor**[2]

moos n, v ▷ **moo**

moose n large N American deer

moot adj (**-er, -est**) debatable ▶ v (**-s, -ing, -ed**) bring up for discussion

mooted v ▷ **moot**

mooter adj ▷ **moot**

mootest adj ▷ **moot**

mooting v ▷ **moot**

moots v ▷ **moot**

mop n (pl **-s**) long stick with twists of cotton or a sponge on the end, used for cleaning ▶ v (**-s, -pping, -pped**) clean or soak up with or as if with a mop

mope v (**-pes, -ping, -ped**) be gloomy and apathetic

moped n (pl **-s**) light motorized cycle ▶ v ▷ **mope**

mopeds v ▷ **mope**

mopes v ▷ **mope**

moping v ▷ **mope**

mopoke n (pl **-s**) small spotted owl of Australia and New Zealand

mopokes n ▷ **mopoke**

mopped v ▷ **mop**

mopping v ▷ **mop**

mops n, v ▷ **mop**

moraine n (pl **-s**) accumulated mass of debris deposited by a glacier

moraines n ▷ **moraine**

moral adj concerned with right and wrong conduct ▶ n (pl **-s**) lesson to be obtained from a story or event > **morally** adv

morale n (pl **-s**) degree of confidence or hope of a person or group

morales n ▷ **morale**

moralist n (pl **-s**) person with a strong sense of right and wrong

moralists n ▷ **moralist**

moralities n ▷ **morality**

morality n (pl **-ties**) good moral conduct

moralize v (**-zes, -zing, -zed**) make moral pronouncements

moralized v ▷ **moralize**

moralizes v ▷ **moralize**

moralizing v ▷ **moralize**

morally adv ▷ **moral**

morals n ▷ **moral**

morass n (pl **-es**) marsh

morasses n ▷ **morass**

moray n (pl **-s**) large voracious eel

morays n ▷ **moray**

morbid adj unduly interested in death or unpleasant events

mordant adj sarcastic or scathing ▶ n (pl **-s**) substance used to fix dyes

mordants n ▷ **mordant**

more adj greater in amount or degree ▷ **much** ▶ adv to a greater extent

▶ *pron* greater or additional amount or number

moreover *adv* in addition to what has already been said

mores *pl n* customs and conventions embodying the fundamental values of a community

morgue *n (pl -s)* mortuary

morgues *n* ▷ **morgue**

moribund *adj* without force or vitality

morn *n (pl -s)* *poetic* morning

morning *n (pl -s)* part of the day before noon

mornings *n* ▷ **morning**

morns *n* ▷ **morn**

morocco *n (pl -s)* goatskin leather

moroccos *n* ▷ **morocco**

moron *n (pl -s)* *informal* foolish or stupid person > **moronic** *adj*

moronic *adj* ▷ **moron**

morons *n* ▷ **moron**

morose *adj (-r, -st)* sullen or moody

moroser *adj* ▷ **morose**

morosest *adj* ▷ **morose**

morphia *n* ▷ **morphine**

morphine, morphia *n (pl -s)* drug extracted from opium, used as an anaesthetic and sedative

morphines *n* ▷ **morphine**

morrow *n (pl -s)* *poetic* next day

morrows *n* ▷ **morrow**

morse *n (pl -s)* clasp or fastening

morsel *n (pl -s)* small piece, esp. of food

morsels *n* ▷ **morsel**

morses *n* ▷ **morse**

mortal *adj* subject to death ▶ *n (pl -s)* human being > **mortally** *adv*

mortalities *n* ▷ **mortality**

mortally *adj* ▷ **mortal**

mortals *n* ▷ **mortal**

mortar *n (pl -s)* small cannon with a short range

mortars *n* ▷ **mortar**

mortgage *n (pl -s)* conditional pledging of property, esp. a house, as security for the repayment of a loan ▶ *v* (-ges, -ging, -ged) pledge (property) as security thus

mortgaged *v* ▷ **mortgage**

mortgages *n, v* ▷ **mortgage**

mortgaging *v* ▷ **mortgage**

mortice, mortise *n (pl -s)* hole in a piece of wood or stone shaped to receive a matching projection on another piece

mortices *n* ▷ **mortice**

mortification *n* ▷ **mortify**

mortifications *n* ▷ **mortify**

mortified *v* ▷ **mortify**

mortifies *v* ▷ **mortify**

mortify *v (-fies, -fying, -fied)* humiliate > **mortification** *n (pl -s)*

mortifying *v* ▷ **mortify**

mortise *n* ▷ **mortice**

mortises *n* ▷ **mortice**

mortuaries *n* ▷ **mortuary**

mortuary *n (pl -aries)* building where corpses are kept before burial or cremation

mosaic *n (pl -s)* design or decoration using small pieces of coloured stone or glass

mosaics *n* ▷ **mosaic**

mosque *n (pl -s)* Muslim temple

mosques *n* ▷ **mosque**

mosquito *n (pl -toes, -tos)* blood-sucking flying insect

mosquitoes *n* ▷ **mosquito**

mosquitos *n* ▷ **mosquito**

moss *n (pl -es)* small flowerless plant growing in masses on moist surfaces > **mossy** *adj (-sier, -siest)*

mosses *n* ▷ **moss**

mossier *adj* ▷ **moss**

mossiest *adj* ▷ **moss**

mossy *adj* ▷ **moss**

most *n* greatest number or degree ▶ *adj* greatest in number or degree ▶ *much* ▶ *adv* in the greatest degree

mostly *adv* for the most part, generally

motel *n (pl -s)* roadside hotel for motorists

motels *n* ▷ **motel**

motet *n (pl -s)* short sacred choral song

motets *n* ▷ **motet**

moth *n (pl -s)* nocturnal insect like a

butterfly

mothball n (pl -s) small ball of camphor or naphtalene used to repel moths from stored clothes ▸ v (-ed, -ing, -ed) store (something operational) for future use
mothballed v ▷ **moth**
mothballing v ▷ **moth**
mothballs n, v ▷ **moth**

mother n (pl -s) female parent ▸ adj native or inborn ▸ v (-s, -ing, -ed) look after as a mother > **motherhood** n (pl -s) > **motherly** adj > **motherless** adj
mothered v ▷ **mother**
motherhood n ▷ **mother**
motherhoods n ▷ **mother**
mothering v ▷ **mother**
motherless adj ▷ **mother**
motherly adj ▷ **mother**
mothers n, v ▷ **mother**
moths n ▷ **moth**

motif n (pl -s) (recurring) theme or design
motifs n ▷ **motif**

motion n (pl -s) process, action, or way of moving ▸ v (-s, -ing, -ed) direct (someone) by gesture
motioned v ▷ **motion**
motioning v ▷ **motion**
motions n, v ▷ **motion**

motivate v (-tes, -ting, -ted) give incentive to > **motivation** n (pl -s)
motivated v ▷ **motivate**
motivates v ▷ **motivate**
motivating v ▷ **motivate**
motivation n ▷ **motivate**
motivations n ▷ **motivate**

motive n (pl -s) reason for a course of action ▸ adj causing motion
motives n ▷ **motive**

motley adj miscellaneous

motor n (pl -s) engine, esp. of a vehicle ▸ v (-s, -ing, -ed) travel by car > **motorbike** n (pl -s) > **motorboat** n (pl -s) > **motorcar** n (pl -s) > **motorcycle** n (pl -s) > **motorcyclist** n (pl -s)
motorbike n ▷ **motor**
motorbikes n ▷ **motor**

motorboat n ▷ **motor**
motorboats n ▷ **motor**
motorcar n ▷ **motor**
motorcars n ▷ **motor**
motorcycle n ▷ **motor**
motorcycles n ▷ **motor**
motorcyclist n ▷ **motor**
motorcyclists n ▷ **motor**
motored v ▷ **motor**
motoring v ▷ **motor**

motorist n (pl -s) driver of a car
motorists n ▷ **motorist**
motors n, v ▷ **motor**

motorway n (pl -s) main road for fast-moving traffic
motorways n ▷ **motorway**

mottled adj marked with blotches

motto n (pl -es, -s) saying expressing an ideal or rule of conduct
mottoes n ▷ **motto**
mottos n ▷ **motto**

mould¹ n (pl -s) hollow container in which metal etc is cast ▸ v (-s, -ing, -ed) shape

mould² n (pl -s) fungal growth caused by dampness

mould³ n (pl -s) loose soil
moulded v ▷ **mould¹**

moulder v (-s, -ing, -ed) decay into dust
mouldered v ▷ **moulder**
mouldering v ▷ **moulder**
moulders v ▷ **moulder**
mouldier adj ▷ **mouldy**
mouldiest adj ▷ **mouldy**

moulding n (pl -s) moulded ornamental edging ▸ v ▷ **mould¹**
moulds n ▷ **mould¹, ², 3** ▸ v ▷ **mould¹**

mouldy adj (-dier, -diest) stale or musty; dull or boring

moult v (-s, -ing, -ed) shed feathers, hair, or skin to make way for new growth ▸ n (pl -s) process of moulting
moulted v ▷ **moult**
moulting v ▷ **moult**
moults v, n ▷ **moult**

mound n (pl -s) heap, esp. of earth

or stones

mounds n ▷ mound

mount v (**-s, -ing, -ed**) climb or ascend ▶ n (pl **-s**) backing or support on which something is fixed

mountain n (pl **-s**) hill of great size

> **mountainous** adj full of mountains

mountains n ▷ mountain

mounted v ▷ mount

mounting v ▷ mount

mounts v, n ▷ mount

mourn v (**-s, -ing, -ed**) feel or express sorrow for (a dead person or lost thing)

mourned v ▷ mourn

mourner n (pl **mourners**) person attending a funeral

mourners n ▷ mourner

mournful adj (**-ler, -lest**) sad or dismal

> **mournfully** adv

mournfuller adj ▷ mournful

mournfullest adj ▷ mournful

mournfully adv ▷ mournful

mourning n (pl **-s**) grieving ▶ v ▷ mourn

mournings n ▷ mourning

mourns v ▷ mourn

mouse n (pl **mice**) small long-tailed rodent

mouser n (pl **-s**) cat used to catch mice

mousers n ▷ mouser

mousse n (pl **-s**) dish of flavoured cream whipped and set

mousses n ▷ mousse

mousy adj like a mouse, esp. in hair colour

mouth n (pl **-s**) opening in the head for eating and issuing sounds ▶ v (**-s, -ing, -ed**) form (words) with the lips without speaking

mouthed v ▷ mouth

mouthful n (pl **-s**) amount of food or drink put into the mouth at any one time when eating or drinking

mouthfuls n ▷ mouthful

mouthing v ▷ mouth

mouths n, v ▷ mouth

move v (**-ves, -ving, -ved**) change in place or position ▶ n (pl **-s**) moving

> **movable, moveable** adj

moved v ▷ move

movement n (pl **-s**) action or process of moving

movements n ▷ movement

moves v, n ▷ move

movie n (pl **-s**) informal cinema film

movies n ▷ movie

moving v ▷ move

mow v (**-s, -ing, -ed** or **mown**) cut (grass or crops)

mowed v ▷ mow

mower n (pl **-s**) machine for cutting grass

mowers n ▷ mower

mowing v ▷ mow

mown v ▷ mow

mows v ▷ mow

> **moz** n (**mozes**). Moz is an old Australian slang word for a jinx or hex. This is an unusual word that is worth remembering as it can be very useful if you have a Z but little chance to play it on a crowded board. Moz scores 14 points.

much adj (**more, most**) large amount or degree of ▶ n large amount or degree ▶ adv (**more, most**) to a great degree

mucilage n (pl **-s**) gum or glue

mucilages n ▷ mucilage

muck n (pl **-s**) dirt, filth > **mucky** adj

mucks n ▷ mucks

mucky adj ▷ mucks

mucus n (pl **-s**) slimy secretion of the mucous membranes

mucuses n ▷ mucus

mud n (pl **-s**) wet soft earth

> **muddy** adj

muddier adj ▷ mud

muddiest adj ▷ mud

muddle v (**-les, -ling, -led**) (often foll. by **up**) confuse ▶ n (pl **-s**) state of confusion

muddled v ▷ muddle

muddles v, n ▷ muddle

muddling v ▷ muddle

muddy adj (**-ddier, -ddiest**) ▷ mud

mudguard n (pl -s) cover over a wheel to prevent mud or water being thrown up by it

mudguards n ▷ mudguard

muds n ▷ mud

muesli n (pl -s) mixture of grain, nuts, and dried fruit, eaten with milk

mueslis n ▷ muesli

muezzin n (pl -s) official who summons Muslims to prayer

muezzins n ▷ muezzin

muff[1] n (pl -s) tube-shaped covering to keep the hands warm

muff[2] v (-s, -ing, -ed) bungle (an action)

muffed v ▷ muff

muffin n (pl -s) light round flat yeast cake

muffing v ▷ muff

muffins n ▷ muffin

muffle v (-les, -ling, -led) wrap up for warmth or to deaden sound

muffled v ▷ muffle

muffler n (pl -s) BRIT scarf

mufflers n ▷ muffle

muffles n, v ▷ muffle

muffling v ▷ muffle

muffs n ▷ muff[1] ▶ v ▷ muff[2]

mufti n (pl -s) civilian clothes worn by a person who usually wears a uniform

muftis n ▷ mufti

mug[1] n (pl -s) large drinking cup

mug[2] n (pl -s) slang face ▶ v (-s, -gging, -gged) informal attack in order to rob > **mugger** n (pl -s)

mug[3] v (-s, -gging, -gged) (foll. by up) informal study hard

mugged v ▷ mug[2,3]

mugger n ▷ mug[2]

muggers v ▷ mug[2]

muggier adj ▷ muggy

muggiest adj ▷ muggy

mugging v ▷ mug[2,3]

muggins n informal stupid or gullible person

muggy adj (-gier, -giest) (of weather) damp and stifling

mugs n ▷ mug[1,2]

mulatto n (pl -tos, -toes) child of one Black and one White parent

mulattoes adj ▷ mulatto

mulattos adj ▷ mulatto

mulberries n ▷ mulberry

mulberry n (pl -rries) tree whose leaves are used to feed silkworms

mulch n (pl -es) mixture of wet straw, leaves, etc, used to protect the roots of plants ▶ v (-es, -ing, -ed) cover (land) with mulch

mulched v ▷ mulch

mulches n, v ▷ mulch

mulching v ▷ mulch

mule[1] n (pl -s) offspring of a horse and a donkey > **mulish** adj obstinate

mule[2] n backless shoe or slipper

mules n ▷ mule[1,2]

mulga n (pl -s) Australian acacia shrub growing in desert regions

mulgas n ▷ mulga

mulish adj ▷ mule[1]

mull v (-s, -ing, -ed) think (over) or ponder > **mulled** adj (of wine or ale) flavoured with sugar and spices and served hot

mullah n (pl -s) Muslim scholar, teacher, or religious leader

mullahs n ▷ mullah

mulled v, adj ▷ mull

mullet[1] n (pl -s) edible sea fish

mullet[2] n (pl -s) haircut in which the hair is short at the top and sides and long at the back

mullets n ▷ mullet[1,2]

mulling v ▷ mull

mullion n (pl -s) vertical dividing bar in a window > **mullioned** adj

mullioned adj ▷ mullion

mullions n ▷ mullion

mulloway n (pl -s) large Australian sea fish, valued for sport and food

mulloways n ▷ mulloway

mulls v ▷ mull

multiple adj having many parts ▶ n (pl -s) quantity which contains another an exact number of times

multiples n ▷ multiple

multiplication n ▷ multiply

multiplications n ▷ multiply

multiplied v ▷ multiply

multiplies v ▷ multiply

multiply v (-lies, -lying, -lied) (cause to) increase in number, quantity, or degree ▷ **multiplication** n (pl -s)

multiplying v ▷ multiply

mum n (pl -s) informal mother

mumble v (-les, -ling, -led) speak indistinctly, mutter

mumbled v ▷ mumble

mumbles v ▷ mumble

mumbling v ▷ mumble

mummer n (pl -s) actor in a traditional English folk play or mime

mummers n ▷ mummer

mummies n ▷ mummy

mummy[1] n (pl -mmies) body embalmed and wrapped for burial in ancient Egypt

mummy[2] n (pl -mmies) ▷ mother

mumps n infectious disease with swelling in the glands of the neck

mums n ▷ mum

munch v (-es, -ing, -ed) chew noisily and steadily

munched v ▷ munch

munches v ▷ munch

munching v ▷ munch

mundane adj everyday

mural n (pl -s) painting on a wall

murals n ▷ mural

murder n (pl -s) unlawful intentional killing of a human being ▷ v (-s, -ing, -ed) kill in this way ▷ **murderer**, **murderess** n (pl -s) ▷ **murderous** adj

murdered v ▷ murder

murderer n ▷ murder

murderers n ▷ murder

murderess n ▷ murder

murderesses n ▷ murder

murdering v ▷ murder

murderous adj ▷ murder

murders v, n ▷ murder

murk n (pl -s) thick darkness

murkier adj ▷ murky

murkiest adj ▷ murky

murks n ▷ murk

murky adj (-kier, -kiest) dark or gloomy

murmur v (-s, -ing, -ed) speak or say in a quiet indistinct way ▷ n (pl -s) continuous low indistinct sound

murmured v ▷ murmur

murmuring v ▷ murmur

murmurs v, n ▷ murmur

muscle n (pl -s) tissue in the body which produces movement by contracting

muscles n ▷ muscle

muscular adj with well-developed muscles

muse v (-ses, -sing, -sed) ponder quietly

mused v ▷ muse

muses v ▷ muse

museum n (pl -s) building where natural, artistic, historical, or scientific objects are exhibited and preserved

museums n ▷ museum

mush n (pl -es) soft pulpy mass > **mushy** adj (-shier, -shiest)

mushes n ▷ mush

mushier adj ▷ mush

mushiest adj ▷ mush

mushroom n (pl -s) edible fungus with a stem and cap ▷ v (-s, -ing, -ed) grow rapidly

mushroomed v ▷ mushroom

mushrooming v ▷ mushroom

mushrooms n, v ▷ mushroom

mushy (-shier, -shiest) adj ▷ mush

music n (pl -s) art form using a melodious and harmonious combination of notes ▷ n (pl -s) play or film with songs and dancing > **musician** n (pl -s)

musical adj of or like music > **musically** adv

musically adv ▷ musical

musician n ▷ music

musicians n ▷ music

musics n ▷ music

musing v ▷ muse

musk n (pl -s) scent obtained from a gland of the musk deer or produced synthetically > **musky** adj (-kier, -kiest)

musket n (pl -s) HIST long-barrelled gun > **musketeer** n (pl -s)

musketeer n ▷ musket

musketeers n ▷ musket

musketries n ▷ musketry

musketry n (pl -ries) (use of) muskets

muskets n ▷ musket

muskier adj ▷ musk

muskiest adj ▷ musk

muskrat n (pl -s) N American beaver-like rodent

muskrats n ▷ muskrat

musks n ▷ musk

musky adj (-kier, -kiest) ▷ musk

muslin n (pl -s) fine cotton fabric

muslins n ▷ muslin

mussel n (pl -s) edible shellfish with a dark hinged shell

mussels n ▷ mussel

must¹ v used as an auxiliary to express obligation, certainty, or resolution ▶ n (pl -s) essential or necessary thing

must² n (pl -s) newly pressed grape juice

mustang n (pl -s) wild horse of SW USA

mustangs n ▷ mustang

mustard n (pl -s) paste made from the powdered seeds of a plant, used as a condiment

mustards n ▷ mustard

muster v (-s, -ing, -ed) assemble ▶ n (pl -s) assembly of military personnel

mustered v ▷ muster

mustering v ▷ muster

musters v, n ▷ muster

mustier adj ▷ musty

mustiest adj ▷ musty

mustiness n ▷ musty

mustinesses n ▷ musty

musts n ▷ must¹, ²

musty adj (-tier, -tiest) smelling mouldy and stale > **mustiness** n (pl -es)

mutabilities n ▷ mutable

mutability n ▷ mutable

mutable adj liable to change
> **mutability** n (pl -ties)

mutant n (pl -s) mutated animal, plant, etc

mutants n ▷ mutant

mutate v (-tes, -ting, -ted) (cause to) undergo mutation

mutated v ▷ mutate

mutates v ▷ mutate

mutating v ▷ mutate

mutation n (pl -s) (genetic) change

mutations n ▷ mutation

mute adj (-r, -st) silent ▶ n (pl -s) person who is unable to speak
> **mutely** adv

muted adj (of sound or colour) softened

mutely adv ▷ mute

muter adj ▷ mute

mutes n ▷ mute

mutest adj ▷ mute

muti n (pl -s) S AFR informal medicine, esp. herbal medicine

mutilate v (-tes, -ting, -ted) deprive of a limb or other part > **mutilation** n (pl -s)

mutilated v ▷ mutilate

mutilates v ▷ mutilate

mutilating v ▷ mutilate

mutilation n ▷ mutilate

mutilations n ▷ mutilate

mutineer n ▷ mutiny

mutineers n ▷ mutiny

mutinied v ▷ mutiny

mutinies n ▷ mutiny

mutinous n ▷ mutiny

mutiny n (pl -nies) rebellion against authority, esp. by soldiers or sailors ▶ v (-nies, -nying, -nied) commit mutiny
> **mutineer** n (pl -s) > **mutinous** adj

mutinying n ▷ mutiny

mutis n ▷ muti

mutt n (pl -s) slang mongrel dog

mutter v (-s, -ing, -ed) utter or speak indistinctly ▶ n (pl -s) muttered sound or grumble

muttered v ▷ mutter

muttering v ▷ mutter

mutters v, n ▷ **mutter**
mutton n (pl -s) flesh of sheep, used as food
muttons n ▷ **mutton**
mutts n ▷ **mutt**
mutual adj felt or expressed by each of two people about the other ▷ **mutually** adv
mutually adv ▷ **mutual**

> **mux** v (**muxes, muxing, muxed**). Mux is an old American word meaning to make a mess of something. This word is very useful not only because it contains an X, but because its verb forms can enable you to clear your rack of unpromising letters. Mux scores 12 points.

> **muzjik** n (**muzjiks**). A muzjik is a Russian peasant. This is a great high-scoring word, combining Z, J and K. If you can play the plural using all of your tiles, you'll get a bonus of 50 points. Muzjik scores 28 points.

muzzier adj ▷ **muzzy**
muzziest adj ▷ **muzzy**
muzzle n (pl -s) animal's mouth and nose ▷ v (**-les, -ling, -led**) prevent from being heard or noticed
muzzled v ▷ **muzzle**
muzzles n, v ▷ **muzzle**
muzzling v ▷ **muzzle**
muzzy adj (**-zzier, -zziest**) confused or muddled
my adj belonging to me
myall n (pl -s) Australian acacia with hard scented wood
myalls n ▷ **myall**
mycologies n ▷ **mycology**
mycology n (pl -gies) study of fungi
myna, mynah, mina n (pl -s) Asian bird which can mimic human speech
mynah n ▷ **myna**
mynahs n ▷ **myna**
mynas n ▷ **myna**
myopia n (pl -s) short-sightedness
> **myopic** ▶ adj

myopias n ▷ **myopia**
myopic adj ▷ **myopia**
myriad adj innumerable ▶ n (pl -s) large indefinite number
myriads n ▷ **myriad**
myrrh n (pl -s) aromatic gum used in perfume, incense, and medicine
myrrhs n ▷ **myrrh**
myrtle n (pl -s) flowering evergreen shrub
myrtles n ▷ **myrtle**
myself pron ▷ **I**
mysteries n ▷ **mystery**
mysterious adj ▷ **mystery**
mysteriously adv ▷ **mystery**
mystery n (pl -ries) strange or inexplicable event or phenomenon
> **mysterious** adj **mysteriously** adv
mystic n (pl -s) person who seeks spiritual knowledge ▶ adj mystical
> **mysticism** n (pl -s)
mystical adj having a spiritual or religious significance beyond human understanding
mysticism n ▷ **mystic**
mysticisms n ▷ **mystic**
mystics n ▷ **mystic**
mystification v ▷ **mystify**
mystifications v ▷ **mystify**
mystified v ▷ **mystify**
mystifies v ▷ **mystify**
mystify v (**-fies, -fying, -fied**) bewilder or puzzle > **mystification** n (pl -s)
mystifying v ▷ **mystify**
mystique n (pl -s) aura of mystery or power
mystiques n ▷ **mystique**
myth n (pl -s) tale with supernatural characters, usu. of how the world and mankind began > **mythical, mythic** adj
mythic adj ▷ **myth**
mythical adj ▷ **myth**
myths n ▷ **myth**

Nn

Along with R and T, N is one of the most common consonants in Scrabble. As you'll often have it on your rack, it's well worth learning what N can do in different situations. N is useful when you need short words, as it begins two-letter words with every vowel except I, and with Y as well. There are plenty of three-letter words starting with N, but there aren't many high-scoring ones. Remember words like **nab** (5 points), **nag** (4), **nap** (5), **nay** (6), **new** (6), **nib** (5), **nob** (5), **nod** (4) and **now** (6).

na *interj* Na is a Scots word for **no** or **not**. This word can be very convenient when you need to form words in different directions. Na scores 2 points.

naan *n (pl -s)* slightly leavened Indian bread in a large flat leaf shape
naans *n* ▷ **naan**

naartjie *n (pl -s)* S AFR tangerine
naartjies *n* ▷ **naartjie**

nab *v (-s, -bbing, -bbed)* informal arrest (someone)
nabbed *v* ▷ **nab**
nabbing *v* ▷ **nab**
nabs *v* ▷ **nab**

nadir *n (pl -s)* point in the sky opposite the zenith
nadirs *n* ▷ **nadir**
naevi *n* ▷ **naevus**

naevus *n (pl -vi)* birthmark or mole

naff *adj (-er, -est)* BRIT slang lacking quality or taste
naffer *adj* ▷ **naff**
naffest *adj* ▷ **naff**

nag[1] *v (-s, -gging, -gged)* scold or find fault constantly ▶ *n (pl -s)* person who nags >**nagging** *adj*, *n (pl -s)*
nag[2] *n (pl -s)* informal old horse
nagged *v* ▷ **nag**[1]
nagging *v, adj n* ▷ **nag**[1]

naggings *n* ▷ **nag**[1]
nags *v* ▷ **nag**[1] ▶ *n* ▷ **nag**[1, 2]

naiad *n (pl -s)* GREEK MYTH nymph living in a lake or river
naiads *n* ▷ **naiad**

nail *n (pl -s)* pointed piece of metal with a head, which a hammer to join two objects together ▶ *v (-s, -ing, -ed)* attach (something) with nails
nailed *v* ▷ **nail**
nailing *v* ▷ **nail**
nails *n, v* ▷ **nail**

naive *adj (-r, -st)* innocent and gullible >**naively** *adv* >**naivety** *n (pl -ties)*
naively *adv* ▷ **naive**
naiver *adj* ▷ **naive**
naivest *adj* ▷ **naive**
naiveties *n* ▷ **naive**
naivety *n* ▷ **naive**

naked *adj (-er, -est)* without clothes >**nakedness** *n (pl -es)*
nakeder *adj* ▷ **naked**
nakedest *adj* ▷ **naked**
nakedness *n* ▷ **naked**
nakednesses *n* ▷ **naked**

name *n (pl -s)* word by which a person or thing is known ▶ *v (-mes, -ming, -med)* give a name to
named *v* ▷ **name**

nameless *adj* without a name

namely adv that is to say

names n, v ▷ **name**

namesake n (pl -s) person with the same name as another

namesakes n ▷ **namesake**

naming v ▷ **name**

nannies n ▷ **nanny**

nanny n (pl -nnies) woman whose job is looking after young children

nap¹ n (pl -s) short sleep ▶ v (-s, -pping, -pped) have a short sleep

nap² n (pl -s) raised fibres of velvet or similar cloth

nap³ n (pl -s) card game similar to whist

napalm n (pl -s) highly inflammable jellied petrol, used in bombs

napalms n ▷ **napalm**

nape n (pl -s) back of the neck

napes n ▷ **nape**

naphtha n (pl -s) liquid mixture distilled from coal tar or petroleum, used as a solvent and in petrol

naphthas n ▷ **naphtha**

napkin n (pl -s) piece of cloth or paper for wiping the mouth or protecting the clothes while eating

napkins n ▷ **napkin**

napped v ▷ **nap¹**

nappies n ▷ **nappy**

napping v ▷ **nap¹**

nappy n (pl -ppies) piece of absorbent material fastened round a baby's lower torso to absorb urine and faeces

naps n ▷ **nap¹** v ▷ **nap¹**

narcoses n ▷ **narcosis**

narcosis n (pl -s) effect of a narcotic

narcotic n (pl -s) ▶ adj (of) a drug, such as morphine or opium, which produces numbness and drowsiness, used medicinally but addictive

narcotics n ▷ **narcotic**

nark slang v (-s, -ing, -ed) annoy ▶ n (pl -s) informer or spy

narked v ▷ **nark**

narkier adj ▷ **narky**

narkiest adj ▷ **narky**

narking v ▷ **nark**

narks v, n ▷ **nark**

narky adj slang (-kier, -kiest) irritable or complaining

narrate v (-tes, -ting, -ted) tell (a story) > **narration** n (pl -s) > **narrator** n (pl -s)

narrated v ▷ **narrate**

narrates v ▷ **narrate**

narrating v ▷ **narrate**

narration n ▷ **narrate**

narrations n ▷ **narrate**

narrator n ▷ **narrate**

narrators n ▷ **narrate**

narrow adj (-er, -est) small in breadth in comparison to length ▶ v (-s, -ing, -ed) make or become narrow > **narrowly** adv > **narrowness** n (pl -es)

narrowed v ▷ **narrow**

narrower adj ▷ **narrow**

narrowest adj ▷ **narrow**

narrowing v ▷ **narrow**

narrowly adv ▷ **narrow**

narrowness n ▷ **narrow**

narrownesses n ▷ **narrow**

narrows v ▷ **narrow** ▶ pl n narrow part of a strait, river, or current

narwhal n (pl -s) arctic whale with a long spiral tusk

narwhals n ▷ **narwhal**

nasal adj of the nose > **nasally** adv

nasally adv ▷ **nasal**

nascent adj starting to grow or develop

nastier adj ▷ **nasty**

nastiest adj ▷ **nasty**

nastily adv ▷ **nasty**

nastiness n ▷ **nasty**

nastinesses n ▷ **nasty**

nasty adj (-tier, -tiest) unpleasant > **nastily** adv > **nastiness** n (pl -es)

natal adj of or relating to birth

nation n (pl -s) people of one or more cultures or races organized as a single state

national adj characteristic of a particular nation ▶ n (pl -s) citizen of a nation > **nationally** adv

nationally adv ▷ **national**

nationals n ▷ **national**

nations n ▷ **nation**
native adj relating to a place where a person was born ▶ n (pl -s) person born in a specified place
natives n ▷ **native**
nativities n ▷ **nativity**
nativity n (pl -ties) birth or origin
natter informal v (-s, -ing, -ed) talk idly or chatter ▶ n (pl -s) long idle chat
nattered v ▷ **natter**
nattering v ▷ **natter**
natters v, n ▷ **natter**
nattier adj ▷ **natty**
nattiest adj ▷ **natty**
natty adj (-tier, -ttiest) informal smart and spruce
natural adj normal or to be expected ▶ n (pl -s) person with an inborn talent or skill
naturals n ▷ **natural**
nature n (pl -s) whole system of the existence, forces, and events of the physical world that are not controlled by human beings
natures n ▷ **nature**
naturism n (pl -s) nudism ▷ **naturist** n (pl -s)
naturisms n ▷ **naturism**
naturist n ▷ **naturism**
naturists n ▷ **naturism**
naught n (pl -s) lit nothing
naughtier adj ▷ **naughty**
naughtiest adj ▷ **naughty**
naughtily adv ▷ **naughty**
naughtiness n ▷ **naughty**
naughtinesses n ▷ **naughty**
naughts n ▷ **naught**
naughty adj (-tier, -tiest) disobedient or mischievous ▷ **naughtily** adv ▷ **naughtiness** n (pl -es)
nausea n (pl -s) feeling of being about to vomit
nauseas n ▷ **nausea**
nauseate v (-tes, -ting, -ted) make (someone) feel sick
nauseated v ▷ **nauseate**
nauseates v ▷ **nauseate**
nauseating v ▷ **nauseate**

nauseous adj as if about to vomit
nautical adj of the sea or ships
nautili n ▷ **nautilus**
nautilus n (pl -luses, -li) shellfish with many tentacles
nautiluses n ▷ **nautilus**
naval adj ▷ **navy**
nave n (pl -s) long central part of a church
navel n (pl -s) hollow in the middle of the abdomen where the umbilical cord was attached
navels n ▷ **navel**
naves n ▷ **nave**
navies n ▷ **navy**
navigate v (-tes, -ting, -ted) direct or plot the path or position of a ship, aircraft, or car ▷ **navigation** n (pl -s) ▷ **navigator** n (pl -s)
navigated v ▷ **navigate**
navigates v ▷ **navigate**
navigating v ▷ **navigate**
navigation n ▷ **navigate**
navigations n ▷ **navigate**
navigator n ▷ **navigate**
navigators n ▷ **navigate**
navvies n ▷ **navvy**
navvy n (pl -vvies) BRIT labourer employed on a road or a building site
navy n (pl -vies) branch of a country's armed services comprising warships with their crews and organization ▶ adj very dark blue
nay interj obs no

> **ne** adv. Ne is an old word meaning **not.** This handy little word can be very helpful when you are trying to form several words at once. Ne scores 2 points.

near prep, adv adj (-er, -est) indicating a place or time not far away ▶ adj almost being the thing specified ▶ v (-s, -ing, -ed) draw close (to) ▷ **nearness** n (pl -es)
nearby adj not far away
neared v ▷ **near**
nearer adj ▷ **near**
nearest adj ▷ **near**

nearing v ▷ near
nearly adv almost
nearness n ▷ near
nearnesses n ▷ near
nears v ▷ near
nearside n (pl -s) side of a vehicle that is nearer the kerb
nearsides n ▷ nearside
neat adj (-er, -est) tidy and clean
> **neatly** adv ▷ **neatness** n (pl -es)
neater adj ▷ neat
neatest adj ▷ neat
neatly adv ▷ neat
neatness n ▷ neat
neatnesses n ▷ neat
nebula n (pl -lae) ASTRONOMY hazy cloud of particles and gases
> **nebulous** adj vague and unclear
nebulae n ▷ nebula
nebulous adj ▷ nebula
neck n (pl -s) part of the body joining the head to the shoulders ▶ v (-s, -ing, -ed) slang kiss and cuddle
necked v ▷ neck
necking v ▷ neck
necklace n (pl -s) decorative piece of jewellery worn around the neck
necklaces n ▷ necklace
necks n, v ▷ neck
nectar n (pl -s) sweet liquid collected from flowers by bees
nectars n ▷ nectar
née prep indicating the maiden name of a married woman
need v (-s, -ing, -ed) require or be in want of ▶ n (pl -s) condition of lacking something
needed v ▷ need
needful adj necessary or required
needier adj ▷ needy
neediest adj ▷ needy
needing v ▷ need
needle n (pl -s) thin pointed piece of metal with an eye through which thread is passed for sewing ▶ v (-les, -ling, -led) informal goad or provoke
needled v ▷ needle
needles n, v ▷ needle

needless adj unnecessary
needling v ▷ needle
needs v, n ▷ need ▶ adv (preceded or foll. by must) necessarily
needy adj (-dier, -diest) poor, in need of financial support
negate v (-tes, -ting, -ted) invalidate
> **negation** n (pl -s)
negated v ▷ negate
negates v ▷ negate
negating v ▷ negate
negation n ▷ negate
negations n ▷ negate
negative adj expressing a denial or refusal ▶ n (pl -s) negative word or statement
negatives n ▷ negative
neglect v (-s, -ing, -ed) take no care of ▶ n (pl -s) neglecting or being neglected > **neglectful** adj
neglected v ▷ neglect
neglectful adj ▷ neglect
neglecting v ▷ neglect
neglects v, n ▷ neglect
negligee n (pl -s) woman's lightweight usu. lace-trimmed dressing gown
negligees n ▷ negligee
neigh n (pl -s) loud high-pitched sound made by a horse ▶ v (-s, -ing, -ed) make this sound
neighed v ▷ neigh
neighing v ▷ neigh
neighs n, v ▷ neigh
neither adj, pron not one nor the other ▶ conj not
nemeses n ▷ nemesis
nemesis n (pl -ses) retribution or vengeance
neolith n (pl -s) stone implement from the Neolithic age
neoliths n ▷ neolith
neon n (pl -s) CHEM colourless odourless gaseous element used in illuminated signs and lights
neons n ▷ neon
neophyte n (pl -s) beginner or novice
neophytes n ▷ neophyte
nephew n (pl -s) son of one's sister

or brother

nephews n ▷ nephew

nepotism n (pl -s) favouritism in business shown to relatives and friends

nepotisms n ▷ nepotism

nerd n (pl -s) slang boring person obsessed with a particular subject

nerds n ▷ nerd

nerve n (pl -s) cordlike bundle of fibres that conducts impulses between the brain and other parts of the body

nerves n ▷ nerve ▶ pl n anxiety or tension

nervier adj ▷ nervy

nerviest adj ▷ nervy

nervous adj apprehensive or worried > **nervously** adv > **nervousness** n (pl -es)

nervously adv ▷ nervous

nervousness n ▷ nervous

nervousnesses n ▷ nervous

nervy adj (-vier, -viest) excitable or nervous

nest n (pl -s) place or structure in which birds or certain animals lay eggs or give birth to young ▶ v (-s, -ing, -ed) make or inhabit a nest

nested v ▷ nest

nesting v ▷ nest

nestle v (-les, -ling, -led) snuggle

nestled v ▷ nestle

nestles v ▷ nestle

nestling n (pl -s) bird too young to leave the nest ▶ v ▷ nestle

nestlings n ▷ nestling

nests v, n ▷ nest

net[1] n (pl -s) fabric of meshes of string, thread, or wire with many openings ▶ v (-s, -tting, -tted) catch (a fish or animal) in a net

net[2], **nett** adj left after all deductions ▶ v (-s, -tting, -tted) yield or earn as a clear profit

netball n (pl -s) team game in which a ball has to be thrown through a net hanging from a ring at the top of a pole

netballs n ▷ netball

nether adj lower

nets v ▷ net[1, 2]

nets n ▷ net[1]

nett adj ▷ net[2]

netted v ▷ net[1, 2]

netting v ▷ net[1, 2] ▶ n (pl -s) material made of net

nettings n ▷ netting

nettle n (pl -s) plant with stinging hairs on the leaves

nettled adj irritated or annoyed

nettles n ▷ nettle

network n (pl -s) system of intersecting lines, roads, etc

networks n ▷ network

neural adj of a nerve or the nervous system

neuritis n (pl -tises) inflammation of a nerve or nerves

neuritises n ▷ neuritis

neuroses n ▷ neurosis

neurosis n (pl -ses) mental disorder producing hysteria, anxiety, depression, or obsessive behaviour

neurotic adj emotionally unstable ▶ n (pl -s) neurotic person

neurotics n ▷ neurotic

neuter adj belonging to a particular class of grammatical inflections in some languages ▶ v (-s, -ing, -ed) castrate (an animal)

neutered v ▷ neuter

neutering v ▷ neuter

neuters n ▷ neuter

neutral adj taking neither side in a war or dispute ▶ n (pl -s) neutral person or nation > **neutrality** n (pl -ties)

neutralities n ▷ neutral

neutrality n ▷ neutral

neutrals n ▷ neutral

neutrino n (pl -nos) elementary particle with no mass or electrical charge

neutrinos n ▷ neutrino

neutron n (pl -s) electrically neutral elementary particle of about the same mass as a proton

neutrons n ▷ neutron

never adv at no time

new adj (**-er**, **-est**) not existing before (foll. by **to**) ▶ adv recently

newbie informal n (pl **-s**) person new to a job, club, etc

newbies n ▷ newbie

newborn adj recently or just born

newcomer n (pl **-s**) recent arrival or participant

newcomers n ▷ newcomer

newel n (pl **-s**) post at the top or bottom of a flight of stairs that supports the handrail

newels n ▷ newel

newer adj ▷ new

newest adj ▷ new

newness n (pl **-es**) quality of being new

newnesses n ▷ newness

news n important or interesting new happenings

newsier adj ▷ newsy

newsiest adj ▷ newsy

newsreel n (pl **-s**) short film giving news

newsreels n ▷ newsreel

newsroom n (pl **-s**) room where news is received and prepared for publication or broadcasting

newsrooms n ▷ newsroom

newsy adj (**-sier**, **-siest**) full of news

newt n (pl **-s**) small amphibious creature with a long slender body and tail

newton n (pl **-s**) unit of force

newtons n ▷ newton

newts n ▷ newt

next adj, adv immediately following

nexus n (pl **nexus**) connection or link

nib n (pl **-s**) writing point of a pen

nibble v (**-les**, **-ling**, **-led**) take little bites (of) ▶ n (pl **-les**) little bite

nibbled v ▷ nibble

nibbles v, n ▷ nibble

nibbling v ▷ nibble

nibs n ▷ nib

nice adj (**-r**, **-st**) pleasant > **nicely** adv > **niceness** n (pl **-es**)

nicely adv ▷ nice

niceness n ▷ nice

nicenesses n ▷ nice

nicer adj ▷ nice

nicest adj ▷ nice

niceties n ▷ nicety

nicety n (pl **-ties**) subtle point

niche n (pl **-s**) hollow area in a wall

niches n ▷ niche

nick v (**-s**, **-ing**, **-ed**) make a small cut in ▶ n (pl **-s**) small cut

nicked v ▷ nick

nickel n (pl **-s**) CHEM silvery-white metal often used in alloys

nickels n ▷ nickel

nicking v ▷ nick

nickname n (pl **-s**) familiar name given to a person or place ▶ v (**-mes**, **-ming**, **-med**) call by a nickname

nicknamed v ▷ nickname

nicknames n, v ▷ nickname

nicknaming v ▷ nickname

nicks v, n ▷ nick

nicotine n (pl **-s**) poisonous substance found in tobacco

nicotines n ▷ nicotine

niece n (pl **-s**) daughter of one's sister or brother

nieces n ▷ niece

niftier adj ▷ nifty

niftiest adj ▷ nifty

nifty adj (**-tier**, **-tiest**) informal neat or smart

niggle v (**-les**, **-ling**, **-led**) worry slightly ▶ n (pl **-s**) small worry or doubt

niggled v ▷ niggle

niggles v, n ▷ niggle

niggling v ▷ niggle

nigh adv, prep lit near

night n (pl **-s**) time of darkness between sunset and sunrise

nightcap n (pl **-s**) drink taken just before bedtime

nightcaps n ▷ nightcap

nightie n (pl **-s**) informal nightdress

nighties n ▷ nightie

nightjar n (pl **-s**) nocturnal bird with a harsh cry

nightjars n ▷ **nightjar**

nightly adj, adv (happening) each night

nights n ▷ **night**

nihilism n (pl -s) rejection of all established authority and institutions > **nihilist** n (pl -s) > **nihilistic** adj

nihilisms n ▷ **nihilism**

nihilist n ▷ **nihilism**

nihilistic adj ▷ **nihilism**

nihilists n ▷ **nihilism**

nil n (pl -s) nothing, zero

nils n ▷ **nil**

nimbi n ▷ **nimbus**

nimble adj (-r, -st) agile and quick > **nimbly** adv

nimbler adj ▷ **nimble**

nimblest adj ▷ **nimble**

nimbly adv ▷ **nimble**

nimbus n (pl -bi, -buses) dark grey rain cloud

nimbuses n ▷ **nimbus**

nine adj, n (pl -s) one more than eight

nines n ▷ **nine**

ninepins n game of skittles

nines n ▷ **nine**

nineteen adj, n (pl -s) ten and nine > **nineteenth** adj, n (pl -s)

nineteens n ▷ **nineteen**

nineteenth adj, n ▷ **nineteen**

nineteenths n ▷ **nineteen**

nineties n ▷ **ninety**

ninetieth adj, n ▷ **ninety**

ninetieths n ▷ **ninety**

ninety adj, n (pl -ties) ten times nine > **ninetieth** adj, n (pl -s)

ninth adj, n (pl -s) (of) number nine in a series

ninths n ▷ **ninth**

niobium n (pl -s) CHEM white superconductive metallic element

niobiums n ▷ **niobium**

nip¹ v (-s, -pping, -pped) informal hurry ▶ n (pl -s) pinch or light bite

nip² n (pl nips) small alcoholic drink

nipped v ▷ **nip¹**

nipper n (pl -s) BRIT, AUST & NZ informal small child

nippers n ▷ **nipper**

nippier adj ▷ **nippy**

nippiest adj ▷ **nippy**

nipping v ▷ **nip¹**

nipple n (pl -s) projection in the centre of a breast

nipples n ▷ **nipple**

nippy adj informal (-pier, -piest) frosty or chilly

nips v ▷ **nip¹** ▶ n ▷ **nip¹, ²**

nirvana n (pl -s) BUDDHISM HINDUISM absolute spiritual enlightenment and bliss

nirvanas n ▷ **nirvana**

nit n (pl -s) egg or larva of a louse informal ▷ **nitwit**

nitrate n (pl -s) compound of nitric acid, used as a fertilizer

nitrates n ▷ **nitrate**

nitric, nitrous, nitrogenous adj of or containing nitrogen

nitrogen n (pl -s) CHEM colourless odourless gas that forms four fifths of the air

nitrogenous n ▷ **nitric**

nitrogens n ▷ **nitrogen**

nitrous adj ▷ **nitric**

nits n ▷ **nit**

nitwit n (pl -s) informal stupid person

nitwits n ▷ **nitwit**

> **nix** n (nixes). A nix is a water sprite in Germanic mythology. This is a handy little word, combining X with two of the most common tiles in the game. If you have an X on your rack, look out for opportunities on the board to play this, as there's most likely an N or I available. Nix scores 10 points.

no interj expresses denial, disagreement, or refusal ▶ adj not any, not a ▶ adv not at all ▶ n (pl noes, nos) answer or vote of 'no'

nob n (pl -s) CHIEFLY BRIT slang person of wealth or social distinction

nobble v (-les, -ling, -led) BRIT slang attract the attention of (someone) in order to talk to him or her

nobbled v ▷ **nobble**
nobbles v ▷ **nobble**
nobbling v ▷ **nobble**
nobelium n (pl -s) CHEM artificially-produced radioactive element
nobeliums n ▷ **nobelium**
nobilities n ▷ **nobility**
nobility n (pl -ties) quality of being noble > **nobleman, noblewoman** (pl **-men**)
noble adj (**-r, -st**) showing or having high moral qualities ▶ n (pl **-s**) member of the nobility > **nobly** adv
nobleman n ▷ **nobility**
noblemen n ▷ **nobility**
nobler adj ▷ **noble**
nobles n ▷ **noble**
noblest adj ▷ **noble**
noblewoman n ▷ **nobility**
noblewomen n ▷ **nobility**
nobly adv ▷ **noble**
nobodies n ▷ **nobody**
nobody pron no person ▶ n (pl **-dies**) person of no importance
nobs n ▷ **nob**
nocturne n (pl **-s**) short dreamy piece of music
nocturnes n ▷ **nocturne**
nod v (**-s, -dding, -dded**) lower and raise (one's head) briefly in agreement or greeting ▶ n act of nodding
nodded v ▷ **nod**
nodding v ▷ **nod**
noddle n (pl s) CHIEFLY BRIT informal the head
noddles n ▷ **noddle**
node n (pl **-s**) point on a plant stem from which leaves grow
nodes n ▷ **node**
nods v, n ▷ **nod**
nodule n (pl **-s**) small knot or lump
nodules n ▷ **nodule**
noel n (pl **-s**) Christmas carol
noels n ▷ **noel**
noes n ▷ **no**
noggin n (pl **-s**) informal head
noggins n ▷ **noggin**
noise n (pl **-s**) sound, usu. a loud

or disturbing one > **noiseless** adj
noiseless adj ▷ **noise**
noises n ▷ **noise**
noisier adj ▷ **noisy**
noisiest adj ▷ **noisy**
noisily adv ▷ **noisy**
noisome adj (of smells) offensive
noisy adj (**-sier, -siest**) making a lot of noise > **noisily** adv
nomad n (pl **-s**) member of a tribe with no fixed dwelling place, wanderer > **nomadic** adj
nomadic adj ▷ **nomad**
nomads n ▷ **nomad**
nominal adj in name only > **nominally** adv
nominally adv ▷ **nominal**
nominate v (**-tes, -ting, -ted**) suggest as a candidate > **nomination** n (pl **-s**)
nominated v ▷ **nominate**
nominates v ▷ **nominate**
nominating v ▷ **nominate**
nomination n ▷ **nominate**
nominations n ▷ **nominate**
nominee n (pl **-s**) candidate
nominees n ▷ **nominee**
nonagon n (pl **-s**) geometric figure with nine sides
nonagons n ▷ **nonagon**
nonce n (pl **-s**) for the present
nonces n ▷ **nonce**
none pron not any
nonevent n (pl **-s**) disappointing or insignificant occurrence
nonevents n ▷ **nonevent**
nonsense n (pl **-s**) something that has or makes no sense > **nonsensical** adj
nonsenses n ▷ **nonsense**
nonsensical adj ▷ **nonsense**
nonstick adj coated with a substance that food will not stick to when cooked
nonstop adj, adv without a stop
nontoxic adj not poisonous
noodles pl n long thin strips of pasta
nook n (pl **-s**) sheltered place
nooks n ▷ **nook**

noon n (pl -s) twelve o'clock midday

noonday adj happening at noon

noons n ▷ noon

noose n (pl -s) loop in the end of a rope, tied with a slipknot

nooses n ▷ noose

nor conj and not

norm n (pl -s) standard that is regarded as normal

normal adj usual, regular, or typical
> **normally** adv ▷ normality n (pl -ties)
> **normalize** v (-izes, -izing, -ized)

normalities n ▷ normal

normality n ▷ normal

normalized v ▷ normal

normalizes v ▷ normal

normalizing v ▷ normal

normally adv ▷ normal

norms n ▷ norm

north n (pl -s) direction towards the North Pole, opposite south ▶ adj to or in the north ▶ adv in, to, or towards the north > **northerly** adj
> **northern** ▷ northward > adj, adv
> **northwards** adv

northerly adj ▷ north

northern adj ▷ north

norths n ▷ north

northward adj, adv ▷ north

northwards adv ▷ north

nos n ▷ no

nose n (pl -s) organ of smell, used also in breathing ▶ v (-ses, -sing, -sed) move forward slowly and carefully

nosed v ▷ nose

nosegay n (pl -s) small bunch of flowers

nosegays n ▷ nosegay

noses n, v ▷ nose

nosey, nosy adj informal (-sier, -siest) prying or inquisitive > **nosiness** n (pl -es)

nosh n (pl -es) BRIT, AUST & NZ slang food ▶ v (-es, -ing, -ed) eat

noshed v ▷ nosh

noshes n, v ▷ nosh

noshing v ▷ nosh

nosier adj ▷ nosey

nosiest adj ▷ nosey

nosiness n ▷ nosey

nosinesses n ▷ nosey

nosing v ▷ nose

nostril n (pl -s) one of the two openings at the end of the nose

nostrils n ▷ nostril

nostrum n (pl -s) quack medicine

nostrums n ▷ nostrum

nosy adj (-sier, -siest) ▷ nosey

not adv expressing negation, refusal, or denial

notable adj worthy of being noted, remarkable ▶ n (pl -s) person of distinction > **notably** adv

notables n ▷ notable

notably adv ▷ notable

notaries n ▷ notary

notary n (pl -ries) person authorized to witness the signing of legal documents

notation n (pl -s) representation of numbers or quantities in a system by a series of symbols

notations n ▷ notation

notch n (pl -es) V-shaped cut ▶ v (-es, -ing, -ed) make a notch in (foll. by up)

notched v ▷ notch

notches n, v ▷ notch

notching v ▷ notch

note n (pl -s) short letter ▶ v (-tes, -ting, -ted) notice, pay attention to

notebook n (pl -s) book for writing in

notebooks n ▷ notebook

noted v ▷ note ▶ adj well-known

notes n, v ▷ note

nothing pron not anything ▶ adv not at all

notice n (pl -s) observation or attention ▶ v (-ces, -cing, -ced) observe, become aware of

noticed v ▷ notice

notices n, v ▷ notice

noticing v ▷ notice

notification n ▷ notify

notifications *n* ▷ notify
notified *v* ▷ notify
notifies *v* ▷ notify
notify *v* (-fies, -fying, -fied) inform
> **notification** *n* (*pl* -s)
notifying *v* ▷ notify
noting *v* ▷ note
notion *n* (*pl* -s) idea or opinion
notional *adj* speculative, imaginary,
or unreal
notions *n* ▷ notion
nougat *n* (*pl* -s) chewy sweet
containing nuts and fruit
nougats *n* ▷ nougat
nought *n* (*pl* -s) figure o
noughts *n* ▷ nought
noun *n* (*pl* -s) word that refers to a
person, place, or thing
nouns *n* ▷ noun
nourish *v* (-shes, -shing, -shed) feed
> **nourishment** *n* (*pl* -s)
nourished *v* ▷ nourish
nourishes *v* ▷ nourish
nourishment *n* ▷ nourish
nourishments *n* ▷ nourish
nova *n* (*pl* -vae, -vas) star that
suddenly becomes brighter and then
gradually decreases to its original
brightness
novae *n* ▷ nova
novas *n* ▷ nova
novel[1] *n* (*pl* -s) long fictitious story in
book form
novel[2] *adj* fresh, new, or original
novelist *n* (*pl* -s) writer of novels
novelists *n* ▷ novelist
novella *n* (*pl* -s, -llae) short
novel
novellae *n* ▷ novella
novellas *n* ▷ novella
novels *n* ▷ novel[1]
novelties *n* ▷ novelty
novelty *n* (*pl* -ties) newness
novena *n* (*pl* -s) RC CHURCH set of
prayers or
services on nine consecutive
days
novenas *n* ▷ novena

novice *n* (*pl* -s) beginner
novices *n* ▷ novice
now *adv* at or for the present time
▶ *conj* seeing that, since
nowadays *adv* in these times
nowhere *adv* not anywhere

nox *n* (**noxes**). In chemistry, nox
is short for nitrogen oxide. This is
an unusual word which can come
in useful in the later stages of the
game when there isn't much space
left, or when you have an X but can't
form a longer word with it. Nox
scores 10 points.

noxious *adj* poisonous or
harmful
nozzle *n* (*pl* -s) projecting spout
through which fluid is
discharged
nozzles *n* ▷ nozzle

nth *adv*. In mathematics, nth
represents an unspecified ordinal
number. Nth is a good word to
remember for awkward situations
on the board, as it's one of very few
three-letter words that doesn't
contain a vowel. Nth scores 6
points.

nu *n* (**nus**). Nu is the 13th letter in
the Greek alphabet. This word is
worth remembering, as it can be
really useful when you want to
form short words in the process
of playing a longer one. Nu scores
2 points.

nuance *n* (*pl* -s) subtle difference in
colour, meaning, or tone
nuances *n* ▷ nuance
nub *n* (*pl* -s) point or gist (of a story etc)
nubile *adj* (of a young woman) sexually
attractive
nubs *n* ▷ nub
nuclear *adj* of nuclear weapons or
energy
nuclei *n* ▷ nucleus
nucleus *n* (*pl* -clei) centre, esp. of an
atom or cell
nude *adj* (-r, -st) naked ▶ *n* (*pl* -s)

naked figure in painting, sculpture, or photography > **nudity** n (pl -**ties**)

nuder adj ▷ **nude**

nudes n ▷ **nude**

nudest adj ▷ **nude**

nudge v (-**dges**, -**dging**, -**dged**) push gently, esp. with the elbow ► n (pl -**s**) gentle push or touch

nudged v ▷ **nudge**

nudges v, n ▷ **nudge**

nudging v ▷ **nudge**

nudism n (pl -**s**) practice of not wearing clothes > **nudist** n (pl -**s**)

nudisms n ▷ **nudism**

nudist n ▷ **nudism**

nudists n ▷ **nudism**

nudities n ▷ **nude**

nudity n ▷ **nude**

nugatory adj of little value

nugget n (pl -**s**) small lump of gold in its natural state ► v (-**s**, -**tting**, -**tted**) NZ & S AFR polish footwear

nuggets n, v ▷ **nugget**

nuggetted v ▷ **nugget**

nuggetting v ▷ **nugget**

nuisance n (pl -**s**) something or someone that causes annoyance or bother

nuisances n ▷ **nuisance**

nuke slang v (-**kes**, -**king**, -**ked**) attack with nuclear weapons ► n (pl -**s**) nuclear weapon

nuked v ▷ **nuke**

nukes v, n ▷ **nuke**

nuking v ▷ **nuke**

null adj not legally valid > **nullity** n (pl -**s**)

nullified v ▷ **nullify**

nullifies v ▷ **nullify**

nullify v (-**fies**, -**fying**, -**fied**) make ineffective

nullifying v ▷ **nullify**

nullities n ▷ **null**

nullity n ▷ **null**

numb adj (-**er**, -**est**) without feeling, as through cold, shock, or fear ► v (-**s**, -**ing**, -**ed**) make numb > **numbly** adv > **numbness** n (pl -**es**)

numbat n (pl -**s**) small Australian marsupial with a long snout and tongue

numbats n ▷ **numbat**

numbed v ▷ **numb**

number¹ adj ▷ **numb**

number² n (pl -**s**) sum or quantity ► v (-**s**, -**ing**, -**ed**) count

numbered v ▷ **number**

numbering v ▷ **number**

numbers n, v ▷ **number**

numbest adj ▷ **numb**

numbing v ▷ **numb**

numbly adv ▷ **numb**

numbness n ▷ **numb**

numbnesses n ▷ **numb**

numbs v ▷ **numb**

numeracies n ▷ **numerate**

numeracy n ▷ **numerate**

numeral n (pl -**s**) word or symbol used to express a sum or quantity

numerals n ▷ **numeral**

numerate adj able to do basic arithmetic > **numeracy** n (pl -**cies**)

numerous adj existing or happening in large numbers

numskulls n ▷ **numskull**

nun n (pl -**s**) female member of a religious order

nuncio n (pl -**s**) RC CHURCH pope's ambassador

nuncios n ▷ **nuncio**

nunneries n ▷ **nunnery**

nunnery n (pl -**ries**) convent

nuns n ▷ **nun**

nuptial adj relating to marriage

nuptials pl n wedding

nurse n (pl -**s**) person employed to look after sick people, usu. in a hospital ► v (-**ses**, -**sing**, -**sed**) look after (a sick person)

nursed v ▷ **nurse**

nurseries n ▷ **nursery**

nursery n (pl -**ries**) room where children sleep or play

nurses n, v ▷ **nurse**

nursing v ▷ **nurse**

nurture n (pl -**s**) act or process of

promoting the development of a child or young plant ▸ v (**-res, -ring, -red**) promote or encourage the development of

nurtured v ▷ nurture
nurtures n, v ▷ nurture
nurturing v ▷ nurture

nut n (pl **-s**) fruit consisting of a hard shell and a kernel

nuthatch n (pl **-es**) small songbird
nuthatches n ▷ nuthatch

nutmeg n (pl **-s**) spice made from the seed of a tropical tree
nutmegs n ▷ nutmeg

nutria n (pl **-s**) fur of the coypu
nutrias n ▷ nutria

nutrient n (pl **-s**) substance that provides nourishment
nutrients n ▷ nutrient

nuts n ▷ nut

nutter n (pl **-s**) BRIT slang insane person
nutters n ▷ nutter
nuttier adj ▷ nutty
nuttiest adj ▷ nutty

nutty adj (**-ttier, -ttiest**) containing or resembling nuts

nuzzle v (**-les, -ling, -led**) push or rub gently with the nose or snout
nuzzled v ▷ nuzzle
nuzzles v ▷ nuzzle
nuzzling v ▷ nuzzle

ny adj, adv. Ny is an old spelling of **nigh**. This word can be useful when you're forming one word adjacent to another, and so need to form two-letter words where the two words meet. Ny is also unusual in that it doesn't contain a vowel. Ny scores 5 points.

nylon n (pl **-s**) synthetic material used for clothing etc
nylons n ▷ nylon ▸ pl n stockings made of nylon

nymph n (pl **-s**) mythical spirit of nature, represented as a beautiful young woman

nymphet n (pl **-s**) sexually precocious young girl
nymphets n ▷ nymphet
nymphs n ▷ nymph

Oo

With eight Os in the bag, you're likely to have at least one on your rack during a game. There are plenty of good two-letter words starting with O. It's worth knowing that O will form a two-letter word in front of every other vowel except **a**, as well as in front of Y. O also combines well with X, with **ox** (9 points) as the obvious starting point, and several words that refer to **oxygen** (17), including **oxo** (10) and **oxy** (13). Don't forget the short everyday words that begin with O. While **on** and **or** (2 each) won't earn you many points, they can be very helpful when you are trying to score in more than one direction at a time. **Of** (5 each) and **oh** (5 each) can also prove very useful.

oaf n (pl -s) stupid or clumsy person
> **oafish** adj

oafish adj ▷ **oaf**

oafs n ▷ **oaf**

oak n (pl -s) deciduous forest tree
> **oaken** adj

oaken adj ▷ **oak**

oaks n ▷ **oak**

oakum n (pl -s) fibre obtained by unravelling old rope

oakums n ▷ **oakum**

oar n (pl -s) pole with a broad blade, used for rowing a boat

oars n ▷ **oar**

oases n ▷ **oasis**

oasis n (pl -ses) fertile area in a desert

oast n (pl -s) CHIEFLY BRIT oven for drying hops

oasts n ▷ **oast**

oat n (pl -s) hard cereal grown as food
▶ pl grain of this cereal

oath n (pl -s) solemn promise, esp. to be truthful in court

oaths n ▷ **oath**

oatmeal adj pale brownish-cream

oats n ▷ **oat**

obduracies n ▷ **obdurate**

obduracy n ▷ **obdurate**

obdurate adj hardhearted or stubborn
> **obduracy** n (pl -cies)

obedience n ▷ **obedient**

obediences n ▷ **obedient**

obedient adj obeying or willing to obey > **obedience** n (pl -s)
> **obediently** adv

obediently adv ▷ **obedient**

obelisk n (pl -s) four-sided stone column tapering to a pyramid at the top

obelisks n ▷ **obelisk**

obese adj (-r, -st) very fat > **obesity** n (pl -ties)

obeser adj ▷ **obese**

obesest adj ▷ **obese**

obesities n ▷ **obese**

obesity n ▷ **obese**

obey v (-s, -ing, -ed) carry out instructions or orders

obeyed v ▷ **obey**

obeying v ▷ **obey**

obeys v ▷ **obey**

obituaries n ▷ **obituary**

obituarist n ▷ **obituary**

obituarists n ▷ **obituary**

obituary n (pl -ies) announcement of someone's death, esp. in a newspaper

>obituarist n (pl -s)

object¹ n (pl -s) physical thing

object² v (-s, -ing, -ed) express disapproval ▶ objection n (pl -s)
> objector n (pl -s)

objected v ▷ object²

objecting v ▷ object²

objection n ▷ object²

objections n ▷ object²

objector n ▷ object²

objectors n ▷ object²

objects n, v ▷ object¹, ²

oblation n (pl -s) religious offering

oblations n ▷ oblation

oblige v (-ges, -ging, -ged) compel (someone) morally or by law to do something

obliged v ▷ oblige

obliges v ▷ oblige

obliging adj ready to help other people ▶ v ▷ oblige ▷ obligingly adv

obligingly adv ▷ oblige

oblique adj (-r, -st) slanting ▶ n (pl -s) the symbol (/) ▷ obliquely adv

obliquely adv ▷ oblique

obliquer n ▷ oblique

obliques n ▷ oblique

obliquest adj ▷ oblique

oblivion n (pl -s) state of being forgotten

oblivions n ▷ oblivion

oblong adj having two long sides, two short sides, and four right angles ▶ n (pl -s) oblong figure

oblongs n ▷ oblong

obloquies n ▷ obloquy

obloquy n (pl -quies) verbal abuse

oboe n (pl -s) double-reeded woodwind instrument ▶ oboist n (pl -s)

oboes n ▷ oboe

oboist n ▷ oboe

oboists n ▷ oboe

obscene adj (-r, -st) portraying sex offensively ▶ obscenity n (pl -ies)

obscener adj ▷ obscene

obscenest adj ▷ obscene

obscenities n ▷ obscene

obscenity n ▷ obscene

obscure adj (-r, -st) not well known ▶ v (-res, -ring, -red) make (something) obscure ▷ obscurity n (pl -ties)

obscured v ▷ obscure

obscurer adj ▷ obscure

obscures v ▷ obscure

obscurest adj ▷ obscure

obscuring v ▷ obscure

obscurities n ▷ obscure

obscurity n ▷ obscure

observable adj ▷ observe

observe v (-ves, -ving, -ved) see or notice ▶ observable adj

observed v ▷ observe

observer n (pl -s) person who observes, esp. one who watches someone or something carefully

observers n ▷ observer

observes v ▷ observe

observing v ▷ observe

obsess v (-es, -ing, -ed) preoccupy (someone) compulsively
> obsessed adj ▷ obsessive adj
> obsession n (pl -s)

obsessed v, adj ▷ obsess

obsesses v ▷ obsess

obsessing v ▷ obsess

obsession n ▷ obsess

obsessions n ▷ obsess

obsessive adj ▷ obsess

obsidian n (pl -s) dark glassy volcanic rock

obsidians n ▷ obsidian

obsolete adj no longer in use

obstacle n (pl -s) something that makes progress difficult

obstacles n ▷ obstacle

obstruct v (-s, -ing, -ed) block with an obstacle ▶ obstruction n (pl -s)
> obstructive adj

obstructed v ▷ obstruct

obstructing v ▷ obstruct

obstruction n ▷ obstruct

obstructions n ▷ obstruct

obstructive adj ▷ obstruct

obstructs v ▷ obstruct

obtain v (-s, -ing, -ed) acquire intentionally ▷ obtainable adj

obtainable *adj* ▷ **obtain**
obtained *v* ▷ **obtain**
obtaining *v* ▷ **obtain**
obtains *v* ▷ **obtain**
obtrude *v* (**-des, -ding, -ded**) push
oneself or one's ideas on others
obtruded *v* ▷ **obtrude**
obtrudes *v* ▷ **obtrude**
obtruding *v* ▷ **obtrude**
obtuse *adj* (**-r, -st**) mentally slow
>**obtuseness** *n* (*pl* **-es**)
obtuseness *n* ▷ **obtuse**
obtusenesses *n* ▷ **obtuse**
obtuser *adj* ▷ **obtuse**
obtusest *adj* ▷ **obtuse**
obverse *n* (*pl* **-s**) opposite way of
looking at an idea
obverses *n* ▷ **obverse**
obviate *v* (**-tes, -ting, -ted**) make
unnecessary
obviated *v* ▷ **obviate**
obviates *v* ▷ **obviate**
obviating *v* ▷ **obviate**
obvious *adj* easy to see or understand,
evident >**obviously** *adv*
obviously *adv* ▷ **obvious**
ocarina *n* (*pl* **-s**) small oval wind
instrument
ocarinas *n* ▷ **ocarina**
occasion *n* (*pl* **-s**) time at which a
particular thing happens ▶ *v* (**-s, -ing,
-ed**) cause
occasioned *v* ▷ **occasion**
occasioning *v* ▷ **occasion**
occasions *n, v* ▷ **occasion**
occident *n* (*pl* **occidents**) *lit* west
>**occidental** *adj*
occidental *adj* ▷ **occident**
occidents *n* ▷ **occident**
occiput *n* (*pl* **-s**) back of the head
occiputs *n* ▷ **occiput**
occlude *v* (**-des, -ding, -ded**) obstruct
>**occlusion** *n* (*pl* **-s**)
occluded *v* ▷ **occlude**
occludes *v* ▷ **occlude**
occluding *v* ▷ **occlude**
occlusion *n* ▷ **occlude**
occlusions *n* ▷ **occlude**

occult *adj* relating to the supernatural
occupant *n* (*pl* **-s**) person occupying a
specified place
occupants *n* ▷ **occupant**
occupied *v* ▷ **occupy**
occupier *n* ▷ **occupy**
occupiers *n* ▷ **occupy**
occupies *v* ▷ **occupy**
occupy *v* (**-pies, -pying, -pied**) live or
work in (a building) >**occupier** *n* (*pl* **-s**)
occur *v* (**-s, -rring, -rred**) happen
occurred *v* ▷ **occur**
occurring *v* ▷ **occur**
occurs *v* ▷ **occur**
ocean *n* (*pl* **-s**) vast area of sea between
continents >**oceanic** *adj*
oceanic *adj* ▷ **ocean**
oceans *n* ▷ **ocean**
ocelot *n* (*pl* **-s**) American wild cat with
a spotted coat
ocelots *n* ▷ **ocelot**
oche *n* (*pl* **-s**) DARTS mark on the floor
behind which a player must stand
oches *n* ▷ **oche**
ochre *adj, n* (*pl* **-s**) brownish-yellow
(earth)
ochres *n* ▷ **ochre**
octagon *n* (*pl* **-s**) geometric figure
with eight sides >**octagonal** *adj*
octagonal *adj* ▷ **octagon**
octagons *n* ▷ **octagon**
octane *n* (*pl* **-s**) hydrocarbon found
in petrol
octanes *n* ▷ **octane**
octave *n* (*pl* **-s**) MUSIC (interval
between the first and) eighth note
of a scale
octaves *n* ▷ **octave**
octet *n* (*pl* **-s**) group of eight performers
octets *n* ▷ **octet**
octopus *n* (*pl* **-es**) sea creature with a
soft body and eight tentacles
octopuses *n* ▷ **octopus**
ocular *adj* relating to the eyes or sight
odd (**-er, -est**) *adj* unusual
odder *adj* ▷ **odd**
oddest *adj* ▷ **odd**
oddities *n* ▷ **oddity**

oddity n (pl **-ties**) odd person or thing

oddments pl n things left over

oddness n (pl **-es**) quality of being odd

oddnesses n ▷ oddness

odds pl n (ratio showing) the probability of something happening

ode n (pl **-s**) lyric poem, usu. addressed to a particular subject

odes n ▷ ode

odious adj offensive

odium n (pl **-s**) widespread dislike

odiums n ▷ odium

odorous adj ▷ odour

odour n (pl **-s**) particular smell

> **odorous** adj > **odourless** adj

odourless adj ▷ odour

odours n ▷ odour

odyssey n (pl **-s**) long eventful journey

odysseys n ▷ odyssey

oe n (**oes**) Oe is a Scots word for a grandchild. This is a good word to remember, as it combines two of the most common letters in the game without using any consonants. Oe scores 2 points.

oedema n (pl **-mata**) MED abnormal swelling

oedemata n ▷ oedema

of prep belonging to

off prep away from ▶ adv away ▶ adj not operating ▶ n (pl **-s**) CRICKET side of the field to which the batsman's feet point

offal n (pl **-s**) edible organs of an animal, such as liver or kidneys

offals n ▷ offal

offcut n (pl **-s**) piece remaining after the required parts have been cut out

offcuts n ▷ offcut

offence n (pl **-s**) (cause of) hurt feelings or annoyance

offences n ▷ offence

offend v (**-s**, **-ing**, **-ed**) hurt the feelings of, insult

offended v ▷ offend

offender n (pl **-s**) person who commits a crime

offenders n ▷ offender

offending v ▷ offend

offends v ▷ offend

offer v (**-s**, **-ing**, **-ed**) present (something) for acceptance or rejection ▶ n (pl **-s**) instance of offering something

offered v ▷ offer

offering n (pl **-s**) thing offered ▶ v ▷ offer

offerings n ▷ offering

offers v, n ▷ offer

offhand adj casual, curt ▶ adv without preparation

office n (pl **-s**) room or building where people work at desks

officer n (pl **-s**) person in authority in the armed services

officers n ▷ officer

offices n ▷ office

official adj of a position of authority ▶ n (pl **-s**) person who holds a position of authority ▶ **officially** adv

officially adv ▷ official

officials n ▷ official

offing n (pl **-s**) area of the sea visible from the shore

offings n ▷ offing

offs n ▷ off

offset v (**-sets**, **-setting**, **-set**) cancel out, compensate for

offsets n ▷ offset

offsetting v ▷ offset

offshoot n (pl **-s**) something developed from something else

offshoots n ▷ offshoot

offside adj, adv SPORT (positioned) illegally ahead of the ball

oft adv poetic often

often adv frequently, much of the time

ogle v (**-les**, **-ling**, **-led**) stare at (someone) lustfully

ogled v ▷ ogle

ogles v ▷ ogle

ogling v ▷ ogle

ogre n (pl **-s**) giant that eats human flesh

ogres n ▷ ogre

oh interj exclamation of surprise,

pain, etc

ohm n (pl **-s**) unit of electrical resistance

ohms n ▷ **ohm**

oi interj. Oi is something people shout to attract attention. This is a good word to remember, as it combines two of the most common letters in the game without using any consonants. Oi scores 2 points.

oil n (pl **-s**) viscous liquid, insoluble in water and usu. flammable ▶ pl oil-based paints used in art ▶ v (**-s, -ing, -ed**) lubricate (a machine) with oil ▷ adj **oily** (**-lier, -liest**)

oiled v ▷ **oil**

oilfield n (**-s**) area containing oil reserves

oilfields n ▷ **oilfield**

oilier adj ▷ **oil**

oiliest adj ▷ **oil**

oiling v ▷ **oil**

oils n, v ▷ **oil**

oilskin n (pl **-s**) (garment made from) waterproof material

oilskins n ▷ **oilskin**

oily adj ▷ **oil**

ointment n (pl **-s**) greasy substance used for healing skin or as a cosmetic

ointments n ▷ **ointment**

okapi n (pl **-s**) African animal related to the giraffe but with a shorter neck

okapis n ▷ **okapi**

okay informal interj expression of approval ▶ v (**-s, -ing, -ed**) approve (something) ▶ n (pl **-s**) approval

okayed v ▷ **okay**

okaying v ▷ **okay**

okays v, n ▷ **okay**

okra n (pl **-s**) tropical plant with edible green pods

okras n ▷ **okra**

old adj (**-er, -est**) having lived or existed for a long time

olden adj old

older adj ▷ **old**

oldest adj ▷ **old**

oldie n (pl **-s**) informal old but popular

song or film

oldies n ▷ **oldie**

oleander n (pl **-s**) Mediterranean flowering evergreen shrub

oleanders n ▷ **oleander**

olive n (pl **-s**) small green or black fruit used as food or pressed for its oil ▶ adj greyish-green

olives n ▷ **olive**

omelette n (pl **-s**) dish of eggs beaten and fried

omelettes n ▷ **omelette**

omen n (pl **-s**) happening or object thought to foretell success or misfortune

omens n ▷ **omen**

ominous adj worrying, seeming to foretell misfortune

omission n ▷ **omit**

omissions n ▷ **omit**

omit v (**-s, -tting, -tted**) leave out ▷ **omission** n (pl **-s**)

omits v ▷ **omit**

omitted v ▷ **omit**

omitting v ▷ **omit**

omnibus n (pl **-es**) several books or TV or radio programmes made into one

omnibuses n ▷ **omnibus**

omnivore n (pl **-s**) omnivorous animal

omnivores n ▷ **omnivore**

on prep indicating position above, attachment, closeness, etc ▶ adv in operation ▶ adj operating ▶ n CRICKET side of the field on which the batsman stands

once adv on one occasion ▶ conj as soon as

oncogene n (pl **-s**) gene that can cause cancer when abnormally activated

oncogenes n ▷ **oncogene**

oncoming adj approaching from the front

one adj single, lone ▶ n (pl **-s**) number or figure 1 ▶ pron any person

oneness n (pl **-es**) unity

onenesses n ▷ **oneness**

onerous adj (of a task) difficult to carry out

ones n ▷ one

oneself pron ▷ one

ongoing adj in progress, continuing

onion n (pl -s) strongly flavoured edible bulb

onions n ▷ onion

online adj (of a computer) directly controlled by a central processor

onlooker n (pl -s) person who watches without taking part

onlookers n ▷ onlooker

only adj alone of its kind ▸ adv exclusively ▸ conj but

onset n (pl -s) beginning

onsets n ▷ onset

onto prep to a position on

ontological adj ▷ ontology

ontologies n ▷ ontology

ontology n (pl -gies) branch of philosophy concerned with existence ▷ **ontological** adj

onus n (pl -es) responsibility or burden

onuses n ▷ onus

onward adj directed or moving forward ▸ adv (also **onwards**) ahead, forward

onwards adv ▷ onward

onyx n (pl -es) type of quartz with coloured layers

onyxes n ▷ onyx

| **oo** n (**oos**). Oo is a Scots word for **wool**. Oo is a good word to remember, as it combines two of the most common letters in the game without using any consonants. Oo scores two points.

oodles pl n informal great quantities

ooze[1] v (-zes, -zing, -zed) flow slowly ▸ n (pl -s) sluggish flow ▷ **oozy** adj (-zier, -ziest)

ooze[2] n (-s) soft mud at the bottom of a lake or river

oozed v ▷ ooze

oozes v, n ▷ ooze[1, 2]

oozier adj ▷ ooze[1]

ooziest adj ▷ ooze[1]

oozing v ▷ ooze[1]

oozy adj ▷ ooze[1]

opacities n ▷ opaque

opacity n ▷ opaque

opal n (pl -s) iridescent precious stone

opals n ▷ opal

opaque adj (-r, -st) not able to be seen through, not transparent ▷ **opacity** n (-ties)

opaquer adj ▷ opaque

opaquest adj ▷ opaque

open adj (-er, -est) not closed ▸ v (-s, -ing, -ed) (cause to) become open ▸ n (pl -s) SPORT competition which all may enter

opened v ▷ open

opener n instrument for opening containers

openest adj ▷ open

opening n (pl -s) opportunity ▸ adj first ▸ v ▷ open

openings n ▷ opening

openly adv without concealment

opens v, n ▷ open

opera[1] n (pl -s) drama in which the text is sung to an orchestral accompaniment ▷ **operatic** adj

opera[2] n ▷ opus

operas n ▷ opera[1]

operate v (-tes, -ting, -ted) (cause to) work ▷ **operator** n (pl -s)

operated v ▷ operate

operates v ▷ operate

operatic adj ▷ opera[1]

operating v ▷ operate

operator n ▷ operate

operators n ▷ operate

operetta n (pl -s) light-hearted comic opera

operettas n ▷ operetta

opiate n (pl -s) narcotic drug containing opium

opiates n ▷ opiate

opine v (-nes, -ning, -ned) old-fashioned express an opinion

opined v ▷ opine

opines v ▷ opine

opining v ▷ opine

opinion n (pl -s) personal belief or judgment

opinions n ▷ opinion

opium n (pl -s) addictive narcotic drug made from poppy seeds
  opiums n ▷ opium

opossum n (pl -s) small marsupial of America or Australasia
  opossums n ▷ opossum

opponent n (pl -s) person one is working against in a contest, battle, or argument
  opponents n ▷ opponent

oppose v (-ses, -sing, -sed) work against
  opposed v ▷ oppose
  opposes v ▷ oppose
  opposing v ▷ oppose

opposite adj situated on the other side ▶ n (pl -s) person or thing that is opposite ▶ prep facing ▶ adv on the other side
  opposites n ▷ opposite

oppress v (-es, -ing, -ed) control by cruelty or force > **oppression** n (pl -s) > **oppressor** n (pl -s)
  oppressed v ▷ oppress
  oppresses v ▷ oppress
  oppressing v ▷ oppress
  oppression n ▷ oppress
  oppressions n ▷ oppress
  oppressor n ▷ oppress
  oppressors n ▷ oppress

opt v (-s, -ing, -ed) show a preference, choose
  opted v ▷ opt

optic adj relating to the eyes or sight > **optical** adj
  optical adj ▷ optic

optician n (pl -s) (also **ophthalmic optician**) person qualified to prescribe glasses (also **dispensing optician**)
  opticians n ▷ optician

optics n science of sight and light

optima n ▷ optimum

optimal adj ▷ optimum

optimism n (pl -s) tendency to take the most hopeful view > **optimist** n (pl -s) > **optimistic** adj > **optimistically** adv
  optimisms n ▷ optimism

optimist n ▷ optimism

optimistic adj ▷ optimism

optimistically adv ▷ optimism

optimists n ▷ optimism

optimize v (-zes, -zing, -zed) make the most of
  optimized v ▷ optimize
  optimizes v ▷ optimize
  optimizing v ▷ optimize

optimum n (pl -ma, -mums) best possible conditions ▶ adj most favourable > **optimal** adj
  optimums n ▷ optimum

opting v ▷ opt

option n (pl -s) choice

optional adj possible but not compulsory
  options n ▷ option

opts v ▷ opt

opulence n ▷ opulent

opulences n ▷ opulent

opulent adj having or indicating wealth > **opulence** n (-s)

opus n (pl **opuses**, **opera**) artistic creation, esp. a musical work
  opuses n ▷ opus

or conj used to join alternatives

oracle n (pl -s) shrine of an ancient god > **oracular** adj
  oracles n ▷ oracle
  oracular adj ▷ oracle

oral adj spoken ▶ n (pl -s) spoken examination > **orally** adv
  orally adv ▷ oral
  orals n ▷ oral

orange n (pl -s) reddish-yellow citrus fruit ▶ adj reddish-yellow
  orangeries n ▷ orangery

orangery n (pl -ries) greenhouse for growing orange trees
  oranges n ▷ orange

oration n (pl -s) formal speech
  orations n ▷ oration

orator n (pl -s) skilful public speaker
  oratorical adj ▷ oratory
  oratories n ▷ oratory¹, ²

oratorio n (pl -s) musical composition for choir and orchestra, usu. with a

religious theme
oratorios n ▷ oratorio
orators n ▷ orator
oratory¹ n (pl -ries) art of making speeches > **oratorical** adj
oratory² n (pl -ries) small private chapel
orb n (pl -s) ceremonial decorated sphere with a cross on top, carried by a monarch
orbit n (pl -s) curved path of a planet, satellite, or spacecraft around another body ▶ v (-s, -ing, -ed) move in an orbit around > **orbital** adj
orbital adj ▷ orbit
orbited v ▷ orbit
orbiting v ▷ orbit
orbits n, v ▷ orbit
orbs n ▷ orb
orchard n (pl -s) area where fruit trees are grown
orchards n ▷ orchard
orchid n (pl -s) plant with flowers that have unusual lip-shaped petals
orchids n ▷ orchid
ordain v (-s, -ing, -ed) make (someone) a member of the clergy
ordained v ▷ ordain
ordaining v ▷ ordain
ordains n ▷ ordain
ordeal n (pl -s) painful or difficult experience
ordeals n ▷ ordeal
order n (pl -s) instruction to be carried out ▶ v (-s, -ing, -ed) give an instruction to
ordered v ▷ order
ordering v ▷ order
orderlies n ▷ orderly
orderliness n ▷ orderly
orderlinesses n ▷ orderly
orderly adj well-organized ▶ n (pl -lies) male hospital attendant > **orderliness** n (pl -es)
orders n, v ▷ order
ordinarily adv ▷ ordinary
ordinary adj usual or normal > **ordinarily** adv

ordnance n (pl -s) weapons and military supplies
ordnances n ▷ ordnance
ordure n (pl -s) excrement
ordures n ▷ ordure
ore n (pl -s) (rock containing) a mineral which yields metal
oregano n (pl -s) sweet-smelling herb used in cooking
oreganos n ▷ oregano
ores n ▷ ore
organ n (pl -s) part of an animal or plant that has a particular function, such as the heart or lungs
organdie n (pl -s) fine cotton fabric
organdies n ▷ organdie
organic adj of or produced from animals or plants CHEM > **organically** adv
organically adv ▷ organic
organism n (-s) any living animal or plant
organisms n ▷ organism
organist n (pl -s) organ player
organists n ▷ organist
organize v (-zes, -zing, -zed) make arrangements for > **organizer** n (pl -s)
organized v ▷ organize
organizer n ▷ organize
organizers n ▷ organize
organizes v ▷ organize
organizing v ▷ organize
organs n ▷ organ
orgasm n (pl -s) most intense point of sexual pleasure > **orgasmic** adj
orgasmic adj ▷ orgasm
orgasms n ▷ orgasm
orgiastic adj ▷ orgy
orgies n ▷ orgy
orgy n (pl -gies) party involving promiscuous sexual activity > **orgiastic** adj
orient¹, **orientate** v (-s, -ing, -ed) position (oneself) according to one's surroundings > **orientation** n (pl -s)
orient² n (pl -s) lit east > **oriental** adj
oriental adj ▷ orient²

orientate v ▷ **orient**
orientated v ▷ **orient**
orientates v ▷ **orient**
orientating v ▷ **orient**
orientation n ▷ **orient**
orientations n ▷ **orient**
oriented v ▷ **orient**
orienting v ▷ **orient**
orients n ▷ **orient**
orifice n (pl -s) opening or hole
orifices n ▷ **orifice**
origami n (pl -s) Japanese decorative
art of paper folding
origamis n ▷ **origami**
origin n (pl -s) point from which
something develops
original adj first or earliest ▶ n (pl
-s) first version, from which others
are copied > **originality** n (pl -ies)
> **originally** adv
originalities n ▷ **original**
originality n ▷ **original**
originally adv ▷ **original**
originals n ▷ **original**
origins n ▷ **origin**
oriole n (pl -s) tropical or American
songbird
orioles n ▷ **oriole**
ormolu n (pl -s) gold-coloured alloy
used for decoration
ormolus n ▷ **ormolu**
ornament n (pl -s) decorative
object ▶ v (-s, -ing, -ed) decorate
> **ornamental** adj > **ornamentation** n
(pl -s)
ornamental adj ▷ **ornament**
ornamentation n ▷ **ornament**
ornamentations n ▷ **ornament**
ornamented v ▷ **ornament**
ornamenting v ▷ **ornament**
ornaments n, v ▷ **ornament**
ornate adj highly decorated, elaborate
orphan n (pl -s) child whose parents
are dead
orphaned adj having no living parents
orphans n ▷ **orphan**
orreries n ▷ **orrery**

orrery n (pl -ries) mechanical model of
the solar system
orris n (pl -es) kind of iris (also **orris
root**)
orrises n ▷ **orris**
orthodox adj conforming to
established views > **orthodoxy** n
(pl -xies)
orthodoxies n ▷ **orthodox**
orthodoxy n ▷ **orthodox**
oryx n (pl -es) large African antelope
oryxes n ▷ **oryx**

> **os** n (**ossa**). Os is a technical word
> for **bone**. This word won't score
> many points on its own, but will
> allow you to connect a word
> beginning with O to one ending
> in S (e.g. most plurals). Os scores
> 2 points.

osier n (pl -s) willow tree
osiers n ▷ **osier**
osmium n (pl -s) CHEM heaviest known
metallic element
osmiums n ▷ **osmium**
osmoses n ▷ **osmosis**
osmosis n (pl -ses) movement of a
liquid through a membrane from
a lower to a higher concentration
> **osmotic** adj
osmotic adj ▷ **osmosis**
osprey n (pl -s) large fish-eating bird
of prey
ospreys n ▷ **osprey**
ossification n ▷ **ossify**
ossifications n ▷ **ossify**
ossified v ▷ **ossify**
ossifies v ▷ **ossify**
ossify v (-fies, -fying, -fied) (cause to)
become bone, harden > **ossification** n
(pl -s)
ossifying v ▷ **ossify**
ostrich n (pl -es) large African bird that
runs fast but cannot fly
ostriches n ▷ **ostrich**
other adj remaining in a group of
which one or some have been specified
▶ n (pl -s) other person or thing
others n ▷ **other**

otiose adj not useful

otter n (pl **-s**) small brown freshwater mammal that eats fish
otters n ▷ otter

ottoman n (pl **-mans**) storage chest with a padded lid for use as a seat
ottomans n ▷ ottoman

ou n (**ous**). Ou is a South African slang word for a man. This word doesn't score many points, but is very useful when you are trying to form words in more than one direction. Ou scores 2 points.

ouch interj exclamation of sudden pain

ought v used to express: obligation

ounce n (pl **-s**) unit of weight equal to one sixteenth of a pound (28.4 grams)
ounces n ▷ ounce

our adj belonging to us

ours pron thing(s) belonging to us
ourselves pron ▷ we

ousel n (pl **-s**) ▷ dipper
ousels n ▷ ousel

oust v (**-s**, **-ing**, **-ed**) force (someone) out, expel
ousted v ▷ oust
ousting v ▷ oust
ousts v ▷ oust

out adv, adj denoting movement or distance away from, a state of being used up or extinguished, public availability, etc ▶ v (**-s**, **-ing**, **-ed**) informal name (a public figure) as being homosexual

outback n (pl **-s**) remote bush country of Australia
outbacks n ▷ outback

outbid v (**-bids**, **-bidding**, **-bid**, **-bidden**) offer a higher price than
outbidden v ▷ outbid
outbidding v ▷ outbid
outbids v ▷ outbid

outbreak n (pl **-s**) sudden occurrence (of something unpleasant)
outbreaks n ▷ outbreak

outburst n (pl **-s**) sudden expression of emotion
outbursts n ▷ outburst

outcast n (pl **-s**) person rejected by a particular group
outcasts n ▷ outcast

outclass v (**-es**, **-ing**, **-ed**) surpass in quality
outclassed v ▷ outclass
outclasses v ▷ outclass
outclassing v ▷ outclass

outcome n (pl **-s**) result
outcomes n ▷ outcome

outcries n ▷ outcry

outcrop n (pl **-s**) part of a rock formation that sticks out of the earth
outcrops n ▷ outcrop

outcry n (pl **-cries**) vehement or widespread protest

outdid v ▷ outdo

outdo v (**-does**, **-doing**, **-did**, **-done**) surpass in performance
outdoes v ▷ outdo
outdoing v ▷ outdo
outdone v ▷ outdo

outdoor adj ▷ outdoors

outdoors adv in(to) the open air ▶ n (pl the open air ▷ **outdoor** adj
outed v ▷ out

outer adj on the outside

outface v (**-ces**, **-cing**, **-ced**) subdue or disconcert (someone) by staring
outfaced v ▷ outface
outfaces v ▷ outface
outfacing v ▷ outface

outfield n (pl **-s**) CRICKET area far from the pitch
outfields n ▷ outfield

outfit n (pl **-s**) matching set of clothes
outfits n ▷ outfit

outflank v (**-s**, **-ing**, **-ed**) get round the side of (an enemy army)
outflanked v ▷ outflank
outflanking v ▷ outflank
outflanks v ▷ outflank

outgoing adj leaving
outgrew v ▷ outgrow

outgrow v (**-grows**, **-growing**, **-grew**, **-grown**) become too large or too old for
outgrowing v ▷ outgrow

outgrown v ▷ outgrow

outgrows v ▷ outgrow

outhouse n (pl -s) building near a main building

outhouses n ▷ outhouse

outing n (pl -s) leisure trip ▶ v ▷ out

outings n ▷ outing

> **outjinx** v (outjinxes, outjinxing, outjinxed). Outjinx means to outmanoeuvre. If someone else plays **jinx**, you can outjinx them by adding O, U and T! If you can form the whole word using all of your letters, you'll get a 50-point bonus. Outjinx scores 21 points.

outlaw n (pl -s) HIST criminal deprived of legal protection, bandit ▶ v (-s, -ing, -ed) make illegal

outlawed v ▷ outlaw

outlawing v ▷ outlaw

outlaws n, v ▷ outlaw

outlay n (pl -s) expenditure

outlays n ▷ outlay

outlet n (pl -s) means of expressing emotion

outlets n ▷ outlet

outline n (pl -s) short general explanation ▶ v (-nes, -ning, -ned) summarize

outlined v ▷ outline

outlines n, v ▷ outline

outlining v ▷ outline

outlook n (pl -s) attitude

outlooks n ▷ outlook

outlying adj distant from the main area

outmoded adj no longer fashionable or accepted

outpost n (pl -s) outlying settlement

outposts n ▷ outpost

output n (pl -s) amount produced ▶ v (-puts, -putting, -putted) COMPUTERS produce (data) at the end of a process

outputs n, v ▷ output

outputted v ▷ output

outputting v ▷ output

outrage n (pl -s) great moral indignation ▶ v (-ges, -ging, -ged)

offend morally

outraged v ▷ outrage

outrages n, v ▷ outrage

outraging v ▷ outrage

outran v ▷ outrun

outré adj shockingly eccentric

outrider n (pl -s) motorcyclist acting as an escort

outriders n ▷ outrider

outright adj, adv absolute(ly)

outrun v (-runs, -running, -ran, -run) run faster than

outrunning v ▷ outrun

outruns v ▷ outrun

outs v ▷ out

outset n (pl -s) beginning

outsets n ▷ outset

outshine v (-shines, -shining, -shone) surpass (someone) in excellence

outshines v ▷ outshine

outshining v ▷ outshine

outshone v ▷ outshine

outside prep, adj, adv indicating movement to or position on the exterior ▶ adj unlikely ▶ n (pl -s) external area or surface

outsider n (pl -s) person outside a specific group

outsiders n ▷ outsider

outsides n ▷ outside

outsize, outsized adj larger than normal

outsized adj ▷ outsize

outsmart v (-s, -ing, -ed) informal outwit

outsmarted v ▷ outsmart

outsmarting v ▷ outsmart

outsmarts v ▷ outsmart

outspan v (-s, -nning, -nned) S AFR relax

outspanned v ▷ outspan

outspanning v ▷ outspan

outspans v ▷ outspan

outstrip v (-s, -pping, -pped) surpass

outstripped v ▷ outstrip

outstripping v ▷ outstrip

outstrips v ▷ outstrip

outtake n (pl -**s**) unreleased take from a recording session, film, or TV programme
outtakes n ▷ **outtake**

outward adj apparent ▶ adv (also **outwards**) away from somewhere > **outwardly** adv
outwardly adv ▷ **outward**

outweigh v (-**s**, -**ing**, -**ed**) be more important, significant, or influential than
outweighed v ▷ **outweigh**
outweighing v ▷ **outweigh**
outweighs v ▷ **outweigh**

outwit v (-**s**, -**tting**, -**tted**) get the better of (someone) by cunning
outwits v ▷ **outwit**
outwitted v ▷ **outwit**
outwitting v ▷ **outwit**

ouzel n (pl -**s**) ▷ **dipper**
ouzels n ▷ **ouzel**
ova n ▷ **ovum**

oval adj egg-shaped ▶ n (pl -**s**) anything that is oval in shape
ovals n ▷ **oval**

ovarian adj ▷ **ovary**
ovaries n ▷ **ovary**

ovary n (pl -**ries**) female egg-producing organ > **ovarian** adj

ovation n (pl -**s**) enthusiastic round of applause
ovations n ▷ **ovation**

oven n (pl -**s**) heated compartment or container for cooking or for drying or firing ceramics
ovens n ▷ **oven**

over prep, adv indicating position on the top of, movement to the other side of, amount greater than, etc ▶ adj finished ▶ n (pl -**s**) CRICKET series of six balls bowled from one end

overall adj, adv in total ▶ n (pl -**s**) coat-shaped protective garment ▶ pl protective garment consisting of trousers with a jacket or bib and braces attached
overalls n ▷ **overall**

overarm adj, adv (thrown) with the arm above the shoulder

overawe v (-**wes**, -**wing**, -**wed**) affect (someone) with an overpowering sense of awe
overawed v ▷ **overawe**
overawes v ▷ **overawe**
overawing v ▷ **overawe**
overcame v ▷ **overcome**

overcast adj (of the sky) covered by clouds

overcoat n (pl -**s**) heavy coat
overcoats n ▷ **overcoat**

overcome v (-**comes**, -**coming**, -**came**, -**come**) gain control over after an effort
overcomes v ▷ **overcome**
overcoming v ▷ **overcome**
overdid v ▷ **overdo**

overdo v (-**does**, -**doing**, -**did**, -**done**) do to excess
overdoes v ▷ **overdo**
overdoing v ▷ **overdo**
overdone v ▷ **overdo**

overdose n (pl -**s**) excessive dose of a drug ▶ v (-**ses**, -**sing**, -**sed**) take an overdose
overdosed n ▷ **overdose**
overdoses n, v ▷ **overdose**
overdosing v ▷ **overdose**

overdraw v (-**draws**, -**drawing**, -**drew**, -**drawn**) withdraw more money than is in (one's bank account)
overdrawing v ▷ **overdraw**
overdrawn v ▷ **overdraw**
overdraws v ▷ **overdraw**
overdrew v ▷ **overdraw**

overdue adj still due after the time allowed

overhaul v (-**s**, -**ing**, -**ed**) examine and repair ▶ n (pl -**s**) examination and repair
overhauled v ▷ **overhaul**
overhauling v ▷ **overhaul**
overhauls v, n ▷ **overhaul**

overhead adv, adj above one's head

overhear v (-**hears**, -**hearing**, -**heard**) hear (a speaker or remark) unintentionally or without the

speaker's knowledge
overheard v ▷ **overhear**
overhearing v ▷ **overhear**
overhears v ▷ **overhear**
overkill n (pl **-s**) treatment that is greater than required
overkills n ▷ **overkill**
overland adj, adv by land
overlap v (**-s, -pping, -pped**) share part of the same space or period of time (as) ▶ n (pl **-s**) area overlapping
overlapped v ▷ **overlap**
overlapping v ▷ **overlap**
overlaps v, n ▷ **overlap**
overleaf adv on the back of the current page
overlook v (**-s, -ing, -ed**) fail to notice
overlooked v ▷ **overlook**
overlooking v ▷ **overlook**
overlooks v ▷ **overlook**
overly adv excessively
overran v ▷ **overrun**
overridden v ▷ **override**
override v (**-rides, -riding, -rode, -ridden**) overrule
overrides v ▷ **override**
overriding v ▷ **override**
overrode v ▷ **override**
overrule v (**-les, -ling, -led**) reverse the decision of (a person with less power)
overruled v ▷ **overrule**
overrules v ▷ **overrule**
overruling v ▷ **overrule**
overrun v (**-runs, -running, -ran, -run**) spread over (a place) rapidly
overrunning v ▷ **overrun**
overruns v ▷ **overrun**
overs n ▷ **over**
oversaw v ▷ **oversee**
overseas adv, adj to, of, or from a distant country
oversee v (**-sees, -seeing, -saw, -seen**) watch over from a position of authority > **overseer** n (**-s**)
overseeing v ▷ **oversee**
overseen v ▷ **oversee**
overseer n ▷ **oversee**

overseers n ▷ **oversee**
oversees v ▷ **oversee**
overstay v (**-s, -ing, -ed**) stay longer than one's host or hostess would like
overstayed v ▷ **overstay**
overstaying v ▷ **overstay**
overstays v ▷ **overstay**
overt adj open, not hidden > **overtly** adv
overtake v (**-takes, -taking, -took, -taken**) move past (a vehicle or person) travelling in the same direction
overtaken v ▷ **overtake**
overtakes v ▷ **overtake**
overtaking v ▷ **overtake**
overtime n, adv (pl **-s**) (paid work done) in addition to one's normal working hours
overtimes n ▷ **overtime**
overtly adv ▷ **overt**
overtone n (pl **-s**) additional meaning
overtones n ▷ **overtone**
overtook v ▷ **overtake**
overture n (pl **-s**) MUSIC orchestral introduction ▶ pl opening moves in a new relationship
overtures n ▷ **overture**
overturn v (**-s, -ing, -ed**) turn upside down
overturned v ▷ **overturn**
overturning v ▷ **overturn**
overturns v ▷ **overturn**
ovoid adj egg-shaped
ovulate v (**-tes, -ting, -ted**) produce or release an egg cell from an ovary > **ovulation** n (**-s**)
ovulated v ▷ **ovulate**
ovulates v ▷ **ovulate**
ovulating v ▷ **ovulate**
ovulation n ▷ **ovulate**
ovulations n ▷ **ovulate**
ovum n (pl **ova**) unfertilized egg cell
owe v (**owes, owing, owed**) be obliged to pay (a sum of money) to (a person)
owed v ▷ **owe**
owes v ▷ **owe**
owing v ▷ **owe**

owl n (pl **-s**) night bird of prey
> **owlish** adj
  owlish adj ▷ **owl**
  owls n ▷ **owl**

own adj used to emphasize possession
▶ v (**-s**, **-ing**, **-ed**) possess > **owner** n (pl
-s) > **ownership** n (pl **-s**)
  owned v ▷ **own**
  owner n ▷ **own**
  owners n ▷ **own**
  ownership n ▷ **own**
  ownerships n ▷ **own**
  owning v ▷ **own**
  owns v ▷ **own**

ox n (pl **oxen**) castrated bull
  oxen n ▷ **ox**

oxide n (pl **-s**) compound of oxygen and
one other element
  oxides n ▷ **oxide**

oxidize v (**-zes**, **-zing**, **-zed**) combine

chemically with oxygen, as in burning
or rusting
  oxidized v ▷ **oxidize**
  oxidizes v ▷ **oxidize**
  oxidizing v ▷ **oxidize**

oxygen n (pl **-s**) CHEM gaseous element
essential to life and combustion
  oxygens n ▷ **oxygen**
  oxymora n ▷ **oxymoron**

oxymoron n (pl **-mora**, **-morons**)
figure of speech that combines two
apparently contradictory ideas
  oxymorons n ▷ **oxymoron**

oyez interj HIST shouted three times by
a public crier, listen

oyster n (pl **-s**) edible shellfish
  oysters n ▷ **oyster**

ozone n (pl **-s**) strong-smelling form
of oxygen
  ozones n ▷ **ozone**

Pp

P forms a two-letter word in front of every vowel except U, which makes it very useful for joining a new word to one already on the board. It also forms several three-letter words with X: **pax, pix, pox** (12 points each) and **pyx** (15).

pa n (pl **-s**) NZ (formerly) a fortified Maori settlement

pace n (pl **-s**) single step in walking ▶ v (**-ces, -cing, -ced**) walk up and down, esp. in anxiety

paced v ▷ **pace**

paces n, v ▷ **pace**

pacification n ▷ **pacify**

pacifications n ▷ **pacify**

pacified v ▷ **pacify**

pacifies v ▷ **pacify**

pacifism n ▷ **pacifist**

pacifisms n ▷ **pacifist**

pacifist n (pl **-s**) person who refuses on principle to take part in war > **pacifism** n (pl **-s**)

pacifists n ▷ **pacifist**

pacify v (**-fies, -fying, -fied**) soothe, calm > **pacification** n (pl **-s**)

pacifying v ▷ **pacify**

pacing v ▷ **pace**

pack v (**-s, -ing, -ed**) put (clothes etc) together in a suitcase or bag ▶ n (pl **-s**) bag carried on a person's or animal's back

package n (pl **-s**) small parcel ▶ v (**-ges, -ging, -ged**) put into a package > **packaging** n (pl **-s**)

packaged v ▷ **package**

packages n, v ▷ **package**

packaging v, n ▷ **package**

packagings n ▷ **package**

packed v ▷ **pack**

packet n (pl **-s**) small container (and contents)

packets n ▷ **packet**

packing v ▷ **pack**

packs v, n ▷ **pack**

pact n (pl **-s**) formal agreement

pacts n ▷ **pact**

pad n (pl **-s**) piece of soft material used for protection, support, absorption of liquid, etc ▶ v (**padding, padded**) protect or fill with soft material

padded v ▷ **pad**

paddies n ▷ **paddy**

padding n (pl **-s**) soft material used to pad something ▶ v ▷ **pad**

paddings n ▷ **pad**

paddle¹ n (pl **-s**) short oar with a broad blade at one or each end ▶ v (**-les, -ling, -led**) move (a canoe etc) with a paddle

paddle² v (**-les, -ling, -led**) walk barefoot in shallow water

paddled v ▷ **paddle¹, ²**

paddles n, v ▷ **paddle¹, ²**

paddling v ▷ **paddle¹, ²**

paddock n (pl **-s**) small field or enclosure for horses

paddocks n ▷ **paddock**

paddy n (pl **-ies**) BRIT informal fit of temper

padlock n (pl **-s**) detachable lock with a hinged hoop fastened over a ring on the object to be secured

padlocks n ▷ **padlock**

padre n (pl **-s**) chaplain to the armed

forces

padres n ▷ **padre**

pads v, n ▷ **pad**

paean n (pl -s) song of triumph or thanksgiving

paeans n ▷ **paean**

paella n (pl -s) Spanish dish of rice, chicken, shellfish, and vegetables

paellas n ▷ **paella**

pagan n (pl -s) ▶ adj (person) not belonging to one of the world's main religions

pagans n ▷ **pagan**

page¹ n (pl -s) (one side of) a sheet of paper forming a book etc

page² n (also **pageboy**) small boy who attends a bride at her wedding ▶ v (-ges, -ging, -ged) summon (someone) by bleeper or loudspeaker, in order to pass on a message

pageant n (pl -s) parade or display of people in costume, usu. illustrating a scene from history > **pageantry** n (pl -ries)

pageantries n ▷ **pageant**

pageantry n ▷ **pageant**

pageants n ▷ **pageant**

paged v ▷ **page²**

pages n, v ▷ **page¹, ²**

paging v ▷ **page²**

pagoda n (pl -s) pyramid-shaped Asian temple or tower

pagodas n ▷ **pagoda**

paid v ▷ **pay**

pail n (pl -s) (contents of) a bucket

pails n ▷ **pail**

pain n (pl -s) physical or mental suffering ▶ pl trouble, effort > **painful** adj > **painfully** adv > **painless** adj > **painlessly** adv

painful adj ▷ **pain**

painfully adv ▷ **pain**

painless adj ▷ **pain**

painlessly adv ▷ **pain**

pains n ▷ **pain**

paint n (pl -s) coloured substance, spread on a surface with a brush or roller ▶ v (-s, -ing, -ed) colour or

coat with paint ▶ **painter** n (pl -s) > **painting** n (pl -s)

painted v ▷ **paint**

painter¹ n ▷ **paint**

painter² n (pl -s) rope at the front of a boat, for tying it up

painters n ▷ **paint painter²**

painting v, n ▷ **paint**

paintings n ▷ **paint**

pair n (pl -s) set of two things matched for use together ▶ v (-s, -ing, -ed) group or be grouped in twos

paired v ▷ **pair**

pairing v ▷ **pair**

pairs n, v ▷ **pair**

pakeha n (pl -s) NZ New Zealander who is not of Maori descent

pakehas n ▷ **pakeha**

pal n (pl -s) informal old-fashioned in NZ friend

palace n (pl -s) residence of a king, bishop, etc

palaces n ▷ **palace**

palagi n (pl -s) NZ Samoan name for a pakeha

palagis n ▷ **palagi**

palate n (pl -s) roof of the mouth

palates n ▷ **palate**

palatial adj like a palace, magnificent

palaver n (pl -s) time-wasting fuss

palavers n ▷ **palaver**

pale¹ adj (-er, -est) light, whitish ▶ v (-les, -ling, -led) become pale

pale² n (pl -s) wooden or metal post used in fences

paled v ▷ **pale¹**

paler adj ▷ **pale¹**

pales v ▷ **pale¹, ²**

palest adj ▷ **pale¹**

palette n (pl -s) artist's flat board for mixing colours on

palettes n ▷ **palette**

paling n (pl -s) wooden or metal post used in fences ▶ n ▷ **pale**

palings n ▷ **paling**

palisade n (pl -s) fence made of wooden posts driven into the ground

palisades n ▷ **palisade**

pall¹ n (pl -s) cloth spread over a coffin

pall² v (-s, -ing, -ed) become boring

palled v ▷ **pall²**

pallet¹ n (pl -s) portable platform for storing and moving goods

pallet² n straw-filled mattress or bed

pallets n ▷ **pallet¹, ²**

palliate v (-tes, -ting, -ted) lessen the severity of (something) without curing it

palliated v ▷ **palliate**

palliates v ▷ **palliate**

palliating v ▷ **palliate**

pallid adj (-er, -est) pale, esp. because ill or weak > **pallor** n (pl -s)

pallider adj ▷ **pallid**

pallidest adj ▷ **pallid**

pallier adj ▷ **pally**

palliest adj ▷ **pally**

palling v ▷ **pall²**

pallor n ▷ **pallid**

pallors n ▷ **pallid**

palls n ▷ **pall¹** ▶ v ▷ **pall²**

pally adj (-lier, -liest) informal on friendly terms

palm¹ n (pl -s) inner surface of the hand

palm² n (pl -s) tropical tree with long pointed leaves growing out of the top of a straight trunk

palms n ▷ **palm¹, ²**

palmtop adj (of a computer) small enough to be held in the hand ▶ n (pl -s) computer small enough to be held in the hand

palmtops n ▷ **palmtop**

palomino n (pl -s) gold-coloured horse with a white mane and tail

palominos n ▷ **palomino**

palpable adj obvious > **palpably** adv

palpably adv ▷ **palpable**

palpate v (-tes, -ting, -ted) MED examine (an area of the body) by touching

palpated v ▷ **palpate**

palpates v ▷ **palpate**

palpating v ▷ **palpate**

pals n ▷ **pal**

palsied adj affected with palsy

palsies n ▷ **palsy**

palsy n (pl -sies) paralysis

paltrier adj ▷ **paltry**

paltriest adj ▷ **paltry**

paltry adj (-rier, -riest) insignificant

pampas pl n vast grassy plains in S America

pamper v (-s, -ing, -ed) treat (someone) with great indulgence, spoil

pampered v ▷ **pamper**

pampering v ▷ **pamper**

pampers v ▷ **pamper**

pamphlet n (pl -s) thin paper-covered booklet

pamphlets n ▷ **pamphlet**

pan¹ n (pl -s) wide long-handled metal container used in cooking ▶ v (-s, -nning, -nned) sift gravel from (a river) in a pan to search for gold

pan² v (-s, -nning, -nned) (of a film camera) be moved slowly so as to cover a whole scene or follow a moving object

panacea n (pl -s) remedy for all diseases or problems

panaceas n ▷ **panacea**

panache n (pl -s) confident elegant style

panaches n ▷ **panache**

pancake n (pl -s) thin flat circle of fried batter

pancakes n ▷ **pancake**

pancreas n (pl -es) large gland behind the stomach that produces insulin and helps digestion > **pancreatic** adj

pancreases n ▷ **pancreas**

pancreatic adj ▷ **pancreas**

panda n (pl -s) large black-and-white bearlike mammal from China

pandas n ▷ **panda**

pandemic adj (of a disease) occurring over a wide area

pander¹ v (-s, -ing, -ed) (foll. by to) indulge (a person his or her desires)

pander² n (pl -s) old-fashioned person who procures a sexual partner for someone

pandered v ▷ pander

pandering v ▷ pander

panders v, n ▷ pander[1, 2]

pane n (pl **-s**) sheet of glass in a window or door

panel n (pl **-s**) flat distinct section of a larger surface, for example in a door ▶ v (**-s, -lling, -lled**) cover or decorate with panels

panelled v ▷ panel

panels n ▷ panel

panes n ▷ pane

pang n (pl **-s**) sudden sharp feeling of pain or sadness

pangolin n (pl **-s**) animal of tropical countries with a scaly body and a long snout for eating ants and termites (also **scaly anteater**)

pangolins n ▷ pangolin

pangs n ▷ pang

panic n (pl **-s**) sudden overwhelming fear, often affecting a whole group of people ▶ v (**-s, -cking, -cked**) feel or cause to feel panic > **panicky** adj (**-ier, -iest**)

panicked v ▷ panic

panickier adj ▷ panic

panickiest adj ▷ panic

panicking v ▷ panic

panicky adj ▷ panic

panics n, v ▷ panic

pannier n (pl **-s**) bag fixed on the back of a cycle

panniers n ▷ pannier

panoplies n ▷ panoply

panoply n (pl **-ies**) magnificent array

panorama n (pl **-s**) wide unbroken view of a scene > **panoramic** adj

panoramas n ▷ panorama

panoramic adj ▷ panorama

pansies n ▷ pansy

pansy n (pl **-sies**) small garden flower with velvety purple, yellow, or white petals

pant v (**-s, -ing, -ed**) breathe quickly and noisily during or after exertion

panted v ▷ pant

pantheon n (pl **-s**) (in ancient Greece and Rome) temple built to honour all the gods

pantheons n ▷ pantheon

panther n (pl **-s**) leopard, esp. a black one

panthers n ▷ panther

panties pl n women's underpants

pantile n (pl **-s**) roofing tile with an S-shaped cross section

pantiles n ▷ pantile

panting v ▷ pant

pantries n ▷ pantry

pantry n (pl **-ries**) small room or cupboard for storing food

pants pl n undergarment for the lower part of the body ▶ v ▷ pant

pap n (pl **-s**) soft food for babies or invalids

papacies n ▷ papacy

papacy n (pl **-cies**) position or term of office of a pope

papal adj of the pope

papaya n (pl **-s**) large sweet West Indian fruit

papayas n ▷ papaya

paper n (pl **-s**) material made in sheets from wood pulp or other fibres ▶ pl personal documents ▶ v (**-s, -ing, -ed**) cover (walls) with wallpaper

papered v ▷ paper

papering v ▷ paper

papers n, v ▷ paper

papoose n (pl **-s**) Native American child

papooses n ▷ papoose

paprika n (pl **-s**) mild powdered seasoning made from red peppers

paprikas n ▷ paprika

paps n ▷ pap

papyri n ▷ papyrus

papyrus n (pl **-ri, -ruses**) tall water plant

papyruses n ▷ papyrus

par n (pl **-s**) usual or average condition

parable n (pl **-s**) story that illustrates a religious teaching

parables n ▷ parable

parabola n (pl **-s**) regular curve resembling the course of an object thrown forward and up > **parabolic** adj
parabolas n ▷ parabola
parabolic adj ▷ parabola

parade n (pl **-s**) procession or march ▶ v (**-des**, **-ding**, **-ded**) display or flaunt
paraded v ▷ parade
parades n, v ▷ parade

paradigm n (pl **-s**) example or model
paradigms n ▷ paradigm
parading v ▷ parade

paradise n heaven
paradises n ▷ paradise

paradox n (pl **-xes**) statement that seems self-contradictory but may be true > **paradoxical** adj > **paradoxically** adv
paradoxes n ▷ paradox
paradoxical adj ▷ paradox
paradoxically adv ▷ paradox

paraffin n (pl **-s**) BRIT & S AFR liquid mixture distilled from petroleum and used as a fuel or solvent
paraffins n ▷ paraffin

paragon n (pl **-s**) model of perfection
paragons n ▷ paragon

parakeet n (pl **-s**) small long-tailed parrot
parakeets n ▷ parakeet

parallax n (pl **-es**) apparent change in an object's position due to a change in the observer's position
parallaxes n ▷ parallax

parallel adj separated by an equal distance at every point ▶ n (pl **-s**) line separated from another by an equal distance at every point ▶ v (**-s**, **-ing**, **-ed**) correspond to
paralleled v ▷ parallel
paralleling v ▷ parallel
parallels n, v ▷ parallel

paralyse v (**-ses**, **-sing**, **-sed**) affect with paralysis
paralysed v ▷ paralyse
paralysing v ▷ paralyse

paramour n (pl **-s**) old-fashioned lover, esp. of a person married to someone else

paramours n ▷ paramour

paranoia n (pl **-s**) mental illness causing delusions of grandeur or persecution informal > **paranoid**, **paranoiac** adj, n (pl **-s**)
paranoiac adj, n ▷ paranoia
paranoiacs n ▷ paranoia
paranoias n ▷ paranoia
paranoid adj, n ▷ paranoia
paranoids n ▷ paranoia

parapet n (pl **-s**) low wall or railing along the edge of a balcony or roof
parapets n ▷ parapet

parasite n (pl **-s**) animal or plant living in or on another > **parasitic** adj
parasites n ▷ parasite
parasitic adj ▷ parasite

parasol n (pl **-s**) umbrella-like sunshade
parasols n ▷ parasol

parboil v (**-s**, **-ing**, **-ed**) boil until partly cooked
parboiled v ▷ parboil
parboiling v ▷ parboil
parboils v ▷ parboil

parcel n (pl **-s**) something wrapped up, package ▶ v (**-s**, **-lling**, **-lled**) (often foll. by **up**) wrap up
parcelled v ▷ parcel
parcelling v ▷ parcel
parcels n, v ▷ parcel

parch v (**-es**, **-ing**, **-ed**) make very hot and dry
parched v ▷ parch
parches v ▷ parch
parching v ▷ parch

pardon v (**-s**, **-ing**, **-ed**) forgive, excuse ▶ n (pl **-s**) forgiveness > **pardonable** adj
pardonable adj ▷ pardon
pardoned v ▷ pardon
pardoning v ▷ pardon
pardons v, n ▷ pardon

pare v (**-res**, **-ring**, **-red**) cut off the skin or top layer of
pared v ▷ pare

parent n (pl **-s**) father or mother > **parental** adj > **parenthood** n (pl **-s**)

parental adj ▷ **parent**
parenthood n ▷ **parent**
parenthoods n ▷ **parent**
parents n ▷ **parent**
pares v ▷ **pare**
pariah n (pl -s) social outcast
pariahs n ▷ **pariah**
parietal adj of the walls of a body cavity such as the skull
paring v ▷ **pare** ▶ n (pl -s) piece pared off
parings n ▷ **paring**
parish n (pl -es) area that has its own church and a priest or pastor
parishes n ▷ **parish**
parities n ▷ **parity**
parity n (pl -ties) equality or equivalence
park n (pl -s) area of open land for recreational use by the public ▶ v (-s, -ing, -ed) stop and leave (a vehicle) temporarily
parka n (pl -s) large waterproof jacket with a hood
parkas n ▷ **parka**
parked v ▷ **park**
parkier adj ▷ **parky**
parkiest adj ▷ **parky**
parking v ▷ **park**
parks n, v ▷ **park**
parky adj (-kier, -kiest) BRIT informal (of the weather) chilly
parlance n (pl -s) particular way of speaking, idiom
parlances n ▷ **parlance**
parley n (pl -s) meeting between leaders or representatives of opposing forces to discuss terms ▶ v (-s, -ing, -ed) have a parley
parleyed v ▷ **parley**
parleying v ▷ **parley**
parleys n, v ▷ **parley**
parlour n (pl -s) old-fashioned living room for receiving visitors
parlours n ▷ **parlour**
parlous adj old-fashioned dire
parodied v ▷ **parody**
parodies n, v ▷ **parody**

parody n (pl -dies) exaggerated and amusing imitation of someone else's style ▶ v (-dies, -dying, -died) make a parody of
parodying v ▷ **parody**
parole n (pl -s) early freeing of a prisoner on condition that he or she behaves well ▶ v (-les, -ling, -led) put on parole
paroled v ▷ **parole**
paroles n, v ▷ **parole**
paroling v ▷ **parole**
paroxysm n (pl -s) uncontrollable outburst of rage, delight, etc
paroxysms n ▷ **paroxysm**
parquet n (pl -s) floor covering made of wooden blocks arranged in a geometric pattern > **parquetry** n (pl -ies)
parquetries n ▷ **parquet**
parquetry n ▷ **parquet**
parquets n ▷ **parquet**
parried v ▷ **parry**
parries v ▷ **parry**
parrot n (pl -s) tropical bird with a short hooked beak and an ability to imitate human speech ▶ v (-s, -ing, -ed) repeat (someone else's words) without thinking
parroted v ▷ **parrot**
parroting v ▷ **parrot**
parrots n, v ▷ **parrot**
parry v (-ries, -rying, -ried) ward off (an attack)
parrying v ▷ **parry**
pars n ▷ **par**
parse v (-ses, -sing, -sed) analyse (a sentence) in terms of grammar
parsed v ▷ **parse**
parses v ▷ **parse**
parsing v ▷ **parse**
parsley n (pl -s) herb used for seasoning and decorating food
parsleys n ▷ **parsley**
parsnip n (pl -s) long tapering cream-coloured root vegetable
parsnips n ▷ **parsnip**
parson n (pl -s) Anglican parish priest

parsons n ▷ **parson**

part n (pl -**s**) one of the pieces that make up a whole ▶ v (-**s**, -**ing**, -**ed**) divide or separate

partake v (-**takes**, -**taking**, -**took**, -**taken**) (foll. by **of**) take (food or drink)

partaken v ▷ **partake**

partakes v ▷ **partake**

partaking v ▷ **partake**

parted v ▷ **part**

partial adj not complete > **partiality** n (pl -**ties**) > **partially** adv

partialities n ▷ **partial**

partiality n ▷ **partial**

partially adv ▷ **partial**

particle n (pl -**s**) extremely small piece or amount

particles n ▷ **particle**

parties n ▷ **party**

parting n (pl -**s**) occasion when one person leaves another ▶ v ▷ **part**

partings n ▷ **parting**

partisan n (pl -**s**) strong supporter of a party or group ▶ adj prejudiced or one-sided

partisans n ▷ **partisan**

partly adv not completely

partner n (pl -**s**) either member of a couple in a relationship or activity ▶ v (-**s**, -**ing**, -**ed**) be the partner of

partnered v ▷ **partner**

partnering v ▷ **partner**

partners n, v ▷ **partner**

partook v ▷ **partake**

parts n, v ▷ **part**

party n (pl -**ties**) social gathering for pleasure

parvenu n (pl -**s**) person newly risen to a position of power or wealth

parvenus n ▷ **parvenu**

pas n ▷ **pa**

pascal n (pl -**s**) unit of pressure

pascals n ▷ **pascal**

paspalum n (pl -**s**) AUST & NZ type of grass with wide leaves

paspalums n ▷ **paspalum**

pass v (-**es**, -**ing**, -**ed**) go by, past, or through SPORT ▶ n (pl -**es**) successful

result in a test or examination

passable adj (just) acceptable

passage n (pl -**s**) channel or opening providing a way through

passages n ▷ **passage**

passbook n (pl -**s**) book issued by a bank or building society for keeping a record of deposits and withdrawals

passbooks n ▷ **passbook**

passé adj out-of-date

passed v ▷ **pass**

passes v, n ▷ **pass**

passim adv LATIN everywhere, throughout

passing adj brief or transitory ▶ v ▷ **pass**

passion n (pl -**s**) intense sexual love > **passionate** adj

passionate adj ▷ **passion**

passions n ▷ **passion**

passive adj not playing an active part > **passivity** n (pl -**ties**)

passivities n ▷ **passive**

passivity n ▷ **passive**

passport n (pl -**s**) official document of nationality granting permission to travel abroad

passports n ▷ **passport**

password n (pl -**s**) secret word or phrase that ensures admission

passwords n ▷ **password**

past adj of the time before the present ▶ n (pl -**s**) period of time before the present ▶ adv by, along ▶ prep beyond

pasta n (pl -**s**) type of food, such as spaghetti, that is made in different shapes from flour and water

pastas n ▷ **pasta**

paste n (pl -**s**) moist soft mixture, such as toothpaste ▶ v (-**tes**, -**ting**, -**ted**) fasten with paste

pasted v ▷ **paste**

pastel n (pl -**s**) coloured chalk crayon for drawing ▶ adj pale and delicate in colour

pastels n ▷ **pastel**

pastes n, v ▷ **paste**

pastiche n (pl -**s**) work of art that

mixes styles or copies the style of another artist

pastiches n ▷ pastiche

pastier adj ▷ pasty¹

pasties n ▷ pasty²

pastiest adj ▷ pasty¹

pastille n (pl -s) small fruit-flavoured and sometimes medicated sweet

pastilles n ▷ pastille

pastime n (pl -s) activity that makes time pass pleasantly

pastimes n ▷ pastime

pasting n (pl -s) informal heavy defeat ▶ v ▷ paste

pastings n ▷ pasting

pastor n (pl -s) member of the clergy in charge of a congregation

pastoral adj of or depicting country life

pastors n ▷ pastor

pastrami n (pl -s) highly seasoned smoked beef

pastramis n ▷ pastrami

pastries n ▷ pastry

pastry n (pl -ries) baking dough made of flour, fat, and water

pasts n ▷ past

pasture n (pl -s) grassy land for farm animals to graze on

pastures n ▷ pasture

pasty¹ adj (-tier, -tiest) (of a complexion) pale and unhealthy

pasty² n (pl -ries) round of pastry folded over a savoury filling

pat¹ v (-s, -tting, -tted) tap lightly ▶ n (pl -s) gentle tap or stroke

pat² adj quick, ready, or glib

patch n (pl -es) piece of material sewn on a garment ▶ v (-es, -ing, -ed) mend with a patch

patched v ▷ patch

patches n, v ▷ patch

patchier adj ▷ patchy

patchiest adj ▷ patchy

patching v ▷ patch

patchy adj (-chier, -chiest) of uneven quality or intensity

pate n (pl -s) old-fashioned head

pâté n (pl -s) spread of finely minced liver etc

patella n (pl -ae) kneecap

patellae n ▷ patella

patent n (pl -s) document giving the exclusive right to make or sell an invention ▶ adj open to public inspection ▶ v (-s, -ing, -ed) obtain a patent for

patented v ▷ patent

patenting v ▷ patent

patently adv obviously

patents n, v ▷ patent

paternal adj fatherly

pates n ▷ pate

pâtés n ▷ pâté

path n (pl -s) surfaced walk or track

pathetic adj causing feelings of pity or sadness > **pathetically** adv

pathetically adv ▷ pathetic

pathogen n (pl -s) thing that causes disease > **pathogenic** adj

pathogenic adj ▷ pathogen

pathogens n ▷ pathogen

pathos n (pl -es) power of arousing pity or sadness

pathoses n ▷ pathos

paths n ▷ path

patience n (pl -s) quality of being patient

patiences n ▷ patience

patient adj enduring difficulties or delays calmly ▶ n (pl -s) person receiving medical treatment

patients n ▷ patient

patina n (pl -s) fine layer on a surface

patinas n ▷ patina

patio n (pl -os) paved area adjoining a house

patios n ▷ patio

patois n (pl patois) regional dialect, esp. of French

patriot n (pl -s) person who loves his or her country and supports its interests > **patriotic** adj > **patriotism** n (pl -s)

patriotic adj ▷ patriot

patriotism n ▷ patriot

patriotisms n ▷ patriot

patriots n ▷ patriot
patrol n (pl -s) regular circuit by a guard ▶ v (-s, -lling, -lled) go round on guard, or reconnoitring
patrolled v ▷ patrol
patrolling v ▷ patrol
patrols n, v ▷ patrol
patron n (pl -s) person who gives financial support to charities, artists, etc
patrons n ▷ patron
pats v, n ▷ pat¹
patted v ▷ pat¹
patter¹ v (-s, -ing, -ed) make repeated soft tapping sounds ▶ n (pl -s) quick succession of taps
patter² n (pl -s) glib rapid speech
pattered v ▷ patter¹
pattering v ▷ patter¹
pattern n (pl -s) arrangement of repeated parts or decorative designs
patterns n ▷ pattern
patters v, n ▷ patter¹, ²
patties n ▷ patty
patting v ▷ pat¹
patty n (pl -ties) small flattened cake of minced food
paucities n ▷ paucity
paucity n (pl -ties) scarcity
paunch n (pl -es) protruding belly
paunches n ▷ paunch
pauper n (pl -s) very poor person
paupers n ▷ pauper
pause v (-ses, -sing, -sed) stop for a time ▶ n (pl -s) stop or rest in speech or action
paused v ▷ pause
pauses v, n ▷ pause
pausing v ▷ pause
pave v (-ves, -ving, -ved) form (a surface) with stone or brick
paved v ▷ pave
pavement n (pl -s) paved path for pedestrians
pavements n ▷ pavement
paves v ▷ pave
pavilion n (pl -s) building on a playing field etc
pavilions n ▷ pavilion

paving v ▷ pave
paw n (pl -s) animal's foot with claws and pads ▶ v (-s, -ing, -ed) scrape with the paw or hoof
pawed v ▷ paw
pawing v ▷ paw
pawn¹ v (-s, -ing, -ed) deposit (an article) as security for money borrowed
pawn² n (pl -s) chessman of the lowest value
pawned v ▷ pawn¹
pawning v ▷ pawn¹
pawns v, n ▷ pawn¹, ²
paws n, v ▷ paw

> **pax** n (**paxes**). A pax is a period of peace, especially when there is one dominant nation. If you have a P and an X on your rack, there is likely to be an A available on the board. Pax gives a decent score for a three-letter word, so watch out for chances to play it on a bonus square. Pax scores 12 points.

pay v (-s, -ing, **paid**) give money etc in return for goods or services ▶ n (pl -s) wages or salary
payable adj due to be paid
payee n (pl -s) person to whom money is paid or due
payees n ▷ payee
paying v ▷ pay
payload n (pl -s) passengers or cargo of an aircraft
payloads n ▷ payload
payment n (pl -s) act of paying
payments n ▷ payment
payola n (pl -s) CHIEFLY US informal bribe to get special treatment, esp. to promote a commercial product
payolas n ▷ payola
pays v ▷ pay

> **pe** n (**pes**). Pe is the 17th letter in the Hebrew alphabet. This is a very handy word because it allows you to connect words beginning with P to those ending in E, or vice versa and E is the most common tile in the game. Pe scores 4 points.

pea n (pl **-s**) climbing plant with seeds growing in pods

peace n (pl **-s**) calm, quietness
> **peaceful** adj > **peacefully** adv
peaceful adj > **peace**
peacefully adv > **peace**
peaces n > **peace**

peach n (pl **-es**) soft juicy fruit with a stone and a downy skin ▶ adj pinkish-orange
peaches n > **peach**

peacock n (pl **-s**) large male bird with a brilliantly coloured fanlike tail
> **peahen** n fem (pl **-s**)
peacocks n > **peacock**
peahen n > **peacock**
peahens n > **peacock**

peak n (pl **-s**) pointed top, esp. of a mountain ▶ v (**-s, -ing, -ed**) form or reach a peak ▶ adj of or at the point of greatest demand > **peaked** adj
peaked adj, v > **peak**
peakier adj > **peaky**
peakiest adj > **peaky**
peaking v > **peak**
peaks n, v > **peak**

peaky adj (**-kier, -kiest**) pale and sickly

peal n (pl **-s**) long loud echoing sound, esp. of bells or thunder ▶ v (**-s, -ing, -ed**) sound with a peal or peals
pealed v > **peal**
pealing v > **peal**
peals n, v > **peal**

peanut n (pl **-s**) pea-shaped nut that ripens underground ▶ pl informal trifling amount of money
peanuts n > **peanut**

pear n (pl **-s**) sweet juicy fruit with a narrow top and rounded base

pearl n (pl **-s**) hard round shiny object found inside some oyster shells and used as a jewel > **pearly** adj (**-lier, -liest**)
pearlier adj > **pearl**
pearliest adj > **pearl**
pearls n > **pearl**
pearly adj > **pearl**
pears n > **pear**

peas n > **pea**

peasant n (pl **-s**) person working on the land, esp. in poorer countries or in the past
peasants n > **peasant**

peat n (pl **-s**) decayed vegetable material found in bogs, used as fertilizer or fuel
peats n > **peat**

pebble n (pl **-s**) small roundish stone
> **pebbly** adj (**-lier, -liest**)
pebbles n > **pebble**
pebblier adj > **pebble**
pebbliest adj > **pebble**
pebbly adj > **pebble**

pecan n (pl **-s**) edible nut of a N American tree
pecans n > **pecan**

peck v (**-s, -ing, -ed**) strike or pick up with the beak ▶ n (pl **-s**) pecking movement
pecked v > **peck**
pecking v > **peck**

peckish adj informal slightly hungry
pecks v, n > **peck**

pecs pl n informal pectoral muscles

pectin n (pl **-s**) substance in fruit that makes jam set
pectins n > **pectin**

pectoral adj of the chest or thorax ▶ n (pl **-s**) pectoral muscle or fin
pectorals n > **pectoral**

peculiar adj strange

pedal n (pl **-s**) foot-operated lever used to control a vehicle or machine, or to modify the tone of a musical instrument ▶ v (**-s, -lling, -lled**) propel (a bicycle) by using its pedals
pedalled v > **pedal**
pedalling v > **pedal**
pedals n > **pedal**

pedant n (pl **-s**) person who is excessively concerned with details and rules, esp. in academic work
> **pedantic** adj > **pedantry** n (pl **-ries**)
pedantic adj > **pedant**
pedantries n > **pedant**
pedantry n > **pedant**

pedants n ▷ pedant
peddle v (-les, -ling, -led) sell (goods) from door to door
peddled v ▷ peddle
peddler n (pl -s) person who sells illegal drugs
peddlers n ▷ peddler
peddles v ▷ peddle
peddling v ▷ peddle
pedestal n (pl -s) base supporting a column, statue, etc
pedestals n ▷ pedestal
pedicure n (pl -s) medical or cosmetic treatment of the feet
pedicures n ▷ pedicure
pedigree n (pl -s) register of ancestors, esp. of a purebred animal
pedigrees n ▷ pedigree
pediment n (pl -s) triangular part over a door etc
pediments n ▷ pediment
pedlar n (pl -s) person who sells goods from door to door
pedlars n ▷ pedlar
pee informal v (-s, -ing, peed) urinate ▶ n (-s) act of urinating
peed v ▷ pee
peeing v ▷ pee
peek v, n (pl -s) peep or glance
peeks n ▷ peek
peel v (-s, -ing, -ed) remove the skin or rind of (a vegetable or fruit) ▶ n (pl -s) rind or skin ▶ **peelings** pl n
peeled v ▷ peel
peeling v ▷ peel
peelings n ▷ peel
peels v, n ▷ peel
peep¹ v (-s, -ing, -ed) look slyly or quickly ▶ n (pl -s) peeping look
peep² v (-s, -ing, -ed) make a small shrill noise ▶ n (-s) small shrill noise
peeped v ▷ peep¹, ²
peeping v ▷ peep¹, ²
peeps v, n ▷ peep¹, ²
peer¹ n (pl -s), fem **peeress** (pl -es) (in Britain) member of the nobility
peer² v (-s, -ing, -ed) look closely and intently

peerage n BRIT whole body of peers
peerages n ▷ peerage
peered v ▷ peer²
peeress n ▷ peer¹
peeresses n ▷ peer¹
peering v ▷ peer²
peerless adj unequalled, unsurpassed
peers n ▷ peer¹ ▶ v ▷ peer²
pees v, n ▷ pee
peeved adj informal annoyed
peevish adj fretful or irritable
> **peevishly** adv
peevishly adv ▷ peevish
peewee n (pl -s) black-and-white Australian bird
peewees n ▷ peewee
peewit n (pl -s) ▷ lapwing
peewits n ▷ peewit
peg n (pl -s) pin or clip for joining, fastening, marking, etc ▶ v (-s, -gging, -gged) fasten with pegs
pegged v ▷ peg
pegging v ▷ peg
pegs n, v ▷ peg
peignoir n (pl -s) woman's light dressing gown
peignoirs n ▷ peignoir
pelican n (pl -s) large water bird with a pouch beneath its bill for storing fish
pelicans n ▷ pelican
pellagra n (pl -s) disease caused by lack of vitamin B
pellagras n ▷ pellagra
pellet n (pl -s) small ball of something
pellets n ▷ pellet
pellucid adj very clear
pelmet n (pl -s) ornamental drapery or board, concealing a curtain rail
pelmets n ▷ pelmet
pelt¹ v (-s, -ing, -ed) throw missiles at
pelt² n (pl -s) skin of a fur-bearing animal
pelted v ▷ pelt¹
pelting v ▷ pelt¹
pelts v, n ▷ pelt¹, ²
pelvic adj ▷ pelvis
pelvis n (pl -es) framework of bones at

the base of the spine, to which the hips are attached > **pelvic** adj

pelvises n ▷ pelvis

pen¹ n (pl -**s**) instrument for writing in ink ▶ v (-**s**, -**nning**, -**nned**) write or compose

pen² n small enclosure for domestic animals ▶ v (-**s**, -**nning**, -**nned**) put or keep in a pen

pen³ n (pl -**s**) female swan

penal adj of or used in punishment

penalize (-**zes**, -**zing**, -**zed**) v impose a penalty on

penalized v ▷ penalize

penalizes v ▷ penalize

penalizing v ▷ penalize

penalties n ▷ penalty

penalty n (pl -**ties**) punishment for a crime or offence

penance n (pl (pl -**s**) voluntary self-punishment to make amends for wrongdoing

penances n ▷ penance

pence n BRIT ▷ penny

penchant n (pl -**s**) inclination or liking

penchants n ▷ penchant

pencil n (pl -**s**) thin cylindrical instrument containing graphite, for writing or drawing ▶ v (-**s**, -**lling**, -**lled**) draw, write, or mark with a pencil

pencilled v ▷ pencil

pencilling v ▷ pencil

pencils n, v ▷ pencil

pendant n (pl -**s**) ornament worn on a chain round the neck

pendants n ▷ pendant

pendent adj hanging

pending prep while waiting for ▶ adj not yet decided or settled

pendulum n (pl -**s**) suspended weight swinging to and fro, esp. as a regulator for a clock

pendulums n ▷ pendulum

penguin n (pl -**s**) flightless black-and-white sea bird of the southern hemisphere

penguins n ▷ penguin

penis n (pl -**es**) organ of copulation and

urination in male mammals

penises n ▷ penis

penitence n ▷ penitent

penitences n ▷ penitent

penitent adj feeling sorry for having done wrong ▶ n (pl -**s**) someone who is penitent ▶ **penitence** n (pl -**s**)

penitents n ▷ penitent

penknife n (pl -**knives**) small knife with blade(s) that fold into the handle

penknives n ▷ penknife

pennant n (pl -**s**) long narrow flag

pennants n ▷ pennant

penned v ▷ pen¹, ²

pennies n ▷ penny

penning v ▷ pen¹, ²

penny n (pl **pence, pennies**) British bronze coin worth one hundredth of a pound

pens n ▷ pen¹, ², ³

pension¹ n (pl -**s**) regular payment to people above a certain age, retired employees, widows, etc > **pensionable** adj

pension² n (pl -**s**) boarding house in Europe

pensionable adj ▷ pension

pensioners n ▷ pension

pensions n ▷ pension¹, ²

pensive adj deeply thoughtful, often with a tinge of sadness

pentagon n (pl -**s**) geometric figure with five sides > **pentagonal** adj

pentagonal adj ▷ pentagon

pentagons n ▷ pentagon

penumbra n (pl -**brae**, -**bras**) (in an eclipse) the partially shadowed region which surrounds the full shadow

penumbrae n ▷ penumbra

penumbras n ▷ penumbra

penuries n ▷ penury

penurious adj ▷ penury

penury n (pl -**ries**) extreme poverty > **penurious** adj

peonies n ▷ peony

peony n (pl -**nies**) garden plant with showy red, pink, or white flowers

people pl n n persons generally ▶ n (pl

-s) race or nation ▶ v (-les, -ling, -led)
provide with inhabitants
peopled v ▷ **people**
peoples n, v ▷ **people**
peopling v ▷ **people**
pep n (pl -s) informal high spirits,
energy, or enthusiasm
pepper n (pl -s) sharp hot condiment
made from the fruit of an East Indian
climbing plant ▶ v (-s, -ing, -ed)
season with pepper
peppered v ▷ **pepper**
pepperier adj ▷ **peppery**
pepperiest adj ▷ **peppery**
peppering v ▷ **pepper**
peppers n, v ▷ **pepper**
peppery adj (-rier, -riest) tasting
of pepper
peps n ▷ **pep**
peptic adj relating to digestion or the
digestive juices
per prep for each
perceive v (-ves, -ving, -ved) become
aware of (something) through the
senses
perceived v ▷ **perceive**
perceives v ▷ **perceive**
perceiving v ▷ **perceive**
perch[1] n (pl -es) resting place for a bird
▶ v (-es, -ing, -ed) alight, rest, or place
on or as if on a perch
perch[2] n (pl -es) any of various edible
fishes
perched v ▷ **perch**[1, 2]
perches n, v ▷ **perch**[1, 2]
perching v ▷ **perch**[1, 2]
perfect adj (-er, -est) having all the
essential elements ▶ n (pl -s) GRAMMAR
perfect tense ▶ v (-s, -ing, -ed)
improve > **perfectly** adv
perfected n ▷ **perfect**
perfecter adj ▷ **perfect**
perfectest adj ▷ **perfect**
perfecting v ▷ **perfect**
perfectly adv ▷ **perfect**
perfects n, v ▷ **perfect**
perforce adv of necessity
perform v (-s, -ing, -ed) carry out

(an action) > **performance** n (pl -s)
> **performer** n (pl -s)
performance n ▷ **perform**
performances n ▷ **perform**
performed v ▷ **perform**
performer n ▷ **perform**
performers n ▷ **perform**
performing v ▷ **perform**
performs v ▷ **perform**
perfume n (pl -s) liquid cosmetic worn
for its pleasant smell ▶ v (-es, -ing,
-ed) give a pleasant smell to
perfumed v ▷ **perfume**
perfumes n, v ▷ **perfume**
perfuming v ▷ **perfume**
pergola n (pl -s) arch or framework of
trellis supporting climbing plants
pergolas n ▷ **pergola**
perhaps adv possibly, maybe
peril n (pl -s) great danger > **perilous** adj
> **perilously** adv
perilous adj ▷ **peril**
perilously adv ▷ **peril**
perils n ▷ **peril**
period n (pl -s) particular portion of
time us ▶ adj (of furniture, dress, a
play, etc) dating from or in the style of
an earlier time
periodic adj recurring at intervals
periods n ▷ **period**
perish v (-es, -ing, -ed) be destroyed
or die
perished v ▷ **perish**
perishes v ▷ **perish**
perjuries n ▷ **perjury**
perjury n (pl -ies) act or crime of lying
while under oath in a court
perk n (pl -s) informal incidental
benefit gained from a job, such as a
company car
perkier adj ▷ **perk**
perkiest adj ▷ **perk**
perks n ▷ **perk**
perky adj (-kier, -kiest) lively or
cheerful
perm n (pl -s) long-lasting curly
hairstyle produced by treating the hair
with chemicals ▶ v (-s, -ing, -ed) give

(hair) a perm

permeate v (-tes, -ting, -ted)
pervade or pass through the whole of
(something)
permeated v ▷ permeate
permeates v ▷ permeate
permeating v ▷ permeate
permed v ▷ perm
perming v ▷ perm
permissible adj ▷ permit
permit v (-s, -tting, -tted) give
permission, allow ▶ n (pl -s) document
giving permission to do something
> **permissible** adj
permits v, n ▷ permit
permitted v ▷ permit
permitting v ▷ permit
perms n, v ▷ perm
peroxide n (pl -s) hydrogen peroxide
used as a hair bleach
peroxides n ▷ peroxide
perplex v (-es, -ing, -ed) puzzle,
bewilder > **perplexity** n (pl -ties)
perplexed v ▷ perplex
perplexes v ▷ perplex
perplexing v ▷ perplex
perplexities n ▷ perplex
perplexity n ▷ perplex
perquisite n (pl -s) formal ▷ perk
perries n ▷ perry
perry n (pl -rries) alcoholic drink made
from fermented pears
persist v (-s, -ing, -ed) continue to
be or happen, last > **persistent** adj
> **persistently** adv > **persistence** n
(pl -s)
persisted v ▷ persist
persistence adj ▷ persist
persistences adj ▷ persist
persistent adj ▷ persist
persistently adv ▷ persist
persisting v ▷ persist
persists v ▷ persist
person n (pl -s) human being
persona n (pl -nae) someone's
personality as presented to others
personae n ▷ persona
personal adj individual or private

persons n ▷ person
perspiration n ▷ perspire
perspirations n ▷ perspire
perspire v (-res, -ring, -red) sweat
> **perspiration** n (pl -s)
perspired v ▷ perspire
perspires v ▷ perspire
perspiring v ▷ perspire
persuade v (-des, -ding, -ded) make
(someone) do something by argument,
charm, etc > **persuasive** adj
persuaded v ▷ persuade
persuades v ▷ persuade
persuading v ▷ persuade
persuasive adj ▷ persuade
pert adj (-er, -est) saucy and cheeky
pertain v (-s, -ing, -ed) belong or be
relevant (to)
pertained v ▷ pertain
pertaining v ▷ pertain
pertains v ▷ pertain
perter adj ▷ pert
pertest adj ▷ pert
perturb v (-s, -ing, -ed) disturb greatly
> **perturbation** n (pl -s)
perturbation n ▷ perturb
perturbation n ▷ perturb
perturbed v ▷ perturb
perturbing v ▷ perturb
perturbs v ▷ perturb
perusal n ▷ peruse
perusals n ▷ peruse
peruse v (-ses, -sing, -sed) read in a
careful or leisurely manner > **perusal** n
(pl -s)
perused v ▷ peruse
peruses v ▷ peruse
perusing v ▷ peruse
pervade v (-des, -ding, -ded)
spread right through (something)
> **pervasive** adj
pervaded v ▷ pervade
pervades v ▷ pervade
pervading v ▷ pervade
pervasive adj ▷ pervade
perverse adj (-r, -st) deliberately
doing something different from
what is thought normal or proper

> **perversely** adv ▷ **perverse** **perversity** n (pl -ties)
perversely n ▷ **perverse**
perverser adj ▷ **perverse**
perversest adj ▷ **perverse**
perversities n ▷ **perverse**
perversity n ▷ **perverse**
pervert v (-s, -ing, -ed) use or alter for a wrong purpose ▶ n (pl -s) person who practises sexual perversion
perverted v ▷ **pervert**
perverting v ▷ **pervert**
perverts v, n ▷ **pervert**
pervious adj able to be penetrated, permeable
peseta n (pl -s) former monetary unit of Spain
pesetas n ▷ **peseta**
pessaries n ▷ **pessary**
pessary n (pl -ries) appliance worn in the vagina, either to prevent conception or to support the womb
pest n (pl -s) annoying person
pester v (-s, -ing, -ed) annoy or nag continually
pestered v ▷ **pester**
pestering v ▷ **pester**
pesters v ▷ **pester**
pestle n (pl -s) club-shaped implement for grinding things to powder in a mortar
pestles n ▷ **pestle**
pests n ▷ **pest**
pet n (pl -s) animal kept for pleasure and companionship ▶ adj particularly cherished ▶ v (-s, -tting, -tted) treat as a pet
petal n (pl -s) one of the brightly coloured outer parts of a flower
> **petalled** adj
petalled adj ▷ **petal**
petals n ▷ **petal**
petard n (pl -s) being the victim of one's own schemes
petards n ▷ **petard**
petite adj (of a woman) small and dainty
petition n (pl -s) formal request,

esp. one signed by many people and presented to parliament ▶ v (-s, -ing, -ed) present a petition to
> **petitioner** n (pl -s)
petitioned v ▷ **petition**
petitioner n ▷ **petition**
petitioners n ▷ **petition**
petitioning v ▷ **petition**
petitions n, v ▷ **petition**
petrel n (pl -s) sea bird with a hooked bill and tubular nostrils
petrels n ▷ **petrel**
petrification n ▷ **petrify**
petrifications n ▷ **petrify**
petrified v ▷ **petrify**
petrifies v ▷ **petrify**
petrify v (-fies, -fying, -fied) frighten severely > **petrification** n (pl -s)
petrol n (pl -s) flammable liquid obtained from petroleum, used as fuel in internal-combustion engines
petrols n ▷ **petrol**
pets n, v ▷ **pet**
petted v ▷ **pet**
pettier adj ▷ **petty**
pettiest adj ▷ **petty**
pettiness n ▷ **petty**
pettinesses n ▷ **petty**
petting v ▷ **pet**
petty adj (-ttier, -ttiest) unimportant, trivial > **pettiness** n (pl -es)
petulance n ▷ **petulant**
petulances n ▷ **petulant**
petulant adj childishly irritable or peevish > **petulance** n (pl -s)
> **petulantly** adv
petulantly adv ▷ **petulant**
petunia n (pl -s) garden plant with funnel-shaped flowers
petunias n ▷ **petunia**
pew n (pl -s) fixed benchlike seat in a church
pews n ▷ **pew**
pewter n (pl -s) greyish metal made of tin and lead
pewters n ▷ **pewter**
phalanx n (pl -es) closely grouped mass of people

phalanxes n ▷ phalanx

phalli n ▷ phallus

phallic adj ▷ phallic

phallus n (pl -es, -lli) penis, esp. as a symbol of reproductive power in primitive rites > **phallic** adj

phalluses n ▷ phallus

phantasm n (pl -s) unreal vision, illusion > **phantasmal** adj

phantasmal adj ▷ phantasm

phantasms n ▷ phantasm

phantom n (pl -s) ghost

phantoms n ▷ phantom

pharmacies n ▷ pharmacy

pharmacy n (pl -cies) preparation and dispensing of drugs and medicines

pharynges n ▷ pharynx

pharynx n (pl -nges, -nxes) cavity forming the back part of the mouth

pharynxes n ▷ pharynx

phase n (pl -s) any distinct or characteristic stage in a development or chain of events ▶ v (-ses, -sing, -sed) arrange or carry out in stages or to coincide with something else

phased v ▷ phase

phases n, v ▷ phase

phasing v ▷ phase

pheasant n (pl -s) game bird with bright plumage

pheasants n ▷ pheasant

phenol n (pl -s) chemical used in disinfectants and antiseptics

phenols n ▷ phenol

phial n (pl -s) small bottle for medicine etc

phials n ▷ phial

philtre n (pl -s) magic drink supposed to arouse love in the person who drinks it

philtres n ▷ philtre

phlegm n (pl -s) thick yellowish substance formed in the nose and throat during a cold

phlegms n ▷ phlegm

phlox n (pl phlox, -xes) flowering garden plant

phloxes n ▷ phlox

phobia n (pl -s) intense and unreasoning fear or dislike

phobias n ▷ phobia

phoenix n (pl -es) legendary bird said to set fire to itself and rise anew from its ashes

phoenixes n ▷ phoenix

phone n, v (-nes, -ning, -ned) informal telephone

phoned v ▷ phone

phones v ▷ phone

phonetic adj of speech sounds > **phonetically** adv

phonetically adv ▷ phonetic

phoney, phony informal adj (-nier, -niest) not genuine ▶ n (pl -neys, -nies) phoney person or thing

phoneys n ▷ phoney

phonier adj ▷ phoney

phonies n ▷ phoney

phoniest adj ▷ phoney

phoning v ▷ phone

phony adj ▷ phoney

photos n ▷ photo

phrase n (pl -s) group of words forming a unit of meaning, esp. within a sentence ▶ v (-ses, -sing, -sed) express in words

phrased v ▷ phrase

phrases n, v ▷ phrase

phrasing v ▷ phrase

physical adj of the body, as contrasted with the mind or spirit > **physically** adv

physically adv ▷ physical

physics n science of the properties of matter and energy

physique n (pl -s) person's bodily build and muscular development

physiques n ▷ physique

pi n (pl -s) MATHS ratio of the circumference of a circle to its diameter

pianist n ▷ piano¹

pianists n ▷ piano¹

piano¹ n (pl -s) musical instrument with strings which are struck by hammers worked by a keyboard (also **pianoforte**) (pl -s) > **pianist** n (pl -s)

piano² adv MUSIC quietly

pianoforte n ▷ **piano¹**

pianofortes n ▷ **piano¹**

pianos n ▷ **piano¹**

piazza n (pl **-s**) square or marketplace, esp. in Italy

piazzas n ▷ **piazza**

pic n (pl **-s**, **pix**) informal photograph or illustration

picador n (pl **-s**) mounted bullfighter with a lance

picadors n ▷ **picador**

piccolo n (pl **-os**) small flute

piccolos n ▷ **piccolo**

pick¹ v (**-s**, **-ing**, **-ed**) choose ▶ n (pl **-s**) choice

pick² n (pl **-s**) tool with a curved iron crossbar and wooden shaft, for breaking up hard ground or rocks

pickaxe n (pl **-s**) large pick

pickaxes n ▷ **pickaxe**

picked v ▷ **pick¹**

picket n (pl **-s**) person or group standing outside a workplace to deter would-be workers during a strike ▶ v (**-s**, **-ing**, **-ed**) form a picket outside (a workplace)

picketed v ▷ **picket**

picketing v ▷ **picket**

pickets n, v ▷ **picket**

picking v ▷ **pick¹**

pickings pl n money easily acquired

pickle n (pl **-s**) food preserved in vinegar or salt water ▶ v (**-les**, **-ling**, **-led**) preserve in vinegar or salt water

pickled adj (of food) preserved ▶ n ▷ **pickle**

pickles n, v ▷ **pickle**

pickling v ▷ **pickle**

picks n, v ▷ **pick¹, ²**

picnic n (pl **-s**) informal meal out of doors ▶ v (**-s**, **-cking**, **-cked**) have a picnic

picnicked v ▷ **picnic**

picnicking v ▷ **picnic**

picnics n, v ▷ **picnic**

pics n ▷ **pic**

picture n (pl **-s**) drawing or painting

▶ pl cinema ▶ v (**-res**, **-ring**, **-red**) visualize, imagine

pictured v ▷ **picture**

pictures n, v ▷ **picture**

picturing v ▷ **picture**

piddle v (**-les**, **-ling**, **-led**) informal urinate

piddled v ▷ **piddle**

piddles v ▷ **piddle**

piddling v ▷ **piddle**

pidgin n (pl **-s**) language, not a mother tongue, made up of elements of two or more other languages

pidgins n ▷ **pidgin**

pie n (pl **-s**) dish of meat, fruit, etc baked in pastry

piebald adj, n (pl **-s**) (horse) with irregular black-and-white markings

piebalds n ▷ **piebald**

piece n (pl **-s**) separate bit or part

pieces n ▷ **piece**

pied adj having markings of two or more colours

pier n (pl **-s**) platform on stilts sticking out into the sea

pierce v (**-ces**, **-cing**, **-ced**) make a hole in or through with a sharp instrument

pierced v ▷ **pierce**

pierces v ▷ **pierce**

piercing adj (of a sound) shrill and high-pitched ▶ v ▷ **pierce**

pierrot n (pl **-s**) pantomime clown with a whitened face

pierrots n ▷ **pierrot**

piers n ▷ **pier**

pies n ▷ **pie**

pieties n ▷ **piety**

piety n (pl **-ties**) deep devotion to God and religion

piffle n (pl **-s**) informal nonsense

piffles n ▷ **piffle**

pig n (pl **-s**) animal kept and killed for pork, ham, and bacon

pigeon¹ n (pl **-s**) bird with a heavy body and short legs, sometimes trained to carry messages

pigeon² n informal concern or responsibility

pigeons *n* ▷ **pigeon**[1, 2]
piggeries *n* ▷ **piggery**
piggery *n* (*pl* -ries) place for keeping and breeding pigs
piggier *adj* ▷ **piggy**
piggiest *adj* ▷ **piggy**
piggish, piggy (-ggier, -ggiest) *adj* informal dirty
piggy *adj* ▷ **piggish**
pigment *n* (*pl* -s) colouring matter, paint or dye ▷ **pigmentation** *n* (*pl* -s)
pigmentation *n* ▷ **pigment**
pigmentations *n* ▷ **pigment**
pigments *n* ▷ **pigment**
pigmies *n* ▷ **pigmy**
pigmy *n* (*pl* -mies) ▷ **pygmy**
pigs *n* ▷ **pig**
pigtail *n* (*pl* -s) plait of hair hanging from the back or either side of the head
pigtails *n* ▷ **pigtail**
pike[1] *n* (*pl* -s) large predatory freshwater fish
pike[2] *n* (*pl* -s) HIST long-handled spear
pikelet *n* (*pl* -s) AUST & NZ small thick pancake
pikelets *n* ▷ **pikelet**
piker *n* (*pl* -s) AUST & NZ *slang* shirker
pikers *n* ▷ **piker**
pikes *n* ▷ **pike**[1, 2]
pilaf *n* ▷ **pilau**
pilaff *n* ▷ **pilau**
pilaffs *n* ▷ **pilau**
pilafs *n* ▷ **pilau**
pilaster *n* (*pl* -s) square column, usu. set in a wall
pilasters *n* ▷ **pilaster**
pilau, pilaf, pilaff *n* (*pl* -s) Middle Eastern dish of meat, fish, or poultry boiled with rice, spices, etc
pilchard *n* (*pl* -s) small edible sea fish of the herring family
pilchards *n* ▷ **pilchard**
pile[1] *n* (*pl* -s) number of things lying on top of each other ▷ *v* (-les, -ling, -led) collect into a pile
pile[2] *n* (*pl* -s) beam driven into the ground, esp. as a foundation for building

pile[3] *n* (*pl* -s) fibres of a carpet or a fabric, esp. velvet, that stand up from the weave
piled *v* ▷ **pile**[1]
piles *pl n* swollen veins in the rectum, haemorrhoids ▶ *v*, *n* ▷ **pile**[1, 2, 3]
pilfer *v* (-s, -ing, -ed) steal in small quantities
pilfered *v* ▷ **pilfer**
pilfering *v* ▷ **pilfer**
pilfers *v* ▷ **pilfer**
pilgrim *n* (*pl* -s) person who journeys to a holy place ▷ **pilgrimage** *n* (*pl* -s)
pilgrimage *n* ▷ **pilgrim**
pilgrimages *n* ▷ **pilgrim**
pilgrims *n* ▷ **pilgrim**
piling *v* ▷ **pile**[1]
pill *n* (*pl* -s) small ball of medicine swallowed whole
pillage *v* (-ges, -ging, -ged) steal property by violence in war ▶ *n* (*pl* -s) violent seizure of goods, esp. in war
pillaged *v* ▷ **pillage**
pillages *v*, *n* ▷ **pillage**
pillaging *v* ▷ **pillage**
pillar *n* (*pl* -s) upright post, usu. supporting a roof
pillars *n* ▷ **pillar**
pillion *n* (*pl* -s) seat for a passenger behind the rider of a motorcycle
pillions *n* ▷ **pillion**
pilloried *v* ▷ **pillory**
pillories *n*, *v* ▷ **pillory**
pillory *n* (*pl* -ries) HIST frame with holes for the head and hands in which an offender was locked and exposed to public abuse ▶ *v* (-ries, -rying, -ried) ridicule publicly
pillow *n* (*pl* -s) stuffed cloth bag for supporting the head in bed ▶ *v* (-s, -ing, -ed) rest as if on a pillow
pillowed *v* ▷ **pillow**
pillowing *v* ▷ **pillow**
pillows *n*, *v* ▷ **pillow**
pills *n* ▷ **pill**
pilot *n* (*pl* -s) person qualified to fly an aircraft or spacecraft ▶ *adj* experimental and preliminary ▶ *v* (-s,

-ing, -ed act as the pilot of
piloted v ▷ pilot
piloting v ▷ pilot
pilots n, v ▷ pilot
pimento n (pl -tos) mild-tasting red pepper
pimentos n ▷ pimento
pimp n (pl -s) man who gets customers for a prostitute in return for a share of his or her earnings ▶ v (-s, -ing, -ed) act as a pimp
pimped v ▷ pimp
pimping v ▷ pimp
pimple n (pl -s) small pus-filled spot on the skin ▶ **pimply** adj (-lier, -liest)
pimples n ▷ pimple
pimplier v ▷ pimple
pimpliest v ▷ pimple
pimply v ▷ pimple
pimps n, v ▷ pimp
pin n (pl -s) short thin piece of stiff wire with a point and head, for fastening things ▶ v (-s, -nning, -nned) fasten with a pin
pinafore n (pl -s) apron
pinafores n ▷ pinafore
pinball n (pl -s) electrically operated table game in which a small ball is shot through various hazards
pinballs n ▷ pinball
pincers pl n tool consisting of two hinged arms, for gripping
pinch v (-es, -ing, -ed) squeeze between finger and thumb ▶ n (pl -es) act of pinching
pinched v ▷ pinch
pinches n, v ▷ pinch
pinching v ▷ pinch
pine¹ n (pl -s) evergreen coniferous tree
pine² v (-nes, -ning, -ned) (foll. by for) feel great longing for, pining
pined v ▷ pine²
pines n, v ▷ pine¹, ²
ping v (-s, -ing, -ed) ▶ n (pl -s) (make) a short high-pitched sound
pinged v ▷ ping
pinging v ▷ ping
pings v, n ▷ ping

pining v ▷ pine²
pinion¹ n (pl -s) bird's wing ▶ v (-s, -ing, -ed) immobilize (someone) by tying or holding his or her arms
pinion² n (pl -s) small cogwheel
pinioned v ▷ pinion
pinioning v ▷ pinion
pinions n, v ▷ pinion¹, ²
pink n (pl -s) pale reddish colour ▶ adj (-er, -est) of the colour pink ▶ v (-s, -ing, -ed) (of an engine) make a metallic noise because not working properly, knock
pinked v ▷ pink
pinker adj ▷ pink
pinkest adj ▷ pink
pinking v ▷ pink
pinks n, v ▷ pink
pinnacle n (pl -s) highest point of fame or success
pinnacles n ▷ pinnacle
pinned v ▷ pin
pinning v ▷ pin
pinotage n (pl -s) blended red wine of S Africa
pinotages n ▷ pinotage
pinpoint v (-s, -ing, -ed) locate or identify exactly
pinpointed v ▷ pinpoint
pinpointing v ▷ pinpoint
pinpoints v ▷ pinpoint
pins n, v ▷ pin
pint n (pl -s) liquid measure, 1/8 gallon (.568 litre)
pints n ▷ pint
pioneer n (pl -s) explorer or early settler of a new country ▶ v (-s, -ing, -ed) be the pioneer or leader of
pioneered v ▷ pioneer
pioneering v ▷ pioneer
pioneers n, v ▷ pioneer
pious adj deeply religious, devout
pip¹ n (pl -s) small seed in a fruit
pip² n high-pitched sound used as a time signal on radio
pipe n (pl -s) tube for conveying liquid or gas ▶ pl bagpipes ▶ v (-pes, -ping, -ped) play on a pipe

piped v ▷ pipe

pipeline n (pl -s) long pipe for transporting oil, water, etc

pipelines n ▷ pipeline

piper n (pl -s) player on a pipe or bagpipes

pipers n ▷ piper

pipes n, v ▷ pipe

pipette n (pl -s) slender glass tube used to transfer or measure fluids

pipettes n ▷ pipette

pipi n (pl -s) AUST mollusc often used as bait

piping n (pl -s) system of pipes ▶ v ▷ pipe

pipings n ▷ piping

pipis n ▷ pipi

pipit n (pl -s) small brownish songbird

pipits n ▷ pipit

pippin n (pl -s) type of eating apple

pippins n ▷ pippin

pips n ▷ pip¹, ²

pips n ▷ pip¹, ²

piquancies n ▷ piquant

piquancy n ▷ piquant

piquant adj having a pleasant spicy taste ▷ **piquancy** n (pl -cies)

pique n (pl -s) feeling of hurt pride, baffled curiosity, or resentment ▶ v (-ques, -quing, -qued) hurt the pride of

piqué n (pl -s) stiff ribbed cotton fabric

piqued v ▷ pique

piques n, v ▷ pique

piqués n ▷ piqué

piquet n (pl -s) card game for two

piquets n ▷ piquet

piquing v ▷ pique

piracies n ▷ pirate

piracy n ▷ pirate

piranha n (pl -s) small fierce freshwater fish of tropical America

piranhas n ▷ piranha

pirate n (pl -s) sea robber ▶ v (-tes, -ting, -ted) sell or reproduce (artistic work etc) illegally ▷ **piracy** n (pl -cies) > **piratical** adj

pirated v ▷ pirate

pirates n, v ▷ pirate

piratical adj ▷ pirate

pirating v ▷ pirate

pis n ▷ pi

piste n (pl -s) ski slope

pistes n ▷ piste

pistil n (pl -s) seed-bearing part of a flower

pistils n ▷ pistil

pistol n (pl -s) short-barrelled handgun

pistols n ▷ pistol

piston n (pl -s) cylindrical part in an engine that slides to and fro in a cylinder

pistons n ▷ piston

pit n (pl -s) deep hole in the ground ▶ v (-s, -tting, -tteds) mark with small dents or scars

pitch¹ v (-es, -ing, -ed) throw, hurl ▶ n (pl -es) area marked out for playing sport

pitch² n dark sticky substance obtained from tar

pitched v ▷ pitch¹

pitcher n (pl -s) large jug with a narrow neck

pitchers n ▷ pitcher

pitches n, v ▷ pitch¹

pitching v ▷ pitch¹

piteous, pitiable adj arousing pity

pitfall n (pl -s) hidden difficulty or danger

pitfalls n ▷ pitfall

pith n (pl -s) soft white lining of the rind of oranges etc

pithier adj ▷ pithy

pithiest adj ▷ pithy

piths n ▷ pith

pithy adj (-thier, -thiest) short and full of meaning

pitiable adj ▷ piteous

pitied v ▷ pity

pities n, v ▷ pity

pitiful adj arousing pity ▶ **pitifully** adv

pitifully adv ▷ pitiful

pitiless adj feeling no pity or mercy > **pitilessly** adv

pitilessly adv ▷ pitiless

piton n (pl -s) metal spike used in climbing to secure a rope

pitons n ▷ **piton**

pits n, v ▷ **pit**

pittance n (pl -s) very small amount of money

pittances n ▷ **pittance**

pitted v ▷ **pit**

pitting v ▷ **pit**

pity n (pl -ies) sympathy or sorrow for others' suffering ▶ v (-ties, -tying, -tied) feel pity for

pitying v ▷ **pity**

pivot n (pl -s) central shaft on which something turns ▶ v (-s, -ing, -ed) provide with or turn on a pivot

pivotal adj of crucial importance

pivoted v ▷ **pivot**

pivoting v ▷ **pivot**

pivots n, v ▷ **pivot**

pix n informal ▷ **pic**

pixie n (pl -s) (in folklore) fairy

pixies n ▷ **pixie**

pizza n (pl -s) flat disc of dough covered with a wide variety of savoury toppings and baked

pizzas n ▷ **pizza**

placard n (pl -s) notice that is carried or displayed in public

placards n ▷ **placard**

placate v (-tes, -ting, -ted) make (someone) stop feeling angry or upset
> **placatory** adj

placated v ▷ **placate**

placates v ▷ **placate**

placating v ▷ **placate**

placatory adj ▷ **placate**

place n (pl -s) particular part of an area or space ▶ v (-ces, -cing, -ced) put in a particular place

placebo n (pl -bos, -boes) sugar pill etc given to an unsuspecting patient instead of an active drug

placeboes n ▷ **placebo**

placebos n ▷ **placebo**

placed v ▷ **place**

placenta n (pl -tas, -tae) organ formed in the womb during pregnancy,

providing nutrients for the fetus
> **placental** adj

placentae n ▷ **placenta**

placental adj ▷ **placenta**

placentas n ▷ **placenta**

places n, v ▷ **place**

placid adj (-er, -est) not easily excited or upset, calm ▷ **placidity** n (pl -ties)

placider adj ▷ **placid**

placidest adj ▷ **placid**

placidities n ▷ **placid**

placidity n ▷ **placid**

placing v ▷ **place**

plague n (pl -s) fast-spreading fatal disease ▶ v (-gues, -guing, -gued) trouble or annoy continually

plagued v ▷ **plague**

plagues n, v ▷ **plague**

plaguing v ▷ **plague**

plaice n (pl plaice) edible European flatfish

plaid n (pl -s) long piece of tartan cloth worn as part of Highland dress

plaids n ▷ **plaid**

plain (-er, -est) adj easy to see or understand ▶ n (pl -s) large stretch of level country ▷ **plainly** adv
> **plainness** n (pl -es)

plainer adj ▷ **plain**

plainest adj ▷ **plain**

plainly adj ▷ **plain**

plainness n ▷ **plain**

plainnesses n ▷ **plain**

plains n ▷ **plain**

plait n (pl -s) intertwined length of hair ▶ v (-s, -ing, -ed) intertwine separate strands in a pattern

plaited v ▷ **plait**

plaiting v ▷ **plait**

plaits n, v ▷ **plait**

plan n (pl -s) way thought out to do or achieve something ▶ v (-s, -nning, -nned) arrange beforehand
> **planner** n (pl -s)

plane[1] n (pl -s) aeroplane ▶ adj perfectly flat or level ▶ v (-nes, -ning, -ned) glide or skim

plane[2] n (pl -s) tool for smoothing

wood ▶ v (-nes, -ning, -ned) smooth (wood) with a plane

plane³ n (pl -s) tree with broad leaves

planed v ▷ **plane¹, ²**

planes n, v ▷ **plane¹, ², 3**

planet n (pl -s) large body in space that revolves round the sun or another star > **planetary** adj

planetary adj ▷ **planet**

planets n ▷ **planet**

plangent adj (of sounds) mournful and resounding

planing v ▷ **plane¹, 2**

plank n (pl -s) long flat piece of sawn timber

planks n ▷ **plank**

plankton n (pl -s) minute animals and plants floating in the surface water of a sea or lake

planktons n ▷ **plankton**

planned v ▷ **plan**

planner n ▷ **plan**

planners n ▷ **plan**

planning v ▷ **plan**

plans n, v ▷ **plan**

plant n (pl -s) living organism that grows in the ground and has no power to move ▶ v (-s, -ing, -ed) put in the ground to grow

plantain¹ n (pl -s) low-growing wild plant with broad leaves

plantain² n (-s) tropical fruit like a green banana

plantains n ▷ **plantain¹, 2**

planted v ▷ **plant**

planter n (pl -s) owner of a plantation

planters n ▷ **planter**

planting v ▷ **plant**

plants n, v ▷ **plant**

plaque n (pl -s) inscribed commemorative stone or metal plate

plaques n ▷ **plaque**

plasma n (pl -s) clear liquid part of blood

plasmas n ▷ **plasma**

plaster n (pl -s) mixture of lime, sand, etc for coating walls ▶ v (-s, -ing, -ed) cover with plaster

plastering v ▷ **plaster**

plasters n, v ▷ **plaster**

plastic n (pl -s) synthetic material that can be moulded when soft but sets in a hard long-lasting shape ▶ adj made of plastic

plastics n ▷ **plastic**

plate n (pl -s) shallow dish for holding food ▶ v (-tes, -ting, -ted) cover with a thin coating of gold, silver, or other metal ▶ **plateful** n (pl -s)

plateau n (pl -s, -x) area of level high land

plateaus n ▷ **plateau**

plateaux n ▷ **plateau**

plated v ▷ **plate**

plateful n ▷ **plate**

platefuls n ▷ **plate**

platen n (pl -s) roller of a typewriter, against which the paper is held

platens n ▷ **platen**

plates n, v ▷ **plate**

platform n (pl -s) raised floor

platforms n ▷ **platform**

plating v ▷ **plate**

platinum n (pl -s) CHEM valuable silvery-white metal

platinums n ▷ **platinum**

platonic adj (of a relationship) friendly or affectionate but not sexual

platoon n (pl -s) smaller unit within a company of soldiers

platoons n ▷ **platoon**

platter n (pl -s) large dish

platters n ▷ **platter**

platypus n (pl -es) Australian egg-laying amphibious mammal, with dense fur, webbed feet, and a ducklike bill (also **duck-billed platypus**)

platypuses n ▷ **platypus**

plaudits pl n expressions of approval

play v (-s, -ing, -ed) occupy oneself in (a game or recreation) ▶ n (pl -s) story performed on stage or broadcast

playboy n (pl -s) rich man who lives only for pleasure

playboys n ▷ **playboy**

played v ▷ **play**

player n (pl -s) person who plays a

game or sport

players n ▷ **player**

playful adj lively

playing v ▷ **play**

plays v, n ▷ **play**

plaza n (pl -**s**) open space or square

plazas n ▷ **plaza**

plea n (pl -**s**) serious or urgent request, entreaty

plead v (-**s**, -**ing**, -**ed**) ask urgently or with deep feeling

pleaded v ▷ **plead**

pleading v ▷ **plead**

pleads v ▷ **plead**

pleas n ▷ **plea**

pleasant adj (-**er**, -**est**) pleasing, enjoyable > **pleasantly** adv

pleasanter adj ▷ **pleasant**

pleasantest adj ▷ **pleasant**

pleasantly adv ▷ **pleasant**

please v (-**ses**, -**sing**, -**sed**) give pleasure or satisfaction to ▶ adv polite word of request > **pleased** adj > **pleasing** adj

pleased v, adj ▷ **please**

pleases v ▷ **please**

pleasing v, adj ▷ **please**

pleasure n (pl -**s**) feeling of happiness and satisfaction

pleasures n ▷ **pleasure**

pleat n (pl -**s**) fold made by doubling material back on itself ▶ v (-**s**, -**ing**, -**ed**) arrange (material) in pleats

pleated v ▷ **pleat**

pleating v ▷ **pleat**

pleats n, v ▷ **pleat**

plebeian adj of the lower social classes ▶ n (pl -**s**) (also **pleb**) member of the lower social classes

plebeians n ▷ **plebeian**

plectra n ▷ **plectrum**

plectrum n (pl -**rums**, -**ra**) small implement for plucking the strings of a guitar etc

plectrums n ▷ **plectrum**

pledge n (pl -**s**) solemn promise ▶ v (-**ges**, -**ging**, -**ged**) promise solemnly

pledged v ▷ **pledge**

pledges n, v ▷ **pledge**

pledging v ▷ **pledge**

plenary adj (of a meeting) attended by all members

plenties n ▷ **plenty**

plenty n (pl -**ties**) large amount or number

pleonasm n (pl -**s**) use of more words than necessary

pleonasms n ▷ **pleonasm**

plethora n (pl -**s**) excess

plethoras n ▷ **plethora**

pleurisies n ▷ **pleurisy**

pleurisy n (pl -**sies**) inflammation of the membrane covering the lungs

pliabilities n ▷ **pliable**

pliability n ▷ **pliable**

pliable adj easily bent > **pliability** n (pl -**ties**)

pliancies n ▷ **pliant**

pliancy n ▷ **pliant**

pliant adj pliable > **pliancy** n (pl -**cies**)

plied v ▷ **ply**

pliers pl n tool with hinged arms and jaws for gripping

plies v, n ▷ **ply**

plight¹ n (pl -**s**) difficult or dangerous situation

plight² v (-**s**, -**ing**, -**ed**) promise formally

plighted v ▷ **plight²**

plighting v ▷ **plight²**

plights n, v ▷ **plight¹, ²**

plinth n (pl -**s**) slab forming the base of a statue, column, etc

plinths n ▷ **plinth**

plod v (-**s**, -**dding**, -**dded**) walk with slow heavy steps ▶ **plodder** n (pl -**s**)

plodded v ▷ **plod**

plodder n ▷ **plod**

plodders n ▷ **plod**

plodding v ▷ **plod**

plods v ▷ **plod**

plonk¹ v (-**s**, -**ing**, -**ed**) put (something) down heavily and carelessly

plonk² n (pl -**s**) informal cheap inferior wine

plonked v ▷ **plonk¹**

plonking v ▷ plonk¹
plonks v, n ▷ plonk¹, ²

plop n (pl -s) sound of an object falling into water without a splash ▶ v (-s, -pping, -pped) make this sound
plopped v ▷ plop
plopping v ▷ plop
plops n, v ▷ plop

plot¹ n (pl -s) secret plan to do something illegal or wrong ▶ v (-s, -tting, -tted) plan secretly, conspire

plot² n (-s) small piece of land
plots n, v ▷ plot¹, ²
plotted v ▷ plot¹
plotting v ▷ plot¹

plough n (pl -s) agricultural tool for turning over soil ▶ v (-s, -ing, -ed) turn over (earth) with a plough
> **ploughman** n (pl -men)
ploughed v ▷ plough
ploughing v ▷ plough
ploughman n ▷ plough
ploughmen n ▷ plough
ploughs n, v ▷ plough

plover n (pl -s) shore bird with a straight bill and long pointed wings
plovers n ▷ plover

ploy n (pl -s) manoeuvre designed to gain an advantage
ploys n ▷ ploy

pluck v (-s, -ing, -ed) pull or pick off ▶ n (pl -s) courage
plucked v ▷ pluck
pluckier adj ▷ plucky
pluckiest adj ▷ plucky
pluckily adj ▷ plucky
plucking v ▷ pluck
plucks v, n ▷ pluck

plucky adj (-kier, -kiest) brave
> **pluckily** adv

plug n (pl -s) thing fitting into and filling a hole ▶ v (-s, -gging, -gged) block or seal (a hole or gap) with a plug
plugged v ▷ plug
plugging v ▷ plug
plugs n, v ▷ plug

plum n (pl -s) oval usu. dark red fruit with a stone in the middle ▶ adj dark

purplish-red

plumage n (pl -s) bird's feathers
plumages n ▷ plumage

plumb v (-s, -ing, -ed) understand (something obscure) ▶ adv exactly
plumbed v ▷ plumb

plumber n (pl -s) person who fits and repairs pipes and fixtures for water and drainage systems
plumbers n ▷ plumber

plumbing n pipes and fixtures used in water and drainage systems ▶ v ▷ plumb
plumbs v ▷ plumb

plume n (pl -s) feather, esp. one worn as an ornament
plumes n ▷ plume

plummet v (-s, -ing, -ed) plunge downward
plummeted v ▷ plummet
plummeting v ▷ plummet
plummets v ▷ plummet

plump¹ adj (-er, -est) moderately or attractively fat > **plumpness** n (pl -es)

plump² v (-s, -ing, -ed) sit or fall heavily and suddenly
plumped v ▷ plump²
plumper adj ▷ plump¹
plumpest adj ▷ plump¹
plumping v ▷ plump²
plumpness n ▷ plump¹
plumpnesses n ▷ plump¹
plumps v ▷ plump²
plums n ▷ plum

plunder v (-s, -ing, -ed) take by force, esp. in time of war ▶ n (pl -s) things plundered, spoils
plundered v ▷ plunder
plundering v ▷ plunder
plunders v, n ▷ plunder

plunge v (-ges, -ging, -ged) put or throw forcibly or suddenly (into) ▶ n (pl -s) plunging, dive
plunged v ▷ plunge

plunger n (pl -s) rubber suction cup used to clear blocked pipes
plungers n ▷ plunger
plunges v, n ▷ plunge

plunging v ▷ plunge

plural adj of or consisting of more than one ► n (pl -s) word indicating more than one

plurals n ▷ plural

plus prep, adj indicating addition ► adj more than zero ► n (pl -es) sign (+) denoting addition

pluses n ▷ plus

plush n (pl -es) fabric with long velvety pile ► adj (-er, -est) (also **plushy**; -ier, -iest) luxurious

plusher adj ▷ plush

plushes n ▷ plush

plushest adj ▷ plush

plushier adj ▷ plush

plushiest adj ▷ plush

ply¹ v (-ies, -ying, -ied) work at (a job or trade)

ply² n (pl -ies) thickness of wool, fabric, etc

plying v ▷ ply¹

plywood n (pl -s) board made of thin layers of wood glued together

plywoods n ▷ plywood

poach¹ v (-es, -ing, -ed) catch (animals) illegally on someone's land

poach² v (-es, -ing, -ed) simmer (food) gently in liquid

poached v ▷ poach

poacher n (pl -s) person who catches animals illegally on someone else's land

poachers n ▷ poacher

poaches v ▷ poach

poaching v ▷ poach

pocket n (pl -s) small bag sewn into clothing for carrying things ► v (-s, -ing, -ed) put into one's pocket ► adj small

pocketed v ▷ pocket

pocketing v ▷ pocket

pockets n, v ▷ pocket

pod n (pl -s) long narrow seed case of peas, beans, etc

podgier adj ▷ podgy

podgiest adj ▷ podgy

podgy adj (-gier, -giest) short and fat

podia n ▷ podium

podium n (pl -diums, -dia) small raised platform for a conductor or speaker

podiums n ▷ podium

pods n ▷ pod

poem n (pl -s) imaginative piece of writing in rhythmic lines

poems n ▷ poem

poep n (pl -s) AFR slang emission of gas from the anus

poeps n ▷ poep

poesies n ▷ poesy

poesy n (pl -sies) obs poetry

poet n (pl -s) writer of poems

poetic, poetical adj of or like poetry > **poetically** adv

poetical adj ▷ poetic

poetically adv ▷ poetic

poetries n ▷ poetry

poetry n (pl -ries) poems

poets n ▷ poet

pogrom n (pl -s) organized persecution and massacre

pogroms n ▷ pogrom

poignancies n ▷ poignant

poignancy n ▷ poignant

poignant adj sharply painful to the feelings > **poignancy** n (pl -cies)

point n (pl -s) main idea in a discussion, argument, etc ► v (-s, -ing, -ed) show the direction or position of something or draw attention to it by extending a finger or other pointed object towards it

pointed adj having a sharp end ► v ▷ point > **pointedly** adv

pointedly adv ▷ pointed

pointer n (pl -s) helpful hint

pointers n ▷ pointer

pointing v ▷ point

points n, v ▷ point

poise n (pl -s) calm dignified manner

poised adj absolutely ready

poises n ▷ poise

poison n (pl -s) substance that kills or injures when swallowed or absorbed

▶ v (-s, -ing, -ed) give poison to
> **poisoner** n (pl -s) > **poisonous** adj
poisoned v ▷ poison
poisoner n ▷ poison
poisoners n ▷ poison
poisoning v ▷ poison
poisonous adj ▷ poison
poisons n, v ▷ poison
poke v (-kes, -king, -ked) jab or prod with one's finger, a stick, etc ▶ n (pl -s) poking
poked v ▷ poke
poker[1] n (pl -s) metal rod for stirring a fire
poker[2] n (pl -s) card game in which players bet on the hands dealt
pokers n ▷ poker[1, 2]
pokes v, n ▷ poke
pokier adj ▷ poky
pokiest adj ▷ poky
poking v ▷ poke
poky adj (-kier, -kiest) small and cramped
polar adj of or near either of the earth's poles
polarization n ▷ polarize
polarizations n ▷ polarize
polarize v (-zes, -zing, -zed) form or cause to form into groups with directly opposite views > **polarization** n (pl -s)
polarized v ▷ polarize
polarizes v ▷ polarize
polarizing v ▷ polarize
polder n (pl -s) land reclaimed from the sea, esp. in the Netherlands
polders n ▷ polder
pole[1] n (pl -s) long rounded piece of wood etc
pole[2] n (pl -s) point furthest north or south on the earth's axis of rotation
poleaxe v (-xes, -xing, -xed) hit or stun with a heavy blow
poleaxed v ▷ poleaxe
poleaxes v ▷ poleaxe
poleaxing v ▷ poleaxe
polecat n (pl -s) small animal of the weasel family
polecats n ▷ polecat

polemic n (pl -s) fierce attack on or defence of a particular opinion, belief, etc > **polemical** adj
polemical adj ▷ polemic
polemics n ▷ polemic
poles n ▷ pole[1, 2]
police n organized force in a state which keeps law and order ▶ v (-ces, -cing, -ced) control or watch over with police or a similar body
policed v ▷ police
polices v ▷ police
policies n ▷ policy[1, 2]
policing v ▷ police
policy[1] n (pl -cies) plan of action adopted by a person, group, or state
policy[2] n (pl -ies) document containing an insurance contract
polio n (pl -s) disease affecting the spinal cord, which often causes paralysis (also **poliomyelitis**)
polios n ▷ polio
polish v (-es, -ing, -ed) make smooth and shiny by rubbing ▶ n (pl -es) substance used for polishing
polished adj accomplished ▶ v ▷ polish
polishes v, n ▷ polish
polishing v ▷ polish
polite adj showing consideration for others in one's manners, speech, etc > **politely** adv > **politeness** n (pl -es)
politely adv ▷ polite
politeness n ▷ polite
politic adj wise and likely to prove advantageous
politics n winning and using of power to govern society
polka n (pl -s) lively 19th-century dance
polkas n ▷ polka
poll n (pl -s) (also **opinion poll**) questioning of a random sample of people to find out general opinion ▶ v (-s, -ing, -ed) receive (votes)
polled v ▷ poll
pollen n (pl -s) fine dust produced by flowers to fertilize other flowers
pollens n ▷ pollen

polling v ▷ **poll**

polls n, v ▷ **poll**

pollster n (pl **-s**) person who conducts opinion polls

pollsters n ▷ **pollster**

pollute v (**-tes, -ting, -ted**) contaminate with something poisonous or harmful ▷ **pollution** n (pl **-s**)

polluted v ▷ **pollute**

pollutes v ▷ **pollute**

polluting v ▷ **pollute**

pollution n ▷ **pollute**

pollutions n ▷ **pollute**

polo n (pl **-s**) game like hockey played by teams of players on horseback

polonium n (pl **-s**) CHEM radioactive element that occurs in trace amounts in uranium ores

poloniums n ▷ **polonium**

polos n ▷ **polo**

poltroon n (pl **-s**) obs utter coward

poltroons n ▷ **poltroon**

polygamies n ▷ **polygamy**

polygamist n ▷ **polygamy**

polygamists n ▷ **polygamy**

polygamous adj ▷ **polygamy**

polygamy n (pl **-mies**) practice of having more than one husband or wife at the same time ▷ **polygamous** adj ▷ **polygamist** n (pl **-s**)

polyglot adj, n (pl **-s**) (person) able to speak or write several languages

polyglots n ▷ **polyglot**

polygon n (pl **-s**) geometrical figure with three or more angles and sides ▷ **polygonal** adj

polygonal adj ▷ **polygon**

polygons n ▷ **polygon**

polymer n (pl **-s**) chemical compound with large molecules made of simple molecules of the same kind

polymers n ▷ **polymer**

polyp n (pl **-s**) small simple sea creature with a hollow cylindrical body

polyps n ▷ **polyp**

pom n (pl **-s**) AUST & NZ slang person from England (also **pommy**) (pl **-mies**)

pomander n (pl **-s**) (container for) a mixture of sweet-smelling petals, herbs, etc

pomanders n ▷ **pomander**

pommel n (pl **-s**) raised part on the front of a saddle

pommels n ▷ **pommel**

pommies n ▷ **pom**

pommy n ▷ **pom**

pomp n (pl **-s**) stately display or ceremony

pompom n (pl **-s**) decorative ball of tufted wool, silk, etc

pompoms n ▷ **pompom**

pomposities n ▷ **pompous**

pomposity n ▷ **pompous**

pompous adj foolishly serious and grand, self-important ▷ **pompously** adv ▷ **pomposity** n (pl **-ties**)

pompously adv ▷ **pompous**

pomps n ▷ **pomp**

poms n ▷ **pom**

poncho n (pl **-s**) loose circular cloak with a hole for the head

ponchos n ▷ **poncho**

pond n (pl **-s**) small area of still water

ponder v (**-s, -ing, -ed**) think thoroughly or deeply (about)

pondered v ▷ **ponder**

pondering v ▷ **ponder**

ponders v ▷ **ponder**

ponds n ▷ **pond**

pong n, v (pl **-s**) informal (give off) a strong unpleasant smell

pongs n ▷ **pong**

ponies n ▷ **pony**

pontiff n (pl **-s**) the Pope

pontiffs n ▷ **pontiff**

pontoon[1] n (pl **-s**) floating platform supporting a temporary bridge

pontoon[2] n (pl **-s**) gambling card game

pontoons n ▷ **pontoon**[1, 2]

pony n (pl **-nies**) small horse

ponytail n (pl **-s**) long hair tied in one bunch at the back of the head

ponytails n ▷ **ponytail**

poodle n (pl -s) dog with curly hair often clipped fancifully

poodles n ▷ poodle

pool¹ n (pl -s) small body of still water

pool² n (pl -s) shared fund or group of workers or resources ▶ v (-s, -ing, -ed) put in a common fund

pooled v ▷ pool²

pooling v ▷ pool²

pools n, v ▷ pool¹, ²

poop n (pl -s) raised part at the back of a sailing ship

poops n ▷ poop

poor adj having little money and few possessions

poorlier adj ▷ poorly

poorliest adj ▷ poorly

poorly adv in a poor manner ▶ adj (-lier, -liest) not in good health

pop¹ v (-s, -pping, -pped) make or cause to make a small explosive sound informal ▶ n small explosive sound BRIT

pop² n (pl -s) music of general appeal, esp. to young people

pop³ n (pl -s) informal father

popcorn n (pl -s) grains of maize heated until they puff up and burst

popcorns n ▷ popcorn

pope n (pl -s) head of the Roman Catholic Church

popes n ▷ pope

poplar n (pl -s) tall slender tree

poplars n ▷ poplar

poplin n (pl -s) ribbed cotton material

poplins n ▷ poplin

poppadom n (pl -s) thin round crisp Indian bread

poppadoms n ▷ poppadom

popped v ▷ pop¹

poppies n ▷ poppy

popping v ▷ pop¹

poppy n (pl -ppies) plant with a large red flower

pops n ▷ pop

populace n (pl -s) the ordinary people

populaces n ▷ populace

popular adj widely liked and admired > popularly adv > popularity n (pl -ties)

popularities n ▷ popular

popularity n ▷ popular

popularly adv ▷ popular

populate v (-tes, -ting, -ted) live in, inhabit

populated v ▷ populate

populates v ▷ populate

populating v ▷ populate

populous adj densely populated

porch n (pl -es) covered approach to the entrance of a building

porches n ▷ porch

porcine adj of or like a pig

pore n (pl -s) tiny opening in the skin or in the surface of a plant

pores n ▷ pore

pork n (pl -s) pig meat

porker n (pl -s) pig raised for food

porkers n ▷ porker

porks n ▷ pork

pornos n ▷ porn

porns n ▷ porn

porosities n ▷ porous

porosity n ▷ porous

porous adj allowing liquid to pass through gradually > porosity n (pl -ties)

porphyries n ▷ porphyry

porphyry n (pl -ries) reddish rock with large crystals in it

porpoise n (pl -s) fishlike sea mammal

porpoises n ▷ porpoise

porridge n (pl -s) breakfast food made of oatmeal cooked in water or milk

porridges n ▷ porridge

port¹ n (pl -s) (town with) a harbour

port² n (pl -s) left side of a ship or aircraft when facing the front of it

port³ n (pl -s) strong sweet wine, usu. red

port⁴ n (pl -s) opening in the side of a ship

portabilities n ▷ portable

portability n ▷ portable

portable adj easily carried > portability n (pl -ies)

portal n (pl -s) large imposing doorway or gate

portals n ▷ portal

portend v (-s, -ing, -ed) be a sign of

portended v ▷ portend

portending v ▷ portend

portends n ▷ portend

portent n (pl -s) sign of a future event

portents n ▷ portent

porter¹ n (pl -s) man who carries luggage

porter² n (pl -s) doorman or gatekeeper of a building

porters n ▷ porter¹, ²

porthole n (pl -s) small round window in a ship or aircraft

portholes n ▷ porthole

portico n (pl -es, -s) porch or covered walkway with columns supporting the roof

porticoes n ▷ portico

porticos n ▷ portico

portion n (pl -s) part or share

portions n ▷ portion

portlier adj ▷ portly

portliest adj ▷ portly

portly adj (-lier, -liest) rather fat

portrait n (pl -s) picture of a person

portraits n ▷ portrait

portray v (-s, -ing, -ed) describe or represent by artistic means, as in writing or film > portrayal n (pl -s)

portrayal n ▷ portray

portrayals n ▷ portray

portrayed v ▷ portray

portraying v ▷ portray

portrays v ▷ portray

ports n ▷ port¹, ², ³, ⁴

pose v (-ses, -sing, -sed) place in or take up a particular position to be photographed or drawn ► n (pl -s) position while posing

posed v ▷ pose

poser n (pl -s) puzzling question

posers n ▷ poser

poses v, n ▷ pose

poseur n (pl -s) person who behaves in an affected way to impress others

poseurs n ▷ poseur

posh adj informal smart, luxurious

posies n ▷ posy

posing v ▷ pose

posit v (-s, -ing, -ed) lay down as a basis for argument

posited v ▷ posit

positing v ▷ posit

position n (pl -s) place ► v (-s, -ing, -ed) place

positioned v ▷ position

positioning v ▷ position

positions n, v ▷ position

positive adj feeling no doubts, certain > positively adv

positively adv ▷ positive

positron n (pl -s) PHYSICS particle with same mass as electron but positive charge

positrons n ▷ positron

posits v ▷ posit

posse n (pl -s) US group of men organized to maintain law and order

posses n ▷ posse

possess v (-es, -ing, -ed) have as one's property > possessor n (pl -s)

possessed v ▷ possess

possesses v ▷ possess

possessing v ▷ possess

possessor n ▷ possess

possessors n ▷ possess

possibility n ▷ possible

possible adj able to exist, happen, or be done ► n (pl -s) person or thing that might be suitable or chosen > possibility n (pl -ties)

possibles n ▷ possible

possibly adv perhaps, not necessarily

possums n ▷ possum

post¹ n (pl -s) official system of delivering letters and parcels ► v (-s, -ing, -ed) send by post > postal adj

post² n (pl -s) length of wood, concrete, etc fixed upright to support or mark something ► v (-s, -ing, -ed) put up (a notice) in a public place

post³ n (pl -s) job ► v (-s, -ing, -ed) send (a person) to a new place to work

postage n charge for sending a letter or parcel by post

postages n ▷ postage
postal adj ▷ post¹
postbag n (pl -s) postman's bag
  postbags n ▷ postbag
postcard n (pl -s) card for sending a
  message by post without an envelope
  postcards n ▷ postcard
postcode n system of letters and
  numbers used to aid the sorting of mail
  postcodes n ▷ postcode
postdate v (-tes, -ting, -ted) write a
  date on (a cheque) that is later than the
  actual date
  postdated v ▷ postdate
  postdates v ▷ postdate
  postdating v ▷ postdate
  posted v ▷ post¹, ², ³
poster n (pl -s) large picture or notice
  stuck on a wall
postern n (pl -s) small back door or gate
  posterns n ▷ postern
  posters n ▷ poster
postie n (pl -s) SCOT, AUST & NZ informal
  postman
  posties n ▷ postie
  posting v ▷ post¹, ², ³
postman, postwoman n (pl -men,
  -women) person who collects and
  delivers post
postmark n (pl -s) official mark
  stamped on letters showing place and
  date of posting
  postmarks n ▷ postmark
  postmen n ▷ postman
postpone v (-nes, -ning, -ned) put
  off to a later time ▶ **postponement** n
  (pl -s)
  postponed v ▷ postpone
  postponement n ▷ postpone
  postponements n ▷ postpone
  postpones v ▷ postpone
  postponing v ▷ postpone
  posts n, v ▷ post¹, ², ³
posture n (pl -s) position or way in
  which someone stands, walks, etc
  ▶ v (-res, -ring, -red) behave in an
  exaggerated way to get attention
  postured v ▷ posture

postures n, v ▷ posture
posturing v ▷ posture
postwomen n ▷ postman
posy n (pl -sies) small bunch of flowers
pot¹ n (pl -s) round deep container ▶ pl
  informal large amount ▶ v (-s, -tting,
  -tted) plant in a pot
pot² n slang cannabis
potable adj drinkable
potash n (pl -es) white powdery
  substance obtained from ashes and
  used as fertilizer
  potashes n ▷ potash
potato n (pl -es) roundish starchy
  vegetable that grows underground
  potatoes n ▷ potato
poteen n (in Ireland) illegally
  made alcoholic drink
  poteens n ▷ poteen
  potencies n ▷ potent
  potency n ▷ potent
potent adj having great power or
  influence ▶ **potency** n (pl -cies)
pothole n (pl -s) hole in the surface
  of a road
  potholes n ▷ pothole
potion n (pl -s) dose of medicine or
  poison
  potions n ▷ potion
potoroo n (pl -s) Australian leaping
  rodent
  potoroos n ▷ potoroo
  pots n ▷ pot¹
pottage n (pl -s) old-fashioned thick
  soup or stew
  pottages n ▷ pottage
potted adj grown in a pot ▶ v ▷ pot¹
potter¹ n (pl -s) person who makes
  pottery
potter² v (-s, -ing, -ed) be busy in a
  pleasant but aimless way
  pottered v ▷ potter²
  potteries n ▷ pottery
  pottering v ▷ potter²
  potters n, v ▷ potter¹, ²
pottery n (pl -ries) articles made from
  baked clay
  pottier adj ▷ potty

potties n ▷ **potty²**

pottiest adj ▷ **potty**

potting v ▷ **pot¹**

potty¹ adj (**-tier, -tiest**) informal crazy or silly

potty² n (pl **-tties**) bowl used by a small child as a toilet

pouch n (pl **-es**) small bag

pouches n ▷ **pouch**

pouf, pouffe n (pl **-s**) large solid cushion used as a seat

pouffe n ▷ **pouf**

pouffes n ▷ **pouf**

poufs n ▷ **pouf**

poultice n (pl **-s**) moist dressing, often heated, applied to inflamed skin

poultices n ▷ **poultice**

poultries n ▷ **poultry**

poultry n (pl **-ries**) domestic fowls

pounce v (**-ces, -cing, -ced**) spring upon suddenly to attack or capture ▶ n (pl **-s**) pouncing

pounced v ▷ **pounce**

pounces v, n ▷ **pounce**

pouncing v ▷ **pounce**

pound¹ n (pl **-s**) monetary unit of Britain and some other countries

pound² v (**-s, -ing, -ed**) hit heavily and repeatedly

pound³ n (pl **-s**) enclosure for stray animals or officially removed vehicles

pounded v ▷ **pound²**

pounding v ▷ **pound²**

pounds n, v ▷ **pound¹, 3**

pour v (**-s, -ing, -ed**) flow or cause to flow out in a stream

poured v ▷ **pour**

pouring v ▷ **pour**

pours v ▷ **pour**

pout v (**-s, -ing, -ed**) thrust out one's lips, look sulky ▶ n (pl **-s**) pouting look

pouted v ▷ **pout**

pouting v ▷ **pout**

pouts v, n ▷ **pout**

poverties n ▷ **poverty**

poverty n (pl **-ties**) state of being without enough food or money

powder n (pl **-s**) substance in the form of tiny loose particles ▶ v (**-s, -ing, -ed**) apply powder to ▷ **powdery** adj (**-rier, -riest**)

powdered adj, v ▷ **powder**

powderier adj ▷ **powder**

powderiest adj ▷ **powder**

powdering v ▷ **powder**

powders n, v ▷ **powder**

power n (pl **-s**) ability to do or act > **powerful** adj > **powerless** adj

powered adj having or operated by mechanical or electrical power

powerful adj ▷ **power**

powerless adj ▷ **power**

powers n ▷ **power**

powwow n (pl **-s**) informal talk or conference

powwows n ▷ **powwow**

pox n (pl **-es**) disease in which skin pustules form

poxes n ▷ **pox**

> **poz** adj. Poz is an old-fashioned short form of **positive**. This is a good word for a crowded board towards the end of the game, especially if you can form another word in the process, or form it on a bonus square. Poz scores 24 points.

practice n (pl **-s**) something done regularly or habitually

practices n ▷ **practice**

practise v (**-ses, -sing, -sed**) do repeatedly so as to gain skill

practised v ▷ **practise**

practises v ▷ **practise**

practising v ▷ **practise**

prairie n (pl **-s**) large treeless area of grassland, esp. in N America and Canada

prairies n ▷ **prairie**

praise v (**-ses, -sing, -sed**) express approval or admiration of (someone or something) ▶ n (pl **-s**) something said or written to show approval or admiration > **praiseworthy** adj

praised v ▷ **praise**

praises v, n ▷ **praise**

praiseworthy adj ▷ **praise**

praising v ▷ praise
praline n (pl -s) sweet made of nuts and caramelized sugar
pralines n ▷ praline
pram n (pl -s) four-wheeled carriage for a baby, pushed by hand
prams n ▷ pram
prance v (-ces, -cing, -ced) walk with exaggerated bouncing steps
pranced v ▷ prance
prances v ▷ prance
prancing v ▷ prance
prang v, n (pl -s) slang (have) a crash in a car or aircraft
prangs n ▷ prang
prank n (pl -s) mischievous trick
pranks n ▷ prank
prat n (pl -s) BRIT, AUST & NZ informal stupid person
prats n ▷ prat
prattle v (-les, -ling, -led) chatter in a childish or foolish way ▶ n (pl -s) childish or foolish talk
prattled v ▷ prattle
prattles v, n ▷ prattle
prattling v ▷ prattle
prawn n (pl -s) edible shellfish like a large shrimp
prawns n ▷ prawn
praxis n (pl -es) practice as opposed to theory
praxises n ▷ praxis
pray v (-s, -ing, -ed) say prayers
prayed v ▷ pray
prayer n (pl -s) thanks or appeal addressed to one's God
prayers n ▷ prayer
praying v ▷ pray
prays v ▷ pray
preach v (-es, -ing, -ed) give a talk on a religious theme as part of a church service
preached v ▷ preach
preacher n (pl -s) person who preaches, esp. in church
preachers n ▷ preacher
preaches v ▷ preach
preaching v ▷ preach

preamble n (pl -s) introductory part to something said or written
preambles n ▷ preamble
precede v (-des, -ding, -ded) go or be before
preceded v ▷ precede
precedes v ▷ precede
preceding v ▷ precede
precept n (pl -s) rule of behaviour
>**preceptive** adj
preceptive adj ▷ precept
precepts n ▷ precept
precinct n (pl -s) BRIT, AUST & S AFR area in a town closed to traffic ▶ pl surrounding region
precincts n ▷ precinct
precious adj of great value and importance
précis n (pl précis) short written summary of a longer piece ▶ v (-ses, -sing, -sed) make a précis of
precise adj (-r, -st) exact, accurate in every detail >**precisely** adv
>**precision** n (pl -s)
précised v ▷ précis
precisely adv ▷ precise
preciser adj ▷ precise
précises n ▷ précis
precisest adj ▷ precise
précising v ▷ précis
precision n ▷ precise
precisions n ▷ precise
preclude v (-des, -ding, -ded) make impossible to happen
precluded v ▷ preclude
precludes v ▷ preclude
precluding v ▷ preclude
predate v (-tes, -ting, -ted) occur at an earlier date than
predated v ▷ predate
predates v ▷ predate
predating v ▷ predate
predator n (pl -s) predatory animal
predict v (-s, -ing, -ed) tell about in advance, prophesy >**predictable** adj
>**prediction** n (pl -s)
predictable adj ▷ predict
predicted v ▷ predict

predicting v ▷ **predict**

prediction n ▷ **predict**

predictions n ▷ **predict**

predicts v ▷ **predict**

preen v (-s, -ing, -ed) (of a bird) clean or trim (feathers) with the beak

preened v ▷ **preen**

preening v ▷ **preen**

preens v ▷ **preen**

prefab n (pl -s) prefabricated house

prefabs n ▷ **prefab**

preface n (pl -s) introduction to a book ▶ v (-ces, -cing, -ced) serve as an introduction to (a book, speech, etc) > **prefatory** adj

prefaced v ▷ **preface**

prefaces n, v ▷ **preface**

prefacing v ▷ **preface**

prefatory adj ▷ **preface**

prefect n (pl -s) senior pupil in a school, with limited power over others

prefects n ▷ **prefect**

prefer v (-s, -rring, -rred) like better > **preference** n (pl -s)

preference n ▷ **prefer**

preferences n ▷ **prefer**

preferred v ▷ **prefer**

preferring v ▷ **prefer**

prefers v ▷ **prefer**

prefix n (pl -es) letter or group of letters put at the beginning of a word to make a new word, such as un- in unhappy ▶ v (-es, -ing, -ed) put as an introduction or prefix (to)

prefixed v ▷ **prefix**

prefixes n, v ▷ **prefix**

prefixing v ▷ **prefix**

pregnancies n ▷ **pregnant**

pregnancy n ▷ **pregnant**

pregnant adj carrying a fetus in the womb > **pregnancy** n (pl -cies)

prelate n (pl -s) bishop or other churchman of high rank

prelates n ▷ **prelate**

prelude n (pl -s) introductory movement in music

preludes n ▷ **prelude**

premier n (pl -s) prime minister ▶ adj

chief, leading > **premiership** n (pl -s)

première n (pl -s) first performance of a play, film, etc

premières n ▷ **première**

premiers n ▷ **premier**

premiership n ▷ **premier**

premierships n ▷ **premier**

premise, premiss n (pl -s or -es) statement assumed to be true and used as the basis of reasoning

premises n ▷ **premise**

premises pl n house or other building and its land

premium n (pl -s) additional sum of money, as on a wage or charge

premiums n ▷ **premium**

prenatal adj before birth, during pregnancy

prepaid adj paid for in advance

prepare v (-res, -ring, -red) make or get ready

prepared adj willing ▶ v ▷ **prepare**

prepares v ▷ **prepare**

preparing v ▷ **prepare**

prepuce n (pl -s) retractable fold of skin covering the tip of the penis, foreskin

prepuces n ▷ **prepuce**

presage v (-ges, -ging, -ged) be a sign or warning of

presaged v ▷ **presage**

presages v ▷ **presage**

presaging v ▷ **presage**

presence n (pl -s) fact of being in a specified place

presences n ▷ **presence**

present[1] adj being in a specified place ▶ n (pl -s) present time or tense

present[2] n something given to bring pleasure to another person ▶ v (-s, -ing, -ed) introduce formally or publicly > **presentation** n (pl -s)

presented v ▷ **present**[2]

presenting v ▷ **present**[2]

presents n, v ▷ **present**[1, 2]

preservation n ▷ **preserve**

preservations n ▷ **preserve**

preserve v (-ves, -ving, -ved) keep from being damaged, changed, or ended ▶ n (pl -s) area of interest restricted to a particular person or group > **preservation** n (pl -s)

preserved v ▷ preserve

preserves v, n ▷ preserve

preserving v ▷ preserve

preside v (-des, -ding, -ded) be in charge, esp. of a meeting

presided v ▷ preside

presides v ▷ preside

presiding v ▷ preside

press v (-es, -ing, -ed) apply force or weight to ▶ n (pl -es) printing machine

pressed v ▷ press

presses n ▷ press

presses v, n ▷ press

pressing adj urgent ▶ v ▷ press

pressure n (pl -s) force produced by pressing

pressures n ▷ pressure

prestige n (pl -s) high status or respect resulting from success or achievements > **prestigious** adj

prestiges n ▷ prestige

prestigious adj ▷ prestige

presto adv music very quickly

presume v (-mes, -ing, -med) suppose to be the case

presumed v ▷ presume

presumed v ▷ presume

presumes v ▷ presume

presuming v ▷ presume

pretence n (pl -s) behaviour intended to deceive, pretending

pretences n ▷ pretence

pretend v (-s, -ing, -ed) claim or give the appearance of (something untrue) to deceive or in play

pretended v ▷ pretend

pretending v ▷ pretend

pretends v ▷ pretend

pretext n (pl -s) false reason given to hide the real one

pretexts n ▷ pretext

prettier adj ▷ pretty

prettiest adj ▷ pretty

prettily adv ▷ pretty

prettiness n ▷ pretty

prettinesses n ▷ pretty

pretty adj (-tier, -tiest) pleasing to look at ▶ adv fairly, moderately > **prettily** adv > **prettiness** n (pl -es)

pretzel n (pl -s) brittle salted biscuit

pretzels n ▷ pretzel

prevail v (-s, -ing, -ed) gain mastery

prevailed v ▷ prevail

prevails v ▷ prevail

prevent v (-s, -ing, -ed) keep from happening or doing > **preventable** adj > **prevention** n (pl -s) > **preventive** adj, n (pl -s)

preventable adj ▷ prevent

prevented v ▷ prevent

preventing v ▷ prevent

prevention n ▷ prevent

preventions n ▷ prevent

preventive adj, n ▷ prevent

preventives n ▷ prevent

prevents v ▷ prevent

preview n (pl -s) advance showing of a film or exhibition before it is shown to the public

previews n ▷ preview

previous adj coming or happening before > **previously** adv

previously adv ▷ previous

prey n (pl -s) animal hunted and killed for food by another animal

preys n ▷ prey

price n (pl -s) amount of money for which a thing is bought or sold ▶ v (-ces, -cing, -ced) fix or ask the price of

priced v ▷ price

prices n, v ▷ price

pricey adj (-cier, -ciest) informal expensive

pricier adj ▷ pricey

priciest adj ▷ pricey

pricing v ▷ price

prick v (-s, -ing, -ed) pierce lightly with a sharp point ▶ n (pl -s) sudden sharp pain caused by pricking

pricked v ▷ prick

pricking v ▷ prick

prickle n (pl -s) thorn or spike on a plant ▶ v (-les, -ling, -led) have

a tingling or pricking sensation
> **prickly** adj (**-lier, -liest**)
prickled v ▷ **prickle**
prickles n, v ▷ **prickle**
pricklier adj ▷ **prickle**
prickliest adj ▷ **prickle**
prickling v ▷ **prickle**
prickly adj ▷ **prickle**
pricks v, n ▷ **prick**
pride n (pl **-s**) feeling of pleasure and
satisfaction when one has done well
prides n ▷ **pride**
pried v ▷ **pry**
pries v ▷ **pry**
priest n (pl **-s**) (in the Christian church)
a person who can administer the
sacraments and preach **priestess** n
fem (pl **-es**) > **priesthood** n (pl **-s**)
> **priestly** adj (**-lier, -liest**)
priestess n ▷ **priest**
priestesses n ▷ **priest**
priesthood n ▷ **priest**
priesthoods n ▷ **priest**
priestlier adj ▷ **priest**
priestliest adj ▷ **priest**
priestly adj ▷ **priest**
priests n ▷ **priest**
prig n (pl **-s**) self-righteous person
who acts as if superior to others
> **priggish** adj > **priggishness** n (pl **-es**)
priggish adj ▷ **prig**
priggishness n ▷ **prig**
priggishnesses n ▷ **prig**
prigs n ▷ **prig**
prim adj (**-mmer, -mmest**) formal,
proper, and rather prudish > **primly** adv
primacies n ▷ **primacy**
primacy n (pl **-cies**) state of being first
in rank, grade, etc
primaeval adj ▷ **primeval**
primal adj of basic causes or origins
primarily adv ▷ **primary**
primary adj chief, most important
> **primarily** adv
primate[1] n (pl **-s**) member of an order
of mammals including monkeys and
humans
primate[2] n (pl **-s**) archbishop

primates n ▷ **primate**[1, 2]
prime adj main, most important
▶ n (pl **-s**) time when someone is at
his or her best or most vigorous ▶ v
(**-mes, -ming, -med**) give (someone)
information in advance to prepare
them for something
primed v ▷ **prime**
primer n (pl **-s**) special paint applied to
bare wood etc before the main paint
primers n ▷ **primer**
primes n, v ▷ **prime**
primeval adj of the earliest age of
the world
priming v ▷ **prime**
primly adv ▷ **prim**
primmer adj ▷ **prim**
primmest adj ▷ **prim**
primrose n (pl **-s**) pale yellow spring
flower
primroses n ▷ **primrose**
primula n (pl **-s**) type of primrose with
brightly coloured flowers
primulas n ▷ **primula**
prince n (pl **-s**) male member of a royal
family, esp. the son of the king or queen
princelier adj ▷ **princely**
princeliest adj ▷ **princely**
princely adj (**-lier, -liest**) of or like
a prince
princes n ▷ **prince**
princess n (pl **-es**) female member of
a royal family, esp. the daughter of the
king or queen
princesses n ▷ **princess**
print v (**-s, -ing, -ed**) reproduce
(a newspaper, book, etc) in large
quantities by mechanical or electronic
means ▶ n (pl **-s**) printed words etc
> **printing** n (pl **-s**)
printed v ▷ **print**
printer n (pl **-s**) person or company
engaged in printing
printers n ▷ **printer**
printing n, v ▷ **print**
printings n ▷ **print**
prints v, n ▷ **print**
prior[1] adj earlier

prior² n (pl -**s**) head monk in a priory

prioress n (pl -**es**) deputy head nun in a convent

prioresses n ▷ **prioress**

priories n ▷ **priory**

priorities n ▷ **priority**

priority n (pl -**ties**) most important thing that must be dealt with first

priors n ▷ **prior²**

priors n ▷ **prior**

priory n (pl -**ries**) place where certain orders of monks or nuns live

prise v (-**ses**, -**sing**, -**sed**) force open by levering

prised v ▷ **prise**

prises v ▷ **prise**

prising v ▷ **prise**

prism n (pl -**s**) transparent block usu. with triangular ends and rectangular sides, used to disperse light into a spectrum or refract it in optical instruments

prisms n ▷ **prism**

prison n (pl -**s**) building where criminals and accused people are held

prisoner n (pl -**s**) person held captive

prisoners n ▷ **prisoner**

prisons n ▷ **prison**

prissier adj ▷ **prissy**

prissiest adj ▷ **prissy**

prissily adv ▷ **prissy**

prissy adj (-**sier**, -**siest**) prim, correct, and easily shocked > **prissily** adv

pristine adj clean, new, and unused

privacies n ▷ **privacy**

privacy n ▷ **private**

private adj for the use of one person or group only ▶ n (pl -**s**) soldier of the lowest rank > **privately** adv > **privacy** n (pl -**cies**)

privately adv ▷ **private**

privates n ▷ **private**

privet n (pl -**s**) bushy evergreen shrub used for hedges

privets n ▷ **privet**

privier adj ▷ **privy**

privies n ▷ **privy**

priviest adj ▷ **privy**

privy adj (-**vier**, -**viest**) sharing knowledge of something secret ▶ n (pl -**ies**) obs toilet, esp. an outside one

prize¹ n (pl -**s**) reward given for success in a competition etc ▶ adj winning or likely to win a prize

prize² v (-**zes**, -**zing**, -**zed**) value highly

prize³ v ▷ **prize**

prized v ▷ **prize**

prizes n, v ▷ **prize¹, prize²**

prizing v ▷ **prize²**

pro¹ adv, prep in favour of

pro² n (pl -**s**) informal professional

probabilities n ▷ **probable**

probability n ▷ **probable**

probable adj likely to happen or be true > **probability** n (pl -**ties**)

probably adv in all likelihood

probate n (pl -**s**) process of proving the validity of a will

probates n ▷ **probate**

probe v (-**bes**, -**bing**, -**bed**) search into or examine closely ▶ n (pl -**s**) surgical instrument used to examine a wound, cavity, etc

probed v ▷ **probe**

probes v, n ▷ **probe**

probing v ▷ **probe**

probities n ▷ **probity**

probity n (pl -**ties**) honesty, integrity

problem n (pl -**s**) something difficult to deal with or solve > **problematic, problematical,** adj

problematic adj ▷ **problem**

problematical adj ▷ **problem**

problems n ▷ **problem**

proceed v (-**s**, -**ing**, -**ed**) start or continue doing

proceeded v ▷ **proceed**

proceeding v ▷ **proceed**

proceeds pl n money obtained from an event or activity ▶ v ▷ **proceed**

process n (pl -**es**) series of actions or changes ▶ v (-**es**, -**ing**, -**ed**) handle or prepare by a special method of manufacture > **processor** n (pl -**s**)

processes n, v ▷ **process**

processing v ▷ **process**

processor n ▷ **process**
processors n ▷ **process**
proclaim v (-s, -ing, -ed) declare publicly ▷ **proclamation** n (pl -s)
proclaimed v ▷ **proclaim**
proclaiming v ▷ **proclaim**
proclaims v ▷ **proclaim**
proclamation n ▷ **proclaim**
proclamations n ▷ **proclaim**
procure v (-res, -ring, -red) get, provide ▷ **procurement** n (pl -s)
procured v ▷ **procure**
procurement n ▷ **procure**
procurements n ▷ **procure**
procurer, procuress n (pl -s, -es) person who obtains people to act as prostitutes
procurers n ▷ **procurer**
procures v ▷ **procure**
procuress n ▷ **procurer**
procuresses n ▷ **procurer**
procuring v ▷ **procure**
prod v (-s, -dding, -dded) poke with something pointed ▶ n (pl -s) prodding
prodded v ▷ **prod**
prodding v ▷ **prod**
prodigal adj recklessly extravagant, wasteful ▷ **prodigality** n (pl -s)
prodigalities n ▷ **prodigal**
prodigality n ▷ **prodigal**
prodigies n ▷ **prodigy**
prodigy n (pl -gies) person with some marvellous talent
prods v, n ▷ **prod**
produce v (-ces, -cing, -ced) bring into existence ▶ n (pl -s) food grown for sale
produced v ▷ **produce**
producer n (pl -s) person with control over the making of a film, record, etc
producers n ▷ **producer**
produces v, n ▷ **producer**
producing v ▷ **producer**
product n (pl -s) something produced
products n ▷ **product**
profane adj showing disrespect for religion or holy things ▶ v (-nes, -ning, -ned) treat (something sacred)

irreverently, desecrate
profaned v ▷ **profane**
profanes v ▷ **profane**
profaning v ▷ **profane**
profess v (-es, -ing, -ed) state or claim (something as true), sometimes falsely ▷ **professed** adj supposed
professed v, adj ▷ **profess**
professes v ▷ **profess**
professing v ▷ **profess**
proffer v (-s, -ing, -ed) offer
proffered v ▷ **proffer**
proffering v ▷ **proffer**
proffers v ▷ **proffer**
profile n (pl -s) outline, esp. of the face, as seen from the side
profiles n ▷ **profile**
profit n (pl -s) money gained ▶ v (-s, -ing, -ed) gain or benefit
profited v ▷ **profit**
profiting v ▷ **profit**
profits n, v ▷ **profit**
profound adj (-er, -est) showing or needing great knowledge ▷ **profundity** n (pl -ties)
profounder adj ▷ **profound**
profoundest adj ▷ **profound**
profundities n ▷ **profound**
profundity n ▷ **profound**
profuse adj plentiful ▷ **profusion** n (pl -s)
profusion n ▷ **profuse**
profusions n ▷ **profuse**
progenies n ▷ **progeny**
progeny n (pl -nies) children
program n (pl -s) sequence of coded instructions for a computer ▶ v (-s, -mming, -mmed) arrange (data) so that it can be processed by a computer ▷ **programmer** n (pl -s) ▷ **programmable** adj
programmable adj ▷ **program**
programmed v ▷ **program**
programmer n ▷ **program**
programmers n ▷ **program**
programming v ▷ **program**
programs n, v ▷ **program**
progress n (pl -es) improvement, development ▶ v (-es, -ing, -ed)

become more advanced or skilful
> **progression** n (pl -**s**)
progressed v ▷ **progress**
progresses v ▷ **progress**
progressing v ▷ **progress**
progression n ▷ **progress**
progressions n ▷ **progress**

prohibit v (-**s**, -**ing**, -**ed**) forbid or
prevent from happening
prohibited v ▷ **prohibit**
prohibiting v ▷ **prohibit**
prohibits v ▷ **prohibit**

project n (pl **projects**) planned
scheme to do or examine something
over a period ▶ v (-**s**, -**ing**, -**ed**) make
a forecast based on known data
> **projection** n (pl -**s**)
projected v ▷ **project**
projecting v ▷ **project**
projection n ▷ **project**
projections n ▷ **project**
projects n, v ▷ **project**

prolapse n (pl -**s**) slipping down of
an internal organ of the body from its
normal position
prolapses n ▷ **prolapse**

prole adj, n (pl -**s**) CHIEFLY BRIT slang
proletarian
proles n ▷ **prole**

prolific adj very productive
> **prolifically** adv
prolifically adv ▷ **prolific**

prolix adj (of speech or a piece of
writing) overlong and boring

prologue n (pl -**s**) introduction to a
play or book
prologues n ▷ **prologue**

prolong v (-**s**, -**ing**, -**ed**) make
(something) last longer
> **prolongation** n (pl -**s**)
prolongation n ▷ **prolong**
prolongations n ▷ **prolong**
prolonged v ▷ **prolong**
prolonging v ▷ **prolong**
prolongs v ▷ **prolong**

promise v (-**ses**, -**sing**, -**sed**) say
that one will definitely do or not do
something ▶ n (pl -**s**) undertaking to

do or not to do something
promised v ▷ **promise**
promises v ▷ **promise**

promo n (pl -**os**) informal short film to
promote a product
promos v ▷ **promo**

promote v (-**tes**, -**ting**, -**ted**) help to
make (something) happen or increase
> **promotion** n (pl -**s**) > **promotional** adj
promoted v ▷ **promote**

promoter n (pl -**s**) person who
organizes or finances an event etc
promoters n ▷ **promoter**
promotes v ▷ **promote**
promoting v ▷ **promote**
promotion n ▷ **promote**
promotional adj ▷ **promote**
promotions n ▷ **promote**

prompt v (-**s**, -**ing**, -**ed**) cause (an
action) ▶ adj done without delay ▶ adv
exactly > **promptness** n (pl -**es**)
prompted v ▷ **prompt**
prompter n ▷ **prompter**

prompter, prompt n (pl -**s**) person
offstage who prompts actors
prompting v ▷ **prompt**

promptly adv immediately, without
delay
promptness n ▷ **prompt**
promptnesses n ▷ **prompt**
prompts v, n ▷ **prompt**
proms n ▷ **prom**

prone adj (-**r**, -**st**) (foll. by **to**) likely to do
or be affected by (something)
proner adj ▷ **prone**
pronest adj ▷ **prone**

prong n (pl -**s**) one spike of a fork or
similar instrument > **pronged** adj
pronged adj ▷ **prong**
prongs n ▷ **prong**

pronoun n (pl -**s**) word, such as she or
it, used to replace a noun
pronouns n ▷ **pronoun**

pronto adv informal at once

proof n (pl -**s**) evidence that shows that
something is true or has happened
▶ adj able to withstand
proofs n ▷ **proof**

prop¹ v (-s, -pping, -pped) support (something) so that it stays upright or in place ▶ n (pl -s) pole, beam, etc used as a support

prop² n (pl -s) movable object used on the set of a film or play

prop³ n (pl -s) *informal* propeller

propane n (pl -s) flammable gas found in petroleum and used as a fuel

propanes n ▷ propane

propel v (-s, -lling, -lled) cause to move forward

propelled v ▷ propel

propelling v ▷ propel

propels v ▷ propel

proper adj (-er, -est) real or genuine > properly adv

properer adj ▷ proper

properest adj ▷ proper

properly adv ▷ proper

properties n ▷ property

property n (pl -ties) something owned

prophecies n ▷ prophecy

prophecy n (pl -cies) prediction

prophesied v ▷ prophesy

prophesies v ▷ prophesy

prophesy v (-sies, -sying, -sied) foretell

prophesying v ▷ prophesy

prophet n (pl -s) person supposedly chosen by God to spread His word > prophetic adj > prophetically adv

prophetic adj ▷ prophet

prophetically adv ▷ prophet

prophets n ▷ prophet

proposal n ▷ propose

proposals n ▷ propose

propose v (-ses, -sing, -sed) put forward for consideration > proposal n (pl -s)

proposed v ▷ propose

proposes v ▷ propose

proposing v ▷ propose

propound v (-s, -ing, -ed) put forward for consideration

propounded v ▷ propound

propounding v ▷ propound

propounds v ▷ propound

propped v ▷ prop¹

propping v ▷ prop¹

props v, n ▷ prop¹, ², ³

propulsion n ▷ propel

prorogation n ▷ prorogue

prorogations n ▷ prorogue

prorogue v (-gues, -guing, -gued) suspend (parliament) without dissolving it > prorogation n (pl -s)

prorogued v ▷ prorogue

prorogues v ▷ prorogue

proroguing v ▷ prorogue

pros n ▷ pro

prosaic adj lacking imagination, dull > prosaically adv

prosaically adv ▷ prosaic

prose n (pl -s) ordinary speech or writing in contrast to poetry

proses n ▷ prose

prospect n (pl -s) something anticipated *old-fashioned* ▶ pl probability of future success ▶ v (-s, -ing, -ed) explore, esp. for gold > prospector n (pl -s)

prospected v ▷ prospect

prospecting v ▷ prospect

prospector n ▷ prospect

prospectors n, v ▷ prospect

prospects n, v ▷ prospect

prosper v (-s, -ing, -ed) be successful > prosperous adj

prospered v ▷ prosper

prospering v ▷ prosper

prosperous adj ▷ prosper

prospers v ▷ prosper

prostate n (pl -s) gland in male mammals that surrounds the neck of the bladder

prostates n ▷ prostate

protea n (pl -s) African shrub with showy flowers

protean adj constantly changing

proteas n ▷ protea

protect v (-s, -ing, -ed) defend from trouble, harm, or loss > protection n (pl -s)

protected v ▷ protect

protecting v ▷ protect

protection n ▷ protect

protections n ▷ protect

protects v ▷ protect

protégé, fem **protégée** n (pl -s) person who is protected and helped by another

protégées n ▷ protégé

protégés n ▷ protégé

protein n (pl -s) any of a group of complex organic compounds that are essential for life

proteins n ▷ protein

protest n (pl -s) declaration or demonstration of objection ▶ v (-s, -ing, -ed) object, disagree

protested v ▷ protest

protesting v ▷ protest

protests n, v ▷ protest

protocol n (pl -s) rules of behaviour for formal occasions

protocols n ▷ protocol

proton n (pl -s) positively charged particle in the nucleus of an atom

protons n ▷ proton

protrude v (-des, -ding, -ded) stick out, project > **protrusion** n (pl -s)

protruded v ▷ protrude

protrudes v ▷ protrude

protruding v ▷ protrude

protrusion n ▷ protrude

protrusions n ▷ protrude

proud adj (-er, -est) feeling pleasure and satisfaction > **proudly** adv

prouder adj ▷ proud

proudest adj ▷ proud

proudly adv ▷ proud

prove v (-ves, -ving, -ved or -ven) establish the validity of

proved v ▷ prove

proven adj known from experience to work ▶ v ▷ prove

proverb n (pl -s) short saying that expresses a truth or gives a warning > **proverbial** adj

proverbial adj ▷ proverb

proverbs n ▷ proverb

proves v ▷ prove

provide v (-des, -ding, -ded) make available > **provider** n (pl -s)

provided v ▷ provide

provider n ▷ provide

providers n ▷ provide

provides v ▷ provide

providing v ▷ provide

province n (pl -s) area governed as a unit of a country or empire ▶ pl parts of a country outside the capital

provinces n ▷ province

proving v ▷ prove

proviso n (pl -s, -es) condition, stipulation

provisoes n ▷ proviso

provisos n ▷ proviso

provocation n ▷ provoke

provocations n ▷ provoke

provocative adj ▷ provoke

provoke v (-kes, -king, -ked) deliberately anger > **provocation** n (pl -s) > **provocative** adj

provoked v ▷ provoke

provokes v ▷ provoke

provoking v ▷ provoke

provost n (pl -s) head of certain university colleges in Britain

provosts n ▷ provost

prow n (pl -s) bow of a vessel

prowess n (pl -es) superior skill or ability

prowesses n ▷ prowess

prowl v (-s, -ing, -ed) move stealthily around a place as if in search of prey or plunder ▶ n (pl -s) prowling

prowled v ▷ prowl

prowler n (pl -s) person who moves stealthily around a place as if in search of prey or plunder

prowlers n ▷ prowl

prowling v ▷ prowl

prowls v, n ▷ prowl

prows n ▷ prow

proxies n ▷ proxy

proxy n (pl -xies) person authorized to act on behalf of someone else

prude n (pl -s) person who is excessively modest, prim, or proper > **prudish** adj > **prudery** n (pl -ries)

prudence n ▷ prudent

prudences n ▷ prudent

prudent adj cautious, discreet, and

sensible > **prudence** n (pl **-s**)
pruderies n ▷ **prude**
prudery n ▷ **prude**
prudes n ▷ **prude**
prudish adj ▷ **prude**
prune¹ n (pl **-s**) dried plum
prune² v (**-nes, -ning, -ned**) cut off dead parts or excessive branches from (a tree or plant)
pruned v ▷ **prune**
prunes n, v ▷ **prune¹, ²**
pruning v ▷ **prune**
prurience n ▷ **prurient**
pruriences n ▷ **prurient**
prurient adj excessively interested in sexual matters > **prurience** n (pl **-s**)
pry v (**pries, prying, pried**) make an impertinent or uninvited inquiry into a private matter
prying v ▷ **pry**
psalm n (pl **-s**) sacred song
psalmist n (pl **-s**) writer of psalms
psalmists n ▷ **psalmist**
psalms n ▷ **psalm**
psalter n (pl **-s**) book containing (a version of) psalms from the Bible
psalteries n ▷ **psalter**
psalters n ▷ **psalter**
psaltery n (pl **-ries**) ancient instrument played by plucking strings
pseud n (pl **-s**) informal pretentious person
pseuds n ▷ **pseud**

> **psi** n (**psis**). Psi is the 23rd letter of the Greek alphabet. This word can be useful if you have a difficult rack, especially if you can form another word at the same time. Psi scores 5 points.

psyche n ▷ **psyche**
psyche n (pl **-s**) human mind or soul
psychic adj (also **psychical**) having mental powers which cannot be explained by natural laws ▶ n (pl **-s**) person with psychic powers
psychics n ▷ **psychic**
psycho n (pl **-s**) informal psychopath
psychos n ▷ **psycho**

ptomaine n (pl **-s**) any of a group of poisonous alkaloids found in decaying matter
ptomaines n ▷ **ptomaine**
pub n (pl **-s**) building with a bar licensed to sell alcoholic drinks
pubertal adj ▷ **puberty**
puberties n ▷ **puberty**
puberty n (pl **-ties**) beginning of sexual maturity > **pubertal** adj
pubic adj of the lower abdomen
public adj of or concerning the people as a whole ▶ n (pl **-s**) the community, people in general > **publicly** adv
publican n (pl **-s**) BRIT, AUST & NZ person who owns or runs a pub
publicans n ▷ **publican**
publication n ▷ **publish**
publications n ▷ **publish**
publicly adv ▷ **public**
publics n ▷ **public**
publish v (**-es, -ing, -ed**) produce and issue (printed matter) for sale > **publication** n (pl **-s**) > **publisher** n (pl **-s**)
published v ▷ **publish**
publisher n ▷ **publish**
publishers n ▷ **publish**
publishes v ▷ **publish**
publishing v ▷ **publish**
pubs n ▷ **pub**
puce adj (**-r, -st**) purplish-brown
pucer adj ▷ **puce**
pucest adj ▷ **puce**
puck¹ n (pl **-s**) small rubber disc used in ice hockey
puck² n (pl **-s**) mischievous or evil spirit > **puckish** adj
pucker v (**-s, -ing, -ed**) gather into wrinkles ▶ n (pl **-s**) wrinkle or crease
puckered v ▷ **pucker**
puckering v ▷ **pucker**
puckers v, n ▷ **pucker**
puckish adj ▷ **puck²**
pucks n ▷ **puck¹, ²**
pudding n (pl **-s**) dessert, esp. a cooked one served hot
puddings n ▷ **pudding**
puddle n (pl **-s**) small pool of water,

esp. of rain

puddles n ▷ **puddle**

puerile adj silly and childish

puff n (pl -s) (sound of) a short blast of breath, wind, etc ▶ v (-s, -ing, -ed) blow or breathe in short quick draughts > **puffy** adj (-fier, -fiest)

puffball n (pl -s) ball-shaped fungus

puffballs n ▷ **puffball**

puffed v ▷ **puff**

puffier adj ▷ **puff**

puffiest adj ▷ **puff**

puffin n (pl -s) black-and-white sea bird with a brightly-coloured beak

puffing v ▷ **puff**

puffins n ▷ **puffin**

puffs n, v ▷ **puff**

puffy adj ▷ **puff**

pug n (pl -s) small snub-nosed dog

pugilism n ▷ **pugilist**

pugilisms n ▷ **pugilist**

pugilist n (pl -s) boxer > **pugilism** n (pl -s) > **pugilistic** adj

pugilistic adj ▷ **pugilist**

pugilists n ▷ **pugilist**

pugs n ▷ **pug**

puke slang v (-kes, -king, -ked) vomit ▶ n (pl -s) act of vomiting

puked v ▷ **puke**

pukes v, n ▷ **puke**

puking v ▷ **puke**

pull v (-s, -ing, -ed) exert force on (an object) to move it towards the source of the force ▶ n (pl -s) act of pulling

pulled v ▷ **pull**

pullet n (pl -s) young hen

pullets n ▷ **pullet**

pulley n (pl -s) wheel with a grooved rim in which a belt, chain, or piece of rope runs in order to lift weights by a downward pull

pulleys n ▷ **pulley**

pulling v ▷ **pull**

pullover n (pl -s) sweater that is pulled on over the head

pullovers n ▷ **pullover**

pulls v, n ▷ **pull**

pulp n (pl -s) soft wet substance made

from crushed or beaten matter ▶ v (-s, -ing, -ed) reduce to pulp

pulped v ▷ **pulp**

pulping v ▷ **pulp**

pulpit n (pl -s) raised platform for a preacher

pulpits n ▷ **pulpit**

pulps n, v ▷ **pulp**

pulsar n (pl -s) small dense star which emits regular bursts of radio waves

pulsars n ▷ **pulsar**

pulsate v ▷ **pulse**[1]

pulsated v ▷ **pulse**[1]

pulsates v ▷ **pulse**[1]

pulsating v ▷ **pulse**[1]

pulsation n ▷ **pulse**[1]

pulsations n ▷ **pulse**[1]

pulse[1] n (pl -s) regular beating of blood through the arteries at each heartbeat ▶ **pulsate** v (-s, -ing, -ed) throb, quiver > **pulsation** n (pl -s)

pulse[2] n (pl -s) edible seed of a podbearing plant such as a bean or pea

pulses n ▷ **pulse**[1, 2]

puma n (pl -s) large American wild cat with a greyish-brown coat

pumas n ▷ **puma**

pumice n (pl -s) light porous stone used for scouring

pumices n ▷ **pumice**

pummel v (-s, -lling, -lled) strike repeatedly with or as if with the fists

pummelled v ▷ **pummel**

pummelling v ▷ **pummel**

pummels v ▷ **pummel**

pump[1] n (pl -s) machine used to force a liquid or gas to move in a particular direction ▶ v (-s, -ing, -ed) raise or drive with a pump

pump[2] n (pl -s) light flat-soled shoe

pumped v ▷ **pump**

pumping v ▷ **pump**

pumpkin n (pl -s) large round fruit with an orange rind, soft flesh, and many seeds

pumpkins n ▷ **pumpkin**

pumps n, v ▷ **pump**[1, 2]

pun n (pl -s) use of words to exploit

double meanings for humorous effect ▶ v (-s, -nning, -nned) make puns

punch¹ v (-es, -ing, -ed) strike at with a clenched fist ▶ n (pl -es) blow with a clenched fist *informal*

punch² n (pl -es) tool or machine for shaping, piercing, or engraving ▶ v (-es, -ing, -ed) pierce, cut, stamp, shape, or drive with a punch

punch³ n (pl -es) drink made from a mixture of wine, spirits, fruit, sugar, and spices

punched v ▷ punch¹, ²
punches v, n ▷ punch
punchier adj ▷ punchy
punchiest adj ▷ punchy
punching v ▷ punch¹, ²
punchy adj (-chier, -chiest) forceful

punctual adj arriving or taking place at the correct time > **punctuality** n (pl -ties) > **punctually** adv
punctualities n ▷ punctual
punctuality n ▷ punctual
punctually adv ▷ punctual

puncture n (pl -s) small hole made by a sharp object, esp. in a tyre ▶ v (-res, -ring, -red) pierce a hole in
punctured v ▷ puncture
punctures n, v ▷ puncture
puncturing v ▷ puncture

pundit n (pl -s) expert who speaks publicly on a subject
pundits n ▷ pundit
pungencies n ▷ pungent
pungency n ▷ pungent

pungent adj having a strong sharp bitter flavour > **pungency** n (pl -cies)
punier adj ▷ puny
puniest adj ▷ puny

punish v (-es, -ing, -ed) cause (someone) to suffer or undergo a penalty for some wrongdoing > **punishment** n (pl -s)
punished v ▷ punish
punishes v ▷ punish
punishment n ▷ punish
punishments n ▷ punish

punitive adj relating to punishment

punk n (pl -s) anti-Establishment youth movement and style of rock music of the late 1970s
punks n ▷ punk
punned v ▷ pun

punnet n (pl -s) small basket for fruit
punnets n ▷ punnet
punning v ▷ pun
puns n, v ▷ pun

punt¹ n (pl -s) open flat-bottomed boat propelled by a pole ▶ v (-s, -ing, -ed) travel in a punt

punt² SPORT n (pl -s) kick of a ball before it touches the ground when dropped from the hands ▶ v (-s, -ing, -ed) kick (a ball) in this way

punt³ n (pl -s) former monetary unit of the Irish Republic
punted v ▷ punt

punter n (pl -s) person who bets
punters n ▷ punter
punting v ▷ punt
punts n, v ▷ punt¹, ², ³

puny adj (-nier, -niest) small and feeble

pup n (pl -s) young of certain animals, such as dogs and seals

pupa n (pl -e, -s) insect at the stage of development between a larva and an adult
pupae n ▷ pupa
pupas n ▷ pupa

pupil¹ n (pl -s) person who is taught by a teacher

pupil² n (pl -s) round dark opening in the centre of the eye
pupils n ▷ pupil¹, ²

puppet n (pl -s) small doll or figure moved by strings or by the operator's hand > **puppeteer** n (pl -s)
puppeteer n ▷ puppet
puppeteers n ▷ puppet
puppets n ▷ puppet
puppies n ▷ puppy

puppy n (pl -pies) young dog
pups n ▷ pup

purchase v (-ses, -sing, -sed) obtain by payment ▶ n (pl -s) thing that is bought > **purchaser** n (pl -s)

purchased v ▷ **purchase**
purchaser n ▷ **purchase**
purchasers n ▷ **purchase**
purchases v, n ▷ **purchase**
purchasing v ▷ **purchase**
purdah n (pl **-s**) Muslim and Hindu custom of keeping women in seclusion, with clothing that conceals them completely when they go out
purdahs n ▷ **purdah**
pure adj (**-r, -st**) unmixed, untainted > **purely** adv > **purity** n (pl **-ies**)
purée n (pl **-s**) pulp of cooked food ▶ v (**-s, -réeing, -réed**) make into a purée
puréed v ▷ **purée**
puréeing v ▷ **purée**
purées n, v ▷ **purée**
purely adv ▷ **pure**
purer adj ▷ **pure**
purest adj ▷ **pure**
purge v (**-ges, -ging, -ged**) rid (a thing or place) of (unwanted things or people) ▶ n (pl **-s**) purging
purged v ▷ **purge**
purges v, n ▷ **purge**
purging v ▷ **purge**
purification n ▷ **purify**
purifications n ▷ **purify**
purified v ▷ **purify**
purifies v ▷ **purify**
purify v (**-fies, -fying, -fied**) make or become pure > **purification** n (pl **-s**)
purifying v ▷ **purify**
purist n (pl **-s**) person concerned with strict obedience to the traditions of a subject
purists n ▷ **purist**
puritan n (pl **-s**) person with strict moral and religious principles > **puritanical** adj > **puritanism** n (pl **-s**)
puritanical adj ▷ **puritan**
puritanism n ▷ **puritan**
puritanisms n ▷ **puritan**
puritans n ▷ **puritan**
purities n ▷ **pure**
purity n ▷ **pure**
purl n (pl **-s**) stitch made by knitting a plain stitch backwards ▶ v (**-s, -ing,**

-ed) knit in purl
purled v ▷ **purl**
purlieus pl n lit outskirts
purling v ▷ **purl**
purloin v (**-s, -ing, -ed**) steal
purloined v ▷ **purloin**
purloining v ▷ **purloin**
purloins v ▷ **purloin**
purls n, v ▷ **purl**
purple adj, n (pl **-s**) (of) a colour between red and blue
purples n ▷ **purple**
purport v (**-s, -ing, -ed**) claim (to be or do something) ▶ n (pl **-s**) apparent meaning, significance
purported v ▷ **purport**
purporting v ▷ **purport**
purports v, n ▷ **purport**
purpose n (pl **-s**) reason for which something is done or exists
purposes n ▷ **purpose**
purr v (**-s, -ing, -ed**) (of cats) make low vibrant sound, usu. when pleased ▶ n (pl **-s**) this sound
purred v ▷ **purr**
purring v ▷ **purr**
purrs v, n ▷ **purr**
purse n (pl **-s**) small bag for money ▶ v (**-ses, -sing, -sed**) draw (one's lips) together into a small round shape
pursed v ▷ **purse**
purser n (pl **-s**) ship's officer who keeps the accounts
pursers n ▷ **purser**
purses n, v ▷ **purse**
pursing v ▷ **purse**
pursue v (**-sues, -suing, -sued**) chase > **pursuer** n (pl **-s**)
pursued v ▷ **pursue**
pursuer n ▷ **pursue**
pursuers n ▷ **pursue**
pursues v ▷ **pursue**
pursuing v ▷ **pursue**
pursuit n (pl **-s**) pursuing
pursuits n ▷ **pursuit**
purulent adj of or containing pus
purvey v (**-s, -ing, -ed**) supply (provisions) > **purveyor** n (pl **-s**)

purveyed v ▷ purvey

purveying v ▷ purvey

purveyor n ▷ purvey

purveyors n ▷ purvey

purveys v ▷ purvey

purview n (pl -s) scope or range of activity or outlook

purviews n ▷ purview

pus n (pl -es) yellowish matter produced by infected tissue

puses n ▷ pus

push v(-es, -ing, -ed) move or try to move by steady force informal ▶ n (pl -es) act of pushing

pushed v ▷ push

pusher n (pl -s) person who sells illegal drugs

pushers n ▷ pusher

pushes v, n ▷ push

pushier adj ▷ pushy

pushiest adj ▷ pushy

pushing v ▷ push

pushy adj (-shier, -shiest) too assertive or ambitious

puss, pussy n (pl -es, -ies) informal cat

pusses n ▷ puss

pussies n ▷ puss

pustule n (pl -s) pimple containing pus

pustules n ▷ pustule

put v(puts, putting, put) cause to be (in a position, state, or place) ▶ n (pl -s) throw in putting the shot

putative adj reputed, supposed

putrefaction n ▷ putrefy

putrefactions n ▷ putrefy

putrefied v ▷ putrefy

putrefies v ▷ putrefy

putrefy v(-fies, -fying, -fied) rot and produce an offensive smell >**putrefaction** n (pl -s)

putrefying v ▷ putrefy

putrid adj rotten and foul-smelling

puts v, n ▷ put

putsch n (pl -es) sudden violent attempt to remove a government from power

putsches n ▷ putsch

putt GOLF n (pl -s) stroke on the putting green to roll the ball into or near the hole ▶ v (-s, -ing, -ed) strike (the ball) in this way

putted n, v ▷ putt

putter n (pl -s) golf club for putting

putters n ▷ putter

putties n ▷ putty

putting n ▷ put putt

putts v, n ▷ putt

putty n (pl -ies) adhesive used to fix glass into frames and fill cracks in woodwork

puzzle v(-les, -ling, -led) perplex and confuse or be perplexed or confused ▶ n (pl -s) problem that cannot be easily solved >**puzzlement** n (pl -s) >**puzzling** adj

puzzled v ▷ puzzle

puzzlement n ▷ puzzle

puzzlements n ▷ puzzle

puzzles v, n ▷ puzzle

puzzling v, adj ▷ puzzle

pygmies n ▷ pygmy

pygmy n (pl -ies) something that is a very small example of its type ▶ adj (p-) very small

pyjamas pl n loose-fitting trousers and top worn in bed

pylon n (pl -s) steel tower-like structure supporting electrical cables

pylons n ▷ pylon

pyramid n (pl -s) solid figure with a flat base and triangular sides sloping upwards to a point >**pyramidal** adj

pyramidal adj ▷ pyramid

pyramids n ▷ pyramid

pyre n (pl -s) pile of wood for burning a corpse on

pyres n ▷ pyre

python n (pl -s) large nonpoisonous snake that crushes its prey

pythons n ▷ python

pyx n (pyxes) A pyx is a container used for testing the weight of coins. This word can also be spelt **pix**. It's a great word to know as it earns a good score and doesn't use any vowels very helpful if you have a difficult rack. Pyx scores 15 points.

Qq

With a value of 10 points, Q is one of the best tiles to have on your rack. It can, however, be a difficult letter to use, especially if you don't have a U to play it with. It's therefore a good idea to remember the short words beginning with Q that don't need a U. This is easy, as there's only one two-letter word starting with Q: **qi** (11 points). There are three three-letter words, only one of which needs a U: **qua** (12). The other two are **qat** and **qis** (12 each). If you do have a U, remember **quiz** (22), which is a very useful word. If you have a blank tile for the second Z, you may be able to form its plural or verb inflections: **quizzes** (24), **quizzed** (25) and **quizzing** (26). This is especially worth remembering in case someone else plays quiz. Don't forget **quartz** (24) either.

qat n (**qats**). Qat is a shrub that grows in Africa and Arabia. This is a great word as it combines Q with two of the most common letters in the game, and this is very handy if there isn't a U on your rack or the board. Qat scores 12 points.

qi n (**qis**). In Chinese medicine, qi is vital energy believed to circulate in the body. This is an exceptionally useful word, as it's the only two-letter word containing Q, and doesn't contain a U. The plural is one of only three three-letter words that begin with Q. As I is one of the more common tiles on the board, it's highly likely that you will be able to play qi if you have a Q. Qi scores 11 points.

qua prep. Qua means in the capacity of. This is the only three-letter word beginning with Q that needs a U, and is useful when you have a U, or there is a U on the board, but don't have any promising tiles to go with it. Qua scores 12 points.

quack[1] v (**-s, -ing, -ed**) (of a duck)

utter a harsh guttural sound ▶ n (pl **-s**) sound made by a duck

quack[2] n (pl **-s**) unqualified person who claims medical knowledge
   quacked v ▷ **quack**[1]
   quacking v ▷ **quack**[1]
   quacks v ▷ **quack**[1] ▶ n ▷ **quack**[1, 2]

quad n (pl **-s**) ▷ **quadrangle** ▶ adj ▷ **quadraphonic**

quadrangle n (pl **-s**) (also **quad**) rectangular courtyard with buildings on all four sides > **quadrangular** adj
   quadrangles n ▷ **quadrangle**
   quadrangular adj ▷ **quadrangle**

quadrant n (pl **-s**) quarter of a circle
   quadrants n ▷ **quadrant**

quadraphonic adj (also **quad**) using four independent channels to reproduce or record sound

quadratic MATHS n (pl **-s**) equation in which the variable is raised to the power of two, but nowhere raised to a higher power ▶ adj of the second power
   quadratics n ▷ **quadratic**

quadrennial adj occurring every

four years

quadrilateral *adj* having four sides
▶ *n* (*pl* -s) polygon with four sides
   quadrilaterals *n* ▷ quadrilateral

quadrille *n* (*pl* -s) square dance for four couples
   quadrilles *n* ▷ quadrille

quadriplegia *n* (*pl* -s) paralysis of all four limbs
   quadriplegias *n* ▷ quadriplegia

quadruped *n* (*pl* -s) any animal with four legs
   quadrupeds *n* ▷ quadruped

quadruple *v* (-les, -ling, -led) multiply by four ▶ *adj* four times as much or as many
   quadrupled *v* ▷ quadruple
   quadruples *v* ▷ quadruple

quadruplet *n* (*pl* -s) one of four offspring born at one birth
   quadruplets *n* ▷ quadruplet
   quadrupling *v* ▷ quadruple
   quads *n* ▷ quad

quaff *v* (-s, -ing, -ed) drink heartily or in one draught
   quaffed *v* ▷ quaff
   quaffing *v* ▷ quaff
   quaffs *v* ▷ quaff

quagmire *n* (*pl* -s) soft wet area of land
   quagmires *n* ▷ quagmire

quail[1] *n* (*pl* -s) small game bird of the partridge family

quail[2] *v* (-s, -ing, -ed) shrink back with fear
   quailed *v* ▷ quail
   quailing *v* ▷ quail
   quails *n* ▷ quail[1] ▶ *v* ▷ quail[2]

quaint *adj* (-er, -est) attractively unusual, esp. in an old-fashioned style
   > **quaintly** *adv*
   quainter *adj* ▷ quaint
   quaintest *adj* ▷ quaint
   quaintly *adv* ▷ quaint

quake *v* (-kes, -king, -ked) shake or tremble with or as if with fear ▶ *n* (*pl* -s) *informal* earthquake
   quaked *v*, *n* ▷ quake
   quakes *v* ▷ quake

quaking *v* ▷ quake

qualification *n* (*pl* -s) official record of achievement in a course or examination
   qualifications *n* ▷ qualification
   qualified *v*, *adj* ▷ qualify
   qualifies *v* ▷ qualify

qualify *v* (-fies, -fying, -fied) provide or be provided with the abilities necessary for a task, office, or duty
   > **qualified** *adj*
   qualifying *v* ▷ qualify

qualitative *adj* of or relating to quality
   qualities *n* ▷ quality

quality *n* (*pl* -ties) degree or standard of excellence ▶ *adj* excellent or superior

qualm *n* (*pl* -s) pang of conscience
   qualms *n* ▷ qualm
   quandaries *n* ▷ quandary

quandary *n* (*pl* -ries) difficult situation or dilemma

quandong *n* (*pl* -s) small Australian tree with edible fruit and nuts used in preserves
   quandongs *n* ▷ quandong

quango *n* (*pl* -s) CHIEFLY BRIT quasi-autonomous nongovernmental organization: any highly independent official body set up by a government
   quangos *n* ▷ quango
   quanta *n* ▷ quantum

quantifiable *adj* ▷ quantify
   quantification *n* ▷ quantify
   quantifications *n* ▷ quantify
   quantified *v* ▷ quantify
   quantifies *v* ▷ quantify

quantify *v* (-fies, -fying, -fied) discover or express the quantity of
   > **quantifiable** *adj* > **quantification** *n* (*pl* -s)
   quantifying *v* ▷ quantify

quantitative *adj* of or relating to quantity
   quantities *n* ▷ quantity

quantity *n* (*pl* -ties) specified or definite amount or number

quantum n (pl **-ta**) desired or required amount, esp. a very small one

quarantine n (pl **-s**) period of isolation of people or animals to prevent the spread of disease ▶ v (**-nes**, **-ning**, **-ned**) isolate in or as if in quarantine

quarantined v ▷ quarantine

quarantines n, v ▷ quarantine

quarantining v ▷ quarantine

quark n (pl **-s**) PHYSICS subatomic particle thought to be the fundamental unit of matter

quarks n ▷ quark

quarrel n (pl **-s**) angry disagreement ▶ v (**-s**, **-lling**, **-lled**) have a disagreement or dispute
> **quarrelsome** adj

quarrelled v ▷ quarrel

quarrelling v ▷ quarrel

quarrels n, v ▷ quarrel

quarrelsome adj ▷ quarrel

quarried v ▷ quarry¹

quarries n ▷ quarry¹, ², v ▷ quarry¹

quarry¹ n (pl **-ries**) place where stone is dug from the surface of the earth ▶ v (**-ries**, **-rying**, **-ried**) extract (stone) from a quarry

quarry² n (pl **-ries**) person or animal that is being hunted

quart n (pl **-s**) unit of liquid measure equal to two pints (1.136 litres)

quarter n (pl **-s**) one of four equal parts of something ▶ v (**-s**, **-ing**, **-ed**) divide into four equal parts

quarterdeck n (pl **-s**) NAUT rear part of the upper deck of a ship

quarterdecks n ▷ quarterdeck

quartered v ▷ quarter

quarterfinal n (pl **-s**) round before the semifinal in a competition

quarterfinals n ▷ quarterfinal

quartering v ▷ quarter

quarterlies n ▷ quarterly

quarterly adj occurring, due, or issued at intervals of three months ▶ n (pl **-lies**) magazine issued every three months ▶ adv once every three months

quartermaster n (pl **-s**)

military officer responsible for accommodation, food, and equipment

quartermasters n ▷ quartermaster

quarters n, v ▷ quarter

quartet n (pl **-s**) group of four performers

quartets n ▷ quartet

quarto n (pl **-s**) book size in which the sheets are folded into four leaves

quartos n ▷ quarto

quarts n ▷ quart

quartz n (pl **-es**) hard glossy mineral

quartzes n ▷ quartz

quasar n (pl **-s**) extremely distant starlike object that emits powerful radio waves

quasars n ▷ quasar

quash v (**-shes**, **-shing**, **-shed**) annul or make void

quashed v ▷ quash

quashes v ▷ quash

quashing v ▷ quash

quatrain n (pl **-s**) stanza or poem of four lines

quatrains n ▷ quatrain

quaver v (**-s**, **-ing**, **-ed**) (of a voice) quiver or tremble ▶ n (pl **-s**) MUSIC note half the length of a crotchet

quavered v ▷ quaver

quavering v ▷ quaver

quavers v, n ▷ quaver

quay n (pl **-s**) wharf built parallel to the shore

quays n ▷ quay

queasier adj ▷ queasy

queasiest adj ▷ queasy

queasiness n ▷ queasy

queasinesses n ▷ queasy

queasy adj (**-sier**, **-siest**) having the feeling that one is about to vomit
> **queasiness** n (pl **-es**)

queen n (pl **-s**) female sovereign who is the official ruler or head of state
> **queenly** adj

queenly adj ▷ queen

queens n ▷ queen

queer adj (**-er**, **-est**) not normal or usual

queerer adj ▷ queer

queerest adj ▷ queer

quell v (-s, -ing, -ed) suppress

quelled v ▷ quell

quelling v ▷ quell

quells v ▷ quell

quench v (-es, -ing, -ed) satisfy (one's thirst)

quenched v ▷ quench

quenches v ▷ quench

quenching v ▷ quench

queried v ▷ query

queries n, v ▷ query

quern n (pl -s) stone hand mill for grinding corn

querns n ▷ quern

querulous adj complaining or whining > querulously adv

querulously adv ▷ querulous

query n (pl -ries) question, esp. one raising doubt ▶ v (-ries, -rying, -ried) express uncertainty, doubt, or an objection concerning (something)

querying v ▷ query

quest n (pl -s) long and difficult search ▶ v (-s, -ing, -ed) (foll. by for or after) go in search of

quested v ▷ quest

questing v ▷ quest

question n (pl -s) form of words addressed to a person in order to obtain an answer ▶ v (-s, -ing, -ed) put a question or questions to (a person)

questionable adj of disputable value or authority > questionably adv

questionably adv ▷ questionable

questioned v ▷ question

questioning v ▷ question

questionnaire n (pl -s) set of questions on a form, used to collect information from people

questionnaires n ▷ questionnaire

questions n, v ▷ question

quests n, v ▷ quest

quetzal or **quezal** n (quetzals, quezales, quezals). The quetzal is a crested bird of Central and South America. This is a great word if you can get the tiles for it, so it's well worth remembering both spellings and the three plural forms. If you can use all your letters to play quetzal or quezals, you'll earn a bonus of 50 points. Quetzal scores 25 points.

queue n (pl -s) line of people or vehicles waiting for something ▶ v (-ues, -uing or -ueing) (-ued) (often foll. by up) form or remain in a line while waiting

queued v ▷ queue

queueing v ▷ queue

queues n, v ▷ queue

queuing v ▷ queue

quibble v (-les, -ling, -led) make trivial objections ▶ n (pl -s) trivial objection

quibbled v ▷ quibble

quibbles v, n ▷ quibble

quibbling v ▷ quibble

quiche n (pl -s) savoury flan with an egg custard filling to which vegetables etc are added

quiches n ▷ quiche

quick adj (-er, -est) speedy, fast ▶ n (pl -s) area of sensitive flesh under a nail ▶ adv informal in a rapid manner > quickly adv

quicken v (-s, -ing, -ed) make or become faster

quickened v ▷ quicken

quickening v ▷ quicken

quickens v ▷ quicken

quicker adj ▷ quick

quickest adj ▷ quick

quicklime n (pl -s) white solid used in the manufacture of glass and steel

quicklimes n ▷ quicklime

quickly adv ▷ quick

quicks n ▷ quick

quicksand n (pl -s) deep mass of loose wet sand that sucks anything on top of it into it

quicksands n ▷ quicksand

quicksilver n (pl -s) mercury

quicksilvers n ▷ quicksilver

quickstep n (pl -s) fast modern ballroom dance

quicksteps n ▷ **quickstep**
quid n (pl **quid, -s**) BRIT slang pound (sterling)
quids n ▷ **quid**
quiescence n ▷ **quiescent**
quiescences n ▷ **quiescent**
quiescent adj quiet, inactive, or dormant ▷ **quiescence** n (pl **-s**)
quiescences n ▷ **quiescent**
quiet adj (**-er, -est**) with little noise ▶ n (pl **-s**) quietness ▶ v (**-s, -ing, -ed**) make or become quiet ▷ **quietly** adv ▷ **quietness** n (pl **-es**)
quieted v ▷ **quiet**
quieten v (**-s, -ing, -ed**) (often foll. by **down**) make or become quiet
quieter adj ▷ **quiet**
quietest adj ▷ **quiet**
quieting v ▷ **quiet**
quietism n (pl **-s**) passivity and calmness of mind towards external events
quietisms n ▷ **quietism**
quietly adv ▷ **quiet**
quietness n ▷ **quiet**
quietnesses n ▷ **quiet**
quiets v, n ▷ **quiet**
quietude n (**-s**) quietness, peace, or tranquillity
quietudes n ▷ **quietude**
quiff n (pl **-s**) tuft of hair brushed up above the forehead
quiffs n ▷ **quiff**
quill n (pl **-s**) pen made from the feather of a bird's wing or tail
quills n ▷ **quill**
quilt n (**-s**) padded covering for a bed
quilted adj consisting of two layers of fabric with a layer of soft material between them
quilts n ▷ **quilt**
quin n (pl **-s**) quintuplet
quince n (pl **-s**) acid-tasting pear-shaped fruit
quinces n ▷ **quince**
quinine n (pl **-s**) bitter drug used as a tonic and formerly to treat malaria
quinines n ▷ **quinine**
quinquennial adj occurring every

five years
quins n ▷ **quin**
quinsies n ▷ **quinsy**
quinsy n (pl **-sies**) inflammation of the throat or tonsils
quintessence n (pl **-s**) most perfect representation of a quality or state ▷ **quintessential** adj
quintessences n ▷ **quintessence**
quintessential adj ▷ **quintessence**
quintet n (pl **-s**) group of five performers
quintets n ▷ **quintet**
quintuplet n (pl **-s**) one of five offspring born at one birth
quintuplets n ▷ **quintuplet**

quinze n (**quinzes**). Quinze is a card game. This is a high-scoring word, and if you can use all of your tiles to form the plural, you'll get a 50-point bonus. Quinze scores 24 points.

quip n (pl **-s**) witty saying ▶ v (**-s, -pping, -pped**) make a quip
quipped v ▷ **quip**
quipping v ▷ **quip**
quips n, v ▷ **quip**
quire n (pl **-s**) set of 24 or 25 sheets of paper
quires n ▷ **quire**
quirk n (pl **-s**) peculiarity of character ▷ **quirky** adj (**-kier, -kiest**)
quirkier adj ▷ **quirk**
quirkiest adj ▷ **quirk**
quirks n ▷ **quirk**
quirky adj ▷ **quirk**
quisling n (pl **-s**) traitor who aids an occupying enemy force
quislings n ▷ **quisling**
quit v (**quits, quitting, quit**) stop (doing something)
quite adv somewhat ▶ interj expression of agreement
quits adj informal on an equal footing ▶ v ▷ **quit**
quitter n (pl **-s**) person who lacks perseverance
quitters n ▷ **quitter**
quitting v ▷ **quit**

quiver[1] v (**-s, -ing, -ed**) shake with a tremulous movement ▸ n (pl **-s**) shaking or trembling

quiver[2] n (pl **-s**) case for arrows

quivered v ▷ **quiver**[1]

quivering v ▷ **quiver**[1]

quivers v ▷ **quiver**[1] & n ▷ **quiver**[1, 2]

> **quixote** n (quixotes). A quixote is an impractically idealistic person. This is a high-scoring word; if you have all the letters to play it, and can place them on the board, you'll score a 50-point bonus for using all of your tiles. Quixote scores 23 points.

quixotic adj romantic and unrealistic > **quixotically** adv

quixotically adv ▷ **quixotic**

quiz n (pl **-zzes**) entertainment in which the knowledge of the players is tested by a series of questions ▸ v (**-zzes, -zzing, -zzed**) investigate by close questioning

quizzed v ▷ **quiz**

quizzes n, v ▷ **quiz**

quizzical adj questioning and mocking > **quizzically** adv

quizzically adv ▷ **quizzical**

quizzing v ▷ **quiz**

quod n (pl **-s**) BRIT slang jail

quods n ▷ **quod**

quoit n (pl **-s**) large ring used in the game of quoits ▸ pl game in which

quoits are tossed at a stake in the ground in attempts to encircle it

quoits n ▷ **quoit**

quokka n (pl **-s**) small Australian wallaby

quokkas n ▷ **quokka**

quorum n (pl **-s**) minimum number of people required to be present at a meeting before any transactions can take place

quorums n ▷ **quorum**

quota n (pl **-s**) share that is due from, due to, or allocated to a group or person

quotable adj ▷ **quote**

quotas n ▷ **quota**

quotation n (pl **-s**) written or spoken passage repeated exactly in a later work, speech, or conversation

quotations n ▷ **quotation**

quote v (**-tes, -ting, -ted**) repeat (words) exactly from (an earlier work, speech, or conversation) ▸ n (pl **-s**) informal quotation > **quotable** adj

quoted v ▷ **quote**

quotes v, n ▷ **quote**

quoth v obs said

quotidian adj daily

quotient n (pl **-s**) result of the division of one number or quantity by another

quotients n ▷ **quotient**

quoting v ▷ **quote**

Rr

R is one of the most common consonants in Scrabble, along with N and T. Despite this, however, there is only one two-letter word beginning with R: **re** (2 points). This is worth remembering, as you won't need to waste time trying to think of others. There are some good three-letter words with R, however, some of which are quite unusual: **raj, rax, rex** (10 each), **rez** (12 each). Also, don't forget common words like **raw, ray** and **row** (6 each).

rabbi n (pl -s) Jewish spiritual leader
> **rabbinical** adj
rabbinical adj ▷ **rabbi**
rabbis n ▷ **rabbi**

rabbit n (pl -s) small burrowing mammal with long ears
rabbits n ▷ **rabbit**

rabble n (pl -s) disorderly crowd of noisy people
rabbles n ▷ **rabble**

rabid adj (-er, -est) fanatical
> **rabidly** adv
rabider adj ▷ **rabid**
rabidest adj ▷ **rabid**
rabidly adv ▷ **rabid**

rabies n usu. fatal viral disease transmitted by dogs and certain other animals

raccoon n (pl -s) small N American mammal with a long striped tail
raccoons n ▷ **raccoon**

race¹ n (pl -s) contest of speed ▶ pl meeting for horse racing ▶ v (-ces, -cing, -ced) compete with in a race
> **racer** n (pl -s) ▷ **racecourse** n (pl -s)
> **racehorse** n (pl -s) ▷ **racetrack** n (pl -s)

race² n (pl -s) group of people of common ancestry with distinguishing physical features, such as skin colour
> **racial** adj
racecourse n ▷ **race¹**

racecourses n ▷ **race¹**
raced n, v ▷ **race¹**
racehorse n ▷ **race¹**
racehorses n ▷ **race¹**

raceme n (pl -s) cluster of flowers along a central stem, as in the foxglove
racemes n ▷ **raceme**
racer n ▷ **race¹**
racers n ▷ **race¹**
races n, v ▷ **race¹, ²**
racetrack n ▷ **race¹**
racetracks n ▷ **race¹**
racial adj ▷ **race²**
racialism n ▷ **racism**
racialisms n ▷ **racism**
racialist adj, n ▷ **racism**
racialists n ▷ **racism**
racier adj ▷ **racy**
raciest adj ▷ **racy**
racing v ▷ **race¹**

racism, racialism n (pl -s) hostile attitude or behaviour to members of other races, based on a belief in the innate superiority of one's own race
> **racist, racialist** adj, n (pl -s)
racisms n ▷ **racism**
racist n ▷ **racism**
racists n ▷ **racism**

rack n (pl -s) framework for holding particular articles, such as coats or luggage HIST ▶ v (-s, -ing, -ed) cause

great suffering to
racked v ▷ **rack**
racket[1] n (pl -s) noisy disturbance
racket[2], **racquet** n (-s) bat with strings stretched in an oval frame, used in tennis etc
rackets n ball game played in a paved walled court ▶ ▷ **racket**[1, 2]
racking v ▷ **rack**
racks n, v ▷ **rack**
racquet n ▷ **racket**[2]
racquets n ▷ **racket**[2]
racy adj (-cier, -ciest) slightly shocking
radar n (pl -s) device for tracking distant objects by bouncing high-frequency radio pulses off them
radars n ▷ **radar**
radial adj spreading out from a common central point
radiance n ▷ **radiant**
radiances n ▷ **radiant**
radiant adj looking happy
>**radiance** n (-s)
radiate v (-tes, -ting, -ted) spread out from a centre
radiated v ▷ **radiate**
radiates v ▷ **radiate**
radiating v ▷ **radiate**
radiator n (-s) BRIT arrangement of pipes containing hot water or steam to heat a room
radiators n ▷ **radiator**
radical adj fundamental ▶ n (pl -s) person advocating fundamental (political) change ▶ **radically** adv
>**radicalism** n (-s)
radicalism n ▷ **radical**
radicalisms n ▷ **radical**
radically adv ▷ **radical**
radicals n ▷ **radical**
radicle n (pl -s) small or developing root
radicles n ▷ **radicle**
radii n ▷ **radius**
radio n (pl -s) use of electromagnetic waves for broadcasting, communication, etc ▶ v (-s, -ing, -ed) transmit (a message) by radio

radioed v ▷ **radio**
radioing v ▷ **radio**
radios n, v ▷ **radio**
radish n (pl -es) small hot-flavoured root vegetable eaten raw in salads
radishes n ▷ **radish**
radium n (pl -s) CHEM radioactive metallic element
radiums n ▷ **radium**
radius n (pl **radii**, **radiuses**) (length of) a straight line from the centre to the circumference of a circle
radiuses n ▷ **radius**
radon n (pl -s) CHEM radioactive gaseous element
radons n ▷ **radon**
raffia n (pl -s) prepared palm fibre for weaving mats etc
raffias n ▷ **raffia**
raffish adj slightly disreputable
raffle n (pl -s) lottery with goods as prizes ▶ v (-les, -ling, -led) offer as a prize in a raffle
raffled v ▷ **raffle**
raffles n, v ▷ **raffle**
raffling v ▷ **raffle**
raft n (pl -s) floating platform of logs, planks, etc
rafter n (pl -s) one of the main beams of a roof
rafters n ▷ **rafter**
rafts n ▷ **raft**
rag[1] n (pl -s) informal ▶ pl tattered clothing
rag[2] BRIT v (-s, -gging, -gged) tease ▶ adj, n (pl -s) (of) events organized by students to raise money for charities
rage n (pl -s) violent anger or passion ▶ v (-ges, -ging, -ged) speak or act with fury
raged v ▷ **rage**
rages n, v ▷ **rage**
ragged adj dressed in shabby or torn clothes ▶ v ▷ **rag**[2]
ragging v ▷ **rag**[2]
raging v ▷ **rage**
raglan adj (of a sleeve) joined to a garment by diagonal seams from the

ragout n (pl **-s**) richly seasoned stew of meat and vegetables

ragouts n ▷ **ragout**

rags n, v ▷ **rag¹, ²**

ragtime n (pl **-s**) style of jazz piano music

ragtimes n ▷ **ragtime**

raid n (pl **-s**) sudden surprise attack or search ▶ v (**-s, -ing, -ed**) make a raid on ▷ **raider** n (pl **-s**)

raided v ▷ **raid**

raider n ▷ **raid**

raiders n ▷ **raid**

raiding v ▷ **raid**

raids n, v ▷ **raid**

rail¹ n (pl **-s**) horizontal bar, esp. as part of a fence or track

rail² v (**-s, -ing, -ed**) (foll. by **at** or **against**) complain bitterly or loudly

rail³ n (pl **-s**) small marsh bird

railed v ▷ **rail²**

railing n (pl **-s**) fence made of rails supported by posts ▶ v ▷ **rail²**

railings n ▷ **railing**

railleries n ▷ **raillery**

raillery n (pl **-ies**) teasing or joking

rails n, v ▷ **rail¹, ³** v ▷ **rail²**

railway n (pl **-s**) track of iron rails on which trains run

railways n ▷ **railway**

raiment n (pl **-s**) obs clothing

raiments n ▷ **raiment**

rain n (pl **-s**) water falling in drops from the clouds ▶ v (**-s, -ing, -ed**) fall or pour down as rain ▶ **rainy** adj (**-nier, -niest**)

rainbow n (pl **-s**) arch of colours in the sky

rainbows n ▷ **rainbow**

raincoat n (pl **-s**) water-resistant overcoat

raincoats n ▷ **raincoat**

rained v ▷ **rain**

rainfall n (pl **-s**) amount of rain

rainfalls n ▷ **rainfall**

rainier adj ▷ **rainy**

rainiest adj ▷ **rainy**

raining v ▷ **rain**

rains n, v ▷ **rain**

rainy adj ▷ **rain**

raise v (**-ses, -sing, -sed**) lift up

raised v ▷ **raise**

raises v ▷ **raise**

raisin n (pl **-s**) dried grape

raising v ▷ **raise**

raisins n ▷ **raisin**

> **raj** n (**rajes**). Raj is an Indian word for government. This word can be very useful when there isn't much space on the board. If you can't play raj, remember that it's just **jar** backwards you might be able to fit that in somewhere. Raj scores 10 points.

raja, rajah n (pl **-s**) HIST Indian prince or ruler

rajah n ▷ **raja**

rajahs n ▷ **raja**

rajas n ▷ **raja**

rake¹ n (pl **-s**) tool with a long handle and a crosspiece with teeth, used for smoothing earth or gathering leaves, hay, etc ▶ v (**-kes, -king, -ked**) gather or smooth with a rake

rake² n (pl **-s**) dissolute or immoral man

raked v ▷ **rake¹**

rakes n ▷ **rake¹, ²** ▶ v ▷ **rake¹**

raking v ▷ **rake¹**

rakish adj dashing or jaunty

rallied v ▷ **rally**

rallies n, v ▷ **rally**

rally n (pl **-llies**) large gathering of people for a meeting ▶ v (**-llies, -llying, -llied**) bring or come together after dispersal or for a common cause

rallying v ▷ **rally**

ram n (pl **-s**) male sheep ▶ v (**-s, -mming, -mmed**) strike against with force

ramble v (**-les, -ling, -led**) walk without a definite route ▶ n (pl **-s**) walk, esp. in the country

rambled v ▷ **ramble**

rambler n (pl **-s**) person who rambles

ramblers n ▷ **rambler**

rambles v, n ▷ ramble
rambling v ▷ ramble
ramekin n (pl **-s**) small ovenproof dish for a single serving of food
ramekins n ▷ ramekin
rammed v ▷ ram
ramming v ▷ ram
ramp n (pl **-s**) slope joining two level surfaces
rampage v (**-ges, -ging, -ged**) dash about violently
rampaged v ▷ rampage
rampages v ▷ rampage
rampaging v ▷ rampage
rampant adj growing or spreading uncontrollably
rampart n (pl **-s**) mound or wall for defence
ramparts n ▷ rampart
ramps n ▷ ramp
rams n, v ▷ ram
ran v ▷ run
ranch n (pl **-es**) large cattle farm in the American West > **rancher** n (pl **-s**)
rancher n ▷ ranch
ranchers n ▷ ranch
ranches n ▷ ranch
rancid adj (of butter, bacon, etc) stale and having an offensive smell > **rancidity** n (pl **-ies**)
rancidity n ▷ rancid
rancorous adj ▷ rancour
rancour n (pl **-s**) deep bitter hate > **rancorous** adj
rancours n ▷ rancour
rand n (pl **-s**) monetary unit of S Africa
randier adj ▷ randy
randiest adj ▷ randy
random adj made or done by chance or without plan
rands n ▷ rand
randy adj (**-ier, -iest**) informal sexually aroused
rang v ▷ ring[1]
range n (pl **-s**) limits of effectiveness or variation ▶ v (**-ges, -ging, -ged**) vary between one point and another
ranged v ▷ range

ranger n (pl **-s**) official in charge of a nature reserve etc
rangers n ▷ ranger
ranges n, v ▷ range
rangier adj ▷ rangy
rangiest adj ▷ rangy
ranging v ▷ range
rangy adj (**-ier, -iest**) having long slender limbs
rank[1] n (pl **-s**) relative place or position ▶ v (**-s, -ing, -ed**) have a specific rank or position
rank[2] adj complete or absolute
ranked v ▷ rank
ranking v ▷ rank
rankle v (**-les, -ling, -led**) continue to cause resentment or bitterness
rankled v ▷ rankle
rankles v ▷ rankle
rankling v ▷ rankle
ranks n, v ▷ rank[1]
ransack v (**-s, -ing, -ed**) search thoroughly
ransacked v ▷ ransack
ransacking v ▷ ransack
ransacks v ▷ ransack
ransom n (pl **-s**) money demanded in return for the release of someone who has been kidnapped
ransoms n ▷ ransom
rant v (**-s, -ing, -ed**) talk in a loud and excited way > **ranter** n (pl **-s**)
ranted v ▷ rant
ranter n ▷ rant
ranters n ▷ rant
ranting v ▷ rant
rants v ▷ rant
rap v (**-s, -pping, -pped**) hit with a sharp quick blow ▶ n (pl **-s**) quick sharp blow > **rapper** n (pl **-s**)
rape[1] v (**-pes, -ping, -ped**) force to submit to sexual intercourse ▶ n (pl **-s**) act of raping > **rapist** n (pl **-s**)
rape[2] n (pl **-s**) plant with oil-yielding seeds, also used as fodder
raped v ▷ rape[1]
rapes v ▷ rape[1] ▶ n ▷ rape[1, 2]
rapid adj (**-er, -est**) quick, swift

> **rapidly** adv > **rapidity** n (pl **-ties**)
rapider adj > **rapid**
rapidest adj > **rapid**
rapidities n > **rapid**
rapidity n > **rapid**
rapidly adv > **rapid**
rapids pl n part of a river with a fast turbulent current
rapier n (pl **-s**) fine-bladed sword
rapiers n > **rapier**
raping v > **rape**[1]
rapist n > **rape**[1]
rapists n > **rape**[1]
rapped v > **rap**
rapper n > **rap**
rappers n > **rap**
rapping v > **rap**
rapport n (pl **-s**) harmony or agreement
rapports n > **rapport**
raps v, n > **rap**
rapt adj engrossed or spellbound
rapture n (pl **-s**) ecstasy
> **rapturous** adj
raptures n > **rapture**
rapturous adj > **rapture**
rare[1] adj (**-r**, **-st**) uncommon > **rarity** n (pl **-ties**)
rare[2] adj (**-r**, **-st**) (of meat) lightly cooked
rarebit n (pl **-s**) dish of melted cheese on toast
rarebits n > **rarebit**
rarefied adj highly specialized, exalted
rarely adv seldom
rarer adj > **rare**[1]
rarest adj > **rare**[1]
raring adj enthusiastic, willing, or ready to
rarities n > **rare**[1]
rarity n > **rare**[1]
rascal n (pl **-s**) rogue > **rascally** adj (**-lier**, **-liest**)
rascallier adj > **rascal**
rascalliest adj > **rascal**
rascally adj > **rascal**
rascals n > **rascal**
rash[1] adj (**-er**, **-est**) hasty, reckless, or incautious > **rashly** adv

rash[2] n (pl **-es**) eruption of spots or patches on the skin
rasher n (pl **-s**) thin slice of bacon
▶ adj > **rash**[1]
rashers n > **rasher**
rashes n > **rash rash**[2]
rashest adj > **rash**[1]
rashly adv > **rash**[1]
rasp n (pl **-s**) harsh grating noise ▶ v (**-s**, **-ing**, **-ed**) speak in a grating voice
rasped v > **rasp**
rasping v > **rasp**
rasps n, v > **rasp**
rat n (pl **-s**) small rodent informal ▶ v (**-s**, **-tting**, **-tted**) informal inform (on)
ratafia n (pl **-s**) liqueur made from fruit
ratafias n > **ratafia**
ratchet n (pl **-s**) set of teeth on a bar or wheel allowing motion in one direction only
ratchets n > **ratchet**
rate n (pl **-s**) degree of speed or progress ▶ pl local tax on business ▶ v (**-tes**, **-ting**, **-ted**) consider or value
> **ratepayer** n (pl **-s**)
rateable adj able to be rated
rated v > **rate**
ratepayer n > **rate**
ratepayers n > **rate**
rates n, v > **rate**
rather adv to some extent
ratification n > **ratify**
ratifications n > **ratify**
ratified v > **ratify**
ratifies v > **ratify**
ratify v (**-fies**, **-fying**, **-fied**) give formal approval to > **ratification** n (pl **-s**)
ratifying v > **ratify**
rating n (pl **-s**) valuation or assessment ▶ pl size of the audience for a TV programme ▶ v > **rating**
ratings n > **rating**
ratio n (pl **-s**) relationship between two numbers or amounts expressed as a proportion
ration n (pl **-s**) fixed allowance of food etc ▶ v (**-s**, **-ing**, **-ed**) limit to a certain

amount per person
rational adj reasonable, sensible
> **rationally** adv > **rationality** n (pl -ies)
rationalities n ▷ **rationality**
rationality n ▷ **rational**
rationally adv ▷ **rational**
rationed v ▷ **ration**
rationing v ▷ **ration**
rations n, v ▷ **ration**
ratios n ▷ **ratio**
rats n ▷ **rat**
rattan n (pl -s) climbing palm with
jointed stems used for canes
rattans n ▷ **rattan**
ratted v ▷ **rat**
rattier adj ▷ **ratty**
rattiest adj ▷ **ratty**
ratting ▷ **rat**
rattle v (-tles, -tling, -led) give out a
succession of short sharp sounds ▶ n
(pl -s) short sharp sound
rattled v ▷ **rattle**
rattles v, n ▷ **rattle**
rattling v ▷ **rattle**
ratty adj (-tier, -tiest) BRIT & NZ
informal bad-tempered, irritable
raucous adj hoarse or harsh
raunchier adj ▷ **raunchy**
raunchiest adj ▷ **raunchy**
raunchy adj (-chier, -chiest) slang
earthy, sexy
ravage v (-ges, -ging, -ged) cause
extensive damage to
ravaged v ▷ **ravage**
ravages pl n damaging effects ▶ v
▷ **ravage**
ravaging v ▷ **ravage**
rave v (-ves, -ving, -ved) talk wildly
or with enthusiasm ▶ n (pl -s) slang
large-scale party with electronic
dance music
raved v ▷ **rave**
ravel v (-s, -lling, -lled) tangle or
become entangled
ravelled v ▷ **ravel**
ravelling v ▷ **ravel**
ravels v ▷ **ravel**
raven n (pl -s) black bird like a large

crow ▶ adj (of hair) shiny black
ravenous adj very hungry
ravens n ▷ **raven**
raves v, n ▷ **rave**
ravine n (pl -s) narrow steep-sided
valley worn by a stream
ravines n ▷ **ravine**
raving adj delirious ▶ v ▷ **rave**
ravioli pl n small squares of pasta with
a savoury filling
ravish v (-es, -ing, -ed) enrapture
ravished v ▷ **ravish**
ravishes v ▷ **ravish**
ravishing adj, v ▷ **ravish**
raw adj (-er, -est) uncooked
rawer adj ▷ **raw**
rawest adj ▷ **raw**
rawhide n (pl -s) untanned hide
rawhides n ▷ **rawhide**

> **rax** v (raxes, raxing, raxed). Rax is
> a Scots word that means to stretch
> or extend. This is a good word to
> have ready when you have an X on
> your rack, as there is probably an A
> or R on the board already. The verb
> forms can also help you to get a
> better score. Rax scores 10 points.

ray¹ n (pl -s) single line or narrow beam
of light
ray² n (pl -s) large sea fish with a flat
body and a whiplike tail
rayon n (pl -s) (fabric made of) a
synthetic fibre
rayons n ▷ **rayon**
rays n ▷ **ray¹, ²**
raze v (-zes, -zing, -zed) destroy
(buildings or a town) completely
razed v ▷ **raze**
razes v ▷ **raze**
razing v ▷ **raze**
razor n (pl -s) sharp instrument for
shaving
razors n ▷ **razor**

> **re** n (res). Re is a musical note.
> This is the only two-letter word
> beginning with R, and so is a good
> one to remember. Re is very useful
> as it allows you to connect a word

beginning with R to one ending in E, or vice versa, and R and E are two of the most common tiles in the game. Re scores 2 points.

reach v (-es, -ing, -ed) arrive at ► n (pl -es) distance that one can reach; ► pl stretch of a river ► **reachable** adj

reachable adj ▷ **reach**

reached v ▷ **reach**

reaches v, n ▷ **reach**

reaching v ▷ **reach**

react v (-s, -ing, -ed) act in response (to)

reacted v ▷ **react**

reacting v ▷ **react**

reaction n (pl -s) physical or emotional response to a stimulus

reactions n ▷ **reaction**

reactive adj chemically active

reactor n (pl -s) apparatus in which a nuclear reaction is maintained and controlled to produce nuclear energy

reactors n ▷ **reactor**

reacts v ▷ **react**

read v (-s, -ing, read) look at and understand or take in (written or printed matter) ► n matter suitable for reading ► **reading** n (pl -s)

readable adj enjoyable to read

reader n (pl -s) person who reads

readers n ▷ **reader**

readier adj ▷ **ready**

readiest adj ▷ **ready**

readily adv ▷ **ready**

readiness n ▷ **ready**

readinesses n ▷ **ready**

reading n, v ▷ **read**

readings n ▷ **read**

readjust v (-s, -ing, -ed) adapt to a new situation ► **readjustment** n (pl -s)

readjusted v ▷ **readjust**

readjusting v ▷ **readjust**

readjustment n ▷ **readjust**

readjustments n ▷ **readjust**

readjusts v ▷ **readjust**

reads v ▷ **read**

ready adj (-dier, -diest) prepared for use or action ► **readily** adv

> **readiness** n (pl -es)

reagent n (pl -s) chemical substance that reacts with another, used to detect the presence of the other reagents n ▷ **reagent**

reagents n ▷ **reagent**

real adj (-er, -est) existing in fact

realities n ▷ **reality**

reality n (pl -ies) state of things as they are

realization n ▷ **realize**

realizations n ▷ **realize**

realize v (-s, -zing, -zed) become aware of or grasp the significance of

> **realization** n (pl -s)

realized v ▷ **realize**

realizes v ▷ **realize**

realizing v ▷ **realize**

really adv very ► interj exclamation of dismay, doubt, or surprise

realm n (pl -s) kingdom

realms n ▷ **realm**

ream n (pl -s) twenty quires of paper, generally 500 sheets ► pl informal large quantity (of written matter)

reams n ▷ **ream**

reap v (-s, -ing, -ed) cut and gather (a harvest) ► **reaper** n (pl -s)

reaped v ▷ **reap**

reaper n ▷ **reap**

reapers n ▷ **reap**

reaping v ▷ **reap**

reappear v (-s, -ing, -ed) appear again

> **reappearance** n (pl -s)

reappearance n ▷ **reappear**

reappearances n ▷ **reappear**

reappeared v ▷ **reappear**

reappearing v ▷ **reappear**

reappears v ▷ **reappear**

reaps v ▷ **reap**

rear[1] n (pl -s) back part ► **rearmost** adj

rear[2] v (-s, -ing, -ed) care for and educate (children)

reared v ▷ **rear**

rearing v ▷ **rear**

rearmost adj ▷ **rear**[1]

rears n ▷ **rear**[1] ► v ▷ **rear**[2]

reason n (pl -s) cause or motive ► v (-s, -ing, -ed) think logically in forming conclusions

reasoned v ▷ reason

reasoning v ▷ reason

reasons n, v ▷ reason

reassess v (-es, -ing, -ed) reconsider the value or importance of

reassessed v ▷ reassess

reassesses v ▷ reassess

reassessing v ▷ reassess

reassurance n ▷ reassure

reassurances n ▷ reassure

reassure v (-res, -ring, -red) restore confidence to > **reassurance** n (pl -s)

reassured v ▷ reassure

reassures v ▷ reassure

reassuring v ▷ reassure

rebate n (pl -s) discount or refund

rebates n ▷ rebate

rebel v (-s, -lling, -lled) revolt against the ruling power ▶ n (pl -s) person who rebels > **rebellious** adj

rebelled v ▷ rebel

rebelling v ▷ rebel

rebellious adj ▷ rebel

rebels v, n ▷ rebel

rebore, reboring n (pl -s) boring of a cylinder to restore its true shape

rebores v ▷ rebore

reboring n ▷ rebore

reborings n ▷ rebore

rebound v (-s, -ing, -ed) spring back

rebounded v ▷ rebound

rebounding v ▷ rebound

rebounds v, n ▷ rebound

rebuff v (-s, -ing, -ed) reject or snub ▶ n (pl -s) blunt refusal, snub

rebuffed v ▷ rebuff

rebuffing v ▷ rebuff

rebuffs v, n ▷ rebuff

rebuke v (-kes, -king, -ked) scold sternly ▶ n (pl -s) stern scolding

rebuked v ▷ rebuke

rebukes v ▷ rebuke

rebuking v ▷ rebuke

rebus n (pl -es) puzzle consisting of pictures and symbols representing words or syllables

rebuses n ▷ rebus

rebut v (-s, -tting, -tted) prove that (a claim) is untrue > **rebuttal** n (pl -s)

rebuts v ▷ rebut

rebuttal n ▷ rebut

rebuttals n ▷ rebut

rebutted v ▷ rebut

rebutting v ▷ rebut

recall v (-s, -ing, -ed) recollect or remember ▶ n (pl (pl -s) ability to remember

recalled v ▷ recall

recalling v ▷ recall

recalls v, n ▷ recall

recant v (-s, -ing, -ed) withdraw (a statement or belief) publicly > **recantation** n (pl -s)

recantation n ▷ recant

recantations n ▷ recant

recanted v ▷ recant

recanting v ▷ recant

recants v ▷ recant

recap informal v (-s, -pping, -pped) recapitulate ▶ n (pl -s) recapitulation

recapped v ▷ recap

recapping v ▷ recap

recaps v, n ▷ recap

recce CHIEFLY BRIT slang v (-s, -ceing, -ced or -cced) reconnoitre ▶ n (pl -s) reconnaissance

recced v ▷ recce

recceed v ▷ recce

recceing v ▷ recce

recces v, n ▷ recce

recede v (-des, -ding, -ded) move to a more distant place

receded v ▷ recede

recedes v ▷ recede

receding v ▷ recede

receipt n (pl -s) written acknowledgment of money or goods received

receipts n ▷ receipt

receive v (-ves, -ving, -ved) take, accept, or get

received adj generally accepted ▶ v ▷ receive

receiver n (pl -s) part of telephone that is held to the ear

receivers n ▷ receiver
receives v ▷ receive
receiving v ▷ receive
recent adj (-er, -est) having happened lately > **recently** adv
recenter adj ▷ recent
recentest adj ▷ recent
recently adv ▷ recent
recess n (pl -es) niche or alcove
recessed adj hidden or placed in a recess
recesses n ▷ recess
recipe n (pl -s) directions for cooking a dish
recipes n ▷ recipe
recital n (pl -s) musical performance by a soloist or soloists
recitals n ▷ recital
recite v (-tes, -ting, -ted) repeat (a poem etc) aloud to an audience
recited v ▷ recite
recites v ▷ recite
reciting v ▷ recite
reckless adj heedless of danger > **recklessly** adv > **recklessness** n (pl -s)
recklessly adv ▷ reckless
recklessness n ▷ reckless
recklessnesses n ▷ reckless
reckon v (-s, -ing, -ed) consider or think > **reckoning** n (pl -s)
reckoned v ▷ reckon
reckoning v, n ▷ reckon
reckonings n ▷ reckon
reckons n ▷ reckon
reclaim v (-s, -ing, -ed) regain possession of > **reclamation** n (pl -s)
reclaimed v ▷ reclaim
reclaiming v ▷ reclaim
reclaims v ▷ reclaim
reclamation n ▷ reclaim
reclamations n ▷ reclaim
recline v (-nes, -ning, -ned) rest in a leaning position > **reclining** adj
reclined v ▷ recline
reclines v ▷ recline
reclining v, adj ▷ recline
recluse n (pl -s) person who avoids other people > **reclusive** adj

recluses n ▷ recluse
reclusive adj ▷ recluse
recoil v (-s, -ing, -ed) jerk or spring back ▶ n (pl -s) backward jerk
recoiled v ▷ recoil
recoiling v ▷ recoil
recoils v, n ▷ recoil
record n (pl -s) document or other thing that preserves information ▶ v (-s, -ing, -ed) put in writing > **recording** n (pl -s)
recorded v ▷ record
recorder n (pl -s) person or machine that records, esp. a video, cassette, or tape recorder
recorders n ▷ recorder
recording v, n ▷ record
recordings n ▷ record
records n, v ▷ record
recount v (-s, -ing, -ed) tell in detail
recounted v ▷ recount
recounting v ▷ recount
recounts v ▷ recount
recoup v (-s, -ing, -ed) regain or make good (a loss)
recouped v ▷ recoup
recouping v ▷ recoup
recoups v ▷ recoup
recourse n (pl -s) source of help
recourses n ▷ recourse
recover v (-s, -ing, -ed) become healthy again > **recovery** n (pl -ies) > **recoverable** adj
recoverable adj ▷ recover
recovered v ▷ recover
recoveries n ▷ recover
recovering v ▷ recover
recovers v ▷ recover
recovery v ▷ recover
recruit v (-s, -ing, -ed) enlist (new soldiers, members, etc) ▶ n (pl -s) newly enlisted soldier > **recruitment** n (pl -s)
recruited v ▷ recruit
recruiting v ▷ recruit
recruitment n ▷ recruit
recruitments n ▷ recruit
recruits v, n ▷ recruit

recta n ▷ **rectum**
rectification n ▷ **rectify**
rectifications n ▷ **rectify**
rectified v ▷ **rectify**
rectifier n ▷ **rectify**
rectifiers n ▷ **rectify**
rectifies v ▷ **rectify**
rectify v (-ies, -ying, -ied) put right, correct > **rectification** n (pl -s) > **rectifier** n (pl -s)
rectifying v ▷ **rectify**
recto n (pl -s) right-hand page of a book
rector n (pl -s) clergyman in charge of a parish
rectories n ▷ **rectory**
rectors n ▷ **rector**
rectory n (pl -ies) rector's house
rectos n ▷ **recto**
rectum n (pl -tums, -ta) final section of the large intestine
rectums n ▷ **rectum**
recur v (-s, -rring, -rred) happen again > **recurrence** n (pl -s) repetition > **recurrent** adj
recurred v ▷ **recur**
recurrence n ▷ **recur**
recurrences n ▷ **recur**
recurrent adj ▷ **recur**
recurring v ▷ **recur**
recurs v ▷ **recur**
recyclable adj ▷ **recycle**
recycle v (-les, -ling, -led) reprocess (used materials) for further use > **recyclable** adj
recycled v ▷ **recycle**
recycles v ▷ **recycle**
recycling v ▷ **recycle**
red adj (-dder, -ddest) of a colour varying from crimson to orange and seen in blood, fire, etc ▶ n (pl -s) red colour > **reddish** adj > **redness** n (pl -es)
redbrick adj (of a university in Britain) founded in the late 19th or early 20th century
redcoat n (pl -s) HIST British soldier
redcoats n ▷ **redcoat**
redden v (-s, -ing, -ed) make or become red

reddened v ▷ **redden**
reddening v ▷ **redden**
reddens v ▷ **redden**
redder adj ▷ **red**
reddest adj ▷ **red**
reddish adj ▷ **red**
redeem v (-s, -ing, -ed) make up for > **redeemable** adj > **redemption** n (pl -s) > **redemptive** adj
redeemable adj ▷ **redeem**
redeemed v ▷ **redeem**
redeeming v ▷ **redeem**
redeems v ▷ **redeem**
redemption adj ▷ **redeem**
redemptions adj ▷ **redeem**
redemptive adj ▷ **redeem**
redeploy v (-s, -ing, -ed) assign to a new position or task > **redeployment** n (pl -s)
redeployed v ▷ **redeploy**
redeploying v ▷ **redeploy**
redeployment n ▷ **redeploy**
redeploys v ▷ **redeploy**
redness n ▷ **red**
rednesses n ▷ **red**
redolent adj reminiscent (of)
redouble v (-les, -ling, -led) increase, multiply, or intensify
redoubled v ▷ **redouble**
redoubles v ▷ **redouble**
redoubling v ▷ **redouble**
redoubt n (pl -s) small fort defending a hilltop or pass
redoubts n ▷ **redoubt**
redound v (-s, -ing, -ed) cause advantage or disadvantage (to)
redounded v ▷ **redound**
redounding v ▷ **redound**
redounds v ▷ **redound**
redox n (pl -es) chemical reaction in which one substance is reduced and the other is oxidized
redoxes n ▷ **redox**
redress v (-es, -ing, -ed) make amends for ▶ n (pl -es) compensation or amends
redressed v ▷ **redress**
redresses v, n ▷ **redress**

redressing v ▷ redress
reds n ▷ red
reduce v (-ces, -cing, -ced) bring down, lower ▷ reducible adj ▷ reduction n (pl -s)
reduced v ▷ reduce
reduces v ▷ reduce
reducible adj ▷ reduce
reducing v ▷ reduce
reduction n ▷ reduce
reductions n ▷ reduce
reed n (pl -s) tall grass that grows in swamps and shallow water
reedier adj ▷ reedy
reediest n ▷ reedy
reeds n ▷ reed
reedy (-dier, -diest) adj harsh and thin in tone
reef¹ n (pl -s) ridge of rock or coral near the surface of the sea
reef² n (pl -s) part of a sail which can be rolled up to reduce its area ▶ v (-s, -ing, -ed) take in a reef of
reefed v ▷ reef²
reefer n (pl -s) short thick jacket worn esp. by sailors
reefers n ▷ reefer
reefing v ▷ reef²
reefs n ▷ reef¹, ² ▶ v ▷ reef¹, ²
reek v (-s, -ing, -ed) smell strongly ▶ n (pl -s) strong unpleasant smell
reeked v ▷ reek
reeking v ▷ reek
reeks v, n ▷ reek
reel¹ n (pl -s) cylindrical object on which film, tape, thread, or wire is wound
reel² v (-s, -ing, -ed) stagger, sway, or whirl
reel³ n (pl -s) lively Scottish dance
reeled v ▷ reel²
reeling v ▷ reel²
reels n ▷ reel¹, ³ ▶ v ▷ reel²
ref n (pl -s) informal referee in sport
refer v (-s, -rring, -rred) (foll. by to) allude (to) ▷ referral n (pl -s)
referee n (pl -s) umpire in sports, esp. soccer or boxing ▶ v (-s, -ing, -eed) act

as referee of
refereed v ▷ referee
refereeing v ▷ referee
referees n, v ▷ referee
referral n ▷ refer
referrals n ▷ refer
referred v ▷ refer
referring v ▷ refer
refers v ▷ refer
refill v (-s, -ing, -ed) fill again ▶ n (pl -s) second or subsequent filling
refilled v ▷ refill
refilling v ▷ refill
refills v, n ▷ refill
refine v (-nes, -ning, -ned) purify
refined adj cultured or polite ▶ v ▷ refine
refineries n ▷ refinery
refinery n (pl -ries) place where sugar, oil, etc is refined
refines v ▷ refine
refining v ▷ refine
reflect v (-s, -ing, -ed) throw back, esp. rays of light, heat, etc
reflected v ▷ reflect
reflecting v ▷ reflect
reflections n ▷ reflect
reflects v ▷ reflect
reflex n (pl -es) involuntary response to a stimulus or situation ▶ adj (of a muscular action) involuntary
reflexes n ▷ reflex
reform n (pl -s) improvement ▶ v (-s, -ing, -ed) improve ▷ reformer n (pl -s)
reformed v ▷ reform
reformer n ▷ reform
reformers n ▷ reform
reforming v ▷ reform
reforms n, v ▷ reform
refract v (-s, -ing, -ed) change the course of (light etc) passing from one medium to another ▷ refraction n (pl -s) ▷ refractive adj ▷ refractor n (pl -s)
refracted v ▷ refract
refracting v ▷ refract
refraction n ▷ refract
refractions n ▷ refract
refractive adj ▷ refract

refractor n ▷ **refract**
refractors n ▷ **refract**
refracts v ▷ **refract**
refrain[1] v (**-s**, **-ing**, **-ed**) keep oneself from doing
refrain[2] n (pl **-s**) frequently repeated part of a song
refrained v ▷ **refrain**[1]
refraining v ▷ **refrain**[1]
refrains v ▷ **refrain**[1] ▶ n ▷ **refrain**[2]
refresh v (**-es**, **-ing**, **-ed**) revive or reinvigorate, as through food, drink, or rest > **refresher** n (pl **-s**)
refreshed v ▷ **refresh**
refresher n ▷ **refresh**
refreshers n ▷ **refresh**
refreshes v ▷ **refresh**
refrigerator n (pl **-s**) ▷ **fridge**
refs n ▷ **ref**
refuge n (pl **-s**) (source of) shelter or protection
refugee n (pl **-s**) person who seeks refuge, esp. in a foreign country
refugees n ▷ **refugee**
refuges n ▷ **refuge**
refund v (**-s**, **-ing**, **-ed**) pay back ▶ n (pl **-s**) return of money
refunded v ▷ **refund**
refunding v ▷ **refund**
refunds v, n ▷ **refund**
refusal n (pl **-s**) denial of anything demanded or offered
refusals n ▷ **refusal**
refuse[1] v (**-ses**, **-sing**, **-sed**) decline, deny, or reject
refuse[2] n (pl **-s**) rubbish or useless matter
refused v ▷ **refuse**[1]
refuses v ▷ **refuse**[1] ▶ n ▷ **refuse**[2]
refusing v ▷ **refuse**[1]
refutation n ▷ **refute**
refutations n ▷ **refute**
refute v (**-tes**, **-ting**, **-ted**) disprove > **refutation** n (pl **-s**)
refuted v ▷ **refute**
refutes v ▷ **refute**
refuting v ▷ **refute**
regain v (**-s**, **-ing**, **-ed**) get back or recover

regained v ▷ **regain**
regaining v ▷ **regain**
regains v ▷ **regain**
regal adj of or like a king or queen > **regally** adv
regale v (**-les**, **-ling**, **-led**) entertain (someone) with stories etc
regaled v ▷ **regale**
regales v ▷ **regale**
regalia pl n ceremonial emblems of royalty or high office
regaling v ▷ **regale**
regally adv ▷ **regal**
regard v (**-s**, **-ing**, **-ed**) consider ▶ n (pl **-s**) respect or esteem ▶ pl expression of goodwill
regarded v ▷ **regard**
regards v, n ▷ **regard**
regatta n (pl **-s**) meeting for yacht or boat races
regattas n ▷ **regatta**
regencies n ▷ **regency**
regency n (pl **-ies**) status or period of office of a regent
regent n (pl **-s**) ruler of a kingdom during the absence, childhood, or illness of its monarch ▶ adj ruling as a regent
regents n ▷ **regent**
reggae n (pl **-s**) style of Jamaican popular music with a strong beat
reggaes n ▷ **reggae**
regicide n (pl **-s**) killing of a king
regicides n ▷ **regicide**
regime n (pl **-s**) system of government
regimen n (pl **-s**) prescribed system of diet etc
regimens n ▷ **regimen**
regiment n (pl **-s**) organized body of troops as a unit of the army > **regimental** adj > **regimentation** n (pl **-s**)
regimental adj ▷ **regiment**
regimentation n ▷ **regiment**
regimentations n ▷ **regiment**
regiments n ▷ **regiment**
regimes n ▷ **regime**

region n (pl **-s**) administrative division
of a country ▷ **regional** adj

regional adj ▷ **region**

regions n ▷ **region**

register n (pl **-s**) (book containing)
an official list or record of things ▶ v
(**-s, -ing, -ed**) enter in a register or set
down in writing ▷ **registration** n (pl **-s**)

registered v ▷ **register**

registering v ▷ **register**

registers n, v ▷ **register**

registration n ▷ **register**

regress v (**-es, -ing, -ed**) revert to a
former worse condition

regressed v ▷ **regress**

regresses v ▷ **regress**

regressing v ▷ **regress**

regret v (**-s, -tting, -tted**) feel sorry
about ▶ n (pl **-s**) feeling of repentance,
guilt, or sorrow ▷ **regretful** adj
▷ **regrettable** adj

regretful adj ▷ **regret**

regrets v ▷ **regret**

regrettable adj ▷ **regret**

regretted v ▷ **regret**

regretting v ▷ **regret**

regular adj normal, customary,
or usual ▶ n (pl **-s**) regular soldier
▷ **regularity** n (pl **-ties**) ▷ **regularize**
(**-zes, -zing, -zed**) ▷ **regularly** adv

regularities n ▷ **regular**

regularity n ▷ **regular**

regularize v ▷ **regular**

regularized v ▷ **regular**

regularizes v ▷ **regular**

regularizing v ▷ **regular**

regularly adv ▷ **regular**

regulars n ▷ **regular**

regulate v (**-tes, -ting, -ted**) control,
esp. by rules

regulated v ▷ **regulate**

regulates v ▷ **regulate**

regulating v ▷ **regulate**

rehash v (**-es, -ing, -ed**) rework or
reuse ▶ n (pl **-es**) old ideas presented
in a new form

rehashed v ▷ **rehash**

rehashes v, n ▷ **rehash**

rehashing v ▷ **rehash**

rehearsal n ▷ **rehearse**

rehearsals n ▷ **rehearse**

rehearse v (**-ses, -sing, -sed**) practise
(a play, concert, etc) ▷ **rehearsal** n
(pl **-s**)

rehearsed v ▷ **rehearse**

rehearses v ▷ **rehearse**

rehearsing v ▷ **rehearse**

rehouse v (**-ses, -sing, -sed**) provide
with a new (and better) home

rehoused v ▷ **rehouse**

rehouses v ▷ **rehouse**

rehousing v ▷ **rehouse**

reign n (pl **-s**) period of a sovereign's
rule ▶ v (**-s, -ing, -ed**) rule (a country)

reigned v ▷ **reign**

reigning v ▷ **reign**

reigns n, v ▷ **reign**

rein v (**-s, -ing, -ed**) check or manage
with reins

reindeer n (pl **-deer, -deers**) deer of
arctic regions with large branched
antlers

reindeers n ▷ **reindeer**

reined v ▷ **rein**

reining v ▷ **rein**

reins pl n narrow straps attached to
a bit to guide a horse ▶ v ▷ **rein**

reject v (**-s, -ing, -ed**) refuse to
accept or believe ▶ n (pl **-s**) person or
thing rejected as not up to standard
▷ **rejection** n (pl **-s**)

rejected v ▷ **reject**

rejecting v ▷ **reject**

rejection n ▷ **reject**

rejections n ▷ **reject**

rejects v, n ▷ **reject**

rejig v (**-s, -gging, -gged**) re-equip (a
factory or plant)

rejigged v ▷ **rejig**

rejigging v ▷ **rejig**

rejigs v ▷ **rejig**

rejoice v (**-ces, -cing, -ced**) feel or
express great happiness

rejoiced v ▷ **rejoice**

rejoices v ▷ **rejoice**

rejoicing v ▷ **rejoice**

rejoin¹ v (-s, -ing, -ed) join again
rejoin² v (-s, -ing, -ed) reply
  rejoined v ▷ **rejoin¹, ²**
  rejoining v ▷ **rejoin¹, ²**
  rejoins v ▷ **rejoin¹, ²**
relapse v (-ses, -sing, -sed) fall back
  into bad habits, illness, etc ▶ n (pl -s)
  return of bad habits, illness, etc
  relapsed v ▷ **relapse**
  relapses v, n ▷ **relapse**
  relapsing v ▷ **relapse**
relate v (-tes, -ting, -ted) establish a
  relation between > **related** adj
  related adj, v ▷ **relate**
  relates v ▷ **relate**
  relating v ▷ **relate**
relation n (pl -s) connection between
  things ▶ pl social or political dealings
  relations n ▷ **relation**
relative adj dependent on relation to
  something else, not absolute ▶ n (pl -s)
  person connected by blood or marriage
  > **relatively** adv
  relatively adv ▷ **relative**
  relatives n ▷ **relative**
relax v (-es, -ing, -ed) make or
  become looser, less tense, or less rigid
  > **relaxing** adj > **relaxation** n (pl -s)
  relaxation n ▷ **relax**
  relaxations n ▷ **relax**
  relaxed v ▷ **relax**
  relaxes v ▷ **relax**
  relaxing v, adj ▷ **relax**
relay n (pl -s) fresh set of people or
  animals relieving others ▶ v (-s, -ing,
  -ed) pass on (a message)
  relayed v ▷ **relay**
  relaying v ▷ **relay**
  relays n, v ▷ **relay**
release v (-ses, -sing, -sed) set free ▶ n
  (pl -s) setting free
  released v ▷ **release**
  releases v, n ▷ **release**
  releasing v ▷ **release**
relegate v (-tes, -ting, -ted) put in a
  less important position > **relegation** n
  (pl -s)
  relegated v ▷ **relegate**

  relegates v ▷ **relegate**
  relegating v ▷ **relegate**
  relegation n ▷ **relegate**
  relegations n ▷ **relegate**
relent v (-s, -ing, -ed) give up a harsh
  intention, become less severe
  relented v ▷ **relent**
  relenting v ▷ **relent**
  relents v ▷ **relent**
  relevance n ▷ **relevant**
  relevances n ▷ **relevant**
relevant adj to do with the matter in
  hand > **relevance** n (pl -s)
  reliabilities n ▷ **reliable**
  reliability n ▷ **reliable**
reliable adj able to be trusted,
  dependable > **reliably** adv
  > **reliability** n (pl -ies)
  reliably adv ▷ **reliable**
reliance n (pl -s) dependence,
  confidence, or trust > **reliant** adj
  reliances n ▷ **reliance**
  reliant adj ▷ **reliance**
  relic n (pl -s) something that has
  survived from the past ▶ pl remains
  or traces
  relics n ▷ **relic**
  relict n (pl -s) obs widow
  relicts n ▷ **relict**
  relied v ▷ **rely**
  relief n (pl -s) gladness at the end or
  removal of pain, distress, etc
  reliefs n ▷ **relief**
  relies v ▷ **rely**
relieve v (-ves, -ving, -ved) bring
  relief to
  relieved v ▷ **relieve**
  relieves v ▷ **relieve**
  relieving v ▷ **relieve**
religion n (pl -s) system of belief in
  and worship of a supernatural power
  or god
  religions n ▷ **religion**
relish v (-es, -ing, -ed) enjoy, like very
  much ▶ n (pl -es) liking or enjoyment
  relished v ▷ **relish**
  relishes v, n ▷ **relish**
  relishing v ▷ **relish**

relocate v (-tes, -ting, -ted) move to a new place to live or work
> **relocation** n (pl -s)
relocated v ▷ relocate
relocates v ▷ relocate
relocating v ▷ relocate
relocation n ▷ relocate
relocations n ▷ relocate

rely v (-ies, -ying, -ied) depend (on)
relying v ▷ rely

remain v (-s, -ing, -ed) continue
remained v ▷ remain
remaining v ▷ remain
remains pl n relics, esp. of ancient buildings ▶ v ▷ remain

remand v (-s, -ing, -ed) send back into custody or put on bail before trial
remanded v ▷ remand
remanding v ▷ remand
remands v ▷ remand

remark v (-s, -ing, -ed) make a casual comment (on) ▶ n (pl -s) observation or comment
remarked v ▷ remark
remarking v ▷ remark
remarks n, v ▷ remark

remedial adj intended to correct a specific disability, handicap, etc
remedied v ▷ remedy
remedies n, v ▷ remedy

remedy n (pl -ies) means of curing pain or disease ▶ v (-ies, -ying, -ied) put right
remedying v ▷ remedy

remember v (-s, -ing, -ed) retain in or recall to one's memory
remembered v ▷ remember
remembering v ▷ remember
remembers v ▷ remember

remind v (-s, -ing, -ed) cause to remember
reminded v ▷ remind

reminder n (pl -s) something that recalls the past
reminders n ▷ reminder
reminding v ▷ remind
reminds v ▷ remind

remiss adj negligent or careless

remit v (-s, -tting, -tted) send (money) for goods, services, etc, esp. by post ▶ n (pl -s) area of competence or authority
remits v, n ▷ remit
remitted v ▷ remit
remitting v ▷ remit

remnant n (pl -s) small piece, esp. of fabric, left over
remnants n ▷ remnant

remorse n (pl -s) feeling of sorrow and regret for something one did
> **remorseful** adj
remorseful adj ▷ remorse
remorses n ▷ remorse

remote adj (-er, -est) far away, distant
> **remotely** adv
remotely adv ▷ remote
remoter adj ▷ remote
remotest adj ▷ remote

remould v (-s, -ing, -ed) BRIT renovate (a worn tyre) ▶ n (pl -s) BRIT renovated tyre
remoulded v ▷ remould
remoulding v ▷ remould
remoulds v, n ▷ remould
removable adj ▷ remove

removal n (pl -s) removing, esp. changing residence
removals n ▷ removal

remove v (-ves, -ving, -ved) take away or off ▶ n (pl -s) degree of difference > **removable** adj
removed v ▷ remove
removes v, n ▷ remove
removing v, n ▷ remove

renal adj of the kidneys

rend v (-s, -ing, rent) tear or wrench apart

render v (-s, -ing, -ed) cause to become
rendered v ▷ render
rendering v ▷ render
renders v ▷ render
rending v ▷ rend
rends v ▷ rend

renegade n (pl -s) person who deserts a cause
renegades n ▷ renegade

renege v (-ges, -ging, -ged) go back (on a promise etc)
reneged v ▷ renege
reneges v ▷ renege
reneging v ▷ renege

renew v (-s, -ing, -ed) begin again
>**renewable** adj >**renewal** n (pl -s)
renewable adj ▷ renew
renewal n ▷ renew
renewals n ▷ renew
renewed v ▷ renew
renewing v ▷ renew
renews v ▷ renew

rennet n (pl -s) substance for curdling milk to make cheese
rennets n ▷ rennet

renounce v (-ces, -cing, -ced) give up (a belief, habit, etc) voluntarily
>**renunciation** n (pl -s)
renounced v ▷ renounce
renounces v ▷ renounce
renouncing v ▷ renounce

renovate v (-tes, -ting, -ted) restore to good condition >**renovation** n (pl -s)
renovated v ▷ renovate
renovates v ▷ renovate
renovating v ▷ renovate
renovation n ▷ renovate
renovations n ▷ renovate

renown n (pl -s) widespread good reputation
renowned adj famous
renowns n ▷ renown

rent¹ v (-s, -ing, -ed) give or have use of in return for regular payments ▶ n (pl -s) regular payment for use of land, a building, machine, etc
rent² n (pl -s) tear or fissure ▶ v ▷ rend
rental n (pl -s) sum payable as rent
rentals n ▷ rental
rented v ▷ rent¹
renting v ▷ rent¹
rents v ▷ rent¹ ▶ n ▷ rent¹, ²
renunciation n ▷ renounce
renunciations n ▷ renounce
rep¹ n (pl -s)
rep² n (pl -s) representative

repair¹ v (-s, -ing, -ed) restore to good condition, mend ▶ n (pl -s) act of repairing
repair² v (-s, -ing, -ed) go (to)
repaired v ▷ repair¹, ²
repairing v ▷ repair¹, ²
repairs v ▷ repair¹, ², ▶ n ▷ repair¹

repartee n (pl -s) interchange of witty retorts
repartees n ▷ repartee

repast n (pl -s) meal
repasts n ▷ repast

repay v (-s, -ing, -paid) pay back, refund >**repayable** adj >**repayment** n (pl -s)
repayable adj ▷ repay
repaying v ▷ repay
repayment n ▷ repay
repayments n ▷ repay
repays v ▷ repay

repeal v (-s, -ing, -ed) cancel (a law) officially ▶ n (pl -s) act of repealing
repealed v ▷ repeal
repealing v ▷ repeal
repeals v, n ▷ repeal

repeat v (-s, -ing, -ed) say or do again ▶ n (pl -s) act or instance of repeating
>**repeatedly** adv
repeated v ▷ repeat
repeatedly adv ▷ repeat

repeater n (pl -s) firearm that may be discharged many times without reloading
repeaters n ▷ repeater
repeating v ▷ repeat
repeats v, n ▷ repeat

repel v (-s, -lling, -lled) be disgusting to
repelled v ▷ repel
repelling v ▷ repel
repels v ▷ repel

repent v (-s, -ing, -ed) feel regret for (a deed or omission) >**repentance** n (pl -s) >**repentant** adj
repentance n ▷ repent
repentances n ▷ repent
repentant adj ▷ repent
repented v ▷ repent

repenting v ▷ **repent**

repents v ▷ **repent**

rephrase v (-ses, -sing, -sed) express in different words

rephrased v ▷ **rephrase**

rephrases v ▷ **rephrase**

rephrasing v ▷ **rephrase**

repine v (-nes, -ning, -ned) fret or complain

repined v ▷ **repine**

repines v ▷ **repine**

repining v ▷ **repine**

replace v (-ces, -cing, -ced) substitute for ▷ **replacement** n (pl -s)

replaced v ▷ **replace**

replacement n ▷ **replace**

replacements n ▷ **replace**

replaces v ▷ **replace**

replacing v ▷ **replace**

replay n (pl -s) immediate reshowing on TV of an incident in sport, esp. in slow motion ▶ v (-s, -ing, -ed) play (a match, recording, etc) again

replayed v ▷ **replay**

replaying v ▷ **replay**

replays n, v ▷ **replay**

replete adj filled or gorged

replica n (pl -s) exact copy

replicas n ▷ **replica**

replied v ▷ **reply**

replies v, n ▷ **reply**

reply v (-ies, -ying, -ied) answer or respond ▶ n (pl -ies) answer or response

replying v ▷ **reply**

report v (-s, -ing, -ed) give an account of ▶ n (pl -s) account or statement

reported v ▷ **report**

reporter n (pl -s) person who gathers news for a newspaper, TV, etc

reporters n ▷ **reporter**

reporting v ▷ **report**

reports v, n ▷ **report**

repose n (pl -s) peace ▶ v (-ses, -sing, -sed) lie or lay at rest

reposed v ▷ **repose**

reposes n, v ▷ **repose**

reposing v ▷ **repose**

repress v (-es, -ing, -ed) keep (feelings) in check ▷ **repression** n (pl -s) ▷ **repressive** adj

repressed v ▷ **repress**

represses v ▷ **repress**

repressing v ▷ **repress**

repression n ▷ **repress**

repressions n ▷ **repress**

repressive adj ▷ **repress**

reprieve v (-ves, -ving, -ved) postpone the execution of (a condemned person) ▶ n (pl -s) (document granting) postponement or cancellation of a punishment

reprieved v ▷ **reprieve**

reprieves v, n ▷ **reprieve**

reprieving v ▷ **reprieve**

reprint v (-s, -ing, -ed) print further copies of (a book) ▶ n (pl -s) reprinted copy

reprinted v ▷ **reprint**

reprinting v ▷ **reprint**

reprints v, n ▷ **reprint**

reprisal n (pl -s) retaliation

reprisals n ▷ **reprisal**

reproach n, v (-es, -ing, -ed) blame, rebuke ▷ **reproachful** adj ▷ **reproachfully** adv

reproached v ▷ **reproach**

reproaches v ▷ **reproach**

reproachful adj ▷ **reproach**

reproachfully adv ▷ **reproach**

reproaching v ▷ **reproach**

reproof n (pl -s) severe blaming of someone for a fault

reproofs n ▷ **reproof**

reprove v (-ves, -ving, -ved) speak severely to (someone) about a fault

reproved v ▷ **reprove**

reproves v ▷ **reprove**

reproving v ▷ **reprove**

reps n ▷ **rep**[1, 2]

reptile n (pl -s) cold-blooded egg-laying vertebrate with horny scales or plates, such as a snake or tortoise ▷ **reptilian** adj

reptiles n ▷ **reptile**

reptilian adj ▷ **reptile**

republic n (pl -s) form of government in which the people or their elected representatives possess the supreme power
republics n ▷ republic
repulse v (-ses, -sing, -sed) be disgusting to ▶ n (pl -s) driving back
repulsed v ▷ repulse
repulses v, n ▷ repulse
repulsing v ▷ repulse
repute n (pl -s) reputation
reputed adj supposed > **reputedly** adv
reputedly adv ▷ reputed
reputes n ▷ repute
request v (-s, -ing, -ed) ask ▶ n (pl -s) asking
requested v ▷ request
requesting v ▷ request
requests v, n ▷ request
requiem n (pl -s) Mass for the dead
requiems n ▷ requiem
require v (-res, -ring, -red) want or need
required v ▷ require
requires v ▷ require
requiring v ▷ require
requite v (-tes, -ting, -ted) return to someone (the same treatment or feeling as received)
requited v ▷ requite
requites v ▷ requite
requiting v ▷ requite
reredos n (pl -es) ornamental screen behind an altar
reredoses n ▷ reredos
resat v ▷ resit
rescind v (-s, -ing, -ed) annul or repeal
rescinded v ▷ rescind
rescinding v ▷ rescind
rescinds v ▷ rescind
rescue v (-ues, -uing, -ued) deliver from danger or trouble, save ▶ n (pl -s) rescuing > **rescuer** n (pl -s)
rescued v ▷ rescue
rescuer n ▷ rescue
rescuers n ▷ rescue
rescues v, n ▷ rescue
rescuing v ▷ rescue

research n (pl -es) systematic investigation to discover facts or collect information ▶ v (-es, -ing, -ed) carry out investigations > **researcher** n (pl -s)
researched v ▷ research
researcher n ▷ research
researchers n ▷ research
researches n, v ▷ research
researching v ▷ research
resemblance n ▷ resemble
resemblances n ▷ resemble
resemble v (-les, -ling, -led) be or look like > **resemblance** n (pl -s)
resembled v ▷ resemble
resembles v ▷ resemble
resembling v ▷ resemble
resent v (-s, -ing, -ed) feel bitter about > **resentful** adj > **resentment** n (pl -s)
resented v ▷ resent
resentful adj ▷ resent
resenting v ▷ resent
resentment n ▷ resent
resentments n ▷ resent
resents v ▷ resent
reserve v (-ves, -ving, -ved) set aside, keep for future use ▶ n (pl -s) something, esp. money or troops, kept for emergencies SPORT
reserved adj not showing one's feelings, lacking friendliness ▶ v ▷ reserve
reserves v, n ▷ reserve
reserving v ▷ reserve
reside v (-des, -ding, -ded) dwell permanently
resided v ▷ reside
resident n (pl -s) person who lives in a place ▶ adj living in a place
residents n ▷ resident
resides v ▷ reside
residing v ▷ reside
residual adj ▷ residue
residue n (pl -s) what is left, remainder > **residual** adj
residues n ▷ residue
resign v (-s, -ing, -ed) give up office, a job, etc

resigned adj content to endure ▶ v
▷ **resign**
  resigning v ▷ **resign**
  resigns v ▷ **resign**
resin n (pl -s) sticky substance from
plants, esp. pines > **resinous** adj
  resinous adj ▷ **resin**
  resins n ▷ **resin**
resist v (-s, -ing, -ed) withstand or
oppose > **resistant** adj > **resistible** adj
  resistant adj ▷ **resist**
  resisted v ▷ **resist**
  resistible adj ▷ **resist**
  resisting v ▷ **resist**
resistor n (pl -s) component of an
electrical circuit producing resistance
  resistors n ▷ **resistor**
  resists v ▷ **resist**
resit v (-s, -tting, -sat) take (an exam)
again ▶ n (pl -s) exam that has to be
taken again
  resits v, n ▷ **resit**
  resitting v ▷ **resit**
resolute adj firm in purpose
> **resolutely** adv
  resolutely adv ▷ **resolute**
resolve v (-ves, -ving, -ved) decide
with an effort of will
  resolved adj determined ▶ v
  ▷ **resolve**
  resolves v ▷ **resolve**
  resolving v ▷ **resolve**
resort v (-s, -ing, -ed) have recourse
(to) for help etc ▶ n (pl -s) place for
holidays
  resorted v ▷ **resort**
  resorting v ▷ **resort**
  resorts v, n ▷ **resort**
resound v (-s, -ing, -ed) echo or ring
with sound
  resounded v ▷ **resound**
  resounds v ▷ **resound**
resource n (pl -s) thing resorted
to for support ▶ pl sources of
economic wealth > **resourceful** adj
> **resourcefulness** n
  resourceful adj ▷ **resource**
  resourcefulness n ▷ **resource**

resources n ▷ **resource**
respect n (pl -s) consideration ▶ v
(-s, -ing, -ed) treat with esteem
> **respecter** n (pl -s) > **respectful** adj
  respected v ▷ **respect**
  respecter n ▷ **respect**
  respecters n ▷ **respect**
  respectful adj ▷ **respect**
  respects n, v ▷ **respect**
respire v (-res, -ring, -red) breathe
  respired v ▷ **respire**
  respires v ▷ **respire**
  respiring v ▷ **respire**
respite n (pl -s) pause, interval of rest
  respites n ▷ **respite**
respond v (-s, -ing, -ed) answer
  responded v ▷ **respond**
  responding v ▷ **respond**
  responds v ▷ **respond**
response n (pl -s) answer
  responses n ▷ **response**
rest[1] n (pl -s) freedom from exertion
etc ▶ v (-s, -ing, -ed) take a rest
> **restful** adj > **restless** adj
rest[2] n what is left ▶ v (-s, -ing, -ed)
remain, continue to be
  rested v ▷ **rest**[1, 2]
restful (-ller, -llest) adj ▷ **rest**[1]
  restfuller adj ▷ **restful**
  restfullest adj ▷ **restful**
  resting v ▷ **rest**[1, 2]
restive adj restless or impatient
restless adj ▷ **rest**[1]
restoration n ▷ **restore**
  restorations n ▷ **restore**
restore v (-res, -ring, -red) return (a
building, painting, etc) to its original
condition > **restoration** n (pl -s)
> **restorer** n (pl -s)
  restored v ▷ **restore**
  restorer n ▷ **restore**
  restorers n ▷ **restore**
  restores v ▷ **restore**
  restoring v ▷ **restore**
restrain v (-s, -ing, -ed) hold
(someone) back from action
  restraining v ▷ **restrain**
  restrains v ▷ **restrain**

restrict v (-s, -ing, -ed) confine to certain limits > **restriction** n (pl -s) > **restrictive** adj
restricted v ▷ restrict
restricting v ▷ restrict
restriction n ▷ restrict
restrictions n ▷ restrict
restrictive adj ▷ restrict
restricts v ▷ restrict
rests n, v ▷ rest¹, ²

result n (pl -s) outcome or consequence ▶ v (-s, -ing, -ed) (foll. by **from**) be the outcome or consequence (of) > **resultant** adj
resultant adj ▷ result
resulted v ▷ result
resulting v ▷ result
results n, v ▷ result

resume v (-mes, -ming, -med) begin again > **resumption** n (pl -s)

résumé n (pl -s) summary
resumed v ▷ resume
résumés n ▷ résumé
resumes v ▷ resume
resuming v ▷ resume
resumption n ▷ resume
resumptions n ▷ resume

retail n (pl -s) selling of goods individually or in small amounts to the public ▶ adv by retail ▶ v (-s, -ing, -ed) sell or be sold retail
retailed v ▷ retail

retailer n (pl -s) person or company that sells goods to the public
retailers n ▷ retailer
retailing v ▷ retail
retails n, v ▷ retail

retain v (-s, -ing, -ed) keep in one's possession
retained v ▷ retain

retainer n (pl -s) fee to retain someone's services
retainers n ▷ retainer
retaining v ▷ retain
retains v ▷ retain

retard v (-s, -ing, -ed) delay or slow (progress or development) > **retardation** n (pl -s)

retardation n ▷ retard
retardations n ▷ retard

retarded adj underdeveloped, esp. mentally ▶ v ▷ retard
retarding v ▷ retard
retards v ▷ retard

retch v (-es, -ing, -ed) try to vomit
retched v ▷ retch
retches v ▷ retch
retching v ▷ retch

rethink v (-s, -ing, -thought) consider again, esp. with a view to changing one's tactics
rethinking v ▷ rethink
rethinks v ▷ rethink
rethought v ▷ rethink
reticence n ▷ reticent
reticences n ▷ reticent

reticent adj uncommunicative, reserved > **reticence** n (pl -s)

retina n (pl -nas, -nae) light-sensitive membrane at the back of the eye
retinae n ▷ retina
retinas n ▷ retina

retinue n (pl -s) band of attendants
retinues n ▷ retinue

retire v (-res, -ring, -red) (cause to) give up office or work, esp. through age > **retirement** n (pl -s)

retired adj having retired from work etc ▶ v ▷ retire
retirement n ▷ retire
retirements n ▷ retire
retires v ▷ retire
retiring adj shy ▶ v ▷ retire

retort¹ v (-s, -ing, -ed) reply quickly, wittily, or angrily ▶ n (pl -s) quick, witty, or angry reply

retort² n (pl -s) glass container with a bent neck used for distilling
retorted v ▷ retort¹
retorting v ▷ retort¹
retorts n, v ▷ retort¹, ² ▶ v ▷ retort¹

retouch v (-es, -ing, -ed) restore or improve by new touches, esp. of paint
retouched v ▷ retouch
retouches v ▷ retouch
retouching v ▷ retouch

retrace v (-ces, -cing, -ced) go back over (a route etc) again
retraced v ▷ retrace
retraces v ▷ retrace
retracing v ▷ retrace
retract v (-s, -ing, -ed) withdraw (a statement etc) ▷ retraction n (pl -s)
retracted v ▷ retract
retracting v ▷ retract
retraction n ▷ retract
retractions n ▷ retract
retracts v ▷ retract
retread v (-s, -ing, -ed) ▶ n (pl -s) ▷ remould
retreaded v ▷ retread
retreading v ▷ retread
retreads v, n ▷ retread
retreat v (-s, -ing, -ed) move back from a position, withdraw ▶ n (pl -s) act of or military signal for retiring or withdrawal
retreated v ▷ retreat
retreating v ▷ retreat
retreats v, n ▷ retreat
retrench v (-es, -ing, -ed) reduce expenditure, cut back ▷ retrenchment n (pl -s)
retrenched v ▷ retrench
retrenches v ▷ retrench
retrenching v ▷ retrench
retrenchment n ▷ retrench
retrenchments n ▷ retrench
retrial n (pl -s) second trial of a case or defendant in a court of law
retrials n ▷ retrial
retrievable adj ▷ retrieve
retrieval n ▷ retrieve
retrievals n ▷ retrieve
retrieve v (-ves, -ving, -ved) fetch back again ▷ retrievable adj ▷ retrieval n (pl -s)
retrieved v ▷ retrieve
retrievers n ▷ retrieve
retrieves v ▷ retrieve
retrieving v ▷ retrieve
retsina n (pl -s) Greek wine flavoured with resin
retsinas n ▷ retsina
return v (-s, -ing, -ed) go or come back

▶ n (pl -s) returning ▷ returnable adj
returnable adj ▷ return
returned v ▷ return
returning v ▷ return
returns v, n ▷ return
reunion n (pl -s) meeting of people who have been apart
reunions n ▷ reunion
reunite v (-tes, -ting, -ted) bring or come together again after a separation
reunited v ▷ reunite
reunites v ▷ reunite
reuniting v ▷ reunite
reusable adj ▷ reuse
reuse v (-ses, -sing, -sed) use again ▷ reusable adj
reused v ▷ reuse
reuses v ▷ reuse
reusing v ▷ reuse
rev informal n (pl -s) revolution (of an engine) ▶ v (-s, -vving, -vved) (foll. by up) increase the speed of revolution of (an engine)
revaluation n ▷ revalue
revaluations n ▷ revalue
revalue v (-ues, -uing, -ued) adjust the exchange value of (a currency) upwards ▷ revaluation n (pl -s)
revalued v ▷ revalue
revalues v ▷ revalue
revaluing v ▷ revalue
revamp v (-s, -ing, -ed) renovate or restore
revamped v ▷ revamp
revamping v ▷ revamp
revamps v ▷ revamp
reveal v (-s, -ing, -ed) make known ▷ revelation n (pl -s)
revealed v ▷ reveal
revealing v ▷ reveal
reveals v ▷ reveal
reveille n (pl -s) morning bugle call to waken soldiers
reveilles n ▷ reveille
revel v (-s, -lling, -lled) take pleasure (in) ▷ reveller n (pl -s)
revelation n ▷ revel
revelations n ▷ revel

revelled v ▷ revel
reveller n ▷ revel
revellers n ▷ revel
revelling v ▷ revel
revelries n ▷ revelry
revelry n (pl -s) festivity
revels pl n merrymaking ▶ v ▷ revel
revenge n (pl -s) retaliation for wrong done ▶ v (-ges, -ging, -ged) make retaliation for > **revengeful** adj
revenged v ▷ revenge
revengeful adj ▷ revenge
revenges n, v ▷ revenge
revenging v ▷ revenge
revenue n (pl -s) income, esp. of a state
revenues n ▷ revenue
revere v (-s, -ing, -ed) be in awe of and respect greatly
revered v ▷ revere
reverent adj showing reverence > **reverently** adv
reverently adv ▷ reverent
reveres v ▷ revere
reverie n (pl -s) absent-minded daydream
reveries n ▷ reverie
revering v ▷ revere
revers n (pl -s) turned back part of a garment, such as the lapel
reversal n ▷ reverse
reversals n ▷ reverse
reverse v (-ses, -sing, -sed) turn upside down, or the other way round ▶ n (pl -s) opposite ▶ adj opposite or contrary > **reversal** n (pl -s) > **reversible** adj
reversed v ▷ reverse
reverses v, n ▷ reverse
reversible adj ▷ reverse
reversing v ▷ reverse
reversion n ▷ revert
reversions n ▷ revert
revert v (-s, -ing, -ed) return to a former state > **reversion** n (pl -s)
reverted v ▷ revert
reverting v ▷ revert
reverts v ▷ revert
review n (pl -s) critical assessment of

a book, concert, etc ▶ v (-s, -ing, -ed) hold or write a review of
reviewed v ▷ review
reviewer n (pl -s) writer of reviews
reviewers n ▷ reviewer
reviewing v ▷ review
reviews n, v ▷ review
revile v (-les, -ling, -led) be abusively scornful of
reviled v ▷ revile
reviles v ▷ revile
reviling v ▷ revile
revise v (-ses, -sing, -sed) change or alter > **revision** n (pl -s)
revised v ▷ revise
revises v ▷ revise
revising v ▷ revise
revision n ▷ revise
revisions n ▷ revise
revival n (pl -s) reviving or renewal > **revivalism** n (pl -s) > **revivalist** n (pl -s)
revivalism n ▷ revival
revivalisms n ▷ revival
revivalist n ▷ revival
revivalists n ▷ revival
revivals n ▷ revival
revive v (-ves, -ving, -ved) bring or come back to life, vigour, use, etc
revived v ▷ revive
revives v ▷ revive
reviving v ▷ revive
revocation n ▷ revoke
revocations n ▷ revoke
revoke v (-kes, -king, -ked) cancel (a will, agreement, etc) > **revocation** n (pl -s)
revoked v ▷ revoke
revokes v ▷ revoke
revoking v ▷ revoke
revolt n (pl -s) uprising against authority ▶ v (-s, -ing, -ed) rise in rebellion
revolted v ▷ revolt
revolts n, v ▷ revolt
revolve v (-ves, -ving, -ved) turn round, rotate
revolved v ▷ revolve
revolves v ▷ revolve
revolving v ▷ revolve
revolver n (pl -s) repeating pistol
revolvers n ▷ revolver

revolves v ▷ revolve

revolving v ▷ revolve

revs n, v ▷ rev

revue n (pl -s) theatrical entertainment with topical sketches and songs

revues n ▷ revue

revved v ▷ rev

revving v ▷ rev

reward n (pl -s) something given in return for a service ▶ v (-s, -ing, -ed) pay or give something to (someone) for a service, information, etc

rewarded v ▷ reward

rewarding v ▷ reward

rewards n, v ▷ reward

rewind v (-s, -ing, -wound) run (a tape or film) back to an earlier point in order to replay

rewinding v ▷ rewind

rewinds v ▷ rewind

rewire v (-res, -ring, -red) provide (a house, engine, etc) with new wiring

rewired v ▷ rewire

rewires v ▷ rewire

rewiring v ▷ rewire

rewound v ▷ rewind

rewrite v (-tes, -ting, -wrote, -written) write again in a different way ▶ n (pl -s) something rewritten

rewrites v, n ▷ rewrite

rewriting v ▷ rewrite

rewritten v ▷ rewrite

rewrote v ▷ rewrite

| **rex** n (rexes) Rex is a Latin word for **king**. This is a very useful word, as it combines X with two of the most common letters on the board, making it one to look for when you get an X. Rex scores 10 points.

| **rez** n (rezes) Rez is a short informal word for **reservation**. Combining Z with two of the most common tiles on the board, this is one of the first words to think about when you draw a Z and don't have the letters for a longer word. Rez scores 12 points.

rhapsodic adj ▷ rhapsody

rhapsodies n ▷ rhapsody

rhapsody n (pl -ies) freely structured emotional piece of music ▷ **rhapsodic** adj

rhea n (pl -s) S American three-toed ostrich

rheas n ▷ rhea

rhenium n (pl -s) CHEM silvery-white metallic element with a high melting point

rheniums n ▷ rhenium

rheostat n (pl -s) instrument for varying the resistance of an electrical circuit

rheostats n ▷ rheostat

rhesus n (pl -es) small long-tailed monkey of S Asia

rhesuses n ▷ rhesus

rhetoric n (pl -s) art of effective speaking or writing

rhetorics n ▷ rhetoric

rhinos n ▷ rhino

rhizome n (pl -s) thick underground stem producing new plants

rhizomes n ▷ rhizome

| **rho** n (rhos). Rho is the 17th letter of the Greek alphabet. It's useful to remember words that start with RH, as there are quite a few that can come in useful. If you or someone else plays rho, remember that it could be expanded to **rhodium**, **rhombus** or **rhomboid**. Rho scores 6 points.

rhodium n (pl -s) CHEM hard metallic element

rhodiums n ▷ rhodium

rhombi n ▷ rhombus

rhomboid n (pl -s) parallelogram with adjacent sides of unequal length

rhomboids n ▷ rhomboid

rhombus n (pl -buses, -bi) parallelogram with sides of equal length but no right angles, diamond-shaped figure

rhombuses n ▷ rhombus

rhubarb n (pl -s) garden plant of which the fleshy stalks are cooked as fruit

rhubarbs n ▷ rhubarb

rhy n (**rhys**). Rhy is an alternative spelling of **rye**. This is a useful word as it doesn't contain a vowel, and so can be helpful when you have a poor combination of tiles on your rack. Rhy scores 9 points.

rhyme n (pl -s) sameness of the final sounds at the ends of lines of verse, or in words ▶ v (-mes, -ming, -med) make a rhyme

rhymed v ▷ rhyme

rhymes n, v ▷ rhyme

rhyming v ▷ rhyme

rhythm n (pl -s) any regular movement or beat > rhythmic, rhythmical adj > rhythmically adv

rhythmic adj ▷ rhythm

rhythmical adj ▷ rhythm

rhythmically adv ▷ rhythm

rhythms n ▷ rhythm

rib¹ n (pl -s) one of the curved bones forming the framework of the upper part of the body ▶ v (-s, -bbing, -bbed) provide or mark with ribs > ribbed adj > ribbing n (pl -s)

rib² v (-s, -bbing, -bbed) informal tease or ridicule > ribbing n (pl -s)

ribald adj humorously or mockingly rude or obscene > ribaldry n (pl -s)

ribaldries n ▷ ribald

ribaldry n ▷ ribald

ribbed v, adj ▷ rib¹, ²

ribbing n, v ▷ rib¹, ²

ribbings n ▷ rib¹, ²

ribbon n (pl -s) narrow band of fabric used for trimming, tying, etc

ribbons n ▷ ribbon

ribcage n (pl -s) bony structure of ribs enclosing the lungs

ribcages n ▷ ribcage

ribs n, v ▷ rib¹, ²

rice n (pl -s) cereal plant grown on wet ground in warm countries

rices n ▷ rice

rich adj (-er, -est) owning a lot of money or property, wealthy > richness n (pl -es)

richer adj ▷ rich

riches pl n wealth

richest adj ▷ rich

richly adv elaborately

richness n ▷ rich

richnesses n ▷ rich

rick¹ n (pl -s) stack of hay etc

rick² v, n (-s, -ing, -ed) sprain or wrench

ricked v ▷ rick²

ricketier adj ▷ rickety

ricketiest adj ▷ rickety

rickets n disease of children marked by softening of the bones, bow legs, etc, caused by vitamin D deficiency

rickety adj (-tier, -tiest) shaky or unstable

ricking v ▷ rick²

ricks n ▷ rick¹ ▶ v ▷ rick²

rickshaw n (pl -s) light two-wheeled man-drawn Asian vehicle

rickshaws n ▷ rickshaw

ricochet v (-s, -ing, -ed) (of a bullet) rebound from a solid surface ▶ n (pl -s) such a rebound

ricocheted v ▷ ricochet

ricocheting v ▷ ricochet

ricochets v, n ▷ ricochet

rid v (-s, -dding, rid) clear or relieve (of)

ridden v ▷ ride ▶ adj afflicted by or affected by the thing specified

ridding v ▷ rid

riddle¹ n (pl -s) question made puzzling to test one's ingenuity

riddle² v (-les, -ling, -led) pierce with many holes ▶ n (pl -s) coarse sieve for gravel etc

riddled v ▷ riddle²

riddles n ▷ riddle¹, ² ▶ v ▷ riddle²

riddling v ▷ riddle²

ride v (-des, -ding, rode, ridden) sit on and control or propel (a horse, bicycle, etc) ▶ n (pl -s) journey on a horse etc, or in a vehicle

rider n (pl -s) person who rides

riders n ▷ rider

rides v, n ▷ ride

ridge n (pl -s) long narrow hill > ridged adj

ridged adj ▷ ridge

ridges n ▷ ridge

ridicule n (pl **-s**) treatment of a person or thing as ridiculous ▶ v (**-les**, **-ling**, **-led**) laugh at, make fun of

ridiculed v ▷ ridicule

ridicules n, v ▷ ridicule

ridiculing v ▷ ridicule

riding[1] v ▷ ride

riding[2] n (pl **-s**) (in Canada) parliamentary constituency

ridings n ▷ riding[2]

rids v ▷ rid

riesling n (pl **-s**) type of white wine

rieslings n ▷ riesling

rife adj (**-r**, **-st**) widespread or common

rifer adj ▷ rife

rifest adj ▷ rife

riff n (pl **-s**) JAZZ ROCK short repeated melodic figure

riffle v (**-les**, **-ling**, **-led**) flick through (pages etc) quickly

riffled v ▷ riffle

riffles v ▷ riffle

riffling v ▷ riffle

riffraff n (pl **-s**) rabble, disreputable people

riffraffs n ▷ riffraff

riffs n ▷ riff

rifle[1] n (pl **-s**) firearm with a long barrel

rifle[2] v (**-les**, **-ling**, **-led**) search and rob

rifled v ▷ rifle[2]

rifles n ▷ rifle[1] ▶ v ▷ rifle[2]

rifling v ▷ rifle[2]

rift n (pl **-s**) break in friendly relations

rifts n ▷ rift

rig v (**-s**, **-gging**, **-gged**) arrange in a dishonest way ▶ n (pl **-s**) apparatus for drilling for oil and gas

rigged v ▷ rig

rigging n ship's spars and ropes ▶ v ▷ rig

right[1] adj (**-er**, **-est**) just ▶ adv properly ▶ n (pl **-s**) claim, title, etc allowed or due ▶ v (**-s**, **-ing**, **-ed**) bring or come back to a normal or correct state > **rightly** adv > **rightful** adj > **rightfully** adv

righted v ▷ right

righter adj ▷ right

rightest adj ▷ right

rightful adj ▷ right

rightfully adv ▷ right

righting v ▷ right

rightist n (pl **-s**) ▶ adj (person) on the political right

rightists n ▷ rightist

rightly adv ▷ right

rights n, v ▷ right

rigid adj (**-er**, **-est**) inflexible or strict > **rigidly** adv > **rigidity** n (pl **-s**)

rigider adj ▷ rigid

rigidest adj ▷ rigid

rigidities n ▷ rigid

rigidity n ▷ rigid

rigidly adv ▷ rigid

rigorous adj harsh, severe, or stern

rigour n (pl **-s**) harshness, severity, or strictness

rigours n ▷ rigour

rigs v, n ▷ rig

rile v (**-les**, **-ling**, **-led**) anger or annoy

riled v ▷ rile

riles v ▷ rile

riling v ▷ rile

rill n (pl **-s**) small stream

rills n ▷ rill

rim n (pl **-s**) edge or border > **rimmed** adj

rime n (pl **-s**) lit hoarfrost

rimes n ▷ rime

rimmed v ▷ rim

rims n ▷ rim

rimu n (pl **-s**) NZ New Zealand tree whose wood is used for building and furniture

rimus n ▷ rimu

rind n (pl **-s**) tough outer coating of fruits, cheese, or bacon

rinds n ▷ rind

ring[1] v (**-s**, **-ing**, **rang**, **rung**) give out a clear resonant sound, as a bell ▶ n (pl **-s**) ringing

ring[2] n (pl **-s**) circle of gold etc, esp. for a finger ▶ v (**-s**, **-ing**, **-ed**) put a ring round

ringed v ▷ ring[1, 2]

ringer n (pl -s) BRIT, AUST & NZ slang person or thing apparently identical to another

ringers n ▷ **ringer**

ringing v ▷ **ring**[1, 2]

ringlet n (pl -s) curly lock of hair

ringlets n ▷ **ringlet**

rings n, v ▷ **ring**[1, 2]

ringside n (pl -s) row of seats nearest a boxing or circus ring

ringsides n ▷ **ringside**

ringtail n (pl -s) AUST possum with a curling tail used to grip branches while climbing

ringtails n ▷ **ringtail**

ringworm n (pl -s) fungal skin disease in circular patches

ringworms n ▷ **ringworm**

rink n (pl -s) sheet of ice for skating or curling

rinks n ▷ **rink**

rinse v (-ses, -sing, -sed) remove soap from (washed clothes, hair, etc) by applying clean water ▶ n (pl -s) rinsing

rinsed v ▷ **rinse**

rinses v, n ▷ **rinse**

rinsing v, n ▷ **rinse**

riot n (pl -s) disorderly unruly disturbance ▶ v (-s, -ing, -ed) take part in a riot

rioted v ▷ **riot**

rioting v ▷ **riot**

riotous adj unrestrained

riots n, v ▷ **riot**

rip v (-s, -pping, -pped) tear violently informal ▶ n (pl -s) split or tear

riparian adj of or on the banks of a river

ripcord n (pl -s) cord pulled to open a parachute

ripcords n ▷ **ripcord**

ripe adj (-r, -st) ready to be reaped, eaten, etc

ripen v (-s, -ing, -ed) grow ripe

ripened v ▷ **ripen**

ripening v ▷ **ripen**

ripens v ▷ **ripen**

riper adj ▷ **ripe**

ripest adj ▷ **ripe**

riposte n (pl -s) verbal retort ▶ v (-tes, -ting, -ted) make a riposte

riposted v ▷ **riposte**

ripostes n, v ▷ **riposte**

riposting v ▷ **riposte**

ripped v ▷ **rip**

ripping v ▷ **rip**

ripple n (pl -s) slight wave or ruffling of a surface ▶ v (-les, -ling, -led) flow or form into little waves (on)

rippled v ▷ **ripple**

ripples n, v ▷ **ripple**

rippling v ▷ **ripple**

rips v, n ▷ **rip**

rise v (-ses, -sing, rose, risen) get up from a lying, sitting, or kneeling position ▶ n (pl -s) rising

risen v ▷ **rise**

riser n (pl -s) person who rises, esp. from bed

risers n ▷ **riser**

rises v, n ▷ **rise**

risible adj causing laughter, ridiculous

rising n (pl -s) revolt ▶ adj increasing in rank or maturity ▶ v ▷ **rise**

risings n ▷ **rising**

risk n (pl -s) chance of disaster or loss ▶ v (-s, -ing, -ed) act in spite of the possibility of (injury or loss)

risked v ▷ **risk**

riskier adj ▷ **risky**

riskiest adj ▷ **risky**

risking v ▷ **risk**

risks n, v ▷ **risk**

risky adj (-kier, -kiest) full of risk, dangerous

risotto n (pl -s) dish of rice cooked in stock with vegetables, meat, etc

risottos n ▷ **risotto**

risqué adj bordering on indecency

rissole n (pl -s) cake of minced meat, coated with breadcrumbs and fried

rissoles n ▷ **rissole**

rite n (pl -s) formal practice or custom, esp. religious

rites n ▷ **rite**

ritual n (pl -s) prescribed order of rites ▶ adj concerning rites > **ritually** adv

ritually adv ▷ ritual

rituals n ▷ ritual

ritzier adj ▷ ritzy

ritziest adj ▷ ritzy

ritzy adj (-zier, -ziest) slang luxurious or elegant

rival n (pl -s) person or thing that competes with or equals another for favour, success, etc ▸ adj in the position of a rival ▸ v (-s, -lling, -lled) (try to) equal

rivalled v ▷ rival

rivalling v ▷ rival

rivalries n ▷ rivalry

rivalry n (pl -s) keen competition

rivals v, n ▷ rival

riven adj split apart

river n (pl -s) large natural stream of water

rivers n ▷ river

rivet n (pl -s) bolt for fastening metal plates, the end being put through holes and then beaten flat ▸ v (-s, -ing, -ed) fasten with rivets

riveted v ▷ rivet

riveting adj very interesting and exciting ▸ v ▷ rivet

rivets n, v ▷ rivet

rivulet n (pl -s) small stream

rivulets n ▷ rivulet

> **riz** v. Riz is the past tense of **rise** in some US dialects. This unusual word can be very useful if you get a Z in the later stages of the game, as you will probably be able to find either I or R on the board already. Riz scores 12 points.

roach n (pl -es) Eurasian freshwater fish

roaches n ▷ roach

road n (pl -s) way prepared for passengers, vehicles, etc

roadie n (pl -s) BRIT, AUST & NZ informal person who transports and sets up equipment for a band

roadies n ▷ roadie

roads n ▷ road

roadside n (pl -s) ▸ adj (area) beside a road

roadsides n ▷ roadside

roadway n (pl -s) the part of a road used by vehicles

roadways n ▷ roadway

roam v (-s, -ing, -ed) wander about

roamed v ▷ roam

roaming v ▷ roam

roams v ▷ roam

roan adj (of a horse) having a brown or black coat sprinkled with white hairs ▸ n (pl -s) roan horse

roans n ▷ roan

roar v (-s, -ing, -ed) make or utter a loud deep hoarse sound like that of a lion ▸ n (pl -s) such a sound

roared v ▷ roar

roaring v ▷ roar

roars v, n ▷ roar

roast v (-s, -ing, -ed) cook by dry heat, as in an oven ▸ n (pl -s) roasted joint of meat ▸ adj roasted

roasted v ▷ roast

roasting informal adj extremely hot ▸ n (pl -s) severe criticism or scolding ▸ v ▷ roast

roastings n ▷ roasting

roasts v, n ▷ roast

rob v (-s, -bbing, -bbed) steal from > **robber** n (pl -s) > **robbery** n (pl -ies)

robbed v ▷ rob

robber n ▷ rob

robberies n ▷ rob

robbers n ▷ rob

robbery n ▷ rob

robbing v ▷ rob

robe n (pl -s) long loose outer garment ▸ v (-bes, -bing, -bed) put a robe on

robed v ▷ robe

robes v, n ▷ robe

robin n (pl -s) small brown bird with a red breast

robing v ▷ robe

robins n ▷ robin

robot n (pl -s) automated machine, esp. one performing functions in a human manner > **robotic** adj

robotic adj ▷ robot

robotics n science of designing and using robots

robots n ▷ robot

robs v ▷ rob

robust adj (-er, -est) very strong and healthy > **robustly** adv > **robustness** n (pl -s)

robuster adj ▷ robust

robustest adj ▷ robust

robustly adv ▷ robust

robustness n ▷ robust

robustnesses n ▷ robust

roc n (pl -s) monstrous bird of Arabian mythology

rock[1] n (pl -s) hard mineral substance that makes up part of the earth's crust, stone

rock[2] v (-s, -ing, -ed) (cause to) sway to and fro ▶ n style of pop music with a heavy beat

rocked v ▷ rock[2]

rocker n (pl -s) rocking chair

rockeries n ▷ rockery

rockers n ▷ rocker

rockery n (pl -ies) mound of stones in a garden for rock plants

rocket n (pl -s) self-propelling device powered by the burning of explosive contents (used as a firework, weapon, etc) ▶ v (-s, -ing, -ed) move fast, esp. upwards, like a rocket

rocketed v ▷ rocket

rocketing v ▷ rocket

rockets n, v ▷ rocket

rockier adj ▷ rocky[1] rocky[2]

rockiest adj ▷ rocky[1] rocky[2]

rocking v ▷ rock[2]

rocks n ▷ rock[1] ▶ v ▷ rock[2]

rocky[1] adj (-kier, -kiest) having many rocks

rocky[2] adj (-kier, -kiest) shaky or unstable

rococo adj (of furniture, architecture, etc) having much elaborate decoration in an early 18th-century style

rocs n ▷ roc

rod n (pl -s) slender straight bar, stick

rode v ▷ ride

rodent n (pl -s) animal with teeth specialized for gnawing, such as a rat, mouse, or squirrel

rodents n ▷ rodent

rodeo n (pl -s) display of skill by cowboys, such as bareback riding

rodeos n ▷ rodeo

rods n ▷ rod

roe[1] n (pl -s) mass of eggs in a fish, sometimes eaten as food

roe[2] n (pl -s) small species of deer

roentgen n (pl -s) unit measuring a radiation dose

roentgens n ▷ roentgen

roes n ▷ roe[1], roe[2]

rogue n (pl -s) dishonest or unprincipled person ▶ adj (of a wild beast) having a savage temper and living apart from the herd > **roguish** adj

rogues n ▷ rogue

roguish adj ▷ rogue

roister v (-s, -ing, -ed) make merry noisily or boisterously

roistered v ▷ roister

roistering v ▷ roister

roisters v ▷ roister

> **rok** n (roks). Rok is an alternative spelling of **roc**. This uncommon word can be helpful if you have a K without the tiles needed for a longer word. Rok scores 7 points.

role n (pl -s) task or function

roles n ▷ role

roll v (-s, -ing, -ed) move by turning over and over ▶ n (pl -s) act of rolling over or from side to side

rolled v ▷ roll

roller n (pl -s) rotating cylinder used for smoothing or supporting a thing to be moved, spreading paint, etc

rollers n ▷ roller

rolling v ▷ roll

rolls v, n ▷ roll

roman n roman type or print

romance n (pl -s) love affair

romances n ▷ romance

romantic adj of or dealing with love

▶ n (pl -s) romantic person or artist > **romantically** adv > **romanticism** n (pl -s)

romantically adv ▷ **romantic**

romanticism n ▷ **romantic**

romanticisms n ▷ **romantic**

romantics n ▷ **romantic**

romp v (-s, -ing, -ed) play wildly and joyfully ▶ n (pl -s) boisterous activity

romped v ▷ **romp**

rompers pl n child's overalls

romping v ▷ **romp**

romps v, n ▷ **romp**

rondo n (pl -s) piece of music with a leading theme continually returned to

rondos n ▷ **rondo**

roo n (pl -s) AUST informal kangaroo

rood n (pl -s) CHRISTIANITY the Cross

roods n ▷ **rood**

roof n (pl -s) outside upper covering of a building, car, etc ▶ v put a roof on

roofs n ▷ **roofs**

rooibos n (pl -es) S AFR tea prepared from the dried leaves of an African plant

rooiboses n ▷ **rooibos**

rook[1] n (pl -s) Eurasian bird of the crow family

rook[2] n (pl -s) chess piece shaped like a castle

rookeries n ▷ **rookery**

rookery n (pl -ies) colony of rooks, penguins, or seals

rookie n (pl -s) informal new recruit

rookies n ▷ **rookie**

rooks n ▷ **rook**

room n (pl -s) enclosed area in a building ▶ pl lodgings

roomier adj ▷ **roomy**

roomiest adj ▷ **roomy**

rooms n ▷ **room**

roomy adj (-ier, -iest) spacious

roos n ▷ **roo**

roost n (pl -s) perch for fowls ▶ v (-s, -ing, -ed) perch

roosted v ▷ **roost**

rooster n (pl -s) domestic cock

roosters n ▷ **rooster**

roosting v ▷ **roost**

roosts v, n ▷ **roost**

root[1] n (pl -s) part of a plant that grows down into the earth obtaining nourishment ▶ pl person's sense of belonging ▶ v (-s, -ing, -ed) establish a root and start to grow

root[2] v (-s, -ing, -ed) dig or burrow

rooted v ▷ **root**[1, 2]

rooting v ▷ **root**[1, 2]

rootless adj having no sense of belonging

roots n ▷ **root**[1] ▶ v ▷ **root**[1, 2]

rope n (pl -s) thick cord

ropes n ▷ **rope**

ropey, ropy adj (-pier, -piest) BRIT informal inferior or inadequate

ropier adj ▷ **ropey**

ropiest adj ▷ **ropey**

ropy adj ▷ **ropey**

rorqual n (pl -s) toothless whale with a dorsal fin

rorquals n ▷ **rorqual**

rort AUST informal n (pl -s) dishonest scheme ▶ v (-s, -ing, -ed) take unfair advantage of something

rorted v ▷ **rort**

rorting v ▷ **rort**

rorts n, v ▷ **rort**

rosaries n ▷ **rosary**

rosary n (pl -ies) series of prayers

rose[1] n (pl -s) shrub or climbing plant with prickly stems and fragrant flowers ▶ adj pink

rose[2] v ▷ **rise**

rosé n (pl -s) pink wine

roseate adj rose-coloured

rosehip n (pl -s) berry-like fruit of a rose plant

rosehips n ▷ **rosehip**

rosella n (pl -s) type of Australian parrot

rosellas n ▷ **rosella**

rosemaries n ▷ **rosemary**

rosemary n (pl -ies) fragrant flowering shrub

roses n ▷ **rose**[1]

rosés n ▷ **rosé**

rosette n (pl -s) rose-shaped ornament, esp. a circular bunch of ribbons

rosettes n ▷ rosette

rosewood n (pl -s) fragrant wood used to make furniture

rosewoods n ▷ rosewood

rosier adj ▷ rosy

rosiest adj ▷ rosy

rosin n (pl -s) resin used for treating the bows of violins etc

rosins n ▷ rosin

roster n (pl -s) list of people and their turns of duty

rosters n ▷ roster

rostra n ▷ rostrum

rostrum n (pl -trums, -tra) platform or stage

rostrums n ▷ rostrum

rosy adj (-sier, -siest) pink-coloured

rot v (-s, -tting, -tted) decompose or decay ▶ n (pl -s) decay informal

rota n (pl -s) list of people who take it in turn to do a particular task

rotary adj revolving

rotas n ▷ rota

rotate v (-tes, -ting, -ted) (cause to) move round a centre or on a pivot ▷ rotation n (pl -s)

rotated v ▷ rotate

rotates v ▷ rotate

rotating v ▷ rotate

rotation n ▷ rotate

rotations n ▷ rotate

rote n (pl -s) mechanical repetition

rotes n ▷ rote

rotor n (pl -s) revolving portion of a dynamo, motor, or turbine

rotors n ▷ rotor

rots v, n ▷ rot

rotted v ▷ rot

rotten adj (-er, -est) decaying informal

rottener adj ▷ rotten

rottenest adj ▷ rotten

rotter n (pl -s) CHIEFLY BRIT slang despicable person

rotters n ▷ rotter

rotting v ▷ rot

rotund adj round and plump ▷ rotundity n (pl -ies)

rotunda n (pl -s) circular building or room, esp. with a dome

rotundas n ▷ rotunda

rotundities n ▷ rotund

rotundity n ▷ rotund

rouble n (pl -s) monetary unit of Russia, Belarus, and Tajikistan

roubles n ▷ rouble

roué n (pl -s) man given to immoral living

roués n ▷ roué

rouge n (pl -s) red cosmetic used to colour the cheeks

rouges n ▷ rouge

rough adj (-er, -est) uneven or irregular ▶ v (-s, -ing, -ed) make rough ▶ n (pl -s) rough state or area ▷ **roughen** (v, -ing, -ed) ▷ **roughly** adv ▷ **roughness** n (pl -s)

roughage n (pl -s) indigestible constituents of food which aid digestion

roughages n ▷ roughage

roughed v ▷ rough

roughen v ▷ rough

roughened v ▷ rough

roughening v ▷ rough

roughens v ▷ rough

rougher adj ▷ rough

roughest adj ▷ rough

roughing v ▷ rough

roughly adv ▷ rough

roughness n ▷ rough

roughnesses n ▷ rough

roughs v, n ▷ rough

roulette n (pl -s) gambling game played with a revolving wheel and a ball

roulettes n ▷ roulette

round adj (-er, -est) spherical, cylindrical, circular, or curved ▶ adv, prep indicating an encircling movement, presence on all sides, etc ▶ v (-s, -ing, -ed) move round ▶ n (pl -s) customary course, as of a milkman

rounded v ▷ round

roundel n (pl -s) small disc

roundels n ▷ roundel

rounder adj ▷ round

rounders n bat-and-ball team game

roundest adj ▷ round

rounding v ▷ round

roundly adv thoroughly

rounds v, n ▷ round

rouse¹ v (-ses, -sing, -sed) wake up

rouse² v (-ses, -sing, -sed) (foll. by **on**) AUST scold or rebuke

roused v ▷ rouse¹, ²

rouses v ▷ rouse¹, ²

rousing v ▷ rouse¹, ²

rout n (pl -s) overwhelming defeat ▶ v (-s, -ing, -ed) defeat and put to flight

route n (pl -s) roads taken to reach a destination

routed v ▷ rout

routes n ▷ route

routine n (pl -s) usual or regular method of procedure ▶ adj ordinary or regular

routines n ▷ routine

routing v ▷ rout

routs n, v ▷ rout

roux n (pl roux) fat and flour cooked together as a basis for sauces

rove v (-ves, -ving, -ved) wander

roved v ▷ rove

rover n (pl -s) wanderer, traveller

rovers n ▷ rover

roves v ▷ rove

roving v ▷ rove

row¹ n (pl -s) straight line of people or things

row² v (-s, -ing, -ed) propel (a boat) by oars ▶ n (-s) spell of rowing

row³ informal n (-s) dispute ▶ v (-s, -ing, -ed) quarrel noisily

rowan n (pl -s) tree producing bright red berries, mountain ash

rowans n ▷ rowan

rowdier adj ▷ rowdy

rowdies n ▷ rowdy

rowdiest adj ▷ rowdy

rowdy adj (-dier, -diest) disorderly, noisy, and rough ▶ n (pl -dies) person like this

rowed v ▷ row², ³

rowel n (pl -s) small spiked wheel on a spur

rowels n ▷ rowel

rowing v ▷ row², ³

rowlock n (pl -s) device on a boat that holds an oar in place

rowlocks n ▷ rowlock

rows n ▷ row¹, ², ³ ▶ v ▷ row¹, ²

royal adj (-er, -est) of, befitting, or supported by a king or queen ▶ n (pl -s) informal member of a royal family
> royally adv

royalist n (pl -s) supporter of monarchy

royalists n ▷ royalist

royaller adj ▷ royal

royallest adj ▷ royal

royally adv ▷ royal

royals n ▷ royal

royalties n ▷ royalty

royalty n (pl -ies) royal people

rub v (-s, -bbing, -bbed) apply pressure and friction to (something) with a circular or backwards-and-forwards movement ▶ n (-s) act of rubbing

rubato adv, n (pl -s) MUSIC (with) expressive flexibility of tempo

rubatos n ▷ rubato

rubbed v ▷ rub

rubber¹ n (pl -s) strong waterproof elastic material, orig. made from the dried sap of a tropical tree, now usu. synthetic ▶ adj made of or producing rubber > rubbery adj (-rier, -riest)

rubber² n (pl -s) match consisting of three games of bridge, whist, etc

rubberier adj ▷ rubber¹

rubberiest adj ▷ rubber¹

rubbers n ▷ rubber¹, ²

rubbery adj ▷ rubber¹

rubbing v ▷ rub

rubbish n (pl -es) waste matter
> rubbishy adj

rubbishes n ▷ rubbish

rubbishy adj ▷ rubbish

rubble n (pl -s) fragments of broken stone, brick, etc

rubbles n ▷ rubble

rubella n (pl -s) German measles

rubellas ▷ rubella

rubicund adj ruddy

rubidium n (pl -s) CHEM soft highly reactive radioactive element

rubidiums ▷ rubidium

rubies n ▷ ruby

rubric n (pl -s) heading or explanation inserted in a text

rubrics n ▷ rubric

rubs v, n ▷ rub

ruby n (pl -ies) red precious gemstone ▷ adj deep red

ruck[1] n (pl -s) rough crowd of common people

ruck[2] n, v (-s, -ing, -ed) wrinkle or crease

rucked v ▷ ruck[2]

rucking v ▷ ruck[2]

rucks n ▷ ruck[1, 2] ▷ v ▷ ruck[2]

rucksack n (pl -s) BRIT, AUST & S AFR large pack carried on the back

rucksacks n ▷ rucksack

ructions pl n informal noisy uproar

rudder n (pl -s) vertical hinged piece at the stern of a boat or the rear of an aircraft, for steering

rudders n ▷ rudder

ruddier adj ▷ ruddy

ruddiest adj ▷ ruddy

ruddy adj (-dier, -diest) of a fresh healthy red colour

rude adj (-r, -st) impolite or insulting ▷ **rudely** adv ▷ **rudeness** n (pl -s)

rudely adv ▷ rude

rudeness n ▷ rude

rudenesses n ▷ rude

ruder adj ▷ rude

rudest adj ▷ rude

rue[1] v (rues, ruing, rued) feel regret for

rue[2] n (pl -s) plant with evergreen bitter leaves

rued v ▷ rue[1]

rueful adj regretful or sorry ▷ **ruefully** adv

ruefully adv ▷ rueful

rues v ▷ rue[1] ▷ rue[2]

ruff n (pl -s) starched and frilled collar

ruffian n (pl -s) violent lawless person

ruffians ▷ ruffian

ruffle v (-les, -ling, -led) disturb the calm of ▷ n (pl -s) frill or pleat

ruffled v ▷ ruffle

ruffles v, n ▷ ruffle

ruffling v ▷ ruffle

ruffs n ▷ ruff

rug n (pl -s) small carpet

rugbies n ▷ rugby

rugby n (pl -ies) form of football played with an oval ball which may be handled by the players

rugged adj rocky or steep

rugger n (pl -s) CHIEFLY BRIT informal rugby

ruggers n ▷ rugger

rugs n ▷ rug

ruin v (-s, -ing, -ed) destroy or spoil completely ▷ n (pl -s) destruction or decay

ruined v ▷ ruin

ruing v ▷ rue[1]

ruining v ▷ ruin

ruinous adj causing ruin ▷ **ruinously** adv

ruinously adv ▷ ruinous

ruins v, n ▷ ruin

rule n (pl -s) statement of what is allowed, for example in a game or procedure ▷ v (-les, -ling, -led) govern

ruled v ▷ rule

ruler n (pl -s) person who governs

rulers n ▷ ruler

rules n, v ▷ rule

ruling n (pl -s) formal decision ▷ v ▷ rule

rulings n ▷ ruling

rum n (pl -s) alcoholic drink distilled from sugar cane

rumba n (pl -s) lively ballroom dance of Cuban origin

rumbas n ▷ rumba

rumble v (-les, -ling, -led) make a low continuous noise ▷ n (pl -s) deep resonant sound

rumbled v ▷ rumble

rumbles v, n ▷ rumble

rumbling v ▷ rumble
ruminant adj, n (pl -s) cud-chewing (animal, such as a cow, sheep, or deer)
ruminants n ▷ ruminant
ruminate v (-tes, -ting, -ted) chew the cud
ruminated v ▷ ruminate
ruminates v ▷ ruminate
ruminating v ▷ ruminate
rummage v (-ges, -ging, -ged) search untidily and at length ▶ n (pl -s) untidy search through a collection of things
rummaged v ▷ rummage
rummages v, n ▷ rummage
rummaging v ▷ rummage
rummies n ▷ rummy
rummy n (pl -ies) card game in which players try to collect sets or sequences
rumour n (pl -s) unproved statement
rumoured adj suggested by rumour
rumours n ▷ rumour
rump n (pl -s) buttocks
rumple v (-les, -ling, -led) make untidy, crumpled, or dishevelled
rumpled v ▷ rumple
rumples v ▷ rumple
rumpling v ▷ rumple
rumps n ▷ rump
rumpus n (pl -es) noisy commotion
rumpuses n ▷ rumpus
rums n ▷ rum
run v (runs, running, ran, run) move with a more rapid gait than walking ▶ n (pl -s) act or spell of running
rune n (pl -s) any character of the earliest Germanic alphabet > **runic** adj
runes n ▷ rune
rung[1] n (pl -s) crossbar on a ladder
rung[2] v ▷ ring[1]
rungs n ▷ rung[1]
runic adj ▷ rune
runnel n (pl -s) small brook
runnels n ▷ runnel
runner n (pl -s) competitor in a race
runners n ▷ runner
runnier adj ▷ runny
runniest adj ▷ runny
running adj continuous ▶ n (pl -s) act

of moving or flowing quickly ▶ v ▷ run
runnings n ▷ running
runny adj (-nier, -niest) tending to flow
runs v, n ▷ run
runt n (pl -s) smallest animal in a litter
runts n ▷ runt
runway n (pl -s) hard level roadway where aircraft take off and land
runways n ▷ runway
rupee n (pl -s) monetary unit of India and Pakistan
rupees n ▷ rupee
rupture n (pl -s) breaking, breach ▶ v (-res, -ring, -red) break, burst, or sever
ruptured v ▷ rupture
ruptures n, v ▷ rupture
rupturing v ▷ rupture
rural adj in or of the countryside
ruse n (pl -s) stratagem or trick
ruses n ▷ ruse
rush[1] v (-es, -ing, -ed) move or do very quickly ▶ n (pl -es) sudden quick or violent movement ▶ pl first unedited prints of a scene for a film ▶ adj done with speed, hasty
rush[2] n (pl -es) marsh plant with a slender pithy stem
rushed v ▷ rush[1]
rushes v, n ▷ rush[1, 2]
rushier adj ▷ rushy
rushiest adj ▷ rushy
rushing v ▷ rush[1]
rushy adj (-shier, -shiest) full of rushes
rusk n (pl -s) hard brown crisp biscuit, used esp. for feeding babies
rusks n ▷ rusk
russet adj reddish-brown ▶ n (pl -s) apple with rough reddish-brown skin
russets n ▷ russet
rust n (pl -s) reddish-brown coating formed on iron etc that has been exposed to moisture ▶ adj reddish-brown ▶ v (-s, -ing, -ed) become coated with rust
rusted v ▷ rust
rustic adj of or resembling country people ▶ n (pl -s) person from the

country
rustics n ▷ **rustic**
rustier adj ▷ **rusty**
rustiest adj ▷ **rusty**
rusting v ▷ **rust**
rustle¹ v, n (pl **-s**) (make) a low whispering sound
rustle² v (**-les**, **-ling**, **-led**) us steal (cattle)
rustled v ▷ **rustle**
rustler n (pl **-s**) us cattle thief
rustlers n ▷ **rustler**
rustles n, v ▷ **rustle**
rustling v ▷ **rustle**
rusts n, v ▷ **rust**
rusty adj (**-tier**, **-tiest**) coated with rust
rut¹ n (pl **-s**) furrow made by wheels

rut² n (pl **-s**) recurrent period of sexual excitability in male deer ▶ v (**-s**, **-tting**, **-tted**) be in a period of sexual excitability
ruthless adj pitiless, merciless > **ruthlessly** adv ▷ **ruthlessness** n (pl **-es**)
ruthlessly adv ▷ **ruthless**
ruthlessness n ▷ **ruthless**
ruthlessnesses n ▷ **ruthless**
ruts n ▷ **rut¹, ²** ▶ v ▷ **rut²**
rutted v ▷ **rut²**
rutting v ▷ **rut²**
rye n (pl **-s**) kind of grain used for fodder and bread
ryes n ▷ **rye**

Ss

S begins only four two-letter words, **sh** (5 points), **si**, **so** and **st** (2 each). These are easy to remember, and it's worth noting that two of them, **sh** and **st**, don't use any vowels. Interestingly, there are quite a few three-letter words beginning with S that don't contain vowels, some of which give good scores. These are **shh** (9), **shy** (9), **sky** (10), **sly** (6), **sny** (6), **spy** (8), **sty** (6), **swy** (9) and **syn** (6). S also forms a number of three-letter words with X. These are easy to remember as they use every vowel except U: **sax**, **sex**, **six** and **sox** (10 each). Apart from the two- and three-letter words, don't forget **squeeze** (25), which uses the two highest-scoring tiles in the game.

sabbath *n (pl -s)* day of worship and rest: Saturday for Jews, Sunday for Christians
  sabbaths *n ▷ sabbath*
sable *n (pl -s)* dark fur from a small weasel-like Arctic animal ▷ *adj* black
  sables *n ▷ sable*
sabot *n (pl -s)* wooden shoe traditionally worn by peasants in France
sabotage *n (pl -s)* intentional damage done to machinery, systems, etc ▷ *v (-ges, -ging, -ged)* damage intentionally
  sabotaged *v ▷ sabotage*
  sabotages *n, v ▷ sabotage*
  sabotaging *v ▷ sabotage*
saboteur *n (pl -s)* person who commits sabotage
  saboteurs *n ▷ saboteur*
  sabots *n ▷ sabot*
sabre *n (pl -s)* curved cavalry sword
  sabres *n ▷ sabre*
sac *n (pl -s)* pouchlike structure in an animal or plant
sachet *n (pl -s)* small envelope or bag containing a single portion
  sachets *n ▷ sachet*
sack¹ *n (pl -s)* large bag made of coarse material ▷ *v (-s, -ing, -ed)* informal dismiss
sack² *n (pl -s)* plundering of a captured town ▷ *v (-s, -ing, -ed)* plunder (a captured town)
  sacked *v ▷ sack¹, ²*
  sacking *v ▷ sack¹, ²*
  sacks *v, n ▷ sack¹, ²*
  sacra *n ▷ sacrum*
sacred *adj* holy
  sacristies *n ▷ sacristy*
sacristy *n (pl -ties)* room in a church where sacred objects are kept
sacrum *n (pl -cra)* wedge-shaped bone at the base of the spine
  sacs *n ▷ sac*
sad *adj (-dder, -ddest)* sorrowful, unhappy ▷ **sadly** *adv* ▷ **sadness** *n (pl -es)*
sadden *v (-s, -ing, -ed)* make sad
  saddened *v ▷ sadden*
  saddening *v ▷ sadden*
  saddens *v ▷ sadden*
  sadder *adj ▷ sad*
  saddest *adj ▷ sad*
saddle *n (pl -les)* rider's seat on a horse or bicycle ▷ *v (-les, -ling, -led)* put a saddle on (a horse)
  saddled *v ▷ saddle*
saddler *n (pl -s)* maker or seller of

saddles
saddlers n ▷ **saddler**
saddles n, v ▷ **saddle**
saddling v ▷ **saddle**
saddo n (pl **-s, -es**) BRIT informal socially inadequate or pathetic person
saddoes n ▷ **saddo**
saddos n ▷ **saddo**
sadism n (pl **-s**) gaining of (sexual) pleasure from inflicting pain ▷ **sadist** n (pl **-s**) ▷ **sadistic** adj ▷ **sadistically** adv
sadisms n ▷ **sadism**
sadist n ▷ **sadism**
sadistic adj ▷ **sadism**
sadistically adv ▷ **sadism**
sadists n ▷ **sadism**
sadly adv ▷ **sad**
sadness n ▷ **sad**
sadnesses n ▷ **sad**
safari n (pl **-s**) expedition to hunt or observe wild animals, esp. in Africa
safaris n ▷ **safari**
safe adj (**-r, -st**) secure, protected ▷ n (pl **-s**) strong lockable container ▷ **safely** adv
safely adv ▷ **safe**
safer adj ▷ **safe**
safes n ▷ **safe**
safest adj ▷ **safe**
safeties n ▷ **safety**
safety n (pl **-ties**) state of being safe
saffron n (pl **-s**) orange-coloured flavouring obtained from a crocus ▷ adj orange
saffrons n ▷ **saffron**
sag v (**-s, -gging, -gged**) sink in the middle ▷ n (pl **-s**) droop
saga n (pl **-s**) legend of Norse heroes
sagas n ▷ **saga**
sage[1] n (pl **-s**) very wise man ▷ adj (**-r, -st**) lit wise ▷ **sagely** adv
sage[2] n (pl **-s**) aromatic herb with grey-green leaves
sagely adv ▷ **sage**[1]
sager adj ▷ **sage**[1]
sages n ▷ **sage**[1, 2]
sagest adj ▷ **sage**[1]
sagged v ▷ **sag**
sagging v ▷ **sag**

sago n (pl **-s**) starchy cereal from the powdered pith of the sago palm tree
sagos n ▷ **sago**
sags v, n ▷ **sag**
said v ▷ **say**
sail n (pl **-s**) sheet of fabric stretched to catch the wind for propelling a sailing boat ▷ v (**-s, -ing, -ed**) travel by water
sailed v ▷ **sail**
sailing v ▷ **sail**
sailor n (pl **-s**) member of a ship's crew
sailors n ▷ **sailor**
sails n, v ▷ **sail**
saint n (pl **-s**) CHRISTIANITY person venerated after death as specially holy ▷ **saintly** adj ▷ **saintliness** n (pl **-es**)
saintliness n ▷ **saint**
saintlinesses n ▷ **saint**
saintly adj ▷ **saint**
saints n ▷ **saint**
sake[1] n (pl **-s**) benefit
sake[2], **saki** n (pl **-s**) Japanese alcoholic drink made from fermented rice
sakes n ▷ **sake**[1, 2]
saki n ▷ **sake**[2]
sakis n ▷ **sake**[2]
salaam n (pl **-s**) low bow of greeting among Muslims
salaams n ▷ **salaam**
salad n (pl **-s**) dish of raw vegetables, eaten as a meal or part of a meal
salads n ▷ **salad**
salami n (pl **-s**) highly spiced sausage
salamis n ▷ **salami**
salaried adj ▷ **salary**
salaries n ▷ **salary**
salary n (pl **-ries**) fixed regular payment, usu. monthly, to an employee ▷ **salaried** adj
sale n (pl **-s**) exchange of goods for money ▷ **saleable** adj fit or likely to be sold
saleable adj ▷ **sale**
sales n ▷ **sale**
salesman, saleswoman (pl **-men**) ▷ **salesperson** (pl **-people**) n person who sells goods
salesmen n ▷ **salesman**
salespeople n ▷ **salesman**

salesperson n ▷ **salesman**
saleswoman n ▷ **salesman**
saleswomen n ▷ **salesman**
salient adj prominent, noticeable ▶ n (pl -**s**) MIL projecting part of a front line
salients n ▷ **salient**
saline adj containing salt > **salinity** n (pl -**ties**)
salinities n ▷ **saline**
salinity n ▷ **saline**
saliva n (pl -**s**) liquid that forms in the mouth, spittle > **salivary** adj
salivary adj ▷ **saliva**
salivas n ▷ **saliva**
salivate v (-**tes**, -**ting**, -**ted**) produce saliva
salivated v ▷ **salivate**
salivates v ▷ **salivate**
salivating v ▷ **salivate**
sallee n (pl -**s**) AUST SE Australian eucalyptus with a pale grey bark
sallees n ▷ **sallee**
sallied v ▷ **sally**
sallies n, v ▷ **sally**
sallow adj (-**er**, -**est**) of an unhealthy pale or yellowish colour
sallower adj ▷ **sallow**
sallowest adj ▷ **sallow**
sally n (pl -**lies**) witty remark ▶ v (-**lies**, -**lying**, -**lied**) rush out
sallying v ▷ **sally**
salmon n (pl -**s**) large fish with orange-pink flesh valued as food ▶ adj orange-pink
salmons n ▷ **salmon**
salon n (pl -**s**) commercial premises of a hairdresser, beautician, etc
salons n ▷ **salon**
saloon n (pl -**s**) two-door or four-door car with body closed off from rear luggage area
saloons n ▷ **saloon**
salt n (pl -**s**) white crystalline substance used to season food ▶ v (-**s**, -**ing**, -**ed**) season or preserve with salt > **salty** adj (-**tier**, -**tiest**)
saltbush n (pl -**es**) shrub that grows in alkaline desert regions
saltbushes n ▷ **saltbush**

salted v ▷ **salt**
saltier adj ▷ **salt**
saltiest adj ▷ **salt**
salting v ▷ **salt**
saltire n (pl -**s**) HERALDRY diagonal cross on a shield
saltires n ▷ **saltire**
salts n, v ▷ **salt**
salty adj ▷ **salt**
saluki n (pl -**s**) tall hound with a silky coat
salukis n ▷ **saluki**
salutary adj producing a beneficial result
salute n (pl -**s**) motion of the arm as a formal military sign of respect ▶ v (-**tes**, -**ting**, -**ted**) greet with a salute
saluted v ▷ **salute**
salutes n, v ▷ **salute**
saluting v ▷ **salute**
salvage n (pl -**s**) saving of a ship or other property from destruction ▶ v (-**ges**, -**ging**, -**ged**) save from destruction or waste
salvaged v ▷ **salvage**
salvages n, v ▷ **salvage**
salvaging v ▷ **salvage**
salve n (pl -**s**) healing or soothing ointment ▶ v (-**ves**, -**ving**, -**ved**) soothe or appease
salved v ▷ **salve**
salver n (pl -**s**) (silver) tray on which something is presented
salvers n ▷ **salver**
salves n, v ▷ **salve**
salvia n (pl -**s**) plant with blue or red flowers
salvias n ▷ **salvia**
salving v ▷ **salve**
salvo n (pl -**s**, -**es**) simultaneous discharge of guns etc
salvoes n ▷ **salvo**
salvos n ▷ **salvo**
samba n (pl -**s**) lively Brazilian dance
sambas n ▷ **samba**
same adj identical, not different, unchanged > **sameness** n (pl -**es**)
sameness n ▷ **same**
samenesses n ▷ **same**

samovar n (pl -s) Russian tea urn
samovars n ▷ samovar
sampan n (pl -s) small boat with oars
used in China
sampans n ▷ sampan
samphire n (pl -s) plant found on rocks
by the seashore
samphires n ▷ samphire
sample n (pl -s) part taken as
representative of a whole ▶ v (-les,
-ling, -led) take and test a sample of
> **sampling** n (pl -s)
sampled v ▷ sample
sampler n (pl -s) piece of embroidery
showing the embroiderer's skill
samplers n ▷ sampler
samples v, n ▷ sample
sampling v, n ▷ sample
samplings n ▷ sample
samurai n (pl -rai) member of an
ancient Japanese warrior caste
sancta n ▷ sanctum
sanctified v ▷ sanctify
sanctifies v ▷ sanctify
sanctify v (-fies, -fying, -fied) make
holy
sanctifying v ▷ sanctify
sanction n (pl -s) permission,
authorization ▶ v (-s, -ing, -ed) allow,
authorize
sanctioned v ▷ sanction
sanctioning v ▷ sanction
sanctions n, v ▷ sanction
sanctities n ▷ sanctity
sanctity n (pl -ties) sacredness,
inviolability
sanctum n (pl -tums, -ta) sacred place
sanctums n ▷ sanctum
sand n (pl -s) substance consisting of
small grains of rock, esp. on a beach or
in a desert ▶ v (-s, -ing, -ed) smooth
with sandpaper
sandal n (pl -s) light shoe consisting of
a sole attached by straps
sandals n ▷ sandal
sandbag n (pl -s) bag filled with sand,
used as protection against gunfire or
flood water
sandbags n ▷ sandbag

sanded v ▷ sand
sander n (pl -s) power tool for
smoothing surfaces
sanders n ▷ sander
sandier adj ▷ sandy
sandiest adj ▷ sandy
sanding v ▷ sand
sands n, v ▷ sand ▶ pl n stretches of
sand forming a beach or desert
sandwich n (pl -es) two slices of bread
with a layer of food between ▶ v (-es,
-ing, -ed) insert between two other
things
sandwiched v ▷ sandwich
sandwiches n, v ▷ sandwich
sandwiching v ▷ sandwich
sandy adj (-dier, -diest) covered
with sand
sane adj (-r, -st) of sound mind
> **sanity** n (pl -ties)
saner adj ▷ sane
sanest adj ▷ sane
sang v ▷ sing
sangoma n (pl -s) s AFR witch doctor
or herbalist
sangomas n ▷ sangoma
sanguine adj cheerful, optimistic
sanitary adj promoting health by
getting rid of dirt and germs
sanities n ▷ sane
sanity n ▷ sane
sank v ▷ sink
sap¹ n (pl -s) moisture that circulates
in plants
sap² v (saps, sapping, sapped)
undermine
sapient adj lit wise, shrewd
sapling n (pl -s) young tree
saplings n ▷ sapling
sapped v ▷ sap²
sapper n (pl -s) soldier in an
engineering unit
sappers n ▷ sapper
sapphire n (pl -s) blue precious stone
▶ adj deep blue
sapphires n ▷ sapphire
sapping v ▷ sap²
saps n ▷ sap¹ ▶ v ▷ sap²
sarcasm n (pl -s) (use of) bitter

or wounding ironic language
> sarcastic adj > sarcastically adv

sarcasms n ▷ sarcasm

sarcastic adj ▷ sarcasm

sarcastically adv ▷ sarcasm

sardine n (pl -s) small fish of the herring family, usu. preserved tightly packed in tins

sardines n ▷ sardine

sardonic adj mocking or scornful
> sardonically adv

sardonically adv ▷ sardonic

saree n ▷ sari

sarees n ▷ sari

sari, saree n (pl -s) long piece of cloth draped around the body and over one shoulder, worn by Hindu women

saris n ▷ sari

sarmie n (pl -s) S AFR slang sandwich

sarmies n ▷ sarmie

sarnie n (pl -s) slang sandwich

sarnies n ▷ sarnie

sarong n (pl -s) long piece of cloth tucked around the waist or under the armpits, worn esp. in Malaysia

sarongs n ▷ sarong

sash¹ n (pl -es) decorative strip of cloth worn round the waist or over one shoulder

sash² n (pl -es) wooden frame containing the panes of a window

sashes n ▷ sash¹, ²

sat v ▷ sit

satanic adj of Satan

satanism n (pl -s) worship of Satan

satanisms n ▷ satanism

satay, saté n (pl -s) Indonesian and Malaysian dish consisting of pieces of chicken, pork, etc. grilled on skewers and served with peanut sauce

satays n ▷ satay

satchel n (pl -s) bag, usu. with a shoulder strap, for carrying books

satchels n ▷ satchel

sate v (-tes, -ting, -ted) satisfy (a desire or appetite) fully

sated v ▷ sate

sates v ▷ sate

satiate v (-tes, -ting, -ted) provide

with more than enough, so as to disgust

satiated v ▷ satiate

satiates v ▷ satiate

satiating v ▷ satiate

satieties n ▷ satiety

satiety n (pl -ties) feeling of having had too much

satin n (pl -s) silky fabric with a glossy surface on one side

sating v ▷ sate

satins n ▷ satin

satiny adj of or like satin

satire n (pl -s) use of ridicule to expose vice or folly > satirical adj > satirist n (pl -s)

satires n ▷ satire

satirical adj ▷ satire

satirist n ▷ satire

satirists n ▷ satire

satirize v (-zes, -zing, -zed) ridicule by means of satire

satirized v ▷ satirize

satirizes v ▷ satirize

satirizing v ▷ satirize

satisfaction n ▷ satisfy

satisfactions n ▷ satisfy

satisfactory adj ▷ satisfy

satisfied v ▷ satisfy

satisfies v ▷ satisfy

satisfy v (-fies, -fying, -fied) please, content > satisfaction n (pl -s)
> satisfactory adj

satisfying v ▷ satisfy

satsuma n (pl -s) kind of small orange

satsumas n ▷ satsuma

saturate v (-tes, -ting, -ted) soak thoroughly > saturation n (pl -s)

saturated v ▷ saturate

saturates v ▷ saturate

saturating v ▷ saturate

saturation n ▷ saturate

saturations n ▷ saturate

satyr n (pl -s) woodland god, part man, part goat

satyrs n ▷ satyr

sauce n (pl -s) liquid added to food to enhance flavour

saucepan n (pl -s) cooking pot with a

long handle

saucepans n ▷ **saucepan**

saucer n (pl -**s**) small round dish put under a cup

saucers n ▷ **saucer**

sauces n ▷ **sauce**

saucier adj ▷ **saucy**

sauciest adj ▷ **saucy**

saucily adv ▷ **saucy**

saucy adj (-**cier**, -**ciest**) impudent > **saucily** adv

sauna n (pl -**s**) Finnish-style steam bath

saunas n ▷ **sauna**

saunter v (-**s**, -**ing**, -**ed**) walk in a leisurely manner, stroll ▶ n (pl -**s**) leisurely walk

sauntered v ▷ **saunter**

sauntering v ▷ **saunter**

saunters v, n ▷ **saunter**

sausage n (pl -**s**) minced meat in an edible tube-shaped skin

sausages n ▷ **sausage**

sauté v (-**tés**, -**téing** or -**téeing**, -**téed**) fry quickly in a little fat

sautéed v ▷ **sauté**

sautéeing v ▷ **sauté**

sautéing v ▷ **sauté**

sautés v ▷ **sauté**

savage adj (-**r**, -**st**) wild, untamed ▶ n (pl -**s**) uncivilized person ▶ v (-**ges**, -**ging**, -**ged**) attack ferociously > **savagely** adv > **savagery** n (pl -**ries**)

savaged v ▷ **savage**

savagely adv ▷ **savage**

savager adj ▷ **savage**

savageries n ▷ **savage**

savagery n ▷ **savage**

savages n, v ▷ **savage**

savagest adj ▷ **savage**

savaging v ▷ **savage**

savanna n ▷ **savannah**

savannah, savanna n (pl -**s**) extensive open grassy plain in Africa

savannahs n ▷ **savanna**

savannas n ▷ **savanna**

save v (-**ves**, -**ving**, -**ved**) rescue or preserve from harm, protect ▶ n (pl -**s**)

SPORT act of preventing a goal > **saver** n (pl -**s**)

saved v ▷ **save**

saveloy n (pl -**s**) BRIT, AUST & NZ spicy smoked sausage

saveloys n ▷ **saveloy**

saver n ▷ **save**

savers n ▷ **save**

saves v, n ▷ **save**

saving v ▷ **save** ▶ n (pl -**s**) economy

savings n money put by for future use

saviour n (pl -**s**) person who rescues another

saviours n ▷ **saviour**

savories n ▷ **savory**

savory n (pl -**ries**) aromatic herb used in cooking

savour v (-**s**, -**ing**, -**ed**) enjoy, relish (foll. by **of**) ▶ n (pl -**s**) characteristic taste or odour

savoured v ▷ **savour**

savourier adj ▷ **savoury**

savouries n ▷ **savoury**

savouriest adj ▷ **savoury**

savouring v ▷ **savour**

savours v, n ▷ **savour**

savoury adj (-**rier**, -**riest**) salty or spicy ▶ n (pl -**ries**) savoury dish served before or after a meal

savoy n (pl -**s**) variety of cabbage

savoys n ▷ **savoy**

savvied v ▷ **savvy**

savvies v, n ▷ **savvy**

savvy slang v (-**vies**, -**vying**, -**vied**) understand ▶ n (pl -**vies**) understanding, intelligence

savvying v ▷ **savvy**

saw[1] n (pl -**s**) cutting tool with a toothed metal blade ▶ v (-**s**, -**ing**, -**ed**, -**ed** or **sawn**) cut with a saw

saw[2] v ▷ **see**[1]

saw[3] n (pl -**s**) wise saying, proverb

sawdust n (pl -**s**) fine wood fragments made in sawing

sawdusts n ▷ **sawdust**

sawed v ▷ **saw**[1]

sawfish n (pl -**es**) fish with a long toothed snout

sawfishes n ▷ **sawfish**

sawing v ▷ **saw**[1]

sawmill n (pl -**s**) mill where timber is sawn into planks

sawmills n ▷ **sawmill**

sawn v ▷ **saw**[1]

saws n ▷ **saw**[1], 3 ▷ v ▷ **saw**[1]

sawyer n (pl -**s**) person who saws timber for a living

sawyers n ▷ **sawyer**

saxes n ▷ **sax**

say v (-**s**, -**ing**, said) speak or utter ▷ n (pl -**s**) right or chance to speak

saying n (pl -**s**) maxim, proverb ▷ v ▷ **say**

sayings n ▷ **saying**

says v, n ▷ **say**

> **saz** (**sazes**). A saz is a Turkish musical instrument. This is a very useful word, and one to remember for when you get a Z in the later stages of the game, with little space left on the board. Saz scores 12 points.

scab n (pl -**s**) crust formed over a wound

scabbard n (pl -**s**) sheath for a sword or dagger

scabbards n ▷ **scabbard**

scabbier adj ▷ **scabby**

scabbiest adj ▷ **scabby**

scabby adj (-**bier**, -**biest**) covered with scabs

scabies n itchy skin disease

scabrous adj rough and scaly

scabs n ▷ **scab**

scaffold n (pl -**s**) temporary platform for workmen

scaffolds n ▷ **scaffold**

scalar n (pl -**s**) ▷ adj (variable quantity) having magnitude but no direction

scalars n ▷ **scalar**

scald v (-**s**, -**ing**, -**ed**) burn with hot liquid or steam ▷ n (pl -**s**) injury by scalding

scalded v ▷ **scald**

scalding v ▷ **scald**

scalds v, n ▷ **scald**

scale[1] n (pl -**s**) one of the thin overlapping plates covering fishes and reptiles ▷ v (-**les**, -**ling**, -**led**) remove scales from > **scaly** adj (-**lier**, -**liest**)

scale[2] n (pl -**s**) (often pl) weighing instrument

scale[3] n (pl -**s**) graduated table or sequence of marks at regular intervals, used as a reference in making measurements ▷ v (-**les**, -**ling**, -**led**) climb

scaled v ▷ **scale**[1], 3

scalene adj (of a triangle) with three unequal sides

scales n ▷ **scale**[1], 2, 3 ▷ v ▷ **scale**[1], 3

scalier adj ▷ **scale**[1]

scaliest adj ▷ **scale**[1]

scaling v ▷ **scale**[1], 3

scallop n (pl -**s**) edible shellfish with two fan-shaped shells

scallops n ▷ **scallop**

scalp n (pl -**s**) skin and hair on top of the head ▷ v (-**s**, -**ing**, -**ed**) cut off the scalp of

scalped v ▷ **scalp**

scalpel n (pl -**s**) small surgical knife

scalpels n ▷ **scalpel**

scalping v ▷ **scalp**

scalps n, v ▷ **scalp**

scaly adj ▷ **scale**[1]

scam n (pl -**s**) informal dishonest scheme

scamp n (pl -**s**) mischievous child

scamper v (-**s**, -**ing**, -**ed**) run about hurriedly or in play ▷ n (pl -**s**) scampering

scampered v ▷ **scamper**

scampering v ▷ **scamper**

scampers v, n ▷ **scamper**

scampi pl n large prawns

scamps n ▷ **scamp**

scams n ▷ **scam**

scan v (-**s**, -**nning**, -**nned**) scrutinize carefully ▷ n (pl -**s**) scanning

scandal n (pl -**s**) disgraceful action or event > **scandalous** adj

scandalous adj ▷ **scandal**

scandals n ▷ **scandal**

scandium n (pl -**s**) CHEM rare silvery-white metallic element

scandiums n ▷ **scandium**

scanned v ▷ **scan**

scanner n (pl -**s**) electronic device used

for scanning

scanners n ▷ **scanner**

scanning v ▷ **scan**

scans v, n ▷ **scan**

scansion n (pl -s) metrical scanning of verse

scansions n ▷ **scansion**

scant adj (-er, -est) barely sufficient, meagre

scanter adj ▷ **scant**

scantest adj ▷ **scant**

scantier adj ▷ **scanty**

scantiest adj ▷ **scanty**

scantily n ▷ **scanty**

scanty adj (-tier, -tiest) barely sufficient or not sufficient > **scantily** adv

scapula n (pl -lae, -las) shoulder blade > **scapular** adj

scapulae n ▷ **scapula**

scapular adj ▷ **scapula**

scapulas n ▷ **scapula**

scar n (pl -s) mark left by a healed wound ▶ v (-s, -rring, -rred) mark or become marked with a scar

scarab n (pl -s) sacred beetle of ancient Egypt

scarabs n ▷ **scarab**

scarce adj (-r, -st) insufficient to meet demand > **scarcity** n (pl -ties)

scarcely adv hardly at all

scarcer adj ▷ **scarce**

scarcest adj ▷ **scarce**

scarcities n ▷ **scarce**

scarcity n ▷ **scarce**

scare v (-res, -ring, -red) frighten or be frightened ▶ n (pl -s) fright, sudden panic

scared v ▷ **scare**

scares v, n ▷ **scare**

scarf[1] n (pl scarves, -s) piece of material worn round the neck, head, or shoulders

scarf[2] n (pl -s) joint between two pieces of timber made by notching the ends and fastening them together ▶ v (-s, -ing, -ed) join in this way

scarfed v ▷ **scarf**[2]

scarfing v ▷ **scarf**[2]

scarfs n ▷ **scarf**[1, 2] ▶ v ▷ **scarf**[2]

scarier adj ▷ **scary**

scariest adj ▷ **scary**

scarification n ▷ **scarify**

scarifications n ▷ **scarify**

scarified v ▷ **scarify**

scarifies v ▷ **scarify**

scarify v (-fies, -fying, -fied) scratch or cut slightly all over > **scarification** n (pl -s)

scarifying v ▷ **scarify**

scaring v ▷ **scare**

scarlet adj, n (pl -s) brilliant red

scarlets n ▷ **scarlet**

scarp n (pl -s) steep slope

scarper v (-s, -ing, -ed) BRIT slang run away

scarpered v ▷ **scarper**

scarpering v ▷ **scarper**

scarpers n ▷ **scarper**

scarps n ▷ **scarp**

scarred v ▷ **scar**

scarring v ▷ **scar**

scars n, v ▷ **scar**

scarves n ▷ **scarf**[1]

scary adj (-rier, -riest) informal frightening

scat[1] v (-s, -tting, -tted) informal go away

scat[2] n (pl -s) jazz singing using improvised vocal sounds instead of words

scathing adj harshly critical

scats n ▷ **scat**[2] ▶ v ▷ **scat**[1]

scatted v ▷ **scat**[1]

scatter v (-s, -ing, -ed) throw about in various directions

scattered v ▷ **scatter**

scattering v ▷ **scatter**

scatters v ▷ **scatter**

scattier adj ▷ **scatty**

scattiest adj ▷ **scatty**

scatting v ▷ **scat**[1]

scatty adj (-tier, -tiest) informal empty-headed

scavenge v (-ges, -ging, -ged) search for (anything usable) among discarded material

scavenged v ▷ **scavenge**

scavenges v ▷ **scavenge**
scavenging v ▷ **scavenge**
scenario n (pl **-rios**) summary of the plot of a play or film
scenarios n ▷ **scenario**
scene n (pl **-s**) place of action of a real or imaginary event
sceneries n ▷ **scenery**
scenery n (pl **-ries**) natural features of a landscape
scenes n ▷ **scene**
scenic adj picturesque
scent n (pl **-s**) pleasant smell ▶ v (**-s**, **-ing**, **-ed**) detect by smell
scented v ▷ **scent**
scenting v ▷ **scent**
scents n, v ▷ **scent**
sceptic n (pl **-s**) person who habitually doubts generally accepted beliefs > **sceptical** adj > **sceptically** adv > **scepticism** n (pl **-s**)
sceptical adj ▷ **sceptic**
sceptically adv ▷ **sceptic**
scepticism n ▷ **sceptic**
scepticisms n ▷ **sceptic**
sceptics n ▷ **sceptic**
sceptre n (pl **-s**) ornamental rod symbolizing royal power
sceptres n ▷ **sceptre**
schedule n (pl **-s**) plan of procedure for a project ▶ v (**-les**, **-ling**, **-led**) plan to occur at a certain time
scheduled v ▷ **schedule**
schedules n, v ▷ **schedule**
scheduling v ▷ **schedule**
schema n (pl **-mata**) overall plan or diagram
scheme n (pl **-s**) systematic plan ▶ v (**-mes**, **-ming**, **-med**) plan in an underhand manner > **scheming** adj, n (pl **-s**)
schemed v ▷ **scheme**
schemes n, v ▷ **scheme**
scheming v, adj n ▷ **scheme**
schemings n ▷ **scheme**
scherzi n ▷ **scherzo**
scherzo n (pl **-zos**, **-zi**) brisk lively piece of music
scherzos n ▷ **scherzo**

schism n (pl **-s**) (group resulting from) division in an organization > **schismatic** adj, n (pl **-s**)
schismatic adj ▷ **schism**
schismatics n ▷ **schism**
schisms n ▷ **schism**
schist n (pl **-s**) crystalline rock which splits into layers
schists n ▷ **schist**
schizoid adj abnormally introverted ▶ n (pl **-s**) schizoid person
schizoids n ▷ **schizoid**
schmaltz n (pl **-es**) excessive sentimentality > **schmaltzy** adj (**-zier**, **-ziest**)
schmaltzes n ▷ **schmaltz**
schmaltzier adj ▷ **schmaltz**
schmaltziest adj ▷ **schmaltz**
schmaltzy adj ▷ **schmaltz**
schnapps n (pl **-es**) strong alcoholic spirit
schnappses n ▷ **schnapps**
scholar n (pl **-s**) learned person
scholars n ▷ **scholar**
school¹ n (pl **-s**) place where children are taught or instruction is given in a subject ▶ v (**-s**, **-ing**, **-ed**) educate or train
school² n (pl **-s**) shoal of fish, whales, etc
schooled v ▷ **school¹**
schoolie n (pl **-s**) Aust schoolteacher or high-school student
schoolies n ▷ **schoolie**
schooling v ▷ **school¹**
schools n ▷ **school¹, ²** ▶ v ▷ **school¹**
schooner n (pl **-s**) sailing ship rigged fore-and-aft
schooners n ▷ **schooner**
sciatic adj of the hip
sciatica n (pl **-s**) severe pain in the large nerve in the back of the leg
sciaticas n ▷ **sciatica**
science n (pl **-s**) systematic study and knowledge of natural or physical phenomena
sciences n ▷ **science**
scimitar n (pl **-s**) curved oriental sword
scimitars n ▷ **scimitar**

scion n (pl -s) descendant or heir
 scions n ▷ scion

scissors pl n cutting instrument with two crossed pivoted blades

scoff¹ v (-s, -ing, -ed) express derision

scoff² v (-s, -ing, -ed) informal eat rapidly
 scoffed v ▷ scoff¹, ²
 scoffing v ▷ scoff¹, ²
 scoffs v ▷ scoff¹, ²

scold v (-s, -ing, -ed) find fault with, reprimand ▶ n (pl -s) person who scolds
 > **scolding** n (pl -s)
 scolded v ▷ scold
 scolding v, n ▷ scold
 scoldings n ▷ scold
 scolds v, n ▷ scold

sconce n (pl -s) bracket on a wall for holding candles or lights
 sconces n ▷ sconce

scone n (pl -s) small plain cake baked in an oven or on a griddle
 scones n ▷ scone

scoop n (pl -s) shovel-like tool for ladling or hollowing out ▶ v (-s, -ing, -ed) take up or hollow out with or as if with a scoop
 scooped v ▷ scoop
 scooping v ▷ scoop
 scoops n, v ▷ scoop

scoot v (-s, -ing, -ed) slang leave or move quickly
 scooted v ▷ scoot

scooter n (pl -s) child's vehicle propelled by pushing on the ground with one foot
 scooters n ▷ scooter
 scooting v ▷ scoot
 scoots v ▷ scoot

scope n (pl -s) opportunity for using abilities
 scopes n ▷ scope

scorch v (-es, -ing, -ed) burn on the surface ▶ n (pl -es) slight burn
 scorched v ▷ scorch

scorcher n (pl -s) informal very hot day
 scorchers n ▷ scorcher
 scorches v, n ▷ scorch
 scorching v ▷ scorch

score n (pl -s) points gained in a game or competition ▶ v (-res, -ring, -red) gain (points) in a game
 scored v ▷ score
 scores n, v ▷ score ▶ pl n lots
 scoring v ▷ score

scorn n (pl -s) open contempt ▶ v (-s, -ing, -ed) despise ▶ scornful adj
 > **scornfully** adv
 scorned v ▷ scorn
 scornful adj ▷ scorn
 scornfully adv ▷ scorn
 scorning v ▷ scorn
 scorns n, v ▷ scorn

scorpion n (pl -s) small lobster-shaped animal with a sting at the end of a jointed tail
 scorpions n ▷ scorpion

scotch v (-es, -ing, -ed) put an end to
 scotched v ▷ scotch
 scotches v ▷ scotch
 scotching v ▷ scotch

scour¹ v (-s, -ing, -ed) clean or polish by rubbing with something rough

scour² v (-s, -ing, -ed) search thoroughly and energetically
 scoured v ▷ scour¹, ²

scourer n (pl -s) small rough nylon pad used for cleaning pots and pans
 scourers n ▷ scourer

scourge n (pl -s) person or thing causing severe suffering ▶ v (-ges, -ging, -ged) cause severe suffering to
 scourged v ▷ scourge
 scourges n, v ▷ scourge
 scourging v ▷ scourge
 scouring v ▷ scour¹, ²
 scours v ▷ scour¹, ²

scout n (pl -s) person sent out to reconnoitre ▶ v (-s, -ing, -ed) act as a scout
 scouted v ▷ scout
 scouting v ▷ scout
 scouts n, v ▷ scout

scowl v (-s, -ing, -ed) ▶ n (pl -s) (have) an angry or sullen expression
 scowled v ▷ scowl
 scowling v ▷ scowl
 scowls v, n ▷ scowl

scrabble v (-les, -ling, -led) scrape at with the hands, feet, or claws

scrabbled v ▷ scrabble

scrabbles v ▷ scrabble

scrabbling v ▷ scrabble

scrag n (pl -s) thin end of a neck of mutton

scraggier adj ▷ scraggy

scraggiest adj ▷ scraggy

scraggy adj (-gier, -giest) thin, bony

scrags n ▷ scrag

scram v (-s, -mming, -mmed) informal go away quickly

scramble v (-les, -ling, -led) climb or crawl hastily or awkwardly ▶ n (pl -les) scrambling

scrambled v ▷ scramble

scrambles v, n ▷ scramble

scrambling v ▷ scramble

scrammed v ▷ scram

scramming v ▷ scram

scrams v ▷ scram

scrap[1] n (pl -s) small piece ▶ v (-s, -pping, -pped) discard as useless

scrap[2] n (pl -s) ▶ v (-s, -pping, -pped) informal fight or quarrel

scrape v (-pes, -ping, -ped) rub with something rough or sharp ▶ n (pl -s) act or sound of scraping > **scraper** n (pl -s)

scraped v ▷ scrape

scraper n ▷ scrape

scrapers n ▷ scrape

scrapes v, n ▷ scrape

scraping v ▷ scrape

scrapped v ▷ scrap[1, 2]

scrappier adj ▷ scrappy

scrappiest adj ▷ scrappy

scrapping v ▷ scrap[1, 2]

scrappy adj (-ppier, -ppiest) fragmentary, disjointed

scraps v, n ▷ scrap[1, 2] ▶ pl n leftover food

scratch v (-es, -ing, -ed) mark or cut with claws, nails, or anything rough or sharp ▶ n (pl -es) wound, mark, or sound made by scratching ▶ adj put together at short notice > **scratchy** adj (-chier, -chiest)

scratched v ▷ scratch

scratches v, n ▷ scratch

scratchier adj ▷ scratch

scratchiest adj ▷ scratch

scratching v ▷ scratch

scratchy adj ▷ scratch

scrawl v (-s, -ing, -ed) write carelessly or hastily ▶ n (pl -s) scribbled writing

scrawled v ▷ scrawl

scrawling v ▷ scrawl

scrawls v, n ▷ scrawl

scrawnier adj ▷ scrawny

scrawniest adj ▷ scrawny

scrawny adj (-nier, -niest) thin and bony

scream v (-s, -ing, -ed) utter a piercing cry, esp. of fear or pain ▶ n (pl -s) shrill piercing cry

screamed v ▷ scream

screaming v ▷ scream

screams v, n ▷ scream

scree n (pl -s) slope of loose shifting stones

screech v (-es, -ing, -ed) ▶ n (pl -es) (utter) a shrill cry

screeched v ▷ screech

screeches v, n ▷ screech

screeching v ▷ screech

screed n (pl -s) long tedious piece of writing

screeds n ▷ screed

screen n (pl -s) surface of a television set, VDU, etc, on which an image is formed ▶ v (-s, -ing, -ed) shelter or conceal with or as if with a screen

screened v ▷ screen

screening v ▷ screen

screens n, v ▷ screen

screes n ▷ scree

screw n (pl -s) metal pin with a spiral ridge along its length, twisted into materials to fasten them together ▶ v (-s, -ing, -ed) turn (a screw)

screwed v ▷ screw

screwier adj ▷ screwy

screwiest adj ▷ screwy

screwing v ▷ screw

screws n, v ▷ screw

screwy adj (-wier, -wiest) informal crazy or eccentric

scribble v (-les, -ling, -led) write hastily or illegibly ▶ n (pl -s) something scribbled
scribbled v ▷ scribble
scribbles v, n ▷ scribble
scribbling v ▷ scribble
scribe n (pl -s) person who copied manuscripts before the invention of printing
scribes n ▷ scribe
scrimp v (-s, -ing, -ed) be very economical
scrimped v ▷ scrimp
scrimping v ▷ scrimp
scrimps v ▷ scrimp
scrip n (pl -s) certificate representing a claim to stocks or shares
scrips n ▷ scrip
script n (pl -s) text of a film, play, or TV programme
scripts n ▷ script
scrofula n (pl -s) tuberculosis of the lymphatic glands > **scrofulous** adj
scrofulas n ▷ scrofula
scrofulous adj ▷ scrofula
scroggin n (pl -s) nz mixture of nuts and dried fruits
scroggins n ▷ scroggin
scroll n (pl -s) roll of parchment or paper ▶ v (-s, -ing, -ed) move (text) up or down on a VDU screen
scrolled v ▷ scroll
scrolling v ▷ scroll
scrolls n, v ▷ scroll
scrota n ▷ scrotum
scrotum n (pl -ta, -tums) pouch of skin containing the testicles
scrotums n ▷ scrotum
scrounge v (-ges, -ging, -ged) informal get by cadging or begging > **scrounger** n (pl -s)
scrounged v ▷ scrounge
scrounger n ▷ scrounge
scroungers n ▷ scrounge
scrounges v ▷ scrounge
scrounging v ▷ scrounge
scrub[1] v (-s, -bbing, -bbed) clean by rubbing, often with a hard brush and water ▶ n (pl -s) scrubbing

scrub[2] n (pl -s) stunted trees
scrubbed v ▷ scrub[1]
scrubbier adj ▷ scrubby
scrubbiest adj ▷ scrubby
scrubbing v ▷ scrub[1]
scrubby adj (-bbier, -bbiest) covered with scrub
scrubs v ▷ scrub[1] ▶ n ▷ scrub[1, 2]
scruff[1] n (pl -s) nape (of the neck)
scruff[2] n (pl -s) informal untidy person
scruffier adj ▷ scruffy
scruffiest adj ▷ scruffy
scruffs n ▷ scruff[1, 2]
scruffy adj (-fier, -fiest) unkempt or shabby
scrum, scrummage n (pl -s) RUGBY restarting of play in which opposing packs of forwards push against each other to gain possession of the ball
scrummage n ▷ scrum
scrummages n ▷ scrum
scrums n ▷ scrum
scrunch v (-es, -ing, -ed) crumple or crunch or be crumpled or crunched ▶ n (pl -es) act or sound of scrunching
scrunched v ▷ scrunch
scrunches v, n ▷ scrunch
scrunching v ▷ scrunch
scruple n (pl -s) doubt produced by one's conscience or morals ▶ v (-les, -ling, -led) have doubts on moral grounds
scrupled v ▷ scruple
scruples n, v ▷ scruple
scrupling v ▷ scruple
scrutinies n ▷ scrutiny
scrutiny n (pl -nies) close examination
scud v (-s, -dding, -dded) move along swiftly
scudded v ▷ scud
scudding v ▷ scud
scuds v ▷ scud
scuff v (-s, -ing, -ed) drag (the feet) while walking ▶ n (pl -s) mark caused by scuffing
scuffed v ▷ scuff
scuffing v ▷ scuff
scuffle v (-les, -ling, -led) fight in a disorderly manner ▶ n (pl -s) disorderly

struggle

scuffled v ▷ **scuffle**

scuffles v, n ▷ **scuffle**

scuffling v ▷ **scuffle**

scuffs v, n ▷ **scuff**

scull n (pl **-s**) small oar ▷ v (**-s, -ing, -ed**) row (a boat) using sculls

sculled v ▷ **scull**

sculleries n ▷ **scullery**

scullery n (pl **-ries**) small room where washing-up and other kitchen work is done

sculling v ▷ **scull**

sculls n, v ▷ **scull**

scum n (pl **-s**) impure or waste matter on the surface of a liquid > **scummy** adj (**-mier, -miest**)

scummier adj ▷ **scum**

scummiest adj ▷ **scum**

scummy adj ▷ **scum**

scums n ▷ **scum**

scungier adj ▷ **scungy**

scungiest adj ▷ **scungy**

scungy adj (**-gier, -giest**) AUST & NZ informal sordid or dirty

scupper v (**-s, -ing, -ed**) informal defeat or ruin

scuppered v ▷ **scupper**

scuppering v ▷ **scupper**

scuppers v ▷ **scupper**

scurf n (pl **-s**) flaky skin on the scalp

scurfs n ▷ **scurf**

scurried v ▷ **scurry**

scurries v, n ▷ **scurry**

scurry v (**-ries, -rying, -ried**) move hastily ▷ n (pl **-ries**) act or sound of scurrying

scurrying v ▷ **scurry**

scurvies v ▷ **scurvy**

scurvy n (pl **-vies**) disease caused by lack of vitamin C

scut n (pl **-s**) short tail of the hare, rabbit, or deer

scuts n ▷ **scut**

scuttle¹ n (pl **-s**) fireside container for coal

scuttle² v (**-les, -ling, -led**) run with short quick steps ▷ n (pl **-s**) hurried run

scuttle³ v (**-les, -ling, -led**) make a hole

in (a ship) to sink it

scuttled v ▷ **scuttle**², ³

scuttles n ▷ **scuttle**¹, ² v ▷ **scuttle**², 3

scuttling v ▷ **scuttle**², ³

scythe n (pl **-s**) long-handled tool with a curved blade for cutting grass ▷ v (**-thes, -thing, -thed**) cut with a scythe

scythed v ▷ **scythe**

scythes n, v ▷ **scythe**

scything v ▷ **scythe**

sea n (pl **-s**) mass of salt water covering three quarters of the earth's surface

seaboard n (pl **-s**) coast

seaboards n ▷ **seaboard**

seafood n (pl **-s**) edible saltwater fish or shellfish

seafoods n ▷ **seafood**

seagull n (pl **-s**) gull

seagulls n ▷ **seagull**

seal¹ n (pl **-s**) piece of wax, lead, etc with a special design impressed upon it, attached to a letter or document as a mark of authentication ▷ v (**-s, -ing, -ed**) close with or as if with a seal

seal² n (pl **-s**) amphibious mammal with flippers as limbs > **sealskin** n (pl **-s**)

sealant n (pl **-s**) any substance used for sealing

sealants n ▷ **sealant**

sealed v ▷ **seal**¹

sealing v ▷ **seal**¹

seals n ▷ **seal**¹, ² v ▷ **seal**¹

sealskin n ▷ **seal**²

sealskins n ▷ **seal**²

seam n (pl **-s**) line where two edges are joined, as by stitching ▷ v (**-s, -ing, -ed**) mark with furrows or wrinkles > **seamless** adj

seaman n (pl **-men**) sailor

seamed v ▷ **seam**

seamen n ▷ **seaman**

seamier adj ▷ **seamy**

seamiest adj ▷ **seamy**

seaming v ▷ **seam**

seamless adj ▷ **seam**

seams n, v ▷ **seam**

seamy adj (**-mier, -miest**) sordid

seance n (pl -s) meeting at which spiritualists attempt to communicate with the dead
seances n ▷ seance

seaplane n (pl -s) aircraft designed to take off from and land on water
seaplanes n ▷ seaplane

sear v (-s, -ing, -ed) scorch, burn the surface of

search v (-es, -ing, -ed) examine closely in order to find something ▶ n (pl -es) searching
searched v ▷ search
searches v, n ▷ search
seared v ▷ sear

searing adj (of pain) very sharp ▶ v ▷ sear
sears v ▷ sear
seas n ▷ sea

seasick adj suffering from nausea caused by the motion of a ship
> **seasickness** n (pl -es)
seasickness n ▷ seasick
seasicknesses n ▷ seasick

seaside n (pl -s) area, esp. a holiday resort, on the coast
seasides n ▷ seaside

season n (pl -s) one of four divisions of the year, each of which has characteristic weather conditions ▶ v (-s, -ing, -ed) flavour with salt, herbs, etc
seasonal adj depending on or varying with the seasons
seasoned adj experienced ▶ v ▷ season
seasons n, v ▷ season

seat n (pl -s) thing designed or used for sitting on ▶ v (-s, -ing, -ed) cause to sit
seated v ▷ seat
seating v ▷ seat
seats n, v ▷ seat

seaweed n (pl -s) plant growing in the sea
seaweeds n ▷ seaweed

secede v (-des, -ding, -ded) withdraw formally from a political alliance or federation > **secession** n (pl -s)
seceded v ▷ secede
secedes v ▷ secede

seceding v ▷ secede
secession n ▷ secede
secessions n ▷ secede

seclude v (-des, -ding, -ded) keep (a person) from contact with others
secluded adj private, sheltered ▶ v ▷ seclude > **seclusion** n (pl -s)
secludes v ▷ seclude
secluding v ▷ seclude
seclusion n ▷ secluded
seclusions n ▷ secluded

second[1] adj coming directly after the first ▶ n (pl -s) person or thing coming second ▶ v (-s, -ing, -ed) express formal support for (a motion proposed in a meeting) > **secondly** adv

second[2] n (pl -s) sixtieth part of a minute of an angle or time

second[3] v (-s, -ing, -ed) transfer (a person) temporarily to another job
> **secondment** n (pl -s)
seconded v ▷ second[1, 3]
seconding v ▷ second[1, 3]
secondly adv ▷ second[1]
secondment n ▷ second[3]
secondments n ▷ second[3]
seconds v ▷ second[1, 2] ▶ n ▷ second[1, 2] ▶ pl n inferior goods

secrecies n ▷ secret
secrecy n ▷ secret

secret adj kept from the knowledge of others ▶ n (pl -s) something kept secret
> **secretly** adv > **secrecy** n (pl -cies)

secrete[1] v (-tes, -ting, -ted) (of an organ, gland, etc) produce and release (a substance) > **secretion** n (pl -s)
> **secretory** adj

secrete[2] v (-tes, -ting, -ted) hide or conceal
secreted v ▷ secrete[1, 2]
secretes v ▷ secrete[1, 2]
secreting v ▷ secrete[1, 2]
secretion n ▷ secrete[1]
secretions n ▷ secrete[1]
secretly adv ▷ secret
secretory adj ▷ secrete[1]
secrets n ▷ secret

sect n (pl -s) subdivision of a religious or political group, esp. one with extreme beliefs

section n (pl -s) part cut off ▶ v (-s, -ing, -ed) cut or divide into sections > **sectional** adj

sectional adj ▷ **section**

sectioned v ▷ **section**

sectioning v ▷ **section**

sections n, v ▷ **section**

sector n (pl -s) part or subdivision

sectors n ▷ **sector**

sects n ▷ **sect**

secular adj worldly, as opposed to sacred

secure adj (-r, -st) free from danger ▶ v (-res, -ring, -red) obtain > **securely** adv

secured v ▷ **secure**

securely adv ▷ **secure**

securer adj ▷ **secure**

secures v ▷ **secure**

securest adj ▷ **secure**

securing v ▷ **secure**

securities n ▷ **security**

security n (pl -ties) precautions against theft, espionage, or other danger

sedan n (pl -s) US, AUST & NZ two-door or four-door car with the body closed off from the rear luggage area

sedans n ▷ **sedan**

sedate[1] adj (-r, -st) calm and dignified > **sedately** adv

sedate[2] v (-tes, -ting, -ted) give a sedative drug to > **sedation** n (pl -s)

sedated v ▷ **sedate**[2]

sedately adv ▷ **sedate**[1]

sedater adj ▷ **sedate**[1]

sedates v ▷ **sedate**[2]

sedatest adj ▷ **sedate**[1]

sedating v ▷ **sedate**[2]

sedation n ▷ **sedate**[2]

sedations n ▷ **sedate**[2]

sedative adj having a soothing or calming effect ▶ n (pl -s) sedative drug

sedatives n ▷ **sedative**

sedge n (pl -s) coarse grasslike plant growing on wet ground

sedges n ▷ **sedge**

sediment n (pl -s) matter which settles to the bottom of a liquid

> **sedimentary** adj

sedimentary adj ▷ **sediment**

sediments n ▷ **sediment**

sedition n (pl -s) speech or action encouraging rebellion against the government > **seditious** adj

seditions n ▷ **sedition**

seditious adj ▷ **sedition**

seduce v (-ces, -cing, -ced) persuade into sexual intercourse > **seducer**, **seductress** n (pl -s, -es) > **seduction** n (pl -s) > **seductive** adj

seduced v ▷ **seduce**

seducer n ▷ **seduce**

seducers n ▷ **seduce**

seduces v ▷ **seduce**

seducing v ▷ **seduce**

seduction n ▷ **seduce**

seductions n ▷ **seduce**

seductive adj ▷ **seduce**

seductress n ▷ **seduce**

seductresses n ▷ **seduce**

sedulous adj diligent or persevering > **sedulously** adv

sedulously adv ▷ **sedulous**

see[1] v (-s, -ing, saw, seen) perceive with the eyes or mind

see[2] n (pl -s) diocese of a bishop

seed n (pl -s) mature fertilized grain of a plant ▶ v (-s, -ing, -ed) sow with seed

seeded v ▷ **seed**

seedier adj ▷ **seedy**

seediest adj ▷ **seedy**

seeding v ▷ **seed**

seedling n (pl -s) young plant raised from a seed

seedlings n ▷ **seedling**

seeds n, v ▷ **seed**

seedy adj (-dier, -diest) shabby

seeing conj in view of the fact that ▶ v ▷ **see**[1]

seek v (-s, -ing, sought) try to find or obtain

seeking v ▷ **seek**

seeks v ▷ **seek**

seem v (-s, -ing, -ed) appear to be

seemed v ▷ **seem**

seeming adj apparent but not real > **seemingly** adv, v ▷ **seem**

seemingly adv ▷ **seeming**
seemlier adj ▷ **seemly**
seemliest adj ▷ **seemly**
seemly adj (-lier, -liest) proper or fitting
seems v ▷ **seem**
seen v ▷ **see**[1]
seep v (-s, -ing, -ed) trickle through slowly, ooze ▷ **seepage** n (pl -s)
seepage n ▷ **seep**
seepages n ▷ **seep**
seeped v ▷ **seep**
seeping v ▷ **seep**
seeps v ▷ **seep**
seer n (pl -s) prophet
seers n ▷ **seer**
sees n ▷ **see**[2] ▷ v ▷ **see**[1]
seesaw n (pl -s) plank balanced in the middle so that two people seated on either end ride up and down alternately ▷ v (-s, -ing, -ed) move up and down
seesawed v ▷ **seesaw**
seesawing v ▷ **seesaw**
seesaws n, v ▷ **seesaw**
seethe v (-thes, -thing, -thed) be very agitated
seethed v ▷ **seethe**
seethes v ▷ **seethe**
seething v ▷ **seethe**
segment n (pl -s) one of several sections into which something may be divided ▷ v (-s, -ing, -ed) divide into segments ▷ **segmentation** n (pl -s)
segmentation n ▷ **segment**
segmentations n ▷ **segment**
segmented v ▷ **segment**
segmenting v ▷ **segment**
segments n, v ▷ **segment**
seine n (pl -s) large fishing net that hangs vertically from floats
seines n ▷ **seine**
seismic adj relating to earthquakes
seize v (-zes, -zing, -zed) take hold of forcibly or quickly (usu. foll. by **up**)
seized v ▷ **seize**
seizes v ▷ **seize**
seizing v ▷ **seize**
seizure n (pl -s) sudden violent attack

of an illness
seizures n ▷ **seizure**
seldom adv not often, rarely
select v (-s, -ing, -ed) pick out or choose ▷ adj chosen in preference to others ▷ **selector** n (pl -s)
selected v ▷ **select**
selecting v ▷ **select**
selector n ▷ **select**
selectors n ▷ **select**
selects v ▷ **select**
selenium n (pl -s) CHEM nonmetallic element with photoelectric properties
seleniums n ▷ **selenium**
self n (pl **selves**) distinct individuality or identity of a person or thing
selfish adj caring too much about oneself and not enough about others ▷ **selfishly** adv ▷ **selfishness** n (pl -es)
selfishly adv ▷ **selfish**
selfishness n ▷ **selfish**
selfishnesses n ▷ **selfish**
selfless adj unselfish
selfsame adj the very same
sell v (-s, -ing, **sold**) exchange (something) for money (foll. by **for**) ▷ n (pl -s) manner of selling ▷ **seller** n (pl -s)
seller n ▷ **sell**
sellers n ▷ **sell**
selling v ▷ **sell**
sellout n (pl -s) performance of a show etc for which all the tickets are sold
sellouts n ▷ **sellout**
sells v, n ▷ **sell**
selvage, selvedge n (pl -s) edge of cloth, woven so as to prevent unravelling
selvages n ▷ **selvage**
selvedge n ▷ **selvage**
selvedges n ▷ **selvage**
selves n ▷ **self**
semantic adj relating to the meaning of words
semen n (pl -s) sperm-carrying fluid produced by male animals
semens n ▷ **semen**
semester n (pl -s) either of two divisions of the academic year
semesters n ▷ **semester**

semi n (pl -s) BRIT & S AFR informal
semidetached house

seminal adj original and influential

seminar n (pl -s) meeting of a group of
students for discussion

seminaries n ▷ **seminary**

seminars n ▷ **seminar**

seminary n (pl -ries) college for priests

semis n ▷ **semi**

semitone n (pl -s) smallest interval
between two notes in Western music

semitones n ▷ **semitone**

semolina n (pl -s) hard grains of wheat
left after the milling of flour, used to
make puddings and pasta

semolinas n ▷ **semolina**

senate n (pl -s) upper house of some
parliaments

senates n ▷ **senate**

senator n (pl -s) member of a senate
▷ **senatorial** adj

senatorial adj ▷ **senator**

senators n ▷ **senator**

send v (-s, -ing, sent) cause (a person
or thing) to go to or be taken or
transmitted to a place

sending v ▷ **send**

sendoff n (pl -s) demonstration of good
wishes at a person's departure

sendoffs n ▷ **sendoff**

sends v ▷ **send**

sendup n (pl -s) informal imitation

sendups n ▷ **sendup**

senile adj mentally or physically weak
because of old age ▷ **senility** n (pl -ties)

senilities n ▷ **senile**

senility n ▷ **senile**

senior adj superior in rank or standing
▷ n (pl -s) senior person ▷ **seniority** n
(pl -ties)

seniorities n ▷ **senior**

seniority n ▷ **senior**

seniors n ▷ **senior**

senna n (pl -s) tropical plant

sennas n ▷ **senna**

señor n (pl -ores) Spanish term of
address equivalent to sir or Mr

señora n (pl -s) Spanish term of address
equivalent to madam or Mrs

señoras n ▷ **señora**

señorita n (pl -s) Spanish term of
address equivalent to madam or Miss

señoritas n ▷ **señorita**

señors n ▷ **señor**

sense n (pl -s) any of the faculties of
perception or feeling (sight, hearing,
touch, taste, or smell) ▷ v (-ses, -sing,
-sed) perceive ▷ **senseless** adj

sensed v ▷ **sense**

senseless adj ▷ **sense**

senses n, v ▷ **sense**

sensible adj (-r, -st) having or showing
good sense ▷ **sensibly** adv

sensibler adj ▷ **sensible**

sensiblest adj ▷ **sensible**

sensibly adv ▷ **sensible**

sensing v ▷ **sense**

sensor n (pl -s) device that detects or
measures the presence of something,
such as radiation

sensors n ▷ **sensor**

sensory adj of the senses or sensation

sensual adj giving pleasure to the
body and senses rather than the mind
▷ **sensually** adv **sensuality** n (pl -ties)
▷ **sensualist** n (pl -s)

sensualist n ▷ **sensual**

sensualists n ▷ **sensual**

sensualities n ▷ **sensual**

sensuality n ▷ **sensual**

sensually adj ▷ **sensual**

sensuous adj pleasing to the senses
▷ **sensuously** adv

sensuously adv ▷ **sensuous**

sent v ▷ **send**

sentence n (pl -s) sequence of words
capable of standing alone as a
statement, question, or command ▷ v
(-ces, -cing, -ced) pass sentence on (a
convicted person)

sentenced v ▷ **sentence**

sentences n, v ▷ **sentence**

sentencing n, v ▷ **sentence**

sentience n ▷ **sentient**

sentiences n ▷ **sentient**

sentient adj capable of feeling
▷ **sentience** n (pl -s)

sentinel n (pl -s) sentry

sentinels n ▷ sentinel
sentries n ▷ sentry
sentry n (pl -tries) soldier on watch
sepal n (pl -s) leaflike division of the calyx of a flower
sepals n ▷ sepal
separable adj ▷ separate
separate v (-tes, -ting, -ted) act as a barrier between ▶ adj not the same, different ▷ **separable** adj
> **separately** adv
separated v ▷ separate
separately adv ▷ separate
separates v ▷ separate
separating v ▷ separate
sepia adj, n (pl -s) reddish-brown (pigment)
sepias n ▷ sepia
sepses n ▷ sepsis
sepsis n (pl -ses) poisoning caused by pus-forming bacteria
septet n (pl -s) group of seven performers
septets n ▷ septet
septic adj (of a wound) infected
sequel n (pl -s) novel, play, or film that continues the story of an earlier one
sequels n ▷ sequel
sequence n (pl -s) arrangement of two or more things in successive order
> **sequential** adj
sequences n ▷ sequence
sequential adj ▷ sequence
sequin n (pl -s) small ornamental metal disc on a garment ▷ **sequined** adj
sequined adj ▷ sequin
sequins n ▷ sequin
sequoia n (pl -s) giant Californian coniferous tree
sequoias n ▷ sequoia
seraglio n (pl -s) harem of a Muslim palace
seraglios n ▷ seraglio
seraph n (pl -s, -aphim) member of the highest order of angels ▷ **seraphic** adj
seraphic adj ▷ seraph
seraphim n ▷ seraph
seraphs n ▷ seraph
serenade n (pl -s) music played or sung to a woman by a lover ▶ v (-des, -ding, -ded) sing or play a serenade to (someone)
serenaded v ▷ serenade
serenades n, v ▷ serenade
serenading v ▷ serenade
serene adj (-r, -st) calm, peaceful
> **serenely** adv ▷ **serenity** n (pl -ties)
serenely adv ▷ serene
serener adj ▷ serene
serenest adj ▷ serene
serenities n ▷ serene
serenity n ▷ serene
serf n (pl -s) medieval farm labourer who could not leave the land he worked on
> **serfdom** n (pl -s)
serfdom n ▷ serf
serfdoms n ▷ serf
serfs n ▷ serf
serge n (pl -s) strong woollen fabric
sergeant n (pl -s) noncommissioned officer in the army
sergeants n ▷ sergeant
serges n ▷ serge
serial n (pl -s) story or play produced in successive instalments ▶ adj of or forming a series
serials n ▷ serial
series n (pl series) group or succession of related things, usu. arranged in order
serious adj giving cause for concern
> **seriously** adv ▷ **seriousness** n (pl -es)
seriously adv ▷ serious
seriousness n ▷ serious
seriousnesses n ▷ serious
sermon n (pl -s) speech on a religious or moral subject by a clergyman in a church service
sermons n ▷ sermon
serpent n (pl -s) lit snake
serpents n ▷ serpent
serrated adj having a notched or sawlike edge
serried adj in close formation
serum n (pl -s) watery fluid left after blood has clotted
serums n ▷ serum
servant n (pl -s) person employed to do

household work for another
servants n ▷ servant

serve v (-s, -ing, -ed) work for (a
person, community, or cause) ▶ n (pl -s)
TENNIS ETC act of serving the ball
served v ▷ serve

server n (pl -s) player who serves in
racket games
servers n ▷ server
serves n, v ▷ serve

service n (pl -s) system that provides
something needed by the public ▶ v
(-ces, -cing, -ced) overhaul (a machine
or vehicle)
serviced v ▷ service
services n, v ▷ service ▶ pl n armed
forces
servicing v ▷ service

servile adj too eager to obey people,
fawning > **servility** n ▷ servile

servilities n ▷ servile
servility n ▷ servile
serving v ▷ serve

sesame n (pl -s) plant cultivated for
its seeds and oil, which are used in
cooking
sesames n ▷ sesame

session n (pl -s) period spent in an
activity
sessions n ▷ session

set v (-s, -tting, set) put in a specified
position or state ▶ n (pl -s) scenery
used in a play or film ▶ adj fixed or
established beforehand

set² n (pl -s) number of things or people
grouped or belonging together

setback n (pl -s) anything that delays
progress
setbacks n ▷ setback
sets v ▷ set¹ ▶ n ▷ set¹, ²

sett, set n (p -s) badger's burrow

settee n (pl -s) couch
settees n ▷ settee

setter n (pl -s) long-haired gun dog
setters n ▷ setter

setting n (pl -s) background or
surroundings ▶ v ▷ set
settings n ▷ setting

settle¹ v (-les, -ling, -led) arrange or

put in order

settle² n (pl -s) long wooden bench
with high back and arms
settled v ▷ settle¹

settler n (pl -s) colonist
settlers n ▷ settler
settles v ▷ settle¹ ▶ n ▷ settle²
settling v ▷ settle¹
setts n ▷ sett

setup n (pl -s) way in which anything is
organized or arranged
setups n ▷ setup

seven adj, n (pl -s) one more than six
sevens n ▷ seven

seventh adj, n (pl -s) (of) number seven
in a series
sevenths n ▷ seventh
seventies n ▷ seventy
seventieth n ▷ seventy
seventieths n ▷ seventy

seventy adj, n (pl -ties) ten times seven
> **seventieth** adj, n (pl -s)

sever v (-s, -ing, -ed) cut through or off
> **severance** n (pl -s)

several adj some, a few
severance n ▷ sever
severances n ▷ sever

severe adj (-r, -st) strict or harsh
> **severely** adv > **severity** n (pl -ties)
severed v ▷ sever
severely adv ▷ severe
severer adj ▷ severe
severest adj ▷ severe
severing v ▷ sever
severities n ▷ severe
severity n ▷ severe
severs v ▷ sever

sew v (-s, -ing, -ed, sewn or -ed) join
with thread repeatedly passed through
with a needle

sewage n (pl -s) waste matter or
excrement carried away in sewers
sewages n ▷ sewage
sewed v ▷ sew

sewer n (pl -s) drain to remove waste
water and sewage > **sewerage** n (pl -s)
system of sewers
sewerage n ▷ sewer
sewerages n ▷ sewer

sewers n ▷ **sewer**

sewing v ▷ **sew**

sewn v ▷ **sew**

sews v ▷ **sew**

sex n (pl **-es**) state of being male or female ▶ v (**-es**, **-ing**, **-ed**) find out the sex of > **sexual** adj > **sexually** adv > **sexuality** n (pl **-ties**)

■ **sexed** v ▷ **sex**

■ **sexes** n, v ▷ **sex**

■ **sexier** adj ▷ **sexy**

■ **sexiest** adj ▷ **sexy**

■ **sexing** v ▷ **sex**

sexism n (pl **-s**) discrimination on the basis of a person's sex > **sexist** adj, n (pl **-s**)

■ **sexisms** n ▷ **sexism**

■ **sexist** n ▷ **sexism**

■ **sexists** n ▷ **sexism**

sextant n (pl **-s**) navigator's instrument for measuring angles, as between the sun and horizon, to calculate one's position

■ **sextants** n ▷ **sextant**

sextet n (pl **-s**) group of six performers

■ **sextets** n ▷ **sextet**

sexton n (pl **-s**) official in charge of a church and churchyard

■ **sextons** n ▷ **sexton**

■ **sexual** adj ▷ **sex**

■ **sexualities** n ▷ **sex**

■ **sexuality** n ▷ **sex**

■ **sexually** adv ▷ **sex**

sexy adj (**-xier**, **-xiest**) sexually exciting or attractive

> **sez** v. Sez is an short informal form of **says**. This word can be very useful when there isn't much space on the board, as it gives a good score. Sez scores 12 points.

> **sh** interj. Sh is a sound people make to request silence or quiet. This is one of two two-letter words beginning with S that do not contain a vowel. It's useful when you want to connect a word beginning with H to one ending in S or vice versa. Sh scores 5 points.

■ **shabbier** adj ▷ **shabby**

■ **shabbiest** adj ▷ **shabby**

shabbily adv ▷ **shabby**

shabbiness n ▷ **shabby**

shabbinesses n ▷ **shabby**

shabby adj (**-bier**, **-biest**) worn or dilapidated in appearance > **shabbily** adv > **shabbiness** n (pl **-es**)

shack n (pl **-s**) rough hut

shackle n (pl **-s**) one of a pair of metal rings joined by a chain, for securing a person's wrists or ankles ▶ v (**-les**, **-ling**, **-led**) fasten with shackles

■ **shackled** v ▷ **shackle**

■ **shackles** n, v ▷ **shackle**

■ **shackling** v ▷ **shackle**

■ **shacks** n ▷ **shack**

shad n (pl **-s**) herring-like fish

shade n (pl **-s**) relative darkness ▶ v (**-des**, **-ding**, **-ded**) screen from light > **shady** adj (**-dier**, **-diest**) situated in or giving shade

■ **shaded** v ▷ **shade**

■ **shades** n, v ▷ **shade** ▶ pl n slang sunglasses

■ **shadier** adj ▷ **shade**

■ **shadiest** adj ▷ **shade**

■ **shading** v ▷ **shade**

shadow n (pl **-s**) dark shape cast on a surface when something stands between a light and the surface ▶ v (**-s**, **-ing**, **-ed**) cast a shadow over > **shadowy** adj (**-wier**, **-wiest**)

■ **shadowed** v ▷ **shadow**

■ **shadowier** adj ▷ **shadow**

■ **shadowiest** adj ▷ **shadow**

■ **shadowing** v ▷ **shadow**

■ **shadows** n, v ▷ **shadow**

■ **shadowy** adj ▷ **shadow**

■ **shads** n ▷ **shad**

shady adj ▷ **shade**

shaft n (pl **-s**) long narrow straight handle of a tool or weapon

■ **shafts** n ▷ **shaft**

shag¹ n (pl **-s**) coarse shredded tobacco ▶ adj (of a carpet) having a long pile

shag² n (pl **-s**) kind of cormorant

■ **shaggier** adj ▷ **shaggy**

■ **shaggiest** adj ▷ **shaggy**

shaggy adj (**-ggier**, **-ggiest**) covered with rough hair or wool

shagreen n (pl -s) sharkskin

shagreens n ▷ shagreen

shags n ▷ shag[1, 2]

shah n (pl -s) formerly, ruler of Iran

shahs n ▷ shah

shake v (-kes, -king, shook, -ken) move quickly up and down or back and forth ▶ n (pl -s) shaking

shaken v ▷ shake

shakes v, n ▷ shake

shakier adj ▷ shaky

shakiest adj ▷ shaky

shakily adv ▷ shaky

shaking v ▷ shake

shaky adj (-kier, -kiest) unsteady > shakily adv

shale n (pl -s) flaky sedimentary rock

shales n ▷ shale

shall v (past tense should) used as an auxiliary to make the future tense or to indicate intention, obligation, or inevitability

shallot n (pl -s) kind of small onion

shallots n ▷ shallot

shallow adj (-er, -est) not deep > shallowness n (pl -es)

shallower adj ▷ shallow

shallowest adj ▷ shallow

shallowness n ▷ shallow

shallownesses n ▷ shallow

shallows pl n area of shallow water

sham n (pl -s) thing or person that is not genuine ▶ adj not genuine ▶ v (-s, -mming, -mmed) fake, feign

shamble v (-les, -ling, -led) walk in a shuffling awkward way

shambled v ▷ shamble

shambles n (pl disorderly event or place ▶ v ▷ shamble

shambling v ▷ shamble

shame n (pl -s) painful emotion caused by awareness of having done something dishonourable or foolish ▶ v (-es, -ming, -med) cause to feel shame ▶ interj S AFR informal exclamation of sympathy or endearment

shamed v ▷ shame

shameful adj causing or deserving

shame > **shamefully** adv

shamefully adv ▷ shameful

shames n, v ▷ shame

shaming v ▷ shame

shammed v ▷ sham

shammies n ▷ shammy

shamming v ▷ sham

shammy n (pl -mies) informal piece of chamois leather

shampoo n (pl -s) liquid soap for washing hair, carpets, or upholstery ▶ v (-s, -ing, -ed) wash with shampoo

shampooed v ▷ shampoo

shampooing v ▷ shampoo

shampoos n, v ▷ shampoo

shamrock n (pl -s) clover leaf, esp. as the Irish emblem

shamrocks n ▷ shamrock

shams n, v ▷ sham

shandies n ▷ shandy

shandy n (pl -dies) drink made of beer and lemonade

shanghai v (-hais, -haiing, -haied) force or trick (someone) into doing something ▶ n (pl -s) AUST & NZ catapult

shanghaied v ▷ shanghai

shanghaiing v ▷ shanghai

shanghais v, n ▷ shanghai

shank n (pl -s) lower leg

shanks n ▷ shank

shanties n ▷ shanty[1, 2]

shantung n (pl -s) soft Chinese silk with a knobbly surface

shantungs n ▷ shantung

shanty[1] n (pl -ties) shack or crude dwelling

shanty[2] n (pl -ties) sailor's traditional song

shape n (pl -s) outward form of an object ▶ v (-pes, -ping, -ped) form or mould > **shapeless** adj

shaped v ▷ shape

shapeless adj ▷ shape

shapelier adj ▷ shapely

shapeliest adj ▷ shapely

shapely adj (-lier, -liest) having an attractive shape

shapes n, v ▷ shape

shaping v ▷ shape

shard n (pl -s) broken piece of pottery or glass

shards n ▷ **shard**

share¹ n (pl -s) part of something that belongs to or is contributed by a person ▶ v (-res, -ring, -red) give or take a share of (something) ▷ **shareholder** n (pl -s)

share² n (pl -s) blade of a plough

shared v ▷ **share¹**

shareholder n ▷ **share¹**

shareholders n ▷ **share¹**

shares v ▷ **share¹** ▶ n ▷ **share¹, ²**

sharing v ▷ **share¹**

shark n (pl -s) large usu. predatory sea fish

sharks n ▷ **shark**

sharp adj having a keen cutting edge or fine point ▶ adv promptly ▶ n (pl -s) MUSIC symbol raising a note one semitone above natural pitch ▷ **sharply** adv > **sharpness** n (pl -es)

sharpen v (-s, -ing, -ed) make or become sharp or sharper ▷ **sharpener** n (pl -s)

sharpened v ▷ **sharpen**

sharpener n ▷ **sharpen**

sharpeners n ▷ **sharpen**

sharpening v ▷ **sharpen**

sharpens v ▷ **sharpen**

sharply adv ▷ **sharp**

sharpness n ▷ **sharp**

sharps n ▷ **sharp**

shatter v (-s, -ing, -ed) break into pieces

shattering v ▷ **shatter**

shatters v ▷ **shatter**

shave v (-ves, -ving, -ved, -ved or shaven) remove (hair) from (the face, head, or body) with a razor or shaver ▶ n (pl -s) shaving

shaved v ▷ **shave**

shaven v ▷ **shave**

shaver n (pl -s) electric razor

shavers n ▷ **shaver**

shaves v, n ▷ **shave**

shaving v ▷ **shave**

shavings pl n parings

shawl n (pl -s) piece of cloth worn over a woman's head or shoulders or wrapped around a baby

shawls n ▷ **shawl**

she pron refers to: female person or animal previously mentioned

sheaf n (pl sheaves) bundle of papers

shear v (-s, -ing, -ed, -ed or shorn) clip hair or wool from ▷ **shearer** n (pl -s)

sheared v ▷ **shear**

shearer n ▷ **shear**

shearers n ▷ **shear**

shearing v ▷ **shear**

shears pl n large scissors or a cutting tool shaped like these ▶ v ▷ **shear**

sheath n (pl -s) close-fitting cover, esp. for a knife or sword

sheathe v (-thes, -thing, -thed) put into a sheath

sheathed v ▷ **sheathe**

sheathes v ▷ **sheathe**

sheathing v ▷ **sheathe**

sheaths n ▷ **sheath**

sheaves n ▷ **sheaf**

shebeen n (pl -s) SCOT, IRISH G S AFR place where alcohol is sold illegally

shebeens n ▷ **shebeen**

shed¹ n (pl -s) building used for storage or shelter or as a workshop

shed² v (-s, -dding, shed) pour forth (tears)

shedding v ▷ **shed²**

sheds n ▷ **shed¹** ▶ v ▷ **shed²**

sheen n (pl -s) glistening brightness on the surface of something

sheens n ▷ **sheen**

sheep n (pl sheep) ruminant animal bred for wool and meat

sheepdog n (pl -s) dog used for herding sheep

sheepdogs n ▷ **sheepdog**

sheepish adj embarrassed because of feeling foolish ▷ **sheepishly** adv

sheepishly adv ▷ **sheepish**

sheer¹ adj (-er, -est) absolute, complete

sheer² v (-s, -ing, -ed) change course suddenly

sheered v ▷ **sheer²**

sheerer adj ▷ **sheer¹**

sheerest adj ▷ **sheer¹**

sheering v ▷ **sheer²**

sheers v ▷ **sheer²**

sheet¹ n (pl -**s**) large piece of cloth used as an inner bed cover

sheet² n (pl -**s**) rope for controlling the position of a sail

sheets n ▷ **sheet¹, ²**

sheikdom n ▷ **sheikh**

sheikdoms n ▷ **sheikh**

sheikh, sheik n (pl -**s**) Arab chief ▷ **sheikdom, sheikdom** n (pl -**s**)

sheikhdom n ▷ **sheikh**

sheikhdoms n ▷ **sheikh**

sheikhs n ▷ **sheikh**

sheiks n ▷ **sheikh**

sheila n (pl -**s**) AUST & NZ slang girl or woman

sheilas n ▷ **sheila**

shekel n (pl -**s**) monetary unit of Israel

shekels n ▷ **shekel** ▷ pl n informal money

shelf n (pl -**ves**) board fixed horizontally for holding things

shell n (pl -**s**) hard outer covering of an egg, nut, or certain animals ▷ v (-**s**, -**lling**, -**lled**) take the shell from

shellac n (pl -**s**) resin used in varnishes ▷ v (-**s**, -**cking**, -**cked**) coat with shellac

shellacked v ▷ **shellac**

shellacking v ▷ **shellac**

shellacs n, v ▷ **shellac**

shelled v ▷ **shell**

shelling v ▷ **shell**

shells n, v ▷ **shell**

shelter n (pl -**s**) structure providing protection from danger or the weather ▷ v (-**s**, -**ing**, -**ed**) give shelter to

sheltered v ▷ **shelter**

sheltering v ▷ **shelter**

shelters n, v ▷ **shelter**

shelve¹ v (-**ves**, -**ving**, -**ved**) put aside or postpone

shelve² v (-**ves**, -**ving**, -**ved**) slope

shelved v ▷ **shelve¹, ²**

shelves n ▷ **shelve¹, ²** ▷ n ▷ **shelf**

shelving n (pl -**s**) (material for) shelves ▷ v ▷ **shelve¹, ²**

shepherd n (pl -**s**) person who tends

sheep ▷ v (-**s**, -**ing**, -**ed**) guide or watch over (people) ▷ **shepherdess** n fem (pl -**es**)

shepherded v ▷ **shepherd**

shepherdess n ▷ **shepherd**

shepherdesses n ▷ **shepherd**

shepherding v ▷ **shepherd**

shepherds n, v ▷ **shepherd**

sherbet n (pl -**s**) BRIT, AUST & NZ fruit-flavoured fizzy powder

sherbets n ▷ **sherbet**

sheriff n (pl -**s**) (in the US) chief law enforcement officer of a county

sheriffs n ▷ **sheriff**

sherries n ▷ **sherry**

sherry n (pl -**ries**) pale or dark brown fortified wine

> **shh** interj. Shh is a sound people make to request silence or quiet. As it doesn't contain a vowel, shh can help you to clear an unpromising rack. Shh scores 9 points.

shied v ▷ **shy¹, ²**

shield n (pl -**s**) piece of armour carried on the arm to protect the body from blows or missiles ▷ v (-**s**, -**ing**, -**ed**) protect

shielded v ▷ **shield**

shielding v ▷ **shield**

shields n, v ▷ **shield**

shies v ▷ **shy¹, ²** n ▷ **shy²**

shift v (-**s**, -**ing**, -**ed**) move ▷ n (pl -**s**) shifting

shifted v ▷ **shift**

shiftier adj ▷ **shifty**

shiftiest adj ▷ **shifty**

shiftiness n ▷ **shifty**

shiftinesses n ▷ **shifty**

shifting v ▷ **shift**

shifts v, n ▷ **shift**

shifty adj (-**tier**, -**tiest**) evasive or untrustworthy ▷ **shiftiness** n (pl -**es**)

shilling n (pl -**s**) former British coin, replaced by the 5p coin

shillings n ▷ **shilling**

shimmer v (-**s**, -**ing**, -**ed**) ▷ n (pl -**s**) (shine with) a faint unsteady light

shimmered v ▷ **shimmer**

shimmering v ▷ **shimmer**

shimmers v, n ▷ **shimmer**

shin n (pl **-s**) front of the lower leg ▶ v (**-s, -nning, -nned**) climb by using the hands or arms and legs

shinbone n (pl **-s**) tibia

shinbones n ▷ **shinbone**

shindig n (pl **-s**) informal noisy party

shindigs n ▷ **shindig**

shine v (**-s, -ing, shone**) give out or reflect light ▶ n (pl **-s**) brightness or lustre ▷ **shiny** adj (**-nier, -niest**)

shiner n (pl **-s**) informal black eye

shiners n ▷ **shiner**

shines v, n ▷ **shine**

shingle¹ n (pl **-s**) wooden roof tile ▶ v (**-les, -ling, -led**) cover (a roof) with shingles

shingle² n (pl **-s**) coarse gravel found on beaches

shingled v ▷ **shingle**¹

shingles n disease causing a rash of small blisters along a nerve ▷ **shingle**¹, ² v ▷ **shingle**¹

shingling v ▷ **shingle**¹

shinier adj ▷ **shine**

shiniest adj ▷ **shine**

shining v ▷ **shine**

shinned v ▷ **shin**

shinning v ▷ **shin**

shins n, v ▷ **shin**

shinties n ▷ **shinty**

shinty n (pl **-ties**) game like hockey

shiny adj ▷ **shine**

ship n (pl **-s**) large seagoing vessel ▶ v (**-s, -pping, -pped**) send or transport by carrier, esp. a ship

shipment n (pl **-s**) act of shipping cargo

shipments n ▷ **shipment**

shipped v ▷ **ship**

shipping n (pl **-s**) freight transport business ▶ v ▷ **ship**

shippings n ▷ **shipping**

ships n, v ▷ **ship**

shipyard n (pl **-s**) place where ships are built

shipyards n ▷ **shipyard**

shire n (pl **-s**) BRIT county

shires n ▷ **shire**

shirk v (**-s, -ing, -ed**) avoid (duty or work) ▷ **shirker** n (pl **-s**)

shirked v ▷ **shirk**

shirker n ▷ **shirk**

shirkers n ▷ **shirk**

shirking v ▷ **shirk**

shirks v ▷ **shirk**

shirt n (pl **-s**) garment for the upper part of the body

shirtier adj ▷ **shirty**

shirtiest adj ▷ **shirty**

shirts n ▷ **shirt**

shirty adj (**-tier, -tiest**) CHIEFLY BRIT slang bad-tempered or annoyed

shiver¹ v (**-s, -ing, -ed**) tremble, as from cold or fear ▶ n (pl **-s**) shivering

shiver² v (**-s, -ing, -ed**) splinter into pieces

shivered v ▷ **shiver**¹

shivering v ▷ **shiver**¹, ²

shivers v ▷ **shiver**¹, ² n ▷ **shiver**¹

shoal¹ n (pl **-s**) large number of fish swimming together

shoal² n (pl **-s**) stretch of shallow water

shoals n ▷ **shoal**¹, ²

shock¹ v (**-s, -ing, -ed**) horrify, disgust, or astonish ▶ n (pl **-s**) sudden violent emotional disturbance ▷ **shocker** n (pl **-s**)

shock² n (pl **-s**) bushy mass (of hair)

shocked v ▷ **shock**¹

shocker n ▷ **shock**¹

shockers n ▷ **shock**¹

shocking adj causing horror, disgust, or astonishment ▶ v ▷ **shock**¹

shocks v ▷ **shock**¹ n ▷ **shock**¹, ²

shod v ▷ **shoe**

shoddier adj ▷ **shoddy**

shoddiest adj ▷ **shoddy**

shoddy adj (**-dier, -diest**) made or done badly

shoe n (pl **-s**) outer covering for the foot, ending below the ankle ▶ v (**shoes, shoeing, shod**) fit with a shoe or shoes

shoehorn n (pl **-s**) smooth curved implement inserted at the heel of a shoe to ease the foot into it

shoehorns n ▷ **shoehorn**

shoeing v ▷ **shoe**

shoes n, v ▷ **shoe**

shone v ▷ **shine**

shonkier adj ▷ **shonky**

shonkiest adj ▷ **shonky**

shonky adj (-kier, -kiest) AUST & NZ informal unreliable or unsound

shoo interj go away! ▶ v (-s, -ing, -ed) drive away as by saying 'shoo'

shooed v ▷ **shoo**

shooing v ▷ **shoo**

shook v ▷ **shake**

shoos v ▷ **shoo**

shoot v (-s, -ing, shot) hit, wound, or kill with a missile fired from a weapon ▶ n (pl -s) new branch or sprout of a plant

shooting v ▷ **shoot**

shoots v, n ▷ **shoot**

shop n (pl -s) place for sale of goods and services ▶ v (-s, -pping, -pped) visit a shop or shops to buy goods

shopped v ▷ **shop**

shopping v ▷ **shop**

shops n, v ▷ **shop**

shore[1] n (pl -s) edge of a sea or lake

shore[2] v (-res, -ring, -red) (foll. by up) prop or support

shored v ▷ **shore**[2]

shores n ▷ **shore**[1] ▶ v ▷ **shore**[2]

shoring v ▷ **shore**[2]

shorn v ▷ **shear**

short adj (-er, -est) not long ▶ adv abruptly ▶ n (pl -s) drink of spirits

shortage n (pl -s) deficiency

shortages n ▷ **shortage**

shorten v (-s, -ing, -ed) make or become shorter

shortened v ▷ **shorten**

shortening v ▷ **shorten**

shortens v ▷ **shorten**

shorter adj ▷ **short**

shortest adj ▷ **short**

shortly adv soon

shorts n ▷ **short** ▶ pl n short trousers

shot n (pl -s) shooting ▶ v ▷ **shoot**

shotgun n (pl -s) gun for firing a charge of shot at short range

shotguns n ▷ **shotgun**

shots n ▷ **shot**

should v ▷ **shall**

shoulder n (pl -s) part of the body to which an arm, foreleg, or wing is attached ▶ v (-s, -ing, -ed) bear (a burden or responsibility)

shouldered v ▷ **shoulder**

shouldering v ▷ **shoulder**

shoulders n, v ▷ **shoulder**

shout n (pl -s) loud cry informal ▶ v (-s, -ing, -ed) cry out loudly

shouted v ▷ **shout**

shouting v ▷ **shout**

shouts n, v ▷ **shout**

shove v (-ves, -ving, -ved) push roughly ▶ n (pl -s) rough push

shoved v ▷ **shove**

shovel n (pl -s) tool for lifting or moving loose material ▶ v (-s, -lling, -lled) lift or move as with a shovel

shovelled v ▷ **shovel**

shovelling v ▷ **shovel**

shovels n, v ▷ **shovel**

shoves v, n ▷ **shove**

shoving v ▷ **shove**

show v (-s, -ing, -ed, shown or showed) make, be, or become noticeable or visible ▶ n (pl -s) public exhibition

showcase n (pl -s) situation in which something is displayed to best advantage

showcases n ▷ **showcase**

showdown n (pl -s) confrontation that settles a dispute

showdowns n ▷ **showdown**

showed v ▷ **show**

shower n (pl -s) kind of bath in which a person stands while being sprayed with water ▶ v (-s, -ing, -ed) wash in a shower ▶ **showery** adj (-rier, -riest)

showered v ▷ **shower**

showerier adj ▷ **shower**

showeriest adj ▷ **shower**

showering v ▷ **shower**

showers n, v ▷ **shower**

showery adj ▷ **shower**

showier adj ▷ **showy**

showiest adj ▷ **showy**

showily adv ▷ **showy**

showing v ▷ **show**

showman n (pl **-men**) man skilled at presenting anything spectacularly
> **showmanship** n (pl **-s**)
showmanship n ▷ **showman**
showmanships n ▷ **showman**
showmen n ▷ **showman**
shown v ▷ **show**

showoff n (pl **-s**) informal person who shows off
showoffs n ▷ **showoff**

showroom n (pl **-s**) room in which goods for sale are on display
showrooms n ▷ **showroom**
shows v, n ▷ **show**

showy adj (**-wier, -wiest**) gaudy
> **showily** adv
shrank v ▷ **shrink**

shrapnel n (pl **-s**) artillery shell filled with pellets which scatter on explosion
shrapnels n ▷ **shrapnel**

shred n (pl **-s**) long narrow strip torn from something ▶ v (**-s, -dding, -dded** or **shred**) tear to shreds
shredded v ▷ **shred**
shredding v ▷ **shred**
shreds n, v ▷ **shred**

shrew n (pl **-s**) small mouselike animal
> **shrewish** adj

shrewd adj (**-er, -est**) clever and perceptive > **shrewdly** adv
> **shrewdness** n (pl **-es**)
shrewder adj ▷ **shrewd**
shrewdest adj ▷ **shrewd**
shrewdly adv ▷ **shrewd**
shrewdness n ▷ **shrewd**
shrewdnesses n ▷ **shrewd**
shrewish adj ▷ **shrew**
shrews n ▷ **shrew**

shriek n (pl **-s**) shrill cry ▶ v (**-s, -ing, -ed**) utter (with) a shriek
shrieked v ▷ **shriek**
shrieking v ▷ **shriek**
shrieks n, v ▷ **shriek**

shrike n (pl **-s**) songbird with a heavy hooked bill
shrikes n ▷ **shrike**

shrill adj (**-er, -est**) (of a sound) sharp and high-pitched > **shrillness** n (pl **-es**)

> **shrilly** adv
shriller adj ▷ **shrill**
shrillest adj ▷ **shrill**
shrillness n ▷ **shrill**
shrillnesses n ▷ **shrill**
shrilly adv ▷ **shrill**

shrimp n (pl **-s**) small edible shellfish informal
shrimps n ▷ **shrimp**

shrine n (pl **-s**) place of worship associated with a sacred person or object
shrines n ▷ **shrine**

shrink v (**-s, -ing, shrank** or **shrunk**, **shrunk** or **shrunken**) become or make smaller ▶ n (pl **-s**) slang psychiatrist
shrinking v ▷ **shrink**
shrinks v, n ▷ **shrink**

shrivel v (**-s, -lling, -lled**) shrink and wither
shrivelled v ▷ **shrivel**
shrivelling v ▷ **shrivel**
shrivels v ▷ **shrivel**

shroud n (pl **-s**) piece of cloth used to wrap a dead body ▶ v (**-s, -ing, -ed**) conceal
shrouded v ▷ **shroud**
shrouding v ▷ **shroud**
shrouds n, v ▷ **shroud**

shrub n (pl **-s**) woody plant smaller than a tree
shrubs n ▷ **shrub**

shrug v (**-s, -gging, -gged**) raise and then drop (the shoulders) as a sign of indifference, ignorance, or doubt ▶ n (pl **-s**) shrugging
shrugged v ▷ **shrug**
shrugging v ▷ **shrug**
shrugs v, n ▷ **shrug**

shrunk v ▷ **shrink**
shrunken v ▷ **shrink**

shudder v (**-s, -ing, -ed**) shake or tremble violently, esp. with horror ▶ n (pl **-s**) shaking or trembling
shuddered v ▷ **shudder**
shuddering v ▷ **shudder**
shudders v, n ▷ **shudder**

shuffle v (**-les, -lling, -led**) walk without lifting the feet ▶ n (pl **-s**)

shuffling
shuffled v ▷ **shuffle**
shuffles v, n ▷ **shuffle**
shuffling v ▷ **shuffle**
shun v (-s, -nning, -nned) avoid
shunned v ▷ **shun**
shunning v ▷ **shun**
shuns v ▷ **shun**
shush interj be quiet!
shut v (-s, -tting, shut) bring together
or fold, close
shutdown n (pl -s) closing of a factory
or shop
shutdowns n ▷ **shutdown**
shuts v ▷ **shut**
shutter n (pl -s) hinged doorlike cover
for closing off a window
shutters n ▷ **shutter**
shutting v ▷ **shut**
shuttle n (pl -s) vehicle going to and fro
over a short distance ▶ v (-les, -ling,
-led) travel by or as if by shuttle
shuttled v ▷ **shuttle**
shuttles n, v ▷ **shuttle**
shuttling v ▷ **shuttle**
shy[1] adj (-er, -est) not at ease in
company (foll. by of) ▶ v (shies, shying,
shied) start back in fear ▷ **shyly** adv
> **shyness** n (pl -es)
shy[2] v (shies, shying, shied) throw ▶ n
(pl shies) throw
shyer adj ▷ **shy**[1]
shyest adj ▷ **shy**[1]
shying v ▷ **shy**[1, 2]
shyly adv ▷ **shy**[1]
shyness n ▷ **shy**[1]
shynesses n ▷ **shy**[1]

> **si** n (**sis**). Si means the same as **te**
> (a musical note). This is an unusual
> word which can be helpful when
> you want to form words in more
> than one direction. Si scores 2
> points.

sibilant adj hissing ▶ n (pl -s) consonant

pronounced with a hissing sound
sibilants n ▷ **sibilant**
sibling n (pl -s) brother or sister
siblings n ▷ **sibling**
sibyl n (pl -s) (in ancient Greece and
Rome) prophetess
sibyls n ▷ **sibyl**
sic adv LATIN thus: used to indicate that
an odd spelling or reading is in fact
accurate
sick adj (-er, -est) vomiting or likely to
vomit> **sickness** n (pl -es)
sicken v (-s, -ing, -ed) make nauseated
or disgusted
sickened v ▷ **sicken**
sickening v ▷ **sicken**
sickens v ▷ **sicken**
sicker adj ▷ **sick**
sickest adj ▷ **sick**
sickle n (pl -s) tool with a curved blade
for cutting grass or grain
sickles n ▷ **sickle**
sicklier adj ▷ **sickly**
sickliest adj ▷ **sickly**
sickly adj (-lier, -liest) unhealthy, weak
sickness n ▷ **sick**
sicknesses n ▷ **sick**
side n (pl -s) line or surface that borders
anything ▶ adj at or on the side
sidekick n (pl -s) informal close friend
or associate
sidekicks n ▷ **sidekick**
sideline n (pl -s) subsidiary interest or
source of income
sidelines n ▷ **sideline**
sidelong adj sideways ▶ adv obliquely
sidereal adj of or determined with
reference to the stars
sides n ▷ **side**
sidestep v (-s, -pping, -pped) dodge
(an issue)
sidestepped v ▷ **sidestep**
sidestepping v ▷ **sidestep**
sidesteps v ▷ **sidestep**
sidewalk n (pl -s) us paved path for
pedestrians, at the side of a road
sidewalks n ▷ **sidewalk**
sideways adv to or from the side
siding n (pl -s) short stretch of railway

track on which trains or wagons are shunted from the main line

sidings n ▷ **siding**

sidle v (**-les**, **-ling**, **-led**) walk in a furtive manner

sidled v ▷ **sidle**

sidles v ▷ **sidle**

sidling v ▷ **sidle**

siege n (pl **-s**) surrounding and blockading of a place

sieges n ▷ **siege**

sienna n (pl **-s**) reddish- or yellowish-brown pigment made from natural earth

siennas n ▷ **sienna**

sierra n (pl **-s**) range of mountains in Spain or America with jagged peaks

sierras n ▷ **sierra**

siesta n (pl **-s**) afternoon nap, taken in hot countries

siestas n ▷ **siesta**

sieve n (pl **-s**) utensil with mesh through which a substance is sifted or strained ▶ v (**-ves**, **-ving**, **-ved**) sift or strain through a sieve

sieved v ▷ **sieve**

sieves n, v ▷ **sieve**

sieving v ▷ **sieve**

sift v (**-s**, **-ing**, **-ed**) remove the coarser particles from a substance with a sieve

sifted v ▷ **sift**

sifting v ▷ **sift**

sifts v ▷ **sift**

sigh n (pl **-s**) long audible breath expressing sadness, tiredness, relief, or longing ▶ v (**-s**, **-ing**, **-ed**) utter a sigh

sighed v ▷ **sigh**

sighing v ▷ **sigh**

sighs n, v ▷ **sigh**

sight n (pl **-s**) ability to see ▶ v (**-s**, **-ing**, **-ed**) catch sight of

sighted v ▷ **sight**

sighting v ▷ **sight**

sights n, v ▷ **sight**

sign n (pl **-s**) indication of something not immediately or outwardly observable ▶ v (**-s**, **-ing**, **-ed**) write (one's name) on (a document or letter) to show its authenticity or one's

agreement

signal n (pl **-s**) sign or gesture to convey information ▶ adj formal very important ▶ v (**-s**, **-lling**, **-lled**) convey (information) by signal > **signally** adv

signalled v ▷ **signal**

signalling v ▷ **signal**

signally adv ▷ **signal**

signals n, v ▷ **signal**

signed v ▷ **sign**

signet n (pl **-s**) small seal used to authenticate documents

signets n ▷ **signet**

signification n ▷ **signify**

significations n ▷ **signify**

signified v ▷ **signify**

signifies v ▷ **signify**

signify v (**-fies**, **-fying**, **-fied**) indicate or suggest > **signification** n (pl **-s**)

signifying v ▷ **signify**

signing n (pl **-s**) system of communication by gestures, used by deaf people ▶ v ▷ **sign**

signings n ▷ **signing**

signor n (pl **-s**) Italian term of address equivalent to sir or Mr

signora n (pl **-s**) Italian term of address equivalent to madam or Mrs

signoras n ▷ **signora**

signors n ▷ **signor**

signpost n (pl **-s**) post bearing a sign that shows the way

signposts n ▷ **signpost**

signs n, v ▷ **sign**

silage n (pl **-s**) fodder crop harvested while green and partially fermented in a silo or plastic bags

silages n ▷ **silage**

silence n (pl **-s**) absence of noise or speech ▶ v (**-ces**, **-cing**, **-ced**) make silent > **silent** adj > **silently** adv

silenced v ▷ **silence**

silencer n (pl **-s**) device to reduce the noise of an engine exhaust or gun

silencers n ▷ **silencer**

silences n, v ▷ **silence**

silencing v ▷ **silence**

silent adj ▷ **silence**

silently adv ▷ **silence**

silica n (pl -s) hard glossy mineral found as quartz and in sandstone
silicas n ▷ silica

silicon n (pl -s) CHEM brittle nonmetallic element widely used in chemistry and industry

silicone n (pl -s) tough synthetic substance made from silicon and used in lubricants, paints, and resins
silicones n ▷ silicone
silicons n ▷ silicon

silk n (pl -s) fibre made by the larva (**silkworm**) of a certain moth
silken adj ▷ silk
silks n ▷ silk

silky, silken adj or like silk

sill n (pl -s) ledge at the bottom of a window or door
sillier adj ▷ silly
silliest adj ▷ silly
silliness n ▷ silly
sillinesses n ▷ silly
sills n ▷ sill

silly adj (-lier, -liest) foolish > silliness n (pl -es)

silo n (pl -los) pit or airtight tower for storing silage or grains
silos n ▷ silo

silt n (pl -s) mud deposited by moving water ▶ v (-s, -ing, -ed) (foll. by up) fill or be choked with silt
silted v ▷ silt
silting v ▷ silt
silts n, v ▷ silt

silvan adj ▷ sylvan

silver n (pl -s) white precious metal ▶ adj made of or of the colour of silver
silvers n ▷ silver

sim n (pl -s) computer game that simulates an activity such as flying or playing a sport

simian adj, n (pl -s) (of or like) a monkey or ape
simians n ▷ simian

similar adj alike but not identical > similarity n (pl -ties) > similarly adv
similarities n ▷ similar
similarity n ▷ similar
similarly adv ▷ similar

simile n (pl -s) figure of speech comparing one thing to another, using 'as' or 'like'
similes n ▷ simile

simmer v (-s, -ing, -ed) cook gently at just below boiling point
simmered v ▷ simmer
simmering v ▷ simmer
simmers v ▷ simmer

simper v (-s, -ing, -ed) smile in a silly or affected way ▶ n (pl -s) simpering smile
simpered v ▷ simper
simpering v ▷ simper
simpers v, n ▷ simper

simple adj (-r, -st) easy to understand or do > **simply** adv > **simplicity** n (pl -ties)
simpler adj ▷ simple
simplest adj ▷ simple
simplicities n ▷ simple
simplicity n ▷ simple
simplification n ▷ simplify
simplifications n ▷ simplify
simplified v ▷ simplify
simplifies v ▷ simplify

simplify v (-fies, -fying, -fied) make less complicated > **simplification** n (pl -s)
simplifying v ▷ simplify
simply adv ▷ simple
sims n ▷ sim

simulate v (-tes, -ting, -ted) make a pretence of > **simulation** n (pl -s) > **simulator** n (pl -s)
simulated v ▷ simulate
simulates v ▷ simulate
simulating v ▷ simulate
simulation n ▷ simulate
simulations n ▷ simulate
simulator n ▷ simulate
simulators n ▷ simulate

sin¹ n (pl -s) breaking of a religious or moral law ▶ v (-s, -nning, -nned) commit a sin > **sinner** n (pl -s)

sin² n MATHS sine

since prep during the period of time after ▶ conj from the time when ▶ adv from that time

sincere adj (-r, -st) without pretence

or deceit > **sincerely** adv > **sincerity** n
(pl **-ties**)
sincerely adv > **sincere**
sincerer adj > **sincere**
sincerest adj > **sincere**
sincerities n > **sincere**
sincerity n > **sincere**
sine n (pl **-s**) (in trigonometry) ratio of
the length of the opposite side to that
of the hypotenuse in a right-angled
triangle
sinecure n (pl **-s**) paid job with
minimal duties
sinecures n > **sinecure**
sines n > **sine**
sinew n (pl **-s**) tough fibrous tissue
joining muscle to bone > **sinewy** adj
(**-wier**, **-wiest**)
sinewier adj > **sinew**
sinewiest adj > **sinew**
sinews n > **sinew**
sinewy adj > **sinew**
sinful adj guilty of sin > **sinfully** adv
sinfully adv > **sinful**
sing v (**-s**, **-ing**, **sang**, **sung**) make
musical sounds with the voice
singe v (**-ges**, **-geing**, **-ged**) burn the
surface of ▶ n (pl **-s**) superficial burn
singed v > **singe**
singeing v > **singe**
singer n (pl **-s**) person who sings, esp.
professionally
singers n > **singer**
singes v, n > **singe**
singing v > **singe**
single adj one only ▶ n (pl **-s**) single
thing ▶ v (**-les**, **-ling**, **-led**) (foll. by **out**)
pick out from others > **singly** adv
singled v > **single**
singles n, v > **single** ▶ pl n game
between two players
singlet n (pl **-s**) sleeveless vest
singlets n > **singlet**
singling v > **single**
singly adv > **single**
sings v > **single**
singsong n (pl **-s**) informal singing
session ▶ adj (of the voice) repeatedly
rising and falling in pitch

singsongs n > **singsong**
singular adj (of a word or form)
denoting one person or thing ▶ n (pl **-s**)
singular form of a word > **singularity** n
(pl **-ties**) > **singularly** adv
singularities n > **singular**
singularity n > **singular**
singularly adv > **singular**
singulars n > **singular**
sinister adj threatening or suggesting
evil or harm
sink v (**-s**, **-ing**, **sank**, **sunk** or **sunken**)
submerge (in liquid) ▶ n (pl **-s**) fixed
basin with a water supply and
drainage pipe
sinker n (pl **-s**) weight for a fishing line
sinkers n > **sinker**
sinking v > **sink**
sinks v, n > **sink**
sinned v > **sin**[1]
sinner n (pl **-s**) > **sin**[1]
sinners n > **sin**[1]
sinning v > **sin**[1]
sins n, v > **sin**[1]
sinuous adj curving > **sinuously** adv
sinuously adv > **sinuous**
sinus n (pl **-nuses**) hollow space in a
bone, esp. an air passage opening into
the nose
sinuses n > **sinus**
sip v (**-s**, **-pping**, **-pped**) drink in small
mouthfuls ▶ n (pl **-s**) amount sipped
siphon n (pl **-s**) bent tube which uses
air pressure to draw liquid from a
container ▶ v (**-s**, **-ing**, **-ed**) draw
off thus
siphoned v > **siphon**
siphoning v > **siphon**
siphons n, v > **siphon**
sipped v > **sip**
sipping v > **sip**
sips v, n > **sip**
sir n (pl **-s**) polite term of address for
a man
sire n (pl **-s**) male parent of a horse or
other domestic animal ▶ v (**-res**, **-ring**,
-red) father
sired v > **sire**
siren n (pl **-s**) device making a loud

wailing noise as a warning
sirens n ▷ **siren**
sires n, v ▷ **sire**
siring v ▷ **sire**
sirloin n (pl -s) prime cut of loin of beef
sirloins n ▷ **sirloin**
sirocco n (pl -s) hot wind blowing from N Africa into S Europe
siroccos n ▷ **sirocco**
sirs n ▷ **sir**
sis interj s AFR informal exclamation of disgust
sisal n (pl -s) (fibre of) plant used in making ropes
sisals n ▷ **sisal**
siskin n (pl -s) yellow-and-black finch
siskins n ▷ **siskin**
sissier adj ▷ **sissy**
sissies n ▷ **sissy**
sissiest adj ▷ **sissy**
sissy adj (-sier, -siest) ▶ n (pl -ssies) weak or cowardly (person)
sister n (pl -s) girl or woman with the same parents as another person ▶ adj closely related, similar > **sisterly** adj
sisterly adj ▷ **sister**
sisters n ▷ **sister**
sit v (-s, -tting, sat) rest one's body upright on the buttocks
sitar n (pl -s) Indian stringed musical instrument
sitars n ▷ **sitar**
sitcom n (pl -s) informal situation comedy
sitcoms n ▷ **sitcom**
site n (pl -s) place where something is, was, or is intended to be located ▷ **website** ▶ v (-tes, -ting, -ted) provide with a site
sited v ▷ **site**
sites n, v ▷ **site**
siting v ▷ **site**
sits v ▷ **sit**
sitting v ▷ **sit**
situate v (-tes, -ting, -ted) place
situated v ▷ **situate**
situates v ▷ **situate**
situating v ▷ **situate**
six adj, n (pl -es) one more than five

sixes n ▷ **six**
sixteen adj, n (pl -s) six and ten
> **sixteenth** adj, n (pl -s)
sixteens n ▷ **sixteen**
sixteenth ▷ **sixteen**
sixteenths n ▷ **sixteen**
sixth adj, n (pl -s) (of) number six in a series
sixths n ▷ **sixth**
sixties n ▷ **sixty**
sixtieth n ▷ **sixty**
sixtieths n ▷ **sixty**
sixty adj, n (pl -ies) six times ten > **sixtieth** adj, n (pl -s)
sizable adj ▷ **sizeable**
size¹ n (pl -s) dimensions, bigness ▶ v (-zes, -zing, -zed) arrange according to size
size² n (pl -s) gluey substance used as a protective coating
sizeable, sizable adj quite large
sized v ▷ **size¹**
sizes n ▷ **size¹, ²** v ▷ **size¹**
sizing v ▷ **size¹**
sizzle v (-les, -ling, -led) make a hissing sound like frying fat
sizzled v ▷ **sizzle**
sizzles v ▷ **sizzle**
sizzling v ▷ **sizzle**
skanky adj slang dirty or unattractive
skate¹ n (pl -s) boot with a steel blade or sets of wheels attached to the sole for gliding over ice or a hard surface ▶ v (-tes, -ting, -ted) glide on or as if on skates
skate² n (pl -s) large marine flatfish
skated v ▷ **skate¹**
skates n ▷ **skate¹, ²** v ▷ **skate¹**
skating v ▷ **skate¹**
skein n (pl -s) yarn wound in a loose coil
skeins n ▷ **skein**
skeletal adj ▷ **skeleton**
skeleton n (pl -s) framework of bones inside a person's or animal's body ▶ adj reduced to a minimum > **skeletal** adj
skeletons n ▷ **skeleton**
sketch n (pl -es) rough drawing ▶ v (-es, -ing, -ed) make a sketch (of)
sketched v ▷ **sketch**

sketches n, v ▷ **sketch**
sketchier adj ▷ **sketchy**
sketchiest adj ▷ **sketchy**
sketching v ▷ **sketch**
sketchy adj (-chier, -chiest) incomplete or inadequate
skew v (-s, -ing, -ed) make slanting or crooked ▶ adj slanting or crooked
skewed v ▷ **skew**
skewer n (pl -s) pin to hold meat together during cooking ▶ v (-s, -ing, -ed) fasten with a skewer
skewered v ▷ **skewer**
skewering v ▷ **skewer**
skewers n, v ▷ **skewer**
skewing v ▷ **skew**
skews v ▷ **skew**
ski n (pl -s) one of a pair of long runners fastened to boots for gliding over snow or water ▶ v (**skis, skiing, skied**) travel on skis ▶ **skier** n (pl -s)
skid v (-s, -dding, -dded) (of a moving vehicle) slide sideways uncontrollably ▶ n (pl -s) skidding
skidded v ▷ **skid**
skidding v ▷ **skid**
skids v, n ▷ **skid**
skied v ▷ **ski**
skier n ▷ **ski**
skiers n ▷ **ski**
skies n ▷ **sky**
skiff n (pl -s) small boat
skiffs n ▷ **skiff**
skiing v ▷ **ski**
skilful adj having or showing skill
> **skilfully** adv
skilfully adv ▷ **skilful**
skill n (pl -s) special ability or expertise
> **skilled** adj
skilled adj ▷ **skill**
skillet n (pl -s) small frying pan or shallow cooking pot
skillets n ▷ **skillet**
skills n ▷ **skill**
skim v (-s, -mming, -mmed) remove floating matter from the surface of (a liquid)
skimmed v ▷ **skim**
skimming v ▷ **skim**

skimp v (-s, -ing, -ed) not invest enough time, money, material, etc
skimped v ▷ **skimp**
skimpier adj ▷ **skimpy**
skimpiest adj ▷ **skimpy**
skimping v ▷ **skimp**
skimps v ▷ **skimp**
skimpy adj (-pier, -piest) scanty or insufficient
skims v ▷ **skim**
skin n (pl -s) outer covering of the body ▶ v (-s, -nning, -nned) remove the skin of ▷ **skinless** adj
skinhead n (pl -s) youth with very short hair
skinheads n ▷ **skinhead**
skinless adj ▷ **skin**
skinned v ▷ **skin**
skinnier adj ▷ **skinny**
skinniest adj ▷ **skinny**
skinning v ▷ **skin**
skinny adj (-nnier, -nniest) thin
skins n, v ▷ **skin**
skint adj BRIT slang having no money
skip¹ v (-s, -pping, -pped) leap lightly from one foot to the other ▶ n (pl -s) skipping
skip² n (pl -s) large open container for builders' rubbish
skipped v ▷ **skip**¹
skipper n (pl -s) ▶ v (-s, -ing, -ed) captain
skippered v ▷ **skipper**
skippering v ▷ **skipper**
skippers n, v ▷ **skipper**
skipping v ▷ **skip**¹
skips v ▷ **skip**¹ ▶ n ▷ **skip**¹, ²
skirl n (pl -s) sound of bagpipes
skirls n ▷ **skirl**
skirmish n (pl -es) brief or minor fight or argument ▶ v (-es, -ing, -ed) take part in a skirmish
skirmished v ▷ **skirmish**
skirmishes n, v ▷ **skirmish**
skirmishing v ▷ **skirmish**
skirt n (pl -s) woman's garment hanging from the waist ▶ v (-s, -ing, -ed) border
skirted v ▷ **skirt**
skirting v ▷ **skirt**

skirts n, v ▷ skirt
skis n, v ▷ ski
skit n (pl -s) brief satirical sketch
skite v (-tes, -ting, -ted) ▶ n (pl -s) AUST
G-NZ boast
skited v ▷ skite
skites v, n ▷ skite
skiting v ▷ skite
skits n ▷ skit
skittish adj playful or lively
skittle n (pl -s) bottle-shaped object
used as a target in some games
skittles n ▷ skittle ▶ pl n game in
which players try to knock over skittles
by rolling a ball at them
skive v (-ves, -ving, -ved) BRIT informal
evade work or responsibility
skived v ▷ skive
skives v ▷ skive
skiving v ▷ skive
skivvies n ▷ skivvy
skivvy n (pl -vies) BRIT female servant
who does menial work
skua n (pl -s) large predatory gull
skuas n ▷ skua
skulk v (-s, -ing, -ed) move stealthily
skulked v ▷ skulk
skulking v ▷ skulk
skulks v ▷ skulk
skull n (pl -s) bony framework of the
head
skullcap n (pl -s) close-fitting brimless
cap
skullcaps n ▷ skullcap
skulls n ▷ skull
skunk n (pl -s) small black-and-white N
American mammal which emits a foul-
smelling fluid when attacked
skunks n ▷ skunk
sky n (pl skies) upper atmosphere as
seen from the earth
skylark n (pl -s) lark that sings while
soaring at a great height
skylarks n ▷ skylark
skylight n (pl -s) window in a roof
or ceiling
skylights n ▷ skylight
slab n (pl -s) broad flat piece
slabs n ▷ slab

slack adj (-er, -est) not tight ▶ n (pl -s)
slack part ▶ v (-s, -ing, -ed) neglect
one's work or duty ▷ slacker n (pl -s)
> slackness n (pl -es)
slacked v ▷ slack
slacken v (-s, -ing, -ed) make or
become slack
slackened v ▷ slacken
slackening v ▷ slacken
slackens v ▷ slacken
slacker n, adj ▷ slack
slackers n ▷ slack
slackest adj ▷ slack
slacking v ▷ slack
slackness n ▷ slack
slacknesses n ▷ slack
slacks n, v ▷ slack ▶ pl n informal
trousers
slag n (pl -s) waste left after metal is
smelted ▶ v (-s, -gging, -gged) (foll. by
off) BRIT, AUST G-NZ slang criticize
slagged v ▷ slag
slagging v ▷ slag
slags n, v ▷ slag
slain v ▷ slay
slake v (-kes, -king, -ked) satisfy (thirst
or desire)
slaked v ▷ slake
slakes v ▷ slake
slaking v ▷ slake
slalom n (pl -s) skiing or canoeing race
over a winding course
slaloms n ▷ slalom
slam v (-s, -mming, -mmed) shut, put
down, or hit violently and noisily ▶ n (pl
-s) act or sound of slamming
slammed v ▷ slam
slamming v ▷ slam
slams v, n ▷ slam
slander n (pl -s) false and malicious
statement about a person ▶ v
(-s, -ing, -ed) utter slander about
> slanderous adj
slandered v ▷ slander
slandering v ▷ slander
slanderous adj ▷ slander
slanders n, v ▷ slander
slang n (pl -s) very informal language
> slangy adj (-gier, -giest)

slangier adj ▷ **slang**
slangiest adj ▷ **slang**
slangs n ▷ **slang**
slangy adj ▷ **slang**
slant v (-s, -ing, -ed) lean at an angle, slope ▶ n (pl -s) slope ▷ **slanting** adj
slanted v ▷ **slant**
slanting v, adj ▷ **slant**
slants v, n ▷ **slant**
slap n (pl -s) blow with the open hand or a flat object ▶ v (-s, -pping, -pped) strike with the open hand or a flat object
slapdash adj careless and hasty
slapped v ▷ **slap**
slapping v ▷ **slap**
slaps n, v ▷ **slap**
slash v (-es, -ing, -ed) cut with a sweeping stroke ▶ n (pl -es) sweeping stroke
slashed v ▷ **slash**
slashes v, n ▷ **slash**
slashing v ▷ **slash**
slat n (pl -s) narrow strip of wood or metal
slate[1] n (pl -s) rock which splits easily into thin layers
slate[2] v (-tes, -ting, -ted) informal criticize harshly
slated v ▷ **slate**[2]
slates n ▷ **slate**[1] ▶ v ▷ **slate**[2]
slating v ▷ **slate**[2]
slats n ▷ **slat**
slattern n (pl -s) old-fashioned slovenly woman ▷ **slatternly** adj
slatternly adv ▷ **slattern**
slatterns n ▷ **slattern**
slave n (pl -s) person owned by another for whom he or she has to work ▶ v (-ves, -ing, -ved) work like a slave
slaved v ▷ **slave**
slaver n (pl -s) person or ship engaged in the slave trade ▶ v (-s, -ing, -ed) dribble saliva from the mouth
slavered v ▷ **slaver**
slaveries n ▷ **slavery**
slavering v ▷ **slaver**
slavers n, v ▷ **slaver**
slavery n (pl -ries) state or condition of being a slave

slaves n, v ▷ **slave**
slaving v ▷ **slave**
slavish adj of or like a slave
slay v (-s, -ing, slew, slain) kill
slaying v ▷ **slay**
slays v ▷ **slay**
sleaze n ▷ **sleazy**
sleazes n ▷ **sleazy**
sleazier adj ▷ **sleazy**
sleaziest adj ▷ **sleazy**
sleazy adj (-zier, -ziest) run-down or sordid ▷ **sleaze** n (pl -s)
sled n (pl -s) ▶ v (-s, -dding, -dded) (travel by) sledge
sledded v ▷ **sled**
sledding v ▷ **sled**
sledge[1] n (pl -s) carriage on runners for sliding on snow ▶ v (-ges, -ging, -ged) travel by sledge
sledge[2], **sledgehammer** n (pl -s) heavy hammer with a long handle
sledged v ▷ **sledge**[1]
sledgehammer n ▷ **sledge**
sledgehammers n ▷ **sledge**
sledges n ▷ **sledge**[1, 2] ▶ v ▷ **sledge**[1]
sledging v ▷ **sledge**[1]
sleds n, v ▷ **sled**
sleek adj (-er, -est) glossy, smooth, and shiny
sleeker adj ▷ **sleek**
sleekest adj ▷ **sleek**
sleep n (pl -s) state of rest characterized by unconsciousness ▶ v (-s, -ing, slept) be in or as if in a state of sleep ▷ **sleepy** adj (-pier, -piest) ▷ **sleepily** adv ▷ **sleepiness** n (pl -es) ▷ **sleepless** adj
sleeper n (pl -s) railway car fitted for sleeping in
sleepers n ▷ **sleeper**
sleepier adj ▷ **sleep**
sleepiest adj ▷ **sleep**
sleepily adv ▷ **sleep**
sleepiness n ▷ **sleep**
sleepinesses n ▷ **sleep**
sleeping v ▷ **sleep**
sleepless adj ▷ **sleep**
sleepout n (pl -s) NZ small building for sleeping in

sleepouts n ▷ **sleepout**
sleeps n, v ▷ **sleep**
sleepy adj ▷ **sleep**
sleet n (pl -s) rain and snow or hail falling together
sleets n ▷ **sleet**
sleeve n (pl -s) part of a garment which covers the arm ▷ **sleeveless** adj
sleeveless adj ▷ **sleeve**
sleeves n ▷ **sleeve**
sleigh n (pl -s) ▷ v (-s, -ing, -ed) sledge
sleighed v ▷ **sleigh**
sleighing v ▷ **sleigh**
sleighs n, v ▷ **sleigh**
slender adj (-er, -est) slim
slenderer adj ▷ **slender**
slenderest adj ▷ **slender**
slept v ▷ **sleep**
sleuth n (pl -s) detective
sleuths n ▷ **sleuth**
slew¹ v ▷ **slay**
slew² v (-s, -ing, -ed) twist or swing round
slewed v ▷ **slew²**
slewing v ▷ **slew²**
slews v ▷ **slew²**
slice n (pl -s) thin flat piece cut from something ▷ v (-ces, -cing, -ced) cut into slices
sliced v ▷ **slice**
slices n, v ▷ **slice**
slicing v ▷ **slice**
slick adj (-er, -est) persuasive and glib ▷ n (pl -s) patch of oil on water ▷ v (-s, -ing, -ed) make smooth or sleek
slicked v ▷ **slick**
slicker adj ▷ **slick**
slickest adj ▷ **slick**
slicking v ▷ **slick**
slicks n, v ▷ **slick**
slid v ▷ **slide**
slide v (-des, -ding, slid) move smoothly along (a surface) ▷ n (pl -s) sliding
slides v, n ▷ **slide**
sliding v ▷ **slide**
slier adj ▷ **sly**
sliest adj ▷ **sly**
slight adj (-er, -est) small in quantity or extent ▷ v (-s, -ing, -ed) ▷ n (pl -s) snub

> **slightly** adv
slighted v ▷ **slight**
slighter adj ▷ **slight**
slightest adj ▷ **slight**
slighting v ▷ **slight**
slightly adv ▷ **slight**
slights v, n ▷ **slight**
slim adj (-mmer, -mmest) not heavy or stout, thin ▷ v (-s, -mming, -mmed) make or become slim by diet and exercise ▷ **slimmer** n (pl -s)
slime n (pl -s) unpleasant thick slippery substance
slimes n ▷ **slime**
slimier adj ▷ **slimy**
slimiest adj ▷ **slimy**
slimmed v ▷ **slim**
slimmer adj, n ▷ **slim**
slimmers n ▷ **slim**
slimmest adj ▷ **slim**
slimming v ▷ **slim**
slims v ▷ **slim**
slimy adj (-mier, -miest) of, like, or covered with slime
sling¹ n (pl -s) bandage hung from the neck to support an injured hand or arm ▷ v (-s, -ing, slung) throw
sling² n (pl -s) sweetened drink with a spirit base
slinging v ▷ **sling¹**
slings n ▷ **sling¹, ²** v ▷ **sling¹**
slink v (-s, -ing, slunk) move furtively or guiltily
slinkier adj ▷ **slinky**
slinkiest adj ▷ **slinky**
slinking v ▷ **slink**
slinks v ▷ **slink**
slinky adj (-kier, -kiest) (of clothes) figure-hugging
slip¹ v (-s, -pping, -pped) lose balance by sliding ▷ n (pl -s) slipping
slip² n (pl -s) small piece (of paper)
slip³ n (pl -s) clay mixed with water used for decorating pottery
slipknot n (pl -s) knot tied so that it will slip along the rope round which it is made
slipknots n ▷ **slipknot**
slipped v ▷ **slip¹**

slipper n (pl **-s**) light shoe for indoor wear
slipperier adj ▷ **slippery**
slipperiest adj ▷ **slippery**
slippers n ▷ **slipper**
slippery adj (**-rier, -riest**) so smooth or wet as to cause slipping or be difficult to hold
slippier adj ▷ **slippy**
slippiest adj ▷ **slippy**
slipping v ▷ **slip**¹
slippy adj (**-pier, -ppiest**) informal slippery
slips n ▷ **slip**¹, ², ³ ▷ v ▷ **slip**¹
slipshod adj (of an action) careless
slipway n (pl **-s**) launching slope on which ships are built or repaired
slipways n ▷ **slipway**
slit n (pl **-s**) long narrow cut or opening ▷ v (**-s, -tting, slit**) make a long straight cut in
slither v (**-s, -ing, -ed**) slide unsteadily
slithered v ▷ **slither**
slithering v ▷ **slither**
slithers v ▷ **slither**
slits n, v ▷ **slit**
slitting v ▷ **slit**
sliver n (pl **-s**) small thin piece
slivers n ▷ **sliver**
slob n (pl **-s**) informal lazy and untidy person > **slobbish** adj
slobber v (**-s, -ing, -ed**) dribble or drool > **slobbery** adj
slobbered v ▷ **slobber**
slobbering v ▷ **slobber**
slobbers v ▷ **slobber**
slobbery adj ▷ **slobber**
slobbish adj ▷ **slob**
slobs n ▷ **slob**
sloe n (pl **-s**) sour blue-black fruit
sloes n ▷ **sloe**
slog v (**-s, -gging, -gged**) work hard and steadily ▷ n (pl **-s**) long and exhausting work or walk
slogan n (pl **-s**) catchword or phrase used in politics or advertising
slogans n ▷ **slogan**
slogged v ▷ **slog**
slogging v ▷ **slog**

slogs v, n ▷ **slog**
sloop n (pl **-s**) small single-masted ship
sloops n ▷ **sloop**
slop v (**-s, -pping, -pped**) splash or spill ▷ n (pl **-s**) spilt liquid
slope v (**-pes, -ping, -ped**) slant ▷ n (pl **-s**) sloping surface
sloped v ▷ **slope**
slopes v, n ▷ **slope** ▷ pl n hills
sloping v ▷ **slope**
slopped v ▷ **slop**
sloppier adj ▷ **sloppy**
sloppiest adj ▷ **sloppy**
slopping v ▷ **slop**
sloppy adj (**-pier, -ppiest**) careless or untidy
slops v, n ▷ **slop** ▷ pl n liquid refuse and waste food used to feed animals
slosh v (**-es, -ing, -ed**) splash carelessly ▷ n (pl **-es**) splashing sound
sloshed adj slang drunk ▷ v ▷ **slosh**
sloshes v, n ▷ **slosh**
sloshing v ▷ **slosh**
slot n (pl **-s**) narrow opening for inserting something ▷ v (**-s, -tting, -tted**) make a slot or slots in
sloth n (pl **-s**) slow-moving animal of tropical America
slothful adj lazy or idle
sloths n ▷ **sloth**
slots n, v ▷ **slot**
slotted v ▷ **slot**
slotting v ▷ **slot**
slouch v (**-es, -ing, -ed**) sit, stand, or move with a drooping posture ▷ n (pl **-es**) drooping posture
slouched v ▷ **slouch**
slouches v, n ▷ **slouch**
slouching v ▷ **slouch**
slough¹ n (pl **-s**) bog
slough² v (**-s, -ing, -ed**) (of a snake) shed (its skin) or (of a skin) be shed
sloughed v ▷ **slough**²
sloughing v ▷ **slough**²
sloughs n ▷ **slough**¹ ▷ v ▷ **slough**²
sloven n (pl **-s**) habitually dirty or untidy person
slovenlier adj ▷ **slovenly**
slovenliest adj ▷ **slovenly**

slovenly adj (-lier, -liest) dirty or untidy
slovens n ▷ sloven
slow adj (-er, -est) taking a longer time than is usual or expected ▶ v (-s, -ing, -ed) reduce the speed (of) > **slowly** adv > **slowness** n (pl -es)
slowed v ▷ slow
slower adj ▷ slow
slowest adj ▷ slow
slowing v ▷ slow
slowly adv ▷ slow
slowness n ▷ slow
slownesses n ▷ slow
slows v ▷ slow
slowworm n (pl -s) small legless lizard
slowworms n ▷ slowworm
sludge n (pl -s) thick mud
sludges n ▷ sludge
slug¹ n (pl -s) land snail with no shell
slug² n (pl -s) bullet informal
slug³ v (-gging, -gged) hit hard ▶ n (pl -s) heavy blow
sluggard n (pl -s) lazy person
sluggards n ▷ sluggard
slugged v ▷ slug³
slugging v ▷ slug³
sluggish adj slow-moving, lacking energy > **sluggishly** adv > **sluggishness** n (pl -es)
sluggishly adv ▷ sluggish
sluggishness n ▷ sluggish
sluggishnesses n ▷ sluggish
slugs n ▷ slug¹, ², ³ v ▷ slug³
sluice n (pl -s) channel carrying off water ▶ v (-ces, -cing, -ced) pour a stream of water over or through
sluiced v ▷ sluice
sluices n, v ▷ sluice
sluicing v ▷ sluice
slum n (pl -s) squalid overcrowded house or area ▶ v (-s, -mming, -mmed) temporarily and deliberately experience poorer places or conditions than usual
slumber v (-s, -ing, -ed) ▶ n (pl -s) lit sleep
slumbered v ▷ slumber
slumbering v ▷ slumber

slumbers v, n ▷ slumber
slummed v ▷ slum
slumming v ▷ slum
slump v (-s, -ing, -ed) (of prices or demand) decline suddenly ▶ n (pl -s) sudden decline in prices or demand
slumped v ▷ slump
slumping v ▷ slump
slumps v, n ▷ slump
slung v ▷ sling¹
slunk v ▷ slink
slur v (-s, -rring, -rred) pronounce or utter (words) indistinctly ▶ n (pl -s) slurring of words
slurp informal v (-s, -ing, -ed) eat or drink noisily ▶ n (pl -s) slurping sound
slurped v ▷ slurp
slurping v ▷ slurp
slurps v, n ▷ slurp
slurred v ▷ slur
slurries n ▷ slurry
slurring v ▷ slur
slurry n (pl -ries) muddy liquid mixture
slurs v, n ▷ slur
slush n (pl -es) watery muddy substance > **slushy** adj (-shier, -shiest)
slushes n ▷ slush
slushier adj ▷ slush
slushiest adj ▷ slush
slushy adj ▷ slush
sly adj (slyer or slier, slyest or sliest) crafty > **slyly** adv > **slyness** n (pl -es)
slyer adj ▷ sly
slyest adj ▷ sly
slyly adv ▷ sly
slyness n ▷ sly
slynesses n ▷ sly
smack¹ v (-s, -ing, -ed) slap sharply ▶ n (pl -s) sharp slap ▶ adv informal squarely or directly
smack² n (pl -s) slight flavour or trace ▶ v (-s, -ing, -ed) have a slight flavour or trace (of)
smack³ n (pl -s) small single-masted fishing boat
smacked v ▷ smack¹, ²
smacker n (pl -s) slang loud kiss
smackers n ▷ smacker

smacking v ⊳ **smack**[1, 2]
smacks n ⊳ **smack**[1, 2, 3] ▶ v
⊳ **smack**[1, 2]
small adj (**-er, -est**) not large in size, number, or amount ▶ n (pl **-s**) narrow part of the lower back ⊳ **smallness** n (pl **-es**)
smaller adj ⊳ **small**
smallest adj ⊳ **small**
smallness n ⊳ **small**
smallnesses n ⊳ **small**
smallpox n (pl **-es**) contagious disease with blisters that leave scars
smallpoxes n ⊳ **smallpox**
smalls n ⊳ **small** ▶ pl n informal underwear
smarmier adj ⊳ **smarmy**
smarmiest adj ⊳ **smarmy**
smarmy adj (**-mier, -miest**) informal unpleasantly suave or flattering
smart adj (**-er, -est**) well-kept and neat ▶ v (**-s, -ing, -ed**) feel or cause stinging pain ▶ n (pl **-s**) stinging pain > **smartly** adv ⊳ **smartness** n (pl **-es**)
smarted v ⊳ **smart**
smarten v (**-s, -ing, -ed**) make or become smart
smartened v ⊳ **smarten**
smartening v ⊳ **smarten**
smartens v ⊳ **smarten**
smarter adj ⊳ **smart**
smartest adj ⊳ **smart**
smarting v ⊳ **smart**
smartly adv ⊳ **smart**
smartness n ⊳ **smart**
smartnesses n ⊳ **smart**
smarts v, n ⊳ **smart**
smash v (**-es, -ing, -ed**) break violently and noisily ▶ n (pl **-es**) act or sound of smashing
smashed v ⊳ **smash**
smasher n (pl **-s**) informal attractive person or thing
smashers n ⊳ **smasher**
smashes v, n ⊳ **smash**
smashing adj informal excellent ▶ v ⊳ **smash**
smear v (**-s, -ing, -ed**) spread with a greasy or sticky substance ▶ n (pl **-s**)

dirty mark or smudge
smeared v ⊳ **smear**
smearing v ⊳ **smear**
smears v, n ⊳ **smear**
smell v (**-s, -ing, smelt** or **-ed**) perceive (a scent or odour) by means of the nose ▶ n (pl **-s**) ability to perceive odours by the nose
smelled v ⊳ **smell**
smellier adj ⊳ **smelly**
smelliest adj ⊳ **smelly**
smelling v ⊳ **smell**
smells v, n ⊳ **smell**
smelly adj (**-lier, -liest**) having a nasty smell
smelt[1] v (**-s, -ing, -ed**) extract (a metal) from (an ore) by heating
smelt[2] n (pl **smelt**) small fish of the salmon family
smelt[3] v ⊳ **smell**
smelted v ⊳ **smelt**[1]
smelter n (pl **-s**) industrial plant where smelting is carried out
smelters n ⊳ **smelter**
smelting v ⊳ **smelt**[1]
smelts v ⊳ **smelt**[1]
smile n (pl **-s**) turning up of the corners of the mouth to show pleasure, amusement, or friendliness ▶ v (**-les, -ing, -led**) give a smile
smiled v ⊳ **smile**
smiles n, v ⊳ **smile**
smiley n (pl **-s**) symbol depicting a smile or other facial expression, used in e-mail
smileys n ⊳ **smiley**
smiling v ⊳ **smile**
smirch v (**-es, -ing, -ed**) stain ▶ n (pl **-es**) stain
smirched v ⊳ **smirch**
smirches v, n ⊳ **smirch**
smirching v ⊳ **smirch**
smirk n (pl **-s**) smug smile ▶ v (**-s, -ing, -ed**) give a smirk
smirked v ⊳ **smirk**
smirking v ⊳ **smirk**
smirks n, v ⊳ **smirk**
smite v (**-tes, -ting, smote, smitten**) old-fashioned strike hard

smites v ▷ smite

smith n (pl -s) worker in metal

smithies n ▷ smithy

smiths n ▷ smith

smithy n (pl -thies) blacksmith's workshop

smiting v ▷ smite

smitten v ▷ smite

smock n (pl -s) loose overall ▶ v (-s, -ing, -ed) gather (material) by sewing in a honeycomb pattern > **smocking** n (pl -s)

smocked v ▷ smock

smocking v, n ▷ smock

smockings n ▷ smock

smocks n, v ▷ smock

smog n (pl -s) mixture of smoke and fog

smogs n ▷ smog

smoke n (pl -s) cloudy mass that rises from something burning ▶ v (-kes, -king, -ked) give off smoke > **smokeless** adj > **smoker** n (pl -s) > **smoky** adj (-kier, -kiest)

smoked v ▷ smoke

smokeless adj ▷ smoke

smoker n ▷ smoke

smokers n ▷ smoke

smokes n, v ▷ smoke

smokier adj ▷ smoke

smokiest adj ▷ smoke

smoking v ▷ smoke

smoky adj ▷ smoke

smooch informal v (-es, -ing, -ed) kiss and cuddle ▶ n (pl -es) smooching

smooched v ▷ smooch

smooches v, n ▷ smooch

smooching v, n ▷ smooch

smooth adj (-er, -est) even in surface, texture, or consistency ▶ v (-s, -ing, -ed) make smooth > **smoothly** adv

smoothed v ▷ smooth

smoother adj ▷ smooth

smoothest adj ▷ smooth

smoothie n (pl -thies) informal charming but possibly insincere man

smoothies n ▷ smoothie

smoothing v ▷ smooth

smoothly adv ▷ smooth

smooths v ▷ smooth

smote v ▷ smite

smother v (-s, -ing, -ed) suffocate or stifle

smothered v ▷ smother

smothering v ▷ smother

smothers v ▷ smother

smoulder v (-s, -ing, -ed) burn slowly with smoke but no flame

smouldered v ▷ smoulder

smouldering v ▷ smoulder

smoulders v ▷ smoulder

smudge v (-ges, -ging, -ged) make or become smeared or soiled ▶ n (pl -s) dirty mark > **smudgy** adj (-gier, -giest)

smudged v ▷ smudge

smudges v, n ▷ smudge

smudgier adj ▷ smudge

smudgiest adj ▷ smudge

smudging v ▷ smudge

smudgy adj ▷ smudge

smug adj (-gger, -ggest) self-satisfied > **smugly** adv > **smugness** n (pl -es)

smugger adj ▷ smug

smuggest adj ▷ smug

smuggle v (-les, -ling, -led) import or export (goods) secretly and illegally > **smuggler** n (pl -s)

smuggled v ▷ smuggle

smuggler n ▷ smuggle

smugglers n ▷ smuggle

smuggles v ▷ smuggle

smuggling v ▷ smuggle

smugly adv ▷ smug

smugness n ▷ smug

smugnesses n ▷ smug

smut n (pl -s) obscene jokes, pictures, etc > **smutty** adj (-tier, -ttiest)

smuts n ▷ smut

smuttier adj ▷ smut

smuttiest adj ▷ smut

smutty adj ▷ smut

snack n (pl -s) light quick meal

snacks n ▷ snack

snaffle n (pl -s) jointed bit for a horse ▶ v (-les, -ling, -led) BRIT, AUST & NZ slang steal

snaffled v ▷ snaffle

snaffles n, v ▷ snaffle

snaffling v ▷ snaffle

snag n (pl -s) difficulty or disadvantage ▶ v (-s, -gging, -gged) catch or tear on a point
snagged v ▷ **snag**
snagging v ▷ **snag**
snags n, v ▷ **snag**

snail n (pl -s) slow-moving mollusc with a spiral shell
snails n ▷ **snail**

snake n (pl -s) long thin scaly limbless reptile ▶ v (-kes, -king, -ked) move in a winding course like a snake
snaked v ▷ **snake**
snakes n, v ▷ **snake**
snakier adj ▷ **snaky**
snakiest adj ▷ **snaky**
snaking v ▷ **snake**

snaky adj (-kier, -kiest) twisted or winding

snap v (-s, -pping, -pped) break suddenly ▶ n (pl -s) act or sound of snapping ▶ adj made on the spur of the moment
snapped v ▷ **snap**

snapper n (pl -s) food fish of Australia and New Zealand with a pinkish body covered with blue spots
snappers n ▷ **snapper**
snappier adj ▷ **snappy**
snappiest adj ▷ **snappy**
snapping v ▷ **snap**
snappish adj ▷ **snappy**

snappy adj (-pier, -piest) (also **snappish**) irritable
snaps v, n ▷ **snap**

snapshot n (pl -s) informal photograph
snapshots n ▷ **snapshot**

snare n (pl -s) trap with a noose ▶ v (-res, -ring, -red) catch in or as if in a snare
snared v ▷ **snare**
snares n, v ▷ **snare**
snaring v ▷ **snare**

snarl[1] v (-s, -ing, -ed) (of an animal) growl with bared teeth ▶ n (pl -s) act or sound of snarling

snarl[2] n (pl -s) tangled mess ▶ v (-s, -ing, -ed) make tangled
snarled v ▷ **snarl**[1,2]

snarling v ▷ **snarl**[1,2]
snarls n, v ▷ **snarl**[1,2]

snatch v (-es, -ing, -ed) seize or try to seize suddenly ▶ n (pl -es) snatching
snatched v ▷ **snatch**
snatches v, n ▷ **snatch**
snatching v ▷ **snatch**
snazzier adj ▷ **snazzy**
snazziest adj ▷ **snazzy**

snazzy adj (-zier, -ziest) informal stylish and flashy

sneak v (-s, -ing, -ed) move furtively ▶ n (pl -s) cowardly or underhand person ▷ **sneaky** adj (-kier, -kiest)
sneaked v ▷ **sneak**

sneakers pl n canvas shoes with rubber soles
sneakier adj ▷ **sneak**
sneakiest adj ▷ **sneak**

sneaking adj slight but persistent ▶ v ▷ **sneak**
sneaks v, n ▷ **sneak**
sneaky adj ▷ **sneak**

sneer n (pl -s) contemptuous expression or remark ▶ v (-s, -ing, -ed) show contempt by a sneer
sneered v ▷ **sneer**
sneering v ▷ **sneer**
sneers n, v ▷ **sneer**

sneeze v (-zes, -zing, -zed) expel air from the nose suddenly, involuntarily, and noisily ▶ n (pl -s) act or sound of sneezing
sneezed v ▷ **sneeze**
sneezes v, n ▷ **sneeze**
sneezing v ▷ **sneeze**

snicker n (pl -s) ▶ v (-s, -ing, -ed) ▷ **snigger**
snickered v ▷ **snicker**
snickering v ▷ **snicker**
snickers n, v ▷ **snicker**

snide adj (-r, -st) critical in an unfair and nasty way
snider adj ▷ **snide**
snidest adj ▷ **snide**

sniff v (-s, -ing, -ed) inhale through the nose in short audible breaths ▶ n (pl -s) act or sound of sniffing
sniffed v ▷ **sniff**

sniffing v ▷ sniff

sniffle v (-les, -ling, -led) sniff repeatedly, as when suffering from a cold ▶ n (pl -s) slight cold

sniffled v ▷ sniffle

sniffles v, n ▷ sniffle

sniffling v ▷ sniffle

sniffs v, n ▷ sniff

snifter n (pl -s) informal small quantity of alcoholic drink

snifters v ▷ snifter

snigger n (pl -s) sly disrespectful laugh, esp. one partly stifled ▶ v (-s, -ing, -ed) utter a snigger

sniggered v ▷ snigger

sniggering v ▷ snigger

sniggers n, v ▷ snigger

snip v (-s, -pping, -pped) cut in small quick strokes with scissors or shears ▶ n (pl -s) informal bargain

snipe n (pl -s) wading bird with a long straight bill ▶ v (-pes, -ping, -ped) (foll. by **at**) shoot at (a person) from cover

sniped v ▷ snipe

sniper n (pl -s) person who shoots at someone from cover

snipers n ▷ sniper

snipes n, v ▷ snipe

sniping v ▷ snipe

snipped v ▷ snip

snippet n (pl -s) small piece

snippets n ▷ snippet

snipping v ▷ snip

snips v, n ▷ snip

snitch informal v (-es, -ing, -ed) act as an informer ▶ n (pl -es) informer

snitched v ▷ snitch

snitches v, n ▷ snitch

snitching v ▷ snitch

snivel v (-s, -lling, -lled) cry in a whining way

snivelled v ▷ snivel

snivelling v ▷ snivel

snivels v ▷ snivel

snob n (pl -s) person who judges others by social rank ▶ **snobbery** n (pl -ries) > **snobbish** adj

snobberies n ▷ snob

snobbery n ▷ snob

snobbish adj ▷ snob

snobs n ▷ snob

snoek n (pl -s) S AFR edible marine fish

snoeks n ▷ snoek

snood n (pl -s) pouch, often of net, loosely holding a woman's hair at the back

snoods n ▷ snood

snook n (pl -s) gesture of contempt

snooker n (pl -s) game played on a billiard table ▶ v (-s, -ing, -ed) leave (a snooker opponent) in a position such that another ball blocks the target ball

snookered v ▷ snooker

snookering v ▷ snooker

snookers n, v ▷ snooker

snooks n ▷ snook

snoop informal v (-s, -ing, -ed) pry ▶ n (pl -s) snooping > **snooper** n (pl -s)

snooped v ▷ snoop

snooper n ▷ snoop

snoopers n ▷ snoop

snooping v ▷ snoop

snoops v, n ▷ snoop

snootier adj ▷ snooty

snootiest adj ▷ snooty

snooty adj (-tier, -tiest) informal haughty

snooze informal v (-zes, -zing, -zed) take a brief light sleep ▶ n (pl -s) brief light sleep

snoozed v ▷ snooze

snoozes v, n ▷ snooze

snoozing v ▷ snooze

snore v (-res, -ring, -red) make snorting sounds while sleeping ▶ n (pl -s) sound of snoring

snored v ▷ snore

snores v, n ▷ snore

snoring v ▷ snore

snorkel n (pl -s) tube allowing a swimmer to breathe while face down on the surface of the water ▶ v (-s, -lling, -lled) swim using a snorkel

snorkelled v ▷ snorkel

snorkelling v ▷ snorkel

snorkels n, v ▷ snorkel

snort v (-s, -ing, -ed) exhale noisily through the nostrils ▶ n (pl -s) act or

sound of snorting
snorted v ▷ snort
snorting v ▷ snort
snorts v, n ▷ snort
snot n (pl -s) slang mucus from the nose
snots n ▷ snot
snout n (pl -s) animal's projecting nose and jaws
snouts n ▷ snout
snow n (pl -s) frozen vapour falling from the sky in flakes ▶ v (-s, -ing, -ed) fall as or like snow ▷ **snowy** adj (-wier, -wiest)
snowball n (pl -s) snow pressed into a ball for throwing ▶ v (-s, -ing, -ed) increase rapidly
snowballed v ▷ snowball
snowballing v ▷ snowball
snowballs n, v ▷ snowball
snowdrop n (pl -s) small white bell-shaped spring flower
snowdrops n ▷ snowdrop
snowed v ▷ snow
snowier adj ▷ snow
snowiest adj ▷ snow
snowing v ▷ snow
snowman n (pl -men) figure shaped out of snow
snowmen n ▷ snowman
snows n, v ▷ snow
snowy adj ▷ snow
snub v (-s, -bbing, -bbed) insult deliberately ▶ n (pl -s) deliberate insult ▶ adj (of a nose) short and blunt
snubbed v ▷ snub
snubbing v ▷ snub
snubs v, n ▷ snub
snuff¹ n (pl -s) powdered tobacco for sniffing up the nostrils
snuff² v (-s, -ing, -ed) extinguish (a candle)
snuffed v ▷ snuff²
snuffing v ▷ snuff²
snuffle v (-les, -ling, -led) breathe noisily or with difficulty
snuffled v ▷ snuffle
snuffles v ▷ snuffle
snuffling v ▷ snuffle
snuffs n ▷ snuff¹ ▶ v ▷ snuff²

snug adj (-gger, -ggest) warm and comfortable ▶ n (pl -s) (in Britain and Ireland) small room in a pub ▷ **snugly** adv
snugger adj ▷ snug
snuggest adj ▷ snug
snuggle v (-les, -ling, -led) nestle into a person or thing for warmth or from affection
snuggled v ▷ snuggle
snuggles v ▷ snuggle
snuggling v ▷ snuggle
snugly adv ▷ snug
snugs n ▷ snug

> **sny** n (**snys**) Sny is a Canadian word for a side channel of a river. This word doesn't contain a vowel, so it can help you to clear an awkward rack. Sny scores 6 points.

so adv to such an extent ▶ conj in order that ▶ interj exclamation of surprise, triumph, or realization
soak v (-s, -ing, -ed) make wet ▶ n (pl -s) soaking ▷ **soaking** n (pl -s) adj
soaked v ▷ soak
soaking v, n adj ▷ soak
soakings n ▷ soak
soaks v, n ▷ soak
soap n (pl -s) compound of alkali and fat, used with water as a cleaning agent ▶ v (-s, -ing, -ed) apply soap to ▷ **soapy** adj (-pier, -piest)
soaped v ▷ soap
soapier adj ▷ soap
soapiest adj ▷ soap
soaping v ▷ soap
soaps n, v ▷ soap
soapy adj ▷ soap
soar v (-s, -ing, -ed) rise or fly upwards
soared v ▷ soar
soaring v ▷ soar
soars v ▷ soar
sob v (-s, -bbing, -bbed) weep with convulsive gasps ▶ n (pl -s) act or sound of sobbing
sobbed v ▷ sob
sobbing v ▷ sob
sober adj (-er, -est) not drunk ▶ v (-s, -ing, -ed) make or become sober

> **soberly** adv

sobered v ▷ sober

soberer adj ▷ sober

soberest adj ▷ sober

sobering v ▷ sober

soberly adv ▷ sober

sobers v ▷ sober

sobrieties n ▷ sobriety

sobriety n (pl **-ties**) state of being sober

sobs v, n ▷ sob

soccer n (pl **-s**) football played by two teams of eleven kicking a spherical ball

soccers n ▷ soccer

sociabilities n ▷ sociable

sociability n ▷ sociable

sociable adj friendly or companionable
> **sociability** n (pl **-ties**) > **sociably** adv

sociably adv ▷ sociable

social adj living in a community ▸ n (pl **-s**) informal gathering • **socially** adv

socially adv ▷ social

socials n ▷ social

societies n ▷ society

society n (pl **-ties**) human beings considered as a group

sock[1] n (pl **-s**) knitted covering for the foot

sock[2] slang v (**-s, -ing, -ed**) hit hard ▸ n (pl **-s**) hard blow

socked v ▷ sock[2]

socket n (pl **-s**) hole or recess into which something fits

sockets n ▷ socket

socking v ▷ sock[2]

socks v ▷ sock[2] ▸ n ▷ sock[1, 2]

sod n (pl **-s**) (piece of) turf

soda n (pl **-s**) compound of sodium

sodas n ▷ soda

sodden adj soaked

sodium n (pl **-s**) CHEM silvery-white metallic element

sodiums n ▷ sodium

sods n ▷ sod

sofa n (pl **-s**) couch

sofas n ▷ sofa

soft adj (**-er, -est**) easy to shape or cut
> **softly** adv

soften v (**-s, -ing, -ed**) make or become soft or softer

softened v ▷ soften

softening v ▷ soften

softens v ▷ soften

softer adj ▷ soft

softest adj ▷ soft

softly adv ▷ soft

software n (pl **-s**) computer programs

softwares n ▷ software

softwood n (pl **-s**) wood of a coniferous tree

softwoods n ▷ softwood

soggier adj ▷ soggy

soggiest adj ▷ soggy

sogginess n ▷ soggy

sogginesses n ▷ soggy

soggy adj (**-ggier, -ggiest**) soaked
> **sogginess** n (pl **-es**)

soigné, fem **soignée** adj well-groomed, elegant

soignée adj ▷ soigné

soil[1] n (pl **-s**) top layer of earth

soil[2] v (**-s, -ing, -ed**) make or become dirty

soiled v ▷ soil

soiling v ▷ soil

soils n ▷ soil[1] ▸ v ▷ soil[2]

soiree n (pl **-s**) evening party or gathering

soirees n ▷ soiree

sojourn n (pl **-s**) temporary stay ▸ v (**-s, -ing, -ed**) stay temporarily

sojourned v ▷ sojourn

sojourning v ▷ sojourn

sojourns n, v ▷ sojourn

solace n, v (**-ces, -cing, -ced**) comfort in distress

solaced v ▷ solace

solaces v ▷ solace

solacing v ▷ solace

solar adj of the sun

solaria n ▷ solarium

solarium n (pl **-riums, -ria**) place with beds and ultraviolet lights used for acquiring an artificial suntan

solariums n ▷ solarium

sold v ▷ sell

solder n (pl **-s**) soft alloy used to join two metal surfaces ▸ v (**-s, -ing, -ed**) join with solder

soldered v ▷ solder
soldering v ▷ solder
solders n, v ▷ solder
soldier n (pl **-s**) member of an army
▶ v (**-s**, **-ing**, **-ed**) serve in an army
▷ **soldierly** adj
soldiered v ▷ soldier
soldiering v ▷ soldier
soldierly adj ▷ soldier
soldiers n, v ▷ soldier
sole¹ adj one and only
sole² n (pl **-s**) underside of the foot
▶ v (**-les**, **-ling**, **-led**) provide (a shoe)
with a sole
sole³ n (pl **-s**) small edible flatfish
solecism n (pl **-s**) minor grammatical
mistake
solecisms n ▷ solecism
soled v ▷ sole²
solely adv only, completely
solemn adj (**-er**, **-est**) serious, deeply
sincere ▷ **solemnly** adv ▷ **solemnity** n
(pl **-ties**)
solemner adj ▷ solemn
solemnest adj ▷ solemn
solemnities n ▷ solemn
solemnity n ▷ solemn
solemnly adv ▷ solemn
solenoid n (pl **-s**) coil of wire
magnetized by passing a current
through it
solenoids n ▷ solenoid
soles n ▷ sole²,³ ▶ v ▷ sole²
solicit v (**-s**, **-ing**, **-ed**) request
▷ **solicitation** n (pl **-s**)
solicitation n ▷ solicit
solicitations n ▷ solicit
solicited v ▷ solicit
soliciting v ▷ solicit
solicits v ▷ solicit
solid adj (**-er**, **-est**) (of a substance)
keeping its shape ▶ n (pl **-s**) three-
dimensional shape ▷ **solidity** n (pl
-ties) ▷ **solidly** adv
solider adj ▷ solid
solidest adj ▷ solid
solidified v ▷ solidify
solidifies v ▷ solidify
solidify v (**-fies**, **-fying**, **-fied**) make or

become solid or firm
solidifying v ▷ solidify
solidities n ▷ solid
solidity n ▷ solid
solidly adv ▷ solid
solids n ▷ solid
soling v ▷ sole²
solitary adj alone, single
solitude n (pl **-s**) state of being alone
solitudes n ▷ solitude
solo n (pl **-s**) music for one performer
▶ adj done alone ▶ adv by oneself, alone
▷ **soloist** n (pl **-s**)
soloist n ▷ solo
soloists n ▷ solo
solos n ▷ solo
solstice n (pl **-s**) either the shortest (in
winter) or longest (in summer) day
of the year
solstices n ▷ solstice
solubilities n ▷ soluble
solubility n ▷ soluble
soluble adj able to be dissolved
▷ **solubility** n (pl **-ties**)
solution n (pl **-s**) answer to a problem
solutions n ▷ solution
solvable adj ▷ solve
solve v (**-ves**, **-ving**, **-ved**) find the
answer to (a problem) ▷ **solvable** adj
solved v ▷ solve
solvencies n ▷ solvent
solvency n ▷ solvent
solvent adj having enough money
to pay one's debts ▶ n (pl **-s**) liquid
capable of dissolving other substances
▷ **solvency** n (pl **-cies**)
solvents n ▷ solvent
solves v ▷ solve
solving v ▷ solve
sombre adj (**-r**, **-st**) dark, gloomy
sombrer adj ▷ sombre
sombrero n (pl **-s**) wide-brimmed
Mexican hat
sombreros n ▷ sombrero
sombrest adj ▷ sombre
some adj unknown or unspecified
▶ pron certain unknown or unspecified
people or things
somebodies n ▷ somebody

somebody pron some person ▶ n (pl **-dies**) important person

somehow adv in some unspecified way

someone pron somebody

sometime adv at some unspecified time ▶ adj former

somewhat adv to some extent, rather

son n (pl **-s**) male offspring

sonar n (pl **-s**) device for detecting underwater objects by the reflection of sound waves

sonars n ▷ sonar

sonata n (pl **-s**) piece of music in several movements for one instrument with or without piano

sonatas n ▷ sonata

song n (pl **-s**) music for the voice

songbird n (pl **-s**) any bird with a musical call

songbirds n ▷ songbird

songs n ▷ song

songster, songstress n (pl **-s, -es**) singer

songsters n ▷ songster

songstress n ▷ songster

songstresses n ▷ songster

sonic adj of or producing sound

sonnet n (pl **-s**) fourteen-line poem with a fixed rhyme scheme

sonnets n ▷ sonnet

sonorities n ▷ sonorous

sonority n ▷ sonorous

sonorous adj (of sound) deep or resonant > **sonorously** adv > **sonority** n (pl **-ties**)

sonorously adv ▷ sonorous

sons n ▷ son

soon adv in a short time

sooner adv rather

soot n (pl **-s**) black powder formed by the incomplete burning of an organic substance > **sooty** adj (**-tier, -tiest**)

soothe v (**-thes, -thing, -thed**) make calm

soothed v ▷ soothe

soothes v ▷ soothe

soothing v ▷ soothe

sootier adj ▷ soot

sootiest adj ▷ soot

soots n ▷ soot

sooty adj ▷ soot

sop n (pl **-s**) concession to pacify someone ▶ v (**-s, -pping, -pped**) mop up or absorb (liquid)

sophist n (pl **-s**) person who uses clever but invalid arguments

sophists n ▷ sophist

sopped v ▷ sop

soppier adj ▷ soppy

soppiest adj ▷ soppy

sopping adj completely soaked ▶ v. ▷ sop

soppy adj (**-pier, -piest**) informal oversentimental

soprano n (pl **-s**) (singer with) the highest female or boy's voice

sopranos n ▷ soprano

sops n, v ▷ sop

sorbet n (pl **-s**) flavoured water ice

sorbets n ▷ sorbet

sorcerer n (pl **-s**) magician >**sorceress** n fem (pl **-s**)

sorcerers n ▷ sorcerer

sorceress n ▷ sorcerer

sorceresses n ▷ sorcerer

sorceries n ▷ sorcery

sorcery n (pl **-ries**) witchcraft or magic

sordid adj (**-er, -est**) dirty, squalid > **sordidly** adv > **sordidness** n (pl **-es**)

sordider adj ▷ sordid

sordidest adj ▷ sordid

sordidly adv ▷ sordid

sordidness n ▷ sordid

sordidnesses n ▷ sordid

sore adj (**-r, -st**) painful ▶ n (pl **-s**) painful area on the body ▶ adv obs greatly > **soreness** n (pl **-es**)

sorely adv greatly

soreness n ▷ sore

sorenesses n ▷ sore

sorer adj ▷ sore

sores n ▷ sore

sorest adj ▷ sore

sorghum n (pl **-s**) kind of grass cultivated for grain

sorghums n ▷ sorghum

sorrel n (pl **-s**) bitter-tasting plant

sorrels n ▷ sorrel

sorrier adj ▷ **sorry**
sorriest adj ▷ **sorry**
sorrow n (pl -s) grief or sadness ▶ v
(-s, -ing, -ed) grieve ▷ **sorrowful** adj
▷ **sorrowfully** adv
sorrowed v ▷ **sorrow**
sorrowful adj ▷ **sorrow**
sorrowfully adv ▷ **sorrow**
sorrowing v ▷ **sorrow**
sorrows n, v ▷ **sorrow**
sorry adj (-rier, -riest) feeling pity
or regret
sort n (pl -s) group all sharing certain
qualities or characteristics ▶ v (-s,
-ing, -ed) arrange according to kind
sorted v ▷ **sort**
sortie n (pl -s) relatively short return
trip
sorties n ▷ **sortie**
sorting v ▷ **sort**
sorts n, v ▷ **sort**
sot n (pl -s) habitual drunkard
sots n ▷ **sot**
soufflé n (pl -s) light fluffy dish made
with beaten egg whites and other
ingredients
soufflés n ▷ **soufflé**
sough v (-s, -ing, -ed) (of the wind)
make a sighing sound
soughed v ▷ **sough**
soughing v ▷ **sough**
soughs v ▷ **sough**
sought v ▷ **seek**
souk n (pl -s) marketplace in Muslim
countries, often open-air
souks n ▷ **souk**
soul n (pl -s) spiritual and immortal part
of a human being
soulful adj full of emotion
soulless adj lacking human qualities,
mechanical
souls n ▷ **soul**
sound[1] n (pl -s) something heard, noise
▶ v (-s, -ing, -ed) make or cause to
make a sound
sound[2] adj (-er, -est) in good condition
▷ **soundly** adv
sound[3] v (-s, -ing, -ed) find the depth
of (water etc)

sound[4] n (pl -s) channel or strait
sounded v ▷ **sound**[1, 3]
sounder adj ▷ **sound**[2]
soundest adj ▷ **sound**[2]
sounding v ▷ **sound**[1, 3]
soundly adv ▷ **sound**[2]
sounds n ▷ **sound**[1, 4] ▲ v ▷ **sound**[1, 3]
soup n (pl -s) liquid food made from
meat, vegetables, etc ▷ **soupy** adj
(-pier, -piest)
soupçon n (pl -s) small amount
soupçons n ▷ **soupçon**
soupier adj ▷ **soup**
soupiest adj ▷ **soup**
soups n ▷ **soup**
soupy adj ▷ **soup**
source n (pl -s) origin or starting point
sources n ▷ **source**
sour adj (-er, -est) sharp-tasting ▶ v
(-s, -ing, -ed) make or become sour
▷ **sourly** adv **sourness** n (pl -s)
soured v ▷ **sour**
sourer adj ▷ **sour**
sourest adj ▷ **sour**
souring v ▷ **sour**
sourly adv ▷ **sour**
sourness n ▷ **sour**
sournesses n ▷ **sour**
sours v ▷ **sour**
souse v (-ses, -sing, -sed) plunge
(something) into liquid
soused v ▷ **souse**
souses v ▷ **souse**
sousing v ▷ **souse**
soutane n (pl -s) Roman Catholic
priest's cassock
soutanes n ▷ **soutane**
south n (pl -s) direction towards the
South Pole, opposite north ▶ adj to or
in the south ▶ adv in, to, or towards the
south ▷ **southerly** adj **southern** adj
▷ **southward** adj, adv **southwards** adv
southerly adj ▷ **south**
southern adj ▷ **south**
southpaw n (pl -s) informal left-handed
person, esp. a boxer
southpaws n ▷ **southpaw**
souths n ▷ **south**
southward adj, adv ▷ **south**

southwards adv ▷ **south**
souvenir n (pl **-s**) keepsake, memento
souvenirs n ▷ **souvenir**
soviet n (pl **-s**) formerly, elected council at various levels of government in the USSR ▷ adj
soviets n ▷ **soviet**
sow¹ v (-s, -ing, -ed, sown or -ed) scatter or plant (seed) in or on (the ground)
sowed v ▷ **sow**¹
sowing v ▷ **sow**¹
sown v ▷ **sow**¹
sows n ▷ **sow**² ▶ v ▷ **sow**¹

sox pl n. Sox is an informal word for **socks**. This is a good word to remember for when you find an X on your rack without the space or tiles to play a longer word. Sox scores 10 points.

soya n (pl **-s**) plant whose edible bean is used for food and as a source of oil
soyas n ▷ **soya**
sozzled adj BRIT, AUST & NZ slang drunk
spa n (pl **-s**) resort with a mineral-water spring
space n (pl **-s**) unlimited expanse in which all objects exist and move ▶ v (-ces, -cing, -ced) place at intervals
spaced v ▷ **space**
spaces n, v ▷ **space**
spacing v ▷ **space**
spacious adj having a large capacity or area
spade¹ n (pl **-s**) tool for digging
spade² n (pl **-s**) playing card of the suit marked with black leaf-shaped symbols
spades n ▷ **spade**¹ ▶ ²
span n (pl **-s**) space between two points ▶ v (-s, -nning, -nned) stretch or extend across
spangle n (pl **-les**) small shiny metallic ornament ▶ v (-les, -ling, -led) decorate with spangles
spangled v ▷ **spangle**
spangles n, v ▷ **spangle**
spangling v ▷ **spangle**

spaniel n (pl **-s**) dog with long ears and silky hair
spaniels n ▷ **spaniel**
spank v (-s, -ing, -ed) slap with the open hand, on the buttocks or legs ▶ n (pl **-s**) such a slap ▶ **spanking** n (pl **-s**)
spanked v ▷ **spank**
spanking adj informal outstandingly fine or smart ▶ v ▷ **spank** ▶ n ▷ **spank**
spankings n ▷ **spank**
spanks v, n ▷ **spank**
spanned v ▷ **span**
spanner n (pl **-s**) tool for gripping and turning a nut or bolt
spanners n ▷ **spanner**
spanning v ▷ **span**
spans n, v ▷ **span**
spar¹ n (pl **-s**) pole used as a ship's mast, boom, or yard
spar² v (-s, -rring, -rred) box or fight using light blows for practice
spare adj extra ▶ n (pl **-s**) duplicate kept in case of damage or loss ▶ v (-res, -ring, -red) refrain from punishing or harming
spared v ▷ **spare**
spares n, v ▷ **spare**
sparing adj economical ▶ v ▷ **spare**
spark n (pl **-s**) fiery particle thrown out from a fire or caused by friction ▶ v (-s, -ing, -ed) give off sparks
sparked v ▷ **spark**
sparkie n (pl **-s**) NZ informal electrician
sparkies n ▷ **sparkie**
sparking v ▷ **spark**
sparkle v (-les, -ling, -led) glitter with many points of light ▶ n (pl **-s**) sparkling points of light
sparkled v ▷ **sparkle**
sparkler n (pl **-s**) hand-held firework that emits sparks
sparklers n ▷ **sparkler**
sparkles v, n ▷ **sparkle**
sparks v, n ▷ **spark**
sparred v ▷ **spar**²
sparring v ▷ **spar**²
sparrow n (pl **-s**) small brownish bird
sparrows n ▷ **sparrow**
spars n ▷ **spar**¹ ▶ v ▷ **spar**²

sparse adj (**-r, -st**) thinly scattered
> **sparsely** adv ▷ **sparse** n (pl **-es**)
sparseness n ▷ **sparse**
sparsenesses n ▷ **sparse**
sparser adj ▷ **sparse**
sparsest adj ▷ **sparse**

spartan adj strict and austere

spas n ▷ **spa**

spasm n (pl **-s**) involuntary muscular contraction
spasms n ▷ **spasm**

spastic n (pl **-s**) person with cerebral palsy ▶ adj suffering from cerebral palsy
spastics n ▷ **spastic**

spat¹ n (pl **-s**) slight quarrel

spat² v ▷ **spit¹**

spate n (pl **-s**) large number of things happening within a period of time
spates n ▷ **spate**

spatial adj of or in space

spats pl n coverings formerly worn over the ankle and instep ▶ n ▷ **spat¹**

spatter v (**-s, -ing, -ed**) scatter or be scattered in drops over (something)
▶ n (pl **-s**) spattering sound
spattered v ▷ **spatter**
spattering v ▷ **spatter**
spatters n, v ▷ **spatter**

spatula n (pl **-s**) utensil with a broad flat blade for spreading or stirring
spatulas n ▷ **spatula**

spawn n (pl **-s**) jelly-like mass of eggs of fish, frogs, or molluscs ▶ v (**-s, -ing, -ed**) (of fish, frogs, or molluscs) lay eggs
spawned v ▷ **spawn**
spawning v ▷ **spawn**
spawns n, v ▷ **spawn**

spay v (**-s, -ing, -ed**) remove the ovaries from (a female animal)
spayed v ▷ **spay**
spaying v ▷ **spay**
spays v ▷ **spay**

speak v (**-s, -ing, spoke, spoken**) say words, talk

speaker n (pl **-s**) person who speaks, esp. at a formal occasion
speakers n ▷ **speaker**
speaking v ▷ **speaker**

speaks v ▷ **speak**

spear¹ n (pl **-s**) weapon consisting of a long shaft with a sharp point ▶ v (**-s, -ing, -ed**) pierce with or as if with a spear

spear² n (pl **-s**) slender shoot
speared v ▷ **spear¹**
spearing v ▷ **spear¹**
spears n ▷ **spear¹, ²** ▶ v ▷ **spear¹**

spec n (pl **-s**) informal speculation

special adj distinguished from others of its kind ▶ **specially** adv
specially adv ▷ **special**

specie n coins as distinct from paper money

species n (pl **-cies**) group of plants or animals that are related closely enough to interbreed naturally

specific adj particular, definite ▶ n (pl **-s**) drug used to treat a particular disease > **specifically** adv
specifically adv ▷ **specific**
specifics n ▷ **specific**
specified v ▷ **specify**
specifies v ▷ **specify**

specify v (**-fies, -fying, -fied**) refer to or state specifically
specifying v ▷ **specify**

specimen n (pl **-s**) individual or part typifying a whole
specimens n ▷ **specimen**

specious adj apparently true, but actually false

speck n (pl **-s**) small spot or particle

speckle n (pl **-s**) small spot ▶ v (**-les, -ling, -led**) mark with speckles
speckled v ▷ **speckle**
speckles n, v ▷ **speckle**
speckling v ▷ **speckle**
specks n ▷ **speck**

specs pl n informal ▷ **spectacles** ▶ n ▷ **spec**

spectate v (**-tes, -ting, -ted**) watch
spectated v ▷ **spectate**
spectates v ▷ **spectate**
spectating v ▷ **spectate**
spectra n ▷ **spectrum**
spectral adj ▷ **spectre**
spectre n (pl **-s**) ghost > **spectral** adj

spectres n ▷ **spectre**

spectrum n (pl **-tra**) range of different colours, radio waves, etc in order of their wavelengths

sped v ▷ **speed**

speech n (pl **-es**) act, power, or manner of speaking

speeches n ▷ **speech**

speed n (pl **-s**) swiftness ▶ v (**-s**, **-ing**, **sped** or **-ed**) go quickly

speeded v ▷ **speed**

speedier adj ▷ **speedy**

speediest adj ▷ **speedy**

speedily adv ▷ **speedy**

speeding v ▷ **speed**

speeds n, v ▷ **speed**

speedway n (pl **-s**) track for motorcycle racing

speedways n ▷ **speedway**

speedy adj (**-dier**, **-diest**) prompt > **speedily** adv

spell v (**-s**, **-ing**, **spelt** or **-ed**) give in correct order the letters that form (a word)

spell² n (pl **-s**) formula of words supposed to have magic power

spell³ n (pl **-s**) period of time of weather or activity

spelled v ▷ **spell¹**

spelling n (pl **-s**) way a word is spelt ▶ v ▷ **spell¹**

spellings n ▷ **spelling**

spells v ▷ **spell¹** ▶ n ▷ **spell², 3**

spelt v ▷ **spell¹**

spend v (**-s**, **-ing**, **spent**) pay out (money)

spending v ▷ **spend**

spends v ▷ **spend**

spent v ▷ **spend**

sperm n (pl **-s** or **sperm**) male reproductive cell

sperms n ▷ **sperm**

spew v (**-s**, **-ing**, **-ed**) vomit

spewed v ▷ **spew**

spewing v ▷ **spew**

spews v ▷ **spew**

sphagnum n (pl **-s**) moss found in bogs

sphagnums n ▷ **sphagnum**

sphere n (pl **-s**) perfectly round solid

object > **spherical** adj

spheres n ▷ **sphere**

spherical adj ▷ **sphere**

sphinx n (pl **-es**) enigmatic person

sphinxes n ▷ **sphinx**

spice n (pl **-s**) aromatic substance used as flavouring ▶ v (**-ces**, **-cing**, **-ced**) flavour with spices

spiced v ▷ **spice**

spices n, v ▷ **spice**

spicier adj ▷ **spicy**

spiciest adj ▷ **spicy**

spicing v ▷ **spice**

spicy adj (**-cier**, **-ciest**) flavoured with spices

spider n (pl **-s**) small eight-legged creature which spins a web to catch insects for food > **spidery** adj

spiders n ▷ **spider**

spidery adj ▷ **spider**

spied v ▷ **spy**

spiel n (pl **-s**) speech made to persuade someone to do something

spiels n ▷ **spiel**

spies v, n ▷ **spy**

spigot n (pl **-s**) stopper for, or tap fitted to, a cask

spigots n ▷ **spigot**

spike n (pl **-s**) sharp point ▶ v (**-kes**, **-king**, **-ked**) put spikes on > **spiky** adj (**-kier**, **-kiest**)

spiked v ▷ **spike**

spikes n, v ▷ **spike** ▶ pl n sports shoes with spikes for greater grip

spikier adj ▷ **spike**

spikiest adj ▷ **spike**

spiking v ▷ **spike**

spiky adj ▷ **spike**

spill v (**-s**, **-ing**, **spilt** or **spilled**) pour from or as if from a container ▶ n (pl **-s**) fall > **spillage** n (pl **-s**)

spill² n (pl **-s**) thin strip of wood or paper for lighting pipes or fires

spillage n ▷ **spill¹**

spillages n ▷ **spill¹**

spilled v ▷ **spill¹**

spilling v ▷ **spill¹**

spills n ▷ **spill¹, 2** ▷ v ▷ **spill¹**

spilt v ▷ **spill¹**

spin v (-s, -nning, spun) revolve or cause to revolve rapidly ▶ n (pl -s) revolving motion ▷ **spinner** n (pl -s)

spinach n (pl -es) dark green leafy vegetable
spinaches n ▷ spinach

spinal adj of the spine

spindle n (pl -s) rotating rod that acts as an axle
spindles n ▷ spindle
spindlier adj ▷ spindly
spindliest adj ▷ spindly

spindly adj (-lier, -liest) long, slender, and frail

spine n (pl -s) backbone
spines n ▷ spine

spinet n (pl -s) small harpsichord
spinets n ▷ spinet
spinier adj ▷ spiny
spiniest adj ▷ spiny

spinifex n (pl -es) coarse spiny Australian grass
spinifexes n ▷ spinifex

spinner n ▷ spin
spinners n ▷ spin

spinney n (pl -s) CHIEFLY BRIT small wood
spinneys n ▷ spinney
spinning v ▷ spin
spins v, n ▷ spin

spinster n (pl -s) unmarried woman
spinsters n ▷ spinster

spiny adj (-nier, -niest) covered with spines

spiral n (pl -s) continuous curve formed by a point winding about a central axis at an ever-increasing distance from it ▶ v (-s, -lling, -lled) move in a spiral ▶ adj having the form of a spiral
spiralled v ▷ spiral
spiralling v ▷ spiral
spirals n, v ▷ spiral

spire n (pl -s) pointed part of a steeple
spires n ▷ spire

spirit¹ n (pl -s) nonphysical aspect of a person concerned with profound thoughts ▶ v (-s, -ing, -ed) carry away mysteriously

spirit² n (pl -s) liquid obtained by distillation

spirited adj lively ▶ v ▷ **spirit¹**
spiriting v ▷ spirit¹
spirits n ▷ spirit¹, ², ▶ pl n emotional state ▶ v ▷ spirit¹

spit¹ v (-s, -tting, spat) eject (saliva or food) from the mouth ▶ n (pl -s) saliva

spit² n (pl -s) sharp rod on which meat is skewered for roasting

spite n (pl -s) deliberate nastiness ▶ v (-tes, -ting, -ted) annoy or hurt from spite ▷ **spiteful** adj ▷ **spitefully** adv
spited v ▷ spite
spiteful adj ▷ spite
spitefully adv ▷ spite
spites n, v ▷ spite

spitfire n (pl -s) person with a fiery temper
spitfires n ▷ spitfire
spiting v ▷ spite
spits n ▷ spit¹, ², ▶ v ▷ spit¹
spitting v ▷ spit¹

spittle n (pl -s) fluid produced in the mouth, saliva
spittles n ▷ spittle

spittoon n (pl -s) bowl to spit into
spittoons n ▷ spittoon

spiv n (pl -s) BRIT, AUST & NZ slang smartly dressed man who makes a living by shady dealings
spivs n ▷ spiv

splash v (-es, -ing, -ed) scatter liquid on (something) ▶ n (pl -es) splashing sound
splashed v ▷ splash
splashes v, n ▷ splash
splashing v, n ▷ splash

splatter v (-s, -ing, -ed) ▶ n (pl -s) splash
splattered v ▷ splatter
splattering v ▷ splatter
splatters v, n ▷ splatter

splay v (-s, -ing, -ed) spread out, with ends spreading in different directions
splayed v ▷ splay
splaying v ▷ splay
splays v ▷ splay

spleen n (pl -s) abdominal organ which filters bacteria from the blood
spleens n ▷ spleen

splendid adj (-er, -est) excellent
> **splendidly** adv > **splendour** n (pl -s)
splendider adj > **splendid**
splendidest adj > **splendid**
splendidly adv > **splendid**
splendour n > **splendid**
splendours n > **splendid**
splice v (-ces, -cing, -ced) join by
interweaving or overlapping ends
spliced v > **splice**
splices v > **splice**
splicing v > **splice**
splint n (pl -s) rigid support for a
broken bone
splinter n (pl -s) thin sharp piece
broken off, esp. from wood ▶ v (-s, -ing,
-ed) break into fragments
splintered v > **splinter**
splintering v > **splinter**
splinters n, v > **splinter**
splints n > **splint**
split v (-s, -tting, split) break into
separate pieces ▶ n (pl -s) crack or
division caused by splitting
splits v, n > **split** ▶ pl n act of sitting
with the legs outstretched in opposite
directions
splitting v > **split**
splodge n (pl -s) ▶ v (-ges, -ging, -ged)
> **splotch**
splodged v > **splodge**
splodges n, v > **splodge**
splodging v > **splodge**
splotch n (pl -s) ▶ v (-ches, -ching,
-ched) splash, daub
splotched v > **splotch**
splotches n, v > **splotch**
splotching v > **splotch**
splurge v (-ges, -ging, -ged) spend
money extravagantly ▶ n (pl -s) bout of
extravagance
splurged v > **splurge**
splurges v, n > **splurge**
splurging v > **splurge**
splutter v (-s, -ing, -ed) utter with
spitting or choking sounds ▶ n (pl -s)
spluttering
spluttered v > **splutter**
spluttering v > **splutter**

splutters v, n > **splutter**
spoil v (-s, -ing, -spoilt or -ed) damage
spoiled v > **spoil**
spoiling v > **spoil**
spoils pl n booty ▶ v > **spoil**
spoilt v > **spoil**
spoke[1] v > **speak**
spoke[2] n (pl -s) bar joining the hub of a
wheel to the rim
spoken v > **speak**
spokes n > **spoke**[2]
sponge n (pl -s) sea animal with a
porous absorbent skeleton ▶ v (-ges,
-ging, -ged) wipe with a sponge
> **spongy** adj (-gier, -giest)
sponged v > **sponge**
sponger n (pl -s) slang person who
sponges on others
spongers n > **sponger**
sponges n, v > **sponge**
spongier adj > **sponge**
spongiest adj > **sponge**
sponging v > **sponge**
spongy adj > **sponge**
sponsor n (pl -s) person who promotes
something ▶ v (-s, -ing, -ed) act as a
sponsor for > **sponsorship** n (pl -s)
sponsored v > **sponsor**
sponsoring v > **sponsor**
sponsors n, v > **sponsor**
sponsorship n > **sponsor**
sponsorships n > **sponsor**
spoof n (pl -s) mildly satirical parody
spoofs n > **spoof**
spook n (pl -s) informal ghost
> **spooky** adj (-kier, -kiest)
spookier adj > **spook**
spookiest adj > **spook**
spooks n > **spook**
spooky adj > **spook**
spool n (pl -s) cylinder round which
something can be wound
spools n > **spool**
spoon n (pl -s) shallow bowl attached to
a handle for eating, stirring, or serving
food ▶ v (-s, -ing, -ed) lift with a spoon
> **spoonful** n (pl -s)
spooned v > **spoon**
spoonful n > **spoon**

spoonfuls n ▷ spoon
spooning v ▷ spoon
spoons n, v ▷ spoon
spoor n (pl -s) trail of an animal
spoors n ▷ spoor
sporadic adj intermittent, scattered
> **sporadically** adv
  sporadically adv ▷ sporadic
spore n (pl -s) minute reproductive
body of some plants
spores n ▷ spore
sporran n (pl -s) pouch worn in front
of a kilt
sporrans n ▷ sporran
sport n (pl -s) activity for pleasure,
competition, or exercise ▶ v (-s, -ing,
-ed) wear proudly
sported v ▷ sport
sportier adj ▷ sporty
sportiest adj ▷ sporty
sporting adj of sport ▶ v ▷ sport
sportive adj playful
sports n, v ▷ sport
sporty adj (-tier, -tiest) fond of sport
spot n (pl -s) small mark on a surface
informal ▶ v (-s, -tting, -tted) notice
spotless adj absolutely clean
> **spotlessly** adv
  spotlessly adv ▷ spotless
spots n, v ▷ spot
spotted v ▷ spot
spottier adj ▷ spotty
spottiest adj ▷ spotty
spotting v ▷ spot
spotty adj (-tier, -tiest) with spots
spouse n (pl -s) husband or wife
spouses n ▷ spouse
spout v (-s, -ing, -ed) pour out in a
stream or jet slang ▶ n (pl -s) projecting
tube or lip for pouring liquids
spouted v ▷ spout
spouting v ▷ spout
spouts v, n ▷ spout
sprain v (-s, -ing, -ed) injure (a joint) by
a sudden twist ▶ n (pl -s) such an injury
sprained v ▷ sprain
spraining v ▷ sprain
sprains v, n ▷ sprain
sprang v ▷ spring

sprat n (pl -s) small sea fish
sprats n ▷ sprat
sprawl v (-s, -ing, -ed) lie or sit with
the limbs spread out ▶ n (pl -s) part of
a city that has spread untidily over a
large area
sprawled v ▷ sprawl
sprawling v ▷ sprawl
sprawls v, n ▷ sprawl
spray¹ n (pl -s) device for producing
fine drops of liquid ▶ v (-s, -ing, -ed)
scatter in fine drops
spray² n (pl -s) branch with buds,
leaves, flowers, or berries
sprayed v ▷ spray¹
spraying v ▷ spray¹
sprays v ▷ spray¹ ▶ n ▷ spray¹, ²
spread v (-s, -ing, spread) open out or
be displayed to the fullest extent ▶ n (pl
-s) spreading informal
spreading v ▷ spread
spreads v, n ▷ spread
spree n (pl -s) session of
overindulgence, usu. in drinking or
spending money
sprees n ▷ spree
sprier adj ▷ spry
spriest adj ▷ spry
sprig n (pl -s) twig or shoot
sprigs n ▷ sprig
spring v (-s, -ing, sprang or sprung,
sprung) move suddenly upwards or
forwards in a single motion, jump
▶ n (pl -s) season between winter and
summer
springer n (pl -s) small spaniel
springers n ▷ springer
springier adj ▷ springy
springiest adj ▷ springy
springing v ▷ spring
springs v, n ▷ springs
springy adj (-gier, -giest) elastic
sprinkle v (-les, -ling, -led) scatter
(liquid or powder) in tiny drops
or particles over (something)
> **sprinkler** n (pl -s)
  sprinkled v ▷ sprinkle
sprinkler n ▷ sprinkle
sprinklers n ▷ sprinkle

squints v, n ▷ **squint**
squire n (pl **-s**) country gentleman, usu. the main landowner in a community
squires v ▷ **squire**
squirm v (**-s**, **-ing**, **-ed**) wriggle, writhe ▶ n (pl **-s**) wriggling movement
squirmed v ▷ **squirm**
squirming v ▷ **squirm**
squirms v, n ▷ **squirm**
squirrel n (pl **-s**) small bushy-tailed tree-living animal
squirrels n ▷ **squirrel**
squirt v (**-s**, **-ing**, **-ed**) force (a liquid) or (of a liquid) be forced out of a narrow opening ▶ n (pl **-s**) jet of liquid
squirted v ▷ **squirt**
squirting v ▷ **squirt**
squirts n, v ▷ **squirt**
squish v (**-es**, **-ing**, **-ed**) ▶ n (pl **-es**) (make) a soft squelching sound
> **squishy** adj (**-shier**, **-shiest**)
squished v ▷ **squish**
squishes n, v ▷ **squish**
squishier adj ▷ **squish**
squishiest adj ▷ **squish**
squishing v ▷ **squish**
squishy adj ▷ **squish**

> **squiz** n (**quizzes**). Squiz is an informal word for a look or glance. This is a useful word to remember, both for when you have the most of the tiles to form it and when someone else plays the word **quiz** which you can then add an S to for a good score. Squiz scores 23 points.

> **st** interj. St is a sound people make to request silence or quiet. This is one of two two-letter words beginning with S that do not contain a vowel. It's useful when you want to connect a word beginning with H to one ending in T or vice versa. St scores 2 points.

stab v (**-s**, **-bbing**, **-bbed**) pierce with something pointed ▶ n (pl **-s**) stabbing
stabbed v ▷ **stab**
stabbing v ▷ **stab**
stabilities n ▷ **stable²**
stability n ▷ **stable²**

stable¹ n (pl **-s**) building in which horses are kept ▶ v (**-les**, **-ling**, **-led**) put or keep (a horse) in a stable
stable² adj (**-r**, **-st**) firmly fixed or established ▶ **stability** n (pl **-ties**)
stabled v ▷ **stable¹**
stabler adj ▷ **stable²**
stables n, v ▷ **stable¹**
stablest adj ▷ **stable²**
stabling v ▷ **stable¹**
stabs v, n ▷ **stab**
staccato adv MUSIC with the notes sharply separated ▶ adj consisting of short abrupt sounds
stack n (pl **-s**) ordered pile ▶ v (**-s**, **-ing**, **-ed**) pile in a stack
stacked v ▷ **stack**
stacking v ▷ **stack**
stacks n, v ▷ **stack**
stadia n ▷ **stadium**
stadium n (pl **-diums**, **-dia**) sports arena with tiered seats for spectators
stadiums n ▷ **stadium**
staff¹ n (pl **-s**) people employed in an organization ▶ v (**-s**, **-ing**, **-ed**) supply with personnel
staff² n (pl **staves**) set of five horizontal lines on which music is written
staffed v ▷ **staff¹**
staffing v ▷ **staff¹**
staffs n, v ▷ **staff¹**
stag n (pl **-s**) adult male deer
stage n (pl **-s**) step or period of development ▶ v (**-ges**, **-ging**, **-ged**) put (a play) on stage
staged v ▷ **stage**
stages n, v ▷ **stage**
stagey adj (**-gier**, **-giest**) overtheatrical
stagger v (**-s**, **-ing**, **-ed**) walk unsteadily ▶ n (pl **-s**) staggering
staggered v ▷ **stagger**
staggering v ▷ **stagger**
staggers v, n ▷ **stagger**
stagier adj ▷ **stagey**
stagiest adj ▷ **stagey**
staging v ▷ **stage**
stagnant adj (of water or air) stale from not moving
stagnate v (**-tes**, **-ting**, **-ted**) be

stagnant > **stagnation** n (pl -s)
stagnated v ▷ stagnate
stagnates v ▷ stagnate
stagnating v ▷ stagnate
stagnation n ▷ stagnate
stagnations n ▷ stagnate
stags n ▷ stag
staid adj (-er, -est) sedate, serious, and rather dull
staider adj ▷ staid
staidest adj ▷ staid
stain v (-s, -ing, -ed) discolour, mark ▶ n (pl -s) discoloration or mark > **stainless** adj
stained v ▷ stain
staining v ▷ stain
stainless adj ▷ stain
stains v, n ▷ stain
stairs pl n flight of steps between floors, usu. indoors
stake[1] n (pl -s) pointed stick or post driven into the ground as a support or marker ▶ v (-kes, -king, -ked) support or mark out with stakes
stake[2] n (pl -s) money wagered ▶ v (-kes, -king, -ked) wager, risk
staked v ▷ stake[1, 2]
stakes v ▷ stake[1, 2] ▶ n ▷ stake[1, 2]
staking v ▷ stake[1, 2]
stale adj (-r, -st) not fresh > **staleness** n (pl -es)
staleness n ▷ stale
stalenesses n ▷ stale
staler adj ▷ stale
stalest adj ▷ stale
stalk[1] n (pl -s) plant's stem
stalk[2] v (-s, -ing, -ed) follow or approach stealthily
stalked v ▷ stalk[2]
stalker n (pl -s) person who follows or stealthily approaches a person or an animal
stalkers n ▷ stalker
stalking v ▷ stalk[2]
stalks n ▷ stalk[1] ▷ v ▷ stalk[2]
stall[1] n (pl -s) small stand for the display and sale of goods ▶ v (-s, -ing, -ed) stop (a motor vehicle or engine) or (of a motor vehicle or engine) stop

accidentally
stall[2] v (-s, -ing, -ed) employ delaying tactics
stalled v ▷ stall[1, 2]
stalling v ▷ stall[1, 2]
stallion n (pl -s) uncastrated male horse
stallions n ▷ stallion
stalls n ▷ stall[1] ▷ v ▷ stall[1, 2] ▶ pl n ground-floor seats in a theatre or cinema
stalwart adj strong and sturdy ▶ n (pl -s) stalwart person
stalwarts n ▷ stalwart
stamen n (pl -s) pollen-producing part of a flower
stamens n ▷ stamen
stamina n (pl -s) enduring energy and strength
staminas n ▷ stamina
stammer v (-s, -ing, -ed) speak or say with involuntary pauses or repetition of syllables ▶ n (pl -s) tendency to stammer
stammered v ▷ stammer
stammering v ▷ stammer
stammers v, n ▷ stammer
stamp n (pl -s) piece of gummed paper stuck to an envelope or parcel to show that the postage has been paid ▶ v (-s, -ing, -ed) bring (one's foot) down forcefully
stamped v ▷ stamp
stampede n (pl -s) sudden rush of frightened animals or of a crowd ▶ v (-des, -ding, -ded) (cause to) take part in a stampede
stampeded v ▷ stampede
stampedes n, v ▷ stampede
stampeding v ▷ stampede
stamping v ▷ stamp
stamps n, v ▷ stamp
stance n (pl -s) attitude
stances n ▷ stance
stanch v (-es, -ing, -ed) ▷ staunch[2]
stanched v ▷ stanch
stanches v ▷ stanch
stanching v ▷ stanch
stand v (-s, -ing, stood) be in, rise to, or place in an upright position ▶ n (pl -s)

stall for the sale of goods
standard n (pl **-s**) level of quality ▶ adj usual, regular, or average
standards n ▷ standard
standing adj permanent, lasting ▶ n (pl **-s**) reputation or status ▶ v ▷ stand
standings n ▷ standing
stands v, n ▷ stand
stank v ▷ stink
stanza n (pl **-s**) verse of a poem
stanzas n ▷ stanza
staple[1] n (pl **-s**) U-shaped piece of metal used to fasten papers or secure things ▶ v (**-les, -ling, -led**) fasten with staples
staple[2] adj of prime importance, principal ▶ n (pl **-s**) main constituent of anything
stapled v ▷ staple[1]
stapler n (pl **-s**) small device for fastening papers together
staplers n ▷ stapler
staples n ▷ staple[1, 2] ▶ v ▷ staple[1]
stapling v ▷ staple[1]
star n (pl **-s**) hot gaseous mass in space, visible in the night sky as a point of light ▶ v (**-s, -rring, -rred**) feature or be featured in a leading role ▶ adj leading, famous
starch n (pl **-es**) carbohydrate forming the main food element in bread, potatoes, etc, and used mixed with water for stiffening fabric ▶ v (**-es, -ing, -ed**) stiffen (fabric) with starch
starched v ▷ starch
starches n, v ▷ starch
starchier adj ▷ starchy
starchiest adj ▷ starchy
starching v ▷ starch
starchy adj (**-chier, -chiest**) containing starch
stardom n (pl **-s**) status of a star in the entertainment or sports world
stardoms n ▷ stardom
stare v (**-res, -ring, -red**) look or gaze fixedly (at) ▶ n (pl **-s**) fixed gaze
stared v ▷ stare
stares v, n ▷ stare
starfish n (pl **-es**) star-shaped sea creature
starfishes n ▷ starfish
staring v ▷ stare
stark adj (**-er, -est**) harsh, unpleasant, and plain ▶ adv completely
starker adj ▷ stark
starkest adj ▷ stark
starling n (pl **-s**) songbird with glossy black speckled feathers
starlings n ▷ starling
starred v ▷ star
starrier adj ▷ starry
starriest adj ▷ starry
starring v ▷ star
starry adj (**-rier, -riest**) full of or like stars
stars n, v ▷ star ▶ pl n astrological forecast, horoscope
start v (**-s, -ing, -ed**) take the first step, begin ▶ n (pl **-s**) first part of something
started v ▷ start
starter n (pl **-s**) first course of a meal
starters n ▷ starter
starting v ▷ start
startle v (**-les, -ling, -led**) slightly surprise or frighten
startled v ▷ startle
startles v ▷ startle
startling v ▷ startle
starts v, n ▷ start
starvation n ▷ starve
starvations n ▷ starve
starve v (**-ves, -ving, -ved**) die or suffer or cause to die or suffer from hunger
> **starvation** n (pl **-s**)
starved v ▷ starve
starves v ▷ starve
starving v ▷ starve
stash informal v (**-es, -ing, -ed**) store in a secret place ▶ n (pl **-es**) secret store
stashed v ▷ stash
stashes v, n ▷ stash
stashing v ▷ stash
state n (pl **-s**) condition of a person or thing ▶ adj of or concerning the State ▶ v (**-tes, -ting, -ted**) express in words
stated v ▷ state
statelier adj ▷ stately
stateliest adj ▷ stately

stately *adj* (-lier, -liest) dignified or grand
states *n*, *v* ▷ **state**
static *adj* stationary or inactive ▶ *n* (*pl* -s) crackling sound or speckled picture caused by interference in radio or television reception (also **static electricity**)
statics *n* ▷ **static**
stating *v* ▷ **state**
station *n* (*pl* -s) place where trains stop for passengers ▶ *v* (-s, -ing, -ed) assign (someone) to a particular place
stationed *v* ▷ **station**
stationing *v* ▷ **station**
stations *n*, *v* ▷ **station**
statuaries *n* ▷ **statuary**
statuary *n* (*pl* -ries) statues collectively
statue *n* (*pl* -s) large sculpture of a human or animal figure
statues *n* ▷ **statue**
stature *n* (*pl* -s) person's height
statures *n* ▷ **stature**
status *n* (*pl* -ses) social position
statuses *n* ▷ **status**
statute *n* (*pl* -s) written law
> **statutory** *adj* required or authorized by law
statutes *n* ▷ **statute**
statutory *adj* ▷ **statute**
staunch[1] *adj* (-er, -est) loyal, firm
staunch[2], **stanch** *v* (-ches, -ching, -ched) stop (a flow of blood)
staunched *v* ▷ **staunch**[2]
stauncher *adj* ▷ **staunch**[1]
staunches *v* ▷ **staunch**[2]
staunchest *adj* ▷ **staunch**[1]
staunching *v* ▷ **staunch**[2]
stave *n* (*pl* -s) one of the strips of wood forming a barrel
staves *n* ▷ **stave** ▷ **staff**[2]
stay[1] *v* (-s, -ing, -ed) remain in a place or condition ▶ *n* (*pl* -s) period of staying in a place
stay[2] *n* (*pl* -s) prop or buttress
stay[3] *n* (*pl* -s) rope or wire supporting a ship's mast
stayed *v* ▷ **stay**[1]
staying *v* ▷ **stay**[1]

stays *n* ▷ **stay**[1, 2, 3] ▶ *v* ▷ **stay**[1] ▶ *pl n* corset
stead *n* (*pl* -s) in someone's place
steadied *v* ▷ **steady**
steadier *adj* ▷ **steady**
steadiest *adj* ▷ **steady**
steadily *adv* ▷ **steady**
steadiness *n* ▷ **steady**
steadinesses *n* ▷ **steady**
steads *n* ▷ **stead**
steady *adj* (-dier, -diest) not shaky or wavering ▶ *v* (-dies, -dying, -died) make steady ▶ *adv* in a steady manner
> **steadily** *adv* > **steadiness** *n* (*pl* -es)
steadying *v* ▷ **steady**
steak *n* (*pl* -s) thick slice of meat, esp. beef
steaks *n* ▷ **steak**
steal *v* (-s, -ing, stole, stolen) take unlawfully or without permission
stealing *v* ▷ **steal**
steals *v* ▷ **steal**
stealth *n* (*pl* -s) secret or underhand behaviour ▶ *adj* (of technology) able to render an aircraft almost invisible to radar > **stealthy** *adj* (-thier, -thiest)
> **stealthily** *adv*
stealthier *adj* ▷ **stealth**
stealthiest *adj* ▷ **stealth**
stealthily *adv* ▷ **stealth**
stealths *n* ▷ **stealth**
stealthy *adj* ▷ **stealth**
steam *n* (*pl* -s) vapour into which water changes when boiled ▶ *v* (-s, -ing, -ed) give off steam
steamed *v* ▷ **steam**
steamer *n* (*pl* -s) steam-propelled ship
steamers *n* ▷ **steamer**
steaming *v* ▷ **steam**
steams *n*, *v* ▷ **steam**
steed *n* (*pl* -s) *lit* horse
steeds *n* ▷ **steed**
steel *n* (*pl* -s) hard malleable alloy of iron and carbon ▶ *v* (-s, -ing, -ed) prepare (oneself) for something unpleasant
> **steely** *adj* (-lier, -liest)
steeled *v* ▷ **steel**
steelier *adj* ▷ **steel**
steeliest *adj* ▷ **steel**

steeling v ▷ **steel**

steels n, v ▷ **steel**

steely adj ▷ **steel**

steep¹ adj (-er, -est) sloping sharply > **steeply** adv > **steepness** n (pl -es)

steep² v (-s, -ing, -ed) soak or be soaked in liquid

steeped v ▷ **steep²**

steeper adj ▷ **steep¹**

steepest adj ▷ **steep¹**

steeping v ▷ **steep²**

steeple n (pl -s) church tower with a spire

steeples n ▷ **steeple**

steeply n ▷ **steep¹**

steepness n ▷ **steep¹**

steepnesses n ▷ **steep¹**

steeps v ▷ **steep²**

steer¹ v (-s, -ing, -ed) direct the course of (a vehicle or ship)

steer² n (pl -s) castrated male ox

steerage n (pl -s) cheapest accommodation on a passenger ship

steerages n ▷ **steerage**

steered v ▷ **steer¹**

steering v ▷ **steer¹**

steers v ▷ **steer¹**² ▷ n ▷ **steer²**

stein n (pl -s) earthenware beer mug

steins n ▷ **stein**

stellar adj of stars

stem¹ n (pl -s) long thin central part of a plant ▷ v (-s, -mming, -mmed) originate from

stem² v (-s, -mming, -mmed) stop (the flow of something)

stemmed v ▷ **stem¹, ²**

stemming v ▷ **stem¹, ²**

stems v ▷ **stem¹, ²** ▷ n ▷ **stem¹**

stench n (pl -es) foul smell

stenches n ▷ **stench**

stencil n (pl -s) thin sheet with cut-out pattern through which ink or paint passes to form the pattern on the surface below ▷ v (-s, -lling, -lled) make (a pattern) with a stencil

stencilled v ▷ **stencil**

stencilling v ▷ **stencil**

stencils n, v ▷ **stencil**

stent n (pl -s) surgical implant used to keep an artery open

stents n ▷ **stent**

step v (-s, -pping, -pped) move and set down the foot, as when walking ▷ n (pl -s) stepping

stepped v ▷ **step**

steppes pl n wide grassy treeless plains in Russia and Ukraine

stepping v ▷ **step**

steps pl n stepladder ▷ n, v ▷ **step**

stereo adj ▷ **stereophonic** ▷ n (pl -s) stereophonic record player

stereos n ▷ **stereo**

sterile adj free from germs > **sterility** n (pl -ties)

sterilities n ▷ **sterile**

sterility n ▷ **sterile**

sterling n (pl -s) British money system ▷ adj genuine and reliable

sterlings n ▷ **sterling**

stern¹ adj (-er, -est) severe, strict > **sternly** adv > **sternness** n (pl -es)

stern² n (pl -s) rear part of a ship

sterna n ▷ **sternum**

sterner adj ▷ **stern¹**

sternest adj ▷ **stern¹**

sternly adv ▷ **stern¹**

sternness n ▷ **stern¹**

sternnesses n ▷ **stern¹**

sterns n ▷ **stern²**

sternums n ▷ **sternum**

steroid n (pl -s) organic compound containing a carbon ring system, such as many hormones

steroids n ▷ **steroid**

stew n (pl -s) food cooked slowly in a closed pot ▷ v (-s, -ing, -ed) cook slowly in a closed pot

steward n (pl -s) person who looks after passengers on a ship or aircraft

> **stewardess** n fem (pl -es)

stewardess n ▷ **steward**

stewardesses n ▷ **steward**

stewards n ▷ **steward**

stewed v ▷ **stew**

stewing v ▷ **stew**

stews n, v ▷ **stew**

stick¹ n (pl -s) long thin piece of wood

stick² v (-s, -ing, stuck) push (a pointed

object) into (something)

sticker n (pl -s) adhesive label or sign
  stickers n ▷ sticker
  stickier adj ▷ sticky
  stickiest adj ▷ sticky
  sticking v ▷ stick²

stickler n (pl -s) person who insists on something
  sticklers n ▷ stickler
  sticks n ▷ stick¹ ▶ v ▷ stick²

stickup n (pl -s) slang robbery at gunpoint
  stickups n ▷ stickup

sticky adj (-kier, -kiest) covered with an adhesive substance
  sties n ▷ sty

stiff adj (-er, -est) not easily bent or moved ▶ n (pl -s) slang corpse
  > **stiffly** adv **stiffness** n (pl -es)

stiffen v (-s, -ing, -ed) make or become stiff
  stiffened v ▷ stiffen
  stiffening v ▷ stiffen
  stiffens v ▷ stiffen
  stiffer adj ▷ stiff
  stiffest adj ▷ stiff
  stiffly adv ▷ stiff
  stiffness n ▷ stiff
  stiffnesses n ▷ stiff
  stiffs n ▷ stiff

stifle v (-les, -ling, -led) suppress
  stifled v ▷ stifle
  stifles v ▷ stifle
  stifling v ▷ stifle

stigma n (pl -mas, -mata) mark of social disgrace
  stigmas n ▷ stigma

stigmata pl n marks resembling the wounds of the crucified Christ ▶ n
  ▷ stigma

stile n (pl -s) set of steps allowing people to climb a fence
  stiles n ▷ stile

stiletto n (pl -s) high narrow heel on a woman's shoe
  stilettos n ▷ stiletto

still¹ adv now or in the future as before
  ▶ adj (-er, -est) motionless ▶ n (pl -s) photograph from a film scene ▶ v (-s,

-ing, -ed) make still > **stillness** n (pl -es)

still² n (pl -s) apparatus for distilling alcoholic drinks
  stilled v ▷ still¹
  stiller adj ▷ still¹
  stillest adj ▷ still¹
  stilling v ▷ still¹
  stillness n ▷ still¹
  stillnesses n ▷ still¹
  stills n ▷ still¹, ² ▶ v ▷ still¹

stilted adj stiff and formal in manner

stilts pl n pair of poles with footrests for walking raised from the ground

stimuli n ▷ stimulus

stimulus n (pl -li) something that rouses a person or thing to activity

sting v (-s, -ing, stung) (of certain animals or plants) wound by injecting with poison ▶ n (pl -s) wound or pain caused by or as if by stinging
  stingier adj ▷ stingy
  stingiest adj ▷ stingy
  stinginess n ▷ stingy
  stinginesses n ▷ stingy
  stinging v ▷ sting
  stings v, n ▷ sting

stingy adj (-gier, -giest) mean or miserly > **stinginess** n (pl -es)

stink n (pl -s) strong unpleasant smell
  ▶ v (-s, -ing, stank or stunk, stunk) give off a strong unpleasant smell
  stinking v ▷ stink
  stinks n, v ▷ stink

stint v (-s, -ing, -ed) (foll. by on) be miserly with (something) ▶ n (pl -s) allotted amount of work
  stinted v ▷ stint
  stinting v ▷ stint
  stints v, n ▷ stint

stipend n (pl -s) regular allowance or salary, esp. that paid to a clergyman
  > **stipendiary** adj receiving a stipend
  stipendiary adj ▷ stipend
  stipends n ▷ stipend

stipple v (-les, -ling, -led) paint, draw, or engrave using dots
  stippled v ▷ stipple
  stipples v ▷ stipple
  stippling v ▷ stipple

stir v (**-s, -rring, -rred**) mix up (a liquid) by moving a spoon etc around in it ▶ n (pl **-s**) a stirring
stirred v ▷ stir
stirring v ▷ stir

stirrup n (pl **-s**) metal loop attached to a saddle for supporting a rider's foot
stirrups n ▷ stirrup
stirs v, n ▷ stir

stitch n (pl **-es**) link made by drawing thread through material with a needle ▶ v (**-es, -ing, -ed**) sew
stitched v ▷ stitch
stitches n, v ▷ stitch
stitching v ▷ stitch

stoat n (pl **-s**) small mammal of the weasel family, with brown fur that turns white in winter
stoats n ▷ stoat

stock n (pl **-s**) total amount of goods available for sale in a shop ▶ adj kept in stock, standard ▶ v (**-s, -ing, -ed**) keep for sale or future use
stockade n (pl **-s**) enclosure or barrier made of stakes
stockades n ▷ stockade
stocked v ▷ stock
stockier adj ▷ stocky
stockiest adj ▷ stocky

stocking n (pl **-s**) close-fitting covering for the foot and leg ▶ v ▷ stock
stockings n ▷ stocking

stockist n (pl **-s**) dealer who stocks a particular product
stockists n ▷ stockist

stocks n HIST instrument of punishment consisting of a wooden frame with holes into which the hands and feet of the victim were locked ▶ n, v ▷ stock

stocky adj (**-kier, -kiest**) (of a person) broad and sturdy

stodge n (pl **-s**) BRIT, AUST & NZ heavy starchy food
stodges n ▷ stodge
stodgier adj ▷ stodgy
stodgiest adj ▷ stodgy
stodgy adj (**-gier, -giest**) (of food) heavy and starchy

stoep n (pl **-s**) S AFR verandah
stoeps n ▷ stoep

stoic n (pl **-s**) person who suffers hardship without showing his or her feelings ▶ adj (also **stoical**) suffering hardship without showing one's feelings > **stoically** adv > **stoicism** n (pl **-s**)
stoical adj ▷ stoic
stoically adv ▷ stoic
stoicism n ▷ stoic
stoicisms n ▷ stoic
stoics n ▷ stoic

stoke v (**-kes, -king, -ked**) feed and tend (a fire or furnace) > **stoker** n (pl **-s**)
stoked v ▷ stoke
stoker n ▷ stoke
stokers n ▷ stoke
stokes v ▷ stoke
stoking v ▷ stoke

stole¹ v ▷ steal
stole² n (pl **-s**) long scarf or shawl
stolen v ▷ steal
stoles n ▷ stole²

stolid adj (**-er, -est**) showing little emotion or interest > **stolidly** adv
stolider adj ▷ stolid
stolidest adj ▷ stolid
stolidly adv ▷ stolid

stomach n (pl **-s**) organ in the body which digests food ▶ v (**-s, -ing, -ed**) put up with
stomached v ▷ stomach
stomaching v ▷ stomach
stomachs n, v ▷ stomach

stomp v (**-s, -ing, -ed**) informal tread heavily
stomped v ▷ stomp
stomping v ▷ stomp
stomps v ▷ stomp

stone n (pl **-s**) material of which rocks are made ▶ v (**-nes, -ning, -ned**) throw stones at
stoned adj slang under the influence of alcohol or drugs ▶ v ▷ stone
stones n, v ▷ stone
stonier adj ▷ stony
stoniest adj ▷ stony
stonily adv ▷ stony

stoning v ▷ **stone**

stony adj (**-nier**, **-niest**) of or like stone
>**stonily** adv

stood v ▷ **stand**

stooge n (pl **-es**) actor who feeds lines
to a comedian or acts as the butt of
his jokes

stooges n ▷ **stooge**

stool n (pl **-s**) chair without arms
or back

stools n ▷ **stool**

stoop v (**-s**, **-ing**, **-ed**) bend (the body)
forward and downward ▶ n (pl **-s**)
stooping posture

stooped v ▷ **stoop**

stooping v ▷ **stoop**

stoops v, n ▷ **stoop**

stop v (**-s**, **-pping**, **-pped**) cease or
cause to cease from doing (something)
▶ n (pl **-s**) stopping or being stopped
>**stoppage** n (pl **-s**)

stopcock n (pl **-s**) valve to control or
stop the flow of fluid in a pipe

stopcocks n ▷ **stopcock**

stopgap n (pl **-s**) temporary substitute

stopgaps n ▷ **stopgap**

stopover n (pl **-s**) short break in a
journey

stopovers n ▷ **stopover**

stoppage n ▷ **stop**

stoppages n ▷ **stop**

stopped v ▷ **stop**

stopper n (pl **-s**) plug for closing a
bottle etc

stoppers n ▷ **stopper**

stopping v ▷ **stop**

stops v, n ▷ **stop**

storage n (pl **-s**) storing

storages n ▷ **storage**

store v (**-res**, **-ring**, **-red**) collect and
keep (things) for future use ▶ n (pl
-s) shop

stored v ▷ **store**

stores v, n ▷ **store** ▶ n pl stock of
provisions

storey n (pl **-s**) floor or level of a building

storeys n ▷ **storey**

stories n ▷ **story**

storing v ▷ **store**

stork n (pl **-s**) large wading bird

storks n ▷ **stork**

storm n (pl **-s**) violent weather with
wind, rain, or snow ▶ v (**-s**, **-ing**, **-ed**)
attack or capture (a place) suddenly

stormed v ▷ **storm**

stormier adj ▷ **stormy**

stormiest adj ▷ **stormy**

storming v ▷ **storm**

storms n, v ▷ **storm**

stormy adj (**-mier**, **-miest**)
characterized by storms

story n (pl **-ries**) description of a
series of events told or written for
entertainment

stoup n (pl **-s**) small basin for holy
water

stoups n ▷ **stoup**

stout adj (**-er**, **-est**) fat ▶ n (pl **-s**) strong
dark beer >**stoutly** adv

stouter adj ▷ **stout**

stoutest adj ▷ **stout**

stoutly adv ▷ **stout**

stouts n ▷ **stout**

stove n (pl **-s**) apparatus for cooking
or heating

stoves n ▷ **stove**

stow v (**-s**, **-ing**, **-ed**) pack or store

stowaway n (pl **-s**) person who
hides on a ship or aircraft in order to
travel free

stowaways n ▷ **stowaway**

stowed v ▷ **stow**

stowing v ▷ **stow**

stows v ▷ **stow**

straddle v (**-les**, **-ling**, **-led**) have one
leg or part on each side of (something)

straddled v ▷ **straddle**

straddles v ▷ **straddle**

straddling v ▷ **straddle**

strafe v (**-fes**, **-fing**, **-fed**) attack (an
enemy) with machine guns from
the air

strafed v ▷ **strafe**

strafes v ▷ **strafe**

strafing v ▷ **strafe**

straggle v (**-les**, **-ling**, **-led**) go or
spread in a rambling or irregular way
>**straggler** n (pl **-s**) >**straggly** adj

(-lier, -liest)
straggled v ▷ straggle
straggler n ▷ straggle
stragglers v ▷ straggle
straggles v ▷ straggle
stragglier adj ▷ straggle
straggliest adj ▷ straggle
straggling v ▷ straggle
straggly adj ▷ straggle
straight adj (-er, -est) not curved or crooked ▶ adv in a straight line ▶ n (pl -s) straight part, esp. of a racetrack
> **straighten** (-s, -ing, -ed)
straighten v ▷ straight
straightened v ▷ straight
straightening v ▷ straight
straightens v ▷ straight
straighter adj ▷ straight
straightest adj ▷ straight
straights n ▷ straight
strain v (-s, -ing, -ed) cause (something) to be used or tested beyond its limits ▶ n (pl -s) tension or tiredness
strain² n (pl -s) breed or race
strained adj not natural, forced ▶ v ▷ strain¹
strainer n (pl -s) sieve
strainers n ▷ strainer
straining v ▷ strain¹
strains n ▷ strain¹, ² ▶ v ▷ strain¹
strait n (pl -s) position of acute difficulty
straits n ▷ strait ▶ n pl narrow channel connecting two areas of sea
strand¹ v (-s, -ing, -ed) run aground ▶ n (pl -s) poetic shore
strand² n (pl -s) single thread of string, wire, etc
stranded v ▷ strand¹
stranding v ▷ strand¹
strands n ▷ strand¹, ² ▶ v ▷ strand¹
strange adj (-r, -st) odd or unusual
> **strangely** adv ▷ **strangeness** n (pl -es)
strangely adv ▷ strange
strangeness n ▷ strange
strangenesses n ▷ strange
stranger n (pl -s) person who is not known or is new to a place or

experience ▶ adj ▷ strange
strangers n ▷ stranger
strangest adj ▷ strange
strangle v (-les, -ling, -led) kill by squeezing the throat > **strangler** n (pl -s)
strangled v ▷ strangle
strangler n ▷ strangle
stranglers n ▷ strangle
strangles v ▷ strangle
strangling v ▷ strangle
strap n (pl -s) strip of flexible material for lifting, fastening, or holding in place ▶ v (-s, -pping, -pped) fasten with a strap or straps
strapped v ▷ strap
straps n, v ▷ strap
strata n ▷ stratum
strategies n ▷ strategy
strategist n ▷ strategy
strategists n ▷ strategy
strategy n (pl -gies) overall plan
> **strategist** n (pl -s)
stratum n (pl -ta) layer, esp. of rock
straw n (pl -s) dried stalks of grain
straws n ▷ straw
stray v (-s, -ing, -ed) wander ▶ adj having strayed ▶ n (pl -s) stray animal
strayed v ▷ stray
straying v ▷ stray
strays v, n ▷ stray
streak n (pl -s) long band of contrasting colour or substance ▶ v (-s, -ing, -ed) mark with streaks > **streaker** n (pl -s)
> **streaky** adj (-kier, -kiest)
streaked v ▷ streak
streaker n ▷ streak
streakers n ▷ streak
streakier adj ▷ streak
streakiest adj ▷ streak
streaking v ▷ streak
streaks n, v ▷ streak
streaky adj ▷ streak
stream n (pl -s) small river ▶ v (-s, -ing, -ed) flow steadily
streamed v ▷ stream
streamer n (pl -s) strip of coloured paper that unrolls when tossed
streamers n ▷ streamer

streaming v ▷ stream
streams n, v ▷ stream
street n (pl -s) public road, usu. lined with buildings
streets n ▷ street
strength n quality of being strong > **strengthen** v (-s, -ing, -ed)
strengthen v ▷ strength
strengthened v ▷ strength
strengthening v ▷ strength
strengthens v ▷ strength
strengths n ▷ strength
stress n (pl -es) tension or strain ▶ v (-es, -ing, -ed) emphasize
stressed v ▷ stress
stresses n, v ▷ stress
stressing v ▷ stress
stretch v (-es, -ing, -ed) extend or be extended ▶ n (pl -es) stretching > **stretchy** adj (-chier, -chiest)
stretched v ▷ stretch
stretches v, n ▷ stretch
stretchier adj ▷ stretch
stretchiest adj ▷ stretch
stretching v ▷ stretch
stretchy adj ▷ stretch
strew v (-s, -ing, -ed or strewn) scatter (things) over a surface
strewed v ▷ strew
strewing v ▷ strew
strewn v ▷ strew
strews v ▷ strew
striated adj having a pattern of scratches or grooves
stricken adj seriously affected by disease, grief, pain, etc
strict adj (-er, -est) stern or severe > **strictly** adv > **strictness** n (pl -es)
stricter adj ▷ strict
strictest adj ▷ strict
strictly adv ▷ strict
strictness n ▷ strict
strictnesses n ▷ strict
stridden v ▷ stride
stride v (-des, -ding, strode, stridden) walk with long steps ▶ n (pl -s) long step
stridencies n ▷ strident
stridency n ▷ strident

strident adj loud and harsh
> **stridently** adv > **stridency** n (pl -cies)
stridently adv ▷ strident
strides v, n ▷ stride ▶ n pl progress
striding v ▷ stride
strife n (pl -s) conflict, quarrelling
strifes n ▷ strife
strike v (-kes, -king, struck) cease work as a protest ▶ n (pl -s) stoppage of work as a protest
striker n (pl -s) striking worker
strikers n ▷ striker
strikes v, n ▷ strike
striking adj impressive ▶ v ▷ strike
string n (pl -s) thin cord used for tying ▶ v (-s, -ing, strung) provide with a string or strings
stringed adj (of a musical instrument) having strings that are plucked or played with a bow
stringier adj ▷ stringy
stringiest adj ▷ stringy
stringing v ▷ string
strings n, v ▷ string ▶ n pl restrictions or conditions
stringy adj (-gier, -giest) like string
strip v (-s, -pping, -pped) take (the covering or clothes) off
strip² n (pl -s) long narrow piece
stripe n (pl -s) long narrow band of contrasting colour or substance > **striped, stripy, stripey** adj (-pier, -piest)
striped adj ▷ stripe
stripes n ▷ stripe
stripey adj ▷ stripe
stripier adj ▷ stripe
stripiest adj ▷ stripe
stripped v ▷ strip¹
stripper n (pl -s) person who performs a striptease
strippers n ▷ stripper
stripping v ▷ strip¹
strips v ▷ strip¹ ▶ n ▷ strip²
stripy adj ▷ stripe
strive v (-ves, -ving, strove, striven) make a great effort
striven v ▷ strive
strives v ▷ strive

striving v ▷ **strive**

strobes n ▷ **strobe**

stroke v (-kes, -king, -ked) touch or caress lightly with the hand ▶ n (pl -s) light touch or caress with the hand

stroked v ▷ **stroke**

strokes v, n ▷ **stroke**

stroking v ▷ **stroke**

stroll v (-s, -ing, -ed) walk in a leisurely manner ▶ n (pl -s) leisurely walk

strolled v ▷ **stroll**

strolling v ▷ **stroll**

strolls v, n ▷ **stroll**

strong adj (-er, -est) having physical power ▷ **strongly** adv

stronger adj ▷ **strong**

strongest adj ▷ **strong**

strongly adv ▷ **strong**

strop n (pl -s) leather strap for sharpening razors

stroppier adj ▷ **stroppy**

stroppiest adj ▷ **stroppy**

stroppy adj (-pier, -piest) slang angry or awkward

strops n ▷ **strop**

strove v ▷ **strive**

struck v ▷ **strike**

strudel n (pl -s) thin sheet of filled dough rolled up and baked, usu. with an apple filling

strudels n ▷ **strudel**

struggle v (-les, -ling, -led) work, strive, or make one's way with difficulty ▶ n (pl -s) striving

struggled v ▷ **struggle**

struggles v, n ▷ **struggle**

struggling v ▷ **struggle**

strum v (-s, -mming, -mmed) play (a guitar or banjo) by sweeping the thumb or a plectrum across the strings

strummed v ▷ **strum**

strumming v ▷ **strum**

strumpet n (pl -s) old-fashioned prostitute

strumpets n ▷ **strumpet**

strums v ▷ **strum**

strung v ▷ **string**

strut v (-s, -tting, -tted) walk pompously, swagger ▶ n (pl -s) bar supporting a structure

struts v, n ▷ **strut**

strutted v ▷ **strut**

strutting v ▷ **strut**

stub n (pl -s) short piece left after use ▶ v (-s, -bbing, -bbed) strike (the toe) painfully against an object

stubbed v ▷ **stub**

stubbier adj ▷ **stubby**

stubbiest adj ▷ **stubby**

stubbing v ▷ **stub**

stubble n (pl -s) short stalks of grain left in a field after reaping > **stubbly** adj (-lier, -liest)

stubbles n ▷ **stubble**

stubblier adj ▷ **stubble**

stubbliest adj ▷ **stubble**

stubbly adj ▷ **stubble**

stubborn adj (-er, -est) refusing to agree or give in > **stubbornly** adv > **stubbornness** n (pl -es)

stubborner adj ▷ **stubborn**

stubbornest adj ▷ **stubborn**

stubbornly adv ▷ **stubborn**

stubbornness n ▷ **stubborn**

stubbornnesses n ▷ **stubborn**

stubby adj (-bbier, -bbiest) short and broad

stubs n, v ▷ **stub**

stucco n (pl -es) plaster used for coating or decorating walls

stuccoes n ▷ **stucco**

stuck v ▷ **stick²**

stud¹ n (pl -s) small piece of metal attached to a surface for decoration ▶ v (-s, -dding, -dded) set with studs

stud² n (pl -s) male animal, esp. a stallion, kept for breeding

studded v ▷ **stud¹**

studding v ▷ **stud¹**

student n (pl -s) person who studies a subject, esp. at university

students n ▷ **student**

studied adj carefully practised or planned ▶ v ▷ **study**

studies v, n ▷ **study**

studio n (pl -s) workroom of an artist or photographer

studios n ▷ studio
studious adj fond of study
> **studiously** adv
  studiously adv ▷ studious
  studs n ▷ stud¹ ² & stud¹
study v (-dies, -dying, -died) be
  engaged in learning (a subject) ▶ n (pl
  -dies) act or process of studying
  studying v ▷ study
stuff n (pl -s) substance or material
  ▶ v (-s, -ing, -ed) pack, cram, or fill
  completely
  stuffed v ▷ stuff
  stuffier adj ▷ stuffy
  stuffiest adj ▷ stuffy
stuffing n (pl -s) seasoned mixture with
  which food is stuffed ▶ v ▷ stuff
  stuffings n ▷ stuffing
  stuffs n, v ▷ stuff
stuffy adj (-fier, -fiest) lacking fresh air
stumble v (-les, -ling, -led) trip and
  nearly fall ▶ n (pl -s) stumbling
  stumbled v ▷ stumble
  stumbles n ▷ stumble
  stumbling v ▷ stumble
stump n (pl -s) base of a tree left when
  the main trunk has been cut away ▶ v
  (-s, -ing, -ed) baffle
  stumped v ▷ stump
  stumpier adj ▷ stumpy
  stumpiest adj ▷ stumpy
  stumping v ▷ stump
  stumps n, v ▷ stump
stumpy adj (-pier, -piest) short and
  thick
stun v (-s, -nning, -nned) shock or
  overwhelm
  stung v ▷ sting
  stunk v ▷ stink
  stunned v ▷ stun
stunning adj very attractive or
  impressive ▶ v ▷ stun
  stuns v ▷ stun
stunt¹ v (-s, -ing, -ed) prevent or
  impede the growth of > **stunted** adj
stunt² n (pl -s) acrobatic or dangerous
  action
  stunted v, adj ▷ stunt¹
  stunting v ▷ stunt¹

  stunts v ▷ stunt¹ ▶ n ▷ stunt²
stupefaction n ▷ stupefy
  stupefactions n ▷ stupefy
  stupefied v ▷ stupefy
  stupefies v ▷ stupefy
stupefy v (-fies, -fying, -fied)
  make insensitive or lethargic
  > **stupefaction** n (pl -s)
  stupefying v ▷ stupefy
stupid adj (-er, -est) lacking
  intelligence > **stupidity** n (pl -ties)
  > **stupidly** adv
  stupider adj ▷ stupid
  stupidest adj ▷ stupid
  stupidities n ▷ stupid
  stupidity n ▷ stupid
  stupidly adv ▷ stupid
stupor n (pl -s) dazed or unconscious
  state
  stupors n ▷ stupor
  sturdier adj ▷ sturdy
  sturdiest adj ▷ sturdy
  sturdily adv ▷ sturdy
sturdy adj (-dier, -diest) healthy and
  robust > **sturdily** adv
sturgeon n (pl -s) fish from which
  caviar is obtained
  sturgeons n ▷ sturgeon
stutter v (-s, -ing, -ed) speak with
  repetition of initial consonants ▶ n (pl
  -s) tendency to stutter
  stuttered v ▷ stutter
  stuttering v ▷ stutter
  stutters v, n ▷ stutter
sty n (pl sties) pen for pigs
stye n (pl styes) inflammation at the
  base of an eyelash
  styes n ▷ stye
style n (pl -s) shape or design ▶ v (-les,
  -ling, -led) shape or design
  styled v ▷ style
  styles n, v ▷ style
  styli n ▷ stylus
  styling v ▷ style
stylish adj smart, elegant, and
  fashionable > **stylishly** adv
  stylishly adv ▷ stylish
stylist n (pl -s) hairdresser
  stylists n ▷ stylist

stylize v (-zes, -zing, -zed) cause to conform to an established stylistic form
stylized v ▷ stylize
stylizes v ▷ stylize
stylizing v ▷ stylize

stylus n (pl -li, -luses) needle-like device on a record player that rests in the groove of the record and picks up the sound signals
styluses n ▷ stylus

stymie v (-mies, -mieing, -mied) hinder or thwart
stymied v ▷ stymie
stymieing v ▷ stymie
stymies v ▷ stymie

styptic n (pl -s) ▶ adj (drug) used to stop bleeding
styptics n ▷ styptic

suave adj smooth and sophisticated in manner ▶ **suavely** adv
suavely adv ▷ suave

sub n (pl -s) subeditor ▶ v (-s, -bbing, -bbed) act as a substitute
subbed v ▷ sub
subbing v ▷ sub

subdue v (-dues, -duing, -dued) overcome
subdued v ▷ subdue
subdues v ▷ subdue
subduing v ▷ subdue

subject n (pl -s) person or thing being dealt with or studied ▶ adj being under the rule of a monarch or government ▶ v (-s, -ing, -ed) (foll. by **to**) cause to undergo ▶ **subjection** n (pl -s)
subjected v ▷ subject
subjecting v ▷ subject
subjection n ▷ subject
subjections n ▷ subject
subjects n, v ▷ subject

sublet v (-s, -letting, -let) rent out (property rented from someone else)
sublets v ▷ sublet
subletting v ▷ sublet

sublime adj (-r, -st) of high moral, intellectual, or spiritual value ▶ v (-mes, -ming, -med) CHEM change from a solid to a vapour without first melting ▶ **sublimely** adv
sublimed v ▷ sublime
sublimely adv ▷ sublime
sublimer adj ▷ sublime
sublimes v ▷ sublime
sublimest adj ▷ sublime
subliming v ▷ sublime

submerge v (-ges, -ging, -ged) put or go below the surface of water or other liquid ▶ **submersion** n (pl -s)
submerged v ▷ submerge
submerges v ▷ submerge
submerging v ▷ submerge
submersion n ▷ submerge
submersions n ▷ submerge

submit v (-s, -tting, -tted) surrender
submits v ▷ submit
submitted v ▷ submit
submitting v ▷ submit

suborn v (-s, -ing, -ed) formal bribe or incite (a person) to commit a wrongful act
suborned v ▷ suborn
suborning v ▷ suborn
suborns v ▷ suborn

subpoena n (pl -s) writ requiring a person to appear before a lawcourt ▶ v (-nas, -naing, -naed) summon (someone) with a subpoena
subpoenaed v ▷ subpoena
subpoenaing v ▷ subpoena
subpoenas n, v ▷ subpoena

subside v (-des, -ding, -ded) become less intense
subsided v ▷ subside
subsides v ▷ subside
subsidies n ▷ subsidy
subsiding v ▷ subside

subsidy n (pl -dies) financial aid

subsist v (-s, -ing, -ed) manage to live ▶ **subsistence** n (pl -s)
subsisted v ▷ subsist
subsistence n ▷ subsist
subsistences n ▷ subsist
subsisting v ▷ subsist
subsists v ▷ subsist

subsonic adj moving at a speed less than that of sound

subsume v (-mes, -ming, -med) include (an idea, case, etc) under a larger classification or group
subsumed v ▷ subsume
subsumes v ▷ subsume
subsuming v ▷ subsume

subtitle n (pl -s) secondary title of a book ▶ v (-les, -ling, -led) provide with a subtitle or subtitles
subtitled v ▷ subtitle
subtitles n, v ▷ subtitle
subtitling v ▷ subtitle

subtle adj (-r, -st) not immediately obvious ▶ **subtly** adv ▶ **subtlety** n (pl -ties)
subtler adj ▷ subtle
subtlest adj ▷ subtle
subtleties n ▷ subtle
subtlety n ▷ subtle
subtly adv ▷ subtle

subtract v (-s, -ing, -ed) take (one number or quantity) from another ▶ **subtraction** n (pl -s)
subtracted v ▷ subtract
subtracting v ▷ subtract
subtraction n ▷ subtract
subtractions n ▷ subtract
subtracts v ▷ subtract

suburb n (pl -s) residential area on the outskirts of a city
suburban adj of or inhabiting a suburb
suburbia n (pl -s) suburbs and their inhabitants
suburbias n ▷ suburbia
suburbs n ▷ suburb

subversion n ▷ subvert
subversions n ▷ subvert
subversive adj, n ▷ subvert
subversives n ▷ subvert

subvert v (-s, -ing, -ed) overthrow the authority of ▶ **subversion** n (pl -s) ▶ **subversive** adj, n (pl -s)
subverted v ▷ subvert
subverting v ▷ subvert
subverts v ▷ subvert

subway n (pl -s) passage under a road or railway
subways n ▷ subway

succeed v (-s, -ing, -ed) accomplish an aim

succeeded v ▷ succeed
succeeding v ▷ succeed
succeeds v ▷ succeed

success n (pl -es) achievement of something attempted
successes n ▷ success

succinct adj (-er, -est) brief and clear ▶ **succinctly** adv
succincter adj ▷ succinct
succinctest adj ▷ succinct
succinctly adv ▷ succinct

succour v (-s, -ing, -ed) ▶ n (pl -s) help in distress
succoured v ▷ succour
succouring v ▷ succour
succours v, n ▷ succour

succumb v (-s, -ing, -ed) (foll. by to) give way (to something overpowering)
succumbed v ▷ succumb
succumbing v ▷ succumb
succumbs v ▷ succumb

such adj of the kind specified ▶ pron such things

suchlike pron such or similar things

suck v (-s, -ing, -ed) draw (liquid or air) into the mouth ▶ n (pl -s) sucking
sucked v ▷ suck

sucker n (pl -s) slang person who is easily deceived or swindled
suckers n ▷ sucker
sucking v ▷ suck

suckle v (-les, -ling, -led) feed at the breast
suckled v ▷ suckle
suckles v ▷ suckle

suckling n (pl -s) unweaned baby or young animal ▶ v ▷ suckle
sucklings n ▷ suckling
sucks v, n ▷ suck

sucrose n (pl -s) chemical name for sugar
sucroses n ▷ sucrose

suction n (pl -s) ▷ suction
suctions n ▷ suction

sudden adj done or occurring quickly and unexpectedly ▶ **suddenly** adv ▶ **suddenness** n (pl -es)
suddenly adv ▷ sudden

suds pl n froth of soap and water, lather

sue v (**-ues, -uing, -ued**) start legal proceedings against
sued v ▷ **sue**
suede n (pl **-s**) leather with a velvety finish on one side
suedes n ▷ **suede**
sues v ▷ **sue**
suet n (pl **-s**) hard fat obtained from sheep and cattle, used in cooking
suets n ▷ **suet**
suffer v (**-s, -ing, -ed**) undergo or be subjected to ▷ **sufferer** n (pl **-s**)
> **suffering** n (pl **-s**) > **sufferance** n (pl **-s**)
sufferance n ▷ **suffer**
sufferances n ▷ **suffer**
suffered v ▷ **suffer**
sufferer n ▷ **suffer**
sufferers n ▷ **suffer**
suffering n, v ▷ **suffer**
sufferings n ▷ **suffer**
suffers v ▷ **suffer**
suffice v (**-ces, -cing, -ced**) be enough for a purpose
sufficed v ▷ **suffice**
suffices v ▷ **suffice**
sufficing v ▷ **suffice**
suffix n (pl **-es**) letter or letters added to the end of a word to form another word, such as -s and -ness in dogs and softness
suffixes n ▷ **suffix**
suffrage n (pl **-s**) right to vote in public elections
suffrages n ▷ **suffrage**
suffuse v (**-ses, -sing, -sed**) spread through or over (something)
> **suffusion** n (pl **-s**)
suffused v ▷ **suffuse**
suffuses v ▷ **suffuse**
suffusing v ▷ **suffuse**
suffusion n ▷ **suffuse**
suffusions n ▷ **suffuse**
sugar n (pl **-s**) sweet crystalline carbohydrate found in many plants and used to sweeten food and drinks
▶ v (**-s, -ing, -ed**) sweeten or cover with sugar > **sugary** adj (**-rier, -riest**)
sugared v ▷ **sugar**

sugarier adj ▷ **sugar**
sugariest adj ▷ **sugar**
sugaring v ▷ **sugar**
sugars n, v ▷ **sugar**
sugary adj ▷ **sugar**
suggest v (**-s, -ing, -ed**) put forward (an idea) for consideration
suggested v ▷ **suggest**
suggesting v ▷ **suggest**
suggests v ▷ **suggest**
suicidal adj liable to commit suicide
> **suicidally** adv
suicidally adv ▷ **suicide**
suicide n (pl **-s**) killing oneself intentionally
suicides n ▷ **suicide**
suing v ▷ **sue**
suit n (pl **-s**) set of clothes designed to be worn together ▶ v (**-s, -ing, -ed**) be appropriate for
suitabilities n ▷ **suitable**
suitability n ▷ **suitable**
suitable adj appropriate or proper
> **suitably** adv > **suitability** n (pl **-ties**)
suitably adv ▷ **suitable**
suitcase n (pl **-s**) portable travelling case for clothing
suitcases n ▷ **suitcase**
suite n (pl **-s**) set of connected rooms in a hotel
suited v ▷ **suit**
suites n ▷ **suite**
suiting v ▷ **suit**
suitor n (pl **-s**) old-fashioned man who is courting a woman
suitors n ▷ **suitor**
suits n, v ▷ **suit**
sulk v (**-s, -ing, -ed**) be silent and sullen because of resentment or bad temper
▶ n (pl **-s**) resentful or sullen mood
> **sulky** adj (**-kier, -kiest**) > **sulkily** adv
sulked v ▷ **sulk**
sulkier adj ▷ **sulk**
sulkiest adj ▷ **sulk**
sulkily adv ▷ **sulk**
sulking v ▷ **sulk**
sulks v, n ▷ **sulk**
sulky adj ▷ **sulk**
sullen adj (**-er, -est**) unwilling to

talk or be sociable > **sullenly** adv
> **sullenness** n (pl -es)
sullener adj > **sullen**
sullenest adj > **sullen**
sullenly adv > **sullen**
sullenness n > **sullen**
sullennesses n > **sullen**
sullied v > **sully**
sullies v > **sully**
sully v (-lies, -lying, -lied) ruin
(someone's reputation)
sullying v > **sully**
sulphate n (pl -s) salt or ester of
sulphuric acid
sulphates n > **sulphate**
sulphide n (pl -s) compound of sulphur
with another element
sulphides n > **sulphide**
sulphite n (pl -s) salt or ester of
sulphurous acid
sulphites n > **sulphite**
sulphur n (pl -s) CHEM pale yellow
nonmetallic element
sulphurs n > **sulphur**
sultan n (pl -s) sovereign of a Muslim
country
sultana n (pl -s) kind of raisin
sultanas n > **sultana**
sultans n > **sultan**
sultrier adj > **sultry**
sultriest adj > **sultry**
sultry adj (-trier, -triest) (of weather or
climate) hot and humid
sum n (pl -s) result of addition, total
summaries n > **summary**
summarily adv > **summary**
summary n (pl -ries) brief account
giving the main points of something
▶ adj done quickly, without formalities
> **summarily** adv
summer n (pl -s) warmest season of
the year, between spring and autumn
> **summery** adj (-rier, -riest)
summerier adj > **summer**
summeriest adj > **summer**
summers n > **summer**
summery adj > **summer**
summit n (pl -s) top of a mountain
or hill

summits n > **summit**
summon v (-s, -ing, -ed) order
(someone) to come
summoned v > **summon**
summoning v > **summon**
summons n (pl -es) command
summoning someone ▶ v (-es, -ing,
-ed) order (someone) to appear in
court ▶ v > **summon**
summonsed v > **summons**
summonses v, n > **summons**
summonsing v > **summons**
sumo n (pl -s) Japanese style of
wrestling
sumos n > **sumo**
sump n (pl -s) container in an internal-
combustion engine into which oil
can drain
sumps n > **sump**
sums n > **sum**
sun n (pl -s) star around which the
earth and other planets revolve ▶ v (-s,
-nning, -nned) expose (oneself) to the
sun's rays > **sunless** adj
sunbathe v (-thes, -thing, -thed) lie in
the sunshine in order to get a suntan
sunbathed v > **sunbathe**
sunbathes v > **sunbathe**
sunbathing v > **sunbathe**
sunbeam n (pl -s) ray of sun
sunbeams n > **sunbeam**
sunburn n (pl -s) painful reddening of
the skin caused by overexposure to the
sun > **sunburnt, sunburned** adj
sunburned adj > **sunburn**
sunburns n > **sunburn**
sunburnt adj > **sunburn**
sundae n (pl -s) ice cream topped with
fruit etc
sundaes n > **sundae**
sundial n (pl -s) device showing the
time by means of a pointer that casts a
shadow on a marked dial
sundials n > **sundial**
sundown n (pl -s) sunset
sundowns n > **sundown**
sundries pl n several things of various
sorts
sundry adj several, various

sung v ▷ **sing**

sunk v ▷ **sink**

sunken v ▷ **sink**

sunless adj ▷ **sun**

sunned v ▷ **sun**

sunnier adj ▷ **sunny**

sunniest adj ▷ **sunny**

sunning v ▷ **sun**

sunny adj (**-nier, -niest**) full of or exposed to sunlight

sunrise n (pl **-s**) daily appearance of the sun above the horizon

sunrises n ▷ **sunrise**

suns n, v ▷ **sun**

sunset n (pl **-s**) daily disappearance of the sun below the horizon

sunsets n ▷ **sunset**

sunshine n (pl **-s**) light and warmth from the sun

sunshines n ▷ **sunshine**

sunspot n (pl **-s**) dark patch appearing temporarily on the sun's surface

sunspots n ▷ **sunspot**

suntan n (pl **-s**) browning of the skin caused by exposure to the sun

suntans n ▷ **suntan**

sup v (**-s, -pping, -pped**) take (liquid) by sips ▷ n (pl **-s**) sip

super adj informal excellent

superb adj excellent, impressive, or splendid ▷ **superbly** adv

superbly adv ▷ **superb**

superbug n (pl **-s**) informal bacterium resistant to antibiotics

superbugs n ▷ **superbug**

superior adj greater in quality, quantity, or merit ▷ n (pl **-s**) person of greater rank or status ▷ **superiority** n (pl **-ties**)

superiorities n ▷ **superior**

superiority n ▷ **superior**

superiors n ▷ **superior**

superman n (pl **-men**) man with great physical or mental powers

supermen n ▷ **superman**

supine adj lying flat on one's back

supped v ▷ **sup**

supper n (pl **-s**) light evening meal

suppers n ▷ **supper**

supping v ▷ **sup**

supplant v (**-s, -ing, -ed**) take the place of, oust

supplanted v ▷ **supplant**

supplanting v ▷ **supplant**

supplants v ▷ **supplant**

supple adj (**-r, -st**) (of a person) moving and bending easily and gracefully ▷ **suppleness** n (pl **-es**)

suppleness n ▷ **supple**

supplenesses n ▷ **supple**

suppler adj ▷ **supple**

supplest adj ▷ **supple**

supplied v ▷ **supply**

supplier n ▷ **supply**

suppliers n ▷ **supply**

supplies pl n food or equipment ▷ v ▷ **supply**

supply v (**-lies, -lying, -lied**) provide with something required ▷ n (pl **-lies**)

supplying v ▷ **supplier**

supplying v ▷ **supply**

support v (**-s, -ing, -ed**) bear the weight of ▷ n (pl **-s**) supporting ▷ **supportive** adj

supported v ▷ **support**

supporting v ▷ **support**

supportive adj ▷ **support**

supports v, n ▷ **support**

suppose v (**-ses, -sing, -sed**) presume to be true

supposed adj presumed to be true without proof, doubtful ▷ v ▷ **suppose** ▷ **supposedly** adv

supposedly adv ▷ **supposed**

supposes v ▷ **suppose**

supposing v ▷ **suppose**

suppress v (**-es, -ing, -ed**) put an end to ▷ **suppression** n (pl **-s**)

suppressed v ▷ **suppress**

suppresses v ▷ **suppress**

suppressing v ▷ **suppress**

suppression n ▷ **suppress**

suppressions n ▷ **suppress**

supreme adj highest in authority, rank, or degree

supremo n (pl **-s**) informal person in

overall authority

supremos n ▷ **supremo**

sups n, v ▷ **sup**

suq n (**suqs**) A suq is an open-air marketplace in Arabic-speaking countries. This unusual word can be very useful. Usually, when you have a Q and a U, you will be looking to play words with QU in them. But look out for opportunities to use suq instead. Suq scores 12 points.

surd n (pl -s) MATHS number that cannot be expressed in whole numbers

surds n ▷ **surd**

sure adj (-r, -st) free from uncertainty or doubt ▶ adv, interj informal certainly

surely adv it must be true that

surer adj ▷ **sure**

surest adj ▷ **sure**

sureties n ▷ **surety**

surety n (pl -ties) person who takes responsibility, or thing given as a guarantee, for the fulfilment of another's obligation

surf n (pl -s) foam caused by waves breaking on the shore ▶ v (-s, -ing, -ed) take part in surfing ▶ **surfer** n (pl -s)

surface n (pl -s) outside or top of an object ▶ v (-ces, -cing, -ced) rise to the surface

surfaced v ▷ **surface**

surfaces n, v ▷ **surface**

surfacing v ▷ **surface**

surfed v ▷ **surf**

surfeit n (pl -s) excessive amount

surfeits n ▷ **surfeit**

surfer n ▷ **surf**

surfers n ▷ **surf**

surfing n (pl -s) sport of riding towards the shore on a surfboard on the crest of a wave ▶ v ▷ **surf**

surfings n ▷ **surfing**

surfs n, v ▷ **surf**

surge n (pl -s) sudden powerful increase ▶ v (-ges, -ging, -ged) increase suddenly

surged v ▷ **surge**

surgeon n (pl -s) doctor who specializes in surgery

surgeons n ▷ **surgeon**

surgeries n ▷ **surgery**

surgery n (pl -ries) treatment in which the patient's body is cut open in order to treat the affected part ▷ **surgical** adj ▷ **surgically** adv

surges n, v ▷ **surge**

surgical adj ▷ **surgery**

surgically adv ▷ **surgery**

surging v ▷ **surge**

surlier adj ▷ **surly**

surliest adj ▷ **surly**

surliness n ▷ **surly**

surlinesses n ▷ **surly**

surly adj (-lier, -liest) ill-tempered and rude ▶ **surliness** n (pl -es)

surmise v (-ises, -ising, -ised) ▶ n (pl -s) guess, conjecture

surmised v ▷ **surmise**

surmises n, v ▷ **surmise**

surmising v ▷ **surmise**

surmount v (-s, -ing, -ed) overcome (a problem) ▷ **surmountable** adj

surmountable adj ▷ **surmount**

surmounted v ▷ **surmount**

surmounting v ▷ **surmount**

surmounts v ▷ **surmount**

surname n (pl -s) family name

surnames n ▷ **surname**

surpass v (-es, -ing, -ed) be greater than or superior to

surpassed v ▷ **surpass**

surpasses v ▷ **surpass**

surpassing v ▷ **surpass**

surplice n (pl -s) loose white robe worn by clergymen and choristers

surplices n ▷ **surplice**

surplus n (pl -es) amount left over in excess of what is required

surpluses n ▷ **surplus**

surprise n (pl -ses) unexpected event ▶ v (-ses, -sing, -sed) cause to feel amazement or wonder

surprised v ▷ **surprise**

surprises n, v ▷ **surprise**

surprising v ▷ **surprise**

surreal adj bizarre ▷ **surrealist** n (pl -s) adj ▷ **surrealistic** adj

surrealist n, adj ▷ **surreal**

surrealistic adj ▷ surreal

surrealists n ▷ surreal

surround v (-s, -ing, -ed) be, come, or place all around (a person or thing) ▶ n (pl -s) border or edging

surrounded v ▷ surround

surrounding v ▷ surround

surrounds v, n ▷ surround

survey v (-s, -ing, -ed) view or consider in a general way ▶ n (pl -s) surveying >**surveyor** n (pl -s)

surveyed v ▷ survey

surveying v ▷ survey

surveyor n ▷ survey

surveyors n ▷ survey

surveys v, n ▷ survey

survival n (pl -s) condition of having survived

survivals n ▷ survival

survive v (-ves, -ing, -ved) continue to live or exist after (a difficult experience) >**survivor** n (pl -s)

survived v ▷ survive

survives v ▷ survive

surviving v ▷ survive

survivor n ▷ survive

survivors n ▷ survive

sushi n (pl -s) Japanese dish of small cakes of cold rice with a topping of raw fish

sushis n ▷ sushi

suspect v (-s, -ing, -ed) believe (someone) to be guilty without having any proof ▶ adj not to be trusted ▶ n (pl -s) person who is suspected

suspected v ▷ suspect

suspecting v ▷ suspect

suspects v, n ▷ suspect

suspend v (-s, -ing, -ed) hang from a high place

suspended v ▷ suspend

suspending v ▷ suspend

suspends v ▷ suspend

suspense n (pl -s) state of uncertainty while awaiting news, an event, etc

suspenses n ▷ suspense

sustain v (-s, -ing, -ed) maintain or prolong

sustained v ▷ sustain

sustaining v ▷ sustain

sustains v ▷ sustain

suture n (pl -s) stitch joining the edges of a wound

sutures n ▷ suture

suzerain n (pl -s) state or sovereign with limited authority over another self-governing state >**suzerainty** n (pl -ties)

suzerains n ▷ suzerain

suzerainties n ▷ suzerain

suzerainty n ▷ suzerain

svelte adj (-r, -st) attractively or gracefully slim

svelter adj ▷ svelte

sveltest adj ▷ svelte

swab n (pl -s) small piece of cotton wool used to apply medication, clean a wound, etc ▶ v (-s, -bbing, -bbed) clean (a wound) with a swab

swabbed v ▷ swab

swabbing v ▷ swab

swabs v, n ▷ swab

swaddle v (-les, -ling, -led) wrap (a baby) in swaddling clothes

swaddled v ▷ swaddle

swaddles v ▷ swaddle

swaddling v ▷ swaddle

swag n (pl -s) slang stolen property

swagger v (-s, -ing, -ed) walk or behave arrogantly ▶ n (pl -s) arrogant walk or manner

swaggered v ▷ swagger

swaggering v ▷ swagger

swaggers v, n ▷ swagger

swagman n (pl -men) AUST HIST tramp who carries his belongings in a bundle on his back

swagmen n ▷ swagman

swags n ▷ swag

swain n (pl -s) poetic suitor

swains n ▷ swain

swallow[1] v (-s, -ing, -ed) cause to pass down one's throat ▶ n (pl -s) swallowing

swallow[2] n (pl -s) small migratory bird with long pointed wings and a forked tail

swallowed v ▷ swallow[1]

swallowing v ▷ **swallow**[1]
swallows v ▷ **swallow**[1] ▷ n
▷ **swallow**[1, 2]
swam v ▷ **swim**

swamp n (pl -s) watery area of land,
bog ▶ v (-s, -ing, -ed) cause (a boat) to
fill with water and sink ▷ **swampy** adj
(-ier, -iest)
swamped v ▷ **swamp**
swampier adj ▷ **swamp**
swampiest adj ▷ **swamp**
swamping v ▷ **swamp**
swamps n, v ▷ **swamp**
swampy adj ▷ **swamp**

swan n (pl -s) large usu. white water
bird with a long graceful neck ▶ v
(-s, -nning, -nned) informal wander
about idly

swank slang v (-s, -ing, -ed) show off or
boast ▶ n (pl -s) showing off or boasting
swanked v ▷ **swank**
swankier adj ▷ **swanky**
swankiest adj ▷ **swanky**
swanking v ▷ **swank**
swanks v, n ▷ **swank**

swanky adj (-kier, -kiest) slang
expensive and showy, stylish
swanned n ▷ **swan**
swanning n ▷ **swan**
swans n, v ▷ **swan**

swap v (-s, -pping, -pped) exchange
(something) for something else ▶ n (pl
-s) exchange
swapped v ▷ **swap**
swapping v ▷ **swap**
swaps v, n ▷ **swap**

sward n (pl -s) stretch of short grass
swards n ▷ **sward**

swarm[1] n (pl -s) large group of bees or
other insects ▶ v (-s, -ing, -ed) move
in a swarm

swarm[2] v (-s, -ing, -ed) (foll. by up)
climb (a ladder or rope) by gripping
with the hands and feet
swarmed v ▷ **swarm**[1, 2]
swarming v ▷ **swarm**[1, 2]
swarms v ▷ **swarm**[1, 2] ▶ n ▷ **swarm**[1]
swarthier adj ▷ **swarthy**
swarthiest adj ▷ **swarthy**

swarthy adj (-thier, -thiest) dark-
complexioned

swastika n (pl -s) symbol in the shape
of a cross with the arms bent at right
angles, used as the emblem of Nazi
Germany
swastikas n ▷ **swastika**

swat v (-s, -tting, -tted) hit sharply ▶ n
(pl -s) sharp blow

swatch n (pl -es) sample of cloth
swatches n ▷ **swatch**

swath n (pl -s) ▷ **swathe**

swathe v (-thes, -thing, -thed) wrap
in bandages or layers of cloth ▶ n (pl
-s) long strip of cloth wrapped around
something (also **swath**)
swathed v ▷ **swathe**
swathes v, n ▷ **swathe**
swathing v ▷ **swathe**
swaths n ▷ **swath**
swats v, n ▷ **swat**
swatted v ▷ **swat**
swatting v ▷ **swat**

sway v (-s, -ing, -ed) swing to and fro
or from side to side ▶ n (pl -s) power
or influence
swayed v ▷ **sway**
swaying v ▷ **sway**
sways v, n ▷ **sway**

swear v (-s, -ing, swore, sworn) use
obscene or blasphemous language
swearing v ▷ **swear**
swears v ▷ **swear**

sweat n (pl -s) salty liquid given off
through the pores of the skin ▶ v (-s,
-ing, -ed) have sweat coming through
the pores ▷ **sweaty** adj (-tier, -tiest)
sweated v ▷ **sweat**

sweater n (pl -s) (woollen) garment for
the upper part of the body
sweaters n ▷ **sweater**
sweatier adj ▷ **sweat**
sweatiest adj ▷ **sweat**
sweating v ▷ **sweat**
sweats n, v ▷ **sweat**
sweaty adj ▷ **sweat**

swede n (pl -s) kind of turnip
swedes n ▷ **swede**

sweep v (-s, -ing, swept) remove dirt

from (a floor) with a broom ▶ n (pl -s) sweeping

sweeping adj wide-ranging ▶ v ▷ **sweep**

sweeps v, n ▷ **sweep**

sweet adj (-er, -est) tasting of or like sugar ▶ n (pl -s) shaped piece of food consisting mainly of sugar > **sweetly** adv > **sweetness** n (pl -es) > **sweeten** v (-s, -ing, -ed)

sweetened v ▷ **sweet**

sweetening v ▷ **sweet**

sweetens v ▷ **sweet**

sweetly adv ▷ **sweet**

sweetness n ▷ **sweet**

sweetnesses n ▷ **sweet**

sweets n ▷ **sweet**

swell v (-lls, -lling, -lled, swollen or swelled) expand or increase ▶ n (pl -s) swelling or being swollen ▶ adj (-er, -est) us slang excellent or fine

swelled v ▷ **swell**

sweller adj ▷ **swell**

swellest adj ▷ **swell**

swelling n (pl -s) enlargement of part of the body, caused by injury or infection ▶ v ▷ **swell**

swells v, n ▷ **swell**

swelter v (-s, -ing, -ed) feel uncomfortably hot

sweltered v ▷ **swelter**

swelters v ▷ **swelter**

swept v ▷ **sweep**

swerve v (-ves, -ving, -ved) turn aside from a course sharply or suddenly ▶ n (pl -s) swerving

swerved v ▷ **swerve**

swerves v, n ▷ **swerve**

swerving v ▷ **swerve**

swift adj (-er, -est) moving or able to move quickly ▶ n (pl -s) fast-flying bird with pointed wings > **swiftly** adv > **swiftness** n (pl -es)

swifter adj ▷ **swift**

swiftest adj ▷ **swift**

swiftly adv ▷ **swift**

swiftness n ▷ **swift**

swiftnesses n ▷ **swift**

swifts n ▷ **swift**

swig n (pl -s) large mouthful of drink ▶ v (-s, -gging, -gged) drink in large mouthfuls

swigged v ▷ **swig**

swigging v ▷ **swig**

swigs n, v ▷ **swig**

swill v (-s, -ing, -ed) drink greedily ▶ n (pl -s) sloppy mixture containing waste food, fed to pigs

swilled v ▷ **swill**

swilling v ▷ **swill**

swills v, n ▷ **swill**

swim v (-s, -mming, swam, swum) move along in water by movements of the limbs ▶ n (pl -s) act or period of swimming > **swimmer** n (pl -s)

swimmer n ▷ **swim**

swimmers n ▷ **swim**

swimming v ▷ **swim**

swims v, n ▷ **swim**

swindle v (-les, -ling, -led) cheat (someone) out of money ▶ n (pl -s) instance of swindling > **swindler** n (pl -s)

swindled v ▷ **swindle**

swindler n ▷ **swindle**

swindlers n ▷ **swindle**

swindles v, n ▷ **swindle**

swindling v ▷ **swindle**

swine n (pl -s) contemptible person

swines n ▷ **swine**

swing v (-s, -ing, swung) move to and fro, sway ▶ n (pl -s) swinging

swinging v ▷ **swing**

swings v, n ▷ **swing**

swipe v (-pes, -ping, -ped) strike (at) with a sweeping blow ▶ n (pl -s) hard blow

swiped v ▷ **swipe**

swipes v, n ▷ **swipe**

swiping v ▷ **swipe**

swirl v (-s, -ing, -ed) turn with a whirling motion ▶ n (pl -s) whirling motion

swirled v ▷ **swirl**

swirling v ▷ **swirl**

swirls v, n ▷ **swirl**

swish v (-es, -ing, -ed) move with a whistling or hissing sound ▶ n (pl -es)

whistling or hissing sound ▶ *adj* (**-er,
-est**) *informal* fashionable, smart
swished *v* ▷ **swish**
swisher *adj* ▷ **swish**
swishes *n, v* ▷ **swish**
swishest *adj* ▷ **swish**
swishing *v* ▷ **swish**
switch *n* (*pl* **-es**) device for opening and
closing an electric circuit ▶ *v* (**-ches,
-ching, -ched**) change abruptly
switched *v* ▷ **switch**
switches *n, v* ▷ **switch**
switching *v* ▷ **switch**
swivel *v* (**-s, -lling, -lled**) turn on a
central point ▶ *n* (*pl* **-s**) coupling device
that allows an attached object to
turn freely
swivelled *v* ▷ **swivel**
swivelling *v* ▷ **swivel**
swivels *v* ▷ **swivel**
swollen *v* ▷ **swell**
swoon *v* (**-s, -ing, -ed**) ▶ *n* (*pl* **-s**) faint
swooned *v* ▷ **swoon**
swooning *v* ▷ **swoon**
swoons *v, n* ▷ **swoon**
swoop *v* (**-s, -ing, -ed**) sweep down
or pounce on suddenly ▶ *n* (*pl* **-s**)
swooping
swooped *v* ▷ **swoop**
swooping *v* ▷ **swoop**
swoops *v, n* ▷ **swoop**
swop *v* (**-s, -pping, -pped**) ▶ *n* (*pl* **-s**)
▷ **swap**
swopped *v* ▷ **swop**
swopping *v* ▷ **swop**
swops *v, n* ▷ **swop**
sword *n* (*pl* **-s**) weapon with a long
sharp blade
swords *n* ▷ **sword**
swore *v* ▷ **swear**
sworn *v* ▷ **swear** ▶ *adj* bound by or as
if by an oath
swot *informal v* (**-s, -tting, -tted**) study
hard ▶ *n* (*pl* **-s**) person who studies
hard
swots *v, n* ▷ **swot**
swotted *v* ▷ **swot**
swotting *v* ▷ **swot**
swum *v* ▷ **swim**

swung *v* ▷ **swing**

swy *n* (**swys**) Swy is an Australian
gambling game. This is a very
unusual word which doesn't
contain a vowel, so it can be useful
in helping you to clear a difficult
rack. Swy scores 9 points.

sybarite *n* (*pl* **-s**) lover of luxury
> **sybaritic** *adj*
sybarites *n* ▷ **sybarite**
sybaritic *adj* ▷ **sybarite**
sycamore *n* (*pl* **-s**) tree with five-
pointed leaves and two-winged fruits
sycamores *n* ▷ **sycamore**
syllabi *n* ▷ **syllabus**
syllabic *adj* ▷ **syllable**
syllable *n* (*pl* **-s**) part of a word
pronounced as a unit > **syllabic** *adj*
syllables *n* ▷ **syllable**
syllabub *n* (*pl* **-s**) dessert of beaten
cream, sugar, and wine
syllabubs *n* ▷ **syllabub**
syllabus *n* (*pl* **-buses, -bi**) list of
subjects for a course of study
syllabuses *n* ▷ **syllabus**
sylph *n* (*pl* **-s**) slender graceful girl or
woman > **sylphlike** *adj*
sylphlike *adj* ▷ **sylph**
sylphs *n* ▷ **sylph**
sylvan *n* *lit* relating to woods and
trees
symbol *n* (*pl* **-s**) sign or thing
that stands for something else
> **symbolic** *adj* **symbolically** *adv*
symbolic *adj* ▷ **symbol**
symbolically *adv* ▷ **symbol**
symbols *n* ▷ **symbol**
symmetrical *adj* ▷ **symmetry**
symmetrically *adv* ▷ **symmetry**
symmetries *n* ▷ **symmetry**
symmetry *n* (*pl* **-tries**) state of having
two halves that are mirror images
of each other > **symmetrical** *adj*
> **symmetrically** *adv*
sympathies *n* ▷ **sympathy**
sympathy *n* (*pl* **-thies**) compassion for
someone's pain or distress
symphonic *adj* ▷ **symphony**
symphonies *n* ▷ **symphony**

symphony *n* (*pl* **-nies**) composition for orchestra, with several movements ▷ **symphonic** *adj*

symptom *n* (*pl* **-s**) sign indicating the presence of an illness ▷ **symptomatic** *adj*

symptomatic *adj* ▷ **symptom**

symptoms *n* ▷ **symptom**

> **syn** *adv*. Syn is a Scots word for **since**. This is a good word to remember for when you have a shortage of vowels. Syn scores 6 points.

sync, synch *informal* ▷ *v* (*pl*) synchronization ▷ *v* (**-s, -ing, -ed**) synchronize

synced *v* ▷ **sync**

synched *v* ▷ **sync**

synching *v* ▷ **sync**

synchs *n, v* ▷ **sync**

syncing *v* ▷ **sync**

syncope *n* (*pl* **-s**) MED a faint

syncopes *n* ▷ **syncope**

syncs *n, v* ▷ **sync**

syndrome *n* (*pl* **-s**) combination of symptoms indicating a particular disease

syndromes *n* ▷ **syndrome**

synergies *n* ▷ **synergy**

synergy *n* (*pl* **-gies**) potential ability for people or groups to be more successful working together than on their own

synod *n* (*pl* **-s**) church council

synods *n* ▷ **synod**

synonym *n* (*pl* **-s**) word with the same meaning as another ▷ **synonymous** *adj*

synonymous *adj* ▷ **synonym**

synonyms *n* ▷ **synonym**

synopses *n* ▷ **synopsis**

synopsis *n* (*pl* **-ses**) summary or outline

syntactic *adj* ▷ **syntax**

syntax *n* (*pl* **-es**) GRAMMAR way in which words are arranged to form phrases and sentences ▷ **syntactic** *adj*

syntaxes *n* ▷ **syntax**

syphilis *n* (*pl* **-es**) serious sexually transmitted disease ▷ **syphilitic** *adj*

syphilises *n* ▷ **syphilis**

syphilitic *adj* ▷ **syphilis**

syphon *n* (*pl* **-s**) ▷ *v* (**-s, -ing, -ed**) ▷ **siphon**

syphoned *v* ▷ **syphon**

syphoning *v* ▷ **syphon**

syphons *n, v* ▷ **syphon**

syringe *n* (*pl* **-s**) device for withdrawing or injecting fluids, consisting of a hollow cylinder, a piston, and a hollow needle ▷ *v* (**-ges, -ging, -ged**) wash out or inject with a syringe

syringed *v* ▷ **syringe**

syringes *n* ▷ **syringe**

syringing *v* ▷ **syringe**

syrup *n* (*pl* **-s**) solution of sugar in water ▷ **syrupy** *adj* (**-pier, -piest**)

syrupier *adj* ▷ **syrup**

syrupiest *adj* ▷ **syrup**

syrups *n* ▷ **syrup**

syrupy *adj* ▷ **syrup**

system *n* (*pl* **-s**) method or set of methods ▷ **systematic** *adj* ▷ **systematically** *adv*

systematic *adj* ▷ **system**

systematically *adv* ▷ **system**

systematization *n*

systemic *adj* affecting the entire animal or body

systems *n* ▷ **system**

systole *n* (*pl* **-s**) regular contraction of the heart as it pumps blood ▷ **systolic** *adj*

systoles *n* ▷ **systole**

systolic *adj* ▷ **systole**

Tt

T is one of the most common consonants in Scrabble. There are only four two-letter words that begin with T, but they are easy to remember as there is one for every vowel except U. Like S, T begins a number of three-letter words that don't use vowels, which are well worth remembering. These are: **thy** (6 points), **try** (6), **tsk** (7), **twp** (8) and **tyg** (7). There are also some useful three-letter words using X: **tax**, **tix** and **tux** (10 each). If you have an X during a game, remember words like **text** (11), **texts** (12), **textile** (14), **textual** (14) and **texture** (14). The last three of these have seven letters, and so will earn you 50-point bonuses if you use all your tiles to form them.

ta interj informal thank you

tab n (pl -s) small flap or projecting label

tabard n (pl -s) short sleeveless tunic decorated with a coat of arms, worn in medieval times
　tabards n ▷ tabard
　tabbies n ▷ tabby

tabby n (pl -bies) ▷ adj (cat) with dark stripes on a lighter background

tabla n (pl -bla, -blas) one of a pair of Indian drums played with the hands
　tablas n ▷ tabla

table n (pl -s) piece of furniture with a flat top supported by legs ▷ v (-les, -ling, -led) submit (a motion) for discussion by a meeting

tableau n (pl -x) silent motionless group arranged to represent some scene
　tableaux n ▷ tableau
　tabled v ▷ table
　tables n, v ▷ table

tablet n (pl -s) pill of compressed medicinal substance
　tablets n ▷ tablet
　tabling v ▷ table

tabloid n (pl -s) small-sized newspaper with many photographs and a concise, usu. sensational style
　tabloids n ▷ tabloid

taboo n (pl -s) prohibition resulting from religious or social conventions ▷ adj forbidden by a taboo
　taboos n ▷ taboo
　tabs n ▷ tab

tabular adj arranged in a table

tabulate v (-tes, -ting, -ted) arrange (information) in a table > **tabulation** n (pl -s)
　tabulated v ▷ tabulate
　tabulates v ▷ tabulate
　tabulating v ▷ tabulate
　tabulation n ▷ tabulate
　tabulations n ▷ tabulate

tacit adj implied but not spoken > **tacitly** adv
　tacitly adv ▷ tacit

taciturn adj habitually uncommunicative > **taciturnity** n (pl -ties)
　taciturnities n ▷ taciturn
　taciturnity n ▷ taciturn

tack¹ n (pl -s) short nail with a large head ▷ v (-s, -ing, -ed) fasten with tacks

tack² n (pl **-s**) course of a ship sailing obliquely into the wind ▶ v (**-s, -ing, -ed**) sail into the wind on a zigzag course

tack³ n (pl **-s**) riding harness for horses

tacked v ▷ **tack¹, ²**

tackier adj ▷ **tacky¹, ²**

tackies, takkies pl n (sing **tacky**) S AFR informal tennis shoes or plimsolls

tackiest adj ▷ **tacky¹, ²**

tacking v ▷ **tack¹, ²**

tackle v (**-les, -ling, -led**) deal with (a task) ▶ n (pl **-s**) SPORT act of attempting to get the ball from an opposing player

tackled v ▷ **tackle**

tackles v, n ▷ **tackle**

tackling v ▷ **tackle**

tacks ▷ **tack¹, ², ³** ▶ v¹, ²

tacky¹ adj (**-kier, -kiest**) slightly sticky

tacky² adj (**-kier, -kiest**) informal vulgar and tasteless

tacky³ sing n ▷ **tackies**

taco n (pl **-s**) MEXICAN COOKERY tortilla fried until crisp, served with a filling

tacos n ▷ **taco**

tact n (pl **-s**) skill in avoiding giving offence > **tactful** adj > **tactfully** adv > **tactless** adj > **tactlessly** adv

tactful adj ▷ **tact**

tactfully adv ▷ **tact**

tactic n (pl **-s**) method or plan to achieve an end ▶ **tactical** adj > **tactician** n (pl **-s**)

tactical adj ▷ **tactic**

tactician n ▷ **tactic**

tacticians n ▷ **tactic**

tactics pl n art of directing military forces in battle ▶ n ▷ **tactic**

tactile adj of or having the sense of touch

tactless adj ▷ **tact**

tactlessly adv ▷ **tact**

tacts n ▷ **tact**

tadpole n (pl **-s**) limbless tailed larva of a frog or toad

tadpoles n ▷ **tadpole**

taffeta n (pl **-s**) shiny silk or rayon fabric

taffetas n ▷ **taffeta**

tag¹ n (pl **-s**) label bearing information ▶ v (**-s, -gging, -gged**) attach a tag to

tag² n (pl **-s**) children's game where the person being chased becomes the chaser upon being touched ▶ v (**-s, -gging, -gged**) touch and catch in this game

tagged v ▷ **tag¹, ²**

tagging v ▷ **tag¹, ²**

tags n, v ▷ **tag¹, ²**

tail n (pl **-s**) rear part of an animal's body, usu. forming a flexible appendage ▶ adj at the rear ▶ v (**-s, -ing, -ed**) informal follow (someone) secretly > **tailless** adj

tailback n (pl **-s**) BRIT queue of traffic stretching back from an obstruction

tailbacks n ▷ **tailback**

tailed v ▷ **tail**

tailing v ▷ **tail**

tailless adj ▷ **tail**

tailor n (pl **-s**) person who makes men's clothes ▶ v (**-s, -ing, -ed**) adapt to suit a purpose

tailored v ▷ **tailor**

tailoring v ▷ **tailor**

tailors n, v ▷ **tailor**

tails adv with the side of a coin uppermost that does not have a portrait of a head on it ▶ pl n informal tail coat ▶ n, v ▷ **tail**

tailspin n (pl **-s**) uncontrolled spinning dive of an aircraft

tailspins n ▷ **tailspin**

tailwind n (pl **-s**) wind coming from the rear

tailwinds n ▷ **tailwind**

taint v (**-s, -ing, -ed**) spoil with a small amount of decay, contamination, or other bad quality ▶ n (pl **-s**) something that taints

tainted v ▷ **taint**

tainting v ▷ **taint**

taints v, n ▷ **taint**

taipan n (pl **-s**) large poisonous Australian snake

taipans n ▷ **taipan**

taj n (**tajes**) A taj is a tall conical cap worn by some Muslims. This unusual word can be helpful if you are struggling to use J because there aren't any good opportunities for longer words on the board. Taj scores 10 points.

take v (**takes, taking, took, taken**) remove from a place ▶ n (pl **-s**) one of a series of recordings from which the best will be used

takeaway n (pl **-s**) shop or restaurant selling meals for eating elsewhere
takeaways n ▷ **takeaway**
taken v ▷ **take**

takeoff n (pl **-s**) (of an aircraft) act of leaving the ground
takeoffs n ▷ **takeoff**

takeover n (pl **-s**) act of taking control of a company by buying a large number of its shares
takeovers n ▷ **takeover**
takes v, n ▷ **take**

taking adj charming ▶ v ▷ **take**
takings pl n money received by a shop
takkies pl n ▷ **tackies**

talc n (pl **-s**) talcum powder
talcs n ▷ **talc**

tale n (pl **-s**) story

talent n (pl **-s**) natural ability
>**talented** adj
talented adj ▷ **talent**
talents n ▷ **talent**
tales n ▷ **tale**

talisman n (pl **-s**) object believed to have magic power >**talismanic** adj
talismanic adj ▷ **talisman**
talismans n ▷ **talisman**

talk v (**-s, -ing, -ed**) express ideas or feelings by means of speech ▶ n (pl **-s**) speech or lecture

talkback n (pl **-s**) NZ broadcast in which telephone comments or questions from the public are transmitted live
talkbacks n ▷ **talkback**
talked v ▷ **talk**

talker n (pl **-s**) person who talks
talkers n ▷ **talker**
talking v ▷ **talk**
talks v, n ▷ **talk**

tall (**-er, -est**) adj higher than average
tallboy n (pl **-s**) high chest of drawers
tallboys n ▷ **tallboy**
taller adj ▷ **tall**
tallest adj ▷ **tall**
tallied v ▷ **tally**
tallies v, n ▷ **tally**

tallow n (pl **-s**) hard animal fat used to make candles
tallows n ▷ **tallow**

tally v (**-lies, -lying, -lied**) (of two things) correspond ▶ n (pl **-lies**) record of a debt or score
tallying v ▷ **tally**

talon n (pl **-s**) bird's hooked claw
talons n ▷ **talon**

tamarind n (pl **-s**) tropical tree
tamarinds n ▷ **tamarind**

tamarisk n (pl **-s**) evergreen shrub with slender branches and feathery flower clusters
tamarisks n ▷ **tamarisk**

tame adj (**-r, -est**) (of animals) brought under human control ▶ v (**-mes, -ming, -med**) make tame >**tamely** adv
tamed v ▷ **tame**
tamely adv ▷ **tame**

tamer n (pl **-s**) person who tames wild animals ▶ adj ▷ **tame**
tamers n ▷ **tamer**
tames v ▷ **tame**
tamest adj ▷ **tame**
taming v ▷ **tame**

tamp v (**-s, -ing, -ed**) pack down by repeated taps
tamped v ▷ **tamp**

tamper v (**-s, -ing, -ed**) (foll. by **with**) interfere
tampered v ▷ **tamper**
tampering v ▷ **tamper**
tampers v ▷ **tamper**
tamping v ▷ **tamp**

tampon n (pl **-s**) absorbent plug of cotton wool inserted into the vagina

during menstruation
tampons n ▷ tampon
tamps v ▷ tamp
tan n (pl -s) brown coloration of the skin from exposure to sunlight ▶ v (-s, -nning, -nned) (of skin) go brown from exposure to sunlight ▶ adj (-nner, -nnest) yellowish-brown
tandem n (pl -s) bicycle for two riders, one behind the other
tandems n ▷ tandem
tandoori adj (of food) cooked in an Indian clay oven
tang n (pl -s) strong taste or smell > **tangy** adj (-gier, -giest)
tangent n (pl -s) line that touches a curve without intersecting it
tangents n ▷ tangent
tangible adj able to be touched > **tangibly** adv
tangibly adv ▷ tangible
tangier adj ▷ tang
tangiest adj ▷ tang
tangle n (pl -les) confused mass or situation ▶ v (-les, -ling, -led) twist together in a tangle
tangled v ▷ tangle
tangles n, v ▷ tangle
tangling v ▷ tangle
tango n (pl -gos) S American dance ▶ v (-goes, -going, -goed) dance a tango
tangoed v ▷ tango
tangoes v ▷ tango
tangoing v ▷ tango
tangos v ▷ tango
tangs n ▷ tang
tangy adj ▷ tang
taniwha n (pl -s) NZ mythical Maori monster that lives in water
taniwhas n ▷ taniwha
tank n (pl -s) container for liquids or gases
tankard n (pl -s) large beer-mug, often with a hinged lid
tankards n ▷ tankard
tanker n (pl -s) ship or truck for carrying liquid in bulk
tankers n ▷ tanker

tanks n ▷ tank
tanned v ▷ tan
tanner adj ▷ tan
tanneries n ▷ tannery
tannery n (pl -ries) place where hides are tanned
tannest adj ▷ tan
tannin n (pl -s) vegetable substance used in tanning
tanning v ▷ tan
tannins n ▷ tannin
tans n, v ▷ tan
tansies n ▷ tansy
tansy n (pl -sies) yellow-flowered plant
tantalum n (pl -s) CHEM hard greyish-white metallic element
tantalums n ▷ tantalum
tantrum n (pl -s) childish outburst of temper
tantrums n ▷ tantrum
tap[1] n (-ps, -pping, -pped) knock lightly and usu. repeatedly ▶ n (pl -s) light knock
tap[2] n (pl -s) valve to control the flow of liquid from a pipe or cask ▶ v (-s, -pping, -pped) listen in on (a telephone call) secretly by making an illegal connection
tape n (pl -s) narrow long strip of material ▶ v (-pes, -ping, -ped) record on magnetic tape
taped v ▷ tape
taper v (-s, -ing, -ed) become narrower towards one end ▶ n (pl -s) long thin candle
tapered v ▷ taper
tapering v ▷ taper
tapers v, n ▷ taper
tapes n, v ▷ tape
tapestries n ▷ tapestry
tapestry n (pl -tries) fabric decorated with coloured woven designs
tapeworm n (pl -s) long flat parasitic worm living in the intestines of vertebrates
tapeworms n ▷ tapeworm
taping v ▷ tape
tapioca n (pl -s) beadlike starch made

from cassava root, used in puddings
tapiocas n ▷ tapioca

tapir n (pl -s) piglike mammal of tropical America and SE Asia, with a long snout
tapirs n ▷ tapir
tapped v ▷ tap¹, ²

tappet n (pl -s) short steel rod in an engine, transferring motion from one part to another
tappets n ▷ tappet
tapping v ▷ tap¹, ²

taproot n (pl -s) main root of a plant, growing straight down
taproots n ▷ taproot
taps n, v ▷ tap¹, ²

tar n (pl -rs) thick black liquid distilled from coal etc ▶ v (-s, -rring, -rred) coat with tar
tardier adj ▷ tardy
tardiest adj ▷ tardy
tardily adv ▷ tardy
tardiness n ▷ tardy
tardinesses n ▷ tardy

tardy adj (-dier, -diest) slow or late
> **tardily** adv ▷ **tardiness** n (pl -es)

tare n (pl -s) type of vetch plant
tares n ▷ tare

target n (pl -s) object or person a missile is aimed at ▶ v (-s, -ing, -ed) aim or direct
targeted v ▷ target
targeting v ▷ target
targets n, v ▷ target

tariff n (pl -s) tax levied on imports
tariffs n ▷ tariff

tarn n (pl -s) small mountain lake

tarnish v (-es, -ing, -ed) make or become stained or less bright ▶ n (pl -es) discoloration or blemish
tarnished v ▷ tarnish
tarnishes v, n ▷ tarnish
tarnishing v ▷ tarnish
tarns n ▷ tarn

tarot n (pl -s) special pack of cards used mainly in fortune-telling
tarots n ▷ tarot

tarragon n (pl -s) aromatic herb

tarragons n ▷ tarragon
tarred v ▷ tar
tarried v ▷ tarry
tarries v ▷ tarry
tarring v ▷ tar

tarry v (-ries, -rying, -ried) old-fashioned linger or delay
tarrying v ▷ tarry
tars n, v ▷ tar
tarsi n ▷ tarsus

tarsus n (pl -si) bones of the heel and ankle collectively

tart¹ n (pl -s) pie or flan with a sweet filling

tart² adj (-er, -est) sharp or bitter
> **tartly** adv ▷ **tartness** n (pl -es)

tart³ n (pl -s) informal sexually provocative or promiscuous woman

tartan n (pl -s) design of straight lines crossing at right angles, esp. one associated with a Scottish clan
tartans n ▷ tartan

tartar¹ n (pl -s) hard deposit on the teeth

tartar² n (pl -s) fearsome or formidable person
tartars n ▷ tartar¹, ²
tarter adj ▷ tart²
tartest adj ▷ tart²
tartly adv ▷ tart²
tartness n ▷ tart²
tartnesses n ▷ tart²
tarts n ▷ tart¹, ³

task n (pl -s) (difficult or unpleasant) piece of work to be done
tasks n ▷ task

tassel n (pl -s) decorative fringed knot of threads
tassels n ▷ tassel

taste n (pl -s) sense by which the flavour of a substance is distinguished in the mouth ▶ v (-tes, -ting, -ted) distinguish the taste of (a substance)
tasted v ▷ taste

tasteful adj having or showing good taste > **tastefully** adv

tastefully adv ▷ tasteful
tastes n, v ▷ taste

unsteadily
teetered v ▷ teeter
teetering v ▷ teeter
teeters v ▷ teeter
teeth n ▷ tooth
teethe v (-thes, -thing, -thed) (of a baby) grow his or her first teeth
teethed v ▷ teethe
teethes v ▷ teethe
teething v ▷ teethe
teetotal adj drinking no alcohol >**teetotaller** n (pl -s)
teetotaller n ▷ teetotal
teetotallers n ▷ teetotal
telegram n (pl -s) formerly, a message sent by telegraph
telegrams n ▷ telegram
televise v (-ses, -sing, -sed) broadcast on television
televised v ▷ televise
televises v ▷ televise
televising v ▷ televise
telex n (pl -es) international communication service using teleprinters ▶ v (-es, -ing, -ed) transmit by telex
telexed v ▷ telex
telexes n, v ▷ telex
telexing v ▷ telex
tell v (-s, -ing, told) make known in words
teller n (pl -s) narrator
tellers n ▷ teller
tellies n ▷ telly
telling adj having a marked effect ▶ v ▷ tell
tells v ▷ tell
telltale n (pl -s) person who reveals secrets ▶ adj revealing
telltales n ▷ telltale
telly n (pl -lies) informal television
temerities n ▷ temerity
temerity n (pl -ties) boldness or audacity
temp BRIT informal n (pl -s) temporary employee, esp. a secretary ▶ v (-s, -ing, -ed) work as a temp
temped v ▷ temp

temper n (pl -s) outburst of anger ▶ v (-s, -ing, -ed) make less extreme
tempera n (pl -s) painting medium for powdered pigments
temperas n ▷ tempera
tempered v ▷ temper
tempering v ▷ temper
tempers n, v ▷ temper
tempest n (pl -s) violent storm
tempests n ▷ tempest
tempi n ▷ tempo
temping v ▷ temp
template n (pl -s) pattern used to cut out shapes accurately
templates n ▷ template
temple¹ n (pl -s) building for worship
temple² n (pl -s) region on either side of the forehead
temples n ▷ temple¹,²
tempo n (pl -pi, -pos) rate or pace
temporal adj of time
tempos n ▷ tempo
temps n, v ▷ temp
tempt v (-s, -ing, -ed) entice (a person) to do something wrong >**tempter, temptress** n (pl -s, -es)
tempted v ▷ tempt
tempter n ▷ tempt
tempters n ▷ tempt
tempting adj attractive or inviting ▶ v ▷ tempt
temptress n ▷ tempt
temptresses n ▷ tempt
tempts v ▷ tempt
ten adj, n (pl -s) one more than nine
tenable adj able to be upheld or maintained
tenancies n ▷ tenant
tenancy n ▷ tenant
tenant n (pl -s) person who rents land or a building >**tenancy** n (pl -cies)
tenants n ▷ tenant
tench n (pl -es) freshwater game fish of the carp family
tenches n ▷ tench
tend¹ v (-s, -ing, -ed) be inclined
tend² v (-s, -ing, -ed) take care of
tended v ▷ tend¹,²

tendencies n ▷ **tendency**
tendency n (pl -**cies**) inclination to act in a certain way > **tendentious** adj biased, not impartial
tendentious adj ▷ **tendency**
tender¹ adj (-**er**, -**est**) not tough > **tenderly** adv > **tenderness** n (pl -**es**)
tender² v (-**s**, -**ing**, -**ed**) offer ▶ n (pl -**s**) such an offer
tender³ n (pl -**s**) small boat that brings supplies to a larger ship in a port
tendered v ▷ **tender**²
tenderer n ▷ **tender**¹
tenderest adj ▷ **tender**¹
tendering v ▷ **tender**²
tenderly adv ▷ **tender**¹
tenderness n ▷ **tender**¹
tendernesses n ▷ **tender**¹
tenders n ▷ **tender**²,³ ▶ v ▷ **tender**²
tending v ▷ **tend**¹,²
tendon n (pl -**s**) strong tissue attaching a muscle to a bone
tendons n ▷ **tendon**
tendril n (pl -**s**) slender stem by which a climbing plant clings
tendrils n ▷ **tendril**
tends v ▷ **tend**¹,²
tenement n (pl -**s**) (esp. in Scotland or the US) building divided into several flats
tenements n ▷ **tenement**
tenet n (pl -**s**) doctrine or belief
tenets n ▷ **tenet**
tenner n (pl -**s**) BRIT informal ten-pound note
tenners n ▷ **tenner**
tennis n (pl -**es**) game in which players use rackets to hit a ball back and forth over a net
tennises n ▷ **tennis**
tenon n (pl -**s**) projecting end on a piece of wood fitting into a slot in another
tenons n ▷ **tenon**
tenor n (pl -**s**) (singer with) the second highest male voice ▶ adj (of a voice or instrument) between alto and baritone

tenors n ▷ **tenor**
tens n ▷ **ten**
tense¹ adj (-**r**, -**st**) emotionally strained ▶ v (-**ses**, -**sing**, -**sed**) make or become tense
tense² n (pl -**s**) GRAMMAR form of a verb showing the time of action
tensed v ▷ **tense**¹
tenser adj ▷ **tense**¹
tenses n ▷ **tense**² ▶ v ▷ **tense**¹
tensest adj ▷ **tense**¹
tensile adj of tension
tensing v ▷ **tense**¹
tension n (pl -**s**) hostility or suspense
tensions n ▷ **tension**
tent n (pl -**s**) portable canvas shelter
tentacle n (pl -**s**) flexible organ of many invertebrates, used for grasping, feeding, etc
tentacles n ▷ **tentacle**
tenth adj, n (pl -**s**) (of) number ten in a series
tenths n ▷ **tenth**
tents n ▷ **tent**
tenuous adj slight or flimsy > **tenuously** adv
tenuously adv ▷ **tenuous**
tenure n (pl -**s**) (period of) the holding of an office or position
tenures n ▷ **tenure**
tepee n (pl -**s**) cone-shaped tent, formerly used by Native Americans
tepees n ▷ **tepee**
tepid adj (-**er**, -**est**) slightly warm
tepider adj ▷ **tepid**
tepidest adj ▷ **tepid**
tequila n (pl -**s**) Mexican alcoholic drink
tequilas n ▷ **tequila**
term n (pl -**s**) word or expression ▶ v (-**s**, -**ing**, -**ed**) name or designate
termed v ▷ **term**
terminal adj (of an illness) ending in death ▶ n (pl -**s**) place where people or vehicles begin or end a journey > **terminally** adv
terminally adv ▷ **terminal**
terminals n ▷ **terminal**

terming v ▷ **term**

termini n ▷ **terminus**

terminus n (pl -ni, -nuses) railway or bus station at the end of a line

terminuses n ▷ **terminus**

termite n (pl -s) white antlike insect that destroys timber

termites n ▷ **termite**

terms n, v ▷ **term** ▶ pl n conditions

tern n (pl -s) gull-like sea bird with a forked tail and pointed wings

ternary adj consisting of three parts

terns n ▷ **tern**

terrace n (pl -s) row of houses built as one block ▶ v (-ces, -cing, -ced) form into or provide with a terrace

terraced v ▷ **terrace**

terraces n, v ▷ **terrace** ▶ pl n (also **terracing**) tiered area in a stadium where spectators stand

terracing v ▷ **terrace**

terrain n (pl -s) area of ground, esp. with reference to its physical character

terrains n ▷ **terrain**

terrapin n (pl -s) small turtle-like reptile

terrapins n ▷ **terrapin**

terrazzo n (pl -s) floor of marble chips set in mortar and polished

terrazzos n ▷ **terrazzo**

terrible adj very serious > **terribly** adv

terribly adv ▷ **terrible**

terrier n (pl -s) any of various breeds of small active dog

terriers n ▷ **terrier**

terries n ▷ **terry**

terrific adj great or intense

terrified v, adj ▷ **terrify**

terrifies v ▷ **terrify**

terrify v (-fies, -fying, -fied) fill with fear > **terrified** adj ▷ **terrifying** adj

terrifying v, adj ▷ **terrify**

terrine n (pl -s) earthenware dish with a lid

terrines n ▷ **terrine**

terror n (pl -s) great fear

terrors n ▷ **terror**

terry n (pl -ries) fabric with small loops

covering both sides, used esp. for making towels

terse adj (-r, -st) neat and concise
> **tersely** adv

tersely adv ▷ **terse**

terser adj ▷ **terse**

tersest adj ▷ **terse**

tertiary adj third in degree, order, etc

test v (-s, -ing, -ed) try out to ascertain the worth, capability, or endurance of ▶ n (pl -s) critical examination
> **testing** adj

testator n, fem, **testatrix** n (pl -s, -xes) maker of a will

testators n ▷ **testator**

testatrix n ▷ **testator**

testatrixes n ▷ **testator**

tested v ▷ **test**

testes n ▷ **testis**

testicle n (pl -s) either of the two male reproductive glands

testicles n ▷ **testicle**

testier adj ▷ **testy**

testiest adj ▷ **testy**

testified v ▷ **testify**

testifies v ▷ **testify**

testify v (-fies, -fying, -fied) give evidence under oath

testifying v ▷ **testify**

testily adv ▷ **testy**

testiness n ▷ **testy**

testinesses n ▷ **testy**

testing v, adj ▷ **test**

testis n (pl -tes) testicle

tests v, n ▷ **test**

testy adj (-tier, -tiest) irritable or touchy > **testily** adv > **testiness** n (pl -es)

tetanus n (pl -es) acute infectious disease producing muscular spasms and convulsions

tetanuses n ▷ **tetanus**

tether n (pl -s) rope or chain for tying an animal to a spot ▶ v (-s, -ing, -ed) tie up with rope

tethered v ▷ **tether**

tethering v ▷ **tether**

tethers n, v ▷ **tether**

text n (pl **-s**) main body of a book as distinct from illustrations etc ▶ v (**-s, -ing, -ed**) send a text message to (someone) > **textual** adj

textbook n (pl **-s**) standard book on a particular subject ▶ adj perfect
textbooks n ▷ textbook
texted v ▷ text
textile n (pl **-s**) fabric or cloth, esp. woven
textiles n ▷ textile
texting v ▷ text
texts n, v ▷ text
textual adj ▷ text
textural adj ▷ texture
texture n (pl **-s**) structure, feel, or consistency ▶ **textured** adj > **textural** adj
textured adj ▷ texture
textures n ▷ texture
thallium n (pl **-s**) CHEM highly toxic metallic element
thalliums n ▷ thallium
than conj, prep used to introduce the second element of a comparison
thane n (pl **-s**) HIST Anglo-Saxon or medieval Scottish nobleman
thanes n ▷ thane
thank v (**-s, -ing, -ed**) express gratitude to
thanked v ▷ thank
thankful adj grateful
thanking v ▷ thank
thanks pl n words of gratitude ▶ interj polite expression of gratitude ▶ v ▷ thank
that adj, pron used to refer to something already mentioned or familiar, or further away ▶ conj used to introduce a clause ▶ pron used to introduce a relative clause
thatch n (pl **-es**) roofing material of reeds or straw ▶ v (**-ches, -ching, -ched**) roof (a house) with reeds or straw
thatched v ▷ thatch
thatches n, v ▷ thatch
thatching v ▷ thatch

thaw v (**-s, -ing, -ed**) make or become unfrozen ▶ n (pl **-s**) thawing
thawed v ▷ thaw
thawing v ▷ thaw
thaws n, v ▷ thaw
the adj the definite article, used before a noun
theatre n (pl **-s**) place where plays etc are performed
theatres n ▷ theatre
thee pron obs objective form of **thou**
theft n (pl **-s**) act or an instance of stealing
thefts n ▷ theft
their adj of or associated with them
theirs pron (thing or person) belonging to them
theism n (pl **-s**) belief in a God or gods > **theist** n (pl **-s**) adj > **theistic** adj
theisms n ▷ theism
theist n, adj ▷ theism
theistic adj ▷ theism
theists n ▷ theism
them pron refers to people or things other than the speaker or those addressed
thematic adj ▷ theme
theme n (pl **-s**) main idea or subject being discussed > **thematic** adj
themes n ▷ theme
themselves pron ▷ they
then adv at that time
thence adv from that place or time
theologian n ▷ theology
theologians n ▷ theology
theological adj ▷ theology
theologically adv ▷ theology
theologies n ▷ theology
theology n (pl **-gies**) study of religions and religious beliefs > **theologian** n (pl **-s**) > **theological** adj > **theologically** adv
theorem n (pl **-s**) proposition that can be proved by reasoning
theorems n ▷ theorem
theories n ▷ theory
theorist n ▷ theory
theorists n ▷ theory

theorize v (-zes, -zing, -zed) form theories, speculate
  theorized v ▷ **theorize**
  theorizes v ▷ **theorize**
  theorizing v ▷ **theorize**
theory n (pl -ries) set of ideas to explain something > **theorist** n (pl -s)
  therapies n ▷ **therapy**
  therapist n ▷ **therapy**
  therapists n ▷ **therapy**
therapy n (pl -pies) curing treatment > **therapist** n (pl -s)
there adv in or to that place
thereby adv by that means
therm n (pl -s) unit of measurement of heat
thermal adj of heat ▶ n (pl -s) rising current of warm air
  thermals n ▷ **thermal**
  therms n ▷ **therm**
  these adj, pron ▷ **this**
  theses n ▷ **thesis**
thesis n (pl **theses**) written work submitted for a degree
thespian n (pl -s) actor or actress ▶ adj of the theatre
  thespians n ▷ **thespian**
they pron refers to: people or things other than the speaker or people addressed
thiamine n (pl -s) vitamin found in the outer coat of rice and other grains
  thiamines n ▷ **thiamine**
thick adj (-er, -est) of great or specified extent from one side to the other > **thickly** adv
thicken v (-s, -ing, -ed) make or become thick or thicker
  thickened v ▷ **thicken**
  thickening v ▷ **thicken**
  thickens v ▷ **thicken**
  thicker adj ▷ **thick**
  thickest adj ▷ **thick**
thicket n (pl -s) dense growth of small trees
  thickets n ▷ **thicket**
  thickly adv ▷ **thick**
thickset adj stocky in build

thief n (pl **thieves**) person who steals
thieve v (-ves, -ving, -ved) steal
  > **thieving** adj
  thieved v ▷ **thieve**
  thieves v ▷ **thieve** ▶ n ▷ **thief**
  thieving v, adj ▷ **thieve**
thigh n (pl -s) upper part of the human leg
  thighs n ▷ **thigh**
thimble n (pl -s) cap protecting the end of the finger when sewing
  thimbles n ▷ **thimble**
thin adj (-nner, -nnest) not thick ▶ v (-s, -nning, -nned) make or become thin > **thinly** adv > **thinness** n (pl -es)
thine pron, adj obs (something) of or associated with you (thou)
thing n (pl -s) material object
  things n ▷ **thing** ▶ pl n possessions, clothes, etc
think v (-s, -ing, **thought**) consider, judge, or believe > **thinker** n (pl -s) > **thinking** adj, n (pl -s)
  thinker n ▷ **think**
  thinkers n ▷ **think**
thinking v, adj ▷ **think**
  thinkings n ▷ **think**
  thinks v ▷ **think**
  thinly adv ▷ **thin**
  thinned v ▷ **thin**
  thinner adj ▷ **thin**
  thinness n ▷ **thin**
  thinnesses n ▷ **thin**
  thinnest adj ▷ **thin**
  thinning v ▷ **thin**
  thins v ▷ **thin**
third adj of number three in a series ▶ n (pl -s) one of three equal parts
  thirds n ▷ **third**
thirst n (pl -s) desire to drink ▶ v (-s, -ing, -ed) feel thirst ▷ **thirsty** adj (-tier, -tiest) > **thirstily** adv
  thirsted v ▷ **thirst**
  thirstier adj ▷ **thirst**
  thirstiest adj ▷ **thirst**
  thirstily adv ▷ **thirst**
  thirsting v ▷ **thirst**
  thirsts n, v ▷ **thirst**

thirsty adj (-**tier**, -**tiest**) ▷ thirst
thirteen adj, n (pl -**s**) three plus ten
>**thirteenth** adj, n (pl -**s**)
thirteens n ▷ thirteen
thirteenth n ▷ thirteen
thirteenths n ▷ thirteen
thirties n ▷ thirty
thirtieth n ▷ thirty
thirtieths n ▷ thirty
thirty adj, n (pl -**ties**) three times ten
>**thirtieth** adj, n (pl -**s**)
this adj, pron used to refer to a thing
or person nearby, just mentioned, or
about to be mentioned ▶ adj used to
refer to the present time
thistle n (pl -**s**) prickly plant with dense
flower heads
thistles n ▷ thistle
thither adv obs to or towards that
place
thong n (pl -**s**) thin strip of leather etc
thongs n ▷ thong
thoraces n ▷ thorax
thoracic adj ▷ thorax
thorax n (pl -**xes**, -**races**) part of
the body between the neck and the
abdomen >**thoracic** adj
thoraxes n ▷ thorax
thorn n (pl -**s**) prickle on a plant
>**thorny** adj (-**nier**, -**niest**)
thornier adj ▷ thorn
thorniest adj ▷ thorn
thorns n ▷ thorn
thorny adj ▷ thorn
thorough adj complete
>**thoroughly** adv >**thoroughness** n
(pl -**es**)
thoroughly adv ▷ thorough
thoroughness n ▷ thorough
thoroughnesses n ▷ thorough
those adj, pron ▷ that
thou pron obs you
though conj despite the fact that ▶ adv
nevertheless
thought v ▷ think ▶ n (pl -**s**) thinking
>**thoughtful** adj considerate
thoughtful adj ▷ thought
thoughts n ▷ thought

thousand adj, n (pl -**s**) ten hundred
thousands n ▷ thousand
thrall n (pl -**s**) state of being in the
power of another person
thralls n ▷ thrall
thrash v (-**es**, -**ing**, -**ed**) beat, esp. with
a stick or whip
thrashed v ▷ thrash
thrashes v ▷ thrash
thread n (pl -**s**) fine strand or yarn ▶ v
(-**s**, -**ing**, -**ed**) pass thread through
threaded v ▷ thread
threading v ▷ thread
threads n, v ▷ thread
threat n (pl -**s**) declaration of intent
to harm
threaten v (-**s**, -**ing**, -**ed**) make or be
a threat to
threatened v ▷ threaten
threatening v ▷ threaten
threatens v ▷ threaten
threats n ▷ threat
three adj, n (pl -**s**) one more than two
threes n ▷ three
threnodies n ▷ threnody
threnody n (pl -**dies**) lament for
the dead
thresh v (-**es**, -**ing**, -**ed**) beat (wheat
etc) to separate the grain from the
husks and straw
threshed v ▷ thresh
threshes v ▷ thresh
threshing v ▷ thresh
threw v ▷ throw
thrice adv lit three times
thrift n (pl -**s**) wisdom and caution
with money >**thrifty** adj
thrifts n ▷ thrift
thrifty adj ▷ thrift
thrill n (pl -**s**) sudden feeling of
excitement ▶ v (-**s**, -**ing**, -**ed**) (cause
to) feel a thrill >**thrilling** adj
thrilled v ▷ thrill
thriller n (pl -**s**) book, film, etc with an
atmosphere of mystery or suspense
thrillers n ▷ thriller
thrilling v, adj ▷ thrill
thrills n, v ▷ thrill

thrive v (-ves, -ving, -ved or throve, thrived or thriven) flourish or prosper

thrived v ▷ thrive

thriven v ▷ thrive

thrives v ▷ thrive

thriving v ▷ thrive

throat n (pl -s) passage from the mouth and nose to the stomach and lungs

throatier adj ▷ throaty

throatiest adj ▷ throaty

throats n ▷ throat

throaty adj (-tier, -tiest) (of the voice) hoarse

throb v (-s, -bbing, -bbed) pulsate repeatedly ▶ n (pl -s) throbbing

throbbed v ▷ throb

throbbing v ▷ throb

throbs v, n ▷ throb

throes pl n violent pangs or pains

throne n (pl -s) ceremonial seat of a monarch or bishop

thrones n ▷ throne

throng n (pl -s) v (-s, -ing, -ed) crowd

thronged v ▷ throng

thronging v ▷ throng

throngs n, v ▷ throng

throstle n (pl -s) song thrush

throstles n ▷ throstle

throttle n (pl -s) device controlling the amount of fuel entering an engine ▶ v (-les, -ling, -led) strangle

throttled v ▷ throttle

throttles n, v ▷ throttle

throttling v ▷ throttle

through prep from end to end or side to side of ▶ adj finished

throve v ▷ thrive

throw v (-s, -ing, threw, thrown) hurl through the air ▶ n (pl -s) throwing

throwing v ▷ throw

thrown v ▷ throw

throws v, n ▷ throw

thrush[1] n (pl -es) brown songbird

thrush[2] n (pl -es) fungal disease of the mouth or vagina

thrushes n ▷ thrush[1, 2]

thrust v (-s, -ing, thrust) push

forcefully ▶ n (pl -s) forceful stab

thrusting v ▷ thrust

thrusts v, n ▷ thrust

thud n (pl -s) dull heavy sound ▶ v (-s, -dding, -dded) make such a sound

thudded v ▷ thud

thudding v ▷ thud

thuds n, v ▷ thud

thug n (pl -s) violent man, esp. a criminal > **thuggery** n (pl -ries) > **thuggish** adj

thuggeries n ▷ thug

thuggery n ▷ thug

thuggish adj ▷ thug

thugs n ▷ thug

thumb n (pl -s) short thick finger set apart from the others ▶ v (-s, -ing, -ed) touch or handle with the thumb

thumbed v ▷ thumb

thumbing v ▷ thumb

thumbs n, v ▷ thumb

thump n (pl -s) (sound of) a dull heavy blow ▶ v (-s, -ing, -ed) strike heavily

thumped v ▷ thump

thumping v ▷ thump

thumps n, v ▷ thump

thunder n (pl -s) loud noise accompanying lightning ▶ v (-s, -ing, -ed) rumble with thunder > **thunderous** adj > **thundery** (-rier, -riest) adj

thundered v ▷ thunder

thunderier adj ▷ thunder

thunderiest adj ▷ thunder

thundering v ▷ thunder

thunderous adj ▷ thunder

thunders v, n ▷ thunder

thundery adj (-rier, -riest) ▷ thunder

thus adv therefore

thwack v (-s, -ing, -ed) ▶ n (pl -s) whack

thwacked v ▷ thwack

thwacking v ▷ thwack

thwacks v, n ▷ thwack

thwart v (-s, -ing, -ed) foil or frustrate ▶ n (pl -s) seat across a boat

thwarted v ▷ thwart

thwarting v ▷ thwart

thwarts v, n ▷ **thwart**

thy adj obs of or associated with you (thou)

thyme n (pl -s) aromatic herb

thymes n ▷ **thyme**

thymi n ▷ **thymus**

thymus n (pl -muses, -mi) small gland at the base of the neck

thymuses n ▷ **thymus**

thyroid adj, n (pl -s) (of) a gland in the neck controlling body growth

thyroids n ▷ **thyroid**

thyself pron obs ▷ **thou**

> **ti** n (**tis**). Ti means the same as **te**. This is a useful word when you want to form words in more than one direction. Ti scores 2 points.

tiara n (pl -s) semicircular jewelled headdress

tiaras n ▷ **tiara**

tibia n (pl -e, -s) inner bone of the lower leg > **tibial** adj

tibiae n ▷ **tibia**

tibial adj ▷ **tibia**

tibias n ▷ **tibia**

tic n (pl -s) spasmodic muscular twitch

tick[1] n (pl -s) mark (✓) used to check off or indicate the correctness of something ▶ v (-s, -ing, -ed) mark with a tick

tick[2] n (pl -s) tiny bloodsucking parasitic animal

tick[3] n (pl -s) informal credit or account

ticked v ▷ **tick**[1]

ticket n (pl -s) card or paper entitling the holder to admission, travel, etc ▶ v (-s, -ing, -ed) attach or issue a ticket to

ticketed v ▷ **ticket**

ticketing v ▷ **ticket**

tickets n, v ▷ **ticket**

ticking n (pl -s) strong material for mattress covers ▶ v ▷ **tick**[1]

tickings n ▷ **ticking**

tickle v (-les, -ling, -led) touch or stroke (a person) to produce laughter ▶ n (pl -s) tickling

tickled v ▷ **tickle**

tickles v, n ▷ **tickle**

tickling v ▷ **tickle**

ticklish adj sensitive to tickling

ticks v ▷ **tick**[1] ▶ n ▷ **tick**[1, 2, 3]

ticktack n (pl -s) BRIT bookmakers' sign language

ticktacks n ▷ **ticktack**

tics n ▷ **tic**

tidal adj ▷ **tide**

tiddler n (pl -s) informal very small fish

tiddlers n ▷ **tiddler**

tiddlier adj ▷ **tiddly**[1, 2]

tiddliest adj ▷ **tiddly**[1, 2]

tiddly[1] adj (-lier, -liest) tiny

tiddly[2] adj (-lier, -liest) informal slightly drunk

tide n (pl -s) rise and fall of the sea caused by the gravitational pull of the sun and moon > **tidal** adj

tides n ▷ **tide**

tidied v ▷ **tidy**

tidier adj ▷ **tidy**

tidies v ▷ **tidy**

tidiest adj ▷ **tidy**

tidily adv ▷ **tidy**

tidiness n ▷ **tidy**

tidinesses n ▷ **tidy**

tidings pl n news

tidy adj (-dier, -diest) neat and orderly ▶ v (-dies, -dying, -died) put in order > **tidily** adv > **tidiness** n (pl -es)

tidying v ▷ **tidy**

tie v (ties, tying, tied) fasten or be fastened with string, rope, etc ▶ n (pl -s) long narrow piece of material worn knotted round the neck

tied v ▷ **tie** ▶ adj BRIT (of a cottage etc) rented to the tenant only as long as he or she is employed by the owner

tier n (pl -s) one of a set of rows placed one above and behind the other

tiers n ▷ **tier**

ties v, n ▷ **tie**

tiff n (pl -s) petty quarrel

tiffs n ▷ **tiff**

tiger n (pl -s) large yellow-and-black striped Asian cat

tigers n ▷ **tiger**

tight adj (-er, -est) stretched or drawn

taut >**tightly** adv
tighten v (-s, -ing, -ed) make or become tighter or tighter
tightened v ▷ **tighten**
tightening v ▷ **tighten**
tightens v ▷ **tighten**
tighter adj ▷ **tight**
tightest adj ▷ **tight**
tightly adv ▷ **tight**
tights pl n one-piece clinging garment covering the body from the waist to the feet
tigress n (pl -es) female tiger
tigresses n ▷ **tigress**
tiki n (pl -s) NZ small carving of a grotesque person worn as a pendant
tikis n ▷ **tiki**
tikka adj INDIAN COOKERY marinated in spices and dry-roasted
tilde n (pl -s) mark (~) used in Spanish to indicate that the letter 'n' is to be pronounced in a particular way
tildes n ▷ **tilde**
tile n (pl -s) flat piece of ceramic, plastic, etc used to cover a roof, floor, or wall ▶ v (-les, -ling, -led) cover with tiles ▷ **tiled** adj
tiled v, adj ▷ **tile**
tiles n, v ▷ **tile**
tiling n (pl -s) tiles collectively ▶ v ▷ **tile**
tilings n ▷ **tiling**
till¹ conj, prep until
till² v (-s, -ing, -ed) cultivate (land) >**tillage** n (pl -s)
till³ n (pl -s) drawer for money, usu. in a cash register
tillage n ▷ **till**²
tillages n ▷ **till**²
tilled v ▷ **till**²
tiller n (pl -s) lever to move a rudder of a boat
tillers n ▷ **tiller**
tilling v ▷ **till**²
tills v ▷ **till**² ▶ n ▷ **till**³
tilt v (-s, -ing, -ed) slant at an angle ▶ n (pl -s) slope
tilted v ▷ **tilt**
tilting v ▷ **tilt**

tilts v, n ▷ **tilt**
timber n (pl -s) wood as a building material >**timbered** adj
timbered adj ▷ **timber**
timbers n ▷ **timber**
timbre n (pl -s) distinctive quality of sound of a voice or instrument
timbres n ▷ **timbre**
time n (pl -s) past, present, and future as a continuous whole ▶ v (-mes, -ming, -med) note the time taken by
timed v ▷ **time**
timeless adj unaffected by time
timelier adj ▷ **timely**
timeliest adj ▷ **timely**
timely adj (-lier, -liest) at the appropriate time
times n, v ▷ **time**
timid adj (-er, -est) easily frightened >**timidly** adv > **timidity** n (pl -dies)
timider adj ▷ **timid**
timidest adj ▷ **timid**
timidities n ▷ **timid**
timidity n ▷ **timid**
timidly adv ▷ **timid**
timing v ▷ **time**
timorous adj timid
timpani pl n set of kettledrums >**timpanist** n (pl -s)
timpanist n ▷ **timpani**
timpanists n ▷ **timpani**
tin n (pl -s) soft metallic element
tincture n (pl -s) medicinal extract in a solution of alcohol
tinctures n ▷ **tincture**
tinder n (pl -s) dry easily-burning material used to start a fire >**tinderbox** n (pl -es)
tinderbox n ▷ **tinder**
tinderboxes n ▷ **tinder**
tinders n ▷ **tinder**
tine n (pl -s) prong of a fork or antler
tines n ▷ **tine**
ting n (pl -s) high metallic sound, as of a small bell
tinge n (pl -s) slight tint ▶ v (-ges, -geing, -ged) give a slight tint or trace to

tinged v ▷ tinge

tinges n, v ▷ tinge

tinging v ▷ tinge

tingle v (**-les, -ling, -led**) ▶ n (pl **-s**) (feel) a prickling or stinging sensation ▷ tingle

tingles v, n ▷ tingle

tingling v ▷ tingle

tings n ▷ ting

tinier adj ▷ tiny

tiniest adj ▷ tiny

tinker n (pl **-s**) travelling mender of pots and pans ▶ v (**-s, -ing, -ed**) fiddle with (an engine etc) in an attempt to repair it

tinkered v ▷ tinker

tinkering v ▷ tinker

tinkers n, v ▷ tinker

tinkle v (**-les, -ling, -led**) ring with a high tinny sound like a small bell ▶ n (pl **-s**) this sound or action

tinkled v ▷ tinkle

tinkles v, n ▷ tinkle

tinkling v ▷ tinkle

tinned adj (of food) preserved by being sealed in a tin

tinny adj (**-nier, -niest**) (of sound) thin and metallic

tinpot adj informal worthless or unimportant

tins n ▷ tin

tinsel n (pl **-s**) decorative metallic strips or threads

tinsels n ▷ tinsel

tint n (pl **-s**) (pale) shade of a colour ▶ v (**-s, -ing, -ed**) give a tint to

tinted v ▷ tint

tinting v ▷ tint

tints n, v ▷ tint

tiny adj (**-nier, -niest**) very small

tip¹ n (pl **-s**) narrow or pointed end of anything ▶ v (**-s, -pping, -pped**) put a tip on

tip² n (pl **-s**) money given in return for service ▶ v (**-s, -pping, -pped**) give a tip to

tip³ v (**-s, -pping, -pped**) tilt or overturn ▶ n (pl **-s**) rubbish dump

tipped v ▷ tip¹, ², ³

tipping v ▷ tip¹, ², ³

tipple v (**-les, -ling, -led**) drink alcohol habitually, esp. in small quantities ▶ n (pl **-s**) alcoholic drink >**tippler** n (pl **-s**)

tippled v ▷ tipple

tippler n ▷ tipple

tipplers n ▷ tipple

tipples v, n ▷ tipple

tippling v ▷ tipple

tips n, v ▷ tip¹, ², ³

tipsier adj ▷ tipsy

tipsiest adj ▷ tipsy

tipster n (pl **-s**) person who sells tips about races

tipsters n ▷ tipster

tipsy adj (**-sier, -siest**) slightly drunk

tiptoe v (**-toes, -toeing, -toed**) walk quietly with the heels off the ground

tiptoed v ▷ tiptoe

tiptoeing v ▷ tiptoe

tiptoes v ▷ tiptoe

tiptop adj of the highest quality or condition

tirade n (pl **-s**) long angry speech

tirades n ▷ tirade

tire v (**-res, -ring, -red**) reduce the energy of, as by exertion >**tiring** adj

tired adj (**-er, -est**) exhausted ▶ v ▷ tire

tireder adj ▷ tired

tiredest adj ▷ tired

tireless adj energetic and determined

tires v ▷ tire

tiresome adj boring and irritating

tiring v, adj ▷ tire

tissue n (pl **-s**) substance of an animal body or plant

tissues n ▷ tissue

tit¹ n (pl **-s**) any of various small songbirds

tit² n (pl **-s**) slang female breast

titanic adj huge or very important

titanium n (pl **-s**) CHEM strong light metallic element used to make alloys

titaniums n ▷ titanium

titbit n (pl **-s**) tasty piece of food

titbits n ▷ titbit

tithe n (pl **-s**) esp. formerly, one tenth

of one's income or produce paid to the church as a tax

tithes n ▷ **tithe**

titian adj (of hair) reddish-gold

titivate v (-tes, -ting, -ted) smarten up

titivated v ▷ **titivate**
titivates v ▷ **titivate**
titivating v ▷ **titivate**

title n (pl -s) name of a book, film, etc

titled adj aristocratic

titles n ▷ **title**

tits n ▷ **tit**[1, 2]

titter v (-s, -ing, -ed) laugh in a suppressed way ▶ n (pl -s) suppressed laugh

tittered v ▷ **titter**
tittering v ▷ **titter**
titters v, n ▷ **titter**

titular adj in name only

tix pl n Tix is an informal word for **tickets**. This is a good word if you are struggling to use an X towards the end of a game.

tizzies n ▷ **tizzy**

tizzy n (pl -zzies) informal confused or agitated state

to prep indicating movement towards, equality or comparison, etc ▶ adv to a closed position

toad n (pl -s) animal like a large frog

toadied v ▷ **toady**
toadies n, v ▷ **toady**
toads n ▷ **toad**

toady n (pl -dies) ingratiating person ▶ v (-dies, -dying, -died) be ingratiating

toadying v ▷ **toady**

toast[1] n (pl -s) sliced bread browned by heat ▶ v (-s, -ing, -ed) brown (bread) by heat

toast[2] n (pl -s) tribute or proposal of health or success marked by people raising glasses and drinking together ▶ v (-s, -ing, -ed) drink a toast to

toasted v, n ▷ **toast**[1, 2]

toaster n (pl -s) electrical device for toasting bread

toasters n ▷ **toaster**

toasting n, v ▷ **toast**[1, 2]

toasts n, v ▷ **toast**[1, 2]

tobacco n (pl -s, -es) plant with large leaves dried for smoking

tobaccoes n ▷ **tobacco**
tobaccos n ▷ **tobacco**

toboggan n (pl -s) narrow sledge for sliding over snow ▶ v (-s, -ing, -ed) ride a toboggan

tobogganed v ▷ **toboggan**
tobogganing v ▷ **toboggan**
toboggans n, v ▷ **toboggan**

toccata n (pl -s) rapid piece of music for a keyboard instrument

toccatas n ▷ **toccata**

today n (pl -s) this day ▶ adv on this day

todays n ▷ **today**
toddies n ▷ **toddy**

toddle v (-les, -ling, -led) walk with short unsteady steps

toddled v ▷ **toddle**

toddler n (pl -s) child beginning to walk

toddlers n ▷ **toddler**
toddles v ▷ **toddle**
toddling v ▷ **toddle**

toddy n (pl -dies) sweetened drink of spirits and hot water

toe n (pl -s) digit of the foot ▶ v (toes, toeing, toed) touch or kick with the toe

toed v ▷ **toe**
toeing v ▷ **toe**
toes n, v ▷ **toe**

toff n (pl -s) BRIT slang well-dressed or upper-class person

toffee n (pl -s) chewy sweet made of boiled sugar

toffees n ▷ **toffee**
toffs n ▷ **toff**

tofu n (pl -s) soft food made from soya-bean curd

tofus n ▷ **tofu**

tog n (pl -s) unit for measuring the insulating power of duvets

toga n (pl -s) garment worn by citizens

of ancient Rome

togas *n* ▷ **toga**

together *adv* in company ▶ *adj informal* organized

toggle *n (pl -s)* small bar-shaped button inserted through a loop for fastening

toggles *n* ▷ **toggle**

togs *n* ▷ **tog**

toil *n (pl -s)* hard work ▶ *v (-s, -ing, -ed)* work hard

toiled *v* ▷ **toil**

toilet *n (pl -s)* (room with) a bowl connected to a drain for receiving and disposing of urine and faeces

toiletries *n* ▷ **toiletry**

toiletry *n (pl -ries)* object or cosmetic used to clean or groom oneself

toilets *n* ▷ **toilet**

toiling *v* ▷ **toil**

toils *n, v* ▷ **toil**

token *n (pl -s)* sign or symbol ▶ *adj* nominal or slight

tokenism *n (pl -s)* policy of making only a token effort, esp. to comply with a law

tokenisms *n* ▷ **tokenism**

tokens *n* ▷ **token**

told *v* ▷ **tell**

tolerate *v (-tes, -ting, -ted)* allow to exist or happen

tolerated *v* ▷ **tolerate**

tolerates *v* ▷ **tolerate**

tolerating *v* ▷ **tolerate**

toll¹ *v (-s, -ing, -ed)* ring (a bell) slowly and regularly, esp. to announce a death ▶ *n (pl -s)* tolling

toll² *n (pl -s)* charge for the use of a bridge or road

tolled *v* ▷ **toll¹**

tolling *v* ▷ **toll¹**

tolls *n* ▷ **toll¹, ²** ▶ *v* ▷ **toll¹**

tom *n (pl -s)* male cat

tomahawk *n (pl -s)* fighting axe of the Native Americans

tomahawks *n* ▷ **tomahawk**

tomato *n (pl -es)* red fruit used in salads and as a vegetable

tomatoes *n* ▷ **tomato**

tomb *n (pl -s)* grave

tombola *n (pl -s)* lottery with tickets drawn from a revolving drum

tombolas *n* ▷ **tombola**

tomboy *n (pl -s)* girl who acts or dresses like a boy

tomboys *n* ▷ **tomboy**

tombs *n* ▷ **tomb**

tome *n (pl -s)* large heavy book

tomes *n* ▷ **tome**

tomorrow *adv, n (pl -s)* (on) the day after today

tomorrows *n* ▷ **tomorrow**

toms *n* ▷ **tom**

ton *n (pl -s)* unit of weight equal to 2240 pounds or 1016 kilograms or, in the US, 2000 pounds or 907 kilograms

tonal *adj MUSIC* written in a key
> **tonality** *n (pl -ties)*

tonalities *n* ▷ **tonal**

tonality *n* ▷ **tonal**

tone *n (pl -s)* sound with reference to its pitch, volume, etc us *MUSIC (also* **whole tone)** ▶ *v (-nes, -ning, -ned)* harmonize (with) > **toneless** *adj*

toned *v* ▷ **tone**

toneless *adj* ▷ **tone**

tones *n, v* ▷ **tone**

tongs *pl n* large pincers for grasping and lifting

tongue *n (pl -s)* muscular organ in the mouth, used in speaking and tasting

tongues *n* ▷ **tongue**

tonic *n (pl -s)* medicine to improve body tone ▶ *adj* invigorating

tonics *n* ▷ **tonic**

tonight *adv, n (pl -s)* (in or during) the night or evening of this day

tonights *n* ▷ **tonight**

toning *v* ▷ **tone**

tonnage *n (pl -s)* weight capacity of a ship

tonnages *n* ▷ **tonnage**

tonne *n (pl -s)* unit of weight equal to 1000 kilograms

tonnes *n* ▷ **tonne**

tons *n* ▷ **ton**

tonsil n (pl -**s**) small gland in the throat
tonsils n ▷ **tonsil**

tonsure n (pl -**s**) shaving of all or the top of the head as a religious or monastic practice ▷ **tonsured** adj
tonsured adj ▷ **tonsure**
tonsures n ▷ **tonsure**

too adv also, as well
took v ▷ **take**

tool n (pl -**s**) implement used by hand
tools n ▷ **tool**

toot n (pl -**s**) short hooting sound ▶ v (-**s**, -**ing**, -**ed**) (cause to) make such a sound
tooted v ▷ **toot**

tooth n (pl **teeth**) bonelike projection in the jaws of most vertebrates for biting and chewing ▷ **toothless** adj
toothless adj ▷ **tooth**
tooting v ▷ **toot**
tooths n, v ▷ **toot**

top[1] n (pl -**s**) highest point or part ▶ adj at or of the top ▶ v (-**s**, -**pping**, -**pped**) form a top on

top[2] n (pl -**s**) toy which spins on a pointed base

topaz n (pl -**es**) semiprecious stone in various colours
topazes n ▷ **topaz**

topee, topi n (pl -**s**) lightweight hat worn in tropical countries
topees n ▷ **topee**
topi n ▷ **topee**
topiaries n ▷ **topiary**

topiary n (pl -**ries**) art of trimming trees and bushes into decorative shapes

topic n (pl -**s**) subject of a conversation, book, etc

topical adj relating to current events ▷ **topicality** n (pl -**ties**)
topicalities n ▷ **topical**
topicality n ▷ **topical**
topics n ▷ **topic**
topis n ▷ **topee**

topless adj (of a costume or woman) with no covering for the breasts

topmost adj highest or best

topological adj ▷ **topology**
topologies n ▷ **topology**

topology n (pl -**gies**) geometry of the properties of a shape which are unaffected by continuous distortion ▷ **topological** adj
topped n ▷ **top**[1]

topping n (pl -**s**) sauce or garnish for food ▶ v ▷ **top**[1]
toppings n ▷ **topping**

topple v (-**les**, -**ling**, -**led**) (cause to) fall over
toppled v ▷ **topple**
topples v ▷ **topple**
toppling v ▷ **topple**
tops n ▷ **top**[1, 2] & v ▷ **top**[1]

topsoil n (pl -**s**) surface layer of soil
topsoils n ▷ **topsoil**

toque n (pl -**s**) small round hat
toques n ▷ **toque**

tor n (pl -**s**) high rocky hill

torch n (pl -**es**) small portable battery-powered lamp ▶ v (-**es**, -**ing**, -**ed**) informal deliberately set (a building) on fire
torched v ▷ **torch**
torches n, v ▷ **torch**
torching v ▷ **torch**
tore v ▷ **tear**[2]

toreador n (pl -**s**) bullfighter
toreadors n ▷ **toreador**
tories n ▷ **tory**

torment v (-**s**, -**ing**, -**ed**) cause (someone) great suffering ▶ n (pl -**s**) great suffering ▷ **tormentor** n (pl -**s**)
tormented v ▷ **torment**
tormenting v ▷ **torment**
tormentor n ▷ **torment**
tormentors n ▷ **torment**
torments v, n ▷ **torment**
torn v ▷ **tear**[2]

tornado n (pl -**s**, -**es**) violent whirlwind
tornadoes n ▷ **tornado**
tornados n ▷ **tornado**

torpedo n (pl -**es**) self-propelled underwater missile ▶ v (-**es**, -**ing**, -**ed**) attack or destroy with or as if with

torpedoes
torpedoed v ▷ torpedo
torpedoes n, v ▷ torpedo
torpedoing v ▷ torpedo
torpid adj sluggish and inactive
torpor n (pl -s) torpid state
torpors n ▷ torpor
torque n (pl -s) force causing rotation
torques n ▷ torque
torrent n (pl -s) rushing stream
torrents n ▷ torrent
torrid adj (-er, -est) very hot and dry
torrider adj ▷ torrid
torridest adj ▷ torrid
tors n ▷ tor
torsion n (pl -s) twisting of a part by
  equal forces being applied at both ends
  but in opposite directions
torsions n ▷ torsion
torso n (pl -s) trunk of the human body
torsos n ▷ torso
tort n (pl -s) LAW civil wrong or injury
  for which damages may be claimed
tortilla n (pl -s) thin Mexican pancake
tortillas n ▷ tortilla
tortoise n (pl -s) slow-moving land
  reptile with a dome-shaped shell
tortoises n ▷ tortoise
torts n ▷ tort
tortuous adj winding or twisting
torture v (-res, -ring, -red) cause
  (someone) severe pain or mental
  anguish ▶ n (pl -s) severe physical or
  mental pain ▶ **torturer** n (pl -s)
tortured v ▷ torture
torturer n ▷ torture
torturers n ▷ torture
tortures v, n ▷ torture
torturing v ▷ torture
tory n (pl -ries) untraconservative or
  reactionary
toss v (-es, -ing, -ed) throw lightly ▶ n
  (pl -es) tossing
tossed v ▷ toss
tosses v, n ▷ toss
tossing v ▷ toss
tot¹ n (pl -s) small child
tot² v (-s, -tting, -tted) add (numbers)

together
total n (pl -s) whole, esp. a sum of parts
  ▶ adj complete ▶ v (-s, -lling, -lled)
  amount to ▶ **totally** adv > **totality** n
  (pl -ties)
totalities n ▷ total
totality n ▷ total
totalled v ▷ total
totalling v ▷ total
totally adv ▷ total
totals n, v ▷ total
tote v (-tes, -ting, -ted) carry (a
  gun etc)
toted v ▷ tote
totem n (pl -s) tribal badge or emblem
totems n ▷ totem
totes v ▷ tote
toting v ▷ tote
tots n ▷ tot¹ ▶ v ▷ tot²
totted v ▷ tot²
totter v (-s, -ing, -ed) move unsteadily
tottered v ▷ totter
tottering v ▷ totter
totters v ▷ totter
totting v ▷ tot²
toucan n (pl -s) tropical American bird
  with a large bill
toucans n ▷ toucan
touch v (-es, -ing, -ed) come into
  contact with ▶ n (pl -es) sense by
  which an object's qualities are
  perceived when they come into
  contact with part of the body ▶ adj of a
  non-contact version of particular sport
touché interj acknowledgment of
  the striking home of a remark or
  witty reply
touched adj emotionally moved ▶ v
  ▷ touch
touches v, n ▷ touch
touchier adj ▷ touchy
touchiest adj ▷ touchy
touching adj emotionally moving
  ▶ v ▷ touch
touchy adj (-chier, -chiest) easily
  offended
tough adj (-er, -est) strong or resilient
  ▶ n (pl -s) informal rough violent person

>**toughness** n (pl -es)

toughen v (-s, -ing, -ed) make or become tough or tougher

toughened v ▷ toughen

toughening v ▷ toughen

toughens v ▷ toughen

tougher adj ▷ tough

toughest adj ▷ tough

toughness n ▷ tough

toughnesses n ▷ tough

toughs n ▷ tough

toupee n (pl -s) small wig

toupees n ▷ toupee

tour n (pl -s) journey visiting places of interest along the way ▶ v (-s, -ing, -ed) make a tour (of)

toured v ▷ tour

touring v ▷ tour

tourism n (pl -s) tourist travel as an industry

tourisms n ▷ tourism

tourist n (pl -s) person travelling for pleasure

tourists n ▷ tourist

touristy adj informal often derogatory full of tourists or tourist attractions

tours n, v ▷ tour

tousled adj ruffled and untidy

tout v (-s, -ing, -ed) seek business in a persistent manner ▶ n (pl -s) person who sells tickets for a popular event at inflated prices

touted v ▷ tout

touting v ▷ tout

touts v, n ▷ tout

tow¹ v (-s, -ing, -ed) drag, esp. by means of a rope ▶ n (pl -s) towing

tow² n (pl -s) fibre of hemp or flax

toward n ▷ towards

towards, toward prep in the direction of

towbar n (pl -s) metal bar on a car for towing vehicles

towbars n ▷ towbar

towed v ▷ tow¹

towel n (pl -s) cloth for drying things

towels n ▷ towel

tower n (pl -s) tall structure, often forming part of a larger building

towers n ▷ tower

towing v ▷ tow¹

town n (pl -s) group of buildings larger than a village

towns n ▷ town

township n (pl -s) small town

townships n ▷ township

towpath n (pl -s) path beside a canal or river, originally for horses towing boats

towpaths n ▷ towpath

tows n ▷ tow¹, ² ▶ v ▷ tow¹

toxaemia n (pl -s) blood poisoning

toxaemias n ▷ toxaemia

toxic adj poisonous >**toxicity** n (pl -ties)

toxicities n ▷ toxic

toxicity n ▷ toxic

toxin n (pl -s) poison of bacterial origin

toxins n ▷ toxin

toy n (pl -s) something designed to be played with ▶ adj (of a dog) of a variety much smaller than is normal for that breed

toys n ▷ toy

trace v (-ces, -cing, -ced) track down and find ▶ n (pl -s) track left by something >**traceable** adj

traceable adj ▷ trace

traced v ▷ trace

tracer n (pl -s) projectile which leaves a visible trail

traceries n ▷ tracery

tracers n ▷ tracer

tracery n (pl -ries) pattern of interlacing lines

traces v, n ▷ trace ▶ n strap by which a horse pulls a vehicle

trachea n (pl -cheae) windpipe

tracheae n ▷ trachea

tracing n (pl -s) traced copy ▶ v ▷ trace

track n (pl -s) rough road or path ▶ v (-s, -ing, -ed) follow the trail or path of

tracked v ▷ track

tracking v ▷ track

tracks n, v ▷ track

tract¹ n (pl **-s**) wide area

tract² n (pl **-s**) pamphlet, esp. a religious one

traction n (pl **-s**) pulling, esp. by engine power

tractions n ▷ **traction**

tractor n (pl **-s**) motor vehicle with large rear wheels for pulling farm machinery

tractors n ▷ **tractor**

tracts n ▷ **tract¹, ²**

trade n (pl **-s**) buying, selling, or exchange of goods ▶ v (**-des, -ding, -ded**) buy and sell ▷ **trader** n (pl **-s**)
> **trading** n ▷ **trade**

traded v ▷ **trade**

trader n ▷ **trade**

traders n ▷ **trade**

trades n, v ▷ **trade**

trading v, n ▷ **trade**

tradings n ▷ **trad**

traduce v (**-ces, -cing, -ced**) slander

traduced v ▷ **traduce**

traduces v ▷ **traduce**

traducing v ▷ **traduce**

traffic n (pl **-s**) vehicles coming and going on a road ▶ v (**-s, -king, -ked**) trade, usu. illicitly ▷ **trafficker** n (pl **-s**)

trafficked v ▷ **traffic**

trafficker n ▷ **traffic**

traffickers n ▷ **traffic**

trafficking v ▷ **traffic**

traffics n, v ▷ **traffic**

tragedies n ▷ **tragedy**

tragedy n (pl **-dies**) shocking or sad event

tragic adj of or like a tragedy
> **tragically** adv
> **tragically** adv ▷ **tragic**

trail n (pl **-s**) path, track, or road ▶ v (**-s, -ing, -ed**) drag along the ground

trailed v ▷ **trail**

trailer n (pl **-s**) vehicle designed to be towed by another vehicle

trailers n ▷ **trailer**

trailing v ▷ **trail**

trails n, v ▷ **trail**

train v (**-s, -ing, -ed**) instruct in a skill

▶ n (pl **-s**) line of railway coaches or wagons drawn by an engine

trained v ▷ **train**

trainee n (pl **-s**) person being trained

trainees n ▷ **trainee**

trainer n (pl **-s**) person who trains an athlete or sportsman

trainers n ▷ **trainer**

training v ▷ **train**

trains v, n ▷ **train**

traipse v (**-ses, -sing, -sed**) informal walk wearily

traipsed v ▷ **traipse**

traipses v ▷ **traipse**

traipsing v ▷ **traipse**

trait n (pl **-s**) characteristic feature

traitor n (pl **-s**) person guilty of treason or treachery ▷ **traitorous** adj

traitorous adj ▷ **traitor**

traitors n ▷ **traitor**

traits n ▷ **trait**

tram n (pl **-s**) public transport vehicle powered by an overhead wire and running on rails laid in the road

tramp v (**-s, -ing, -ed**) travel on foot, hike ▶ n (pl **-s**) homeless person who travels on foot

tramped v ▷ **tramp**

tramping v ▷ **tramp**

trample v (**-les, -ling, -led**) tread on and crush

trampled v ▷ **trample**

tramples v ▷ **trample**

trampling v ▷ **trample**

tramps v ▷ **tramp**

trams n ▷ **tram**

trance n (pl **-s**) unconscious or dazed state

trances n ▷ **trance**

tranche n (pl **-s**) portion of something large, esp. a sum of money

tranches n ▷ **tranche**

tranquil adj (**-ler, -lest**) calm and quiet > **tranquilly** adv > **tranquillity** n (pl **-ties**)

tranquiller adj ▷ **tough**

tranquillest adj ▷ **tough**

tranquillities n ▷ **tranquil**

tranquillity n ▷ **tranquil**
tranquilly adv ▷ **tranquil**
transact v (-s, -ing, -ed) conduct or negotiate (a business deal)
transacted v ▷ **transact**
transacting v ▷ **transact**
transacts v ▷ **transact**
transept n (pl -s) either of the two shorter wings of a cross-shaped church
transepts n ▷ **transept**
transfer v (-fers, -ferring, -ferred) move or send from one person or place to another ▶ n (pl -s) transferring
>**transferable** adj
transferable adj ▷ **transfer**
transferred v ▷ **transfer**
transferring v ▷ **transfer**
transfers v, n ▷ **transfer**
transfix v (-es, -ing, -ed) astound or stun
transfixed v ▷ **transfix**
transfixes v ▷ **transfix**
transfixing v ▷ **transfix**
transit n (pl -s) movement from one place to another
transits n ▷ **transit**
transmit v (-mits, -mitting, -mitted) pass (something) from one person or place to another >**transmittable** adj >**transmitter** n (pl -s)
transmits v ▷ **transmit**
transmittable adj ▷ **transmit**
transmitted v ▷ **transmit**
transmitter n ▷ **transmit**
transmitters n ▷ **transmit**
transmitting v ▷ **transmit**
transom n (pl -s) horizontal bar across a window
transoms n ▷ **transom**
trap n (pl -s) device for catching animals ▶ v (-s, -pping, -pped) catch
trapdoor n (pl -s) door in floor or roof
trapdoors n ▷ **trapdoor**
trapeze n (pl -s) horizontal bar suspended from two ropes, used by circus acrobats
trapezes n ▷ **trapeze**
trapped n ▷ **trap**

trapper n (pl -s) person who traps animals for their fur
trappers n ▷ **trapper**
trapping v ▷ **trap**
traps n, v ▷ **trap**
trash n (pl -es) anything worthless >**trashy** adj (-shier, -shiest)
trashes n ▷ **trash**
trashier adj ▷ **trash**
trashiest adj ▷ **trash**
trashy adj ▷ **trash**
trauma n (pl -mata, -s) emotional shock >**traumatic** adj >**traumatize** v (-zes, -zing, -zed)
traumas n ▷ **trauma**
traumata n ▷ **trauma**
traumatic adj ▷ **trauma**
traumatized v ▷ **trauma**
traumatizes v ▷ **trauma**
traumatizing v ▷ **trauma**
travail n (pl -s) lit labour or toil
travails n ▷ **travail**
travel v (-s, -lling, -lled) go from one place to another, through an area, or for a specified distance ▶ n (pl -s) travelling, esp. as a tourist **traveller** n (pl -s)
travelled v ▷ **travel**
traveller n ▷ **travel**
travellers n ▷ **travel**
travelling v ▷ **travel**
travels v, n ▷ **travel** ▶ pl n (account of) travelling
traverse v (-ses, -sing, -sed) move over or back and forth over
traversed v ▷ **traverse**
traverses v ▷ **traverse**
traversing v ▷ **traverse**
travesties n ▷ **travesty**
travesty n (pl -ties) grotesque imitation or mockery
trawl n (pl -s) net dragged at deep levels behind a fishing boat ▶ v (-s, -ing, -ed) fish with such a net
trawled v ▷ **trawl**
trawler n (pl -s) trawling boat
trawlers n ▷ **trawler**
trawling v ▷ **trawl**

trawls n, v ▷ **trawl**

tray n (pl -s) flat board, usu. with a rim, for carrying things

trays n ▷ **tray**

treacle n (pl -s) thick dark syrup produced when sugar is refined
> **treacly** adj (-lier, -liest)

treacles n ▷ **treacle**

treaclier adj ▷ **treacle**

treacliest adj ▷ **treacle**

treacly adj ▷ **treacle**

tread v (-s, -ing, trod, trodden or trod) set one's foot on ▶ n (pl -s) way of walking or dancing

treading v ▷ **tread**

treadle n (pl -s) lever worked by the foot to turn a wheel

treadles n ▷ **treadle**

treads v, n ▷ **tread**

treason n (pl -s) betrayal of one's sovereign or country > **treasonable** adj

treasonable adj ▷ **treason**

treasons n ▷ **treason**

treasure n (pl -s) collection of wealth, esp. gold or jewels ▶ v (-res, -ring, -red) prize or cherish

treasured v ▷ **treasure**

treasures n, v ▷ **treasure**

treasuries n ▷ **treasury**

treasuring v ▷ **treasure**

treasury n (pl -ries) storage place for treasure

treat v (-s, -ing, -ed) deal with or regard in a certain manner ▶ n (pl -s) pleasure, entertainment, etc given or paid for by someone else

treated v ▷ **treat**

treaties n ▷ **treaty**

treating v ▷ **treat**

treatise n (pl -s) formal piece of writing on a particular subject

treatises n ▷ **treatise**

treats v, n ▷ **treat**

treaty n (pl -ties) signed contract between states

treble adj triple ▶ n (pl -s) (singer with or part for) a soprano voice ▶ v (-les, -ling, -led) increase three times

> **trebly** adv

trebled v ▷ **treble**

trebles n, v ▷ **treble**

trebling v ▷ **treble**

trebly adv ▷ **treble**

tree n (pl -s) large perennial plant with a woody trunk > **treeless** adj

treeless adj ▷ **tree**

trees n ▷ **tree**

trefoil n (pl -s) plant, such as clover, with a three-lobed leaf

trefoils n ▷ **trefoil**

trek n (pl -s) long difficult journey, esp. on foot ▶ v (-s, -kking, -kked) make such a journey

trekked v ▷ **trek**

trekking v ▷ **trek**

treks n, v ▷ **trek**

trellis n (pl -ises) framework of horizontal and vertical strips of wood

trellises n ▷ **trellis**

tremble v (-les, -ling, -led) shake or quiver ▶ n (pl -les) trembling
> **trembling** adj

trembled v ▷ **tremble**

trembles v, n ▷ **tremble**

trembling v, adj ▷ **tremble**

tremolo n (pl -s) MUSIC quivering effect in singing or playing

tremolos n ▷ **tremolo**

tremor n (pl -s) involuntary shaking

tremors n ▷ **tremor**

trench n (pl -s) long narrow ditch, esp. one used as a shelter in war

trencher n (pl -s) HIST wooden plate for serving food

trenchers n ▷ **trencher**

trenches n ▷ **trench**

trend n (pl -s) general tendency or direction

trendier adj ▷ **trendy**

trendies n ▷ **trendy**

trendiest adj ▷ **trendy**

trendiness n ▷ **trendy**

trendinesses n ▷ **trendy**

trends n ▷ **trend**

trendy adj (-dier, -diest) ▶ n (pl -dies) informal consciously fashionable (person) > **trendiness** n (pl **-es**)

trespass v (**-es, -ing, -ed**) go onto another's property without permission ▶ n (pl **-es**) trespassing > **trespasser** n (pl **-s**)

trespassed v ▷ trespass

trespasser n ▷ trespass

trespassers n ▷ trespass

trespasses v, n ▷ trespass

trespassing v ▷ trespass

tresses pl n long flowing hair

trestle n (pl **-s**) board fixed on pairs of spreading legs, used as a support

trestles n ▷ trestle

trevallies n ▷ trevally

trevally n (pl **-lies**) AUST & NZ any of various food and game fishes

trews pl n close-fitting tartan trousers

triad n (pl **-s**) group of three

triads n ▷ triad

trial n (pl **-s**) investigation of a case before a judge

trials n ▷ trial ▶ pl n sporting competition for individuals

triangle n (pl **-s**) geometric figure with three sides > **triangular** adj

triangles n ▷ triangle

triangular adj ▷ triangle

tribal adj ▷ tribe

tribe n (pl **-s**) group of clans or families believed to have a common ancestor > **tribal** adj

tribes n ▷ tribe

tribunal n (pl **-s**) board appointed to inquire into a specific matter

tribunals n ▷ tribunal

tribune n (pl **-s**) people's representative, esp. in ancient Rome

tribunes n ▷ tribune

tribute n (pl **-s**) sign of respect or admiration

tributes n ▷ tribute

trice n (pl **-s**) moment

triceps n (pl **-pses**) muscle at the back of the upper arm

tricepses n ▷ triceps

trices n ▷ trice

trick n (pl **-s**) deceitful or cunning

action or plan ▶ v (**-s, -ing, -ed**) cheat or deceive > **trickery** n (pl **-ries**) > **trickster** n (pl **-s**)

tricked v ▷ trick

trickeries n ▷ trickery

trickery n ▷ trick

trickier adj ▷ tricky

trickiest adj ▷ tricky

tricking v ▷ trick

trickle v (**-les, -ling, -led**) (cause to) flow in a thin stream or drops ▶ n (pl **-s**) gradual flow

trickled v ▷ trickle

trickles v, n ▷ trickle

trickling v ▷ trickle

tricks n, v ▷ trick

trickster n ▷ trick

tricksters n ▷ trick

tricky adj (**-kier, -kiest**) difficult, needing careful handling

tricycle n (pl **-s**) three-wheeled cycle

tricycles n ▷ tricycle

trident n (pl **-s**) three-pronged spear

tridents n ▷ trident

tried v ▷ try

tries v, n ▷ try

trifle n (pl **-s**) insignificant thing or amount

trifles n ▷ trifle

trifling adj insignificant

trigger n (pl **-s**) small lever releasing a catch on a gun or machine ▶ v (**-s, -ing, -ed**) (usu. foll. by **off**) set (an action or process) in motion

triggered v ▷ trigger

triggering v ▷ trigger

triggers n, v ▷ trigger

trike n (pl **-s**) informal tricycle

trikes n ▷ trike

trilbies n ▷ trilby

trilby n (pl **-bies**) man's soft felt hat

trill n (pl **-s**) MUSIC rapid alternation between two notes ▶ v (**-s, -ing, -ed**) play or sing a trill

trilled v ▷ trill

trilling v ▷ trill

trillion n (pl **-s**) one million million, 10^{12}

trillions n ▷ trillion

trills n, v ▷ **trill**

trilogies n ▷ **trilogy**

trilogy n (pl **-gies**) series of three related books, plays, etc

trim adj (**-mmer**, **-mmest**) neat and smart ▶ v (**-s**, **-mming**, **-mmed**) cut or prune into good shape ▶ n (pl **-s**) decoration

trimaran n (pl **-s**) three-hulled boat

trimarans n ▷ **trimaran**

trimmed v ▷ **trim**

trimmer adj ▷ **trim**

trimmest adj ▷ **trim**

trimming n (pl **-s**) decoration ▶ v ▷ **trim**

trims v, n ▷ **trim**

trinities n ▷ **trinity**

trinity n (pl **-ties**) group of three

trinket n (pl **-s**) small or worthless ornament or piece of jewellery

trinkets n ▷ **trinket**

trio n (pl **-s**) group of three

trios n ▷ **trio**

trip n (pl **-s**) journey to a place and back, esp. for pleasure ▶ v (**-s**, **-pping**, **-pped**) (cause to) stumble

tripe n (pl **-s**) stomach of a cow used as food

tripes n ▷ **tripe**

triple adj having three parts ▶ v (**-les**, **-ling**, **-led**) increase three times

tripled v ▷ **triple**

triples v ▷ **triple**

triplet n (pl **-s**) one of three babies born at one birth

triplets n ▷ **triplet**

tripling n ▷ **triple**

tripod n (pl **-s**) three-legged stand, stool, etc

tripods n ▷ **tripod**

tripos n (pl **-poses**) final examinations for an honours degree at Cambridge University

triposes n ▷ **tripos**

tripped v ▷ **trip**

tripper n (pl **-s**) tourist

trippers n ▷ **tripper**

tripping v ▷ **trip**

trips n, v ▷ **trip**

triptych n (pl **-s**) painting or carving on three hinged panels, often forming an altarpiece

triptychs n ▷ **triptych**

trite adj (of a remark or idea) commonplace and unoriginal

tritium n (pl **-s**) radioactive isotope of hydrogen

tritiums n ▷ **tritium**

triumph n (pl **-s**) (happiness caused by) victory or success ▶ v (**-s**, **-ing**, **-ed**) be victorious or successful

triumphed v ▷ **triumph**

triumphing v ▷ **triumph**

triumphs n, v ▷ **triumph**

trivet n (pl **-s**) metal stand for a pot or kettle

trivets n ▷ **trivet**

trivia pl n trivial things or details

trivial adj of little importance

> **trivially** adv > **triviality** n (pl **-ties**)

trivialities n ▷ **trivial**

triviality n ▷ **trivial**

trivially adv ▷ **trivial**

trod v ▷ **tread**

trodden v ▷ **tread**

troika n (pl **-s**) Russian vehicle drawn by three horses abreast

troikas n ▷ **troika**

troll n (pl **-s**) giant or dwarf in Scandinavian folklore

trolley n (pl **-s**) small wheeled table for food and drink

trolleys n ▷ **trolley**

trollop n (pl **-s**) old-fashioned promiscuous or slovenly woman

trollops n ▷ **trollop**

trolls n ▷ **troll**

trombone n (pl **-s**) brass musical instrument with a sliding tube

> **trombonist** n (pl **-s**)

trombones n ▷ **trombone**

trombonist n ▷ **trombone**

trombonists n ▷ **trombone**

troop n (pl **-s**) large group ▶ v (**-s**, **-ing**, **-ed**) move in a crowd

trooped v ▷ **troop**

trooper n (pl **-s**) cavalry soldier
  troopers n ▷ **trooper**
  trooping v ▷ **troop**
  troops n, v ▷ **troop** ▶ pl n soldiers

trope n (pl **-s**) figure of speech
  tropes n ▷ **trope**
  trophies n ▷ **trophy**

trophy n (pl **-phies**) cup, shield, etc given as a prize

tropic n (pl **-s**) either of two lines of latitude at 23½°N (**tropic of Cancer**) or 23½°S (**tropic of Capricorn**) ▶ pl n part of the earth's surface between these lines

tropical adj of or in the tropics
  tropics n ▷ **tropic**

trot v (**-s, -tting, -tted**) (of a horse) move at a medium pace, lifting the feet in diagonal pairs ▶ n (pl **-s**) trotting

troth n (pl **-s**) obs pledge of devotion, esp. a betrothal
  troths n ▷ **troth**
  trots v, n ▷ **trot**
  trotted v ▷ **trot**

trotter n (pl **-s**) pig's foot
  trotters n ▷ **trotter**
  trotting v ▷ **trot**

trouble n (pl **-s**) (cause of) distress or anxiety ▶ v (**-les, -ling, -led**) (cause to) worry ▶ **troubled** adj
  > **troublesome** adj
  troubled v, adj ▷ **trouble**
  troubles n, v ▷ **trouble**
  troublesome adj ▷ **trouble**
  troubling v ▷ **trouble**

trough n (pl **-s**) long open container, esp. for animals' food or water
  troughs n ▷ **trough**

trounce v (**-ces, -cing, -ced**) defeat utterly
  trounced v ▷ **trounce**
  trounces v ▷ **trounce**
  trouncing v ▷ **trounce**

troupe n (pl **-s**) company of performers
  > **trouper** n (pl **-s**)
  trouper n ▷ **troupe**
  troupers n ▷ **troupe**
  troupes n ▷ **troupe**

trouser adj of trousers

trousers pl n two-legged outer garment with legs reaching usu. to the ankles

trout n (pl **trout, trouts**) game fish related to the salmon
  trouts n ▷ **trout**

trowel n (pl **-s**) hand tool with a wide blade for spreading mortar, lifting plants, etc
  trowels n ▷ **trowel**
  truancies n ▷ **truant**
  truancy n ▷ **truant**

truant n (pl **-s**) pupil who stays away from school without permission
  > **truancy** n (pl **-cies**)
  truants n ▷ **truant**

truce n (pl **-s**) temporary agreement to stop fighting
  truces n ▷ **truce**

truck[1] n (pl **-s**) large vehicle for transporting loads by road

trucker n (pl **-s**) truck driver
  truckers n ▷ **trucker**
  trucks n ▷ **truck**

trudge v (**-ges, -ging, -ged**) walk heavily or wearily ▶ n (pl **-s**) long tiring walk
  trudged v ▷ **trudge**
  trudges v, n ▷ **trudge**
  trudging v ▷ **trudge**

true adj (**truer, truest**) in accordance with facts ▶ **truly** adv
  truer adj ▷ **true**
  truest adj ▷ **true**

truffle n (pl **-s**) edible underground fungus
  truffles n ▷ **truffle**

trug n (pl **-s**) BRIT long shallow basket used by gardeners
  trugs n ▷ **trug**

truism n (pl **-s**) self-evident truth
  truisms n ▷ **truism**

truly adv ▷ **true**

trump[1] n (pl **-s**) ▶ adj (card) of the suit outranking the others ▶ v (**-s, -ing, -ed**) play a trump card on (another card)

trump² n (pl -s) lit (sound of) a trumpet
trumped v ▷ **trump¹**
trumpet n (pl -s) valved brass instrument with a flared tube ▶ v (-s, -ing, -ed) proclaim loudly >**trumpeter** n ▷

trumpeted v ▷ **trumpet**
trumpeter n ▷ **trumpet**
trumpeters n ▷ **trumpet**
trumpeting v ▷ **trumpet**
trumpets n, v ▷ **trumpet**
trumping v ▷ **trump¹**
trumps n ▷ **trump¹, ²** ▶ pl n suit outranking the others ▶ v ▷ **trump¹**
truncate v (-tes, -ting, -ted) cut short
truncated v ▷ **truncate**
truncates v ▷ **truncate**
truncating v ▷ **truncate**
trundle v (-les, -ling, -led) move heavily on wheels
trundled v ▷ **trundle**
trundles v ▷ **trundle**
trundling v ▷ **trundle**
trunk n (pl -s) main stem of a tree
trunks n ▷ **trunk** ▶ pl n man's swimming shorts
truss v (-es, -ing, -ed) tie or bind up ▶ n (pl -es) device for holding a hernia in place
trussed v ▷ **truss**
trusses v, n ▷ **truss**
trussing v ▷ **truss**
trust v (-s, -ing, -ed) believe in and rely on ▶ n (pl -s) confidence in the truth, reliability, etc of a person or thing
trusted v ▷ **trust**
trustee n (pl -s) person holding property on another's behalf
trustees n ▷ **trustee**
trustful, trusting adj inclined to trust others
trustier adj ▷ **trusty**
trustiest adj ▷ **trusty**
trusting v ▷ **trust** ▶ adj ▷ **trustful**
trusts n, v ▷ **trust**
trusty adj (-tier, -tiest) faithful or reliable

truth n (pl -s) state of being true
truthful adj honest >**truthfully** adv
truthfully adv ▷ **truthful**
truths n ▷ **truth**
try v (**tries, trying, tried**) make an effort or attempt ▶ n (pl **tries**) attempt or effort
trying adj informal difficult or annoying ▶ v ▷ **try**
tryst n (pl -s) arrangement to meet
trysts n ▷ **tryst**
tsar, czar n (pl -s) HIST Russian emperor
tsars n ▷ **tsar**

> **tsk** interj. Tsk is a sound people make to show disapproval. This is a useful word because it enables you to play K without using vowels, which is handy if your rack is low on vowel tiles. Tsk scores 7 points.

tsunami n (pl -mis, -mi) tidal wave, usu. caused by an earthquake under the sea
tsunamis n ▷ **tsunami**
tuatara n (pl -s) large lizard-like New Zealand reptile
tuataras n ▷ **tuatara**
tub n (pl -s) open, usu. round container
tuba n (pl -s) valved low-pitched brass instrument
tubas n ▷ **tuba**
tubbier adj ▷ **tubby**
tubbiest adj ▷ **tubby**
tubby adj (-bbier, -bbiest) (of a person) short and fat
tube n (pl -s) hollow cylinder
tuber n (pl -s) fleshy underground root of a plant such as a potato >**tuberous** adj
tubercle n (pl -s) small rounded swelling
tubercles n ▷ **tubercle**
tuberous adj ▷ **tuber**
tubers n ▷ **tuber**
tubes n ▷ **tube**
tubing n (pl -s) length of tube
tubs n ▷ **tub**
tubular adj of or shaped like a tube

tuck v (-s, -ing, -ed) push or fold into a small space ▶ n (pl -s) stitched fold
  tucked v ▷ **tuck**

tucker n (pl -s) AUST & NZ informal food
  tuckers n ▷ **tucker**
  tucking v ▷ **tuck**
  tucks v, n ▷ **tuck**

tufa n (pl -s) porous rock formed as a deposit from springs
  tufas n ▷ **tufa**

tuffet n (pl -s) small mound or seat
  tuffets n ▷ **tuffet**

tuft n (pl -s) bunch of feathers, grass, hair, etc held or growing together at the base
  tufts n ▷ **tuft**

tug v (-s, -gging, -gged) pull hard ▶ n (pl -s) hard pull
  tugged v ▷ **tug**
  tugging v ▷ **tug**
  tugs v, n ▷ **tug**

tuition n (pl -s) instruction, esp. received individually or in a small group
  tuitions n ▷ **tuition**

tulip n (pl -s) plant with bright cup-shaped flowers
  tulips n ▷ **tulip**

tulle n (pl -s) fine net fabric of silk etc
  tulles n ▷ **tulle**

tumble v (-les, -ling, -led) (cause to) fall, esp. awkwardly or violently ▶ n (pl -s) fall
  tumbled v ▷ **tumble**

tumbler n (pl -s) stemless drinking glass
  tumblers n ▷ **tumbler**
  tumbles v, n ▷ **tumble**
  tumbling v ▷ **tumble**
  tumbrel n ▷ **tumbril**
  tumbrels n ▷ **tumbril**

tumbril, tumbrel n (pl -s) farm cart used during the French Revolution to take prisoners to the guillotine
  tumbrils n ▷ **tumbril**
  tummies n ▷ **tummy**

tummy n (pl -mies) informal stomach

tumour n (pl -s) abnormal growth in or on the body
  tumours n ▷ **tumour**
  tumuli n ▷ **tumulus**

tumult n (pl -s) uproar or commotion
  >**tumultuous** ▶ adj
  tumults n ▷ **tumult**
  tumultuous adj ▷ **tumult**

tumulus n (pl -li) burial mound
  tun n (pl -s) large beer cask

tuna n (pl -s) large marine food fish
  tunas n ▷ **tuna**

tundra n (pl -s) vast treeless Arctic region with permanently frozen subsoil
  tundras n ▷ **tundra**

tune n (pl -s) (pleasing) sequence of musical notes ▶ v (-s, -nes, -ning, -ned) adjust (a musical instrument) so that it is in tune >**tuneful** adj > **tunefully** adv >**tuneless** adj > **tuner** n (pl -s)
  tuned v ▷ **tune**
  tuneful adj ▷ **tune**
  tunefully adv ▷ **tune**
  tuneless adj ▷ **tune**
  tuner n ▷ **tune**
  tuners n ▷ **tune**
  tunes n, v ▷ **tune**

tungsten n (pl -s) CHEM greyish-white metal
  tungstens n ▷ **tungsten**

tunic n (pl -s) close-fitting jacket forming part of some uniforms
  tunics n ▷ **tunic**
  tuning v ▷ **tune**

tunnel n (pl -s) underground passage ▶ v (-s, -lling, -lled) make a tunnel (through)
  tunnelled v ▷ **tunnel**
  tunnelling v ▷ **tunnel**
  tunnels n, v ▷ **tunnel**
  tunnies n ▷ **tunny**

tunny n (pl -nnies) tuna
  tuns n ▷ **tun**

tup n (pl -s) male sheep
  tups n ▷ **tup**

turban n (pl -s) Muslim, Hindu, or Sikh man's head covering, made by winding cloth round the head

turbans n ▷ **turban**

turbid adj muddy, not clear

turbine n (pl **-s**) machine or generator driven by gas, water, etc turning blades

turbines n ▷ **turbine**

turbot n (pl **-s**) large European edible flatfish

turbots n ▷ **turbot**

tureen n (pl **-s**) serving dish for soup

tureens n ▷ **tureen**

turf n (pl **-s**, **-ves**) short thick even grass ▶ v (**-s**, **-ing**, **-ed**) cover with turf

turfed v ▷ **turf**

turfing v ▷ **turf**

turfs n, v ▷ **turf**

turgid adj (**-er**, **-est**) (of language) pompous

turgider adj ▷ **turgid**

turgidest adj ▷ **turgid**

turkey n (pl **-s**) large bird bred for food

turkeys n ▷ **turkey**

turmeric n (pl **-s**) yellow spice obtained from the root of an Asian plant

turmerics n ▷ **turmeric**

turmoil n (pl **-s**) agitation or confusion

turmoils n ▷ **turmoil**

turn v (**-s**, **-ing**, **-ed**) change the position or direction of ▶ n (pl **-s**)

turning ▷ **turner** n (pl **-s**)

turncoat n (pl **-s**) person who deserts one party or cause to join another

turncoats n ▷ **turncoat**

turned v ▷ **turn**

turner n ▷ **turn**

turners n ▷ **turn**

turning n (pl **-s**) road or path leading off a main route ▶ v ▷ **turn**

turnings n ▷ **turning**

turnip n (pl **-s**) root vegetable with orange or white flesh

turnips n ▷ **turnip**

turnout n (pl **-s**) number of people appearing at a gathering

turnouts n ▷ **turnout**

turnover n (pl **-s**) total sales made by a business over a certain period

turnovers n ▷ **turnover**

turnpike n (pl **-s**) BRIT road where a toll is collected at barriers

turnpikes n ▷ **turnpike**

turns v, n ▷ **turn**

turnup n (pl **-s**) turned-up fold at the bottom of a trouser leg

turnups n ▷ **turnup**

turps n turpentine oil

turret n (pl **-s**) small tower

turrets n ▷ **turret**

turtle n (pl **-s**) sea tortoise

turtles n ▷ **turtle**

turves n ▷ **turf**

tusk n (pl **-s**) long pointed tooth of an elephant, walrus, etc

tusks n ▷ **tusk**

tussle n (pl **-s**) ▶ v (**-les**, **-ling**, **-led**) fight or scuffle

tussled v ▷ **tussle**

tussles n, v ▷ **tussle**

tussling v ▷ **tussle**

tussock n (pl **-s**) tuft of grass

tussocks n ▷ **tussock**

tutelage n (pl **-s**) instruction or guidance, esp. by a tutor ▷ **tutelary** ▶ adj

tutelages n ▷ **tutelage**

tutelary adj ▷ **tutelage**

tutor n (pl **-s**) person teaching individuals or small groups ▶ v (**-s**, **-ing**, **-ed**) act as a tutor to

tutored v ▷ **tutor**

tutorial n (pl **-s**) period of instruction with a tutor

tutorials n ▷ **tutorial**

tutoring v ▷ **tutor**

tutors n, v ▷ **tutor**

tutu n (pl **-s**) short stiff skirt worn by ballerinas

tutus n ▷ **tutu**

> **tux** n (**tuxes**). Tux is a short form of **tuxedo**. This is a very useful word, as U and T are common tiles, so look for opportunities to play it when you get an X. Tux scores 10 points.

tuxedo n (pl **-s**) US & AUST dinner jacket

tuxedos n ▷ **tuxedo**

twaddle n (pl -s) silly or pretentious talk or writing

twaddles n ▷ **twaddle**

twain n (pl -s) obs two

twains n ▷ **twain**

twang n (pl -s) sharp ringing sound ▶ v (-s, -ing, -ed) (cause to) make a twang

twanged v ▷ **twang**

twanging v ▷ **twang**

twangs n, v ▷ **twang**

tweak v (-s, -ing, -ed) pinch or twist sharply ▶ n (pl -s) tweaking

tweaked v ▷ **tweak**

tweaking v ▷ **tweak**

tweaks v, n ▷ **tweak**

twee adj informal (-r, -st) too sentimental, sweet, or pretty

tweed n (pl -s) thick woollen cloth > **tweedy** adj (-dier, -diest)

tweedier adj ▷ **tweed**

tweediest adj ▷ **tweed**

tweeds n ▷ **tweed** ▶ pl n suit of tweed

tweedy n (-dier, -diest) ▷ **tweed**

tweer adj ▷ **twee**

tweest adj ▷ **twee**

tweet n (pl -s) ▶ v (-s, -ing, -ed) chirp

tweeted v ▷ **tweet**

tweeter n (pl -s) loudspeaker reproducing high-frequency sounds

tweeters n ▷ **tweeter**

tweeting v ▷ **tweet**

tweets n, v ▷ **tweet**

tweezers pl n small pincer-like tool

twelfth adj, n (pl -s) (of) number twelve in a series

twelfths n ▷ **twelfth**

twelve adj, n (pl -s) two more than ten

twelves n ▷ **twelve**

twenties n ▷ **twenty**

twentieth adj, n ▷ **twenty**

twentieths n ▷ **twenty**

twenty adj, n (pl -ties) two times ten > **twentieth** adj, n (pl -s)

twerp n (pl -s) informal silly person

twerps n ▷ **twerp**

twice adv two times

twiddle v (-les, -ling, -led) fiddle or twirl in an idle way

twiddled v ▷ **twiddle**

twiddles v ▷ **twiddle**

twiddling v ▷ **twiddle**

twig¹ n (pl -s) small branch or shoot

twig² v (-s, -gging, -gged) informal realize or understand

twigged v ▷ **twig¹**

twigging v ▷ **twig¹**

twigs n ▷ **twig¹** ▶ v ▷ **twig²**

twilight n (pl -s) soft dim light just after sunset

twilights n ▷ **twilight**

twill n (pl -s) fabric woven to produce parallel ridges

twills n ▷ **twill**

twin n (pl -s) one of a pair, esp. of two children born at one birth ▶ v (-s, -nning, -nned) pair or be paired

twine n (pl -es) string or cord ▶ v (-nes, -ning, -ned) twist or coil round

twined v ▷ **twine**

twines n, v ▷ **twine**

twinge n (pl -s) sudden sharp pain or emotional pang

twinges n ▷ **twinge**

twining v ▷ **twine**

twinkle v (-les, -ling, -led) shine brightly but intermittently ▶ n (pl -les) flickering brightness

twinkled v ▷ **twinkle**

twinkles v, n ▷ **twinkle**

twinkling v ▷ **twinkle**

twinned v ▷ **twin**

twinning v ▷ **twin**

twins n, v ▷ **twin**

twirl v (-s, -ing, -ed) turn or spin around quickly

twirled v ▷ **twirl**

twirling v ▷ **twirl**

twirls v ▷ **twirl**

twist v (-s, -ing, -ed) turn out of the natural position ▶ n (pl -s) twisting

twisted adj (of a person) cruel or perverted ▶ v ▷ **twist**

twister n (pl -s) BRIT informal swindler

twisters n ▷ **twister**

twisting v ▷ **twist**

twists v, n ▷ **twist**

twit[1] v (-s, -tting, -tted) poke fun at (someone)

twit[2] n (pl -s) informal foolish person

twitch v (-es, -ing, -ed) move spasmodically ▶ n (pl -es) nervous muscular spasm

twitched v ▷ twitch

twitches v, n ▷ twitch

twitching v ▷ twitch

twits n ▷ twit[2] ▶ v ▷ twit[1]

twitted v ▷ twit[1]

twitter v (-s, -ing, -ed) (of birds) utter chirping sounds ▶ n (pl -s) act or sound of twittering

twittered v ▷ twitter

twittering v, n ▷ twitter

twitters v, n ▷ twitter

twitting v ▷ twit[1]

two adj, n (pl -s) one more than one

twos n ▷ two

> **twp** adj. This is a Welsh word that means stupid or daft. This is a useful word because it contains no vowels, and can thus help when you have an awkward rack. Twp scores 8 points.

tycoon n (pl -s) powerful wealthy businessman

tycoons n ▷ tycoon

> **tyg** n (tygs). A tyg is a cup with more than one handle. This word is useful because it uses no vowels, and can thus help you when you are short of them. Tyg scores 7 points.

tying v ▷ tie

tyke n (pl -s) BRIT, AUST & NZ informal small cheeky child

tykes n ▷ tyke

type n (pl -s) class or category ▶ v (-pes, -ping, -ped) print with a typewriter or word processor

typecast v (-s, -ing, typecast) continually cast (an actor or actress) in similar roles

typecasting v ▷ typecast

typecasts v ▷ typecast

typed v ▷ type

types n, v ▷ type

typhoon n (pl -s) violent tropical storm

typhoons n ▷ typhoon

typhus n (pl -uses) infectious feverish disease

typhuses n ▷ typhus

typical adj true to type, characteristic > **typically** adv

typically adv ▷ typical

typified v ▷ typify

typifies v ▷ typify

typify v (-fies, -fying, -fied) be typical of

typifying v ▷ typify

typing v ▷ type

typist n (pl -s) person who types with a typewriter or word processor

typists n ▷ typist

tyrannies n ▷ tyranny

tyranny n (pl -nies) tyrannical rule

tyrant n (pl -s) oppressive or cruel ruler

tyrants n ▷ tyrant

tyre n (pl -s) rubber ring, usu. inflated, over the rim of a vehicle's wheel to grip the road

tyres n ▷ tyre

tyro n (pl -ros) novice or beginner

tyros n ▷ tyro

> **tzaddiq** n (tzaddiqim, tzaddiqs). A tzaddiq is a Hasidic Jewish leader. This is a fantastic word if you can get the necessary tiles. If someone has played add, you might be able to form it around that; if you can form the whole word using all your tiles you'll earn a 50-point bonus. Tzaddiq scores 27 points.

Uu

U can be a difficult tile to use effectively. Although there are quite a few two-letter words beginning with U, most of them are quite unusual, and so difficult to remember. Only **up** (4 points) and **us** (2) are immediately obvious, so it's well worth learning words like **ug** (3), **uh** (5), **um** (4), and **un**, and **ut** (2 each). Three-letter words beginning with U can also be difficult to remember. If you are trying to use a Q, X or Z, bear in mind that there aren't any valid three-letter words with these letters that start with U. Knowing this can save you valuable time. It's also helpful to remember that there aren't any particularly high-scoring two- or three-letter words starting with U.

udder *n* (*pl* **-s**) large baglike milk-producing gland of cows, sheep, or goats
udders *n* ▷ udder

ug *v* (**ugs, ugging, ugged**). Ug is an old word meaning to loathe. The different verb forms of this word can be useful, and remember that if someone plays ug or its inflections, you can put B, L, M or T in front of it to form another valid word. Ug scores 3 points.

ugh *interj*. Ugh is a sound that people make when they dislike something or are disgusted by it. Together with uke, this is the highest-scoring three-letter word starting with U. Ugh scores 7 points.

uglier *adj* ▷ ugly
ugliest *adj* ▷ ugly
ugliness *n* ▷ ugly
uglinesses *n* ▷ ugly
ugly *adj* (**-lier, -liest**) of unpleasant appearance ▷ **ugliness** *n* (*pl* **-es**)
uh *interj*. Uh is a sound that people make when they are unsure about something. This useful little word

can help when you are trying to form words in more than one direction. Uh scores 5 points.

uke *n* (**ukes**). Uke is a short form of ukulele. Together with ugh, this is the highest-scoring three-letter word starting with U. Uke scores 7 points.

ukelele *n* ▷ ukulele
ukeleles *n* ▷ ukulele
ukulele, ukelele *n* (*pl* **-s**) small guitar with four strings
ukuleles *n* ▷ ukulele

ulcer *n* (*pl* **-s**) open sore on the surface of the skin or mucous membrane.
▷ **ulceration** *n* (*pl* **-s**)
ulceration *n* ▷ ulcer
ulcerations *n* ▷ ulcer

ulcerous *adj* of, like, or characterized by ulcers
ulcers *n* ▷ ulcer

ulna *n* (*pl* **-nae, -nas**) inner and longer of the two bones of the human forearm
ulnae *n* ▷ ulna
ulnas *n* ▷ ulna

ulterior *adj* (of an aim, reason, etc) concealed or hidden
ultimate *adj* final in a series or process

> **ultimately** adv
ultimately adv ▷ **ultimate**
ululate v (**-tes, -ting, -ted**) howl or wail > **ululation** n (pl **-s**)
ululated v ▷ **ululate**
ululates v ▷ **ululate**
ululating v ▷ **ululate**
ululation n ▷ **ululate**
ululations n ▷ **ululate**

| **um** interj. Um is a sound people make when hesitating in speech. If someone plays this word, remember that lots of words end in UM (dictum, podium and rostrum, for example) and look out for chances to play them. Um scores 4 points.

umber adj dark brown to reddish-brown
umbrella n (pl **-s**) portable device used for protection against rain, consisting of a folding frame covered in material attached to a central rod
umbrellas n ▷ **umbrella**
umpire n (pl **-s**) official who rules on the playing of a game ▶ v (**-res, -ring, -red**) act as umpire in (a game)
umpired v ▷ **umpire**
umpires n, v ▷ **umpire**
umpiring v ▷ **umpire**
umpteen adj informal very many > **umpteenth** adj
umpteenth adj ▷ **umpteen**

| **un** pron. Un is a dialect word for one. If someone plays this, remember that you can form lots of words by placing letters after UN. Un scores 2 points.

unable adj lacking the necessary power, ability, or authority to (do something)
unarmed adj without weapons
unaware adj not aware or conscious
unawares adv by surprise
unbend v (**-s, -ing, unbent**) informal become less strict or more informal in one's attitudes or behaviour > **unbending** adj

unbending v, adj ▷ **unbend**
unbends v ▷ **unbend**
unbent v ▷ **unbend**
unbidden adj not ordered or asked
unborn adj not yet born
unbosom v (**-s, -ing, -ed**) relieve (oneself) of (secrets or feelings) by telling someone
unbosomed v ▷ **unbosom**
unbosoming v ▷ **unbosom**
unbosoms v ▷ **unbosom**
unburden v (**-s, -ing, -ed**) relieve (one's mind or oneself) of a worry by confiding in someone
unburdened v ▷ **unburden**
unburdening v ▷ **unburden**
unburdens v ▷ **unburden**
uncannier adj ▷ **uncanny**
uncanniest adj ▷ **uncanny**
uncannily adv ▷ **uncanny**
uncanny adj (**-nier, -niest**) weird or mysterious > **uncannily** adv
uncle n (pl **-s**) brother of one's father or mother
unclean adj lacking moral, spiritual, or physical cleanliness
uncles n ▷ **uncle**
uncommon adj (**-er, -est**) not happening or encountered often > **uncommonly** adv
uncommoner adj ▷ **uncommon**
uncommonest adj ▷ **uncommon**
uncommonly adv ▷ **uncommon**
uncouth adj (**-er, -est**) lacking in good manners, refinement, or grace
uncouther adj ▷ **uncouth**
uncouthest adj ▷ **uncouth**
uncover v (**-s, -ing, -ed**) reveal or disclose
uncovered v ▷ **uncover**
uncovering v ▷ **uncover**
uncovers v ▷ **uncover**
unction n (pl **-s**) act of anointing with oil in sacramental ceremonies
unctions n ▷ **unction**
unctuous adj pretending to be kind and concerned
under prep, adv indicating movement

to or position beneath the underside or base ▶ *prep* less than

underage *adj* below the required or standard age

underarm *adj* SPORT denoting a style of throwing, bowling, or serving in which the hand is swung below shoulder level ▶ *adv* SPORT in an underarm style

undercut *v* (**-cuts, -cutting, -cut**) charge less than (a competitor) to obtain trade
undercuts *v* ▷ undercut
undercutting *v* ▷ undercut

underdog *n* (*pl* **-s**) person or team in a weak or underprivileged position
underdogs *n* ▷ underdog

undergo *v* (**-goes, -going, -went, -gone**) experience, endure, or sustain
undergoes *v* ▷ undergo
undergoing *v* ▷ undergo
undergone *v* ▷ undergo

underlain *v* ▷ underlie
underlay *v* ▷ underlie

underlie *v* (**-lies, -lying, -lay, underlain**) lie or be placed under
>**underlying** *adj* fundamental or basic
underlies *v* ▷ underlie
underlying *v, adj* ▷ underlie

underpin *v* (**-pins, -pinning, -pinned**) give strength or support to
underpinned *v* ▷ underpin
underpinning *v* ▷ underpin
underpins *v* ▷ underpin

undertow *n* (*pl* **-s**) strong undercurrent flowing in a different direction from the surface current
undertows *n* ▷ undertow
underwent *v* ▷ undergo
undid *v* ▷ undo

undo *v* (**-does, -doing, -did, -done**) open, unwrap >**undone** *adj*
undoes *v* ▷ undo

undoing *n* (*pl* **-s**) cause of someone's downfall ▶ *v* ▷ undo
undoings *n* ▷ undoing
undone *v, adj* ▷ undo

undue *adj* greater than is reasonable,

excessive >**unduly** *adv*

undulate *v* (**-tes, -ting, -ted**) move in waves >**undulation** *n* (*pl* **-s**)
undulated *v* ▷ undulate
undulates *v* ▷ undulate
undulating *v* ▷ undulate
undulation *n* ▷ undulate
undulations *n* ▷ undulate

unduly *adv* ▷ undue

undying *adj* never ending, eternal

unearth *v* (**-s, -ing, -ed**) reveal or discover by searching
unearthed *v* ▷ unearth
unearthing *v* ▷ unearth
unearths *v* ▷ unearth

unease *n* (*pl* **-s**) feeling of anxiety
uneases *n* ▷ unease

uneasier *adj* ▷ uneasy
uneasiest *adj* ▷ uneasy
uneasily *adv* ▷ uneasy
uneasiness *n* ▷ uneasy
uneasinesses *n* ▷ uneasy

uneasy *adj* (**-sier, -siest**) (of a person) anxious or apprehensive >**uneasily** *adv* >**uneasiness** *n* (*pl* **-es**)

unerring *adj* never mistaken, consistently accurate

unfair *adj* (**-er, -est**) not right, fair, or just >**unfairly** *adv* >**unfairness** *n* (*pl* **-es**)
unfairer *adj* ▷ unfair
unfairest *adj* ▷ unfair
unfairly *adv* ▷ unfair
unfairness *n* ▷ unfair
unfairnesses *n* ▷ unfair

unfit *adj* unqualified or unsuitable

unfold *v* (**-s, -ing, -ed**) open or spread out from a folded state
unfolded *v* ▷ unfold
unfolding *v* ▷ unfold
unfolds *v* ▷ unfold

unfrock *v* (**-s, -ing, -ed**) deprive (a priest in holy orders) of his or her priesthood
unfrocked *v* ▷ unfrock
unfrocking *v* ▷ unfrock
unfrocks *v* ▷ unfrock

ungainlier *adj* ▷ ungainly

ungainliest adj ▷ ungainly

ungainly adj (-lier, -liest) lacking grace when moving

ungodlier adj ▷ ungodly

ungodliest adj ▷ ungodly

ungodly adj (-lier, -liest) informal unreasonable or outrageous

unguent n (pl -s) lit ointment

unguents n ▷ unguent

unhand v (-s, -ing, -ed) old-fashioned or lit release from one's grasp

unhanded v ▷ unhand

unhanding v ▷ unhand

unhands v ▷ unhand

unhappier adj ▷ unhappy

unhappiest adj ▷ unhappy

unhappily adv ▷ unhappy

unhappiness n ▷ unhappy

unhappinesses n ▷ unhappy

unhappy adj (-pier, -piest) sad or depressed > **unhappily** adv > **unhappiness** n (pl -es)

unhinge v (-ges, -ging, -ged) derange or unbalance (a person or his or her mind)

unhinged v ▷ unhinge

unhinges v ▷ unhinge

unhinging v ▷ unhinge

unicorn n (pl -s) imaginary horselike creature with one horn growing from its forehead

unicorns n ▷ unicorn

unification n ▷ unify

unifications n ▷ unify

unified v ▷ unify

unifies v ▷ unify

uniform n (pl -s) special identifying set of clothes for the members of an organization, such as soldiers ▶ adj regular and even throughout, unvarying > **uniformly** adv > **uniformity** n (pl -ties)

uniformities n ▷ uniform

uniformity n ▷ uniform

uniformly adv ▷ uniform

uniforms n ▷ uniform

unify v (-fies, -fying, -fied) make or become one > **unification** n (pl -s)

unifying v ▷ unify

union n (pl -s) uniting or being united

unions n (pl -s) member or supporter of a trade union

unionist n ▷ unionist

unionists n ▷ unionist

unionization n ▷ unionize

unionizations n ▷ unionize

unionize v (-zes, -zing, -zed) organize (workers) into a trade union > **unionization** n (pl -s)

unionized v ▷ unionize

unionizes v ▷ unionize

unionizing v ▷ unionize

unions n ▷ union

unique adj being the only one of a particular type > **uniquely** adv

uniquely adv ▷ unique

unisex adj designed for use by both sexes

unison n (pl -s) complete agreement

unisons n ▷ unison

unit n (pl -s) single undivided entity or whole

unitary adj consisting of a single undivided whole

unite v (-tes, -ting, -ted) make or become an integrated whole

united v ▷ unite

unites v ▷ unite

unities n ▷ unity

uniting v ▷ unite

units n ▷ unit

unity n (pl -ties) state of being one

universe n (pl -s) whole of all existing matter, energy, and space

universes n ▷ universe

unkempt adj (of the hair) not combed

unknown adj not known ▶ n (pl -s) unknown person, quantity, or thing

unknowns n ▷ unknown

unleaded adj (of petrol) containing less tetraethyl lead, in order to reduce environmental pollution

unless conj except under the circumstances that

unlike adj dissimilar or different ▶ prep not like or typical of

unlikely adj improbable

unload v (-s, -ing, -ed) remove (cargo) from (a ship, truck, or plane)
unloaded v ▷ unload
unloading v ▷ unload
unloads v ▷ unload

unmask v (-s, -ing, -ed) remove the mask or disguise from
unmasked v ▷ unmask
unmasking v ▷ unmask
unmasks v ▷ unmask

unmoved adj not affected by emotion, indifferent

unnerve v (-ves, -ving, -ved) cause to lose courage, confidence, or self-control
unnerved v ▷ unnerve
unnerves v ▷ unnerve
unnerving v ▷ unnerve

unpack v (-s, -ing, -ed) remove the contents of (a suitcase, trunk, etc)
unpacked v ▷ unpack
unpacking v ▷ unpack
unpacks v ▷ unpack

unpick v (-s, -ing, -ed) undo (the stitches) of (a piece of sewing)
unpicked v ▷ unpick
unpicking v ▷ unpick
unpicks v ▷ unpick

unravel v (-vels, -velling, -velled) reduce (something knitted or woven) to separate strands
unravelled v ▷ unravel
unravelling v ▷ unravel
unravels v ▷ unravel

unrest n (pl -s) rebellious state of discontent
unrests n ▷ unrest

unroll v (-s, -ing, -ed) open out or unwind (something rolled or coiled) or (of something rolled or coiled) become opened out or unwound
unrolled v ▷ unroll
unrolling v ▷ unroll
unrolls v ▷ unroll

unrulier adj ▷ unruly
unruliest adj ▷ unruly
unruly adj (-lier, -liest) difficult to control or organize

unseat v (-s, -ing, -ed) throw or displace from a seat or saddle
unseated v ▷ unseat
unseating v ▷ unseat
unseats v ▷ unseat

unsociable adj ▷ unsocial

unsocial adj (also **unsociable**) avoiding the company of other people

unsound adj unhealthy or unstable

unstable adj (-r, -st) lacking stability or firmness
unstabler adj ▷ unstable
unstablest adj ▷ unstable

unsuited adj not appropriate for a particular task or situation
untidier adj ▷ untidy
untidiest adj ▷ untidy
untidily adv ▷ untidy
untidiness n ▷ untidy
untidinesses n ▷ untidy

untidy adj (-dier, -diest) messy and disordered > **untidily** adv
> **untidiness** n (pl -es)

untie v (-ties, -tying, -tied) open or free (something that is tied)
untied v ▷ untie
unties v ▷ untie

until conj up to the time that ▶ prep in or throughout the period before
untimelier adj ▷ untimely
untimeliest adj ▷ untimely

untimely adj (-lier, -liest) occurring before the expected or normal time

unto prep old-fashioned to

untold adj incapable of description

untoward adj causing misfortune or annoyance

untrue adj (-r, -st) incorrect or false
untruer adj ▷ untrue
untruest adj ▷ untrue

untruth n (pl -s) statement that is not true, lie
untruths n ▷ untruth

untying v ▷ untie

unusual adj uncommon or extraordinary > **unusually** adv
unusually adv ▷ unusual

unwieldier adj ▷ unwieldy

unwieldiest adj ▷ **unwieldy**

unwieldy adj (**-dier, -diest**) too heavy, large, or awkward to be easily handled

unwind v (**-s, -ing, unwound**) relax after a busy or tense time

unwinding v ▷ **unwind**

unwinds v ▷ **unwind**

unwonted adj out of the ordinary

unworthier adj ▷ **unworthy**

unworthiest adj ▷ **unworthy**

unworthy adj (**-thier, -thiest**) not deserving or worthy

unwound v ▷ **unwind**

unwrap v (**-s, -pping, -pped**) remove the wrapping from (something)

unwrapped v ▷ **unwrap**

unwrapping v ▷ **unwrap**

unwraps v ▷ **unwrap**

up prep, adv indicating movement to or position at a higher place ▶ adv indicating readiness, intensity or completeness, etc ▶ adj of a high or higher position ▶ v (**-s, -pping, -pped**) increase or raise ▶ adv (also **upwards**) from a lower to a higher place, level, or condition

upbeat adj informal cheerful and optimistic ▶ n (pl **-s**) MUSIC unaccented beat

upbeats n ▷ **upbeat**

upbraid v (**-s, -ing, -ded**) scold or reproach

upbraided v ▷ **upbraid**

upbraiding v ▷ **upbraid**

upbraids v ▷ **upbraid**

update v (**-tes, -ting, -ted**) bring up to date

updated v ▷ **update**

updates v ▷ **update**

updating v ▷ **update**

upend v (**-s, -ing, -ed**) turn or set (something) on its end

upended v ▷ **upend**

upending v ▷ **upend**

upends v ▷ **upend**

upfront adj open and frank ▶ adv, adj (of money) paid out at the beginning of a business arrangement

upgrade v (**-des, -ding, -ded**) promote (a person or job) to a higher rank

upgraded v ▷ **upgrade**

upgrades v ▷ **upgrade**

upgrading v ▷ **upgrade**

upheaval n (pl **-s**) strong, sudden, or violent disturbance

upheavals n ▷ **upheaval**

upheld v ▷ **uphold**

uphill adj sloping or leading upwards ▶ adv up a slope ▶ n (pl **-s**) S AFR difficulty

uphills n ▷ **uphill**

uphold v (**-s, -ing, upheld**) maintain or defend against opposition ▷ **upholder** n (pl **-s**)

upholder n ▷ **uphold**

upholders n ▷ **uphold**

upholding v ▷ **uphold**

upholds v ▷ **uphold**

upkeep n (pl **-s**) act, process, or cost of keeping something in good repair

upkeeps n ▷ **upkeep**

upland adj of or in an area of high or relatively high ground

uplands pl n area of high or relatively high ground

uplift v (**-s, -ing, -ed**) raise or lift up ▶ n (pl **-s**) act or process of improving moral, social, or cultural conditions ▷ **uplifting** adj

uplifted v ▷ **uplift**

uplifting v, adj ▷ **uplift**

uplifts v, n ▷ **uplift**

upload v (**-s, -ing, -ed**) transfer (data or a program) from one's own computer into the memory of another computer

uploaded v ▷ **upload**

uploading v ▷ **upload**

uploads v ▷ **upload**

upon prep on

upped v ▷ **up**

upper adj higher or highest in physical position, wealth, rank, or status ▶ n (pl **-s**) part of a shoe above the sole

uppers n ▷ **upper**

upping v ▷ **up**

uppish, uppity adj BRIT informal snobbish, arrogant, or presumptuous

uppity adj ▷ uppish

upright adj vertical or erect ▶ adv vertically or in an erect position ▶ n (pl -s) vertical support, such as a post
> **uprightness** n (pl -es)

uprightness n ▷ upright

uprightnesses n ▷ upright

uprights n ▷ upright

uprising n (pl -s) rebellion or revolt

uprisings n ▷ uprising

uproar n (pl -s) disturbance characterized by loud noise and confusion

uproars n ▷ uproar

uproot v (-s, -ing, -ed) pull up by or as if by the roots

uprooted v ▷ uproot

uprooting v ▷ uproot

uproots v ▷ uproot

ups v ▷ up

upset adj emotionally or physically disturbed or distressed ▶ v (-s, -tting, upset) tip over ▶ n (pl -s) unexpected defeat or reversal > **upsetting** adj

upsets v, n ▷ upset

upsetting v, adj ▷ upset

upshot n (pl -s) final result or conclusion

upshots n ▷ upshot

upstage adj at the back half of the stage ▶ v (-ges, -ging, -ged) informal draw attention to oneself from (someone else)

upstaged v ▷ upstage

upstages v ▷ upstage

upstaging v ▷ upstage

upstairs adv to or on an upper floor of a building

upstart n (pl -s) person who has risen suddenly to a position of power and behaves arrogantly

upstarts n ▷ upstart

upstream adv, adj in or towards the higher part of a stream

upsurge n (pl -s) rapid rise or swell

upsurges n ▷ upsurge

uptake n (pl -s) informal quick or slow to understand or learn

uptakes n ▷ uptake

uptight adj informal nervously tense, irritable, or angry

upturn n (pl -s) upward trend or improvement > **upturned** adj facing upwards

upturned adj ▷ upturn

upturns n ▷ upturn

upward adj directed or moving towards a higher place or level

upwards adv ▷ up

> **ur** interj. Ur is a sound people make when hesitating in speech. If someone plays this, you may be able to use it to form words that begin with UR. Ur is also handy for connecting words beginning with U to those ending in R. Ur scores 2 points.

uranium n (pl -s) CHEM radioactive silvery-white metallic element, used chiefly as a source of nuclear energy

uraniums n ▷ uranium

urban adj of or living in a city or town

urbane adj (-r, -st) characterized by courtesy, elegance, and sophistication
> **urbanity** n (pl -ties)

urbaner adj ▷ urbane

urbanest adj ▷ urbane

urbanities n ▷ urbane

urbanity n ▷ urbane

urbanization n ▷ urbanize

urbanizations n ▷ urbanize

urbanize v (-zes, -zing, -zed) make (a rural area) more industrialized and urban > **urbanization** n (pl -s)

urbanized v ▷ urbanize

urbanizes v ▷ urbanize

urbanizing v ▷ urbanize

urchin n (pl -s) mischievous child

urchins n ▷ urchin

urethra n (pl -rae) canal that carries urine from the bladder out of the body

urethrae n ▷ urethra

urge n (pl -s) strong impulse, inner drive, or yearning ▶ v (-ges, -ging,

-ged) plead with or press (a person to do something)

urged v ▷ urge

urgencies n ▷ urgent

urgency n ▷ urgent

urgent adj requiring speedy action or attention > **urgency** n (pl -cies) > **urgently** adv

urgently adv ▷ urgent

urges n, v ▷ urge

urging v ▷ urge

urinal n (pl -s) sanitary fitting used by men for urination

urinals n ▷ urine

urinary adj ▷ urine

urinate v (-tes, -ting, -ted) discharge urine > **urination** n (pl -s)

urinated v ▷ urinate

urinates v ▷ urinate

urinating v ▷ urinate

urination n ▷ urinate

urinations n ▷ urinate

urine n (pl -s) pale yellow fluid excreted by the kidneys to the bladder and passed as waste from the body > **urinary** adj

urines n ▷ urine

urn n (pl -s) vase used as a container for the ashes of the dead

urns n ▷ urn

ursine adj of or like a bear

us pron ▷ **we**

usable adj able to be used

usage n (pl -s) regular or constant use

usages n ▷ usage

use v (-ses, -sing, -sed) put into service or action ▶ n (pl -s) using or being used > **user** n (pl -s) > **useful** adj > **usefully** adv > **usefulness** n (pl -es) > **useless** adj > **uselessly** adv > **uselessness** n (pl -es)

used adj second-hand ▶ v ▷ use

useful adj ▷ use

usefully adv ▷ use

usefulness n ▷ use

usefulnesses n ▷ use

useless adj ▷ use

uselessly adv ▷ use

uselessness n ▷ use

uselessnesses n ▷ use

user n ▷ use

username n (pl -s) COMPUTERS name entered into a computer for identification purposes

usernames n ▷ username

users n ▷ user

uses v, n ▷ use

usher n (pl -s) official who shows people to their seats, as in a church ▶ v (-s, -ing, -ed) conduct or escort

ushered v ▷ usher

ushering v ▷ usher

ushers n, v ▷ usher

using v ▷ use

usual adj of the most normal, frequent, or regular type

usually adv most often, in most cases

usurer n ▷ usury

usurers n ▷ usury

usuries n ▷ usury

usurp v (-s, -ing, -ed) seize (a position or power) without authority > **usurpation** n (pl -s) > **usurper** n (pl -s)

usurpation n ▷ usurp

usurpations n ▷ usurp

usurped v ▷ usurp

usurper n ▷ usurp

usurpers n ▷ usurp

usurping v ▷ usurp

usurps v ▷ usurp

usury n (pl -ries) practice of lending money at an extremely high rate of interest > **usurer** n (pl -s)

ut n (**uts**). Ut is a musical note. This unusual word is useful for connecting words beginning with U to those ending with T. Ut scores 2 points.

ute n (pl -s) AUST & NZ informal utility truck

utensil n (pl -s) tool or container for practical use

utensils n ▷ utensil

uteri n ▷ uterus

uterine adj ▷ uterus

uterus n (pl **uteri**) womb > **uterine** adj

utes n ▷ ute

utilities n ▷ utility

utility n (pl -ties) usefulness ▶ adj designed for use rather than beauty

utilization n ▷ utilize

utilizations n ▷ utilize

utilize v (-zes, -zing, -zed) make practical use of ▷ **utilization** n (pl -ties)

utilized v ▷ utilize

utilizes v ▷ utilize

utilizing v ▷ utilize

utmost, uttermost adj, n (pl -s) (of) the greatest possible degree or amount

utmosts n ▷ utmost

utopia n (pl -s) any real or imaginary society, place, or state considered to be perfect or ideal ▷ **utopian** adj

utopian adj ▷ utopia

utopias n ▷ utopia

utter[1] v (-s, -ing, -ed) express (something) in sounds or words

utter[2] adj total or absolute ▷ **utterly** adv

uttered v ▷ utter[1]

uttering v ▷ utter[1]

utterly adv ▷ utter[2]

uttermost adj, n (pl -s) ▷ utmost

utters v ▷ utter[1]

uvula n (pl -s) small fleshy part of the soft palate that hangs in the back of the throat ▷ **uvular** adj

uvular adj ▷ uvula

uvulas n ▷ uvula

uxorious adj excessively fond of or dependent on one's wife

Vv

If you have a V on your rack, the first thing to remember is that there are no valid two-letter words beginning with V. In fact, there are no two-letter words that end in V either, so you can't form any two-letter words using V. Remembering this will stop you wasting time trying to think of some. While V is useless for two-letter words, it does start some good three-letter words. **Vex** and **vox** (13 points each) are the best of these, while **vaw**, **vow** and **vly** (9 each) are also useful.

vac n **vacs**. Vac is a short form of vacuum cleaner. This word can prove useful when you have a V but not much space to play it in. Remember that if you have the letters for vac, you might be able to form **cave** using an E that is already on the board. Vac scores 8 points.

vacancies n ▷ **vacancy**

vacancy n (pl **-cies**) unfilled job

vacant adj (of a toilet, room, etc) unoccupied > **vacantly** adv

vacantly adv ▷ **vacant**

vacate v (**-tes**, **-ting**, **-ted**) cause (something) to be empty by leaving

vacated v ▷ **vacate**

vacates v ▷ **vacate**

vacating v ▷ **vacate**

vacation n time when universities and law courts are closed

vacations n ▷ **vacation**

vaccine n (pl **-s**) substance designed to cause a mild form of a disease to make a person immune to the disease itself

vaccines n ▷ **vaccine**

vacua n ▷ **vacuum**

vacuous adj not expressing intelligent thought > **vacuity** n (pl **-ties**)

vacuum n (pl **-cuums**, **-cua**) empty space from which all or most air or gas

has been removed ▷ v (**-s**, **-ing**, **-ed**) clean with a vacuum cleaner

vacuumed v ▷ **vacuum**

vacuuming v ▷ **vacuum**

vacuums n ▷ **vacuum**

vagabond n (pl **-s**) person with no fixed home, esp. a beggar

vagabonds n ▷ **vagabond**

vagaries n ▷ **vagary**

vagary n (pl **-ries**) unpredictable change

vagina n (pl **-s**) (in female mammals) passage from the womb to the external genitals > **vaginal** adj

vaginal adj ▷ **vagina**

vaginas n ▷ **vagina**

vagrancies n ▷ **vagrancy**

vagrancy n ▷ **vagrant**

vagrant n (pl **-s**) person with no settled home ▷ adj wandering > **vagrancy** n (pl **-cies**)

vagrants n ▷ **vagrant**

vague adj (**-guer**, **-guest**) not clearly explained > **vaguely** adv

vaguely adv ▷ **vague**

vaguer adj ▷ **vague**

vaguest adj ▷ **vague**

vain adj (**-er**, **-est**) excessively proud, esp. of one's appearance

vainer adj ▷ **vain**

vainest adj ▷ **vain**
valance n (pl **-s**) piece of drapery round the edge of a bed
valances n ▷ **valance**
vale n (pl **-s**) lit valley
valence n (pl **-s**) molecular bonding between atoms
valences n ▷ **valence**
valencies n ▷ **valency**
valency n (pl **-cies**) power of an atom to make molecular bonds
valerian n (pl **-s**) herb used as a sedative
valerians n ▷ **valerian**
vales n ▷ **vale**
valet n (pl **-s**) man's personal male servant
valets n ▷ **valet**
valiant adj brave or courageous
valid adj (**-er, -est**) soundly reasoned ▷ **validity** n (pl **-ies**)
validate v (**-tes, -ting, -ted**) make valid ▷ **validation** n (pl **-s**)
validated v ▷ **validate**
validates v ▷ **validate**
validating v ▷ **validate**
validation n ▷ **validate**
validations n ▷ **validate**
valider adj ▷ **valid**
validest adj ▷ **valid**
validities n ▷ **valid**
validity n ▷ **valid**
valise n (pl **-s**) old-fashioned small suitcase
valises n ▷ **valise**
valley n (pl **-s**) low area between hills, often with a river running through it
valleys n ▷ **valley**
valour n (pl **-s**) lit bravery
valours n ▷ **valour**
valuable adj having great worth
value n (pl **-s**) importance, usefulness ▶ pl moral principles ▶ v (**-ues, -uing, -ued**) assess the worth or desirability of ▷ **valueless** adj ▷ **valuer** n (pl **-s**)
valued v ▷ **value**
valueless adj ▷ **value**
valuer n ▷ **value**

valuers n ▷ **value**
values n, v ▷ **value**
valuing v ▷ **value**
valve n (pl **-s**) device to control the movement of fluid through a pipe ▷ **valvular** adj
valves n ▷ **valve**
valvular adj ▷ **valve**
vamp¹ n (pl **-s**) informal sexually attractive woman who seduces men
vamp² v (**-s, -ing, -ed**) make (a story, piece of music, etc) seem new by inventing additional parts
vamped v ▷ **vamp²**
vamping v ▷ **vamp²**
vampire n (pl **-s**) (in folklore) corpse that rises at night to drink the blood of the living
vampires n ▷ **vampire**
vamps n, v ▷ **vamp¹, ²**
van¹ n (pl **-s**) motor vehicle for transporting goods
van² n (pl **-s**) ▷ **vanguard**
vanadium n (pl **-s**) CHEM metallic element, used in steel
vanadiums n ▷ **vanadium**
vandal n (pl **-s**) person who deliberately damages property ▷ **vandalism** n (pl **-s**) ▷ **vandalize** v (**-zes, -zing, -zed**)
vandalism n ▷ **vandal**
vandalisms n ▷ **vandal**
vandalize n ▷ **vandal**
vandalized n ▷ **vandal**
vandalizes n ▷ **vandal**
vandalizing v ▷ **vandal**
vandals n ▷ **vandal**
vane n (pl **-s**) flat blade on a rotary device such as a weathercock or propeller
vanes n ▷ **vane**
vanguard n (pl **-s**) unit of soldiers leading an army
vanguards n ▷ **vanguard**
vanilla n (pl **-s**) seed pod of a tropical climbing orchid, used for flavouring
vanillas n ▷ **vanilla**

vanish v (-es, -ing, -ed) disappear
suddenly or mysteriously
  vanished v ▷ vanish
  vanishes v ▷ vanish
  vanishing v ▷ vanish
  vanities n ▷ vanity
vanity n (pl -ies) (display of) excessive
pride
vanquish v (-es, -ing, -ed) lit defeat
(someone) utterly
  vanquished v ▷ vanquish
  vanquishes v ▷ vanquish
  vanquishing v ▷ vanquish
  vans n ▷ van[1, 2]
vantage n position that gives
one an overall view
  vantages n ▷ vantage
vapid adj (-er, -est) lacking character,
dull
  vapider adj ▷ vapid
  vapidest adj ▷ vapid
vaporize v ▷ vapour
  vaporized v ▷ vapour
  vaporizer n ▷ vapour
  vaporizers n ▷ vapour
  vaporizes v ▷ vapour
  vaporizing v ▷ vapour
  vaporous adj ▷ vapour
vapour n (pl -s) moisture suspended
in air as steam or mist ▷ **vaporize** v
(-zes, -zing, -zed) ▷ **vaporizer** n (pl -s)
▷ **vaporous** adj
  vapours n ▷ vapour
variabilities n ▷ variable
variability n ▷ variable
variable adj not always the same,
changeable ▶ n (pl -s) MATHS
expression with a range of values
▷ **variability** n (pl -ies)
  variables n ▷ variable
variant adj differing from a standard
or type ▶ n (pl -s) something that
differs from a standard or type
  variants n ▷ variant
  varied v, adj ▷ vary
  varies v ▷ vary
  varieties n ▷ variety
variety n (pl -ies) state of being diverse

or various
various adj of several kinds
  variously adv
  variously adv ▷ various
varnish n (pl -es) solution of oil and
resin, put on a surface to make it hard
and glossy ▶ v (-es, -ing, -ed) apply
varnish to
  varnished v ▷ varnish
  varnishes n, v ▷ varnish
  varnishing v ▷ varnish
vary v (-ries, -rying, -ried) change
▷ **varied** adj
  varying v ▷ vary
vascular adj BIOL relating to vessels
vase n (pl -s) ornamental jar, esp. for
flowers
  vases n ▷ vase
vassal n HIST man given land
by a lord in return for military service
▷ **vassalage** n (pl -s)
  vassalage n ▷ vassal
  vassalages n ▷ vassal
  vassals n ▷ vassal
vast adj (-er, -est) extremely large
▷ **vastly** adv ▷ **vastness** n (pl -es)
  vaster adj ▷ vast
  vastest adj ▷ vast
  vastly adv ▷ vast
  vastness n ▷ vast
  vastnesses n ▷ vast
vat n (pl -s) large container for
liquids
  vats n ▷ vat
vault[1] n (pl -s) secure room for storing
valuables
vault[2] v (-s, -ing, -ed) jump over
(something) by resting one's hand(s)
on it. ▶ n such a jump
  vaulted adj having an arched roof ▶ v
▷ vault[2]
  vaulting v ▷ vault[2]
  vaults n, v ▷ vault[1, 2]
vaunt v (-s, -ing, -ed) describe or
display (success or possessions)
boastfully ▷ **vaunted** adj
  vaunted adj, v ▷ vaunt
  vaunting v ▷ vaunt

vaunts v ▷ vaunt

vaw n (**vaws**) Vaw is a letter of the Hebrew alphabet. This is a very unusual word that can be useful when you are short of options. If you have the tiles for vaw, look out for opportunities to play **wave** or **wavy** using an E or Y that is already on the board. Vaw scores 9 points.

veal n (pl -s) calf meat

veals n ▷ veal

vector n (pl -s) MATHS quantity that has size and direction, such as force

vectors n ▷ vector

veer v (-s, -ing, -ed) change direction suddenly

veered v ▷ veer

veering v ▷ veer

veers v ▷ veer

veg n (**veges**) Veg is a short form of **vegetable**. If someone plays this, look out for opportunities to form **vegan** or **vegetate** from it. Veg scores 7 points.

vegan n (pl -s) person who eats no meat, fish, eggs, or dairy products ▶ adj suitable for a vegan > **veganism** n (pl -s)

veganism n ▷ vegan

veganisms n ▷ vegan

vegans n ▷ vegan

vegetate v (-tes, -ting, -ted) live a dull boring life with no mental stimulation

vegetated v ▷ vegetate

vegetates v ▷ vegetate

vegetating v ▷ vegetate

vehemence n ▷ vehement

vehemences n ▷ vehement

vehement adj expressing strong feelings > **vehemence** n (pl -s) > **vehemently** adv

vehemently adv ▷ vehement

vehicle n (pl -s) machine, esp. with an engine and wheels, for carrying people or objects > **vehicular** adj

vehicles n ▷ vehicle

vehicular adj ▷ vehicle

veil n (pl -s) piece of thin cloth covering the head or face ▶ v (-s, -ing, -ed) cover with or as if with a veil

veiled adj disguised ▶ v ▷ veil

veiling v ▷ veil

veils v ▷ veil

vein n (pl -s) tube that takes blood to the heart > **veined** adj

veined adj ▷ vein

veins n ▷ vein

veld, veldt n (pl -s) high grassland in southern Africa

velds n ▷ veld

veldts n ▷ veld

vellum n (pl -s) fine calfskin parchment

vellums n ▷ vellum

velocities n ▷ velocity

velocity n (pl -ties) speed of movement in a given direction

velour, velours n (pl -s) fabric similar to velvet

velours n ▷ velour

velvet n (pl -s) fabric with a thick soft pile

velvetier adj ▷ velvety

velvetiest adj ▷ velvety

velvets n ▷ velvet

velvety adj (-tier, -tiest) soft and smooth

venal adj easily bribed

vend v (-s, -ing, -ed) sell > **vendor** n (pl -s)

vended v ▷ vend

vendetta n (pl -s) prolonged quarrel between families, esp. one involving revenge killings

vendettas n ▷ vendetta

vending v ▷ vend

vendor n ▷ vend

vendors n ▷ vend

vends v ▷ vend

veneer n (pl -s) thin layer of wood etc covering a cheaper material

veneers n ▷ veneer

venerate v (-tes, -ting, -ted) hold (a person) in deep respect > **veneration** n (pl -s)

venerated v ▷ venerate

venerates v ▷ **venerate**

venerating v ▷ **venerate**

veneration n ▷ **venerate**

venerations n ▷ **venerate**

vengeful adj wanting revenge

venial adj (of a sin or fault) easily forgiven

venison n (pl **-s**) deer meat

venisons n ▷ **venison**

venom n (pl **-s**) malice or spite >**venomous** adj

venomous adj ▷ **venom**

venoms n ▷ **venom**

venous adj ANAT of veins

vent¹ n (pl **-s**) outlet releasing fumes or fluid ▶ v (**-s**, **-ing**, **-ed**) express (an emotion) freely

vent² n (pl **-s**) vertical slit in a jacket

vented v ▷ **vent**¹

venting v ▷ **vent**¹

ventral adj relating to the front of the body

vents n, v ▷ **vent**¹, ²

venture n (pl **-s**) risky undertaking, esp. in business ▶ v (**-res**, **-ring**, **-red**) do something risky

ventured v ▷ **venture**

ventures n, v ▷ **venture**

venturing v ▷ **venture**

venue n (pl **-s**) place where an organized gathering is held

venues n ▷ **venue**

veracious adj ▷ **veracity**

veracities n ▷ **veracity**

veracity n (pl **-ties**) habitual truthfulness >**veracious** adj

veranda n ▷ **verandah**

verandah, veranda n (pl **-s**) open porch attached to a house

verandahs n ▷ **verandah**

verandas n ▷ **verandah**

verb n (pl **-s**) word that expresses the idea of action, happening, or being

verbal adj spoken >**verbally** adv

verbally adv ▷ **verbal**

verbatim adv, adj word for word

verbena n (pl **-s**) plant with sweet-smelling flowers

verbenas n ▷ **verbena**

verbiage n (pl **-s**) excessive use of words

verbiages n ▷ **verbiage**

verbose adj (**-r**, **-st**) speaking at tedious length >**verbosity** n (pl **-ties**)

verboser adj ▷ **verbose**

verbosest adj ▷ **verbose**

verbosities n ▷ **verbose**

verbosity n ▷ **verbose**

verbs n ▷ **verb**

verdant adj lit covered in green vegetation

verdict n (pl **-s**) decision of a jury

verdicts n ▷ **verdict**

verdure n (pl **-s**) lit flourishing green vegetation

verdures n ▷ **verdure**

verge n (pl **-s**) grass border along a road

verger n (pl **-s**) C of E church caretaker

vergers n ▷ **verger**

verges n ▷ **verge**

verifiable adj ▷ **verify**

verification n ▷ **verify**

verifications n ▷ **verify**

verified v ▷ **verify**

verifies v ▷ **verify**

verify v (**-fies**, **-fying**, **-fied**) check the truth or accuracy of >**verifiable** adj >**verification** n (pl **-s**)

verifying v ▷ **verify**

verily adv obs in truth

verities n ▷ **verity**

verity n (pl **-ies**) true statement or principle

vermin pl n (pl (pl **-s**) animals, esp. insects and rodents, that spread disease or cause damage >**verminous** adj

verminous adj ▷ **vermin**

vermins n ▷ **vermin**

vermouth n (pl **-s**) wine flavoured with herbs

vermouths n ▷ **vermouth**

vernal adj occurring in spring

vernier n (pl **-s**) movable scale on a graduated measuring instrument for taking readings in fractions

verniers n ▷ **vernier**

veronica n (pl -s) plant with small blue, pink, or white flowers
veronicas n ▷ **veronica**
verruca n (pl -s) wart, usu. on the foot
verrucas n ▷ **verruca**
verse n (pl -s) group of lines forming part of a song or poem
verses n ▷ **verse**
version n (pl -s) form of something, such as a piece of writing, with some differences from other forms
versions n ▷ **version**
verso n (pl -s) left-hand page of a book
versos n ▷ **verso**
versus prep in opposition to or in contrast with
vertebra n (pl -rae) one of the bones that form the spine > **vertebral** adj
vertebrae n ▷ **vertebra**
vertebral adj ▷ **vertebra**
vertex n (pl -texes, -tices) MATHS point on a geometric figure where the sides form an angle
vertexes n ▷ **vertex**
vertical adj straight up and down ▶ n (pl -s) vertical direction
verticals n ▷ **vertical**
vertices n ▷ **vertex**
vertiginous adj ▷ **vertigo**
vertigo n (pl -gos) dizziness, usu. when looking down from a high place > **vertiginous** adj
vertigoes n ▷ **vertigo**
vervain n (pl -s) plant with spikes of blue, purple, or white flowers
vervains n ▷ **vervain**
verve n (pl -s) enthusiasm or liveliness
verves n ▷ **verve**
very adv more than usually, extremely ▶ adj absolute, exact
vesicle n (pl -s) BIOL sac or small cavity, esp. one containing fluid
vesicles n ▷ **vesicle**
vespers pl n RC CHURCH (service of) evening prayer
vessel n (pl -s) ship
vessels n ▷ **vessel**
vest n (pl -s) undergarment worn on the top half of the body ▶ v (-s, -ing, -ed) (foll. by **in** or **with**) give (authority) to (someone)
vested v ▷ **vest**
vestige n (pl -s) small amount or trace > **vestigial** adj
vestiges n ▷ **vestige**
vestigial adj ▷ **vestige**
vesting v ▷ **vest**
vestries n ▷ **vestry**
vestry n (pl -ies) room in a church used as an office by the priest or minister
vests n, v ▷ **vest**
vet[1] n (pl -s) ▶ veterinary surgeon ▶ v (-s, -tting, -tted) check the suitability of
vet[2] n US, AUST & NZ military veteran
vetch n (pl -es) climbing plant with a beanlike fruit used as fodder
vetches n ▷ **vetch**
veteran n (pl -s) person with long experience in a particular activity, esp. military service ▶ adj long-serving
veterans n ▷ **veteran**
veto n (pl -es) official power to cancel a proposal ▶ v (-es, -ing, -ed) enforce a veto against
vetoed v ▷ **veto**
vetoes n, v ▷ **veto**
vetoing v ▷ **veto**
vets n, v ▷ **vet**[1, 2]
vetted v ▷ **vet**[1]
vetting v ▷ **vet**[1]
vex v (-es, -ing, -ed) frustrate, annoy
vexation n (pl -s) something annoying > **vexatious** adj
vexations n ▷ **vexation**
vexatious adj ▷ **vexation**
vexed v ▷ **vex**
vexes v ▷ **vex**
vexing v ▷ **vex**
via prep by way of
viabilities n ▷ **viable**
viability n ▷ **viable**
viable adj able to be put into practice > **viability** n (pl -ties)
viaduct n (pl -s) bridge over a valley

viaducts n ▷ viaduct
vial n (pl -s) ▷ phial
vials n ▷ vial
viands pl n obs food
vibes pl n informal emotional reactions between people
vibrant adj vigorous in appearance, energetic
vibrate v (-tes, -ting, -ted) move back and forth rapidly ▷ vibration (pl -s)
vibrated v ▷ vibrate
vibrates v ▷ vibrate
vibrating v ▷ vibrate
vibration n ▷ vibrate
vibrations n ▷ vibrate
vibrato n (pl -s) music rapid fluctuation in the pitch of a note
vibrator n (pl -s) device that produces vibratory motion, used for massage or as a sex aid ▷ vibratory adj
vibrators n ▷ vibrator
vibratos n ▷ vibrato
vicar n (pl -s) C of E member of the clergy in charge of a parish
vicarage n (pl -s) vicar's house
vicarages n ▷ vicarage
vicars n ▷ vicar
vice¹ n (pl -s) immoral or evil habit or action
vice² n (pl -s) tool with a pair of jaws for holding an object while working on it
vice³ adj serving in place of
viceregal adj ▷ viceroy
viceroy n (pl -s) governor of a colony who represents the monarch ▷ viceregal adj
viceroys n ▷ viceroy
vices n ▷ vice¹, ²
vicinities n ▷ vicinity
vicinity n (pl -ties) surrounding area
vicious adj cruel and violent ▷ viciously adv
viciously adv ▷ vicious
victim n (pl -s) person or thing harmed or killed
victims n ▷ victim
victor n (pl -s) person who has defeated an opponent, esp. in war or in sport

victories n ▷ victory
victorious adj ▷ victory
victors n ▷ victor
victory n (pl -ries) winning of a battle or contest ▷ victorious adj
victuals pl n old-fashioned food and drink
vicuña n (pl -s) S American animal like the llama
vicuñas n ▷ vicuña
video n (pl -s) video cassette (recorder) ▶ v (-s, -ing, -ed) record (a TV programme or event) on video ▶ adj relating to or used in producing television images
videoed v ▷ video
videoing v ▷ video
videos n, v ▷ video
vie v (vies, vying, vied) compete (with someone)
vied v ▷ vie
vies v ▷ vie
view n (pl -s) opinion or belief ▶ v (-s, -ing, -ed) think of (something) in a particular way
viewdata n (pl -s)® videotext service linking users to a computer by telephone
viewed v ▷ view
viewer n person who watches television
viewers n ▷ viewer
viewing v ▷ view
views n, v ▷ view
vigil n (pl -s) night-time period of staying awake to look after a sick person, pray, etc
vigilance n ▷ vigilant
vigilances n ▷ vigilant
vigilant adj watchful in case of danger ▷ vigilance n (pl -s)
vigils n ▷ vigil
vignette n (pl -s) concise description of the typical features of something
vignettes n ▷ vignette
vigorous adj ▷ vigour
vigorously adv ▷ vigour
vigour n (pl -s) physical or mental

energy > **vigorous** adj > **vigorously** adv
vigours n > **vigour**
viking n (pl -s) HIST seafaring raider and settler from Scandinavia
vikings n > **viking**
vile (-r, -st) adj very wicked > **vilely** adv
> **vileness** n (pl -s)
vilely adv > **vile**
vileness n > **vile**
vilenesses n > **vile**
viler adj > **vile**
vilest adj > **vile**
vilification n > **vilify**
vilifications n > **vilify**
vilified v > **vilify**
vilifies v > **vilify**
vilify v (-fies, -fying, -fied) attack the character of > **vilification** n (pl -s)
vilifying v > **vilify**
villa n (pl -s) large house with gardens
village n (pl -s) small group of houses in a country area > **villager** n (pl -s)
villager n > **village**
villagers n > **village**
villages n > **village**
villain n (pl -s) wicked person
> **villainous** adj > **villainy** n (pl -nies)
villainies n > **villain**
villainous adj > **villain**
villains n > **villain**
villainy n > **villain**
villas n > **villa**
villein n (pl -s) HIST peasant bound in service to his lord
villeins n > **villein**

> **vim** (**vims**). Vim means vigour or energy. This word can be helpful when you're stuck with unpromising letters, and gives a reasonable score for a three-letter word. Vim scores 8 points.

vine n (pl -s) climbing plant, esp. one producing grapes
vinegar n (pl -s) acid liquid made from wine, beer, or cider > **vinegary** adj
vinegars n > **vinegar**
vinegary adj > **vinegar**

vines n > **vine**
vineyard n (pl -s) plantation of grape vines, esp. for making wine
vineyards n > **vineyard**
vino n (pl -s) informal wine
vinos n > **vino**
vintage n (pl -s) wine from a particular harvest of grapes ▶ adj best and most typical
vintages n > **vintage**
vintner n (pl -s) dealer in wine
vintners n > **vintner**
vinyl n (pl -s) type of plastic, used in mock leather and records
vinyls n > **vinyl**
viol n (pl -s) early stringed instrument preceding the violin
viola¹ n (pl -s) stringed instrument lower in pitch than a violin
viola² n (pl -s) variety of pansy
violas n > **viola**¹, ²
violate v (-tes, -ting, -ted) break (a law or agreement) > **violation** n
> **violator** n
violated v > **violate**
violates v > **violate**
violating v > **violate**
violation n > **violate**
violations n > **violate**
violator n > **violate**
violators n > **violate**
violence n (pl -s) use of physical force, usu. intended to cause injury or destruction > **violent** adj
> **violently** adv
violences n > **violence**
violent adj > **violence**
violently adv > **violent**
violet n (pl -s) plant with bluish-purple flowers ▶ adj bluish-purple
violets n > **violet**
violin n (pl -s) small four-stringed musical instrument played with a bow.
> **violinist** n (pl -s)
violinist n > **violin**
violinists n > **violin**
violins n > **violin**
viols n > **viol**

viper n (pl **-s**) poisonous snake
vipers n ▷ **viper**
virago n (pl **-goes**, **-gos**) aggressive woman
viragoes n ▷ **virago**
viragos n ▷ **virago**
viral adj of or caused by a virus
virgin n (pl **-s**) person, esp. a woman, who has not had sexual intercourse ▶ adj not having had sexual intercourse > **virginity** n (pl **-ties**)
virginal adj like a virgin ▶ n early keyboard instrument like a small harpsichord
virginities n ▷ **virginity**
virginity n ▷ **virgin**
virgins n ▷ **virgin**
virile adj having the traditional male characteristics of physical strength and a high sex drive > **virility** n (pl **-ties**)
virilities n ▷ **virile**
virility n ▷ **virile**
virologies n ▷ **virology**
virology n (pl **-gies**) study of viruses
virtual adj having the effect but not the form of > **virtually** adv practically, almost
virtually adv ▷ **virtual**
virtue n (pl **-s**) moral goodness
virtues n ▷ **virtue**
virtuosi n ▷ **virtuoso**
virtuosities n ▷ **virtuoso**
virtuosity n ▷ **virtuoso**
virtuoso n (pl **-sos**, **-si**) person with impressive esp. musical skill > **virtuosity** n (pl **-ies**)
virtuosos n ▷ **virtuoso**
virtuous adj morally good > **virtuously** adv
virtuously adv ▷ **virtuous**
virulent adj very infectious
virus n (pl **-es**) microorganism that causes disease in humans, animals, and plants
viruses n ▷ **virus**
visa n (pl **-s**) permission to enter a country, granted by its government and shown by a stamp on one's passport

visage n (pl **-s**) lit face
visages n ▷ **visage**
visas n ▷ **visa**
viscera pl n large abdominal organs
visceral adj instinctive
viscid adj sticky
viscose n (pl **-s**) synthetic fabric made from cellulose
viscoses n ▷ **viscose**
viscosities n ▷ **viscous**
viscosity n ▷ **viscous**
viscount n (pl **-s**) British nobleman ranking between an earl and a baron
viscounts n ▷ **viscount**
viscous adj thick and sticky > **viscosity** n (pl **-ties**)
visible adj able to be seen > **visibly** adv
visibly adv ▷ **visible**
vision n (pl **-s**) ability to see
visions n ▷ **vision**
visit v (**-s**, **-ing**, **-ed**) go or come to see ▶ n instance of visiting > **visitor** n (pl **-s**)
visited v ▷ **visit**
visiting v ▷ **visit**
visitor n ▷ **visit**
visitors n ▷ **visit**
visits v ▷ **visit**
visor n (pl **-s**) transparent part of a helmet that pulls down over the face
visors n ▷ **visor**
vista n (pl **-s**) (beautiful) extensive view
vistas n ▷ **vista**
visual adj done by or used in seeing
vital adj essential or highly important > **vitally** adv
vitalities n ▷ **vitality**
vitality n (pl **-ties**) physical or mental energy
vitally adv ▷ **vital**
vitals pl n bodily organs necessary to maintain life
vitamin n (pl **-s**) one of a group of substances that are essential in the diet for specific body processes
vitamins n ▷ **vitamin**
vitiate v (**-tes**, **-ting**, **-ted**) spoil the effectiveness of

vitiated v ▷ vitiate
vitiates v ▷ vitiate
vitiating v ▷ vitiate
vitreous adj like or made from glass
vitriol n (pl -s) language expressing bitterness and hatred > **vitriolic** adj
vitriolic adj ▷ vitriol
vitriols n ▷ vitriol
viva¹ interj long live (a person or thing)
viva² n (pl -s) BRIT examination in the form of an interview
vivace adv MUSIC in a lively manner
vivas n ▷ viva²
vivid adj (-er, -est) very bright
> **vividly** adv > **vividness** n (pl -es)
vivider adj ▷ vivid
vividest adj ▷ vivid
vividly adv ▷ vivid
vividness n ▷ vivid
vividnesses n ▷ vivid
vixen n (pl -s) female fox
vixens n ▷ vixen
vizier n (pl -s) high official in certain Muslim countries
viziers n ▷ vizier
vizor n (pl -s) ▷ visor
vizors n ▷ vizor

> **vly** n (**vlys**) Vly is a South African word meaning an area of low marshy ground. This is a good word to remember because it doesn't contain any vowels, making it useful when you are short of vowel tiles. Vly scores 9 points.

vocal adj relating to the voice
vocalist n (pl -s) singer
vocalists n ▷ vocalist
vocalization n ▷ vocalize
vocalizations n ▷ vocalize
vocalize v (-zes, -zing, -zed) express with or use the voice > **vocalization** n (pl -s)
vocalized v ▷ vocalize
vocalizes v ▷ vocalize
vocalizing v ▷ vocalize
vocally adv ▷ vocal
vocals pl n singing part of a piece of pop music > **vocally** adv

vocation n (pl -s) profession or trade
vocations n ▷ vocation
vodka n (pl -s) (Russian) spirit distilled from potatoes or grain
vodkas n ▷ vodka
vogue n (pl -s) popular style
vogues n ▷ vogue
voice n (pl -s) (quality of) sound made when speaking or singing ▶ v (-ces, -cing, -ced) express verbally
> **voiceless** adj
voiced v ▷ voice
voiceless adj ▷ voice
voices n, v ▷ voice
voicing v ▷ voice
void adj not legally binding ▶ n (pl -s) empty space ▶ v (-s, -ing, -ed) make invalid
voided v ▷ void
voiding v ▷ void
voids n, v ▷ void
voile n (pl -s) light semitransparent fabric
voiles n ▷ voile
volatile adj liable to sudden change, esp. in behaviour > **volatility** n (pl -ties)
volatilities n ▷ volatile
volatility n ▷ volatile
volcanic adj ▷ volcano
volcano n (pl -noes, -nos) mountain with a vent through which lava is ejected > **volcanic** adj
volcanoes n ▷ volcano
volcanos n ▷ volcano
vole n (pl -s) small rodent
voles n ▷ vole
volition n (pl -s) ability to decide things for oneself
volitions n ▷ volition
volley n (pl -s) simultaneous discharge of ammunition ▶ v (-s, -ing, -ed) discharge (ammunition) in a volley
volleyed v ▷ volley
volleying v ▷ volley
volleys n, v ▷ volley
volt n (pl -s) unit of electric potential
voltage n (pl -s) electric potential difference expressed in volts

voltages n ▷ voltage
volts n ▷ volt
volubilities n ▷ voluble
volubility n ▷ voluble
voluble adj talking easily and at length
> **volubility** n (pl **-ties**) > **volubly** adv
volubly adv ▷ voluble
volume n (pl **-s**) size of the space
occupied by something
volumes n ▷ volume
volute n (pl **-s**) spiral or twisting turn,
form, or object
volutes n ▷ volute
vomit v (**-s, -ing, -ed**) eject (the
contents of the stomach) through the
mouth ▶ n (pl **-s**) matter vomited
vomited v ▷ vomit
vomiting v ▷ vomit
vomits v, n ▷ vomit
voodoo n (pl **-s**) religion involving
ancestor worship and witchcraft,
practised by Black people in the West
Indies, esp. in Haiti.
voodoos n ▷ voodoo
vortex n (pl **-texes, -tices**) whirlpool
vortexes n ▷ vortex
vortices n ▷ vortex
vote n (pl **-s**) choice made by a
participant in a shared decision, esp.
in electing a candidate ▶ v (**-tes,
-ting, -ted**) make a choice by a vote
▶ **voter** n (pl **-s**)
voted v ▷ vote
voter n ▷ vote
voters n ▷ vote
votes n, v ▷ vote
voting v ▷ vote
votive adj done or given to fulfil a vow
vouch v (**-es, -ing, -ed**) give one's
personal assurance about
vouched v ▷ vouch
voucher n (pl **-s**) ticket used instead of
money to buy specified goods
vouchers n ▷ voucher
vouches v ▷ vouch
vouching v ▷ vouch
vow n (pl **-s**) solemn and binding promise
▶ pl formal promises made when

marrying or entering a religious order
▶ v (**-s, -ing, -ed**) promise solemnly
vowed v ▷ vow
vowel n (pl **-s**) speech sound made
without obstructing the flow of breath
vowels n ▷ vowel
vowing v ▷ vow
vows n, v ▷ vow

> **vox** n (**voces**) Vox means a voice
> or sound. Along with **vex**, this is
> the highest-scoring three-letter
> word beginning with V. Vox scores
> 13 points.

voyage n (pl **-s**) long journey by sea or
in space ▶ v (**-ges, -ging, -ged**) make a
voyage > **voyager** n (pl **-s**)
voyaged v ▷ voyage
voyager n ▷ voyage
voyagers n ▷ voyager
voyages n, v ▷ voyage
voyaging v ▷ voyage
voyeur n (pl **-s**) person who
obtains pleasure from watching
people undressing or having sex
> **voyeurism** n (pl **-s**)
voyeurism n ▷ voyeur
voyeurisms n ▷ voyeur
voyeurs n ▷ voyeur

> **vug** n (**vugs**) A vug is a small cavity
> in a rock. This is a very unusual word
> that can be useful when you have an
> uninspiring combination of letters.
> Vug scores 7 points.

vulgar adj (**-er, -est**) showing lack of
good taste, decency, or refinement
> **vulgarly** adv > **vulgarity** n (pl **-ties**)
vulgarer adj ▷ vulgar
vulgarest adj ▷ vulgar
vulgarities n ▷ vulgar
vulgarly adv ▷ vulgar
vulpine adj of like a fox
vulture n (pl **-s**) large bird that feeds on
the flesh of dead animals
vultures n ▷ vulture
vulva n (pl **-vae**) woman's external
genitals
vulvae n ▷ vulva
vying v ▷ vie

Ww

W is a useful tile to have on your rack as it earns 4 points on its own and produces a number of high-scoring short words. There are, however, only two two-letter words begin with W: **we** and **wo** (5 points each). If you know this, though, you won't waste time looking for others. There are lots of everyday three-letter words that earn good scores: **wax** (13) with its two old-fashioned variants **wex** and **wox** (also 13 each). There are lots of everyday **way**, **who**, **why**, **wow** and **wry** (9 each). Don't forget **wok** (10) either, which can be as useful on the Scrabble board as in the kitchen!

wackier adj ▷ **wacky**

wackiest adj ▷ **wacky**

wackiness n ▷ **wacky**

wackinesses n ▷ **wacky**

wacky adj (**-ckier, -ckiest**) informal eccentric or funny ▶ **wackiness** n (pl **-es**)

wad n (pl **-s**) small mass of soft material

waddies n ▷ **waddy**

wadding n (pl **-s**) soft material used for padding or stuffing

waddings n ▷ **wadding**

waddle v (**-les, -ling, -led**) walk with short swaying steps ▶ n (pl **-s**) swaying walk

waddled v, n ▷ **waddle**

waddles v ▷ **waddle**

waddling v ▷ **waddle**

waddy n (pl **-ies**) heavy wooden club used by Australian Aborigines

wade v (**-des, -ding, -ded**) walk with difficulty through water or mud

waded v ▷ **wade**

wader n (pl **-s**) long-legged water bird ▶ pl angler's long waterproof boots

waders n ▷ **wader**

wades v ▷ **wade**

wadi n (pl **-s**) (in N Africa and Arabia) river which is dry except in the wet season

wading v ▷ **wade**

wadis n ▷ **wadi**

wads n ▷ **wad**

wafer n (pl **-s**) thin crisp biscuit

wafers n ▷ **wafer**

waffle¹ informal v (**-les, -ling, -led**) speak or write in a vague wordy way ▶ n (pl **-s**) vague wordy talk or writing

waffle² n (pl **-s**) square crisp pancake with a gridlike pattern

waffled v ▷ **waffle**¹

waffles v, n ▷ **waffle**¹, ²

waffling v ▷ **waffle**¹

waft v (**-s, -ing, -ed**) drift or carry gently through the air ▶ n (pl **-s**) something wafted

wafted v ▷ **waft**

wafting v ▷ **waft**

wafts v, n ▷ **waft**

wag v (**-s, -ging, -gged**) move rapidly from side to side ▶ n (pl **-s**) wagging movement

wage n (pl **-s**) (often pl) payment for work done, esp. when paid weekly ▶ v (**-ges, -ging, -ged**) engage in (an activity)

waged v ▷ **wage**

wager n, v (**-s, -ing, -ed**) bet on the

outcome of something

wagered v ▷ **wager**

wagering v ▷ **wager**

wagers n, v ▷ **wager**

wages n, v ▷ **wage**

wagged v ▷ **wag**

wagging v ▷ **wag**

waggle v (**-les, -ling, -led**) move with a rapid shaking or wobbling motion

waggled v ▷ **waggle**

waggles v ▷ **waggle**

waggling v ▷ **waggle**

waggon n ▷ **wagon**

waggons n ▷ **wagon**

waging v ▷ **wage**

wagon, waggon n (pl **-s**) four-wheeled vehicle for heavy loads

wagons n ▷ **wagon**

wags v ▷ **wag**

wagtail n (pl **-s**) small long-tailed bird

wagtails n ▷ **wagtail**

wahoo n (pl **-s**) food and game fish of tropical seas

wahoos n ▷ **wahoo**

waif n (pl **-s**) young person who is, or seems, homeless or neglected

waifs n ▷ **waif**

wail v (**-s, -ing, -ed**) cry out in pain or misery ▶ n (pl **-s**) mournful cry

wailed v ▷ **wail**

wailing v ▷ **wail**

wails v, n ▷ **wail**

wain n (pl **-s**) poetic farm wagon

wains n ▷ **wain**

wainscot, wainscoting n (pl **-s**) wooden lining of the lower part of the walls of a room

wainscoting n ▷ **wainscot**

wainscots n ▷ **wainscot**

wainscots n ▷ **wainscot**

waist n (pl **-s**) part of the body between the ribs and hips

waists n ▷ **waist**

wait v (**-s, -ing, -ed**) remain inactive in expectation (of something) ▶ n (pl **-s**) act or period of waiting

waited v ▷ **wait**

waiter n (pl **-s**) man who serves in a

restaurant etc ▷ **waitress** n fem (pl **-es**)

waiters n ▷ **waiter**

waiting v ▷ **wait**

waitress n ▷ **waiter**

waitresses n ▷ **waiter**

waits v, n ▷ **wait**

waive v (**-ves, -ving, -ved**) refrain from enforcing (a law, right, etc)

waived v ▷ **waive**

waiver n (pl **-s**) act or instance of voluntarily giving up a claim, right, etc

waivers n ▷ **waiver**

waives v ▷ **waive**

waiving v ▷ **waive**

waka n (pl **-s**) NZ Maori canoe

wakas n ▷ **waka**

wake¹ v (**-kes, -king, woke, woken**) rouse from sleep or inactivity ▶ n (pl **-s**) vigil beside a corpse the night before the funeral ▷ **wakeful** adj

wake² n (pl **-s**) track left by a moving ship

wakeful adj ▷ **wake**¹

waken v (**-s, -ing, -ed**) wake

wakened v ▷ **waken**

wakening v ▷ **waken**

wakens v ▷ **waken**

wakes n ▷ **wake**¹, ²

waking v ▷ **wake**¹

walk v (**-s, -ing, -ed**) move on foot with at least one foot always on the ground ▶ n (pl **-s**) act or instance of walking ▷ **walker** n (pl **-s**)

walked v ▷ **walk**

walker n ▷ **walk**

walkers n ▷ **walk**

walking v ▷ **walk**

walkout n (pl **-s**) strike

walkouts n ▷ **walkout**

walkover n (pl **-s**) easy victory

walkovers n ▷ **walkover**

walks v, n ▷ **walk**

wall n (pl **-s**) structure of brick, stone, etc used to enclose, divide, or support ▶ v (**-s, -ing, -ed**) enclose or seal with a wall or walls

wallabies n ▷ **wallaby**

wallaby n (pl **-bies**) marsupial like a

small kangaroo

wallaroo n (pl **-s**) large stocky Australian kangaroo of rocky regions

wallaroos n ▷ wallaroo

walled v ▷ wall

wallet n (pl **-s**) small folding case for paper money, documents, etc

wallets n ▷ wallet

walleye n (pl **-s**) fish with large staring eyes (also **dory**)

walleyes n ▷ walleye

wallies n ▷ wally

walling v ▷ wall

wallop informal v (**-s**, **-ing**, **-ed**) hit hard ▶ n (pl **-s**) hard blow

walloped v ▷ wallop

wallops v, n ▷ wallop

wallow v (**-s**, **-ing**, **-ed**) revel in an emotion ▶ n (pl **-s**) act or instance of wallowing

wallowed v ▷ wallow

wallowing v ▷ wallow

wallows v, n ▷ wallow

walls n, v ▷ wall

wally n (pl **-ies**) BRIT slang stupid person

walnut n (pl **-s**) edible nut with a wrinkled shell

walnuts n ▷ walnut

walrus n (pl **-es**) large sea mammal with long tusks

walruses n ▷ walrus

waltz n (pl **-es**) ballroom dance ▶ v (**-zes**, **-zing**, **-zed**) dance a waltz

waltzed v ▷ waltz

waltzes n, v ▷ waltz

waltzing v ▷ waltz

wampum n (pl **-s**) shells woven together, formerly used by Native Americans for money and ornament

wampums n ▷ wampum

wan adj (**-nner**, **-nnest**) pale and sickly looking

wand n (pl **-s**) thin rod, esp. one used in performing magic tricks

wander v (**-s**, **-ing**, **-ed**) move about without a definite destination or aim ▶ n (pl **-s**) act or instance of wandering

> **wanderer** n (pl **-s**)

wandered v ▷ wander

wanderer n ▷ wander

wanderers n ▷ wander

wandering v ▷ wander

wanders v, n ▷ wander

wands n ▷ wand

wane v (**-nes**, **-ning**, **-ned**) decrease gradually in size or strength

waned v ▷ wane

wanes v ▷ wane

wangle v (**-les**, **-ling**, **-led**) informal get by devious methods

wangled v ▷ wangle

wangles v ▷ wangle

wangling v ▷ wangle

waning v ▷ wane

wanner adj ▷ wan

wannest adj ▷ wan

want v (**-s**, **-ing**, **-ed**) need or long for ▶ n (pl **-s**) act or instance of wanting

wanted adj sought by the police ▶ v ▷ want

wanting adj lacking ▶ v ▷ want

wanton adj (**-er**, **-est**) without motive, provocation, or justification

wantoner adj ▷ wanton

wantonest adj ▷ wanton

wants v, n ▷ want

war n (pl **-s**) fighting between nations ▶ adj of, like, or caused by war ▶ v (**-s**, **-rring**, **-rred**) conduct a war

> **warring** v

waratah n (pl **-s**) Australian shrub with crimson flowers

waratahs n ▷ waratah

warble v (**-les**, **-ling**, **-led**) sing in a trilling voice

warbled v ▷ warble

warbler n (pl **-s**) any of various small songbirds

warblers n ▷ warbler

warbles v ▷ warble

warbling v ▷ warble

ward n (pl **-s**) room in a hospital for patients needing a similar kind of care

warden n (pl **-s**) person in charge of a building and its occupants

wardens n ▷ **warden**
warder n (pl -s) prison officer
>**wardress** n fem (pl -es)
warders n ▷ **warder**
wardress n ▷ **warder**
wardresses n ▷ **warder**
wardrobe n (pl -s) cupboard for hanging clothes in
wardrobes n ▷ **wardrobe**
wardroom n (pl -s) officers' quarters on a warship
wardrooms n ▷ **wardroom**
wards n ▷ **ward**
ware n (pl -s) articles of a specified type or material ▶ pl goods for sale
wares n ▷ **ware**
warfare n (pl -s) fighting or hostilities
warfares n ▷ **warfare**
warhead n (pl -s) explosive front part of a missile
warheads n ▷ **warhead**
warier adj ▷ **wary**
wariest adj ▷ **wary**
warily adv ▷ **wary**
wariness n ▷ **wary**
warinesses n ▷ **wary**
warlike adj of or relating to war
warlock n (pl -s) man who practises black magic
warlocks n ▷ **warlock**
warm adj (-er, -est) moderately hot ▶ v (-s, -ing, -ed) make or become warm
>**warmly** adv
warmed v ▷ **warm**
warmer adj ▷ **warm**
warmest adj ▷ **warm**
warming v ▷ **warm**
warmly adv ▷ **warm**
warms v ▷ **warm**
warmth n (pl -s) mild heat
warmths n ▷ **warmth**
warn v (-s, -ing, -ed) make aware of possible danger or harm
warned v ▷ **warn**
warning n (pl -s) something that warns ▶ v ▷ **warn**
warnings n ▷ **warning**
warns v ▷ **warn**

warp v (-s, -ing, -ed) twist out of shape ▶ n (pl -s) state of being warped
warped v ▷ **warp**
warping v ▷ **warp**
warps v, n ▷ **warp**
warrant n (pl -s) (document giving) official authorization ▶ v (-s, -ing, -ed) make necessary
warranted v ▷ **warrant**
warranties n ▷ **warranty**
warranting v ▷ **warrant**
warrants n, v ▷ **warrant**
warranty n (pl -ties) (document giving) a guarantee
warred v ▷ **war**
warren n (pl -s) series of burrows in which rabbits live
warrens n ▷ **warren**
warrigal AUST n (pl -s) dingo ▶ adj wild
warrigals n ▷ **warrigal**
warring v ▷ **war**
warrior n (pl -s) person who fights in a war
warriors n ▷ **warrior**
wars n, v ▷ **war**
warship n (pl -s) ship designed and equipped for naval combat
warships n ▷ **warship**
wart n (pl -s) small hard growth on the skin
warts n ▷ **wart**
wary adj (-rier, -riest) watchful or cautious >**warily** adv >**wariness** n (pl -es)
was v ▷ **be**
wash v (-es, -ing, -ed) clean (oneself, clothes, etc) with water and usu. soap informal ▶ n (pl -es) act or process of washing >**washable** adj
washable adj ▷ **wash**
washed v ▷ **wash**
washer n (pl -s) ring put under a nut or bolt or in a tap as a seal
washers n ▷ **washer**
washes v, n ▷ **wash**
washing n (pl -s) clothes to be washed ▶ v ▷ **wash**
washings n ▷ **washing**

washout n (pl -s) informal complete failure

washouts n ▷ washouts

wasp n (pl -s) stinging insect with a slender black-and-yellow striped body

waspish adj bad-tempered

wasps n ▷ wasp

wastage n (pl -s) loss by wear or waste

wastages n ▷ wastage

waste v (-tes, -ting, -ted) use pointlessly or thoughtlessly ▶ n (pl -s) act of wasting or state of being wasted ▶ pl desert ▶ adj rejected as worthless or surplus to requirements

wasted v ▷ waste

wasteful adj extravagant > **wastefully** adv

wastefully adv ▷ waste

waster, wastrel n (pl -s) layabout

wasters n ▷ waster

wastes v, n ▷ waste

wasting v ▷ waste

wastrel n ▷ waster

wastrels n ▷ waster

watch v (-es, -ing, -ed) look at closely ▶ n (pl -es) portable timepiece for the wrist or pocket > **watchable** adj > **watcher** n (pl -s)

watchable adj ▷ watch

watchdog n (pl -s) dog kept to guard property

watchdogs n ▷ watchdog

watched v ▷ watch

watcher n ▷ watch

watchers n ▷ watch

watches v, n ▷ watch

watchful adj vigilant or alert > **watchfully** adv

watchfully adv ▷ watchful

watching v ▷ watch

watchman n (pl -men) man employed to guard a building or property

watchmen n ▷ watchman

water n (pl -s) clear colourless tasteless liquid that falls as rain and forms rivers etc ▶ v (-s, -ing, -ed) put water on or into > **watery** adj (-rier, -riest)

watered v ▷ water

waterier adj ▷ watery

wateriest adj ▷ watery

watering v ▷ water

waters n, v ▷ water

watery adj ▷ water

watt n (pl -s) unit of power

wattage n (pl -s) electrical power expressed in watts

wattages n ▷ wattage

wattle n (pl -s) branches woven over sticks to make a fence making fences

wattles n ▷ wattle

watts n ▷ watt

wave v (-ves, -ving, -ved) move the hand to and fro as a greeting or signal ▶ n (pl -s) moving ridge on water > **wavy** adj (-vier, -viest)

waved v ▷ wave

waver v (-s, -ing, -ed) hesitate or be irresolute > **waverer** n (pl -s)

wavered v ▷ waver

waverer n ▷ waver

waverers n ▷ waver

wavering v ▷ waver

wavers v ▷ waver

waves v, n ▷ wave

wavier adj ▷ wave

waviest adj ▷ wave

waving v ▷ wave

wavy adj ▷ wave

wax[1] n (pl -es) solid shiny fatty or oily substance used for sealing, making candles, etc ▶ v (-es, -ing, -ed) coat or polish with wax > **waxy** adj (-xier, -xiest)

wax[2] v (-es, -ing, -ed) increase in size or strength

waxed v ▷ wax[1, 2]

waxen adj made of or like wax

waxes n, v ▷ wax[1, 2]

waxier adj ▷ wax

waxiest adj ▷ wax

waxing v ▷ wax[1, 2]

waxwork n (pl -s) lifelike wax model of a (famous) person ▶ pl place exhibiting these

waxworks n ▷ waxwork

waxy adj ▷ wax[1]

way n (pl **-s**) manner or method

wayfarer n lit traveller

wayfarers n ▷ **wayfarer**

waylaid v ▷ **waylay**

waylay v (**-lays**, **-laying**, **-laid**) lie in wait for and accost or attack

waylaying v ▷ **waylay**

waylays v ▷ **waylay**

ways n ▷ **way**

wayside adj, n (pl **-s**) (situated by) the side of a road

waysides n ▷ **wayside**

wayward adj erratic, selfish, or stubborn > **waywardness** n (pl **-es**)

waywardnesses n ▷ **wayward**

we pron (used as the subject of a verb) the speaker or writer and one or more others

weak adj (**-er**, **-est**) lacking strength

weaken v (**-s**, **-ing**, **-ed**) make or become weak

weakened v ▷ **weaken**

weakening v ▷ **weaken**

weakens v ▷ **weaken**

weaker adj ▷ **weak**

weakest adj ▷ **weak**

weakling n feeble person or animal

weaklings n ▷ **weakling**

weakly adv feebly

weakness n (**-es**) being weak

weaknesses n ▷ **weakness**

weal n (pl **-s**) raised mark left on the skin by a blow

weals n ▷ **weal**

wealth n (pl **-s**) state of being rich > **wealthy** adj (**-thier**, **-thiest**)

wealthier adj ▷ **wealth**

wealthiest adj ▷ **wealth**

wealthy adj ▷ **wealth**

wean v (**-s**, **-ing**, **-ed**) accustom (a baby or young mammal) to food other than mother's milk

weaned v ▷ **wean**

weaning v ▷ **wean**

weans v ▷ **wean**

weapon n (pl **-s**) object used in fighting

weaponries n ▷ **weapon**

weaponry n (pl **-ies**) weapons collectively

weapons n ▷ **weapon**

wear v (**-s**, **-ing**, wore, worn) have on the body as clothing or ornament ▶ n (pl **-s**) clothes suitable for a particular time or purpose > **wearer** n (pl **-s**)

wearer n ▷ **wear**

wearers n ▷ **wear**

wearied v ▷ **weary**

wearier adj ▷ **weary**

wearies v ▷ **weary**

weariest adj ▷ **weary**

wearily adv ▷ **weary**

weariness n ▷ **weary**

wearinesses n ▷ **weary**

wearing v ▷ **wear**

wears n, v ▷ **wear**

weary adj (**-rier**, **-riest**) tired or exhausted ▶ v (**-ies**, **-ying**, **-ied**) make or become weary > **wearily** adv > **weariness** n (pl **-es**)

wearying v ▷ **weary**

weasel n (pl **-s**) small carnivorous mammal with a long body and short legs

weasels n ▷ **weasel**

weather n day-to-day atmospheric conditions of a place ▶ v (**-s**, **-ing**, **-ed**) (cause to) be affected by the weather

weathered v ▷ **weather**

weathering v ▷ **weather**

weathers v, n ▷ **weather**

weave v (**-s**, **-ving**, wove or weaved) (woven or weaved) make (fabric) by interlacing (yarn) on a loom > **weaver** n (pl **-s**)

weaved v ▷ **weave**

weaver n ▷ **weave**

weavers n ▷ **weave**

weaves n ▷ **weave**

web n (pl **-s**) net spun by a spider > **webbed** adj

webbed adj ▷ **web**

webbing n (pl **-s**) strong fabric woven in strips

webbings n ▷ **web**

webcam n (pl -s) camera that transmits images over the Internet

webcams n ▷ webcam

webcast n (pl -s) broadcast of an event over the Internet

webcasts n ▷ webcast

weblog n (pl -s) person's online journal (also **blog**)

weblogs n ▷ weblog

webs n ▷ web

website n (pl -s) group of connected pages on the World Wide Web

websites n ▷ website

wed v (-s, -dding, -dded or wed) marry

wedded v ▷ wed

wedding n (pl -s) act or ceremony of marriage ▶ v ▷ wed

weddings n ▷ wedding

wedge n (pl wedges) piece of material thick at one end and thin at the other ▶ v (-ges, -ging, -ged) fasten or split with a wedge

wedged v ▷ wedge

wedges n, v ▷ wedge

wedging v ▷ wedge

wedlock n (pl -s) marriage

wedlocks n ▷ wedlock

wee adj (-r, -st) BRIT, AUST & NZ informal small or short

weed n (pl -s) plant growing where undesired ▶ v (-s, -ing, -ed) clear of weeds

weeded v ▷ weed

weedier adj ▷ weedy

weediest adj ▷ weedy

weeding v ▷ weed

weeds n, v ▷ weed ▶ pl n obs widow's mourning clothes

weedy adj (-dier, -diest) informal (of a person) thin and weak

week n (pl -s) period of seven days, esp. one beginning on a Sunday

weekday n (pl -s) any day of the week except Saturday or Sunday

weekdays n ▷ weekday

weekend n (pl -s) Saturday and Sunday

weekends n ▷ weekend

weeklies n ▷ weekly

weekly adj, adv happening, done, etc once a week ▶ n (pl -ies) newspaper or magazine published once a week

weeks n ▷ week

weep v (-s, -ing, wept) shed tears

weepier adj ▷ weepy

weepiest adj ▷ weepy

weeping v ▷ weep

weeps v ▷ weep

weepy adj (-pier, -piest) liable to cry

weer adj ▷ wee

weest adj ▷ wee

weevil n (pl -s) small beetle which eats grain etc

weevils n ▷ weevil

weft n (pl -s) cross threads in weaving

wefts n ▷ weft

weigh v (-s, -ing, -ed) have a specified weight

weighed v ▷ weigh

weighing v ▷ weigh

weighs v ▷ weigh

weight n (pl -s) heaviness of an object ▶ v (-s, -ing, -ed) add weight to > **weightless** adj > **weightlessness** n

weighted v ▷ weight

weightier adj ▷ weighty

weightiest adj ▷ weighty

weightily adv ▷ weighty

weightless adj ▷ weight

weightlessness n ▷ weight

weights n, v ▷ weight

weighty adj (-tier, -tiest) important or serious > **weightily** adv

weir n (pl -s) river dam

weird (-er, -est) adj strange or bizarre

weirder adj ▷ weird

weirdest adj ▷ weird

weirdo n (pl -os) informal peculiar person

weirdos n ▷ weirdo

weirs n ▷ weir

welch v (-es, -ing, -ed) ▷ welsh

welched v ▷ welch

welches v ▷ welch

welching v ▷ welch

welcome v (-mes, -ming, -med)

greet with pleasure ▶ n (pl **-s**) kindly
greeting ▶ adj received gladly
welcomed v ▷ **welcome**
welcomes v, n ▷ **welcome**
welcoming v ▷ **welcome**

weld v (**-s, -ing, -ed**) join (pieces of
metal or plastic) by softening with
heat ▶ n (pl **-s**) welded joint ▶ **welder** n
(pl **-s**)
welded v ▷ **weld**
welder n ▷ **weld**
welders n ▷ **weld**
welding v ▷ **weld**
welds v, n ▷ **weld**

welfare n (pl **-s**) wellbeing
welfares n ▷ **welfare**

well¹ adv (**better, best**) satisfactorily
▶ adj in good health ▶ interj
exclamation of surprise, interrogation,
etc

well² n (pl **-s**) hole sunk into the earth
to reach water, oil, or gas ▶ v (**-s, -ing,
-ed**) flow upwards or outwards
welled v ▷ **well²**

wellies pl n BRIT & AUST informal
wellingtons
welling v ▷ **well²**
wells n, v ▷ **well²**

welsh v (**-es, -ing, -ed**) fail to pay a
debt or fulfil an obligation
welshed v ▷ **welsh**
welshes v ▷ **welsh**
welshing v ▷ **welsh**

welt n (pl **-s**) raised mark on the skin
produced by a blow

welter n (pl **-s**) jumbled mass
welters n ▷ **welter**
welts n ▷ **welt**

wen n (pl **-s**) cyst on the scalp

wench n (pl **-es**) facetious young
woman
wenches n ▷ **wench**

wend v (**-s, -ing, -ed**) go or travel
wended v ▷ **wend**
wending v ▷ **wend**
wends v ▷ **wend**
wens n ▷ **wen**
went v ▷ **go**

wept v ▷ **weep**

were v form of the past tense of **be** used
after we, you, they, or a plural noun ▷ **be**

werewolf n (pl **-wolves**) (in folklore)
person who can turn into a wolf
werewolves n ▷ **werewolf**

west n (pl **-s**) (direction towards) the
part of the horizon where the sun
sets ▶ adj to or in the west ▶ adv in,
to, or towards the west ▷ **westerly**
> **westward** adj, adv > **westwards** adv
westerly adj ▷ **west**

western adj of or in the west ▶ n (pl
-s) film or story about cowboys in the
western US
westerns n ▷ **western**
wests n ▷ **west**
westward adj ▷ **west**
westwards adv ▷ **west**

wet adj (**-tter, -ttest**) covered or
soaked with water or another liquid
BRIT informal ▶ n moisture or rain BRIT
informal ▶ v (**-s, -tting, wet** or **wetted**)
make wet

wetland n (pl **-s**) area of marshy land
wetlands n ▷ **wetland**
wetted v ▷ **wet**
wetter adj ▷ **wet**
wettest adj ▷ **wet**
wetting v ▷ **wet**

wex n (**wexes**). Wex is an old word
for **wax**. This gives a very good
score for a three-letter word, and
is a good one to look for when you
have an X. Wex scores 13 points.

whack v (**-s, -ing, -ed**) strike with a
resounding blow ▶ n (pl **-s**) such a blow
whacked adj exhausted ▶ v ▷ **whack**
whacking adj informal huge ▶ v
▷ **whack**
whacks v, n ▷ **whack**

whale n (pl **-s**) large fish-shaped sea
mammal

whaler n ship or person involved in
whaling
whalers n ▷ **whaler**
whales n ▷ **whale**

whaling n (pl **-s**) hunting of whales for

food and oil

whalings n ▷ whaling

wharf n (pl **wharves, wharfs**) platform at a harbour for loading and unloading ships

wharfie n (pl **-s**) AUST person employed to load and unload ships

wharfies n ▷ wharfie

wharfs n ▷ wharf

wharves n ▷ wharf

what pron which thing ▶ interj exclamation of anger, surprise, etc ▶ adv in which way, how much

whatnot n (pl **-s**) informal similar unspecified things

whatnots n ▷ whatnot

wheat n (pl **-s**) grain used in making flour, bread, and pasta > **wheaten** adj

wheatear n (pl **-s**) small songbird

wheatears n ▷ wheatear

wheaten adj ▷ wheat

wheats n ▷ wheat

wheedle v (**-les, -ling, -led**) coax or cajole

wheedled v ▷ wheedle

wheedles v ▷ wheedle

wheedling v ▷ wheedle

wheel n (pl **-s**) disc that revolves on an axle ▶ v (**-s, -ing, -ed**) push or pull (something with wheels)

wheeled v ▷ wheel

wheeling v ▷ wheel

wheels n, v ▷ wheel

wheeze v (**-zes, -zing, -zed**) breathe with a hoarse whistling noise ▶ n (pl **-s**) wheezing sound > **wheezy** adj (**-zier, -ziest**)

wheezed v ▷ wheeze

wheezes v, n ▷ wheeze

wheezier adj ▷ wheeze

wheeziest adj ▷ wheeze

wheezing v ▷ wheeze

wheezy adj ▷ wheeze

whelk n (pl **-s**) edible snail-like shellfish

whelks n ▷ whelk

whelp n (pl **-s**) pup or cub ▶ v (**-s, -ing, -ed**) (of an animal) give birth

whelped v ▷ whelp

whelping v ▷ whelp

whelps n, v ▷ whelp

when adv at what time? ▶ conj at the time that ▶ pron at which time

whence adv, conj obs from what place or source

whenever adv, conj at whatever time

where adv in, at, or to what place? ▶ pron in, at, or to which place ▶ conj in the place at which

whereas conj but on the other hand

whereby pron by which

wherever conj, adv at whatever place

whet v (**-s, -tting, -tted**) sharpen (a tool)

whether conj used to introduce an indirect question or a clause expressing doubt or choice

whets v ▷ whet

whetted v ▷ whet

whetting v ▷ whet

whey n (pl **-s**) watery liquid that separates from the curd when milk is clotted

wheys n ▷ whey

which adj, pron used to request or refer to a choice from different possibilities ▶ pron used to refer to a thing already mentioned

whiff n (pl **-s**) puff of air or odour

whiffs n ▷ whiff

whig n (pl **-s**) member of a British political party of the 18th–19th centuries that sought liberal reform

whigs n ▷ whig

while conj at the same time that ▶ n (pl **-s**) period of time

whiles n ▷ while

whilst conj while

whim n (pl **-s**) sudden fancy

whimper v (**-s, -ing, -ed**) cry in a soft whining way ▶ n (pl **-s**) soft plaintive whine

whimpered v ▷ whimper

whimpering v ▷ whimper

whimpers v, n ▷ whimper

whims n ▷ whim

whimsies n ▷ whimsy

whimsy n (pl -ies) capricious idea

whin n (pl -s) BRIT gorse

whine n (pl -s) high-pitched plaintive cry ▶ v (-nes, -ning, -ned) make such a sound ▷ **whining** n, adj (pl -s)
whined v ▷ whine
whines n, v ▷ whine

whinge BRIT, AUST & NZ informal v (-ges, -geing, -ged) complain ▶ n (pl -s) complaint
whinged v ▷ whinge
whingeing v ▷ whinge
whinges v, n ▷ whinge

whining v, n adj ▷ whine
whinings n ▷ whine
whinnied v ▷ whinny
whinnies v, n ▷ whinny

whinny (-nnies, -nnying, -nnied) neigh softly ▶ n (pl -nnies) soft neigh
whinnying v ▷ whinny
whins n ▷ whin

whip n (pl -s) cord attached to a handle, used for beating animals or people ▶ v (-s, -pping, -pped) strike with a whip, strap, or cane
whipped v ▷ whip

whippet n (pl -s) racing dog like a small greyhound
whippets n ▷ whippet
whipping v ▷ whip
whips v, n ▷ whip
whir v ▷ whirr

whirl v (-s, -ing, -ed) spin or revolve ▶ n (pl -s) whirling movement
whirled v ▷ whirl
whirling v ▷ whirl
whirls v, n ▷ whirl

whirr, whir n (pl -s) prolonged soft buzz ▶ v (-s, -rring, -rred) (cause to) make a whirr
whirred v ▷ whirr
whirring v ▷ whirr
whirrs n, v ▷ whirr
whirs n ▷ whirr

whisk v (-s, -ing, -ed) move or remove quickly ▶ n (pl -s) egg-beating utensil
whisked v ▷ whisk

whisker n (pl -s) any of the long stiff hairs on the face of a cat or other mammal ▶ pl hair growing on a man's face
whiskers n ▷ whisker

whiskey n (pl -s) Irish or American whisky
whiskeys n ▷ whiskey
whiskies n ▷ whisky
whisking v, v ▷ whisk
whisks n ▷ whisk

whisky n (pl -ies) spirit distilled from fermented cereals

whisper v (-s, -ing, -ed) speak softly, without vibration of the vocal cords ▶ n (pl -s) soft voice
whispered v ▷ whisper
whispering v ▷ whisper
whispers v, n ▷ whisper

whist n (pl -s) card game in which one pair of players tries to win more tricks than another pair

whistle v (-les, -ling, -led) produce a shrill sound, esp. by forcing the breath through pursed lips ▶ n (pl -s) whistling sound ▷ **whistling** n, adj (pl -s)
whistled v ▷ whistle
whistles v, n ▷ whistle
whistling v, n ▷ whistle
whistlings n ▷ whistle
whists n ▷ whist

whit n (pl -s) not the slightest amount

white adj (-r, -st) of the colour of snow ▶ n (pl -s) colour of snow ▷ **whiteness** n (pl -es) ▷ **whitish** adj

whiten v (-s, -ing, -ed) make or become white or whiter
whitened v ▷ white
whiteness n ▷ white
whitenesses n ▷ white
whitening n ▷ white
whitens v ▷ whiten
whiter adj ▷ white
whites n ▷ white
whitest adj ▷ white

whither adv obs to what place

whiting n (pl -s) edible sea fish
whitings n ▷ whiting

whitish adj ▷ white
whittle v (-les, -ling, -led) cut or carve (wood) with a knife
whittled v ▷ whittle
whittles v ▷ whittle
whittling v ▷ whittle
whiz v ▷ whizz
whizz, whiz v (-es, -ing, -ed) make a loud buzzing sound *informal* ▶ n (pl -es) loud buzzing sound *informal*
whizzed v ▷ whizz
whizzes v, n ▷ whizz
whizzing v ▷ whizz
who pron which person
whoever pron any person who
whole adj containing all the elements or parts ▶ n (pl -s) complete thing or system > **wholly** adv
wholes n ▷ whole
wholly adv ▷ whole
whom pron ▷ who
whoop v, n (pl -s) shout or cry to express excitement
whoopee interj *informal* cry of joy
whoops n ▷ whoop
whopper n (pl -s) *informal* anything unusually large > **whopping** adj
whoppers n ▷ whopper
whopping adj ▷ whopper
whore n (pl -s) prostitute
whores n ▷ whore
whorl n (pl -s) ring of leaves or petals
whorls n ▷ whorl
whose pron of whom or of which
why adv for what reason ▶ pron because of which
wick n (pl -s) cord through a lamp or candle which carries fuel to the flame
wicked (-er, -est) adj morally bad > **wickedly** adv **wickedness** n (pl -s)
wickedly adv ▷ wicked
wickedness n ▷ wicked
wickednesses n ▷ wicked
wicker adj made of woven cane > **wickerwork** n (pl -s)
wickerwork n ▷ wicker
wickerworks n ▷ wicker
wicket n (pl -s) set of three cricket

stumps and two bails
wickets n ▷ wicket
wicks n ▷ wick
wide adj (-r, -st) large from side to side ▶ adv to the full extent > **widely** adv
widely adv ▷ wide
widen v (-s, -ing, -ed) make or become wider
widened v ▷ widen
widening v ▷ widen
widens v ▷ widen
wider adj ▷ wide
widest adj ▷ wide
widgeon n (pl -s) ▷ wigeon
widgeons n ▷ widgeon
widow n (pl -s) woman whose husband is dead and who has not remarried > **widowed** adj **widowhood** n (pl -s)
widowed adj ▷ widow
widower n (pl -s) man whose wife is dead and who has not remarried
widowers n ▷ widower
widowhood n ▷ widow
widowhoods n ▷ widow
widows n ▷ widow
width n (pl -s) distance from side to side
widths n ▷ width
wield v (-s, -ing, -ed) hold and use (a weapon)
wielded v ▷ wield
wielding v ▷ wield
wields v ▷ wield
wife n (pl wives) woman to whom a man is married
wig n (pl -s) artificial head of hair
wigeon n (pl -s) duck found in marshland
wigeons n ▷ wigeon
wiggle v (-les, -ling, -led) move jerkily from side to side ▶ n (pl -les) wiggling movement
wiggled v ▷ wiggle
wiggles v, n ▷ wiggle
wiggling v ▷ wiggle
wigs n ▷ wig
wigwam n (pl -s) Native American's tent

wigwams n ▷ wigwam

wild adj (-er, -est) (of animals) not tamed or domesticated ▷ **wildly** adv ▷ **wildness** n (pl -es)

wildcat n (pl -s) European wild animal like a large domestic cat

wildcats n ▷ wildcat

wilder adj ▷ wild

wildest adj ▷ wild

wildlife n (pl -s) wild animals and plants collectively

wildlifes n ▷ wildlife

wildly adv ▷ wild

wildness n ▷ wild

wildnesses n ▷ wild

wilds pl n desolate or uninhabited place

wiles pl n tricks or ploys

wilful adj headstrong or obstinate ▷ **wilfully** adv

wilfully adv ▷ wilful

wilier adj ▷ wily

wiliest adj ▷ wily

will[1] v (past **would**) used as an auxiliary to form the future tense or to indicate intention, ability, or expectation

will[2] n (pl -s) strong determination ▷ v (-s, -ing, -ed) use one's will in an attempt to do (something)

willed v ▷ will[2]

willing adj ready or inclined (to do something) ▷ v ▷ will[2] ▷ **willingly** adv ▷ **willingness** n (pl -es)

willingly adv ▷ willing

willingness n ▷ willing

willingnesses n ▷ willing

willow n (pl -s) tree with thin flexible branches

willowier adj ▷ willowy

willowiest adj ▷ willowy

willows n ▷ willow

willowy adj (-wier, -wiest) slender and graceful

wills n, v ▷ will[2]

wilt v (-s, -ing, -ed) (cause to) become limp or lose strength

wilted v ▷ wilt

wilting v ▷ wilt

wilts v ▷ wilt

wily (-lier, -liest) adj crafty or sly

wimp n (pl -s) informal feeble ineffectual person

wimple n (pl -s) garment framing the face, worn by medieval women and now by nuns

wimples n ▷ wimple

wimps n ▷ wimp

win v (-s, -nning, won) come first in (a competition, fight, etc) ▷ n (pl -s) victory, esp. in a game ▷ **winner** n (pl -s)

wince v (-ces, -cing, -ced) draw back, as if in pain ▷ n (pl -s) wincing

winced v ▷ wince

winces v, n ▷ wince

winch n (pl -es) machine for lifting or hauling using a cable or chain wound round a drum ▷ v (-es, -ing, -ed) lift or haul using a winch

winched v ▷ winch

winches n, v ▷ winch

winching v ▷ winch

wincing v ▷ wince

wind[1] n (pl -s) current of air ▷ v (-s, -ing, -ed) render short of breath ▷ **windy** adj (-dier, -diest)

wind[2] v (-s, -ing, wound) coil or wrap around

winded v ▷ wind[1]

windfall n (pl -s) unexpected good luck

windfalls n ▷ windfall

windier adj ▷ wind[1]

windiest adj ▷ wind[1]

winding v ▷ wind[1, 2]

windlass n (pl -es) winch worked by a crank

windlasses n ▷ windlass

windmill n (pl -s) machine for grinding or pumping driven by sails turned by the wind

windmills n ▷ windmill

window n (pl -s) opening in a wall to let in light or air

windows n ▷ window

windpipe n (pl -s) tube linking the throat and the lungs

windpipes n ▷ windpipe

winds n, v ▷ wind¹, ²

windsock n (pl -s) cloth cone on a mast at an airfield to indicate wind direction

windsocks n ▷ windsock

windward adj, n (pl -s) (of or in) the direction from which the wind is blowing

windwards n ▷ windward

windy adj ▷ wind¹

wine n (pl -s) alcoholic drink made from fermented grapes

wines n ▷ wine

wing n (pl -s) one of the limbs or organs of a bird, insect, or bat that are used for flying ▶ pl sides of a stage ▶ v (-s, -ing, -ed) fly ▷ **winged** adj

winged v, adj ▷ wing

winger n (pl -s) SPORT player positioned on the side of the pitch

wingers n ▷ winger

winging v ▷ wing

wings n, v ▷ wing

wink v (-s, -ing, -ed) close and open (an eye) quickly as a signal ▶ n (pl -s) winking

winked v ▷ wink

winking v ▷ wink

winkle n (pl -s) shellfish with a spiral shell

winkles n ▷ winkle

winks v, n ▷ wink

winner n ▷ win

winners n ▷ win

winning adj gaining victory ▶ v ▷ win

winnings pl n sum won, esp. in gambling

winnow v (-s, -ing, -ed) (pl -s) separate (chaff) from (grain)

winnowed v ▷ winnow

winnowing v ▷ winnow

winnows v, n ▷ winnow

winsome adj (-r, -st) charming or winning

winsomer adj ▷ winsome

winsomest adj ▷ winsome

winter n (pl -s) coldest season ▶ v (-s, -ing, -ed) spend the winter

wintered v ▷ winter

wintering v ▷ winter

winters n, v ▷ winter

wintrier adj ▷ wintry

wintriest adj ▷ wintry

wintry adj (-rier, -riest) of or like winter

wipe v (-pes, -ping, -ped) clean or dry by rubbing ▶ n (pl -s) wiping

wiped v ▷ wipe

wipes v, n ▷ wipe

wiping v ▷ wipe

wire n (pl -s) thin flexible strand of metal obs ▶ v (-res, -ring, -red) equip with wires

wired v ▷ wire

wireless n (pl -es) old-fashioned ▷ **radio** ▶ adj (of a computer network) connected by radio rather than by cables or fibre optics

wirelesses n ▷ wireless

wires n, v ▷ wire

wirier adj ▷ wiry

wiriest adj ▷ wiry

wiring n (pl -s) system of wires ▶ v ▷ wire

wirings n ▷ wiring

wiry adj (-rier, -riest) lean and tough

wisdom n (pl -s) good sense and judgment

wisdoms n ▷ wisdom

wise¹ adj (-r, -st) having wisdom ▶ **wisely** adv

wise² n (pl -s) obs manner

wiseacre n (pl -s) person who wishes to seem wise

wisely adv ▷ wise¹

wiser adj ▷ wise¹

wises n ▷ wise²

wisest adj ▷ wise¹

wish v (-es, -ing, -ed) want or desire ▶ n (pl -es) expression of a desire

wishbone n (pl -s) V-shaped bone above the breastbone of a fowl

wishbones n ▷ wishbone

wished v ▷ wish

wishes v, n ▷ wish

wishful adj too optimistic

wishing v ▷ wish

wisp n (pl -s) light delicate streak
  >**wispy** adj (-pier, -piest)
  wispier adj ▷ wisp
  wispiest adj ▷ wisp
  wisps n ▷ wisp
  wispy adj ▷ wisp
wisteria n (pl -s) climbing shrub with blue or purple flowers
  wisterias n ▷ wisteria
wistful adj sadly longing
  >**wistfully** adv
  wistfully adv ▷ wistful
wit n (pl -s) ability to use words or ideas in a clever and amusing way
witch n (pl -es) person, usu. female, who practises (black) magic
  witches n ▷ witch
with prep indicating presence alongside, possession, means of performance, characteristic manner, etc
withdraw v (-drawing, -drew, -drawn) take or move out or away
  >**withdrawal** n (pl -s)
  withdrawal n ▷ withdraw
  withdrawals n ▷ withdraw
  withdraws v ▷ withdraw
  withdrew v ▷ withdraw
wither v (-s, -ing, -ed) wilt or dry up
  withered v ▷ wither
  withers n ▷ wither ▸ pl n ridge between a horse's shoulder blades
  withheld v ▷ withhold
withhold v (-s, -ing, -held) refrain from giving
  withholding v ▷ withhold
  withholds v ▷ withhold
within prep, adv in or inside
without prep not accompanied by, using, or having
witless adj foolish
witness n (pl -es) person who has seen something happen ▸ v (-es, -ing, -ed) see at first hand
  witnessed v ▷ witness
  witnesses n, v ▷ witness
  witnessing v ▷ witness
  wits n ▷ wit

witter v (-s, -ing, -ed) CHIEFLY BRIT chatter pointlessly or at unnecessary length
  wittered v ▷ witter
  wittering v ▷ witter
  witters v ▷ witter
  wittier adj ▷ witty
  wittiest adj ▷ witty
  wittily adv ▷ witty
witty adj (-ttier, -ttiest) clever and amusing >**wittily** adv
wives n ▷ wife

> **wiz** n (wizzes) Wiz is a short form of **wizard**. This is the highest-scoring three-letter word beginning with W, and can be especially useful when there isn't much room to manoeuvre. Wiz scores 15 points.

wizard n (pl -s) magician >**wizardry** n (pl -ries)
  wizardries n ▷ wizard
  wizardry n ▷ wizard
  wizards n ▷ wizard
wizened adj shrivelled or wrinkled

> **wo** n (wos) Wo is an old-fashioned spelling of **woe**. This unusual word is handy for joining words ending in W to those beginning in O. Wo scores 5 points.

woad n (pl -s) blue dye obtained from a plant, used by the ancient Britons as a body dye
  woads n ▷ woad
wobble v (-les, -ling, -led) move unsteadily ▸ n (pl -s) wobbling movement or sound >**wobbly** adj (-lier, -liest)
  wobbled v ▷ wobble
  wobbles v, n ▷ wobble
  wobblier adj ▷ wobble
  wobbliest adj ▷ wobble
  wobbling v ▷ wobble
  wobbly adj ▷ wobble
wodge n (pl -s) informal thick lump or chunk
  wodges n ▷ wodge
woe n (pl -s) grief

woeful adj extremely sad
>**woefully** adv

woefully adv ▷ **woeful**
woes n ▷ **woe**

wok n (pl **-s**) bowl-shaped Chinese cooking pan, used for stir-frying
woke v ▷ **wake**[1]
woken v ▷ **wake**[1]
woks n ▷ **wok**

wold n (pl **-s**) high open country
wolds n ▷ **wold**

wolf n (pl **wolves**) wild predatory canine mammal ▶ v eat ravenously
wolves n ▷ **wolf**

woman n (pl **women**) adult human female >**womanhood** n (pl **-s**)
womanhood n ▷ **woman**
womanhoods n ▷ **woman**

womanish adj effeminate

womanly adj having qualities traditionally associated with a woman

womb n (pl **-s**) hollow organ in female mammals where babies are conceived and develop

wombat n (pl **-s**) small heavily-built burrowing Australian marsupial
wombats n ▷ **wombat**
wombs n ▷ **womb**
women n ▷ **woman**
won v ▷ **win**

wonder v (**-s, -ing, -ed**) be curious about ▶ n ▶ adj wonderful thing
▶ adj spectacularly successful
>**wonderment** n (pl **-s**)
wondered v ▷ **wonder**
wondering v ▷ **wonder**
wonderment n ▷ **wonder**
wonderments n ▷ **wonder**
wonders v, n ▷ **wonder**

wondrous adj old-fashioned wonderful
wonkier adj ▷ **wonky**
wonkiest adj ▷ **wonky**

wonky adj (**-kier, -kiest**) BRIT, AUST & NZ informal shaky or unsteady

wont adj accustomed ▶ n (pl **-s**) custom
wonts n ▷ **wont**

woo v (**-s, -ing, -ed**) try to persuade

old-fashioned

wood n (pl **-s**) substance trees are made of, used in carpentry and as fuel
>**woody** adj (**-dier, -diest**)

woodbine n (pl **-s**) honeysuckle
woodbines n ▷ **woodbine**

woodcock n (pl **-s**) game bird
woodcocks n ▷ **woodcock**

woodcut n (pl **-s**) (print made from) an engraved block of wood
woodcuts n ▷ **woodcut**

wooded adj covered with trees

wooden adj made of wood
woodier adj ▷ **wood**
woodiest adj ▷ **wood**

woodland n (pl **-s**) forest
woodlands n ▷ **woodland**
woods n ▷ **wood**

woodwind adj, n (pl **-s**) (of) a type of wind instrument made of wood
woodwinds n ▷ **woodwind**

woodworm n insect larva that bores into wood
woodworms n ▷ **woodworm**
woody adj ▷ **wood**
wooed v ▷ **woo**

woof[1] n (pl **-s**) cross threads in weaving
woof[2] n (pl **-s**) barking noise made by a dog

woofer n (pl **-s**) loudspeaker reproducing low-frequency sounds
woofers n ▷ **woofer**
woofs n ▷ **woof**[1, 2]
wooing v ▷ **woo**

wool n (pl **-s**) soft hair of sheep, goats, etc >**woollen** adj
woollen adj ▷ **wool**
woollier adj ▷ **woolly**
woolliest adj ▷ **woolly**

woolly adj (**-lier, -liest**) of or like wool
▶ n knitted woollen garment
wools n ▷ **wool**

woomera n (pl **-s**) notched stick used by Australian Aborigines to aid the propulsion of a spear
woomeras n ▷ **woomera**
woos v ▷ **woo**
woozier adj ▷ **woozy**

wooziest adj ▷ **woozy**

woozy adj (**-zier**, **-ziest**) informal weak, dizzy, and confused

word n (pl **-s**) smallest single meaningful unit of speech or writing ▶ v (**-s**, **-ing**, **-ed**) express in words

worded v ▷ **word**

wordier adj ▷ **wordy**

wordiest adj ▷ **wordy**

wording n (pl **-s**) choice and arrangement of words ▶ v ▷ **word**

wordings n ▷ **wording**

words n, v ▷ **word**

wordy adj (**-dier**, **-diest**) using too many words

wore v ▷ **wear**

work n (pl **-s**) physical or mental effort directed to making or doing something ▶ pl factory informal ▶ adj of or for work ▶ v (**-s**, **-ing**, **-ed**) (cause to) do work **workable** adj > **worker** n (pl **-s**)

workable adj > **work**

worked v ▷ **work**

worker n ▷ **work**

workers n ▷ **work**

working v ▷ **work**

workman n (pl **-men**) manual worker

workmen n ▷ **workman**

works n, v ▷ **work**

workshop n (pl **-s**) room or building for a manufacturing process

workshops n ▷ **workshop**

worktop n (pl **-s**) surface in a kitchen, used for food preparation

worktops n ▷ **worktop**

world n (pl **-s**) the planet earth ▶ adj of the whole world

worldlier adj ▷ **worldly**

worldliest adj ▷ **worldly**

worldly adj (**-ier**, **-iest**) not spiritual

worlds n ▷ **world**

worm n (pl **-s**) small limbless invertebrate animal informal COMPUTERS n illness caused by parasitic worms in the intestines ▶ v (**-s**, **-ing**, **-ed**) rid of worms > **wormy** adj (**-mier**, **-miest**)

wormed v ▷ **worm**

wormier adj ▷ **worm**

wormiest adj ▷ **worm**

worming v ▷ **worm**

worms n, v ▷ **worm**

wormwood n (pl **-s**) bitter plant

wormwoods n ▷ **wormwood**

wormy adj ▷ **worm**

worn v ▷ **wear**

worried v, adj ▷ **worry**

worries v, n ▷ **worry**

worry v (**-ries**, **-rying**, **-ried**) (cause to) be anxious or uneasy ▶ n (pl **-ies**) (cause of) anxiety or concern > **worried** adj > **worrying** adj, n

worrying v, adj ▷ **worry**

worse adj, adv ▷ **bad**

worsen v (**-s**, **-ing**, **-ed**) make or grow worse

worsened v ▷ **worsen**

worsening v ▷ **worsen**

worsens v ▷ **worsen**

worship v (**-s**, **-pping**, **-pped**) show religious devotion to ▶ n (pl **-s**) act or instance of worshipping > **worshipper** n (pl **-s**)

worshipped v ▷ **worship**

worshipper n ▷ **worship**

worshippers n ▷ **worship**

worshipping v ▷ **worship**

worships v, n ▷ **worship**

worst adj, adv ▷ **bad** ▶ n worst thing

worsted n (pl **-s**) type of woollen yarn or fabric

worsteds n ▷ **worsted**

worth prep having a value of ▶ n (pl **-s**) value or price **worthless** adj

worthier adj ▷ **worthy**

worthiest adj ▷ **worthy**

worthily adv ▷ **worthy**

worthiness n ▷ **worthy**

worthinesses n ▷ **worthy**

worthless adj ▷ **worth**

worths n ▷ **worth**

worthy adj (**-thier**, **-thiest**) deserving admiration or respect ▶ n informal notable person > **worthily** adv > **worthiness** n (pl **-es**)

would v ▷ **will**[1]

wound[1] n (pl -s) injury caused by violence ▶ v (-s, -ing, -ed) inflict a wound on

wound[2] v ▷ **wind**[2]

wounded v ▷ **wound**[1]

wounding v ▷ **wound**[1]

wounds n, v ▷ **wound**[1]

wove v ▷ **weave**

woven v ▷ **weave**

wow interj exclamation of astonishment ▶ v (pl ▷) informal astonishing person or thing

wows n ▷ **wow**

wowser n (pl -s) AUST & NZ slang puritanical person

wowsers n ▷ **wowser**

> **wox** n (**woxes**). Wox is an old past tense of the verb **wax**. This gives a very good score for a three-letter word, and is a good one to look for when you have an X. Wox scores 13 points.

wrack n (pl -s) seaweed

wracks n ▷ **wrack**

wraith n (pl -s) ghost

wraiths n ▷ **wraith**

wrangle v (-les, -ling, -led) argue noisily ▶ n (pl -s) noisy argument

wrangled v ▷ **wrangle**

wrangles v, n ▷ **wrangle**

wrangling v ▷ **wrangle**

wrap v (-s, -pping, -pped) fold (something) round (a person or thing) so as to cover ▶ n (pl -s) garment wrapped round the shoulders

wrapped v ▷ **wrap**

wrapper n (pl -s) cover for a product

wrappers n ▷ **wrapper**

wrapping n (pl -s) material used to wrap ▶ v ▷ **wrap**

wrappings n ▷ **wrapping**

wraps n, v ▷ **wrap**

wrasse n (pl -s) colourful sea fish

wrasses n ▷ **wrasse**

wrath n (pl -s) intense anger
> **wrathful** adj

wrathful adj ▷ **wrath**

wraths n ▷ **wrath**

wreak v (-s, -ing, -ed) cause (chaos)

wreaked v ▷ **wreak**

wreaking v ▷ **wreak**

wreaks v ▷ **wreak**

wreath n (pl -s) twisted ring or band of flowers or leaves used as a memorial or tribute

wreathed adj surrounded or encircled

wreaths n ▷ **wreath**

wreck v (-s, -ing, -ed) destroy ▶ n (pl -s) remains of something that has been destroyed or badly damaged, esp. a ship ▷ **wrecker** n (pl -s)

wreckage n (pl -s) wrecked remains

wreckages n ▷ **wreckage**

wrecked v ▷ **wreck**

wrecker n ▷ **wreck**

wreckers n ▷ **wreck**

wrecking v ▷ **wreck**

wrecks v, n ▷ **wreck**

wren n (pl -s) small brown songbird

wrench v (-es, -ing, -ed) twist or pull violently ▶ n (pl -es) violent twist or pull

wrenched v ▷ **wrench**

wrenches v, n ▷ **wrench**

wrenching v ▷ **wrench**

wrens n ▷ **wren**

wrest v (-s, -ing, -ed) twist violently

wrested v ▷ **wrest**

wresting v ▷ **wrest**

wrestle v (-les, -ling, -led) fight, esp. as a sport, by grappling with and trying to throw down an opponent > **wrestler** n (pl -s) > **wrestling** n (pl -s)

wrestled v ▷ **wrestle**

wrestler n ▷ **wrestle**

wrestlers n ▷ **wrestle**

wrestles v ▷ **wrestle**

wrestling v, n ▷ **wrestle**

wrestlings n ▷ **wrestle**

wrests v ▷ **wrest**

wretch n (pl -es) despicable person

wretched adj (-er, -est) miserable or unhappy > **wretchedly** adv
> **wretchedness** n (pl -es)

wretcheder adj ▷ **wretched**

wretchedest adj ▷ **wretched**
wretchedly adv ▷ **wretched**
wretchedness n ▷ **wretched**
wretchednesses n ▷ **wretched**
wretches n ▷ **wretch**
wrier adj ▷ **wry**
wriest adj ▷ **wry**
wriggle v (-les, -ling, -led) move with
a twisting action ▶ n (pl -s) wriggling
movement
wriggled v ▷ **wriggle**
wriggles v, n ▷ **wriggle**
wriggling v ▷ **wriggle**
wright n (pl -s) maker
wrights n ▷ **wright**
wring v (-s, -ing, wrung) twist, esp. to
squeeze liquid out of
wringing v ▷ **wring**
wrings v ▷ **wring**
wrinkle n (pl -s) slight crease, esp. one
in the skin due to age ▶ v (-les, -ling,
-led) make or become slightly creased
> **wrinkly** adj (-lier, -liest)
wrinkled v ▷ **wrinkle**
wrinkles n, v ▷ **wrinkle**
wrinklier adj ▷ **wrinkle**
wrinkliest adj ▷ **wrinkle**
wrinkling v ▷ **wrinkle**
wrinkly adj ▷ **wrinkle**
wrist n (pl -s) joint between the hand
and the arm
wrists n ▷ **wrist**
writ n (pl -s) written legal command
write v (-tes, -ting, wrote, written)
mark paper etc with symbols or words
> **writing** n
(pl -s)

writer n (pl -s) author
writers n ▷ **writer**
writhe v (-thes, -thing, -thed) twist
or squirm in or as if in pain
writhed v ▷ **writhe**
writhes v ▷ **writhe**
writhing v ▷ **writhe**
writing v ▷ **write**
writings n ▷ **write**
writs n ▷ **writ**
written v ▷ **write**
wrong adj incorrect or mistaken
▶ adv in a wrong manner ▶ n (pl -s)
something immoral or unjust ▶ v (-s,
-ing, -ed) treat unjustly > **wrongly** adv
> **wrongful** adj > **wrongfully** adv
wronged v ▷ **wrong**
wrongful adj ▷ **wrong**
wrongfully adv ▷ **wrong**
wronging v ▷ **wrong**
wrongly adv ▷ **wrong**
wrongs n, v ▷ **wrong**
wrote v ▷ **write**
wrought v lit ▷ **work** ▶ adj (of metals)
shaped by hammering or beating
wrung v ▷ **wring**
wry adj (wrier, wriest or wryer,
wryest) drily humorous > **wryly** adv
wryer adj ▷ **wry**
wryest adj ▷ **wry**
wryly adv ▷ **wry**

wye n (wyes) Wye is the letter Y. If
you have W and Y on your rack, look
for an E on the board that will allow
you to play this especially if you can
land on a bonus square as a result.
Wye scores 9 points.

X x

Worth 8 points on its own, X is one of the best tiles in the game. It doesn't, however, start many two- and three-letter words. There are only two valid two-letter words, **xi** and **xu** (9 points each) beginning with X, and only one three-letter word, **xis**. Therefore, if you have an X on your rack and need to play short words, you're probably better off thinking of words that end in X or have X in them rather than those that start with X.

xebec *n* (**xebecs**). A xebec is an Algerian ship. This is a good high-scoring word. If you have an X, you'll probably only need one E as well as B and C to play it, as there is likely to be an available E on the board already. Xebec scores 16 points.

xenon *n* (*pl* **-s**) CHEM colourless odourless gas found in very small quantities in the air
xenons *n* ▷ **xenon**
xylem *n* (*pl* **-s**) plant tissue that conducts water and minerals from the roots to all other parts
xylems *n* ▷ **xylem**

Yy

Y is a useful tile to have on your rack. It's worth 4 points on its own, and so often gives you good scores. There are only four two-letter words beginning with Y, but these are easy to remember as there's one for every vowel except I: **ya**, **ye**, **yo** and **yu** (5 points each). There are quite a few useful three-letter words: **yew** (9) and **yob** (8) and remember that yob was originally **boy** backwards: if you can't fit in yob, you may be able to use boy instead. And while his half-brother the **zo** (or **dzo** or **dso** or **zho**) gets all the attention, don't forget that the **yak** (10) earns quite a decent score!

ya *interj* S AFR yes

yabbies *n* ▷ **yabby**

yabby *n* (*pl* -**bies**) AUST small freshwater crayfish

yacht *n* (*pl* -**s**) large boat with sails or an engine, used for racing or pleasure cruising > **yachting** *n* (*pl* -**s**) > **yachtsman** *n* (*pl* -**men**) > **yachtswoman** *n* (*pl* -**women**)

yachting *n* ▷ **yacht**

yachtings *n* ▷ **yacht**

yachts *n* ▷ **yacht**

yachtsman *n* ▷ **yacht**

yachtsmen *n* ▷ **yacht**

yachtswoman *n* ▷ **yacht**

yachtswomen *n* ▷ **yacht**

yak[1] *n* (*pl* -**s**) Tibetan ox with long shaggy hair

yak[2] *v* (-**s**, -**kking**, -**kked**) *slang* talk continuously about unimportant matters

yakka *n* (*pl* -**s**) AUST & NZ *informal* work

yakkas *n* ▷ **yakka**

yakked *v* ▷ **yak**[2]

yakking *v* ▷ **yak**[2]

yaks *n* ▷ **yak**[1] *or* ▷ **yak**[2]

yam *n* (*pl* -**s**) tropical root vegetable

yams *n* ▷ **yam**

yank *v* (-**s**, -**ing**, -**ed**) pull or jerk

suddenly ▶ *n* (*pl* -**s**) sudden pull or jerk

yanked *v* ▷ **yank**

yanking *v* ▷ **yank**

yanks *v*, *n* ▷ **yank**

yap *v* (-**s**, -**pping**, -**pped**) bark with a high-pitched sound *informal* ▶ *n* (*pl* -**s**) high-pitched bark

yapped *v* ▷ **yap**

yapping *v* ▷ **yap**

yaps *v* ▷ **yap**

yard[1] *n* (*pl* -**s**) unit of length equal to 36 inches or about 91.4 centimetres > **yardstick** *n* (*pl* -**s**) standard against which to judge other people or things

yard[2] *n* (*pl* -**s**) enclosed area, usu. next to a building and often used for a particular purpose

yards *n* ▷ **yard**[1, 2]

yardstick *n* ▷ **yard**[1]

yardsticks *n* ▷ **yard**[1]

yarmulke *n* (*pl* -**s**) skullcap worn by Jewish men

yarmulkes *n* ▷ **yarmulke**

yarn *n* (*pl* -**s**) thread used for knitting or making cloth

yarns *n* ▷ **yarn**

yashmak *n* (*pl* -**s**) veil worn by a Muslim woman to cover her face in public

yashmaks n ▷ yashmak

yaw v (-s, -ing, -ed) (of an aircraft or ship) turn to one side or from side to side while moving

yawed v ▷ yaw

yawing v ▷ yaw

yawl n (pl -s) two-masted sailing boat

yawls n ▷ yawl

yawn v (-s, -ing, -ed) open the mouth wide and take in air deeply, often when sleepy or bored ▶ n (pl -s) act of yawning > **yawning** adj

yawned v ▷ yawn

yawning v, adj ▷ yawn

yawns v, n ▷ yawn

yaws v ▷ yaw

ye pron obs you

year n (pl -s) time taken for the earth to make one revolution around the sun, about 365 days

yearling n (pl -s) animal between one and two years old

yearlings n ▷ yearling

yearly adj, adv (happening) every year or once a year

yearn v (-s, -ing, -ed) want (something) very much > **yearning** n (pl -s) adj

yearned v ▷ yearn

yearning v, n ▷ yearn

yearnings n ▷ yearn

yearns v ▷ yearn

years n ▷ year

yeast n (pl -s) fungus used to make bread rise and to ferment alcoholic drinks > **yeasty** adj

yeasts n ▷ yeast

yebo interj s AFR informal yes

yell v (-s, -ing, -ed) shout or scream in a loud or piercing way ▶ n (pl -s) loud cry of pain, anger, or fear

yelled v ▷ yell

yelling v ▷ yell

yellow n (pl -s) the colour of gold, a lemon, etc ▶ adj (-er, -est) of this colour ▶ v (-s, -ing, -ed) make or become yellow

yellowed v ▷ yellow

yellower adj ▷ yellow

yellowest adj ▷ yellow

yellowing v ▷ yellow

yellows n, v ▷ yellow

yells v, n ▷ yell

yelp v (-s, -ing, -ed) ▶ n (pl -s) (give) a short sudden cry

yelped v ▷ yelp

yelping v ▷ yelp

yelps v, n ▷ yelp

yen¹ n (pl yen) monetary unit of Japan

yen² n (pl yen) informal longing or desire

yeoman n (pl -men) HIST farmer owning and farming his own land

yeomen n ▷ yeoman

yes interj expresses consent, agreement, or approval

yet conj nevertheless, still ▶ adv up until then or now

yeti n (pl yetis) large apelike creature said to live in the Himalayas

yetis n ▷ yeti

yew n (pl -s) evergreen tree with needle-like leaves and red berries

yews n ▷ yew

> **yex** v (**yexes, yexing, yexed**). Yex is a Scots word that means to hiccup or cough. This word gives you a good score, and the verb forms offer the chance to expand it if someone else plays it, or if you get the chance later on. Yex scores 13 points.

yield v (-s, -ing, -ed) produce or bear ▶ n (pl -s)

yielded v ▷ yield

yielding adj submissive ▶ v ▷ yield

yields v, n ▷ yield

> **yo** interj. Yo is an informal greeting. This is useful for connecting words ending in Y with ones beginning in O. Yo scores 5 points.

yob n (pl -s) slang bad-mannered aggressive youth

yobbo n (pl -es or -s) yob

yobbees n ▷ yobbo

yobbos n ▷ yobbo

yobs n ▷ yob

yodel v (**-s, -lling, -lled**) sing with abrupt changes between a normal and a falsetto voice

yodelled v ▷ yodel

yodelling v ▷ yodel

yodels v ▷ yodel

yoga n (pl **-s**) Hindu method of exercise and discipline aiming at spiritual, mental, and physical wellbeing

yogas n ▷ yoga

yoghurt n ▷ yogurt

yoghurts n ▷ yogurt

yogi n (pl **-s**) person who practises yoga

yogis n ▷ yogi

yogurt, yoghurt n (pl **-s**) slightly sour custard-like food made from milk that has had bacteria added to it, often sweetened and flavoured with fruit

yogurts n ▷ yogurt

> **yok** n (**yoks**). A yok is a noisy laugh. This unusual word is useful if there isn't much space on the board, as there's likely to be an O available to form it around. Yok scores 10 points.

yoke n (pl **-s**) wooden bar put across the necks of two animals to hold them together lit ▶ v (**-kes, -king, -ked**) put a yoke on

yoked v ▷ yoke

yokel n (pl **yokels**) offens person who lives in the country and is usu. simple and old-fashioned

yokels n, v ▷ yokel

yokes n, v ▷ yoke

yoking v ▷ yoke

yolk n (pl **-s**) yellow part of an egg that provides food for the developing embryo

yolks n ▷ yolk

yonder adj, adv (situated) over there

yonks pl n informal very long time

yore n (pl **-s**) lit a long time ago

yores n ▷ yore

you pron refers to: the person or people addressed

young adj in an early stage of life or growth ▶ pl n young people in general

your adj of, belonging to, or associated with you ▷ yourself pron

yours pron something belonging to you

yourself pron ▷ your

youth n (pl **-s**) time of being young > **youthful** adj > **youthfulness** n (pl **-es**)

youthful adj ▷ youth

youthfulness n ▷ youth

youthfulnesses adj ▷ youth

youths n ▷ youth

yowl v, n (pl **-s**) (produce) a loud mournful cry

yowls n ▷ yowl

yttrium n (pl **-s**) CHEM silvery metallic element used in various alloys

yttriums n ▷ yttrium

> **yu** n (**yus**). Yu is a Chinese word that means precious jade. This word is good for connecting words ending in Y with ones beginning in U. Yu scores 5 points.

yucca n (pl **-s**) tropical plant with spikes of white leaves

yuccas n ▷ yucca

yuckier adj ▷ yucky

yuckiest adj ▷ yucky

yucky adj (**-kier, -kiest**) slang disgusting, nasty

> **yuk** interj. Yuk is a noise people make to express disgust or dislike. This funny little word is worth remembering as it give a good score and uses an unpromising combination of letters. Yuk scores 10 points.

yuppie n (pl **-s**) young highly-paid professional person, esp. one who has a materialistic way of life ▶ adj typical of or reflecting the values of yuppies

yuppies n ▷ yuppie

Zz

Scoring the same as Q but easier to use, Z is the most valuable tile in Scrabble. There is only one two-letter word beginning with Z, **zo** (11 points), but remembering this will save you wasting time looking for others. There some very good three-letter words starting with Z, however. These include another variant of **zo**, **zho** (15), as well as **zax** and **zex** (19 each), **zap** (14), **zip** (14) and **zoo** (12).

zanier adj ▷ **zany**

zaniest adj ▷ **zany**

> **zanja** n (**zanjas**). A zanja is an irrigation canal. This unusual word is very useful because of its combination of J and Z. As there are many As in the game, if you are lucky enough to get J and Z together, you may well be able to play this somewhere. Zanja scores 21 points.

> **zanjero** n (**zanjeros**). A zanjero is a supervisor of irrigation canals. If you can use all your tiles to play zanjero, you'll earn a 50-letter bonus. Zanjero scores 23 points.

zany adj (**-nier, -niest**) comical in an endearing way

zap v (**-s, -pping, -pped**) slang kill (by shooting)

zapped v ▷ **zap**

zapping v ▷ **zap**

zaps v ▷ **zap**

> **zax** n (**zaxes**). A zax a small axe for cutting slates. This is great word combining X and Z. If you get a Z late in the game, check if X has already been played, and whether there is an opportunity to form zax or **zex**. Zax scores 19 points.

zeal n (**-s**) great enthusiasm or eagerness

zealot n (**pl -s**) fanatic or extreme enthusiast

zealots n ▷ **zealot**

zealous adj extremely eager or enthusiastic ▷ **zealously** adv

zealously adv ▷ **zealous**

zeals n ▷ **zeal**

zebra n (**pl -s**) black-and-white striped African animal of the horse family

zebras n ▷ **zebra**

zebu n (**pl -s**) Asian ox with a humped back and long horns

zebus n ▷ **zebu**

> **zed** n (**zeds**). Zed is the letter Z. This is a handy word when you have a Z but no space or letters for a longer word. Zed scores 13 points.

> **zee** n (**zees**). Zee is the American pronunciation of the letter Z. This word can be very useful because E is the most common tile in Scrabble, so keep it in mind if you draw a Z. Zee scores 12 points.

zenith n (**pl -s**) highest point of success or power

zeniths n ▷ **zenith**

zephyr n (**pl -s**) soft gentle breeze

zephyrs n ▷ **zephyr**

zeppelin n (**pl -s**) HIST large cylindrical airship

zeppelins n ▷ zeppelin
zero n (pl **-s**, **-es**) (symbol representing) the number o ▶ adj having no measurable quantity or size
zeroes n ▷ zero
zeros n ▷ zero
zest n (pl **-s**) enjoyment or excitement
zests n ▷ zest

> **zeuxite** n (**zeuxites**). Zeuxite is a mineral. This unusual word is great if you have the letters for it. If you can use all of your tiles to play zeuxite, you'll get a 50-point bonus. Zeuxite scores 23 points.

> **zex** n (**zexes**). Zex means the same as zax. If you get a Z late in the game, check if X has already been played, and whether there is an opportunity to form zax. Zex scores 19 points.

> **zho** n (**zhos**). Zho is one of several spelling for a Tibetan animal bred from yaks and cattle. The other forms are **dso**, **dzo** and **zo**, and it's worth remembering all of them. Zho scores 15 points.

zigzag n (pl **-s**) line or course having sharp turns in alternating directions ▶ v (**-zags**, **-zagging**, **-zagged**) move in a zigzag ▶ adj formed in or proceeding in a zigzag
zigzagged v ▷ zigzag
zigzagging v ▷ zigzag
zigzags n, v ▷ zigzag
zinc n (pl **-s**) CHEM bluish-white metallic element used in alloys and to coat metal
zincs n ▷ zinc
zing n (pl **-s**) informal quality in something that makes it lively or interesting
zings n ▷ zing
zip n (pl **-s**) fastener with two rows of teeth that are closed or opened by a small clip pulled between them ▶ v (**-s**, **-pping**, **-pped**) fasten with a zip
zipped v ▷ zip
zipping v ▷ zip

zips n, v ▷ zip
zircon n (pl **-s**) mineral used as a gemstone and in industry
zircons n ▷ zircon

> **zit** n (**zits**). A zit is a pimple. This nasty little word can be very useful during a game, especially when there's not much space left on the board. Zit scores 12 points.

zither n (pl **-s**) musical instrument consisting of strings stretched over a flat box and plucked to produce musical notes
zithers n ▷ zither

> **zo** n (**zos**). Zo is one of several spelling for a Tibetan animal bred from yaks and cattle. The other forms are **dso**, **dzo** and **zho**, and it's worth remembering all of them. If someone plays zo and you have a D, remember that you can form dzo from it. Zo is the only two-letter word beginning with Z, and scores 11 points.

zodiac n (pl **-s**) imaginary belt in the sky within which the sun, moon, and planets appear to move, divided into twelve equal areas, called signs of the zodiac, each named after a constellation
zodiacs n ▷ zodiac
zombi n ▷ zombie
zombie, zombi n (pl **-s**) person who appears to be lifeless, apathetic, or totally lacking in independent judgment
zombies n ▷ zombie
zombis n ▷ zombie
zonal adj ▷ zone
zone n (pl **-s**) area with particular features or properties ▶ v (**-nes**, **-ning**, **-ned**) divide into zones > **zonal** adj
zoned v ▷ zone
zones n, v ▷ zone
zoning v ▷ zone
zoo n (pl **-s**) place where live animals are kept for show
zoological adj ▷ zoology

zoologies *n* ▷ zoology
zoologist *n* ▷ zoology
zoologists *n* ▷ zoology
zoology *n* (*pl* **-gies**) study of animals
> **zoologist** *n* (*pl* **-s**) > **zoological** *adj*
zoom *v* (**-s, -ing, -ed**) move or rise
very rapidly
zoomed *v* ▷ zoom
zooming *v* ▷ zoom
zooms *v* ▷ zoom
zoos *n* ▷ zoo

> **zootaxy** *n* (**zootaxies**). Zootaxy
is the scientific classification of
animals. If you're lucky enough to
have the letters for this word, you
can earn a 50-point bonus by using
all of your tiles to form it. Zootaxy
scores 26 points.

zucchini *n* (*pl* **-s**) US & AUST courgette
zucchinis *n* ▷ zucchini
zulu *n* (*pl* **-s**) member of a tall Black
people of southern Africa
zulus *n* ▷ zulu
zygote *n* (*pl* **-s**) fertilized egg cell
zygotes *n* ▷ zygote